M000309601

AL ALABAMA

Houghton Mifflin Harcourt

The AMERICANS

BEGINNINGS TO 1914

Gerald A. Danzer

J. Jorge Klor de Alva

Larry S. Krieger

Louis E. Wilson

Nancy Woloch

Authors and Consultants

Gerald A. Danzer, Ph.D.
Gerald A. Danzer is Professor of History at the University of Illinois at Chicago. He served from 1992 to 1994 as Chair of the Council for Effective Teaching and Learning at UIC and was Director of the Chicago Neighborhood History Project. Dr. Danzer's area of specialization is historical geography, in which he has written *Discovering American History Through Maps and Views* and numerous other publications. Before entering university teaching, Dr. Danzer taught high school history in the Chicago area. Dr. Danzer received his Ph.D. in history from Northwestern University.

J. Jorge Klor de Alva, J.D. and Ph.D.
J. Jorge Klor de Alva is President of Apollo International, Inc., a global education provider. Formerly he was president of the University of Phoenix. Before that he was Class of 1940 Professor of Comparative Ethnic Studies and Anthropology at the University of California at Berkeley and former Professor of Anthropology at Princeton University. Dr. Klor de Alva's interests include interethnic relations, historical ethnography, and educational reform. His publications include *The Aztec Image of Self* and *Society and Interethnic Images: Discourse and Practice in the New World, 1492–1992*, as well as more than ten other books and more than seventy scholarly articles. Dr. Klor de Alva earned his J.D. from the University of California at Berkeley and his Ph.D. in history/anthropology from the University of California at Santa Cruz.

Larry S. Krieger, B.A., M.A., M.A.T.
Larry S. Krieger is the Social Studies Supervisor for Grades K–12 in Montgomery Township Public Schools in New Jersey. For 26 years he has been a world history teacher in public schools. He has also introduced many innovative in-service programs, such as "Putting the Story Back in History," and has co-authored several successful history textbooks. Mr. Krieger earned his B.A. and M.A.T. from the University of North Carolina and his M.A. from Wake Forest University.

Louis E. Wilson, Ph.D.
Louis E. Wilson is Associate Professor and from 1989 through 1998 was the Chair of the Afro-American and African Studies Department at Smith College. In 1999, Dr. Wilson was a Senior Fulbright History Professor at the University of Cape Town, South Africa. Previously Dr. Wilson was on the faculty at the University of Colorado, Boulder, and was a senior Fulbright Scholar at the University of Ghana, Legon. Dr. Wilson is the author of *The Krobo People of Ghana to 1892: A Political, Social, and Economic History* and *Genealogical and Militia Data on Blacks, Indians, and Mustees from Military American Revolutionary War Records.* He is also one of the authors of *Houghton Mifflin Social Studies.* Dr. Wilson is currently writing a book entitled *Forgotten Patriots: African Americans and Native Americans in the American Revolution from Rhode Island.* In 1991, Dr. Wilson received The Blackwell Fellowship and Prize as Outstanding Black New England Scholar. Dr. Wilson received his Ph.D. in history from the University of California at Los Angeles.

Nancy Woloch, Ph.D.
Nancy Woloch teaches history at Barnard College, where she has been on the faculty since 1988. Dr. Woloch's main scholarly interest is the history of women in the United States, and in this area she has published *Women and the American Experience* and *Early American Women: A Documentary History, 1600–1900*. She is also the author of *Muller v. Oregon* and the co-author of *The American Century*. Dr. Woloch was the recipient of two National Endowment for the Humanities Fellowships. She received her Ph.D. in history and American studies from Indiana University.

This book contains material written by **John S. Bowes** that originally appeared in *The Americans* © 1985 and © 1991.

Senior Consultant
Dr. Robert Dallek
Presidential historian and biographer
Washington, D.C.

Constitution Consultant
Melvin Dubnick
Professor of Political Science
Rutgers University, Trenton
Trenton, New Jersey

Contributing Writer
Miriam Greenblatt
Educational Writer and Consultant
Highland Park, Illinois

Multicultural Advisory Board
The multicultural advisers reviewed the manuscript for appropriateness content.

Pat A. Brown
Director of the Indianapolis Public Schools Office of African-Centered Multicultural Education
Indianapolis Public Schools
Indianapolis, Indiana

Ogle B. Duff
Associate Professor of English
University of Pittsburgh
Pittsburgh, Pennsylvania

Mary Ellen Maddox
Black Education Commission Director, Los Angeles Unified School District
Los Angeles, California

Jon Reyhner
Associate Professor and Coordinator of the Bilingual Multicultural Ed. Program
Northern Arizona University
Flagstaff, Arizona

Curtis L. Walker
Executive Officer, Office of Equity and Compliance
Pittsburgh Public Schools
Pittsburgh, Pennsylvania

Ruben Zepeda
Compliance Advisor, Language Acquisition and Curriculum Development
Los Angeles, California

2015 Edition

Printed in the U.S.A.

ISBN 978-0-544-12761-6

5 6 7 8 9 10 0918 22 21 20 19 18 17 16 15 14
4500487223 ^ B C D E F G

Consultants and Reviewers

Content Consultants
The content consultants reviewed the manuscript for historical depth and accuracy and for clarity of presentation.

Catherine Clinton
Fellow of the W. E. B. Du Bois Institute
Harvard University
Cambridge, Massachusetts

Theodore Karaminski
Professor of History
Loyola University
Chicago, Illinois

Joseph Kett
Professor of History
University of Virginia
Charlottesville, Virginia

Jack Rakove
Professor of History
Stanford University
Stanford, California

Harvard Sitkoff
Professor of History
University of New Hampshire
Durham, New Hampshire

Teacher Consultants
The following educators contributed ideas and activities for the program.

Edmund Austin
William Tennant High School
Warminster, Pennsylvania

William Brown
Retired,
Northeast High School
Philadelphia, Pennsylvania

Larry Bruno
Denby High School
Detroit, Michigan

Suzanne Cook
Scarborough High School
Houston, Texas

John Devine
Elgin High School
Elgin, Illinois

George Dyche
West Aurora High School
Aurora, Illinois

Steve Ellison
Petaluma High School
Petaluma, California

Betsy Fitzgerald
Erskine Academy
South China, Maine

Michael Fleming
Jupiter High School
Jupiter, Florida

Thomas J. Flynn
Turner High School
Kansas City, Kansas

Dominic Fruscello
West Genesee High School
Camillus, New York

Craig T. Grace
Lanier High School
West Austin, Texas

Cynthia M. Greene
Ridley High School
Folsom, Pennsylvania

Patti Harrold
Edmond Memorial High School
Edmond, Oklahoma

Korri Kinney
Meridian High School
Meridian, Idaho

Don A. Lee
Mira Mesa High School
San Diego, California

Dr. Carol D. McCree
DeBakey Health Prof. High School
Houston, Texas

Harry McCown
Hazelwood West High School
Hazelwood, Missouri

Lou Morrison
Lake Weir High School
Ocala, Florida

Theresa C. Noonan
West Irondequoit High School
Rochester, New York

Gloria Remijio
Del Valle High School
El Paso, Texas

Diane M. Rodgers
Crooksville High School
Crooksville, Ohio

James Rosenberg
Retired, Crystal Lake South High School
Crystal Lake, Illinois

John Seeley
Westminster High School
Westminster, California

Brenda G. Smith
Instructional Supervisor, Social Studies, Colorado Springs District 11
Colorado Springs, Colorado

Steve Smith
Clayton High School
Clayton, North Carolina

Ruby Thompson
Athens Drive High School
Raleigh, North Carolina

Linda Tillis
South Oak Cliff High School
Dallas, Texas

Mark A. Van Hecke
Anchor Bay High School
New Baltimore, Michigan

Joshua Weiner
Benson High School
Portland, Oregon

Teacher Review Panels
The following educators provided ongoing review during the development of prototypes, the table of contents, and key components of the program.

FLORIDA TEACHER PANEL

David Debs
Mandarin High School
Jacksonville, Florida

Ronald Eckstein
Hudson High School
Hudson, Florida

Sharman Feliciani
Land O'Lakes High School
Land O'Lakes, Florida

Flossie Gautier
Bay High School
Panama City, Florida

Glenn Hallick
Vanguard High School
Ocala, Florida

Mary Kenney
Astronaut High School
Titusville, Florida

Lou Morrison
Lake Weir High School
Ocala, Florida

Brenda Sims Palmer
Lehigh High School
Lehigh Acres, Florida

Marsee Perkins
Maynard Evans High School
Orlando, Florida

Kent Rettig
Pensacola High School
Pensacola, Florida

Jim Sutton
Edgewater High School
Orlando, Florida

ILLINOIS TEACHER PANEL

Rosemary Albright
Conant High School
Hoffman Estates, Illinois

Jeff Anhut
Wheaton Warrenville South High School
Wheaton, Illinois

James Crider
Downers Grove South High School
Downers Grove, Illinois

John Devine
Elgin High School
Elgin, Illinois

George Dyche
West Aurora High School
Aurora, Illinois

Diane Ring
St. Charles High School
St. Charles, Illinois

Jim Rosenberg
Crystal Lake South High School
Crystal Lake, Illinois

Pam Zimmerman
Stevenson High School
Lincolnshire, Illinois

CALIFORNIA TEACHER PANEL

Elaine Deatherage
Hiram Johnson High School
Sacramento, California

Steve Ellison
Petaluma High School
Petaluma, California

Judy Horrigan
Moreno Valley High School
Moreno Valley, California

Don Lee
Mira Mesa High School
San Diego, California

Russom Mesfun
Fremont High School
Oakland, California

Randy Sanford
Hueneme High School
Oxnard, California

John Seeley
Westminster High School
Westminster, California

Kathleen Torosian
Herbert Hoover High School
Fresno, California

Glenda Watanabe
Banning High School
Los Angeles, California

TEXAS TEACHER PANEL

Patricia Brison
Bellaire High School
Houston, Texas

Brian Greeney
Stratford High School
Spring Branch, Texas

Jim Lee
Lamar High School
Arlington, Texas

Janie Maldonado
Lanier High School
Austin, Texas

Leonore Murray
Lubbock High School
Lubbock, Texas

Deborah Pennington
The Woodlands High School
Conroe, Texas

Gloria Remijio
Dell Valley High School
Yselta, Texas

H.V. Stafford
MacArthur High School
Aldine, Texas

Dawn Stapp
Lee Freshman High School
Midland, Texas

Manuscript Reviewers
The educators listed in the next column reviewed the prototype chapter and the manuscript of the entire book.

Arman Afshani
North Tonawanda High School
North Tonawanda, New York

Debra Brown
Eisenhower High School
Houston, Texas

Dianne Bumgarner
Ashbrook High School
Mt. Holly, North Carolina

Sherry Burgin
Garland High School
Garland, Texas

Maurice Bush
South Point High School
Crouse, North Carolina

(*continued on RC2*)

Student Board
The following students reviewed prototype materials for the book.

John Afordakos
Chantilly High School
Fairfax County, Virginia

Marisha Cook
Rockford East High School
Rockford, Illinois

Matthew Cornejo
New Bedford High School
New Bedford, Massachusetts

(*continued on RC2*)

HISTORY® is the leading destination for revealing, award-winning, original non-fiction series and event-driven specials that connect history with viewers in an informative, immersive and entertaining manner across multiple platforms. HISTORY is part of A&E Television Networks (AETN), a joint venture of Hearst Corporation, Disney/ABC Television Group and NBC Universal, an award-winning, international media company that also includes, among others, A&E Network™, BIO™, and History International™.

HISTORY programming greatly appeals to educators and young people who are drawn into the visual stories our documentaries tell. Our Education Department has a long-standing record in providing teachers and students with curriculum resources that bring the past to life in the classroom. Our content covers a diverse variety of subjects, including American and world history, government, economics, the natural and applied sciences, arts, literature and the humanities, health and guidance, and even pop culture.

The HISTORY website, located at **www.history.com**, is the definitive historical online source that delivers entertaining and informative content featuring broadband video, interactive timelines, maps, games, podcasts and more.

"We strive to engage, inspire and encourage the love of learning..."

Since its founding in 1995, HISTORY has demonstrated a commitment to providing the highest quality resources for educators. We develop multimedia resources for K–12 schools, two- and four-year colleges, government agencies, and other organizations by drawing on the award-winning documentary programming of A&E Television Networks. We strive to engage, inspire and encourage the love of learning by connecting with students in an informative and compelling manner. To help achieve this goal, we have formed a partnership with Houghton Mifflin Harcourt.

The Idea Book for Educators

Classroom resources that bring the past to life

Live webcasts

HISTORY Take a Veteran to School Day

In addition to premium video-based resources, **HISTORY** has extensive offerings for teachers, parents, and students to use in the classroom and in their in-home educational activities, including:

- ***The Idea Book for Educators*** is a biannual teacher's magazine, featuring guides and info on the latest happenings in history education to help keep teachers on the cutting edge.
- **HISTORY Classroom (www.history.com/classroom)** is an interactive website that serves as a portal for history educators nationwide. Streaming videos on topics ranging from the Roman aqueducts to the civil rights movement connect with classroom curricula.
- **HISTORY email newsletters** feature updates and supplements to our award-winning programming relevant to the classroom with links to teaching guides and video clips on a variety of topics, special offers, and more.
- **Live webcasts** are featured each year as schools tune in via streaming video.
- **HISTORY Take a Veteran to School Day** connects veterans with young people in our schools and communities nationwide.

In addition to **HOUGHTON MIFFLIN HARCOURT**, our partners include the *Library of Congress*, the *Smithsonian Institution, National History Day*, *The Gilder Lehrman Institute of American History,* the *Organization of American Historians*, and many more. HISTORY video is also featured in museums throughout America and in over 70 other historic sites worldwide.

For more information go to hmhsocialstudies.com

UNIT
1
American Beginnings to 1783

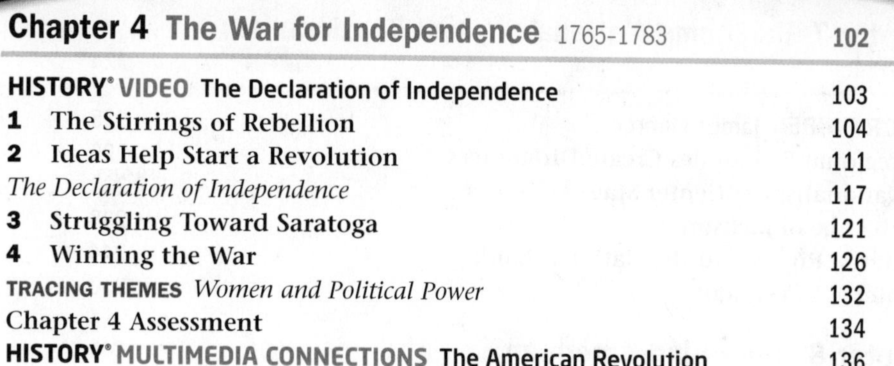

UNIT 2
1781–1850
A New Nation

For more information go to hmhsocialstudies.com

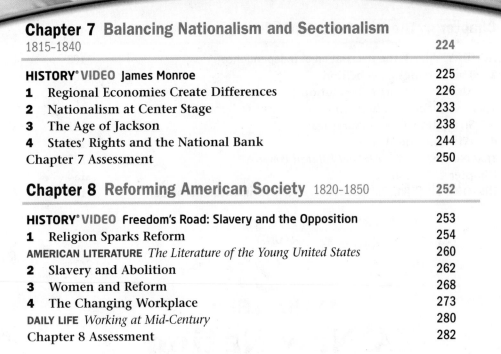

UNIT
3
1825–1877
An Era of Growth and Disunion

Chapter 10 The Union in Peril 1850-1861 320

Chapter 11 The Civil War 1861-1865 354

Chapter 12 Reconstruction and Its Effects 1865-1877 394

For more information go to hmhsocialstudies.com

UNIT

4

1877–1917

Migration and Industrialization

For more information go to hmhsocialstudies.com

UNIT

5

1890–1920

Modern America Emerges

Available @ hmhsocialstudies.com

- Strategies for Taking Standardized Tests
- Economics Handbook

Houghton Mifflin Harcourt

The history of a nation is shaped as much by geography as by people and events. Paying attention to the following themes of geography can help you recognize when geographic forces are at work in the story of the United States.

LOCATION

Geographers speak of absolute location—the latitude and longitude of an area—and of relative location—where one area is in relation to another. In absolute terms, the city of San Francisco lies at 37°45' North latitude and 122°26' West longitude. This information allows you to pinpoint San Francisco on a map. In relative terms, San Francisco lies at the western edge of North America and looks out across the vast Pacific Ocean. This information helps explain San Francisco's history as a port city where people and ideas have come together.

Critical Thinking **Locate your city or town on both a political and a physical map. How has location influenced the history of your city or town?**

PLACE

Place, in geography, refers to what an area looks like in physical and human terms. An area's landforms, soil, climate, and resources are aspects of place. So are the numbers and cultures of the population. San Francisco's natural harbor has made the city an international port. It is connected to the American River—where gold was discovered in 1848. Its position along a major fault line has subjected it to periodic earthquakes, the most disastrous in 1906. During its history, San Francisco has attracted people from North America, Europe, Asia, and various Pacific islands, making its population one of the most diverse in the United States.

Critical Thinking **What is unique about the place where you live and the people who live there? What past events contributed to its uniqueness?**

REGION

Geographers use the idea of region to show what places in close proximity to one another have in common. As a part of the Pacific Coast region, San Francisco shares with Seattle, Washington, and Portland, Oregon, a mild, rainy climate and an economic interest in international shipping. As a part of California, San Francisco shares economic and environmental concerns of the state as a whole.

Critical Thinking **To what region or regions does your area belong? How have the characteristics and concerns of your region changed over the last generation?**

MOVEMENT

One place or region can influence another through the movement of people, materials, and even ideas. San Francisco has been the site of many important movements of people and cultures. It has been a port of entry for immigrants, many of them Asian. It also lies along the path that Spanish missionaries trod in their quest to convert native peoples.

Critical Thinking **When and by what groups was your area settled? What trends in movement today may shape the future of your area?**

HUMAN-ENVIRONMENT INTERACTION

Wherever people live, they affect the environment in the way they modify their natural surroundings. They build shelters and clear trees. They turn the earth inside out to extract its resources. People in the San Francisco Bay area have built bridges in order to move around more easily. People have also modified the bay itself, reducing its area by about one-third as they filled in tidelands for development.

Critical Thinking **How have people in your area modified their surroundings? What consquences might these modifications have?**

Among the important themes in U.S. history are the promise of technology, the rights enjoyed by Americans, and the roles of women in the 21st century. As you study U.S. history, you will encounter these and other themes again and again. The Americans *focuses on nine themes, described on these pages. What do you think are the important issues raised by each theme?*

DIVERSITY AND THE NATIONAL IDENTITY

E Pluribus Unum—From the Many, One. Pick up a dollar bill and you'll find this Latin motto on the Great Seal of the United States. From the first settlement, this has been a land of many peoples, cultures, and faiths. This mixing of ethnic, racial, and religious groups has produced a rich and uniquely American culture. It has also led to competition and conflict. Today, the United States is more diverse than ever, yet the nation's motto remains *E Pluribus Unum*.

Critical Thinking **How do you think America today is enriched by its diversity?**

AMERICA IN WORLD AFFAIRS

From the earliest colonial times, the United States has been influenced by the events, people, and forms of government in other nations—and America has influenced world affairs. Today, relationships between the United States and other countries are more critical than ever, as modern communications and transportation have drawn the world closer together. As America continues to participate in world affairs, questions of trade, diplomacy, and regional conflict will grow in importance.

Critical Thinking **What do you think America's role in the world should be in the 21st century?**

ECONOMIC OPPORTUNITY

America has always been a land of economic opportunity. Blessed with fertile land and abundant resources, this has been a country where anyone who has worked hard has had a chance to prosper. Indeed, American history is full of heartening "rags-to-riches" success stories. Just as inspiring are the heroic struggles of women and minorities who fought to improve their economic prospects. As your generation enters the work force, you and your friends will have the opportunity to write your own success stories.

Critical Thinking **What do you think are the most exciting economic opportunities for Americans today?**

SCIENCE AND TECHNOLOGY

Americans have always had a deep respect for the power of science and technology to improve life. In the past two centuries, new inventions, new technologies, and scientific breakthroughs have transformed the United States—and continue to appear at a dizzying pace. Which ones will change your life? You can be sure that some will, and in ways that no one can yet predict.

Critical Thinking **How do you think science and technology will change American life in the 21st century?**

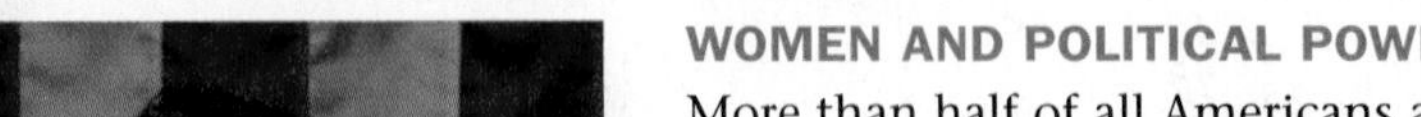

WOMEN AND POLITICAL POWER

More than half of all Americans are women, but only recently have their contributions and concerns found their way into history books. American women have helped shape the social and political history of every era. In their private roles as wives and mothers, they have strengthened families and raised America's children. In their more public roles as workers, reformers, and crusaders for equal rights, they have attacked the nation's worst social ills and challenged barriers to women's full participation in American life.

Critical Thinking **What do you think is the most important goal for American women today?**

IMMIGRATION AND MIGRATION

Seeking a better life seems to be part of the American character. This nation was first established by and has remained a magnet for immigrants. One out of every ten people living in the United States today was born in another country. Moreover, every year one out of every six Americans moves to a new address.

Critical Thinking **Why do you think people continue to have the dream of immigrating to the United States?**

STATES' RIGHTS

The power struggle between states and the federal government has caused controversy since the country's beginning. In 1861 the conflict led to the Civil War, in which Southern states acted upon the belief that they had the right to nullfy acts of the federal government and even to leave the Union if they chose to do so. Throughout the history of this country, state and federal governments have squared off on this and other constitutional issues.

Critical Thinking **When do you think a state has the right to challenge a federal law?**

VOTING RIGHTS

When Americans first began their experiment with democracy, only white men with property could vote or hold office. Over the past two centuries, women, African Americans, and other groups have fought for and won the right to vote and participate in government. Today the challenge is getting people to exercise the right to vote. In 2000, only 50.7 percent of eligible voters cast ballots in the presidential election.

Critical Thinking **What do you think can be done to bring more Americans into the democratic process?**

CIVIL RIGHTS

The American system of government is based on a simple but revolutionary idea: Every citizen has certain rights and liberties. Among them are the right to participate in government and to exercise such liberties as freedom of speech and worship. Deciding who should have what rights, how these rights should be exercised, and how to protect a person's civil rights is anything but easy. Defining and protecting our civil rights are not likely to get any easier.

Critical Thinking **What issue of civil rights do you think is most critical in the United States today?**

AL Alabama

Alabama State Capitol, Montgomery

Offshore drilling platform

Sunset at Mobile Bay

As you read the following pages and work through the unpacking of Alabama United States History I: Beginnings to the Industrial Revolution Course of Study, you will discover the big ideas and key concepts that your teacher expects you to learn and understand.

You will see two things:

1 > What the standard actually says

2 **What does it mean?** an explanation to help you understand the big ideas within the standard

Alabama United States History I: Beginnings to the Industrial Revolution

>1. Compare effects of economic, geographic, social, and political conditions before and after European explorations of the fifteenth through seventeenth centuries on Europeans, American colonists, Africans, and indigenous Americans.

- **Describing the influence of the Crusades, Renaissance, and Reformation on European exploration**
- **Comparing European motives for establishing colonies, including mercantilism, religious persecution, poverty, oppression, and new opportunities**
- **Analyzing the course of the Columbian Exchange for its impact on the global economy**
- **Explaining triangular trade and the development of slavery in the colonies**

What does it mean?

Compare the effects of European explorations of the fifteenth through the seventeenth centuries on Europeans, American colonists, Africans, and Native Americans. Describe how events in Europe affected exploration in the Americas, and compare the reasons why Europeans established colonies in America. Explain how the Colombian Exchange—an exchange of plants, animals, and diseases—occurred during this time. Understand how trade affected the development of slavery in the colonies. Go to Chapter 1, *Three Worlds Meet, 1200 B.C.–A.D. 1506;* as well as Chapter 3, *The Colonies Come of Age, 1650–1760,* for help.

Camellia

Yellowhammer

>2. Compare regional differences among early New England, Middle, and Southern colonies regarding economics, geography, culture, government, and American Indian relations.

- **Explaining the role of essential documents in the establishment of colonial governments, including the Magna Carta, the English Bill of Rights, and the Mayflower Compact**
- **Explaining the significance of the House of Burgesses and New England town meetings in colonial politics**
- **Describing the impact of the Great Awakening on colonial society**

What does it mean?

Identify differences in way of life among colonies in different regions. Analyze how the geography of an area influenced the ways colonists could earn a living. Explain how the values and beliefs that immigrants brought with them shaped the culture where they settled, particularly the concepts in the Magna Carta, English Bill of Rights, and Mayflower Compact on which colonists based their governments and political practices. Describe the effects of the Great Awakening, a powerful religious revival that swept through the colonies. Contrast the treatment of Native Americans in different regions. Go to Chapter 2, *The American Colonies Emerge, 1492–1681;* and Chapter 3, *The Colonies Come of Age, 1650–1760,* for help.

>3. Trace the chronology of events leading to the American Revolution, including the French and Indian War, passage of the Stamp Act, the Boston Tea Party, the Boston Massacre, passage of the Intolerable Acts, the Battles of Lexington and Concord, the publication of *Common Sense*, and the signing of the Declaration of Independence.

- **Explaining the role of key revolutionary leaders, including George Washington, John Adams, Thomas Jefferson, Patrick Henry, Samuel Adams, Paul Revere, Crispus Attucks, and the Marquis de Lafayette**
- **Explaining the significance of revolutionary battles, including Bunker Hill, Trenton, Saratoga, and Yorktown**
- **Summarizing major ideas of the Declaration of Independence, including theories of John Locke, Charles de Montesquieu, and Jean-Jacques Rousseau**
- **Comparing perspectives of differing groups in society and their roles in the American Revolution, including men, women, white settlers, free and enslaved African Americans, and American Indians**
- **Describing how provisions of the Treaty of Paris of 1783 affected relations of the United States with European nations and American Indians**

What does it mean?

Summarize key events that pushed the colonies ever closer to revolution. Explain how the ideas of influential thinkers of the time inspired the colonists to seek independence. Describe the roles of American leaders and key battles in achieving independence. Recognize that differing views led groups of colonists to play different roles in the struggle for independence. Explain how the terms of the treaty that ended the American Revolution shaped relations of the new United States with European nations and Native Americans. Go to Chapter 4, *The War for Independence, 1768–1783,* for help.

Old Depot Museum, Selma

Natural Bridge Park

>4. Describe the political system of the United States based on the Constitution of the United States.

- **Interpreting the Preamble to the Constitution of the United States; separation of powers; federal system; elastic clause; the Bill of Rights; and the Thirteenth, Fourteenth, Fifteenth, and Nineteenth Amendments as key elements of the Constitution of the United States**
- **Describing inadequacies of the Articles of Confederation**
- **Distinguishing personalities, issues, ideologies, and compromises related to the Constitutional Convention and the ratification of the Constitution of the United States, including the role of the Federalist papers**
- **Identifying factors leading to the development and establishment of political parties, including Alexander Hamilton's economic policies, conflicting views of Thomas Jefferson and Alexander Hamilton, George Washington's Farewell Address, and the election of 1800**

What does it mean?

Understand the meaning of key clauses in the Constitution of the United States and its amendments. Describe the political system that the Constitution created. Identify the weaknesses of the Articles of Confederation that revealed the need for a new constitution. Describe the views and personalities of the leaders who wrote the new constitution and promoted or opposed its ratification. Explain the difficult issues they faced and the compromises they made to achieve a workable constitution that most Americans would accept. Contrast the views of American leaders on political parties. Go to Chapter 5, *Shaping a New Nation, 1781–1788;* as well as Chapter 6, *Launching the New Nation, 1789–1816,* for help.

>5. Explain key cases that helped shape the United States Supreme Court, including *Marbury versus Madison, McCullough versus Maryland, and Cherokee Nation versus Georgia*.

- **Explaining concepts of loose and strict interpretations of the Constitution of the United States**

What does it mean?

Explain how decisions in landmark cases helped define the power of the United States Supreme Court and its role as a branch of government. Describe the difference between strict and loose interpretation of the Constitution. Go to Chapter 6, *Launching the New Nation, 1789–1816;* as well as Chapter 7, *Balancing Nationalism and Sectionalism, 1815–1840,* for help.

>6. Describe relations of the United States with Britain and France from 1781 to 1823, including the XYZ Affair, the War of 1812, and the Monroe Doctrine.

What does it mean?

Describe how relations between the United States and Britain and France changed between 1781 and 1823. Explain how the XYZ Affair—when in 1797 three French agents attempted to bribe American negotiators in order to profit from diplomatic negotiations—further strained United States relations with France. Trace events leading to the War of 1812. Examine how the Monroe Doctrine—stating that the United States would protect the Western Hemisphere from further European expansion—asserted new power for the young United States in international relations. Go to Chapter 6, *Launching the New Nation, 1789–1816;* and Chapter 7, *Balancing Nationalism and Sectionalism, 1815–1840,* for help.

>7. Describe causes, courses, and consequences of United States' expansionism prior to the Civil War, including the Treaty of Paris of 1783, the Land Ordinance of 1785, the Northwest Ordinance of 1787, the Louisiana Purchase, the Indian Removal Act, the Trail of Tears, Manifest Destiny, the Mexican War and Cession, Texas Independence, the acquisition of Oregon, the California Gold Rush, and the Western Trails.

What does it mean?

Trace the sequence of events as the United States expanded its territory westward. Understand how a belief in Manifest Destiny—or that the United States was destined to stretch across the North American continent—inspired westward expansion. Explain how key ordinances (laws) and agreements with other nations allowed this expansion. Analyze the effects of expansion, especially on Native American. Go to Chapter 9, *Expanding Markets and Moving West, 1825–1847; as well as* Chapter 5, *Shaping a New Nation, 1781–1788;* Chapter 6, *Launching the New Nation, 1789–1816;* and Chapter 7, *Balancing Nationalism and Sectionalism, 1815–1840,* for help.

>8. Compare major events in Alabama from 1781 to 1823, including statehood as part of the expanding nation, acquisition of land, settlement, and the Creek War, to those of the developing nation.

What does it mean?

Understand how major events in Alabama from 1781 to 1823 fit with developments in the nation as a whole. Provide details about how the United States acquired land from other nations (treaties, etc.) and from Native Americans (treaties, forced removal, etc.) to form what is now Alabama. Describe the settlement of the area and the process leading to statehood in 1819. Go to Unit 2, "Focus on Alabama," for help.

Bellingrath Gardens, Theodore

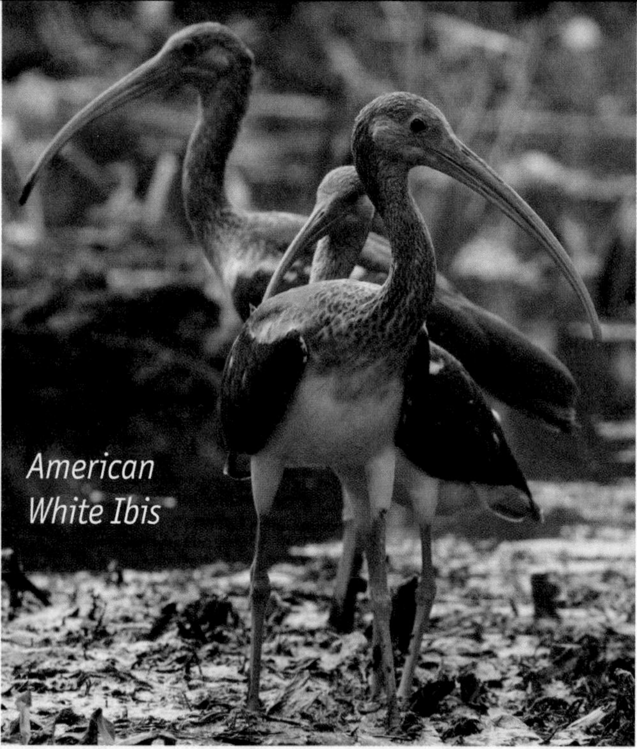
American White Ibis

>9. Explain dynamics of economic nationalism during the Era of Good Feelings, including transportation systems, Henry Clay's American System, slavery and the emergence of the plantation system, and the beginning of industrialism in the Northeast.

What does it mean?

Describe the Era of Good Feelings, a period of national unity following the War of 1812. Discuss plans to bind the nation together economically, including an expansion of roads and canals, tariffs (import taxes) to protect American companies from foreign competition, and a national bank. Describe the economy of the South based on slavery and organized around plantations, or large farms. Explain the rise of an economy based on factories in the Northeast. Go to Chapter 7, *Balancing Nationalism and Sectionalism, 1815–1840,* for help.

>10. Analyze key ideas of Jacksonian Democracy for their impact on political participation, political parties, and constitutional government.

- **Explaining the spoils system, nullification, extension of voting rights, the Indian Removal Act, and the common man ideal**

What does it mean?

Examine how the ideas of President Andrew Jackson promoted greater participation in politics and government for the "common man." Describe how Jackson's views led to more people being able to vote but also to the political favoritism (the spoils system) and to further claims on Native American lands. Present both sides of the controversy over nullification—the view that states had the power to ignore federal laws with which they disagreed. Go to Chapter 7, *Balancing Nationalism and Sectionalism, 1815–1840,* for help.

>11. Evaluate the impact of American social and political reform on the emergence of a distinct culture.

- **Explaining the impact of the Second Great Awakening on the emergence of a national identity**
- **Explaining the emergence of uniquely American writers**
- **Examples: James Fenimore Cooper, Henry David Thoreau, Edgar Allen Poe**
- **Explaining the influence of Elizabeth Cady Stanton, Dorothea Lynde Dix, and Susan B. Anthony on the development of social reform movements prior to the Civil War**

What does it mean?

Explain how the Second Great Awakening, a religious revival movement in the 1790s, inspired various reform movements. Identify popular American writers of the time and summarize their themes. Describe the work of women reformers in movements such as abolition, temperance, and women's rights. Identify the ways that these new movements contributed to a specific American identity and culture. Go to Chapter 8, *Reforming American Society, 1820–1850,* for help.

>12. Describe the founding of the first abolitionist societies by Benjamin Rush and Benjamin Franklin and the role played by later critics of slavery, including William Lloyd Garrison, Frederick Douglass, Sojourner Truth, Angelina and Sarah Grimké, Henry David Thoreau, and Charles Sumner.

- **Describing the rise of religious movements in opposition to slavery, including objections of the Quakers**
- **Explaining the importance of the Northwest Ordinance of 1787 that banned slavery in new states north of the Ohio River**
- **Describing the rise of the Underground Railroad and its leaders, including Harriet Tubman and the impact of Harriet Beecher Stowe's *Uncle Tom's Cabin,* on the abolitionist movement**

What does it mean?

Understand that abolitionist societies formed to end slavery. Identify leading abolitionists and describe their efforts. Recognize that Quaker beliefs and the religious excitement of the Second Great Awakening fueled antislavery feelings on moral grounds. Discuss the effects of the Northwest Ordinance on slavery in new territories. State the purpose of the Underground Railroad—a network of formerly enslaved people and anti-slavery activists that helped formerly enslaved people reach freedom—and describe its methods and key leaders. Explain how the book *Uncle Tom's Cabin*, by Harriet Beecher Stowe, swayed public opinion about slavery. Go to Chapter 8, *Reforming American Society, 1820–1850;* as well as Chapter 10, *The Union in Peril, 1850–1861,* for help.

>13. Summarize major legislation and court decisions from 1800 to 1861 that led to increasing sectionalism, including the Missouri Compromise of 1820, the Compromise of 1850, the Fugitive Slave Acts, the Kansas-Nebraska Act, and the Dred Scott decision.

- **Describing Alabama's role in the developing sectionalism of the United States from 1819 to 1861, including participation in slavery, secession, and the Indian War, and reliance on cotton**
- **Analyzing the Westward Expansion from 1803 to 1861 to determine its effect on sectionalism, including the Louisiana Purchase, Texas Annexation, and the Mexican Cession**
- **Describing tariff debates and the nullification crisis between 1800 and 1861**
- **Analyzing the formation of the Republican Party for its impact on the 1860 election of Abraham Lincoln as President of the United States**

What does it mean?

Explain how major laws and court decisions fostered sectionalism—greater loyalty to one's region than to the nation. Provide details of key compromises designed to hold the nation together. Understand how Alabama's cotton-based economy led to reliance on slave labor and the desire for more land. Note that threats to this way of life motivated Alabama to side with other slave states. Understand how adding new territories further inflamed sectional conflicts over slavery by making Congress decide whether or not to permit slavery in those territories. Explain the concept of states' rights that underlay attempts to nullify, or declare void, a federal tariff (tax on goods) law. Recognize that the Republican Party formed as a unified voice against slavery, helping its candidate, Abraham Lincoln, win against other parties that were divided on this key issue. Go to Chapter 10, *The Union in Peril, 1850–1865;* as well as Chapter 7, *Balancing Nationalism and Sectionalism, 1815–1840;* Chapter 9, *Expanding Markets and Moving West, 1825–1847;* and Units 2 and 3, "Focus on Alabama," for help.

>14. Describe how the Civil War influenced the United States, including the Anaconda Plan and the major battles of Bull Run, Antietam, Vicksburg, and Gettysburg and Sherman's March to the Sea.

- **Identifying key Northern and Southern Civil War personalities, including Abraham Lincoln, Jefferson Davis, Ulysses S. Grant, Robert E. Lee, Thomas Jonathan "Stonewall" Jackson, and William Tecumseh Sherman**
- **Analyzing the impact of the division of the nation during the Civil War regarding resources, population distribution, and transportation**
- **Explaining reasons for border states' remaining in the Union during the Civil War**
- **Describing nonmilitary events and life during the Civil War, including the Homestead Act, the Morrill Act, Northern draft riots, the Emancipation Proclamation, and the Gettysburg Address**
- **Describing the role of women in American society during the Civil War, including efforts made by Elizabeth Blackwell and Clara Barton**
- **Tracing Alabama's involvement in the Civil War**

What does it mean?

Trace major events in the Civil War. Understand the significance of key battles. Identify important individuals on both sides. Explain how differences in resources, population characteristics, and transportation systems between the North and South affected the ability of each side to wage war. Explain why border states did not secede. Discuss key events in civilian life during the Civil War. Describe how the roles of women expanded during the war due to the absence of men on the homefront. Discuss Alabama's participation in the war and the effects of war on the state. Go to Chapter 11, *The Civil War, 1861–1865;* as well as Chapter 10, *The Union in Peril, 1850–1861;* Chapter 13, *Changes on the Western Frontier, 1877–190;* and Unit 3, "Focus on Alabama," for help.

Montgomery skyline

>15. Compare congressional and presidential reconstruction plans, including African-American political participation.

- **Tracing economic changes in the post-Civil War period for whites and African Americans in the North and South, including the effectiveness of the Freedmen's Bureau**
- **Describing social restructuring of the South, including Southern military districts, the role of carpetbaggers and scalawags, the creation of the black codes, and the Ku Klux Klan**
- **Describing the Compromise of 1877**
- **Summarizing post-Civil War constitutional amendments, including the Thirteenth, Fourteenth, and Fifteenth Amendments**
- **Explaining causes for the impeachment of President Andrew Johnson**
- **Explaining the impact of Jim Crow laws and *Plessey versus Ferguson* on the social and political structure of the New South after Reconstruction**
- **Analyzing political and social motives that shaped the Constitution of Alabama of 1901 to determine their long-term effect on politics and economics in Alabama**

What does it mean?

Compare the plans of Abraham Lincoln, Andrew Johnson, and Congress for rebuilding the South. Point out differences in the terms for readmitting states to the Union and in the views on African Americans. Describe the governments set up in Southern states during Reconstruction, the period of reform between 1865 and 1877. Discuss the work of the Freedman's Bureau in helping newly freed slaves gain an economic foothold. Explain how black codes, the Ku Klux Klan, Jim Crow laws, and *Plessey* v. *Ferguson* hindered full participation of African Americans in politics and society. Identify the conflicts between President Andrew Johnson and Congress that led to impeachment, or charging a public official or president with a crime in Congress. Summarize the changes brought about by the Thirteenth, Fourteenth, and Fifteenth Amendments. Describe the compromise that ended Reconstruction. Analyze the motives for redrawing the Alabama Constitution and the effects on voting rights, political power, and economics of the state. Go to Chapter 12, *Reconstruction and Its Effects, 1865–1877;* as well as Chapter 5, *Shaping a New Nation, 1781–1788;* Chapter 16, *Life at the Turn of the 20th Century, 1877–1917;* and Unit 5, "Focus on Alabama," for help.

Gulf of Mexico beach

Pulpit Rock,
Cheaha Mountain

Alabama: Physical

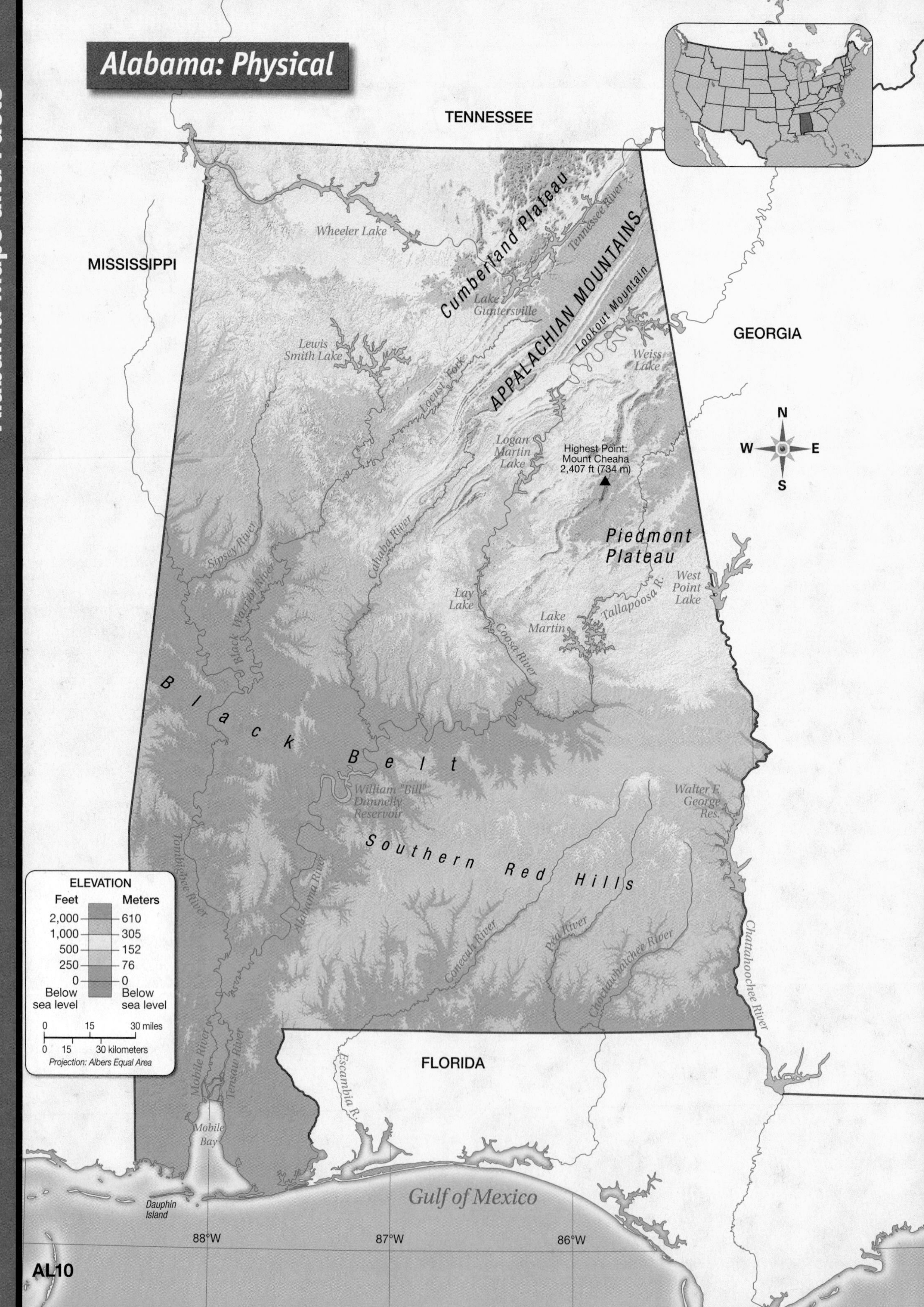
TENNESSEE
MISSISSIPPI
GEORGIA
FLORIDA
Wheeler Lake
Cumberland Plateau
Tennessee River
APPALACHIAN MOUNTAINS
Lake Guntersville
Lookout Mountain
Lewis Smith Lake
Locust Fork
Weiss Lake
Logan Martin Lake
Highest Point: Mount Cheaha 2,407 ft (734 m)
N
W
E
S
Piedmont Plateau
Sipsey River
Black Warrior River
Cahaba River
Lay Lake
West Point Lake
Tallapoosa R.
Lake Martin
Coosa River
Black Belt
William "Bill" Dannelly Reservoir
Walter F. George Res.
Southern Red Hills
Tombigbee River
Alabama River
Conecuh River
Pea River
Choctawhatchee River
Chattahoochee River
ELEVATION
Feet
Meters
2,000
610
1,000
305
500
152
250
76
0
0
Below sea level
Below sea level
0
15
30 miles
0
15
30 kilometers
Projection: Albers Equal Area
Mobile River
Tensaw River
Escambia R.
Mobile Bay
Dauphin Island
Gulf of Mexico
88°W
87°W
86°W

Alabama: Political

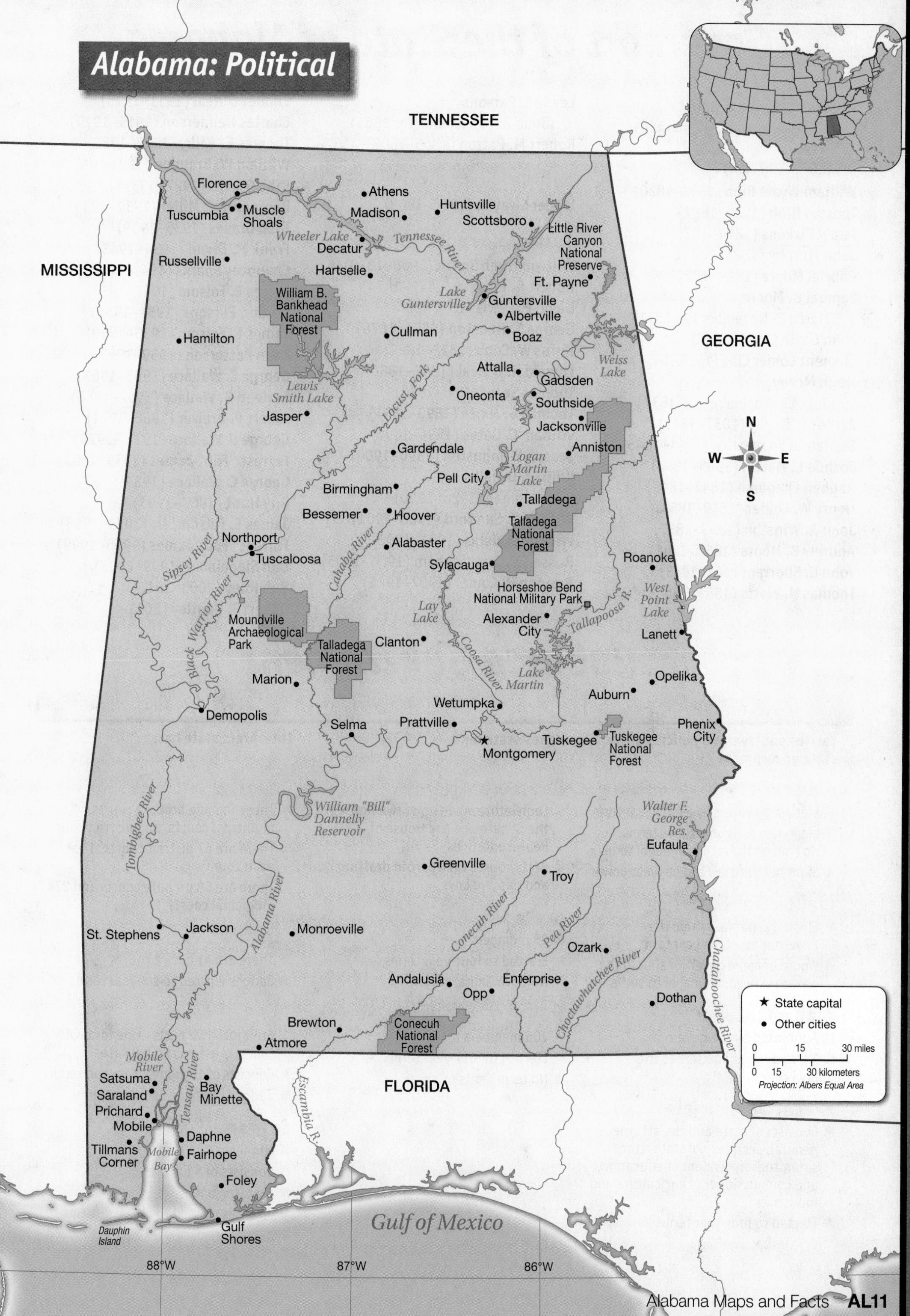
TENNESSEE
MISSISSIPPI
GEORGIA
FLORIDA
Gulf of Mexico
Florence
Tuscumbia
Muscle Shoals
Athens
Huntsville
Madison
Scottsboro
Little River Canyon National Preserve
Wheeler Lake
Decatur
Tennessee River
Russellville
Hartselle
Ft. Payne
William B. Bankhead National Forest
Lake Guntersville
Guntersville
Albertville
Cullman
Boaz
Hamilton
Attalla
Gadsden
Weiss Lake
Lewis Smith Lake
Locust Fork
Oneonta
Southside
Jasper
Jacksonville
Gardendale
Anniston
Logan Martin Lake
Pell City
Birmingham
Talladega
Bessemer
Hoover
Talladega National Forest
Northport
Tuscaloosa
Alabaster
Sipsey River
Cahaba River
Sylacauga
Roanoke
Horseshoe Bend National Military Park
West Point Lake
Black Warrior River
Moundville Archaeological Park
Lay Lake
Alexander City
Tallapoosa R.
Lanett
Clanton
Talladega National Forest
Coosa River
Lake Martin
Marion
Opelika
Auburn
Wetumpka
Demopolis
Selma
Prattville
Phenix City
Montgomery
Tuskegee
Tuskegee National Forest
Tombigbee River
William "Bill" Dannelly Reservoir
Walter F. George Res.
Eufaula
Greenville
Troy
Alabama River
Conecuh River
Pea River
Chattahoochee River
St. Stephens
Jackson
Monroeville
Ozark
Choctawhatchee River
Andalusia
Enterprise
Opp
Dothan
Brewton
Conecuh National Forest
Atmore
Mobile River
Tensaw River
Escambia R.
Satsuma
Saraland
Bay Minette
Prichard
Mobile
Daphne
Tillmans Corner
Mobile Bay
Fairhope
Foley
Dauphin Island
Gulf Shores
88°W
87°W
86°W
N
S
W
E
★ State capital
• Other cities
0 15 30 miles
0 15 30 kilometers
Projection: Albers Equal Area

Alabama Maps and Facts

Governors of the State of Alabama

Territorial Governor

William Wyatt Bibb (1817–1819)

State Governors

William Wyatt Bibb (1819–1820)
Thomas Bibb (1820–1821)
Israel Pickens (1821–1825)
John Murphy (1825–1829)
Gabriel Moore (1829–1831)
Samuel B. Moore (March 3–November 22, 1831)
John Gayle (1831–1835)
Clement Comer Clay (1835–1837)
Hugh McVay (July 17–November 30, 1837)
Arthur P. Bagby (1837–1841)
Benjamin Fitzpatrick (1841–1845)
Joshua L. Martin (1845–1847)
Reuben Chapman (1847–1849)
Henry W. Collier (1849–1853)
John A. Winston (1853–1857)
Andrew B. Moore (1857–1861)
John G. Shorter (1861–1863)
Thomas H. Watts (1863–1865)
Lewis E. Parsons (June 21–December 13, 1865)
Robert M. Patton (1865–1868)

Military Governor

Wager Swayne (1867–1868)

State Governors

William Hugh Smith (1868–1870)
Robert B. Lindsay (1872–1874)
David P. Lewis (1872–1874)
George S. Houston (1874–1878)
Rufus W. Cobb (1878–1882)
Edward A. O'Neal (1882–1886)
Thomas Seay (1886–1890)
Thomas G. Jones (1890–1894)
William C. Oates (1894–1896)
Joseph F. Johnston (1896–1900)
William D. Jelks (December 1–26, 1900)
William J. Samford (1900–1901)
William D. Jelks (1901–1907)
Russell M. Cunningham (1904–1905)
Braxton B. Comer (1907–1911)
Emmet O'Neal (1911–1915)
Charles Henderson (1915–1919)
Thomas E. Kilby (1919–1923)
William W. Brandon (1923–1927)
Bibb Graves (1927–1931)
Benjamin M. Miller (1931–1935)
Bibb Graves (1935–1939)
Frank M. Dixon (1939–1943)
Chauncey Sparks (1943–1947)
James E. Folsom (1947–1951)
Gordon Persons (1951–1955)
James E. Folsom (1955–1959)
John Patterson (1959–1963)
George C. Wallace (1963–1967)
Lurleen B. Wallace (1967–1968)
Albert P. Brewer (1968–1971)
George C. Wallace (1971 –1979)
Forrest "Fob" James (1979–1983)
George C. Wallace (1983–1987)
Guy Hunt (1987–1993)
James E. Folsom, Jr. (1993–1995)
Forrest "Fob" James (1995–1999)
Don Siegelman (1999–2003)
Bob Riley (2003–2011)
Robert J. Bentley (2011–)

Alabama Government

Executive Branch

Carries out laws and policies of state government

Governor

- Elected by voters to a four-year term
- Limited to two consecutive terms, but no limit on the total number of terms
- Signs bills into law and has veto power

Lieutenant Governor

- Elected separately from the Governor to a four-year term
- Would become governor should the governor become unable to serve

Alabama Cabinet

- Appointed by the governor
- Serve as chief advisors to the governor

Executive Officials

- Consists of state auditor, attorney general, secretary of state, treasurer, superintendent of education, and commissioner of agriculture and industries
- Elected to four-year terms

Legislative Branch

Makes state laws

Bicameral System

- Legislature made up of two houses, the Senate and the House of Representatives
- Both houses take part in drafting and passing laws

State Senate

- 35 members
- Elected to four-year terms
- No term limits

House of Representatives

- 105 members
- Elected to four-year terms
- No term limits

Judicial Branch

Interprets state laws

County Courts

- These include probate courts, municipal courts, and district courts
- There are 67 district courts, 1 for each county
- There are 68 probate courts and 274 municipal courts

Circuit Courts

- There are 41 circuit courts
- Judges elected to six-year terms

Appeals Courts

- Split into two parts—one for civil cases, one for criminal cases
- Consists of 10 judges, 5 for each court
- Judges elected to six-year terms

Supreme Court

- Highest state court
- Consists of 9 justices
- No term limits
- Justices elected to six-year terms
- Justices cannot seek re-election after age 70

Alabama State Facts

State amphibian	Red hills salamander
State bird	Yellowhammer
State flower	Camellia
State freshwater fish	Largemouth bass
State fruit	Blackberry
State game bird	Wild turkey
State gemstone	Star blue quartz
State insect	Monarch butterfly
State mammal	Black bear
State mascot and butterfly	Eastern tiger swallowtail
State mineral	Hematite
State nut	Pecan
State reptile	Alabama red-bellied turtle
State saltwater fish	Tarpon
State tree	Southern long-leaf pine
State wildflower	Oak-leaf hydrangea
Capital	Montgomery
Motto	"We Dare Maintain Our Rights"
Song	"Alabama"
Folk dance	Square dance
Year of statehood	1819
Highest natural point	2,407 feet (Mount Cheaha)
Total area	51,701 square miles
National rank in total area	29
Population (2011 estimate)	4,802,740
National rank in population	23
Most populous city	Birmingham
Most populous metropolitan area	Greater Birmingham area
Number of counties	67
Bordering states	Florida, Georgia, Mississippi, Tennessee

State flag

Monarch butterfly

Black bear

UNIT 1

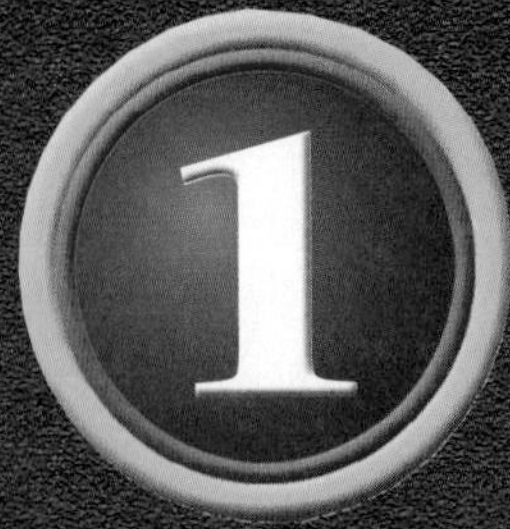

American Beginnings to 1783

CHAPTER 1
Three Worlds Meet
Beginnings to 1500

CHAPTER 2
The American Colonies Emerge
1492–1681

CHAPTER 3
The Colonies Come of Age
1650–1765

CHAPTER 4
The War for Independence
1765–1783

UNIT PROJECT

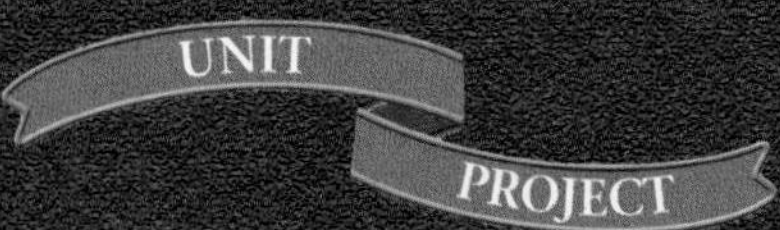

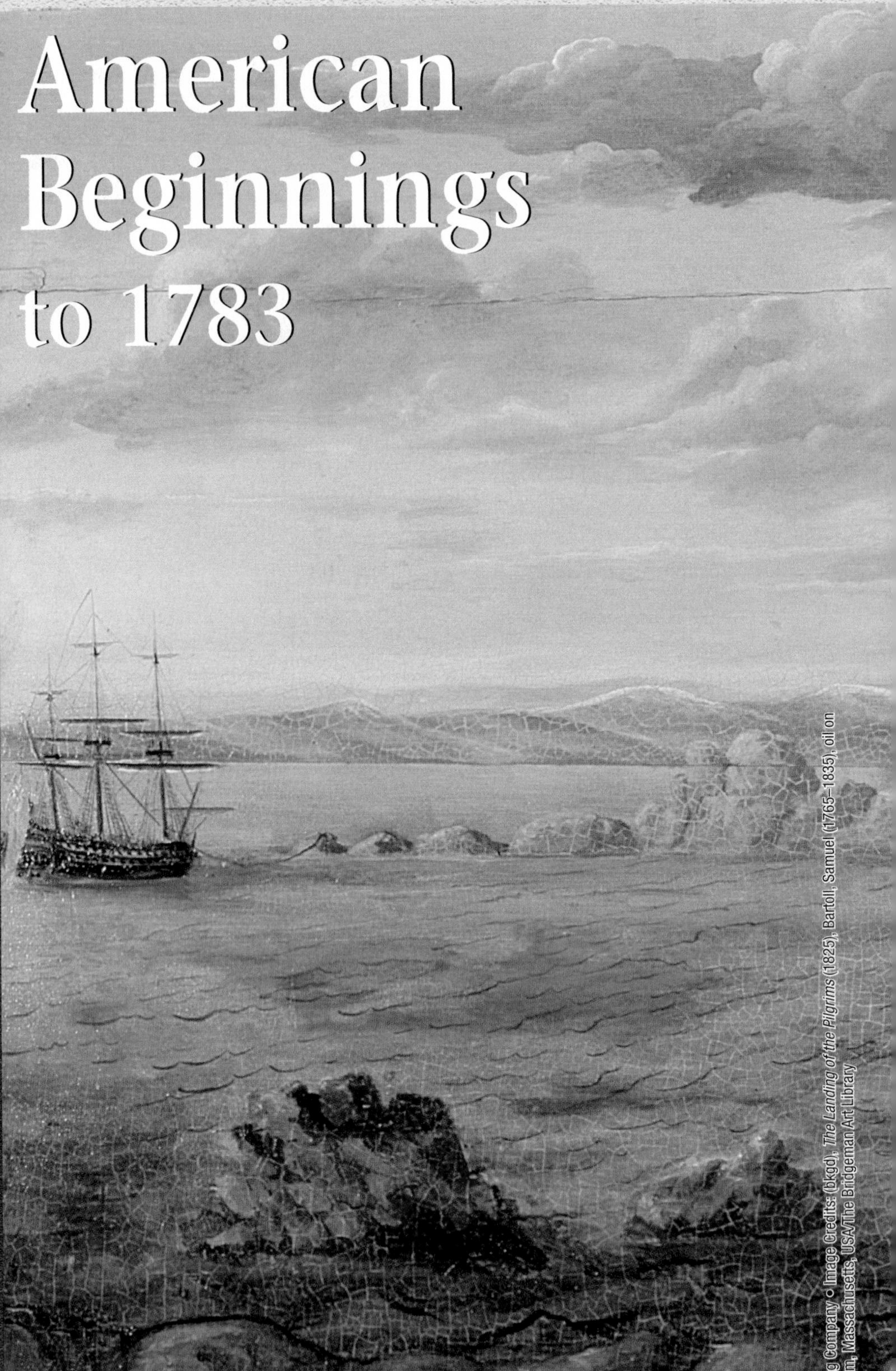

Letter to the Editor

As you read, look for an issue that interests you, such as the effect of colonization on Native Americans or the rights of American colonists. Write a letter to the editor in which you explain your views. Your letter should include reasons and facts.

The Landing of the Pilgrims, by Samuel Bartoll (1825)

1620
Dec 22

ALABAMA *Through the Colonial Era*

The area that is now Alabama has been home to Native American groups for thousands of years. Over time these peoples developed complex societies. During the Middle Woodland period (AD 1–500), for example, Native Americans constructed complicated burial mounds filled with artifacts. Late Woodland (AD 500–1000) peoples used arrows with stone points to hunt better and grew crops that could be stored to support a larger population. During the Mississippian period (AD 1000–1550), Native Americans in present-day Alabama formed larger communities, built walled towns, and established large trade networks.

Spanish explorer Hernando de Soto led an expedition through what is now Alabama in 1540.

Exploring Alabama

Europeans explored the land that is present-day Alabama in the 16th and 17th centuries but experienced conflicts with Native Americans and other difficulties. The first Europeans to set eyes on the land that is now Alabama were Spanish explorers in the early 1500s, but these explorers remained close to the coast. Hernando de Soto led the first extended European exploration in 1540. The Spaniards often fought with the Native Americans they encountered in their search for gold. In October 1540, de Soto's men met resistance from Native Americans led by Chief Tascaluza. Though many Spaniards were killed, the explorers defeated the Native Americans and set fire to their capital, Mabila.

Nearly two decades later, Tristán de Luna y Arellano led a Spanish expedition into Mobile Bay and north following the Alabama River. He established a settlement close to present-day Mobile, but a hurricane wrecked most of his vessels and supplies. After this, Spain showed little interest in the land that is present-day Alabama for more than a century until two more Spanish explorers came in the 1680s to counter French explorations and claims. Spain was unable to prevent the French from exploring and settling in what is now Alabama.

These mounds near Tuscaloosa are remains of the Mississippian culture that thrived in what is today Alabama between 500 and 1,000 years ago. Buildings and houses were built on the tops of the mounds.

European Rivals

Present-day Alabama then became a source of conflict between the British and French who were competing for land and power in North America. A French expedition under the command of Pierre Le Moyne d'Iberville explored the Gulf Coast by ship in 1699. An inland colony was established in 1702, but floods and attacks by Native Americans forced the French to move their settlement south in 1711. This settlement grew to become the city of Mobile. To balance the growing British presence in the Carolina colony and future Georgia colony, the French built Fort Toulouse in 1717 where the Coosa and Tallapoosa rivers meet, near what is now Montgomery.

The French maintained these colonial outposts through the first half of the 18th century. Following France's defeat in the French and Indian War (1754–1763), however, Britain claimed all French territories east of the Mississippi River, including what is now Alabama. The northern part was reserved for Native Americans by the Proclamation of 1763. The rest became known as British West Florida. In the following decade, the British sent several expeditions to survey their new possessions along the Gulf Coast. But the land of present-day Alabama did not remain in British hands for long.

Alabama during the Revolutionary War

The outbreak of the Revolutionary War in 1775 divided the Native Americans of what is now Alabama. The Cherokees, the Chickasaw, and most of the Choctaw supported and even fought for the British. The Catawba fought for the Patriots, but advancing Redcoats burned their villages and seized their cattle. Alabama's large Creek population did not take a unified stance during the war. Some helped the British, but most tried to stay out of the conflict, wanting to protect trade links to both sides.

Spanish forces invaded British West Florida in 1779. The outnumbered British force surrendered after a short campaign. Spanish troops next captured Pensacola, removing the British from the Gulf Coast. The Treaty of Paris ended the Revolutionary War in 1783 and gave most of the land that is now Alabama to the United States. Spain controlled Mobile until 1813, when it was captured by the United States during the War of 1812.

Alexander McGillivray, or Hoboi-Hili-Miko, led some Creeks to ally with Britain during the Revolutionary War. He later negotiated with Spanish and American leaders to preserve Creek lands in what is now Georgia, Florida, and Alabama.

Exploring Further...

Research the history of Alabama during the colonial era (1540–1783) and create a timeline of events. Your timeline should include major developments in the area, such as

- when the Europeans first explored Alabama.
- important expeditions in Alabama.
- major battles fought in the area.
- when control of the area changed hands.

THREE WORLDS MEET

Essential Question

How did the their convergence affect the cultures of North America, Africa, and Europe?

ALABAMA COURSE OF STUDY

1 Compare effects of economic, geographic, social, and political conditions before and after European explorations of the fifteenth through seventeenth centuries on Europeans, American colonists, Africans, and indigenous Americans.

- Describing the influence of the Crusades, Renaissance, and Reformation on European exploration.
- Analyzing the course of the Columbian Exchange for its impact on the global economy.
- Explaining triangular trade and the development of slavery in the colonies.

Native Americans watch for the arrival of a European ship.

AMERICAS

c. 20,000 B.C. Asian peoples begin migrating to America across the Beringia land bridge.

c. 5000 B.C. Corn is raised as a domesticated crop in central Mexico.

1200 B.C. Olmec society, which created this colossal stone head, develops in what is now southern Mexico.

500 B.C. Adena culture begins building large earthen mounds in what is now southern Ohio.

200 B.C.– A.D. 400 Hopewell culture, which created this mica bird claw, flourishes in the Midwest.

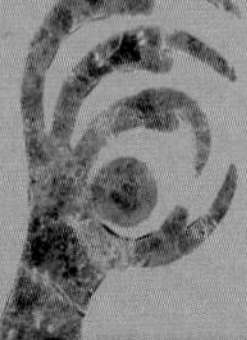

1200 B.C.* | A.D.* | 500

WORLD

1020 B.C. Israel becomes a kingdom.

753 B.C. Rome is founded.

622 Muhammad founds Islam.

* B.C. corresponds to B.C.E., or "before the common era."
A.D. corresponds to C.E., or "common era."

Image Credits: (bkgd) The Granger Collection, New York; 2 (bl), Anthropology Museum, Veracruz University, Jalapa, Mexico/Art Resource, New York; (br), ©Richard A. Cooke/Corbis

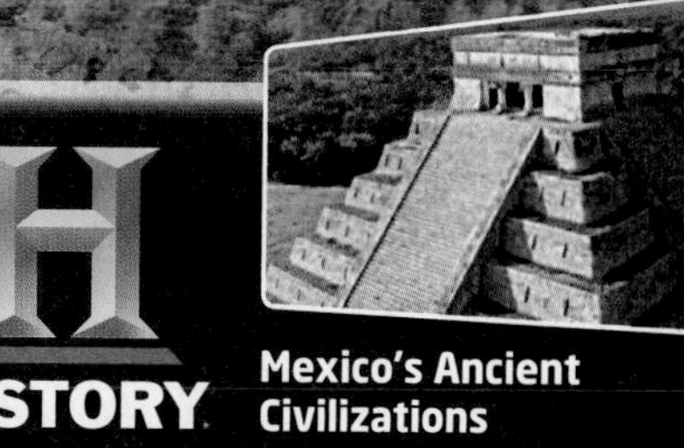

INTERACT
WITH HISTORY

You live on a Caribbean island in the 15th century. Your society hunts game freely, grows crops of great variety, and trades actively with nearby cultures. Now you sense that your world is about to change; the ships you see approaching are like nothing you have encountered before.

Explore the Issues

- How would you react to a people whose appearance and language are unlike anything you have ever known?
- What can happen when one culture imposes its values on another?

1000 Viking Leif Ericson reaches what is now Newfoundland.

1096 The Crusades begin.

1434 Portuguese begin West African slave trade.

1440 Johann Gutenberg develops printing press.

1492 Christopher Columbus first reaches America.

c. 1500 Iroquois League is formed.

1000 — 1500

Image Credits: (bkgd), The Granger Collection, New York; (br), *Portrait of a Man, said to be Christopher Columbus* (born about 1446, died 1506), (1519), Sebastiano del Piombo. Oil on canvas, 42" x 34 3/4", The Metropolitan Museum of Art, gift of J. Pierpont Morgan, 1900 (00.18.2). Photograph copyright ©1979 The Metropolitan Museum of Art; (bl), ©Leonard de Selva/Corbis

SECTION 1

Peopling the Americas

MAIN IDEA	WHY IT MATTERS NOW	Terms & Names
In ancient times, migrating peoples settled the Americas, where their descendants developed complex societies.	**Patterns of immigration have always shaped and continue to shape American history.**	**•nomadic •Olmec •Maya •Aztec •Inca •Hohokam •Anasazi •Adena •Hopewell •Mississippian**

One American's Story

hmhsocialstudies.com
TAKING NOTES

Use the graphic organizer online to take notes on the early civilizations of the Americas.

Thomas Canby, a writer for *National Geographic* magazine, spent a year with archaeologists as they searched for clues about the earliest Americans. As Canby watched the archaeologists unearthing fragile artifacts, a long-lost world came into sharper focus.

A PERSONAL VOICE THOMAS CANBY

"What a wild world it was! To see it properly, we must board a time machine and travel back into the Ice Age. The northern half of North America has vanished, buried beneath ice sheets two miles thick. Stretching south to Kentucky, they buckle earth's crust with their weight. . . . Animals grow oversize. . . . Elephant-eating jaguars stand as tall as lions, beavers grow as big as bears, South American sloths as tall as giraffes. With arctic cold pushing so far southward, walrus bask on Virginia beaches, and musk-oxen graze from Maryland to California."

—"The Search for the First Americans," *National Geographic*, Sept. 1979

Modern depiction of early Americans hunting the woolly mammoth around 20,000 B.C.

This was the world of the first Americans—people who migrated to the Americas from another continent. Centuries later, a different kind of immigration to the Americas would bring together people from three complex societies: the Native American, the European, and the West African. The interaction of these three cultures helped create the present-day culture of the United States. However, it is with the ancient peoples of the Americas that the story of America actually begins.

Ancient Peoples Come to the Americas

The first Americans may have arrived as early as 22,000 years ago. Ice Age glaciers had frozen vast quantities of the earth's water, lowering sea levels enough to expose a land bridge between Asia and Alaska. Ancient hunters trekked across the frozen land, now called Beringia, into North America.

HUNTING AND GATHERING Experts suspect that most of these ancient explorers came by foot. Some groups may have edged down the Pacific coast in boats fashioned from the bones and hides of animals—boats that are much like the kayaks used by modern-day Inuit.

The evidence suggests that the earliest Americans were big-game hunters. Their most challenging and rewarding prey was the woolly mammoth, which provided food, clothing, and bones for making shelters and tools.

As the Ice Age ended around 12,000 to 10,000 years ago, this hunting way of life also ended. Temperatures warmed, glaciers melted, and sea levels rose once again. Travel to the Americas by foot ceased as the ancient land bridge disappeared below the Bering Sea.

Over time, people switched to hunting smaller game, fishing, and gathering nuts, berries, and fruit along with grains, beans, and squash. While many ancient groups established settlements in North America, others continued south through what is now Mexico into South America. Wherever they went, the first Americans developed ways of life to suit their surroundings.

Hunters roaming over 10,000 years ago in what is now southern Arizona may have used this large spearhead to kill a woolly mammoth.

AGRICULTURE DEVELOPS Between 10,000 and 5,000 years ago, a revolution quietly took place in what is now central Mexico. There, people began to plant crops. Some archaeologists believe that maize (corn) was the first plant that ancient Americans developed for human use. Other plants followed—gourds, pumpkins, peppers, beans, and more. Eventually, agricultural techniques spread throughout the Americas.

MAIN IDEA

Analyzing Effects

A What were the effects of agriculture on the hunting and gathering peoples of the Americas?

The introduction of agriculture brought tremendous change. Agriculture made it possible for people to remain in one place and to store surplus food. As their surplus increased, people had more time to develop other skills. From this agricultural base evolved larger, more stable societies and increasingly complex cultures. However, some Native American cultures never adopted agriculture and remained **nomadic,** moving from place to place in search of food and water, while others mixed nomadic and non-nomadic lifestyles. A

Complex Societies Flourish in the Americas

Around 3,000 years ago, the first Americans began to form larger communities and build flourishing civilizations. A closer look at the more prominent of these societies reveals the diversity and complexity of the early American world.

Today, Alaska and Siberia are separated by the Bering Strait, a strip of sea only 55 miles wide. During the last Ice Age, glaciers moved south from the North Pole, freezing up the waters of the Bering Sea and exposing more land. This formed the Beringia land bridge, over which the earliest Americans probably migrated from Asia.

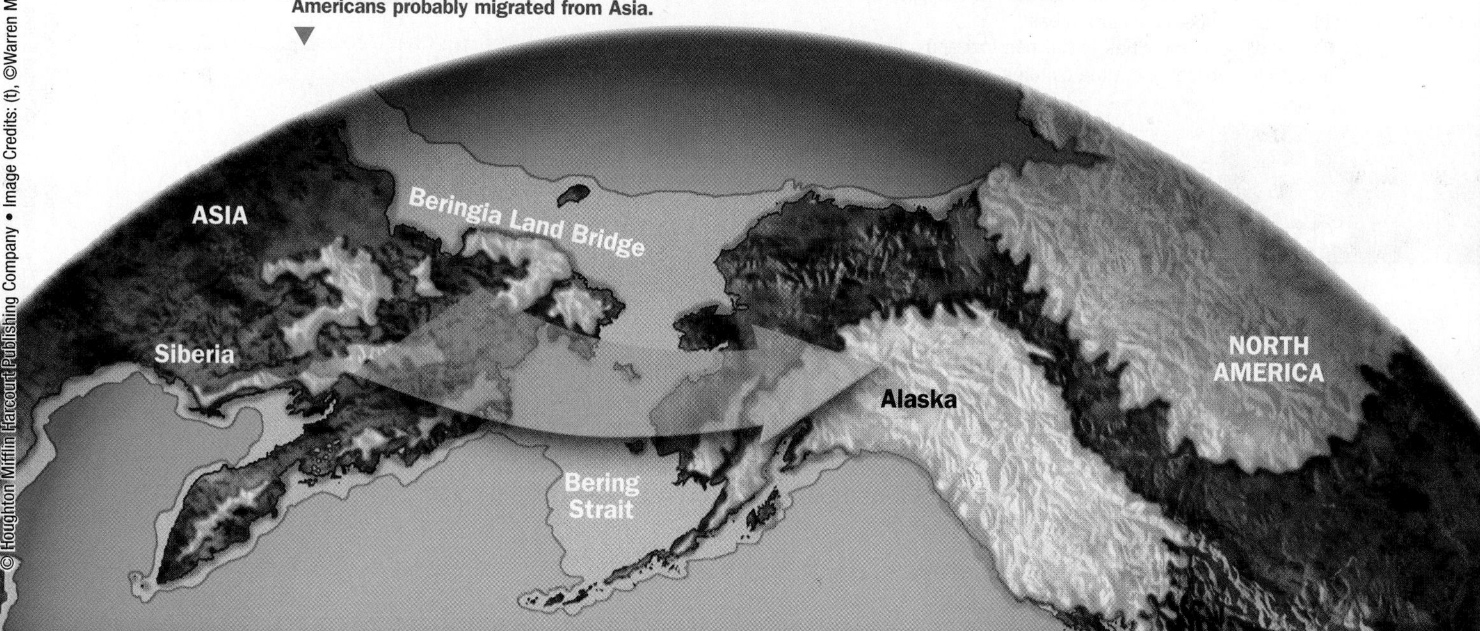

Early North American Cultures

hmhsocialstudies.com INTERACTIVE MAP

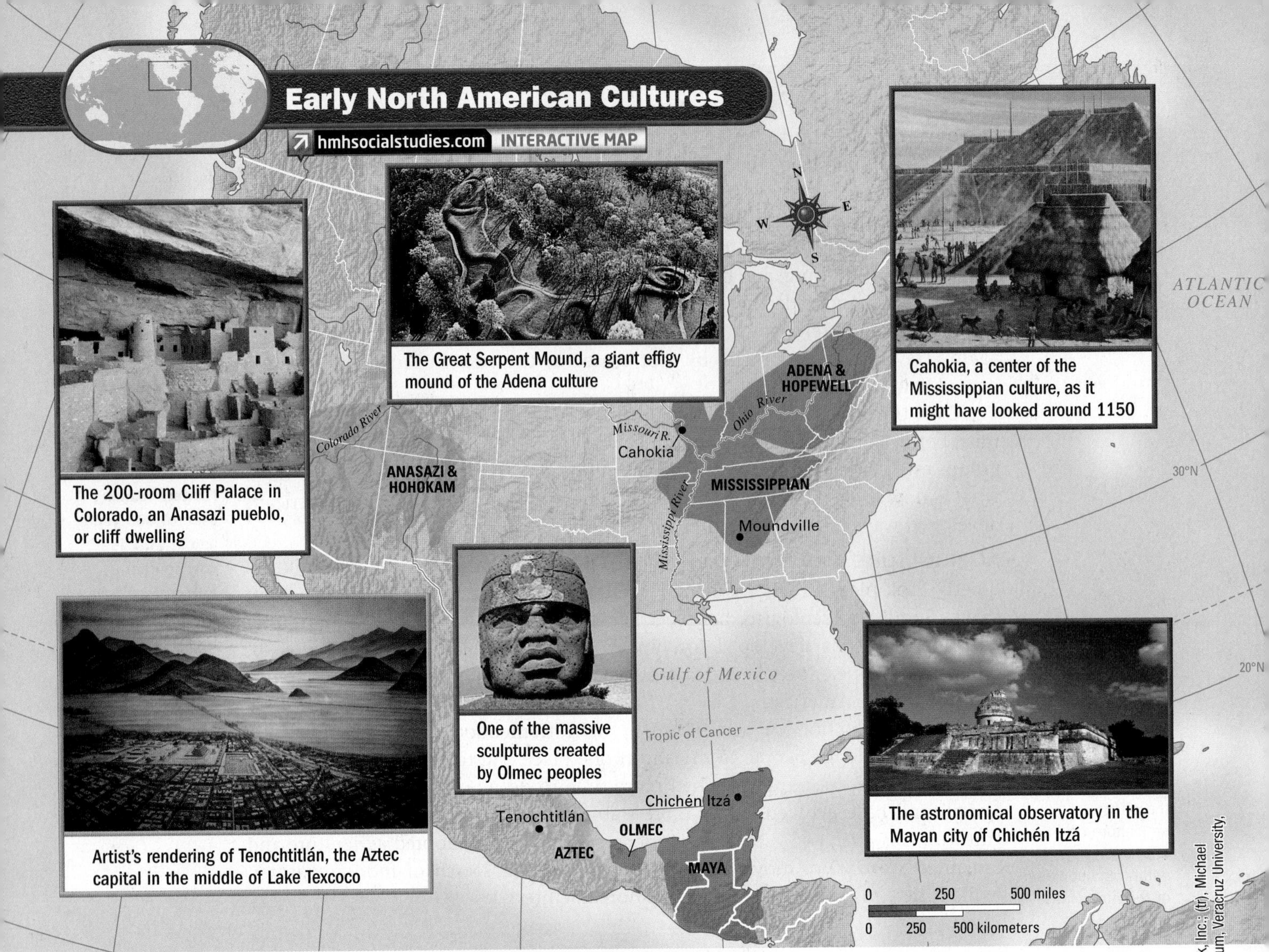

The 200-room Cliff Palace in Colorado, an Anasazi pueblo, or cliff dwelling

The Great Serpent Mound, a giant effigy mound of the Adena culture

Cahokia, a center of the Mississippian culture, as it might have looked around 1150

One of the massive sculptures created by Olmec peoples

Artist's rendering of Tenochtitlán, the Aztec capital in the middle of Lake Texcoco

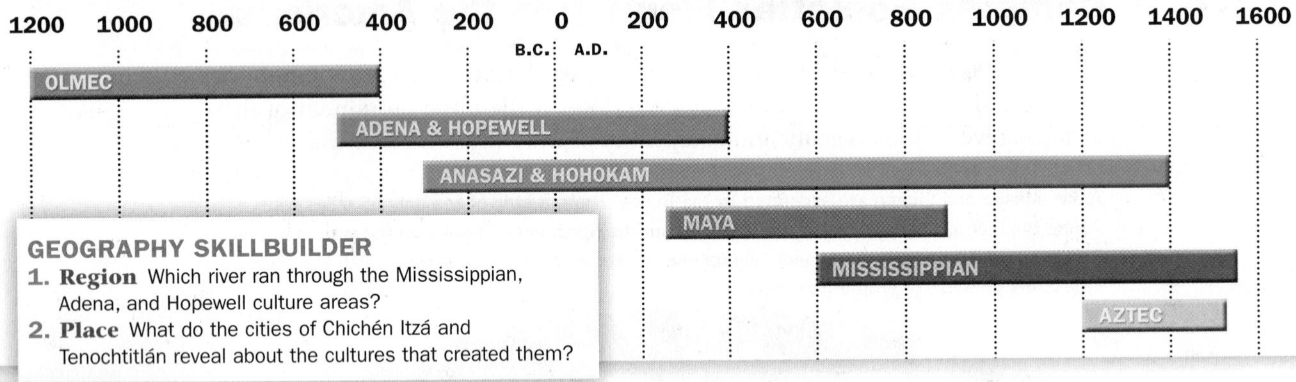

The astronomical observatory in the Mayan city of Chichén Itzá

GEOGRAPHY SKILLBUILDER

1. **Region** Which river ran through the Mississippian, Adena, and Hopewell culture areas?
2. **Place** What do the cities of Chichén Itzá and Tenochtitlán reveal about the cultures that created them?

VIDEO
Secret Mounds of Pre-Historic America

hmhsocialstudies.com

EMPIRES OF MIDDLE AND SOUTH AMERICA Archaeologists believe that the first empire of the Americas emerged as early as 1200 B.C. in what is now southern Mexico. There the **Olmec** peoples created a thriving civilization in the humid rain forest along the coast of the Gulf of Mexico. Other civilizations appeared in the wake of the Olmec's mysterious collapse around 400 B.C. These included the **Maya,** who built a dynamic culture in Guatemala and the Yucatán Peninsula between A.D. 250 and 900, and the **Aztec,** who swept into the Valley of Mexico in the 1200s.

In South America the most prominent of these empire builders were the **Inca**, who around A.D. 1200 created a glittering empire that stretched nearly 2,500 miles along the mountainous western coast of South America.

MAIN IDEA

Summarizing
B What were some of the achievements of the early civilizations of the Americas?

These empires' achievements rivaled those of ancient cultures in other parts of the world. The peoples of these American empires built great cities and ceremonial centers, some with huge palaces, temple-topped pyramids, and central plazas. To record their histories, some of these civilizations invented forms of glyph writing—using symbols or images to express words and ideas. **B**

ANCIENT DESERT FARMERS As early as 3,000 years ago, several North American groups, including the **Hohokam** and the **Anasazi,** introduced crops into the arid deserts of the Southwest. Later, between 300 B.C. and A.D. 1400, each group established its own civilization. The Hohokam settled in the valleys of the Salt and Gila rivers in what is now central Arizona. The Anasazi took to the mesa tops, cliff sides, and canyon bottoms of the Four Corners region—an area where the present-day states of Utah, Colorado, Arizona, and New Mexico meet.

MOUND BUILDERS To the east of the Mississippi River, in a region extending from the Great Lakes to the Gulf of Mexico, another series of complex societies developed. There the **Adena,** the **Hopewell,** and the **Mississippian** societies excelled at trade and at building. Some Adena and Hopewell structures consisted of huge burial mounds filled with finely crafted objects. Other mounds were sculpted into effigies, or likenesses, of animals so large that they can be seen clearly only from the air. People of the Mississippian culture constructed gigantic pyramidal mounds.

Although societies such as the Mississippian and the Aztec still flourished when Christopher Columbus reached American shores in 1492, others had long since disappeared. Despite their fate, these early peoples were the ancestors of the many Native American groups that inhabited North America on the eve of its encounter with the European world.

HISTORICAL SPOTLIGHT

THE "OTHER" PYRAMIDS

The stone pyramids of Egypt, which were used as elaborate tombs for Egyptian kings more than 4,000 years ago, are some of today's most famous structures. However, they were not the only pyramids to tower over the ancient world.

On the American side of the Atlantic, the Maya built giant flat-topped pyramids with stairs leading to rooftop temples, where Mayan priests performed religious ceremonies.

Farther north, at Cahokia, in what is now Illinois, people of the Mississippian culture constructed more than 100 massive earthen mounds. The mounds served as tombs, temples, and foundations for elaborate homes. The largest of these mounds is Monk's Mound, which is 100 feet high and covers about 16 acres at its base.

SECTION 1 ASSESSMENT

1. **TERMS & NAMES** For each term or name, write a sentence explaining its significance.
   - **nomadic**
   - **Olmec**
   - **Maya**
   - **Aztec**
   - **Inca**
   - **Hohokam**
   - **Anasazi**
   - **Adena**
   - **Hopewell**
   - **Mississippian**

MAIN IDEA

2. **TAKING NOTES**
In a chart like the one below, list the early civilizations of the Americas. Include the approximate dates they flourished and their locations.

Civilization	Dates	Location

What are some similarities that you have noticed among these early civilizations?

CRITICAL THINKING

3. **ANALYZING**
How did the development of agriculture affect ancient societies in the Americas?

4. **EVALUATING**
Evaluate the achievements of the ancient cultures of the Americas. Which single accomplishment do you find most remarkable and why?

5. **DRAWING CONCLUSIONS**
Which ancient American empire do you think was most advanced? Support your choice with details from the text. **Think About:**
   - the cultural achievements of each empire
   - the characteristics of modern civilizations

SECTION 2

North American Societies Around 1492

MAIN IDEA	WHY IT MATTERS NOW	Terms & Names
The varied landscapes of North America encouraged the diversity of Native American cultures.	Many modern Native American groups maintain ancient customs of their respective cultures.	• Kashaya Pomo • Kwakiutl • Pueblo • Iroquois • kinship • division of labor

One American's Story

hmhsocialstudies.com
TAKING NOTES
Use the graphic organizer online to take notes about North America's diverse societies.

Essie Parrish, a Native American storyteller and medicine woman, kept alive stories from a time when her people, the **Kashaya Pomo,** flourished along the northern California coast. She invited Robert Oswalt, an anthropologist, to time-travel with her to the 1540s. As Parrish spoke, the centuries rolled back.

A Personal Voice ESSIE PARRISH

> **"In the old days, before the white people came up here, there was a boat sailing on the ocean from the south. Because before that . . . [the Kashaya Pomo] had never seen a boat, they said, 'Our world must be coming to an end. Couldn't we do something? This big bird floating on the ocean is from somewhere, probably from up high. . . .' [T]hey promised Our Father [a feast] saying that destruction was upon them.**
>
> **When they had done so, they watched [the ship] sail way up north and disappear. . . . They were saying that nothing had happened to them—the big bird person had sailed northward without doing anything—because of the promise of a feast. . . . Consequently they held a feast and a big dance."**
>
> —quoted in *Kashaya Texts*

Dressed for a ceremony in the 1950s, spiritual leader Essie Parrish wears a feathered headdress and holds two bead-covered staffs.

The event became part of the Kashaya Pomo's oral history. Stories like this have provided us with a broad picture of the Native American world before it came into contact with the world of European explorers and settlers.

Native Americans Live in Diverse Societies

The native groups of North America were as diverse as the environments in which they lived. The North American continent provided for many different ways of life, from nomadic to the kind of fixed, nonmigratory life of farming communities.

MAIN IDEA

Making Inferences
A How might California's varied landscapes have encouraged diverse ways of life?

CALIFORNIA Not one land, but many lands—that's how the Kashaya Pomo and other native peoples regarded the region that is now California. The land has a long coastline, a lush northwestern rain forest, and a parched southern desert.

The peoples of California adapted to these diverse settings. The Kashaya Pomo hunted waterfowl with slingshots and nets. To the north, the Yurok and Hupa searched the forests for acorns and fished in mountain streams. A

NORTHWEST COAST The waterways and forests of the northwest coast sustained large communities year-round. The sea was of prime importance. On a coastline that stretched from what is now southern Alaska to northern California, peoples such as the **Kwakiutl** (kwä′kē-o͞ot′l), Nootka, and Haida collected shellfish from the beaches and hunted the ocean for whales, sea otters, and seals.

Peoples such as the Kwakiutl decorated masks and boats with magnificent totems, symbols of the ancestral spirits that guided each family. Kwakiutl families also displayed their histories on huge totem poles set in front of their cedar-plank houses. A family's totems announced its wealth and status.

Leading Kwakiutl families also organized potlatches, elaborate ceremonies in which they gave away large quantities of their possessions. A family's reputation depended upon the size of its potlatch—that is, on how much wealth it gave away. A family might spend up to 12 years planning the event.

SOUTHWEST In the dry Southwest, the Pima and Pueblo tribes, descendants of the Hohokam and Anasazi, lived in a harsh environment. By 1300, the **Pueblo** and a related tribe, the Hopi, had left the cliff houses of their Anasazi ancestors. The Pueblo built new settlements near waterways such as the Rio Grande, where they could irrigate their farms. However, the Hopi and the Acoma continued to live near the cliffs and developed irrigation systems.

Vocabulary
adobe: a sun-dried brick of clay and straw

People lived in multistory houses made of adobe or stone and grew corn, beans, melons, and squash. Like their ancestors, they built underground kivas, or ceremonial chambers, for religious ceremonies and councils.

Science & Technology

FORENSIC RECONSTRUCTIONS

Artists are now able to recreate the facial features of ancient peoples. The appearance of Native Americans who died sometime between A.D. 1000 and 1400 have recently been reconstructed from skeletal remains. These remains, removed from a burial site in Virginia, have since been returned to the Monacan tribe. The reconstructions bear a remarkable resemblance to modern Monacans.

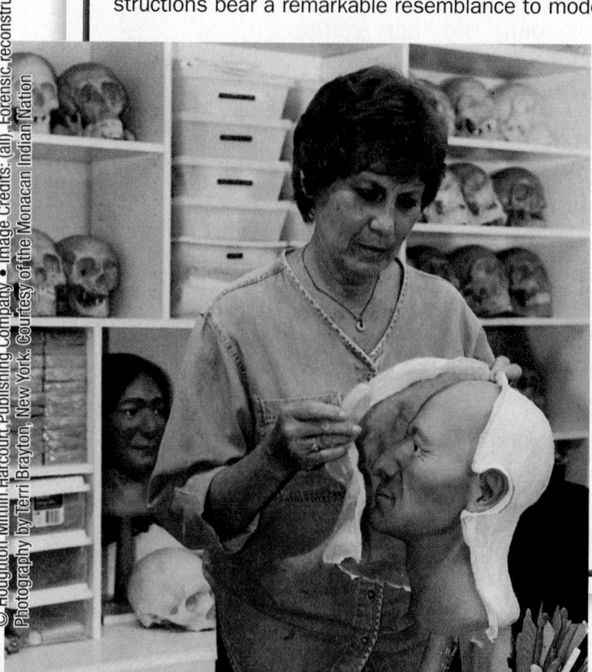

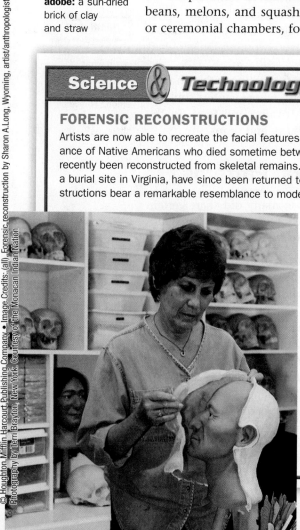

◀ The forensic artist first makes a plaster cast from the original skull. Then the artist uses clay to build up the facial features. Finally, the artist individualizes the head, based on clues about the subject's weight, muscularity, and environment.

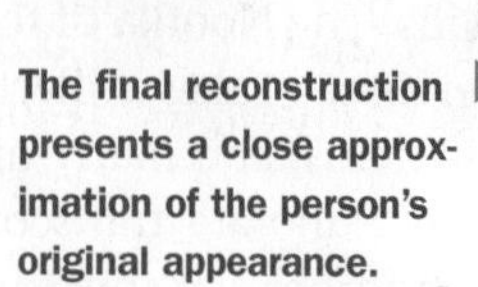

The final reconstruction presents a close approximation of the person's original appearance. ▶

SKILLBUILDER Interpreting Visual Sources
1. What strikes you most about these reconstructed faces?
2. How might forensic reconstructions contribute to our understanding of the past?

SEE SKILLBUILDER HANDBOOK, PAGE R23.

The lyrics to the ritual songs they sang may have resembled the ones recalled by a Hopi chief named Lololomai at the start of the 1900s. "This is the song of the men from my kiva," Lololomai explained. "It tells how in my kiva the chief and his men are praying to make the corn to grow next year for all the people."

A PERSONAL VOICE LOLOLOMAI

"**Thus we, thus we**
The night along,
With happy hearts
Wish well one another.

In the chief's kiva
They, the fathers . . .
Plant the double ear—
Plant the perfect double corn-ear.
So the fields shall shine
With tassels white of perfect corn-ears.

Hither to them, hither come,
Rain that stands and cloud that rushes!"

—quoted in *The Indians' Book*

This kachina doll represented the corn spirit in Hopi religious ceremonies.

EASTERN WOODLANDS The landscape of the Southwest contrasted sharply with the woodlands east of the Mississippi River. Here, hardwood forests stretched from the Great Lakes and the St. Lawrence River in the north to the Gulf of Mexico in the south.

The tribes that lived in the Eastern Woodlands had much in common. Native peoples like the **Iroquois** (ĭr′ə-kwoi′) built villages in forest clearings and blended agriculture with hunting and gathering. They traveled by foot or by canoe. Because of the vast supply of trees, most groups used woodworking tools to craft everything from snowshoes to canoes.

The peoples of the Eastern Woodlands also differed from one another in their languages, customs, and environments. In the Northeast, where winters could be long and harsh, people relied on wild animals for clothing and food. In the warmer Southeast, groups grew such crops as corn, squash, and beans. B

MAIN IDEA

Contrasting

B In what ways did food production differ among Native American societies?

Native Americans Share Cultural Patterns

Although no two Native American societies were alike, many did share certain cultural traits. Patterns of trade, attitudes toward land use, and certain religious beliefs and social values were common to many cultures.

TRADING NETWORKS Trade was one of the biggest factors in bringing Native American peoples into contact with one another. As tribes established permanent settlements, many of these settlements became well known for specific products or skills. The Nootka of the Northwest Coast mastered whaling. The Ojibwa of the upper Great Lakes collected wild rice. The Taos of the Southwest made pottery. These items, and many more, were traded both locally and long-distance.

An elaborate transcontinental trading network enabled one group to trade with another without direct contact. Traders passed along items from far-off, unfamiliar places. Intermediaries carried goods hundreds and sometimes thousands of miles from their source. So extensive was the network of forest trails and river roads that an English sailor named David Ingram claimed in 1568 to have walked along Native American trade routes all the way from Mexico to the Atlantic Coast. C

MAIN IDEA

Forming Generalizations

C In what ways did trade link Native Americans?

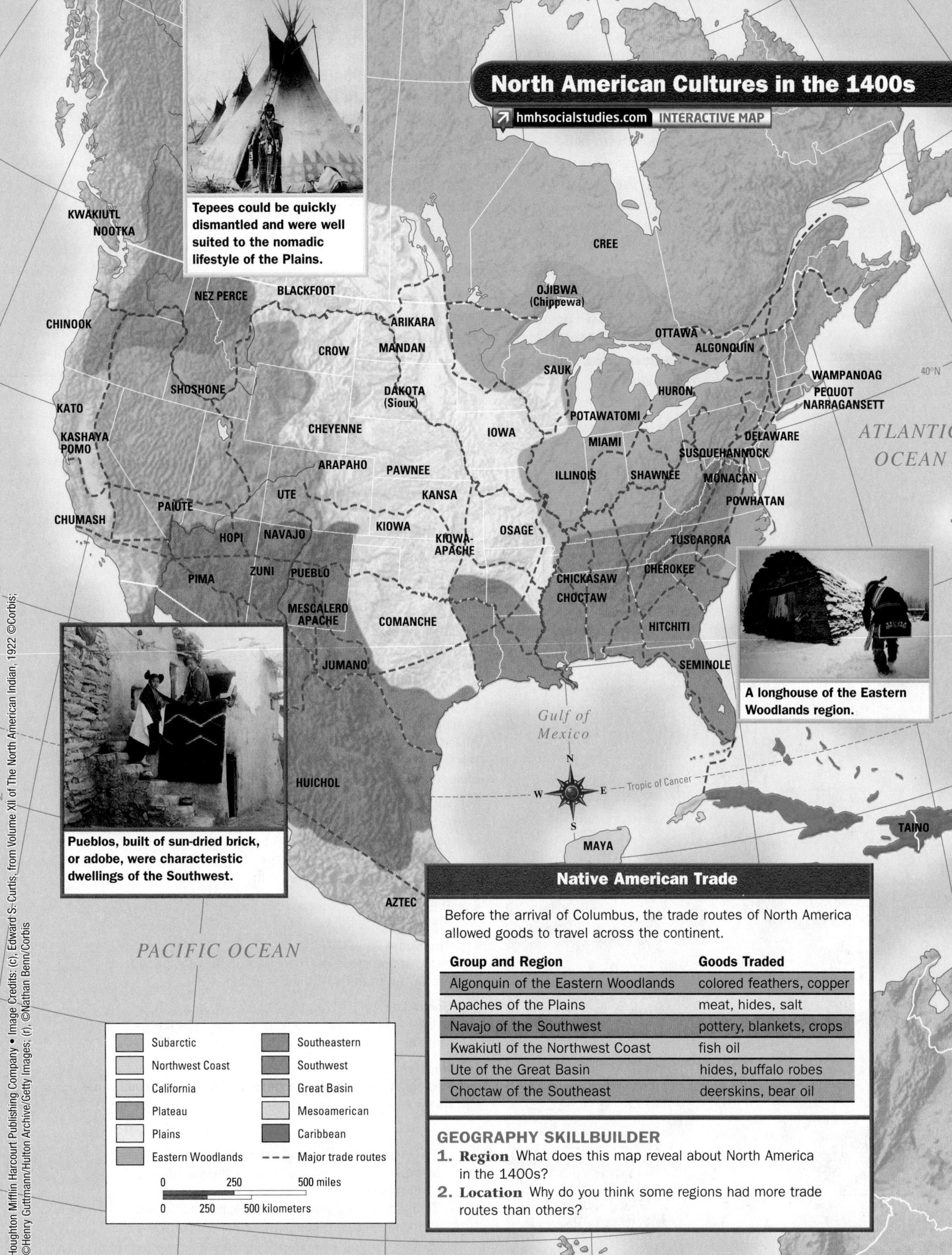

Tepees could be quickly dismantled and were well suited to the nomadic lifestyle of the Plains.

Pueblos, built of sun-dried brick, or adobe, were characteristic dwellings of the Southwest.

A longhouse of the Eastern Woodlands region.

Native American Trade

Before the arrival of Columbus, the trade routes of North America allowed goods to travel across the continent.

Group and Region	Goods Traded
Algonquin of the Eastern Woodlands	colored feathers, copper
Apaches of the Plains	meat, hides, salt
Navajo of the Southwest	pottery, blankets, crops
Kwakiutl of the Northwest Coast	fish oil
Ute of the Great Basin	hides, buffalo robes
Choctaw of the Southeast	deerskins, bear oil

GEOGRAPHY SKILLBUILDER

1. **Region** What does this map reveal about North America in the 1400s?
2. **Location** Why do you think some regions had more trade routes than others?

LAND USE Native Americans traded many things, but land was not one of them. They regarded the land as the source of life, not as a commodity to be sold. "We cannot sell the lives of men and animals," said one Blackfoot chief in the 1800s, "therefore we cannot sell this land." This attitude would lead to many clashes with the Europeans, who believed in private ownership of land.

Vocabulary
commodity: an article of trade or commerce

Native Americans disturbed the land only for the most important activities, such as food gathering or farming. A female shaman, or priestess, from the Wintu of California expressed this age-old respect for the land as she spoke to anthropologist Dorothy Lee.

A PERSONAL VOICE WINTU WOMAN

> **"When we dig roots, we make little holes. When we build houses, we make little holes. . . . We shake down acorns and pinenuts. We don't chop down the trees. We only use dead wood [for fires]. . . . But the white people plow up the ground, pull down the trees, [and. . . the] tree says, 'Don't. I am sore. Don't hurt me.'"**
>
> —quoted in *Freedom and Culture*

RELIGIOUS BELIEFS Nearly all Native Americans thought of the natural world as filled with spirits. Past generations remained alive to guide the living. Every object—both living and non-living—possessed a voice that might be heard if one listened closely. "I hear what the ground says," remarked Young Chief of the Cayuses, who lived in what is now Washington and Oregon, in 1855. "The ground says, 'It is the Great Spirit that placed me here.' The Great Spirit tells me to take care of the Indians. . . " Some cultures believed in one supreme being, known as "Great Spirit," "Great Mystery," "the Creative Power," or "the Creator."

Native American Village Life

John White, one of the first English colonists to arrive in North America, made several drawings of Native American life in the Chesapeake region in 1585. The engraving shown here was copied from White's original drawing and published in 1590. The image shows the village life of the Secotan people, who lived near Roanoke Island, North Carolina.

A Agriculture
A Secotan guards the ripened corn crop to keep away hungry birds and animals. A tobacco field appears to the left of this field, and other corn fields and a pumpkin patch appear below it.

B Hunting
Men hunt for deer.

C The Home
Huts, whose sides can be rolled up for ventilation, are woven from thick plant stems.

D Social Life
Villagers prepare for a community feast. The fire for this feast appears up the path in the heart of the village.

E Religion
Residents dance around a circle of idols in a religious ceremony. Across the main path lies a prayer circle with fire.

SKILLBUILDER Analyzing Primary Sources
1. What Native American work activities are shown in this drawing?
2. Based on the drawing, what appear to be two significant daily concerns of the Secotan?

SOCIAL ORGANIZATION Bonds of **kinship,** or strong ties among family members, ensured the continuation of tribal customs. Elders instructed the young. In exchange, the young honored the elders and their departed ancestors.

The tasks assigned to men and women varied with each society. Among the Iroquois and Hopi, for example, women owned the household items, and families traced their ancestry from mother to grandmother to great-grandmother, and so on. In other Native American cultures, men owned the family possessions and traced their ancestry through their father's kin.

The **division of labor**—the assignment of tasks according to gender, age, or status—formed the basis of social order. Among the Kwakiutl, for example, slaves performed the most menial jobs, while nobles ensured that Kwakiutl law was obeyed.

The basic unit of organization among all Native American groups was the family, which included aunts, uncles, cousins, and other relatives. Some tribes further organized the families into clans, or groups of families descended from a common ancestor. Among the Iroquois, for example, members of a clan often lived together in huge bark-covered longhouses. All families participated in community decision making.

Not all Native American groups lived together for long periods of time. In societies in which people hunted and gathered, groups broke into smaller bands for hunting. On the plains, for example, families searched the grasslands for buffalo. Groups like these reunited only to celebrate important occasions. D

MAIN IDEA

Comparing
D What similarities and differences existed among Native American social structures?

In the late 1400s, on the eve of the encounter with the Europeans, the rhythms of Native American life were well-established. No one could have imagined the changes that were about to transform the Native American societies.

NOW & THEN

SCHEMITZUN

The sights and sounds of the Native American world come alive each August for several days on the Connecticut reservation of Mashantucket. Here, performers and visitors from nearly 500 Native American tribes meet under a massive tent for Schemitzun, the "World Championship of Song and Dance."

Schemitzun was traditionally a dance to celebrate the corn harvest. Today it has become an occasion for Native Americans to meet, share their art and culture, and celebrate their heritage.

SECTION 2 ASSESSMENT

1. **TERMS & NAMES** For each term or name, write a sentence explaining its significance.
   - **Kashaya Pomo**
   - **Kwakiutl**
   - **Pueblo**
   - **Iroquois**
   - **kinship**
   - **division of labor**

MAIN IDEA

2. **TAKING NOTES**
Copy an outline of North America like the one below. Then shade in the areas belonging to each of the following Native American cultures: Northwest Coast, Southwest, and Eastern Woodlands.

Describe how each society adapted to its environment.

CRITICAL THINKING

3. **COMPARING**
In your opinion, were the differences between Native American groups greater than their similarities? Cite specific examples to support your answer. **Think About:**
   - adaptation to physical settings
   - the role of tradition
   - the variety of goods and languages encountered in trading

4. **SYNTHESIZING**
Describe the relationship between the individual and his or her social group in Native American society. Use details from the text to support your description.

5. **HYPOTHESIZING**
Why did Native American societies not wish to buy and sell land?

SECTION 3

West African Societies Around 1492

MAIN IDEA	WHY IT MATTERS NOW	Terms & Names
West Africa in the 1400s was home to a variety of peoples and cultures.	Modern African Americans have strong ancestral ties to the people of West Africa.	• Islam • plantation • Songhai • savanna • Benin • Kongo • lineage

One African's Story

hmhsocialstudies.com TAKING NOTES

Use the graphic organizer online to take notes on the geography, climate, and culture of West Africa.

Leo Africanus was about 18 when he laid eyes on the renowned city of Timbuktu in the West African empire of Songhai. A Muslim born in Granada (in modern Spain) and raised in North Africa, Leo Africanus visited the city with his uncle, who was on a diplomatic mission to the emperor of Songhai. At the time of their journey in 1513, Songhai was one of the largest kingdoms in the world, and the emperor, Askia Muhammad, was rich and powerful. Leo Africanus later described the bustling prosperity of Timbuktu and its lively intellectual climate.

A PERSONAL VOICE LEO AFRICANUS

"Here are many shops of . . . merchants, and especially such as weave linen and cotton cloth. And hither do the Barbary [North African] merchants bring cloth of Europe. . . . Here are great store of doctors, judges, priests, and other learned men, that are bountifully maintained at the king's cost and charges, and hither are brought divers manuscripts or written books out of Barbary, which are sold for more money than any other merchandise."

—*The History and Description of Africa Done into English* by John Pory

These ancient boards from Africa contain sayings from the Qur'an, the holy scripture of Islam.

Leo Africanus provides a glimpse of 16th-century West African life. From this region of Africa, and particularly from the West and West-Central coastal areas, would come millions of people brought to the Americas as slaves. These people would have a tremendous impact on American history and culture.

West Africa Connects with the Wider World

Although geographically isolated from Europe and Asia, West Africa by the 1400s had long been connected to the wider world through trade. For centuries, trade had brought into the region new goods, new ideas, and new beliefs, including those of the Islamic religion. Then, in the mid-1400s, the level of interaction with the world increased with the arrival of European traders on the West African coast.

THE SAHARA HIGHWAY The Timbuktu that Leo Africanus described was the hub of a well-established trading network that connected most of West Africa to the coastal ports of North Africa, and through these ports to markets in Europe and Asia. Leo Africanus and his uncle reached Timbuktu by following ancient trade routes across the Sahara desert. At the crossroads of this trade, cities such as Timbuktu, Gao, and Jenne became busy commercial centers. The empires that controlled these cities and trade routes grew wealthy and powerful.

Traders from North Africa brought more than goods across the Sahara—they also brought their Islamic faith. **Islam,** founded in Arabia in 622 by Muhammad, spread quickly across the Middle East and North Africa. By the 1200s, Islam had become the court religion of the large empire of Mali, and it was later embraced by the rulers of Songhai, including Askia Muhammad. Despite its official status, however, Islam did not yet have much influence over the daily lives and religious practices of most West Africans in the late 1400s. (A)

> **MAIN IDEA**
> **Making Inferences**
> (A) Why would trade have helped spread the Islamic faith?

> **HISTORICAL SPOTLIGHT**
> **ISLAM**
> Like Judaism and Christianity, Islam is monotheistic, or based on the belief in one God. Islam was founded by Muhammad (about A.D. 570–632), who believed the angel Gabriel appeared to him and told him to preach a new religion to the Arabs. This religion became known as Islam, which in Arabic means "surrender" [to Allah]. (Allah is the Arabic name for God.) The followers of Islam are called Muslims, "those who submit to God's will."
> The words that Muhammad claimed he had received from God were recorded in the Qur'an, the holy book of Islam.

THE PORTUGUESE ARRIVE The peoples of West Africa and Europe knew little of each other before the 1400s. This situation began to change as Portuguese mariners made trading contacts along the West African coast. By the 1470s, Portuguese traders had established an outpost on the West African coast near the large Akan goldfields, the source of much West African gold. Other trading outposts soon

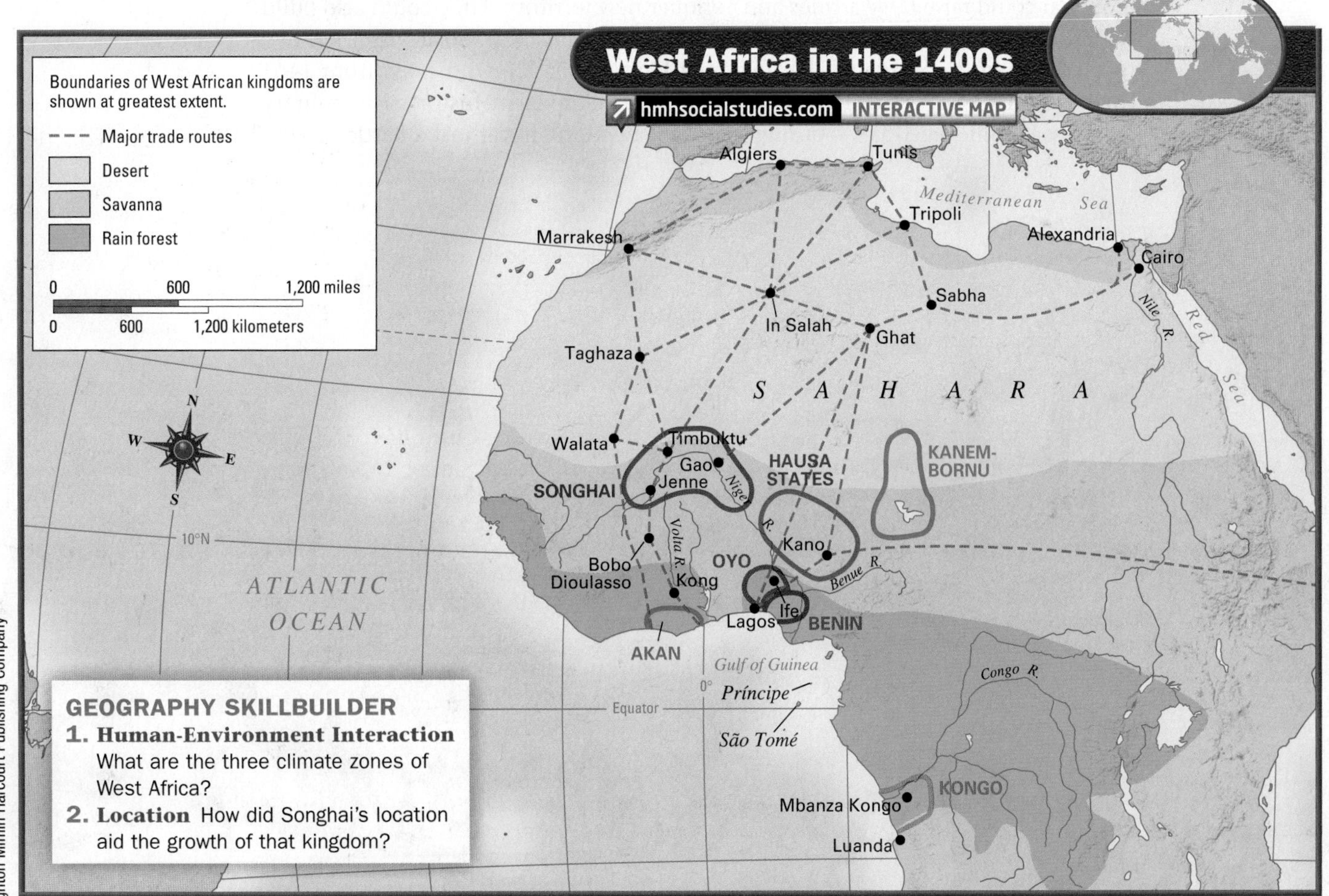

GEOGRAPHY SKILLBUILDER

1. **Human-Environment Interaction** What are the three climate zones of West Africa?
2. **Location** How did Songhai's location aid the growth of that kingdom?

followed. These early contacts between West Africans and Portuguese traders would have two significant consequences for West Africa and the Americas. First, direct trade between the Portuguese and the coastal peoples of West Africa bypassed the old trade routes across the Sahara and pulled the coastal region into a closer relationship with Europe. Second, the Portuguese began the European trade in West African slaves.

In the 1480s the Portuguese claimed two uninhabited islands off the African coast, Príncipe and São Tomé. Discovering that the soil and climate were perfect for growing sugar cane, they established large sugar plantations there. A **plantation** is a farm on which a single crop, usually one that requires much human labor, is grown on a large scale. To work these plantations, the Portuguese began importing slaves from the West African mainland.

At first this trade was limited to a small number of West Africans purchased from village chiefs, usually captives from rival groups. However, the success of the Portuguese slave plantations provided a model that would be reproduced on a larger scale in the Americas—including the British North American colonies. **B**

MAIN IDEA

Summarizing

B How did the Portuguese sugar plantations affect the course of history?

Three African Kingdoms Flourish

In the late 1400s, western Africa was a land of thriving trade, diverse cultures, and many rich and well-ordered states.

SONGHAI From about 600 to 1600, a succession of empires—first Ghana, then Mali, and beginning in the mid-1400s, **Songhai** (sông′hī′)—gained power and wealth by controlling the trans-Sahara trade. The rulers of these empires grew enormously rich by taxing the goods that passed through their realms.

With wealth flowing in from the north-south trade routes, the rulers of Songhai could raise large armies and conquer new territory. They could also build cities, administer laws, and support the arts and education. So it was with two great rulers of the Songhai. The first great king, Sunni Ali, who ruled from 1464 to 1492, made Songhai the largest West African empire in history. His military prowess became legendary—during his entire reign, he never lost a battle.

A desert caravan reaches the fabled Songhai city of Timbuktu. ▼

Another great ruler, Askia Muhammad, was a master organizer, a devout Muslim, and a scholar. He organized Songhai into administrative districts and appointed officials to govern, collect taxes, and regulate trade, agriculture, and fishing. Under his rule, Timbuktu regained its reputation as an important education center as it attracted scholars from all over the Islamic world.

At its height in the 1500s, Songhai's power extended across much of West Africa. However, it did not control the forest kingdoms. Songhai's cavalry might easily thunder across the **savanna,** the region of dry grassland, but it could not penetrate the belt of dense rain forest along the southern coast. Protected by the forest, peoples such as the Akan, Ibo, Edo, Ifi, Oyo, and Yoruba lived in kingdoms that thrived in the 1400s and 1500s.

BENIN Although the forests provided protection from conquest, they nevertheless allowed access for trade. Traders carried goods out of the forests or paddled them along the Niger River to the savanna. The brisk trade with Songhai and North Africa, and later with Portugal, helped the forest kingdoms grow. In the 1400s one of these kingdoms, **Benin,** dominated a large region around the Niger Delta. Leading the expansion was a powerful oba (ruler) named Ewuare. Stories that have been passed down to the present day recall Ewuare's triumphs in the mid-1400s.

A PERSONAL VOICE CHIEF JACOB EGHAREVBA

> "He fought against and captured 201 towns and villages. . . . He took their rulers captive and he caused the people to pay tribute to him. He made good roads in Benin City. . . . In fact the town rose to importance and gained the name of city during his reign. It was he who had the innermost and greatest of the walls and ditches made round the city, and he also made powerful charms and had them buried at each of the nine gateways of the city so as to ward against any evil."
>
> —*A Short History of Benin*

Within this great walled city, Ewuare headed a highly organized government in which districts were governed by appointed chiefs. Through other appointed officials, the oba controlled trade and managed the metal-working industries such as goldsmithing and brass-smithing. He also exchanged ambassadors with Portugal in the late 1400s. Under the patronage of Ewuare and his successors, metalworkers produced stunning and sophisticated works of art, such as bronze sculptures and plaques. C

MAIN IDEA

Comparing

C How was the government in Benin similar to that of Askia Muhammad?

▲ An unknown Yoruba artist in the kingdom of Ife produced this bronze head of a king in the 1100s. The highly developed bronze artistry of Ife was handed down to the kingdom of Benin, which arose later in the same area.

KONGO Within another stretch of rain forest, in West Central Africa, the powerful kingdom of **Kongo** arose on the lower Zaire (Congo) River. In the late 1400s, Kongo consisted of a series of small kingdoms ruled by a single leader called the Manikongo, who lived in what is today Angola. The Manikongo, who could be either a man or a woman, held kingdoms together by a system of royal marriages, taxes, and, when necessary, by war and tribute. By the 1470s, the Manikongo oversaw an empire estimated at over 4 million people.

The Bakongo, the people of Kongo, mined iron ore and produced well-wrought tools and weapons. They also wove palm leaf threads into fabric that reminded Europeans of velvet. The Portuguese sailors who first reached Kongo in 1483 were struck by the similarities between Kongo and their own world. Its system of government—a collection of provinces centralized under one strong king—resembled that of many European nations at the time.

West African Culture

In the late 1400s the world of most West Africans was a local one. Most people lived in small villages, where life revolved around family, the community, and tradition. West African customs varied greatly but followed some common patterns. These patterns would influence the future interactions between Africans and Europeans and shape the experience of enslaved Africans in the Americas.

FAMILY AND GOVERNMENT Bonds of kinship—ties among people of the same **lineage,** or line of common descent—formed the basis of most aspects of life in rural West Africa. Some societies, such as the Akan, were matrilineal—that is, people traced their lineage through their mother's family. These lineage ties determined not only family loyalties but also inheritances and whom people could marry. Societies such as the Ibo also encouraged people to find a mate outside their lineage groups. These customs helped create a complex web of family alliances.

Within a family, age carried rank. The oldest living descendant of the group's common ancestor controlled family members and represented them in councils of the larger groups to which a family might belong. These larger groups shared a common language and history and often a common territory. One leader or chief might speak for the group as a whole. But this person rarely spoke without consulting a council of elders made up of the heads of individual extended families.

RELIGION Religion was important in all aspects of African life. Political leaders claimed authority on the basis of religion. For example, the ruler of the Ife kingdom claimed descent from the first person placed on earth by the "God of the Sky." Religious rituals were also central to the daily activities of farmers, hunters, and fishers. D

MAIN IDEA

Hypothesizing

D Why did political leaders claim authority on the basis of religion?

West Africans believed that nature was filled with spirits and perceived spiritual forces in both living and non-living objects. They also believed that the spirits of ancestors spoke to the village elders in dreams. Although West African peoples might worship a variety of ancestral spirits and lesser gods, most believed in a single creator. The Bakongo, for example, believed in *Nzambi ampungu,* a term that means the "creator of all things," and so understood the Christian or Muslim belief in a supreme god. However, the Bakongo and other cultures could not

Against the ▶ backdrop of centuries-old cliff dwellings built by their ancestors, modern-day Dogon elders in Mali carry out an ancient religious ritual.

understand the Christian and Muslim insistence that West Africans stop worshipping spirits, who were believed to carry out the Creator's work. Out of this difference grew many cultural conflicts.

LIVELIHOOD Throughout West Africa, people supported themselves by age-old methods of farming, herding, hunting, and fishing, and by mining and trading. Almost all groups believed in collective ownership of land. Individuals might farm the land, but it reverted to family or village ownership when not in use.

People on the dry savanna depended on rivers, such as the Niger, to nourish their crops and livestock. On the western coast, along the Senegal and Gambia rivers, farmers converted tangled mangrove swamps into rice fields. This grain—and the skills for growing it—would accompany West Africans to the Americas. E

Developing Historical Perspective
E What agricultural skills did West Africans bring to the Americas?

USE OF SLAVE LABOR West Africans divided tasks by age and by social status. At the lowest rung in some societies were slaves. However, in Africa, people were not born into slavery, nor did slavery necessarily mean a lifetime of servitude. In Africa, slaves could escape their bondage in a number of ways. Sometimes they were adopted into or they married into the family they served. This was a very different kind of servitude from that which evolved in the Americas, where slavery continued from generation to generation and was based on race.

While slavery eventually came to dominate the interaction between Africans and Europeans, it was not the primary concern of the Portuguese sailors who first explored the African coast. At this time, in the late 1400s, a variety of political, social, and economic changes in Europe spurred rulers and adventurers to push outward into unexplored reaches of the ocean.

KENTE CLOTH

Today people of African descent all over the world value as a symbol of Africa the multicolored fabric known as kente cloth. For African Americans who choose to wear kente cloth or display it in their homes, the fabric serves as a tangible link to West African cultures from which their ancestors came.

Artisans of the Asante (Ashanti) people of modern Ghana have woven kente cloth for centuries. Working at looms, they produce long strips of cloth of complex designs and varying colors. These strips are then sewn together into a brilliant fabric that sparkles with reds, greens, blues, golds, and whatever other hues the weavers chose as dyes.

SECTION 3 ASSESSMENT

1. **TERMS & NAMES** For each term or name, write a sentence explaining its significance.
   - **Islam**
   - **Songhai**
   - **Benin**
   - **lineage**
   - **plantation**
   - **savanna**
   - **Kongo**

MAIN IDEA

2. **TAKING NOTES**
   Make an outline using the main topics shown below, and fill it in with factual details related to each topic.

   I. West Africa's Climate Zones
   II. West Africa's Major Geographical Features
   III. Three West African Kingdoms and Their Climate Zones

CRITICAL THINKING

3. **ANALYZING CAUSES**
   What factors helped the trade system flourish in West Africa? Use evidence from the text to support your response. **Think About:**
   - the geography of the region
   - the kinds of goods exchanged
   - the societies that emerged in West Africa

4. **ANALYZING EFFECTS**
   What effects did Portuguese trade routes have on West Africa?

5. **CONTRASTING**
   How did West African slavery differ from the kind of slavery that developed in the Americas?

European Societies Around 1492

MAIN IDEA

Political, economic, and intellectual developments in western Europe in the 1400s led to the Age of Exploration.

WHY IT MATTERS NOW

European settlement in the Americas led to the founding of the United States.

Terms & Names

- **Prince Henry**
- **Renaissance**
- **hierarchy**
- **nuclear family**
- **Crusades**
- **Reformation**

One European's Story

hmhsocialstudies.com TAKING NOTES

Use the graphic organizer online to take notes on changes in western Europe in the 1400s.

During the early decades of the 15th century, **Prince Henry** of Portugal, often called "Henry the Navigator," sent Portuguese ships to explore the west coast of Africa. According to his biographer, Prince Henry's driving motivation was the need to know.

A PERSONAL VOICE GOMES EANES DE ZURARA

"The noble spirit of this Prince . . . was ever urging him both to begin and to carry out very great deeds. For which reason . . . he had also a wish to know the land that lay beyond the isles of Canary and that Cape called Bojador, for that up to his time, neither by writings, nor by the memory of man, was known with any certainty the nature of the land beyond that Cape. . . . it seemed to him that if he or some other lord did not endeavor to gain that knowledge, no mariners or merchants would ever dare to attempt it. . . ."

—*The Chronicle of the Discovery and Conquest of Guinea*

Prince Henry's curiosity was typical of the "noble spirit" of the **Renaissance,** (rĕn′ĭ-säns′) a period when Europeans began investigating all aspects of the physical world. The term *Renaissance* means "rebirth" of the kind of interest in the physical world that had characterized ancient Greece and Rome. With his burning desire for knowledge, Prince Henry helped launch the era of European expansion.

▲ **Prince Henry the Navigator**

The European Social Order

In the late 1400s, most Europeans, like most Native Americans and most Africans, lived in small villages, bound to the land and to ancient traditions.

THE SOCIAL HIERARCHY European communities were based on social **hierarchy,** that is, they were organized according to rank. Monarchs and nobles held most of the wealth and power at the top of the hierarchy. At the bottom labored the peasants, who constituted the majority of the people. The nobility offered their peasants land and protection. In return, the peasants supplied the nobles with livestock or crops—and sometimes with military service.

Within the social structure, few individuals moved beyond the position into which they were born. Europeans generally accepted their lot as part of a larger order ordained by God and reflected in the natural world. Writing in the late 1500s, William Shakespeare expressed the fixed nature of this order in one of his plays.

A PERSONAL VOICE WILLIAM SHAKESPEARE

"The heavens themselves, the planets, and this center [earth]
Observe degree, priority, and place . . .
Take but degree away, untune that string,
And hark! what discord follows. . . ."

—*Troilus and Cressida*

MAIN IDEA

Forming Generalizations

A) Why did artisans and merchants experience social mobility?

One group that did experience social mobility was composed of artisans and merchants, the people who created and traded goods for money. Although this group was relatively small in the 1400s, the profit they earned from trade would eventually make them a valuable source of tax revenue. Monarchs needed them to finance costly overseas exploration and expansion. A)

THE FAMILY IN SOCIETY While Europeans recognized and respected kinship ties, the extended family was not as important for them as it was for Native American and African societies at this time. Instead, life centered around the **nuclear family,** the household made up of a mother and father and their children. As in other societies, gender largely determined the division of labor. Among peasant families, for example, men generally did most of the field labor and herded livestock. Women did help in the fields, but they also handled child care and household labor, such as preparing and preserving the family's food.

History Through Art

JUNE, *FROM* LES TRÈS RICHES HEURES DU DUC DE BERRY

This miniature painting, representing the month of June, is a page from a prayer book calendar made by the Limbourg brothers around the year 1416. The book, made for a younger son of the French king, tells us a great deal about the aristocratic view of the European social order.

In the background, the walls of the city of Paris protect a palace and the royal chapel, buildings that represent the two most powerful institutions in medieval European society: church and aristocracy.

In the foreground, peasants mow the fields in an orderly world of peace and tranquility. However, the image is a fantasy, an idealized vision painted to please the aristocracy. There is no hint of the peasants' grinding poverty or of the violence of the Hundred Years' War that was at that moment devastating northern France.

SKILLBUILDER Interpreting Visual Sources

1. What does the painting tell you about the importance of gender in the division of labor during the 1400s?
2. Why might images of poverty have displeased the aristocracy?

SEE SKILLBUILDER HANDBOOK, PAGE R23.

Christianity Shapes the European Outlook

The Roman Catholic Church was the dominant religious institution in western Europe. The leader of the church—the pope—and his bishops had great political and spiritual authority. In the spiritual realm, church leaders determined most matters of faith. Parish priests interpreted the scriptures and urged the faithful to endure earthly sufferings in exchange for the promise of eternal life in heaven, or salvation. Priests also administered important rituals called the sacraments—such as baptism and communion—that were thought to ensure salvation.

Background
In Christian theology, salvation is the deliverance from the power or penalty of sin.

Hand in hand with the belief in salvation was the call to convert people of other faiths. This missionary call spurred Europe to reach out beyond its borders first to defend, and then to spread, the faith.

CRUSADING CHRISTIANITY By the early 700s, Muslim armies had seized huge areas of Asia and North Africa, along with most of the Iberian Peninsula, where Spain and Portugal sit. To regain this territory, Spanish Christians waged a campaign called the *reconquista,* or reconquest. By 1492, the forces of the combined kingdoms of Queen Isabella of Castile and King Ferdinand of Aragon, who married in 1469, finally drove the Muslims from the peninsula. This victory ended more than seven centuries of religious warfare. A united Spain stood ready to assert itself internationally and to spread Christianity around the globe.

Meanwhile, Christian armies from all over western Europe responded to the church's call to force the Muslims out of the Holy Land around Jerusalem. From 1096 to 1270, Europeans launched the **Crusades,** a series of military expeditions to the Middle East in the name of Christianity.

In the end, these bloody Crusades failed to "rescue" the Holy Land, but they had two consequences that encouraged European exploration and expansion. First, they sparked an increase in trade, as crusaders returned home with a new taste for products from Asia. Second, the Crusades weakened the power of European nobles, many of whom lost their lives or fortunes in the wars. Monarchs were able to take advantage of the nobles' weakened ranks by consolidating their own power. Eventually, monarchs sponsored overseas exploration in order to increase their wealth and power.

DECLINE IN CHURCH AUTHORITY The Crusades had a third long-term consequence: the decline of the power of the pope. The ultimate failure of these campaigns weakened the prestige of the papacy (the office of the pope), which had led the quest. Power struggles in the 1300s and 1400s between the church and European kings further reduced papal authority and tipped the balance of power in favor of the monarchies.

Disagreements over church authority, along with outrage over corrupt practices among the clergy, led to a reform movement in the early 1500s. This movement, known as the **Reformation,** divided Christianity in western Europe between Catholicism and Protestantism. This split deepened the rivalries between European nations during the period of American colonization and sent newly formed Protestant sects across the Atlantic to seek religious freedom. B

MAIN IDEA

Recognizing Effects
B How did religious changes in Europe affect the European colonization of the Americas?

KEY PLAYER

"KING ISABELLA"
1451–1504

Queen Isabella, who played a central role in European exploration by sponsoring Christopher Columbus's voyages to the Americas, made her mark on the Old World as well. As co-ruler of Spain, Isabella participated in her country's religious and military matters.

The queen often defied the pope to ensure that her candidates were appointed to positions in the Spanish church. In addition, Isabella tasted battle more frequently than most rulers, either male or female. The queen rode among her troops in full armor, personally commanding them in Ferdinand's absence. Whenever Isabella appeared, her troops shouted, "Castile, Castile, for our King Isabella!"

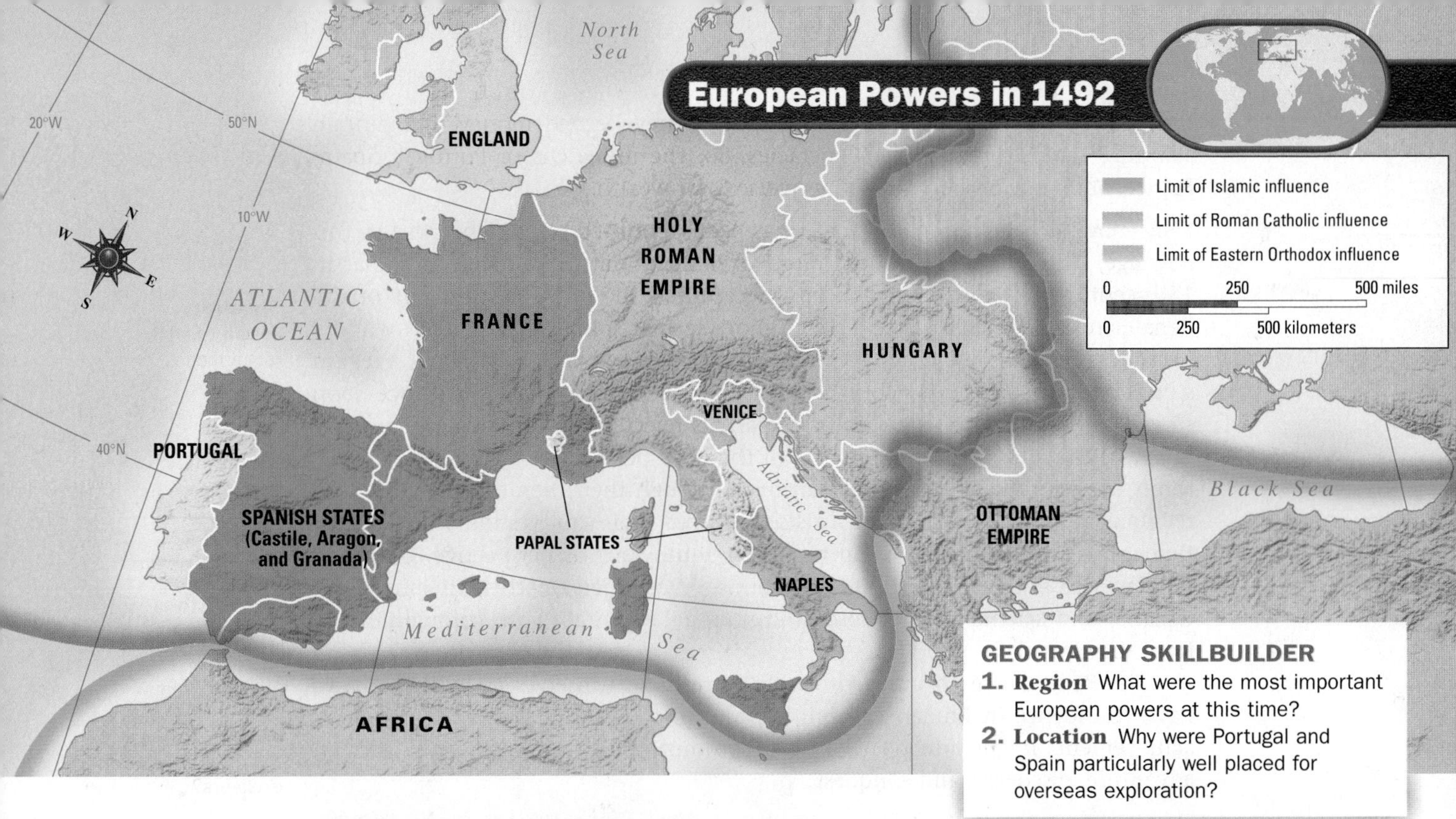

GEOGRAPHY SKILLBUILDER

1. **Region** What were the most important European powers at this time?
2. **Location** Why were Portugal and Spain particularly well placed for overseas exploration?

Changes Come to Europe

As the 1400s began, European societies were still recovering from a series of disasters during the previous century. From 1314 to 1316, heavy rain and disease wiped out crops and livestock. Thousands of peasants died of starvation. Then, beginning in the 1340s, an epidemic of plagues killed over 25 million people—a fourth of Europe's population. Meanwhile, long wars also raged across the continent, including the Hundred Years' War between England and France.

However, amid this turmoil, modern Europe began to take shape. After the plague, Europe experienced vigorous growth and change. The expansion of Europe pushed Europeans to look to other lands.

THE GROWTH OF COMMERCE AND POPULATION The Crusades opened up Asian trade routes and whetted the European appetite for Eastern luxuries, such as silk, porcelain, tea, and rugs. Merchants in Italian city-states were the first to profit from trade with Asia. They traded with the Muslim merchants who controlled the flow of goods through much of the Middle East. As trade opportunities increased, new markets were established and new trade routes were opened.

By the end of the 1400s, Europe's population had rebounded from the plagues. This increase stimulated commerce and encouraged the growth of towns. The return to urban life (which had been largely neglected after the fall of Rome) brought about far-reaching social and cultural change. The new urban middle class would assume increasing political power, especially in Britain and its colonies. (C)

MAIN IDEA

Developing Historical Perspective

(C) In what ways would the revival of the cities have affected European social and cultural life?

THE RISE OF NATIONS The Crusades weakened the nobility and strengthened monarchies. Western European monarchs began exerting more control over their lands by collecting new taxes, raising professional armies, and strengthening central governments. Among the new allies of the monarchs were merchants, who willingly accepted taxes on their newfound wealth in exchange for the protection or expansion of trade. By the late 1400s, four major nations were taking shape in western Europe: Portugal, Spain, France, and England.

Only the king or queen of a unified nation had enough power and resources to finance overseas exploration. Monarchs had a powerful motive to encourage the quest for new lands and trading routes: they needed money to maintain standing armies and large bureaucracies. So, the monarchs of Portugal, Spain, France, and England began looking overseas for wealth.

THE RENAISSANCE "Thank God it has been permitted to us to be born in this new age, so full of hope and promise," exclaimed Matteo Palmieri, a scholar in 15th-century Italy. Palmieri's optimism captured the enthusiastic spirit of the Renaissance. The Renaissance led to a more secular spirit, an interest in worldly pleasures, and a new confidence in human achievement. Starting in Italy, a region stimulated by commercial contact with Asia and Africa, the Renaissance soon spread throughout Europe. Renaissance artists rejected the flat, two-dimensional images of medieval painting in favor of the deep perspectives and fully rounded forms of ancient sculpture and painting. Although their themes were still often religious in nature, Renaissance artists portrayed their subjects more realistically than had medieval artists, using new techniques such as perspective. European scholars reexamined the writings of ancient philosophers, mathematicians, geographers, and scientists. They also studied scholarly Arab works brought home from the Crusades.

The Renaissance encouraged people to regard themselves as individuals, to have confidence in human capabilities, and to look forward to the fame their achievements might bring. This attitude prompted many to seek glory through adventure, discovery, and conquest. D

Vocabulary
secular: worldly rather than spiritual

MAIN IDEA
Drawing Conclusions
D How might Renaissance attitudes and ideas have influenced European explorers?

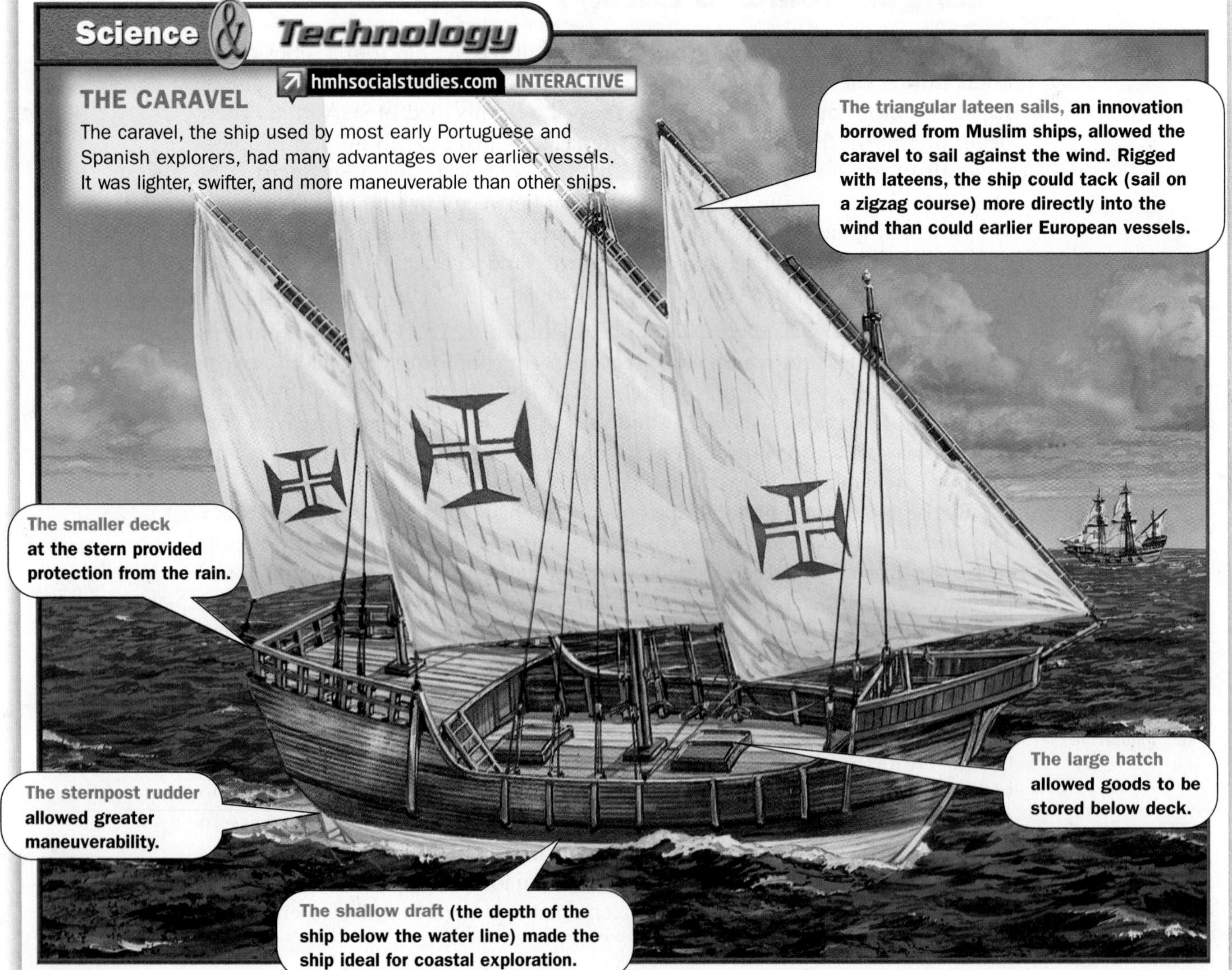

Science & Technology
hmhsocialstudies.com INTERACTIVE
THE CARAVEL
The caravel, the ship used by most early Portuguese and Spanish explorers, had many advantages over earlier vessels. It was lighter, swifter, and more maneuverable than other ships.
The triangular lateen sails, an innovation borrowed from Muslim ships, allowed the caravel to sail against the wind. Rigged with lateens, the ship could tack (sail on a zigzag course) more directly into the wind than could earlier European vessels.
The smaller deck at the stern provided protection from the rain.
The large hatch allowed goods to be stored below deck.
The sternpost rudder allowed greater maneuverability.
The shallow draft (the depth of the ship below the water line) made the ship ideal for coastal exploration.

Europe Enters a New Age of Expansion

Although Marco Polo's journey to China took place in the 1200s, it was not until 1477 that the first printed edition of Polo's account caused renewed interest in the East. Like other European merchants, Polo traveled to Asia by land. The expense and peril of such journeys led Europeans to seek alternative routes. European merchants and explorers listened to the reports of travelers and reexamined the maps drawn by ancient geographers.

SAILING TECHNOLOGY Europeans, however, needed more than maps to guide them through uncharted waters. On the open seas, winds easily blew ships off course. With only the sun, moon, and stars to guide them, few ships ventured beyond the sight of land. To overcome their fears, European ship captains adopted the compass and the astrolabe, navigating tools that helped plot direction. They also took advantage of innovations in sailing technology that allowed ships such as the caravel to sail against the wind.

PORTUGAL TAKES THE LEAD Under Prince Henry the Navigator, Portugal developed and employed these innovations. Although Henry was only an armchair navigator, he earned his nickname by establishing an up-to-date sailing school and by sponsoring the earliest voyages.

For almost 40 years, Prince Henry sent his captains sailing farther and farther south along the west coast of Africa. Portuguese explorations continued after Prince Henry died. Bartolomeu Dias rounded the southern tip of Africa in 1488. Vasco da Gama reached India ten years later. By sailing around Africa to eastern Asia via the Indian Ocean, Portuguese traders were able to cut their costs and increase their profits.

While cartographers redrew their maps to show the route around Africa, an Italian sea captain named Christopher Columbus traveled from nation to nation with his own collection of maps and figures. Columbus believed there was an even shorter route to Asia—one that lay west across the Atlantic.

In Spain an adviser of Queen Isabella pointed out that support of the proposed venture would cost less than a week's entertainment of a foreign official. Isabella was convinced and summoned Columbus to appear before the Spanish court.

ASSESSMENT

1. **TERMS & NAMES** For each term or name, write a sentence explaining its significance.
   - **Prince Henry**
   - **hierarchy**
   - **Crusades**
   - **Reformation**
   - **Renaissance**
   - **nuclear family**

MAIN IDEA

2. **TAKING NOTES**
Re-create the web below on your paper. Fill it in with the changes taking place in western Europe during the 1400s.

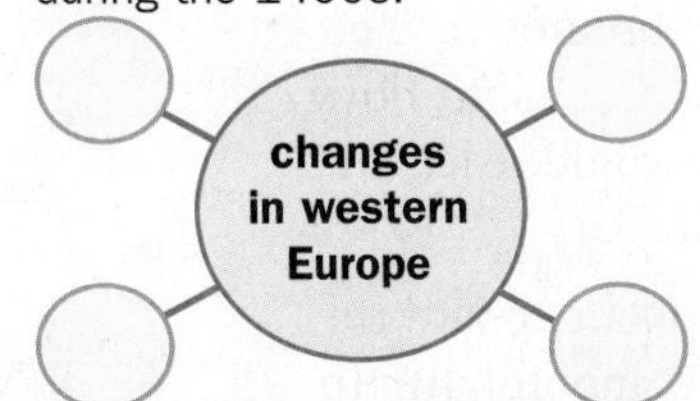

How did these changes help lead to the European Age of Exploration?

CRITICAL THINKING

3. **ANALYZING ISSUES**
Which European event of the late 1400s to early 1500s do you think had the most far-reaching impact on European lives? Explain and support your answer. **Think About:**
   - the importance of religion
   - the role of adventurers and explorers
   - the increase in prosperity

4. **SUMMARIZING**
How did advances in technology open the way for world exploration?

5. **DRAWING CONCLUSIONS**
Why do you think other European nations lagged behind Portugal in the race for overseas exploration? Support your reasons with details from the text.

SECTION 5

Transatlantic Encounters

MAIN IDEA	WHY IT MATTERS NOW	Terms & Names
Columbus's voyages set off a chain of events that brought together the peoples of Europe, Africa, and the Americas.	**The interactions among the people of these three continents laid the foundations for modern multicultural America.**	**• Christopher Columbus • Taino • colonization • Columbian Exchange • Treaty of Tordesillas**

One European's Story

hmhsocialstudies.com TAKING NOTES

Use the graphic organizer online to take notes about Columbus's voyages and their effects.

In January 1492, the Genoese sailor **Christopher Columbus** stood before the Spanish court with a daring plan: he would find a route to Asia by sailing west across the Atlantic Ocean. The plan was accepted, and on August 3, 1492, Columbus embarked on a voyage that changed the course of history. He began his journal by restating the deal he had struck with Spain.

A Personal Voice CHRISTOPHER COLUMBUS

"Based on the information that I had given Your Highnesses about the land of India and about a Prince who is called the Great Khan [of China], which in our language means 'King of Kings,' Your Highnesses decided to send me . . . to the regions of India, to see . . . the peoples and the lands, and to learn of . . . the measures which could be taken for their conversion to our Holy Faith. . . . Your Highnesses . . . ordered that I shall go to the east, but not by land as is customary. I was to go by way of the west, whence until today we do not know with certainty that anyone has gone. . . ."

—*The Log of Christopher Columbus*

Christopher Columbus, around 1519

Although Columbus did not find a route to Asia, his voyage set in motion a process that brought together the American, European, and African worlds.

Columbus Crosses the Atlantic

The *Niña, Pinta,* and *Santa Maria* slid quietly out of a Spanish port in the predawn hours of August 3, 1492. Although they were setting out into the unknown, their crews included no soldiers, priests, or ambassadors—only sailors and cabin boys with a taste for the sea. In a matter of months, Columbus's fleet would reach the sandy shores of what was to Europeans an astonishing new world.

FIRST ENCOUNTERS At about 2 A.M. on October 12, 1492, a lookout aboard the *Pinta* caught sight of two white sand dunes sparkling in the moonlight. In between lay a mass of dark rocks. "*Tierra*! *Tierra*!" he shouted. "Land! Land!"

At dawn Columbus went ashore and caught sight of a group of people who called themselves the **Taino** (tī′nō), or "noble ones." He renamed their island San Salvador, or "Holy Savior," and claimed it for Spain.

On the first day of their encounter, the generosity of the Taino startled Columbus. "They are friendly and well-dispositioned people who bear no arms," he wrote in his log. "They traded and gave everything they had with good will." But after only two days, Columbus offered an assessment of the Taino that had dark implications for the future.

A PERSONAL VOICE CHRISTOPHER COLUMBUS

> **"It would be unnecessary to build . . . [a fort here] because these people are so simple in deeds of arms. . . . If Your Highnesses order either to bring all of them to Castile or to hold them as captivos [slaves] on their own island it could easily be done, because with about fifty men you could control and subjugate them all, making them do whatever you want."**
>
> —quoted in *Columbus: The Great Adventure*

GOLD, LAND, AND RELIGION The search for gold was one of the main reasons for Columbus's journey. On his second day in the Americas, Columbus expressed one of the main reasons he had embarked on his journey. "I have been very attentive," he wrote, "and have tried very hard to find out if there is any gold here." When he did not find gold on San Salvador, he left to look elsewhere. Columbus spent 96 days exploring some small islands in what is now the Bahamas and the coastlines of two other Caribbean islands, known today as Cuba and Hispaniola. All along the way, he bestowed Spanish names on territory he claimed for Spain. "It was my wish to bypass no island without taking possession," he wrote. Columbus also honored his promise to assert Christian domination. "In every place I have entered, islands and lands, I have always planted a cross," he noted on November 16. Less than two weeks later, he predicted, "Your Highnesses will order a city . . . built in these regions [for] these countries will be easily converted." (A)

MAIN IDEA

Summarizing
(A) What activities preoccupied Columbus as he explored the Americas?

SPANISH FOOTHOLDS In early January 1493, Columbus began his trip back to Spain. Convinced that he had landed on islands off Asia known to Europeans as the Indies, Columbus called the people he met *los indios*. The term translated into "Indian," a word mistakenly applied to all the diverse peoples of the Americas.

Columbus's reports thrilled the Spanish monarchs, who funded three more voyages. When he set sail for the Americas in September 1493, Columbus was no longer an explorer but an empire builder. He commanded a fleet of some 17 ships and several hundred armed soldiers. He also brought five priests and more than 1,000 colonists, including *hidalgos,* or members of the minor nobility.

These European soldiers, priests, and colonists, and the many others that followed, would occupy first the Caribbean and then most of the Americas, and impose their will on the Native Americans who lived there. Their arrival on Hispaniola, the island presently divided between Haiti and the Dominican Republic, signaled the start of a cultural clash that would continue for the next five centuries.

HISTORICAL SPOTLIGHT

THE VIKINGS

The first Europeans to reach North America were probably Vikings. About 982, the Norwegian Viking Eric the Red crossed the Atlantic in an open boat and set up two colonies on Greenland. Some fifteen years later, his son, Leif, voyaged farther to a place he called Vinland the Good because of its abundant grapes. Historians now believe that present-day Newfoundland is Leif Ericson's Vinland. In 1963, archaeologists discovered there a half-burned timbered house of Norse design that dates to about the year 1000.

According to Norwegian sagas, or tales of great deeds, another Norwegian expedition followed Leif Ericson's and stayed in Newfoundland for three years. Then the Skraelings, as the saga calls the native peoples, drove away the colonists, and the Vikings never returned.

The Impact on Native Americans

The Taino who greeted Columbus in 1492 could not have imagined the colonization and outbreaks of disease that would soon follow. While the Taino resisted Spanish control, there was little they could do against the viruses and diseases that accompanied the new settlers.

METHODS OF COLONIZATION The European system of **colonization**—the establishment of distant settlements controlled by the parent country—was established long before Columbus set sail for Hispaniola. During the Crusades, Italians from Venice had taken over Arab sugar farms in what is now Lebanon. By the late 1400s, the Portuguese had established plantation colonies on islands off the coast of West Africa, and Spain had colonized the Canary Islands.

From this experience, Europeans learned the advantages of using the plantation system. They also realized the economic benefits of using forced labor. Finally, they learned to use European weapons to dominate a people who had less sophisticated weapons. These tactics would be used in full against the peoples that the Europeans called Indians. B

MAIN IDEA

Summarizing
B Where did Europeans first experiment with the plantation system?

RESISTANCE AND CONQUEST The natives of the Caribbean, however, did not succumb to Columbus and the Spaniards without fighting. In November of 1493, Columbus attempted to conquer the present-day island of St. Croix. Instead of surrendering, the inhabitants defended themselves by firing rounds of poisoned arrows. The Spaniards won easily, but the struggle proved that Native Americans would not yield in the easy conquest predicted by Columbus.

Controlling the Taino who inhabited Hispaniola was even more difficult. After several rebellions, the Taino submitted to Columbus for several years but revolted again in 1495. The Spanish response was swift and cruel. A later settler, the missionary Bartolomé de Las Casas, criticized the Spaniards' brutal response.

A PERSONAL VOICE BARTOLOMÉ DE LAS CASAS

"This tactic begun here . . . [will soon] spread throughout these Indies and will end when there is no more land nor people to subjugate and destroy in this part of the world."

—quoted in *Columbus: The Great Adventure*

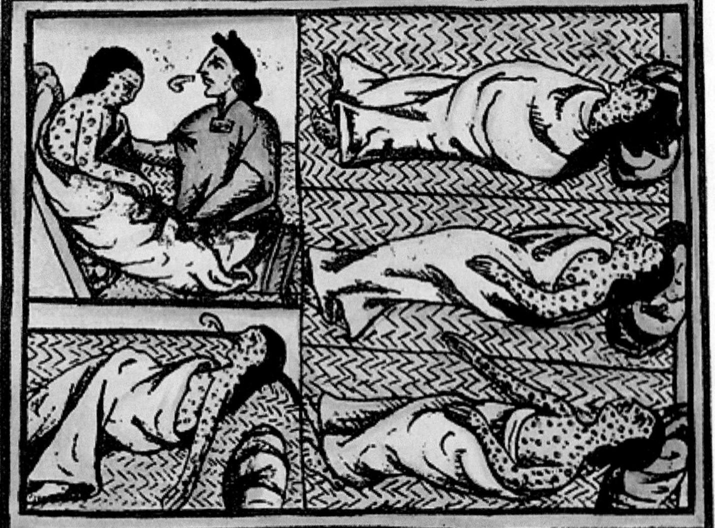

▲
In this series of drawings from an Aztec codex, or book (c. 1575), a medicine man takes care of an Aztec with smallpox, a deadly disease brought to the Americas by Europeans.

DISEASE RAVAGES THE NATIVE AMERICANS European settlers brought deadly diseases such as measles, mumps, chicken pox, smallpox, and typhus, which devastated Native Americans, who had not developed any natural immunity to these diseases. They died by the thousands. According to one estimate, nearly one-third of Hispaniola's estimated 300,000 inhabitants died during Columbus's time there. By 1508, fewer than 100,000 survivors lived on the island. Sixty years later, only two villages were left. These illnesses would soon spread to the rest of the Americas. More surely than any army, disease conquered region after region. C

MAIN IDEA

Analyzing Effects
C How did the arrival of European settlers affect Native American societies?

The Slave Trade Begins

With disease reducing the native work force, European settlers turned to Africa for slaves. In the coming years, European slave ships would haul hundreds of thousands of Africans across the Atlantic to toil in the Americas.

A NEW SLAVE LABOR FORCE The enslavement of Native Americans was a controversial issue among the Spaniards. Unfortunately, the Spanish saw the use of Africans as a possible solution to the colonies' labor shortage. Advised Las Casas, "The labor of one . . . [African] . . . [is] more valuable than that of four Indians; every effort should be made to bring many . . . [Africans] from Guinea."

As more natives died of disease, the demand for Africans grew. The price of enslaved Africans rose, and more Europeans joined the slave trade. African slavery was becoming an essential part of the European-American economic system. D

MAIN IDEA

Forming Generalizations

D Why did European settlers increase their demand for enslaved Africans?

AFRICAN LOSSES The Atlantic slave trade would devastate many African societies, which lost many of their fittest members. Before the slave trade ended in the 1800s, it would drain Africa of at least 12 million people.

The Impact on Europeans

Columbus's voyages had profound effects on Europe as well. Merchants and monarchs saw an opportunity to increase their wealth and influence. Ordinary people saw a chance to live in a new world, relatively free of social and economic constraints. Within a century, thousands of Europeans began crossing the Atlantic in what became one of the biggest voluntary migrations in history.

THE COLUMBIAN EXCHANGE The voyages of Columbus and others led to the introduction of new plants and animals to Europe, Africa, and the Americas. Ships took plants and animals from the Americas back to Europe and to Africa and brought items from the Eastern Hemisphere to the Western Hemisphere. This global transfer of living things, called the **Columbian Exchange,** began with Columbus's first voyage and continues today.

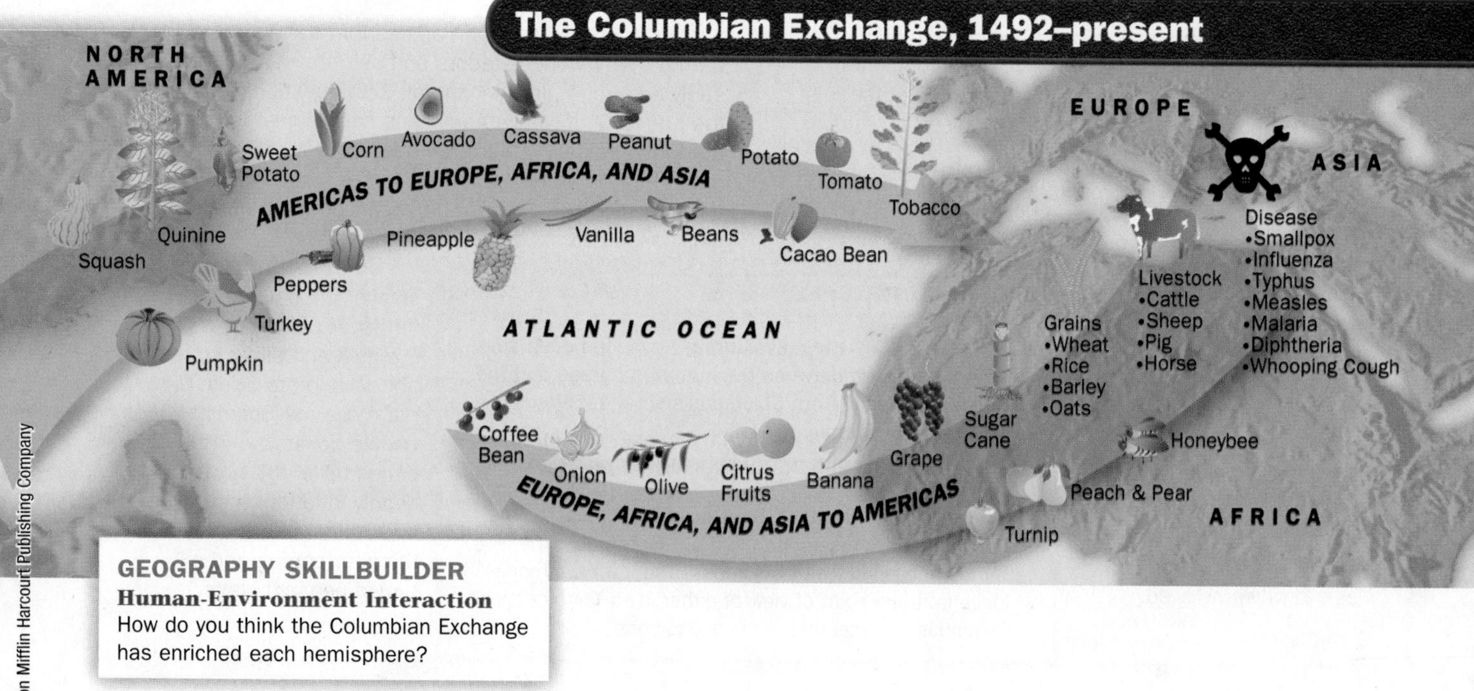

GEOGRAPHY SKILLBUILDER

Human-Environment Interaction

How do you think the Columbian Exchange has enriched each hemisphere?

NATIONAL RIVALRIES Overseas expansion inflamed European rivalries. Portugal, the pioneer in navigation and exploration, deeply resented Spain's sudden conquests. In 1493, Pope Alexander VI, a Spaniard, stepped in to avoid war between the two nations. In the **Treaty of Tordesillas** (tôr′də-sē′əs), signed in 1494, Spain and Portugal agreed to divide the Western Hemisphere between them. Lands to the west of an imaginary vertical line drawn in the Atlantic, including most of the Americas, belonged to Spain. Lands to the east of this line, including Brazil, belonged to Portugal.

The plan proved impossible to enforce. Its only long-lasting effect was to give Portugal a colony—Brazil—in a South America that was largely Spanish. Otherwise, the agreement had no effect on the English, Dutch, or French, all of whom began colonizing the Americas during the early 1600s. E

MAIN IDEA

Making Inferences

E Why might Spain and Portugal have been willing to go to war over the issue of overseas exploration?

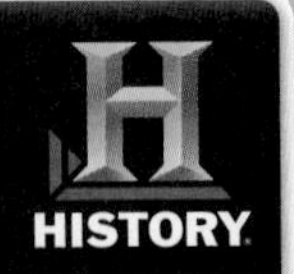

VIDEO
Christopher Columbus: Explorer of the New World

hmhsocialstudies.com

A New Society Is Born

Christopher Columbus lived on Hispaniola until 1500. That year, King Ferdinand and Queen Isabella, dissatisfied with the explorer's inability to maintain order on the island, ordered him to leave. After further travels throughout the Caribbean,

POINT

"Columbus's achievements were historic and heroic."

Many historians argue that Columbus's fateful voyages produced many long-term benefits. As the journalist Paul Gray notes, "Columbus's journey was the first step in a long process that eventually produced the United States of America, . . . a symbol and a haven of individual liberty for people throughout the world."

Other historians suggest that respect is due Columbus for the sheer dimension of the change he caused.

"The Columbian discovery was of greater magnitude than any other discovery or invention in human history. . . . both because of the . . . development of the New World and because of the numerous other discoveries that have stemmed from it," asserts the historian Paolo Emilio Taviani.

Some historians contend that, although millions of Native Americans were enslaved or killed by Europeans and the diseases they brought with them, this does not detract from Columbus's achievements. They argue that sacrifice is often necessary for the sake of progress. Further, they claim that, like any historical figure, Columbus was a man of his time and ought not to be condemned for acting according to the values of the age in which he lived.

COUNTERPOINT

"The legacy of Columbus is primarily one of 'genocide, cruelty, and slavery.'"

Some historians have questioned the traditional view of Columbus as a hero. The historian Hans Konig argues that Columbus's legacy should be deplored rather than celebrated: "The year 1492 opened an era of genocide, cruelty, and slavery on a larger scale than had ever been seen before." Speaking to the experience of Native Americans in particular, the activist Suzan Shown Harjo insists that "this half millennium of land grabs and one-cent treaty sales has been no bargain [for Native Americans]."

Historian Howard Zinn argues that the actions of the European conquistadors and settlers were unnecessarily cruel and plainly immoral. Zinn questions whether the suffering of Native Americans can be justified by European gains: "If there *are* necessary sacrifices to be made for human progress, is it not essential to hold to the principle that those to be sacrificed must make the decision [to be sacrificed] themselves?"

In any event, Konig claims, the balance does not favor Columbus: "all the gold and silver stolen and shipped to Spain did not make the Spanish people richer. . . . They ended up [with] . . . a deadly inflation, a starving population, the rich richer, the poor poorer, and a ruined peasant class."

THINKING CRITICALLY

1. **CONNECT TO TODAY Evaluating** How does each side view the tradeoff between the human progress and the violence resulting from Columbus's voyages? With which side do you agree? Why?

SEE SKILLBUILDER HANDBOOK, PAGE R14.

2. **CONNECT TO HISTORY Developing Historical Perspective** Do research to find out more about the Taino's encounters with Columbus. Then, write a monologue from the point of view of either (1) a Taino or (2) Columbus or a member of his expeditions.

Columbus reluctantly returned to Spain in 1504, where he died two years later. The daring sea captain went to his grave disappointed that he had not reached China.

Neither Columbus nor anyone else could have foreseen the long chain of events that his voyages set in motion. In time, settlers from England would transplant their cultures to colonies in North America. From within these colonies would emerge a new society—and a new nation—based on ideas of representative government and religious tolerance.

The story of the United States of America thus begins with a meeting of North American, African, and European peoples and cultures that radically transformed all three worlds. The upheaval threw unfamiliar peoples and customs together on a grand scale. Although the Europeans tried to impose their ways on Native Americans and Africans, they never completely succeeded. Their need to borrow from the peoples they sought to dominate proved too strong. Furthermore, the Native Americans and Africans resisted giving up their cultural identities. The new nation that emerged would blend elements of these three worlds, as well as others, in a distinctly multicultural society. Throughout the history of the United States, this multiculturalism would be one of its greatest challenges and also one of its greatest assets.

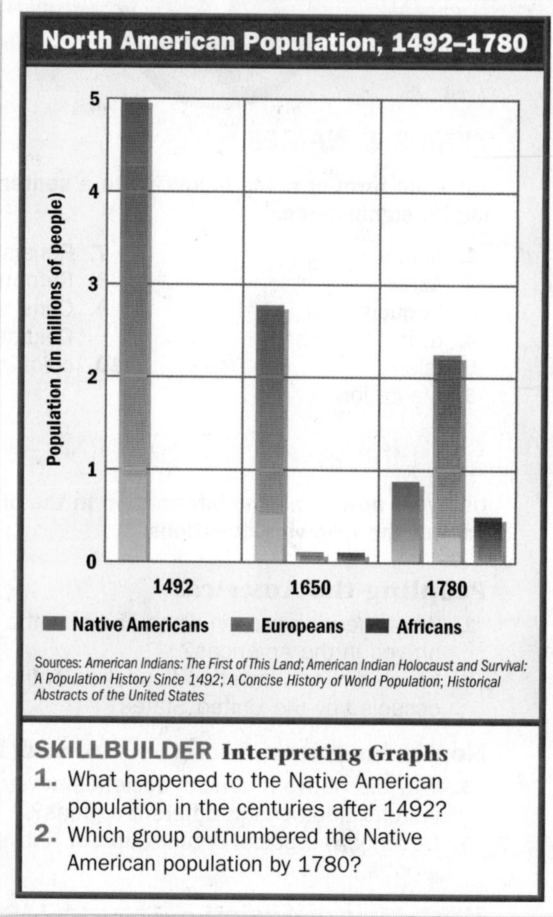

SKILLBUILDER Interpreting Graphs

1. What happened to the Native American population in the centuries after 1492?
2. Which group outnumbered the Native American population by 1780?

ASSESSMENT

1. **TERMS & NAMES** For each term or name, write a sentence explaining its significance.
   - **Christopher Columbus**
   - **colonization**
   - **Columbian Exchange**
   - **Treaty of Tordesillas**
   - **Taino**

MAIN IDEA

2. **TAKING NOTES**
   Create a time line of the major events of Columbus's voyages and interactions with Native Americans. Use the dates already plotted on the time line below as a guide.

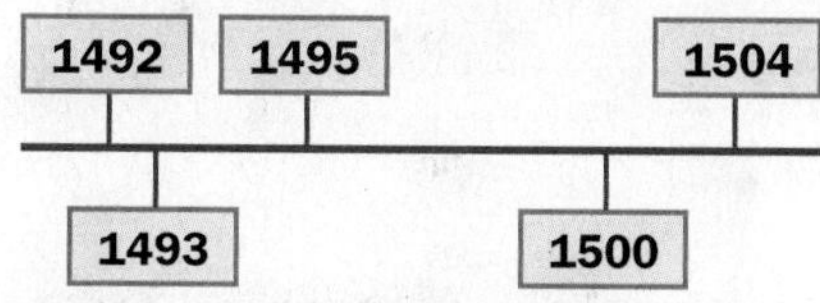

How did the Americas change during Columbus's lifetime as a result of his voyages?

CRITICAL THINKING

3. **DEVELOPING HISTORICAL PERSPECTIVE**
   Why did European explorers believe they could simply claim lands for their home countries, even though these lands were already populated?
4. **SUMMARIZING**
   In the centuries before Columbus's voyages, where had Europeans gained experience in colonization?
5. **ANALYZING EFFECTS**
   What do you think were three of the most important long-term consequences of Columbus's encounters in the Americas?
   Think About:
   - conquering and claiming land
   - forced labor of Native Americans and Africans
   - the Columbian Exchange

CHAPTER 1 ASSESSMENT

TERMS & NAMES

For each term or name below, write a sentence explaining its significance.

1. nomadic
2. Aztec
3. Iroquois
4. division of labor
5. Islam
6. plantation
7. Renaissance
8. Reformation
9. Christopher Columbus
10. colonization

MAIN IDEAS

Use your notes and the information in the chapter to answer the following questions.

Peopling the Americas

1. What theories explain when and how the first people arrived in the Americas?
2. Which ancient societies flourished in the region now occupied by the United States?

North American Societies Around 1492

3. Why did Native American societies develop different cultural traditions in different regions?
4. Describe the social organization of Native American groups.

West African Societies Around 1492

5. Why was Timbuktu such an important city?
6. Which religion did traders from North Africa bring with them to West Africa?

European Societies Around 1492

7. How did religion reinforce the social hierarchy of European societies?
8. How did the Reformation deepen rivalries between European nations?

Transatlantic Encounters

9. What impact did the Columbian Exchange have on people's lives throughout the world?
10. Why did the Spanish want to colonize the Americas?

CRITICAL THINKING

1. **USING YOUR NOTES** In a web like the one shown, describe how trade and commerce affected each region and time period shown.

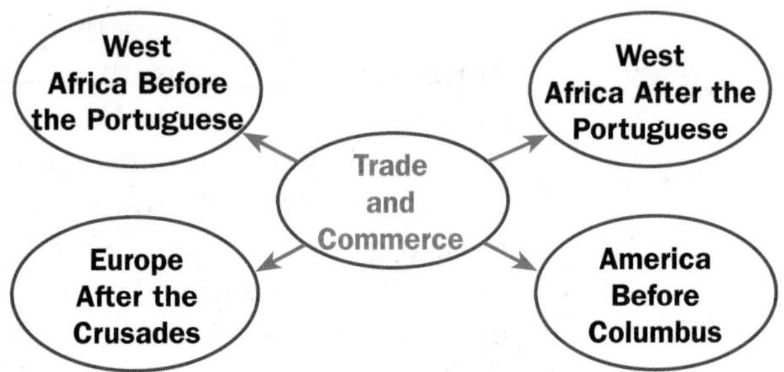

2. **DEVELOPING HISTORICAL PERSPECTIVE** How do you think the contrasting cultural attitudes to land ownership might have affected the relationship between Europeans and Native Americans?

VISUAL SUMMARY THREE WORLDS MEET

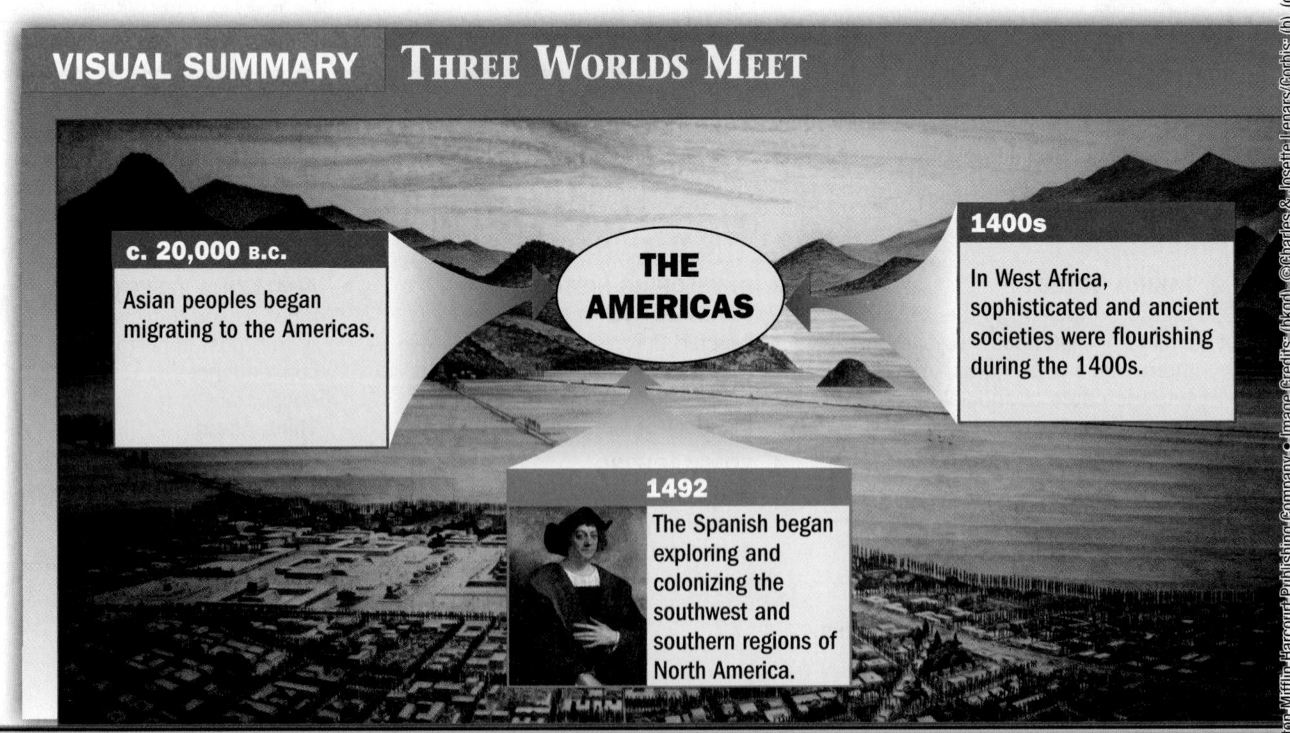

THE AMERICAS
c. 20,000 B.C.
Asian peoples began migrating to the Americas.
1400s
In West Africa, sophisticated and ancient societies were flourishing during the 1400s.
1492
The Spanish began exploring and colonizing the southwest and southern regions of North America.

STANDARDIZED TEST PRACTICE

Use the quotation below and your knowledge of U.S. history to answer questions 1 and 2.

> **"'The earth is our mother. The sky is our father.' This concept of nature . . . is at the center of the Native American world view. . . . The Native American's attitudes toward this landscape have been formulated over a long period of time, a span that reaches back to the end of the Ice Age. . . . [T]he Indian has assumed a deep ethical regard for the earth and sky, a reverence for the natural world. . . . It is this ancient ethic of the Native American that must shape our efforts to preserve the earth and the life upon and within it."**
>
> —N. Scott Momaday, "A First American Views His Land," *National Geographic,* July 1976

1. N. Scott Momaday refers to the Ice Age because—
   - **A** Native Americans' attitudes to the land were formed during the Ice Age.
   - **B** the landscape of the Americas took its present shape during the last Ice Age.
   - **C** that was when European immigrants first arrived in the Americas.
   - **D** he wants to show how long Native Americans have been living in the Americas.

2. In this passage, Momaday describes the "ancient ethic"—Native American reverence for the land—in order to —
   - **F** contrast it with modern attitudes.
   - **G** dismiss it as unimportant.
   - **H** present it as a quaint, old-fashioned idea.
   - **J** suggest that European Americans will never accept it.

3. Why did the Spanish begin importing enslaved Africans?
   - **A** The Spanish were weakened by disease and could not work.
   - **B** There was a labor shortage in the Americas.
   - **C** They wanted to compete with the British colonies.
   - **D** The Spanish wanted colonies in Africa.

4. Unlike some West African and Native American societies at the time, European societies in the 1400s had *not* developed —
   - **F** matrilineal kinship systems.
   - **G** systems of mathematics and astronomy.
   - **H** a centralized religious authority.
   - **J** agriculture.

hmhsocialstudies.com TEST PRACTICE

For additional test practice, go online for:

- Diagnostic tests
- Tutorials

INTERACT WITH HISTORY

Think about the issues you explored at the beginning of the chapter. Now that you know how Native Americans' way of life was changed by the arrival of the Europeans, form small groups and discuss the following question: Would you have resisted or helped the Europeans if you had been a Native American during the days of European colonization?

FOCUS ON WRITING

Imagine that you are one of the Taino people. You have just seen a landing party from Christopher Columbus's expedition arrive on the shores near your village. Based on what you have read in this chapter, write a paragraph describing your first encounter with the expedition, your reactions to the explorers, and your thoughts about further contact.

COLLABORATIVE LEARNING

Organize into pairs and use library or Internet sources to find excerpts from the journals of early explorers such as Columbus or Cabeza de Vaca. After reading, work together to list the assumptions and conclusions drawn by the writer about the new land and peoples he encountered. Write a paragraph explaining how these assumptions affected the interactions between explorers and native peoples.

THE Maya

The Maya developed one of the most advanced civilizations in the Americas, but their story is shrouded in mystery. Around A.D. 250, the Maya began to build great cities in southern Mexico and Central America. They developed a writing system, practiced astronomy, and built magnificent palaces and pyramids with little more than stone tools. Around A.D. 900, however, the Maya abandoned their cities, leaving their monuments to be reclaimed by the jungle and, for a time, forgotten.

Explore some of the incredible monuments and cultural achievements of the ancient Maya online. You can find a wealth of information, video clips, primary sources, and more at hmhsocialstudies.com.

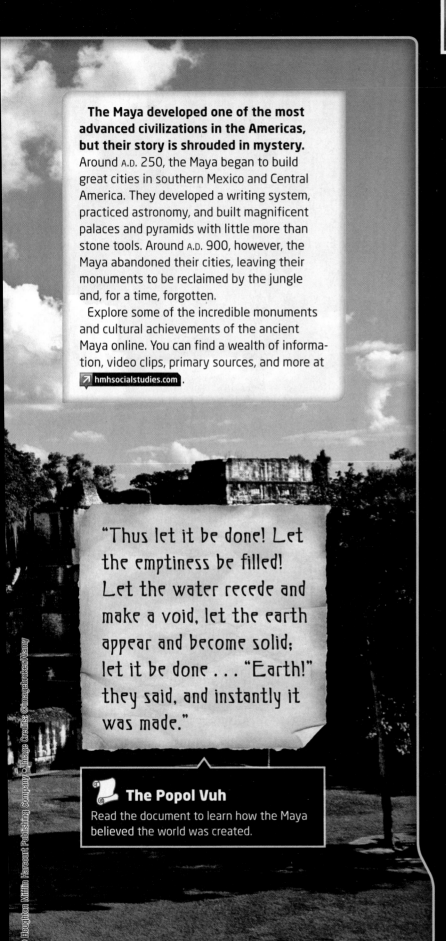

"Thus let it be done! Let the emptiness be filled! Let the water recede and make a void, let the earth appear and become solid; let it be done . . . "Earth!" they said, and instantly it was made."

The Popol Vuh

Read the document to learn how the Maya believed the world was created.

Destroying the Maya's Past

Watch the video to learn how the actions of one Spanish missionary nearly destroyed the written record of the Maya world.

Finding the City of Palenque

Watch the video to learn about the great Maya city of Palenque and the European discovery of the site in the eighteenth century.

Pakal's Tomb

Watch the video to explore how the discovery of the tomb of a great king helped archaeologists piece together the Maya past.

CHAPTER 2

The American Colonies Emerge

Essential Question

How did the their convergence affect the cultures of North America, Africa, and Europe?

ALABAMA COURSE OF STUDY

1 Compare effects of economic, geographic, social, and political conditions before and after European explorations of the fifteenth through seventeenth centuries on Europeans, American colonists, Africans, and indigenous Americans.

• Comparing European motives for establishing colonies, including mercantilism, religious persecution, poverty, oppression, and new opportunities.

2 Compare regional differences among early New England, Middle, and Southern colonies regarding economics, geography, culture, government, and American Indian relations.

• Explaining the role of essential documents in the establishment of colonial governments, including the Magna Carta, the English Bill of Rights, and the Mayflower Compact.

• Explaining the significance of the House of Burgesses and New England town meetings in colonial politics.

17th-century English explorers land in North America.

AMERICAS

1521 Hernándo Cortés conquers the Aztec Empire.

1540 Coronado explores the American southwest.

1565 Spanish settlers establish Saint Augustine, Florida.

1585 English colonists establish a colony at Roanoke Island.

1500 — 1550

WORLD

1517 Martin Luther begins the Protestant Reformation.

1534 Parliament declares Henry VIII head of the English church.

1588 England defeats the Spanish Armada.

Image Credits: (bkgd), ©MPI/HultonArchive/Getty Images; (bl), *Mask, Quetzalcoatl or Tonatiuh, the Sun God* (early 16th century), Aztec. Turquoise and pearl shell. British Museum, London/Photograph ©Werner Forman/Art Resource, New York; (br), ©Gianni Dagli Orti/Corbis

INTERACT WITH HISTORY

It is 1607. You are a colonist about to arrive in the land that England has claimed for itself and named Virginia. Although little is known about this place, you look forward to a life of adventure and prosperity. When you arrive, you are met by Native Americans who ask you why you have come to their land.

Explore the Issues

- As a colonist, how does the presence of another people change your expectations?
- What obligations does a colonist have to natives who already inhabit the land?

1607 John Smith and other colonists establish Jamestown.

1618 The Thirty Years War between Catholics and Protestants begins in central Europe.

1620 English "Pilgrims" found Plymouth Colony.

1630 English Puritans found the Massachusetts Bay Colony.

1649 Oliver Cromwell establishes the Puritan Commonwealth in England.

1650

1660 The English monarchy is restored with the accession of Charles II.

1664 England takes New Amsterdam from the Dutch.

1681 William Penn receives charter for Pennsylvania.

1700

Image Credits: (bkgd), ©MPI/HultonArchive/Getty Images (br), The Granger Collection, New York; (bl), ©Bettmann/Corbis

SECTION 1

Spain's Empire in the Americas

MAIN IDEA

Throughout the 1500s and 1600s, the Spanish conquered Central and portions of North America.

WHY IT MATTERS NOW

Spanish language, religion, and architecture continue to influence the Americas.

Terms & Names

- **Hernándo Cortés**
- **conquistador**
- **New Spain**
- **mestizo**
- ***encomienda***
- **Juan Ponce de León**
- **New Mexico**
- **Popé**

One American's Story

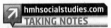

hmhsocialstudies.com TAKING NOTES

Use the graphic organizer online to take notes on how Spain established a profitable empire in the Americas.

In 1519, the native world near Tabasco in southeastern Mexico changed forever. That year, **Hernándo Cortés** led an army into the American mainland, eager to claim new lands for Spain. The peoples of the Tabasco, a province of the mighty Aztec empire, resisted the invaders but were no match for the Spaniards' rifles and cannons.

In surrendering, the natives handed over to the Spaniards 20 women, one of whom came to be called Doña Marina, or Malinche. Malinche easily mastered the Spanish language and soon acted as both translator and guide for Cortés as he fought and negotiated his way through Mexico. She also proved to be a brave and daring warrior. Bernal Díaz del Castillo, one of Cortés's foot soldiers, noted Malinche's courage.

Malinche *(center)* translates for Cortés *(seated)* and three Aztec ambassadors.

A PERSONAL VOICE BERNAL DÍAZ DEL CASTILLO

"Doña Marina . . . possessed such manly valor that, although she had heard every day how the Indians were going to kill us and eat our flesh with chili, and had seen us surrounded in the late battles, and knew that all of us were wounded or sick, yet never allowed us to see any sign of fear in her, only . . . courage."

—quoted in *Notable Latin American Women*

Malinche played a key role in the early stages of the Spanish conquest of the Americas. As the first European settlers in the Americas, the Spanish greatly enriched their empire and left a mark on the cultures of North and South America that still exists today.

The Spanish Claim a New Empire

In the wake of Columbus's voyages, Spanish explorers took to the seas to claim new colonies for Spain. Lured by the prospect of vast lands filled with gold and silver, these explorers, known as **conquistadors** (conquerors), pushed first into the Caribbean region—the islands and coast of Central and South America along the Caribbean Sea. Then they swept through Mexico and south to the tip of South America.

CORTÉS SUBDUES THE AZTEC Soon after landing in Mexico, Cortés learned of the vast and wealthy Mexica, or Aztec, empire, located deep in the region's interior. The Aztec, members of the diverse Nahua peoples of central Mexico, dominated the region. Cortés set off to conquer the Aztec with a force of 600 soldiers, 17 horses, numerous dogs, and 10 cannons. As he marched inland, Cortés, a gifted diplomat as well as military leader, convinced those Nahua who had long resented the spread of Aztec power to join his ranks.

After marching for weeks through 200 miles of difficult mountain passes, Cortés and his legions finally looked on the magnificent Aztec capital of Tenochtitlán. The Spaniards marveled at Tenochtitlán, with its towering temples and elaborate engineering works—including a system that brought fresh water into the city. "We were amazed," Bernal Díaz said of his first glimpse of Tenochtitlán. "Some of our soldiers even asked whether the things we saw were not a dream." While the Aztec city astonished the Spaniards, the capital's glittering gold stock seemed to hypnotize them. "They picked up the gold and fingered it like monkeys," one Native American witness recalled. "They hungered like pigs for that gold." (A)

MAIN IDEA

Analyzing Motives

(A) Why was Cortés interested in the Aztec empire?

KEY PLAYER

HERNÁNDO CORTÉS
1485–1547

Cortés made himself the enemy of the Native Americans, but the daring conquistador had few friends among Spaniards either. Spanish authorities on Cuba, where Cortés owned land, accused him of murdering his wife, Catalina Juárez. "There were ugly accusations, but none proved," wrote Juárez's biographer.

In addition, the Cuban governor, Diego Velázquez, who resented Cortés's arrogance, relieved him of the command of a gold-seeking expedition to the mainland. Cortés left Cuba anyway.

As he fought his way through Mexico, Cortés had to battle not only the Native Americans, but also the Spanish forces that Velázquez had sent to arrest him.

Convinced at first that Cortés was an armor-clad god, the Aztec emperor Montezuma agreed to give the Spanish explorer a share of the empire's existing gold supply. Cortés, who admitted that he and his comrades had "a disease of the heart that only gold can cure," eventually forced the Aztec to mine more gold and silver. In the spring of 1520, the Aztec rebelled against the Spaniards' intrusion. It is believed that, before driving out Cortes's forces, the Aztec stoned Montezuma to death, having come to regard him as a traitor.

HISTORY

VIDEO

The Arrival of the Spanish

hmhsocialstudies.com

While they successfully repelled the Spanish invaders, the natives found they could do little to stop disease. By the time Cortés launched a counterattack in 1521, the Spanish and their native allies overran an Aztec force that was greatly reduced by smallpox and measles. After several months of fighting, the invaders finally sacked and burned Tenochtitlán, and the Aztec surrendered. (B)

MAIN IDEA

Summarizing

(B) What factors enabled the Spaniards to conquer the Aztec?

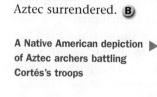

A Native American depiction of Aztec archers battling Cortés's troops

While flames still flickered in the shattered capital, Cortés laid plans for the colony of **New Spain,** whose capital he called Mexico City. Within three years, Spanish churches and homes rose from the foundations of old native temples and palaces in Mexico City. Cathedrals and a university followed.

SPANISH PATTERN OF CONQUEST In building their new American empire, the Spaniards drew from techniques used during the reconquest of Spain from the Moors, a Muslim people from North Africa who had occupied Spain for centuries. When conquering the Moors in the late 1400s, the Spanish lived among them and imposed upon them their Spanish culture.

"You and your people, . . . entering with such speed and fury into my country, . . . as to strike terror into our hearts."

NATIVE AMERICAN CHIEF, TO SPANISH EXPLORER HERNANDO DE SOTO

Spanish settlers in the Americas were mostly men and were known as *peninsulares*. Marriage between peninsulares and native women was common. These marriages created a large **mestizo**—or mixed Spanish and Native American—population. Their descendants live today in Mexico, other Latin American countries, and the United States.

Although the Spanish conquerors lived among and intermarried with the native people, they also oppressed them. In their effort to exploit the land for its precious resources, the Spanish forced the native workers to labor within a system known as ***encomienda,*** in which the natives farmed, ranched, or mined for Spanish landlords, who had received the rights to their labor from Spanish authorities.

The harsh pattern of labor that emerged under the *encomienda* caused priests such as Antonio de Montesinos to demand its end in a sermon delivered in 1511.

A PERSONAL VOICE FRAY ANTONIO DE MONTESINOS

"Tell me, by what right or justice do you hold these Indians in such a cruel and horrible servitude? . . . Why do you keep them so oppressed and exhausted, without giving them enough to eat or curing them of the sicknesses they incur from the excessive labor you give them? . . . Are you not bound to love them as you love yourselves? Don't you understand this? Don't you feel this?"

—quoted in *Reflections, Writing for Columbus*

MAIN IDEA

Analyzing Causes

C Why did the Spanish begin to use African slaves on their plantations in the New World?

In 1542, the Spanish monarchy, which had tried to encourage fair treatment of native subjects, abolished the *encomienda*. To meet their intense labor needs, the Spaniards instead turned to other labor systems and began to use African slaves. C

The Conquistadors Push North

Dreaming of new conquests and more gold, and afraid that European nations might invade their American empire from the north, Spain undertook a series of expeditions into what would become the southeastern and southwestern United States.

EXPLORING FLORIDA In 1513, on Easter Sunday—a day the Spaniards called *pascua florida,* or "feast of flowers"— explorer **Juan Ponce de León** spied a tree-covered beach. In honor of the holiday, he named the land *La Florida*. For almost five decades, the Spanish probed La Florida and the surrounding areas for gold, battling the local residents, disease, and starvation. In 1562, discouraged by the lack of economic success, Spain abandoned further exploration of Florida.

VIDEO
Claiming Florida for Spain

hmhsocialstudies.com

Within months of Spain's departure, a band of French settlers arrived near what is now Jacksonville. Accompanying the settlers were French pirates, or buccaneers, who quickly took interest in Spain's treasure-filled ships sailing from the Gulf of Mexico. Consequently, Spain reversed its decision to abandon Florida and ordered one of its fiercest warriors, Pedro Menéndez de Avilés, to drive the French out of the area.

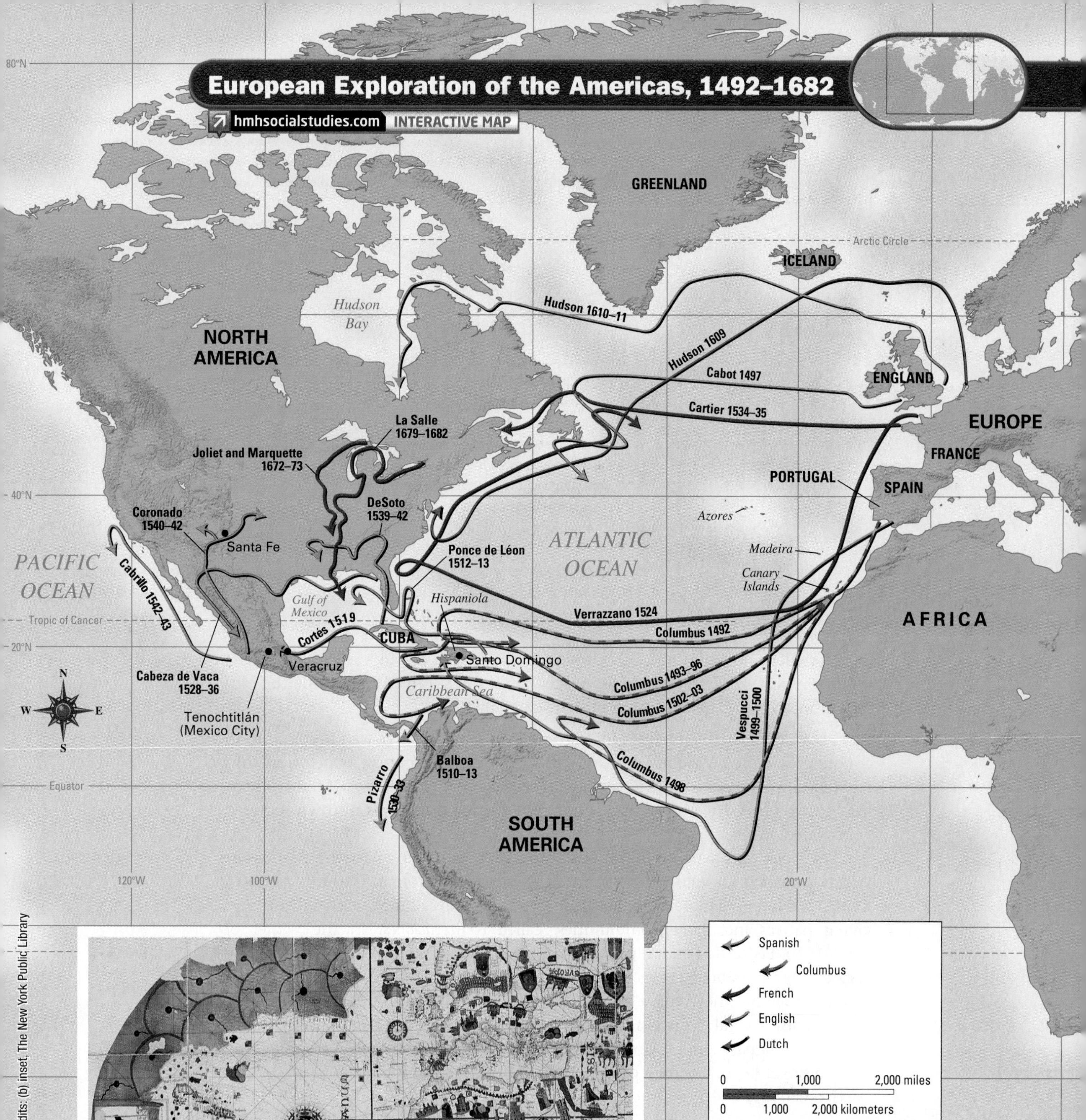

European Exploration of the Americas, 1492–1682

hmhsocialstudies.com INTERACTIVE MAP

Spanish
Columbus
French
English
Dutch

0 1,000 2,000 miles
0 1,000 2,000 kilometers

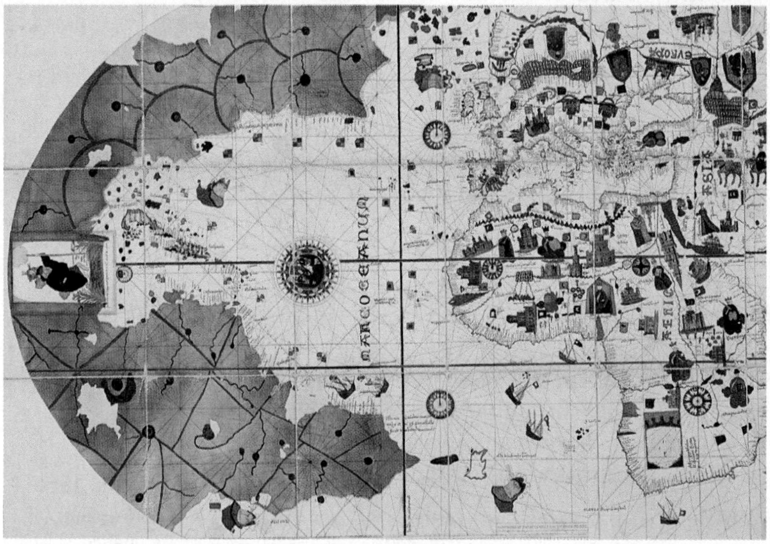

Juan de la Cosa, pilot-navigator on Columbus's ship *Niña*, drew the known world on this oxhide map in 1500.

GEOGRAPHY SKILLBUILDER

1. **Movement** How many voyages to the Americas did Columbus make?
2. **Place** In what years did England and France sail to the Americas and which regions did they explore?

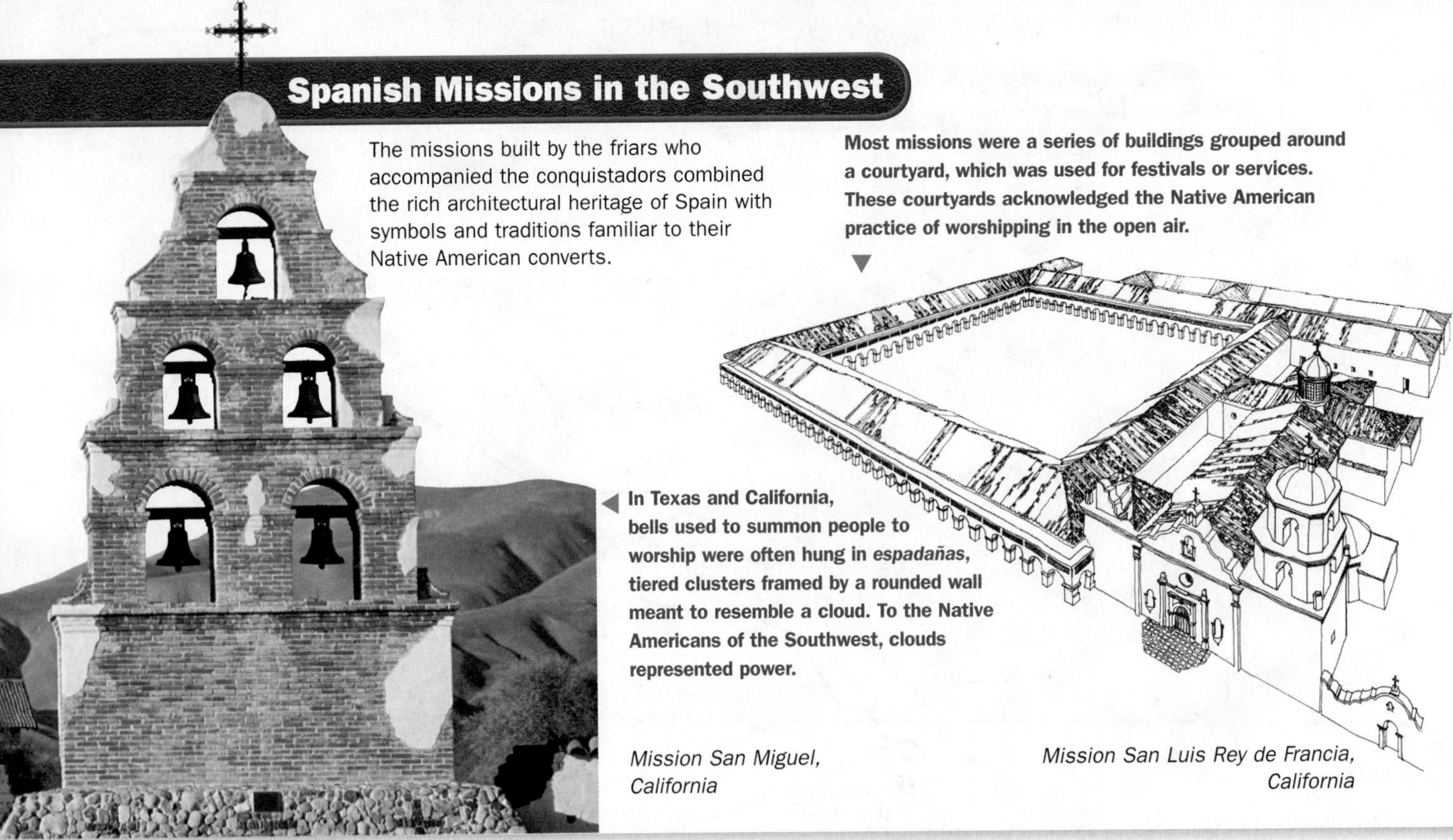

Spanish Missions in the Southwest

The missions built by the friars who accompanied the conquistadors combined the rich architectural heritage of Spain with symbols and traditions familiar to their Native American converts.

Most missions were a series of buildings grouped around a courtyard, which was used for festivals or services. These courtyards acknowledged the Native American practice of worshipping in the open air.

In Texas and California, bells used to summon people to worship were often hung in *espadañas*, tiered clusters framed by a rounded wall meant to resemble a cloud. To the Native Americans of the Southwest, clouds represented power.

Mission San Miguel, California

Mission San Luis Rey de Francia, California

Menéndez de Avilés not only drove out the French but in 1565 established a lonely outpost, which he called St. Augustine. It has survived to become the oldest European-founded city in the present-day United States.

SETTLING THE SOUTHWEST In 1540, in search of another wealthy empire to conquer, Francisco Vásquez de Coronado led the first Spanish expedition into what is now Arizona, New Mexico, Texas, Oklahoma, and Kansas. After wandering for two years, the only precious metal he carried home was his own battered gold-plated armor.

The Spaniards who followed in Coronado's wake came to the Southwest largely to search for veins of silver ore or to spread the Roman Catholic religion. As the native population dwindled from disease, Spanish priests gathered the surviving natives into large communities, called *congregaciónes*. In the winter of 1609–1610, Pedro de Peralta, governor of Spain's northern holdings, called **New Mexico**, led missionary priests and other settlers to a tributary of the upper Rio Grande. Together they built a capital called Santa Fe, or "Holy Faith." In the next two decades, several Christian missions were built among the Pueblos in the area. The hooves of pack mules wore down a 1,500-mile trail known as *el Camino Real*, or "the Royal Road," as they carried goods back and forth between Santa Fe and Mexico City. **D**

MAIN IDEA

Analyzing Motives

D Why did the Spanish build a road between Santa Fe and Mexico City?

Resistance to the Spanish

The Catholic missionaries who settled north of Mexico not only tried to Christianize the peoples they encountered but also attempted to impose Spanish culture on them. The native inhabitants of New Mexico resisted and eventually rebelled against the Spaniards' attempts to transform their lives and beliefs.

Vocabulary

conversion: A change in which a person adopts a new belief, opinion, or religion

CONFLICT IN NEW MEXICO While Spanish priests converted scores of Native Americans in New Mexico, tension marked the relationship between the priests and their new converts. As they sought to transform the Native Americans' cultures, Spanish priests and soldiers smashed and burned objects held sacred by local communities and suppressed many of their ceremonial dances and rituals.

During the 1670s, priests and soldiers around Santa Fe began forcing Native Americans to help support the missions by paying a tribute, an offering of either goods or services. The tribute was usually a bushel of maize or a deer hide, but the Spanish also forced Native Americans to work for them and sometimes abused them physically. Native Americans who practiced their native religion or refused to pay tribute were beaten.

POPÉ'S REBELLION One unfortunate Native American who felt the sting of a Spanish whip was the Pueblo religious leader **Popé.** The priests punished Popé for his worship practices, which they interpreted as witchcraft. The whipping left the Pueblo leader scarred with hatred and ready for rebellion. In 1680, he led a well-organized uprising against the Spanish that involved some 17,000 people from villages all over New Mexico. The triumphant fighters destroyed Spanish churches, executed priests, and drove the Spaniards back into New Spain. "The heathen," one Spanish officer wrote about the uprising, "have concealed a mortal hatred for our holy faith and enmity for the Spanish nation." For the next 14 years—until Spanish armies regained control of the area—the southwest region of the future United States once again belonged to its original inhabitants. E

Analyzing Causes
E Why did the Native Americans of New Mexico revolt against the Spanish settlers?

But Spain would never again have complete control of the Americas. In 1588, England had defeated the Spanish Armada, ending Spain's naval dominance in the Atlantic. In time, England began forging colonies along the eastern shore of North America, thus extending its own empire in the New World.

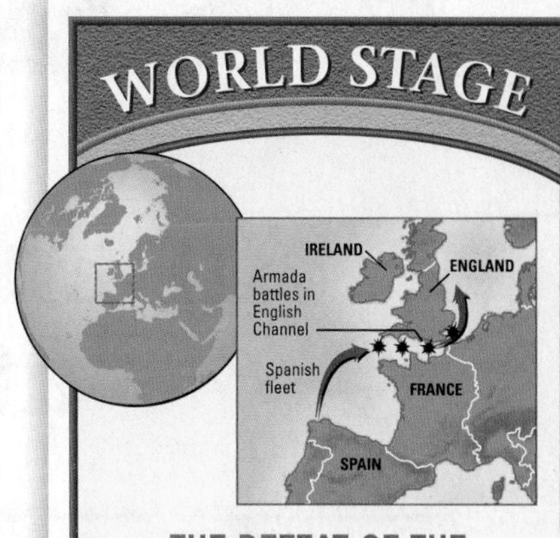

THE DEFEAT OF THE SPANISH ARMADA

To stop English raids on his treasure ships, King Philip II of Spain assembled an armada, or fleet, of about 130 ships, carrying nearly 19,000 soldiers. In the summer of 1588, the Spanish Armada sailed into the English Channel. However, English warships out-maneuvered the vessels, bombarding them with heavy, long-range cannons.

Aiding the English cannons were powerful storms that destroyed much of the Armada. Its defeat dealt a blow to Spain's military power and opened the way for the rest of Europe to venture into the Americas.

SECTION 1 ASSESSMENT

1. **TERMS & NAMES** For each term or name, write a sentence explaining its significance.
   - **Hernándo Cortés**
   - **conquistador**
   - **New Spain**
   - **mestizo**
   - ***encomienda***
   - **Juan Ponce de León**
   - **New Mexico**
   - **Popé**

MAIN IDEA

2. **TAKING NOTES**
   Re-create the web below on your paper and fill in events related to the main idea in the center.

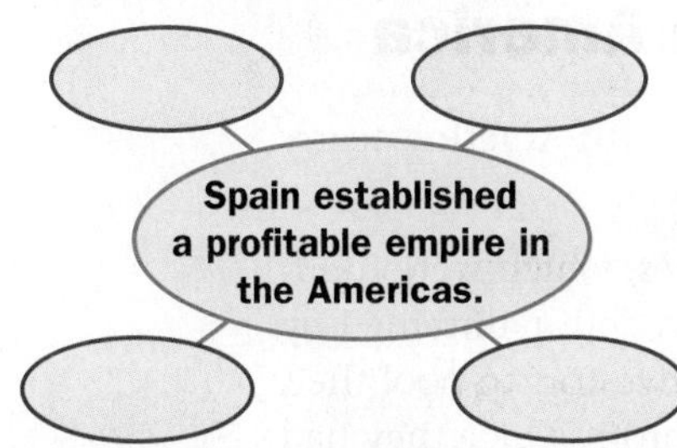

CRITICAL THINKING

3. **EVALUATING IMPACT**
   Do you agree or disagree with this statement: The Spanish conquest of the Aztecs, which led to the creation of Mexico, was neither a triumph nor a defeat? Support your opinion with references to the text.
   Think About:
   - the actions of the conquistadors
   - the effects of disease on the native peoples
   - the *encomienda* system
   - the mestizo population in Mexico today

4. **FORMING GENERALIZATIONS**
   State three main ideas about the Spaniards' exploration and settlement north of Mexico and their interaction with Native Americans there.

5. **MAKING INFERENCES**
   What can you infer from the fact that approximately 17,000 Native Americans from all over New Mexico took part in Popé's rebellion?

SECTION 2

An English Settlement at Jamestown

MAIN IDEA	WHY IT MATTERS NOW	Terms & Names
The first permanent English settlement in North America was founded at Jamestown, Virginia, in 1607.	English colonies in Virginia developed into the present states of the southern United States.	• John Smith • joint-stock companies • Jamestown • Powhatan • headright system • indentured servant • royal colony • Nathaniel Bacon

One American's Story

John Smith craved adventure. In 1600, at age 20, Smith trekked across Europe and helped Hungary fight a war against the Turks. For his heroic battle efforts, the Hungarians offered a knighthood to Smith, who inscribed his coat of arms with the phrase *Vincere est vivere*—"to conquer is to live."

In 1606, the daring and often arrogant adventurer approached the members of the Virginia Company, a group of merchants who were interested in founding an English colony in North America. Smith later recalled the opportunities that he saw open to him and other potential colonists.

A PERSONAL VOICE JOHN SMITH

> "What man who is poor or who has only his merit to advance his fortunes can desire more contentment than to walk over and plant the land he has obtained by risking his life? . . . Here nature and liberty . . . [give] us freely that which we lack or have to pay dearly for in England. . . .
>
> What pleasure can be greater than to grow tired from . . . planting vines, fruits, or vegetables?"
>
> —*The General History of Virginia*

▲ John Smith was a self-proclaimed soldier of fortune, a sea captain, and a poet.

With the help of Smith's leadership and, later, the production of the profitable crop of tobacco, England's small North American settlement survived.

English Settlers Struggle in North America

England's first attempts to carve out a colony of its own in North America nearly collapsed because of disease and starvation.

hmhsocialstudies.com TAKING NOTES

Use the graphic organizer online to take notes on the colonization of Virginia.

THE BUSINESS OF COLONIZATION Unlike Spanish colonies, which were funded by Spanish rulers, English colonies were originally funded and maintained by **joint-stock companies.** Stock companies allowed several investors to pool their wealth in support of a colony that would, hopefully, yield a profit. Once they had obtained a charter, or official permit, a stock company accepted responsibility for maintaining the colony, in return for which they would be entitled to receive back most of the profit that the colony might yield.

In 1606, King James I of England granted a charter to the Virginia Company. The company hoped to found a colony along the eastern shores of North America in territory explored earlier by Sir Walter Raleigh. Raleigh had named the territory Virginia after Elizabeth I (1533–1603), "the virgin queen." The Virginia Company had lured financial supporters by asking for a relatively small investment. Stockholders would be entitled to receive four-fifths of all gold and silver found by the colonists. The king would receive the remaining fifth.

The Virginia Company's three ships—*Susan Constant, Discovery,* and *Godspeed*—with nearly 150 passengers and crew members aboard, reached the shores of Virginia in April of 1607. They slipped into a broad coastal river and sailed inland until they reached a small peninsula. There, the colonists claimed the land as theirs. They named the settlement **Jamestown** and the river the James, in honor of their king.

A DISASTROUS START John Smith sensed trouble from the beginning. As he wrote later, "There was no talk, no hope, no work, but dig gold, wash gold, refine gold, load gold." Smith warned of disaster, but few listened to the arrogant captain, who had made few friends on the voyage over.

Disease from contaminated river water struck first. Hunger soon followed. The colonists, many of whom were unaccustomed to a life of labor, had refused to clear fields, plant crops, or even gather shellfish from the river's edge. One settler later described the terrifying predicament.

HISTORICAL SPOTLIGHT

THE MYSTERY OF ROANOKE

England's first attempt to plant a colony in North America at what is now Roanoke Island remains shrouded in mystery. After one failed attempt in 1585, Sir Walter Raleigh (pictured above) dispatched a second expedition in 1587. Its captain, John White, sailed back to England for supplies. Upon his return to Roanoke in 1590, White found the settlement empty, the colonists vanished. The word "CROATOAN" (a Native American tribe) was carved into a tree. Historians believe that the colonists starved or were either attacked by or joined with local Native American tribes.

A Personal Voice

"Thus we lived for the space of five months in this miserable distress . . . our men night and day groaning in every corner of the fort, most pitiful to hear. If there were any conscience in men, it would make their hearts to bleed to hear the pitiful murmurings and outcries of our sick men for relief, every night and day for the space of six weeks: some departing out of the World, many times three or four in a night; in the morning their bodies being trailed out of their cabins like dogs, to be buried."

—A Jamestown colonist quoted in *A New World*

On a cold winter day in 1607, standing among the 38 colonists who remained alive, John Smith took control of the settlement. "You see that power now rests wholly with me," he announced. "You must now obey this law, . . . he that will not work shall not eat." Smith held the colony together by forcing the colonists to farm. He also persuaded the nearby **Powhatan** people to provide food. Unfortunately, later that winter, a stray spark ignited a gunpowder bag Smith was wearing and set him on fire. Badly burned, Smith headed back to England, leaving Jamestown to fend for itself.

In the spring of 1609, about 600 new colonists arrived with hopes of starting a new life in the colony. The Powhatan, by now alarmed at the growing number of settlers, began to kill the colonists' livestock and destroy their farms. By the following winter, conditions in Jamestown had deteriorated to the point of famine. In what became known as the "starving time," the colonists ate roots, rats, snakes, and even boiled shoe leather. Of those 600 new colonists, only about 60 survived. (A)

MAIN IDEA

Summarizing
(A) What factors contributed to the near failure of Jamestown?

Rediscovering Fort James

hmhsocialstudies.com INTERACTIVE

Erosion turned the Jamestown Peninsula into an island and, for many years, the site of the original Fort James was assumed to be under water. However, in 1996, archaeologists from the Association for the Preservation of Virginia Antiquities discovered artifacts on what they concluded was the original site of the fort.

Since then, archaeologists have discovered armor, weapons, even games used by the first colonists. Archaeologists and historians are constantly learning more and more about this long-buried treasure of American history.

16th-century helmet and breastplate.

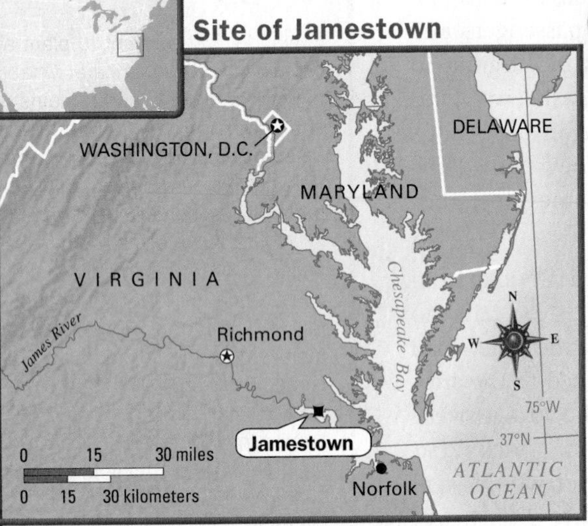

An archaeologist kneels beside holes left from the original palisade fence of Fort James. Note that the palisades were less than one foot in width.

Rounded bulwarks, or watch towers, mounted with cannon were located at each corner of the fort. The range of each cannon was approximately one mile.

The walls of the triangular-shaped fort measured 420 feet on the river side and 300 feet on the other two sides.

A barracks or "bawn" stood along the wall.

Colonists' houses were built about ten feet from the fort's walls. Houses measured sixteen by forty feet and several colonists lived in each.

The main gate, located on the long side, faced the James River.

This illustration re-creates what historians and archaeologists now believe Fort James looked like early in its history.

JAMESTOWN BEGINS TO FLOURISH The surviving colonists decided to abandon the seemingly doomed settlement. However, as they sailed down the James River, they were met by a second English ship whose passengers convinced the fleeing colonists to turn around. Under the watchful eye of new leaders, who did not hesitate to flog or even hang colonists found neglecting their work, Jamestown stabilized and the colony began to expand farther inland along the James River. However, equally important in the colony's growth was the development of a highly profitable crop: tobacco.

"BROWN GOLD" AND INDENTURED SERVANTS Europeans had become aware of tobacco soon after Columbus's first return from the West Indies. In 1612, the Jamestown colonist John Rolfe experimented by cross breeding tobacco from Brazil with a harsh strain of the weed that local Native Americans had grown for years. Rolfe's experiment resulted in a high-quality tobacco strain for which the citizens of England soon clamored. By the late 1620s, colonists exported more than 1.5 million pounds of "brown gold" to England each year. B

MAIN IDEA

Analyzing Events

B Why was tobacco so important to the Jamestown colony?

In order to grow tobacco, the Virginia Company needed a key ingredient that was missing from the colony—field laborers. In an effort to lure settlers to Jamestown, the Virginia Company introduced the **headright system** in 1618. Under this system, anyone who paid for their own or another's passage to Virginia received 50 acres of land. Immigration to the colony jumped.

The headright system yielded huge land grants for anyone who was wealthy enough to transport large numbers of people to Virginia. The Company used the term "plantation" for the group of people who settled the land grant, but eventually, the term was used to refer to the land itself. To work their plantations, many owners imported **indentured servants** from England. In exchange for passage to North America, and food and shelter upon arrival, an indentured servant agreed to a limited term of servitude—usually four to seven years. Indentured servants were usually from the lower classes of English society. C

MAIN IDEA

Contrasting

C How did the conditions of indentured servitude differ from those of the headright system?

THE FIRST AFRICAN LABORERS Another group of laborers—Africans—first arrived in Virginia aboard a Dutch merchant ship in 1619. Records suggest that the Jamestown colonists treated the group of about 20 Africans as indentured servants. After a few years, most of the Africans received land and freedom. Meanwhile, other Africans continued to arrive in the colony in small numbers, but it would be several decades before the English colonists in North America began the systematic use of Africans as slave labor.

ANOTHER PERSPECTIVE

FANTASIES OF THE "NEW WORLD"

By the early 1600s, many Englishmen, weary of wars and living in overcrowded cities, listened eagerly to early reports about Virginia. Playwrights, poets, and adventurers, most of whom had never seen the "New World," turned those reports into fantasies of a "promised land," a place of fair climate, friendly natives, rich harvests, and bright futures.

A play produced in London in 1605 described Virginia as a place where native children wore rubies and diamonds in their coats and caps. In 1606, the English poet Michael Drayton called Virginia "that delicious land" because of its rich soil and fantastic harvests. By 1607, the Virginia Company officers translated those fantasies into advertisements. During the "starving time," Jamestown colonists must have bitterly recalled the promises made in those advertisements.

NOVA BRITANNIA.
OFFERING MOST
Excellent fruites by Planting in
VIRGINIA.
Exciting all ſuch as be well affected
to further the ſame.

LONDON
Printed for SAMVEL MACHAM, and are to be ſold at
his Shop in Pauls Church-yard, at the
Signe of the Bul-head.
1609.

This poster, dated 1609, reflects an attempt to attract settlers to the early Virginia colony.

▲ In this 18th-century engraving, a Virginia planter oversees slaves packing tobacco leaves for shipment to England.

One reason for this was economics. In Virginia, where tobacco served as currency in the early 1600s, an indentured servant could be purchased for 1,000 pounds of tobacco, while a slave might cost double or triple that amount. However, by the late 1600s, a decline in the indentured servant population coupled with an increase in the colonies' overall wealth spurred the colonists to begin importing slaves in huge numbers. While the life of indentured servants was difficult, slaves endured far worse conditions. Servants could eventually become full members of society, but slaves were condemned to a life of harsh labor. D

MAIN IDEA

Summarizing

D What factors led to the importation of African slaves to Virginia?

The Settlers Clash with Native Americans

As the English settlers expanded their settlement, their uneasy relations with the Native Americans worsened. The colonists' desire for more land led to warfare with the original inhabitants of Virginia.

THE ENGLISH PATTERN OF CONQUEST Unlike the Spanish, whose colonists intermarried with Native Americans, the English followed the pattern used when they conquered the Irish during the 1500s and 1600s. England's Laws of Conquest declared, in part, "Every Irishman shall be forbidden to wear English apparel or weapons upon pain of death." The same law also banned marriages between the English and the Irish.

The English brought this pattern of colonization with them to North America. Viewing the Native Americans as being "like the wild Irish," the English settlers had no desire to live among or intermarry with the Native Americans they defeated.

THE SETTLERS BATTLE NATIVE AMERICANS As the English settlers recovered in the years following the starving time, they never forgot the Powhatan's hostility during the starving time. In retaliation, the leaders of Jamestown demanded tributes of corn and labor from the local native peoples. Soldiers pressed these demands by setting Powhatan villages on fire and kidnapping hostages, especially children. One of the kidnapped children, Chief Powhatan's daughter, Pocahontas, married John Rolfe in 1614. This lay the groundwork for a half-hearted peace. However, the peace would not last, as colonists continued to move further into Native American territory and seize more land to grow tobacco. E

MAIN IDEA

Analyzing Causes

E Why were the colonists in conflict with the Powhatan?

By 1622, English settlers had worn out the patience of Chief Opechancanough, Chief Powhatan's brother and successor. In a well-planned attack, Powhatan raiding parties struck at colonial villages up and down the James River, killing more than 340 colonists. The attack forced the Virginia Company to send in more troops and supplies, leaving it nearly bankrupt. In 1624, James I, disgusted by the turmoil in Virginia, revoked the company's charter and made Virginia a **royal colony**—one under direct control of the king. England sent more troops and settlers to strengthen the colony and to conquer the Powhatan. By 1644, nearly 10,000 English men and women lived in Virginia, while the Powhatan population continued to fall.

▲ Pocahontas as she appeared during her visit to England in 1616–1617

Economic Differences Split Virginia

By the 1670s, many of the free white men in Virginia were former indentured servants who, although they had completed their servitude, had little money to buy land. Because they did not own land, they could not vote and therefore enjoyed almost no rights in colonial society. These poor colonists lived mainly on the western outskirts of Virginia, where they constantly fought with Native Americans for land.

HOSTILITIES DEVELOP During the 1660s and 1670s, Virginia's poor settlers felt oppressed and frustrated by the policies of the colony's governor, Sir William Berkeley. More and more, Berkeley levied or imposed high taxes, which were paid mostly by the poorer settlers who lived along Virginia's western frontier. Moreover, the money collected by these taxes was used not for the public good but for the personal profit of the "Grandees," or "planters," the wealthy plantation farmers who had settled along the eastern shores of Virginia. Many of these planters occupied positions in the government, positions that they used to protect their own interests. As hostilities began to develop between the settlers along Virginia's western frontier and the Native Americans who lived there, the settlers demanded to know why money collected in taxes and fines was not being used to build forts for their protection.

Vocabulary

levy: to impose or collect

In 1675, a bloody clash between Virginia's frontier settlers and local natives revealed an underlying tension between the colony's poor whites and its wealthy landowners and sparked a pitched battle between the two classes. In June of 1675, a dispute between the Doeg tribe and a Virginia frontier farmer grew into a bloodbath. A group of frontier settlers who were pursuing Doeg warriors murdered fourteen friendly Susquehannock and then executed five chiefs during a peace conference. Fighting soon broke out between Native Americans and frontier colonists. The colonists pleaded to Governor Berkeley for military support, but the governor, acting on behalf of the wealthy planters, refused to finance a war to benefit the colony's poor frontier settlers.

BACON'S REBELLION Berkeley's refusal did not sit well with a twenty-nine-year-old planter named **Nathaniel Bacon.** Bacon, a tall, dark-haired, hot-tempered son of a wealthy Englishman, detested Native Americans. He called

HISTORICAL SPOTLIGHT

HOUSE OF BURGESSES

The House of Burgesses served as the first representative body in colonial America. The House first met in Jamestown on July 30, 1619, and included two citizens, or burgesses, from each of Virginia's eleven districts.

The House claimed the authority to raise taxes and make laws. However, the English governor had the right to veto any legislation the House passed. While the House represented a limited constituency—since only white male landowners could vote—it contributed to the development of representative government in English America. A century and a half after its founding, the House of Burgesses would supply delegates to the Continental Congress—the revolutionary body that orchestrated the break from Great Britain.

them "wolves" who preyed upon "our harmless and innocent lambs." In 1676, Bacon broke from his old friend Berkeley and raised an army to fight Native Americans on the Virginia frontier. **F**

> **MAIN IDEA**
> **Analyzing Issues**
> **F** Why was Nathaniel Bacon frustrated with Governor Berkeley?

Governor Berkeley quickly declared Bacon's army—one-third of which was made up of landless settlers and debtors—illegal. Hearing this news, Bacon marched on Jamestown in September of 1676 to confront colonial leaders about a number of grievances, including the frontier colonists' lack of representation in the House of Burgesses—Virginia's colonial legislature. Virginia's "rabble," as many planters called the frontier settlers, resented being taxed and governed without their consent. Ironically, 100 years later in 1776, both wealthy and poor colonists would voice this same complaint against Great Britain at the beginning of the American Revolution.

The march turned violent. The rebels set fire to the town as Berkeley and numerous planters fled by ship. However, Bacon had little time to enjoy his victory. He died of illness a month after storming Jamestown. Upon Bacon's death, Berkeley returned to Jamestown and easily subdued the leaderless rebels.

Bacon's Rebellion, as it came to be known, did succeed in drawing King Charles's attention to Berkeley's government, and Charles's commissioners, or investigators, were highly critical of Berkeley's policies. The old governor was recalled to England to explain himself but died before meeting with the king.

Although it spurred the planter class to cling more tightly to power, Bacon's Rebellion exposed the growing power of the colony's former indentured servants. Meanwhile, farther to the north, another group of English colonists, who had journeyed to North America for religious reasons, were steering their own course into the future.

ASSESSMENT

1. **TERMS & NAMES** For each term or name, write a sentence explaining its significance.
   - **John Smith**
   - **joint-stock companies**
   - **Jamestown**
   - **Powhatan**
   - **headright system**
   - **indentured servant**
   - **royal colony**
   - **Nathaniel Bacon**

MAIN IDEA

2. **TAKING NOTES**
   Create a time line of the major developments in the colonization of Virginia, using a form such as the one below.

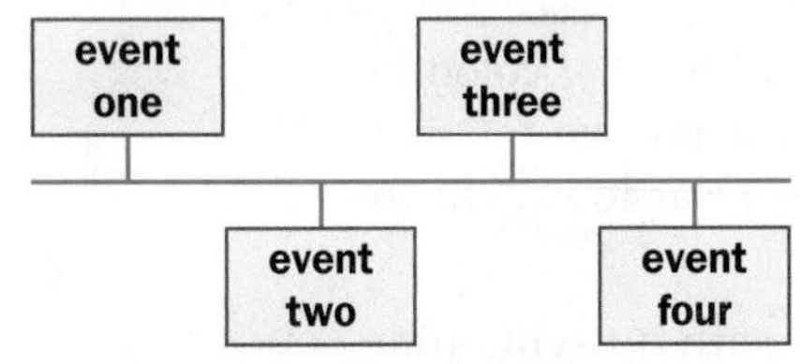

   Which event do you think was the most critical turning point? Why?

CRITICAL THINKING

3. **RECOGNIZING EFFECTS**
   The success of tobacco farming in Virginia had wide-ranging effects. Describe its impact on each of these groups: the Jamestown colonists, indentured servants, the Powhatan, the planters.
   Think About:
   - the headright system and indentured servitude
   - the colonists' need for more land
   - the conflict between rich and poor colonists

4. **ANALYZING PRIMARY SOURCES**
   The following lines appear in Michael Drayton's 1606 poem, "To the Virginian Voyage":

   > **"When as the luscious smell**
   > **of that delicious land**
   > **Above the sea that flows**
   > **The clear wind throws,**
   > **Your hearts to swell"**

   What do these lines tell you about the expectations many colonists had before they arrived in Virginia?

Section 3

Puritan New England

MAIN IDEA

English Puritans came to North America, beginning in 1620.

WHY IT MATTERS NOW

The United States continues to use an expanded form of representative government begun by the Puritans.

Terms & Names

- **Puritans**
- **John Winthrop**
- **Separatist**
- **Plymouth Colony**
- **Massachusetts Bay Colony**
- **Roger Williams**
- **Anne Hutchinson**
- **Pequot War**
- **Metacom**
- **King Philip's War**

One American's Story

hmhsocialstudies.com
TAKING NOTES

Use the graphic organizer online to take notes on the cause-and-effect relationships discussed in this section.

In 1628, at age 16, a young English woman named Anne Dudley married Simon Bradstreet, who, like herself, was one of a group of **Puritans,** church members who wanted to "purify" or reform the Church of England. Simon, Anne, and her parents left England with other Puritans who hoped to create a "holy" community in New England. There Anne became America's first English-speaking poet, whose poems would provide future generations with a glimpse of Puritan life and values. When her house burned to the ground on a July night in 1666, Anne composed a poem to express her sorrow and her resolve to remain strong.

A Personal Voice ANNE BRADSTREET

> **"Then, coming out, beheld a space**
> **The flame consume my dwelling place.**
> **And when I could no longer look,**
> **I blest His name that gave and took."**
>
> —from "Here Follows Some Verses upon the Burning of Our House (July 10th, 1666)"

Anne Dudley Bradstreet's book of poetry, *The Tenth Muse Lately Sprung Up in America,* is regarded as one of the first important works of American literature.

This picture of Anne Bradstreet is from a window in St. Botolph's Church, Lincolnshire, England.

Puritans Create a "New England"

When Anne Bradstreet and her family boarded the *Arbella,* the flagship of the Puritan expedition to America, the English settlement at Jamestown was still struggling to survive. Unlike the profit-minded colonists at Jamestown, however, the Puritans emigrated in order to create a model new society—what **John Winthrop,** their first governor, called a "City upon a Hill."

Puritans cherished their Bibles, passing them down as family treasures from one generation to the next. This Bible belonged to Governor William Bradford of the Plymouth Colony.

hmhsocialstudies.com
INTERACTIVE
Explore Plymouth Colony

PURITANS AND PILGRIMS Puritanism had its origins in the English Reformation. After King Henry VIII (1491–1547) broke with Roman Catholicism in the 1530s, his daughter, Elizabeth I (1533–1603) formed the Anglican church, or the Church of England. Although the Anglican church was free of Catholic control, some church members felt that it had kept too much of the Catholic ritual and tradition. These people were called Puritans because they wanted to purify the Anglican church by eliminating all traces of Roman Catholicism. Puritans embraced the idea that every worshipper should experience God directly through faith, prayer, and study of the Bible. Puritans held ministers in respect as a source of religious and moral instruction, but they objected to the authority of Anglican bishops.

Some Puritans felt they should remain in the Church of England and reform it from within. Other Puritans did not think that was possible, so they formed independent congregations with their own ministers. These **Separatists,** known today as the Pilgrims, fled from England to escape persecution, first to Holland and eventually to America. In 1620, this small group of families founded the **Plymouth Colony,** the second permanent English colony in North America. (A)

MAIN IDEA
Contrasting
(A) How were the Separatists different from other Puritans?

THE MASSACHUSETTS BAY COMPANY Meanwhile, other English Puritans in the 1620s who were discouraged about Anglican reform also turned their thoughts toward New England. Like the Separatists, they too felt the burden of increasing religious persecution, political repression, and dismal economic conditions. John Winthrop wrote to his wife in 1629, "[the Lord will] provide a shelter and a hiding place for us." Winthrop and others believed that this refuge would be in America.

In 1629, Winthrop and some of his well-connected friends obtained a royal charter for a joint-stock enterprise, the Massachusetts Bay Company. Winthrop and the other colonists transferred both the charter and the company's headquarters to New England. This strategy meant that when the Puritans migrated, they took with them the authority for an independent government. (B)

MAIN IDEA
Analyzing Motives
(B) Why did the Puritans leave England?

In September 1630, Winthrop and the other colonists aboard the *Arbella* established the **Massachusetts Bay Colony.** The port town of Boston became their capital. Soon other towns were founded to accommodate the large number of settlers flocking to join the colony. In the first year of the colony's settlement, 17 ships (including the *Arbella*) arrived with about 1,000 English men, women, and children—Puritan and non-Puritan. The migration was greater in size and more thorough in planning than all pre-

HISTORICAL SPOTLIGHT

THE MAYFLOWER COMPACT

Although the Pilgrims aimed for Virginia, their ship, the *Mayflower*, strayed far off course to Cape Cod. The Pilgrims knew that New England lay too far north for their colonial charter to be valid. They were also afraid that non-Pilgrim passengers would challenge their authority. Before departing the ship, the Pilgrim men signed a compact, or agreement, in which they created a civil government and pledged loyalty to the king.

The Mayflower Compact stated that the purpose of their government in America would be to frame "just and equal laws . . . for the general good of the colony." Laws approved by the majority would be binding on Pilgrims and non-Pilgrims alike. The document became a landmark of American democratic government.

This Mayflower Compact was the first governmental document in the new American colonies. It was the basis of the Plymouth colony's government and established democratic ideas that remain in the United States today, such as majority rule and self-government. The Mayflower Compact remained in effect until 1691.

vious expeditions to North America. Eventually, Plymouth Colony was incorporated into the Massachusetts Bay Colony.

"CITY UPON A HILL" In a sermon delivered before the *Arbella* landed, Winthrop expressed the sense of mission that bound the Puritans together.

A PERSONAL VOICE JOHN WINTHROP

> **"We must be knit together in this work; . . . we must uphold [each other] . . . in all meekness, gentleness, patience and liberality [generosity]. We must delight in each other, make others' conditions our own, rejoice together, mourn together, labor and suffer together. . . .**
>
> **So shall we keep the unity of the spirit, in the bond of peace. . . . Ten of us will be able to resist a thousand of our enemies. For we must consider that we [in New England] shall be as a City upon a Hill, the eyes of all people are on us."**
>
> —"A Model of Christian Charity"

Winthrop's vision, however, did not stem from a belief in either social equality or political democracy. Explained Winthrop in his shipboard sermon, God had decreed that "some must be rich, some poor, some high and eminent in power and dignity, others mean [common] and in subjugation."

Although Puritans made no effort to create a democracy, political power was spread more broadly than in England. The Massachusetts Bay Company extended the right to vote to not only stockholders but to all adult males who belonged to the Puritan church, roughly 40 percent of the colony's men. This was a large electorate by the standards of Europe in the 1630s. These "freemen," as they were called, voted annually for members of a lawmaking body called the General Court, which in turn chose the governor. C

MAIN IDEA

Analyzing Issues

C Who could vote in the Massachusetts Bay Colony?

CHURCH AND STATE As this system of self-government evolved, so did the close relationship between the government and the Puritan church. Civic officials were members of the Puritan church who believed that they were God's "elect," or chosen, and had a duty to carry out God's will. Puritan laws criminalized

History Through Art

PURITAN HEADSTONES

Puritans forbade images in their churches but they permitted them in their cemeteries. The images on a headstone were meant not just to memorialize the dead but to remind both young and old that life was brief and should be lived according to the Puritan virtues of piety and hard work.

Central to virtually every Puritan headstone was the image of the winged skull. The skull itself was meant to symbolize the physical reality of death. The wings represented the soul and the possibility of immortality. ▶

The winged skull motif persisted into the 18th century, when the winged skull was either modified to resemble a cherub or was replaced with a carved portrait of the deceased. ▶

SKILLBUILDER **Interpreting Visual Sources**

1. What kind of emotions does the image of the winged skull elicit?
2. How do Puritan headstones compare with other memorials you have seen?

SEE SKILLBUILDER HANDBOOK, PAGE R23.

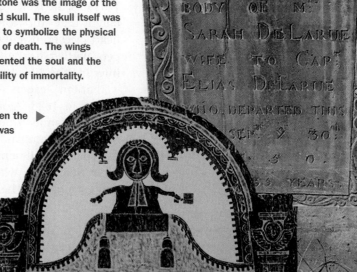

such sins as drunkenness, swearing, theft, and idleness. "No person . . . shall spend his time idly or unprofitably," decreed the General Court in 1633, "under pain of such punishment as the court shall think meet [appropriate] to inflict."

IMPORTANCE OF THE FAMILY Unlike settlers in Virginia, Puritans generally crossed the Atlantic as families rather than as single men or women. "Without family care," declared one minister, "the labor of Magistrates and Ministers . . . is likely to be in great measure unsuccessful." Puritans kept a watchful eye on the actions of husbands, wives, and children, and the community stepped in when necessary. If parents failed to nip disobedience in the bud, they might find their children placed in more "God-fearing" homes. If a husband and wife quarreled too much, a court might intervene as a form of marriage counseling. If they still bickered, one or both might end up in the stocks or the pillory.

Vocabulary
stocks, pillory: devices in which an offender was shackled and held on public display as a form of punishment

Dissent in the Puritan Community

Division soon threatened Massachusetts Bay. Two dissenters, Roger Williams and Anne Hutchinson, challenged the social order upon which the colony was founded.

THE FOUNDING OF PROVIDENCE "Forced religion stinks in the nostrils of God," declared **Roger Williams** in a sermon to his Salem congregation. Williams, an extreme Separatist, expressed two controversial views. First, he declared that the English settlers had no rightful claim to the land unless they purchased it from Native Americans. He called the royal charter that granted the lands a "National Sinne" and demanded that it be revised to reflect Native American claims. Second, Williams declared that government officials had no business punishing settlers for their religious beliefs. He felt every person should be free to worship according to his or her conscience.

The outraged General Court ordered Williams to be arrested and returned to England. Before this order was carried out, Williams fled Massachusetts. In January 1636, he headed southward to the headwaters of Narragansett Bay. There he negotiated with the local Narragansett tribe for land to set up a new colony, which he called Providence. In Providence, later the capital of Rhode Island, Williams guaranteed separation of church and state and religious freedom. D

MAIN IDEA
Contrasting
D What two principles did Providence guarantee that Massachusetts Bay did not?

ANNE HUTCHINSON BANISHED Puritan leaders soon banished another dissenter, **Anne Hutchinson.** To strict Puritans, she posed an even greater threat than Williams. In Bible readings at her home, Hutchinson taught that "the Holy Spirit illumines [enlightens] the heart of every true believer." In other words, worshippers needed neither the church nor its ministers to interpret the Bible for them.

Puritan leaders banished Hutchinson from the colony in 1638. Along with a band of followers, she and her family trudged to Rhode Island. After the death of her husband in 1642, Hutchinson moved with her younger children to the colony of New Netherland (now New York), where the Dutch also practiced religious toleration. The following year, she died in a war fought between the Dutch and Native Americans.

This statue of Anne Hutchinson stands in Boston, Massachusetts. Ironically, she was banished from Massachusetts for leading religious discussions.

Native Americans Resist Colonial Expansion

While Williams and his followers were settling Rhode Island, thousands of other white settlers fanned out to western Massachusetts and to new colonies in New Hampshire and Connecticut. However, as Native Americans saw their lands claimed and cleared for farming, they recognized that the rapid spread of the settlers meant an end to their way of life.

DISPUTES OVER LAND Disputes between the Puritans and Native Americans arose over land use. For every acre a colonial farmer needed to support life, a Native American needed twenty for hunting, fishing, and agriculture. To Native Americans, no one owned the land—it was there for everyone to use. Native Americans saw land treaties with Europeans as agreements in which they received gifts, such as blankets, guns, iron tools, or ornaments, in return for which they agreed to share the land for a limited time. Europeans, however, saw the treaties as a one-time deal in which Native Americans permanently sold their land to new owners. E

MAIN IDEA

Analyzing Issues

E How did Native Americans view land treaties?

THE PEQUOT WAR The first major conflict arose in Connecticut in 1637, when the Pequot nation decided to take a stand against the colonists. The colonists formed an alliance with the Narragansett, old enemies of the Pequot. The result of the **Pequot War** was the near destruction of the Pequot nation. The end came in May 1637, when about 90 English colonists and hundreds of their Native American allies surrounded a Pequot fort on the Mystic River. After setting the fort on fire, the colonists shot Pequot men, women, and children as they tried to escape or surrender. The massacre was so awful that the Narragansett pleaded,

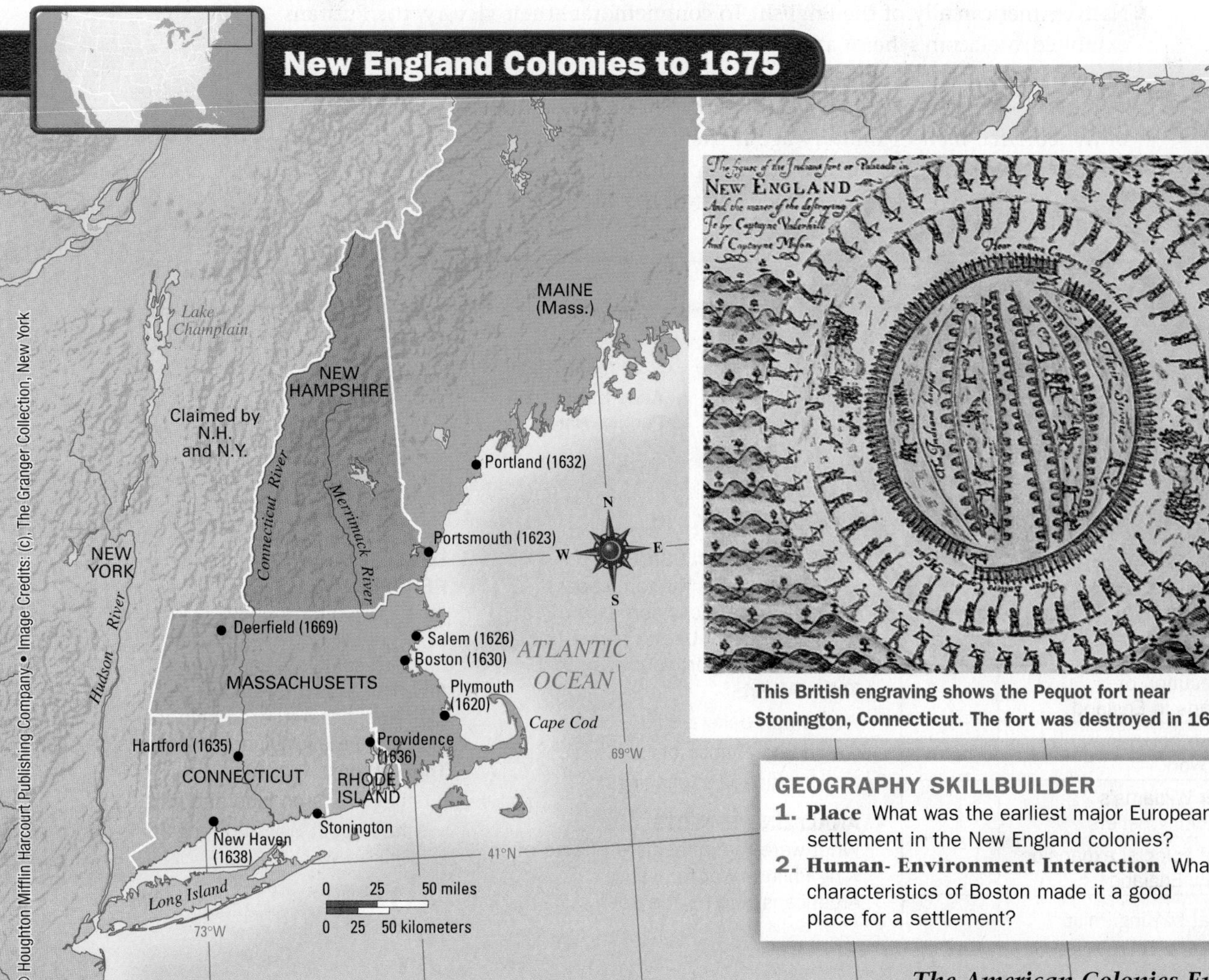

This British engraving shows the Pequot fort near Stonington, Connecticut. The fort was destroyed in 1637.

GEOGRAPHY SKILLBUILDER

1. **Place** What was the earliest major European settlement in the New England colonies?
2. **Human- Environment Interaction** What characteristics of Boston made it a good place for a settlement?

"This is evil, this is evil, too furious, too many killed." The colonists ignored them, until all but a few out of about 500–600 people in the fort had died. Later, the Narraganset leader Miantonomo declared in a speech to the Montauk tribe,

A PERSONAL VOICE MIANTONOMO

"These English have gotten our land, they with scythes cut down grass, and with axes fell the trees; their cows and horses eat the grass, and their hogs spoil our clam banks, and we shall all be starved. . . .

For so are we all Indians as the English are, and say brother to one another; so must we be one as they are, otherwise we shall be all gone shortly."

—quoted in *Changes in the Land*

KING PHILIP'S WAR Deprived of their land and livelihood, many Native Americans had to toil for the English to earn a living. They also had to obey Puritan laws such as no hunting or fishing on Sunday, the Sabbath day. Wampanoag chief **Metacom,** whom the English called King Philip, bristled under these restrictions. In a last-ditch effort to wipe out the invaders, he organized his tribe and several others into an alliance.

The eruption of **King Philip's War** in the spring of 1675 startled the Puritans with its intensity. Using hit-and-run tactics, Native Americans attacked and burned outlying settlements throughout New England. For over a year, the two sides waged a war of mutual brutality and destruction. Finally, food shortages, disease, and heavy casualties wore down the Native Americans' resistance, and they gradually surrendered or fled.

Wampanoag casualties included Metacom, the victim of a bullet fired by a Native American ally of the English. To commemorate their victory, the Puritans exhibited Metacom's head at Plymouth for 20 years. With his defeat, Native American power in southeastern New England was gone forever.

Still, the English paid a high price for their victory. All told, about one-tenth of the colonial men of military age in New England were killed in King Philip's War, a higher proportion of the total population than would be killed in either the American Revolution or the Civil War of the 1860s.

ASSESSMENT

1. **TERMS & NAMES** For each term or name, write a sentence explaining its significance.
   - **Puritans**
   - **John Winthrop**
   - **Separatist**
   - **Plymouth Colony**
   - **Massachusetts Bay Colony**
   - **Roger Williams**
   - **Anne Hutchinson**
   - **Pequot War**
   - **Metacom**
   - **King Philip's War**

MAIN IDEA

2. **TAKING NOTES**
Identify the effects of each of the causes listed in the chart below.

Cause	Effect
Persecution of Puritans in England	
Puritan belief in hard work	
Roger Williams's dissenting beliefs	
Rapid colonial expansion in New England	
Defeat of King Philip	

CRITICAL THINKING

3. **DRAWING CONCLUSIONS**
Why do you think Puritan leaders viewed Anne Hutchinson as a threat to their society? Use evidence from the text to support your answer.
Think About:
   - Puritan beliefs
   - characteristics of Puritan society
   - Hutchinson's teachings

4. **ANALYZING EFFECTS**
What were the immediate effects of King Philip's War for Native Americans and for the settlers?

5. **DEVELOPING HISTORICAL PERSPECTIVE**
Imagine you have been called upon to negotiate between the New England colonists and Native Americans. What would you tell each side about the other to help them overcome their misunderstandings?
Think About:
   - their views on land and religion
   - the Pequot War and King Philip's War

SECTION 4

Settlement of the Middle Colonies

MAIN IDEA	WHY IT MATTERS NOW	Terms & Names
The Dutch settled New Netherland; English Quakers led by William Penn settled Pennsylvania.	The principles of tolerance and equality promoted in the Quaker settlement remain fundamental values in America.	•William Penn •New Netherland •proprietor •Quakers

One American's Story

hmhsocialstudies.com
TAKING NOTES
Use the graphic organizer online to take notes on the similarities and differences between New Netherland and Pennsylvania.

William Penn had frustrated his father, Admiral Sir William Penn. In 1667, at age 22, the younger Penn committed himself to the Society of Friends, or Quakers, a Protestant sect whose religious and social beliefs were radical for the time.

Ironically, his late father would play a key role in helping William Penn realize his dream—establishing a haven for Quakers in America. King Charles II had owed Penn's father money, which the younger Penn asked to be repaid with American land. Charles agreed, and in 1681 he gave Penn a charter for Pennsylvania. Penn had big plans for his colony—a government run on Quaker principles of equality, cooperation, and religious toleration. As he confided to a friend, however, Penn did not reveal the true nature of his plans before receiving the charter.

A PERSONAL VOICE WILLIAM PENN

"**For matters of liberty and privilege, I propose that which is extraordinary, and [I intend] to leave myself and successors no power for doing mischief, [in order] that the will of one man may not hinder the good of a whole country; but to publish those things now and here, as matters stand, would not be wise. . . .**"

—quoted in *A New World*

This chalk drawing shows William Penn around 1695, at about the age of 50.

While Penn only partially realized his "extraordinary" plans, the tolerant Quaker principles on which he established his colony attracted many settlers of different faiths.

The Dutch Found New Netherland

While English Puritans were establishing colonies in New England, the Dutch were founding one to the south. As early as 1609, Henry Hudson—an Englishman employed by the Dutch—sailed up what is now known as the Hudson River. In 1621, the Dutch government granted the newly formed Dutch West India Company permission to colonize **New Netherland** and expand the thriving fur trade. New Amsterdam (now New York City), founded in 1625, became the capital of the colony. In 1655, the Dutch extended their claims by taking over New Sweden, a tiny colony of Swedish and Finnish settlers that had established a rival fur trade along the Delaware River.

A DIVERSE COLONY Although the Dutch company profited from its fur trade, New Netherland was slow to attract Dutch colonists. To encourage settlers to come and stay, the colony opened its doors to a variety of people. Gradually, more Dutch as well as Germans, French, Scandinavians, Jews, and other Europeans settled the area. The colony also included many Africans, free as well as enslaved. By the 1660s, one-fifth of New Netherland's population was of African ancestry.

These settlers generally enjoyed friendlier relations with Native Americans than did the English colonists in New England and Virginia. The Dutch were less interested in conquering the Native Americans than in trading with them for furs. The first Dutch traders had the good sense not to anger the powerful and well-organized Iroquois, who controlled a large territory between Dutch traders to the south and French traders to the north. However, the Dutch did engage in fighting with various Native American groups over land claims and trade rivalries. (A)

MAIN IDEA

Summarizing

(A) What were the important characteristics of the colony of New Netherland?

ENGLISH TAKEOVER To the English, New Netherland had become a "Dutch wedge" separating its northern and southern colonies. In 1664, King Charles II granted his brother James, the duke of York (who later became King James II), permission to drive out the Dutch. When the duke's fleet arrived in New Amsterdam's harbor, Peter Stuyvesant, the autocratic and unpopular Dutch governor, raised a call to arms. The call was largely ignored. Severely outmanned, Stuyvesant surrendered to the English without anyone firing a shot. The duke of York, the new **proprietor,** or owner, of the colony, renamed it New York. The duke later gave a portion of this land to two of his friends, naming the territory New Jersey for the British island of Jersey.

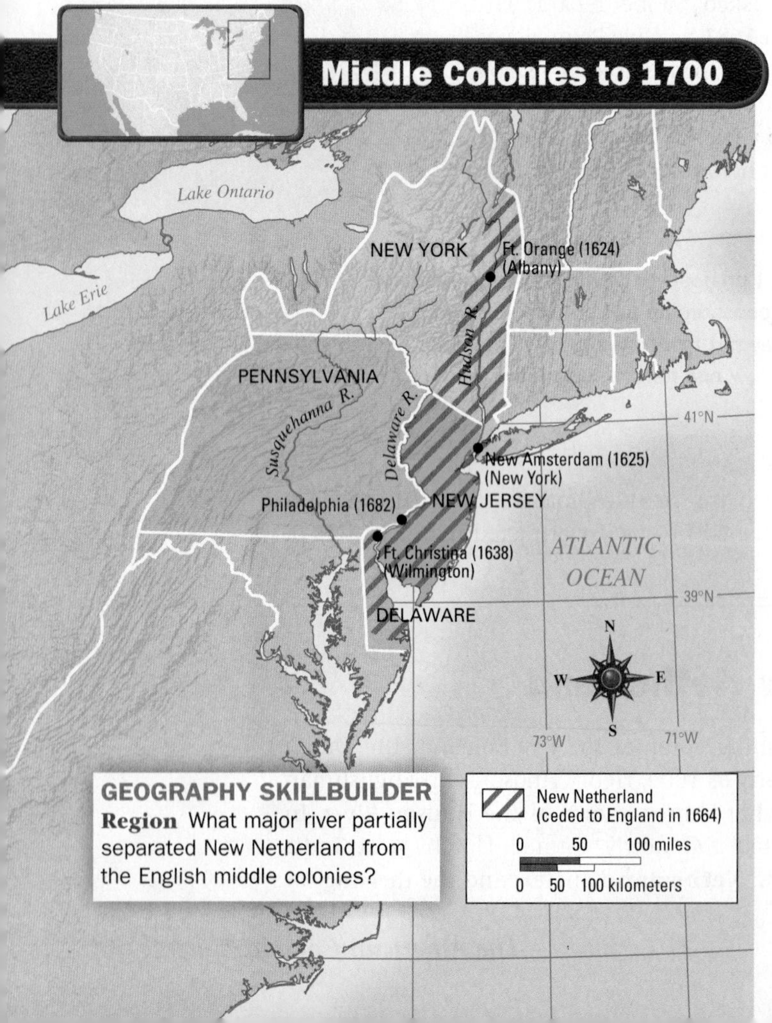

Middle Colonies to 1700

GEOGRAPHY SKILLBUILDER
Region What major river partially separated New Netherland from the English middle colonies?

The Quakers Settle Pennsylvania

The acquisition of New Netherland was an important step in England's quest to extend its American empire after the restoration of the monarchy. The colony that took shape was a marked contrast to England's other North American settlements.

Background
A Commonwealth headed by Oliver Cromwell ruled England from 1649 until 1658. The monarchy was restored under Charles II in 1660.

PENN'S "HOLY EXPERIMENT" William Penn well knew that England in the late 1660s was no place for Quakers. The **Quakers** believed that God's "inner light" burned inside everyone. They held services without formal ministers, allowing any person to speak as the spirit moved him or her. They dressed plainly, refused to defer to persons of rank, and embraced pacifism by opposing war and refusing to serve in the military. For their radical views, they were harassed by Anglicans and Puritans alike. (B)

MAIN IDEA

Comparing

(B) How did Quaker beliefs compare to Puritan beliefs?

COLONIAL MEETINGHOUSES

The Puritans of the northeast, the Quakers of Pennsylvania, and the Anglicans of the southern colonies held profound but often different convictions about community, social responsibility, and individual freedom. These convictions were often expressed in the religious services of each group as well as the architecture of the places of worship where these services were held.

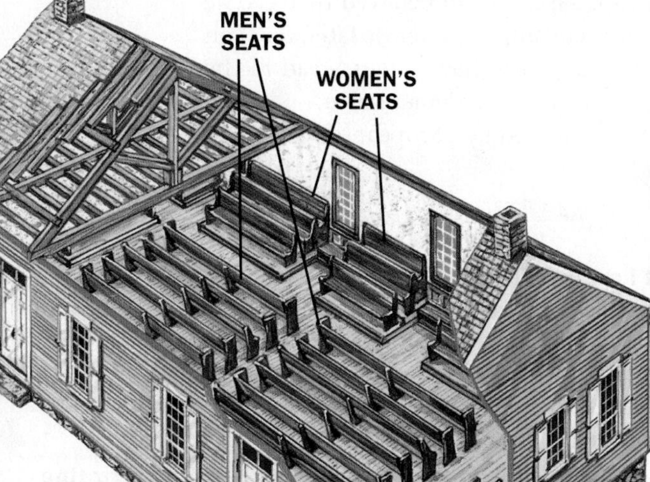

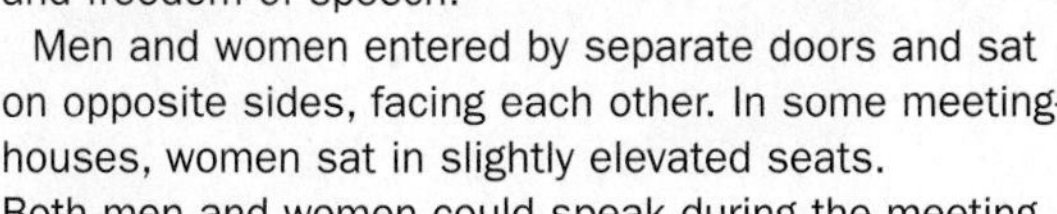

▲ **Quaker Meetinghouse**

Quaker services, which were called "meetings," relied on the inspiration of the "inner light." Meetings reflected a respect for conscience and freedom of speech.

Men and women entered by separate doors and sat on opposite sides, facing each other. In some meetinghouses, women sat in slightly elevated seats. Both men and women could speak during the meeting.

PULPIT

▲ **Puritan Meetinghouse**

Puritan services focused on preaching. Sermons, which sometimes lasted for hours, instructed the individual conscience to be mindful of the common good.

The pulpit was the focal point of the meetinghouse. A plain interior reflected a value for austerity and simplicity. Meetinghouses were also used for town meetings.

◀ **Anglican Church**

The head of the Anglican church was the British monarch. Anglican services valued ritual. Their churches stressed the importance of authority and status.

Anglican churches emphasized the altar through ornamentation and elaborate windows. A screen separated the altar from the congregation. Elaborate pews were reserved for wealthy church members.

SKILLBUILDER Interpreting Visual Sources

1. In what ways do the Puritan and Quaker meetinghouses resemble each other? In what ways are they different?
2. How does the interior of the Anglican church show a respect for hierarchy?

SEE SKILLBUILDER HANDBOOK, PAGE R23.

Penn saw his colony as a "holy experiment" in living, a place without a land-owning aristocracy. He guaranteed every adult male settler 50 acres of land and the right to vote. Penn's plan for government called for a representative assembly and freedom of religion. As a lasting symbol of his Quaker beliefs, Penn also helped plan a capital he called the "City of Brotherly Love," or Philadelphia.

Penn's constitution also provided for a separate assembly for the three southern counties along the Delaware Bay. Delaware thereby gained a somewhat separate existence. However, it continued to have the same governor as Pennsylvania.

NATIVE AMERICAN RELATIONS Like most Quakers, Penn believed that people approached in friendship would respond in friendship—sooner or later. So even before setting foot in North America, Penn arranged to have a letter read to the Lenni Lenapi, or Delaware, the tribe that inhabited his settlement area.

Aware that the Delaware had already been ravaged by European diseases and war, Penn wrote,

> **A PERSONAL VOICE** WILLIAM PENN
>
> **"Now I would have you well observe, that I am very sensible of the unkindness and injustice that has been too much exercised towards you by the people of these parts of the world, who have sought . . . to make great advantages by you, . . . sometimes to the shedding of blood. . . . But I am not such a man. . . . I have great love and regard toward you, and I desire to win and gain your love and friendship by a kind, just, and peaceable life."**
>
> —quoted in *A New World*

MAIN IDEA

Contrasting
Ⓒ How did Penn's attitudes and actions toward the Native Americans differ from those of the Puritans?

To be sure that his colonists treated the native peoples fairly, Penn regulated trade with them and provided for a court composed of both colonists and Native Americans to settle any differences. The Native Americans respected Penn, and for more than 50 years the Pennsylvania colony had no major conflicts with Native Americans who lived in the colony. Ⓒ

William Penn's 1682 treaty with the Native Americans is commemorated in this Edward Hicks painting from the 1840s.

A THRIVING COLONY Penn faced the same challenge as the Dutch West India Company; he needed to attract settlers—farmers, builders, and traders—to create a profitable colony. After initially opening the colony to Quakers, he vigorously recruited immigrants from around western Europe. Glowing advertisements for the colony were printed in German, Dutch, and French. In time, settlers came in numbers, including thousands of Germans who brought with them craft skills and farming techniques that helped the colony to thrive.

Penn himself spent only about four years in Pennsylvania. And, despite the colony's success, he never profited financially as proprietor and died in poverty in 1718. Meanwhile, his idealistic vision had faded but not failed. His own Quakers were a minority in a colony thickly populated by people from all over western Europe. Slavery was introduced and, despite Penn's principles, many prominent Quakers in Pennsylvania owned slaves. However, the principles of equality, cooperation, and religious tolerance on which he founded his vision would eventually become fundamental values of the new American nation.

▲ **Quakers offered silver collars like the one above to local Native Americans as a token of peace.**

THIRTEEN COLONIES Throughout the 1600s and 1700s, other British colonies in North America were founded as well, each for very different reasons. In 1632, King Charles I granted a charter for land north of Chesapeake Bay to George Calvert, the first Lord Baltimore. Calvert's son Cecil, the second Lord Baltimore, named the colony Maryland, after Queen Henrietta Maria, Charles's queen. Lord Baltimore, who was a Roman Catholic, obtained a religious toleration law from Maryland's colonial assembly, and the colony became famous for its religious freedom. In 1663, King Charles II awarded a group of key supporters the land between Virginia and Spanish Florida, a territory that soon became North and South Carolina.

In 1732, an English philanthropist named James Ogelthorpe, and several associates received a charter for a colony they hoped could be a haven for those imprisoned for debt. Ogelthorpe named the colony Georgia, after King George II. Few debtors actually came to Georgia, and Ogelthorpe's policies, which prohibited both slavery and the drinking of rum, were reversed when the British crown assumed direct control of the colony in 1752. By that time, there were thirteen British colonies in North America, but a growing desire for independence would soon put a strain on their relationship with England.

ASSESSMENT

1. **TERMS & NAMES** For each term or name, write a sentence explaining its significance.
   - **William Penn**
   - **New Netherland**
   - **proprietor**
   - **Quakers**

MAIN IDEA

2. **TAKING NOTES**
   Compare the colonies of New Netherland and Pennsylvania, using a Venn diagram such as the one below.

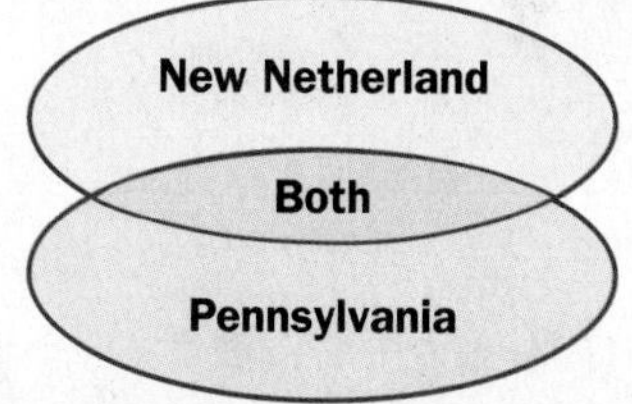

   Write a paragraph comparing and contrasting the two colonies.

CRITICAL THINKING

3. **ANALYZING CAUSES**
   Why was Ogelthorpe's prohibition of slavery reversed?

4. **EVALUATING DECISIONS**
   Both New Netherland and Pennsylvania encouraged settlers to come from all over western Europe. Do you think this was a good decision for these colonies? Why or why not?

5. **DRAWING CONCLUSIONS**
   How did William Penn succeed in achieving his goals for Pennsylvania, and how did he fail? Explain.
   Think About:
   - Penn's actions toward Native Americans
   - Penn's plans for representative government and freedom of religion
   - Quakers who owned slaves

GEOGRAPHY SPOTLIGHT

Surviving in a New World

Early settlers quickly discovered that the "new world" they had chosen to colonize was indeed an extraordinary place, but not in the ways they had expected it to be. Little did colonists know that during the years of colonization, North America was experiencing the worst of what scientists now refer to as the "Little Ice Age." Extremes of cold and heat up and down the eastern seaboard were more severe than they had been in several hundred years. In time, colonists learned about natural resources that were also unknown to them, foods and plants that ultimately saved and sustained their lives.

The Southern Colonies

Jamestown colonists had counted on bartering for food with Native Americans in order to survive, but the Powhatan had little food to spare. The area was being hit with its worst drought in 800 years. The intense heat destroyed crops, and Native Americans were reluctant to trade what little they had.

Average January Temperature: 40–50°F
Average July Temperature: 80–90°F
Rainfall: 20–40 inches per year
Days of Snow Cover: 10–20
Growing Season: 180–210 days
Soil: yellowish and sandy
Crops of Native Peoples: maize (corn), tobacco

The heat created other hardships as well. The swampy Jamestown peninsula bred malaria–bearing mosquitoes, and many colonists died from the disease. Soon, the colonists' drinking water, supplied by the river, became contaminated with salty sea water. Eventually, the colonists' export of tobacco—a crop that Native Americans had been growing for centuries—provided a source of income that attracted more colonists, whose arrival saved the colony.

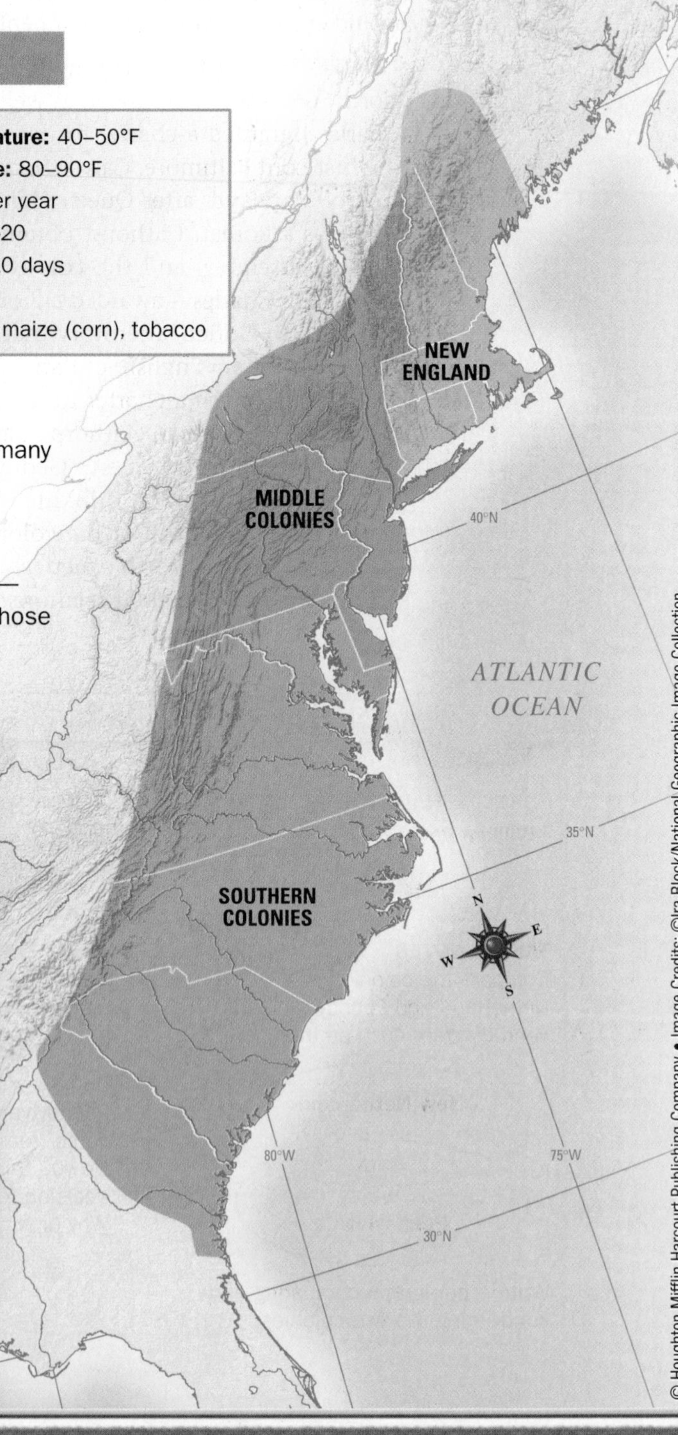

NEW ENGLAND
MIDDLE COLONIES
SOUTHERN COLONIES
ATLANTIC OCEAN
40°N
35°N
30°N
80°W
75°W
N
E
S
W

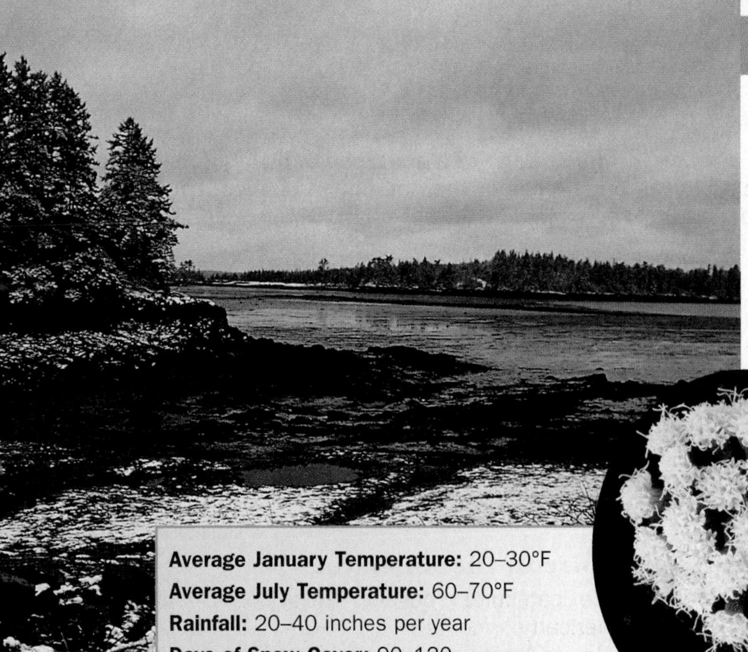

The New England Colonies

Colonists in New England likewise suffered from extreme weather conditions. The first hurricane recorded in North America occurred in Massachusetts Bay in 1635. Colonists noted in astonishment that it "blew down many hundreds of trees . . . overthrew some houses, drove ships from their anchors." Seasonal temperatures were also extreme. In the summer of 1637 a number of colonists died of sunstroke. Yet, the following winter, three feet of snow covered the ground.

To cope with illnesses brought on by the climate, colonists heeded Native Americans and looked to local plants and herbs as medicines. For instance, colonists learned from Native Americans that the Boneset plant (*Eupatorium perfoliatum*), pictured at left, could be used to break fevers and chills and could treat diseases ranging from colds and influenza to malaria and typhoid.

Average January Temperature: 20–30°F
Average July Temperature: 60–70°F
Rainfall: 20–40 inches per year
Days of Snow Cover: 90–120
Growing Season: 120–150 days
Soil: gray to brown, gravelly, stony
Crops of Native Peoples: maize (corn), beans, squash

The Middle Colonies

The Delaware River Valley would later be a rich farmland, but in the mid-1600s it too was affected by severe weather. Late frosts and wet springs caused poor harvests because conditions were too cold and wet for grains to ripen. Swedish colonists near what is now Wilmington, Delaware, reported in 1657 that onslaughts of frigid temperatures froze the Delaware River in a single day. In time, colonists learned from Native Americans about the crops that grew in the rich soil surrounding the Delaware River.

Average January Temperature: 30–40°F
Average July Temperature: 70–80°F
Rainfall: 20–40 inches per year
Days of Snow Cover: 30–40
Growing Season: 150–180 days
Soil: brownish and silty
Crops of Native Peoples: maize (corn), beans, pumpkin

THINKING CRITICALLY

1. **Analyzing Patterns** What seasonal patterns did the colonists in all three regions encounter? How did these patterns affect each colony?
2. **Creating a Diagram** Create an illustrated diagram that explains the interconnections in one of the North American colonies between colonists, Native Americans, and the land itself. Your diagram should include a reference to a particular crisis relating to the land, what the colonists learned from Native Americans, and how this new knowledge helped the colonists to survive.

SEE SKILLBUILDER HANDBOOK, PAGE R30.

CHAPTER 2 ASSESSMENT

VISUAL SUMMARY

THE AMERICAN COLONIES EMERGE: 1513–1681

SPANISH COLONIES

- Hernándo Cortés conquers Mexico (1519–1521)
- Juan Ponce de León establishes Florida (1513)
- Francisco Vasquez de Coronado explores American southwest (1540)
- Pedro de Peralta founds Santa Fe (1609–1610)
- Native Americans led by Popé rebel in southwest (1680)

VIRGINIA

- Virginia Colony is established (1607)
- Colony is saved by export of tobacco (1612)

- First African slaves are brought to North America (1619)
- Settlers clash with Powhatan tribe (1622)
- Settlement burns in Bacon's Rebellion (1676)

NEW ENGLAND

- English Pilgrims establish colony at Plymouth (1620)
- English Puritans establish colony at Boston (1630)
- Roger Williams is banished and founds colony at Providence (1635–1636)
- Anne Hutchinson is banished for heresy (1638)
- Puritans clash with Native Americans in Pequot War (1637) and King Philip's War (1675)

ENGLISH MIDDLE COLONIES

- Dutch found colony of New Netherland (1621)
- English acquire New Netherland and rename it New York (1664)
- William Penn establishes colony of Pennsylvania (1681)
- By the mid-1700s, there are 13 English colonies in North America

TERMS & NAMES

For each term below, write a sentence explaining its connection to the emergence of the American colonies. For each person below, explain his or her role in these colonies.

1. conquistador
2. mestizo
3. Popé
4. John Smith
5. indentured servant
6. John Winthrop
7. Anne Hutchinson
8. Metacom
9. proprietor
10. Quaker

MAIN IDEAS

Use your notes and the information in the chapter to answer the following questions.

Spain's Empire in the Americas

1. How did Mexican culture develop out of both Spanish and Native American elements?
2. How did Native Americans react to Spanish efforts to establish colonies?

An English Settlement at Jamestown

3. Explain how John Rolfe transformed the Virginia colony.
4. What conditions caused tension and warfare between settlers and Native Americans in Virginia?
5. What caused Bacon's Rebellion?

Puritan New England

6. Describe the role of religion in the lives of Puritans living in the Massachusetts Bay Colony.
7. How were the experiences of Roger Williams and Anne Hutchinson similar and different?
8. What caused conflicts between New England colonists and Native Americans?

Settlement of the Middle Colonies

9. Why did New Netherland gain a reputation for diversity?
10. How did Pennsylvania reflect William Penn's Quaker ideals?

CRITICAL THINKING

1. **USING YOUR NOTES** Using a chart like the one below, summarize the way European settlers and Native Americans interacted in the four listed regions.

Region	Interaction
New Mexico	
Virginia	
New England	
Pennsylvania	

2. **FORMING OPINIONS** John Winthrop dreamed that New England would be "like a City upon a Hill" in which "the eyes of all people are on us." In your opinion, what most impressed you positively and negatively about the founding of each North American colony?

STANDARDIZED TEST PRACTICE

Use the map and your knowledge of U.S. history to answer questions 1 and 2.

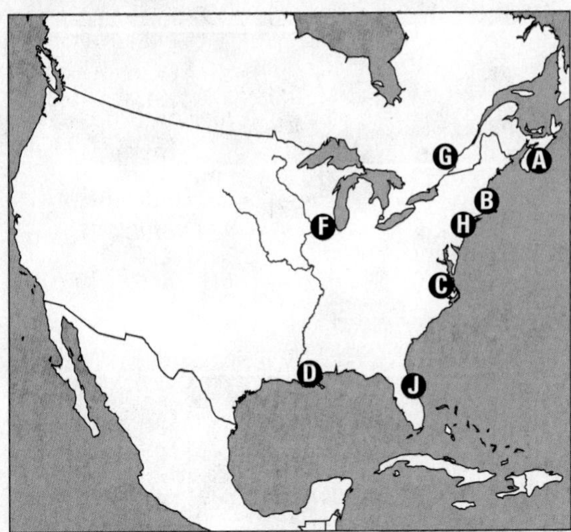

1. Which letter on the map shows the first permanent British settlement in North America?

   A A **C** C
   B B **D** D

2. Which letter shows an area colonized by Spain?

   F F **H** H
   G G **J** J

Use the information in the box and your knowledge of U.S. history to answer question 3.

- William Penn
- Roger Williams
- John Winthrop

3. Of these three colonists, who insisted that Native Americans be paid for land?

   A William Penn and Roger Williams only
   B John Winthrop and Roger Williams only
   C John Winthrop and William Penn only
   D John Winthrop, William Penn, and Roger Williams

4. Anne Hutchinson was banished from Massachusetts because she taught that —

   F colonists should remain loyal to the English king.
   G individuals could interpret the Bible for themselves.
   H the colonists should not trade with local Native Americans.
   J the Puritans should break away from the English church.

For additional test practice, go online for:

- Diagnostic tests
- Tutorials

INTERACT WITH HISTORY

Recall the issues that you explored at the beginning of the chapter. Imagine that it is now 1685 and you are a colonist living in one of the English-speaking colonies. Relatives have written to tell you that they are about to emigrate to North America, and they are asking for your thoughts about sharing the land. Write a letter back in which you describe what you think they should know. Include important details from the history of the colonies that you have read about in this chapter.

FOCUS ON WRITING

You have been living in the Massachusetts Bay Colony for nearly a year. You have been asked by leaders of the colony to write an advertisement that will persuade new settlers to come to Massachusetts. Focus your advertisement on the advantages of living in the Massachusetts Bay Colony.

COLLABORATIVE LEARNING

Use the *Electronic Library of Primary Sources* and other reference materials to research a specific law and punishment in 17th-century America. With a group of students, act out a colonial trial. Each student should know the law and perform his or her part carefully. The rest of the class must decide the verdict and punishment. Then have a class discussion about the value of the law and its punishment.

MULTIMEDIA CONNECTIONS

Ponce de Leon

The Spanish conquistador Juan Ponce de Leon was the first European to set foot on land that later became part of the United States. Ponce de Leon first sailed to the Americas with Christopher Columbus on his second voyage in 1493. Once in the Caribbean region, he helped conquer what is now Puerto Rico and was named ruler of the island. In Puerto Rico, Ponce de Leon heard about a nearby island that supposedly held the legendary Fountain of Youth. Its waters were said to make old people young again. In 1513, Ponce de Leon set out to find the island but instead landed in what is now Florida. He named Florida and claimed it for Spain.

Explore important events in the life of Ponce de Leon online. You can find a wealth of information, video clips, primary sources, activities, and more at hmhsocialstudies.com.

CLICK THROUGH
INTER/ACTIVITIES
hmhsocialstudies.com

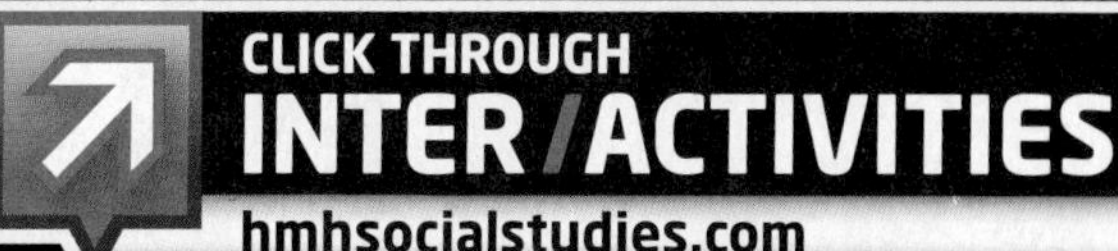

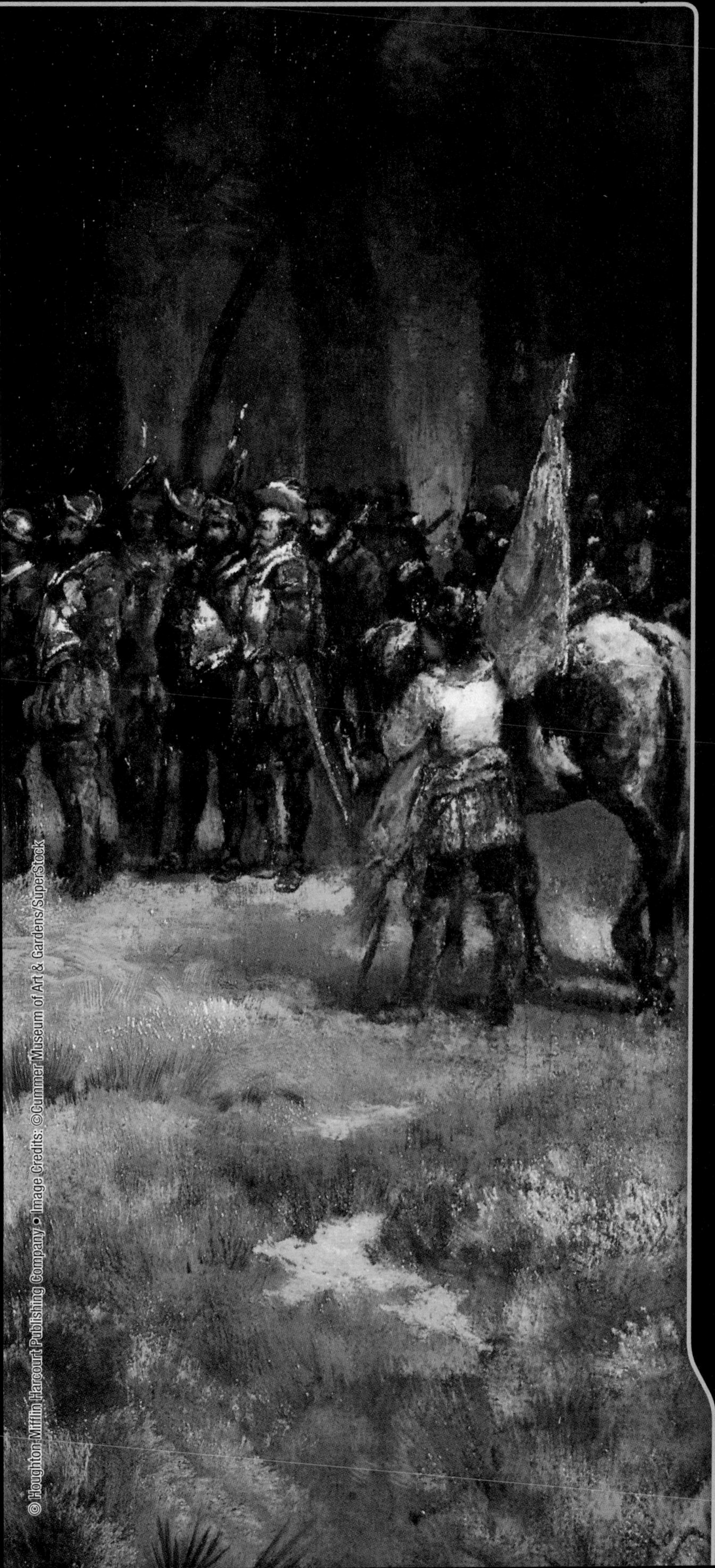

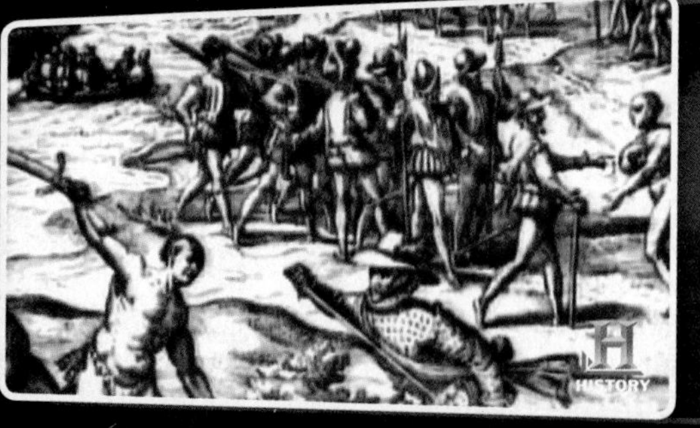

Caribbean Island Encounters

Watch the video to learn about the first encounters between Spanish explorers and the people of the Caribbean.

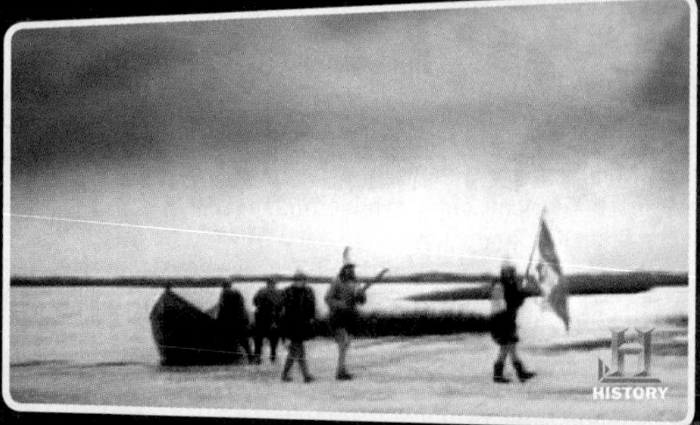

Claiming Florida for Spain

Watch the video to learn about Ponce de Leon's first landing on the coast of what is now Florida.

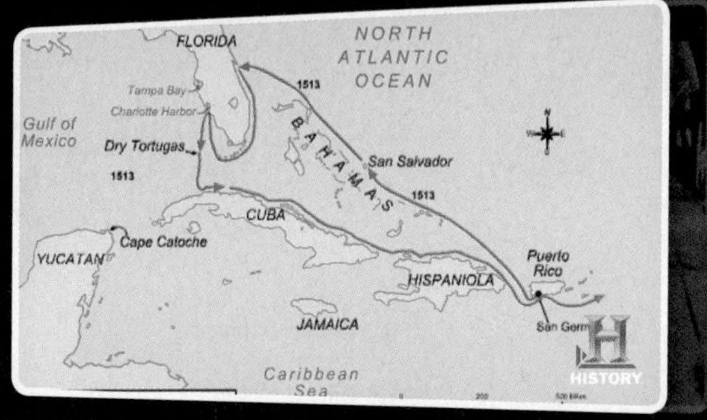

Ponce de Leon's 1513 Route

Study the map to learn about the region of the Americas that Ponce de Leon explored in 1513.

CHAPTER 3 THE COLONIES COME OF AGE

Essential Question

How did the colonies develop economically, socially, and politically?

ALABAMA COURSE OF STUDY

1 Compare effects of economic, geographic, social, and political conditions before and after European explorations of the fifteenth through seventeenth centuries on Europeans, American colonists, Africans, and indigenous Americans.

- Comparing European motives for establishing colonies, including mercantilism, religious persecution, poverty, oppression, and new opportunities.
- Explaining triangular trade and the development of slavery in the colonies.

2 Compare regional differences among early New England, Middle, and Southern colonies regarding economics, geography, culture, government, and American Indian relations.

- Explaining the role of essential documents in the establishment of colonial governments, including the Magna Carta, the English Bill of Rights, and the Mayflower Compact.
- Explaining the significance of the House of Burgesses and New England town meetings in colonial politics.
- Describing the impact of the Great Awakening on colonial society.

View of Boston, around 1764

AMERICAS

1651 English Parliament passes first of the Navigation Acts.

1686 James II creates the Dominion of New England.

1693 The College of William and Mary is chartered in Williamsburg, Virginia.

1650 | 1660 | 1670 | 1680 | 1690 | 1700

WORLD

1652 Dutch settlers establish Cape Town in South Africa.

1660 The English monarchy is restored when Charles II returns from exile.

1688 In England the Glorious Revolution establishes the supremacy of Parliament.

Image Credits: (bkgd), *View of the Long Wharf and the Harbor of Boston* (1764), J. Byron. ©Burstein Collection/Corbis; (br), Courtesy of the Special Collections Research Center, Earl Gregg Swem Library, The College of William and Mary; (bc), ©Bettmann/Corbis

HISTORY

Salem Witch Trials

hmhsocialstudies.com VIDEO

INTERACT WITH HISTORY

The year is 1750. As a hard-working young colonist, you are proud of the prosperity of your new homeland. However, you are also troubled by the inequalities around you—inequalities between the colonies and Britain, between rich and poor, between men and women, and between free and enslaved.

Explore the Issues

- Can prosperity be achieved without exploiting or enslaving others?
- What does freedom mean, beyond the right to make money without government interference?

1707 Act of Union unites England and Wales with Scotland to form Great Britain.

1714 Tea is introduced into the colonies.

1733 Benjamin Franklin publishes *Poor Richard's Almanac.*

1739 In Japan, 84,000 farmers protest heavy taxation.

1754 French and Indian War begins.

1763 Treaty of Paris ends French and Indian War.

1763 Treaty of Paris recognizes British control over much of India.

1710 | 1720 | 1730 | 1740 | 1750 | 1760

Image Credits: (bkgd), *View of the Long Wharf and the Harbor of Boston* (1764), J. Byron. ©Burstein Collection/Corbis; (bl), The Granger Collection, New York; (br), ©Bettmann/Corbis

SECTION 1

England and Its Colonies

MAIN IDEA	WHY IT MATTERS NOW	Terms & Names
England and its largely self-governing colonies prospered under a mutually beneficial trade relationship.	**The colonial system of self-governing colonies was the forerunner of our modern system of self-governing states.**	**• mercantilism • Parliament • Navigation Acts • Dominion of New England • Sir Edmund Andros • Glorious Revolution • salutary neglect**

One American's Story

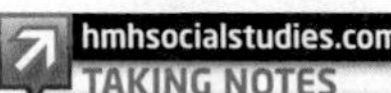

Use the graphic organizer online to take notes on problems between England and its colonies in North America.

With her father fighting for Britain in the West Indies and her mother ill, 17-year-old Eliza Lucas was left to manage the family's South Carolina plantations. On her own, the enterprising Eliza became the first person in the colonies to grow indigo and developed a way of extracting its deep blue dye. Eliza hoped that her indigo crops would add not only to her family's fortune but to that of the British empire.

A PERSONAL VOICE ELIZA LUCAS PINCKNEY

"We please ourselves with the prospect of exporting in a few years a good quantity from hence, and supplying our mother country [Great Britain] with a manufacture for which she has so great a demand, and which she is now supplied with from the French colonies, and many thousand pounds per annum [year] thereby lost to the nation, when she might as well be supplied here, if the matter were applied to in earnest."

—quoted in *South Carolina: A Documentary Profile of the Palmetto State*

African slaves working on an indigo plantation in the West Indies; fresh water in a series of leaching basins extracts the dye from the plant.

English settlers like the Lucases exported raw materials such as indigo dye to England, and in return they imported English manufactured goods. This economic relationship benefited both England and its colonies.

England and Its Colonies Prosper

Although many colonists benefited from the trade relationship with the home country, the real purpose of the colonial system was to enrich Britain.

MERCANTILISM The British interest in establishing colonies was influenced by the theory of **mercantilism,** which held that a country's ultimate goal was self-sufficiency and that all countries were in a competition to acquire the most gold and silver.

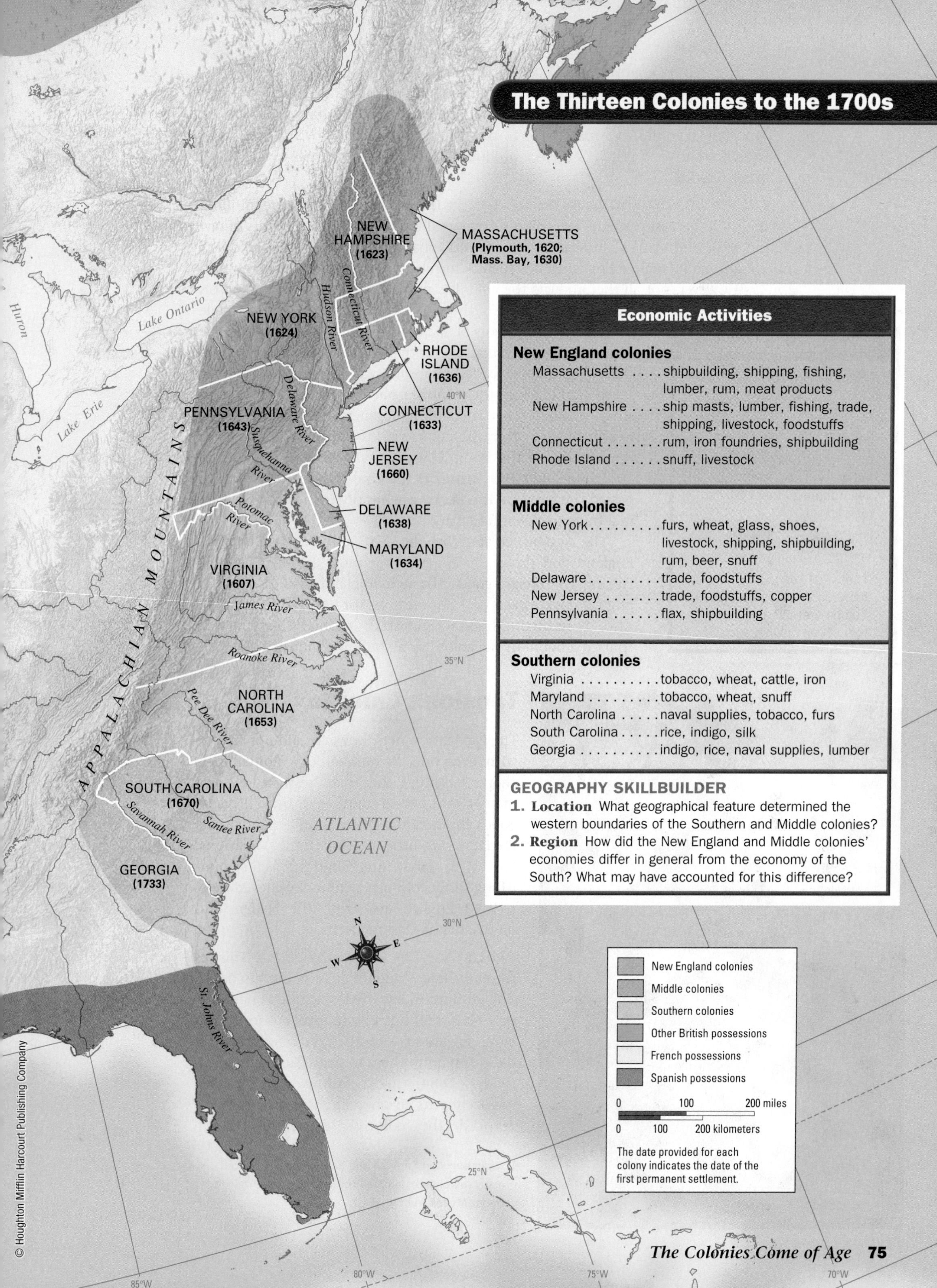

The Thirteen Colonies to the 1700s

Economic Activities

Colony	Economic activities
New England colonies	
Massachusetts	shipbuilding, shipping, fishing, lumber, rum, meat products
New Hampshire	ship masts, lumber, fishing, trade, shipping, livestock, foodstuffs
Connecticut	rum, iron foundries, shipbuilding
Rhode Island	snuff, livestock
Middle colonies	
New York	furs, wheat, glass, shoes, livestock, shipping, shipbuilding, rum, beer, snuff
Delaware	trade, foodstuffs
New Jersey	trade, foodstuffs, copper
Pennsylvania	flax, shipbuilding
Southern colonies	
Virginia	tobacco, wheat, cattle, iron
Maryland	tobacco, wheat, snuff
North Carolina	naval supplies, tobacco, furs
South Carolina	rice, indigo, silk
Georgia	indigo, rice, naval supplies, lumber

GEOGRAPHY SKILLBUILDER

1. **Location** What geographical feature determined the western boundaries of the Southern and Middle colonies?
2. **Region** How did the New England and Middle colonies' economies differ in general from the economy of the South? What may have accounted for this difference?

Inspired by mercantilism, nations concentrated on the balance of trade—the amount of goods sold compared to the amount bought—since a favorable balance meant that more gold was coming in than going out. Thus Britain looked to its American colonies as a market for British goods, a source of raw materials that were not native to Britain, and as a producer of goods and materials to be sold to other nations.

THE NAVIGATION ACTS By the mid-1600s, the American colonies were fulfilling their role, at least partially. The colonists exported to England large amounts of raw materials and staples—lumber, furs, fish, and tobacco. In addition, the colonists bought manufactured English goods such as furniture, utensils, books, and china.

However, not all the products the colonists produced for export ended up on English docks. Some of the colonists' lumber and tobacco made its way into the harbors of Spain, France, and Holland. With the nations of Europe clamoring for their goods, many colonial merchants could not resist the opportunity to increase their wealth.

England viewed the colonists' pursuit of foreign markets as an economic threat. According to mercantilist theory, any wealth flowing from the colonies to another nation came at the expense of the home country. As a result, beginning in 1651, England's **Parliament,** the country's legislative body, passed the **Navigation Acts,** a series of laws restricting colonial trade (see chart at left).

The system created by the Navigation Acts benefited England and proved to be good for most colonists as well. Passing all foreign goods through England yielded jobs for English dockworkers and import taxes for the English treasury. Also, by restricting trade to English or colonial ships, the acts spurred a boom in the colonial shipbuilding industry. (A)

The Navigation Acts

- No country could trade with the colonies unless the goods were shipped in either colonial or English ships.
- All vessels had to be operated by crews that were at least three-quarters English or colonial.
- The colonies could export certain products only to England.
- Almost all goods traded between the colonies and Europe first had to pass through an English port.

MAIN IDEA

Analyzing Effects

(A) What effects did the Navigation Acts have on both Britain and its colonies?

Tensions Emerge

The Navigation Acts, however, did not sit well with everyone. A number of colonial merchants resented the trade restrictions, and many continued to smuggle, or trade illegally, goods to and from other countries. For years England did little to stop these violations. Finally, in 1684, King Charles II acted, punishing those colonists whom he believed most resisted English authority: the leaders and merchants of Massachusetts.

CRACKDOWN IN MASSACHUSETTS Charles certainly had evidence to support his belief. The Puritan leaders of Massachusetts had long professed their hostility to royal authority and even suggested that their corporate charter did not require them to obey Parliament.

In 1684, after failing to persuade Massachusetts to obey English laws, England revoked the colony's corporate charter.

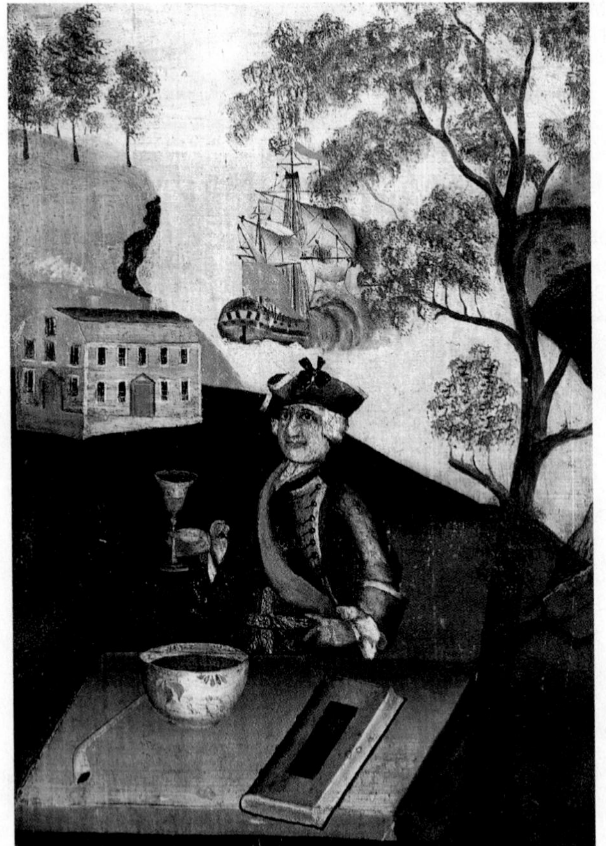

◀ **Trade between England and her colonies benefited many merchants, such as the wealthy New England trader Moses Marcy.**

MAIN IDEA

Developing Historical Perspective
B Why did England take action against Massachusetts?

Massachusetts, the "Puritan utopia," was suddenly a royal colony, under strict control of the crown. **B**

THE DOMINION OF NEW ENGLAND When King James II succeeded his brother Charles in 1685, he immediately aggravated the situation. Seeking to make the colonial governments more obedient, he placed the Northern colonies under a single ruler in Boston. Within three years, the land from southern Maine to New Jersey was united into one vast colony, the **Dominion of New England.**

To rule New England, James picked **Sir Edmund Andros,** a veteran military officer from an aristocratic English family. Andros made his hard-line attitude toward the colonists clear: "You have no more privileges left you, than not to be sold for slaves." Within weeks of arriving in Boston, Andros managed to make thousands of enemies. He angered Puritans by questioning the lawfulness of their religion. He made it clear that the Navigation Acts would be enforced and smugglers prosecuted. Furthermore, he restricted local assemblies and levied taxes without any input from local leaders.

Andros's behavior outraged the Northern colonists. In 1688, the colonists of Massachusetts sent their most prominent minister, Increase Mather, to London to try to get their old charter restored and Andros recalled. However, before Mather could put his diplomatic skills to work, a bloodless revolution in England changed the entire political picture.

THE GLORIOUS REVOLUTION While King James's actions had made him few friends in the colonies, his religious leanings made him even less popular back home. A Roman Catholic who ruled with little respect for Parliament, James had no idea how much his subjects valued their Protestantism and their parliamentary rights. When James fathered a son in 1688, England suddenly faced the possibility of a dynasty of Roman Catholic monarchs.

To head off that possibility, Parliament invited William of Orange, the husband of James's Protestant daughter Mary, to England. William and his army sailed from Holland as James fled the country. In 1689 Parliament voted to offer the throne to William and Mary. In the aftermath of these events, which became known as the **Glorious Revolution,** Parliament passed a series of laws establishing its power over the monarch.

Upon learning of the events in England, the colonists of Massachusetts staged a bloodless rebellion of their own, arresting Andros and his royal councilors. Parliament rapidly restored to their original status the colonies that had been absorbed by the Dominion of New England. In restoring Massachusetts's charter, however, the English government made several changes. The new charter, granted in 1691, called for the king to appoint the governor of Massachusetts and required more religious toleration and non-Puritan representation in the colonial assembly. The Puritans would no longer be able to persecute such groups as the Anglicans—members of the Church of England—and the Quakers.

Background
The Puritans were particularly cruel to Quakers, who were whipped, maimed, tortured, and executed as punishment for their religious customs.

HISTORICAL SPOTLIGHT

MAGNA CARTA AND ENGLISH BILL OF RIGHTS

Two of England's most important documents greatly influenced American governments. The Magna Carta, an English charter signed in 1215, established freedom under the law and *habeas corpus.* The important idea of *habeas corpus* means that citizens cannot be held unless there is proof of a crime.

The English Bill of Rights, established by Parliament during the Glorious Revolution, reinforced the rights declared in the Magna Carta. The document primarily declared illegal some actions of James II, the previous monarch. The English Bill of Rights also reinforced the authority of Parliament and the law, over even a king's desires. Moreover, the document proclaimed the rights to fair elections and freedom of speech.

Since many of the American colonists were English subjects, they maintained their legal traditions when they came to America. Colonial charters, such as the Mayflower Compact and the Virginia Company charters, preserved the rule of law. The ideas of the Magna Carta and Bill of Rights can be seen even in the U.S. Constitution.

English Rulers' Colonial Policies

Charles II (1660–1685)

Angered by Massachusetts's refusal to obey English law, he revoked the colony's charter in 1684 and brought Massachusetts under royal control.

James II (1685–1688)

He consolidated the Northern colonies into the Dominion of New England in 1686 and enlisted Sir Edmund Andros to rule the region.

William and Mary (1689–1702)

They succeeded James II after the Glorious Revolution of 1688 and helped establish the supremacy of Parliament. Parliament then dissolved the Dominion of New England and restored the colonies' charters.

England Loosens the Reins

After 1688, England largely turned its attention away from the colonies and toward France, which was competing with England for control of Europe. The home country still expected the colonies to perform their duties of exporting raw materials and importing manufactured goods. As long as they did this, Parliament saw little reason to devote large amounts of money and large numbers of soldiers to aggressively enforcing its colonial laws.

SALUTARY NEGLECT Ironically, England ushered in its new policy of neglect with an attempt to increase its control over the colonies. In the years immediately following the Glorious Revolution, Parliament strengthened the Navigation Acts in two ways. First, it moved smuggling trials from colonial courts—with juries composed of colonists who often found colonial smugglers innocent—to admiralty courts presided over by English judges. Second, it created the Board of Trade, an advisory board with broad powers to monitor colonial trade.

While England appeared to tighten its colonial grip, in reality it loosened its hold. English officials only lightly enforced the new measures as they settled into an overall colonial policy that became known as **salutary neglect.** Salutary—beneficial—neglect meant that England relaxed its enforcement of most regulations in return for the continued economic loyalty of the colonies. As long as raw materials continued flowing into the homeland and the colonists continued to buy English-produced goods, Parliament did not supervise the colonies closely. C

MAIN IDEA

Synthesizing

C How did both the colonies and Great Britain benefit from the policy of salutary neglect?

THE SEEDS OF SELF-GOVERNMENT This policy of salutary neglect had an important effect on colonial politics as well as economics. In nearly every colony, a governor appointed by the king served as the highest authority. The governor presided over a political structure that included an advisory council, usually appointed by the governor, and a local assembly, elected by eligible colonists (land-owning white males). The governor held a wide range of powers. He had the authority to call and disband the assembly, appoint and dismiss judges, and oversee all aspects of colonial trade.

However, just as England's economic policies were stronger in print than in practice, its colonial governors were not as powerful as they might seem. The colonial assembly, not the king, paid the governor's salary. Using their power of the purse liberally, the colonists influenced the governor in a variety of ways, from the approval of laws to the appointment of judges.

Under England's less-than-watchful eye, the colonies were developing a taste for self-government that would eventually create the conditions for rebellion. Nehemiah Grew, a British mercantilist, voiced an early concern about the colonies' growing self-determination. He warned his fellow subjects in 1707.

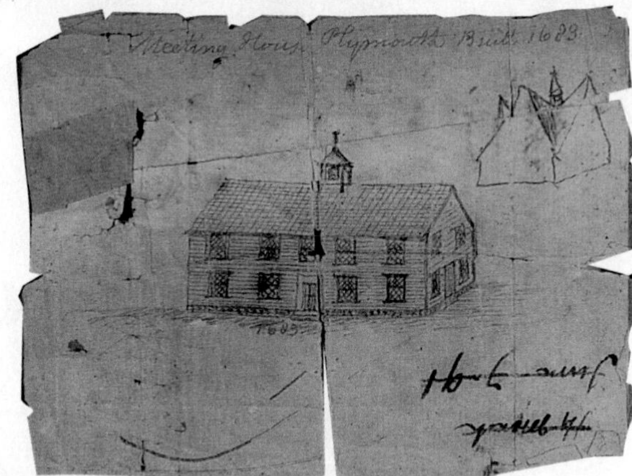

▲ **The sketch above depicts a Puritan meetinghouse built at Plymouth, Massachusetts, in 1683. Meetinghouses served a double purpose, as community halls where people voted on local issues and as religious buildings.**

A PERSONAL VOICE NEHEMIAH GREW

> **"The time may come . . . when the colonies may become populous and with the increase of arts and sciences strong and politic, forgetting their relation to the mother countries, will then confederate and consider nothing further than the means to support their ambition of standing on their [own] legs."**
>
> —quoted in *The Colonial Period of American History*

However, the policy of salutary neglect that characterized British and colonial relations throughout the first half of the 1700s worked in large part because of the colonists' loyalty to Britain. The men and women of the colonies still considered themselves loyal British subjects, eager to benefit the empire as well as themselves. Aside from a desire for more economic and political breathing room, the colonies had little in common with one another that would unite them against Britain. In particular, the Northern and Southern colonies were developing distinct societies, based on sharply contrasting economic systems.

ASSESSMENT

1. TERMS & NAMES For each term or name, write a sentence explaining its significance.

- **mercantilism**
- **Parliament**
- **Navigation Acts**
- **Dominion of New England**
- **Sir Edmund Andros**
- **Glorious Revolution**
- **salutary neglect**

MAIN IDEA

2. TAKING NOTES
Create a problem-solution chart similar to the one below. Fill it in with steps that England took to solve its economic and political problems with the colonists.

Problem	Solutions
Keeping the colonies under economic and political control	1. in 1651 2. in 1686 3. after 1688

Which policy might colonists have resented most and why?

CRITICAL THINKING

3. ANALYZING ISSUES
Reread Grew's warning quoted above. Explain why the British did not want this to happen.
Think About:
- the goals of mercantilism
- what might happen to Great Britain's economy if Grew's prediction came true
- how New England town meetings were examples of Grew's warning

4. SUMMARIZING
How did political events in England affect the lives of the colonists? Use evidence from the text to support your response.

5. PREDICTING EFFECTS
Britain established policies to control the American colonies but was inconsistent in its enforcement of those policies. What results might be expected from such inconsistency?

SECTION 2

The Agricultural South

MAIN IDEA	WHY IT MATTERS NOW	Terms & Names
In the Southern colonies, a predominantly agricultural society developed.	The modern South maintains many of its agricultural traditions.	•cash crop •slave •triangular trade •middle passage •Stono Rebellion

One American's Story

hmhsocialstudies.com TAKING NOTES

Use the graphic organizer online to take notes about Southern society.

In the fall of 1773, Philip Vickers Fithian left his home in Princeton, New Jersey, to tutor the children of Robert Carter III and his wife Frances at their Virginia manor house. Fithian, who kept a journal of his one-year stay there, recalled an evening walk through the plantation.

A PERSONAL VOICE PHILIP VICKERS FITHIAN

> **"We stroll'd down the Pasture quite to the River, admiring the Pleasantness of the evening, & the delightsome Prospect of the River, Hills, Huts on the Summits, low Bottoms, Trees of various Kinds, and Sizes, Cattle & Sheep feeding some near us, & others at a great distance on the green sides of the Hills. . . . I love to walk on these high Hills . . . where I can have a long View of many Miles & see on the Summits of the Hills Clusters of Savin Trees, through these often a little Farm-House, or Quarter for Negroes."**
>
> —*Journal & Letters of Philip Vickers Fithian*

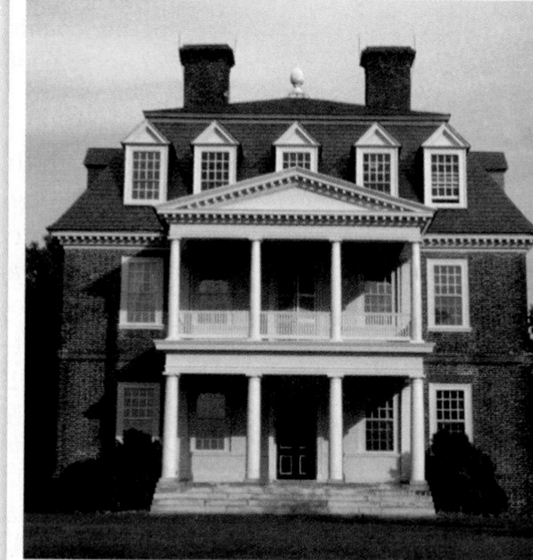

▲ The Shirley plantation house in Virginia is representative of many old Southern mansions. Built in 1723, it was the birthplace of Ann Hill Carter, the mother of Civil War general Robert E. Lee.

Although Fithian's journal goes on to express outrage over the treatment of the slaves, he was fascinated by the plantation system, which had come to dominate the South. The plantation economy led to a largely rural society in which enslaved Africans played an unwilling yet important role.

A Plantation Economy Arises

Since the early days of Jamestown, when the planting of tobacco helped save the settlement, the Southern colonists had staked their livelihood on the fertile soil that stretched from the Chesapeake region to Georgia. Robert Carter, like his father and grandfather before him, specialized in raising a single **cash crop**—one grown primarily for sale rather than for the farmer's own use. In Maryland, Virginia, and North Carolina, farmers grew the broad green leaves of tobacco. In South Carolina and Georgia, rice and later indigo were successful cash crops.

MAIN IDEA

Making Inferences

A How did the geography of the South contribute to the self-sufficiency of Southern plantations?

Throughout the South, plantations developed instead of towns. Because the long and deep rivers allowed access for ocean-going vessels, planters—owners of large profitable plantations—could ship their goods directly to the northern colonies and Europe without the need for city docks and warehouses. Because plantation owners produced most of what they needed on their property, they had little use for shops, bakeries, and markets. There were some cities in the South, including Charles Town (later Charleston), South Carolina, one of the most thriving port cities in the British empire. On the whole, the South developed largely as a rural and self-sufficient society. **A**

Life in Southern Society

As the Southern colonies grew in wealth and population, they also grew in diversity. However, not all groups benefited equally from the South's prosperity.

A DIVERSE AND PROSPEROUS PEOPLE During the 1700s, large numbers of European immigrants traveled to North America in search of a new start. The influx of immigrants helped create a diverse population in both the Northern and Southern colonies. In the South, thousands of Germans settled throughout Maryland and Virginia and as far south as South Carolina. There they raised grain, livestock, and tobacco. A wave of Scots and Scots-Irish also settled in the South, residing mainly along the hills of western North Carolina.

▲ **This folk art painting shows an aristocratic Southern mansion perched high on a hill, dominating the warehouses, mill, slave quarters, and other buildings that helped make the plantation self-sufficient. Along the river, a ship carries the plantation's products to the wider world.**

▲ Detail from *The Country Housewife*, published in London in 1770. Many settlers brought this guidebook with them when they immigrated to the colonies.

While small farmers formed the majority of the Southern population, the planters controlled much of the South's economy. They also controlled its political and social institutions. The activities at the Carter mansion described by Philip Fithian reflected the luxury of planter life. Fithian recalled attending numerous balls, banquets, dance recitals, and parties that continued for several days.

By the mid-1700s, life was good for many Southern colonists, particularly those in the Chesapeake Bay region. Due to a large growth in the entire colonies' export trade, colonial standards of living rose dramatically in the years from 1700 to 1770. Colonists along the Chesapeake, where tobacco prices had rebounded after tumbling during the late 1600s, saw the greatest economic boom. From 1713 to 1774 tobacco exports there almost tripled, and many Chesapeake farmers and merchants prospered. **B**

MAIN IDEA

Analyzing Causes

B Explain how colonial standards of living rose so dramatically in the 18th century.

THE ROLE OF WOMEN Women in Southern society—and Northern society as well—shared a common trait: second-class citizenship. Women had few legal or social rights; for instance, they could not vote or preach. Even daughters of wealthy Southern planters were usually taught only the basics of reading, writing, and arithmetic. Instead, they were mostly educated in the social graces or in domestic tasks, such as canning and preserving food, sewing, and embroidery.

Throughout the day, the average Southern woman worked over a hot fire baking bread or boiling meat. Her outdoor duties included milking the cows, slaughtering pigs for ham and bacon, and tending the garden. She was also expected to sew, wash clothes, and clean. Women of the planter class escaped most of these tasks, as servants handled the household chores. Regardless of class, however, most

NOW & THEN

TOBACCO AND NORTH CAROLINA'S ECONOMY

Tobacco has long been a key element of the Southern economy. The soil and climate of the South are ideal for growing tobacco, which was first harvested for commercial use in 1612. In recent years, however, tobacco revenues have shrunk as North Carolina lessens its dependence on tobacco and develops a more diversified economy.

The focal point of North Carolina's new economy is the Research Triangle, so called for the cluster of major universities in Raleigh, Durham, and Chapel Hill. These universities cooperate in research and development in many areas, including technology and health care. Other new industries, such as computers and telecommunications, are fueling North Carolina's growth.

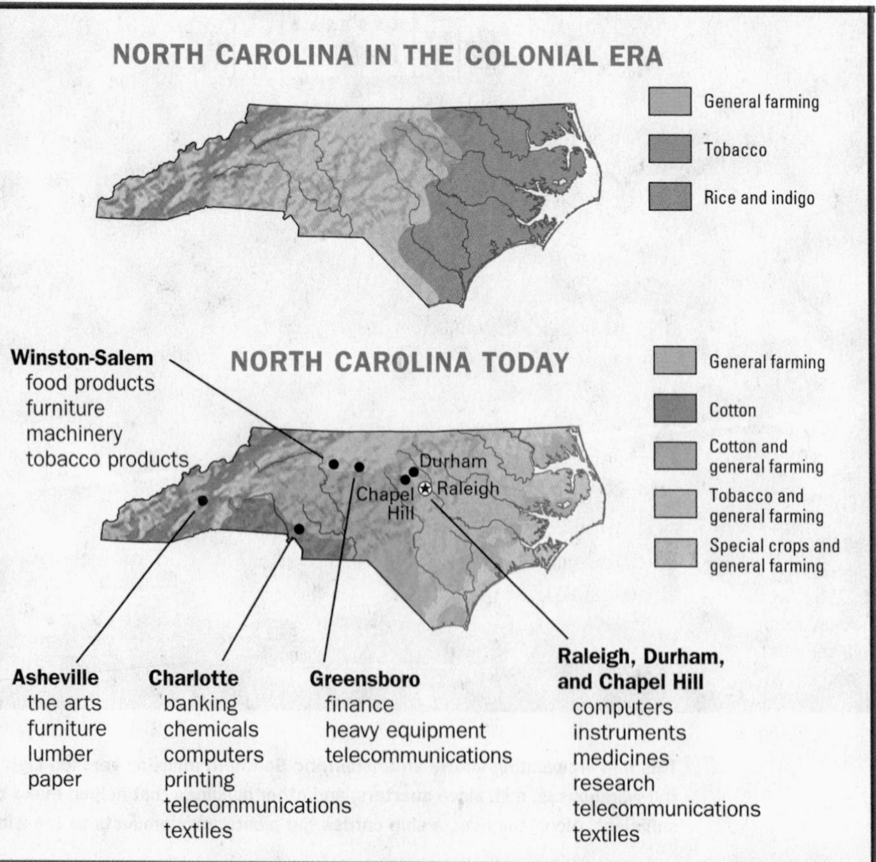

MAIN IDEA

Making Generalizations

C What roles did women play in the Southern household?

women bowed to their husbands' will. An excerpt from Virginia plantation owner William Byrd's diary hints at Lucia Parke Byrd's subservient position: "My wife and I had another scold about mending my shoes," Byrd wrote, "but it was soon over by her submission." **C**

INDENTURED SERVANTS Also low on Southern society's ladder were indentured servants. Many of these young, mostly white men had traded a life of prison or poverty in Europe for a limited term of servitude in North America. They had few rights while in bondage. Those who lived through their harsh years of labor—and many did not—saw their lives improve only slightly as they struggled to survive on the western outskirts of the Southern colonies.

While historians estimate that indentured servants made up a significant portion of the colonial population in the 1600s—between one-half and two-thirds of all white immigrants after 1630—their numbers declined toward the end of the century. With continuing reports of hardship in the New World, many laborers in Europe decided to stay home. Faced with a depleted labor force and a growing agricultural economy, the Southern colonists turned to another group to meet their labor needs: African slaves.

Slavery Becomes Entrenched

The English colonists gradually turned to the use of African **slaves**—people who were considered the property of others—after efforts to meet their labor needs with enslaved Native Americans and indentured servants failed. During the 1600s and 1700s, plantation owners and other colonists would subject hundreds of thousands of Africans to a life of intense labor and cruelty in North America.

THE EVOLUTION OF SLAVERY In the early days of the colonies, the English, like their Spanish counterparts, had forced Native Americans to work for them. However, the English settlers found it increasingly difficult to enslave Native Americans. Aside from being reluctant to learn English labor techniques, Native Americans could easily escape because they had far better knowledge of the local fields and forests than did the colonists.

As the indentured servant population fell, the price of indentured servants rose. As a result, the English colonists turned to African slaves as an alternative. A slave worked for life and thus brought a much larger return on the investment. In addition, most white colonists convinced themselves that Africans' dark skin was a sign of inferiority, and so had few reservations about subjecting them to a life of servitude. Black Africans were also thought better able to endure the harsh physical demands of plantation labor in hot climates. By 1690, nearly 13,000 black slaves toiled in the Southern colonies. By 1750, that number had increased to almost 200,000. **D**

MAIN IDEA

Analyzing Causes

D What were the main reasons that English colonists turned to African slaves to fill their depleted labor force?

THE EUROPEAN SLAVE TRADE Before the English began the large-scale importation of African slaves to their colonies on the American mainland, Africans had been laboring as slaves for years in the West Indies. During the late 1600s, English planters in Jamaica and Barbados imported tens of thousands of African slaves to work their sugar plantations. By 1690, the African population on Barbados was about

WORLD STAGE

SERFS, SLAVES, AND SERVANTS

Many forms of servitude existed throughout Europe and the Americas well into the 19th century. Serfs were peasants who were considered part of a lord's property. Unlike slaves, who could be moved to different locations, serfs were obliged to remain on the land that they farmed for the landowner.

While the institution of serfdom declined in the later Middle Ages, it persisted with remarkable strength in the west and south of England. These were the very regions where many Southern landowners and indentured servants originated.

Serfdom was ended in England in the 1600s, but survived in Russia until 1861. Tsar Alexander's Edict of Emancipation freed the Russian serfs just two years before President Lincoln's Emancipation Proclamation began the process of freeing the American slaves.

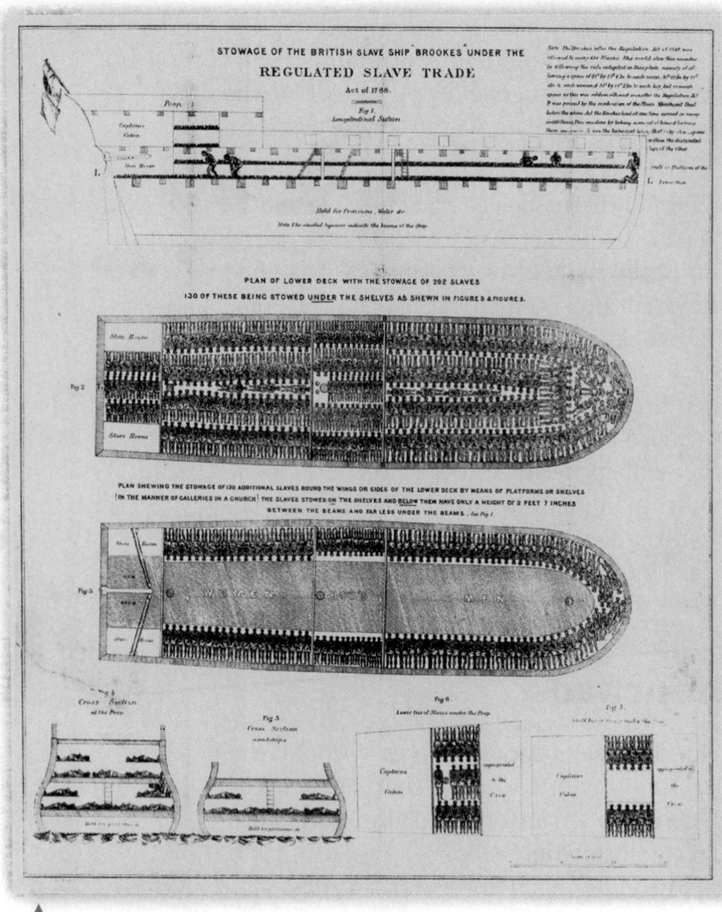

▲ This plan and section of the British slave ship "Brookes" was published in London around 1790 by a leading British antislavery advocate named Thomas Clarkson. The image effectively conveys the degradation and inhumanity of the slave trade, which reduced human beings to the level of merchandise.

60,000—three times the white population.

During the 17th century, Africans had become part of a transatlantic trading network described as the **triangular trade.** This term referred to a three-way trading process: merchants carried rum and other goods from New England to Africa; in Africa they traded their merchandise for enslaved people, whom they transported to the West Indies and sold for sugar and molasses; these goods were then shipped to New England to be distilled into rum. The "triangular" trade, in fact, encompassed a network of trade routes criss-crossing the Northern and Southern colonies, the West Indies, England, Europe, and Africa. The network carried an array of traded goods, from furs and fruit to tar and tobacco, as well as African people. (E)

MAIN IDEA

Developing Historical Perspective

(E) What parts of the world were involved in the triangular trade?

THE MIDDLE PASSAGE The voyage that brought Africans to the West Indies and later to North America was known as the **middle passage,** because it was considered the middle leg of the transatlantic trade triangle. Sickening cruelty characterized this journey. In the bustling ports along West Africa, European traders branded Africans with red-hot irons for identification purposes and packed them into the dark holds of large ships. On board a slave ship, Africans fell victim to whippings and beatings from slavers as well as diseases that swept through the vessel. The smell of blood, sweat, and excrement filled the hold, as the African passengers lived in their own vomit and waste. One African, Olaudah Equiano, recalled the inhumane conditions on his trip from West Africa to the West Indies in 1756 when he was 11 years old.

hmhsocialstudies.com
INTERACTIVE MAP
Learn more about the triangular trade.

A Personal Voice OLAUDAH EQUIANO

> "**The closeness of the place, and the heat of the climate, added to the number in the ship, which was so crowded that each had scarcely room to turn himself, almost suffocated us. This produced copious perspirations, so that the air soon became unfit for respiration from a variety of loathsome smells, and brought on a sickness among the slaves, of which many died . . . .**"
>
> —*The Interesting Narrative of the Life of Olaudah Equiano*

▲ Olaudah Equiano was kidnapped from Africa and sold to a succession of owners before buying his freedom.

Whether they died from disease or from cruel treatment by merchants, or whether they committed suicide, as many did by plunging into the ocean, up to 20 percent or more of the Africans aboard each slave ship perished during the trip to the New World.

SLAVERY IN THE SOUTH Africans who survived their ocean voyage entered an extremely difficult life of bondage in North America. Most slaves—probably 80 to 90 percent—worked in the fields. On large plantations, a white slave owner directed their labor, often through field bosses. On smaller farms, slaves often worked alongside their owner.

The other 10 to 20 percent of slaves worked in the house of their owner or as artisans. Domestic slaves cooked, cleaned, and raised the master's children. While owners did not subject their domestic slaves to the rigors of field labor, they commonly treated them with equal cruelty. Other slaves developed skills as artisans—carpenters, blacksmiths, and bricklayers. Owners often rented these slaves out to work on other plantations.

Whatever their task, slaves led a grueling existence. Full-time work began around age 12 and continued until death. John Ferdinand Smyth, an English traveler, described a typical slave workday.

A Personal Voice JOHN FERDINAND SMYTH

"He (the slave) is called up in the morning at daybreak, and is seldom allowed time enough to swallow three mouthfuls of hominy, or hoecake, but is driven out immediately to the field to hard labor, at which he continues, without intermission, until noon . . . About noon is the time he eats his dinner, and he is seldom allowed an hour for that purpose . . . They then return to severe labor, which continues in the field until dusk in the evening."

—quoted in *Planters and Pioneers*

MAIN IDEA

Making Inferences

F Why weren't slave owners punished if they killed their slaves?

Slave owners whipped and beat those slaves they thought were disobedient or disrespectful. In Virginia, the courts did not consider slave owners guilty of murder for killing their slaves during punishment. F

Africans Cope in Their New World

The Africans who were transported to North America came from a variety of different cultures and spoke varied languages. Forced to labor in a strange new land, these diverse peoples bonded together for support and fought against their plight in numerous ways.

CULTURE AND FAMILY In the midst of the horrors of slavery, Africans developed a way of life based strongly on their cultural heritage. Enslaved people wove baskets and molded pottery as they had done in their homeland. They kept alive their musical traditions and retold the stories of their ancestors. Because slave merchants tore apart many African families, slaves created new families among the people with whom they lived. If a master sold a parent to another plantation, other slaves stepped in to raise the children left behind.

Background

Rice was an important crop in West Africa for centuries before the slave trade began.

The African influence remained particularly strong among the slaves of South Carolina and Georgia. By the mid-1700s, planters in these colonies had imported large numbers of Africans with rice-growing expertise to help develop rice as the colonies' main cash crop. Many of these slaves came from the same region in West Africa.

One of the most important customs that Africans kept alive in North America was their dance. From Maryland to Georgia, slaves continued to practice what became known in the colonies as the ring shout, a circular religious dance. While variations of the dance brought to North America differed throughout the regions in West and Central Africa, the dance paid tribute to the group's ancestors and gods and usually involved loud chants and quick, circular steps. Despite the white colonists' efforts to eradicate it, the ritual endured.

▲ The gourd fiddle and drum, both made by slaves, reflect ways in which enslaved African Americans continued their African traditions.

RESISTANCE AND REVOLT Enslaved Africans also resisted their position of subservience. Throughout the colonies, planters reported slaves faking illness, breaking tools, and staging work slowdowns. One master noted the difficulty in forcing African slaves to accept their lot, commenting that if a slave "must be broke, either from Obstinacy, or, which I am more apt to suppose, from Greatness of Soul, [it] will require . . . hard Discipline. . . . You would really be surpriz'd at their Perseverance . . . they often die before they can be conquer'd."

Some slaves pushed their resistance to open revolt. One such uprising, the **Stono Rebellion,** began on a September Sunday in 1739. That morning, about 20 slaves gathered at the Stono River southwest of Charles Town. Wielding guns and other weapons, they killed several planter families and marched south, beating drums and loudly inviting other slaves to join them in their plan to flee to Spanish-held Florida.

By late Sunday afternoon, a white militia had surrounded the group of escaping slaves. The two sides clashed, and many slaves died in the fighting. Those captured were executed. Despite the rebellion's failure, it sent a chill through many Southern colonists and led to the tightening of harsh slave laws already in place. However, slave rebellions continued into the 1800s.

Despite the severe punishment that escape attempts brought, a number of slaves tried to run away. The runaway notices published in the various newspapers throughout Virginia show that from 1736 to 1801, at least 1,279 enslaved men and women in that state took to flight. Many who succeeded in running away from their masters found refuge with Native American tribes, and marriage between runaway slaves and Native Americans was common.

As the Southern colonies grew, they became ever more dependent on the use of African slavery. This was not the case in the Northern colonies, due mainly to an economy driven by commerce rather than agriculture. This economic distinction spurred the North to develop in ways that differed greatly from the South.

WILLIAMSBURG, Jan. 14, 1766.

RUN from the Subscriber's plantation in *Albemarle* county, a tall slim Negro fellow, named GEORGE; he is marked in the face as the *Gold Coast* slaves generally are, had the usual clothing of labouring Negroes, and is supposed to be harboured at some of the plantations on *Cary's* creek, in *Goochland* county. Also run away from the subscriber's quarter called *Westham*, in *Henrico* county, another Negro fellow, named ROBIN; he is very tall, slim, and of a thin visage, having lost some of his teeth; he formerly belonged to Col. *Benjamin Harrison* of *Berkeley*, and is supposed to be gone in the neighbourhood of his plantation on *Nottoway* river, where he formerly lived. Whoever will convey the former Negro to Mr. *Lucas Powell* in *Albemarle*, and the latter to *William Walker* at *Westham*, shall receive FORTY SHILLINGS for each of them, besides what is allowed by law. As I have been always tender of my slaves, and particularly attentive to the good usage of them, I hope wherever these fellows may be apprehended that they will receive such moderate correction as will deter them from running away for the future; and wherever any of my Negroes are taken up as runaways, I desire the favour of the magistrate, who may be applied to for a certificate, to order them back to their respective overseers, instead of sending them to me in this city.

RO. C. NICHOLAS.

ASSESSMENT

1. **TERMS & NAMES** For each term or name, write a sentence explaining its significance.
   - **cash crop**
   - **slave**
   - **triangular trade**
   - **middle passage**
   - **Stono Rebellion**

MAIN IDEA

2. **TAKING NOTES**
   Fill in a chart like the one below to show the social order of Southern society. In the tiers, name and describe the different social classes, ranging from most powerful at the top to least powerful at the bottom.

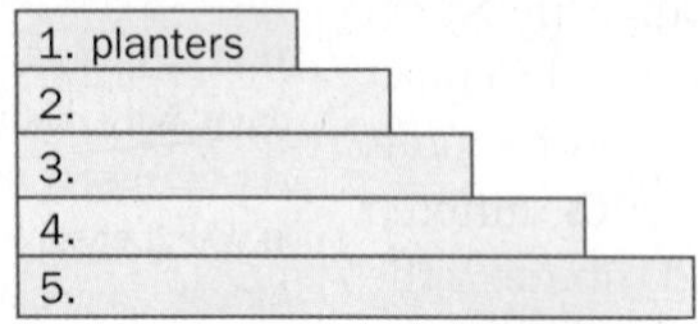

CRITICAL THINKING

3. **DRAWING CONCLUSIONS**
   Why were so many enslaved Africans brought to the Southern colonies? **Think About:**
   - why Native Americans were not used instead
   - why Europeans were not used instead
   - the cash crops of the South
   - the triangular trade

4. **ANALYZING PRIMARY SOURCES**
   The ad shown above is from a Virginia newspaper of the 1730s. What does this ad reveal about the brutality of the slave system?

5. **ANALYZING CAUSES**
   Why did fewer cities develop in the South during the 1700s? Use evidence from the text to support your response.

SECTION 3

The Commercial North

MAIN IDEA

The Northern colonies developed a predominantly urban society, based on commerce and trade.

WHY IT MATTERS NOW

The states that were once the Northern colonies remain predominantly urban today.

Terms & Names

- **Enlightenment**
- **Benjamin Franklin**
- **Jonathan Edwards**
- **Great Awakening**

One American's Story

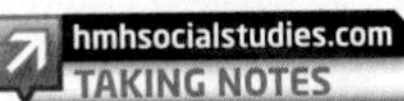
TAKING NOTES

Use the graphic organizer online to take notes about the Northern colonies.

After growing up on a Massachusetts farm, John Adams found city life in Boston distracting. In 1759 he wrote,

John Adams

A PERSONAL VOICE JOHN ADAMS

"Who can study in Boston Streets? I am unable to observe the various Objects that I meet, with sufficient Precision. My Eyes are so diverted with Chimney Sweeps, Carriers of Wood, Merchants, Ladies, Priests, Carts, Horses, Oxen, Coaches, Market men and Women, Soldiers, Sailors, and my Ears with the Rattle Gabble of them all that I cant think long enough in the Street upon any one Thing to start and pursue a Thought."

—The Diary and Autobiography of John Adams

Adams's description illustrates the changes that transformed the New England and Middle colonies during the 18th century. The growth of thriving commercial cities made the North radically different from the agricultural South. In addition, interest in education was on the rise, partially due to intellectual and religious movements. These movements brought about social changes that contributed to the colonies' eventual break with England.

Commerce Grows in the North

The theory of mercantilism held that colonies existed to help the home country amass wealth. However, the American colonies found their own economy prospering more. From 1650 to 1750, the colonies' economy grew twice as fast as Great Britain's economy did. Much of this growth occurred in the New England and middle colonies.

A DIVERSIFIED ECONOMY Unlike farms in the South, those in the New England and middle colonies usually produced several crops instead of a single one. Cold winters and rocky soil restricted New Englanders to small farms. In the more fertile areas of the middle colonies, such as New York and Pennsylvania, farmers raised a variety of crops and livestock, including wheat, corn, cattle, and hogs. They produced so much that they sold their surplus food to the West Indies, where raising sugar cane produced such tremendous profits that planters did not want to waste land growing food for the slaves who worked their fields.

Vocabulary
profit: the money left over after costs are subtracted from income

A diverse commercial economy also developed in the New England and Middle colonies. Grinding wheat, harvesting fish, and sawing lumber became thriving industries. Colonists also manufactured impressive numbers of ships and quantities of iron. By 1760, the colonists had built one-third of all British ships and were producing more iron than England was. While at times the North's economy dipped, many colonists prospered. In particular, the number of merchants grew. By the mid-1700s, merchants were one of the most powerful groups in the North. (A)

MAIN IDEA

Forming Generalizations
(A) What kinds of industries developed in the North?

URBAN LIFE The expansion in trade caused port cities to grow. Only one major port, Charles Town, existed in the South. In contrast, the North boasted Boston, New York City, and Philadelphia. In fact, Philadelphia eventually became the second largest city (after London) in the British empire. Philadelphia was the first large city since ancient Roman times to be laid out on a gridlike street plan. For colonists accustomed to the winding medieval streets of European cities, this kind of rational urban planning must have appeared startling and new. Influenced by Sir Christopher Wren's designs for the rebuilding of London after the Great Fire of 1666, Philadelphia included a number of open squares intended for public use. Both the grid plan and the parklike square would become important elements of American urban design in the centuries to come.

With its parks, police patrols, paved streets, and whale-oil lamps to light the sidewalks, Philadelphia was a sophisticated city. However, the high concentration of people without adequate public services caused problems. Firewood and clean water could be hard to come by, whereas garbage was abundant.

Daily Urban Life in Colonial Times

By the mid-18th century, colonial cities were prosperous and growing. Brick rowhouses were replacing the wooden structures of the 17th century, while large mansions and churches, built of brick or stone, were rising everywhere.

English colonists had brought with them a preference for houses (as opposed to apartments, which were the norm in the cities of other European countries). As in Britain, the size of the house indicated the social position of its occupant.

In contemporary Philadelphia, Elfreth's Alley preserves the scale and appearance of a mid-18th-century city street. A neighborhood like this could have commercial and residential uses. Many people lived above the shops where they worked. ▶

◀ **The house known as Cliveden, also in Philadelphia, was built in 1767. In contrast to the artisan or lower-middle-class housing of Elfreth's Alley, this large, freestanding mansion shows the kind of building that the rich could afford.**

Northern Society Is Diverse

Northern society was composed of diverse groups with sometimes conflicting interests. Groups whose interests clashed with those of the people in power included immigrants, African Americans, and women.

INFLUX OF IMMIGRANTS Even more so than those in the South, the Northern colonies attracted a variety of immigrants. The Germans and the Scots-Irish were the largest non-English immigrant groups. Germans began arriving in Pennsylvania in the 1680s. Most were fleeing economic distress, but some, such as the Mennonites, came to Pennsylvania because of William Penn's policy of religious freedom and because they shared the Quakers' opposition to war.

Colonial Diversity

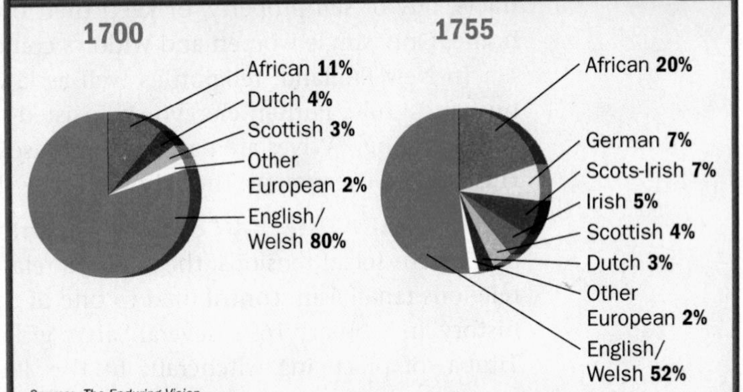

Source: *The Enduring Vision*

SKILLBUILDER Interpreting Graphs
What new ethnic groups had settled in the American colonies by 1755?

SEE SKILLBUILDER HANDBOOK, PAGE R28.

The Scots-Irish—descendants of Scottish Protestants who had colonized northern Ireland in the 1600s—entered mostly through Philadelphia. They commonly arrived as families. Many established farms in frontier areas such as western Pennsylvania, where they often clashed with Native Americans.

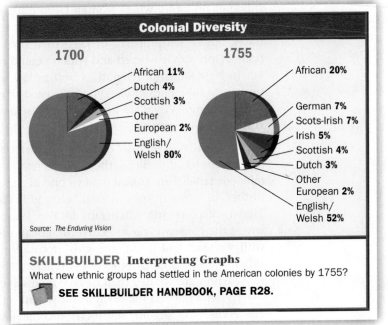

Other ethnic groups included the Dutch in New York, Scandinavians in Delaware, and Jews in such cities as Newport and Philadelphia. The different groups did not always mix. Benjamin Franklin, echoing the sentiments of many English colonists, made the following complaint in 1751.

A PERSONAL VOICE BENJAMIN FRANKLIN

"Why should the [Germans] be suffered to swarm into our Settlements and, by herding together establish their Language and Manners to the Exclusion of ours? Why should Pennsylvania, founded by the English, become a Colony of Aliens, who will shortly be so numerous as to Germanize us instead of our Anglifying them?"

—"Observations Concerning the Increase of Mankind, Peopling of Countries, etc."

MAIN IDEA

Analyzing Effects

B What were the negative and positive effects of the growing ethnic diversity in the colonies?

In spite of this fear of being swamped by non-English speakers, English colonists found ways of getting along with their new neighbors, thus furthering the evolution of a truly diverse American society. **B**

SLAVERY IN THE NORTH Because raising wheat and corn did not require as much labor as raising tobacco or rice, Northerners had less incentive to turn to slavery than did Southerners. However, slavery did exist in New England and was extensive throughout the Middle colonies, as were racial prejudices against blacks—free or enslaved.

While still considered property, most enslaved persons in New England enjoyed greater legal standing than slaves elsewhere in the colonies. They could sue and be sued, and they had the right of appeal to the highest courts. As in the South, however, enslaved persons in the North led harsh lives and were considered less than human beings. Laws forbade them to gather or to carry weapons, and there were no laws to protect them from cruel treatment. Reacting to the harsh conditions, slaves sometimes rebelled. An uprising occurred in 1712 in New York, leading to the execution of 21 people. In 1741, a series of suspicious fires and robberies led New Yorkers to fear another uprising. They decided to make an example of the suspected ringleaders, burning alive 13 persons and hanging 18.

WOMEN IN NORTHERN SOCIETY As in the South, women in the North had extensive work responsibilities but few legal rights. Most people in the colonies still lived on farms, where women faced unceasing labor. A colonial wife had virtually no legal rights. She could not vote. Most women could not enter into contracts, buy or sell property, or keep their own wages if they worked outside the home. Only single women and widows could run their own businesses.

In New England, religion as well as law served to keep women under their husbands' rule. Puritan clergymen insisted that wives must submit to their husbands, saying, "Wives are part of the House and Family, and ought to be under a Husband's Government: they should Obey their own Husbands."

WITCHCRAFT TRIALS IN SALEM The strict limitations on women's roles, combined with social tensions, the strained relations with the Native Americans, and religious fanaticism, contributed to one of the most bizarre episodes in American history. In February 1692, several Salem girls accused a West Indian slave woman, Tituba, of practicing witchcraft. In this Puritan New England town of Salem, where the constant fear of Native American attacks encouraged a preoccupation with violence and death, the girls' accusations drew a great deal of attention. When the girls accused others of witchcraft, the situation grew out of control, as those who were accused tried to save themselves by naming other "witches."

Hysteria gripped the town as more and more people made false accusations. The accusations highlighted social and religious tensions. Many of the accusers were poor and brought charges against richer residents. In addition, a high proportion of victims were women who might be considered too independent.

The accusations continued until the girls dared to charge such prominent citizens as the governor's wife. Finally realizing that they had been hearing false evidence, officials closed the court. The witchcraft hysteria ended—but not before 19 persons had been hanged and another person killed by being crushed to death. Four or five more "witches" died in jail, and about 150 were imprisoned. C

MAIN IDEA

Analyzing Causes

C What were the underlying causes of the Salem witch hunts in 1692?

New Ideas Influence the Colonists

The Salem trials of 1692 caused many people to question the existence of witchcraft. During the 1700s, individuals began to make other changes in the way they viewed the world.

THE ENLIGHTENMENT Since before the Renaissance, philosophers in Europe had been using reason and the scientific method to obtain knowledge. Scientists looked beyond religious doctrine to investigate how the world worked. Influenced by the observations of Nicolaus Copernicus, Galileo Galilei, and Sir Isaac Newton, people determined that the earth revolved around the sun and not vice versa. They also concluded that the world is governed not by chance or miracles but by fixed mathematical laws. These ideas about nature gained prevalence in the 1700s in a movement called the **Enlightenment.**

Enlightenment ideas traveled from Europe to the colonies and spread quickly in numerous books and pamphlets. Literacy was particularly high in New England because the Puritans had long supported public education to ensure that everyone could read the Bible.

One outstanding Enlightenment figure was **Benjamin Franklin.** Franklin embraced the notion of obtaining truth through experimentation and reasoning. For example, his most famous experiment—flying a kite in a thunderstorm—demonstrated that lightning was a form of electrical power.

The Enlightenment also had a profound effect on political thought in the colonies. Colonial leaders such as Thomas Jefferson used reason to conclude that individuals have natural rights, which governments must respect. Enlightenment principles eventually would lead many colonists to question the authority of the British monarchy. D

MAIN IDEA

Forming Generalizations

D Why was the Enlightenment such a revolutionary movement?

THE GREAT AWAKENING By the early 1700s, the Puritan church had lost its grip on society, and church membership was in decline. The new Massachusetts charter of 1691 forced Puritans to allow freedom of worship and banned the practice of permitting only Puritan church members to vote. Furthermore, many people seemed to be doing so well in this world that they paid little attention to the next. As Puritan merchants prospered, they developed a taste for material possessions and sensual pleasures.

VIDEO

Did You Know: Ben Franklin

hmhsocialstudies.com

Jonathan Edwards, of Northampton, Massachusetts, was one member of the clergy who sought to revive the intensity and commitment of the original Puritan vision. Edwards preached that church attendance was not enough for salvation; people must acknowledge their sinfulness and feel God's love for them. In his most famous sermon, delivered in 1741, Edwards vividly described God's mercy.

A Personal Voice
JONATHAN EDWARDS

"**The God that holds you over the pit of hell, much as one holds a spider, or some loathsome insect over the fire, abhors [hates] you, and is dreadfully provoked: His wrath towards you burns like fire; He looks upon you as worthy of nothing else but to be cast into the fire; . . . and yet it is nothing but His hand that holds you from falling into the fire every moment.**"

—"Sinners in the Hands of an Angry God"

Other preachers traveled from village to village, stirring people to rededicate themselves to God. Such traveling preachers attracted thousands, making it necessary for revival meetings to be held outdoors. The resulting religious revival, known as the **Great Awakening,** lasted throughout the 1730s and 1740s.

KEY PLAYERS

BENJAMIN FRANKLIN
1706–1790

Benjamin Franklin was one of the leading champions of Enlightenment ideals in America. Like other scientists and philosophers of the Enlightenment, Franklin believed that human beings could use their intellectual powers to improve their lot.

Franklin's observations and experiments led to a number of inventions, including the lightning rod, bifocals, and a new kind of heating system that became known as the Franklin stove. Inventions like these proved that knowledge derived from scientific experiment could be put to practical use.

Franklin's achievements brought him world renown. In 1756 British scholars elected him to the Royal Society, and in 1772 France honored him with membership in the French Academy of Sciences.

JONATHAN EDWARDS
1703–1758

Descended from a long line of Puritan ministers, Jonathan Edwards denied that humans had the power to perfect themselves. He believed that "however you may have reformed your life in many things," as a sinner you were destined for hell unless you had a "great change of heart."

Edwards was a brilliant thinker who entered Yale College when he was only 13. His preaching was one of the driving forces of the Great Awakening. Ironically, when the religious revival died down, Edwards's own congregation rejected him for being too strict about doctrine. Edwards moved to Stockbridge, Massachusetts, in 1751, where he lived most of his remaining years as missionary to a Native American settlement.

▲ **The British minister George Whitefield was a major force behind the Great Awakening. In his seven journeys to the American colonies between 1738 and 1770, Whitefield preached dramatic sermons that brought many listeners to tears.**

The Great Awakening brought many colonists, as well as Native Americans and African Americans, into organized Christian churches for the first time. As the movement gained momentum, it also challenged the authority of established churches. Some colonists abandoned their old Puritan or Anglican congregations. At the same time, independent denominations, such as the Baptists and Methodists, gained new members. The Great Awakening also led to an increased interest in higher education, as several Protestant denominations founded colleges such as Princeton (originally the College of New Jersey), Brown, Columbia (originally King's College), and Dartmouth to train ministers for their rapidly growing churches.

Vocabulary
denomination: a large group of religious congregations united by shared beliefs

While the Great Awakening and the Enlightenment emphasized opposing aspects of human experience—emotionalism and reason, respectively—they had similar consequences. Both caused people to question traditional authority. Moreover, both stressed the importance of the individual—the Enlightenment by emphasizing human reason, and the Great Awakening by de-emphasizing the role of church authority.

These movements helped lead the colonists to question Britain's authority over their lives. The separation between Britain and the colonies was further hastened by another significant event, a North American war between Great Britain and France, in which the colonists fought on Britain's side.

ASSESSMENT

1. **TERMS & NAMES** For each term or name, write a sentence explaining its significance.
   - **Enlightenment**
   - **Benjamin Franklin**
   - **Jonathan Edwards**
   - **Great Awakening**

MAIN IDEA

2. **TAKING NOTES**
   Re-create the diagram below on your paper and fill it in with historical examples that illustrate the main idea at the top.

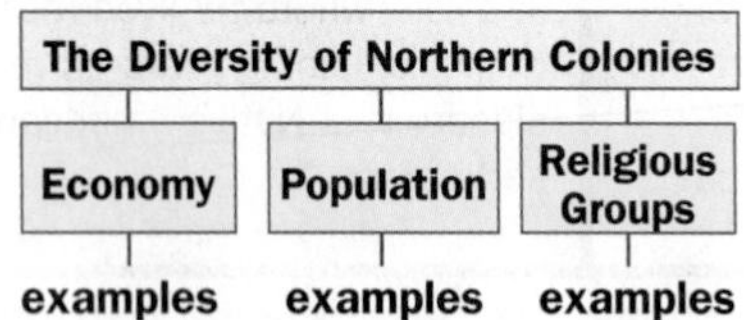

Name the advantages and the disadvantages of this kind of society.

CRITICAL THINKING

3. **COMPARING**
   What positive and negative trends that emerged in the Northern colonies during the 1700s do you think still affect the United States today? Support your responses with details from the text. **Think About:**
   - the growth of cities
   - the influx of immigrants
   - the status of women and African Americans
   - the effects of the Enlightenment and the Great Awakening

4. **MAKING INFERENCES**
   How do you think a person who believed in the ideas of the Enlightenment might have assessed the Salem witchcraft trials? Support your response with reasons.

5. **CONTRASTING**
   In what ways did the Northern colonies differ from the Southern colonies in the 1700s? Use evidence from the text to support your response.

SECTION 4

The French and Indian War

MAIN IDEA

British victory over the French in North America enlarged the British empire but led to new conflicts with the colonists.

WHY IT MATTERS NOW

British victories helped spread the English language throughout North America.

Terms & Names

- **New France**
- **George Washington**
- **French and Indian War**
- **William Pitt**
- **Pontiac**
- **Proclamation of 1763**
- **George Grenville**
- **Sugar Act**

One American's Story

hmhsocialstudies.com
TAKING NOTES

Use the graphic organizer online to take notes on the major events of the French and Indian War.

Joseph Nichols and other Massachusetts men joined British soldiers in fighting the French near the Hudson River in 1758. Yet even though the colonists and the British had united against a common enemy, the two groups held conflicting ideas about authority. On October 31, 1758, Nichols recorded the following dispute.

A PERSONAL VOICE JOSEPH NICHOLS

"About sunrise, the chief officer of the fort came to our regiment and ordered all our men up to the falls to meet the wagons and teams. Our men seemed to be loath to go before they eat. Those that refused to turn out, he drove out, and some he struck with his staff, which caused a great uproar among us. Our people in general declare in case we are so used tomorrow, blows shall end the dispute."

—quoted in *A People's Army*

The British general Edward Braddock met defeat and death near Fort Duquesne in 1755. In the French and Indian War, the colonists and the British fought side by side for nine years.

This "uproar" demonstrates that the British and the colonists differed in their views about authority and individual freedom. During the war between Great Britain and France, these conflicting viewpoints triggered divisions between Great Britain and its colonies that would never heal.

Rivals for an Empire

In the 1750s, France was Great Britain's biggest rival in the struggle to build a world empire, and one major area of contention between them was the rich Ohio River Valley. The colonists favored Great Britain because they still thought of themselves as British; as well, they were eager to expand the colonies westward from the increasingly crowded Atlantic seaboard.

FRANCE'S NORTH AMERICAN EMPIRE France had begun its North American empire in 1534, when Jacques Cartier explored the St. Lawrence River. In 1608, Samuel de Champlain founded the town of Quebec, the first permanent French settlement in North America.

After establishing Quebec, French priests and traders spread into the heart of the continent. In 1682, Robert Cavelier, Sieur de La Salle, claimed the entire Mississippi Valley for France, naming it Louisiana in honor of King Louis XIV. However, by 1754 the European population of **New France,** the French colony in North America, had grown to only about 70,000 (compared to more than 1,000,000 in the British colonies).

From the start, New France differed from the British colonies. Typical French colonists included fur traders and Catholic priests who wanted to convert Native Americans. Neither had a desire to build towns or raise families.

The French colonists also developed friendlier relations with Native Americans than did the British. They relied on Hurons, Ottawas, Ojibwas, and others to do most of the trapping and then traded with them for the furs, which were in great demand in Europe. This trade relationship led to several military alliances. As early as 1609, for example, the Algonquin and other Native Americans used Champlain's help to defeat their traditional enemies, the Mohawk Iroquois. A

MAIN IDEA

Contrasting

A How was the French colony in North America unlike the British colonies?

Britain Defeats an Old Enemy

As the French empire in North America expanded, it collided with the growing British empire. France and Great Britain had already fought two inconclusive wars during the previous half-century. In 1754, the French-British conflict reignited. In that year, the French built Fort Duquesne at the point where the Allegheny and Monongahela rivers join to form the Ohio—the site of modern Pittsburgh. However, the British had previously granted 200,000 acres of land in the Ohio country to a group of wealthy planters. The Virginia governor sent militia, a group of ordinary citizens who performed military duties, to evict the French.

The small band, led by an ambitious 22-year-old officer named **George Washington,** established an outpost called Fort Necessity about 40 miles from Fort Duquesne. In May 1754, Washington's militia attacked a small detachment of French soldiers, and the French swiftly counterattacked. In the battle that followed in July, the French forced Washington to surrender. Although neither side realized it, these battles at Fort Necessity were the opening of the **French and Indian War,** the fourth war between Great Britain and France for control of North America.

EARLY FRENCH VICTORIES A year after his defeat, Washington again headed into battle, this time as an aide to the British general Edward Braddock, whose mission was to drive the French out of the Ohio Valley.

Braddock first launched an attack on Fort Duquesne. As Braddock and nearly 1,500 soldiers neared the fort, French soldiers and their Native American allies ambushed them. The British soldiers, accustomed to enemies who marched in orderly rows rather than ones who fought from behind trees, turned and fled.

HISTORICAL SPOTLIGHT

WASHINGTON'S RESIGNATION

George Washington's military career nearly ended shortly after it started. In 1754, as the British prepared to wage war on France in North America, Washington eagerly awaited a position with the regular British army.

The governor of Virginia offered Washington the rank of captain—a demotion from Washington's position as colonel. Washington angrily rejected the offer as well as a later proposal that he retain the rank of colonel but have the authority and pay of a captain.

The young Virginian's patriotism, however, was too strong. He swallowed his pride and relaunched his military career as a volunteer aide to General Braddock in the spring of 1755.

Washington showed incredible courage, while the weakness of the supposedly invincible British army surprised him and many other colonists. They began to question the competence of the British army, which suffered defeat after defeat during 1755 and 1756.

PITT AND THE IROQUOIS TURN THE TIDE Angered by French victories, Britain's King George II selected new leaders to run his government in 1757. One of these was **William Pitt,** an energetic, self-confident politician. Under Pitt, the reinvigorated British army finally began winning battles, which prompted the powerful Iroquois to support them. Now Britain had some Native American allies to balance those of France.

In September 1759, the war took a dramatic and decisive turn on the Plains of Abraham just outside Quebec. Under the cover of night, British troops under General James Wolfe scaled the high cliffs that protected Quebec. Catching the French and their commander, the Marquis de Montcalm, by surprise, they won a short but deadly battle. The British triumph at Quebec led them to victory in the war.

MAIN IDEA

Summarizing

B How did Great Britain's victory change the balance of power in North America?

The French and Indian War officially ended in 1763 with the Treaty of Paris. Great Britain claimed all of North America east of the Mississippi River. This included Florida, which Britain acquired from Spain, an ally of France. Spain gained the French lands west of the Mississippi, including the city of New Orleans. France kept control of only a few small islands near Newfoundland and in the West Indies. The other losers in the war were Native Americans, who found the victorious British harder to bargain with than the French had been. B

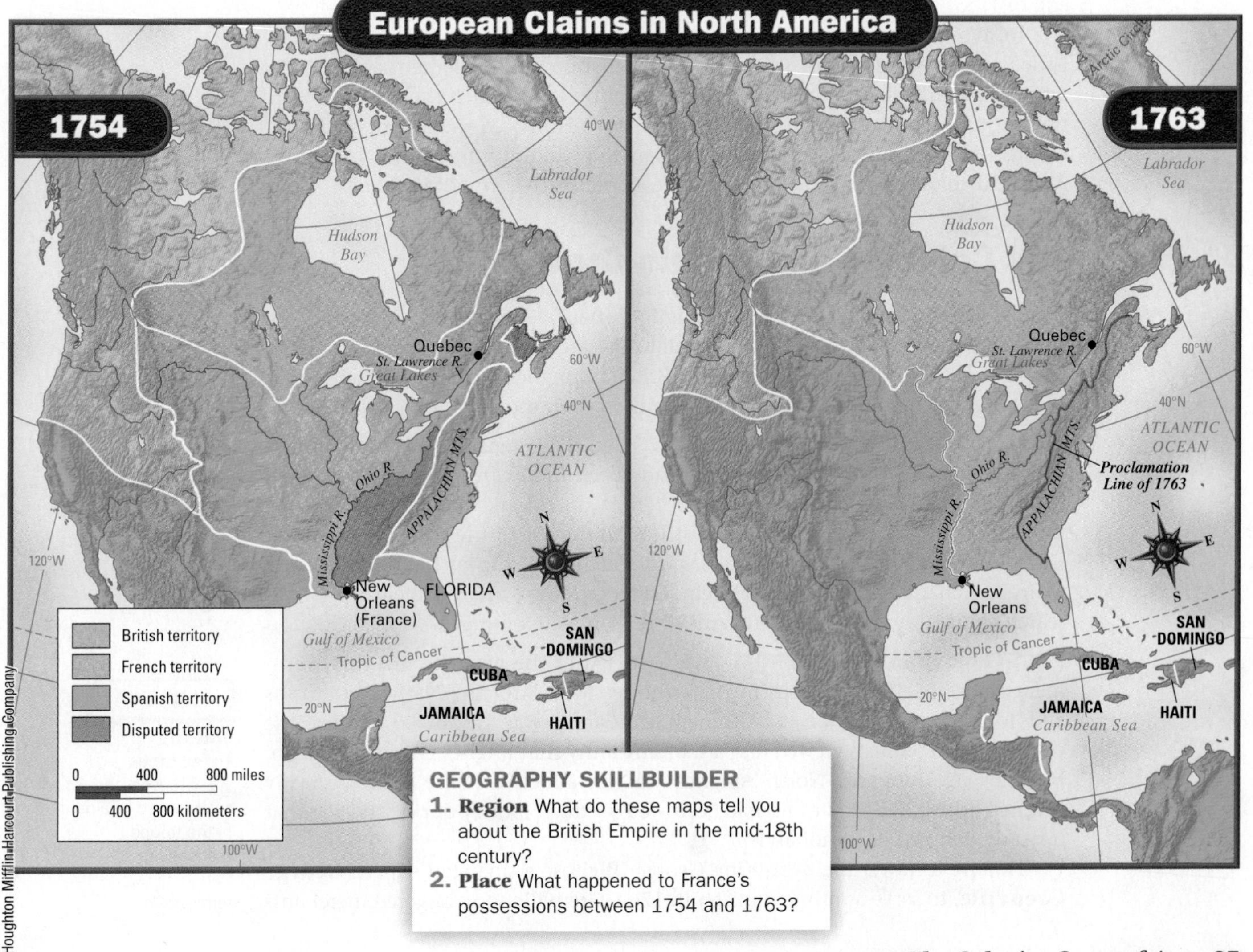

GEOGRAPHY SKILLBUILDER

1. **Region** What do these maps tell you about the British Empire in the mid-18th century?
2. **Place** What happened to France's possessions between 1754 and 1763?

VICTORY BRINGS NEW PROBLEMS Claiming ownership of the Ohio River Valley brought Great Britain trouble. Native Americans feared that the growing number of British settlers crossing the Appalachian mountains would soon drive away the game they depended on for survival. In the spring of 1763, the Ottawa leader **Pontiac** recognized that the French loss was a loss for Native Americans.

A PERSONAL VOICE PONTIAC

> **"When I go to see the English commander and say to him that some of our comrades are dead, instead of bewailing their death, as our French brothers do, he laughs at me and at you. If I ask for anything for our sick, he refuses with the reply that he has no use for us. From all this you can well see that they are seeking our ruin. Therefore, my brothers, we must all swear their destruction and wait no longer."**
>
> —quoted in *Red and White*

▲ Pontiac, the Ottawa chief, depicted in an 18th-century engraving.

Led by Pontiac, Native Americans captured eight British forts in the Ohio Valley and laid siege to two others. In angry response, British officers presented smallpox-infected blankets to two Delaware chiefs during peace negotiations, and the virus spread rapidly among the Native Americans. Weakened by disease and war, most Native American groups negotiated treaties with the British by the end of 1765.

To avoid further conflicts with Native Americans, the British government issued the **Proclamation of 1763,** which banned all settlement west of the Appalachians. This ban established a Proclamation Line, which the colonists were not to cross. (See the map on the previous page.) However, the British could not enforce this ban any more effectively than they could enforce the Navigation Acts, and colonists continued to move west onto Native American lands.

The Colonies and Britain Grow Apart

Because the Proclamation of 1763 sought to halt expansion, it convinced the colonists that the British government did not care about their needs. A second result of the French and Indian War—Britain's financial crisis—brought about new laws that reinforced the colonists' opinion even more.

BRITISH POLICIES ANGER COLONISTS By 1763, tensions between Britain and one colony, Massachusetts, had already been increasing. During the French and Indian War, the British had cracked down on colonial smuggling. In 1761, the royal governor of Massachusetts authorized the use of the writs of assistance, which allowed British customs officials to search any ship or building. Because many merchants worked out of their residences, the writs enabled officials to search colonial homes. The merchants of Boston were outraged.

PROBLEMS RESULTING FROM THE WAR After the war, the British government stationed 10,000 troops in its territories to control the Native Americans and former French subjects. Although this army was meant to protect the colonies, the colonists viewed it as a standing army that might turn against them. Maintaining troops in North America was an added expense on an already strained British budget. Britain had borrowed so much money during the war that it nearly doubled its national debt. (C)

MAIN IDEA

Making Inferences

(C) Why were the colonists so afraid of the troops stationed in Britain's new territories?

Hoping to lower the debt, King George III chose a financial expert, **George Grenville,** to serve as prime minister in 1763. Grenville soon angered merchants

Analyzing *Political Cartoons*

"JOIN, OR DIE"

In 1754 Benjamin Franklin drew this image of a severed snake to encourage the British colonies to unite against the threat posed by French and Indian forces. The design was inspired by a superstition that a sliced snake would revive if the pieces of its body were joined before sunset.

The image, the first political cartoon to be published in an American newspaper, was widely circulated in 1754 and later during the American Revolution. A remarkably direct and simple cartoon, it reveals the beginning of a sense of national identity.

SKILLBUILDER **Analyzing Political Cartoons**

1. Why are there only eight segments of the snake?
2. Why do you think this image was so persuasive to colonists who may never have thought of the separate colonies as parts of a whole?

SEE SKILLBUILDER HANDBOOK, PAGE R24.

throughout the colonies. He began to suspect that the colonists were smuggling goods into the country. In 1764 he prompted Parliament to enact a law known as the **Sugar Act.** The Sugar Act did three things. It halved the duty on foreign-made molasses (in the hopes that colonists would pay a lower tax rather than risk arrest by smuggling). It placed duties on certain imports. Most important, it strengthened the enforcement of the law allowing prosecutors to try smuggling cases in a vice-admiralty court rather than in a more sympathetic colonial court.

By the end of 1764, the colonies and Great Britain were disagreeing more and more about how the colonies should be taxed and governed. These feelings of dissatisfaction soon would swell into outright rebellion.

SECTION 4 ASSESSMENT

1. **TERMS & NAMES** For each term or name, write a sentence explaining its significance.
   - **New France**
   - **George Washington**
   - **French and Indian War**
   - **William Pitt**
   - **Pontiac**
   - **Proclamation of 1763**
   - **George Grenville**
   - **Sugar Act**

MAIN IDEA

2. **TAKING NOTES**
   Create a time line of the major events of the French and Indian War and its aftermath. Use the dates already plotted on the time line below as a guide.

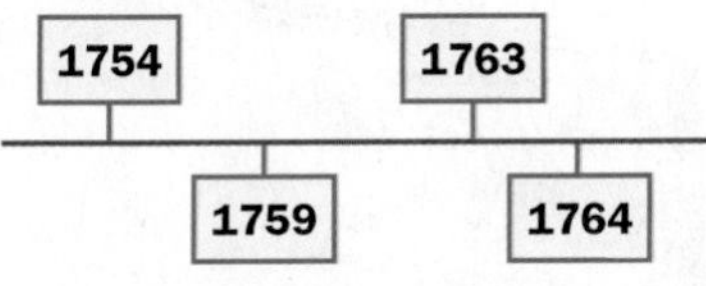

How long was the war? Why do you think it lasted so long?

CRITICAL THINKING

3. **ANALYZING CAUSES**
   How did the French and Indian War lead to tension between the colonists and the British government?
4. **EVALUATING DECISIONS**
   If you had been a Native American living in the Northeast during the French and Indian War, would you have formed a military alliance with France or with Great Britain? Support your choice with reasons.
5. **HYPOTHESIZING**
   What if the outcome of the French and Indian War had been different and France had won? How might this have affected the 13 colonies?
   Think About:
   - the actual outcome of the Treaty of Paris
   - France's patterns of colonization
   - France's relations with Native Americans

DAILY LIFE 1630–1763

Colonial Courtship

The concept of dating among teenagers was nonexistent in colonial times. Young people were considered either children or adults, and as important as marriage was in the colonies, sweethearts were older than one might suspect. The practices of courtship and marriage varied among the different communities.

▼ FRONTIER OR BACKCOUNTRY PEOPLE

Andrew Jackson, depicted with his wife in the painting below, "stole" his wife (she was willing) from her family. Jackson was following a custom of the backcountry people, who lived along the western edge of the colonies.

These colonists, mostly Scots-Irish, based their marriages on the old custom of "abduction"—stealing the bride—often with her consent. Even regular marriages began with the groom and his friends coming to "steal" the bride. Much drinking and dancing accompanied these wild and hilarious weddings.

PURITANS

For Puritans, marriage was a civil contract, not a religious or sacred union. Although adults strictly supervised a couple's courting, parents allowed two unusual practices. One was the use of a courting stick, a long tube into which the couple could whisper while the family was in another room. The other was the practice of "bundling": a young man spent the night in the same bed as his sweetheart, with a large bundling board (shown below) between them.

Before marrying, the couple had to allow for Puritan leaders to voice any objections to the marriage at the meeting house. Passing that, the couple would marry in a very simple civil ceremony and share a quiet dinner.

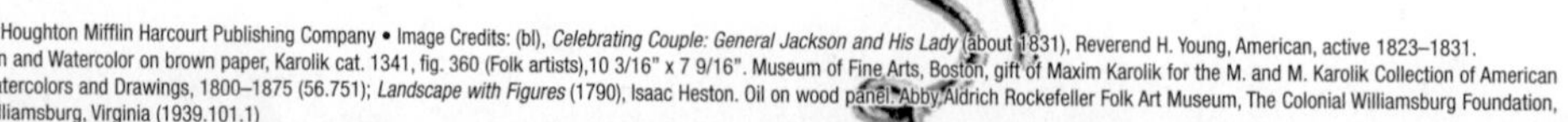

THE SOUTH ▲

Many African slaves married in a "jumping the broomstick" ceremony, in which the bride and groom jumped over a broomstick to seal their union. Although there is disagreement among African-American scholars, some suggest that the above painting depicts a slave wedding on a South Carolina plantation in the late 1700s.

◀ QUAKERS

Quaker couples intent on marrying needed the consent not only of the parents but also of the whole Quaker community. Quakers who wanted to marry had to go through a 16-step courtship phase before they could wed. Quaker women, however, were known to reject men at the last minute.

VIRGINIA ▶

In Virginia, marriage was a sacred union. Since the marriage often involved a union of properties, and love was not necessary, parents were heavily involved in the negotiations. In this illustration from a dance manual (right), a young upper-class couple work to improve their social graces by practicing an elaborate dance step.

DATA FILE

WHO MARRIED?

Puritans:
- 98% of males and 94% of females married
- Grooms were usually a few years older than brides
- Discouraged marriages between first cousins

Virginians:
- 25% of males never married; most females married
- Grooms nearly 10 years older than brides
- Allowed first-cousin marriages

Quakers:
- 16% of women single at age 50
- forbade first-cousin marriages

Frontier People:
- Almost all women and most men married
- Ages of bride and groom about the same
- Youngest group to marry

Average Age at Marriage

Group	Males	Females
Puritan	26	23
Virginians	26	19
Quakers		
in Delaware	31	29
in Penn. & N.J.	26	22
Philadelphians	26	23
Frontier People	21	19
Modern Americans	27	25

Who Could Divorce?

Puritans:	Yes
Virginians:	No
Quakers:	No

Source: David Hackett Fischer, *Albion's Seed*

THINKING CRITICALLY

CONNECT TO HISTORY

1. **Interpreting Data** What was a common characteristic of courtship among Puritans, Quakers, and Virginians?

SEE SKILLBUILDER HANDBOOK, PAGE R22.

CONNECT TO TODAY

2. **Synthesizing** Research modern courtship practices by interviewing your parents or relatives. Write a brief paper comparing and contrasting modern-day and colonial courtship practices.

hmhsocialstudies.com RESEARCH WEB LINKS

CHAPTER  ASSESSMENT

TERMS & NAMES

For each term or name below, write a sentence explaining its significance for the growth of the colonies to the mid-18th century.

1. mercantilism
2. Dominion of New England
3. triangular trade
4. middle passage
5. Stono Rebellion
6. Enlightenment
7. Great Awakening
8. New France
9. Pontiac
10. Proclamation of 1763

MAIN IDEAS

Use your notes and the information in the chapter to answer the following questions.

England and Its Colonies

1. Why did Parliament pass the Navigation Acts?
2. How did the policy of salutary neglect benefit both England and its colonies?

The Agricultural South

3. Which ethnic groups besides the English began to settle in the South?
4. Which social class came to control the economy as well as the political and social institutions of the South?

The Commercial North

5. Why did large, single-crop plantations not develop in the North?
6. What factors contributed to the witchcraft hysteria in late 17th-century Salem?

The French and Indian War

7. How did the goals of the French colonists differ from those of the English colonists?
8. What problems were brought about for Britain by its victory in the French and Indian War?

CRITICAL THINKING

1. **USING YOUR NOTES** In a chart like the one below, show the differences between the Northern and Southern economies that led to the development of two distinct cultural regions.

Northern Economy	Southern Economy

2. **DEVELOPING HISTORICAL PERSPECTIVE** How did immigration contribute to the ethnic diversity of the American colonies after 1700?

3. **ANALYZING EFFECTS** How did the French and Indian War help inspire a sense of unity and shared identity among the colonists?

VISUAL SUMMARY — THE COLONIES COME OF AGE

Trade
The colonies supplied Britain with raw materials and bought Britain's manufactured goods.

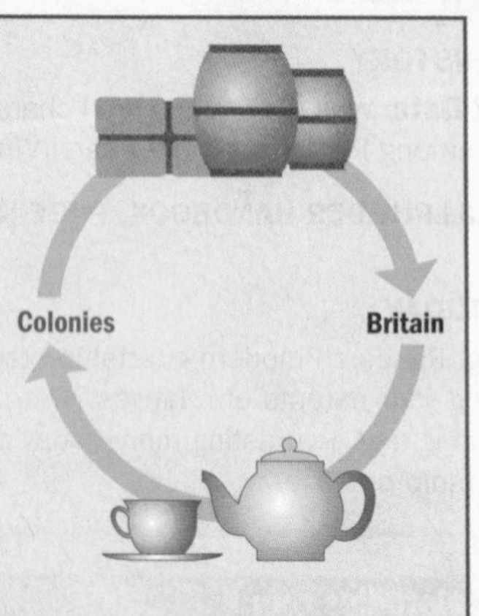

Regional Distinctions
Industry developed in the Northern colonies, while the South became predominantly agricultural.

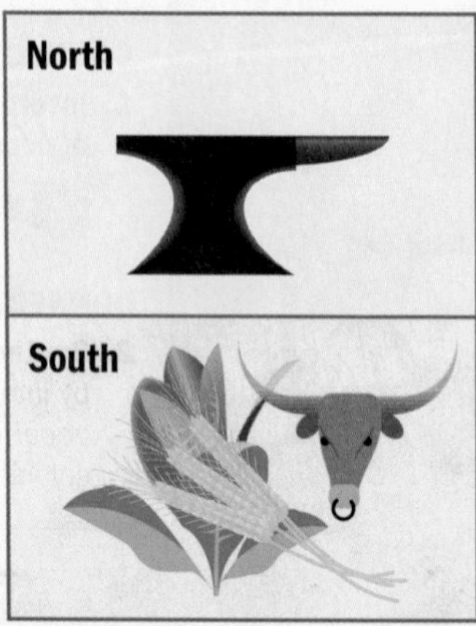

French and Indian War
The British victory in the French and Indian War brought about both territorial expansion and new tensions with the American colonies.

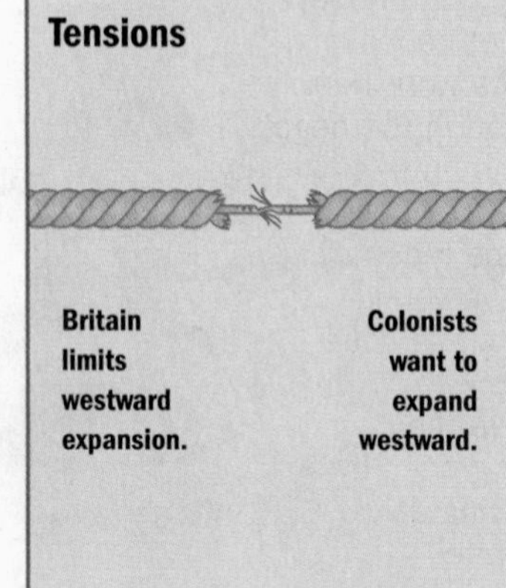

STANDARDIZED TEST PRACTICE

Use the chart and your knowledge of U.S. history to answer questions 1 and 2.

Kings and Queens of England, 1685–1820	
James II	1685–1688
William III & Mary II	1689–1702
Anne	1702–1714
George I	1714–1727
George II	1727–1760
George III	1760–1820

1. Why was the Glorious Revolution of 1688 significant to the colonies?

- **A** William and Mary supported capitalism instead of mercantilism.
- **B** William and Mary practiced Catholicism instead of Anglicanism.
- **C** William and Mary supported the supremacy of Parliament.
- **D** Willam and Mary appointed Sir Edmund Andros to enforce the Navigation Acts.

2. The Treaty of Paris ending the French and Indian War was signed during the reign of —

- **F** Queen Anne
- **G** King George I
- **H** King George II
- **J** King George III

3. In the 1700s an intellectual movement known as the Enlightenment developed in Europe and spread to the colonies. Benjamin Franklin and Thomas Jefferson were among those colonists heavily influenced by Enlightenment ideas. In which of the following ways did the Enlightenment affect the colonists?

- **A** Enlightenment ideas led people to expand the trade in enslaved persons.
- **B** Enlightenment ideas stirred people to rededicate themselves to God.
- **C** Enlightenment ideas persuaded people to establish colonies in order to generate a favorable balance of trade.
- **D** Enlightenment ideas convinced people of the importance of civil rights.

4. Compared to the Southern colonies, the Northern colonies in 1720 were —

- **F** less economically diverse.
- **G** less dependent on trade with England.
- **H** more dependent on slavery.
- **J** more urban.

hmhsocialstudies.com TEST PRACTICE

For additional test practice, go online for:

- Diagnostic tests
- Tutorials

INTERACT WITH HISTORY

Think about the issues you explored at the beginning of the chapter. In a small group, discuss whether or not equality and freedom have been achieved in the United States today. Prepare an oral or visual presentation comparing equality and freedom in the United States today with equality and freedom in the colonies in the early 1700s.

FOCUS ON WRITING

The British Parliament has just enacted the Sugar Act of 1764. As a colonial leader, you need to decide if you are for or against the Sugar Act. Write a pamphlet in which you support or oppose the new tax. Begin by clearly identifying your position and then prepare a clear list of evidence that supports your position. Also, be sure to counter arguments for the opposing viewpoint.

COLLABORATIVE LEARNING

21st CENTURY

Working in small groups, do library or Internet research to learn more about the history of one of the 13 colonies. Create an exhibit documenting the first 100 years of the colony's development. Find images and write text to highlight key events and important people in the early history of the colony.

CHAPTER 4

THE WAR FOR INDEPENDENCE

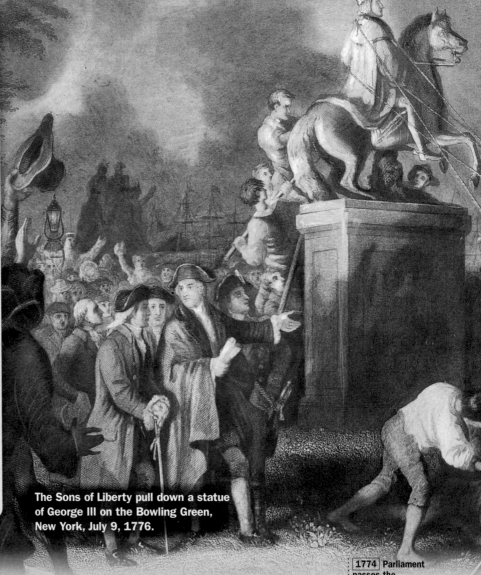

Essential Question

What were the causes and major events of the American revolution and who were the significant individuals involved in the conflict?

ALABAMA COURSE OF STUDY

1 Compare effects of economic, geographic, social, and political conditions before and after European explorations of the fifteenth through seventeenth centuries on Europeans, American colonists, Africans, and indigenous Americans.

3 Trace the chronology of events leading to the American Revolution, including the French and Indian War, passage of the Stamp Act, the Boston Tea Party, the Boston Massacre, passage of the Intolerable Acts, the Battles of Lexington and Concord, the publication of Common Sense, and the signing of the Declaration of Independence.

- Explaining the role of key revolutionary leaders, including George Washington, John Adams, Thomas Jefferson, Patrick Henry, Samuel Adams, Paul Revere, Crispus Attucks, and the Marquis de Lafayette.
- Explaining the significance of revolutionary battles, including Bunker Hill, Trenton, Saratoga, and Yorktown.
- Summarizing major ideas of the Declaration of Independence, including theories of John Locke, Charles de Montesquieu, and Jean-Jacques Rousseau.
- Comparing perspectives of differing groups in society and their roles in the American Revolution, including men, women, white settlers, free and enslaved African Americans, and American Indians.

The Sons of Liberty pull down a statue of George III on the Bowling Green, New York, July 9, 1776.

USA

1765 The British Parliament passes the Stamp Act.

1767 Parliament passes the Townshend Acts.

1770 Five colonists are killed in the "Boston Massacre."

1773 Colonists stage the Boston Tea Party.

1774 Parliament passes the Intolerable Acts.

1774 First Continental Congress convenes.

1768 — 1770 — 1772 — 1774

WORLD

1760 George III becomes king of Great Britain.

1769 Scotland's James Watt patents a steam engine capable of running other machines.

1770 Tukolor Kingdom arises in the former Songhai region of West Africa.

1774 The Reign of Louis XVI begins in France.

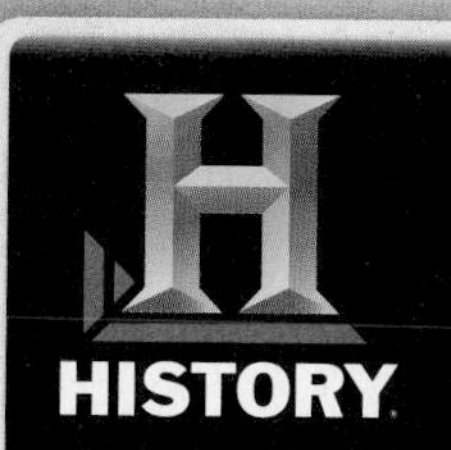

The Declaration of Independence

hmhsocialstudies.com VIDEO

INTERACT WITH HISTORY

It is 1767, and your Boston printing shop may soon be forced to close. British import taxes have all but eliminated your profits. In response to petitions to repeal the tax, the king has instead stationed troops throughout the city. Some of your neighbors favor further petitions, but others urge stronger measures. How do you think the colonists should respond?

Explore the Issues

- Should American colonists obey every law passed in Britain?
- Are colonists entitled to the same rights as all other British subjects?

1776 Thomas Paine publishes *Common Sense.*

1776 The American colonies declare independence.

1777 The colonists' victory at Saratoga marks a turning point in the war.

1781 The British surrender at Yorktown.

1783 Colonists and British sign the Treaty of Paris, ending the war.

1776 | 1778 | 1780 | 1782

1776 Adam Smith's *The Wealth of Nations* is published.

1779 Spain declares war on Britain.

1782 Spain puts down a Native American rebellion in Peru.

Image Credits: (bkgd), The Granger Collection, New York; (bl), ©Leif Skoogfors/Corbis; (br), The Granger Collection, New York; (bc), ©Time & Life Pictures/Getty Images

SECTION 1

The Stirrings of Rebellion

MAIN IDEA

Conflict between Great Britain and the American colonies grew over issues of taxation, representation, and liberty.

WHY IT MATTERS NOW

The events that shaped the American Revolution are a turning point in humanity's fight for freedom.

Terms & Names

- **Stamp Act**
- **Samuel Adams**
- **Townshend Acts**
- **Boston Massacre**
- **committees of correspondence**
- **Boston Tea Party**
- **King George III**
- **Intolerable Acts**
- **martial law**
- **minutemen**

One American's Story

hmhsocialstudies.com TAKING NOTES

Use the graphic organizer online to take notes on the major events of the growing conflict between Great Britain and the American colonies.

On the cold, clear night of March 5, 1770, a mob gathered outside the Customs House in Boston. They heckled the British sentry on guard, calling him a "lobster-back" to mock his red uniform. More soldiers arrived, and the mob began hurling stones and snowballs at them. At that moment, Crispus Attucks, a sailor of African and Native American ancestry, arrived with a group of angry laborers.

A PERSONAL VOICE JOHN ADAMS

"This Attucks . . . appears to have undertaken to be the hero of the night; and to lead this army with banners . . . up to King street with their clubs . . . [T]his man with his party cried, 'Do not be afraid of them. . . .' He had hardiness enough to fall in upon them, and with one hand took hold of a bayonet, and with the other knocked the man down."

—quoted in *The Black Presence in the Era of the American Revolution*

▲ **Crispus Attucks**

Attucks's action ignited the troops. Ignoring orders not to shoot, one soldier and then others fired on the crowd. Five people were killed; several were wounded. Crispus Attucks was, according to a newspaper account, the first to die.

The Colonies Organize to Resist Britain

The uprising at the Customs House illustrated the rising tensions between Britain and its American colonies. In order to finance debts from the French and Indian War, as well as from European wars, Parliament had turned hungry eyes on the colonies' resources.

THE STAMP ACT The seeds of increased tension were sown in March 1765 when Parliament, persuaded by Prime Minister George Grenville, passed the **Stamp Act.** The Stamp Act required colonists to purchase special stamped paper for every legal document, license, newspaper, pamphlet, and almanac, and imposed special "stamp duties" on packages of playing cards and dice. The tax reached into every colonial pocket. Colonists who disobeyed the law were to be tried in the vice-admiralty courts, where convictions were probable.

STAMP ACT PROTESTS When word of the Stamp Act reached the colonies in May of 1765, the colonists united in their defiance. Boston shopkeepers, artisans, and laborers organized a secret resistance group called the Sons of Liberty. One of its founders was Harvard-educated **Samuel Adams,** who, although unsuccessful in business and deeply in debt, proved himself to be a powerful and influential political activist.

Background
A New York branch of the Sons of Liberty was also founded at around the same time as the Boston chapter.

By the end of the summer, the Sons of Liberty were harassing customs workers, stamp agents, and sometimes royal governors. Facing mob threats and demonstrations, stamp agents all over the colonies resigned. The Stamp Act was to become effective on November 1, 1765, but colonial protest prevented any stamps from being sold.

During 1765 and early 1766, the individual colonial assemblies confronted the Stamp Act measure. Virginia's lower house adopted several resolutions put forth by a 29-year-old lawyer named Patrick Henry. These resolutions stated that Virginians could be taxed only by the Virginia assembly—that is, only by their own representatives. Other assemblies passed similar resolutions.

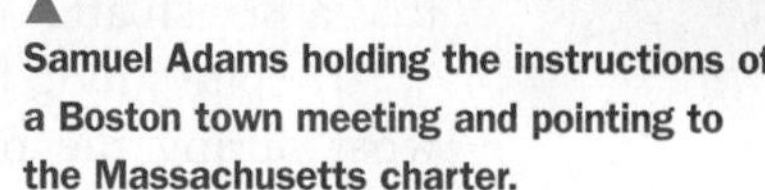
Samuel Adams holding the instructions of a Boston town meeting and pointing to the Massachusetts charter.

The colonial assemblies also made a strong collective protest. In October 1765, delegates from nine colonies met in New York City. This Stamp Act Congress issued a Declaration of Rights and Grievances, which stated that Parliament lacked the power to impose taxes on the colonies because the colonists were not represented in Parliament. More than 10 years earlier, the colonies had rejected Benjamin Franklin's Albany Plan of Union, which called for a joint colonial council to address defense issues. Now, for the first time, the separate colonies began to act as one.

Merchants in New York, Boston, and Philadelphia agreed not to import goods manufactured in Britain until the Stamp Act was repealed. They expected that British merchants would force Parliament to repeal the Stamp Act. The widespread boycott worked. In March 1766, Parliament repealed the Stamp Act; but on the same day, to make its power clear, Parliament issued the Declaratory Act. This act asserted Parliament's full right to make laws "to bind the colonies and people of America . . . in all cases whatsoever."

Vocabulary
boycott: a collective refusal to use, buy, or deal with, especially as an act of protest

THE TOWNSHEND ACTS Within a year after Parliament repealed the Stamp Act, Charles Townshend, the leading government minister at the time, impetuously decided on a new method of gaining revenue from the American colonies. His proposed revenue laws, passed by Parliament in 1767, became known as the **Townshend Acts.** Unlike the Stamp Act, which was a direct tax, these were indirect taxes, or duties levied on imported materials—glass, lead, paint, and paper—as they came into the colonies from Britain. The acts also imposed a three-penny tax on tea, the most popular drink in the colonies.

The colonists reacted with rage and well-organized resistance. Educated Americans spoke out against the Townshend Acts, protesting "taxation without representation." Boston's Samuel Adams called for another boycott of British goods, and American women of every rank in society became involved in the protest. Writer Mercy Otis Warren of Massachusetts urged women to lay their British "female ornaments aside," foregoing "feathers, furs, rich sattins and . . . capes." Wealthy women stopped buying British luxuries and joined other women in spinning bees. These were public displays of spinning and weaving of colonial-made cloth designed to show colonists' determination to boycott British-made cloth. Housewives also boycotted British tea and exchanged recipes for tea made from birch bark and sage. (A)

MAIN IDEA
Comparing
(A) How would you compare reactions to the Townshend Acts with reactions to the Stamp Act?

Conflict intensified in June 1768. British agents in Boston seized the *Liberty*, a ship belonging to local merchant John Hancock. The customs inspector claimed that Hancock had smuggled in a shipment of wine from Madeira and had failed to pay the customs taxes. The seizure triggered riots against customs agents. In response, the British stationed 2,000 "redcoats," or British soldiers—so named for the red jackets they wore—in Boston. **B**

> **MAIN IDEA**
> **Evaluating**
> **B** Do you think that the colonists' reaction to the seizing of the *Liberty* was justified?

Tension Mounts in Massachusetts

The presence of British soldiers in Boston's streets charged the air with hostility. The city soon erupted in clashes between British soldiers and colonists and later in a daring tea protest, all of which pushed the colonists and Britain closer to war.

THE BOSTON MASSACRE One sore point was the competition for jobs between colonists and poorly paid soldiers who looked for extra work in local shipyards during off-duty hours. On the cold afternoon of March 5, 1770, a fist-fight broke out over jobs. That evening a mob gathered in front of the Customs House and taunted the guards. When Crispus Attucks and several dockhands appeared on the scene, an armed clash erupted, killing three men including Attucks, and fatally wounding two more. Instantly, Samuel Adams and other colonial agitators labeled this confrontation the **Boston Massacre,** thus presenting it as a British attack on defenseless citizens.

Despite strong feelings on both sides, the political atmosphere relaxed somewhat during the next two years until 1772, when a group of Rhode Island colonists attacked a British customs schooner that patrolled the coast for smugglers. After the ship accidentally ran aground near Providence, the colonists boarded the vessel and burned it to the waterline. In response, King George named a special commission to seek out the suspects and bring them to England for trial.

History Through *Art*

THE BOSTON MASSACRE

Paul Revere was not only a patriot, he was a silversmith and an engraver as well. One of the best-known of his engravings, depicting the Boston Massacre, is a masterful piece of anti-British propaganda. Widely circulated, Revere's engraving played a key role in rallying revolutionary fervor.

- The sign above the redcoats reads "Butcher's Hall."
- The British commander, Captain Prescott (standing at the far right of the engraving) appears to be inciting the troops to fire, whereas in fact, he tried to calm the situation.
- At the center foreground is a small dog, a detail that gave credence to the rumor that, following the shootings, dogs licked the blood of the victims from the street.

SKILLBUILDER Interpreting Visual Sources

1. According to the details of the engraving, what advantages do the redcoats have that the colonists do not? What point does the artist make through this contrast?
2. How could this engraving have contributed to the growing support for the Patriots' cause?

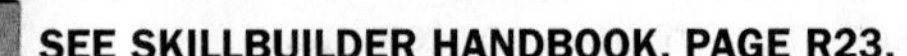

SEE SKILLBUILDER HANDBOOK, PAGE R23.

MAIN IDEA

Analyzing Motives

C Why were the committees of correspondence established?

The plan to haul Americans to England for trial ignited widespread alarm. The assemblies of Massachusetts and Virginia set up **committees of correspondence** to communicate with other colonies about this and other threats to American liberties. By 1774, such committees formed a buzzing communication network linking leaders in nearly all the colonies. **C**

THE BOSTON TEA PARTY Early in 1773, Lord Frederick North, the British prime minister, faced a new problem. The British East India Company, which held an official monopoly on tea imports, had been hit hard by the colonial boycotts. With its warehouses bulging with 17 million pounds of tea, the company was nearing bankruptcy. To save it, North devised the Tea Act, which granted the company the right to sell tea to the colonies free of the taxes that colonial tea sellers had to pay. This action would cut colonial merchants out of the tea trade, because the East India Company could sell its tea directly to consumers for less. North hoped the American colonists would simply buy the cheaper tea; instead, they protested violently.

On the moonlit evening of December 16, 1773, a large group of Boston rebels disguised themselves as Native Americans and proceeded to take action against three British tea ships anchored in the harbor. John Andrews, an onlooker, wrote a letter on December 18, 1773, describing what happened.

A PERSONAL VOICE JOHN ANDREWS

"**They muster'd . . . to the number of about two hundred, and proceeded . . . to Griffin's wharf, where [the three ships] lay, each with 114 chests of the *ill fated* article . . . and before *nine* o'clock in the evening, every chest from on board the three vessels was knock'd to pieces and flung over the sides.**

They say the actors were *Indians* from *Narragansett*. Whether they were or not, . . . they appear'd as *such*, being cloath'd in Blankets with the heads muffled, and copper color'd countenances, being each arm'd with a hatchet or axe. . . ."

—quoted in *1776: Journals of American Independence*

In this incident, later known as the **Boston Tea Party**, the "Indians" dumped 18,000 pounds of the East India Company's tea into the waters of Boston Harbor.

THE INTOLERABLE ACTS **King George III** was infuriated by this organized destruction of British property, and he pressed Parliament to act. In 1774, Parliament responded by passing a series of measures that colonists called the **Intolerable Acts.** One law shut down Boston Harbor because the colonists had refused to pay for the damaged tea. Another, the Quartering Act, authorized British commanders to house soldiers in vacant private homes and other buildings. In addition to these measures, General Thomas Gage, commander in chief of British forces in North America, was appointed the new governor of Massachusetts. To keep the peace, he placed Boston under **martial law,** or rule imposed by military forces. **D**

MAIN IDEA

Analyzing Motives

D What did King George set out to achieve when he disciplined Massachusetts?

The committees of correspondence quickly moved into action and assembled the First Continental Congress. In September 1774, 56 delegates met in Philadelphia and drew up a declaration of colonial rights. They defended the colonies' right to run their own affairs. They supported the protests in Massachusetts and stated that if the British used force against the colonies, the colonies should fight back. They also agreed to reconvene in May 1775 if their demands weren't met.

NOW & THEN

PROPOSITION 13

A more recent tax revolt occurred in California on June 6, 1978, when residents voted in a tax reform law known as Proposition 13. By the late 1970s, taxes in California were among the highest in the nation. The property tax alone was fifty-two percent above the national norm.

Proposition 13, initiated by ordinary citizens, limited the tax on real property to one percent of its value in 1975–1976. It passed with sixty-five percent of the vote.

Because of the resulting loss of revenue, many state agencies were scaled down or cut. In 1984, California voters approved a state lottery that provides supplemental funds for education. Proposition 13 still remains a topic of heated debate.

British Actions and Colonial Reactions, 1765–1775

1765 STAMP ACT		1767 TOWNSHEND ACTS		1770 BOSTON MASSACRE	
British Action	**Colonial Reaction**	**British Action**	**Colonial Reaction**	**British Action**	**Colonial Reaction**
Britain passes the Stamp Act, a tax law requiring colonists to purchase special stamps to prove payment of tax.	Colonists harass stamp distributors, boycott British goods, and prepare a Declaration of Rights and Grievances.	Britain taxes certain colonial imports and stations troops at major colonial ports to protect customs officers.	Colonists protest "taxation without representation" and organize a new boycott of imported goods.	British troops stationed in Boston are taunted by an angry mob. The troops fire into the crowd, killing five colonists.	Colonial agitators label the conflict a massacre and publish a dramatic engraving depicting the violence.

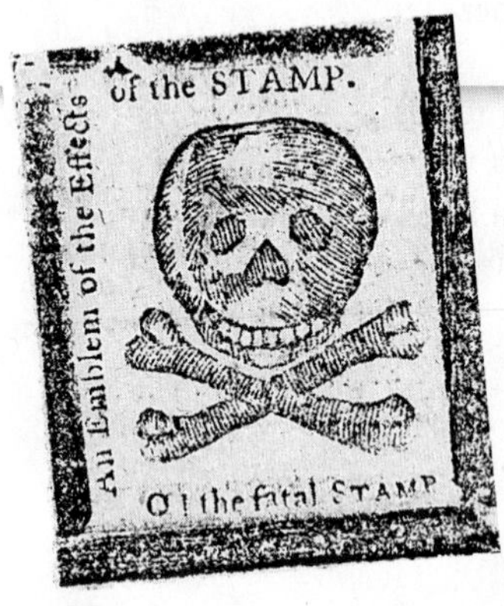

▲ This colonial engraving was meant to warn of the effects of the Stamp Act.

Fighting Erupts at Lexington and Concord

After the First Continental Congress, colonists in many eastern New England towns stepped up military preparations. **Minutemen,** or civilian soldiers, began to quietly stockpile firearms and gunpowder. General Gage soon learned about these activities and prepared to strike back.

TO CONCORD, BY THE LEXINGTON ROAD The spring of 1775 was a cold one in New England. Because of the long winter frosts, food was scarce. General Gage had been forced to put his army on strict rations, and British morale was low. Around the same time, Gage became concerned about reports brought to him concerning large amounts of arms and munitions hidden outside of Boston.

In March, Gage sent agents toward Concord, a town outside of Boston reported to be the site of one of the stockpiles. The agents returned with maps detailing where arms were rumored to be stored in barns, empty buildings, and private homes. The agents also told that John Hancock and Samuel Adams, perhaps the two most prominent leaders of resistance to British authority, were staying in Lexington, a smaller community about five miles east of Concord. As the snows melted and the roads cleared, Gage drew up orders for his men to march along the Lexington Road to Concord, where they would seize and destroy all munitions that they could find.

"THE REGULARS ARE COMING!" As General Gage began to ready his troops quartered in Boston, minutemen were watching. Rumors were that a strike by British troops against resistance activities would come soon, although no one knew exactly when, nor did they know which towns would be targeted.

With Hancock and Adams in hiding, much of the leadership of resistance activity in Boston fell to a prominent young physician named Joseph Warren. Sometime during the afternoon of April 18, Doctor Warren consulted a confidential source close to the British high command. The source informed him that Gage intended to march on Concord by way of Lexington, seize Adams and Hancock, and destroy all hidden munitions. Warren immediately sent for Paul Revere, a member of the Sons of Liberty, and told him to warn Adams and Hancock as well as the townspeople along the way. Revere began to organize a network of riders who would spread the alarm. (E)

MAIN IDEA
Summarizing
(E) What did Warren order Paul Revere to do?

On the night of April 18, Paul Revere, William Dawes, and Samuel Prescott rode out to spread word that 700 British Regulars, or army soldiers, were headed

1773 TEA ACT		1774 INTOLERABLE ACTS		1775 LEXINGTON AND CONCORD	
British Action	**Colonial Reaction**	**British Action**	**Colonial Reaction**	**British Action**	**Colonial Reaction**
Britain gives the East India Company special concessions in the colonial tea business and shuts out colonial tea merchants.	Colonists in Boston rebel, dumping 18,000 pounds of East India Company tea into Boston Harbor.	King George III tightens control over Massachusetts by closing Boston Harbor and quartering troops.	Colonial leaders form the First Continental Congress and draw up a declaration of colonial rights.	General Gage orders troops to march to Concord, Massachusetts, and seize colonial weapons.	Minutemen intercept the British and engage in battle—first at Lexington, and then at Concord.

SKILLBUILDER Interpreting Charts
In what ways did colonial reaction to British rule intensify between 1765 and 1775?

This bottle contains tea that colonists threw into Boston Harbor during the Boston Tea Party.

for Concord. Before long, the darkened countryside rang with church bells and gunshots—prearranged signals to warn the population that the Regulars were coming.

Revere burst into the house where Adams and Hancock were staying and warned them to flee to the backwoods. He continued his ride until he, like Dawes, was detained by British troops. As Revere was being questioned, shots rang out and the British officer realized that the element of surprise had been lost. When more shots rang out, the officer ordered the prisoners released so that he could travel with greater speed to warn the other British troops marching toward Lexington that resistance awaited them there.

The Battle of Lexington, as depicted in a mid-nineteenth-century painting.

A View of the Town of Concord, painted by an unknown artist, shows British troops assembling on the village green.

"A GLORIOUS DAY FOR AMERICA" By the morning of April 19, 1775, the king's troops reached Lexington. As they neared the town, they saw 70 minutemen drawn up in lines on the village green. The British commander ordered the minutemen to leave, and the colonists began to move out without laying down their muskets. Then someone fired, and the British soldiers sent a volley of shots into the departing militia. Eight minutemen were killed and ten more were wounded, but only one British soldier was injured. The Battle of Lexington lasted only 15 minutes.

The British marched on to Concord, where they found an empty arsenal. After a brief skirmish with minutemen, the British soldiers lined up to march back to Boston, but the march quickly became a slaughter. Between 3,000 and 4,000 minutemen had assembled by now, and they fired on the marching troops from behind stone walls and trees. British soldiers fell by the dozen. Bloodied and humiliated, the remaining British soldiers made their way back to Boston.

While the battles were going on, Adams and Hancock were fleeing deeper into the New England countryside. At one point, they heard the sound of musketfire in the distance. Adams remarked that it was a fine day and Hancock, assuming that his companion was speaking of the weather said, "Very pleasant." "I mean," Adams corrected Hancock, "this is a glorious day for America."

ASSESSMENT

1. TERMS & NAMES For each term or name, write a sentence explaining its significance.

- **Stamp Act**
- **Samuel Adams**
- **Townshend Acts**
- **Boston Massacre**
- **committees of correspondence**
- **Boston Tea Party**
- **King George III**
- **Intolerable Acts**
- **martial law**
- **minutemen**

MAIN IDEA

2. TAKING NOTES
Create a cluster diagram like the one shown and fill it in with events that demonstrate the conflict between Great Britain and the American colonies.

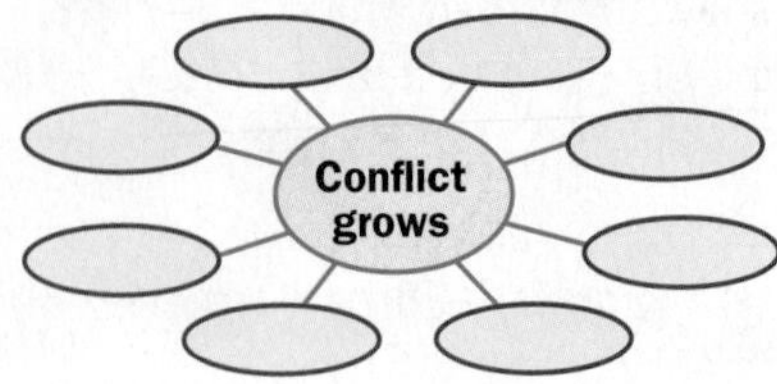

Choose one event to further explain in a paragraph.

CRITICAL THINKING

3. DEVELOPING HISTORICAL PERSPECTIVE
What opinion might a British soldier have had about the Boston Massacre? Explain and support your response. **Think About:**

- the start of the conflict on March 5, 1770
- the behavior of Crispus Attucks and other colonists
- the use of the event as propaganda

4. MAKING GENERALIZATIONS
Explain whether you think the British government acted wisely in its dealings with the colonies between 1765 and 1775. Support your explanation with examples from the text. **Think About:**

- the reasons for British actions
- the reactions of colonists
- the results of British actions

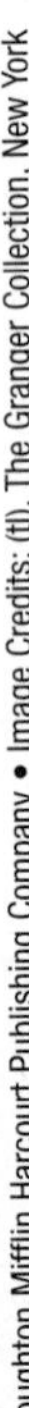

SECTION 2

Ideas Help Start a Revolution

MAIN IDEA	WHY IT MATTERS NOW	Terms & Names
Tensions increased throughout the colonies until the Continental Congress declared independence on July 4, 1776.	**The Declaration of Independence continues to inspire and challenge people everywhere.**	• **Second Continental Congress** • **Olive Branch Petition** • ***Common Sense*** • **Thomas Jefferson** • **Declaration of Independence** • **Patriots** • **Loyalists**

One American's Story

hmhsocialstudies.com TAKING NOTES

Use the graphic organizer online to take notes on the writing and impact of the Declaration of Independence.

William Franklin, son of the famous American writer, scientist, statesman, and diplomat Benjamin Franklin, was royal governor of New Jersey. Despite his father's patriotic sympathies, William remained stubbornly loyal to King George. In a letter written on August 2, 1775, to Lord Dartmouth, he stated his position and that of others who resisted revolutionary views.

William Franklin

A PERSONAL VOICE WILLIAM FRANKLIN

"There is indeed a dread in the minds of many here that some of the leaders of the people are aiming to establish a republic. Rather than submit . . . we have thousands who will risk the loss of their lives in defense of the old Constitution. [They] are ready to declare themselves whenever they see a chance of its being of any avail."

—quoted in *A Little Revenge: Benjamin Franklin and His Son*

Because of William's stand on colonial issues, communication between him and his father virtually ceased. The break between William Franklin and his father exemplified the chasm that now divided American from American.

The Colonies Hover Between Peace and War

In May of 1775, colonial leaders convened a second Continental Congress in Philadelphia to debate their next move. Beyond their meeting hall, however, events continued moving quickly, as minutemen and British soldiers clashed in a bloody battle outside Boston, and an increasingly furious King George readied his country for war.

THE SECOND CONTINENTAL CONGRESS The loyalties that divided colonists sparked endless debates at the **Second Continental Congress.** John Adams of Massachusetts suggested a sweeping, radical plan—that each colony set up its own government and that the Congress declare the colonies independent.

Furthermore, he argued, the Congress should consider the militiamen besieging Boston to be the Continental Army and name a general to lead them. Moderate John Dickinson of Pennsylvania strongly disagreed with Adams's call for revolt. In private, he confronted Adams.

PERSONAL VOICE JOHN DICKINSON

"What is the reason, Mr. Adams, that you New England men oppose our measures of reconciliation? . . . If you don't concur with us in our pacific system, I and a number of us will break off from you in New England, and we will carry on the opposition by ourselves in our own way."

—quoted in *Patriots: The Men Who Started the American Revolution*

The debates raged on into June, but one stubborn fact remained: colonial militiamen were still encamped around Boston. The Congress agreed to recognize them as the Continental Army and appointed as its commander a 43-year-old veteran of the French and Indian War, George Washington. The Congress, acting like an independent government, also authorized the printing of paper money to pay the troops and organized a committee to deal with foreign nations. These actions came just in time. (A)

MAIN IDEA

Evaluating Leadership

(A) Do you think that the Continental Congress was responsible in the actions that it took?

THE BATTLE OF BUNKER HILL Cooped up in Boston, British General Thomas Gage decided to strike at militiamen who had dug in on Breed's Hill, north of the city and near Bunker Hill. On the steamy summer morning of June 17, 1775, Gage sent out nearly 2,400 British troops. The British, sweating in wool uniforms and heavy packs, began marching up Breed's Hill in their customary broad lines. The colonists held their fire until the last minute, then began to shoot down the advancing redcoats. The surviving British troops made a second attack, and then a third. The third assault succeeded, but only because the militiamen ran low on ammunition.

This painting shows "Bunker's Hill" before the battle, as shells from Boston set nearby Charles Town ablaze. At the battle, the British demonstrated a maneuver they used throughout the war: they massed together, were visible for miles, and failed to take advantage of ground cover. ▼

By the time the smoke cleared, the colonists had lost 450 men, while the British had suffered over 1,000 casualties. The misnamed Battle of Bunker Hill would prove to be the deadliest battle of the war.

THE OLIVE BRANCH PETITION By July, the Second Continental Congress was readying the colonies for war while still hoping for peace. Most of the delegates, like most colonists, felt deep loyalty to George III and blamed the bloodshed on the king's ministers. On July 8, 1775, the Congress sent the king the so-called **Olive Branch Petition,** urging a return to "the former harmony" between Britain and the colonies. **B**

MAIN IDEA

Evaluating

B Do you think that the Olive Branch Petition was too little too late?

King George flatly rejected the petition. Furthermore, he issued a proclamation stating that the colonies were in rebellion and urged Parliament to order a naval blockade of the American coast.

The Patriots Declare Independence

In the months after the Olive Branch Petition, a thin document containing the powerful words of an angry citizen began to circulate and change public opinion.

COMMON SENSE In ***Common Sense,*** an anonymous 50-page pamphlet, the colonist Thomas Paine attacked King George III. Paine explained that his own revolt against the king had begun with Lexington and Concord.

A PERSONAL VOICE THOMAS PAINE

> **"No man was a warmer wisher for a reconciliation than myself, before the fatal nineteenth of April, 1775, but the moment the event of that day was made known, I rejected the hardened, sullen tempered Pharaoh of England for ever . . . the wretch, that with the pretended title of Father of his people can unfeelingly hear of their slaughter, and composedly sleep with their blood upon his soul."**
>
> —*Common Sense*

▲ **Thomas Paine's pamphlet *Common Sense* helped to overcome many colonists' doubts about separating from Britain.**

Paine declared that the time had come for colonists to proclaim an independent republic. He argued that independence, which was the American "destiny," would allow America to trade freely with other nations for guns and ammunition and win foreign aid from British enemies. Finally, Paine stated, independence would give Americans the chance to create a better society—one free from tyranny, with equal social and economic opportunities for all.

Common Sense sold nearly 500,000 copies and was widely applauded. In April 1776, George Washington wrote, "I find *Common Sense* is working a powerful change in the minds of many men." **C**

MAIN IDEA

Analyzing Issues

C Why do you think that *Common Sense* was so effective?

DECLARING INDEPENDENCE By early summer 1776, events pushed the wavering Continental Congress toward a decision. North Carolina had declared itself independent, and a majority of Virginians told their delegates that they favored independence. At last, the Congress urged each colony to form its own government. On June 7, Virginia delegate Richard Henry Lee moved that "these United Colonies are, and of a right ought to be, free and independent States."

While talks on this fateful motion were under way, the Congress appointed a committee to prepare a formal declaration explaining the reasons for the colonies' actions. Virginia lawyer **Thomas Jefferson,** known for his broad knowledge and skillfully crafted prose, was chosen to express the committee's points.

PHILOSOPHERS AND THE DECLARATION OF INDEPENDENCE

Although Thomas Jefferson wrote the Declaration of Independence, he was influenced by Enlightenment philosophers, including Charles de Montesquieu and Jean-Jacques Rousseau.

Montesquieu was a French nobleman of the early eighteenth century. Montesquieu declared that the republic was the form of government based on virtue. Montesquieu also explained that separation of powers is necessary to prevent tyranny. These ideas can be seen in the Declaration of Independence's denunciation of King George III as a tyrant and not fit to rule.

Rousseau's ideas were even more central to the Declaration of Independence. Rousseau established the idea of the social contract, or that free people live in society in order to protect their rights. The purpose of the Declaration was to show how King George had broken the social contract with the American colonists.

Jefferson's masterful **Declaration of Independence** drew on the concepts of the English philosopher John Locke, who maintained that people enjoy "natural rights" to life, liberty, and property. Jefferson described these rights as "Life, Liberty and the pursuit of Happiness."

In keeping with Locke's ideas, Jefferson then declared that governments derive "their just powers from the consent of the governed"—that is, from the people. This right of consent gave the people the right "to alter or to abolish" any government that threatened their unalienable rights and to install a government that would uphold these principles. On the basis of this reasoning, the American colonies declared their independence from Britain, listing in the Declaration the numerous ways in which the British king had violated the "unalienable rights" of the Americans. D

MAIN IDEA

Summarizing

D What reasons did Thomas Jefferson give to justify revolt by the colonies?

The Declaration states flatly that "all men are created equal." When this phrase was written, it expressed the common belief that free citizens were political equals. It did not claim that all people had the same abilities or ought to have equal wealth. It was not meant to embrace women, Native Americans, and African-American slaves—a large number of Americans. However, Jefferson's words presented ideals that would later help these groups challenge traditional attitudes.

In his first draft, Jefferson included an eloquent attack on the cruelty and injustice of the slave trade. However, South Carolina and Georgia, the two colonies most dependent on slavery, objected. In order to gain the votes of those two states, Jefferson dropped the offending passage.

On July 2, 1776, the delegates voted unanimously that the American colonies were free, and on July 4, 1776, they adopted the Declaration of Independence. While delegates created a formal copy of the Declaration, the document was read to a crowd in front of the Pennsylvania State House—now called Independence Hall. A rush of pride and anxiety ran through the **Patriots**—the supporters of independence—when they heard the closing vow: "We mutually pledge to each other our Lives, our Fortunes, and our Sacred Honor."

Americans Choose Sides

Americans now faced a difficult, bitter choice: revolution or loyalty to the Crown. This issue divided communities, friends, and even families throughout the colonies.

LOYALISTS AND PATRIOTS The exact number of **Loyalists**—those who opposed independence and remained loyal to the Crown—is unknown. Many with Loyalist sympathies changed sides as the war progressed.

Some Loyalists felt a special tie to the king because they had served as judges, councilors, or governors. Most Loyalists, however, were ordinary people of modest means. They included some people who lived far from the cities and knew little of the events that turned other colonists into revolutionaries. Other people remained loyal because they thought that the British were going to win the war and they wanted to avoid being punished as rebels. Still others were Loyalists because they thought that the crown would protect their rights more effectively than the new colonial governments would. E

MAIN IDEA

Contrasting

E How did the thinking of the Loyalists differ from that of the Patriots?

Patriots drew their numbers from people who saw economic opportunity in an independent America. The Patriot cause embraced farmers, artisans, merchants,

Colonists Choose Sides

Loyalists and Patriots had much to gain and much to lose in the American colonies' struggle for independence. Fortunes, family ties, and religious obligations as well as personal convictions were at stake. For many, the most important issue was that of national identity. Both sides believed that they were fighting for their country as well as being loyal to what was best for America.

PATRIOTS

Nathanael Greene

A pacifist Quaker, Nathanael Greene nonetheless chose to fight against the British.

"I am determined to defend my rights and maintain my freedom or sell my life in the attempt."

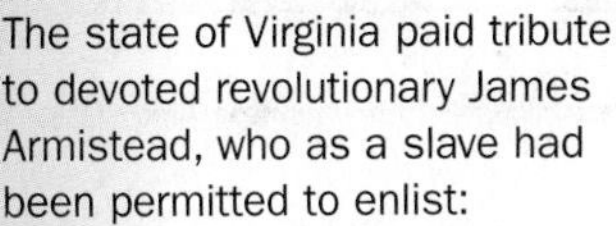

James Armistead

The state of Virginia paid tribute to devoted revolutionary James Armistead, who as a slave had been permitted to enlist:

"At the peril of his life [Armistead] found means to frequent the British camp, and thereby faithfully executed important commissions entrusted to him by the marquis."

Mercy Otis Warren

Patriot Mercy Otis Warren wrote,

"I see the inhabitants of our plundered cities quitting the elegancies of life, possessing nothing but their freedom, I behold faction & discord tearing up an Island we once held dear and a mighty Empire long the dread of distant nations, tott'ring to the very foundation."

LOYALISTS

Charles Inglis

A clergyman of the Church of England, Charles Inglis was loyal to the king and argued against independence:

"By a reconciliation with Britain, [an end] would be put to the present calamitous war, by which many lives have been lost, and so many more must be lost, if it continues."

Joseph Brant

Mohawk chief Joseph Brant fought for the British during the French and Indian War and remained loyal to the crown during the Revolutionary War.

"If we . . . [do] nothing for the British . . . there will be no peace for us. Our throats will be cut by the Red Coat man or by America. . . . We should go and join the father [Britain] . . . this is the only way for us."

Isaac Wilkins

Isaac Wilkins had to leave his home after he opposed sending delegates to the Second Continental Congress.

"I leave America and every endearing connection because I will not raise my hand against my Sovereign, nor will I draw my sword against my country. When I can conscientiously draw it in her favor, my life shall be cheerfully devoted to her service."

Analyzing *Political Cartoons*

MOB RULE

This British cartoon portrays the events of the Boston Tea Party from the Loyalist perspective. While Patriots are dumping tea, a British tax collector, having been tarred and feathered, is having tea poured down his throat. The "Liberty Tree," where a copy of the Stamp Act has been nailed upside down, has been converted into a gallows, a device used for hanging people.

SKILLBUILDER Analyzing Political Cartoons

1. How does the cartoonist make the mob look sinister?
2. What kind of comment does the cartoonist make by suspending a hangman's noose from the "Liberty Tree"? Explain.

SEE SKILLBUILDER HANDBOOK, PAGE R24.

landowners, and elected officials. German colonists in Pennsylvania, Maryland, and Virginia also joined the fight for independence. While Patriots made up nearly half the population, many Americans remained neutral.

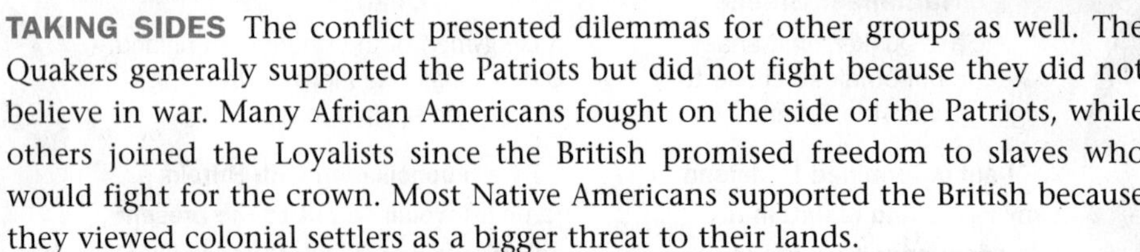

TAKING SIDES The conflict presented dilemmas for other groups as well. The Quakers generally supported the Patriots but did not fight because they did not believe in war. Many African Americans fought on the side of the Patriots, while others joined the Loyalists since the British promised freedom to slaves who would fight for the crown. Most Native Americans supported the British because they viewed colonial settlers as a bigger threat to their lands.

Now the colonies were plunged into two wars—a war for independence and a civil war in which Americans found themselves on opposing sides. The price of choosing sides could be high. In declaring their independence, the Patriots had invited war with the mightiest empire on earth.

SECTION 2 ASSESSMENT

1. **TERMS & NAMES** For each term or name, write a sentence explaining its significance.
   - **Second Continental Congress**
   - **Olive Branch Petition**
   - ***Common Sense***
   - **Thomas Jefferson**
   - **Declaration of Independence**
   - **Patriots**
   - **Loyalists**

MAIN IDEA

2. **TAKING NOTES**
   Re-create the cluster diagram below on your paper. Fill it in with details presenting causes, ideas, and results related to the Declaration of Independence.

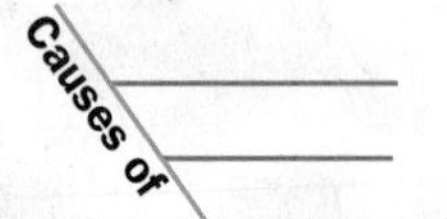

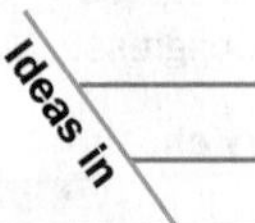

The Declaration of Independence

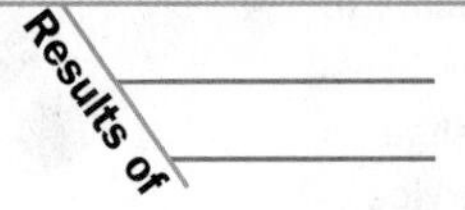

CRITICAL THINKING

3. **HYPOTHESIZING**
   Imagine that King George had accepted the Olive Branch Petition and sought a diplomatic resolution with the Congress. Do you think colonists would still have pressed for independence? **Think About:**
   - the attitudes of the king and Parliament toward the colonies
   - the impact of fighting at Lexington, Concord, and Breed's Hill
   - the writings of Thomas Paine

4. **ANALYZING PRIMARY SOURCES**
   Thomas Paine wrote in the introduction to *Common Sense*:

   > **"The cause of America is in a great measure the cause of all mankind."**

   Evaluate the significance of Paine's statement. **Think About:**
   - Locke's ideas about natural rights
   - Jefferson's ideas about "unalienable rights"

The Declaration of Independence

Thomas Jefferson's Declaration of Independence is one of the most important and influential legal documents of modern times. Although the text frequently refers to eighteenth-century events, its Enlightenment philosophy and politics have continuing relevance today. For more than 200 years the Declaration of Independence has inspired leaders of other independence movements and has remained a crucial document in the struggle for civil rights and human rights.

Th Jefferson

In Congress, July 4, 1776.

A Declaration by the Representatives of the United States of America, in General Congress assembled.

When in the Course of human events, it becomes necessary for one people to dissolve the political bands which have connected them with another, and to assume among the powers of the earth, the separate and equal station to which the Laws of Nature and of Nature's God entitle them, a decent respect to the opinions of mankind requires that they should declare the causes which impel them to the separation.

Jefferson begins the Declaration by attempting to legally and philosophically justify the revolution that was already underway. Here Jefferson is saying that, now that the colonists have begun to separate themselves from British rule, it is time to explain why the colonists have taken this course of action.

We hold these truths to be self-evident, that all men are created equal, that they are endowed by their Creator with certain unalienable Rights, that among these are Life, Liberty and the pursuit of Happiness; that, to secure these rights, Governments are instituted among Men, deriving their just powers from the consent of the governed; that whenever any Form of Government becomes destructive of these ends, it is the Right of the People to alter or to abolish it, and to institute new Government, laying its foundation on such principles and organizing its powers in such form, as to them shall seem most likely to effect their Safety and Happiness. Prudence, indeed, will dictate that Governments long established should not be changed for light and transient causes; and accordingly all experience hath shewn that mankind are more disposed to suffer, while evils are sufferable, than to right themselves by abolishing the forms to which they are accustomed. But when a long train of abuses and usurpations, pursuing invariably the same Object, evinces a design to reduce them under absolute Despotism, it is their right, it is their duty, to throw off such Government, and to provide new Guards for their future security.

These passages reveal the influence of the English philosopher John Locke. In *Two Treatises of Government* (1690), Locke argued that if a government does not allow its citizens to enjoy certain rights and freedoms, the people have a right to replace that government.

Such has been the patient sufferance of these Colonies; and such is now the necessity which constrains them to alter their former Systems of Government. The history of the present King of Great Britain is a history of repeated injuries and usurpations, all having in direct object the establishment of an absolute Tyranny over these States. To prove this, let facts be submitted to a candid world.

He has refused his Assent to Laws, the most wholesome and necessary for the public good.

Here begins the section in which Jefferson condemns the behavior of King George, listing the king's many tyrannical actions that have forced his American subjects to rebel.

He has forbidden his Governors to pass Laws of immediate and pressing importance, unless suspended in their operation till his assent should be obtained; and, when so suspended, he has utterly neglected to attend to them.

He has refused to pass other Laws for the accommodation of large districts of people, unless those people would relinquish the right of Representation in the Legislature, a right inestimable to them, and formidable to tyrants only.

He has called together legislative bodies at places unusual, uncomfortable, and distant from the depository of their public Records, for the sole purpose of fatiguing them into compliance with his measures.

He has dissolved Representative Houses repeatedly, for opposing with manly firmness his invasions on the rights of the people.

He has refused for a long time, after such dissolutions, to cause others to be elected; whereby the Legislative powers, incapable of Annihilation, have returned to the people at large for their exercise; the State remaining in the mean time exposed to all the dangers of invasions from without, and convulsions within.

He has endeavoured to prevent the population of these States; for that purpose obstructing the Laws for Naturalization of Foreigners; refusing to pass others to encourage their migration hither, and raising the conditions of new Appropriations of Lands.

He has obstructed the Administration of Justice, by refusing his Assent to Laws for establishing Judiciary powers.

He has made Judges dependent on his Will alone, for the tenure of their offices, and the amount and payment of their salaries.

He has erected a multitude of New Offices, and sent hither swarms of Officers to harass our people and eat out their substance.

He has kept among us, in times of peace, Standing Armies, without the Consent of our legislatures.

He has affected to render the Military independent of and superior to the Civil power.

He has combined with others to subject us to a jurisdiction foreign to our constitution and unacknowledged by our laws; giving his Assent to their Acts of pretended Legislation:

For quartering large bodies of armed troops among us;

For protecting them, by a mock Trial, from punishment for any Murders which they should commit on the Inhabitants of these States;

For cutting off our Trade with all parts of the world;

For imposing Taxes on us without our Consent;

For depriving us, in many cases, of the benefits of Trial by Jury;

For transporting us beyond Seas to be tried for pretended offenses;

For abolishing the free System of English Laws in a neighboring Province, establishing therein an Arbitrary government, and enlarging its Boundaries so as to render it at once an example and fit instrument for introducing the same absolute rule into these Colonies;

For taking away our Charters, abolishing our most valuable laws, and altering fundamentally the Forms of our Governments;

For suspending our own Legislatures, and declaring themselves invested with power to legislate for us in all cases whatsoever.

He has abdicated Government here, by declaring us out of his Protection and waging War against us.

He has plundered our seas, ravaged our Coasts, burnt our towns, and destroyed the lives of our people.

He is at this time transporting large Armies of foreign Mercenaries to compleat the works of death, desolation, and tyranny, already begun with circumstances of Cruelty & perfidy scarcely paralleled in the most barbarous ages, and totally unworthy the Head of a civilized nation.

HISTORICAL SPOTLIGHT

INDEPENDENCE AND SLAVERY

The Declaration of Independence went through many revisions before the final draft. Jefferson, a slaveholder himself, regretted having to eliminate one passage in particular—a condemnation of slavery and the slave trade. However, in the face of opposition of delegates from Southern states, the anti-slavery passage was deleted.

This is a reference to the 10,000 troops that the British government stationed in North America after the French and Indian War. Although the British government saw the troops as protection for the colonists, the colonists themselves viewed the troops as a standing army that threatened their freedom.

Here Jefferson condemns both the king and Parliament for passing the Intolerable Acts. Most of these laws were intended to punish the people of Massachusetts for the Boston Tea Party. For example, the Quartering Act of 1774 forced colonists to provide lodging for British troops. Another act allowed British soldiers accused of murder to be sent back to England for trial. The Boston Port Bill closed the port of Boston, "cutting off our Trade with all parts of the world."

Here Jefferson refers to the Quebec Act, which extended the boundaries of the province. He then refers to another act that changed the charter of Massachusetts and restricted town meetings.

In Congress, July 4, 1776

The unanimous Declaration of the thirteen united States of America.

He has constrained our fellow Citizens, taken Captive on the high Seas, to bear Arms against their Country, to become the executioners of their friends and Brethren, or to fall themselves by their Hands.

He has excited domestic insurrections amongst us, and has endeavoured to bring on the inhabitants of our frontiers the merciless Indian Savages, whose known rule of warfare is an undistinguished destruction of all ages, sexes and conditions.

In every stage of these Oppressions We have Petitioned for Redress in the most humble terms; Our repeated Petitions have been answered only by repeated injury. A Prince, whose character is thus marked by every act which may define a Tyrant, is unfit to be the ruler of a free people.

Nor have We been wanting in attentions to our British brethren. We have warned them from time to time of attempts by their legislature to extend an unwarrantable jurisdiction over us. We have reminded them of the circumstances of our emigration and settlement here. We have appealed to their native justice and magnanimity, and we have conjured them by the ties of our common kindred, to disavow these usurpations, which would inevitably interrupt our connections and correspondence. They too have been deaf to the voice of justice and of consanguinity. We must, therefore, acquiesce in the necessity, which denounces our Separation, and hold them, as we hold the rest of mankind, Enemies in War, in Peace Friends.

We, therefore, the Representatives of the United States of America, in General Congress, Assembled, appealing to the Supreme Judge of the world for the rectitude of our intentions, do, in the name, and by the Authority of the good People of these Colonies solemnly publish and declare, That these United Colonies are, and of Right ought to be, Free and Independent States; that they are Absolved from all Allegiance to the British Crown, and that all political connection between them and the State of Great Britain is, and ought to be, totally dissolved; and that as Free and Independent States, they have full Power to levy War, conclude Peace, contract Alliances, establish Commerce, and do all other Acts and Things which Independent States may of right do.

ANOTHER PERSPECTIVE

"ALL MEN WOULD BE TYRANTS IF THEY COULD."

Although the Declaration dealt with issues of equality, justice, and independence, it did not address conditions of inequality within the colonies themselves. Husbands dominated their wives, for example, and slaves lived under complete control of their owners. Speaking on behalf of women, Abigail Adams (above) had this to say to her husband John, who served in the Continental Congress:

> "Remember the Ladies, and be more generous and favourable to them than your ancestors. Do not put such unlimited power into the hands of the Husbands. Remember all Men would be tyrants if they could. If particular care . . . is not paid to the Ladies, we are determined to foment a Rebellion."

Here Jefferson turns his attention away from the king and toward the British people. Calling the British the "common kindred" of the colonists, Jefferson reminds them how often the Americans have appealed to their sense of justice. Reluctantly the colonists are now forced to break their political connections with their British kin.

In this final paragraph, the delegates declare independence.

The Declaration ends with the delegates' pledge, or pact. The delegates at the Second Continental Congress knew that, in declaring their independence from Great Britain, they were committing treason—a crime punishable by death. "We must all hang together," Benjamin Franklin reportedly said, as the delegates prepared to sign the Declaration, "or most assuredly we shall all hang separately."

KEY PLAYER

JOHN HANCOCK
1737–1793

Born in Braintree, Massachusetts, and raised by a wealthy uncle, John Hancock became one of the richest men in the colonies. He traveled around Boston in a luxurious carriage and dressed only in the finest clothing. "He looked every inch an aristocrat," noted one acquaintance, "from his dress and powdered wig to his smart pumps of grained leather."

Beneath Hancock's refined appearance, however, burned the heart of a patriot. He was only too glad to lead the Second Continental Congress. When the time came to sign the Declaration of Independence, Hancock scrawled his name in big, bold letters. "There," he reportedly said, "I guess King George will be able to read that."

And for the support of this Declaration, with a firm reliance on the protection of divine Providence, we mutually pledge to each other our Lives, our Fortunes, and our sacred Honor.

[Signed by]

John Hancock **[President of the Continental Congress]**

[Georgia]
Button Gwinnett
Lyman Hall
George Walton

[Rhode Island]
Stephen Hopkins
William Ellery

[Connecticut]
Roger Sherman
Samuel Huntington
William Williams
Oliver Wolcott

[North Carolina]
William Hooper
Joseph Hewes
John Penn

[South Carolina]
Edward Rutledge
Thomas Heyward, Jr.
Thomas Lynch, Jr.
Arthur Middleton

[Maryland]
Samuel Chase
William Paca
Thomas Stone
Charles Carroll

[Virginia]
George Wythe
Richard Henry Lee
Thomas Jefferson
Benjamin Harrison
Thomas Nelson, Jr.
Francis Lightfoot Lee
Carter Braxton

[Pennsylvania]
Robert Morris
Benjamin Rush
Benjamin Franklin
John Morton
George Clymer
James Smith
George Taylor
James Wilson
George Ross

[Delaware]
Caesar Rodney
George Read
Thomas McKean

[New York]
William Floyd
Philip Livingston
Francis Lewis
Lewis Morris

[New Jersey]
Richard Stockton
John Witherspoon
Francis Hopkinson
John Hart
Abraham Clark

[New Hampshire]
Josiah Bartlett
William Whipple
Matthew Thornton

[Massachusetts]
Samuel Adams
John Adams
Robert Treat Paine
Elbridge Gerry

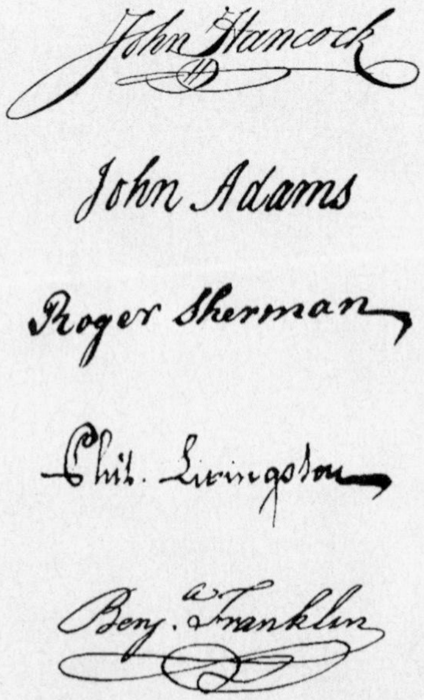

John Hancock

John Adams

Roger Sherman

Phil. Livingston

Benj. Franklin

SECTION 3

Struggling Toward Saratoga

MAIN IDEA	WHY IT MATTERS NOW	Terms & Names
After a series of setbacks, American forces won at Saratoga and survived.	Determination, resilience, and unity have become part of the American character.	• Valley Forge • Trenton • Saratoga • inflation • profiteering

One American's Story

hmhsocialstudies.com
TAKING NOTES

Use the graphic organizer online to take notes on the early battles of the American Revolution.

After the colonists had declared independence, few people thought the rebellion would last. A divided colonial population of about two and a half million people faced a nation of 10 million that was backed by a worldwide empire.

Albigense Waldo worked as a surgeon at **Valley Forge** outside Philadelphia, which served as the site of the Continental Army's camp during the winter of 1777–1778. While British troops occupied Philadelphia and found quarters inside warm homes, the underclothed and underfed Patriots huddled in makeshift huts in the freezing, snow-covered Pennsylvania woods. Waldo, who wrote of his stay at Valley Forge, reported on what was a common sight at the camp.

A PERSONAL VOICE ALBIGENSE WALDO

"Here comes a bowl of beef soup full of dead leaves and dirt. There comes a soldier. His bare feet are seen through his worn-out shoes—his legs nearly naked from the tattered remains of an only pair of stockings—his Breeches [trousers] are not sufficient to cover his nakedness—his Shirt hanging in Strings—his hair disheveled—his face meager."

—quoted in *Valley Forge, the Making of an Army*

The ordeal at Valley Forge marked a low point for General Washington's troops, but even as it occurred, the Americans' hopes of winning began to improve.

General Washington's troops march to Valley Forge. ▼

The War Moves to the Middle States

The British had previously retreated from Boston in March 1776, moving the theater of war to the Middle states. As part of a grand plan to stop the rebellion by isolating New England, the British decided to seize New York City.

DEFEAT IN NEW YORK Two brothers, General William Howe and Admiral Richard Howe, joined forces on Staten Island and sailed into New York harbor in the summer of 1776 with the largest British expeditionary force ever assembled—32,000 soldiers, including thousands of German mercenaries, or soldiers who fight solely for money. The Americans called these troops Hessians, because many of them came from the German region of Hesse.

Washington rallied 23,000 men to New York's defense, but he was vastly outnumbered. Most of his troops were untrained recruits with poor equipment. The battle for New York ended in late August with an American retreat following heavy losses. Michael Graham, a Continental Army volunteer, described the chaotic withdrawal on August 27, 1776.

A PERSONAL VOICE MICHAEL GRAHAM

"It is impossible for me to describe the confusion and horror of the scene that ensued: the artillery flying . . . over the horses' backs, our men running in almost every direction, . . . [a]nd the enemy huzzahing when they took prisoners. . . . At the time, I could not account for how it was that our troops were so completely surrounded but have since understood there was another road across the ridge several miles above Flatbush that was left unoccupied by our troops. Here the British passed and got betwixt them and Brooklyn unobserved. This accounts for the disaster of that day."

—quoted in *The Revolution Remembered: Eyewitness Accounts of the War for Independence*

By late fall, the British had pushed Washington's army across the Delaware River into Pennsylvania. The vast majority of Washington's men had either deserted or had been killed or captured. Fewer than 8,000 men remained under Washington's command, and the terms of their enlistment were due to end on December 31. Washington desperately needed some kind of victory for his men to keep them from going home.

THE BATTLE OF TRENTON Washington resolved to risk everything on one bold stroke set for Christmas night, 1776. In the face of a fierce storm, he led 2,400 men in small rowboats across the ice-choked Delaware River.

By 8 o'clock the next morning, the men had marched nine miles through sleet and snow to the objective—**Trenton,** New Jersey, held by a garrison of Hessians. Lulled into confidence by the storm, most of the Hessians had drunk too much rum the night before and were still sleeping it off. In a surprise attack, the Americans killed 30 of the enemy and took 918 captives and six Hessian cannons.

The Americans were rallied by another astonishing victory eight days later against 1,200 British stationed at Princeton. Encouraged by these victories, Washington marched his army into winter camp near Morristown, in northern New Jersey. (A)

MAIN IDEA

Analyzing Effects

(A) Why were the victories at Trenton and Princeton so important to the Continental Army?

THE FIGHT FOR PHILADELPHIA As the muddy fields dried out in the spring of 1777, General Howe began his campaign to seize the American capital at Philadelphia. His troops sailed from New York to the head of Chesapeake Bay, and landed near the capital in late August. The Continental Congress fled the city while Washington's troops unsuccessfully tried to block the redcoats at nearby Brandywine Creek. The British captured Philadelphia, and the pleasure-loving General Howe settled in to enjoy the hospitality of the city's grateful Loyalists.

VICTORY AT SARATOGA Meanwhile, one of Howe's fellow British generals, General John "Gentleman Johnny" Burgoyne, convinced the London high command to allow him to pursue a complex scheme. Burgoyne's plan was to lead an army down a route of lakes from Canada to Albany, where he would meet Howe's troops as they arrived from New York City. According to Burgoyne's plan, the two generals would then join forces to isolate New England from the rest of the colonies.

Burgoyne set out with 4,000 redcoats, 3,000 mercenaries, and 1,000 Mohawk under his command. His army had to haul 30 wagons containing 138 pieces of artillery along with extra personal items, such as fine clothes and champagne. South of Lake Champlain, swamps and gullies, as well as thick underbrush, bogged down Burgoyne's army. Food supplies ran low.

The Continental Congress had appointed General Horatio Gates to command the Northern Department of the Continental Army. Gates, a popular commander, gathered militiamen and soldiers from all over New York and New England. Burgoyne lost several hundred men every time his forces clashed with the Americans, such as when Ethan Allen and his Green Mountain Boys attacked Burgoyne at Bennington, in what is now Vermont. Even worse, Burgoyne didn't realize that Howe was preoccupied with conquering and occupying Philadelphia and wasn't coming to meet him.

VIDEO
Saratoga: Force Surrender
hmhsocialstudies.com

MAIN IDEA

Summarizing
B What factors contributed to General Burgoyne's defeat at Saratoga?

Massed American troops finally surrounded Burgoyne at **Saratoga,** where he surrendered his battered army to General Gates on October 17, 1777. The surrender at Saratoga dramatically changed Britain's war strategy. From that time on, the British generally kept their troops along the coast, close to the big guns and supply bases of the British fleet. **B**

Revolutionary War, 1775–1778

hmhsocialstudies.com INTERACTIVE MAP

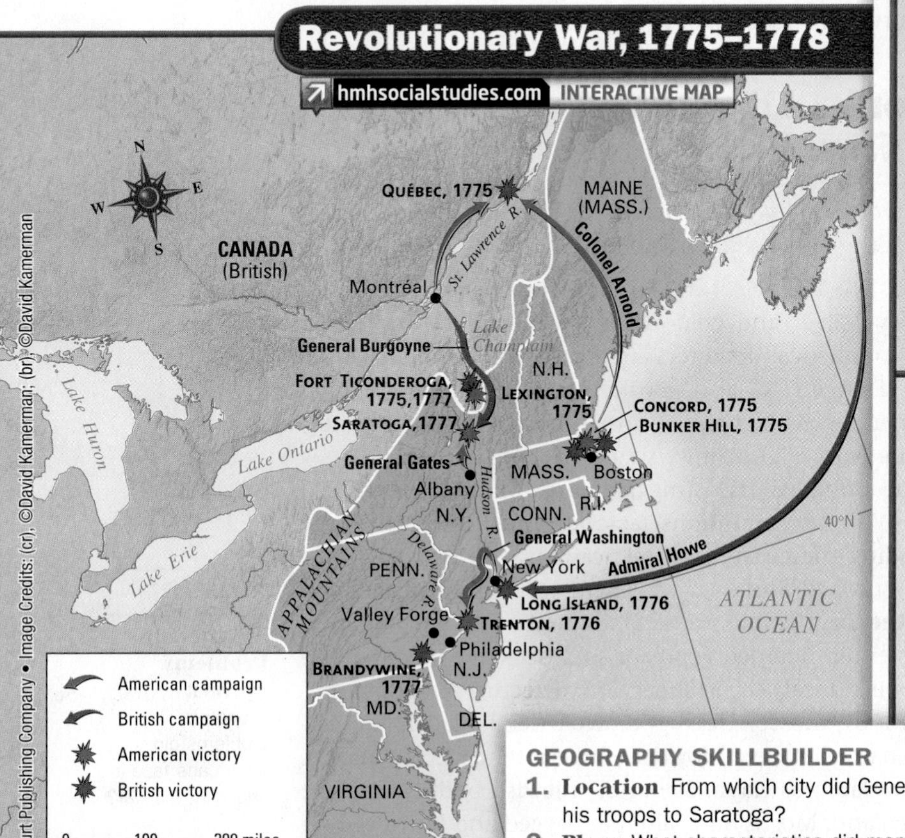

Military Strengths and Weaknesses

UNITED STATES

Strengths	Weaknesses
· familiarity of home ground · leadership of George Washington and other officers · inspiring cause of the independence	· most soldiers untrained and undisciplined · shortage of food and ammunition · inferior navy · no central government to enforce wartime policies

GREAT BRITAIN

Strengths	Weaknesses
· strong, well-trained army and navy · strong central government with available funds · support of colonial Loyalists and Native Americans	· large distance separating Britain from battlefields · troops unfamiliar with terrain · weak military leaders · sympathy of certain British politicans for the American cause

GEOGRAPHY SKILLBUILDER

1. **Location** From which city did General Burgoyne march his troops to Saratoga?
2. **Place** What characteristics did many of the battle sites have in common? Why do you think this was so?

A TURNING POINT Still bitter from their defeat by the British in the French and Indian War, the French had secretly sent weapons to the Patriots since early 1776. The Saratoga victory bolstered French trust in the American army, and France now agreed to support the Revolution. The French recognized American independence and signed an alliance, or treaty of cooperation, with the Americans in February 1778. According to the terms, France agreed not to make peace with Britain unless Britain also recognized American independence. C

MAIN IDEA

Summarizing

C What did France agree to do in its treaty of cooperation with the Americans?

WINTER AT VALLEY FORGE It would take months for French aid to arrive. In the meantime, the British controlled New York and parts of New England. While British troops wintered comfortably in Philadelphia, Washington and his meager Continental Army struggled to stay alive amidst bitter cold and primitive conditions at winter camp in Valley Forge, Pennsylvania. Soldiers suffered from exposure and frostbite, and surgeons like Albigense Waldo worked constantly but often unsuccessfully to save arms and limbs from amputation. Washington's letters to the Congress and his friends were filled with reports of the suffering and endurance of his men.

KEY PLAYER

GEORGE WASHINGTON
1732–1799

During the Revolutionary War, Commander in Chief George Washington became a national hero. An imposing man, Washington stood six feet two inches tall. He was broad-shouldered, calm, and dignified, and he was an expert horseman. But it was Washington's character that won hearts and, ultimately, the war.

Washington roused dispirited men into a fighting force. At Princeton, he galloped on his white horse into the line of fire, shouting and encouraging his men. At Valley Forge, he bore the same cold and privation as every suffering soldier. Time and again, Washington's tactics saved his smaller, weaker force to fight another day. By the end of the war, the entire nation idolized General Washington, and adoring soldiers crowded near him just to touch his boots when he rode by.

A PERSONAL VOICE GEORGE WASHINGTON

> **"To see men without Clothes to cover their nakedness, without Blankets to lay on, without Shoes, by which their Marches might be traced by the blood of their feet, and almost as often without Provision . . . is a mark of patience and obedience which in my opinion can scarcely be paralleled."**
>
> —quoted in *Ordeal at Valley Forge*

Of the 10,000 soldiers who braved wind, snow, and hunger at Valley Forge that winter, more than 2,000 died. Yet those who survived remained at their posts.

Colonial Life During the Revolution

The Revolutionary War touched the life of every American, not just the men on the battlefield.

FINANCING THE WAR When the Congress ran out of hard currency—silver and gold—it borrowed money by selling bonds to American investors and foreign governments, especially France. It also printed paper money called Continentals. As Congress printed more and more money, its value plunged, causing rising prices, or **inflation.**

The Congress also struggled to equip the beleaguered army. With few munitions factories and the British navy blockading the coast, the Americans had to smuggle arms from Europe. Some government officials engaged in **profiteering,** selling scarce goods for a profit. Corrupt merchants either hoarded goods or sold defective merchandise like spoiled meat, cheap shoes, and defective weapons. D

MAIN IDEA

Identifying Problems

D What economic problems did the Americans face in financing the war?

In 1781, the Congress appointed a rich Philadelphia merchant named Robert Morris as superintendent of finance. His associate was Haym Salomon, a Jewish political refugee from Poland. Morris and Salomon begged and borrowed on their personal credit to raise money to provide salaries for the Continental Army. They raised funds from many sources,

▲ Molly Pitcher was the heroine of the battle of Monmouth, New Jersey, in 1778.

including Philadelphia's Quakers and Jews. Due to the efforts of Morris and Salomon, on September 8, 1781, the troops were finally paid in specie, or gold coin.

CIVILIANS AT WAR The demands of war also affected civilians. When men marched off to fight, many wives had to manage farms, shops, and businesses as well as households and families. Some women, such as Benjamin Franklin's daughter, Sarah Franklin Bache of Philadelphia, organized volunteers to mend clothing for the soldiers. Many women made ammunition from their household silver. And hundreds of women followed their husbands to the battlefield, where they washed, mended, and cooked for the troops.

Some women risked their lives in combat. At Fort Washington, New York, Margaret Corbin replaced a gunner who was shot and then was shot herself. Mary Ludwig Hays McCauly took her husband's place at a cannon when he was wounded at the Battle of Monmouth. Known for carrying pitchers of water to the soldiers, McCauly won the nickname "Molly Pitcher." Afterward, General Washington made her a noncommissioned officer for her brave deeds. (E)

MAIN IDEA

Summarizing
(E) In what ways did women contribute to the Revolutionary War?

Thousands of African-American slaves escaped to freedom, some to the cities, where they passed as free people, others to the frontier, where they sometimes joined Native American tribes. About 5,000 African Americans served in the Continental Army, where their courage, loyalty, and talent impressed white Americans. Native Americans remained on the fringes of the Revolution. Some fought for the British but most remained apart from the conflict.

SECTION 3 ASSESSMENT

1. **TERMS & NAMES** For each term or name, write a sentence explaining its significance.
   - **Valley Forge**
   - **Trenton**
   - **Saratoga**
   - **inflation**
   - **profiteering**

MAIN IDEA

2. **TAKING NOTES**
   In a chart like the one below, list each early battle of the American Revolution, its outcome, and why it was important.

Battle	Outcome	Importance

CRITICAL THINKING

3. **HYPOTHESIZING**
   Imagine that Burgoyne and the British had captured Saratoga in 1777. How might the course of the war have changed? **Think About:**
   - the military strength of the British
   - the fighting skills of the Americans
   - French support of the colonists

4. **EVALUATING**
   If you were a woman civilian during the beginning of the American Revolution, what problem caused by the war do you think would affect you the most? **Think About:**
   - inflation and the scarcity of goods
   - the separation of families
   - the demands of the war effort

SECTION 4

Winning the War

MAIN IDEA	WHY IT MATTERS NOW	Terms & Names
Strategic victories in the South and at Yorktown enabled the Americans to defeat the British.	The American defeat of the British established the United States as an independent Nation.	• Yorktown • Friedrich von Steuben • Marquis de Lafayette • Charles Cornwallis • Treaty of Paris • egalitarianism

One American's Story

▲ **The detail of John Trumbull's painting of the British surrender at Yorktown depicts General Charles O'Hara, who stood in for General Cornwallis at the ceremony.**

Colonel William Fontaine of the Virginia militia stood with the American and French armies lining a road near **Yorktown,** Virginia, on the afternoon of October 19, 1781, to witness the formal British surrender. The French were dressed in bright blue coats and white trousers, while the American troops, standing proudly behind their generals, wore rough hunting shirts and faded Continental uniforms. Colonel Fontaine later described the scene.

A PERSONAL VOICE COLONEL WILLIAM FONTAINE

> I had the happiness to see that British army which so lately spread dismay and desolation through all our country, march forth . . . at 3 o'clock through our whole army, drawn up in two lines about 20 yards distance and return disrobed of all their terrors. . . . You could not have heard a whisper or seen the least motion throughout our whole line, but every countenance was erect and expressed a serene cheerfulness.
>
> —quoted in *The Yorktown Campaign and the Surrender of Cornwallis, 1781*

The American Revolution had finally ended, and the Americans had won—a fact that astonished the world. Several years before, in the depths of the Valley Forge winter of 1777–1778, few would have thought such an event possible.

hmhsocialstudies.com
TAKING NOTES

Use the graphic organizer online to write headlines on the significant events discussed in this section.

European Allies Shift the Balance

In February 1778, in the midst of the frozen winter at Valley Forge, American troops began an amazing transformation. **Friedrich von Steuben** (vŏn sto͞o′bən), a Prussian captain and talented drillmaster, volunteered his services to General Washington and went to work "to make regular soldiers out of country bumpkins." Von Steuben taught the colonial soldiers to stand at attention, execute field maneuvers, fire and reload quickly, and wield bayonets. With the help of such European military leaders, the raw Continental Army was becoming an effective fighting force.

LAFAYETTE AND THE FRENCH Around the same time, another military leader, the **Marquis de Lafayette** (mär-kē′ də lăf′ē-ĕt′), a brave, idealistic 20-year-old French aristocrat, offered his assistance. The young Lafayette joined Washington's staff and bore the misery of Valley Forge, lobbied for French reinforcements in France in 1779, and led a command in Virginia in the last years of the war.

The British Move South

After their devastating defeat at Saratoga, the British changed their military strategy; in the summer of 1778 they began to shift their operations to the South. There, the British hoped to rally Loyalist support, reclaim their former colonies in the region, and then slowly fight their way back north.

EARLY BRITISH SUCCESS IN THE SOUTH At the end of 1778, a British expedition easily took Savannah, Georgia, and by the spring of 1779, a royal governor once again commanded Georgia. In 1780, General Henry Clinton, who had replaced Howe in New York, along with the ambitious general **Charles Cornwallis** sailed south with 8,500 men. In their greatest victory of the war, the British captured Charles Town, South Carolina, in May 1780 and marched 5,500 American soldiers off as prisoners of war. Clinton then left for New York, leaving Cornwallis to command the British forces in the South and to conquer South and North Carolina. (A)

> **MAIN IDEA**
> **Summarizing**
> (A) What was the British strategy in the South and how well did it work initially?

For most of 1780, Cornwallis succeeded. As the redcoats advanced, they were joined by thousands of African Americans who had escaped from Patriot slave

Revolutionary War, 1778–1781

hmhsocialstudies.com INTERACTIVE MAP

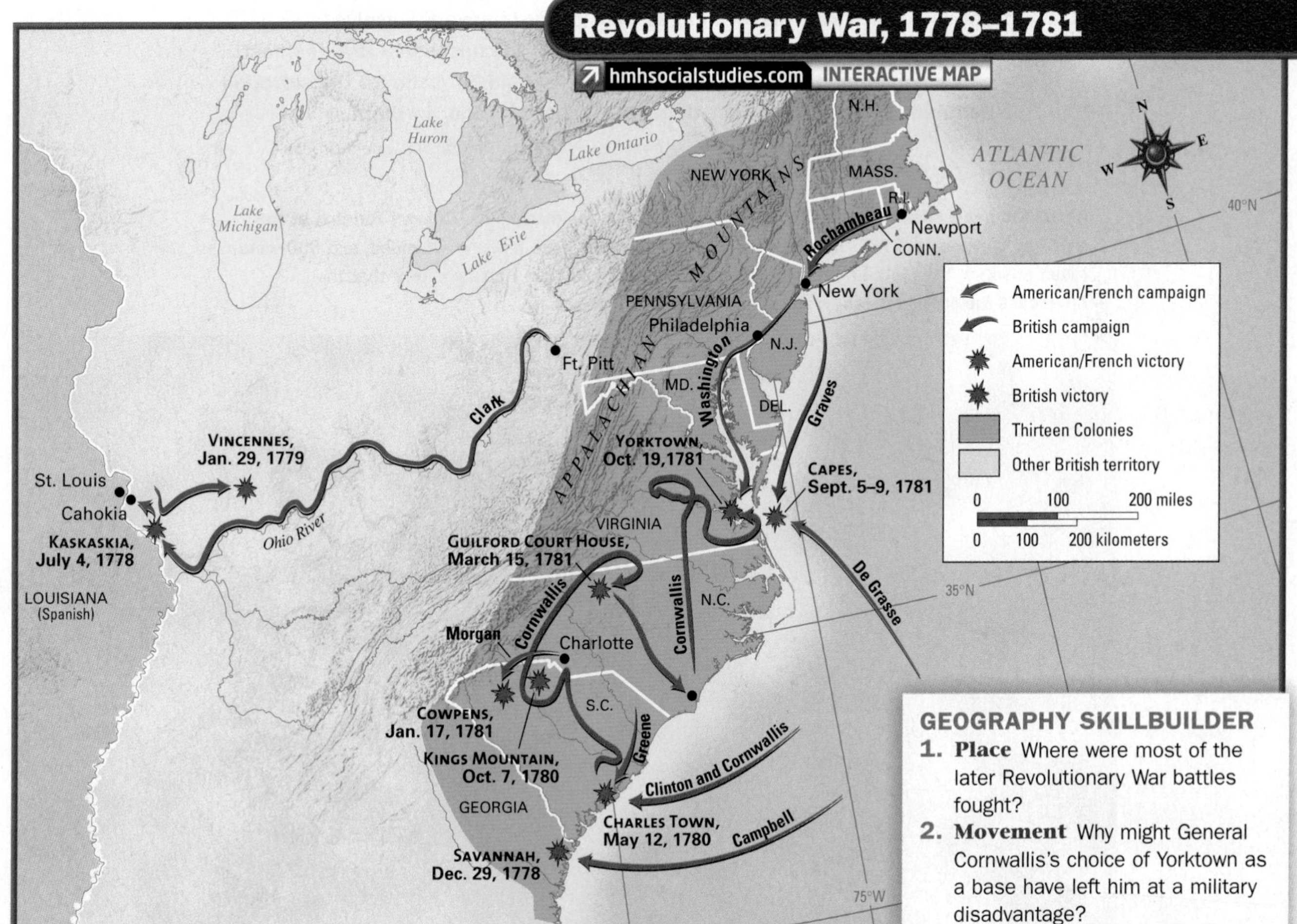

GEOGRAPHY SKILLBUILDER

1. **Place** Where were most of the later Revolutionary War battles fought?
2. **Movement** Why might General Cornwallis's choice of Yorktown as a base have left him at a military disadvantage?

owners to join the British and win their freedom. In August, Cornwallis's army smashed American forces at Camden, South Carolina, and within three months the British had established forts across the state. However, when Cornwallis and his forces advanced into North Carolina, Patriot bands attacked them and cut British communication lines. The continuous harassment forced the redcoats to retreat to South Carolina.

BRITISH LOSSES IN 1781 Washington ordered Nathanael Greene, his ablest general, to march south and harass Cornwallis as he retreated. Greene divided his force into two groups, sending 600 soldiers under the command of General Daniel Morgan to South Carolina. Cornwallis in turn sent Lieutenant Colonel Banastre Tarleton and his troops to pursue Morgan's soldiers.

Morgan and his men led the British on a grueling chase through rough countryside. When the forces met in January 1781 at Cowpens, South Carolina, the British expected the outnumbered Americans to flee; but the Continental Army fought back, and forced the redcoats to surrender.

Angered by the defeat at Cowpens, Cornwallis attacked Greene two months later at Guilford Court House, North Carolina. Cornwallis won the battle, but the victory cost him nearly a fourth of his troops—93 were killed, over 400 were wounded, and 26 were missing. B

Greene had weakened the British, but he worried about the fight for the South. On April 3, 1781, he wrote a letter to Lafayette, asking for help.

MAIN IDEA

Summarizing

B How did generals Morgan and Greene work together to defeat British forces?

A PERSONAL VOICE NATHANAEL GREENE

"[I] wish you to March your force Southward by Alexandria & Fredricksburg to Richmond. . . . It is impossible for the Southern States with all the exertions they can make under the many disadvantages they labour to save themselves. Subsistence is very difficult to be got and therefore it is necessary that the best of troops should be employed. . . . Every exertion should be made for the salvation of the Southern States for on them depend the liberty of the Northern."

—from *The Papers of General Nathanael Greene*, vol. VIII

Daniel Morgan's colonial forces defeated a crack British regiment under Colonel Tarleton at the battle of Cowpens in 1781. More than 300 British soldiers were killed or wounded, and 600 were taken prisoner. This detail from *The Battle of Cowpens* by William Ranney shows that the Americans included both white and African-American soldiers. ▼

After the exhausting battle in the Carolinas, Cornwallis chose to move the fight to Virginia, where he met up with reinforcements. First he tried to capture the divisions led by Lafayette and von Steuben. When that failed, Cornwallis made a fateful mistake: he led his army of 7,500 onto the peninsula between the James and York rivers and camped at Yorktown (see map, Revolutionary War, 1778–1781). Cornwallis planned to fortify Yorktown, take Virginia, and then move north to join Clinton's forces.

hmhsocialstudies.com
INTERACTIVE
Explore the Battle of Yorktown

The British Surrender at Yorktown

A combination of good luck and well-timed decisions now favored the American cause. In 1780, a French army of 6,000 had landed in Newport, Rhode Island, after the British left the city to focus on the South. The French had stationed one fleet there and were operating another in the West Indies. When news of Cornwallis's plans reached him, the Marquis de Lafayette suggested that the American and French armies join forces with the two French fleets and attack the British forces at Yorktown.

VICTORY AT YORKTOWN Following Lafayette's plan, the Americans and the French closed in on Cornwallis. A French naval force defeated a British fleet and then blocked the entrance to the Chesapeake Bay, thereby preventing a British rescue by sea. Meanwhile, about 17,000 French and American troops surrounded the British on the Yorktown peninsula and bombarded them day and night. The siege of Yorktown lasted about three weeks. On October 17, 1781, with his troops outnumbered by more than two to one and exhausted from constant shelling, Cornwallis finally raised the white flag of surrender. C

MAIN IDEA

Analyzing Issues

C How did the French forces contribute to the American victory at Yorktown?

On October 19, a triumphant Washington, the French generals, and their troops assembled to accept the British surrender. After General Charles O'Hara, representing Cornwallis, handed over his sword, the British troops laid down their arms. In his diary, Captain Johann Ewald, a German officer, tried to explain this astonishing turn of events.

HISTORICAL SPOTLIGHT

BENEDICT ARNOLD

In the early years of the Revolution, Benedict Arnold, a popular Patriot soldier and leader, helped defend New England and then served as the American commandant of Philadelphia. In the later years of the war, however, Arnold and his wife, Peggy Shippen Arnold, lived extravagantly. In 1779, Arnold was court-martialed and found guilty of using government supplies for personal use. Angry with Congress, Arnold, with his wife's support, shifted his allegiance to Great Britain.

In 1780, Arnold decided to hand West Point, a strategic fort north of New York City, on the Hudson River, over to the British. To do so, he requested command of the fort. Despite Arnold's tarnished background, Washington granted his request. Fortunately, the Americans discovered the plot, and Arnold escaped to Britain. He died there, scorned by both sides as a traitor.

A PERSONAL VOICE CAPTAIN JOHANN EWALD

> "**With what soldiers in the world could one do what was done by these men, who go about nearly naked and in the greatest privation? Deny the best-disciplined soldiers of Europe what is due them and they will run away in droves, and the general will soon be alone. But from this one can perceive what an enthusiasm—which these poor fellows call 'Liberty'—can do!**"
>
> —*Diary of the American War*

SEEKING PEACE Peace talks began in Paris in 1782. Representatives of four nations—the United States, Great Britain, France, and Spain—joined the negotiations, with each nation looking out for its own interests. Britain hoped to avoid giving America full independence. France supported American independence but feared America's becoming a major power. Spain was interested in acquiring the land between the Appalachian Mountains and the Mississippi River.

Many observers expected the savvy European diplomats to outwit the Americans at the bargaining table. But the Continental Congress chose an able team of negotiators—John Adams, Benjamin Franklin, and John Jay of New York. Together the three demanded that Britain recognize American independence before any other negotiations began. Once Britain agreed to full independence, the talks officially opened.

In September 1783, the delegates signed the **Treaty of Paris,** which confirmed U.S. independence and set the boundaries of the new nation. The United States now stretched from the Atlantic Ocean to the Mississippi River and from Canada to the Florida border.

Some provisions of the treaty promised future trouble. The British made no attempt to protect the land interests of their Native American allies, and the treaty did not specify when the British would evacuate their American forts. On the other side, the Americans agreed that British creditors could collect debts owed them by Americans and promised to allow Loyalists to sue in state courts for recovery of their losses. The state governments, however, later failed to honor this agreement. **D**

MAIN IDEA

Summarizing

D What issues did the Treaty of Paris leave unresolved?

The War Becomes a Symbol of Liberty

With the signing of the Treaty of Paris, all European nations recognized the United States of America. Former British subjects now possessed a new identity as free Americans, loyal to a new ideal. The American Revolution would inspire the world as both a democratic revolution and a war for independence.

THE IMPACT ON AMERICAN SOCIETY Revolutionary ideals set a new course for American society. During the war, class distinctions between rich and poor had begun to blur as the wealthy wore homespun clothing and military leaders showed respect for all of their men. These changes stimulated a rise of **egalitarianism**—a belief in the equality of all people—which fostered a new attitude: the idea that ability, effort, and virtue, not wealth or family, defined one's worth.

The egalitarianism of the 1780s, however, applied only to white males. It did not bring any new political rights to women. A few states made it possible for women to divorce, but common law still dictated that a married woman's property belonged to her husband.

This "A New and Correct Map of the United States of North America," of 1784 was one of the first maps produced to show the boundaries of the new nation. Unfortunately, it contained much inaccurate information, such as the incorrect placement of rivers.

Moreover, most African Americans were still enslaved, and even those who were free usually faced discrimination and poverty. However by 1804, many Northern states had taken steps to outlaw slavery.

The Southern states, where slavery was more entrenched, did not outlaw the practice, but most made it easier for slave owners to free their slaves. Planters in the upper South debated the morality of slavery, and some, like George Washington, freed their slaves. In Maryland and Virginia, the number of free blacks increased from about 4,000 to over 20,000 following the war. The slavery debate generally did not reach the Deep South, although some Southern slaveholders did have grave misgivings.

▲ English potter Josiah Wedgwood designed this antislavery cameo and sent copies of it to Benjamin Franklin.

For Native Americans, the Revolution brought uncertainty. During both the French and Indian War and the Revolution, many Native American communities had either been destroyed or displaced, and the Native American population east of the Mississippi had declined by about 50 percent. Postwar developments further threatened Native American interests, as settlers from the United States moved west and began taking tribal lands left unprotected by the Treaty of Paris. **E**

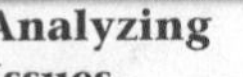

MAIN IDEA

Analyzing Issues

E What were the exceptions to the spirit of egalitarianism that arose after the Revolutionary War?

THE CHALLENGE OF CREATING A GOVERNMENT In adopting the Declaration of Independence, Americans had rejected the British system of government, in which kings and nobles held power. In its place, they set out to build a stable republic, a government of the people. The Continental Congress had chosen a motto for the reverse side of the Great Seal of the United States: "a new order of the ages." Creating this new order forced Americans to address complex questions: Who should participate in government? How should the government answer to the people? How could a government be set up so that opposing groups of citizens would all have a voice?

SECTION 4 ASSESSMENT

1. **TERMS & NAMES** For each term or name, write a sentence explaining its significance.
   - Yorktown
   - Friedrich von Steuben
   - Marquis de Lafayette
   - Charles Cornwallis
   - Treaty of Paris
   - egalitarianism

MAIN IDEA

2. **SUMMARIZING**
   Choose five significant events described in this section. For each, write a newspaper headline that summarizes its significance.

Event	Headline

Choose one of the headlines and write the first paragraph of the article.

CRITICAL THINKING

3. **ANALYZING CAUSES**
   Do you think the colonists could have won independence without aid from foreigners? Explain.
   Think About:
   - the military needs of the Americans and strengths of the French
   - the Americans' belief in their fight for independence
   - von Steuben and de Lafayette

4. **ANALYZING EFFECTS**
   What were the effects of the Revolutionary War on the American colonists? **Think About:**
   - political effects
   - economic effects
   - social effects

5. **EVALUATING**
   In your opinion, what was the single biggest challenge facing the new country?

TRACING THEMES

Women and Political Power

In their families and in the workplace, in speeches and in print, countless American women have worked for justice for all citizens. Throughout the history of the United States, women have played whatever roles they felt were necessary to better this country. They also fought to expand their own political power, a power that throughout much of American history has been denied them.

1770s

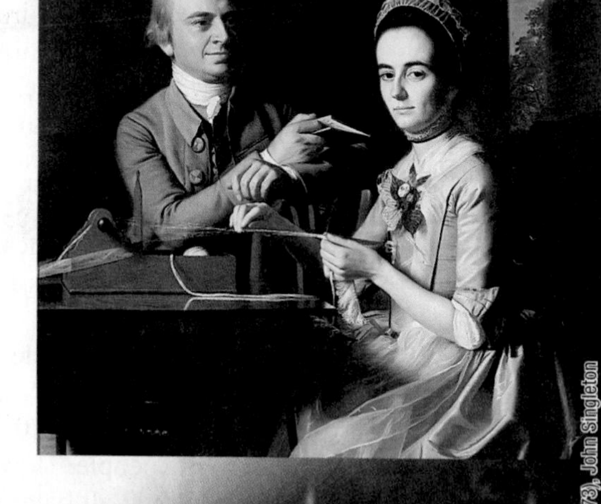

PROTEST AGAINST BRITAIN ▶

In the tense years leading up to the Revolution, American women found ways to participate in the protests against the British. Homemakers boycotted tea and British-made clothing. In the painting at right, Sarah Morris Mifflin, shown with her husband Thomas, spins her own thread rather than use British thread. Some businesswomen, such as printer Mary Goddard, who produced the official copies of the Declaration of Independence, took more active roles.

1848

A WOMAN'S DECLARATION

ELIZABETH CADY
the cruel and unju
the office of her f
child, to find a way
to the abolitionist
ly into the curren
foundation for the
for woman's right
inspiring leader. T
executed the first
Falls, New York, J

SENECA FALLS ▶

As America grew, women became acutely aware of their unequal status in society, particularly their lack of suffrage, or the right to vote.

In 1848, two women—Elizabeth Cady Stanton, shown above, and Lucretia Mott—launched the first woman suffrage movement in the United States at the Seneca Falls Convention in Seneca Falls, New York. During the convention, Stanton introduced her Declaration of Sentiments, in which she demanded greater rights for women, including the right to vote.

1920

THE RIGHT TO VOTE ▶

More than a half-century after organizing for the right to vote, women finally won their struggle. In 1920, the United States adopted the Nineteenth Amendment, which granted women the right to vote.

Pictured to the right is one of the many suffrage demonstrations of the early 1900s that helped garner public support for the amendment.

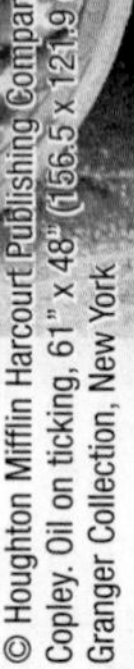

1972–1982

THE EQUAL RIGHTS AMENDMENT MOVEMENT ▶

During the mid-1900s, as more women entered the workforce, many women recognized their continuing unequal status, including the lack of equal pay for equal work. By passing an Equal Rights Amendment, some women hoped to obtain the same social and economic rights as men.

Although millions supported the amendment, many men and women feared the measure would prompt unwanted change. The ERA ultimately failed to be ratified for the Constitution.

2010

WOMEN IN CONGRESS ▲

In spite of the failure of the ERA, many women have achieved strong positions for themselves—politically as well as socially and economically.

In the 111th Congress, 73 women served in the House of Representatives and 17 served in the Senate. Shown above is Nancy Pelosi, the first woman to serve as Speaker of the House.

THINKING CRITICALLY

CONNECT TO HISTORY

1. **Synthesizing** How did women's political status change from 1770 to 2010?

SEE SKILLBUILDER HANDBOOK, PAGE R19.

CONNECT TO TODAY

2. **Researching and Reporting** Think of a woman who has played an important role in your community. What kinds of things did this woman do? What support did she receive in the community? What problems did she run into? Report your findings to the class.

CHAPTER 4 ASSESSMENT

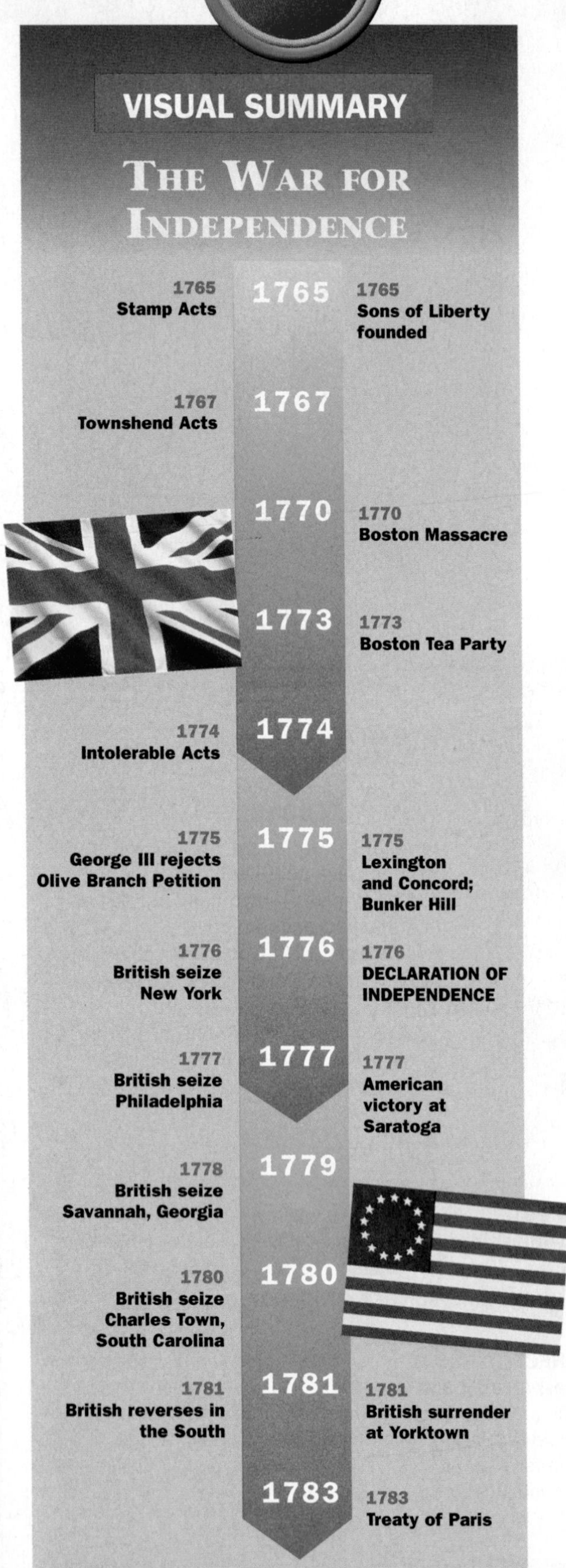

TERMS & NAMES

For each term below, write a sentence explaining its connection to the American Revolution. For each person below, explain his role in the event.

1. Stamp Act
2. Boston Massacre
3. committee of correspondence
4. Olive Branch Petition
5. *Common Sense*
6. Thomas Jefferson
7. Saratoga
8. Valley Forge
9. Marquis de Lafayette
10. Yorktown

MAIN IDEAS

The Stirrings of Rebellion

11. What methods did colonists use to protest actions by Parliament between 1765 and 1775?
12. Describe the causes and the results of the Boston Tea Party.
13. What were the results of fighting at Lexington and Concord?

Ideas Help Start a Revolution

14. What did Jefferson mean, and not mean, by the phrase "all men are created equal"?
15. Why did many colonists not support independence?

Struggling Toward Saratoga

16. Why was the Battle of Trenton significant?
17. What British military plan did the colonial victory at Saratoga ruin?
18. Explain how civilians supported the war effort in the colonies.

Winning the War

19. How did France help the colonies during the American Revolution?
20. Describe three significant challenges facing the United States when the American Revolution ended.

THINKING CRITICALLY

1. **USING YOUR NOTES** Create a dual-path chart showing how the colonies became independent. On one path, list four or more military events, such as battles and changes in command. On the other, list four or more political events, including protests, publication of documents, and legal actions.

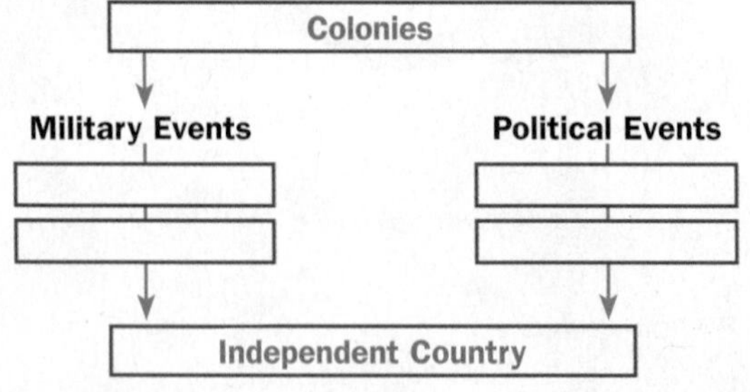

2. **EVALUATING** Review France's role in helping the colonies rebel against Great Britain. Under what conditions, if any, do you think the United States should help other countries?

STANDARDIZED TEST PRACTICE

Use the cartoon below and your knowledge of U.S. history to answer question 1.

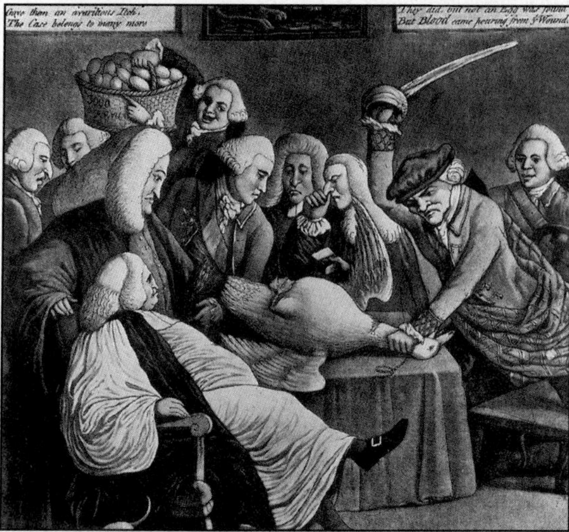

1. This British cartoon was published during the winter of 1775–1776. In it, King George III and his ministers are shown killing the goose that laid the golden egg. The cartoon is criticizing —

   A the killing of British soldiers at Concord and Bunker Hill.
   B King George's response to the Olive Branch Petition.
   C John Locke's theory of natural rights.
   D Thomas Paine's *Common Sense*.

2. The Battle of Trenton was important to the Americans because —

   A it prevented the capture of Philadelphia by the British.
   B it was a badly needed victory that inspired soldiers to reenlist.
   C it prompted the French to sign an alliance with the Americans.
   D it ended a series of British victories in the South.

Use the information in the box and your knowledge of U.S. history to answer question 3.

- Declaration of Independence
- Battles of Lexington and Concord
- Second Continental Congress

3. Which of the following lists the events in chronological order from first to last?

   A Declaration of Independence, Battles of Lexington and Concord, Second Continental Congress
   B Battles of Lexington and Concord, Second Continental Congress, Declaration of Independence
   C Second Continental Congress, Battles of Lexington and Concord, Declaration of Independence
   D Second Continental Congress, Declaration of Independence, Battles of Lexington and Concord

For additional test practice, go online for:

- Diagnostic tests
- Tutorials

INTERACT WITH HISTORY

Recall the issues that you explored at the beginning of the chapter. Imagine that it is 1783, and you have been present at a gathering of your friends who recall the many sacrifices made during the the War for Independence from Great Britain. Write a journal entry in which you try to describe some of those sacrifices. Recall key military events, contributions made by civilians, and key figures who played important roles in the struggle for freedom.

FOCUS ON WRITING

Review the Another Pespective feature that describes Abigail Adams's view of the status of women. Write a letter answering her in which you give some ideas about the status of women after the Revolutionary War.

COLLABORATIVE LEARNING

In a small group read and discuss the "One American's Story" at the beginning of the section. Then consider the following question: What makes someone a patriot? Using stories and images from the Internet, books, magazines, and newspapers, make a list of people you consider to be patriots. List their names as well as the reasons why you chose them on a chart in your classroom.

MULTIMEDIA CONNECTIONS

THE *American* REVOLUTION

The American Revolution led to the formation of the United States of America in 1776. Beginning in the 1760s, tensions grew between American colonists and their British rulers when Britain started passing a series of new laws and taxes for the colonies. With no representation in the British government, however, colonists had no say in these laws, which led to growing discontent. After fighting broke out in 1775, colonial leaders met to decide what to do. They approved the Declaration of Independence, announcing that the American colonies were free from British rule. In reality, however, freedom would not come until after years of fighting.

Explore some of the people and events of the American Revolution online. You can find a wealth of information, video clips, primary sources, activities, and more at hmhsocialstudies.com.

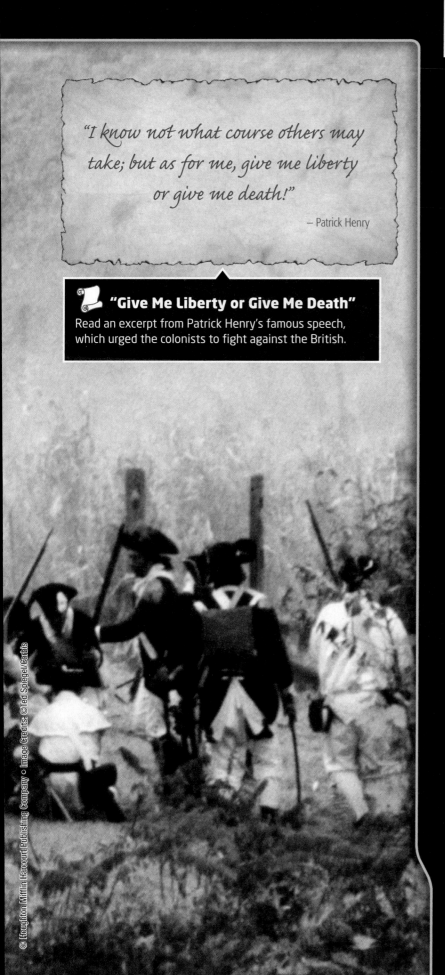

"I know not what course others may take; but as for me, give me liberty or give me death!"

– Patrick Henry

"Give Me Liberty or Give Me Death"

Read an excerpt from Patrick Henry's famous speech, which urged the colonists to fight against the British.

Seeds of Revolution

Watch the video to learn about colonial discontent in the years before the Revolutionary War.

Independence!

Watch the video to learn about the origins of the Declaration of Independence.

Victory!

Watch the video to learn how the American colonists won the Revolutionary War.

A New Nation 1781–1850

CHAPTER 5
Shaping a New Nation
1781–1788

CHAPTER 6
Launching the New Nation
1789–1816

CHAPTER 7
Balancing Nationalism and Sectionalism
1815–1840

CHAPTER 8
Reforming American Society
1820–1850

Constitution

Work with a small group of classmates to create a constitution for your class or school. Explain how laws will be passed and changed.

Signing of the Constitution by Howard Chandler Christy

ALABAMA *Territory and Statehood*

The Treaty of Paris ending the American Revolution placed the area of what is now Alabama under United States control. In 1798 Congress created the Mississippi Territory out of the land from Georgia to the Mississippi River and from Tennessee to the Gulf of Mexico. Wanting to keep a balance of slave and free states, southern political leaders wanted the Mississippi Territory to become two states allowing slavery. In 1817 Congress designated the eastern half of the Mississippi Territory as the Alabama Territory, naming William Wyatt Bibb as governor.

The Creek War

In the early days of the United States, settlers and Native Americans traded and helped each other. Some officials wanted Native Americans to adopt white ways and have a good relationship with the United States. But as the nation grew, tensions over land hurt the relationship between the United States and Native Americans on the frontier.

The Creek War was a tipping point in the relationship between Native Americans and white settlers. White settlement was putting pressure on Creek lands. The trading relationships between settlers and Native Americans were getting worse as the national economy changed. Creeks were divided as to how to deal with the changing frontier. A faction of Creeks known as the Red Sticks wanted to keep Americans from settling in the Mississippi Territory. They were ready to use force if necessary to maintain their lands.

To prevent the Red Sticks from getting ammunition, a Mississippi Territory militia attacked the Red Sticks near Burnt Corn Creek in July 1813. The Red Sticks retaliated on August 30, near what is now Mobile. At least 700 Creek warriors belonging to the Red Sticks group stormed Fort Mims. More that 250 white settlers and pro-American Creeks were killed. General Andrew Jackson rallied American soldiers and Native American allies in response to the Fort Mims massacre. Jackson's force crushed the Red Sticks at the Battle of Horseshoe Bend in March 1814. The United States then forced the Creeks to give up 23 million acres of land.

The Creek War was one of many conflicts between white settlers and Native Americans in the early 19th century. These conflicts destroyed friendly relationships between Native Americans and the United States. Native Americans faced increased pressure to give up their land for white settlement. Federal policy began to view Native Americans as occupiers of the land rather than owners.

Native Americans took up arms against white settlers moving into frontier territory in conflicts such as the Creek War.

Statehood and Native American Removal

More white settlers poured into the Alabama Territory after the Creek War. The white population soared from 1,250 in 1800 to 127,900 by 1820. This mirrored the national trend of westward migration after the War of 1812. Alabama quickly reached the population requirement for statehood and became the 22nd state in 1819. In a close election, territorial governor Bibb became the state's first governor.

Statehood increased the pressure on the Creek, Cherokee, and Choctaw nations living within Alabama's borders. White farmers in Alabama, like those across the South, demanded more land to grow crops. By the 1820s, settlers called for the complete removal of Native Americans from Alabama. When Andrew Jackson was elected president in 1828, Indian Removal soon became official federal policy. In the 1830s, U.S. troops evicted thousands of Native Americans from Alabama and other southern states. Alabama's militia was active in these forced marches west, which claimed the lives of thousands of Native Americans.

Native Americans were forcibly removed from lands in the South. Many Native Americans died of exhaustion and exposure on the thousand-mile forced marches.

Growing Sectionalism

With the removal of Native Americans, Alabama planters devoted more acres to cotton, a crop increasingly in demand for British factories. Steamboats carried huge bales of cotton down the Alabama River to Mobile. From there, the bales were shipped to New England or Europe. Alabama's plantations thrived in the antebellum era, making the state a key part of the South's Cotton Kingdom.

Cotton production required a huge labor force to pick and process the crop. Alabama plantation owners kept large numbers of enslaved African Americans to tend cotton. With cotton and slavery so integral to Alabama's economy, the state played a key role in the sectional divide between North and South that grew worse in the 1840s. The planters who made up Alabama's social and political leadership showed little tolerance for any northern viewpoint that threatened their profits or way of life.

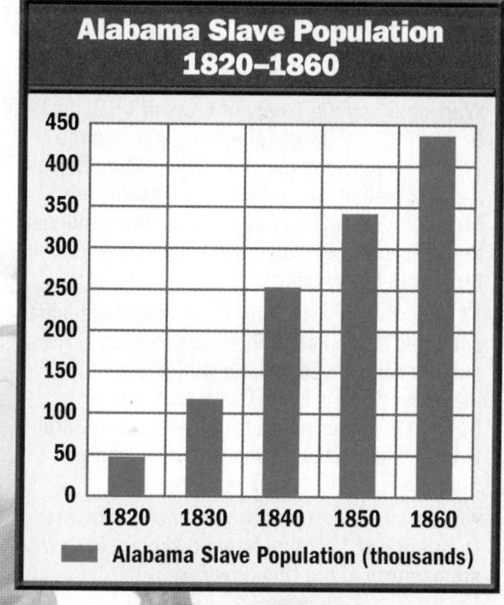

Cotton quickly became the foundation of Alabama's economy in the early 1800s. It was a difficult crop to harvest and required a large labor force.

Exploring Further...

Research the relations between white people and Native Americans in Alabama between 1800 and 1840 and write a one-page report. Your report should include the impact of the following events and developments.

- White migration into Alabama
- Congress appointing superintendents of Indian Affairs, especially Benjamin Hawkins
- The Creek War of 1813–1814
- Alabama's statehood
- Andrew Jackson's election as U.S. president

CHAPTER 5

SHAPING A NEW NATION

Washington *(on the far right)* addressing the Constitutional Congress

Essential Question

What challenges did the new American republic face, and how did the U.S. Constitution reflect those challenges?

ALABAMA COURSE OF STUDY

4 Describe the political system of the United States based on the Constitution of the United States.

- Describing inadequacies of the Articles of Confederation.
- Distinguishing personalities, issues, ideologies, and compromises related to the Constitutional Convention and the ratification of the Constitution of the United States, including the role of the Federalist papers.

7 Describe causes, courses, and consequences of United States' expansionism prior to the Civil War, including the Treaty of Paris of 1783, the Land Ordinance of 1785, the Northwest Ordinance of 1787, the Louisiana Purchase, the Indian Removal Act, the Trail of Tears, Manifest Destiny, the Mexican War and Cession, Texas Independence, the acquisition of Oregon, the California Gold Rush, and the Western Trails.

12 Describe the founding of the first abolitionist societies by Benjamin Rush and Benjamin Franklin and the role played by later critics of slavery, including William Lloyd Garrison, Frederick Douglass, Sojourner Truth, Angelina and Sarah Grimké, Henry David Thoreau, and Charles Sumner.

- Explaining the importance of the Northwest Ordinance of 1787 that banned slavery in new states north of the Ohio River.

USA

WORLD

1782

1784

1781 The Articles of Confederation, which John Dickinson helped write five years earlier, go into effect.

1783 The Treaty of Paris at the end of the Revolutionary War recognizes United States independence.

1784 Russians found colony in Alaska.

1784 Spain closes the Mississippi River to American commerce.

1785 New York state outlaws slavery.

1785 The Treaty of Hopewell concerning Native American lands is signed.

1781 Joseph II allows religious toleration in Austria.

1782 Rama I founds a new dynasty in Siam, with Bangkok as the capital.

1783 Russia annexes the Crimean Peninsula.

1783 Ludwig van Beethoven's first works are published.

1785 Jean-Pierre Blanchard and John Jeffries cross the English Channel in a balloon.

Image Credits: (bkgd), *Washington as Statesman at the Constitutional Convention* (1856), Junius Brutus Stearns. Oil on canvas, 37 1/2" H x 54" W. Virginia Museum of Fine Arts, Richmond, Virginia; gift of Edgar William and Bernice Chrysler Garbisch. Photograph by Ron Jennings; (bc), ©Kevin R. Morris/Corbis; (br), ©Time & Life Pictures/Getty Images; (cl), ©Corbis

HISTORY Shays's Rebellion

hmhsocialstudies.com VIDEO

INTERACT WITH HISTORY

The year is 1787. You have recently helped your fellow patriots overthrow decades of oppressive British rule. However, it is easier to destroy an old system of government than to create a new one. In a world of kings and tyrants, your new republic struggles to find its place.

Explore the Issues

- Which should have more power—the states or the national government?
- How can the new nation avoid a return to tyranny?
- How can the rights of all people be protected?

1786 Daniel Shays leads a rebellion of farmers in Massachusetts.

1786 The Annapolis Convention is held.

1786 The Virginia legislature guarantees religious freedom.

1787 The Northwest Ordinance is passed.

1788 The Constitution, which James Madison helped write at the Pennsylvania State House, is ratified.

1786 — 1788

1786 Charles Cornwallis becomes governor-general of India.

1787 Sierra Leone in Africa becomes a haven for freed American slaves.

1787 War breaks out between Turkey and Russia.

1788 Austria declares war on Turkey.

1788 Bread riots erupt in France.

Image Credits: (bkgd), *Washington as Statesman at the Constitutional Convention* (1856), Junius Brutus Stearns. Oil on canvas, 37 1/2" H x 54" W. Virginia Museum of Fine Arts, Richmond, Virginia; gift of Edgar William and Bernice Chrysler Garbisch. Photograph by Ron Jennings; (b), The Granger Collection, New York

SECTION 1

Experimenting with Confederation

MAIN IDEA	WHY IT MATTERS NOW	Terms & Names
Americans adopted the Articles of Confederation but found the new government too weak to solve the nation's problems.	**The reaction to the weak Articles of Confederation led to a stronger central government that has continued to expand its power.**	**• republic • republicanism • Articles of Confederation • confederation • Land Ordinance of 1785 • Northwest Ordinance of 1787**

One American's Story

hmhsocialstudies.com TAKING NOTES

Use the graphic organizer online to take notes about the Articles of Confederation.

Although John Dickinson had once opposed American independence, he later worked hard to help create a government for the new United States. In 1779 John Dickinson returned to the Continental Congress as a delegate from Delaware. At that time he explained the principles that guided his political decisions.

A PERSONAL VOICE JOHN DICKINSON

"Two rules I have laid down for myself throughout this contest . . . first, on all occasions where I am called upon, as a trustee for my countrymen, to deliberate on questions important to their happiness, disdaining all personal advantages to be derived from a suppression of my real sentiments . . . openly to avow [declare] them; and, secondly, . . . whenever the public resolutions are taken, to regard them though opposite to my opinion, as sacred . . . and to join in supporting them as earnestly as if my voice had been given for them."

—quoted in *The Life and Times of John Dickinson, 1732–1808*

John Dickinson

Dickinson's two rules became guiding principles for the leaders who faced the formidable task of starting a new nation.

Americans Debate Republicanism

The task of creating a new government posed a great challenge. Among many other issues, the relationship between the new states and the national government was difficult to define. The debate over the nature of the new government of the United States would consume the political energies of the new nation.

COLONIES BECOME STATES British settlers in North America had founded not one colony but many, each with its own governor, council, and colonial assembly. This system of distinct, self-governing colonies encouraged people to think of the colony as the primary political unit. Because of this, most people's allegiance was to the colony in which they lived. The Revolutionary War gave the colonies a common goal, but as these colonies became states, they remained reluctant to unite under a strong central government. The challenge was to develop a system of government that balanced the interests of the several states with those of the nation. (A)

MAIN IDEA

Developing Historical Perspective
(A) What relics of the colonial period survived in the new system of government?

UNITY THROUGH A REPUBLIC Eighteenth-century Americans believed that a democracy, or government directly by the people, placed too much power in the hands of the uneducated masses. Therefore, they favored a **republic**—a government in which citizens rule through their elected representatives. However, **republicanism,** the idea that governments should be based on the consent of the people (which should not be confused with the Republicanism of the modern-day political party), meant different things to different Americans.

Some, like John Dickinson, believed that a republic required a virtuous people. The new government could only succeed, they argued, if people placed the good of the nation above their personal interests.

Other Americans, influenced by the writings of the philosopher and economist Adam Smith, believed that a republic would benefit from self-interest. They asserted that if a government allowed independent citizens to pursue their own economic and political interests, the whole nation would benefit.

Background
In *An Inquiry into the Nature and Causes of the Wealth of Nations,* Adam Smith (1723–1790) argued that social order and progress were the natural result of individualism and self-interest.

STATE CONSTITUTIONS As the states created their own constitutions, they wrestled with how to put republican ideals into practice. Many state constitutions shared certain similarities. They limited the powers of government leaders. They guaranteed specific rights for citizens, including freedom of speech, religion, and the press. In general, state constitutions emphasized liberty rather than equality and reflected a fear of centralized authority.

At the same time, state constitutions differed widely in granting the right to vote. Although the new states were more democratic than any western nation at this time, it was still only a very limited democracy by modern standards. African Americans were generally not allowed to vote. Some states granted voting rights to all white males. Other states, like Maryland, continued to make property ownership a requirement for voting.

Despite the more active political role that women had played during the Revolution, they were still denied the right to vote in most states. However, New Jersey gave voting rights to all free property owners but neglected to specify males. Consequently, some New Jersey women gained the right to vote—at least until 1807, when this right was revoked.

POLITICAL PRECEDENTS In a world where most nations were still governed by kings, there were few political systems that could serve as models for the new republic. The nation's founders searched history for political precedents for the

HISTORICAL SPOTLIGHT

REPUBLICAN MOTHERHOOD

An important issue in the early years of the nation was the role that women should play in the republic. In the years before and during the Revolutionary War, many women became politically active, organizing boycotts of British goods and helping raise money for the army. This involvement in public affairs was an important departure for women, who had traditionally been confined to the private sphere of family life.

After the Revolution, as the nation readjusted to peace, the new ideal of republican motherhood helped channel women's newfound political awareness and activism back into the home. Women were expected to raise the next generation of patriots by instilling democratic values in their children.

Political Precedents

ATHENS AND ROME

In the 18th century, American leaders revered the political achievements of ancient Athens and Rome. The Greek city of Athens was acknowledged as the birthplace of democracy, while the early Romans were admired for overthrowing monarchy and establishing a republic. However, Greek democracy, like the democracy of the New England town meeting, was workable only at a local level. It was the democracy of a city, not of a huge nation. Neither Greek democracy nor the Roman republic had endured.

▲ Engraving of the ancient Roman Senate

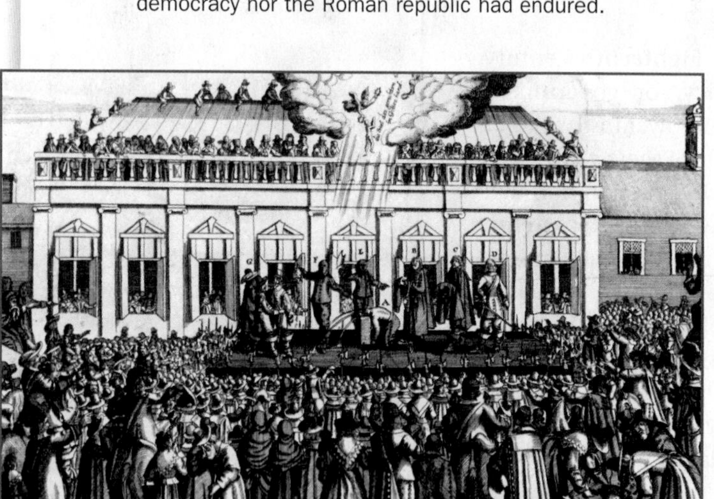

THE ENGLISH COMMONWEALTH

In the mid-17th century the English parliament executed the king and established a republic, which lasted from 1649 to 1660. This republic, called the Commonwealth and Protectorate, was controlled first by Oliver Cromwell and later by his son Richard. The Commonwealth was continually threatened by anarchy and bad leadership and did not long survive Cromwell's death. The failure of the English Commonwealth must have haunted American political leaders as they planned the government of their republic.

◀ The execution of King Charles I

new government. In the previous century, the English had established a short-lived republic after the execution of King Charles I. During the Middle Ages, Italian cities such as Florence, Pisa, Genoa, and Venice had become self-governing city-states. Swiss communities also had resisted royal control, forming alliances that developed into the Swiss Confederation. In ancient times, republics and various democratic systems had existed in Greece and in Rome. However, none of these models could be adapted easily to the political situation of the new United States, with its need to balance the concerns of state and national governments.

The Continental Congress Debates

While the states developed their individual constitutions, the Continental Congress tried to draft one for the states as a whole. However, there was much disagreement over the role of the national government. The delegates had to answer three basic questions.

REPRESENTATION BY POPULATION OR BY STATE? Although the states were equal as political entities, they were unequal in size, wealth, and population. These differences posed a serious dilemma. Should delegates to a new government represent people or states? Should each state elect the same number of representatives regardless of its population? Or should states with large populations have more representatives than states with small populations?

For the time being, the members of the Continental Congress saw themselves as representing independent states. As a result, they made the decision that each state would have one vote regardless of population. (B)

MAIN IDEA

Analyzing Issues

(B) Why did differences between the states cause problems of representation in the new government?

SUPREME POWER: CAN IT BE DIVIDED? Until this time most people assumed that a government could not share supreme power with smaller administrative units, such as provinces or states.

However, the Congress proposed a new type of government in a set of laws called the **Articles of Confederation**—one in which two levels of government shared fundamental powers. State governments were supreme in some matters, while the national government was supreme in other matters. The delegates called this new form of government a **confederation,** or alliance.

In true Enlightenment fashion, John Dickinson hoped that the new system of government would reflect the order and harmony found in nature.

A PERSONAL VOICE JOHN DICKINSON

"Let our government be like that of the solar system. Let the general government be like the sun and the states the planets, repelled yet attracted, and the whole moving regularly and harmoniously in their several orbits."

—from *The Records of the Federal Convention of 1787*

The Articles of Confederation gave the new national government power to declare war, make peace, and sign treaties. It could borrow money, set standards for coins and for weights and measures, establish a postal service, and deal with Native American peoples. The Articles, however, created no separate executive department to carry out and enforce the acts of Congress and no national court system to interpret the meaning of laws. C

MAIN IDEA

Summarizing

C What is a confederation?

WESTERN LANDS: WHO GETS THEM? By 1779, 12 states had agreed to accept the new government, but conflict over western lands delayed final approval for two more years. Some states had claims to lands west of the Appalachian Mountains. Maryland, which had no such claims, feared that states with land claims would expand and overpower smaller states. It refused to approve the Articles until all states turned over their western lands to the United States. Consequently, the landed states gave up their western claims, and with Maryland's approval, the Articles of Confederation went into effect in March 1781.

GOVERNING THE WESTERN LANDS The Confederation Congress then faced the question of how to govern the public lands west of the Appalachians and north of the Ohio River that offered rich land for settlers. Congress passed the **Land Ordinance of 1785,** which established a plan for surveying the land. (See Geography Spotlight, Land Ordinance of 1785.) In the **Northwest Ordinance of 1787,** Congress provided a procedure for dividing the land into territories. The Northwest Ordinance also set requirements for the admission of new states, which seemed to overlook Native American land claims. There were three stages for becoming a state:

1. Congress would appoint a territorial governor and judges.
2. When a territory had 5,000 voting residents, the settlers could write a temporary constitution and elect their own government.
3. When the total population of a territory reached 60,000 free inhabitants, the settlers could write a state constitution, which had to be approved by Congress before it granted statehood.

The Land Ordinance of 1785 and the Northwest Ordinance of 1787 became the Confederation's greatest achievements. These laws established a blueprint for future growth of the nation. D

MAIN IDEA

Contrasting

D What was the basic difference between the Land Ordinance of 1785 and the Northwest Ordinance of 1787?

ANOTHER PERSPECTIVE

JOHN BAPTIST DE COIGNE

John Baptist de Coigne, a Kaskaskia chief, was among a group of Indians from the Northwest Territory who met with leaders of the U.S. government in 1793. He expressed the Native American view of the westward expansion of white settlers during the previous ten years:

"Order your people to be just. They are always trying to get our lands. They come on our lands, they hunt on them; kill our game and kill us. Keep them on one side of the line, and us on the other. Listen, my father, to what we say, and protect the nations of the Wabash and the Mississippi in their lands."

The Confederation Encounters Problems

After its success in dealing with the Northwest Territory, the Confederation encountered overwhelming problems in dealing with more immediate issues. These problems ranged from economic issues, such as taxation and the national debt, to political issues, such as the nature of Congressional representation. In addition to these domestic issues, there were also many foreign-relations problems that the Confederation was powerless to solve.

POLITICAL AND ECONOMIC PROBLEMS The most serious problem was that the country under the Confederation lacked national unity. Each state functioned independently by pursuing its own interests rather than those of the nation as a whole. In addition, the Confederation didn't recognize the differences in population among the states. Each state, regardless of its population, had only one vote in Congress. Thus, the political power of Georgia, with a population of 23,375 in 1770, was equal to that of Massachusetts, with a population of 235,308. Furthermore, the Articles could not be amended without the consent of every state; a single state could stall the amendment process. Therefore, changes in government were difficult to achieve.

The most serious economic problem was the huge debt that the Congress had amassed during the Revolutionary War. The war had cost the nation $190 million—a huge amount of money in those days. The Continental Congress had borrowed from foreign countries and had printed its own paper money. After the war, Continental currency became worthless.

Lacking the power to tax, the Congress requested the states' approval to impose a tariff, or tax on imported goods. It planned to use the revenue to repay foreign loans. However, one state, Rhode Island, rejected the proposed tax, so it was not adopted. Unable to impose taxes, the Confederation Congress also had no control over interstate or foreign trade. **E**

MAIN IDEA

Identifying Problems

E What weakness in the Confederation was highlighted by the actions of Rhode Island?

BORROWERS VERSUS LENDERS Another problem caused by the debt from the Revolution was the struggle between creditors (lenders of money) and debtors (borrowers of money). After the war, wealthy people who had lent money to the states favored high taxes so that the states would be able to pay them back. However, high taxes sent many farmers into debt. When a creditor sued a farmer in court for repayment and won the case, the government seized the farmer's land and animals and sold them at auction.

Debtors and creditors also disagreed over the usefulness of paper money. Debtors wanted to increase the supply of money to lessen its value and enable them to pay off their debts with cheap currency. Creditors, in contrast, wanted to keep the supply of money low so that it would keep its full value. Both groups had much to lose.

Currency, such as this early example from Connecticut, was issued by the colonies and the states.

FOREIGN-RELATIONS PROBLEMS The lack of support from states for national concerns led to foreign-relations problems for the Congress. First, since the United States could not repay its debts to British merchants and would not compensate Loyalists for property losses suffered during the Revolutionary War, Britain refused to evacuate its military forts on the Great Lakes. Furthermore, Spain's presence on the borders of the United States posed another threat to westward expansion. In 1784, Spain closed the Mississippi River to American navigation. This action deprived Western farmers of a means of shipping their crops

Weaknesses of the Articles of Confederation	
• Congress could not enact and collect taxes. • Congress could not regulate interstate or foreign trade. • Regardless of population, each state had only one vote in Congress. • Two-thirds majority—9 out of 13 states needed to agree to pass any law.	• Articles could be amended only if all states approved. • There was no executive branch to enforce the laws of Congress. • There was no national court system to settle legal disputes. • There were 13 separate states that lacked national unity.

SKILLBUILDER Interpreting Charts

1. How many states' votes were needed to approve changes in the Articles of Confederation?
2. Why did the listed weaknesses lead to an ineffective government?

to Eastern markets through New Orleans. Though Northerners were willing to give up navigation rights on the Mississippi in exchange for more profitable trade concessions, Westerners and Southerners insisted on access to the Mississippi. However, Congress was too weak to resolve either of these challenges by Spain and Britain.

The problems the Congress encountered in dealing with foreign nations revealed the basic weaknesses of the Confederation government. Americans' fear of giving the national government too much power had resulted in a government that lacked sufficient power to deal with the nation's problems. The forthcoming Constitutional Convention would change all of this.

ASSESSMENT

1. **TERMS & NAMES** For each term or name, write a sentence explaining its significance.
   - **republic**
   - **republicanism**
   - **Articles of Confederation**
   - **confederation**
   - **Land Ordinance of 1785**
   - **Northwest Ordinance of 1787**

MAIN IDEA

2. **TAKING NOTES**
   In a diagram like the one below, describe the powers given to the national government by the Articles of Confederation.

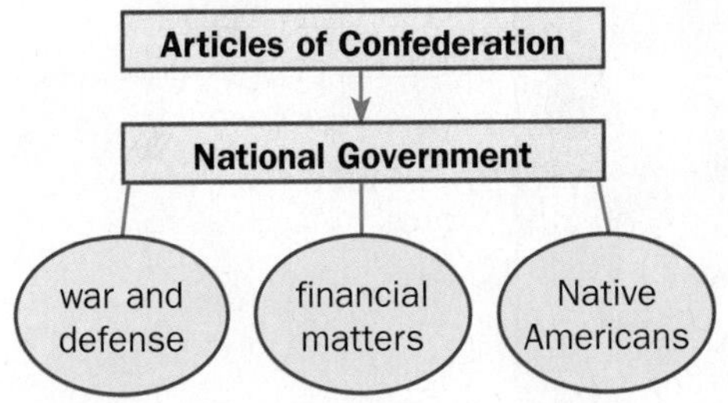

What were the weaknesses of the Articles of Confederation?

CRITICAL THINKING

3. **ANALYZING ISSUES**
   Why were the states afraid of centralized authority and a strong national government?

4. **IDENTIFYING PROBLEMS**
   What was the main problem with the system of representation by state (rather than by population) that was adopted by the Confederation?

5. **HYPOTHESIZING**
   Do you think that the United States would have become a world power if the Articles of Confederation had remained the basis of government? Explain the reasons for your opinion.
   Think About:
   - the power that the Articles gave the states
   - foreign affairs and the Confederation Congress
   - the Confederation Congress's taxation powers

GEOGRAPHY SPOTLIGHT

The Land Ordinance of 1785

▲ Aerial photograph showing how the Land Ordinance transformed the landscape into a patchwork of farms.

When states ceded, or gave up, their western lands to the United States, the new nation became "land rich" even though it was "money poor." Government leaders searched for a way to use the land to fund such services as public education.

The fastest and easiest way to raise money would have been to sell the land in huge parcels. However, only the rich would have been able to purchase land. The Land Ordinance of 1785 made the parcels small and affordable.

The Land Ordinance established a plan for dividing the land. The government would first survey the land, dividing it into townships of 36 square miles, as shown on the map below. Then each township would be divided into 36 sections of 1 square mile, or about 640 acres, each. An individual or a family could purchase a section and divide it into farms or smaller units. A typical farm of the period was equal to one-quarter section, or 160 acres. The minimum price per acre was one dollar.

Government leaders hoped the buyers would develop farms and establish communities. In this way settlements would spread across the western territories in an orderly way. Government surveyors repeated the process thousands of times, imposing frontier geometry on the land.

In 1787, the Congress further provided for the orderly development of the Northwest Territory by passing the Northwest Ordinance, which established how states would be created out of the territory.

▼ The map below shows how an eastern section of Ohio has been subdivided into townships and sections, according to the Land Ordinance of 1785.

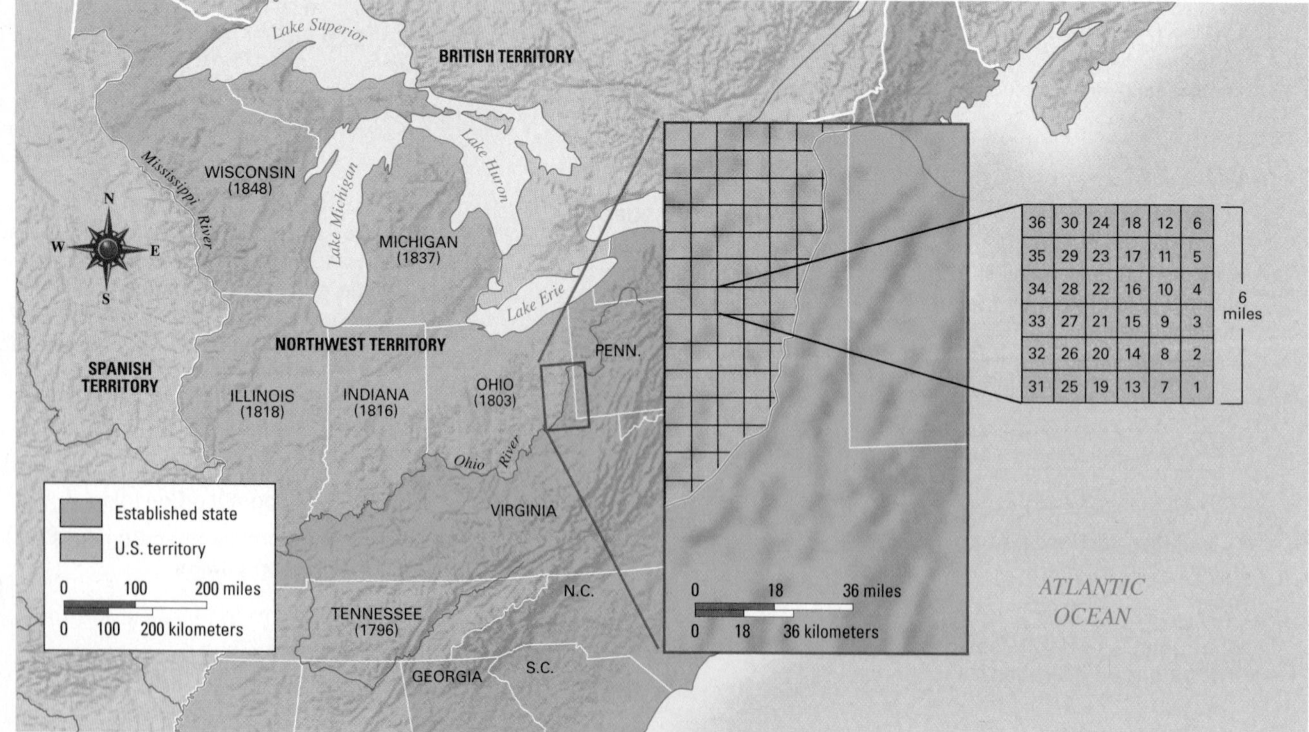

This map shows how a township, now in Meigs County, Ohio, was divided in 1787 into parcels of full square-mile sections and smaller, more affordable plots. The names of the original buyers are written on the full sections. ▶

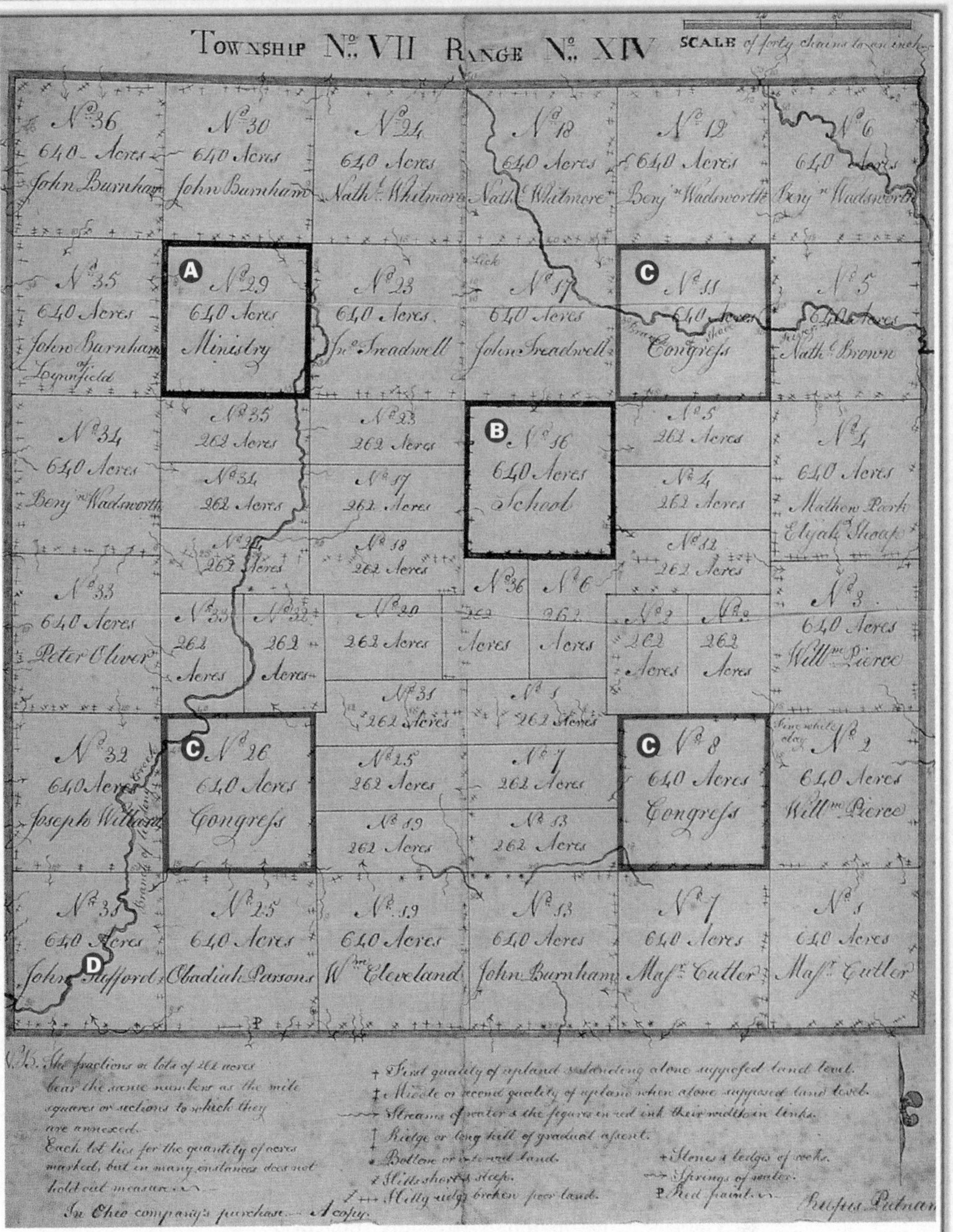

Ⓐ RELIGION To encourage the growth of religion within the township, the surveyors set aside a full section of land. Most of the land within the section was sold to provide funds for a church and a minister's salary. This practice was dropped after a few years because of concern about the separation of church and state.

Ⓑ EDUCATION The ordinance encouraged public education by setting aside section 16 of every township for school buildings. Local people used the money raised by the sale of land within this section to build a school and hire a teacher. This section was centrally located so that students could reach it without traveling too far.

Ⓒ REVENUE Congress reserved two or three sections of each township for sale at a later date. Congress planned to sell the sections then at a tidy profit. The government soon abandoned this practice because of criticism that it should not be involved in land speculation.

Ⓓ WATER Rivers and streams were very important to early settlers, who used them for transportation. Of most interest, however, was a meandering stream, which indicated flat bottomland that was highly prized for its fertility.

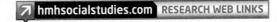

THINKING CRITICALLY

1. **Analyzing Distributions** How did the Land Ordinance of 1785 provide for the orderly development of the Northwest Territory? How did it make land affordable?
2. **Creating a Chart** Create a table that organizes and summarizes the information in the map above. To help you organize your thoughts, pose questions that the map suggests and that a table could help answer.

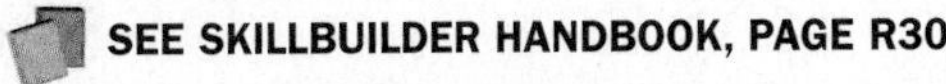
SEE SKILLBUILDER HANDBOOK, PAGE R30.

SECTION 2

Drafting the Constitution

MAIN IDEA

At the Philadelphia convention in 1787, delegates rejected the Articles of Confederation and created a new constitution.

WHY IT MATTERS NOW

The Constitution remains the basis of our government.

Terms & Names

- **Shays's Rebellion**
- **James Madison**
- **Roger Sherman**
- **Great Compromise**
- **Three-Fifths Compromise**
- **federalism**
- **legislative branch**
- **executive branch**
- **judicial branch**
- **checks and balances**
- **electoral college**

One American's Story

Use the graphic organizer online to take notes about issues debated at the Constitutional Convention.

Daniel Shays was angry. A veteran of the Revolutionary War battles at Bunker Hill and Saratoga, he had returned to his farm in western Massachusetts. Because of the heavy debt that he carried, however, he faced debtors' prison. Shays felt that he was the victim of too much taxation.

During the summer and fall of 1786, farmers like Shays kept demanding that the courts be closed so they would not lose their farms to creditors. Their discontent boiled over into mob action in September of 1786 when Daniel Shays led an army of farmers to close the courts. In 1787, Shays's army, 1,200 strong, marched through the snow toward the arsenal at Springfield.

▲ Shays's Rebellion in 1786–1787 not only resulted in the death of four rebels but also unsettled some of the nation's leaders.

State officials hurriedly called out the militia. Four of the rebels were killed and the rest were scattered. Clearly, though, if so many farmers were rebelling, there was something seriously wrong.

Nationalists Strengthen the Government

Shays's Rebellion, as the farmers' protest came to be called, caused panic and dismay throughout the nation. Every state had debt-ridden farmers. Would rebellion spread from Massachusetts elsewhere? Not only was private property in danger, but so was the new nation's reputation. As George Washington himself exclaimed, "What a triumph for our enemies . . . to find that we are incapable of governing ourselves."

It was clearly time to talk about a stronger national government. In order to prevent abuse of power, the states had placed such severe limits on the government that the government was too weak.

Fearing that the new nation was about to disintegrate, George Washington addressed this issue.

A PERSONAL VOICE GEORGE WASHINGTON

"The consequences of . . . [an] inefficient government are too obvious to be dwelt upon. Thirteen sovereignties pulling against each other, and all tugging at the federal head will soon bring ruin on the whole. . . . Let us have [government] by which our lives, liberty, and property will be secured or let us know the worst at once."

CALL FOR CONVENTION One of the nation's biggest problems was trade between the states, which led to quarrels over the taxes that states imposed on one another's goods and disagreements over navigation rights. In September 1786, leaders such as **James Madison** of Virginia and Alexander Hamilton called a meeting of state delegates to discuss issues of interstate trade. Only five states sent representatives to the convention, held in Annapolis, Maryland. Delegates decided to call for another meeting the following year in Philadelphia to deal with trade and other problems.

Meanwhile, the disturbing news of Shays's Rebellion in Massachusetts spread throughout the states. The incident convinced 12 states to send delegates to the Philadelphia convention. (A)

MAIN IDEA

Analyzing Motives

(A) Why do you think news of Shays's Rebellion made states decide to participate in the Philadelphia convention?

CONVENTION HIGHLIGHTS In May 1787, delegates from all the states except Rhode Island gathered at the Philadelphia State House—in the same room in which the Declaration of Independence had been signed 11 years earlier. In spite of the sweltering heat, the windows were tightly closed to prevent outsiders from eavesdropping on the discussions.

Most of the 55 delegates were lawyers, merchants, or planters. Most were rich, well-educated men in their thirties or forties. They included some of the most outstanding leaders of the time, such as Benjamin Franklin, Alexander Hamilton, and George Washington. Washington was elected presiding officer by a unanimous vote.

KEY PLAYERS

JAMES MADISON
1751–1836

The oldest of 12 children, James Madison grew up in Virginia. He was a sickly child who suffered all his life from physical ailments. Because of a weak voice, he decided not to become a minister and thus entered politics.

Madison's Virginia Plan resulted from extensive research on political systems that he had done before the convention. He asked Edmund Randolph, a fellow delegate from Virginia, to present the plan because his own voice was too weak to be heard throughout the assembly.

Besides providing brilliant political leadership, Madison kept a record of the debates that took place at the convention. Because of his plan and his leadership, Madison is known as the "Father of the Constitution."

ROGER SHERMAN
1721–1793

Born in Massachusetts, Roger Sherman spoke a New England dialect that some people found laughable. As a young man, he became a successful merchant. Sherman also studied law and became so active in politics that he had to quit his business.

Sherman helped draft the Declaration of Independence. When he returned to Philadelphia in 1787 for the Constitutional Convention, he was 66 years old. He introduced a plan—later called the Great Compromise—that resolved the issue of state representation in the national legislature. Roger Sherman was the only man to sign the Continental Association of 1774, the Declaration of Independence, the Articles of Confederation, and the Constitution.

Conflict Leads to Compromise

Most of the delegates recognized the need to strengthen the central government. Within the first five days of the meeting, they gave up the idea of revising the Articles of Confederation and decided to form a new government.

BIG STATES VERSUS SMALL STATES One big issue the delegates faced was giving fair representation to both large and small states. Madison's Virginia Plan proposed a bicameral, or two-house, legislature, with membership based on each state's population. The voters would elect members of the lower house, who would then elect members of the upper house.

Delegates from the small states vigorously objected to the Virginia Plan because it gave more power to states with large populations. Small states supported William Paterson's New Jersey Plan, which proposed a single-house congress in which each state had an equal vote.

Proponents of the plans became deadlocked. Finally, **Roger Sherman,** a political leader from Connecticut, suggested the **Great Compromise,** which offered a two-house Congress to satisfy both small and big states. Each state would have equal representation in the Senate, or upper house. The size of the population of each state would determine its representation in the House of Representatives, or lower house. Voters of each state would choose members of the House. The state legislatures would choose members of the Senate.

Sherman's plan pleased those who favored government by the people insofar as it allowed voters to choose representatives. It also pleased those who defended states' rights insofar as it preserved the power of state legislatures. B

MAIN IDEA

Analyzing Issues

B Why was Sherman's compromise a success?

SLAVERY-RELATED ISSUES Representation based on population raised the question of whether slaves should be counted as people. Southern delegates, whose states had many slaves, wanted slaves included in the population count that determined the number of representatives in the House. Northern delegates, whose states had few slaves, disagreed. Not counting Southern slaves would give the Northern states more representatives than the Southern states in the House of Representatives. The delegates eventually agreed to the **Three-Fifths Compromise,** which called for three-fifths of a state's slaves to be counted as population.

The Three-Fifths Compromise settled the political issue but not the economic issue of slavery. Slaveholders, especially in the South, worried that if Congress were given power to regulate foreign trade, it might do away with the

Key Conflicts in the Constitutional Convention

STRONG CENTRAL GOVERNMENT	STRONG STATES
• Authority derives from the people. • The central government should be stronger than the states.	• Authority derives from the states. • The states should remain stronger than the central government.
LARGE STATES	**SMALL STATES**
• Congress should be composed of two houses. • Delegates should be assigned according to population.	• A congress of one house should be preserved. • Each state should have one vote.
NORTH	**SOUTH**
• Slaves should not be counted when deciding the number of delegates. • Slaves should be counted when levying taxes.	• Slaves should be counted when determining congressional representation. • Slaves should not be counted when levying taxes.

slave trade. To resolve this issue, the convention gave Congress the power to regulate trade but prevented it from interfering with the slave trade for at least 20 years. Although the proposal passed, not all the delegates agreed with it. James Madison predicted, "Twenty years will produce all the mischief that can be apprehended from the liberty to import slaves. So long a term will be more dishonorable to the national character than to say nothing about it in the Constitution."

Creating a New Government

After reaching agreement on questions of slavery and representation, the delegates dealt with other issues. They divided power between the states and the national government and separated the national government's power into three branches.

DIVISION OF POWERS The new system of government was a form of **federalism** that divided power between the national government and the state governments. The powers granted to the national government by the Constitution are known as delegated powers, or enumerated powers. These include such powers as control of foreign affairs, providing national defense, regulating trade between the states, and coining money. Powers kept by the states are called reserved powers. These include powers such as providing and supervising education, establishing marriage laws, and regulating trade within a state. C

MAIN IDEA

Summarizing

C Which powers were granted to the national government and to the state governments?

Both levels of government share such important powers as the right to tax, to borrow money, and to pay debts. They also share the power to establish courts.

SEPARATION OF POWERS The delegates protected the rights of the states, but they also granted some powers exclusively to the national government. At the same time, they limited the authority of the government. First, they created three branches of government—a **legislative branch** to make laws, an **executive branch** to carry out laws, and a **judicial branch** to interpret the law.

Then the delegates established a system of **checks and balances** to prevent one branch from dominating the others. (See the chart below.) For example, the president has considerable power, but the Senate has to approve some of the president's decisions. The president can veto acts of Congress, but Congress can override a veto by a

The Checks and Balances of the Federal System

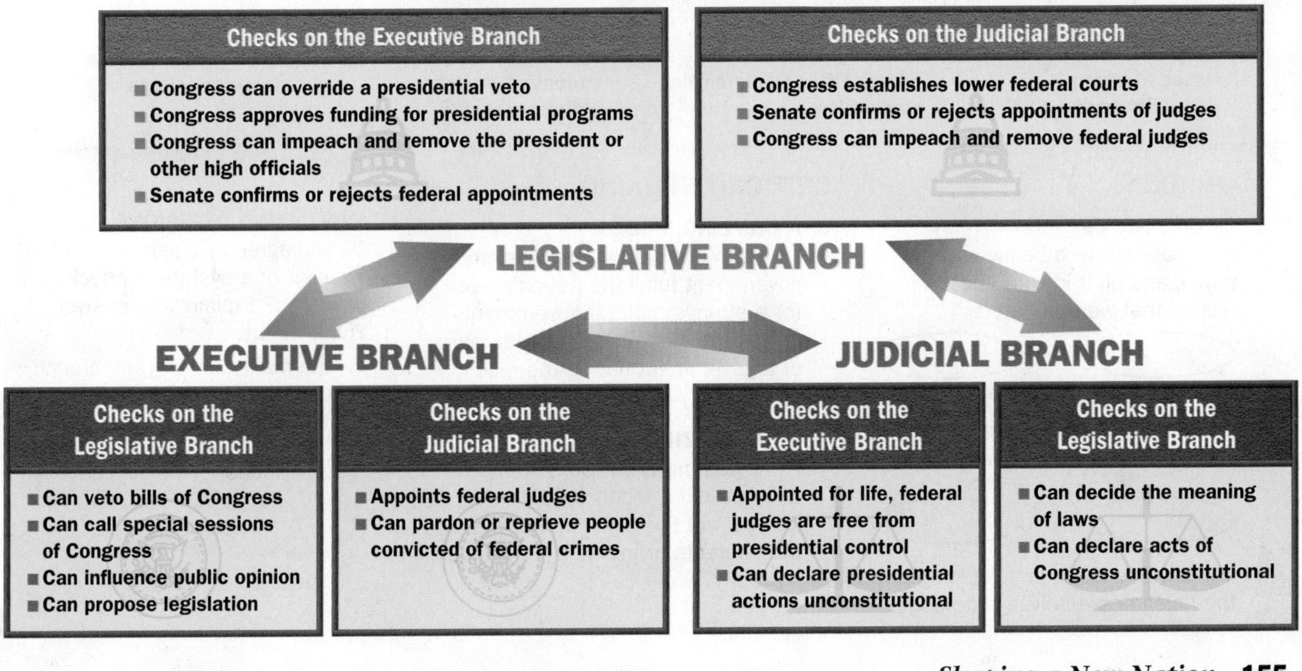

LEGISLATIVE BRANCH

Checks on the Executive Branch	Checks on the Judicial Branch
■ Congress can override a presidential veto ■ Congress approves funding for presidential programs ■ Congress can impeach and remove the president or other high officials ■ Senate confirms or rejects federal appointments	■ Congress establishes lower federal courts ■ Senate confirms or rejects appointments of judges ■ Congress can impeach and remove federal judges

EXECUTIVE BRANCH

Checks on the Legislative Branch	Checks on the Judicial Branch
■ Can veto bills of Congress ■ Can call special sessions of Congress ■ Can influence public opinion ■ Can propose legislation	■ Appoints federal judges ■ Can pardon or reprieve people convicted of federal crimes

JUDICIAL BRANCH

Checks on the Executive Branch	Checks on the Legislative Branch
■ Appointed for life, federal judges are free from presidential control ■ Can declare presidential actions unconstitutional	■ Can decide the meaning of laws ■ Can declare acts of Congress unconstitutional

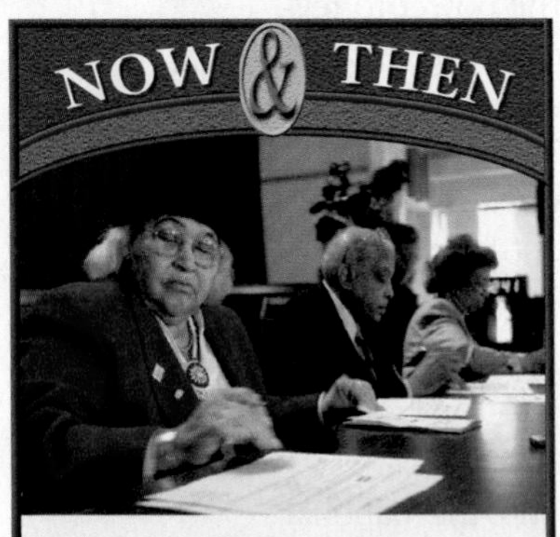

THE ELECTORAL COLLEGE

Distrust of popular sovereignty led the framers of the Constitution to devise a complicated system of electing the president. The creation of an electoral college ensured that a college of electors, or representatives, would have the last say in the vote.

In the 2000 presidential election, the electoral college played a decisive role in choosing the president. Even though Al Gore won the popular vote by a margin of almost 540,000, the electors gave George W. Bush 271 electoral votes—one vote more than the 270 votes needed to win the presidency.

two-thirds vote. The Supreme Court assumes the power to interpret the Constitution, but the president appoints the justices, and Congress can bring them to trial for abuses of power.

The procedure for electing the president reflected two main concerns. Because there were no national political parties and because travel and communication were limited, there was a fear that the popular vote would be divided among many regional candidates. Also, many among the upper classes distrusted and feared the lower classes. Some did not trust the common people to vote wisely; others trusted them to vote the upper class out of power. So the delegates came up with a new system of electing the president. Instead of voters choosing the president directly, each state would choose a number of electors equal to the number of senators and representatives the state had in Congress. The group of electors chosen by the states, known as the **electoral college,** would cast ballots for the candidates.

CREATING THE CONSTITUTION Finally, the delegates provided a means of changing the Constitution through the amendment process. After nearly four months of debate and compromise, the delegates succeeded in creating a constitution that was flexible enough to last through the centuries to come. Yet when George Washington adjourned the convention on September 17, 1787, he was somewhat uncertain about the future of the new plan of government. Washington remarked to a fellow delegate, "I do not expect the Constitution to last for more than 20 years."

The convention's work was over, but the new government could not become a reality until the voters agreed. So the Constitution of the United States of America was sent to the Congress, which submitted it to the states for approval.

ASSESSMENT

1. **TERMS & NAMES** For each term or name, write a sentence explaining its significance.
   - **Shays's Rebellion**
   - **James Madison**
   - **Roger Sherman**
   - **Great Compromise**
   - **Three-Fifths Compromise**
   - **federalism**
   - **legislative branch**
   - **executive branch**
   - **judicial branch**
   - **checks and balances**
   - **electoral college**

MAIN IDEA

2. **TAKING NOTES**
   Re-create the web below on your paper, and fill it in with specific issues that were debated.

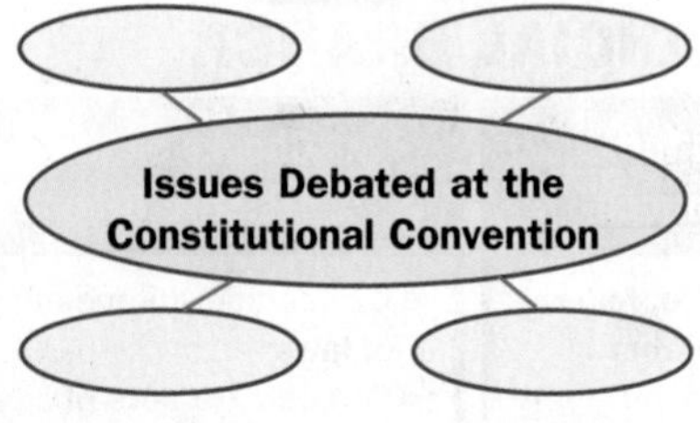

Choose one issue and explain how the delegates resolved that issue.

CRITICAL THINKING

3. **ANALYZING ISSUES**
   In what ways did the new system of government fulfill the nation's need for a stronger central government and at the same time allay its fear of a government having too much power?

4. **SUMMARIZING**
   What was the Great Compromise and how did it reconcile the interests of the small states with the interests of the more populous states?

5. **EVALUATING DECISIONS**
   Do you agree or disagree with the creation of a system of checks and balances? Explain your answer.
   Think About:
   - the main task of each branch
   - how the branches function
   - the efficiency of governmental operations

Ratifying the Constitution

MAIN IDEA	WHY IT MATTERS NOW	Terms & Names
During the debate on the Constitution, the Federalists promised to add a bill of rights in order to get the Constitution ratified.	**The Bill of Rights continues to protect ordinary citizens.**	**• ratification • Federalists • Antifederalists • *The Federalist* • Bill of Rights**

One American's Story

hmhsocialstudies.com TAKING NOTES

Use the graphic organizer online to take notes about the Federalists and the Antifederalists.

When John Jay was in college, he refused to reveal the identity of a student who had broken school property. As he was being interrogated, Jay pointed out that the college rules did not require one student to inform on another.

Years later, Jay argued for ratification of the newly written constitution. He warned how other nations would view the United States if it did not unify itself.

A PERSONAL VOICE JOHN JAY

"What a poor pitiful figure will America make in their eyes! How liable would she become not only to their contempt, but to their outrage; and how soon would dear-bought experience proclaim that when a people or family so divide, it never fails to be against themselves."

—*The Federalist,* Number 4

Whether Jay was defending his peers or his country's Constitution, his strong principles and commitment to unity gave his arguments tremendous force. Men like John Jay played a key role in ratifying the Constitution.

John Jay

Federalists and Antifederalists

The delegates to the Philadelphia convention had spent four months drafting the Constitution. When newspapers printed the full text of the new Constitution, many Americans were shocked by the radical changes it proposed. They had expected the convention to merely amend the Articles of Confederation. Supporters and opponents battled over controversies that threatened to shatter the framers' hope of uniting the states.

"*They . . . divided the powers, that each [branch of the legislature] might be a check upon the other . . . and I presume that every reasonable man will agree to it.*"

ALEXANDER HAMILTON

"*You are not to inquire how your trade may be increased, nor how you are to become a great and powerful people, but how your liberties can be secured. . . .*"

PATRICK HENRY

CONTROVERSIES OVER THE CONSTITUTION The framers set up a procedure for ratification that called for each state to hold a special convention. The voters would elect the delegates to the convention, who would then vote to accept or reject the Constitution. **Ratification**—official approval—required the agreement of at least nine states. This system largely bypassed the state legislatures, whose members were likely to oppose the Constitution, since it reduced the power of the states. It also gave the framers an opportunity to campaign for delegates in their states who would support ratification.

Supporters of the Constitution called themselves **Federalists,** because they favored the new Constitution's balance of power between the states and the national government. Their opponents became known as **Antifederalists** because they opposed having such a strong central government and thus were against the Constitution.

The Federalists insisted that the division of powers and the system of checks and balances would protect Americans from the tyranny of centralized authority. Antifederalists countered with a long list of possible abuses of power by a strong central government. These included a fear that the government would serve the interests of the privileged minority and ignore the rights of the majority. Antifederalists also raised doubts that a single government could manage the affairs of a large country. Their leading argument, however, centered on the Constitution's lack of protection for individual rights. (A)

MAIN IDEA

Analyzing Issues

(A) What were the Antifederalists' major arguments against the Constitution?

THE OPPOSING FORCES Leading Federalists included framers of the Constitution such as George Washington, James Madison, and Alexander Hamilton. They used their experience and powers of persuasion to win support for the document they had drafted. They received heavy support from urban centers, where merchants, skilled workers, and laborers saw the benefit of a national government that could regulate trade. Small states and those with weak economies also favored a strong central government that could protect their interests.

Leading Antifederalists included revolutionary heroes and leaders such as Patrick Henry, Samuel Adams, and Richard Henry Lee. They received support from rural areas, where people feared a strong government that might add to their tax burden. Large states and those with strong economies, such as New York, which had greater freedom under the Articles of Confederation, also were unsupportive of the Constitution at first.

Both sides waged a war of words in the public debate over ratification. ***The Federalist,*** a series of 85 essays defending the Constitution, appeared in New York newspapers between 1787 and 1788. They were published under the pseudonym *Publius,* but were written by Federalist leaders Alexander Hamilton, James Madison, and John Jay. *The Federalist* provided an analysis and an explanation of Constitutional provisions, such as the separation of powers and the limits on the power of majorities, that remain important today.

Letters from the Federal Farmer, most likely written by Richard Henry Lee, was the most widely read Antifederalist publication. Lee listed the rights the Antifederalists believed should be protected, such as freedom of the press and of religion, guarantees against unreasonable searches of people and their homes, and the right to a trial by jury.

The Bill of Rights Leads to Ratification

The proposed U.S. Constitution contained no guarantee that the government would protect the rights of the people or of the states. Some supporters of the Constitution, such as Thomas Jefferson, viewed the Constitution's lack of a bill of rights—a formal summary of citizens' rights and freedoms, as a serious drawback to ratification.

A PERSONAL VOICE THOMAS JEFFERSON

"I like much the general idea of framing a government, which should go on of itself, peaceably, without needing continual recurrence to the State legislatures. . . . I will now tell you what I do not like. First, the omission of a bill of rights. . . . Let me add, that a bill of rights is what the people are entitled to against every government on earth, general or particular; and what no just government should refuse. . . ."

—letter to James Madison from Paris, December 20, 1787

PEOPLE DEMAND A BILL OF RIGHTS Antifederalists argued that since the Constitution weakened the states, the people needed a national bill of rights. They wanted written guarantees that the people would have freedom of speech, of the press, and of religion. They demanded assurance of the right to trial by jury and the right to bear arms.

Federalists insisted that the Constitution granted only limited powers to the national government so that it could not violate the rights of the states or of the people. They also pointed out that the Constitution gave the people the power to protect their rights through the election of trustworthy leaders. In the end, though, the Federalists yielded to people's overwhelming desire and promised to add a bill of rights if the states would ratify the Constitution. B

MAIN IDEA

Summarizing

B What were the arguments made by Antifederalists and Federalists over adding a bill of rights to the Constitution?

RATIFICATION OF THE CONSTITUTION Delaware led the country in ratifying the Constitution in December 1787. In June 1788, New Hampshire fulfilled the requirement for ratification by becoming the ninth state to approve the Constitution. Nevertheless, Virginia and New York had not voted, and the new government needed these very large and influential states.

Powerful adversaries squared off in Virginia. Patrick Henry, Richard Henry Lee, and James Monroe led the opposition. Richard Henry Lee, a prominent political

A parade in New York in 1788 celebrates the new Constitution and features the "Ship of State" float. Alexander Hamilton's name emphasizes the key role he played in launching the new government. ▼

figure of his time, claimed that those in favor of the Constitution were voluntarily placing themselves under the power of an absolute ruler.

A PERSONAL VOICE RICHARD HENRY LEE

"'Tis really astonishing that the same people, who have just emerged from a long and cruel war in defense of liberty, should now agree to fix an elective despotism [absolute power] upon themselves and their posterity."

The struggle for New York pitted John Jay and Alexander Hamilton against a strong Antifederalist majority. Jay, Hamilton, and Madison launched an effective public campaign through *The Federalist.* News of ratification by New Hampshire and Virginia strengthened the Federalists' cause. On July 26, 1788, New York ratified by a vote of 30 to 27. Although Rhode Island did not accept the Constitution until 1790, the new government became a reality in 1789.

SOUTH AFRICA CREATES A BILL OF RIGHTS

On May 8, 1996, South African lawmakers danced in the aisles of South Africa's Parliament. They had just approved a landmark constitution guaranteeing equal rights for blacks and whites in the new South Africa. Included in this constitution was a bill of rights modeled in part on the United States Bill of Rights, though with significant differences.

The South African bill of rights is a much broader and more detailed document than the U.S. Bill of Rights. For example, two pages are devoted to the rights of arrested, detained, and accused persons. One page is devoted to the rights of children. The document forbids discrimination of all kinds and protects the rights of minorities. It also guarantees every citizen the right to freedom of travel within the country, which was often denied blacks under apartheid. In addition, the bill of rights guarantees a range of social and economic rights—including the right to adequate housing, food, water, education, and health care—which were often denied blacks under apartheid.

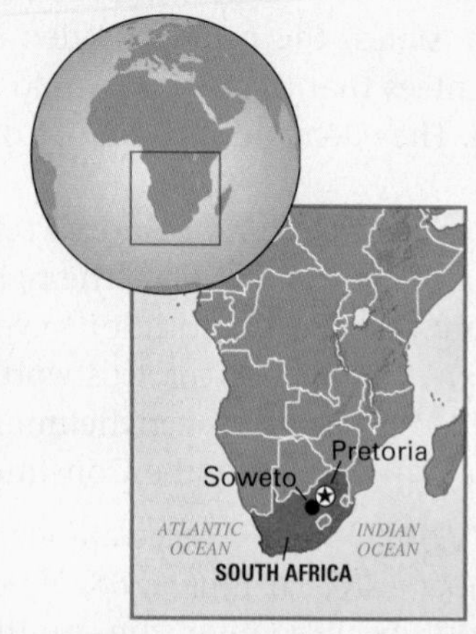

Nelson Mandela, the first black president of South Africa, greets a crowd celebrating the new constitution May 8, 1996. ▼

People outside the polling station in the black township of Soweto waiting to vote in South Africa's first multiracial election. ▶

ADOPTION OF A BILL OF RIGHTS In several states, ratification had hinged on the Federalists' pledge to add a bill of rights. In September 1789, Congress submitted 12 amendments to the state legislatures for ratification. By December 1791, the required three-fourths of the states had ratified ten of the amendments, which became known as the **Bill of Rights.**

The first eight amendments spell out the personal liberties the states had requested. The Ninth and Tenth Amendments impose general limits on the powers of the federal government.

The Bill of Rights

1. Religious and political freedom
2. Right to bear arms
3. Freedom from quartering troops
4. Freedom against unreasonable search and seizure
5. Rights of accused persons
6. Right to a speedy, public trial
7. Right to a trial by jury
8. Limits on fines and punishments
9. Rights of the people
10. Powers of states and the people

- The *First Amendment*—guarantees citizens' rights to freedom of religion, speech, the press, and political activity.
- The *Second* and *Third Amendments*—grant citizens the right to bear arms as members of a militia of citizen-soldiers and prevent the government from housing troops in private homes in peacetime.
- The *Fourth* through *Eighth Amendments*—guarantee fair treatment for individuals suspected or accused of crimes.
- The *Ninth Amendment*—makes it clear that people's rights are not restricted to just those specifically mentioned in the Constitution.
- The *Tenth Amendment*—clarifies that the people and the states have all the powers that the Constitution does not specifically give to the national government or deny to the states.

The protection of rights and freedoms did not apply to all Americans at the time the Bill of Rights was adopted. Native Americans and slaves were excluded. Women were not mentioned in the Constitution. Although some northern states permitted free blacks to vote, the Bill of Rights offered them no protection against whites' discrimination and hostility. The expansion of democracy came from later amendments. Nevertheless, the flexibility of the U.S. Constitution made it a model for governments around the world.

ASSESSMENT

1. **TERMS & NAMES** For each term or name, write a sentence explaining its significance.
   - **ratification**
   - **Federalists**
   - **Antifederalists**
   - ***The Federalist***
   - **Bill of Rights**

MAIN IDEA

2. **TAKING NOTES**
   Use a chart like the one below to show which groups and public figures supported the Federalists and which supported the Antifederalists.

	Public Figures	Groups
Federalists		
Antifederalists		

   Which group would you have supported? Explain why.

CRITICAL THINKING

3. **EVALUATING**
   Do you think the Federalists or the Antifederalists had the more valid arguments? Support your opinion with examples from the text.
   Think About:
   - whom each group represented
   - Americans' experience with the Articles of Confederation
   - Americans' experience with British rule

4. **ANALYZING MOTIVES**
   Why did the Antifederalists demand the Bill of Rights?

5. **HYPOTHESIZING**
   How might the course of American history have changed if the Bill of Rights had forbidden discrimination of all kinds and had protected the rights of minorities?

CHAPTER 5 ASSESSMENT

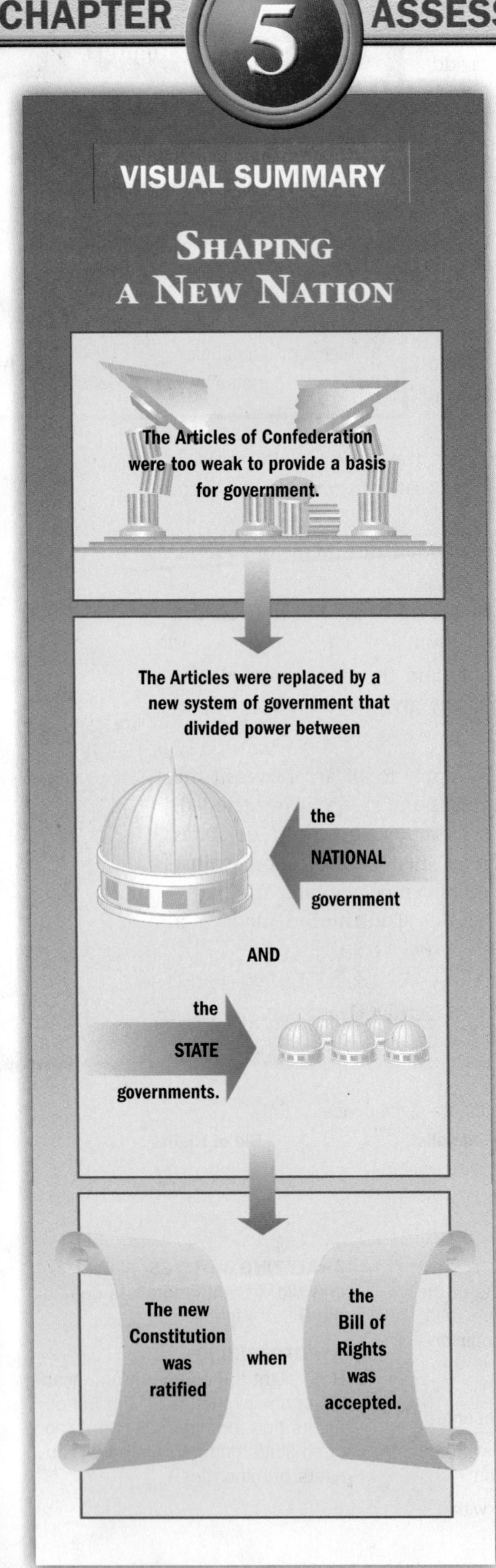

VISUAL SUMMARY
SHAPING A NEW NATION
The Articles of Confederation were too weak to provide a basis for government.
The Articles were replaced by a new system of government that divided power between
the NATIONAL government
AND
the STATE governments.
The new Constitution was ratified
when
the Bill of Rights was accepted.

TERMS & NAMES

For each term or name below, write a sentence explaining its significance for the United States in the 1780s.

1. republic
2. Articles of Confederation
3. Land Ordinance of 1785
4. Shays's Rebellion
5. James Madison
6. checks and balances
7. electoral college
8. Federalist
9. Antifederalist
10. Bill of Rights

MAIN IDEAS

Use your notes and the information in the chapter to answer the following questions.

Experimenting with Confederation

1. Why did the new states prefer a republic rather than a democracy for their government?
2. Why did the states fear a strong central government?
3. In what ways was the confederation too weak to handle the nation's problems?

Drafting the Constitution

4. What issues and events led to the Constitutional Convention?
5. In what ways did compromise play a critical role in the drafting of the Constitution?
6. Why was the slave trade an issue at the Constitutional Convention?
7. Briefly explain the separation of powers established by the Constitution.

Ratifying the Constitution

8. What were the arguments for and against ratifying the Constitution?
9. What was *The Federalist* and what effect did this publication have on ratification?
10. Why did the states ratify the Constitution once a bill of rights was promised?

CRITICAL THINKING

1. **USING YOUR NOTES** In a chart like the one below, list the beliefs and goals of the Federalists and Antifederalists.

	Federalists	Antifederalists
Beliefs		
Goals		

2. **DEVELOPING HISTORICAL PERSPECTIVE** How might the United States have developed if the Articles of Confederation had continued to provide the basis for government?

3. **MAKING INFERENCES** In what ways was the land of the Northwest Territory distributed democratically?

STANDARDIZED TEST PRACTICE

Use the quotation below and your knowledge of United States history to answer questions 1 and 2.

> "**Among the numerous advantages promised by a well-constructed Union, none deserves to be more accurately developed than its tendency to break and control the violence of faction. . . . By a faction, I understand a number of citizens, whether amounting to a majority or a minority of the whole, who are united and actuated by some common impulse of passion, or of interest, adverse to the rights of other citizens, or to the permanent and aggregate interests of the community. . . . A landed interest, a manufacturing interest, a mercantile interest, a moneyed interest, with many lesser interests, grow up of necessity in civilized nations, and divide them into different classes, actuated by different sentiments and views.**"
>
> —James Madison, *The Federalist,* Number 10

1. As used by Madison, the term *faction* means —

A any interest group.
B a religious cult.
C either of the two political parties.
D anyone who does not own property.

2. Madison believed that factions were —

F necessary to the working of government.
G characteristic of British government only.
H extremely destructive and divisive.
J outdated and insignificant.

3. The Constitution was finally ratified because —

A the Federalists agreed to grant additional powers to the states.
B the Federalists agreed to add a Bill of Rights.
C the electoral college voted for ratification.
D the Antifederalists agreed to additional restrictions on the power of the states.

4. Why was it so difficult to devise a system of government for the United States?

F The new nation was too big.
G No one wanted a national government.
H Many feared that a national government would infringe upon the power of the states.
J Some states did not want to rejoin Britain.

hmhsocialstudies.com TEST PRACTICE

For additional test practice, go online for:

- Diagnostic tests
- Tutorials

INTERACT WITH HISTORY

Think about the issues you explored at the beginning of the chapter. Imagine you are living in the 1780s. Write an article for either *The Federalist* or *Letters from the Federal Farmer*, arguing either for or against giving the national government more power.

FOCUS ON WRITING

You are a representative of one of the former colonies and you have just returned from the Constitutional Convention. Write a letter explaining how the U.S. Constitution is an improvement upon the Articles of Confederation. Support your explanation with reasoning and examples from the chapter.

COLLABORATIVE LEARNING

Organize into pairs and choose an issue debated at the Constitutional Convention. Read the section of the Constitution that contains the final compromise as well as documents that show the various sides of the issue before a compromise was reached. Then prepare a debate of the issue to present to the class. Each partner should draft a three-minute speech defending one side of the issue. The opposing partner should give a short rebuttal after each point of view is presented. Have the class evaluate the two sides of the argument before you remind your classmates how the issue was resolved.

The Living Constitution

"The Constitution was not made to fit us like a straightjacket. In its elasticity lies its chief greatness."
President Woodrow Wilson

Purposes of the Constitution

The official charge to the delegates who met in Philadelphia in 1787 was to amend the Articles of Confederation. They soon made a fateful decision, however, to ignore the Articles and to write an entirely new constitution. These delegates—the "framers"—set themselves five purposes to fulfill in their effort to create an effective constitution.

1. Establish Legitimacy

First, the framers of the Constitution had to establish the new government's legitimacy—its right to rule. The patriots' theory of government was set out in the Declaration of Independence, which explained why British rule over the colonies was illegitimate. Now the framers had to demonstrate that their new government met the standards of legitimacy referred to in the Declaration.

For the framers of the Constitution, legitimacy had to be based on a compact or contract among those who are to be ruled. This is why the Constitution starts with the words "We the people of the United States . . . do ordain and establish this Constitution."

2. Create Appropriate Structures

The framers' second purpose was to create appropriate structures for the new government. The framers were committed to the principles of representative democracy. They also believed that any new government must include an important role for state governments and ensure that the states retained some legitimacy to rule within their borders.

To achieve their goals, the framers created the Congress, the presidency, and the judiciary to share the powers of the national government. They also created a system of division of powers between the national government and the state governments.

The original manuscript of the Constitution is now kept in the National Archives in Washington, D.C. ▶

We the People of the United States, in Order to form a more perfect Union, establish Justice, insure domestic Tranquility, provide for the common defence, promote the general Welfare, and secure the Blessings of Liberty to ourselves and our Posterity, do ordain and establish this Constitution for the United States of America.

Article. I.

Section. 1. All legislative Powers herein granted shall be vested in a Congress of the United States, which shall consist of a Senate and House of Representatives.

Section. 2. The House of Representatives shall be composed of Members chosen every second Year by the People of the several States, and the Electors in each State shall have the Qualifications requisite for Electors of the most numerous Branch of the State Legislature.

No Person shall be a Representative who shall not have attained to the Age of twenty five Years, and been seven Years a Citizen of the United States, and who shall not, when elected, be an Inhabitant of that State in which he shall be chosen.

Representatives and direct Taxes shall be apportioned among the several States which may be included within this Union, according to their respective Numbers, which shall be determined by adding to the whole Number of free Persons, including those bound to Service for a Term of Years, and excluding Indians not taxed, three fifths of all other Persons. The actual Enumeration shall be made within three Years after the first Meeting of the Congress of the United States, and within every subsequent Term of ten Years, in such Manner as they shall by Law direct. The Number of Representatives shall not exceed one for every thirty Thousand, but each State shall have at Least one Representative; and until such enumeration shall be made, the State of New Hampshire shall be entitled to chuse three, Massachusetts eight, Rhode Island and Providence Plantations one, Connecticut five, New York six, New Jersey four, Pennsylvania eight, Delaware one, Maryland six, Virginia ten, North Carolina five, South Carolina five, and Georgia three.

When vacancies happen in the Representation from any State, the Executive Authority thereof shall issue Writs of Election to fill such Vacancies.

The House of Representatives shall chuse their Speaker and other Officers; and shall have the sole Power of Impeachment.

Section. 3. The Senate of the United States shall be composed of two Senators from each State, chosen by the Legislature thereof for six Years; and each Senator shall have one Vote.

Immediately after they shall be assembled in Consequence of the first Election, they shall be divided as equally as may be into three Classes. The Seats

RESEARCHING A CONSTITUTIONAL QUESTION

As you study the Constitution, think about a constitutional question that interests you. Here are some possible questions:

- How much, if at all, can the federal government or a state government restrict the sale of firearms?
- Under what conditions does the president have the power to order American troops into battle without congressional approval?
- Under what conditions may a police officer conduct a search of the inside of an automobile?

Once you have chosen a constitutional question, research that question in articles and books on the Constitution. Also check the indexes of well-known newspapers, such as the *New York Times*, for articles that are relevant.

3. Describe and Distribute Power

The framers had as their third purpose to describe governmental powers and to distribute them among the structures they created. The powers of the legislative branch, which are those of Congress, are listed in Article 1, Section 8, of the Constitution. Many of the executive powers belonging to the president are listed in Article 2, Sections 2 and 3. The courts are given judicial powers in Article 3. The words of Article 4 imply that the states retain authority over many public matters.

4. Limit Government Powers

The fourth purpose of the framers was to limit the powers of the structures they created. Limits on the Congress's powers are found in Article 1, Section 9. Some of the limits on the powers of state governments are found in Article 1, Section 10. There the framers enumerate functions that are delegated to the national government and so cannot be directed by the states.

5. Allow for Change

The framers' fifth purpose was to include some means for changing the Constitution. Here they faced a dilemma: they wanted to make certain that the government endured by changing with the times, but they did not want to expose the basic rules of government to so many changes that the system would be unstable. So in Article 5 they created a difficult but not impossible means for amending the Constitution.

How to Read the Constitution

The Constitution is printed on a beige background, while the explanatory notes next to each article, section, or clause are printed on blue. Each article is divided into sections, and the sections are subdivided into clauses. Headings have been added and the spelling and punctuation modernized for easier reading. Portions of the Constitution no longer in use have been crossed out. The Constitutional Insight questions and answers will help you understand significant issues related to the Constitution.

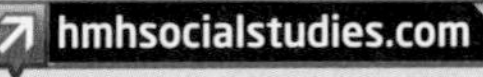

The Constitution

PREAMBLE. *Purpose of the Constitution*

We the people of the United States, in order to form a more perfect Union, establish justice, insure domestic tranquility, provide for the common defense, promote the general welfare, and secure the blessings of liberty to ourselves and our posterity, do ordain and establish this Constitution for the United States of America.

ARTICLE 1. *The Legislature*

SECTION 1. CONGRESS All legislative powers herein granted shall be vested in a Congress of the United States, which shall consist of a Senate and House of Representatives.

SECTION 2. THE HOUSE OF REPRESENTATIVES

1. **ELECTIONS** The House of Representatives shall be composed of members chosen every second year by the people of the several states, and the electors in each state shall have the qualifications requisite for electors of the most numerous branch of the state legislature.

2. **QUALIFICATIONS** No person shall be a Representative who shall not have attained to the age of twenty-five years, and been seven years a citizen of the United States, and who shall not, when elected, be an inhabitant of that state in which he shall be chosen.

3. **NUMBER OF REPRESENTATIVES** Representatives ~~and direct taxes~~ shall be apportioned among the several states which may be included within this Union, according to their respective numbers, ~~which shall be determined by adding to the whole number of free persons, including those bound to service for a term of years, and excluding Indians not taxed, three fifths of all other persons.~~ The actual enumeration shall be made within three years after the first meeting of the Congress of the United States, and within every subsequent term of ten years, in such manner as they shall by law direct. The number of Representatives shall not exceed one for every thirty thousand, but each state shall have at least one Representative; ~~and until such enumeration shall be made, the state of New Hampshire shall be entitled to choose three, Massachusetts eight, Rhode Island and Providence Plantations one, Connecticut five, New York six, New Jersey four, Pennsylvania eight, Delaware one, Maryland six, Virginia ten, North Carolina five, South Carolina five, and Georgia three.~~

4. **VACANCIES** When vacancies happen in the representation from any state, the executive authority thereof shall issue writs of election to fill such vacancies.

5. **OFFICERS AND IMPEACHMENT** The House of Representatives shall choose their Speaker and other officers; and shall have the sole power of impeachment.

PREAMBLE

Constitutional Insight **Preamble**
Why does the Preamble say "We the people of the United States . . . ordain and establish" the new government? The Articles of Confederation was an agreement among the states. But the framers of the Constitution wanted to be sure its legitimacy came from the American people, not from the states, which might decide to withdraw their support at any time. This is a basic principle of the Constitution.

ARTICLE 1

Constitutional Insight **Section 1**
Why does the first article of the Constitution focus on Congress rather than on the presidency or the courts? The framers were intent on stressing the central role of the legislative branch in the new government because it is the branch that most directly represents the people and is most responsive to them.

A CRITICAL THINKING
Do you think Congress is still the branch of the federal government that is most directly responsible to the people? Why or why not?

Constitutional Insight **Section 2.1**
Why are members of the House of Representatives elected every two years? The House of Representatives was designed to be a truly representative body, with members who reflect the concerns and sentiments of their constituents as closely as possible. The framers achieved this timely representation by establishing two years as a reasonable term for members of the House to serve.

B CRITICAL THINKING
Do you think electing members of the House of Representatives every two years is a good idea? Why or why not?

Requirements for Holding Federal Office

POSITION	MINIMUM AGE	RESIDENCY	CITIZENSHIP
Representative	25	state in which elected	7 years
Senator	30	state in which elected	9 years
President	35	14 years in the United States	natural-born
Supreme Court Justice	none	none	none

Section 3. The Senate

1. Numbers The Senate of the United States shall be composed of two Senators from each state, ~~chosen by the legislature thereof,~~ for six years; and each Senator shall have one vote.

2. Classifying Terms Immediately after they shall be assembled in consequence of the first election, they shall be divided as equally as may be into three classes. The seats of the Senators of the first class shall be vacated at the expiration of the second year, of the second class at the expiration of the fourth year, and of the third class at the expiration of the sixth year, so that one third may be chosen every second year; ~~and if vacancies happen by resignation, or otherwise, during the recess of the legislature of any state, the executive thereof may make temporary appointments until the next meeting of the legislature, which shall then fill such vacancies.~~

3. Qualifications No person shall be a Senator who shall not have attained to the age of thirty years, and been nine years a citizen of the United States, and who shall not, when elected, be an inhabitant of that state for which he shall be chosen.

4. Role of Vice-President The Vice-President of the United States shall be President of the Senate, but shall have no vote, unless they be equally divided.

5. Officers The Senate shall choose their other officers, and also a President pro tempore, in the absence of the Vice-President, or when he shall exercise the office of President of the United States.

6. Impeachment Trials The Senate shall have the sole power to try all impeachments. When sitting for that purpose, they shall be on oath or affirmation. When the President of the United States is tried, the Chief Justice shall preside: and no person shall be convicted without the concurrence of two thirds of the members present.

7. Punishment for Impeachment Judgment in cases of impeachment shall not extend further than to removal from office, and disqualification to hold and enjoy any office of honor, trust or profit under the United States; but the party convicted shall nevertheless be liable and subject to indictment, trial, judgment and punishment, according to law.

Section 4. Congressional Elections

1. Regulations The times, places and manner of holding elections for Senators and Representatives shall be prescribed in each state by the legislature thereof; but the Congress may at any time by law make or alter such regulations, except as to the places of choosing Senators.

2. Sessions The Congress shall assemble at least once in every year, ~~and such meeting shall be on the first Monday in December, unless they shall by law appoint a different day.~~

Constitutional Insight **Section 3.1** *Why are members of the Senate elected every six years?* The framers feared the possibility of instability in the government. So they decided that senators should have six-year terms and be elected by the state legislatures rather than directly by the people. The Seventeenth Amendment, as you will see later, changed this. The framers also staggered the terms of the senators so that only one-third of them are replaced at any one time. This stabilizes the Senate still further.

C CRITICAL THINKING

Do you think it is important today for the Senate to have more stability than the House of Representatives? If so, why?

Constitutional Insight **Sections 3.6 and 3.7** *Must an impeached president step down from office?* Not necessarily. An impeachment is a formal accusation of criminal behavior or serious misbehavior. By impeaching the president, the U.S. House of Representatives is officially accusing the nation's chief executive of one or more wrongdoings that warrant possible removal from office. It is then the responsibility of the Senate to conduct a trial to determine whether the president is guilty or not guilty of the charges—and thus whether or not the president must step down. Conviction requires a two-thirds vote of the Senate.

D CRITICAL THINKING

Do you think a president should be put on trial for a crime while he or she is still in office? Explain.

Constitutional Insight Section 5.2
What kinds of rules does Congress make for itself? The Constitution gives each house control over most of its rules of procedure and membership. Rules are important, for they help shape the kinds of laws and policies that pass each body. Senate rules allow a filibuster, whereby a senator holds the floor as long as he or she likes in order to block consideration of a bill he or she dislikes. In recent years, a "cloture" rule has been used to end debate if 60 or more members vote to do so.

In contrast, the House of Representatives has rules to limit debate. A rules committee has the primary task of determining how long a bill on the floor of the House may be discussed and whether any amendments can be offered to the bill. In recent years, the power of the Rules Committee has been limited, but being able to shape the rules remains a powerful tool of members of Congress.

E CRITICAL THINKING
Why do you think the chair of the Rules Committee is in a powerful position?

Constitutional Insight Section 7.1
Why must all bills to raise revenue originate in the House? Because its members all stand for election every two years, the House was expected to be more directly responsive to the people. The tradition of restricting the powers of taxation to the people's representatives dates prior to the English Bill of Rights (1689), which granted to Parliament and withheld from the king the right to raise taxes. When colonists protesting the Stamp Act and the Intolerable Acts protested "no taxation without representation," they were appealing to a longstanding right codified in the English Bill of Rights.

Constitutional Insight Section 7.2
How often do presidents use the veto, and how often is that action overridden? The use of the veto, which is the refusal to approve a bill, depends on many factors, especially the political conditions of the time. Until 1865, only nine presidents exercised the veto for 36 pieces of legislation, including Andrew Jackson who used it 12 times. Since 1865, every president has used the veto power, some on relatively few occasions, others as frequently as over a hundred times. Usually, Congress is unable to produce the votes (those of two-thirds of the members present in each house) needed to override presidential vetoes.

F CRITICAL THINKING
Do you think it should be easier for Congress to override a president's veto? Why or why not?

Section 5. Rules and Procedures

1. Quorum Each house shall be the judge of the elections, returns and qualifications of its own members, and a majority of each shall constitute a quorum to do business; but a smaller number may adjourn from day to day, and may be authorized to compel the attendance of absent members, in such manner, and under such penalties, as each house may provide.

2. Rules and Conduct Each house may determine the rules of its proceedings, punish its members for disorderly behavior, and, with the concurrence of two thirds, expel a member.

3. Congressional Records Each house shall keep a journal of its proceedings, and from time to time publish the same, excepting such parts as may in their judgment require secrecy; and the yeas and nays of the members of either house on any question shall, at the desire of one fifth of those present, be entered on the journal.

4. Adjournment Neither house, during the session of Congress, shall, without the consent of the other, adjourn for more than three days, nor to any other place than that in which the two houses shall be sitting.

Section 6. Payment and Privileges

1. Salary The Senators and Representatives shall receive a compensation for their services, to be ascertained by law, and paid out of the treasury of the United States. They shall in all cases, except treason, felony and breach of the peace, be privileged from arrest during their attendance at the session of their respective houses, and in going to and returning from the same; and for any speech or debate in either house, they shall not be questioned in any other place.

2. Restrictions No Senator or Representative shall, during the time for which he was elected, be appointed to any civil office under the authority of the United States, which shall have been created, or the emoluments whereof shall have been increased, during such time; and no person holding any office under the United States shall be a member of either house during his continuance in office.

Section 7. How a Bill Becomes a Law

1. Tax Bills All bills for raising revenue shall originate in the House of Representatives; but the Senate may propose or concur with amendments as on other bills.

2. Lawmaking Process Every bill which shall have passed the House of Representatives and the Senate shall, before it become a law, be presented to the President of the United States; if he approves he shall sign it, but if not he shall return it with his objections to that house in which it shall have originated, who shall enter the objections at large on their journal, and proceed to reconsider it. If after such reconsideration two thirds of that house shall agree to pass the bill, it shall be sent, together with the objections, to the other house, by which it shall likewise be reconsidered, and if approved by two thirds of that house, it shall become a law. But in all such cases the votes of both houses shall be determined by yeas and nays, and the names of the persons voting for and against the bill shall be entered on the journal of each house respectively. If any bill shall not be returned by the President within ten days (Sundays excepted) after it shall have been presented to him, the same shall be a law, in like manner as if he had signed it, unless the Congress by their adjournment prevent its return, in which case it shall not be a law.

3. ROLE OF THE PRESIDENT Every order, resolution, or vote to which the concurrence of the Senate and House of Representatives may be necessary (except on a question of adjournment) shall be presented to the President of the United States; and before the same shall take effect, shall be approved by him, or being disapproved by him, shall be repassed by two thirds of the Senate and House of Representatives, according to the rules and limitations prescribed in the case of a bill.

How a Bill in Congress Becomes a Law

1. A bill is introduced in the House or the Senate and referred to a standing committee for consideration.

2. A bill may be reported out of committee with or without changes—or it may be shelved.

3. Either house of Congress debates the bill and may make revisions. If passed, the bill is sent to the other house.

4. If the House and the Senate pass different versions of a bill, both versions go to a conference committee to work out the differences.

5. The conference committee submits a single version of the bill to the House and the Senate.

6. If both houses accept the compromise version, the bill is sent to the president to be signed.

7. If the president signs the bill, it becomes law.

8. If the president vetoes the bill, the House and the Senate may override the veto by a vote of two thirds of the members present in each house, and then the bill becomes law.

SKILLBUILDER Interpreting Charts
How is the constitutional principle of checks and balances reflected in the process of a bill's becoming a law?

Constitutional Insight **Section 8** The powers given to Congress are in Section 8 of Article 1. The first 17 clauses of Section 8 are often called the enumerated powers because they name individually Congress's specific powers. These powers deal with issues ranging from taxation and the national debt to calling out the armed forces of the various states to governing the nation's capital district (Washington, D.C.).

The 18th and final clause is different. It gives Congress the power to do what is "necessary and proper" to carry out the enumurated powers. Thus, the enumerated powers of Congress "to lay and collect taxes," "to borrow money," "to regulate commerce," and "to coin money" imply the power to create a bank in order to execute these powers. Early in the country's history, this Elastic Clause, as it has been called, was used by Congress to establish the controversial Bank of the United States in 1791 and the Second Bank of the United States in 1816.

G CRITICAL THINKING
Why do you think the Elastic Clause is still important today?

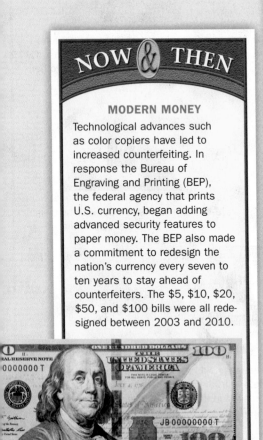

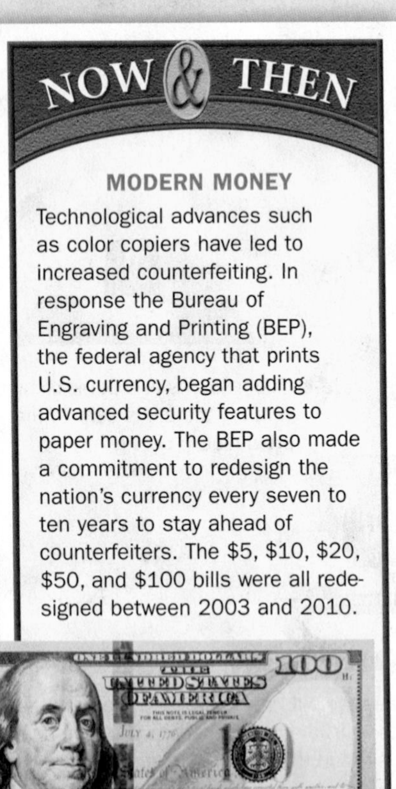

NOW & THEN

MODERN MONEY

Technological advances such as color copiers have led to increased counterfeiting. In response the Bureau of Engraving and Printing (BEP), the federal agency that prints U.S. currency, began adding advanced security features to paper money. The BEP also made a commitment to redesign the nation's currency every seven to ten years to stay ahead of counterfeiters. The $5, $10, $20, $50, and $100 bills were all redesigned between 2003 and 2010.

Section 8. Powers Granted to Congress

1. Taxation The Congress shall have power to lay and collect taxes, duties, imposts and excises, to pay the debts and provide for the common defense and general welfare of the United States; but all duties, imposts and excises shall be uniform throughout the United States;

2. Credit To borrow money on the credit of the United States;

3. Commerce To regulate commerce with foreign nations, and among the several states, and with the Indian tribes;

4. Naturalization, Bankruptcy To establish a uniform rule of naturalization, and uniform laws on the subject of bankruptcies throughout the United States;

5. Money To coin money, regulate the value thereof, and of foreign coin, and fix the standard of weights and measures;

6. Counterfeiting To provide for the punishment of counterfeiting the securities and current coin of the United States;

7. Post Office To establish post offices and post roads;

8. Patents, Copyrights To promote the progress of science and useful arts, by securing for limited times to authors and inventors the exclusive right to their respective writings and discoveries;

9. Federal Courts To constitute tribunals inferior to the Supreme Court;

10. International Law To define and punish piracies and felonies committed on the high seas, and offenses against the law of nations;

11. War To declare war, grant letters of marque and reprisal, and make rules concerning captures on land and water;

12. Army To raise and support armies, but no appropriation of money to that use shall be for a longer term than two years;

13. Navy To provide and maintain a navy;

14. Regulation of Armed Forces To make rules for the government and regulation of the land and naval forces;

15. Militia To provide for calling forth the militia to execute the laws of the Union, suppress insurrections and repel invasions;

16. Regulations for Militia To provide for organizing, arming, and disciplining the militia, and for governing such part of them as may be employed in the service of the United States, reserving to the states respectively the appointment of the officers, and the authority of training the militia according to the discipline prescribed by Congress;

17. District of Columbia To exercise exclusive legislation in all cases whatsoever, over such district (not exceeding ten miles square) as may, by cession of particular states, and the acceptance of Congress, become the seat of the government of the United States, and to exercise like authority over all places purchased by the consent of the legislature of the state in which the same shall be, for the erection of forts, magazines, arsenals, dockyards, and other needful buildings;—and

18. Elastic Clause To make all laws which shall be necessary and proper for carrying into execution the foregoing powers, and all other powers vested by this Constitution in the government of the United States, or in any department or officer thereof.

SECTION 9. POWERS DENIED CONGRESS

~~**1. SLAVE TRADE** The migration or importation of such persons as any of the states now existing shall think proper to admit, shall not be prohibited by the Congress prior to the year one thousand eight hundred and eight, but a tax or duty may be imposed on such importation, not exceeding ten dollars for each person.~~

2. HABEAS CORPUS The privilege of the writ of habeas corpus shall not be suspended, unless when in cases of rebellion or invasion the public safety may require it.

3. ILLEGAL PUNISHMENT No bill of attainder or ex post facto law shall be passed.

4. DIRECT TAXES No capitation, ~~or other direct, tax~~ shall be laid, ~~unless in proportion to the census or enumeration herein before directed to be taken.~~

5. EXPORT TAXES No tax or duty shall be laid on articles exported from any state.

6. NO FAVORITES No preference shall be given by any regulation of commerce or revenue to the ports of one state over those of another: nor shall vessels bound to, or from, one state be obliged to enter, clear, or pay duties in another.

7. PUBLIC MONEY No money shall be drawn from the treasury, but in consequence of appropriations made by law; and a regular statement and account of the receipts and expenditures of all public money shall be published from time to time.

8. TITLES OF NOBILITY No title of nobility shall be granted by the United States: and no person holding any office of profit or trust under them shall, without the consent of the Congress, accept of any present, emolument, office, or title, of any kind whatever, from any king, prince, or foreign state.

SECTION 10. POWERS DENIED THE STATES

1. RESTRICTIONS No state shall enter into any treaty, alliance, or confederation; grant letters of marque and reprisal; coin money; emit bills of credit; make anything but gold and silver coin a tender in payment of debts; pass any bill of attainder, ex post facto law, or law impairing the obligation of contracts, or grant any title of nobility.

2. IMPORT AND EXPORT TAXES No state shall, without the consent of the Congress, lay any imposts or duties on imports or exports, except what may be absolutely necessary for executing its inspection laws; and the net produce of all duties and imposts, laid by any state on imports or exports, shall be for the use of the treasury of the United States; and all such laws shall be subject to the revision and control of the Congress.

Constitutional Insight Section 9

Why didn't the framers include a bill of rights in the original Constitution? Actually, they did. Article 1, Section 9, defines limits on the powers of Congress, just as the first ten amendments (which we call the Bill of Rights) do. While some of the provisions focus on such issues as slavery and taxation, there are three explicit prohibitions dealing with citizens' rights:

- *Writ of habeas corpus.* Section 9, Clause 2 says that, except in time of rebellion or invasion, Congress cannot suspend people's right to a writ of habeas corpus. This means that people cannot be held in prison or jail without being formally charged with a crime.
- *Bill of attainder.* Clause 3 prohibits the passage of any law that convicts or punishes a person directly and without a trial. Any legislative action that would punish someone without recourse to a court of law is called a bill of attainder.
- *Ex post facto law.* The same clause prohibits ex post facto laws. Such a law would punish a person for an act that was legal when it was performed.

The fact that these particular rights were protected by the original document issued by the framers reflects both the framers' experiences during the Revolution and their fear of excessive government power.

H CRITICAL THINKING

Why are American citizens today so intent on having protections against government violations of their rights?

3. Peacetime and War Restraints No state shall, without the consent of Congress, lay any duty of tonnage, keep troops or ships of war in time of peace, enter into any agreement or compact with another state, or with a foreign power, or engage in war, unless actually invaded, or in such imminent danger as will not admit of delay.

ARTICLE 2. *The Executive*

Section 1. The Presidency

1. Terms of Office The executive power shall be vested in a President of the United States of America. He shall hold his office during the term of four years and, together with the Vice-President, chosen for the same term, be elected as follows:

2. Electoral College Each state shall appoint, in such manner as the legislature thereof may direct, a number of electors, equal to the whole number of Senators and Representatives to which the state may be entitled in the Congress; but no Senator or Representative, or person holding an office of trust or profit under the United States, shall be appointed an elector.

~~**3. Former Method of Electing President** The electors shall meet in their respective states, and vote by ballot for two persons, of whom one at least shall not be an inhabitant of the same state with themselves. And they shall make a list of all the persons voted for, and of the number of votes for each; which list they shall sign and certify, and transmit sealed to the seat of the government of the United States, directed to the President of the Senate. The President of the Senate shall, in the presence of the Senate and House of Representatives, open all the certificates, and the votes shall then be counted. The person having the greatest number of votes shall be the President, if such number be a majority of the whole number of electors appointed; and if there be more than one who have such majority, and have an equal number of votes, then the House of Representatives shall immediately choose by ballot one of them for President; and if no person have a majority, then from the five highest on the list the said house shall in like manner choose the President. But in choosing the President, the votes shall be taken by states, the representation from each state having one vote; a quorum for this purpose shall consist of a member or members from two thirds of the states, and a majority of all the states shall be necessary to a choice. In every case, after the choice of the President, the person having the greatest number of votes of the electors shall be the Vice-President. But if there should remain two or more who have equal votes, the Senate shall choose from them by ballot the Vice-President.~~

4. Election Day The Congress may determine the time of choosing the electors, and the day on which they shall give their votes; which day shall be the same throughout the United States.

ARTICLE 2

Constitutional Insight **Section 1.1**
What exactly is "executive power"? We know the president has it, but nowhere is it explicitly defined. It is most often defined as the power to carry out the laws of the land, but of course no one person can handle such a chore alone. A more appropriate definition is found in Section 3 of this article, which empowers the president to "take care that the laws be faithfully executed." In this sense, the president is the chief administrator.

I CRITICAL THINKING
Why is it important to have an executive who is the chief administrator?

5. Qualifications No person except a natural-born citizen, ~~or a citizen of the United States at the time of the adoption of this Constitution,~~ shall be eligible to the office of President; neither shall any person be eligible to that office who shall not have attained to the age of thirty-five years, and been fourteen years a resident within the United States.

6. Succession In case of the removal of the President from office, or of his death, resignation, or inability to discharge the powers and duties of the said office, the same shall devolve on the Vice-President, and the Congress may by law provide for the case of removal, death, resignation, or inability, both of the President and Vice-President, declaring what officer shall then act as President, and such officer shall act accordingly, until the disability be removed, or a President shall be elected.

7. Salary The President shall, at stated times, receive for his services a compensation, which shall neither be increased nor diminished during the period for which he shall have been elected, and he shall not receive within that period any other emolument from the United States, or any of them.

8. Oath of Office Before he enter on the execution of his office, he shall take the following oath or affirmation:—"I do solemnly swear (or affirm) that I will faithfully execute the office of President of the United States, and will to the best of my ability, preserve, protect and defend the Constitution of the United States."

Section 2. Powers of the President

1. Military Powers The President shall be commander in chief of the army and navy of the United States, and of the militia of the several states, when called into the actual service of the United States; he may require the opinion, in writing, of the principal officer in each of the executive departments, upon any subject relating to the duties of their respective offices, and he shall have power to grant reprieves and pardons for offenses against the United States, except in cases of impeachment.

2. Treaties, Appointments He shall have power, by and with the advice and consent of the Senate, to make treaties, provided two thirds of the Senators present concur; and he shall nominate, and by and with the advice and consent of the Senate, shall appoint ambassadors, other public ministers and consuls, judges of the Supreme Court, and all other officers of the United States, whose appointments are not herein otherwise provided for, and which shall be established by law; but the Congress may by law vest the appointment of such inferior officers, as they think proper, in the President alone, in the courts of law, or in the heads of departments.

3. Vacancies The President shall have power to fill up all vacancies that may happen during the recess of the Senate, by granting commissions which shall expire at the end of their next session.

Constitutional Insight **Section 1.6**
What happens when the vice-president succeeds a dead or incapacitated president? Section 1.6 provides that the vice-president shall assume the powers and duties of the presidential office. But until the Twenty-fifth Amendment was added to the Constitution in 1967, there was no explicit statement in the document that the vice-president is to become president. That procedure owes its origin to John Tyler, the tenth president of the United States, who in 1841 succeeded William Henry Harrison—the first president to die in office. Tyler decided to take the oath of office and assume the title of president of the United States. Congress voted to go along with his decision, and the practice was repeated after Lincoln was assassinated. It would take another century for the written provisions of the Constitution to catch up with the practice.

J CRITICAL THINKING
Why is it important to know the order of succession if a president dies in office?

Constitutional Insight **Section 2.1**
Just how much authority does the president have as "commander in chief" of the armed forces? The president has the power to give orders to American military forces. There have been several instances in U.S. history when presidents have used that authority in spite of congressional wishes.

President Harry Truman involved the armed forces of the United States in the Korean War from 1950 to 1953 without a congressional declaration of war.

Reacting to criticism of the Vietnam War, Congress in 1973 enacted the War Powers Resolution, making the president more accountable to Congress for any military actions he or she might take. Every president since Richard Nixon has called the resolution unconstitutional. Nevertheless, every president has reported to Congress within 48 hours of sending troops into an international crisis, as is required by the War Powers Resolution.

K CRITICAL THINKING
Why is it important that the commander in chief of the armed forces of the United States be a civilian (the president) rather than a military general?

Constitutional Insight **Section 3**
Is it necessary for the president to deliver a State of the Union address before a joint session of Congress at the start of each legislative year? The Constitution requires only that the president report to Congress on the state of the Union from time to time, and nowhere does it call for an annual address. In 1913, President Woodrow Wilson wanted to influence Congress to take action without delay on some legislation that he thought was important. Wilson revived the tradition—which had been discontinued by Jefferson—of delivering the State of the Union address in person.

L CRITICAL THINKING
How does the president use the State of the Union address today?

Constitutional Insight **Section 4**
Have high-level public officials ever been impeached? In all of American history, the House has impeached two presidents, and neither had to leave office. In 1868, the Senate found President Andrew Johnson not guilty by one vote after the House impeached him, charging him with violating a Congressional Act. In 1999, senators acquitted President Bill Clinton after the House impeached him with charges of lying under oath and obstructing justice in the attempted cover-up of a White House scandal.

The only other president to come close to impeachment was Richard Nixon. In 1974, the House Judiciary Committee, in what is the first step of the impeachment process, recommended three articles of impeachment against Nixon for his role in the infamous Watergate scandal. Before the full House could vote for or against the articles of impeachment, however, Nixon resigned from office.

M CRITICAL THINKING
Why do you think the framers of the Constitution created such an elaborate and seemingly difficult procedure for removing a sitting president?

SECTION 3. PRESIDENTIAL DUTIES He shall from time to time give to the Congress information of the state of the Union, and recommend to their consideration such measures as he shall judge necessary and expedient; he may, on extraordinary occasions, convene both houses, or either of them, and in case of disagreement between them, with respect to the time of adjournment, he may adjourn them to such time as he shall think proper; he shall receive ambassadors and other public ministers; he shall take care that the laws be faithfully executed, and shall commission all the officers of the United States.

SECTION 4. IMPEACHMENT The President, Vice-President and all civil officers of the United States shall be removed from office on impeachment for, and conviction of, treason, bribery, or other high crimes and misdemeanors.

(above) **Rep. Henry Hyde, chairman of the House Judiciary Committee, swears in Independent Counsel Kenneth Starr during the Committee's hearings on impeachment charges against President Bill Clinton in 1998;** ***(right)*** **President Andrew Johnson is handed the articles of impeachment before his trial in 1868.**

ARTICLE 3. *The Judiciary*

SECTION 1. FEDERAL COURTS AND JUDGES The judicial power of the United States shall be vested in one Supreme Court, and in such inferior courts as the Congress may from time to time ordain and establish. The judges, both of the Supreme and inferior courts, shall hold their offices during good behavior, and shall, at stated times, receive for their services a compensation, which shall not be diminished during their continuance in office.

Section 2. The Courts' Authority

1. General Authority The judicial power shall extend to all cases, in law and equity, arising under this Constitution, the laws of the United States, and treaties made, or which shall be made, under their authority;—to all cases affecting ambassadors, other public ministers and consuls;—to all cases of admiralty and maritime jurisdiction;—to controversies to which the United States shall be a party;—to controversies between two or more states;~~—between a state and citizens of another state;—~~between citizens of different states;—between citizens of the same state claiming lands under grants of different states, ~~and between a state, or the citizens thereof, and foreign states, citizens or subjects.~~

2. Supreme Court In all cases affecting ambassadors, other public ministers and consuls, and those in which a state shall be party, the Supreme Court shall have original jurisdiction. In all the other cases before mentioned, the Supreme Court shall have appellate jurisdiction, both as to law and fact, with such exceptions, and under such regulations, as the Congress shall make.

3. Trial by Jury The trial of all crimes, except in cases of impeachment, shall be by jury; and such trial shall be held in the state where the said crimes shall have been committed; but when not committed within any state, the trial shall be at such place or places as the Congress may by law have directed.

Section 3. Treason

1. Definition Treason against the United States shall consist only in levying war against them, or in adhering to their enemies, giving them aid and comfort. No person shall be convicted of treason unless on the testimony of two witnesses to the same overt act, or on confession in open court.

2. Punishment The Congress shall have power to declare the punishment of treason, but no attainder of treason shall work corruption of blood, or forfeiture except during the life of the person attainted.

ARTICLE 3

***Constitutional Insight* Section 2.1**
What is judicial review? Is it the same as judicial power? Actually, they are not the same. Judicial power is the authority to hear cases involving disputes over the law or the behavior of people. Judicial review, in contrast, is a court's passing judgment on the constitutionality of a law or government action that is being disputed. Interestingly, nowhere does the Constitution mention judicial review. There are places where it is implied (for example, in Section 2 of Article 6), but the only explicit description of the responsibility of the courts is the reference to judicial power in Section 1 of Article 3. The Supreme Court's power to review laws passed by Congress was explicitly affirmed by the Court itself in *Marbury* v. *Madison*.

N CRITICAL THINKING
Why is judicial review, although not mentioned in the Constitution, an important activity of the Supreme Court?

The Supreme Court of the United States as of August 2010. In the front row (*left to right*) are Associate Justices Clarence Thomas and Antonin Scalia, Chief Justice John Roberts, and Associate Justices Anthony Kennedy and Ruth Bader Ginsburg. In the back row (*left to right*) are Associate Justices Sonia Sotomayor, Stephen Breyer, Samuel Alito, and Elena Kagan. ▼

ARTICLE 4. *Relations Among States*

SECTION 1. STATE ACTS AND RECORDS Full faith and credit shall be given in each state to the public acts, records, and judicial proceedings of every other state. And the Congress may by general laws prescribe the manner in which such acts, records, and proceedings shall be proved, and the effect thereof.

SECTION 2. RIGHTS OF CITIZENS

1. **CITIZENSHIP** The citizens of each state shall be entitled to all privileges and immunities of citizens in the several states.
2. **EXTRADITION** A person charged in any state with treason, felony, or other crime, who shall flee from justice, and be found in another state, shall on demand of the executive authority of the state from which he fled, be delivered up, to be removed to the state having jurisdiction of the crime.
3. ~~**FUGITIVE SLAVES** No person held to service or labor in one state, under the laws thereof, escaping into another, shall, in consequence of any law or regulation therein, be discharged from such service or labor, but shall be delivered up on claim of the party to whom such service or labor may be due.~~

SECTION 3. NEW STATES

1. **ADMISSION** New states may be admitted by the Congress into this Union; but no new state shall be formed or erected within the jurisdiction of any other state; nor any state be formed by the junction of two or more states, or parts of states, without the consent of the legislatures of the states concerned as well as of the Congress.
2. **CONGRESSIONAL AUTHORITY** The Congress shall have power to dispose of and make all needful rules and regulations respecting the territory or other property belonging to the United States; and nothing in this Constitution shall be so construed as to prejudice any claims of the United States, or of any particular state.

SECTION 4. GUARANTEES TO THE STATES The United States shall guarantee to every state in this Union a republican form of government, and shall protect each of them against invasion; and on application of the legislature, or of the executive (when the legislature cannot be convened), against domestic violence.

ARTICLE 5. *Amending the Constitution*

The Congress, whenever two thirds of both houses shall deem it necessary, shall propose amendments to this Constitution, or, on the application of the legislatures of two thirds of the several states, shall call a convention for proposing amendments, which, in either case, shall be valid to all intents and purposes, as part of this Constitution, when ratified by the legislatures of three fourths of the several states, or by conventions in three fourths thereof, as the one or the other mode of ratification may be proposed by the Congress; ~~provided that no amendment which may be made prior to the year one thousand eight hundred and eight shall in any manner affect the first and fourth clauses in the ninth section of the first article;~~ and that no state, without its consent, shall be deprived of its equal suffrage in the Senate.

ARTICLE 4

***Constitutional Insight* Section 2.1**
Why do college students attending public universities outside their state of residence have to pay higher tuition fees?
The Supreme Court has interpreted the "privileges and immunities" clause to allow higher tuition fees (and fees for hunting permits, etc.) for nonresidents when a state can give a "substantial reason" for the difference. Since state colleges and universities receive some financial support from the states' taxpayers, the difference is regarded as justified in most states. If a student establishes residency in the state, he or she can pay in-state tuition after one year.

O CRITICAL THINKING
Do you think it is fair that a nonresident must pay higher tuition fees at a state college than a resident of the state must pay? Explain.

***Constitutional Insight* Section 3.1**
Should there be a West Virginia? The Constitution states that "no new state shall be formed or erected within the jurisdiction of any other state" without the permission of the legislature of the state involved and of the Congress. Vermont, Kentucky, Tennessee, and Maine were created from territory taken from existing states, with the approval of the sitting legislatures.

West Virginia, however, is a different story. During the Civil War, the residents of the westernmost counties of Virginia were angry with their state's decision to secede from the Union. They petitioned Congress to have their counties declared a distinct state. Congress agreed, and so the state of West Virginia was created. After the Civil War, the legislature of Virginia gave its formal approval, perhaps because it was in no position to dispute the matter.

P CRITICAL THINKING
Suppose a section of Texas should decide to become a new state today. Could it do this? Why or why not?

ARTICLE 6. *Supremacy of the National Government*

SECTION 1. VALID DEBTS All debts contracted and engagements entered into, before the adoption of this Constitution, shall be as valid against the United States under this Constitution, as under the Confederation.

SECTION 2. SUPREME LAW This Constitution, and the laws of the United States which shall be made in pursuance thereof; and all treaties made, or which shall be made, under the authority of the United States, shall be the supreme law of the land; and the judges in every state shall be bound thereby, anything in the constitution or laws of any state to the contrary notwithstanding.

SECTION 3. LOYALTY TO CONSTITUTION The Senators and Representatives before mentioned, and the members of the several state legislatures, and all executive and judicial officers, both of the United States and of the several states, shall be bound by oath or affirmation to support this Constitution; but no religious test shall ever be required as a qualification to any office or public trust under the United States.

ARTICLE 7. *Ratification*

The ratification of the conventions of nine states shall be sufficient for the establishment of this Constitution between the states so ratifying the same. Done in convention by the unanimous consent of the states present, the seventeenth day of September in the year of our Lord one thousand seven hundred and eighty-seven and of the independence of the United States of America the twelfth. In witness whereof we have hereunto subscribed our names.

George Washington—President and deputy from Virginia

Delaware: *George Read, Gunning Bedford, Jr., John Dickinson, Richard Bassett, Jacob Broom*

Maryland: *James McHenry, Dan of St. Thomas Jenifer, Daniel Carroll*

Virginia: *John Blair, James Madison, Jr.*

North Carolina: *William Blount, Richard Dobbs Spaight, Hugh Williamson*

South Carolina: *John Rutledge, Charles Cotesworth Pinckney, Charles Pinckney, Pierce Butler*

Georgia: *William Few, Abraham Baldwin*

New Hampshire: *John Langdon, Nicholas Gilman*

Massachusetts: *Nathaniel Gorham, Rufus King*

Connecticut: *William Samuel Johnson, Roger Sherman*

New York: *Alexander Hamilton*

New Jersey: *William Livingston, David Brearley, William Paterson, Jonathan Dayton*

Pennsylvania: *Benjamin Franklin, Thomas Mifflin, Robert Morris, George Clymer, Thomas FitzSimons, Jared Ingersoll, James Wilson, Gouverneur Morris*

ARTICLE 6

Constitutional Insight **Section 2** *Just how "supreme" is the "law of the land"?* The Constitution and all federal laws and treaties are the highest law of the land. (To be supreme, federal laws must be constitutional.) All state constitutions and laws and all local laws rank below national law and cannot be enforced if they contradict national law. For example, if the United States enters into a treaty protecting migratory Canadian birds, the states must change their laws to fit the provisions of that agreement. That was the decision of the Supreme Court in the case of *Missouri* v. *Holland* (1920). The state of Missouri argued that the national government could not interfere with its power to regulate hunting within its borders, but the Supreme Court concluded that the treaty was a valid exercise of national power and therefore took priority over state and local laws. The states had to adjust their rules and regulations accordingly.

Q CRITICAL THINKING

What would happen if the national law were not supreme?

ARTICLE 7

Constitutional Insight *Why was ratification by only 9 states sufficient to put the Constitution into effect?* In taking such a momentous step as replacing one constitution (the Articles of Confederation) with another, the framers might have been expected to require the agreement of all 13 states. But the framers were political realists. They knew that they would have a difficult time winning approval from all 13 states. But they also knew that they had a good chance of getting 9 or 10 of the states "on board" and that once that happened, the rest would follow. Their strategy worked, but just barely. Although they had the approval of 9 states by the end of June 1788, 2 of the most important states—Virginia and New York—had not yet decided to ratify. Without the approval of these influential states, the new government would have had a difficult time surviving. Finally, by the end of July, both had given their blessing to the new constitution, but not without intense debate.

And then there was the last holdout—Rhode Island. Not only had Rhode Island refused to send delegates to the Constitutional Convention in 1787, but it turned down ratification several times before finally giving its approval in 1790 under a cloud of economic and even military threats from neighboring states.

R CRITICAL THINKING

Do you think all 50 states would ratify the Constitution today? Why or why not?

The Bill of Rights

and Amendments 11–27

BILL OF RIGHTS

Constitutional Insight **Amendment 1**
Do Americans have an absolute right to free speech? The right to free speech is not without limits. In the case of *Schenck* v. *United States* (1919), Justice Oliver Wendell Holmes wrote that this right does "not protect a man in falsely shouting fire in a theatre and causing a panic." Thus, there are some forms of speech that are not protected by the First Amendment, and Congress is allowed to make laws regarding certain types of expression.

A CRITICAL THINKING
Why is there controversy over freedom of speech today?

Constitutional Insight **Amendment 4**
Can the police search your car without a court-issued search warrant when they stop you for speeding? The answer, according to Supreme Court decisions, depends on whether they have good reasons—called "probable cause"—for doing so. If a state trooper notices bloody clothing on the back seat of a vehicle she stops for a traffic violation, there might be probable cause for her to insist on searching the vehicle. There is probably not sufficient reason for a search if the trooper is merely suspicious of the driver because of the way he is acting. In such cases, the trooper may make a casual request, such as "Do you mind if I look inside your vehicle?" If the answer is no, then according to the Court, the driver has waived his or her constitutional right against unreasonable searches.

B CRITICAL THINKING
Why do you think the right against unreasonable searches and seizures is highly important to most people?

Constitutional Insight **Amendment 5**
Can you be tried twice for the same offense? The prohibition against "double jeopardy" protects you from having the same charge twice brought against you for the same offense, but you can be tried on different charges related to that offense.

C CRITICAL THINKING
What do you think could happen if a person could be tried twice for the same offense?

Amendments 1–10

Proposed by Congress September 25, 1789. Ratified December 15, 1791.

AMENDMENT 1. RELIGIOUS AND POLITICAL FREEDOM (1791)
Congress shall make no law respecting an establishment of religion, or prohibiting the free exercise thereof; or abridging the freedom of speech, or of the press; or the right of the people peaceably to assemble, and to petition the government for a redress of grievances.

AMENDMENT 2. RIGHT TO BEAR ARMS (1791) A well-regulated militia being necessary to the security of a free state, the right of the people to keep and bear arms shall not be infringed.

AMENDMENT 3. QUARTERING TROOPS (1791) No soldier shall, in time of peace, be quartered in any house without the consent of the owner, nor in time of war, but in a manner to be prescribed by law.

AMENDMENT 4. SEARCH AND SEIZURE (1791) The right of the people to be secure in their persons, houses, papers, and effects, against unreasonable searches and seizures, shall not be violated, and no warrants shall issue, but upon probable cause, supported by oath or affirmation, and particularly describing the place to be searched, and the persons or things to be seized.

AMENDMENT 5. RIGHTS OF ACCUSED PERSONS (1791) No person shall be held to answer for a capital or otherwise infamous crime, unless on a presentment or indictment of a grand jury, except in cases arising in the land or naval forces, or in the militia, when in actual service in time of war or public danger; nor shall any person be subject for the same offense to be twice put in jeopardy of life or limb; nor shall be compelled in any criminal case to be a witness against himself, nor be deprived of life, liberty, or property, without due process of law; nor shall private property be taken for public use, without just compensation.

Analyzing *Political Cartoons*

"THE FEDERAL EDIFICE"
This 1788 cartoon celebrated the ratification of the Constitution by New York, the 11th state to ratify it. This left only North Carolina and Rhode Island to complete all 13 pillars of the federal structure.

SKILLBUILDER Analyzing Political Cartoons
1. What details in the cartoon convey the unity of the states who have voted for ratification?
2. How does the cartoonist contrast the states who have voted for ratification with those who have not? What message does this convey?

SEE SKILLBUILDER HANDBOOK, PAGE R24.

AMENDMENT 6. RIGHT TO A SPEEDY, PUBLIC TRIAL (1791) In all criminal prosecutions, the accused shall enjoy the right to a speedy and public trial, by an impartial jury of the state and district wherein the crime shall have been committed, which district shall have been previously ascertained by law, and to be informed of the nature and cause of the accusation; to be confronted with the witnesses against him; to have compulsory process for obtaining witnesses in his favor, and to have the assistance of counsel for his defense.

AMENDMENT 7. TRIAL BY JURY IN CIVIL CASES (1791) In suits at common law, where the value in controversy shall exceed twenty dollars, the right of trial by jury shall be preserved, and no fact tried by a jury shall be otherwise reexamined in any court of the United States, than according to the rules of the common law.

AMENDMENT 8. LIMITS OF FINES AND PUNISHMENTS (1791) Excessive bail shall not be required, nor excessive fines imposed, nor cruel and unusual punishments inflicted.

AMENDMENT 9. RIGHTS OF PEOPLE (1791) The enumeration in the Constitution, of certain rights, shall not be construed to deny or disparage others retained by the people.

AMENDMENT 10. POWERS OF STATES AND PEOPLE (1791) The powers not delegated to the United States by the Constitution, nor prohibited by it to the states, are reserved to the states respectively, or to the people.

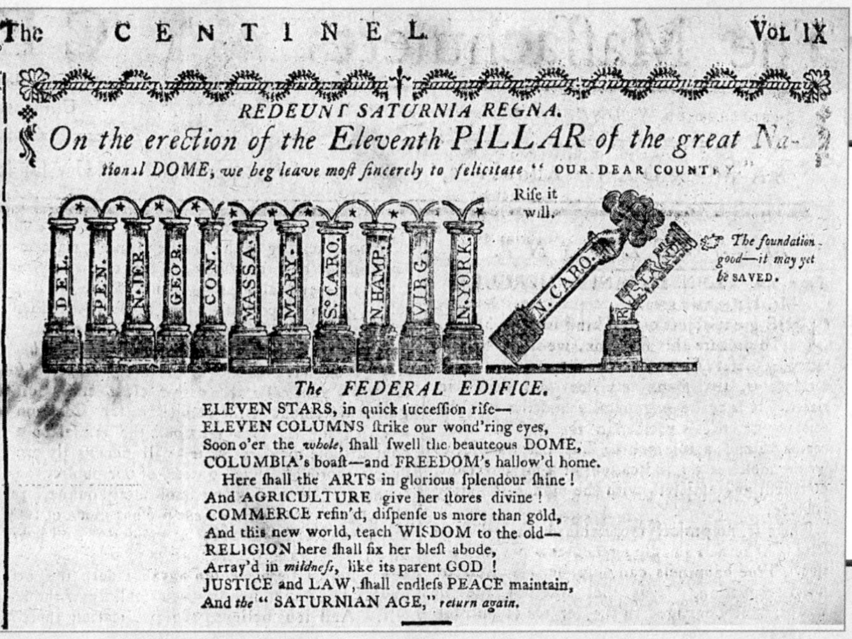

The CENTINEL. VOL IX

REDEUNT SATURNIA REGNA.

On the erection of the Eleventh PILLAR of the great National DOME, we beg leave moſt ſincerely to felicitate "OUR DEAR COUNTRY."

The FEDERAL EDIFICE.

ELEVEN STARS, in quick ſucceſſion riſe—
ELEVEN COLUMNS ſtrike our wond'ring eyes,
Soon o'er the *whole*, ſhall ſwell the beauteous DOME,
COLUMBIA's boaſt—and FREEDOM's hallow'd home.
Here ſhall the ARTS in glorious ſplendour ſhine!
And AGRICULTURE give her ſtores divine!
COMMERCE refin'd, diſpenſe us more than gold,
And this new world, teach WISDOM to the old—
RELIGION here ſhall fix her bleſt abode,
Array'd in *mildneſs*, like its parent GOD!
JUSTICE and LAW, ſhall endleſs PEACE maintain,
And *the* "SATURNIAN AGE," *return again.*

Constitutional Insight **Amendment 6**
What are the Miranda rights? The term comes from the Supreme Court's decision in *Miranda* v. *Arizona* (1966), in which the justices established basic rules that the police must follow when questioning a suspect. If suspected of a crime, you must be told that you have a right to remain silent and that anything you say "can and will" be used against you. You also need to be informed that you have a right to an attorney and that the attorney may be present during questioning.

D CRITICAL THINKING
How do the Miranda rights protect you?

Constitutional Insight **Amendment 7**
What are the "rules of the common law"? The common law is the body of legal practices and decrees developed in England and English-speaking America from A.D. 1066 through the present. It includes Magna Carta (1215), which acknowledges versions of rights affirmed in the Fifth, Sixth, and Seventh Amendments, as well as the English Bill of Rights (1689), which codified rights asserted in the First, Second, Seventh, and Eighth Amendments. The common law also includes the decisions and published opinions of state and federal appeals courts, including the U.S. Supreme Court.

Constitutional Insight **Amendment 9**
Do you have a right to privacy? Until 1965, no such right had ever been explicitly stated by the courts. That year, in the case of *Griswold* v. *Connecticut*, the Court said there is an implied right of American citizens to make certain personal choices without interference from the government; this case concerned the right to use birth control. Years later, in *Roe* v. *Wade* (1973), the same logic was used to declare unconstitutional a Texas law restricting a woman's right to an abortion in the first stages of pregnancy. Since that decision, both the right to privacy and abortion rights have become the focus of major political controversies.

E CRITICAL THINKING
How do you define the right to privacy?

Amendments 11–27

AMENDMENT 11. LAWSUITS AGAINST STATES (1795) Passed by Congress March 4, 1794. Ratified February 7, 1795.

Note: Article 3, Section 2, of the Constitution was modified by the Eleventh Amendment.

The Judicial power of the United States shall not be construed to extend to any suit in law or equity, commenced or prosecuted against one of the United States by citizens of another state, or by citizens or subjects of any foreign state.

AMENDMENT 12. ELECTION OF EXECUTIVES (1804) Passed by Congress December 9, 1803. Ratified June 15, 1804.

Note: A portion of Article 2, Section 1, of the Constitution was superseded by the Twelfth Amendment.

The electors shall meet in their respective states and vote by ballot for President and Vice-President, one of whom, at least, shall not be an inhabitant of the same state with themselves; they shall name in their ballots the person voted for as President, and in distinct ballots the person voted for as Vice-President, and they shall make distinct lists of all persons voted for as President, and of all persons voted for as Vice-President, and of the number of votes for each, which lists they shall sign and certify, and transmit sealed to the seat of the government of the United States, directed to the President of the Senate;—the President of the Senate shall, in the presence of the Senate and House of Representatives, open all the certificates and the votes shall then be counted;—the person having the greatest number of votes for President shall be the President, if such number be a majority of the whole number of electors appointed; and if no person have such majority, then from the persons having the highest numbers not exceeding three on the list of those voted for as President, the House of Representatives shall choose immediately, by ballot, the President. But in choosing the President, the votes shall be taken by states, the representation from each state having one vote; a quorum for this purpose shall consist of a member or members from two thirds of the states, and a majority of all the states shall be necessary to a choice. And if the House of Representatives shall not choose a President whenever the right of choice shall devolve upon them, ~~before the fourth day of March next following,~~ then the Vice-President shall act as President, as in the case of the death or other constitutional disability of the President. The person having the greatest number of votes as Vice-President shall be the Vice-President, if such number be a majority of the whole number of electors appointed, and if no person have a majority, then from the two highest numbers on the list, the Senate shall choose the Vice-President; a quorum for the purpose shall consist of two thirds of the whole number of Senators, and a majority of the whole number shall be necessary to a choice. But no person constitutionally ineligible to the office of President shall be eligible to that of Vice-President of the United States.

AMENDMENT 13. SLAVERY ABOLISHED (1865) Passed by Congress January 31, 1865. Ratified December 6, 1865.

Note: A portion of Article 4, Section 2, of the Constitution was superseded by the Thirteenth Amendment.

Constitutional Insight **Amendment 12**
How did the election of 1800 lead to the Twelfth Amendment? The election ended in a tie vote between the Republican running mates. The election was decided in Jefferson's favor on the House's 36th ballot. Almost immediately Alexander Hamilton and others designed an amendment that established that the presidential electors would vote for both a presidential and a vice-presidential candidate. This amendment prevents a repeat of the problem experienced in the 1800 election.

F CRITICAL THINKING
Why is the Twelfth Amendment important?

ELECTION REFORM

A new wave of electoral reform efforts was triggered by the controversial presidential election of 2000, in which George W. Bush's narrow victory over Al Gore left many Americans questioning the system in which a candidate can lose the popular vote but win the election.

Eliminating or reworking the electoral college has been historically the most frequently proposed constitutional amendment. Other reform proposals have included improving access to polling places by allowing voting on weekend hours or making Election Day a national holiday. Still other proposals would modernize inaccurate polling and counting machines or replace them with computer stations or online voting.

SECTION 1 Neither slavery nor involuntary servitude, except as a punishment for crime whereof the party shall have been duly convicted, shall exist within the United States, or any place subject to their jurisdiction.

SECTION 2 Congress shall have power to enforce this article by appropriate legislation.

AMENDMENT 14. CIVIL RIGHTS (1868) Passed by Congress June 13, 1866. Ratified July 9, 1868.

Note: Article 1, Section 2, of the Constitution was modified by Section 2 of the Fourteenth Amendment.

SECTION 1 All persons born or naturalized in the United States, and subject to the jurisdiction thereof, are citizens of the United States and of the state wherein they reside. No state shall make or enforce any law which shall abridge the privileges or immunities of citizens of the United States; nor shall any state deprive any person of life, liberty, or property, without due process of law; nor deny to any person within its jurisdiction the equal protection of the laws.

SECTION 2 Representatives shall be apportioned among the several states according to their respective numbers, counting the whole number of persons in each state, excluding Indians not taxed. But when the right to vote at any election for the choice of electors for President and Vice-President of the United States, Representatives in Congress, the executive and judicial officers of a state, or the members of the legislature thereof, is denied to any of the male inhabitants of such state, being twenty-one years of age, and citizens of the United States, or in any way abridged, except for participation in rebellion, or other crime, the basis of representation therein shall be reduced in the proportion which the number of such male citizens shall bear to the whole number of male citizens twenty-one years of age in such state.

SECTION 3 No person shall be a Senator or Representative in Congress, or elector of President and Vice-President, or hold any office, civil or military, under the United States, or under any state, who, having previously taken an oath, as a member of Congress, or as an officer of the United States, or as a member of any state legislature, or as an executive or judicial officer of any state, to support the Constitution of the United States, shall have engaged in insurrection or rebellion against the same, or given aid or comfort to the enemies thereof. But Congress may, by a vote of two thirds of each house, remove such disability.

SECTION 4 The validity of the public debt of the United States, authorized by law, including debts incurred for payment of pensions and bounties for services in suppressing insurrection or rebellion, shall not be questioned. But neither the United States nor any state shall assume or pay any debt or obligation incurred in aid of insurrection or rebellion against the United States, or any claim for the loss or emancipation of any slave; but all such debts, obligations and claims shall be held illegal and void.

SECTION 5 The Congress shall have power to enforce, by appropriate legislation, the provisions of this article.

Constitutional Insight **Amendment 14, Section 1** *Which personal status takes priority—that of U.S. citizen or that of state citizen?* The Fourteenth Amendment firmly notes that Americans are citizens of both the nation and the states but that no state can "abridge the privileges or immunities" of U.S. citizens, deprive them "of life, liberty, or property, without due process of law," or deny them "equal protection of the laws."

What does it mean to have "equal protection of the laws"? Equal protection means that the laws are to be applied to all persons in the same way. The legal system may discriminate between persons—treat them differently, or unequally—if there are relevant reasons to do so. For example, a person's income and number of dependents are relevant for how much income tax the person should pay; a person's gender is not. The Supreme Court's 1954 decision in *Brown v. Board of Education of Topeka*, which declared segre-gated public schools unconstitutional, was based on an Equal Protection claim; a child's race is not a relevant reason for the state to assign that child to a particular school.

G CRITICAL THINKING

Do you agree or disagree with the Supreme Court's decision that separate educational facilities are unequal? Explain your position.

The lawyers who successfully challenged segregation in the *Brown* v. *Board of Education* case in 1954 included (*left to right*) George E. C. Hayes, Thurgood Marshall, and James M. Nabrit, Jr.

Amendment 15. Right to Vote (1870) Passed by Congress February 26, 1869. Ratified February 3, 1870.

Section 1 The right of citizens of the United States to vote shall not be denied or abridged by the United States or by any state on account of race, color, or previous condition of servitude.

Section 2 The Congress shall have power to enforce this article by appropriate legislation.

Constitutional Insight **Amendment 15**
Can you be denied the right to vote? The Fifteenth Amendment prohibits the United States or any state from keeping citizens from voting because of race or color or because they were once slaves. However, a person convicted of a crime can be denied the right to vote, as can someone found to be mentally incompetent.

H CRITICAL THINKING
Why do you think so many people do not exercise the right to vote?

Amendment 16. Income Tax (1913) Passed by Congress July 12, 1909. Ratified February 3, 1913.

Note: Article 1, Section 9, of the Constitution was modified by the Sixteenth Amendment.

The Congress shall have power to lay and collect taxes on incomes, from whatever source derived, without apportionment among the several states, and without regard to any census or enumeration.

Constitutional Insight **Amendment 16**
How has the ability of Congress to impose taxes been amended? The Sixteenth Amendment permits a federal income tax and in so doing changes Article 1, Section 9, Clause 4, by stating that Congress has the power to levy an income tax—which is a direct tax—without apportioning such a tax among the states according to their populations.

I CRITICAL THINKING
Do you think Congress should have the power to impose an income tax on the people of the nation? Explain your answer.

Amendment 17. Direct Election of Senators (1913) Passed by Congress May 13, 1912. Ratified April 8, 1913.

Note: Article 1, Section 3, of the Constitution was modified by the Seventeenth Amendment.

Clause 1 The Senate of the United States shall be composed of two Senators from each state, elected by the people thereof, for six years; and each Senator shall have one vote. The electors in each state shall have the qualifications requisite for electors of the most numerous branch of the state legislatures.

Clause 2 When vacancies happen in the representation of any state in the Senate, the executive authority of such state shall issue writs of election to fill such vacancies: Provided, that the legislature of any state may empower the executive thereof to make temporary appointments until the people fill the vacancies by election as the legislature may direct.

Clause 3 This amendment shall not be so construed as to affect the election or term of any Senator chosen before it becomes valid as part of the Constitution.

Constitutional Insight **Amendment 17**
How has the way senators are elected been changed? The Seventeenth Amendment changes Article 1, Section 3, Clause 1, by stating that senators shall be elected by the people of each state rather than by the state legislatures.

J CRITICAL THINKING
Why is the direct election of senators by the people of each state important?

Amendment 18. Prohibition (1919) Passed by Congress December 18, 1917. Ratified January 16, 1919. Repealed by Amendment 21.

~~**Section 1** After one year from the ratification of this article the manufacture, sale, or transportation of intoxicating liquors within, the importation thereof into, or the exportation thereof from the United States and all territory subject to the jurisdiction thereof for beverage purposes is hereby prohibited.~~

~~**Section 2** The Congress and the several states shall have concurrent power to enforce this article by appropriate legislation.~~

~~**Section 3** This article shall be inoperative unless it shall have been ratified as an amendment to the Constitution by the legislatures of the several states, as provided in the Constitution, within seven years from the date of the submission hereof to the states by the Congress.~~

Federal agents enforcing the Eighteenth Amendment prepare to smash containers of illegal whiskey.

Amendment 19. Woman Suffrage (1920) Passed by Congress June 4, 1919. Ratified August 18, 1920.

Clause 1 The right of citizens of the United States to vote shall not be denied or abridged by the United States or by any state on account of sex.

Clause 2 Congress shall have power to enforce this article by appropriate legislation.

Amendment 20. "Lame Duck" Sessions (1933) Passed by Congress March 2, 1932. Ratified January 23, 1933.

Note: Article 1, Section 4, of the Constitution was modified by Section 2 of this amendment. In addition, a portion of the Twelfth Amendment was superseded by Section 3.

Section 1 The terms of the President and Vice-President shall end at noon on the 20th day of January, and the terms of Senators and Representatives at noon on the 3rd day of January, of the years in which such terms would have ended if this article had not been ratified; and the terms of their successors shall then begin.

Section 2 The Congress shall assemble at least once in every year, and such meeting shall begin at noon on the 3rd day of January, unless they shall by law appoint a different day.

Section 3 If, at the time fixed for the beginning of the term of the President, the President elect shall have died, the Vice-President elect shall become President. If a President shall not have been chosen before the time fixed for the beginning of his term, or if the President elect shall have failed to qualify, then the Vice-President elect shall act as President until a President shall have qualified; and the Congress may by law provide for the case wherein neither a President elect nor a Vice-President elect shall have qualified, declaring who shall then act as President, or the manner in which one who is to act shall be selected, and such person shall act accordingly until a President or Vice-President shall have qualified.

Section 4 The Congress may by law provide for the case of the death of any of the persons from whom the House of Representatives may choose a President whenever the right of choice shall have devolved upon them, and for the case of the death of any of the persons from whom the Senate may choose a Vice-President whenever the right of choice shall have devolved upon them.

Section 5 Sections 1 and 2 shall take effect on the 15th day of October following the ratification of this article.

Section 6 This article shall be inoperative unless it shall have been ratified as an amendment to the Constitution by the legislatures of three fourths of the several states within seven years from the date of its submission.

Amendment 21. Repeal of Prohibition (1933) Passed by Congress February 20, 1933. Ratified December 5, 1933.

Section 1 The eighteenth article of amendment to the Constitution of the United States is hereby repealed.

Section 2 The transportation or importation into any state, territory, or possession of the United States for delivery or use therein of intoxicating liquors, in violation of the laws thereof, is hereby prohibited.

Constitutional Insight **Amendment 19**
When did women first get the right to vote in the United States? Women had the right to vote in the state of New Jersey between 1776 and 1807. In the late 19th century, some states and territories began to extend full or limited suffrage to women. Then, in 1920, the Nineteenth Amendment prohibited the United States or any state from denying women the right to vote.

K CRITICAL THINKING
How does the right of women to vote affect politics today?

Constitutional Insight **Amendment 20**
Why is the Twentieth Amendment usually called the "Lame Duck" amendment? A lame duck is a person who continues to hold office after his or her replacement has been elected. Such a person is called a lame duck because he or she no longer has any strong political influence. The Twentieth Amendment reduces the time between the election of a new president and vice-president in November and their assumption of the offices, which it sets at January 20 instead of March 4. It also reduces the time new members of Congress must wait to take their seats from 4 months to about 2 months. They are now seated on January 3 following the November election. As a result, the lame duck period is now quite short.

L CRITICAL THINKING
Why may the framers have specified a longer lame duck period?

Constitutional Insight **Amendment 21**
What is unique about the Twenty-first Amendment? Besides being the only amendment that explicitly repeals another, it was the first, and is so far the only one, to have been ratified by the state convention method outlined in Article 5. Congress, probably fearing that state legislatures would not deal swiftly with the issue of repeal, chose to have each state call a special convention to consider the amendment. The strategy worked well, for the elected delegates to the conventions represented public opinion on the issue and ratified the amendment without delay.

M CRITICAL THINKING
Why is it necessary to pass another amendment to revoke or remove an existing amendment?

CONGRESSIONAL TERM LIMITS

In 1995, the Supreme Court struck down all state laws limiting congressional terms, stating that they were unconstitutional. The Court ruled that only a constitutional amendment—such as the Twenty-second, which limits the president to two terms—could impose term limits on members of Congress.

Proposed constitutional amendments for Congressional term limits were defeated in Congress in 1995 and in 1997.

Constitutional Insight **Amendment 23** *Why were residents of the District of Columbia without a vote in presidential elections?* First, the district was merely an idea at the time the Constitution was written. Second, no one expected the district to include many residents. Third, the framers designed the electoral college on a state framework. By 1960, however, the fact that nearly 800,000 Americans living in the nation's capital could not vote in presidential elections was an embarrassment. The Twenty-third Amendment gives Washington, D.C., residents the right to vote in presidential elections by assigning them electoral votes.

N CRITICAL THINKING
Do you think the District of Columbia should be made a separate state?

Constitutional Insight **Amendment 24** *Why was the poll tax an issue important enough to require an amendment?* The poll tax was used in some places to prevent African-American voters—at least the many who were too poor to pay the tax—from participating in elections. As the civil rights movement gained momentum, the abuse of the poll tax became a major issue, but the national government found it difficult to change the situation because the constitutional provisions in Article 1, Section 4, leave the qualifications of voters in the hands of the states. The Twenty-fourth Amendment changed this by prohibiting the United States or any state from including payment of any tax as a requirement for voting.

O CRITICAL THINKING
What impact do you think the Twenty-fourth Amendment has had on elections?

SECTION 3 This article shall be inoperative unless it shall have been ratified as an amendment to the Constitution by conventions in the several states, as provided in the Constitution, within seven years from the date of the submission hereof to the states by the Congress.

AMENDMENT 22. LIMIT ON PRESIDENTIAL TERMS (1951) Passed by Congress March 21, 1947. Ratified February 27, 1951.

SECTION 1 No person shall be elected to the office of the President more than twice, and no person who has held the office of President, or acted as President, for more than two years of a term to which some other person was elected President shall be elected to the office of the President more than once. ~~But this article shall not apply to any person holding the office of President when this article was proposed by the Congress, and shall not prevent any person who may be holding the office of President, or acting as President, during the term within which this article becomes operative from holding the office of President or acting as President during the remainder of such term.~~

SECTION 2 This article shall be inoperative unless it shall have been ratified as an amendment to the Constitution by the legislatures of three fourths of the several states within seven years from the date of its submission to the states by the Congress.

AMENDMENT 23. VOTING IN DISTRICT OF COLUMBIA (1961) Passed by Congress June 17, 1960. Ratified March 29, 1961.

SECTION 1 The district constituting the seat of government of the United States shall appoint in such manner as Congress may direct: a number of electors of President and Vice-President equal to the whole number of Senators and Representatives in Congress to which the district would be entitled if it were a state, but in no event more than the least populous state; they shall be in addition to those appointed by the states, but they shall be considered, for the purposes of the election of President and Vice-President, to be electors appointed by a state; and they shall meet in the district and perform such duties as provided by the twelfth article of amendment.

SECTION 2 The Congress shall have power to enforce this article by appropriate legislation.

AMENDMENT 24. ABOLITION OF POLL TAXES (1964) Passed by Congress August 27, 1962. Ratified January 23, 1964.

SECTION 1 The right of citizens of the United States to vote in any primary or other election for President or Vice-President, for electors for President or Vice-President, or for Senator or Representative in Congress, shall not be denied or abridged by the United States or any state by reason of failure to pay any poll tax or other tax.

SECTION 2 The Congress shall have power to enforce this article by appropriate legislation.

AMENDMENT 25. PRESIDENTIAL DISABILITY, SUCCESSION (1967) Passed by Congress July 6, 1965. Ratified February 10, 1967.

Note: Article 2, Section 1, of the Constitution was affected by the Twenty-fifth Amendment.

SECTION 1. In case of the removal of the President from office or of his death or resignation, the Vice-President shall become President.

SECTION 2 Whenever there is a vacancy in the office of the Vice-President, the President shall nominate a Vice-President who shall take office upon confirmation by a majority vote of both houses of Congress.

SECTION 3 Whenever the President transmits to the President pro tempore of the Senate and the Speaker of the House of Representatives his written declaration that he is unable to discharge the powers and duties of his office, and until he transmits to them a written declaration to the contrary, such powers and duties shall be discharged by the Vice-President as Acting President.

SECTION 4 Whenever the Vice-President and a majority of either the principal officers of the executive departments or of such other body as Congress may by law provide, transmit to the President pro tempore of the Senate and the Speaker of the House of Representatives their written declaration that the President is unable to discharge the powers and duties of his office, the Vice-President shall immediately assume the powers and duties of the office as Acting President.

Thereafter, when the President transmits to the President pro tempore of the Senate and the Speaker of the House of Representatives his written declaration that no inability exists, he shall resume the powers and duties of his office unless the Vice-President and a majority of either the principal officers of the executive department[s] or of such other body as Congress may by law provide, transmit within four days to the President pro tempore of the Senate and the Speaker of the House of Representatives their written declaration that the President is unable to discharge the powers and duties of his office. Thereupon Congress shall decide the issue, assembling within forty-eight hours for that purpose if not in session. If the Congress, within twenty-one days after receipt of the latter written declaration, or, if Congress is not in session, within twenty-one days after Congress is required to assemble, determines by two thirds vote of both houses that the President is unable to discharge the powers and duties of his office, the Vice-President shall continue to discharge the same as Acting President; otherwise, the President shall resume the powers and duties of his office.

AMENDMENT 26. 18-YEAR-OLD VOTE (1971) Passed by Congress March 23, 1971. Ratified July 1, 1971.

Note: Amendment 14, Section 2, of the Constitution was modified by Section 1 of the Twenty-sixth Amendment.

SECTION 1 The right of citizens of the United States, who are eighteen years of age or older, to vote shall not be denied or abridged by the United States or by any state on account of age.

SECTION 2 The Congress shall have power to enforce this article by appropriate legislation.

AMENDMENT 27. CONGRESSIONAL PAY (1992) Proposed by Congress September 25, 1789. Ratified May 7, 1992.

No law, varying the compensation for the services of the Senators and Representatives, shall take effect, until an election of Representatives shall have intervened.

Constitutional Insight **Amendment 26**
Why was the Twenty-sixth Amendment passed? Granting 18-year-olds the right to vote became an issue in the 1960s, during the Vietnam War, when people questioned the justice of requiring 18-year-old men to submit to the military draft but refusing them the right to vote. In 1970, Congress passed a voting rights act giving 18-year-olds the right to vote in elections. When the constitutionality of this act was challenged, the Supreme Court decided that states had to honor the 18-year-old vote for congressional and presidential elections but could retain higher age requirements for state and local elections. To avoid confusion at the polls, the Twenty-sixth Amendment was passed. It guarantees 18-year-olds the right to vote in national and state elections.

P CRITICAL THINKING
Do you think 18-year-olds should have the right to vote? Why or why not?

(above) **President Richard M. Nixon signs the Twenty-sixth Amendment to the Constitution, adopted in 1971.**

Constitutional Insight **Amendment 27**
How long did it take to ratify this amendment? Although the Twenty-seventh Amendment was one of the 12 amendments proposed in 1789 as part of the Bill of Rights, it was not ratified until 1992. This amendment, which deals with congressional compensation, allows the members of Congress to increase Congressional pay, but delays the increase until after a new Congress is seated.

Q CRITICAL THINKING
Do you think members of Congress should be able to vote themselves a pay increase? Explain your answer.

TRACING THEMES

Voting Rights

When the American colonists declared their independence from Great Britain in 1776, their struggle to create a representative government was just beginning. The state constitutions that were drafted at that time established voting rights, but only for certain citizens. The Articles of Confederation did not address voting rights; therefore, existing state laws remained intact.

Even the new Constitution that replaced the Articles in 1788 did not extend voting rights to many groups of people living in the new United States. As the Constitution has been amended over the years however, things changed. The right to vote was gradually extended to more and more citizens, enabling them to participate in local and national government.

1789

MALE PROPERTY OWNERS ▶

In the early years of the United States, property qualifications were relaxed in some states (Pennsylvania, Delaware, North Carolina, Georgia, and Vermont) to include all male taxpayers. With few exceptions, women were not allowed to vote. Most state constitutions also required that a voting male be at least 21 years of age.

Those who qualified to vote were generally white, although some states allowed free African Americans to vote.

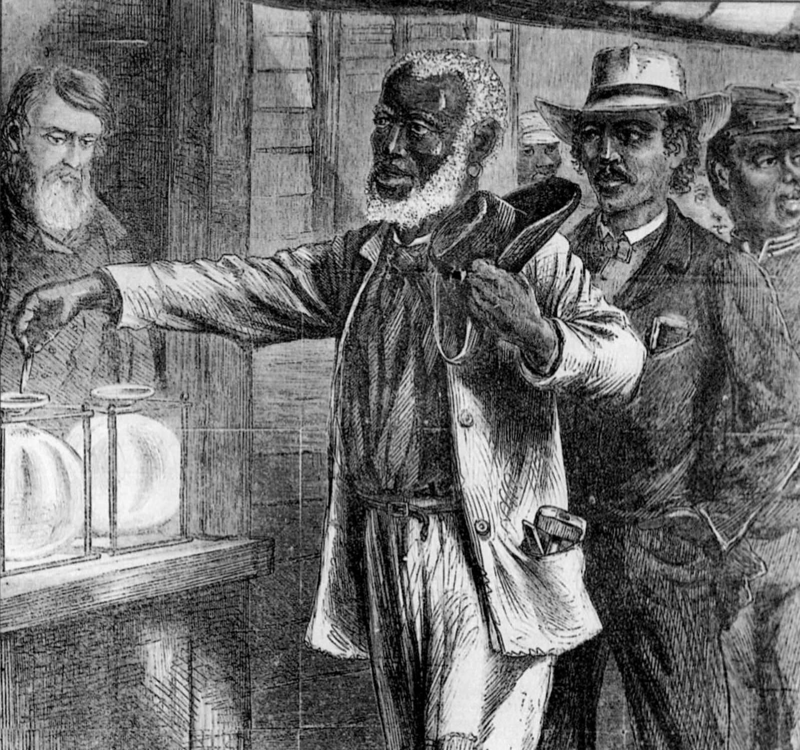

1870

◀ AFRICAN-AMERICAN MALES

The Fifteenth Amendment to the Constitution attempted to guarantee African-American males the right to vote by stating that the right of U.S. citizens "to vote shall not be denied or abridged [limited] by the United States or by any state on account of race, color, or previous condition of servitude." The picture to the left shows African-American males voting in a state election in 1867. African-American males, however, were often kept from voting through the use of poll taxes, which were finally abolished by the Twenty-fourth Amendment in 1964, and literacy tests, which were suspended by the Voting Rights Act of 1965.

1920

◀ WOMAN SUFFRAGE

In 1920, the Nineteenth Amendment, granting voting rights to women, was finally ratified. Elizabeth Cady Stanton, Susan B. Anthony, and many other women, such as those shown at left marching in a woman suffrage parade in 1919, worked tirelessly for women's voting rights.

Four years after ratification of the Nineteenth Amendment, in 1924, citizenship—including the right to vote—was extended to Native Americans.

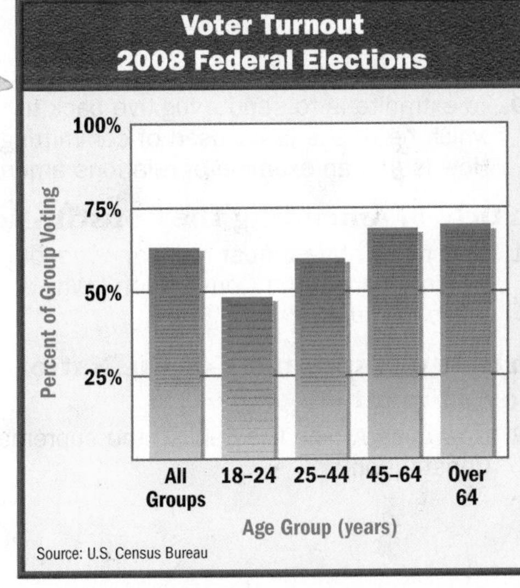

1971

▼ EIGHTEEN-YEAR-OLD VOTE

The Twenty-sixth Amendment, ratified in 1971, granted the right to vote to citizens "eighteen years of age or older." Voting rights for young people had become an issue in the 1960s during the Vietnam War. Many people questioned drafting 18-year-olds to fight but refusing them the right to vote. The picture below shows a young woman exercising her new right to vote.

THINKING CRITICALLY

CONNECT TO HISTORY

1. **Forming Generalizations** What does the information on these pages demonstrate about how voting rights in the United States have changed? How did the Constitution help bring about the changes?

SEE SKILLBUILDER HANDBOOK, PAGE R21.

CONNECT TO TODAY

2. **Interpreting Data** Research voter turnout statistics from a recent election. What age group scored highest? Which scored lowest?

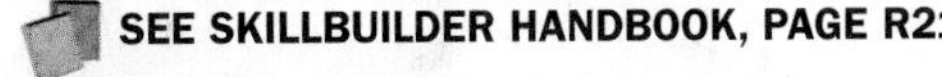

MAIN IDEAS

Article 1. The Legislature

1. Why does the legislative branch of the government represent the people most directly? What is the principal job of this branch?
2. Why are there more members of the House of Representatives than of the Senate?
3. Name four powers Congress has.
4. What powers are denied to Congress? to the states?

Article 2. The Executive

5. What is the main function of the executive branch?
6. Who officially elects the president of the United States? Explain.
7. How can the president lose his or her job before election time?

Article 3. The Judiciary

8. How are Supreme Court justices appointed?
9. What kinds of cases go before the Supreme Court? Why is the Court's decision whether to hear a case important?

Article 4. Relations Among States

10. To extradite is to send a fugitive back to the state in which he or she is accused of committing a crime. How is this an example of relations among states?

Article 5. Amending the Constitution

11. How many states must ratify an amendment for it to become part of the Constitution? Why do you think it takes that many?

Article 6. Supremacy of the National Government

12. How does Article 6 establish the supremacy of the Constitution?

The Amendments

13. Does the First Amendment allow complete freedom of speech—the right to say anything you want at any time, anywhere? Explain your answer.
14. What is the newest amendment? What protection does that amendment give to the American people?

THINKING CRITICALLY

1. **TAKING NOTES** The powers of the federal government are separated among the three branches. Create a chart like the one below that shows how the Constitution's framers used checks and balances to ensure that no one branch of the government could become too much stronger than the others.

Executive	Legislative	Judicial

2. **MAKING INFERENCES** How does the Constitution reflect the fear of too strong a central government?

3. **EVALUATING** The Bill of Rights guarantees a defendant a speedy, public trial. Do you think it is being observed today? Explain.

4. **ANALYZING MOTIVES** Why did the framers make it so difficult to amend the Constitution? Do you agree or disagree with their philosophy? Explain.

5. **DEVELOPING HISTORICAL PERSPECTIVE** The Fifteenth, Nineteenth, and Twenty-sixth amendments give voting rights to specific groups. Why was it necessary for Congress to spell out these groups' rights in amendments?

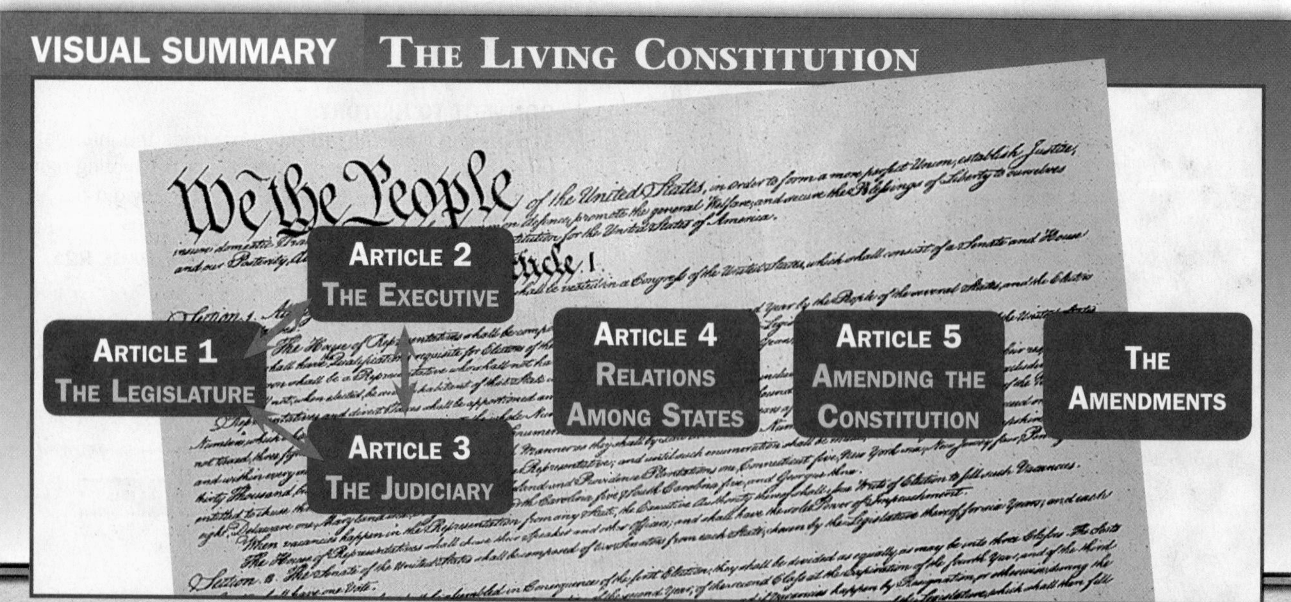

STANDARDIZED TEST PRACTICE

Use the cartoon and your knowledge of U.S. history to answer question 1.

"It's Awful The Way They're Trying To Influence Congress. Why Don't They Serve Cocktails And Make Campaign Contributions Like We Do?"

1. In the Constitutional Convention, the framers adopted certain principles to be embodied in the Constitution. Which of the following Constitutional principles does the cartoon support?

   A The federal government's power should be divided into separate branches.
   B The federal government should be stronger than the state governments.
   C The federal legislature should be responsive to the will of the people.
   D The legislature and the president should check each other's power.

Use the quotation and your knowledge of U.S. history to answer question 2.

> **"[The president] shall have power, by and with the advice and consent of the Senate, to make treaties, provided two thirds of the Senators present concur; and he shall nominate, and by and with the advice and consent of the Senate, shall appoint ambassadors, other public ministers and consuls, judges of the Supreme Court, and all other officers of the United States . . ."**
>
> —U.S. Constitution, Art. 2, Sec. 2, part 2

2. The passage describes checks on the power of—

   F the president.
   G the Senate.
   H the judiciary.
   J the states.

3. Which of the following must ratify Constitutional amendments?

   A Congress
   B the people
   C the states
   D the president

For additional test practice, go online for:

- Diagnostic tests
- Tutorials

FOCUS ON WRITING

Imagine that it is 1787, and you are a citizen of one of the original thirteen states. Your vote is necessary to ratify the new Constitution that has been approved by the convention in Philadelphia. You have studied the seven articles and listened to spirited discussions about how you and your state will be affected. Write a journal entry in which you express your views about this document that is so important for the new United States. Make sure you include references to what you have read and heard about the Constitution.

MULTIMEDIA ACTIVITY

Visit the links for Chapter Assessment to learn more about how bills become law. Because of the process by which bills become laws, problems may occur when the president and a majority of members of Congress are from different political parties. Using the Internet, research bills that were proposed by the president but became stalled in Congress because of party differences. Then divide into groups. Have each group research a different bill. Try to follow the debate and see how party differences affected the discussion. Did the bill pass and become law? Present your findings to the class.

Applying the Constitution

The United States Constitution is admired the world over. But a healthy democracy depends on the continuing participation of its citizens—including you. Here are four projects that will help you learn the rewards and challenges of responsible citizenship.

hmhsocialstudies.com RESEARCH WEB LINKS Visit the links for the Constitution for more information that will help you with these Projects for Citizenship.

PROJECT 1

Becoming an Educated Voter

ENDORSING A CANDIDATE

Choose a campaign for elective office and learn about the issues and the candidates in the campaign. After doing your research, write an endorsement, or a statement in favor, of one of the candidates.

LEARNING ABOUT THE CANDIDATES

✔ **Examine news media and news services.** During campaigns, some services and publications offer endorsements that explain why particular candidates are worthy of support.

✔ **Get information from political parties.** They provide information on the candidates, but their perspective is biased toward their own candidates. The major parties have Internet sites, as do many local groups and individual candidates.

✔ **Contact interest groups,** such as the Sierra Club and the National Association of Manufacturers. They often list candidates' positions on issues and support candidates who share their beliefs.

✔ **Look at databases and voters' guides** published by nonpartisan organizations such as the League of Women Voters and Project Vote Smart.

As you use each source, try to identify any bias. Think about the following questions.

- What does the author of this source stand to gain from supporting a particular candidate?
- Is the information in the source complete and accurate?
- Does the author use loaded or inflammatory language?

PRESENTING YOUR PROJECT

After you have written your endorsement, you might send it to a media outlet, such as a newspaper or a television station, or post it on the Internet. Or you might send it to your local or school newspaper.

PROJECT 2

Expressing Political Opinions

WRITING A LETTER TO THE EDITOR

Identify an issue that concerns you. Then write a letter or send an e-mail message about that issue to the editor of a newspaper or magazine.

WRITING A PERSUASIVE LETTER

✔ **Find an issue** that has been in the news lately and about which you feel strongly.

✔ **Read recent articles,** editorials, and cartoons in newspapers or magazines. Notice how they have addressed this issue.

✔ **Compose a letter** that clearly and concisely explains your views about the issue you have chosen. Your letter should also include reasons and facts that support your opinion on the issue. It might also advocate some specific action to be taken to address the issue.

✔ **Identify the person** to whom you should send your letter, and note any requirements the newspaper or magazine has for writing letters to the editor.

✔ **Edit your letter carefully.** Be sure to use standard grammar, spelling, sentence structure, and punctuation.

PRESENTING YOUR PROJECT

Present the letter you wrote to the rest of the class. When you do, explain why you chose to write about this issue.

A student expresses her political opinions as she addresses an audience.

PROJECT 3

UNDERSTANDING HOW TO LOBBY

PLANNING A LOBBYING CAMPAIGN

Form a committee with other students to organize a lobbying campaign—a campaign to influence legislation or public policy. Create a plan for the campaign that includes materials to be presented to government officials. In creating your plan, keep the following points in mind.

CREATING A LOBBYING PLAN

- ✔ **Establish a clear goal** of what you want to achieve. Make sure all members of the group understand and agree with the established goal.
- ✔ **Identify the appropriate people to lobby**—the people who can best help you to achieve your goal. For example, if your group is planning to lobby to have a bill passed, you would lobby the legislators who will vote on the bill. However, if your group wants to lobby for a local improvement—such as cleaning up an abandoned factory site—you should lobby the local officials who make those decisions.
- ✔ **Gather statistics** and other information that support your case. Explore a variety of resources, including the library, the Internet, and news services. Conduct interviews with appropriate state or local officials. Use the information you gather to develop a brief written report that can be given to the officials you intend to lobby.
- ✔ **Organize public opinion** in favor of your case. Gather signatures on petitions or conduct a letter-writing campaign to encourage people who support your goal to contact government officials. You can also create fliers calling attention to your cause.
- ✔ **Present your case** to government officials firmly but politely. Practice your presentation several times before you actually appear before them.

PRESENTING YOUR PROJECT

Share your lobbying plan with the rest of the class in the form of a written proposal that includes materials, such as petition forms, that you will use in your lobbying effort. If you implement your lobbying plan, describe to the class what response you received from the officials you lobbied.

PROJECT 4

VOLUNTEERING IN YOUR COMMUNITY

MAKING AN ORAL REPORT

Identify a local community organization that you might want to help. Find out what kinds of volunteer activities the organization has, such as answering phones in the office, serving food to the homeless, or cleaning vacant lots. Then volunteer to participate in one of those activities. Prepare an oral report to present to the rest of the class about your experiences as a volunteer. Keep the following points in mind as you choose which organization to help.

A group of young volunteers in the Summer of Service project discusses plans with carpenters.

SUGGESTIONS FOR VOLUNTEERING

- ✔ **Decide what kinds of public service projects might interest you.** You might talk to your parents, a teacher, friends, a local church, or a local political organization to learn what kinds of volunteer services are needed in your community.
- ✔ **Call local community organizations** to find out what kinds of volunteer opportunities they offer and decide whether you would like to volunteer for those projects.
- ✔ **Decide what cause you want to support** and identify an organization that addresses that cause.
- ✔ **Decide what type of work you want to do** and work with that organization.

PRESENTING YOUR PROJECT

Deliver an oral report to your class about your experiences as a volunteer. Explain why you chose the specific volunteer activity that you did. Describe the activity you performed. Then explain what effect your volunteering had as well as whether you felt the experience was a good one.

CHAPTER 6

LAUNCHING THE NEW NATION

Essential Question

What major domestic and foreign problems faced the leaders of the new Republic?

ALABAMA COURSE OF STUDY

4 Describe the political system of the United States based on the Constitution of the United States.

- Identifying factors leading to the development and establishment of political parties, including Alexander Hamilton's economic policies, conflicting views of Thomas Jefferson and Alexander Hamilton, George Washington's Farewell Address, and the election of 1800.

5 Explain key cases that helped shape the United States Supreme Court, including Marbury versus Madison, McCullough versus Maryland, and Cherokee Nation versus Georgia.

6 Describe relations of the United States with Britain and France from 1781 to 1823, including the XYZ Affair, the War of 1812, and the Monroe Doctrine.

13 Summarize major legislation and court decisions from 1800 to 1861 that led to increasing sectionalism, including the Missouri Compromise of 1820, the Compromise of 1850, the Fugitive Slave Acts, the Kansas-Nebraska Act, and the Dred Scott decision.

- Analyzing the Westward Expansion from 1803 to 1861 to determine its effect on sectionalism, including the Louisiana Purchase, Texas Annexation, and the Mexican Cession.

Lake George, New York, in 1817

USA

1789 George Washington is elected president.

1792 George Washington is reelected president.

1794 The Whiskey Rebellion breaks out.

1796 John Adams is elected president.

1800 Thomas Jefferson is elected president.

1790 — 1795 — 1800

WORLD

1789 The French Revolution begins.

1791 Slaves revolt in Saint Domingue, now known as Haiti.

1793 French King Louis XVI is executed in the French Revolution.

1799 Napoleon Bonaparte seizes control of the French government.

1801 Act of Union, uniting Great Britain and Ireland, goes into effect.

Image Credits: (bkgd), *Carter's Tavern at the Head of Lake George* (1817–18), Francis Guy. Oil on canvas, 101cm x 168cm. The Detroit Institute of Arts, Founders' Society Purchase, R.H. Tannahill Foundation Fund/The Bridgeman Art Library; (bl), ©Corbis; (br), ©Paul Almasy/Corbis

Lewis and Clark: Jefferson's Bold Plan

hmhsocialstudies.com VIDEO

INTERACT WITH HISTORY

You are a teacher in a small town on the western frontier in 1789. You ask your students what the new government means to them. A girl whose parents own the general store says that her father worries about taxes. Her brother says that he wants to join the army. A boy from a small farm in the backcountry replies that the government is only for town people.

Explore the Issues

- How can a government win people's trust?
- How can a government build a unified nation out of a people with diverse interests and concerns?

1803 France and the United States sign the Louisiana Purchase.

1804 Thomas Jefferson is reelected president.

1808 James Madison is elected president.

1812 James Madison is reelected.

1814 The Treaty of Ghent ends the War of 1812.

1816 James Monroe is elected president.

1805 | 1810 | 1815

1804 Haiti declares itself independent from France.

1807 Great Britain outlaws the slave trade.

1815 Napoleon is defeated at Waterloo.

Image Credits: (bkgd), *Carter's Tavern at the Head of Lake George* (1817–18), Francis Guy. Oil on canvas, 101cm x 168cm. The Detroit Institute of Arts, Founders' Society Purchase, R.H. Tannahill Foundation Fund/The Bridgeman Art Library; (bl), ©Bettmann/Corbis; (br), Library of Congress Prints and Photographs Division [LC-USZ62-116232]

SECTION 1

Washington Heads the New Government

MAIN IDEA

President Washington transformed the ideas of the Constitution into a real government.

WHY IT MATTERS NOW

The Cabinet, an institution Washington created, is still a key element of every presidential administration.

Terms & Names

- **Judiciary Act of 1789**
- **Alexander Hamilton**
- **Cabinet**
- **Bank of the United States**
- **Democratic-Republicans**
- **two-party system**
- **protective tariff**
- **excise tax**

One American's Story

hmhsocialstudies.com TAKING NOTES

Use the graphic organizer online to take notes on the country's first political parties.

George Washington had no desire to be president after the Constitutional Convention. His dream was to settle down to a quiet life at his Virginia estate, Mount Vernon. The American people had other ideas, though. They wanted a strong national leader of great authority as their first president. As the hero of the Revolution, Washington was the unanimous choice in the first presidential ballot. When the news reached him on April 16, 1789, Washington reluctantly accepted the call to duty. Two days later he set out for New York City to take the oath of office.

A PERSONAL VOICE GEORGE WASHINGTON

"About ten o'clock I bade adieu [farewell] to Mount Vernon, to private life, and to domestic felicity [happiness]; and with a mind oppressed with more anxious and painful sensations than I have words to express, set out for New York . . . with the best dispositions [intentions] to render service to my country in obedience to its call, but with less hope of answering its expectations."

—*The Diaries of George Washington*

George Washington

When Washington took office as the first president of the United States under the Constitution, he and Congress faced a daunting task—to create an entirely new government. The momentous decisions that these early leaders made have resounded through American history.

The New Government Takes Shape

Washington took charge of a political system that was a bold experiment. Never before had a nation tried to base a government on the Enlightenment ideals of republican rule and individual rights. No one knew if a government based on the will of the people could really work.

Although the Constitution provided a strong foundation, it was not a detailed blueprint for governing. To create a working government, Washington and Congress had to make many practical decisions—such as how to raise revenue and provide for defense—with no precedent, or prior example, for American leaders to follow. Perhaps James Madison put it best: "We are in a wilderness without a single footstep to guide us."

JUDICIARY ACT OF 1789 One of the first tasks Washington and Congress tackled was the creation of a judicial system. The Constitution had authorized Congress to set up a federal court system, headed by a Supreme Court, but it failed to spell out the details. What type of additional courts should there be and how many? What would happen if federal court decisions conflicted with state laws?

The **Judiciary Act of 1789** answered these critical questions, creating a judicial structure that has remained essentially intact. This law provided for a Supreme Court consisting of a chief justice and five associate justices. It also set up 3 federal circuit courts and 13 federal district courts throughout the country. (The numbers of justices and courts increased over time.) Section 25 of the Judiciary Act, one of the most important provisions of the law, allowed state court decisions to be appealed to a federal court when constitutional issues were raised. This section guaranteed that federal laws remained "the supreme Law of the Land," as directed by Article 6 of the Constitution. (A)

MAIN IDEA

Analyzing Motives

(A) Why did federal law have to be "the supreme Law of the Land" in the new nation?

WASHINGTON SHAPES THE EXECUTIVE BRANCH At the same time that Congress shaped the judiciary, Washington faced the task of building an executive branch to help him make policies and carry out the laws passed by Congress. In 1789, when Washington took office, the executive branch of government consisted of two officials, the president and the vice-president. To help these leaders govern, Congress created three executive departments: the Department of State, to deal with foreign affairs; the Department of War, to handle military matters; and the Department of the Treasury, to manage finances.

To head these departments, Washington chose capable leaders he knew and trusted. He picked Thomas Jefferson as secretary of state, **Alexander Hamilton** as secretary of the treasury, and Henry Knox, who had served as Washington's general of artillery during the Revolution, as secretary of war. Finally, he chose Edmund Randolph as attorney general, the chief lawyer of the federal government. These department heads soon became the president's chief advisers, or **Cabinet.**

THE CABINET

The Constitution provided the president the right to "require the opinion, in writing, of the principal officer in each of the executive departments." Washington chose to seek those opinions, in person, on a regular basis. In 1793, James Madison called this group the Cabinet, a term used in Britain for advisers to the king.

Since Washington's time the number of departments has increased to 15. In addition to the secretaries of these 15 departments, Cabinet officers include other executive branch officials such as the director of the Central Intelligence Agency, the administrator of the Environmental Protection Agency, and the vice-president. The Cabinet meets at the request of the president and frequency varies from administration to administration.

President Washington *(far right)* meets with his first Cabinet: *(from left to right)* Henry Knox, Thomas Jefferson, Edmund Randolph *(with back turned)*, and Alexander Hamilton.

Hamilton and Jefferson Debate

Hamilton and Jefferson were brilliant thinkers, but they had very different political ideas. The differences between the two also caused bitter disagreements, many of which centered on Hamilton's plan for the economy.

HAMILTON AND JEFFERSON IN CONFLICT Political divisions in the new nation were great. No two men embodied these differences more than Hamilton and Jefferson. Hamilton believed in a strong central government led by a prosperous, educated elite of upper-class citizens. Jefferson distrusted a strong central government and the rich. He favored strong state and local governments rooted in popular participation. Hamilton believed that commerce and industry were the keys to a strong nation. Jefferson favored a society of farmer-citizens.

Overall, Hamilton's vision of America was that of a country much like Great Britain, with a strong central government, commerce, and industry. His views found more support in the North, particularly New England, whereas Jefferson's views won endorsement in the South and the West. (B)

MAIN IDEA

Contrasting

(B) How did Jefferson's and Hamilton's views of government differ?

KEY PLAYERS

THOMAS JEFFERSON
1743–1826

The writer of the Declaration of Independence, Thomas Jefferson began his political career at age 26, when he was elected to Virginia's colonial legislature. In 1779 he was elected governor of Virginia, and in 1785 he was appointed minister to France. He served as secretary of state from 1790 to 1793.

A Southern planter, Jefferson was also an accomplished scholar, the architect of Monticello (his Virginia house), an inventor (of, among other things, a machine that made copies of letters), and the founder of the University of Virginia in 1819. Despite his elite background and his ownership of slaves, he was a strong ally of the small farmer and average citizen.

ALEXANDER HAMILTON
1755–1804

Born into poverty in the British West Indies, Alexander Hamilton was orphaned at age 13 and went to work as a shipping clerk. He later made his way to New York, where he attended King's College (now Columbia University). He joined the army during the Revolution and became an aide to General Washington.

Intensely ambitious, Hamilton quickly moved up in society. Although in his humble origins Hamilton was the opposite of Jefferson, he had little faith in the common citizen and sided with the interests of upper-class Americans. Hamilton said of Jefferson's beloved common people: "Your people, sir, your people is a great beast!"

HAMILTON'S ECONOMIC PLAN As secretary of the treasury, Hamilton's job was to set in order the nation's finances and to put the nation's economy on a firm footing. To do this, he proposed a plan to manage the country's debts and a plan to establish a national banking system.

According to Hamilton's calculations in his *Report on the Public Credit,* the public debt of the United States in 1790 (most of it incurred during the Revolution) was many millions of dollars. The national government was responsible for about two-thirds of this debt, and individual states were responsible for the rest. The new nation owed some of the debt to foreign governments and some to private citizens, including soldiers who had received bonds—certificates that promised payment plus interest—as payment for their service during the war.

Hamilton proposed to pay off the foreign debt and to issue new bonds to cover the old ones. He also proposed that the federal government assume the debts of the states. Although this would increase the federal debt, Hamilton reasoned that assuming state debts would give creditors—the people who

Contrasting Views of the Federal Government	
HAMILTON	**JEFFERSON**
• Concentrating power in federal government	• Sharing power with state and local governments; limited national government
• Fear of mob rule	• Fear of absolute power or ruler
• Republic led by a well-educated elite	• Democracy of virtuous farmers and tradespeople
• Loose interpretation of the Constitution	• Strict interpretation of the Constitution
• National bank constitutional (loose interpretation)	• National bank unconstitutional (strict interpretation)
• Economy based on shipping and manufacturing	• Economy based on farming
• Payment of national and state debts (favoring creditors)	• Payment of only the national debt (favoring debtors)
• Supporters: merchants, manufacturers, landowners, investors, lawyers, clergy	• Supporters: the "plain people" (farmers, tradespeople)

SKILLBUILDER Interpreting Charts

1. Whose view of the federal government was a wealthy person more likely to favor? Why?
2. How do you think Jefferson differed from Hamilton in his view of people and human nature?

originally loaned the money—an incentive to support the new federal government. If the government failed, these creditors would never get their money back. However, this proposal made many people in the South furious. Some Southern states had already paid off most of their debts. Southerners resented assumption of state debts because they thought that they would be taxed to help pay the debts incurred by the Northern states. (C)

MAIN IDEA

Analyzing Issues

(C) Why did the new nation need to pay off its debts?

PLAN FOR A NATIONAL BANK Hamilton's line of reasoning also motivated his proposal for a national bank that would be funded by both the federal government and wealthy private investors. Hamilton hoped to tie wealthy investors to the country's welfare. The **Bank of the United States** would issue paper money and handle tax receipts and other government funds.

Hamilton's proposals aroused a storm of controversy. Opponents of a national bank, including James Madison, claimed that the bank would forge an unhealthy alliance between the government and wealthy business interests. Madison also argued that since the Constitution made no provision for a national bank, Congress had no right to authorize it. This argument began the debate between those who favored a "strict" interpretation of the Constitution, one in which the federal government has very limited powers, and a "loose" interpretation, which favors greater federal powers. The latter group appealed to the so-called elastic clause of the Constitution (Article 1, Section 8, Clause 18), which gives Congress the authority to do whatever is "necessary and proper" to carry out its specific enumerated powers, such as regulating commerce. In the end, however, Hamilton convinced Washington and a majority in Congress to accept his views, and the federal government established the Bank of the United States.

THE DISTRICT OF COLUMBIA To win support for his debt plan from Southern states, Hamilton offered a suggestion: What if the nation's capital were moved from New York City to a new city in the South, on the banks of the Potomac River? This idea pleased Southerners, particularly Virginians such as Madison and Jefferson, who believed that a Southern site for the capital would make the government more responsive to their interests. With this incentive, Virginians agreed to back the debt plan. In 1790, the debt bill passed Congress, along with authorization for the construction of a new national capital in the District of Columbia, located between Maryland and Virginia.

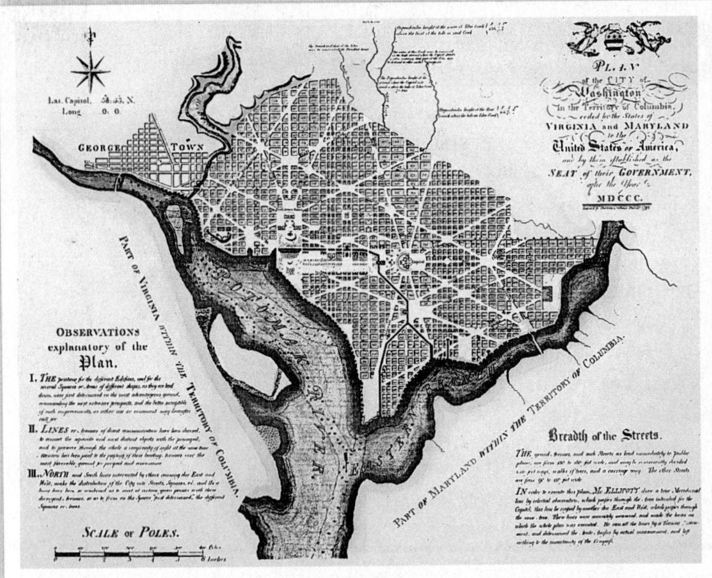

▲ Pierre L'Enfant proposed a federal capital of spacious, tree-lined boulevards, symbolizing the freedom of the young republic.

Pierre L'Enfant, a French engineer, drew up plans for the new capital. L'Enfant was later fired by George Washington for being obstinate. He was replaced by Andrew Ellicott, who redrew L'Enfant's plan, but kept much of the grand vision. An African-American surveyor, Benjamin Banneker, assisted Ellicott with the surveying work. They made their plan on a grand scale, incorporating boulevards, traffic circles, and monuments reminiscent of European capitals. By 1800, the capital had been moved to its new site on the Potomac.

The First Political Parties and Rebellion

President Washington tried to remain above the arguments between Hamilton and Jefferson and to encourage them to work together despite their basic differences. These differences were so great, however, that the two men continued to clash over government policy. Their conflict divided the cabinet and fueled a growing division in national politics.

FEDERALISTS AND DEMOCRATIC-REPUBLICANS The split in Washington's cabinet helped give rise to the country's first political parties. The two parties formed around one of the key issues in American history—the power and size of the federal government in relation to state and local governments. Those who shared Hamilton's vision of a strong central government called themselves Federalists. Those who supported Jefferson's vision of strong state governments called themselves Republicans. No relation to today's Republican Party, Jefferson's Republicans—later called **Democratic-Republicans**—were in fact the ancestors of today's Democratic Party. D

> **MAIN IDEA**
> **Contrasting**
> D How did the Federalists and the Democratic-Republicans differ from each other?

The very existence of political parties worried many leaders, including Washington, who saw parties as a danger to national unity. At the close of his presidency, Washington criticized what he called "the spirit of party."

A PERSONAL VOICE GEORGE WASHINGTON

> **"It serves always to distract the public councils and enfeeble the public administration. It agitates the community with ill-founded jealousies and false alarms; kindles the animosity of one part against another; foments [incites] occasionally riot and insurrection. It opens the door to foreign influence and corruption. . . ."**
>
> —"Farewell Address," 1796

Despite criticism, the two parties continued to develop. The **two-party system** was well established by the time Washington left office.

THE WHISKEY REBELLION During Washington's second term, an incident occurred that reflected the tension between federal and regional interests. In 1789, Congress had passed a **protective tariff,** an import tax on goods produced in Europe. This tax, meant to encourage American production, brought in a great deal of revenue, but Secretary Hamilton wanted more. So he pushed through an **excise tax**—a tax on a product's manufacture, sale, or distribution—to be levied on the manufacture of whiskey.

> **Background**
> In addition to promoting American goods, the Tariff Act of 1789, as well as tariffs that followed, provided the majority of the federal government's revenue until the 20th century.

A group of rebels taking part in the Whiskey Rebellion tar and feather a tax collector.

Most whiskey producers were small frontier farmers. Their major crop was corn. Corn was too bulky to carry across the Appalachian Mountains and sell in the settled areas along the Atlantic. Therefore, the farmers distilled the corn into whiskey, which could be more easily sent to market on the backs of mules.

Since whiskey was the main source of cash for these frontier farmers, Hamilton knew that the excise tax would make them furious. And it did. In 1794, farmers in western Pennsylvania refused to pay the tax. They beat up federal marshals in Pittsburgh, and they even threatened to secede from the Union.

Hamilton looked upon the Whiskey Rebellion as an opportunity for the federal government to show that it could enforce the law along the western frontier. Accordingly, some 15,000 militiamen were called up. Accompanied by Washington part of the way and by Hamilton all the way, the federal troops hiked over the Alleghenies and scattered the rebels without the loss of a single life.

The Whiskey Rebellion was a milestone in the consolidation of federal power in domestic affairs. At the same time, the new government was also facing critical problems and challenges in foreign affairs—particularly in its relations with Europe and with Native American peoples west of the Appalachians.

ASSESSMENT

1. **TERMS & NAMES** For each term or name, write a sentence explaining its significance.
   - **Judiciary Act of 1789**
   - **Alexander Hamilton**
   - **Cabinet**
   - **Bank of the United States**
   - **Democratic-Republicans**
   - **two-party system**
   - **protective tariff**
   - **excise tax**

MAIN IDEA

2. **TAKING NOTES**
   In a chart, list the leaders, beliefs, and goals of the country's first political parties.

Federalists	Democratic-Republicans

If you had lived in that time, which party would you have favored?

CRITICAL THINKING

3. **EVALUATING DECISIONS**
   How would you judge President Washington's decision to put two such opposed thinkers as Hamilton and Jefferson on his Cabinet? **Think About:**
   - both men's merits
   - their philosophies
   - the conflicts that developed

4. **ANALYZING ISSUES**
   How was the Whiskey Rebellion an opportunity for the federal government to demonstrate its authority?

5. **ANALYZING**
   Would you have supported Hamilton's economic plan? Explain why or why not. **Think About:**
   - the money problems the nation faced
   - other problems the nation faced

Young People in the Early Republic

Whether in farms on the frontier or in any of the cities and towns sprouting up throughout the nation, life in the early United States required energy and perseverance. This was especially true for young people, who were expected to shoulder responsibilities that, in our own time, even an adult would find challenging. Children worked alongside adults from the time they could walk and were considered adults at 14. School and leisure-time activities were work oriented and were meant to prepare young people for the challenges that lay ahead.

▲ **EDUCATION**

Country children attended school only when they weren't needed to do chores at home or in the fields. Schoolhouses were one-room log cabins and supplies were scarce. Younger and older children learned their lessons together by reciting spelling, multiplication tables, and verses from the Bible. Schoolmasters, seldom more learned than their students, punished wrong answers and restless behavior with severe beatings.

Some city children were either tutored at home or attended private schools. Girls studied etiquette, sewing, and music. Boys prepared for professional careers. "Professors" punished poor students by beating their hands. There were no laws requiring a child to attend school until the mid-1800s.

◀ **WORK**

Country children were expected to work alongside their parents from the time they were about six. Even when children went to school, they were expected to put in many hours performing such chores as chopping wood, watering the horses, gathering vegetables, and spooling yarn.

City boys as young as eight years old—especially poorer ones—went to work as "apprentices" for a tradesman who taught them such trades as printing, or, like the boys pictured here, dying cloth. Other boys worked in shops or went to sea. Girls learned from their mothers how to sew, spin, mend, and cook.

▼ **LEISURE**

Young people from the country gathered for events that were both entertaining as well as practical, such as the "husking bee" pictured here. Huskers were divided into teams, and the team that stripped the husks off the most ears of corn was the winner. Cheating, though resented, was expected and was usually followed by a fight.

Young people from the city gathered for cultured social events such as the cotillion, or dance, pictured at right. Young men and women were expected to follow the lead of their elders with regard to the strict social codes that determined how one behaved in polite society.

DATA FILE

CHILD MORTALITY

In Puritan America, one out of every two children died before they reached their teens. Child mortality remained high throughout the 18th and 19th centuries. Common causes of death for children were cholera, smallpox, diphtheria, and dysentery.

CHILDREN IN THE MILITARY

From the American Revolution until World War I, boys 14 and younger served in the United States military. Some as young as six were musicians and aides in the army and marines, while others served as deckhands and cartridge carriers in the United States Navy.

CHILDREN AND CAPITAL PUNISHMENT

Colonial law forbade the execution of children under 14, but exceptions were made. In December 1786, in New London, Connecticut, 12-year-old Hannah Ocuish was hanged for killing a six-year-old girl who had accused her of stealing strawberries.

CHILD LABOR

Apprentices who learned a trade could later go into business for themselves, but children who worked in factories had no such future. Virtually every industry in the country depended on child labor. Children worked in mills, mines, factories, and laundries.

Child Labor Data

- **1790:** All of the workers—seven boys and two girls—in the first American textile mill in Pawtucket, Rhode Island, were under the age of 12.
- **1830s:** One third of the labor force in New England was under the age of 16.
- **1842:** For the first time, Massachusetts law limited the workday of children under the age of 12 to ten hours a day.

THINKING CRITICALLY

CONNECT TO HISTORY

1. **Identifying Problems** What types of physical hardships were young people exposed to during this period in history?

 **SEE SKILLBUILDER HANDBOOK, PAGE R5.**

CONNECT TO TODAY

2. **Researching Jobs** In our own day, young people work at many different kinds of jobs. Some have even started their own businesses and have been very successful. Research some of the businesses that youths run on their own and present a report to the class.

RESEARCH WEB LINKS

SECTION 2

Foreign Affairs Trouble the Nation

MAIN IDEA

Events in Europe sharply divided American public opinion in the late 18th century.

WHY IT MATTERS NOW

Foreign policy remains a key element of every presidential administration.

Terms & Names

- **neutrality**
- **Edmond Genêt**
- **Thomas Pinckney**
- **Little Turtle**
- **John Jay**
- **sectionalism**
- **XYZ Affair**
- **Alien and Sedition Acts**
- **nullification**

One American's Story

hmhsocialstudies.com
TAKING NOTES

Use the graphic organizer online to take notes on some of the disputes discussed in this section.

Gouverneur Morris, the man responsible for the final draft of the Constitution, witnessed one of the great events of history—the French Revolution. On July 14, 1789, a mob stormed the Bastille, the infamous Paris prison, releasing the prisoners and killing the prison governor. Not long afterward, while walking on a Paris street, Morris got a close look at revolutionary violence.

A PERSONAL VOICE GOUVERNEUR MORRIS

"[T]he Head and Body of Mr. de Foulon are introduced in Triumph. The Head on a Pike, the Body dragged naked on the Earth. Afterwards this horrible Exhibition is carried thro the different Streets. His crime [was] to have accepted a Place in the Ministry. This mutilated form of an old Man of seventy five is shewn to Bertier, his Son in Law, the Intend't. [another official] of Paris, and afterwards he also is put to Death and cut to Pieces, the Populace carrying about the mangled Fragments with a Savage Joy."

—*quoted from his journal*

French revolutionaries storm the Bastille in Paris, France, on July 14, 1789.

Morris was appointed minister to France in 1792. Despite his horror at the violence around him, Morris remained at his post throughout the bloodiest days of the Revolution. Meanwhile, at home, Americans were divided in their views concerning the events underway in France.

U.S. Response to Events in Europe

Most Americans initially supported the French Revolution because, like the American Revolution, it was inspired by the ideal of republican rule. Heartened by the American struggle against royal tyranny, the French set out to create a government based on the will of the people. The alliance between France and the United States, created by the Treaty of 1778, served as an additional bond between the two nations. Whether or not the United States should support the French Revolution was one of the most important foreign policy questions that the young nation faced.

REACTIONS TO THE FRENCH REVOLUTION Despite the bonds between the nations, Americans soon became divided over the Revolution. In early 1793, a radical group called the Jacobins seized power in France. They beheaded the French king, Louis XVI, and launched the Reign of Terror against their opponents, sending moderate reformers and royalists alike to the guillotine. In an excess of revolutionary zeal, the Jacobins also declared war on other monarchies, including Great Britain.

Because of their alliance with the United States, the French expected American help. The American reaction tended to split along party lines. Democratic-Republicans, such as Thomas Jefferson and James Madison, wanted to honor the 1778 treaty and support France. Federalists, such as Alexander Hamilton, wanted to back the British. President Washington took a middle position. On April 22, 1793, he issued a declaration of **neutrality,** a statement that the United States would support neither side in the conflict. Hamilton and Jefferson came to agree; entering a war was not in the new nation's interest. (A)

MAIN IDEA

Analyzing Motives

(A) Why did the United States want to maintain its neutrality?

Earlier in April, the French had sent a young diplomat, **Edmond Genêt,** to win American support. Before following diplomatic procedure and presenting his credentials to the Washington administration, Genêt began to recruit Americans for the war effort against Great Britain. This violation of American neutrality and diplomatic protocol outraged Washington, who demanded that the French recall Genêt. By then, however, Genêt's political backers had fallen from power in Paris. Fearing for his life, the young envoy remained in the United States and became a U.S. citizen. Although Jefferson protested against Genêt's actions, Federalists called Jefferson a radical because he supported France. Frustrated by these attacks and by his ongoing feud with Hamilton, Jefferson resigned from the cabinet in 1793.

Politics and Style

Events in France not only affected politics in the United States, they influenced styles of clothing as well. Political differences could often be detected by observing different styles of dress and appearance.

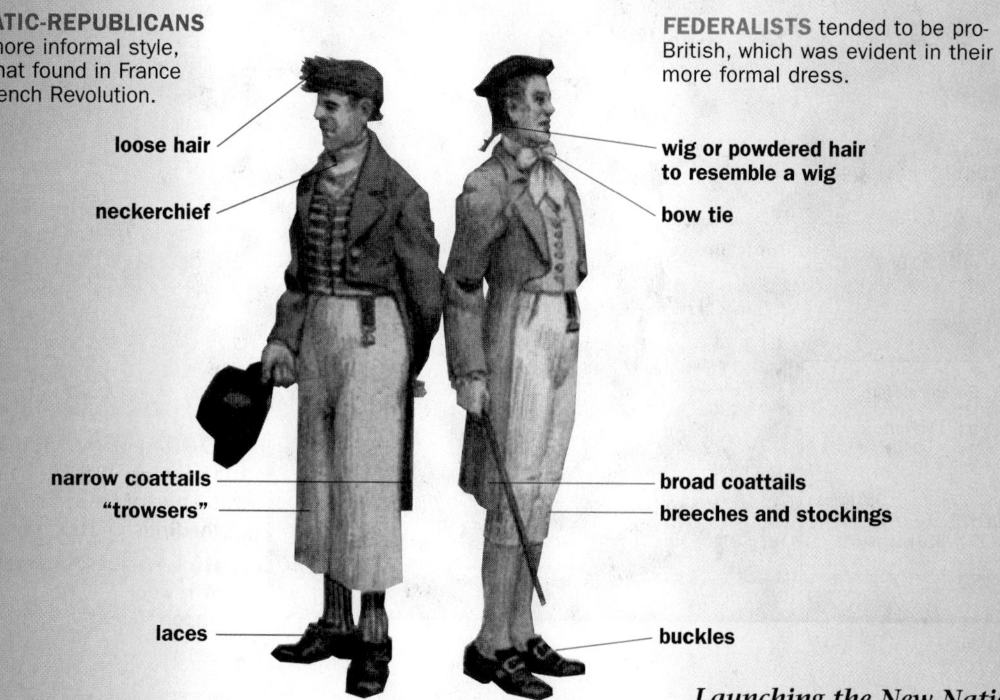

TREATY WITH SPAIN The United States wanted to secure land claims west of the Appalachian mountains and to gain shipping rights on the Mississippi River. To do this, it needed to come to an agreement with Spain, which still held Florida and the Louisiana Territory, a vast area of land west of the Mississippi River.

Negotiations stalled because of the turmoil in Europe. Spain, unlike Britain, signed a treaty with France. Spain then feared British retaliation and suspected that a joint British-American action might be launched against the Louisiana Territory. Suddenly, Spain agreed to meet with U.S. minister to Great Britain **Thomas Pinckney,** and on October 27, 1795, both sides signed a treaty.

Pinckney's Treaty of 1795, also known as the Treaty of San Lorenzo, included virtually every concession that the Americans desired. Spain gave up all claims to land east of the Mississippi (except Florida) and recognized the 31st parallel as the southern boundary of the United States and the northern boundary of Florida. Spain also agreed to open the Mississippi River to traffic by Spanish subjects and U.S. citizens, and to allow American traders to use the port of New Orleans. **B**

MAIN IDEA

Recognizing Effects

B Why did the United States want access to the Mississippi River?

Native Americans Resist White Settlers

Pioneers moving west assumed that the 1783 Treaty of Paris, in which Great Britain had ceded its land rights west of the Appalachians, gave them free rein to settle the area. But the British still maintained forts in the Northwest Territory—an area that included what is now Ohio, Indiana, Illinois, Michigan, and Wisconsin—in direct violation of the treaty. In addition to this continued British presence, the settlers met fierce resistance from the original inhabitants.

British Forts on U.S. Land, 1783–1794

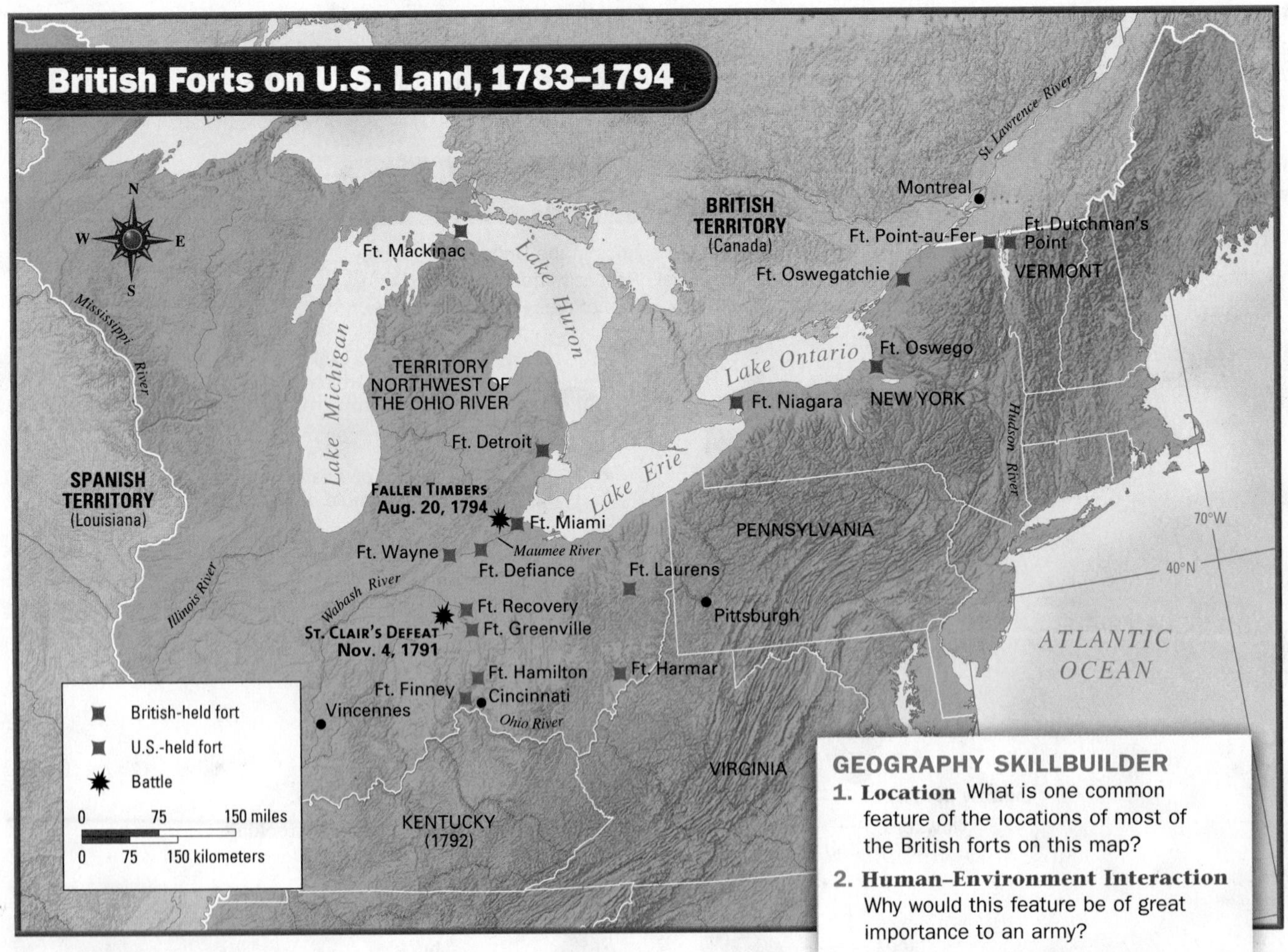

GEOGRAPHY SKILLBUILDER

1. **Location** What is one common feature of the locations of most of the British forts on this map?
2. **Human-Environment Interaction** Why would this feature be of great importance to an army?

▲ The Miami war chief Little Turtle negotiates with General Anthony Wayne.

FIGHTS IN THE NORTHWEST Having been excluded from the negotiations that led to the Treaty of Paris, Native Americans in the Northwest Territory never accepted the provisions. They continued to claim their tribal lands and demanded direct negotiations with the United States. They also took heart from the presence of British troops, who encouraged their resistance. When white settlers moved into their territory, Native Americans often attacked them. (C)

MAIN IDEA

Analyzing Issues

(C) Why did Native Americans demand negotiations with the United States over the Northwest Territory?

To gain control over the area that would become Ohio, the federal government sent an army led by General Josiah Harmar. In 1790, Harmar's troops clashed with a confederacy of Native American groups led by a chieftain of the Miami tribe named **Little Turtle.** The Native Americans won that battle. The following year, the Miami Confederacy inflicted an even worse defeat on a federal army led by General Arthur St. Clair.

BATTLE OF FALLEN TIMBERS Finally, in 1792, Washington appointed General Anthony Wayne to lead federal troops against the Native Americans. Known as "Mad Anthony" for his reckless courage, Wayne spent an entire year drilling his men. Greatly impressed, Little Turtle urged his people to seek peace.

A PERSONAL VOICE LITTLE TURTLE

> **"We have beaten the enemy twice under different commanders. . . . The Americans are now led by a chief who never sleeps. . . . We have never been able to surprise him. . . . It would be prudent to listen to his offers of peace."**
>
> —speech to his allies

The other chiefs did not agree with Little Turtle and replaced him with a less able leader. On August 20, 1794, Wayne defeated the Miami Confederacy at the Battle of Fallen Timbers, near present-day Toledo, Ohio. After the battle, Wayne's army marched defiantly past the British Fort Miami, only two miles away, and then built an American post nearby.

This victory ended Native American resistance in Ohio. The following year, the Miami Confederacy signed the Treaty of Greenville, agreeing to give up most of the land in Ohio in exchange for $20,000 worth of goods and an annual payment of nearly $10,000. This settlement continued a pattern in which settlers and the government paid Native Americans much less for their land than it was worth. Meanwhile, in the Northwest Territory, new sources of conflict were developing between Britain and the United States.

MAIN IDEA

Analyzing Issues

D Why were so many Americans dissatisfied with Jay's treaty with Britain?

JAY'S TREATY At the time of the Battle of Fallen Timbers, **John Jay,** the chief justice of the Supreme Court, was in London to negotiate a treaty with Britain. One of the disputed issues was which nation would control territories west of the Appalachian Mountains. When news of Wayne's victory at Fallen Timbers arrived, the British agreed to evacuate their posts in the Northwest Territory and a treaty was signed on November 19, 1794. The treaty managed to pass the Senate, but many Americans, especially western settlers, were angry at its terms, which allowed the British to continue their fur trade on the American side of the U.S.-Canadian border. **D**

Adams Provokes Criticism

The bitter political fight over Jay's Treaty, along with the growing division between Federalists and Democratic-Republicans, convinced Washington not to seek a third term in office. In his "Farewell Address" he urged the United States to "steer clear of permanent alliances" with other nations. Then, in 1797, Washington retired to his home at Mount Vernon.

In the presidential election of 1796, Americans faced a new situation: a contest between opposing parties. The Federalists nominated Vice-President John Adams for president and Thomas Pinckney for vice-president. The Democratic-Republicans nominated Thomas Jefferson for president and Aaron Burr for vice-president.

In the election, Adams received 71 electoral votes, while Jefferson received 68. Because the Constitution stated that the runner-up should become vice-president, the country found itself with a Federalist president and a Democratic-Republican vice-president. What had seemed sensible when the Constitution was written had become a problem because of the unexpected rise of political parties.

▲ Portrait of a young John Adams by Joseph Badger

The election also underscored the growing danger of **sectionalism**—placing the interests of one region over those of the nation as a whole. Almost all the electors from the southern states voted for Jefferson, while all the electors from the northern states voted for Adams. **E**

MAIN IDEA

Analyzing Issues

E How did political parties affect the results of the election of 1796?

ADAMS TRIES TO AVOID WAR Soon after taking office, President Adams faced his first crisis: a looming war with France. The French government, which regarded the Jay treaty with Britain as a violation of the French-American alliance, refused to receive the new American ambassador and began to seize American ships bound for Britain. Adams sent a three-man delegation consisting of Charles Pinckney, minister to France; future Chief Justice John Marshall; and Elbridge Gerry to Paris to negotiate a solution.

By this time, the Reign of Terror had ceased and the French government consisted of a legislature and and a five-man executive branch called the Directory. French power and prestige were at a high point because of the accomplishments of a young general named Napoleon Bonaparte who had conquered most of western Europe. The Directory had little patience with the concerns of the Americans.

The American delegation planned to meet with the French foreign minister, Talleyrand. Instead, the Directory sent three low-level officials, whom Adams in

Analyzing *Political Cartoons*

"THE PARIS MONSTER"

"*Cinque-tetes*, or the Paris Monster," is the title of this political cartoon satirizing the XYZ Affair. On the right, the five members of the French Directory, or ruling executive body, are depicted as a five-headed monster demanding money. The three American representatives, Elbridge Gerry, Charles Pinckney, and John Marshall, are on the left, exclaiming "Cease bawling, monster! We will not give you six-pence!"

SKILLBUILDER Analyzing Political Cartoons

1. How would you contrast the cartoon's depiction of the American representatives with its depiction of the French Directory?
2. What other details in the cartoon show the cartoonist's attitude toward the French?

SEE SKILLBUILDER HANDBOOK, PAGE R24.

his report to Congress called "X, Y, and Z." These officials demanded a $250,000 bribe as payment for seeing Talleyrand. News of this insult, which became known as the **XYZ Affair,** provoked a wave of anti-French feeling at home. "Millions for defense, but not one cent for tribute" became the slogan of the day. The mood was so anti-French that audiences refused to listen to French music.

In 1798, Congress created a navy department and authorized American ships to seize French vessels. Twelve hundred men marched to the president's residence to volunteer for war. Congress authorized the creation of an army of 50,000 troops and brought George Washington yet again out of retirement to be "Lieutenant General and Commander in Chief of the armies raised or to be raised." While war was never officially declared, for the next two years an undeclared naval war raged between France and the United States.

Vocabulary
alien: belonging to or coming from another country; foreign

Vocabulary
sedition: rebellion against one's country; treason

THE ALIEN AND SEDITION ACTS Anti-French feeling continued to flourish, and many Federalists believed that French agents were everywhere, plotting to overthrow the government. New arrivals from foreign countries were soon held in particular suspicion, especially because many immigrants were active in the Democratic-Republican party. Some of the most vocal critics of the Adams administration were foreign-born. They included French and British radicals as well as recent Irish immigrants who lashed out at anyone who was even faintly pro-British, including the Federalist Adams.

To counter what they saw as a growing threat against the government, the Federalists pushed through Congress in 1798 four measures that became known as the **Alien and Sedition Acts.** Three of these measures, the Alien Acts, raised the residence requirement for American citizenship from five years to 14 years and allowed the president to deport or jail any alien considered undesirable.

The fourth measure, the Sedition Act, set fines and jail terms for anyone trying to hinder the operation of the government or expressing "false, scandalous, and malicious statements" against the government. Under the terms of this act, the federal government prosecuted and jailed a number of Democratic-Republican editors, publishers, and politicians. Outraged Democratic-Republicans called the laws a violation of freedom of speech guaranteed by the First Amendment.

VIRGINIA AND KENTUCKY RESOLUTIONS The two main Democratic-Republican leaders, Jefferson and James Madison, saw the Alien and Sedition Acts as a serious misuse of power on the part of the federal government. They decided to organize opposition to the Alien and Sedition Acts by appealing to the states. Madison drew up resolutions that were adopted by the Virginia legislature, while Jefferson wrote resolutions that were approved in Kentucky. The Kentucky Resolutions in particular asserted the principle of **nullification**—that states had the right to nullify, or consider void, any act of Congress that they deemed unconstitutional. Virginia and Kentucky viewed the Alien and Sedition Acts as unconstitutional violations of First Amendment citizens rights. (F)

The resolutions warned of the dangers that the Alien and Sedition Acts posed to a government of checks and balances guaranteed by the Constitution.

MAIN IDEA

Analyzing Issues

(F) How did the Kentucky Resolutions challenge the authority of the federal government?

A PERSONAL VOICE THOMAS JEFFERSON

> "**Let the honest advocate of confidence [in government] read the alien and sedition acts, and say if the Constitution has not been wise in fixing limits to the government it created, and whether we should be wise in destroying those limits.**"
>
> —8th Resolution, The Virginia and Kentucky Resolutions

Moreover, Virginia and Kentucky claimed the right to declare null and void federal laws going beyond powers granted by the Constitution to the Federal government.

The resolutions also called for other states to adopt similar declarations. No other state did so, however, and the issue died out by the next presidential election. Nevertheless, the resolutions showed that the balance of power between the states and the federal government remained a controversial issue. In fact, the election of 1800 between Federalist John Adams and Republican Thomas Jefferson would center on this critical debate.

THE DEATH OF WASHINGTON Throughout 1799, George Washington remained active, writing letters to recruit possible generals and making plans for the army that might be needed in a possible war against France. However, on December 14, Washington died after catching a severe cold. Washington was buried according to his wishes with a military funeral at Mount Vernon.

Ironically, Washington's death was instrumental in improving relations with France. Napoleon Bonaparte, now first consul of France, hoped to lure American friendship away from the British and back to the French. Napoleon ordered ten days of mourning to be observed in the French armies for the American leader. Soon, Napoleon would offer even greater concessions to the Americans.

ASSESSMENT

1. **TERMS & NAMES** For each term or name, write a sentence explaining its significance.
   - **neutrality**
   - **Edmond Genêt**
   - **Thomas Pinckney**
   - **Little Turtle**
   - **John Jay**
   - **sectionalism**
   - **XYZ Affair**
   - **Alien and Sedition Acts**
   - **nullification**

MAIN IDEA

2. **TAKING NOTES**
   List some of the disputes mentioned in this section. Indicate the dispute and each side's arguments.

Dispute	
One side	**Other side**

Choose one dispute and defend one side's arguments.

CRITICAL THINKING

3. **ANALYZING ISSUES**
   Do you agree with the Democratic-Republicans that the Alien and Sedition Acts were a violation of the First Amendment? Were they necessary? Support your opinion. **Think About:**
   - the intent of the First Amendment
   - what was happening in Europe
   - what was happening in America

4. **EVALUATING DECISIONS**
   Should the United States have officially supported the French revolutionaries against the British? Support your opinion with examples from the text. **Think About:**
   - Federalist and Republican attitudes toward France and Great Britain
   - the Reign of Terror
   - U.S. gratitude to France for its support against Britain

Jefferson Alters the Nation's Course

MAIN IDEA	WHY IT MATTERS NOW	Terms & Names
The United States expanded its borders during Thomas Jefferson's administration.	Part or all of 15 states now occupy the territory Jefferson acquired in the Louisiana Purchase.	• Lewis and Clark • Aaron Burr • John Marshall • Judiciary Act of 1801 • midnight judges • *Marbury* v. *Madison* • judicial review • Louisiana Purchase • Sacajawea

One American's Story

hmhsocialstudies.com
TAKING NOTES
Use the graphic organizer online to take notes on the accomplishments of Jefferson's presidency.

Patrick Gass was born on June 12, 1771 and died on April 2, 1870. During that time, the country grew from the original 13 colonies to 37 states. Gass played a part in that expansion as a participant in the **Lewis and Clark** expedition commissioned by President Jefferson to explore the West. Setting out from St. Louis, Missouri, in 1804, the expedition traveled overland to the Pacific Ocean. Along the way, Gass kept a journal. The following passage is from his journal entry of May 14, 1805.

Patrick Gass

A PERSONAL VOICE PATRICK GASS

"This forenoon we passed a large creek on the North side and a small river on the South. About 4 in the afternoon we passed another small river on the South side near the mouth of which some of the men discovered a large brown bear, and six of them went out to kill it. They fired at it; but having only wounded it, it made battle and was near seizing some of them, but they all fortunately escaped, and at length succeeded in dispatching it."

—*A Journal of the Voyages and Travels of a Corps of Discovery*

By charting unexplored territory, the Lewis and Clark expedition helped lay the foundations for western expansion. It was one of the great achievements of the Jefferson presidency.

Jefferson Wins Presidential Election of 1800

The presidential campaign of 1800 was a bitter struggle between Thomas Jefferson, a Democratic-Republican, and his Federalist opponent, President John Adams. Each party hurled wild charges at the other. To Democratic-Republicans, Adams was a tool of the rich who wanted to turn the executive branch into a British-style monarchy. To Federalists, Jefferson was a dangerous supporter of revolutionary France and an atheist bent on destroying organized religion.

HISTORICAL SPOTLIGHT

BURR AND HAMILTON DUEL

After losing to Jefferson in the election of 1800, Aaron Burr needed to revive his failing political career. Shortly thereafter, Burr read unflattering remarks made about him by Alexander Hamilton, his longtime political enemy. Burr, hoping for publicity, challenged Hamilton to a duel.

Usually, after a challenge was made, differences were resolved peacefully. But Hamilton and Burr did not reconcile. On the morning of July 11, 1804, they threw dice to see who would fire first. Hamilton won but fired into the air. Burr then shot his opponent in the stomach, and Hamilton died the next day. Burr was charged with murder but fled before he was brought to trial. In 1806, he became involved in a failed plot to annex Mexico. Charged with treason, Burr was found not guilty. With further charges pending, he briefly fled to Europe before returning to New York.

ELECTORAL DEADLOCK In the balloting, Jefferson defeated Adams by eight electoral votes. However, since Jefferson's running mate, **Aaron Burr,** received the same number of votes in the electoral college as Jefferson, the House of Representatives was called upon to choose between the two highest vote getters. For six feverish days, the House took one ballot after another—35 ballots in all. Finally, Alexander Hamilton intervened. Hamilton persuaded enough Federalists to cast blank votes to give Jefferson a majority of two votes. Burr then became vice-president. Although Hamilton opposed Jefferson's philosophy of government, he regarded Jefferson as much more qualified for the presidency than Burr was.

The deadlock revealed a flaw in the electoral process as spelled out in the Constitution. As a result, Congress passed the Twelfth Amendment, which called for electors to cast separate ballots for president and vice-president. This system is still in effect today.

The Jefferson Presidency

In his inaugural address, Jefferson extended the hand of peace to his opponents. "Every difference of opinion is not a difference of principle," he said. "We are all [Democratic-] Republicans; we are all Federalists." Nevertheless, Jefferson planned to wage a "peaceful revolution" to restore what he saw as the republican ideals of 1776 against the strong-government policies of Federalism. Under Washington and Adams, Federalists had filled the vast majority of government positions. Jefferson reversed this pattern by replacing some Federalist officials with Democratic-Republican ones. By 1803, the government bureaucracy was more evenly balanced between Democratic-Republicans and Federalists.

SIMPLIFYING THE PRESIDENCY Jefferson believed that a simple government best suited the needs of a republic. In a symbolic gesture, he walked to his own inauguration instead of riding in a carriage. As president, he took off his powdered wig and sometimes wore work clothes and frayed slippers when receiving visitors.

In accord with his belief in decentralized power, Jefferson also tried to shrink the government and cut costs wherever possible. He reduced the size of the army, halted a planned expansion of the navy, and lowered expenses for government social functions. He also rolled back Hamilton's economic program by eliminating all internal taxes and reducing the influence of the Bank of the United States. Jefferson strongly favored free trade rather than government-controlled trade and tariffs. He believed that free trade would benefit the United States because the raw materials and food that Americans were producing were in short supply in Europe. (A)

MAIN IDEA

Drawing Conclusions

(A) How did Jefferson's actions reflect his philosophy of government?

SOUTHERN DOMINANCE OF POLITICS Jefferson was the first president to take office in the new federal capital, Washington, D.C. Though in appearance the city was a primitive place of dirt roads and few buildings, its location between Virginia and Maryland reflected the growing importance of the South in national politics. In fact, Jefferson and the two presidents who followed him—James Madison and James Monroe—all were from Virginia.

This pattern of Southern dominance underscored the declining influence of both New England and the Federalists in national political life. The decline of the Federalists was hastened by Jefferson's political moderation. Also, many Federalists refused to participate in political campaigns because they did not want to appeal to the common people for support. Furthermore, national expansion worked against the Federalists because settlers in the new states tended to vote for the Democratic-Republicans, who represented farmers' interests.

JOHN MARSHALL AND THE SUPREME COURT Federalists continued to exert great influence in the judicial branch, however. Adams had appointed **John Marshall,** a staunch Federalist, as chief justice of the Supreme Court. Marshall served on the Court for more than 30 years, handing down decisions that would strengthen the power of the Supreme Court and the federal government.

Some of Adams's other judicial appointments proved to be less effective, however. Just prior to leaving office, Adams pushed through Congress the **Judiciary Act of 1801,** which increased the number of federal judges by 16. In an attempt to control future federal judicial decisions, Adams filled most of these positions with Federalists. These judges were called **midnight judges** because Adams signed their appointments late on the last day of his administration.

Adams's packing of the courts with Federalists angered Jefferson and the Democratic-Republicans. Since the documents authorizing some of the appointments had not been delivered by the time Adams left office, Jefferson argued that these appointments were invalid.

MARBURY* v. *MADISON This argument led to one of the most important Supreme Court decisions of all time: ***Marbury* v. *Madison*** (1803). William Marbury was one of the midnight judges who had never received his official papers. James Madison was Jefferson's Secretary of State, whose duty it was to deliver the papers. The Judiciary Act of 1789 required the Supreme Court to order that the papers be delivered, and Marbury sued to enforce this provision. Chief Justice Marshall decided that this provision of the act was unconstitutional because the Constitution did not empower the Supreme Court to issue such orders. (See Historic Decisions of the Supreme Court, *Marbury* v. *Madison.*) The decision was later recognized as significant for affirming the principle of **judicial review**—the ability of the Supreme Court to declare an act of Congress unconstitutional. B

MAIN IDEA

Summarizing

B What is judicial review, and why is it important?

The United States Expands West

During Jefferson's presidency, Americans continued their westward migration across the Appalachians. For instance, between 1800 and 1810, the population of Ohio grew from 45,000 to 231,000. Although pioneer life was hard, the pioneers kept coming.

A PERSONAL VOICE F. A. MICHAUX

"The houses that they inhabit are built upon the borders of the river, . . . whence they enjoy the most delightful prospects [views]; still, their mode of building does not correspond with the beauties of the spot, being nothing but miserable log houses, without windows, and so small that two beds occupy the greatest part of them."

—from *Travels to the West of the Allegheny Mountains*

Supplies for the journey west.

Lewis and Clark Expedition, 1804–1806

hmhsocialstudies.com INTERACTIVE MAP

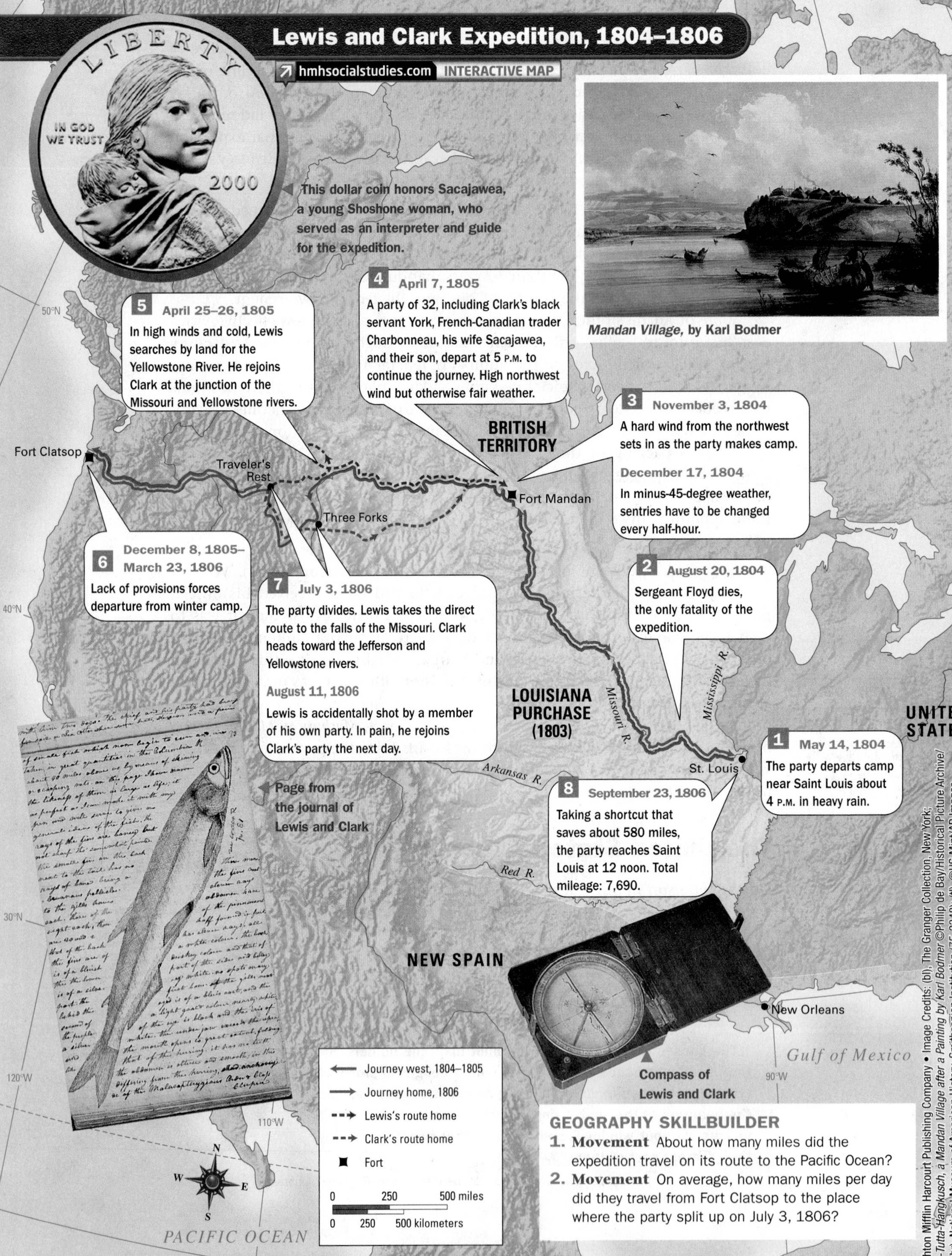

LIBERTY
IN GOD WE TRUST
2000
5 April 25–26, 1805
In high winds and cold, Lewis searches by land for the Yellowstone River. He rejoins Clark at the junction of the Missouri and Yellowstone rivers.
4 April 7, 1805
A party of 32, including Clark's black servant York, French-Canadian trader Charbonneau, his wife Sacajawea, and their son, depart at 5 P.M. to continue the journey. High northwest wind but otherwise fair weather.
3 November 3, 1804
A hard wind from the northwest sets in as the party makes camp.
December 17, 1804
In minus-45-degree weather, sentries have to be changed every half-hour.
2 August 20, 1804
Sergeant Floyd dies, the only fatality of the expedition.
1 May 14, 1804
The party departs camp near Saint Louis about 4 P.M. in heavy rain.
6 December 8, 1805–March 23, 1806
Lack of provisions forces departure from winter camp.
7 July 3, 1806
The party divides. Lewis takes the direct route to the falls of the Missouri. Clark heads toward the Jefferson and Yellowstone rivers.
August 11, 1806
Lewis is accidentally shot by a member of his own party. In pain, he rejoins Clark's party the next day.
8 September 23, 1806
Taking a shortcut that saves about 580 miles, the party reaches Saint Louis at 12 noon. Total mileage: 7,690.
BRITISH TERRITORY
LOUISIANA PURCHASE (1803)
UNITED STATES
NEW SPAIN
Fort Clatsop
Traveler's Rest
Three Forks
Fort Mandan
St. Louis
New Orleans
Missouri R.
Mississippi R.
Arkansas R.
Red R.
Gulf of Mexico
PACIFIC OCEAN
50°N
40°N
30°N
120°W
110°W
90°W
N
S
E
W
Journey west, 1804–1805
Journey home, 1806
Lewis's route home
Clark's route home
Fort
0 250 500 miles
0 250 500 kilometers

This dollar coin honors Sacajawea, a young Shoshone woman, who served as an interpreter and guide for the expedition.

Mandan Village, by Karl Bodmer

Page from the journal of Lewis and Clark

Compass of Lewis and Clark

GEOGRAPHY SKILLBUILDER

1. **Movement** About how many miles did the expedition travel on its route to the Pacific Ocean?
2. **Movement** On average, how many miles per day did they travel from Fort Clatsop to the place where the party split up on July 3, 1806?

Most of the settlers who arrived in Ohio, Kentucky, and Tennessee came through the Cumberland Gap, a natural passage through the Appalachians near where Kentucky, Tennessee, and Virginia meet. A generation earlier, in 1775, Daniel Boone, one of America's great frontier guides, had led the clearing of a road from Virginia, through the Cumberland Gap, into the heart of Kentucky. When it was finished, the Wilderness Road became one of the major routes for westward migration.

THE LOUISIANA PURCHASE In 1800, Napoleon Bonaparte of France persuaded Spain to return the Louisiana Territory, which it had received from France in 1762. When news of the secret transfer leaked out, Americans reacted with alarm. Jefferson feared that a strong French presence in the midcontinent would force the United States into an alliance with Britain. C

MAIN IDEA

Analyzing Issues

C Why was the United States concerned about the Louisiana Territory?

Jefferson wanted to resolve the problem by buying New Orleans and western Florida from the French. He sent James Monroe to join American ambassador Robert Livingston in Paris. Before Monroe arrived, however, Napoleon had abandoned his hopes for an American empire. He had failed to reconquer France's most important island colony, Saint Domingue (now known as Haiti). By the time that Monroe arrived in Paris in April 1803, Napoleon had decided to sell the entire Louisiana Territory to the United States.

With no time to consult their government, Monroe and Livingston went ahead and closed the deal for $15 million. Jefferson, though, was not certain that the purchase was constitutional. As a strict constructionist, he doubted whether the Constitution gave the government the power to acquire new territory. But, after a delay, he submitted the treaty finalizing the purchase, and the Senate ratified it. With the **Louisiana Purchase,** which included all the land drained by the western tributaries of the Mississippi River, the size of the United States more than doubled.

LEWIS AND CLARK Jefferson was eager to explore the new territory. In 1803, he appointed Meriwether Lewis to lead the expedition he called the Corps of Discovery from St. Louis to the Pacific coast. Jefferson ordered the Corps to collect scientific information about unknown plants and animals en route to the Pacific and to learn as much as possible about the Native American tribes encountered along the way. Lewis chose William Clark to be second in command. Starting off with some 50 soldiers and woodsmen, including Patrick Gass, the expedition later became smaller but added a Native American woman, **Sacajawea,** who served as interpreter and guide. The Lewis and Clark expedition took two years and four months and recorded invaluable information about the western territories.

Background

Even before the Louisiana Purchase, Jefferson had planned to explore the West. In February 1803, Congress approved Jefferson's request for funds to finance an expedition.

SECTION 3 ASSESSMENT

1. **TERMS & NAMES** For each term or name, write a sentence explaining its significance.
   - **Lewis and Clark**
   - **Aaron Burr**
   - **John Marshall**
   - **Judiciary Act of 1801**
   - **midnight judges**
   - ***Marbury* v. *Madison***
   - **judicial review**
   - **Louisiana Purchase**
   - **Sacajawea**

MAIN IDEA

2. **TAKING NOTES**
   Make a chart like the one below listing the major accomplishments of Jefferson's presidency and the significance of each.

Event	Significance

CRITICAL THINKING

3. **EVALUATING**
   How did the Louisiana Purchase and the Lewis and Clark expedition affect the expansion of the United States?

4. **ANALYZING ISSUES**
   Why was *Marbury* v. *Madison* such an important case? **Think About:**
   - Judge Marshall's decision
   - its effects on the future

5. **ANALYZING PRIMARY SOURCES**
   How does this sketch—from Patrick Gass's journal—of a man treed by a grizzly bear illustrate fanciful ideas about the West?

SECTION 4

The War of 1812

MAIN IDEA	WHY IT MATTERS NOW	Terms & Names
War broke out again between the United States and Britain in 1812.	The War of 1812 confirmed American independence and strengthened nationalism.	• blockade • impressment • embargo • William Henry Harrison • Tecumseh • war hawk • Andrew Jackson • Treaty of Ghent • armistice

One American's Story

hmhsocialstudies.com TAKING NOTES

Use the graphic organizer online to take notes on why the war hawks wanted war with Great Britain.

During the War of 1812, Samuel Wilson became a symbol for the nation. The owner of a meat-packing business in Troy, New York, he began supplying barrels of salted meat to the army, stamping the barrels with the initials "U.S.," for United States. One of Wilson's employees joked that the letters stood for "Uncle Sam," Wilson's nickname. Soon army recruits were calling themselves "Uncle Sam's soldiers." One of Wilson's great-nephews, Lucius Wilson, spoke about his famous relative in 1917.

A PERSONAL VOICE LUCIUS E. WILSON

"He was the old original Uncle Sam that gave the name to the United States. . . . [He] engaged in many enterprises, employed many hands [workers], had extensive acquaintance, was jolly, genial, generous, and known [as] and called "Uncle Sam" by everyone."

—*Uncle Sam: The Man and the Legend*

▲ **One of the earliest depictions of Uncle Sam**

The story took on the features of a legend. Uncle Sam came to symbolize American values of honesty and hard work. The war during which the phrase caught on was just around the corner for the United States.

The War Hawks Demand War

Jefferson's popularity soared after the Louisiana Purchase, and he won reelection in 1804. During his second term, renewed fighting between Britain and France threatened American shipping. In 1806, Napoleon decided to exclude British goods from Europe. In turn, Great Britain decided that the best way of attacking Napoleon's Europe was to **blockade** it, or seal up its ports and prevent ships from entering or leaving. By 1807, Britain had seized more than 1,000 American ships and confiscated their cargoes, and France had seized about half that number.

GRIEVANCES AGAINST BRITAIN Although both France and Britain engaged in these acts of aggression, Americans focused their anger on the British. One reason was the British policy of **impressment,** the practice of seizing Americans at sea and "impressing," or drafting, them into the British navy. Another reason was the *Chesapeake* incident. In June 1807, the commander of a British warship demanded the right to board and search the U.S. naval frigate *Chesapeake* for British deserters. When the U.S. captain refused, the British opened fire, killing 3 Americans and wounding 18.

Jefferson convinced Congress to declare an **embargo,** a ban on exporting products to other countries. He believed that the Embargo Act of 1807 would hurt Britain and the other European powers and force them to honor American neutrality. The embargo hurt America more than Britain, and in 1809 Congress lifted the ban on foreign trade—except with France and Britain. (A)

MAIN IDEA

Analyzing Issues

(A) What was Jefferson's reasoning behind the embargo of 1807?

TECUMSEH'S CONFEDERACY Another source of trouble appeared in 1809, when General **William Henry Harrison,** the governor of the Indiana Territory, invited several Native American chiefs to Fort Wayne, Indiana, and persuaded them to sign away three million acres of tribal land to the U.S. government.

Not all chiefs gave in. Like Little Turtle and chiefs from other tribes, the Shawnee chief **Tecumseh** believed that the only way for Native Americans to protect their homeland against intruding white settlers was to form a confederacy, a united Native American nation.

Tecumseh was aided by his younger brother, known as the Prophet. Around 1805, the Prophet had started a reform movement within the Shawnee tribe to cast off all traces of the white "civilization," including Christianity. Both the Prophet and Tecumseh warned that the Great Spirit was angry with all of the tribes who had abandoned their traditional practices and beliefs. The time had come to return to those beliefs, they urged, and to implore the aid of the Great Spirit in driving out the invaders.

"The Great Spirit gave this great land to his red children."

TECUMSEH

More practical than his brother, Tecumseh was a brilliant strategist and a skillful diplomat. While continuing to press Harrison to withdraw from Native American land, Tecumseh began negotiations with the British for assistance in what seemed like an inevitable war with the Americans. Throughout 1810 and 1811, Tecumseh traveled throughout the Midwest and the South, trying to win followers to his confederacy. Unfortunately, many tribes had already accepted payment for their lands. Others were reluctant to give up tribal autonomy by joining the kind of confederacy that Tecumseh proposed.

THE WAR HAWKS In November 1811, while Tecumseh was absent, his brother led the Shawnee in an attack on Harrison and his troops. Harrison struck back. On the banks of the Tippecanoe river, he burned the Shawnee capital known as Prophetstown to the ground. Harrison's victory at what came to be known as the Battle of Tippecanoe made him a national hero, but his troops suffered heavy losses. When it was discovered that the Native American confederacy was using arms from British Canada, a group of young congressmen from the South and the West known as the **war hawks** called for war against Britain. Led by Senator John C. Calhoun of South Carolina and Henry Clay of Kentucky, the Speaker of the House of Representatives, the war hawks rallied behind their motto: "On to Canada!" (B)

MAIN IDEA

Analyzing Motives

(B) Why did the war hawks call for the war with Britain?

The War Brings Mixed Results

In the election of 1808, another Virginia Democratic-Republican—James Madison—coasted to victory against a weak Federalist opponent, Charles C. Pinckney. By the spring of 1812, President Madison had decided to go to war against Britain. Madison believed that Britain was trying to strangle American trade and cripple the American economy. Congress approved the war declaration in early June.

THE WAR IN CANADA Declaring war was one thing—but fighting it was another. The American military was unprepared for war. Detroit was captured by the British shortly after war was declared and the Americans suffered numerous setbacks, including a failed attempt to take Montreal. The following year, a fleet commanded by Oliver Hazard Perry defeated a British fleet on Lake Erie, and American soldiers retook Detroit and won several battles. Different Native American groups allied with British or U.S. forces, depending on relationships they had developed before the war. Tecumseh, like many Native Americans, had fought for the British with the hopes of continuing British aid in stopping U.S. expansion. The Shawnee leader was killed at the Battle of the Thames in 1813.

VIDEO
War of 1812: Madison Declares War
hmhsocialstudies.com

THE WAR AT SEA The war was an opportunity for the relatively young U.S. Navy to test its ability. Badly outnumbered with only 16 ships, the United States was aided by its three 44-gun frigates, or warships, the *President,* the *United States,* and the *Constitution.* Known for their speed and ability to sail close to enemy vessels and open fire, these ships sailed alone. Each scored victories against British vessels.

However, the superior numbers of the British navy began to tell. In November of 1812, the British government ordered a blockade of the Chesapeake and Delaware bays (see the map below). As the war progressed and U.S. frigates scored

The War of 1812

hmhsocialstudies.com INTERACTIVE MAP

Lake Champlain, Sept. 11, 1814
U.S. gains control of lake, and British retreat to Canada.

Thames, Oct. 5, 1813
Death of Tecumseh leads to collapse of Native American support for British.

Tippecanoe, Nov. 7, 1811
With British support, Native Americans try to stop U.S. westward expansion but Harrison defeats them.

Put-in-Bay, Sept. 10, 1813
U.S. Naval forces under Oliver Hazard Perry gain control of Lake Erie.

New Orleans, Jan. 8, 1815
After defeating Native Americans in Mississippi Territory, Andrew Jackson moves to defend this city. Battle is fought two weeks after peace treaty was signed at Ghent, Dec. 24, 1814.

Baltimore, Sept. 12–14, 1814
British fail to capture city and withdraw from Chesapeake Bay in October.

Washington, D.C., Aug. 24–25, 1814
British burn Capitol, White House, and other important buildings.

BRITISH TERRITORY (Canada)
Lake Superior
Fort Mackinac July 17, 1812
York (Toronto) April 27, 1813
Montreal
Lake Michigan
Lake Huron
L. Ontario
Fort Erie Aug. 2–Sept. 21, 1814
Boston
Detroit
L. Erie
New York
Fort Dearborn August 15, 1812
Delaware Bay
Chesapeake Bay
Mississippi River
Horseshoe Bend March 27, 1814
British Blockade
Pensacola
SPANISH TERRITORY (Florida)
Gulf of Mexico
ATLANTIC OCEAN
40°N
30°N
90°W
80°W

U.S. forces
British forces
U.S. victory
British victory
Blockade
0 150 300 miles
0 150 300 kilometers

GEOGRAPHY SKILLBUILDER

1. **Location** Why do you think there were a number of battles on the Great Lakes?
2. **Human-Environment Interaction** Why do you think the British blockaded the coast from Boston to Georgia?

more victories against British ships, the blockade was extended along the east coast. By the end of 1813, most American ships were bottled up in port.

BRITISH BURN THE WHITE HOUSE By 1814, the British were raiding and burning towns all along the Atlantic coast. The redcoats brushed aside some hastily assembled American troops and entered Washington, D.C. In retaliation for the U.S. victory at the Battle of York, the capital of Upper Canada, in which U.S. forces burned the governor's mansion and the legislative assembly buildings, the British burned the Capitol, the White House, and other public buildings. On August 24, Madison and other federal officials had to flee from their own capital.

THE BATTLE OF NEW ORLEANS At the same time, a general from Tennessee named **Andrew Jackson** was winning a series of battles that gained him national fame. After a six months' campaign involving four battles, Jackson defeated Native Americans of the Creek tribe at the battle of Horseshoe Bend in March of 1814. The Creeks had earlier been victorious at the battle of Fort Mims in which all but 36 of the fort's 553 inhabitants were killed. Jackson's victory at Horseshoe Bend destroyed the military power of Native Americans in the south.

Ironically, Jackson's greatest victory came after the war was over. On January 8, 1815, Jackson's troops defeated a superior British force at the Battle of New Orleans. Hundreds of British troops died, while just a handful of Americans lost their lives.

THE TREATY OF GHENT Unknown to Jackson, British and American diplomats had already signed a peace agreement. The **Treaty of Ghent,** signed on Christmas Eve 1814, declared an **armistice,** or end to the fighting. Although it did not address the issues of impressment or neutral shipping rights, Americans were eager for peace and welcomed the treaty.

Within a few years, the United States and Great Britain were able to reach agreement on many of the issues left open at Ghent. In 1815, a commercial treaty reopened trade between the two countries. In 1817, the Rush-Bagot agreement limited the number of warships on the Great Lakes. In 1818, a British-American commission set the northern boundary of the Louisiana Territory at the 49th parallel as far west as the Rocky Mountains. The two nations then agreed to a ten-year joint occupation of the Oregon Territory. But at home, Americans were unable to resolve differences that had already begun to divide the nation.

ASSESSMENT

1. **TERMS & NAMES** For each term or name, write a sentence explaining its significance.
   - **blockade**
   - **impressment**
   - **embargo**
   - **William Henry Harrison**
   - **Tecumseh**
   - **war hawk**
   - **Andrew Jackson**
   - **Treaty of Ghent**
   - **armistice**

MAIN IDEA

2. **TAKING NOTES**
In the web below, show the reasons why the war hawks wanted war with Great Britain.

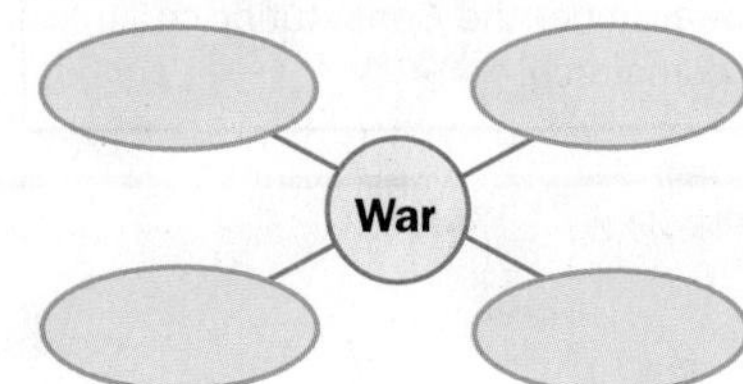

CRITICAL THINKING

3. **EVALUATING**
What was the most important achievement of the U.S. in this period? **Think About:**
   - relations between the U.S. and Britain
   - the results of the war

4. **ANALYZING**
Even though it was fought after an armistice had been signed, why was the Battle of New Orleans an important victory for the Americans?

5. **EVALUATING**
Do you think that Tecumseh's confederacy helped or hurt the cause of Native Americans? **Think About:**
   - the loss of Native American lands
   - the reluctance of certain tribes to join the confederacy
   - Tecumseh's role in the War of 1812

MARBURY v. *MADISON* (1803)

ORIGINS OF THE CASE A few days before Thomas Jefferson's inauguration, outgoing president John Adams appointed William Marbury to be a justice of the peace. But the commission was not delivered to Marbury. Later, Jefferson's new secretary of state, James Madison, refused to give Marbury the commission. Marbury asked the Supreme Court to force Madison to give him his commission.

THE RULING **The Court declared that the law on which Marbury based his claim was unconstitutional, and therefore it refused to order Madison to give Marbury his commission.**

LEGAL REASONING

Writing for the Court, Chief Justice John Marshall decided that Marbury had a right to his commission, and he scolded Madison at length for refusing to deliver it.

However, he then considered Marbury's claim that, under the Judiciary Act of 1789, the Supreme Court should order Madison to deliver the commission. As Marshall pointed out, the powers of the Supreme Court are set by the Constitution, and Congress does not have the authority to alter them. The Judiciary Act attempted to do just that.

Marshall reasoned that, since the Constitution is the "supreme law of the land, no law that goes against the Constitution can be valid."

> **"If . . . the courts are to regard the constitution, and the constitution is superior to any ordinary act of the legislature, the constitution, and not such ordinary act, must govern the case to which they both apply."**

If an act of Congress violates the Constitution, then a judge must uphold the Constitution and declare the act void. In choosing to obey the Constitution, the Supreme Court did declare the Judiciary Act unconstitutional and void, and so refused to grant Marbury's request.

◀ **Chief Justice John Marshall**

LEGAL SOURCES

U.S. CONSTITUTION

U.S. CONSTITUTION, ARTICLE III, SECTION 2 (1789)

"The judicial power shall extend to all cases . . . arising under this Constitution, the laws of the United States, and treaties made . . . under their authority."

U.S. CONSTITUTION, ARTICLE VI, CLAUSE 2 (1789)

"This Constitution, and the laws of the United States which shall be made in pursuance thereof . . . shall be the supreme law of the land; and the judges in every State shall be bound thereby."

RELATED CASES

***FLETCHER* v. *PECK* (1810)**

The Court ruled a state law unconstitutional for the first time.

***COHENS* v. *VIRGINIA* (1821)**

The Court overturned a state court decision for the first time.

***GIBBONS* v. *OGDEN* (1824)**

The Court ruled that the federal Congress—not the states—had the power under the Constitution to regulate interstate commerce.

◀ William Marbury

WHY IT MATTERED

In 1803, interest in Marbury's commission was primarily about partisan politics. The fight was just one skirmish in the ongoing battle between Federalists, such as Adams, and Democratic-Republicans, led by Jefferson and Madison, which had intensified in the election of 1800.

When Jefferson won the election, Adams made a final effort to hinder Jefferson's promised reforms. Before leaving office, he tried to fill the government with Federalists, including the "midnight" justices such as Marbury. Madison's refusal to deliver Marbury's appointment was part of Jefferson's subsequent effort to rid his administration of Federalists.

Marshall's opinion in *Marbury* might seem like a victory for Jefferson because it denied Marbury his commission. However, by scolding Madison and extending the principle of judicial review—the power of courts to decide whether or not specific laws are valid—the Court sent a message to Jefferson and to the Congress that the judiciary had the power to affect legislation. The Marshall Court, however, never declared another act of Congress unconstitutional.

HISTORICAL IMPACT

In striking down part of the Judiciary Act, an act of Congress, Marshall gave new force to the principle of judicial review. The legacy of John Marshall and of *Marbury* is that judicial review has become a cornerstone of American government. One scholar has called it "America's novel contribution to political theory and the practice of constitutional government." As Justice Marshall recognized, judicial review is an essential component of democratic government; by ensuring that Congress exercises only those powers granted by the Constitution, the courts protect the sovereignty of the people.

Perhaps more importantly, the principle of judicial review plays a vital role in our federal system of checks and balances. With *Marbury,* the judicial branch secured its place as one of three coequal branches of the federal government. The judiciary has no power to make laws or to carry them out. However, judges have an important role in deciding what the law is and how it is carried out.

In *City of Boerne* v. *Flores* (1997), for instance, the Supreme Court declared void the Religious Freedom Restoration Act of 1993. Members of Congress had passed the act in an attempt to change the way federal courts apply the First Amendment's Free Exercise Clause. The Supreme Court ruled that Congress does not have the authority to decide what the First Amendment means—in effect, to define its own powers. The Court, and not Congress, is the interpreter of the Constitution.

Through the 2007–2008 term, the Court had rendered 162 decisions striking down—in whole or part—acts of Congress. It had also voided or restricted the enforcement of state laws 1,179 times. That the entire country has with few exceptions obeyed these decisions, no matter how strongly they disagreed, proves Americans' faith in the Supreme Court as the protector of the rule of law.

THINKING CRITICALLY

CONNECT TO HISTORY

1. **Comparing** Read encyclopedia articles about another Marshall Court decision, such as *Fletcher* v. *Peck*, *Cohens* v. *Virginia*, or *Gibbons* v. *Ogden*. Compare that decision with *Marbury* and consider what the two cases and opinions have in common. Write a paragraph explaining the major similarities between the cases.

SEE SKILLBUILDER HANDBOOK, PAGE R8.

CONNECT TO TODAY 

2. Visit the links for Historic Decisions of the Supreme Court to research a recent Supreme Court decision involving judicial review of an act of Congress. Write a case summary in which you describe the law's purpose, the Court's ruling, and the potential impact of the decision.

VISUAL SUMMARY

LAUNCHING THE NEW NATION

GOVERNMENT

- Washington forms the Cabinet.
- The Judiciary Act of 1789 establishes the Supreme Court.
- Hamilton founds the Bank of the United States.
- National capital is established in the District of Columbia.

CONFLICTS

- The Federalist and Democratic-Republican parties emerge.
- The Whiskey Rebellion protests Hamilton's excise tax.
- The Alien and Sedition Acts restrict protest.
- The Virginia and Kentucky Resolutions assert nullification.

TERRITORIES

- The Louisiana Purchase more than doubles the size of the U.S.
- Lewis and Clark explore the new territory.
- Differences between North and South continue to grow.
- More and more settlers push west.

WAR AND PEACE

- Native Americans, aided by the British, fight loss of their lands.
- War hawks urge war with Britain.
- War of 1812 occurs.
- Treaty of Ghent is signed.

TERMS & NAMES

For each term or name below, write a sentence explaining its connection to the new United States.

1. Alexander Hamilton
2. Cabinet
3. neutrality
4. Alien and Sedition Acts
5. John Marshall
6. Louisiana Purchase
7. Meriwether Lewis
8. embargo
9. Tecumseh
10. Andrew Jackson

MAIN IDEAS

Use your notes and the information in the chapter to answer the following questions.

Washington Heads the New Government

1. What were the first steps taken by the Washington administration in building a new government?
2. Why did President Washington want both Thomas Jefferson and Alexander Hamilton to be among his closest advisers?
3. Why was the Whiskey Rebellion a significant event in the early days of the new government?

Foreign Affairs Trouble the Nation

4. What were three major international issues at this time, and how did the United States respond to them?
5. How did the United States manage to stay out of war during this period?
6. How did the expanding nation deal with Native Americans?

Jefferson Alters the Nation's Course

7. What were some of the accomplishments of Jefferson's first administration?
8. How did the Louisiana Purchase change the United States?

The War of 1812

9. What events led to the War of 1812?
10. What did the Treaty of Ghent accomplish?

CRITICAL THINKING

1. **CONTRASTING** Create a chart listing some of the more important differences in the beliefs and goals of the Federalists and the Democratic-Republicans. Whose ideas appeal to you more?

Federalists	Democratic-Republicans

2. **HYPOTHESIZING** What if you had been your current age in 1800? What might have been some of the advantages and disadvantages of growing up in this period? Write two paragraphs describing what you like and dislike about the U.S. at that time. Provide examples from the text in your answer.

STANDARDIZED TEST PRACTICE

Use the cartoon and your knowledge of U.S. history to answer the question below.

1. The British cartoon above entitled "The Fall of Washington—or Maddy [Madison] in full flight" was published in 1814. In it, a character exclaims, "The great Washington fought for Liberty, but we are fighting for shadows." The character is contrasting the Revolutionary War and —

   A Shays's Rebellion.
   B the XYZ Affair.
   C the War of 1812.
   D Washington's declaration of neutrality.

For additional test practice, go online for:

- Diagnostic tests
- Tutorials

INTERACT WITH HISTORY

Recall the issues that you explored at the beginning of the chapter. Imagine that it is now 1814, and one of your former students has written to ask your opinion about how the United States has grown as a nation. Write a response in which you mention events from the chapter that show key challenges and achievements that helped to shape the young republic.

FOCUS ON WRITING

Imagine you are a citizen during the early years of the United States. Select an important issue from that time period. Write a persuasive letter to the federal government in opposition to its decision or policy. In your letter, clearly present why you are opposed to the government's actions and present an alternate plan of action that you feel the government should pursue.

COLLABORATIVE LEARNING

In a small group read and discuss the "One American's Story" at the beginning of Section 3. Then consider the following questions: Who do you think are the explorers of our time? What challenges do they face in their journeys of exploration? Prepare a report and present it to the class.

Lewis and Clark

In 1804 Meriwether Lewis, William Clark, and the 33-man Corps of Discovery began a 8,000-mile journey across uncharted territory. Under orders from President Thomas Jefferson, the expedition mapped a route across the Louisiana Purchase to the Pacific Ocean. From St. Louis, Missouri, they traveled west up the Missouri River, then across the Rocky Mountains, and to the Pacific. They met Native American peoples and cataloged geography, plants, and animals. Not only was their mission one of history's greatest explorations, it also secured an American claim to the Pacific Coast and helped inspire millions to migrate west.

Explore entries from Lewis's journal and other primary sources online. You can find a wealth of information, video clips, activities, and more at hmhsocialstudies.com.

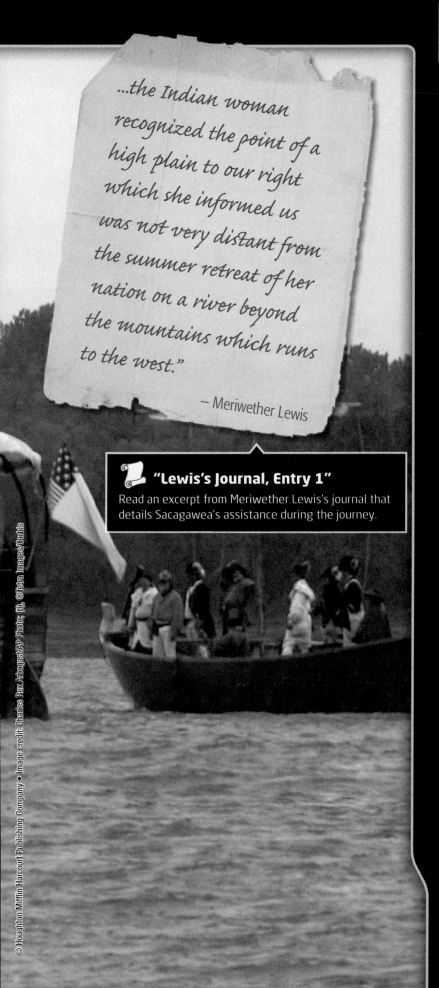

"...the Indian woman recognized the point of a high plain to our right which she informed us was not very distant from the summer retreat of her nation on a river beyond the mountains which runs to the west."

– Meriwether Lewis

"Lewis's Journal, Entry 1"

Read an excerpt from Meriwether Lewis's journal that details Sacagawea's assistance during the journey.

Underway on the Missouri

Watch the video to see how the Corps of Discovery sailed up the Missouri River to begin their expedition.

Making Friends Upriver

Watch the video to see which Native American peoples the Corps met and traded with as they made their journey west.

The Shores of the Pacific

Watch the video to see how the Corps tried to adapt to a different climate and the new peoples that they met along the Pacific coast.

CHAPTER 7

Balancing Nationalism and Sectionalism

Essential Question

How did regional differences contribute to the growing conflict over states' rights versus federal power?

ALABAMA COURSE OF STUDY

5 Explain key cases that helped shape the United States Supreme Court, including Marbury versus Madison, McCullough versus Maryland, and Cherokee Nation versus Georgia.

6 Describe relations of the United States with Britain and France from 1781 to 1823, including the XYZ Affair, the War of 1812, and the Monroe Doctrine.

9 Explain dynamics of economic nationalism during the Era of Good Feelings, including transportation systems, Henry Clay's American System, slavery and the emergence of the plantation system, and the beginning of industrialism in the Northeast.

10 Analyze key ideas of Jacksonian Democracy for their impact on political participation, political parties, and constitutional government.

• Explaining the spoils system, nullification, extension of voting rights, the Indian Removal Act, and the common man ideal.

13 Summarize major legislation and court decisions from 1800 to 1861 that led to increasing sectionalism, including the Missouri Compromise of 1820, the Compromise of 1850, the Fugitive Slave Acts, the Kansas-Nebraska Act, and the Dred Scott decision.

• Describing tariff debates and the nullification crisis between 1800 and 1861.

The port of New Orleans, Louisiana, a major center for the cotton trade

USA

1817 Construction begins on the Erie Canal.

1819 U.S. acquires Florida from Spain.

1820 James Monroe is reelected president.

1820 Congress agrees to the Missouri Compromise.

1824 John Quincy Adams is elected president.

1815 — 1820 — 1825

WORLD

1815 Napoleon is defeated at Waterloo.

1819 Simón Bolívar becomes president of Colombia.

1822 Freed U.S. slaves found Liberia on the west coast of Africa.

1824 Mexico becomes a republic.

Image Credits: (bkgd), Library of Congress Department of Prints and Photographs [LC-USZC4-994]; (b), The Granger Collection, New York

hmhsocialstudies.com VIDEO

INTERACT WITH HISTORY

The year is 1828. You are a senator from a Southern state. Congress has just passed a high tax on imported cloth and iron in order to protect Northern industry. The tax will raise the cost of these goods in the South and will cause Britain to buy less cotton. Southern states hope to nullify, or cancel, such federal laws that they consider unfair.

Explore the Issues

- What might happen if some states enforce laws and others don't?
- How can Congress address the needs of different states?
- What does it mean to be a nation?

1828 Andrew Jackson is elected president.

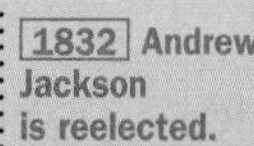

1832 Andrew Jackson is reelected.

1836 Martin Van Buren is elected president.

1838 Removal of the Cherokee along the Trail of Tears begins.

1840 William Henry Harrison is elected president.

1830 | 1835 | 1840

1830 France invades Algeria.

1833 British Parliament takes steps to end employment of children under nine years of age.

1837 Victoria becomes queen of England.

1839 Opium War breaks out in China.

Image Credits: (bkgd), Library of Congress Department of Prints and Photographs [LC-USZC4-994]; (bl), *Andrew Jackson* (Detail), (1845), Thomas Sully. Oil on canvas, 20 3/8" x 17 1/4". ©1996 Board of Trustees, National Gallery of Art, Washington DC, Andrew W. Mellon Foundation; (br), *The Trail of Tears*, Troy Anderson/Marilyn Angel Wynn/Nativestock.com; (bc), The Granger Collection, New York

Regional Economies Create Differences

MAIN IDEA

The North and the South developed different economic systems that led to political differences between the regions.

WHY IT MATTERS NOW

Different regions of the country continue to have differing political and economic interests today.

Terms & Names

- **Eli Whitney**
- **interchangeable parts**
- **mass production**
- **Industrial Revolution**
- **cotton gin**
- **Henry Clay**
- **American System**
- **National Road**
- **Erie Canal**
- **Tariff of 1816**

One American's Story

hmhsocialstudies.com
TAKING NOTES

Use the graphic organizer online to take notes on the different economic systems of the North and South.

In a dramatic presentation in front of President John Adams in 1801, inventor **Eli Whitney** demonstrated the first musket made of **interchangeable parts,** parts that are exactly alike. He assembled a musket from pieces chosen at random from crates full of parts. Whitney had made his musket parts the old-fashioned way, by hand. Nonetheless, his efforts were the first steps toward developing tools with which unskilled workers could make uniform parts.

A PERSONAL VOICE ELI WHITNEY

> **"One of my primary objects is to form the tools so the tools themselves shall fashion the work and give to every part its just proportion—which when once accomplished will give expedition, uniformity, and exactness to the whole. . . . In short, the tools which I contemplate are similar to an engraving on copper plate from which may be taken a great number of impressions exactly alike."**
>
> —quoted in *Eli Whitney and the Birth of American Technology*

▲ **In 1798, Eli Whitney manufactured 10,000 muskets in just two years. At that time, arms factories could produce only around 300 guns a year.**

Better tools sped up the manufacture of goods and improved their reliability. Inventions and ideas such as these would affect different regions of the young nation in different ways.

Another Revolution Affects America

During the 19th century, new approaches to manufacturing, such as Whitney's interchangeable parts, took industry out of American households and artisans' workshops. Factories became the new centers of industry. The factory system (using power-driven machinery and laborers assigned to different tasks) made **mass production**—the production of goods in large quantities—possible. These changes in manufacturing brought about an **Industrial Revolution**—social and economic reorganization that took place as machines replaced hand tools and large-scale factory production developed.

GREAT BRITAIN STARTS A REVOLUTION The Industrial Revolution actually first began in Great Britain. It was in Britain, during the 18th century, that inventors came up with ways to generate power using swiftly flowing streams and bountiful supplies of coal. Inventors then developed power-driven machinery and ways to use this machinery to quickly mass-produce goods such as textiles. British merchants built the first factories. When these factories prospered, their owners had the money to build more factories, invent more labor-saving machines, and industrialize the nation.

THE INDUSTRIAL REVOLUTION IN THE UNITED STATES The primary source of income in America after the War of Independence was international trade, not manufacturing. Farms and plantations produced agricultural products such as grain and tobacco, which were shipped to Great Britain, southern Europe, and the West Indies. However, two events—the passage of President Thomas Jefferson's Embargo Act of 1807 and the War of 1812—turned the attention of Americans toward the development of domestic industries. Jefferson's embargo, which prohibited Americans from shipping goods to Europe, brought to a standstill the once-thriving foreign trade. In fact, by the time Congress repealed the act in 1809, many shipping centers—especially those in New England—had shut down.

MAIN IDEA

Analyzing Effects

A What effects did the Embargo Act of 1807 and the War of 1812 have on Americans involved in shipping and foreign trade?

Then, just as these seaports recovered, the War of 1812 broke out, and the British navy blockaded much of the coastline. With ships unable to get into or out of U.S. harbors, Americans had to invest their capital in ventures other than overseas shipping. **A**

NEW ENGLAND INDUSTRIALIZES Probably nowhere else in the nation was the push to invest in industry as great as in New England. There, citizens had depended heavily upon shipping and foreign trade for income. Agriculture in the region was not highly profitable.

In 1793, a British immigrant named Samuel Slater had established in Pawtucket, Rhode Island, the first successful mechanized textile factory in America. However, Slater's factory and those modeled after it still only mass-produced one part of the textile, or finished cloth: thread.

Then, in 1813, three Bostonians revolutionized the American textile industry by mechanizing all the stages in the manufacture of cloth. Using plans from an English mill, Francis Cabot Lowell, Nathan Appleton, and Patrick Tracy Jackson built a weaving factory in Waltham, Massachusetts, and outfitted it with power machinery. By 1822 Appleton and Jackson had made enough money to build a larger operation. The changes that their factory triggered in the town of Lowell—named for their deceased partner, Francis Cabot Lowell—exemplify the changes wrought by the Industrial Revolution. By the late 1820s, quiet little Lowell had become a booming manufacturing center. Thousands of people—mostly young women who came to Lowell because their families' farms were in decline—journeyed there in search of work. **B**

MAIN IDEA

Summarizing

B How did manufacturing develop in New England?

Samuel Slater's cotton mill drew its power from the Blackstone River in Pawtucket, Rhode Island. ▼

Science & Technology

hmhsocialstudies.com INTERACTIVE

A NEW ENGLAND TEXTILE MILL

In a typical mill, water was channeled to turn the mill wheel, a large wooden cylinder made up of many angled slats. The mill wheel then turned a gear called the main drum. Belts enabled the drum to rotate gears connected to shafts, or heavy iron rods, on each level of the factory. Small gears and belts transferred the power to individual machines.

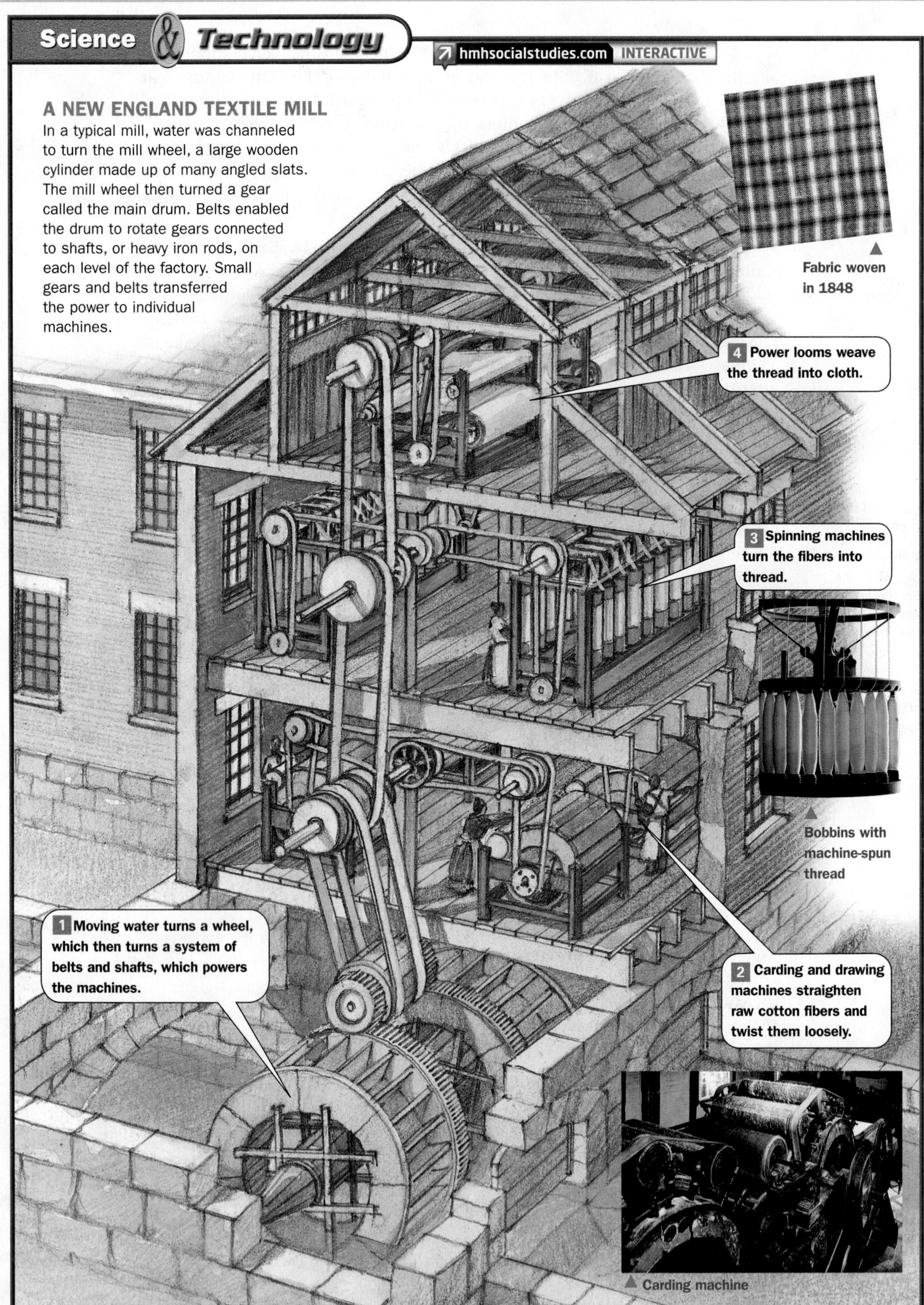

1 Moving water turns a wheel, which then turns a system of belts and shafts, which powers the machines.
2 Carding and drawing machines straighten raw cotton fibers and twist them loosely.
3 Spinning machines turn the fibers into thread.
4 Power looms weave the thread into cloth.

▲ Fabric woven in 1848

▲ Bobbins with machine-spun thread

▲ Carding machine

Two Economic Systems Develop

Northeasterners, prompted by changing economic conditions, invested their capital in factories and manufacturing operations. Cash crops did not grow well in the Northern soil and climate. Southerners, on the other hand, had begun to reap huge profits from cotton by the mid-1790s. The South had little incentive to industrialize. As a result, the North and the South continued to develop two distinct economies, including very different agricultural systems.

AGRICULTURE IN THE NORTH The North had not eliminated agriculture. However, the type of land and the growth of cities in the North encouraged farmers to cultivate smaller farms than Southerners did, and to grow crops that did not require much labor to flourish.

Farmers in the North usually started out growing only what their families needed. Then farming practices in the Old Northwest—the area north of the Ohio River, encompassing what is now the states of Ohio, Indiana, Illinois, Wisconsin, and Michigan—diverged from farming practices in the Northeast. As cities grew, farmers in the Old Northwest discovered that they could raise one or two types of crops or livestock (corn and cattle, for example), and sell what they produced at city markets. They could then purchase from stores whatever else they needed. Such grain crops as corn did not require much labor to grow, nor were they hugely profitable, so there was little demand for slaves. In the Northeast, farms were even smaller than those in the Northwest, so here too there was little demand for slavery.

By the late 1700s, slavery in the North was dying out. Farmers had little economic motivation to use slaves, and an increasing number of Northerners began to voice their religious and political opposition to slavery. Consequently, by 1804 almost all of the Northern states had voluntarily abolished slavery. **C**

MAIN IDEA

Analyzing Causes

C Why was slavery abolished in the North?

COTTON IS KING IN THE SOUTH Eli Whitney's invention of a **cotton gin** (short for "cotton engine") in 1793 had helped to set the South on a different course of development from the North. Short-staple (or short-fiber) cotton was easier to grow but harder to clean than long-staple cotton. Whitney's gin made it possible for Southern farmers to grow short-staple cotton for a profit. Since cotton was in great demand in Britain and, increasingly, in the North, an efficient machine for cleaning the seeds from short-staple cotton proved a major breakthrough. Armed with the cotton gin, poor, nonslaveholding farmers quickly claimed land in the area between the Appalachians and the Mississippi south of the Ohio to begin cultivating this cash-producing crop. Wealthier planters followed, bought up huge areas of land, and then put an enormous slave labor force to work cultivating it. By 1820, this plantation system of farming had transformed Louisiana, Mississippi, and Alabama into a booming Cotton Kingdom. In this way, the cotton gin accelerated the expansion of slavery. **D**

MAIN IDEA

Comparing

D How were the agricultural systems of the North and South different?

SLAVERY BECOMES ENTRENCHED Although slave importation had declined during the American Revolution, by the 1820s the demand for slaves had begun

NOW & THEN

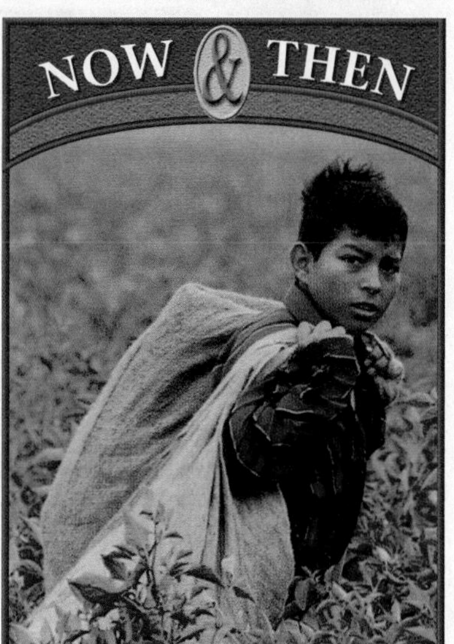

AGRICULTURE AND MIGRATION

Changes in agricultural technology often cause large population movements. Today's agricultural technology enables farmers to plant and grow crops with fewer workers than in the past, but many hands are still needed at harvest time. The United States has about half a million migrant agricultural workers. Whole families may move seasonally following the harvest. Children of migrant workers, like this 11-year old boy in Plainview, Texas, often help in the fields at peak harvest times.

In the early 1800s, the cotton gin led to a mass movement of planters and slaves into Alabama, Mississippi, and Louisiana. Mechanical cotton pickers replaced huge communities of field hands in the 1930s. Many laborers were African Americans, who then migrated from rural to urban areas in search of work.

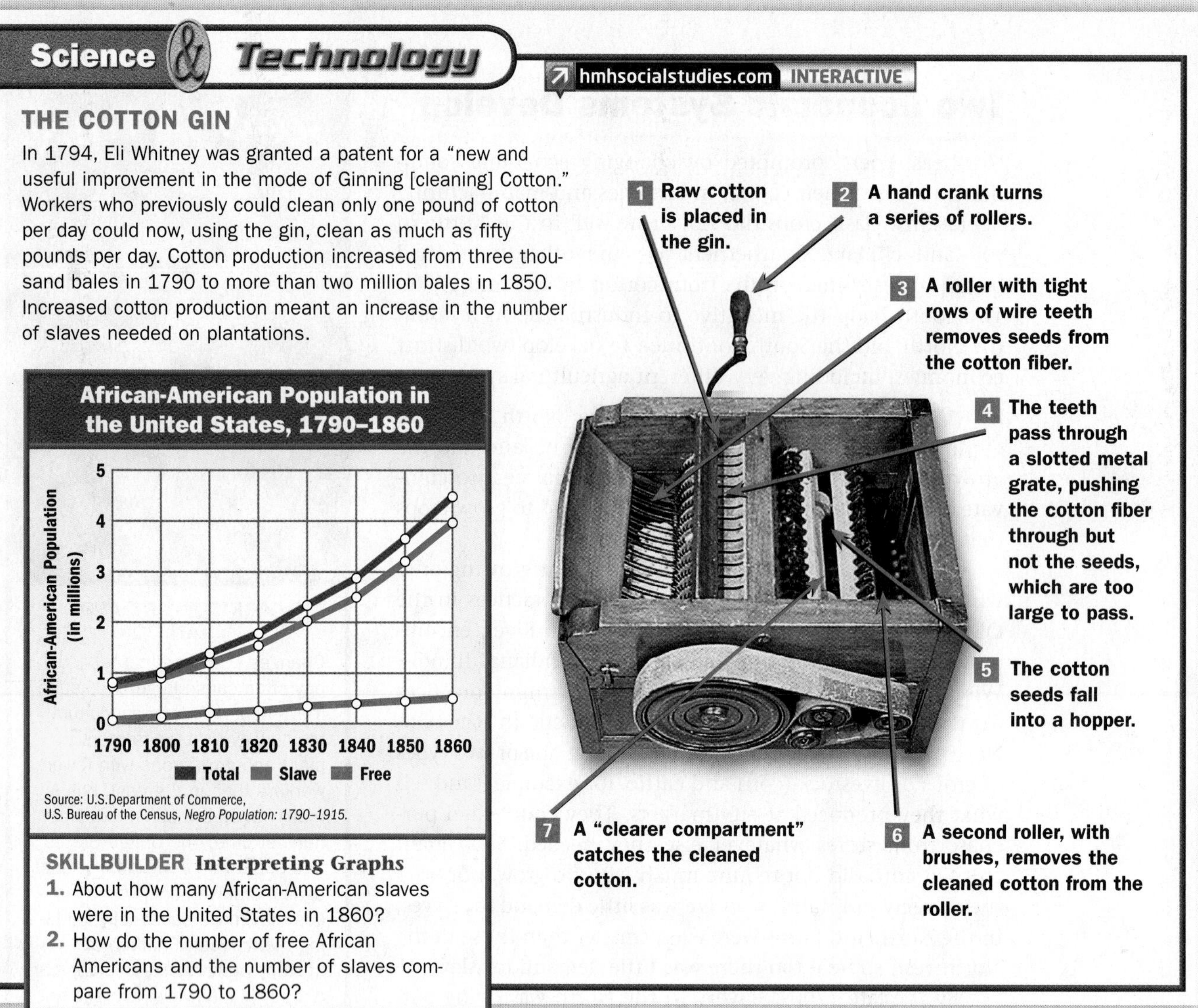
Science & Technology
hmhsocialstudies.com INTERACTIVE
1 Raw cotton is placed in the gin.
2 A hand crank turns a series of rollers.
3 A roller with tight rows of wire teeth removes seeds from the cotton fiber.
4 The teeth pass through a slotted metal grate, pushing the cotton fiber through but not the seeds, which are too large to pass.
5 The cotton seeds fall into a hopper.
6 A second roller, with brushes, removes the cleaned cotton from the roller.
7 A "clearer compartment" catches the cleaned cotton.
African-American Population in the United States, 1790–1860
African-American Population (in millions)
5
4
3
2
1
0
1790 1800 1810 1820 1830 1840 1850 1860
Total Slave Free

THE COTTON GIN

In 1794, Eli Whitney was granted a patent for a "new and useful improvement in the mode of Ginning [cleaning] Cotton." Workers who previously could clean only one pound of cotton per day could now, using the gin, clean as much as fifty pounds per day. Cotton production increased from three thousand bales in 1790 to more than two million bales in 1850. Increased cotton production meant an increase in the number of slaves needed on plantations.

Source: U.S. Department of Commerce, U.S. Bureau of the Census, *Negro Population: 1790–1915*.

SKILLBUILDER Interpreting Graphs

1. About how many African-American slaves were in the United States in 1860?
2. How do the number of free African Americans and the number of slaves compare from 1790 to 1860?

to grow. Increases in cotton production and increases in the number of slaves owned paralleled each other. From 1790 to 1810, cotton production surged from 3,000 bales a year to 178,000 bales, while the number of slaves in the South leapt from 700,000 to 1,200,000. By 1808 slave traders had brought 250,000 additional Africans to the United States—as many as had been brought to the mainland American colonies between 1619 and 1776.

Clay Proposes the American System

As the North and South developed different economies, the creation of a plan to unify the nation became increasingly important. In 1815, President Madison presented such a plan to Congress. He hoped his agenda would both unite the different regions of the country and create a strong, stable economy that would make the nation self-sufficient. His plan included three major points:

- developing transportation systems and other internal improvements
- establishing a protective tariff
- resurrecting the national bank (established during Washington's administration under Hamilton's guidance, and then much reduced in influence under Jefferson)

The plan held promise. Recognizing this, even former critics of the president—Henry Clay and John C. Calhoun—rallied behind it. House Speaker **Henry Clay** began to promote it as the **American System.**

As Clay explained it, the American System would unite the nation's economic interests. An increasingly industrial North would produce the manufactured goods that farmers in the South and West would buy. Meanwhile, a predominantly agricultural South and West would produce most of the grain, meat, and cotton needed in the North. A nationally accepted currency and improved transportation network would facilitate the exchange of goods. With each part of the country sustaining the other, Americans would finally be economically independent of Britain and other European nations. E

MAIN IDEA

Summarizing

E What was the intention of the American System?

ERIE CANAL AND OTHER INTERNAL IMPROVEMENTS For people in different regions to do business with one another and for the economy to grow, they had to communicate, travel, and transport goods. The first steam locomotive in the United States was built in 1825. Railroads offered several advantages over existing modes of transport; they were fast, able to cross almost any terrain, and possible to operate in severe weather. Most transportation at this time, however, was still accomplished using roads and canals. Eventually, better roads and canals would lower costs. But in the short run, they would cost money.

Many states built turnpikes, which paid for themselves through the collection of tolls paid by users who, literally, turned a pike (or spiked pole) to continue their journey along the road. At the same time the federal government experimented with funding highways, which would connect different regions by land. Construction of the **National Road** began in 1811. By 1838 the new road extended from Cumberland, Maryland, to Vandalia, Illinois.

One of the most impressive projects, the **Erie Canal,** stretched 363 miles. The "Big Ditch," as it was called, took eight years to dig, and by 1825 had linked the Hudson River to Lake Erie—or, in effect, the Atlantic Ocean to the Great Lakes. Just 12 years after it had opened, canal tolls had completely paid for its construction. New York City had become the dominant port in the country. In their rush to make similar profits, other states built over 3,000 miles of canals by 1837.

Major Roads, Canals, and Railroads, 1840

hmhsocialstudies.com INTERACTIVE MAP

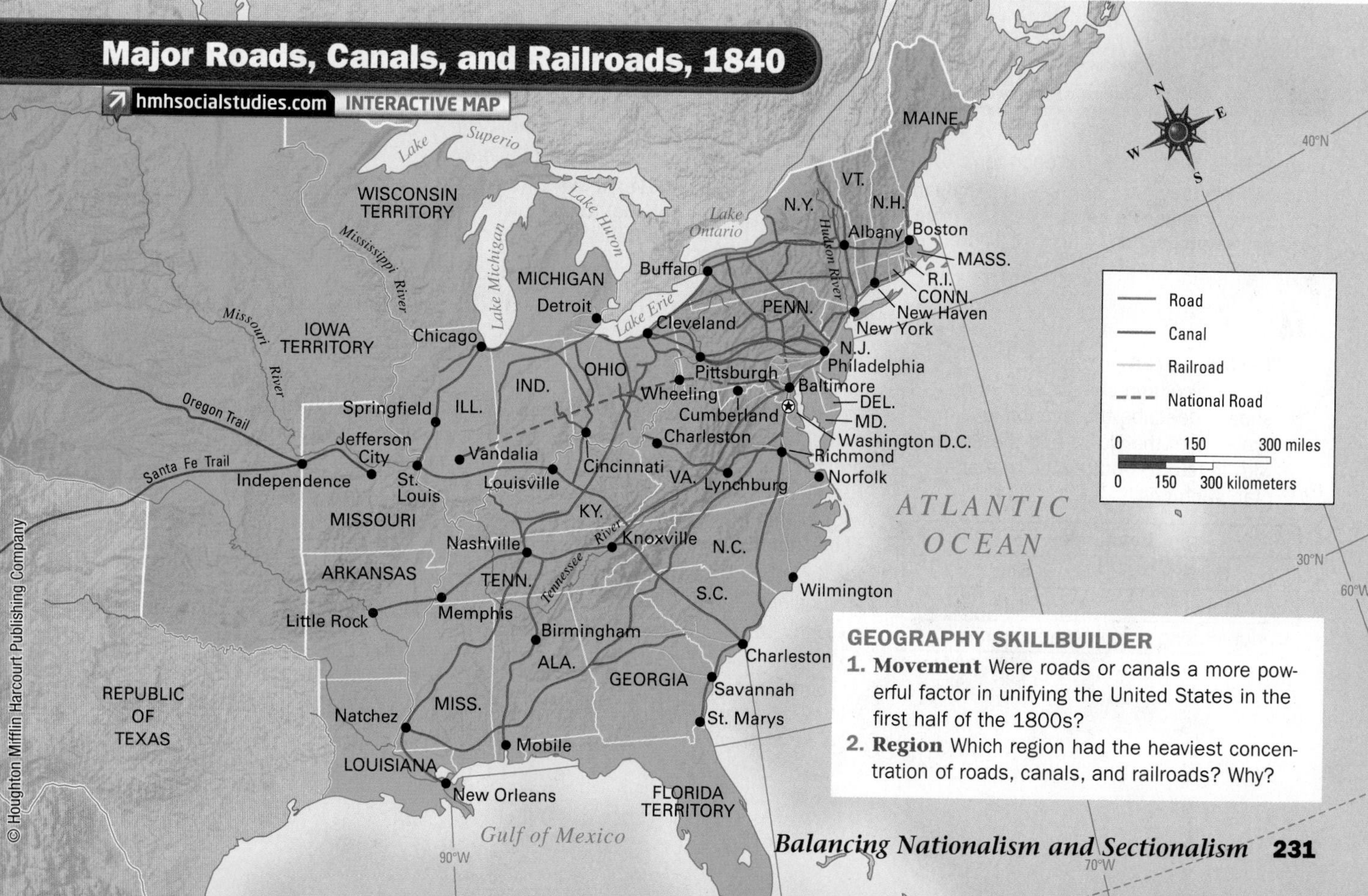

GEOGRAPHY SKILLBUILDER

1. **Movement** Were roads or canals a more powerful factor in unifying the United States in the first half of the 1800s?
2. **Region** Which region had the heaviest concentration of roads, canals, and railroads? Why?

TARIFFS AND THE NATIONAL BANK Why were the tariffs on imports proposed by Madison and promoted by Clay necessary? Ever since the end of the War of 1812, British goods such as iron and textiles—stockpiled during the war—were sold far below the cost of American-made merchandise. Consequently, few bought the more expensive American products. Placing a tariff on imports would increase the cost of foreign goods and thereby eliminate their price advantage. Moreover, tariff revenues would help pay for internal improvements, such as roads, canals, and lighthouses. For these reasons, President James Madison proposed the **Tariff of 1816.**

Most Northeasterners welcomed protective tariffs with relief. However, people in the South and West, whose livelihoods did not depend on manufacturing, were not as eager to tax European imports. They resented any government intervention that would make goods more expensive. Nevertheless, Clay, who was from the West (Kentucky), and Calhoun, a Southerner from South Carolina, managed to sway congressmen from their regions to approve the Tariff of 1816 in the national interest.

Attitudes toward the proposed Second Bank of the United States (BUS) were less divided. Most leaders agreed that a national bank would benefit all. The Second Bank would make available a currency guaranteed to be accepted nationwide, thus making it easier for people in different regions to do business with one another. In 1816, Congress chartered the Second Bank of the United States for a 20-year period.

People were pleased with the way the country was developing. In 1816, they elected James Monroe of Virginia as president. Soon after his inauguration in 1817, Monroe took a goodwill tour of New England, receiving a warm welcome in Boston. The idea of a Republican from Virginia being welcomed in this northern Federalist stronghold impressed the nation. The Boston *Columbian Centinel* declared that Americans had entered an "Era of Good Feelings."

ASSESSMENT

1. **TERMS & NAMES** For each term or name, write a sentence explaining its significance.
   - **Eli Whitney**
   - **interchangeable parts**
   - **mass production**
   - **Industrial Revolution**
   - **cotton gin**
   - **Henry Clay**
   - **American System**
   - **National Road**
   - **Erie Canal**
   - **Tariff of 1816**

MAIN IDEA

2. **TAKING NOTES**
   In a two-column chart like the one shown, describe the economic systems of the North and the South with regard to both agriculture and manufacturing.

Economies	
North	South
Agriculture	Agriculture
Manufacturing	Manufacturing

CRITICAL THINKING

3. **ANALYZING EFFECTS**
   What shifts in population might be attributed to advances in technology and changes in regional economies during America's Industrial Revolution? Support your answer with examples from the text.
   Think About:
   - the industrialization of New England
   - agricultural changes in the South
   - improvements in internal transportation systems

4. **SYNTHESIZING**
   How was the American System expected to unite the nation's economic interests? Provide several examples.

5. **PREDICTING EFFECTS**
   Do you think the invention of the railroad would hasten or slow the construction of new roads and canals? Why?

Nationalism at Center Stage

MAIN IDEA	WHY IT MATTERS NOW	Terms & Names
Nationalism exerted a strong influence in the courts, foreign affairs, and westward expansion in the early 1800s.	Nationalism continues to affect such decisions as whether or not we should involve the country in foreign conflicts and what limits can be placed on business, communications, and other trade.	• *McCulloch* v. *Maryland* • John Quincy Adams • nationalism • Adams-Onís Treaty • Monroe Doctrine • Missouri Compromise

One American's Story

hmhsocialstudies.com
TAKING NOTES
Use the graphic organizer online to take notes about how nationalism influenced the United States.

In 1807 Robert Fulton's boat, the *Clermont*, propelled by a steam engine, cruised the 150 miles up the Hudson River from New York City to Albany in 32 hours. This successful demonstration marked the beginning of the steamboat era. Another one of Fulton's boats was so luxurious that it had a wood-paneled dining room and private bedrooms. Fulton posted regulations on his opulent steamboats.

▲ Like Fulton's *Clermont*, the *Telegraph* was a 19th-century steamboat.

A Personal Voice ROBERT FULTON

"As the steamboat has been fitted up in an elegant style, order is necessary to keep it so; gentlemen will therefore please to observe cleanliness, and a reasonable attention not to injure the furniture; for this purpose no one must sit on a table under the penalty of half a dollar each time, and every breakage of tables, chairs, sofas, or windows, tearing of curtains, or injury of any kind must be paid for before leaving the boat."

—quoted in *Steamboats Come True: American Inventors in Action*

Steamboats carried freight as well as passengers, and this new method of transportation spread quickly to the Ohio and Mississippi rivers. For the next 20 years, the steamboat was one factor that helped to unite the economic life of the North and the South. It thus contributed to the growing national spirit.

The Supreme Court Boosts National Power

In 1808, Robert Fulton and Robert Livingston received a charter from the New York legislature that gave them the exclusive right to run steamboats on rivers in that state. They profited from this state charter, which granted them a monopoly (exclusive legal control of a commercial activity), by charging steamboat operators for licenses to operate on various stretches of river.

One of these operators was Aaron Ogden. Ogden was licensed by Fulton and Livingston under the laws of New York State to run his steamship line between New York and New Jersey. Ogden believed that he was the only operator legally entitled to run a steamboat service on that stretch of the Hudson. Then Thomas Gibbons began to run a similar service in the same area, claiming that he was entitled to do so according to federal law. Ogden took Gibbons to court to stop him. However, in 1824 the Supreme Court ruled that interstate commerce could be regulated only by the federal government. In other words, Ogden's "exclusive" right granted by New York was not legal, since the route crossed state lines.

More important, by clarifying that Congress had authority over interstate commerce, the *Gibbons* v. *Ogden* decision helped to ensure that the federal government has the power to regulate just about everything that crosses state lines. In modern life, that authority means everything from air traffic to television and radio waves to interstate cellular communications. In addition, this decision led to future rulings favoring competition over monopolies. In this way, nationalism exerted a strong influence on the legal system.

▲ John Marshall was appointed Chief Justice of the Supreme Court in 1801 by Federalist President John Adams.

STRENGTHENING GOVERNMENT ECONOMIC CONTROL In ***McCulloch* v. *Maryland*** (1819), as in *Gibbons* v. *Ogden*, Chief Justice John Marshall had also guided the Supreme Court to a ruling that strengthened the federal government's control over the economy. The Court's ruling also supported the national government over the state governments.

Maryland had levied a heavy tax on the local branch of the Bank of the United States, hoping to make it fail. Marshall declared that if this were allowed, states would in effect be overturning laws passed by Congress. The Chief Justice denied the right of Maryland to tax the Bank, stating that "the power to tax is the power to destroy." He declared the Bank of the United States constitutional.

LIMITING STATE POWERS Under Chief Justice Marshall, the Supreme Court made several rulings that blocked state interference in business and commerce—even when this meant overturning state law. In *Fletcher* v. *Peck* (1810), for example, the Court nullified a Georgia law that had violated individuals' constitutional right to enter into contracts. In the *Dartmouth College* v. *Woodward* (1819) decision, the Court declared that the state of New Hampshire could not revise the original charter it had granted to the college's trustees in colonial times. A charter was a contract, the Court said, and the Constitution did not permit states to interfere with contracts. (A)

MAIN IDEA

Summarizing

(A) In what ways did the Supreme Court boost federal power?

Nationalism Shapes Foreign Policy

Chief Justice Marshall guided the Supreme Court to decisions that increased the power of the federal government over the state government. At the same time, Secretary of State **John Quincy Adams** established foreign policy guided by **nationalism**—the belief that national interests should be placed ahead of regional concerns or the interests of other countries.

TERRITORY AND BOUNDARIES Working under President James Monroe, Adams prioritized the security of the nation and expansion of its territory. To further these interests, Adams worked out a treaty with Great Britain to reduce the Great Lakes fleets of both countries to only a few military vessels. The Rush-Bagot

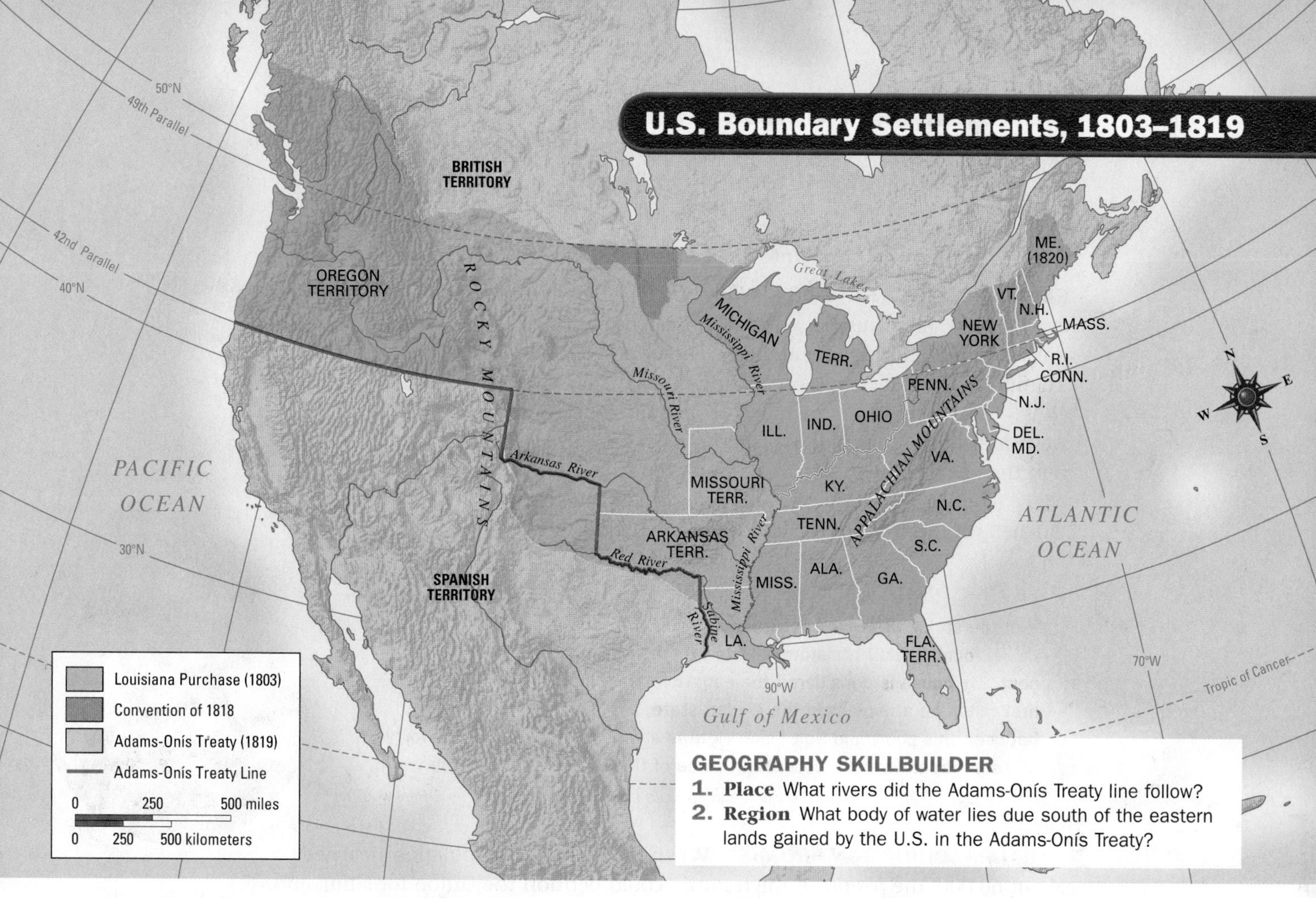

GEOGRAPHY SKILLBUILDER

1. **Place** What rivers did the Adams-Onís Treaty line follow?
2. **Region** What body of water lies due south of the eastern lands gained by the U.S. in the Adams-Onís Treaty?

Treaty (1817) eventually led the United States and Canada to completely demilitarize their common border. Adams also arranged the Convention of 1818, which fixed the U.S. border at the 49th parallel up to the Rocky Mountains. Finally, he reached a compromise with Britain to jointly occupy the Oregon Territory, the territory west of the Rockies, for ten years.

There remained one outstanding piece of business. Most Americans assumed that Spanish Florida would eventually become part of the United States. In 1819, too weak to police its New World territories, Spain ceded Florida to the United States in the **Adams-Onís Treaty** and gave up its claims to the Oregon Territory.

THE MONROE DOCTRINE After Spain and Portugal defeated Napoleon in 1815, these European powers wanted to reclaim their former colonies in Latin America. Meanwhile, the Russians, who had been in Alaska since 1784, were establishing trading posts in what is now California.

With Spain and Portugal trying to move back into their old colonial areas, and with Russia pushing in from the northwest, the United States knew it had to do something. Many Americans were interested in acquiring northern Mexico and the Spanish colony of Cuba. Moreover, the Russian action posed a threat to American trade with China, which brought huge profits.

MAIN IDEA

Synthesizing
B How did the foreign policies of John Quincy Adams and James Monroe serve national interests?

Hence, in his 1823 message to Congress, President Monroe warned all outside powers not to interfere with affairs in the Western Hemisphere. They should not attempt to create new colonies, he said, or try to overthrow the newly independent republics in the hemisphere. The United States would consider such action "dangerous to our peace and safety." At the same time, the United States would not involve itself in European affairs or interfere with existing colonies in the Western Hemisphere. These principles became known as the **Monroe Doctrine**. B

Nationalism Pushes America West

While Presidents Adams and Monroe established policies that expanded U.S. territory, American settlers pushed into the Northwest Territory (present-day Ohio, Indiana, Illinois, Wisconsin, and Michigan), felling forests, turning lush prairies into farms and waterfronts into city centers.

EXPANSION TO THE WEST While some settlers went west to escape debts or even the law, most pushed westward in search of economic gain—for land was not only plentiful and fertile but cheap. There were also social gains to be made. For example, one could change occupations more easily on the frontier. Jim Beckwourth (1798–1867), the son of a white man and an African-American woman, ventured westward with a fur-trading expedition in 1823. He lived among the Crow, who gave him the name "Bloody Arm" because of his skill as a fighter. Later he served as an Army scout. In California in 1850, he decided to settle down and become a rancher, yet this was not the last of his occupations.

A Personal Voice JIM BECKWOURTH

"**In the spring of 1852 I established myself in Beckwourth Valley, and finally found myself transformed into a hotel-keeper and chief of a trading-post. My house is considered the emigrant's landing-place, as it is the first ranch he arrives at in the golden state, and is the only house between this point and Salt Lake. Here is a valley two hundred and forty miles in circumference, containing some of the choicest land in the world.**"

—quoted in *The Life and Adventures of James P. Beckwourth*

Jim Beckwourth

THE MISSOURI COMPROMISE When a territory's population reached about 60,000, the people of the territory could petition the Union for admission, draft a state constitution, elect representatives, and become part of the United States, once Congress approved. In 1819, however, when settlers in Missouri requested admission into the Union, conflict arose. In Missouri, the new spirit of nationalism was challenged by an issue that had previously confronted the framers of the Constitution. That issue was the question of slavery.

Until 1818, the United States had consisted of ten free and ten slave states. The government admitted Illinois as the eleventh free state in 1818. Southerners then expected that Missouri would become the eleventh slave state, thereby maintaining the balance between free states and slave states in Congress. However, New York Congressman James Tallmadge amended the Missouri statehood bill to require Missouri to gradually free its slaves, a bill that passed the House. Southerners, perceiving a threat to their power, blocked the bill's passage in the Senate. As arguments raged, Alabama was then admitted to the Union as a slave state. With 11 free to 11 slave states, Missouri's status became crucial to the delicate balance.

The slaveholding states claimed that Northerners were trying to end slavery. Northerners accused Southerners of plotting to extend the institution into new territories. Hostilities became so intense that at times people on both sides even mentioned civil war and the end of the Union. Indeed, the issues that came to light during these debates foreshadowed the war to come. "We have the wolf by the ears," wrote the aging Thomas Jefferson of this crisis, "and we can neither hold him, nor safely let him go."

Under the leadership of Henry Clay, however, Congress managed to temporarily resolve the crisis with a series of agreements collectively called the **Missouri Compromise.** Maine was admitted as a free state and Missouri as a slave state, thus preserving the sectional balance in the Senate. The rest of the Louisiana Territory was split into two spheres of interest, one for slaveholders and one for free settlers. The dividing line was set at 36° 30′ north latitude. South

The Missouri Compromise, 1820–1821

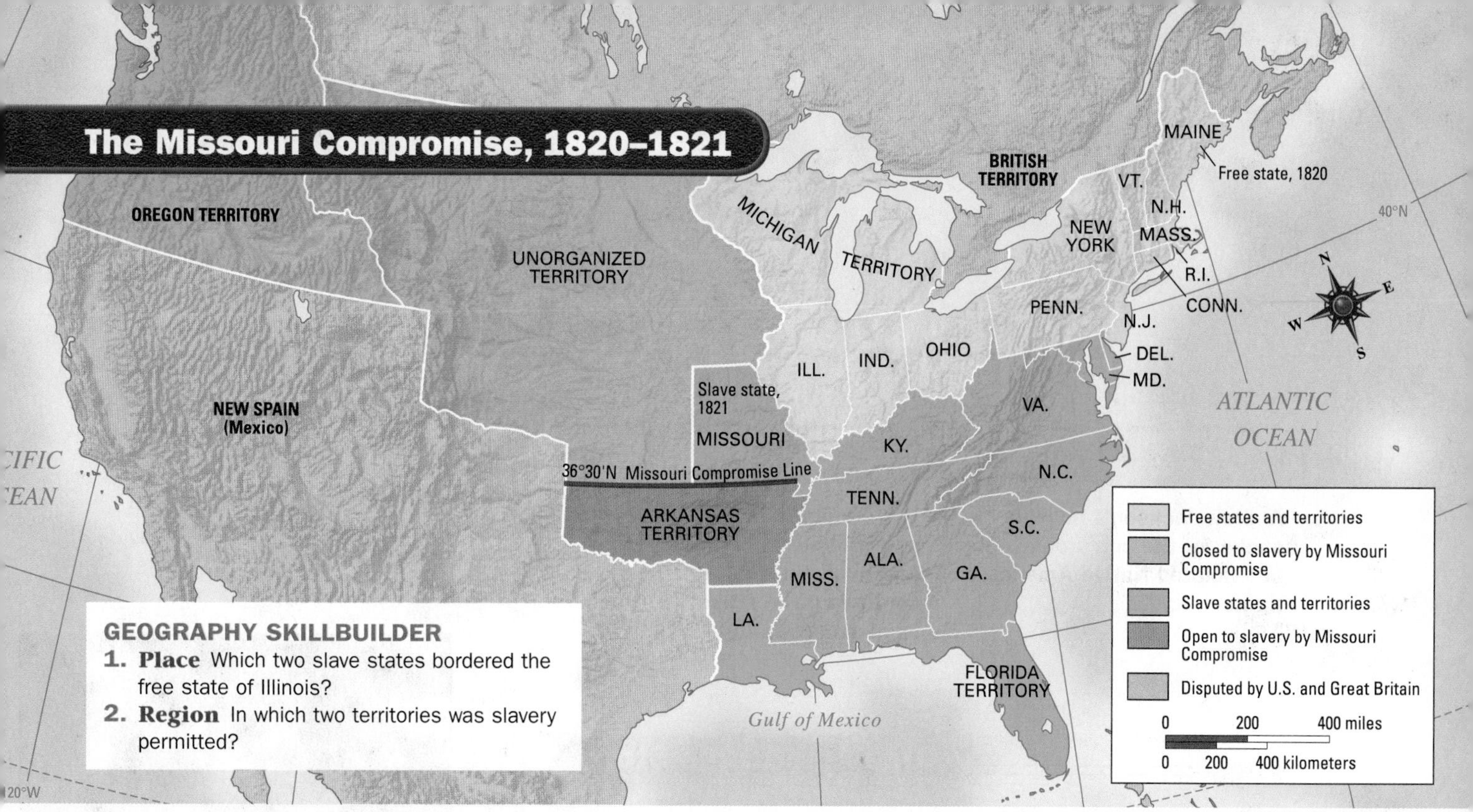

Free states and territories
Closed to slavery by Missouri Compromise
Slave states and territories
Open to slavery by Missouri Compromise
Disputed by U.S. and Great Britain

0 200 400 miles
0 200 400 kilometers

Maine: Free state, 1820
Missouri: Slave state, 1821
36°30'N Missouri Compromise Line

GEOGRAPHY SKILLBUILDER

1. **Place** Which two slave states bordered the free state of Illinois?
2. **Region** In which two territories was slavery permitted?

of the line, slavery was legal. North of the line—except in Missouri—slavery was banned. Thomas Jefferson was among those who feared for the Union's future after the Missouri Compromise. His words would prove prophetic.

A PERSONAL VOICE THOMAS JEFFERSON

> **"This momentous question, like a firebell in the night, awakened and filled me with terror. I considered it at once as the knell of the Union. It is hushed, indeed, for the moment. But this is a reprieve only, not a final sentence."**
>
> —letter to John Holmes, April 22, 1820

President Monroe signed the Missouri Compromise in 1820. For a generation, the problem of slavery in federal territories seemed settled.

ASSESSMENT

1. **TERMS & NAMES** For each term or name, write a sentence explaining its significance.
   - ***McCulloch* v. *Maryland***
   - **nationalism**
   - **Monroe Doctrine**
   - **John Quincy Adams**
   - **Adams-Onís Treaty**
   - **Missouri Compromise**

MAIN IDEA

2. **TAKING NOTES**
   In a diagram like the one shown, write historical examples that illustrate the influence of nationalism.

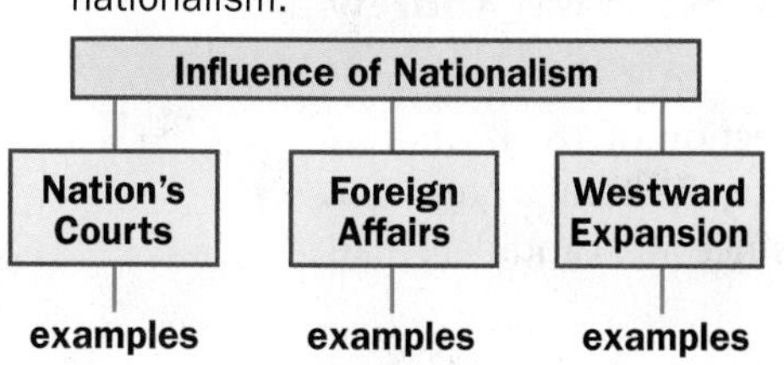

CRITICAL THINKING

3. **HYPOTHESIZING**
   What short- and long-term goals might President Monroe have had in mind when he formulated the Monroe Doctrine in 1823? Support your answer. **Think About:**
   - European nations' presence in the Western Hemisphere
   - the influence of nationalism on foreign policy
   - the nation's westward expansion

4. **SYNTHESIZING**
   What agreements did Congress reach that are regarded collectively as the Missouri Compromise? Why were they important at the time?

5. **EVALUATING**
   From what you know about the Missouri Compromise and the controversy that preceded it, do you think the new spirit of nationalism in the United States was strong or fragile? Support your opinion.

SECTION 3

The Age of Jackson

MAIN IDEA	WHY IT MATTERS NOW	Terms & Names
Andrew Jackson's policies spoke for the common people but violated Native American rights.	**The effects of land losses and persecution faced by Native Americans in the 1800s continue to be reflected in their legal struggles today.**	**• Andrew Jackson • Democratic-Republican Party • spoils system • Indian Removal Act • Trail of Tears**

One American's Story

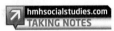

hmhsocialstudies.com TAKING NOTES

Use the graphic organizer online to take notes on key events during the Age of Jackson.

The era of the leaders who had founded the nation passed with Adams's and Jefferson's deaths in 1826. During an extended conversation with John Adams in 1776, Thomas Jefferson had tried to convince him to draft the Declaration of Independence.

▲ **This Gilbert Stuart portrait of John Adams was begun in 1798, when Adams was 63.**

A PERSONAL VOICE JOHN ADAMS

> **"[Adams] said 'I will not.' . . .**
>
> **'What can be your reasons?'**
>
> **'Reason first—You are a Virginian, and a Virginian ought to appear at the head of this business. Reason second—I am obnoxious, suspected, and unpopular. You are very much otherwise. Reason third—You can write ten times better than I can.'**
>
> **'Well,' said Jefferson, 'if you are decided, I will do as well as I can.'"**
>
> —quoted in *John Adams: A Biography in His Own Words*

Thus began a mutual regard that would last for 50 years. On July 4, 1826, exactly 50 years after the delegates approved the Declaration of Independence, both men died. Now the presidency belonged to another generation.

Expanding Democracy Changes Politics

When John Adams died, his son John Quincy Adams was in the second year of his single term as president. He had succeeded James Monroe as president but was not effective as the nation's chief executive. The principal reason was **Andrew Jackson,** his chief political opponent.

TENSION BETWEEN ADAMS AND JACKSON In the election of 1824, Andrew Jackson won the popular vote but lacked the majority of electoral votes. The House of Representatives had to decide the outcome, since no candidate had received a majority of the votes of the electoral college.

Because of his power in the House, Henry Clay could swing the election either way. Clay disliked Jackson personally and mistrusted his lack of political experience. "I cannot believe," Clay commented, "that killing twenty-five hundred Englishmen at New Orleans qualifies [him] for the various difficult and complicated duties of [the presidency]." Adams, on the other hand, agreed with Clay's American System. In the end, Adams was elected president by a majority of the states represented in the House.

Background
The Battle of New Orleans in 1815 made Jackson a national hero. The British attacked Jackson's forces at New Orleans in January 1815. American riflemen mowed down advancing British forces. American casualties totaled 71, compared to Britain's 2,000.

Jacksonians, or followers of Jackson, accused Adams of stealing the presidency. When Adams appointed Clay secretary of state, the Jacksonians claimed that Adams had struck a corrupt bargain. The Jacksonians left the Republican Party to form the **Democratic-Republican Party** (forerunner of today's Democratic Party) and did whatever they could to sabotage Adams's policies.

MAIN IDEA

Predicting Effects
A How might reducing property requirements for voting affect political campaigns?

DEMOCRACY AND CITIZENSHIP During Adams's presidency, most states eased the voting requirements, thereby enlarging the voting population. Fewer states now had property qualifications for voting. In the presidential election of 1824, approximately 350,000 white males voted. In 1828, over three times that number voted, and their votes helped Andrew Jackson. However, certain groups still lacked political power. Free African Americans and women did not enjoy the political freedoms of white males. A

Jackson's New Presidential Style

The expansion of voting rights meant that candidates had to be able to speak to the concerns of ordinary people. Andrew Jackson had this common touch.

JACKSON'S APPEAL TO THE COMMON CITIZEN During the 1828 campaign, Jackson characterized Adams as an intellectual elitist and, by contrast, portrayed himself as a man of humble origins—though he was actually a wealthy plantation owner. Jackson won the election by a landslide. He was so popular that record numbers of people came to Washington to see "Old Hickory" inaugurated.

President-elect Andrew Jackson on his way to Washington, D.C., to be inaugurated in 1829

Mrs. Samuel Harrison Smith described the scene.

VIDEO
Jackson's Personality and Legacy
hmhsocialstudies.com

A PERSONAL VOICE MRS. SAMUEL HARRISON SMITH

"The President, after having been *literally* nearly pressed to death and almost suffocated and torn to pieces by the people in their eagerness to shake hands with Old Hickory [Jackson], had retreated through the back way, or south front, and had escaped to his lodgings at Gadsby's. Cut glass and china to the amount of several thousand dollars had been broken in the struggle to get the refreshments. . . . Ladies fainted, men were seen with bloody noses, and such a scene of confusion took place as is impossible to describe; those who got in could not get out by the door again but had to scramble out of windows."

—from a letter dated March 1829

KEY PLAYER

ANDREW JACKSON
1767–1845

Andrew Jackson thought of himself as a man of the people. The son of Scots-Irish immigrants, he had been born in poverty in the Carolinas. He was the first president since George Washington without a college education.

At the time of his election at the age of 61, however, Jackson had built a highly successful career. He had worked in law, politics, land speculation, cotton planting, and soldiering. Victory at New Orleans in the War of 1812 had made him a hero. His Tennessee home, the Hermitage, was a mansion. Anyone who owned more than a hundred slaves, as Jackson did, was wealthy.

Underlying Jackson's iron will was a fiery temper. He survived several duels, one of which left a bullet lodged near his heart and another of which left his opponent dead. His ire, however, was most often reserved for special-interest groups and those whose power came from privilege.

JACKSON'S SPOILS SYSTEM If Jackson knew how to inspire loyalty and enthusiasm during a campaign, he also knew how to use the powers of the presidency upon gaining office. He announced that his appointees to federal jobs would serve a maximum of four-year terms. Unless there was a regular turnover of personnel, he declared, officeholders would become inefficient and corrupt.

Jackson's administration practiced the **spoils system**—so called from the saying "To the victor belong the spoils of the enemy"—in which incoming officials throw out former appointees and replace them with their own friends. He fired nearly 10 percent of the federal employees, most of them holdovers from the Adams administration, and gave their jobs to loyal Jacksonians. Jackson's friends also became his primary advisers, dubbed his "kitchen cabinet" because they supposedly slipped into the White House through the kitchen. B

MAIN IDEA

Summarizing
B What is the spoils system?

Removal of Native Americans

Since the 1600s, white settlers had held one of two attitudes toward Native Americans. Some whites favored the displacement and dispossession of all Native Americans. Others wished to convert Native Americans to Christianity, turn them into farmers, and absorb them into the white culture.

Since the end of the War of 1812, some Southeastern tribes—the Cherokee, Choctaw, Seminole, Creek, and Chickasaw—had begun to adopt the European culture of their white neighbors. These "five civilized tribes," as they were called by whites, occupied large areas in Georgia, North and South Carolina, Alabama, Mississippi, and Tennessee. Many white planters and miners wanted that land.

INDIAN REMOVAL ACT OF 1830 Jackson thought that assimilation could not work. Another possibility—allowing Native Americans to live in their original areas—would have required too many troops to keep the areas free of white settlers. Jackson believed that the only solution was to move the Native Americans from their lands to areas farther west.

Congress passed the **Indian Removal Act** in 1830. Under this law, the federal government funded negotiation of treaties that would force the Native Americans to move west.

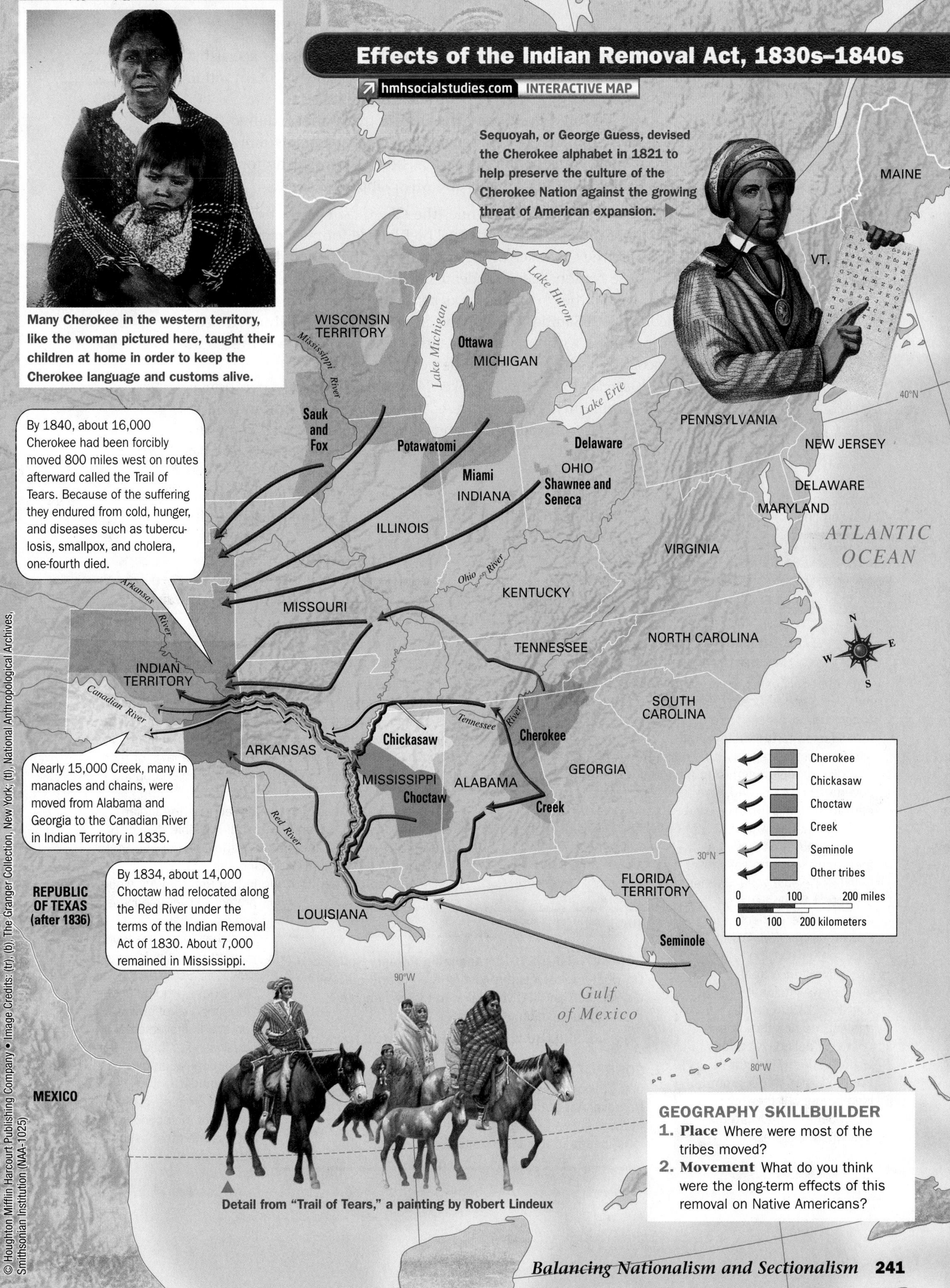

Many Cherokee in the western territory, like the woman pictured here, taught their children at home in order to keep the Cherokee language and customs alive.

Sequoyah, or George Guess, devised the Cherokee alphabet in 1821 to help preserve the culture of the Cherokee Nation against the growing threat of American expansion.

Detail from "Trail of Tears," a painting by Robert Lindeux

GEOGRAPHY SKILLBUILDER

1. **Place** Where were most of the tribes moved?
2. **Movement** What do you think were the long-term effects of this removal on Native Americans?

About 90 treaties were signed. For Jackson, the removal policy was "not only liberal, but generous," but his arguments were mainly based on the rights of states to govern within their own boundaries. C

In 1830, Jackson pressured the Choctaw to sign a treaty that required them to move from Mississippi. In 1831, he ordered U.S. troops to forcibly remove the Sauk and Fox from their lands in Illinois and Missouri. In 1832, he forced the Chickasaw to leave their lands in Alabama and Mississippi.

MAIN IDEA

Analyzing Issues

C Why did Jackson think that Native Americans should be moved west of the Mississippi?

THE CHEROKEE FIGHT BACK Meanwhile, the Cherokee Nation tried to win just treatment through the U.S. legal system. Chief Justice John Marshall refused to rule on the first case the Cherokee brought against Georgia, though, because in his view the Cherokee Nation had no federal standing; it was neither a foreign nation nor a state, but rather a "domestic dependent nation." Undaunted, the Cherokee teamed up with Samuel Austin Worcester, a missionary who had been jailed for teaching Indians without a state license. The Cherokee knew the Court would have to recognize a citizen's right to be heard.

HISTORY

VIDEO

Jackson v. the Cherokee and South Carolina

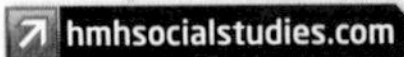

hmhsocialstudies.com

In *Worcester* v. *Georgia* (1832), the Cherokee Nation finally won recognition as a distinct political community. The Court ruled that Georgia was not entitled to regulate the Cherokee nor to invade their lands. Jackson refused to abide by the Supreme Court decision, saying: "John Marshall has made his decision; now let him enforce it."

Cherokee leader John Ross still tried to fight the state in the courts, but other Cherokee began to promote relocation. In 1835, federal agents declared the

POINT

"The Indian Removal Act of 1830 was a terrible injustice."

John Marshall, chief justice of the Supreme Court, believed that the Cherokee had "an unquestionable right" to their territory "until title should be extinguished by voluntary cession to the United States."

In their protest against the Indian Removal Act, the Cherokee people referred to past treaties with the federal government and stated, "We have a perfect and original right to remain without interruption and molestation." Congressman Edward Everett of Massachusetts described Indian removal as "inflicting the pains of banishment from their native land on seventy or eighty thousand human beings." Rejecting claims that the removal was necessary to protect the Indians against white settlers, Everett demanded, "What other power has the Executive over a treaty or law, but to enforce it?"

In their 1832 protest against the Act, the Creek pointedly asked, "Can [our white brethren] exempt us from intrusion in our promised borders, if they are incompetent to our protection where we are?"

COUNTERPOINT

"The Indian Removal Act of 1830 was unfortunate but necessary."

Blame for the displacement of Native Americans was sometimes placed on the states or on the law, which, it was argued, all people must obey. As Secretary of War John Eaton explained to the Creek of Alabama: "It is not your Great Father who does this; but the laws of the Country, which he and every one of his people is bound to regard."

President Andrew Jackson contended that the Indian Removal Act would put an end to "all possible danger of collision between the authorities of the General and State Governments on account of the Indians."

Jackson also claimed that the Indian Removal Act would protect Native Americans against further removal from their lands. He found support for his point of view from Secretary of War Lewis Cass, who defended "the progress of civilization and improvement." Cass wished "that the aboriginal population had accommodated themselves to the inevitable change of their condition," but asserted that "such a wish is vain."

THINKING CRITICALLY

1. **CONNECT TO HISTORY** **Analyzing Primary Sources** On what central issue regarding the Indian Removal Act did Jackson and Native American tribes disagree? Explain your opinion of the Act.

SEE SKILLBUILDER HANDBOOK, PAGE R22.

2. **CONNECT TO TODAY** **Analyzing Issues** Research how one of the five tribes was affected by the Indian Removal Act. Write a proposal for how the U.S. government might today make reparations to the group for land losses in the 19th century.

minority who favored relocation the true representatives of the Cherokee Nation and promptly had them sign the Treaty of New Echota. This treaty gave the last eight million acres of Cherokee land to the federal government in exchange for approximately $5 million and land "west of the Mississippi." The signing of this treaty marked the beginning of the Cherokee exodus. However, when by 1838 nearly 20,000 Cherokee still remained in the East, President Martin Van Buren (Jackson's successor) ordered their forced removal. U.S. Army troops under the command of General Winfield Scott rounded up the Cherokee and drove them into camps to await the journey. **D**

MAIN IDEA

Analyzing Effects

D How did the Cherokee react to the Indian Removal Act?

THE TRAIL OF TEARS Beginning in October and November of 1838, the Cherokee were sent off in groups of about 1,000 each on the long journey. The 800-mile trip was made partly by steamboat and railroad but mostly on foot. As the winter came on, more and more of the Cherokee died en route.

A PERSONAL VOICE TRAIL OF TEARS SURVIVOR

> **"Children cry and many men cry, and all look sad like when friends die, but they say nothing and just put heads down and keep on go towards West. Many days pass and people die very much."**
>
> —quoted in *From the Heart: Voices of the American Indian*

Along the way, government officials stole the Cherokee's money, while outlaws made off with their livestock. The Cherokee buried more than a quarter of their people along what came to be known as the **Trail of Tears.** When they reached their final destination, they ended up on land far inferior to that which they had been forced to leave.

NOW & THEN

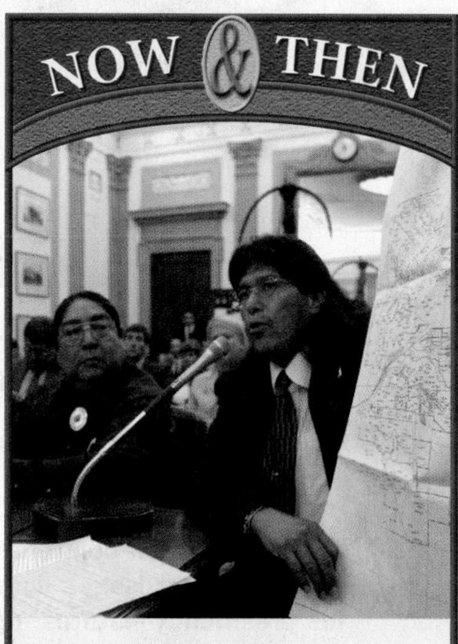

NATIVE AMERICAN LANDS

Native Americans continue to struggle for recognition of land rights.

In the 2002 picture above, Native American leaders testify during a Congressional hearing on the protection of sacred sites. Many of these sites are threatened by development, pollution, or vandalism.

Other present-day Native Americans have won recognition of their land claims. Over the past 30 years, the federal government has settled property disputes with several tribes in Connecticut, Maine, and other states and has provided them with funds to purchase ancestral lands.

SECTION 3 ASSESSMENT

1. **TERMS & NAMES** For each term or name, write a sentence explaining its significance.
   - **Andrew Jackson**
   - **Democratic-Republican Party**
   - **spoils system**
   - **Indian Removal Act**
   - **Trail of Tears**

MAIN IDEA

2. **TAKING NOTES**
   Create a time line like the one shown here, listing key events relating to Jackson's political career.

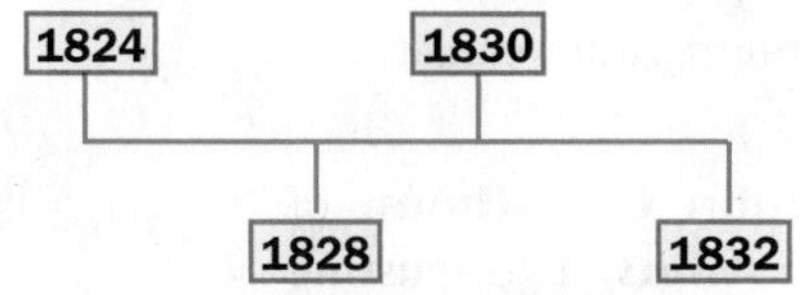

   Do you think Jackson was an effective leader? Why or why not?

CRITICAL THINKING

3. **EVALUATING**
   If you were a U.S. citizen voting in the 1828 presidential election, would you cast your ballot for John Quincy Adams or Andrew Jackson? Support your choice. **Think About:**
   - each candidate's background and political experience
   - each candidate's views of the national bank and tariffs
   - where you might live—the South, the West, or New England

4. **ANALYZING EVENTS**
   In your opinion, what factors set the stage for the Indian Removal Act? Support your answer. **Think About:**
   - the attitude of white settlers toward Native Americans
   - Jackson's justification of the Indian Removal Act
   - why Jackson was able to defy the Supreme Court's ruling in *Worcester* v. *Georgia*

SECTION 4

States' Rights and the National Bank

MAIN IDEA	WHY IT MATTERS NOW	Terms & Names
Andrew Jackson confronted two important issues during his presidency—states' rights and a national bank.	**The conflict between states' rights and federal government control continues to flare up in such arenas as education, commerce, and law enforcement.**	**•Daniel Webster •John C. Calhoun •Tariff of Abominations •Bank of the United States •Whig Party •Martin Van Buren •panic of 1837 •William Henry Harrison •John Tyler**

One American's Story

On January 26, 1830, Massachusetts senator **Daniel Webster** rose in the Senate and delivered one of the great speeches of American history.

A PERSONAL VOICE DANIEL WEBSTER

"When my eyes shall be turned to behold for the last time the sun in heaven, may I not see him shining on the broken and dishonored fragments of a once glorious Union. . . . Let their last feeble and lingering glance rather behold the gorgeous ensign of the republic . . . bearing for its motto, no such miserable interrogatory as 'What is all this worth?' nor those other words of delusion and folly, 'Liberty first and Union afterwards'; but everywhere, spread all over in characters of living light, . . . that other sentiment, dear to every true American heart—Liberty *and* Union, now and forever, one and inseparable!"

—speech delivered in the Senate on January 26 and 27, 1830

▲ **Daniel Webster defended the federal government's power to make laws that applied to all states in the Union.**

"Liberty first and Union afterwards" was favored by John C. Calhoun, one of Webster's greatest opponents in the struggle between states' rights and federal authority. The question of how much power the federal—as opposed to the state—government should have came to a head over the issue of tariffs.

A Tariff Raises the States' Rights Issue

When the War of 1812 ended, British manufacturers wanted to destroy their American competitors by flooding the U.S. market with inexpensive goods. In response, Congress in 1816 passed a tariff to protect the infant American industries. The tariff was increased in 1824 and again in 1828.

hmhsocialstudies.com TAKING NOTES

Use the graphic organizer online to take notes about key issues during Jackson's presidency.

THE NULLIFICATION THEORY Jackson's vice-president, **John C. Calhoun** of South Carolina, called the 1828 tariff a **Tariff of Abominations,** a "disgusting and loathsome" tariff. As an agricultural region dependent on cotton, the South had to compete in the world market. The high tariff on manufactured goods reduced British exports to the United States and forced the South to buy the more expensive Northern manufactured goods. From the South's point of view, the North was getting rich at the expense of the South. One observer remarked that when Southerners "see the flourishing villages of New England they cry, 'We pay for all this.'"

Calhoun was in an unusual and politically dangerous position. He had long been known as a nationalist spokesman, and he had supported the protective tariff of 1816. Calhoun was building a career as a national statesman, having served under both Adams and Jackson as vice-president. The situation in his home state, however, had made him change his views. South Carolina's economy had failed to recover fully from an economic depression. Cotton prices remained low because planters and their slaves were moving to more fertile lands in Alabama and in the lower Mississippi River valley. Some South Carolinians began to wonder if Calhoun really cared about the needs of his state. He soon showed them that he did.

KEY PLAYERS

JOHN C. CALHOUN
1782–1850

John Caldwell Calhoun entered national politics in 1811 when he was elected to the House of Representatives. There he was labeled a War Hawk for his support of the War of 1812. As President Monroe's secretary of war starting in 1817, Calhoun improved the army's organization.

This ambitious and handsome man with dark, flashing eyes served as vice-president under two presidents—John Quincy Adams, elected in 1824, and Andrew Jackson, elected in 1828.

Calhoun had a hard and humorless side. He took a tough position on slavery, arguing that it was not only necessary but even good:

> "There never has yet existed a wealthy and civilized society in which one portion of the community did not . . . live on the labor of the other."

DANIEL WEBSTER
1782–1852

In New England he was known as the "godlike Daniel." New Hampshire native Daniel Webster actually began his career in favor of states' rights. After moving to Boston, Massachusetts, in 1816, however, his views changed. New England's textile manufacturers needed a strong national government to protect their interests. As a lawyer and a congressman, Webster represented Boston's business interests. He argued several landmark cases before the Supreme Court, including *Gibbons* v. *Ogden*.

Webster was best known for his skill as an orator, but he hungered after the presidency. He ran for the highest office twice, never winning. Late in his career he said:

> "I have given my life to law and politics. Law is uncertain and politics is utterly vain."

Calhoun devised a nullification theory, which basically questioned the legality of applying some federal laws in sovereign states. Calhoun's argument was that the United States Constitution was based on a compact among the sovereign states. If the Constitution had been established by 13 sovereign states, he reasoned, then each had the right to nullify, or reject, a federal law that it considered unconstitutional. In 1828 Calhoun wrote down his theory in a document entitled "The South Carolina Exposition," but he did not sign his name to it. Nor did he say what he privately felt. Calhoun believed that if the federal government refused to permit a state to nullify a federal law, the state had the right to withdraw from the Union. (A)

MAIN IDEA
Summarizing
(A) What was Calhoun's nullification theory?

HAYNE AND WEBSTER DEBATE STATES' RIGHTS The tariff question (and the underlying states' rights issue) was discussed in one of the great debates in American history. In January 1830, visitors to the Senate listened to Senator

Robert Hayne of South Carolina debate Senator Daniel Webster of Massachusetts. Hayne delivered a pointed condemnation of the tariff.

A PERSONAL VOICE SENATOR ROBERT HAYNE

"The measures of the federal government . . . will soon involve the whole South in irretrievable ruin. But even this evil, great as it is, is not the chief ground of our complaints. It is the principle involved in the contest—a principle, which substituting the discretion of Congress for the limitations of the constitution, brings the States and the people to the feet of the federal government, and leaves them nothing they can call their own."

—from a speech to Congress, January 21, 1830

On January 26 Webster replied that he could not conceive of a "middle course, between submission to the laws, when regularly pronounced constitutional, on the one hand, and open resistance, which is revolution, or rebellion, on the other."

Once the debates ended, the people wanted to hear President Jackson's position. On April 13, at a public dinner, he clarified his position in a toast: "Our Union: it must be preserved." Calhoun replied with an equally pointed toast: "The Union, next to our liberty, the most dear; may we all remember that it can only be preserved by respecting the rights of the States and distributing equally the benefit and burden of the Union." The two men would not work together again; in fact, Calhoun resigned the vice-presidency in 1832. Jackson would run for reelection with former secretary of state Martin Van Buren.

South Carolinians wore emblems made from palmetto leaves to show their support for nullification. ▼

SOUTH CAROLINA REBELS The issue of states' rights was finally put to a test in 1832 when Congress passed a tariff law that South Carolina legislators still found unacceptable. They responded by declaring the tariffs of 1828 and 1832 "unauthorized by the Constitution" and "null, void, and no law." Then they threatened to secede, or withdraw, from the Union, if customs officials tried to collect duties.

Jackson was furious. Although himself a Southerner and a slaveholder, he believed that South Carolina's action in declaring a federal law null and void flouted the will of the people as expressed in the U.S. Constitution. He declared South Carolina's actions treasonous and threatened to hang Calhoun and march federal troops into South Carolina to enforce the tariff. To make good on his threats, Jackson next persuaded Congress to pass the Force Bill in 1833. This bill allowed the federal government to use the army and navy against South Carolina if state authorities resisted paying proper duties.

A bloody confrontation seemed inevitable until Henry Clay stepped in. In 1833 the Great Compromiser proposed a tariff bill that would gradually lower duties over a ten-year period. For now, the crisis between states' rights and federal authority was controlled, but the issue would continue to cause conflict in the 1840s and 1850s and would be a major cause of the Civil War. (B)

MAIN IDEA

Contrasting

(B) What were Jackson's and Calhoun's differing opinions on states' rights versus federal authority?

Jackson Attacks the National Bank

Although Andrew Jackson never did resort to sending troops into South Carolina, he did wage a very personal war on the **Bank of the United States** (BUS). In fact, during the same year he dealt with the South Carolina crisis, 1832, he vetoed the bill to recharter the Bank.

JACKSON OPPOSES THE BANK The Second Bank's 20-year charter was not due to expire until 1836, but Henry Clay and Daniel Webster wanted to introduce the renewal earlier to make it a campaign issue. They thought that Jackson might veto a new charter and, in so doing, lose some of his support. They underestimated, however, both the public's dislike of the BUS and Jackson's political skill.

Jackson and his allies made certain that the general public came to think of the BUS as a privileged institution. Jacksonians did have some powerful facts to support their opinions. Since all federal tax revenues were deposited in the BUS rather than state or private banks, the Second Bank had an unfair advantage over other banks. Furthermore, BUS stockholders, not average American taxpayers, earned the interest from these deposits. A privileged few were making money that should have benefited all the taxpayers. In addition, the bank's president, Nicholas Biddle, often extended loans to congressmen at much lower rates of interest than the bank gave to the average citizen. C

MAIN IDEA

Analyzing Motives

C What were some of Jackson's reasons for opposing the Second Bank of the United States?

PET BANKS In 1832, Jackson told his running mate, Martin Van Buren, that the BUS was a "monster" that corrupted "our statesmen" and wanted "to destroy our republican institution." "The bank, Mr. Van Buren, is trying to kill me, but *I will kill it.*" After Jackson's reelection in 1832, he tried to kill the BUS before its charter ran out in 1836. He appointed a secretary of the treasury who was willing to place all government funds in certain state banks. The banks were called "pet banks" because of their loyalty to the Democratic Party.

In an attempt to save the BUS, Nicholas Biddle decided to have the bank call in—or demand repayment of—loans. He also refused to make new loans. He hoped that these actions would cause a frustrated public to demand the passage of a new bank charter. Businessmen descended on Washington, D.C., to plead

VIDEO
Jackson v. the Bank of America

hmhsocialstudies.com

Analyzing *Political Cartoons*

"KING ANDREW THE FIRST"

Andrew Jackson once justified his tendency to place personal prerogative above constitutional law or national policy by stating that "One man with courage makes a majority." His critics replied with accusations of tyranny. The *New York American* condemned Jackson as a "maniac," who would "trample the rights of our people under his feet." The Whig convention of 1834 declared, "your president has become your MONARCH."

Both of those sentiments are reflected in this political cartoon which portrays Jackson as a king. Ancient portraits of kings often depicted them grinding their conquered enemies beneath their heels. Notice that beneath Jackson's feet are the torn pages of the Constitution. Notice, too, that in one hand Jackson is holding a scepter, a symbol of kingly power, while in the other he is holding the veto, a symbol of presidential power.

SKILLBUILDER Analyzing Political Cartoons

1. What does this cartoon suggest about Jackson's attitude towards the Constitution?
2. How does this cartoon specifically comment on Jackson's use of presidential power?

SEE SKILLBUILDER HANDBOOK, PAGE R24.

with Jackson for help. Jackson firmly told them they were talking to the wrong man. "Go to Nicholas Biddle," he said.

Pressure from financial leaders finally forced Biddle to adopt a more generous loan policy. However, the entire chain of events had by this time cost Biddle much of his backing. In 1836, when its charter expired, the Second Bank of the United States became just another Philadelphia bank. Five years later, it went out of business.

WHIG PARTY FORMS Jackson's tactics and policies had angered many people, including some members of his own Democratic Party. In 1834 the discontented—including Henry Clay, John Quincy Adams, and Daniel Webster—channeled their frustrations into action; they formed a new political party called the **Whig Party.** The Whigs backed the ideals of the American System, as promoted by Henry Clay. Besides a protective tariff, they wanted to use federal money to construct roads and canals to foster the exchange of goods between regions. The Whigs also backed federal control of the banking system and a nationally accepted currency. D

MAIN IDEA

Analyzing Causes

D Why was this a good time for the formation of the Whig Party?

Van Buren Deals with Jackson's Legacy

When Jackson announced that he would not run for a third term, the Democrats chose Vice-President **Martin Van Buren** as their candidate. The newly formed Whig Party, which in 1836 was not able to agree on a single candidate, ran three regional candidates against him. With Jackson's support Van Buren won the election easily. Along with the presidency, however, Van Buren inherited the dire consequences of Jackson's bank war and money policies.

JACKSON'S LEGACY Many of Jackson's pet banks—where federal funds had been deposited—were wildcat banks. These banks printed bank notes wildly in excess of the gold and silver they had on deposit, and were doomed to fail when many people attempted to redeem their currency for gold or silver.

Since the notes printed by wildcat banks were nearly worthless, the federal government was left holding the bag when people used them to purchase land from the government. Jackson realized what was happening. He caused the Treasury Department to issue an order that made only gold and silver, called specie, acceptable payment for public land. The order went into effect on August 15, 1836, and sent people rushing to banks to trade paper currency for gold and silver. In turn, many banks, which had limited specie, suspended the redemption of bank notes.

By May 1837, New York banks stopped accepting all paper currency. Other banks soon did the same. In the **panic of 1837,** bank closings and the collapse of the credit system cost many people their savings, bankrupted hundreds of businesses, and put more than a third of the population out of work.

Van Buren tried to help by reducing federal spending, but that caused already declining prices to drop further. Then he tried to set up an independent treasury that would use only gold and silver coin. In 1840 Congress established this treasury, but the demand for gold and silver it created only worsened matters. E

MAIN IDEA

Analyzing Causes

E How did Jackson's actions hurt the nation's economy?

POLITICAL ADVERTISEMENTS

In 1840, the campaign slogan "Tippecanoe and Tyler, too" helped William Henry Harrison win the White House. Harrison's party, the Whigs, printed their slogan on ribbons, metal badges, and even dinner plates.

Today, politicians find TV an efficient way to reach a large audience. During the 2000 election cycle, political parties, candidates, and issue advocacy groups spent 77 percent more on TV ads than they had in 1996.

However, critics believe that television ads have a negative impact on the democratic process. Candidates outside the two-party system rarely can afford as many TV ads as the major-party candidates. In 1998, a presidential advisory committee recommended that TV stations voluntarily provide five minutes a day of candidate coverage to help balance this inequality; only seven percent of TV stations participated in 2000.

HARRISON AND TYLER That same year, the Democratic Party candidate Van Buren ran for reelection against Whig Party candidate **William Henry Harrison**—but this time the Whigs had an advantage. They portrayed Harrison, the old war hero, as a man of the people and Van Buren as a pampered, privileged aristocrat. Actually, Van Buren was more of a common man; he was the son of a tavern owner and never earned much money. Harrison, on the other hand, came from a wealthy family and lived in a 16-room mansion.

Harrison won and immediately took steps to enact the Whig program to revitalize the economy, which was still in a severe depression. However, just a month after his inauguration he died of pneumonia.

John Tyler, Harrison's vice-president and successor, opposed many parts of the Whig program for economic recovery. The Whigs had put Tyler on the ballot to pick up Southern votes; they never thought he would play much of a role in government. During the next four years, however, they would see his inclusion on the ticket as a grave mistake—and would begin referring to President Tyler as "His Accidency."

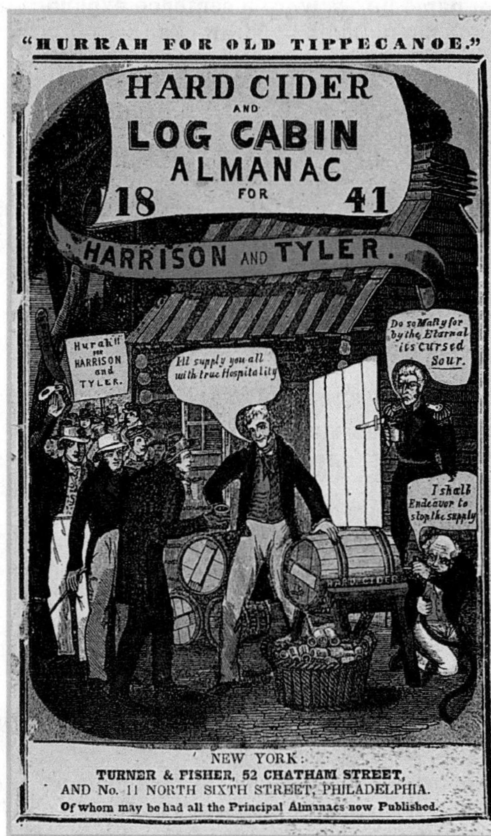

An almanac cover celebrating the election of William Henry Harrison and John Tyler. His campaign symbols, hard cider (an alcoholic beverage) and a log cabin, were meant to show that Harrison was a man of the people.

ASSESSMENT

1. **TERMS & NAMES** For each term or name, write a sentence explaining its significance.
   - **Daniel Webster**
   - **John C. Calhoun**
   - **Tariff of Abominations**
   - **Bank of the United States**
   - **Whig Party**
   - **Martin Van Buren**
   - **panic of 1837**
   - **William Henry Harrison**
   - **John Tyler**

MAIN IDEA

2. **TAKING NOTES**
   In a chart like the one shown, list the key issues that Jackson confronted and the important legacies of his administration.

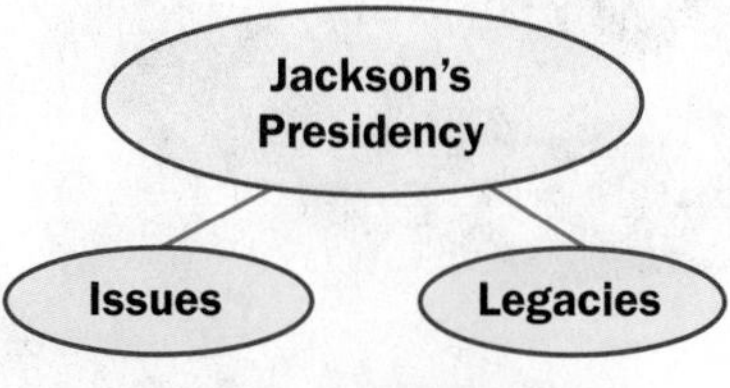

   In what ways does one of these legacies continue today?

THINKING CRITICALLY

3. **FORMING GENERALIZATIONS**
   In what ways do you think the tariff crises of 1828 and 1832 might be considered important milestones in American history before the Civil War? Use evidence from the text to support your response.
   Think About:
   - Calhoun's nullification theory
   - the Hayne-Webster debate
   - why Jackson pushed Congress to pass the Force Bill

4. **ANALYZING ISSUES**
   How do you think Jackson might have countered his critics' accusation that he was acting like a king? Support your answer.

5. **COMPARING**
   Compare the strategy William Henry Harrison used in the 1840 presidential campaign to strategies used in today's political campaigns. In what ways are they alike? Give examples.

CHAPTER 7 ASSESSMENT

TERMS & NAMES

For each term or name below, write a sentence explaining its significance during the early 19th century.

1. Eli Whitney
2. Industrial Revolution
3. John Quincy Adams
4. nationalism
5. Missouri Compromise
6. Andrew Jackson
7. spoils system
8. Trail of Tears
9. Bank of the United States (BUS)
10. Whig Party

MAIN IDEAS

Use your notes and the information in the chapter to answer the following questions.

Regional Economies Create Differences

1. What key changes in technology and methods of organizing manufacturing spurred the Industrial Revolution?
2. How did people in the Northeast, the South, and the West react to the Tariff of 1816?

Nationalism at Center Stage

3. Cite two ways in which the *Gibbons* v. *Ogden* decision set the stage for future Supreme Court rulings.
4. Why did conflict arise when Missouri requested admission into the Union?

The Age of Jackson

5. What changes occurred in the voting population and in voting patterns between the presidential elections of 1824 and 1828?
6. What alternatives did Jackson have in shaping a policy to tackle the problem of Native Americans?

States' Rights and the National Bank

7. What measures was Jackson willing to take in response to South Carolina's threat to secede in 1832?
8. Why did Jackson oppose the Bank of the United States?

CRITICAL THINKING

1. **USING YOUR NOTES** Create a continuum similar to the one below, labeled with *compromise* at one end and *confrontation* at the other. Mark where you think Andrew Jackson, Henry Clay, and John C. Calhoun would fall on the continuum. Support your ratings by citing historical events in which these men played critical roles.

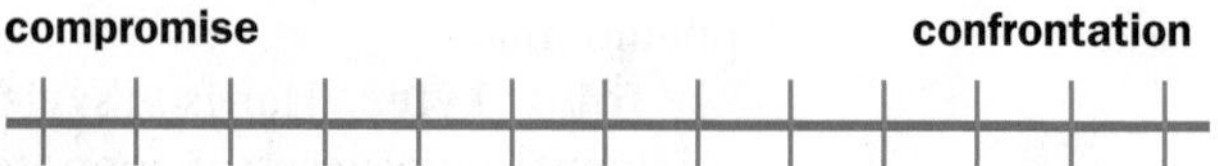

2. **HYPOTHESIZING** What do you think would have happened if the Indian Removal Act of 1830 had not been passed, and Native Americans had remained on their lands? Use evidence to support your answer.

3. **ANALYZING PRIMARY SOURCES** Read the quotation from John C. Calhoun. How does his choice of words reflect issues of the time? Explain your response.

> **"I never use the word 'Nation' in speaking of the United States. We are not a Nation, but a Union, a confederacy of equal and sovereign States."**

VISUAL SUMMARY Balancing Nationalism and Sectionalism

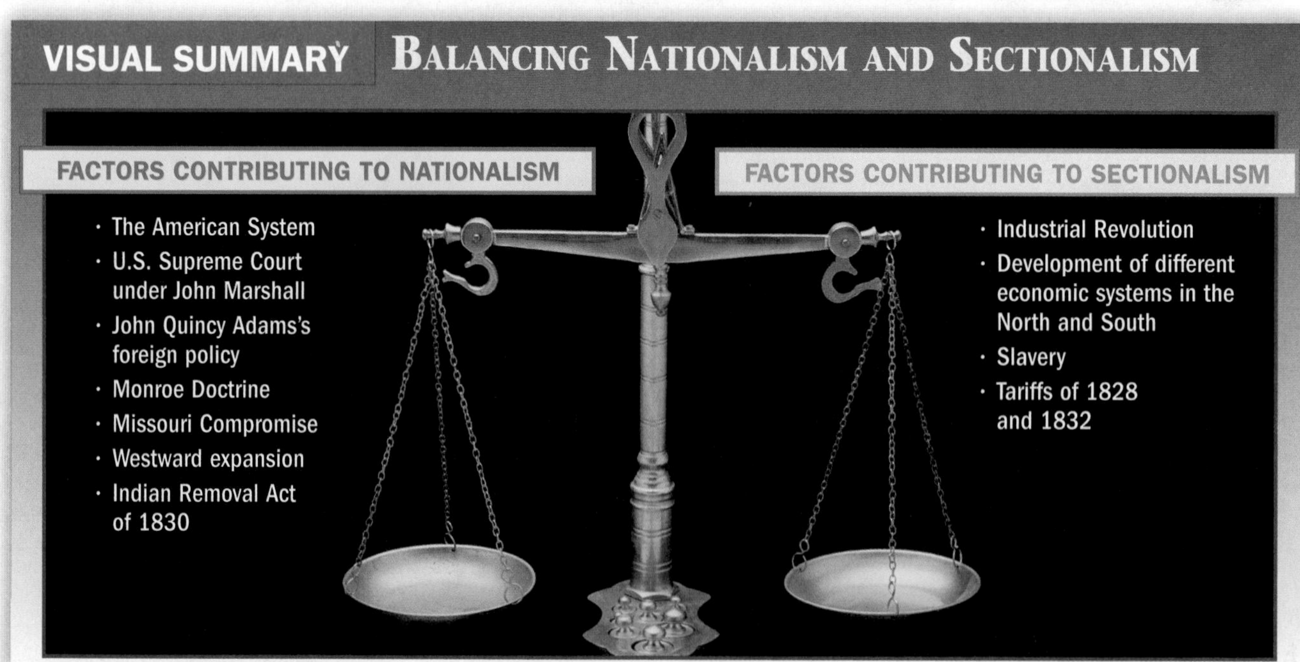

FACTORS CONTRIBUTING TO NATIONALISM
· The American System
· U.S. Supreme Court under John Marshall
· John Quincy Adams's foreign policy
· Monroe Doctrine
· Missouri Compromise
· Westward expansion
· Indian Removal Act of 1830
FACTORS CONTRIBUTING TO SECTIONALISM
· Industrial Revolution
· Development of different economic systems in the North and South
· Slavery
· Tariffs of 1828 and 1832

STANDARDIZED TEST PRACTICE

Use the quotation below and your knowledge of U.S. history to answer question 1.

> **"Every man is equally entitled to protection by law; but when the laws undertake to add to these natural and just advantages artificial distinctions, to grant . . . exclusive privileges, to make the rich richer and the potent more powerful, the humble members of society—the farmers, mechanics, and laborers—who have neither the time nor the means of securing like favors to themselves, have a right to complain of the injustice of their Government. There are no necessary evils in government. Its evils exist only in its abuses. If it would confine itself to equal protection, and, as Heaven does its rains, shower its favors alike on the high and the low, the rich and the poor, it would be an unqualified blessing. In the act [to recharter the Second Bank of the United States] before me there seems to be a wide and unnecessary departure from these just principles."**
>
> —Andrew Jackson, from *A Compilation of the Messages and Papers of the Presidents, 1789–1902*

1. The excerpt suggests that Jackson's vision of government's role in a democracy is to —

A address the rights and concerns of all citizens.
B increase the power of wealthy citizens.
C provide a national bank for its citizens.
D support only the poor citizens.

2. Which reason best explains why the theory of nullification was widely supported in the South?

F Southerners believed that states had the right to determine whether federal laws were constitutional.
G Southerners wanted to continue buying manufactured goods from Britain.
H Southerners wanted to divide the United States into two separate countries.
J Southerners did not want to pay the high tariffs that Congress passed.

3. Two politicians who each were elected president after campaigning as the candidate of the "common man" were —

A John C. Calhoun and Andrew Jackson.
B William Henry Harrison and John Tyler.
C Andrew Jackson and William Henry Harrison.
D Andrew Jackson and Henry Clay.

For additional test practice, go online for:
- Diagnostic tests
- Tutorials

INTERACT WITH HISTORY

Think about the issues you explored at the beginning of the chapter. Now that you know more about nullification and the fight over tariffs and states' rights, form small groups and discuss the following question: Would you have supported the federal or state government?

FOCUS ON WRITING

The clash between supporters of states' rights and the federal government has come to a head. This conflict has divided the nation. Write a persuasive essay arguing for or against states' rights. In your essay, include a clear argument for your position. Use examples to support your point of view.

MULTIMEDIA ACTIVITY

21st CENTURY

Choose a technological development of the early 1800s and create a Web site to advertise it. Visit the Chapter Assessment links for research leads. Possible inventions include the cotton gin, the steam engine, and the spinning mule. Use vivid language to describe how the invention works, what it accomplishes, what kind of labor it requires, and its effects on how people live or work. Include an image of the invention.

hmhsocialstudies.com

CHAPTER 8

REFORMING AMERICAN SOCIETY

Essential Question

What were the causes and effects of the Second Great Awakening and the various reform movements that swept the nation in the first half of the 19th century?

ALABAMA COURSE OF STUDY

11 Evaluate the impact of American social and political reform on the emergence of a distinct culture.

- Explaining the impact of the Second Great Awakening on the emergence of a national identity.
- Explaining the emergence of uniquely American writers.
- Explaining the influence of Elizabeth Cady Stanton, Dorothea Lynde Dix, and Susan B. Anthony on the development of social reform movements prior to the Civil War.

12 Describe the founding of the first abolitionist societies by Benjamin Rush and Benjamin Franklin and the role played by later critics of slavery, including William Lloyd Garrison, Frederick Douglass, Sojourner Truth, Angelina and Sarah Grimké, Henry David Thoreau, and Charles Sumner.

- Describing the rise of religious movements in opposition to slavery, including objections of the Quakers.

This 1834 engraving shows women and children working in a New England textile mill.

USA

1822 Large textile mill opens in Lowell, Massachusetts.

1827 Sojourner Truth is freed from slavery.

1829 David Walker prints *Appeal*, a pamphlet urging slaves to revolt.

1831 Nat Turner leads slave rebellion.

1834 National Trades' Union is formed.

1820 — 1830

WORLD

1820 Revolts break out in Spain and Portugal.

1832 Britain passes its first Reform Bill.

1833 Britain abolishes slavery in its empire.

Image Credits: (bkgd), The Granger Collection, New York; (b), Courtesy of the Lowell Historical Society

HISTORY

Freedom's Road: Slavery and the Opposition

hmhsocialstudies.com VIDEO

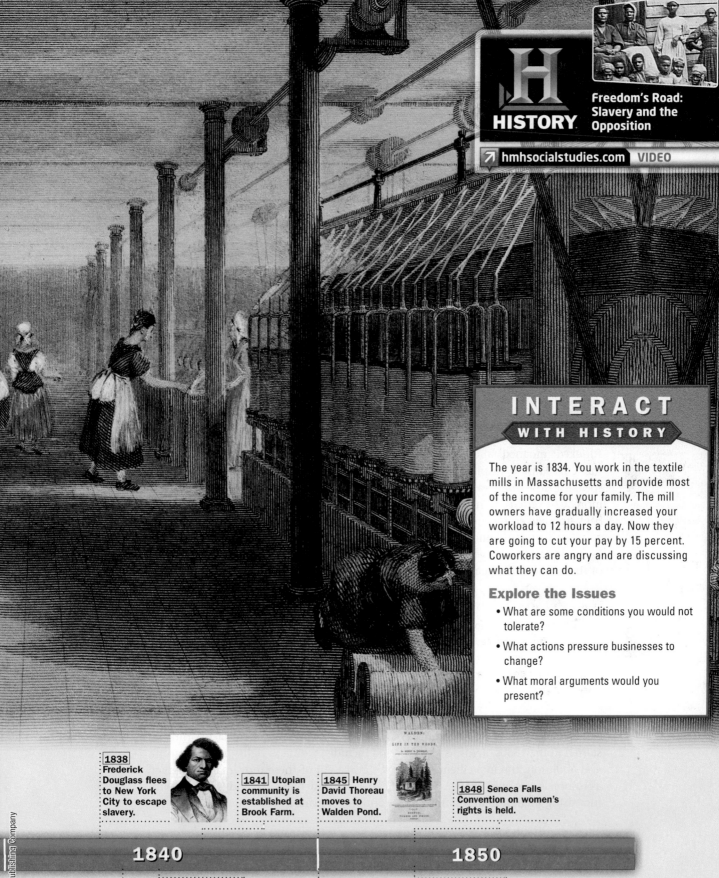

INTERACT WITH HISTORY

The year is 1834. You work in the textile mills in Massachusetts and provide most of the income for your family. The mill owners have gradually increased your workload to 12 hours a day. Now they are going to cut your pay by 15 percent. Coworkers are angry and are discussing what they can do.

Explore the Issues

- What are some conditions you would not tolerate?
- What actions pressure businesses to change?
- What moral arguments would you present?

1838 Frederick Douglass flees to New York City to escape slavery.

1841 Utopian community is established at Brook Farm.

1845 Henry David Thoreau moves to Walden Pond.

1848 Seneca Falls Convention on women's rights is held.

1840

1850

1839 French and British introduce first forms of photography.

1840 World's Anti-Slavery Convention is held in London.

1845 Great Potato Famine begins in Ireland.

1848 Revolutions erupt across Europe, causing many Germans and others to move to America.

Image Credits: (bkgd), The Granger Collection, New York; (bl), ©Paul Almasy/Corbis; (br), The Granger Collection, New York; (cr), ©Hulton Archive/Getty Images; (cl), The Granger Collection, New York

SECTION 1

Religion Sparks Reform

MAIN IDEA	WHY IT MATTERS NOW	Terms & Names
A renewal of religious sentiment—known as the Second Great Awakening—inspired a host of reform movements.	Many modern social and political reform movements grew out of the reform movements of 19th-century America.	• Charles Grandison Finney • Second Great Awakening • revival • Ralph Waldo Emerson • transcendentalism • Henry David Thoreau • civil disobedience • utopian community • Dorothea Dix

One American's Story

Use the graphic organizer online to take notes on the Second Great Awakening.

When **Charles Grandison Finney** preached, his listeners shrieked, moaned, and fainted. The most famous preacher of the era, Finney inspired emotional religious faith, using a speaking style that was as much high drama as prayer or sermon. Converted at the age of 29, Finney traveled by horseback to deliver his message. Finney seated the most likely converts in his audiences on a special "anxious bench," where he could fasten his eyes upon them. He lectured on the depth of the conversion experience.

▲ Charles Grandison Finney

A PERSONAL VOICE CHARLES GRANDISON FINNEY

"I know this is all so much algebra to those who have never felt it. But to those who have experienced the agony of wrestling, prevailing prayer, for the conversion of a soul, you may depend upon it, that soul . . . appears as dear as a child is to the mother who brought it forth with pain."

—*Lectures on Revivals of Religions*

The convert's duty was to spread the word about personal salvation to others. This religious activism—or evangelism—was part of an overall era of reform that started in the 1830s. Reforms of the period included women's rights, school reform, and abolition, the movement to outlaw slavery. All of these movements emerged as responses to rapid changes in American society such as early industrial growth, increasing migration and immigration, and new means of communication.

The Second Great Awakening

Much of the impulse toward reform was rooted in the revivals of the broad religious movement that swept the United States after 1790, known as the **Second Great Awakening.** Finney and his contemporaries were participants in the Second Great Awakening. These preachers rejected the 18th-century Calvinistic belief that God predetermined one's salvation or damnation—whether a person went to heaven or hell. Instead, they emphasized individual responsibility for seeking salvation, and they insisted that people could improve themselves and society.

Religious ideas current in the early 19th century promoted individualism and responsibility, similar to the emphasis of Jacksonian democracy on the power of the common citizen. Christian churches split over these ideas, as various denominations competed to proclaim the message of a democratic God, one who extends the possibility of salvation to all people. The forums for their messages were large gatherings, where some preachers could draw audiences of 20,000 or more at outdoor camps.

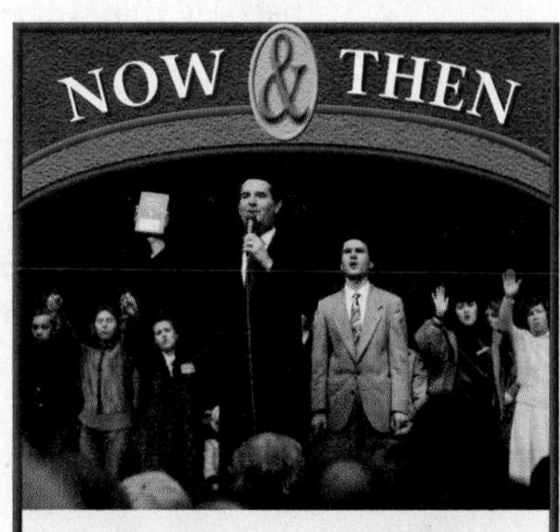

MODERN REVIVALISM

Evangelical Christianity reemerged in several different religious organizations in the late 20th century. One example is the Christian Coalition, a religiously based citizen-action organization with almost 2 million members.

As with the Second Great Awakening, members of these religious organizations often are active in political movements that spring from personal religious beliefs. Indeed, some of the organizations use television much like Finney used the revival meeting to encourage believers to act on their faith.

REVIVALISM Such a gathering was called a **revival,** an emotional meeting designed to awaken religious faith through impassioned preaching and prayer. A revival might last 4 or 5 days. During the day the participants studied the Bible and examined their souls. In the evening they heard emotional preaching that could make them cry out, burst into tears, or tremble with fear.

Revivalism swept across the United States in the early 19th century. Some of the most intense revivals took place in a part of western New York known as the burned-over district because of the religious fires that frequently burned there. Charles Finney fanned these flames, conducting some of his most successful revivals in Rochester, New York. The Rochester revivals earned Finney the reputation of "the father of modern revivalism." Revivalism had a strong impact on the public. According to one estimate, in 1800 just 1 in 15 Americans belonged to a church, but by 1850, 1 in 6 was a member. (A)

MAIN IDEA

Analyzing Effects

(A) How did the Second Great Awakening revolutionize the American religious tradition?

THE AFRICAN-AMERICAN CHURCH The Second Great Awakening also brought Christianity on a large scale to enslaved African Americans. There was a strong democratic impulse in the new churches and a belief that all people—black or white—belonged to the same God. Thus, the camp meetings and the new Baptist or Methodist churches were open to both blacks and whites. Slaves in the rural South—though they were segregated in pews of their own—worshiped in the same churches, heard the same sermons, and sang the same hymns as did the slave owners. Enslaved African Americans, however, interpreted the Christian message as a promise of freedom for their people.

In the East, many free African Americans worshiped in separate black churches, like Richard Allen's Bethel African Church in Philadelphia, which by 1816 would

This early-19th-century tray depicts Lemuel Haynes preaching in his Vermont Congregational Church. ▼

become the African Methodist Episcopal Church. Allen inspired his congregation to strengthen its faith as well as to fight against slavery.

A PERSONAL VOICE RICHARD ALLEN

"**Our only design is to secure to ourselves, our rights and privileges to regulate our affairs temporal and spiritual, the same as if we were white people, and to guard against any oppression which might possibly arise from the improper prejudices or administration of any individual having the exercise of Discipline over us.**"

—quoted in *Segregated Sabbaths*

Membership in the African Methodist Episcopal Church grew rapidly. It became a political, cultural, and social center for African Americans, providing schools and other services that whites denied them.

Eventually the African-American church developed a political voice and organized the first black national convention, held in Philadelphia in September 1830. Richard Allen convened the meeting, in which participants agreed to explore the possible settlement of free African Americans and fugitive slaves in Canada. Allen's convention was the first of what would become an annual convention of free blacks in the North. The African-American church gave its members a deep inner faith, a strong sense of community—and the spiritual support to oppose slavery. B

MAIN IDEA

Summarizing
B How did the African-American church support its followers?

Transcendentalism and Reforms

Many reform-minded individuals sought an alternative to traditional religion but found revivalism too public a forum for religious expression.

TRANSCENDENTALISM By the mid-1800s, some Americans were taking new pride in their emerging culture. **Ralph Waldo Emerson,** a New England writer, nurtured this pride. He led a group practicing **transcendentalism**—a philosophical

History Through Art

A VIEW OF THE MOUNTAIN PASS CALLED THE NOTCH OF THE WHITE MOUNTAINS (CRAWFORD NOTCH) (1839)

This painting by Thomas Cole is an example of the Hudson River school. Like the transcendentalists, its painters celebrated the beauty of the American landscape, and the truth found in personal emotion.
What relationship between humans and nature does Cole's painting portray?

and literary movement that emphasized living a simple life and celebrated the truth found in nature and in personal emotion and imagination.

Exalting the dignity of the individual, the transcendentalists spawned a literary movement that stressed American ideas of optimism, freedom, and self-reliance. Emerson's friend **Henry David Thoreau** put the idea of self-reliance into practice. Abandoning community life, he built himself a cabin on the shore of Walden Pond near Concord, Massachusetts, where he lived alone for two years. (See American Literature, Literature of the Transcendentalists.) In *Walden* (1854), Thoreau advised readers to follow their inner voices.

MAIN IDEA

Synthesizing
C In what way did Thoreau's experience at Walden reflect transcendentalist beliefs?

Because Thoreau believed in the importance of individual conscience, he urged people not to obey laws they considered unjust. Instead of protesting with violence, they should peacefully refuse to obey those laws. This form of protest is called **civil disobedience.** For example, Thoreau did not want to support the U.S. government, which allowed slavery and fought the War with Mexico. Instead of paying taxes that helped finance the war, Thoreau went to jail. C

Thoreau's beliefs also led him to be an abolitionist, or someone who wants to abolish slavery. In addition to refusing to pay taxes to support slavery, Thoreau also spoke out against slavery in the lecture that became "On the Duty of Civil Disobedience." Thoreau was active in the Concord Lyceum in Massachusetts where the abolition cause was debated actively. Moreover, Thoreau spent a large amount of his journal discussing slavery. However, despite his strong convictions against slavery, Thoreau thought that individuals had to decide for themselves to free their slaves and abolish slavery.

UNITARIANISM Rather than appealing to the emotions, Unitarians emphasized reason and appeals to conscience as the paths to perfection. In New England, Unitarians quickly attracted a wealthy and educated following. In place of the dramatic conversions produced by the revivals, Unitarians believed conversion was a gradual process. William Ellery Channing, a prominent Unitarian leader, asserted that the purpose of Christianity was "the perfection of human nature, the elevation of men into nobler beings." Unitarians agreed with revivalists that individual and social reform were both possible and important. D

MAIN IDEA

Contrasting
D How did the Unitarians' approach to religious experience differ from the revivalists'?

Americans Form Ideal Communities

Some of the optimism of religious and social reform also inspired the establishment of **utopian communities,** experimental groups who tried to create a "utopia," or perfect place. These communities varied in their philosophies and living arrangements but shared common goals such as self-sufficiency. One of the best-known utopian communities was established in New Harmony, Indiana. Another was Brook Farm, located near Boston.

In 1841 transcendentalist George Ripley established Brook Farm to "prepare a society of liberal, intelligent and cultivated persons, whose relations with each other would permit a more wholesome and simple life than can be led amidst the pressure of our competitive institutions." A fire destroyed the main building at Brook Farm in 1847, and the community immediately disbanded. Most utopias lasted no more than a few years.

HAWTHORNE AT BROOK FARM

New England writer Nathaniel Hawthorne spent about six months at Brook Farm in 1841. He hoped to find solitude in which to write, but instead spent close to ten hours a day working in the barns and fields. He was forced to conclude that life there was "unnatural and unsuitable" for him.

Ten years after he left Brook Farm, Hawthorne, now considered an established author, wrote *The Blithedale Romance* (1852). A fictional account of communal life based on Brook Farm, the book suggests that striving for perfection may yield unexpected results.

The failure of the utopian communities did not lessen the zeal of the religious reformers. Many became active in humanitarian reform movements, such as the abolition of slavery and improved conditions for women.

SHAKER COMMUNITIES Religious belief spurred other ideal communities. The Shakers, who followed the teachings of Ann Lee, set up their first communities in New York, New England, and on the frontier. Shakers shared their goods with each other, believed that men and women are equal, and refused to fight for any reason. When a person became a Shaker, he or she vowed not to marry or have children. Shakers depended on converts and adopting children to keep their communities going. In the 1840s, the Shakers had 6,000 members—their highest number. In 2009, only about three Shakers remained in the entire United States.

▲ These fine oval wooden boxes were made in the Shaker village in Canterbury, New Hampshire. They were used for storing small items.

Schools and Prisons Undergo Reform

By the mid-19th century, thousands of Americans holding a variety of philosophical positions had joined together to fight the various social ills that troubled the young nation. Some social reformers focused their attention on schools and other institutions.

REFORMING ASYLUMS AND PRISONS In 1831, French writer Alexis de Tocqueville had visited the United States to study its penitentiary system. Observing prisoners who were physically punished or isolated for extended periods, de Tocqueville concluded that "While society in the United States gives the example of the most extended liberty, the prisons of the same country offer the spectacle of the most complete despotism [rigid and severe control]." Reformers quickly took up the cause.

Dorothea Dix was compelled by personal experience to join the movement for social reform. On visiting a Massachusetts house of correction, Dix was horrified to discover that jails often housed mentally ill people.

A PERSONAL VOICE DOROTHEA DIX

"I proceed, gentlemen, briefly to call your attention to the present state of insane persons confined within this Commonwealth. . . . Chained, naked, beaten with rods, and lashed into obedience! . . . Injustice is also done to the convicts: it is certainly very wrong that they should be doomed day after day and night after night to listen to the ravings of madmen and madwomen."

—Report to the Massachusetts Legislature

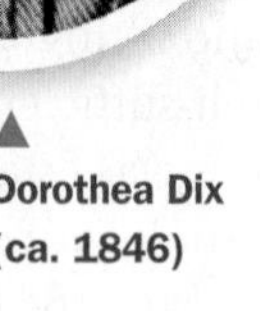

▲ Dorothea Dix (ca. 1846)

In 1843 she sent a report of her findings to the Massachusetts legislature, who in turn passed a law aimed at improving conditions. Between 1845 and 1852, Dix persuaded nine Southern states to set up public hospitals for the mentally ill.

Prison reformers—and Dorothea Dix in her efforts on behalf of the mentally ill—emphasized the idea of rehabilitation, treatment that might reform the sick or imprisoned person to a useful position in society. There was, as revivalists suggested, hope for everyone. (E)

MAIN IDEA

Analyzing Effects

(E) How did the reformers change the treatment of the mentally ill and prisoners?

IMPROVING EDUCATION Before the mid-1800s, no uniform educational policy existed in the United States. School conditions varied across regions. Massachussetts and Vermont were the only states before the Civil War to pass a compulsory school attendance law. Classrooms in the early schools were not divided by grade, so younger and older pupils were thrown together. Few children continued in school beyond the age of ten.

In the 1830s, Americans increasingly began to demand tax-supported public schools. For example, in 1834 Pennsylvania established a tax-supported public school system. Although the system was optional, a storm of opposition erupted from well-to-do taxpayers. They saw no reason to support schools that their children, who were mostly enrolled in private schools, would not attend. Opposition also came from some German immigrants who feared that their children would forget the German language and culture. Within three years, however, about 42 percent of the elementary-school-age children in Pennsylvania were attending public schools.

One remarkable leader in the public school reform movement was Horace Mann of Massachusetts. After a childhood spent partly at work and partly in poor schools, Mann declared, "If we do not prepare children to become good citizens, . . . if we do not enrich their minds with knowledge, then our republic must go down to destruction, as others have gone before it." In 1837 he became the first secretary of the Massachusetts Board of Education. In 12 years of service, Mann established teacher-training programs and instituted curriculum reforms. He also doubled the money that the state spent on schools.

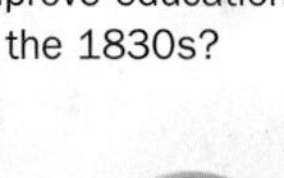

Summarizing

F What efforts were made to improve education in the 1830s?

Other states soon followed Massachusetts's and Pennsylvania's good example. By the 1850s every state had provided some form of publicly funded elementary schools. In states in the far West and in Southern states, however, it took years before public schools were firmly established. **F**

HISTORICAL SPOTLIGHT

MCGUFFEY'S READERS

If you attended school during the mid- to late-1800s, you probably would have used a McGuffey's reader. William H. McGuffey, a teacher and preacher in Ohio, first published his popular grade-school reading books in the 1830s.

The readers, which had sold more than 60 million copies by 1879, taught reading, writing, and arithmetic, as well as the democratic cultural values of hard work, honesty, and love of country. They also contained little moral lessons to live by, such as "Idleness is the nest in which mischief lays its eggs."

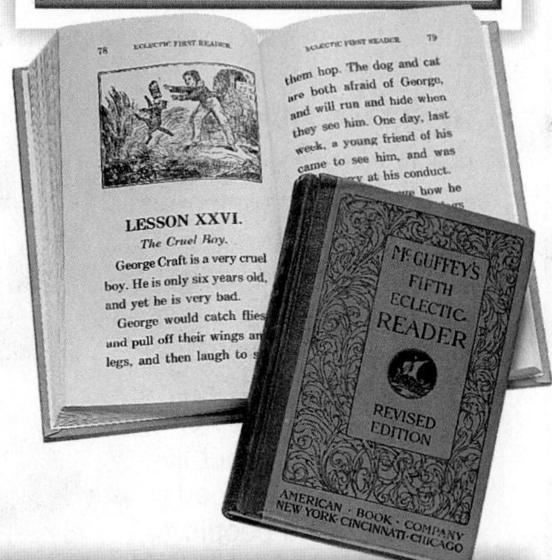

SECTION 1 ASSESSMENT

1. **TERMS & NAMES** For each term or name, write a sentence explaining its significance.
   - **Charles Grandison Finney**
   - **Second Great Awakening**
   - **revival**
   - **Ralph Waldo Emerson**
   - **transcendentalism**
   - **Henry David Thoreau**
   - **civil disobedience**
   - **utopian community**
   - **Dorothea Dix**

MAIN IDEA

2. **TAKING NOTES**
   In a web similar to the one shown, fill in events and ideas that relate to the Second Great Awakening.

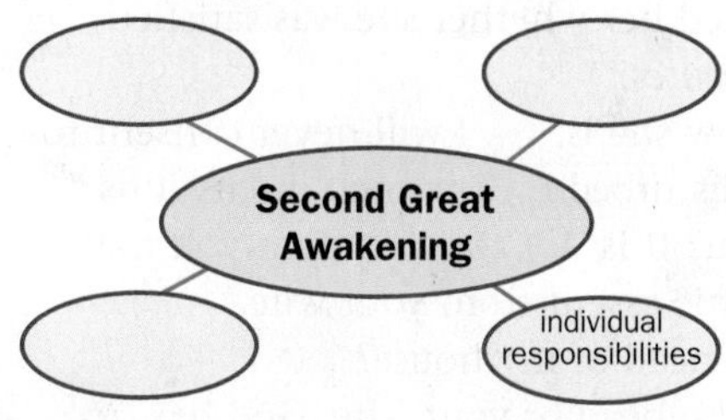

Why did revivalism catch hold in the early 19th century?

CRITICAL THINKING

3. **SYNTHESIZING**
   Consider the philosophical and religious ideas expressed during the Second Great Awakening and other religious reform movements. What were the key values and beliefs that guided 19th-century reformers' actions? **Think About:**
   - concepts of individualism and individual salvation
   - attitudes toward social responsibility
   - the viewpoints of Finney, Channing, and Emerson

4. **ANALYZING ISSUES**
   How do you think the 19th-century reform movements in schools, prisons, and asylums might have influenced reform movements today?

5. **COMPARING**
   Why might the idea of utopian communities appeal to the transcendentalists?

The Literature of the Young United States

1820–1850 In the 19th century, American writers found a distinctive voice. One influential American thinker was Ralph Waldo Emerson. A poet, essayist, and lecturer, Emerson met writers in England who were part of the romantic movement. Romanticism stressed emotional expression in art and literature. Based on these ideas, Emerson developed transcendentalism, emphasizing a simple life not dictated by any organized system of belief. Fellow transcendentalists included Margaret Fuller and Henry David Thoreau. Although most influenced by European romanticism, some transcendentalists found inspiration in Puritan, Buddhist, and Asian traditions.

At the same time as the budding transcendentalist movement, more American writers embraced other romantic styles. James Fenimore Cooper wrote many novels about life on the frontier, appealing to readers' emotional sense of adventure. Edgar Allan Poe also played on emotions of readers by utilizing mystery and suspense. Together, these early American writers developed a unique American voice separate from their European predecessors.

HENRY DAVID THOREAU

Henry David Thoreau believed that people must be free to act by their own idea of right and wrong. His work helped shape many reform movements of his time. In *Walden*, published in 1854, Thoreau wrote about living alone in the woods. Thoreau urged people to reject the greed and materialism that were affecting Americans in their daily lives.

Simplicity, simplicity, simplicity! I say, let your affairs be as two or three, and not a hundred or a thousand; instead of a million count half a dozen, and keep your accounts on your thumb-nail. . . . Simplify, simplify. Instead of three meals a day, if it be necessary eat but one; instead of a hundred dishes, five; and reduce other things in proportion. . . .

When we are unhurried and wise, we perceive that only great and worthy things have any permanent and absolute exis-tence, that petty fears and petty pleasures are but the shadow of the reality. . . .

Time is but the stream I go a-fishing in. I drink at it; but while I drink I see the sandy bottom and detect how shallow it is. Its thin current slides away, but eternity remains. . . .

—*Walden* (published 1854)

MARGARET FULLER

Margaret Fuller was one of the editors of the transcendentalist journal *The Dial*. In 1845, Fuller published *Woman in the Nineteenth Century*, a work that demanded equality and fulfillment for women.

"Is it not enough," cries the irritated trader, "that you have done all you could to break up the national union, and thus destroy the prosperity of our country, but now you must be trying to break up family union, to take my wife away from the cradle and the kitchen-hearth to vote at polls and preach from a pulpit? Of course, if she does such things, she cannot attend to those of her own sphere. She is happy enough as she is. She has more leisure than I have—every means of improvement, every indulgence."

"Have you asked her whether she was satisfied with these *indulgences?*"

"No, but I know she is. . . . I will never consent to have our peace disturbed by any such discussions."

"Consent—you? It is not consent from you that is in question—it is assent from your wife."

"Am not I the head of my house?"

"You are not the head of your wife. God has given her a mind of her own."

—*Woman in the Nineteenth Century* (1845)

JAMES FENIMORE COOPER

Cooper's famous *The Last of the Mohicans* told the story of Hawkeye, or Natty Bumppo, during the French and Indian War. Cooper evokes a sense of sadness at the end of a Native American nation and the loss of American wilderness.

> "Why should Tamenund stay? The pale faces are masters of the earth, and the time of the red men has not yet come again. My day has been too long. In the morning I saw the sons of Unamis happy and strong; and yet, before the night has come, have I lived to see the last warrior of the wise race of the Mohicans."
>
> —*The Last of the Mohicans* (1826)

RALPH WALDO EMERSON

Emerson's poem "Berrying" expresses his celebration of the truth found in nature and in personal emotion and imagination.

> "May be true what I had heard,
> Earth's a howling wilderness
> Truculent with fraud and force,"
> Said I, strolling through the pastures,
> And along the riverside.
> Caught among the blackberry vines,
> Feeding on the Ethiops sweet,
> Pleasant fancies overtook me:
> I said, "What influence me preferred
> Elect to dreams thus beautiful?"
> The vines replied, "And didst thou deem
> No wisdom to our berries went?"
>
> —"Berrying"
> (published 1846)

◀ **EDGAR ALLAN POE**

Poe's short story "The Tell-Tale Heart" exemplifies Poe's mysterious and suspenseful style. In the story, a killer is haunted by the sound of his victim's beating heart.

> Yet the sound increased —and what could I do? It was a low, dull, quick sound —much such a sound as a watch makes when enveloped in cotton. I gasped for breath —and yet the officers heard it not. . . . I paced the floor to and fro with heavy strides, as if excited to fury by the observations of the men —but the noise steadily increased. . . . And still the men chatted pleasantly, and smiled. Was it possible they heard not? Almighty God! —no, no! They heard! —they suspected! —they knew! —they were making a mockery of my horror! . . . I felt that I must scream or die! and now —again! —hark! louder! louder! louder! louder!
>
> "Villains!" I shrieked, "dissemble no more! I admit the deed! —tear up the planks! here, here! —It is the beating of his hideous heart!"
>
> —"The Tell-Tale Heart" (1843)

THINKING CRITICALLY

1. **Comparing and Contrasting** What does each selection reveal about habits and attitudes in 1850s America? Cite details to help explain your answers.

SEE SKILLBUILDER HANDBOOK, PAGE R8.

2. 

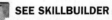

Use the links for American Literature to research and create an annotated book of famous transcendentalist quotations. Well-known examples might include: Emerson's "Hitch your wagon to a star," or Thoreau's "The mass of men lead lives of quiet desperation." The quotations you choose for each writer should contain information on the source of the quotation and a short description of how each quotation expresses transcendentalist beliefs.

Slavery and Abolition

MAIN IDEA	WHY IT MATTERS NOW	Terms & Names
Slavery became an explosive issue, as more Americans joined reformers working to put an end to it.	**The people of the United States continue to be challenged by questions of economic and social inequality.**	**• abolition • William Lloyd Garrison • emancipation • David Walker • Frederick Douglass • Nat Turner • antebellum • gag rule**

One American's Story

hmhsocialstudies.com TAKING NOTES

Use the graphic organizer online to take notes on antislavery and proslavery activities during the years from 1820 to 1850.

James Forten's great-grandfather had been brought from Africa to the American colonies in chains, but James was born free. In 1781, the 15-year-old James went to sea to fight for American independence. Captured by the British and offered passage to England, the patriotic youth refused, saying, "I am here a prisoner for the liberties of my country. I never, NEVER shall prove a traitor to her interests."

By the 1830s Forten had become a wealthy sailmaker in Philadelphia, with a fortune rumored to exceed $100,000. Though some people argued that free blacks should return to Africa, Forten disagreed and responded with sarcasm.

James Forten, a wealthy leader of Philadelphia's free black community, took an active role in a variety of political causes.

A Personal Voice JAMES FORTEN

"Here I have dwelt until I am nearly sixty years of age, and have brought up and educated a family. . . . Yet some ingenious gentlemen have recently discovered that I am still an African; that a continent three thousand miles, and more, from the place where I was born, is my native country. And I am advised to go home. . . . Perhaps if I should only be set on the shore of that distant land, I should recognize all I might see there, and run at once to the old hut where my forefathers lived a hundred years ago."

—quoted in *Forging Freedom: The Formation of Philadelphia's Black Community 1720–1840*

Forten's unwavering belief that he was an American led him to oppose the effort to resettle free blacks in Africa and also pushed him fervently to oppose slavery.

Abolitionists Speak Out

By the 1820s more than 100 antislavery societies were advocating for resettlement of blacks in Africa—based on the belief that African Americans were an inferior race that could not coexist with white society. Yet most free blacks considered America their home, and only about 1,400 blacks emigrated to Africa between

1820 and 1830. As one black pastor from New York angrily proclaimed, "We are natives of this country. We only ask that we be treated as well as foreigners."

African Americans increasingly were joined by whites in public criticism of slavery. White support for **abolition,** the call to outlaw slavery, was fueled by preachers like Charles G. Finney, who termed slavery "a great national sin."

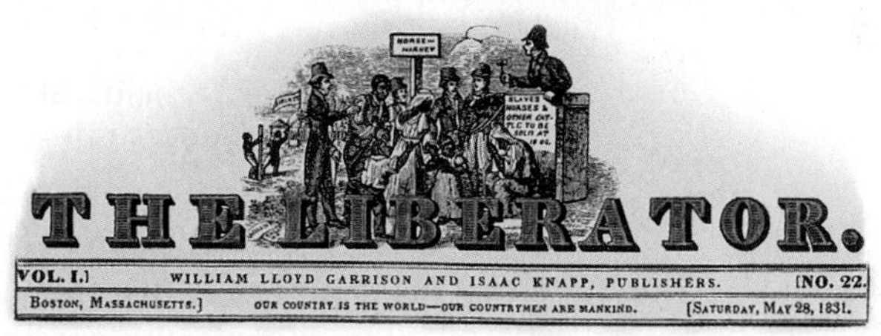
THE LIBERATOR.
VOL. I.] WILLIAM LLOYD GARRISON AND ISAAC KNAPP, PUBLISHERS. [NO. 22.
BOSTON, MASSACHUSETTS.] OUR COUNTRY IS THE WORLD—OUR COUNTRYMEN ARE MANKIND. [SATURDAY, MAY 28, 1831.

▲ **William Lloyd Garrison's newspaper, *The Liberator*, bore the motto: "Our country is the world—Our countrymen are all mankind."**

WILLIAM LLOYD GARRISON The most radical white abolitionist was an editor named **William Lloyd Garrison.** Active in religious reform movements in Massachusetts, Garrison started his own paper, *The Liberator*, in 1831 to deliver an uncompromising message: immediate **emancipation**—the freeing of slaves, with no payment to slaveholders.

A PERSONAL VOICE WILLIAM LLOYD GARRISON

"[I]s there not cause for severity? I *will* be harsh as truth, and as uncompromising as justice. On this subject [immediate emancipation], I do not wish to think or speak or write, with moderation. . . . I am in earnest—I will not equivocate—I will not excuse—I will not retreat a single inch—AND I WILL BE HEARD."

—*The Liberator*

As white abolitionists began to respond to Garrison's ideas, he founded the New England Anti-Slavery Society in 1832, followed by the national American Anti-Slavery Society a year later. Garrison enjoyed core black support; three out of four early subscribers were African Americans. Whites who opposed abolition, however, hated him. Some whites supported abolition but opposed Garrison when he attacked churches and the government for failing to condemn slavery. Garrison alienated whites even more when he associated with fiery abolitionist David Walker.

VIDEO
Frederick Douglass
hmhsocialstudies.com

FREE BLACKS In his *Appeal to the Colored Citizens of the World,* published in 1829, **David Walker,** a free black, advised blacks to fight for freedom rather than to wait for slave owners to end slavery. He wrote, "The man who would not fight . . . ought to be kept with all of his children or family, in slavery, or in chains, to be butchered by his cruel enemies."

Many free blacks, more willing to compromise than Walker, had joined one of many antislavery societies active by the end of the 1820s. In 1850, most of the 434,000 free blacks in the South worked as day laborers, but some held jobs as artisans. Northern free blacks discovered that only the lowest-paying jobs were open to them. Recalling his youth in Rhode Island in the 1830s, William J. Brown wrote, "To drive carriages, carry a market basket after the boss, and brush his boots . . . was as high as a colored man could rise." Frederick Douglass, however, rose above such limitations. (A)

Frederick Douglass, 1851 ▼

MAIN IDEA

Synthesizing
(A) What was radical at the time about Garrison's and Walker's ideas on abolition?

FREDERICK DOUGLASS Born into slavery in 1817, **Frederick Douglass** had been taught to read and write by the wife of one of his owners. Her husband ordered her to stop teaching Douglass, however, because reading "would forever unfit him to be a slave." When Douglass realized that knowledge could be his "pathway from slavery to freedom," he studied even harder.

By 1838, Douglass held a skilled job as a ship caulker in Baltimore. He earned the top wages in the yard but was not allowed to keep any of his earnings. After a disagreement with his owner, Douglass decided to escape. Borrowing the identity of a free black sailor and carrying official papers, he reached New York and tasted freedom for the first time.

Douglass became an eager reader of *The Liberator*, which, he said, "sent a thrill of joy through my soul, such as I had never felt before." When Garrison heard him speak of his experiences, he was so impressed he sponsored Douglass as a lecturer for the American Anti-Slavery Society. A superb speaker, Douglass thrilled huge audiences. "I appear before the immense assembly this evening as a thief and a robber," he would say. "I stole this head, these limbs, this body from my master and ran off with them." Hoping that abolition could be achieved through political actions, Douglass broke with Garrison in 1847 and began his own antislavery newspaper. He named it *The North Star*, after the star that guided runaway slaves to freedom. B

MAIN IDEA

Contrasting

B How did the various antislavery groups differ in approach?

Life Under Slavery

After 1830, Americans hotly debated the issue of slavery, but many African Americans still lived in bondage. In fact, the population of slaves in America had nearly doubled in the years between 1810 and 1830, growing from 1.2 million to roughly 2 million.

The institution of slavery had changed substantially since the 18th century. In those days, most slaves had recently arrived from the Caribbean or Africa and spoke one of several non-English languages. Most of these slaves worked on small farms alongside people with whom they could not easily communicate. By 1830, the majority had been born in America and spoke enough English to be able to communicate with other slaves. The rise of the plantation in the mid-18th century brought further change to the lives of the enslaved.

▲ Planters' children—like Charlotte Helen Middleton, shown with her nurse Lydia in 1857—often were tended by slaves who had been forced to give up their own children.

RURAL SLAVERY On large plantations, men, women, and even children toiled from dawn to dusk in the fields. The whip of the overseer or slave driver compelled them to work faster. Solomon Northup, who was born free and later enslaved, recalled the never-ending labor.

A PERSONAL VOICE SOLOMON NORTHUP

"The hands are required to be in the cotton field as soon as it is light in the morning, and, with the exception of ten or fifteen minutes, which is given them at noon to swallow their allowance of cold bacon, they are not permitted to be a moment idle until it is too dark to see, and when the moon is full, they often times labor till the middle of the night. They do not dare to stop even at dinner time, nor return to the quarters, however late it be, until the order to halt is given by the driver."

—*Twelve Years a Slave*

By 1850 most slaves lived on plantations or large farms that employed ten or more slaves, but many lived on small farms, laboring beside their owners. Others lived and worked in the cities. C

MAIN IDEA

Summarizing

C Describe typical work experiences of rural Southern slaves.

URBAN SLAVERY By the 1830s the promise of cotton wealth had lured many Southern whites into farming, thus creating a shortage of white laborers for such

Southern Plantations

Plantations were virtually self-contained, self-sufficient worlds over which owners ruled with absolute authority. Owners established the boundaries that a slave could not cross without punishment or death. But no boundary protected a slave from the owner's demands or cruel treatment.

Slave quarters, from a photograph taken around 1865

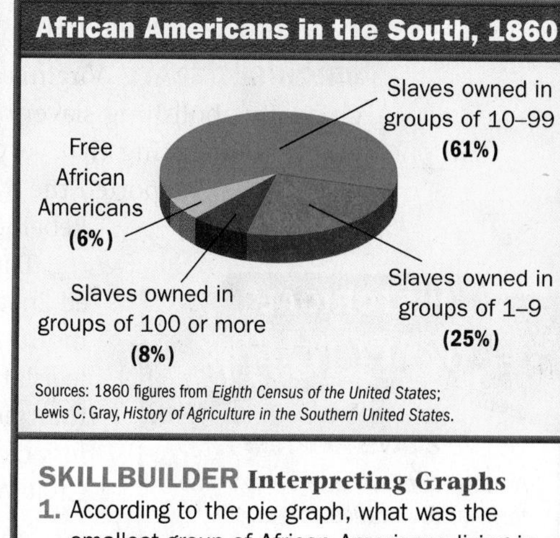

African Americans in the South, 1860

Sources: 1860 figures from *Eighth Census of the United States*; Lewis C. Gray, *History of Agriculture in the Southern United States.*

SKILLBUILDER Interpreting Graphs

1. According to the pie graph, what was the smallest group of African Americans living in the American South in 1860?
2. Under what conditions did 61% of slaves in the South live? Explain.

industries as mining and lumber. As a result, a demand arose for slaves as workers in mills and on ships. Slaves who had developed specialized skills on plantations were now in demand in Southern cities. For example, slaves filled skilled occupations such as blacksmithing or carpentry, resulting in a new class of skilled black laborers. Most slaves lived rurally—2.8 million in 1850, compared with the 400,000 slaves living in cities. However, enslaved blacks could hire themselves out as artisans in Southern cities, often more easily than free blacks in the North, where racial discrimination prevailed.

Many enslaved women and children worked the same jobs as men in Southern industry. Slave owners "hired out" their slaves to factory owners. In return, the slave owners collected the pay of their slaves without having to supervise their activities. Thus, urban slaves spent more time beyond the watchful eye of their slave owners. Frederick Douglass remarked on differences between rural and urban slavery, noting that "a city slave is almost a freeman, compared with a slave on the plantation. He is much better fed and clothed, and enjoys privileges altogether unknown to the slave on the plantation." Douglass also noted that "a vestige of decency" in the cities limited the acts of "atrocious cruelty" to slaves that were common on plantations.

Artist Felix Darley completed this tinted drawing in 1863 for a history book. Nat Turner is shown *(standing)* preaching to his followers.

Still slaves never lost sight of their goal of freedom. For some, it was time to take more drastic and organized action.

NAT TURNER'S REBELLION **Nat Turner** was born into slavery in 1800 in Southampton County, Virginia. A gifted preacher, Turner believed that he had been chosen to lead his people out of bondage. In August, 1831, Turner judged an eclipse of the sun to be a divine signal for action. With nearly 80 followers, Turner's band attacked four plantations and killed almost 60 white inhabitants before being captured by state and federal troops.

Though Turner himself hid out for several weeks, eventually he was captured, tried, and hanged. In the retaliation that followed, whites killed as many as 200 blacks—many of them innocent of any connection with the uprising. Turner's bloody rebellion strengthened the resolve of Southern whites to defend slavery and to control their slaves.

Slave Owners Defend Slavery

In some states, in the aftermath of the Turner rebellion, people argued that the only way to prevent further slave revolts was through emancipation. Others, however, chose to tighten restrictions on all African Americans.

VIRGINIA DEBATE Virginia governor John Floyd wrote of his wish for a "law . . . gradually abolishing slavery in this State." By January 1832 the state legislature was hotly debating that very prospect. "Nothing else could have prompted [the discussions]," reported the *Richmond Enquirer*, "but the bloody massacre [Turner's Rebellion] in the month of August."

The debate over the future of slavery in Virginia resulted in a motion for abolition in the state legislature. The motion lost by a 73 to 58 vote, primarily because the state legislature was balanced toward eastern slaveholders rather than non-slaveholders in the western part of the state. That loss closed the debate on slavery in the **antebellum** (pre-Civil War) South.

BACKLASH FROM REVOLTS In addition to forcing the Virginia debate, whites' fear of future slave revolts had another important effect. Most slave owners believed that education and privilege inspired revolt. Thus, many slave owners pushed their state legislatures to further tighten controls on African Americans. These controls became known as slave codes. D

In 1833, for example, Alabama forbade free and enslaved blacks from preaching the gospel unless "respectable" slaveholders were present. Georgia followed suit. In 1835 North Carolina became the last Southern state to deny the vote to free blacks. In some states, free blacks lost the right to own guns, purchase alcohol, assemble in public, and testify in court. In some Southern cities, African Americans could no longer own property, learn to

HISTORICAL SPOTLIGHT

SLAVE REVOLTS

Armed rebellion was an extreme form of resistance to slavery. Nat Turner's 1831 rebellion was merely the most recent example of slave desperation.

In 1811, more than 300 slaves had rebelled in Louisiana and marched on New Orleans with spikes and axes before a well-trained militia with firearms stopped them. Gabriel Prosser had hatched a plot to take over Richmond in 1800, and Denmark Vesey had led a conspiracy to control Charleston in 1822. Both of these conspiracies were thwarted by the authorities before larger rebellions occurred.

MAIN IDEA

Analyzing Effects

D How did Turner's revolt harden Southern white attitudes about basic liberties for blacks?

read and write, or work independently as carpenters or blacksmiths.

PROSLAVERY DEFENSES Some proslavery advocates used the Bible to defend slavery, citing passages that counseled servants to obey their masters. Slavery, Southern slave owners argued, actually benefited blacks by making them part of a prosperous and Christian civilization. Even Southern white Christian ministers gradually shifted toward accepting slavery during this period. Some had attacked slavery in the early 1800s, but by the 1830s most white ministers in the South agreed that slavery and Christianity could coexist.

Slave owners invented the myth of the happy slave, a cherished addition to the plantation family. To this image they contrasted that of the Northern wage slave, a wage-earning immigrant or free black who worked for pennies in dark and airless factories. George Fitzhugh, a Virginia slave owner, argued that whereas Northern mill owners fired their workers when they became too old or sick to work, Southerners cared for their slaves for a lifetime.

Abolitionists, however, continued to campaign for emancipation. One maneuver was to swamp Congress with petitions to end slavery in the District of Columbia. Southern representatives countered in 1836 by securing the adoption of a **gag rule,** a rule limiting or preventing debate on an issue—which meant that citizens submitting petitions were deprived of their right to have them heard. The gag rule eventually was repealed in 1844.

Nevertheless, as abolitionists' efforts intensified during the 1850s, some turned to violence. The more clear-sighted began to sound the alarm: this turmoil over slavery would lead to a divided nation.

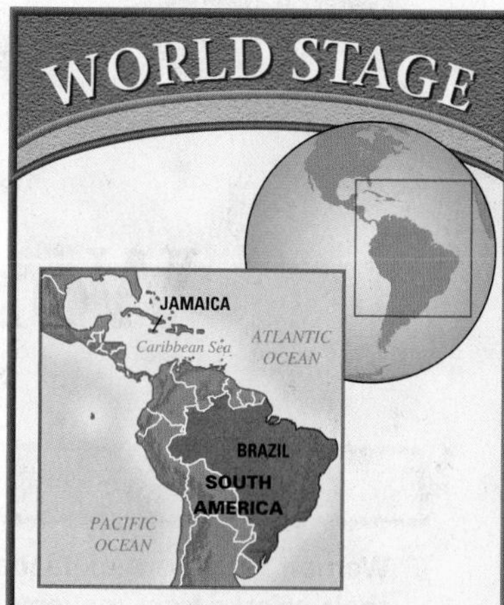

SLAVERY IN THE AMERICAS

Slaves formed a smaller portion of the total population in the American South than in the Caribbean and in Brazil. African slaves formed almost 80 percent of the population of Jamaica, a colony of Great Britain. Because so many slaves in that colony died, slave owners demanded a constant renewal of their supply from Africa, thus maintaining the Atlantic slave trade. Slavery ended in the British empire in 1833.

Brazil also had a large proportion of slaves. During the 1800s slaves made up more than half the colonial population of Brazil and worked primarily on large coffee plantations. Slavery was abolished in Brazil in 1888.

ASSESSMENT

1. **TERMS & NAMES** For each term or name, write a sentence explaining its significance.
   - **abolition**
   - **William Lloyd Garrison**
   - **emancipation**
   - **David Walker**
   - **Frederick Douglass**
   - **Nat Turner**
   - **antebellum**
   - **gag rule**

MAIN IDEA

2. **TAKING NOTES**
   In a two-column chart, list the major antislavery and proslavery actions that occurred from 1820 to 1850.

Antislavery Actions	Proslavery Actions

Which activity do you think was most effective? Explain.

CRITICAL THINKING

3. **SYNTHESIZING**
   Which do you think was a more effective strategy for achieving the abolitionists' goal of eliminating slavery—violence or nonviolence? Why? **Think About:**
   - Garrison's and Walker's remarks
   - Frederick Douglass's views
   - Southerners' reactions to Nat Turner's rebellion

4. **SUMMARIZING**
   What arguments did Southern proslavery whites employ to defend slavery?

5. **COMPARING**
   Compare the similarities and differences between the situations of free blacks in the North and slaves in the South.

SECTION 3

Women and Reform

MAIN IDEA	WHY IT MATTERS NOW	Terms & Names
Women reformers expanded their efforts from movements such as abolition and temperance to include women's rights.	The efforts of 19th-century women reformers inspired both woman suffragists in the early-1900s and present-day feminist movements.	• Elizabeth Cady Stanton • Lucretia Mott • cult of domesticity • Sarah Grimké • Angelina Grimké • temperance movement • Seneca Falls Convention • Sojourner Truth

One American's Story

hmhsocialstudies.com
TAKING NOTES
Use the graphic organizer online to take notes on how women approached the question of inequality.

Elizabeth Cady Stanton timed her marriage in 1840 so that she could accompany her husband to London for the World's Anti-Slavery Convention, where her husband was a delegate. At the antislavery convention, Stanton and the other women delegates received an unpleasant surprise.

A PERSONAL VOICE ELIZABETH CADY STANTON

"Though women were members of the National Anti-Slavery society, accustomed to speak and vote in all its conventions, and to take an equally active part with men in the whole antislavery struggle, and were there as delegates from associations of men and women, as well as those distinctively of their own sex, yet all alike were rejected because they were women."

—quoted in *Elizabeth Cady Stanton*

At the convention, Stanton found a friend in the Quaker abolitionist **Lucretia Mott.** Stanton and Mott vowed "to hold a convention as soon as we returned home, and form a society to advocate the rights of women." They kept their pledge and headed the first women's rights convention, assembled at Seneca Falls, New York, in 1848.

▲ Elizabeth Cady Stanton

Women's Roles in the Mid-1800s

In the early 19th century, women faced limited options. Prevailing customs demanded that women restrict their activities after marriage to the home and family. Housework and child care were considered the only proper activities for married women. Later that tradition became known as the **cult of domesticity.**

By 1850, roughly one in five white women had worked for wages a few years before they were married. About one in ten single white women worked outside

MAIN IDEA

Identifying Problems

A What were the main problems faced by women in the mid-1800s?

the home, earning about half the pay men received to do the same job. Women could neither vote nor sit on juries in the early 1800s, even if they were taxpayers. Typically, when a woman married, her property and any money she earned became her husband's. In many instances, married women lacked guardianship rights over their children. **A**

Women Mobilize for Reform

Despite such limits, women actively participated in all the important reform movements of the 19th century. Many middle-class white women were inspired by the optimistic message of the Second Great Awakening. Women were often shut out of meetings by disapproving men, and responded by expanding their efforts to seek equal rights for themselves.

WOMEN ABOLITIONISTS **Sarah and Angelina Grimké,** daughters of a South Carolina slaveholder, spoke eloquently for abolition. In 1836 Angelina Grimké published *An Appeal to Christian Women of the South,* in which she called upon women to "overthrow this horrible system of oppression and cruelty." Women abolitionists also raised money, distributed literature, and collected signatures for petitions to Congress.

Some men supported women's efforts. William Lloyd Garrison, for example, joined the determined women who had been denied participation in the World's Anti-Slavery Convention in 1840. Garrison said, "After battling so many long years for the liberties of African slaves, I can take no part in a convention that strikes down the most sacred rights of all women." Other men, however, denounced the female abolitionists. The Massachusetts clergy criticized the Grimké sisters for assuming "the place and tone of man as public reformer."

Opposition only served to make women reformers more determined. The abolitionist cause became a powerful spur to other reform causes, as well as to the women's rights movement. **B**

KEY PLAYER

LUCRETIA MOTT
1793–1880

History has it that Lucretia Mott was so talkative as a child that her mother called her Long Tongue. As an adult, she used her considerable public-speaking skills to campaign against slavery.

Mott became interested in women's rights when she learned that her salary as a teacher would be roughly half of what a man might receive. She was a prominent figure at the Seneca Falls Convention, at which she delivered the opening and closing addresses. Mott and her husband later acted on their abolitionist principles by taking in runaway slaves escaping on the Underground Railroad.

MAIN IDEA

Summarizing

B In what ways were women excluded from the abolitionist movement?

WORKING FOR TEMPERANCE The **temperance movement,** the effort to prohibit the drinking of alcohol, was another offshoot of the influence of churches and the women's rights movement. Speaking at a temperance meeting in 1852, Mary C. Vaughan attested to the evils of alcohol.

A PERSONAL VOICE MARY C. VAUGHAN

"There is no reform in which woman can act better or more appropriately than temperance. . . . Its effects fall so crushingly upon her . . . she has so often seen its slow, insidious, but not the less surely fatal advances, gaining upon its victim. . . . Oh! the misery, the utter, hopeless misery of the drunkard's wife!"

—quoted in *Women's America: Refocusing the Past*

In the early 19th century, alcohol flowed freely in America. Liquor helped wash down the salted meat and fish that composed the dominant diet and, until the development of anesthetics in the 1840s, doctors dosed their patients with whiskey or brandy before operating.

Many Americans, however, recognized drunkenness as a serious problem. Lyman Beecher, a prominent Connecticut minister, had begun lecturing against all use of liquor in 1825. A year later, the American Temperance Society was founded. By 1833, some 6,000 local temperance societies dotted the country.

This engraving is from a temperance society tract of around 1840. It depicts a family driven to despair by alcohol.

They held rallies, produced pamphlets, and brought about a decline in the consumption of alcohol that would continue into the 1860s.

EDUCATION FOR WOMEN Until the 1820s, American girls had few educational avenues open to them beyond elementary school. As Sarah Grimké, who ran a school for women with her sister Angelina, complained in *Letters on the Equality of the Sexes and the Condition of Woman* (1838), a woman who knew "chemistry enough to keep the pot boiling, and geography enough to know the location of the different rooms in her house," was considered learned enough.

A PERSONAL VOICE SARAH GRIMKÉ

"During the early part of my life, my lot was cast among the butterflies of the fashionable world, I am constrained to say . . . that their education is miserably deficient. . . . Our brethren may reject my doctrine . . . but I believe they would be 'partakers of the benefit' . . . and would find that woman, as their equal, was unspeakably more valuable than woman as their inferior, both as a moral and an intellectual being."

—*Letters on the Equality of the Sexes and the Condition of Woman*

Sarah Grimké *(above)* and her sister Angelina spoke out against slavery and gender inequality.

In 1821 Emma Willard opened one of the nation's first academically rigorous schools for girls in Troy, New York. The Troy Female Seminary became the model for a new type of women's school. Despite much mockery that "they will be educating cows next," Willard's school prospered.

In 1837 Mary Lyon overcame heated resistance to found another important institution of higher learning for women, Mount Holyoke Female Seminary (later Mount Holyoke College) in South Hadley, Massachusetts. In the same year Ohio's Oberlin College admitted four women to its degree program, thus becoming the nation's first fully coeducational college.

African-American women faced greater obstacles to getting an education. In 1831 white Quaker Prudence Crandall opened a school for girls in Canterbury, Connecticut. Two years later she admitted an African-American girl, but the townspeople protested so vigorously against desegregated education that Crandall decided to admit only African-American students. This aroused even more opposition, and in 1834 Crandall was forced to close the school and leave town. Only after the Civil War would the severely limited educational opportunities for African-American women finally, though slowly, begin to expand. C

MAIN IDEA

Summarizing

C What gains did women make in education in the 1820s and 1830s? Did these gains extend to African-American women?

WOMEN AND HEALTH REFORM In the mid-19th century, educated women also began to work for health reforms. Elizabeth Blackwell, who in 1849 became the first woman to graduate from medical college, later opened the New York Infirmary for Women and Children. In the 1850s, Lyman Beecher's daughter, Catharine, undertook a national survey of women's health. To her dismay, Beecher found three sick women for every healthy one. It was no wonder: women rarely bathed or exercised, and the fashion of the day included corsets so restrictive that breathing sometimes was difficult.

Amelia Bloomer, publisher of a temperance newspaper, rebelled. Bloomer often wore a costume of loose-fitting pants tied at the ankles and covered by a short skirt. Readers besieged her with requests for the sewing pattern. Most women who sewed the "bloomers," however, considered it a daring venture, as many men were outraged by women wearing pants.

▲ Amelia Bloomer adopted the full trousers that became known as bloomers in 1851.

Women's Rights Movement Emerges

The various reform movements of the mid-19th century fed the growth of the women's movement by providing women with increased opportunities to act outside the home.

SENECA FALLS In 1848 Elizabeth Cady Stanton and Lucretia Mott decided to hold a women's rights convention. They announced what would become known as the **Seneca Falls Convention** (for the New York town in which it was held). Stanton and Mott composed an agenda and a detailed statement of grievances. Stanton carefully modeled this "Declaration of Sentiments" on the Declaration of Independence. The second paragraph began with a revision of very familiar words: "We hold these truths to be self-evident: that all men and women are created equal." Some of the resolutions that were also proposed at the convention spoke to the circumstances with which women reformers had struggled.

A Personal Voice

"*Resolved*, That all laws which prevent women from occupying such a station in society as her conscience shall dictate, or which place her in a position inferior to that of man, are contrary to the great precept of nature, and therefore of no force or authority.

***Resolved*, That woman is man's equal—was intended to be so by the Creator, and the highest good of the race demands that she should be recognized as such."**

—Resolutions adopted at Seneca Falls Convention, 1848

Nearly 300 women and men gathered at the Wesleyan Methodist Church for the convention. The participants approved all parts of the declaration unanimously—including several resolutions to encourage women to participate in all public issues on an equal basis with men—except one. The one exception, which still passed by a narrow majority, was the resolution calling for women "to secure to

◀ In 1888, delegates to the First International Council of Women met to commemorate the 40th anniversary of Seneca Falls. Stanton is seated third from the right.

KEY PLAYER

SOJOURNER TRUTH
1797–1883

Sojourner Truth, born Isabella Van Wagener (or Baumfree), became legally free on July 4, 1827, when slavery was abolished in New York. A deeply spiritual woman, Truth became a traveling preacher dedicated to pacifism, abolitionism, and equality. She earned a reputation for tenacity, successfully suing for the return of her youngest son who had been illegally sold into slavery.

Truth was not taught to read or write but dictated her memoirs, published in 1850 as The *Narrative of Sojourner Truth: A Northern Slave.*

After the Emancipation Proclamation, Truth's final cause was to lobby (unsuccessfully) for land distribution for former slaves.

themselves their sacred right to the elective franchise," the right to vote. The vote remained a controversial aim. Some thought suffrage was an extreme solution to a nonexistent problem. As Lucy Stone's sister wrote in 1846, "I can't vote, but what care I for that, I would not if I could." **D**

MAIN IDEA

Contrasting

D How did the Seneca Falls Convention differ from the World's Anti-Slavery Convention held in 1840?

SOJOURNER TRUTH Women reformers made significant contributions to improving social conditions in the mid-19th century. Yet conditions for slaves worsened. Isabella Baumfree, a slave for the first 30 years of her life, took the name **Sojourner Truth** when she decided to sojourn (travel) throughout the country preaching, and later, arguing for abolition. At a women's rights convention in 1851, the tall, muscular black woman was hissed at in disapproval. Because Truth supported abolition, some participants feared her speaking would make their own cause less popular. But Truth won applause with her speech that urged men to grant women their rights.

A PERSONAL VOICE SOJOURNER TRUTH

> **"Look at me! Look at my arm! I have ploughed and planted, and gathered into barns, and no man could head me! And ain't I a woman? I could work as much and eat as much as a man—when I could get it—and bear the lash as well! And ain't I a woman? I have borne thirteen children, and seen most all sold off to slavery, and when I cried out with my mother's grief, none but Jesus heard me! And ain't I a woman?"**
>
> —quoted in *Narrative of Sojourner Truth: A Northern Slave*

As Truth showed, hard work was a central fact of life for most women. In the mid-19th century, this continued to be the case as women entered the emerging industrial workplace. Once there, they continued the calls for women's rights and other social reforms.

SECTION 3 ASSESSMENT

1. **TERMS & NAMES** For each term or name, write a sentence explaining its significance.
   - **Elizabeth Cady Stanton**
   - **Lucretia Mott**
   - **cult of domesticity**
   - **Sarah and Angelina Grimké**
   - **temperance movement**
   - **Seneca Falls Convention**
   - **Sojourner Truth**

MAIN IDEA

2. **TAKING NOTES**
   In a diagram similar to the one shown, fill in historical events, ideas, or people that relate to the main idea.

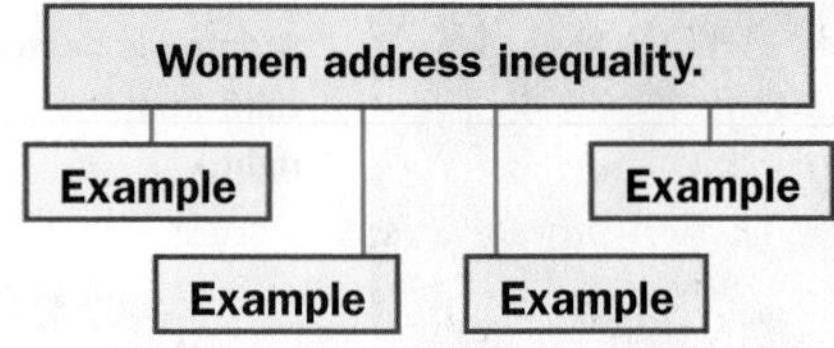

CRITICAL THINKING

3. **ANALYZING ISSUES**
   The Seneca Falls "Declaration of Sentiments" asserted that "Woman is man's equal." In what ways would that change the status women held at that time? Cite facts to support your answer. **Think About:**
   - women's social, economic, and legal status in the mid-1800s
   - married women's domestic roles
   - single women's career opportunities and wages

4. **EVALUATING**
   In what ways did the reform movements affect the lives of women—both white and African American? Use details from the section to support your answer.

5. **DRAWING CONCLUSIONS**
   Why do you think that many of the people who fought for abolition also fought for women's rights?

SECTION 4

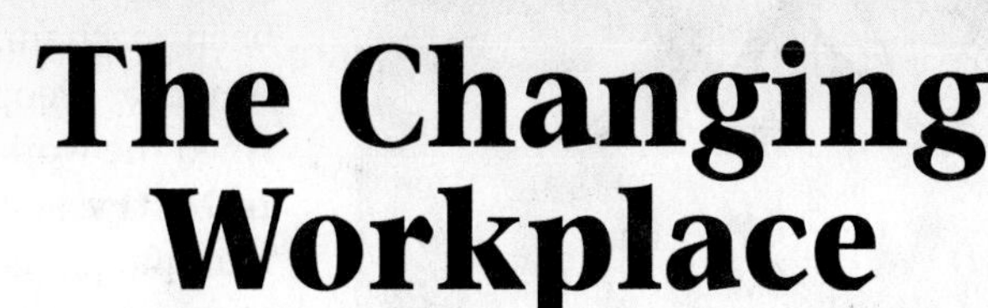

The Changing Workplace

MAIN IDEA

A growing industrial work force faced problems arising from manufacturing under the factory system.

WHY IT MATTERS NOW

The National Trades' Union was the forerunner of America's labor unions today.

Terms & Names

- **cottage industry**
- **master**
- **journeyman**
- **apprentice**
- **strike**
- **National Trades' Union**

One American's Story

hmhsocialstudies.com
TAKING NOTES

Use the graphic organizer online to take notes on the changing workplace in the first half of the nineteenth century.

In 1841 a brief narrative appeared in the *Lowell Offering*, the first journal written by and for female mill workers. A young girl who toiled in the mill—identified only by the initials F.G.A.—wrote about the decision of "Susan Miller" to save her family's farm by working in the Lowell, Massachusetts, textile mills.

At first, Susan found the factory work dispiriting, but she made friends, and was proud of the wages she sent home.

A PERSONAL VOICE F.G.A.

"Every morning the bells pealed forth the same clangor, and every night brought the same feeling of fatigue. But Susan felt. . . that she could bear it for a while. There are few who look upon factory labor as a pursuit for life. It is but a temporary vocation; and most of the girls resolve to quit the Mill when some favorite design is accomplished. Money is their object—not for itself, but for what it can perform."

—*Lowell Offering*, 1841

▲ **A young worker from the mills in Waltham, or Lowell, 1850.**

Just a few decades earlier, work outside the home might not have been an option for girls like Susan. At the same time that women's roles began to expand, changes occurred in the way goods were manufactured.

Industry Changes Work

Before "Susan" and other girls began to leave the farms for New England's textile mills, women had spun and sewn most of their families' clothing from raw fibers. In fact, in the early 19th century almost all clothing manufacturing was produced at home. Moving production from the home to the factory split families, created new communities, and transformed traditional relationships between employers and employees. The textile industry pioneered the new manufacturing techniques that would affect rules and behavior required of most American workers.

▲ Families used spinning wheels to spin yarn, which they wove into cloth on home looms. They sold their cloth to local merchants.

RURAL MANUFACTURING Until the 1820s, only the first step in the manufacture of clothing—the spinning of cotton into thread—had been mechanized widely in America. People then finished the work in a **cottage industry** system in which manufacturers provided the materials for goods to be produced at home. Though women did most of this work, men and children sometimes helped too. The participants in this cottage industry brought the finished articles to the manufacturer, who paid them by the piece and gave them new materials for the next batch of work.

When entrepreneurs like Patrick Jackson, Nathan Appleton, and Francis Cabot Lowell opened their weaving factories in Waltham and later Lowell, Massachusetts, their power looms replaced the cottage industries. Mechanizing the entire process and housing the tools in the same place slashed the production time, as well as the cost, of textile manufacture. By the 1830s, the company that Lowell and his partners had formed owned eight factories in Massachusetts with over 6,000 employees, at an investment of over $6 million.

EARLY FACTORIES Textiles led the way, but other areas of manufacture also shifted from homes to factories. In the early 19th century, skilled artisans had typically produced items that a family could not make for itself—furniture and tools, for example. As in cottage industries, the artisans usually worked in shops attached to their own homes. The most experienced artisans had titles: a **master** might be assisted by a **journeyman,** a skilled worker employed by a master, and assisted by an **apprentice,** a young worker learning a craft. Master artisans and their assistants traditionally handcrafted their products until the 1820s, when manufacturers began using production processes that depended on the use of interchangeable parts.

The rapid spread of factory production revolutionized industry. The cost of making household items and clothing dramatically dropped. In addition, new machines allowed unskilled workers to perform tasks that once had employed trained artisans. Unskilled artisans shifted from farm work to boring and repetitive factory work and to the tight restrictions imposed by factory managers. Nowhere were these restrictions more rigid than in the factory town of Lowell, Massachusetts. (A)

MAIN IDEA

Analyzing Effects

(A) How did factory production change American manufacturing?

Farm Worker to Factory Worker

Under the strict control of female supervisors, a work force—consisting almost entirely of unmarried farm girls—clustered in Lowell and the other mill towns that soon dotted New England. At their boarding houses, the "mill girls" lived under strict curfews. The girls' behavior and church attendance was closely monitored, but despite this scrutiny, most mill girls found time to enjoy the company of their coworkers. By 1828 women made up nine-tenths of the work force in the New England mills, and four out of five of the women were not yet 30 years old.

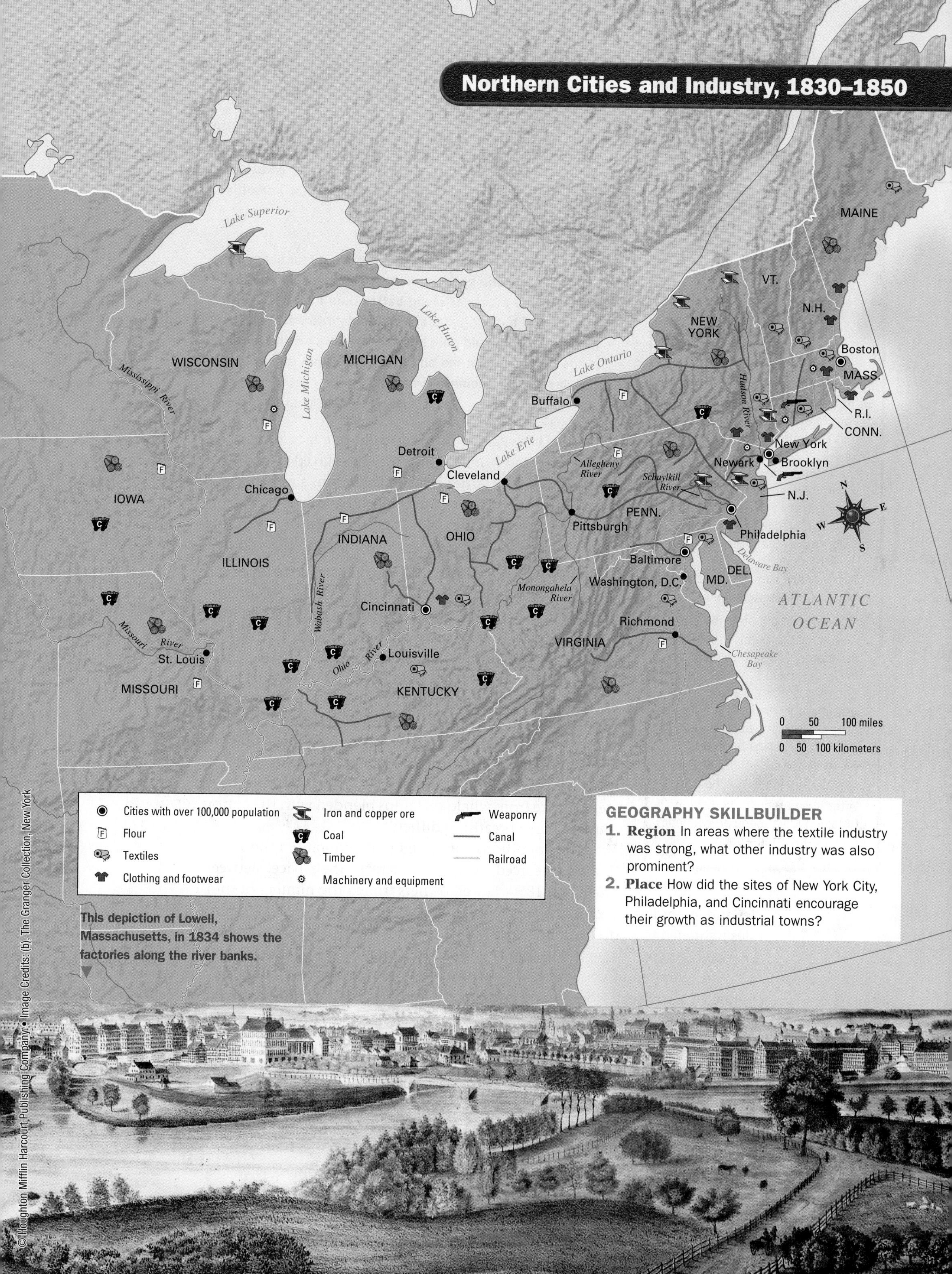

GEOGRAPHY SKILLBUILDER

1. **Region** In areas where the textile industry was strong, what other industry was also prominent?
2. **Place** How did the sites of New York City, Philadelphia, and Cincinnati encourage their growth as industrial towns?

This depiction of Lowell, Massachusetts, in 1834 shows the factories along the river banks. ▼

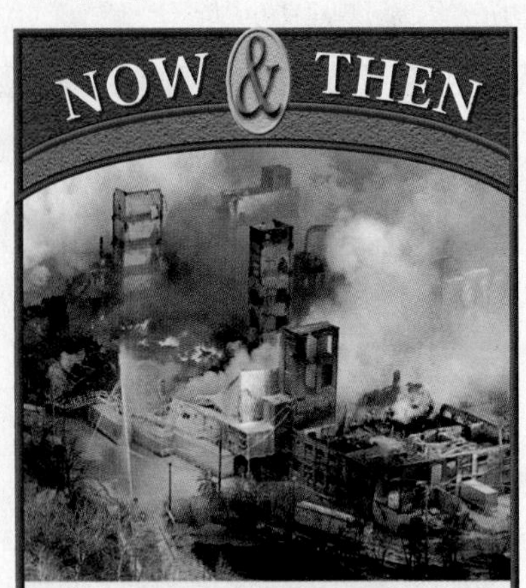

FROM THE ASHES

Malden Mills, the largest employer in Lawrence, Massachusetts (near Lowell) was devastated by fire in December 1995, as shown above.

The mills' owner, septuagenarian Aaron Feuerstein, not only announced that he intended to rebuild but pledged to keep his employees on the payroll during reconstruction.

To much acclaim for his generosity, Mr. Feuerstein said:

> "Everything I did after the fire was in keeping with the ethical standards I've tried to maintain my entire life. . . . Whether I deserve it or not, I guess I became a symbol of what the average worker would like corporate America to be in a time when the American dream has been pretty badly injured."

After it was rebuilt, production of Malden Mills' popular synthetic product—Polartec—doubled.

THE LOWELL MILL Mill owners hired females because they could pay them lower wages than men who did similar jobs. To the girls in the mills, though, textile work offered better pay than their only alternatives: teaching, sewing, and domestic work. In an 1846 letter to her father in New Hampshire, 16-year-old Mary Paul expressed her satisfaction with her situation at Lowell.

A PERSONAL VOICE MARY PAUL

> **"I am at work in a spinning room tending four sides of warp which is one girl's work. The overseer tells me that he never had a girl get along better than I do. . . . I have a very good boarding place, have enough to eat. . . . The girls are all kind and obliging. . . . I think that the factory is the best place for me and if any girl wants employment, I advise them to come to Lowell."**
>
> —quoted in *Women and the American Experience*

Like Mary Paul, who eventually left factory work to pursue other work, most female workers stayed at Lowell for only a few years. Harriet Hanson Robinson, a mill girl who later became involved in the abolition and women's rights movements, applauded the mill girls' influence in carrying "new fashions, new books, new ideas" back to their homes.

CONDITIONS AT LOWELL The workday at Lowell began at 5 A.M., Mary Paul wrote her father, with a bell ringing "for the folks to get up. At seven they are called to the mill. At half past twelve we have dinner, are called back again at one and stay until half past seven."

These hours probably didn't seem long to farm girls, but heat, darkness, and poor ventilation in the factories contributed to discomfort and illness. Overseers would nail windows shut to seal in the humidity they thought prevented the threads from breaking, so that in the summer the weaving rooms felt like ovens. In the winter, pungent smoke from whale-oil lamps blended with the cotton dust to make breathing difficult.

Mill conditions continued to deteriorate in the 1830s. Managers forced workers to increase their pace. Between 1836 and 1850, Lowell owners tripled the number of spindles and looms but hired only 50 percent more workers to operate them. Factory rules tightened too. After gulping a noon meal, workers now had to rush back to the weaving rooms to avoid fines for lateness. Mill workers began to organize. In 1834, the Lowell mills announced a 15 percent wage cut. Eight hundred mill girls conducted a **strike,** a work stoppage in order to force an employer to respond to demands. **B**

MAIN IDEA

Analyzing Causes

B What factors contributed to the worsening conditions workers endured at Lowell beginning in the 1830s?

STRIKES AT LOWELL Under the heading "UNION IS POWER," the Lowell Mills strikers of 1834 issued a proclamation declaring that they would not return to work "unless our wages are continued to us as they have been." For its part, the company threatened to recruit local women to fill the strikers' jobs. Criticized by the Lowell press and clergy, most of the strikers agreed to return to work at reduced wages. The mill owners fired the strike leaders.

In 1836, Lowell mill workers struck again, this time over an increase in their board charges that was equivalent to a 12.5 percent pay cut. Twice as many

▲ Lowell mill workers often lived in company-owned boarding houses.

women participated as had two years earlier. Only 11 years old at the time of the strike, Harriet Hanson later recalled the protest.

A PERSONAL VOICE HARRIET HANSON

"As I looked back at the long line that followed me, I was more proud than I have ever been since at any success I may have achieved, and more proud than I shall ever be again until my own beloved State gives to its women citizens the right of suffrage [voting]."

—quoted in *Women's America: Refocusing the Past*

Again, the company prevailed. It fired the strike leaders and dismissed Harriet Hanson's widowed mother, a boarding-house supervisor. Most of the strikers returned to their spindles and looms.

In the 1840s, the mill girls took their concerns to the political arena. In 1845, Sarah Bagley founded the Lowell Female Labor Reform Association to petition the Massachusetts state legislature for a ten-hour workday. The proposed legislation failed, but the Lowell Association was able to help defeat a local legislator who opposed the bill. C

MAIN IDEA

Evaluating Decisions

C Based on the results, do you think the decision to strike at Lowell was a good one? Explain.

Workers Seek Better Conditions

Conditions for all workers deteriorated during the 1830s. Skilled artisans, who had originally formed unions to preserve their own interests, began to ally themselves with unskilled laborers. When Philadelphia coal workers struck for a 10-hour day and a wage increase in 1835, for example, carpenters, printers, and other artisans joined them in what became the first general strike in the United States.

Although only 1 or 2 percent of U.S. workers were organized, the 1830s and 1840s saw dozens of strikes—many for higher wages, but some for a shorter workday. Employers won most of these strikes because they could easily replace unskilled workers with strikebreakers who would toil long hours for low wages. Many strikebreakers were immigrants who had fled even worse poverty in Europe.

"I regard my work people just as I regard my machinery."

TEXTILE MILL MANAGER, 1840s

IMMIGRATION INCREASES European immigration rose dramatically in the United States between 1830 and 1860. In the decade 1845–1854 alone nearly

3 million immigrants were added to the U.S. population that had numbered just over 20 million. The majority of the immigrants were German or Irish.

Most immigrants avoided the South because slavery limited their economic opportunity. What's more, Southerners were generally hostile to European, particularly Catholic, immigrants. German immigrants clustered in the upper Mississippi Valley and in the Ohio Valley. Most German immigrants had been farmers in Europe, but some became professionals, artisans, and shopkeepers in the United States.

A SECOND WAVE Irish immigrants settled in the large cities of the East. Nearly a million Irish immigrants had settled in America between 1815 and 1844. Between 1845 and 1854 Irish immigration soared after a blight destroyed the peasants' staple crop, potatoes, which led to a famine in Ireland. The Great Potato Famine killed as many as 1 million of the Irish people and drove over 1 million more to new homes in America.

Irish immigrants faced bitter prejudice, both because they were Roman Catholic and because they were poor. Frightened by allegations of a Catholic conspiracy to take over the country, Protestant mobs in New York, Philadelphia, and Boston rampaged through Irish neighborhoods. Native-born artisans, whose wages had fallen because of competition from unskilled laborers and factory production, considered Irish immigrants the most unfair competition of all. Their willingness to work for low wages under terrible conditions made the desperate Irish newcomers easy prey for employers who sought to break strikes with cheap labor.

NATIONAL TRADES' UNION In their earliest attempts to organize, journeymen formed trade unions specific to each trade. For example, journeymen shoemakers

ECONOMIC BACKGROUND

IRISH IMMIGRANTS STRIKE

Smarting from the hostility around them, Irish immigrants soon began to view unions as an opportunity to advance their prospects. In fact, Irish dock workers organized New York City's most famous strike of the 1840s.

When Irish women tailors organized the Ladies Industrial Association in New York City in 1845, their leader, Elizabeth Gray, denounced "tyrant employers."

Though employers retained great power through the 1840s, unions did manage to win a few victories.

This 1848 engraving shows immigants arriving in New York City from Europe.

organized one of the nation's earliest strikes in 1806. During the 1830s, the trade unions in different towns began to join together to establish unions for such trades as carpentry, shoemaking, weaving, printing, and comb making. By means of these unions, the workers sought to standardize wages and conditions throughout each industry.

In a few cities the trade unions united to form federations. In 1834, for example, journeymen's organizations from six industries formed the largest of these unions, the **National Trades' Union,** which lasted until 1837. The trade-union movement faced fierce opposition from bankers and owners, who threatened the unions by forming associations of their own. In addition, workers' efforts to organize were at first hampered by court decisions declaring strikes illegal. D

MAIN IDEA

Evaluating

D Why was the national trade union movement important?

COURT BACKS STRIKERS In 1842, however, the Massachusetts Supreme Court supported workers' right to strike in the case of *Commonwealth v. Hunt.* In this case, Chief Justice Lemuel Shaw declared that Boston's journeymen bootmakers could act "in such a manner as best to subserve their own interests." A prominent American court finally had upheld the rights of labor. Although by 1860 barely 5,000 workers were members of what would now be called labor unions, far larger numbers of workers, 20,000 or more, participated in strikes for improved working conditions and wages.

The religious and social reform movements in the nation in the mid-19th century went hand in hand with economic changes that set in place the foundation for the modern American economy. While some Americans poured their efforts into reforming society, others sought new opportunities for economic growth and expansion. As the nation adjusted to the newly emerging market economy, migration west became a popular option.

▲ **This trade union banner was made for the glass cutters organization around 1840.**

SECTION 4 ASSESSMENT

1. **TERMS & NAMES** For each term or name, write a sentence explaining its significance.
   - **cottage industry**
   - **master**
   - **journeyman**
   - **apprentice**
   - **strike**
   - **National Trades' Union**

MAIN IDEA

2. **TAKING NOTES**
   In a chart like the one shown, name things that contributed to the changing workplace in the first half of the 19th century.

Which of these are still part of the workplace today?

CRITICAL THINKING

3. **ANALYZING ISSUES**
   Do you think the positive effects of mechanizing the manufacturing process outweighed the negative effects? Why or why not?
   Think About:
   - changes in job opportunities for artisans, women, and unskilled male laborers
   - changes in employer-employee relationships
   - working conditions in factories
   - the cost of manufactured goods

4. **EVALUATING DECISIONS**
   If you were working in a factory during the mid-1800s, would you be a striker or a strikebreaker? Support your choice with details from the text.

5. **IDENTIFYING PROBLEMS**
   How did the influx of new immigrants from Germany and Ireland affect circumstances in the American workplace?

DAILY LIFE 1820–1850

Working at Mid-Century

In the years before the Civil War, most workers labored from dawn to dusk, six days a week, without benefits. Although many Northerners criticized the South for exploiting slave labor, Southerners criticized the industrial wage system, mostly in the North, for exploiting free workers. Both North and South used children—cheap labor—for full workdays. While 10-year-old slave children worked in the fields like adults, one Northern mill employed 100 children ages four to ten.

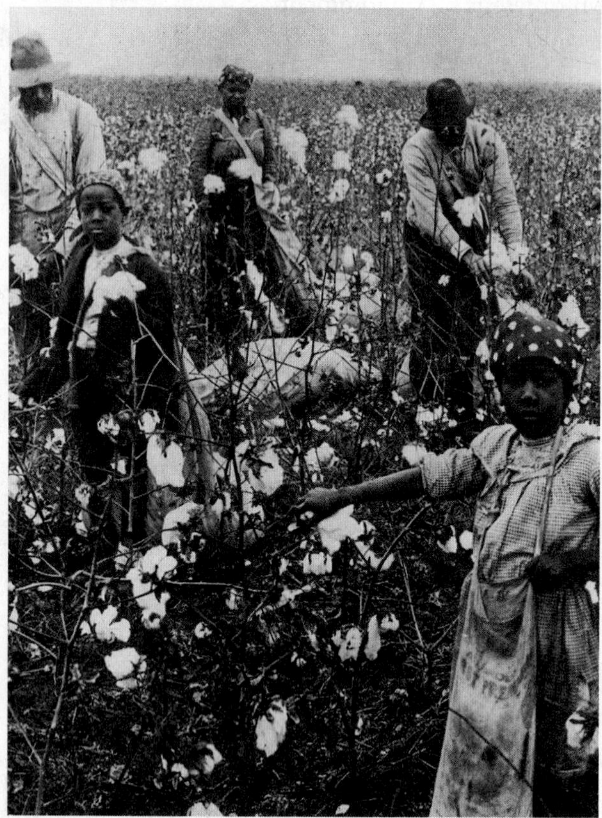

◀ COTTON PLANTATION FIELD SLAVES

The field slave's day during cotton harvest began with a bell an hour before dawn, a quick breakfast, and then a march to the fields. Men, women, and children spent the entire day picking cotton, bundling it, and coming back after dark carrying bales of cotton to the gin house. They then made their own suppers and ate quickly before falling asleep on wooden planks. No other antebellum workers had such harsh, brutal treatment imposed on them. For most field slaves, the master's whip was a constant threat.

Length of Day: pre-dawn until after dark
Type of Labor: picking and bundling cotton
Payment: substandard food and shelter

MILL WORKERS ▶

Approximately 80 percent of textile-mill workers were young women between the ages of 15 and 30. The day began with a bell for a quick breakfast in the boarding house, followed by a march to the factory, and the tending of machines all day. Workers put up with heavy dust, the roar of machines, and hot air with windows nailed shut to keep in the humidity. When competitive pressure increased on the owners, workers had to speed up their work for lower wages. Children made $1 a week; older girls and women, $3; men, $6.

Length of Day: 12 hours
Type of Labor: operating machines
Payment: $1 to $6 a week

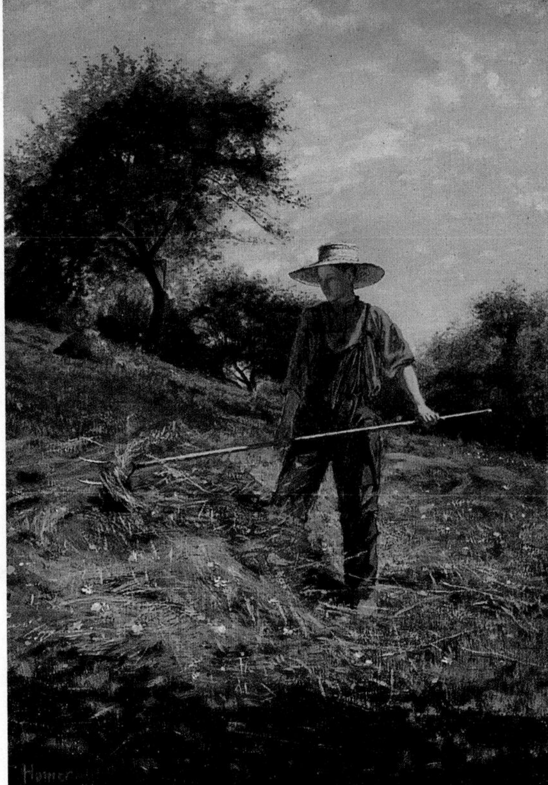

▲ **FARMERS**

Because farmers' livelihoods depended on the weather, soil conditions, and the market prices of crops, their earnings were unpredictable—but usually very low. Generally men spent their days clearing land, plowing, planting, and hoeing the fields, while women raised vegetables for family consumption, helped harvest fields, cared for livestock and for the family, and made clothing.

Length of Day: dawn until after dark
Type of Labor: planting, tending crops, caring for livestock
Payment: dependent on crop prices

DATA FILE

ANNUAL COST OF MAINTAINING A FIELD SLAVE

A typical Southern plantation owner in 1848–1860 would spend the following to take care of a field slave for one year.

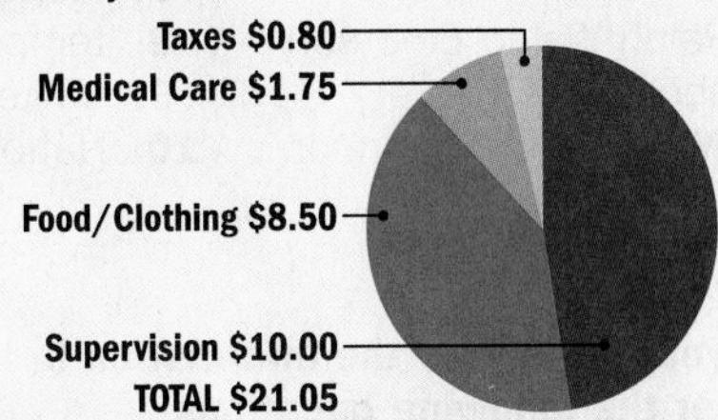

Source: *Slavery and the Southern Economy*, Harold D. Woodman, editor

WORKERS IN THE MID-19TH CENTURY

Average monthly earnings from 1830 to 1850 for a few common occupations:

Job	Year	Monthly Earnings
Artisan	1830	$ 45
Laborer	1830	$ 26
Teacher, male	1840	$ 15
Teacher, female	1840	$ 7
Northern farmhand	1850	$ 13
Southern farmhand	1850	$ 9

Source: *Historical Statistics of the United States*

WORKERS IN THE EARLY 21ST CENTURY

Average monthly salaries for each profession:

Job	Monthly Salary
Teacher—elementary	$ 4,353
Teacher—high school	$ 4,533
Construction worker	$ 3,529
Service worker	$ 2,423

Source: *Occupational Employment and Statistics*, May 2008. U.S. Department of Labor

THINKING CRITICALLY

CONNECT TO HISTORY

1. **Drawing Conclusions** What attitudes about women and children do you see reflected in work patterns during the mid-19th century?

SEE SKILLBUILDER HANDBOOK, PAGE R18.

CONNECT TO TODAY

2. **Researching Children's Rights** Report on labor laws and societal changes that protected children's rights and prevented child labor in factories.

CHAPTER 8 ASSESSMENT

TERMS & NAMES

For each term or name, write a sentence explaining its significance during the mid-19th century.

1. Second Great Awakening
2. revival
3. Ralph Waldo Emerson
4. abolition
5. William Lloyd Garrison
6. Frederick Douglass
7. Elizabeth Cady Stanton
8. temperance movement
9. strike
10. National Trades' Union

MAIN IDEAS

Use your notes and the information in the chapter to answer the following questions.

Religion Sparks Reform

1. What new religious ideas set the stage for the reform movements of the mid-19th century?
2. How did Dorothea Dix contribute to reform?

Slavery and Abolition

3. How did William Lloyd Garrison, Frederick Douglass, and David Walker each propose ending slavery?
4. What steps did white Southerners take to suppress slave revolts?

Women and Reform

5. What was the cult of domesticity?
6. What was the purpose of the Seneca Falls Convention?

The Changing Workplace

7. How did working conditions in the Lowell textile mills present new opportunities and new hazards?
8. Describe the two waves of U.S. immigration in the mid-1800s.

CRITICAL THINKING

1. **USING YOUR NOTES** Use a diagram similar to the one shown below to list the various reform movements that grew out of early-19th-century religious movements.

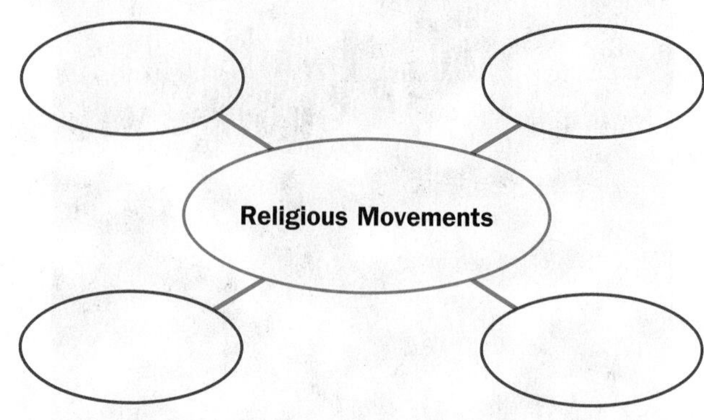

2. **EVALUATING** What was the most important reform of this period? Support your answer with references to the text.

3. **INTERPRETING MAPS** Look at the map Northern Cities and Industry. From the pattern of industries shown on the map, what conclusions can you draw about the kinds of industries that were the first to develop in the West? Support your answer with references to the text.

4. **SYNTHESIZING** What means did the abolitionists use to try to convince the public that slavery should be abolished?

VISUAL SUMMARY REFORMING AMERICAN SOCIETY

RELIGION SPARKS REFORM

The Second Great Awakening brings religious revival, social reform, and a new awareness of what it means to be an American.

WOMEN AND REFORM

Women reformers expand their reform efforts from movements such as abolition and temperance to include women's social and political rights.

SLAVERY AND ABOLITION

Slavery becomes an explosive issue as growing numbers of white and black Americans join reformers working for abolition.

THE CHANGING WORKPLACE

A growing industrial work force faces problems arising from changes in manufacturing and the creation of the factory system.

STANDARDIZED TEST PRACTICE

Use the quotation below and your knowledge of U.S. history to answer question 1.

> **"We affirm that while women are liable to punishment for acts, which the laws call criminal, or while they are taxed in their labor or property for the support of government, they have a self-evident and indisputable right to a direct voice in the enactment of those laws and the formation of that government. . . . Who are citizens? Why males? Why foreigners? because they pay a poll-tax—the intemperate, the vicious, the ignorant, anybody and everybody who has the wit to elude pauperism and guardianship, if they are only *males.* And yet women are to live under this city charter, obey, be taxed to support, and no pauper establishment or guardianship is thought necessary for them . . . How inconsistent is all this!"**
>
> —**Harriot Kezia Hunt,** letter to *"Frederick U. Tracy . . . of the City of Boston, and the Citizens generally, and the Legislature in particular, November 15, 1854."*

1. In this passage, Dr. Harriot Kezia Hunt, an early-19th-century feminist, is asking that —

A women be entitled to vote.
B women pay their share of taxes.
C immigrants be subject to taxation.
D only intelligent people be entitled to vote.

2. The National Trades' Union was supported by all of the following groups *except* —

F factory workers and farmers.
G immigrants.
H business owners and bankers.
J journeymen and apprentices.

Use the quotation below and your knowledge of U.S. history to answer question 3.

> **"What is a man born for but to be a Reformer, a Remaker of what man has made; a renouncer of lies; a restorer of truth and good . . . The power, which is at once spring and regulator in all efforts of reform, is the conviction that there is infinite worthiness in man which will appear at the call of worth, and that all particular reforms are the removing of some impediment. . . . I see at once how paltry is all this generation of unbelievers, and what a house of cards their institutions are, and I see what one brave man, what one great thought executed might effect."**
>
> —**Ralph Waldo Emerson,** "Man the Reformer"

3. How does Emerson characterize his belief in reform?

A All people are capable of positive reform.
B Some people are good; others are not.
C Most people are too selfish for reform.
D Most institutions are ungodly and will fall.

4. The Seneca Falls Convention agenda modeled its resolutions on —

F the cult of domesticity.
G the Declaration of Independence.
H the Fourteenth Amendment.
J the temperance movement.

For additional test practice, go online for:

- Diagnostic tests
- Tutorials

INTERACT WITH HISTORY

Recall the issues that you explored at the beginning of the chapter. Now that you know more about the changing workplace, address some specific actions to address workers' grievances. Work with a small group to develop a plan of action.

FOCUS ON WRITING

Reread the excerpt from the Declaration of Sentiments. Then write a paragraph explaining whether or not the resolutions proposed in the document have been achieved.

MULTIMEDIA ACTIVITY

21st CENTURY

Visit the links for Chapter Assessment to find out more about utopian communities. If you were a utopian reformer, what kind of community would you form? Prepare an oral report that describes your plans for a utopian community.

hmhsocialstudies.com

UNIT 3

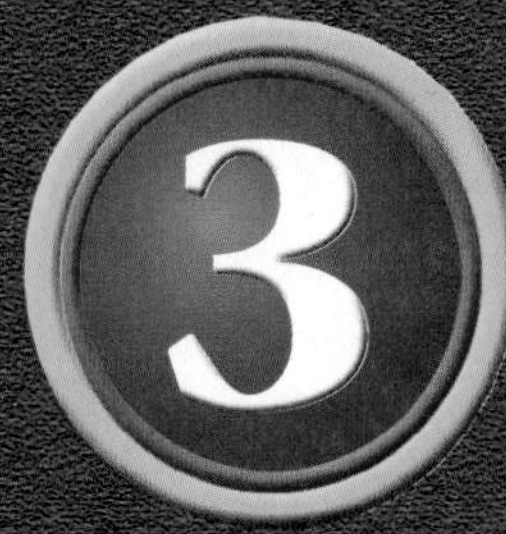

An Era of Growth and Disunion

1825–1877

UNIT PROJECT

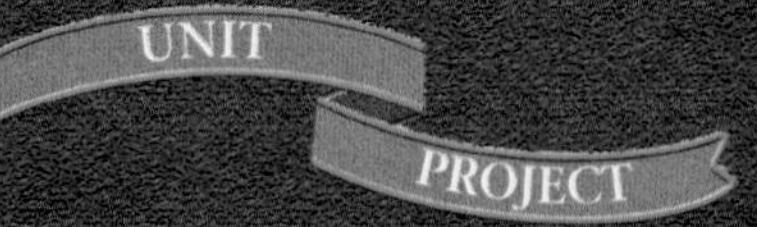

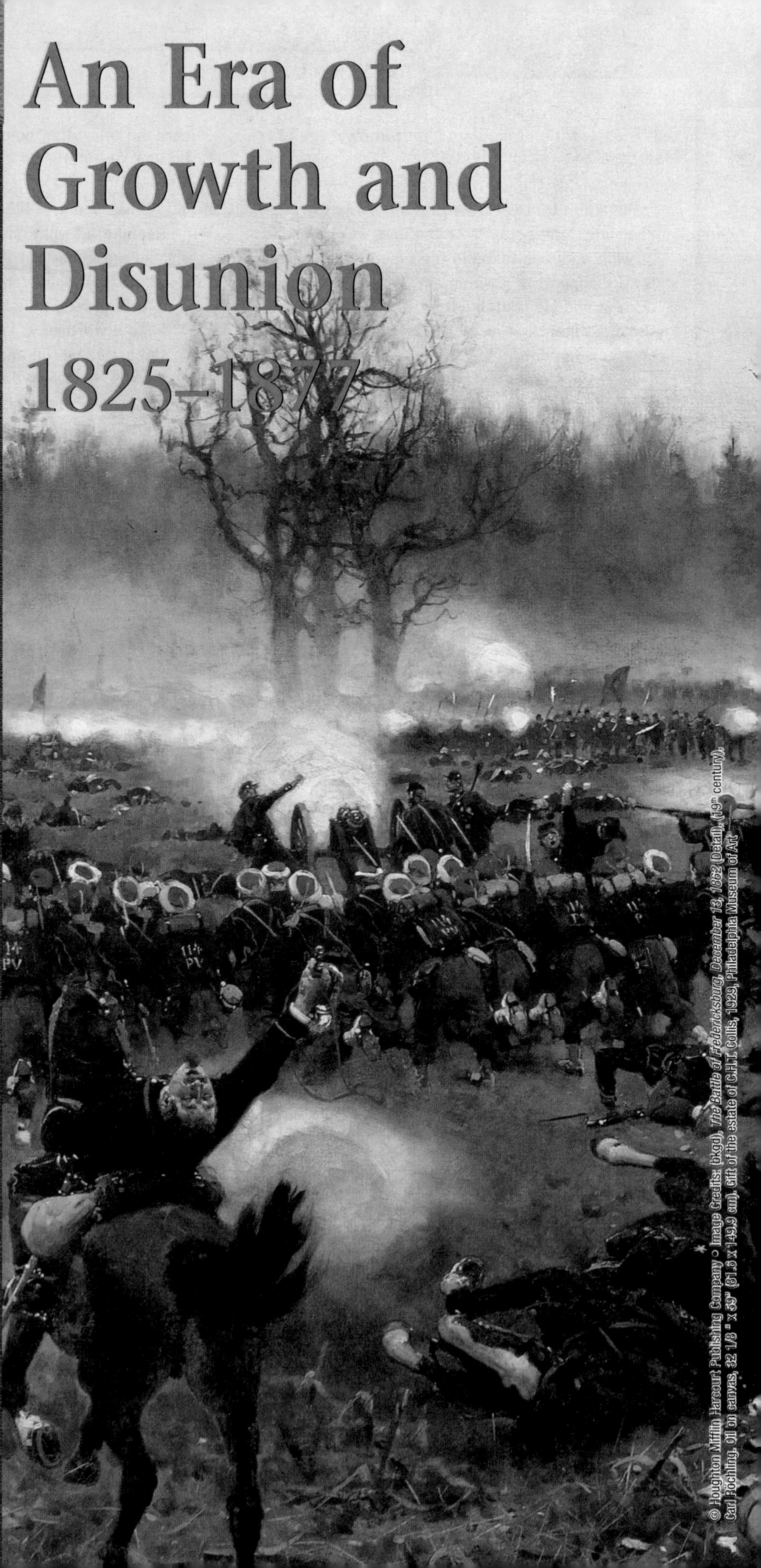

Television News Broadcast

As you read, choose an event that you can present in a television news broadcast. Compile a list of information for a script. Make a list of the visual images that you will use to illustrate your report. Present your news report to the class.

The Battle of Fredericksburg, December 13, 1862 by Carl Rochling

ALABAMA *The Civil War Comes*

In the first half of the 1800s, Alabama's economy was based on cotton, livestock, and slave labor. Alabama was a defender of the Deep South's economic system as sectionalism over slavery grew. Sectionalism, or putting the interests of a region above the interests of the nation, was a powerful force in mid-19th century politics. When northern politicians introduced the Wilmot Proviso in 1849 to exclude slavery from new territories, Alabama Democrats responded with a platform calling for no restrictions on the expansion of slavery. Montgomery attorney William Lowndes Yancey became the leader of the southern rights cause in Alabama at this time.

Inauguration of Jefferson Davis as president of the Confederacy at the Alabama statehouse

Secession

In the 1850s, the anti-slavery Republican Party emerged, and opposition to slavery grew in the North. In a sectionalist response, support for pro-slavery leaders in Alabama and other southern states increased. In 1860 Yancey opposed northern Democrat Stephen Douglas's run for president because of Douglas's support for popular sovereignty, or allowing the residents of territories to vote on allowing slavery. Southern Democrats nominated John C. Breckinridge of Kentucky. Although Breckinridge carried Alabama, Republican Abraham Lincoln swept the North to win the presidency in 1860.

Faced with a president opposed to expanding slavery, Alabamians held a constitutional convention to decide if Alabama should secede. Secession was the ultimate expression of southern sectionalism. Yancey called for immediate secession, while Senator Benjamin Fitzpatrick advised that Alabama secede only if joined by other southern states. Yancey's followers gained a majority, and Alabama delegates voted 61 to 39 in favor of immediately leaving the Union in January 1861.

Union forces defeated Fort Morgan and Confederate ships at the Battle of Mobile Bay in August 1864.

Civil War

In February 1861, Alabama and six other states formed the Confederate States of America. Montgomery was the new capital of the Confederacy. Jefferson Davis took the oath as president on the Alabama statehouse portico. Although the Confederate capital later moved to Virginia, Alabama played an integral role in the war effort. Alabama was a key location for manufacturing weapons for the Confederacy. Also, as many as 122,000 Alabamians served in the Confederate Army.

The war reached Alabama soil early in 1862 when Union forces advanced up the Tennessee River and captured Florence and Huntsville. In the southern part of the state, Confederate sailors used Mobile as a launching point for blockade runners and raiding vessels. The CSS *Alabama* seized or sunk 65 U.S. merchant vessels and sank one Union warship before being destroyed in June 1864. Two months later, Alabama's naval contribution to the Civil War was stopped. Union Admiral David Farragut won control of Mobile Bay by capturing Fort Morgan and Fort Gaines. Union raids destroyed the University of Alabama in Tuscaloosa and the industrial complex in Selma. However, most of Alabama escaped the destruction that other southern states experienced during the Civil War.

African-American representatives to Congress in the Reconstruction period

After the War

The northern victory in the Civil War brought freedom and citizenship to 440,000 African-American Alabamians. The postwar era, however, did not bring racial harmony to the state, due to the lingering turbulence of the Civil War and racist attitudes among the population.

President Andrew Johnson developed a plan to bring the Confederate states back into the Union in 1865. Congress, however, rejected Johnson's plan as too merciful. Congress passed its own Reconstruction plan requiring equal voting rights for those who had been enslaved. Alabama adopted a new constitution allowing African-American suffrage and was readmitted to the Union in 1868. Republicans controlled the state government, and several African Americans were elected to state and local offices, as well as to Congress.

The Ku Klux Klan responded to these reforms with a terror campaign against African Americans and white supporters of the new order. The threat of violence and a national slow-down of the economy lowered support for Alabama's Republican government. White-supremacist Democrats regained control of the state government in 1874 and passed laws denying political and social equality to African Americans.

Exploring Further...

Research a Civil War battle that took place in Alabama, or select a battle in another state if significant numbers of Alabamians were involved. Write a one-page report about the battle that includes the following:

- how many soldiers fought in the battle
- which side won the battle
- how the battle affected the course of the Civil War
- how the battle affected Alabama

CHAPTER 9

EXPANDING MARKETS AND MOVING WEST

Essential Question

What were the causes and consequences of westward expansion?

ALABAMA COURSE OF STUDY

7 Describe causes, courses, and consequences of United States' expansionism prior to the Civil War, including the Treaty of Paris of 1783, the Land Ordinance of 1785, the Northwest Ordinance of 1787, the Louisiana Purchase, the Indian Removal Act, the Trail of Tears, Manifest Destiny, the Mexican War and Cession, Texas Independence, the acquisition of Oregon, the California Gold Rush, and the Western Trails.

9 Explain dynamics of economic nationalism during the Era of Good Feelings, including transportation systems, Henry Clay's American System, slavery and the emergence of the plantation system, and the beginning of industrialism in the Northeast.

13 Summarize major legislation and court decisions from 1800 to 1861 that led to increasing sectionalism, including the Missouri Compromise of 1820, the Compromise of 1850, the Fugitive Slave Acts, the Kansas-Nebraska Act, and the Dred Scott decision.

• Analyzing the Westward Expansion from 1803 to 1861 to determine its effect on sectionalism, including the Louisiana Purchase, Texas Annexation, and the Mexican Cession.

William Ranney's 1853 painting *Advice on the Prairie* is an idealistic image of a family travelling west in the mid-1800s.

USA

1825 The Erie Canal connects the East to the West.

1828 Andrew Jackson is elected president.

1830 Joseph Smith establishes the Mormon Church.

1832 Chief Black Hawk leads Sauk rebellion.

1832 Andrew Jackson is reelected.

1836 Martin Van Buren is elected president.

1825 — 1830 — 1835

WORLD

1828 Uruguay becomes an independent republic.

1830 Revolutions occur in Belgium, France, and Poland.

1833 Santa Anna is elected president of Mexico.

1835 Ferdinand I becomes emperor of Austria.

Image Credits: (bkgd), *Advice on the Prairie* (1853), William Tylee Ranney. Oil on canvas, 38 3/4" x 55 1/4". Private collection/The Bridgeman Art Library; (br), The Granger Collection, New York

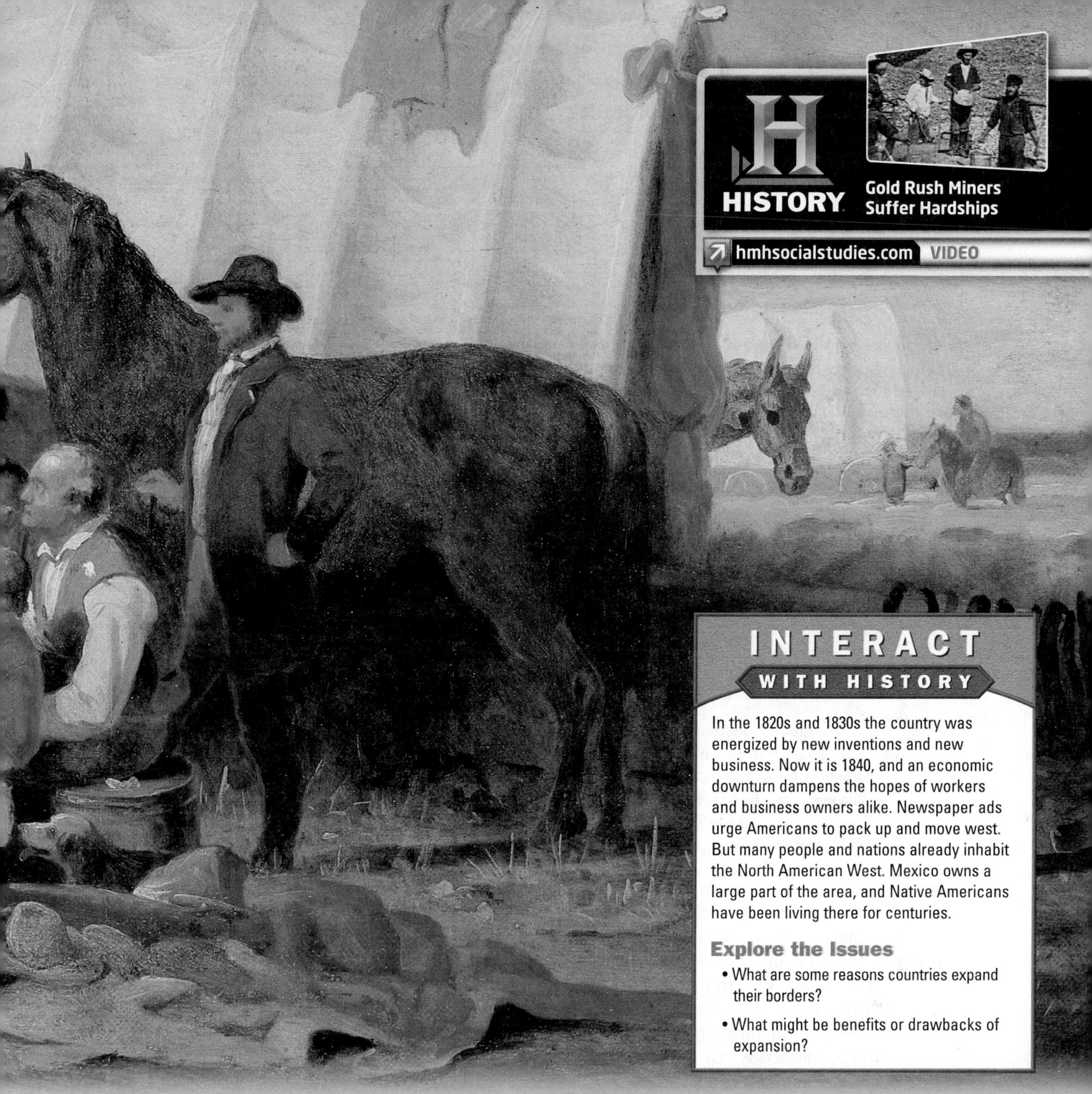

HISTORY Gold Rush Miners Suffer Hardships

hmhsocialstudies.com VIDEO

INTERACT WITH HISTORY

In the 1820s and 1830s the country was energized by new inventions and new business. Now it is 1840, and an economic downturn dampens the hopes of workers and business owners alike. Newspaper ads urge Americans to pack up and move west. But many people and nations already inhabit the North American West. Mexico owns a large part of the area, and Native Americans have been living there for centuries.

Explore the Issues

- What are some reasons countries expand their borders?
- What might be benefits or drawbacks of expansion?

1837 John Deere invents the steel plow.

1841 John Tyler becomes president when President William Henry Harrison dies.

1844 James K. Polk is elected president.

1848 Gold is discovered in California.

1848 Zachary Taylor is elected president.

1840 — 1845 — 1850

1837 Constitutional revolts occur in Lower and Upper Canada.

1840 Benito Juárez begins liberal reform movement in Mexico.

1847 U.S. wins Mexican-American War.

1848 Marx and Engels issue the *Communist Manifesto.*

Image Credits: (bkgd), *Advice on the Prairie* (1853), William Tylee Ranney. Oil on canvas, 38 3/4" x 55 1/4". Private collection/The Bridgeman Art Library; (cl), (cr), (bl), (br), The Granger Collection, New York

The Market Revolution

MAIN IDEA	WHY IT MATTERS NOW	Terms & Names
Technological changes created greater interaction and more economic diversity among the regions of the nation.	The linking of markets continues today, as new technologies are opening the United States to globalized trade.	• Samuel F. B. Morse • specialization • market revolution • capitalism • entrepreneur • telegraph • John Deere • Cyrus McCormick

One American's Story

hmhsocialstudies.com TAKING NOTES

Use the graphic organizer online to take notes on important inventions in the early 19th century.

In 1837, painter and scientist **Samuel F. B. Morse,** with Leonard Gale, built an electromagnetic telegraph. Morse's first model could send signals ten miles through copper wire. Morse asked Congress to fund an experimental telegraphic communication that would travel for 100 miles.

A Personal Voice SAMUEL F. B. MORSE

> "**This mode of instantaneous communication must inevitably become an instrument of immense power, to be wielded for good or for evil. . . . Let the sole right of using the Telegraph belong, in the first place, to the Government, who should grant . . . the right to lay down a communication between any two points for the purpose of transmitting intelligence.**"
>
> —quoted in *Samuel F. B. Morse: His Letters and Journals*

Congress granted Morse $30,000 to build a 40-mile telegraph line between Baltimore and Washington, D.C. In 1844, Morse tapped out in code the words "What hath God wrought?" The message sped from Washington, D.C., over a metal wire in less than a second. As new communication links began to put people into instant communication with one another, new transportation links carried goods and people across vast regions.

▲ **Samuel Morse was a painter before he became famous as an inventor.**

U.S. Markets Expand

In the early 19th century, rural American workers produced their own goods or traded with neighbors to meet almost all of their needs. Farm families were self-sufficient—they grew crops and raised animals for food and made their own clothing, candles, and soap. At local markets, farmers sold wood, eggs, or butter for cash, which they used to purchase the coffee, tea, sugar, or horseshoes they couldn't produce themselves.

By midcentury, however, the United States had become more industrialized, especially in the Northeast, where the rise of textile mills and the factory system changed the lives of workers and consumers. Now, workers spent their earnings on goods produced by other workers. Farmers began to shift from self-sufficiency to **specialization,** raising one or two cash crops that they could sell at home or abroad.

These developments led to a **market revolution,** in which people bought and sold goods rather than making them for their own use. The market revolution created a striking change in the U.S. economy and in the daily lives of Americans. In these decades, goods and services multiplied while incomes rose. In fact, in the 1840s, the national economy grew more than it had in the previous 40 years.

THE ENTREPRENEURIAL SPIRIT The quickening pace of U.S. economic growth depended on **capitalism,** the economic system in which private businesses and individuals control the means of production—such as factories, machines, and land—and use them to earn profits. For example, in 1813, Francis Cabot Lowell and other Boston merchants had put up $400,000 to form the Boston Manufacturing Company, which produced textiles. Other businesspeople supplied their own funds to create capital—the money, property, machines, and factories that fueled America's expanding economy.

These investors, called **entrepreneurs** from a French word that means "to undertake," risked their own money in new industries. They risked losing their investment, but they also stood to earn huge profits if they succeeded. Alexander Mackay, a Scottish journalist who lived in Canada and traveled in the United States, applauded the entrepreneurs' competitive spirit. (A)

MAIN IDEA

Analyzing Causes

(A) What led to the rise of capitalism?

A PERSONAL VOICE ALEXANDER MACKAY

"America is a country in which fortunes have yet to be made. . . . All cannot be made wealthy, but all have a chance of securing a prize. This stimulates to the race, and hence the eagerness of the competition."

—quoted in *The Western World*

NEW INVENTIONS Inventor-entrepreneurs began to develop goods to make life more comfortable for more people. For example, Charles Goodyear developed vulcanized rubber in 1839. Unlike untreated India rubber, the new product didn't freeze in cold weather or melt in hot weather. People first used the product to protect their boots, but, in the early 1900s, it became indispensable in the manufacturing of automobile tires.

A natural place for the growth of industrialization was in producing clothing, a process greatly aided by the invention of the sewing machine. Patented by Elias Howe in 1846, the sewing machine found its first use in shoe factories. Homemakers appreciated I. M. Singer's addition of the foot treadle, which drastically reduced the time it took to sew garments. More importantly,

ECONOMIC BACKGROUND

GOODYEAR AS ENTREPRENEUR

One entrepreneur who developed an industry still vital today was Charles Goodyear (1800–1860). Goodyear took a big risk that paid off for the American public—but left him penniless.

While he was exploring the problem of how to keep rubber elastic and waterproof under extreme temperatures, Goodyear purchased the rights of an inventor who had mixed rubber with sulfur. In 1839, Goodyear discovered that when heated, the mixture toughened into a durable elastic. In 1844, he received a patent for the process, named vulcanization after Vulcan, the mythological god of fire.

Unfortunately, Goodyear earned only scant monetary reward for his discovery, which others stole and used. The inventor was deep in debt when he died in 1860.

I. M. Singer's foot-treadle sewing machine was patented in 1851 and soon dominated the industry.

the foot-treadle sewing machine led to the factory production of clothing. When clothing prices tumbled by more than 75 percent, increasing numbers of working people could afford to buy store-bought clothes.

IMPACT ON HOUSEHOLD ECONOMY While entrepreneurial activity boosted America's industrial output, American agriculture continued to flourish. Workers in industrial cities needed food. To meet this demand, American farmers began to use mechanized farm equipment produced in factories. Farmers, therefore, made significant contributions to the American industrial machine and became important consumers of manufactured items.

Manufactured items grew less expensive as technology advances lowered expenses. For example, a clock that had cost $50 to craft by hand in 1800 could be turned out by machine for half a dollar by midcentury. Falling prices meant that many workers became regular consumers. They purchased new products not only for work, but for comfort as well. B

MAIN IDEA

Analyzing Effects

B Describe the impact of the market revolution on potential customers.

The Economic Revolution

These new inventions, many developed in the United States, contributed immensely to changes in American life. Some inventions simply made life more enjoyable. Other inventions fueled the economic revolution of the midcentury, and transformed manufacturing, transportation and communication.

IMPACT ON COMMUNICATION Improving on a device developed by Joseph Henry, Samuel F. B. Morse, a New England artist, created the **telegraph** in 1837 to carry messages, tapped in code, across copper wire. Within ten years, telegraph lines connected the larger cities on the East Coast.

Businesses used the new communication device to transmit orders and to relay up-to-date information on

NOW & THEN

FROM TELEGRAPH TO INTERNET

What do the telegraph and the Internet have in common? They are both tools for instant communication. The telegraph relied on a network of wires that spanned the country. The Internet—an international network of smaller computer networks—allows any computer user to communicate instantly with any other computer user in the world.

MORSE CODE In 1837 Samuel Morse patents the telegraph, the first instant electronic communicator. Morse taps on a key to send bursts of electricity down a wire to the receiver, where an operator "translates" the coded bursts into understandable language within seconds.

1837

TELEPHONE In 1876 Alexander Graham Bell invents the telephone, which relies on a steady stream of electricity, rather than electrical bursts, to transmit sounds. By 1900, there are over one million telephones in the United States.

1876

MARCONI RADIO In 1895, Guglielmo Marconi, an Italian inventor, sends telegraph code through the air as electromagnetic waves. By the early 1900s, "the wireless" makes voice transmissions possible. Commercial radio stations are broadcasting music and entertainment programs by the 1920s.

1895

prices and sales. The telegraph was a huge success. The new railroads employed the telegraph to keep trains moving regularly and to warn engineers of safety hazards. By 1854, 23,000 miles of telegraph wire crossed the country.

IMPACT ON TRANSPORTATION Better and faster transportation became essential to the expansion of agriculture and industry. Farmers and manufacturers alike sought more direct ways to ship their goods to market. In 1807, Pennsylvanian Robert Fulton had ushered in the steamboat era when his boat, the *Clermont*, made the 150-mile trip up the Hudson River from New York City to Albany, New York, in 32 hours. Ships that had previously only been able to drift southward down the Mississippi with the current could now turn around to make the return trip because they were powered by steam engines. By 1830, 200 steamboats traveled the nation's western rivers, thus slashing freight rates as well as voyage times.

Water transport was particularly important in moving heavy machinery and such raw materials as lead and copper. Where waterways didn't exist, workers excavated them. In 1816, America had a mere 100 miles of canals. Twenty-five years later, the country boasted more than 3,300 miles of canals.

The Erie Canal was the nation's first major canal, and it was used heavily. Shipping charges fell to about a tenth of the cost of sending goods over land. Before the first shovel broke ground on the Erie Canal in 1817, for example, freight charges between Buffalo, New York, and New York City averaged 19 cents a ton per mile. By 1830, that average had fallen to less than 2 cents.

The Erie Canal's success led to dozens of other canal projects. Farmers in Ohio no longer depended on Mississippi River passage to New Orleans. They could now ship their grain via canal and river to New York City, the nation's major port. The canals also opened the heartland of America to world markets by connecting the Northeast to the Midwest.

EMERGENCE OF RAILROADS The heyday of the canals lasted only until the 1860s, due to the rapid emergence of railroads. Although shipping by rail cost significantly more in the 1840s than did shipping by canal, railroads offered the advantage of speed. In addition, trains could operate in the winter, and they brought goods to people who lived inland.

TELEVISION In the late 1800s, scientists begin to experiment with transmitting pictures as well as words through the air. In 1923, Vladimir Zworykin, a Russian-born American scientist, files a patent for the iconoscope, the first television camera tube suitable for broadcasting. In 1924 he files a patent for the kinescope, the picture tube used in receiving television signals. In 1929, Zworykin demonstrated his new television.

1929

COMPUTERS Scientists develop electronically powered computers during the 1940s. In 1951, UNIVAC I (UNIVersal Automatic Computer) becomes the first commercially available computer. In 1964, IBM initiates System/360, a family of mutually compatible computers that allow several terminals to be attached to one computer system.

1964

INTERNET Today, on the Internet, through e-mail (electronic mail) or online conversation, any two people can have instant dialogue. The Internet becomes the modern tool for instant global communication not only of words, but images, too.

By the 1840s, steam engines pulled freight at ten miles an hour—more than four times faster than canal boats traveled. Passengers found such speeds exciting, although early train travel was far from comfortable, as Samuel Breck, a Philadelphia merchant, complained.

A PERSONAL VOICE SAMUEL BRECK

> "**If one could stop when one wanted, and if one were not locked up in a box with 50 or 60 tobacco-chewers; and the engine and fire did not burn holes in one's clothes . . . and the smell of the smoke, of the oil, and of the chimney did not poison one . . . and [one] were not in danger of being blown sky-high or knocked off the rails—it would be the perfection of travelling.**"
>
> —quoted in *American Railroads*

MAIN IDEA

Analyzing Effects

C How did new products, communications methods, and transportation methods help the U.S. economy?

Eventually, railroads grew to be both safe and reliable, and the cost of rail freight gradually came down. By 1850, almost 10,000 miles of track had been laid, and by 1859, railroads carried 2 billion tons of freight a year. **C**

New Markets Link Regions

By the 1840s, improved transportation and communication made America's regions interdependent. Arteries like the National Road, whose construction began in 1811, had also opened up western travel. By 1818, the road extended from Cumberland, Maryland, west to Wheeling, Virginia; by 1838, it reached as far west as Springfield, Illinois.

Growing links between America's regions contributed to the development of regional specialties. The South exported its cotton to England as well as to New England. The West's grain and livestock fed hungry factory workers in eastern cities and in Europe. The East manufactured textiles and machinery.

SOUTHERN AGRICULTURE Most of the South remained agricultural and relied on such crops as cotton, tobacco, and rice. Southerners who had seen the North's "filthy, overcrowded, licentious factories" looked with disfavor on industrialization. Even if wealthy Southerners wanted to build factories, they usually lacked the capital to do so because their money was tied up in land and the slaves required to plant and harvest the crops.

Though the new transportation and communication lines were less advanced in the South, these improvements helped keep Americans from every region in touch with one another. Furthermore, they changed the economic relationships between the regions, creating new markets and interdependencies.

BRITAIN'S COTTON IMPORTS

By 1840, the American South, the world's leading producer of cotton, was also the leading supplier of cotton to Great Britain. In all, Great Britain imported four-fifths of its cotton from the South. Cotton directly or indirectly provided work for one in eight people in Britain, then the world's leading industrial power.

For its part, Britain relied so heavily on Southern cotton that some cotton growers incorrectly assumed that the British would actively support the South during the Civil War. "No power on earth dares make war upon [cotton]," a South Carolina senator boldly declared in 1858. "Cotton is king."

NORTHEAST SHIPPING AND MANUFACTURING Heavy investment in canals and railroads transformed the Northeast into the center of American commerce. After the opening of the Erie Canal in 1825, New York City became the central link between American agriculture and European markets. In fact, more cotton was exported through New York City than through any other American city.

The most striking development of the era, however, was the rise in manufacturing. Although most Americans still lived in rural areas and only 14 percent of workers had manufacturing jobs, these workers produced more and better goods at lower prices than had ever been produced before. **D**

MAIN IDEA

Analyzing Causes

D How did the transportation revolution bind U.S. regions to one another and to the rest of the world?

▲ Cyrus McCormick patented the first successful horse-drawn grain reaper *(above left).* The McCormick company grew into the huge International Harvester Company. Their ads helped persuade farmers to revolutionize farming.

MIDWEST FARMING As the Northeast began to industrialize, many people moved to farm the fertile soil of the Midwest. First, however, they had to work very hard to make the land arable, or fit to cultivate. Many wooded areas had to be cleared before fields could be planted. Then two ingenious inventions allowed farmers to develop the farmland more efficiently and cheaply, and made farming more profitable. In 1837, blacksmith **John Deere** invented the first steel plow. It sliced through heavy soil much more easily than existing plows and therefore took less animal power to pull. Deere's steel plow enabled farmers to replace their oxen with horses.

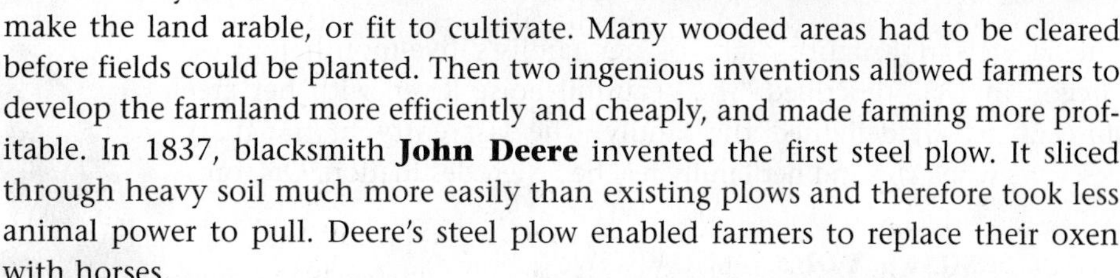

Once harvest time arrived, the mechanical reaper, invented by **Cyrus McCormick,** permitted one farmer to do the work of five hired hands. The reaper was packed in parts and shipped to the farmer, along with a handbook of directions for assembling and operating. Armed with plows and reapers, ambitious farmers could shift from subsistence farming to growing such cash crops as wheat and corn.

Meanwhile, the rapid changes encouraged Southerners as well as Northerners to seek land in the seemingly limitless West.

ASSESSMENT

1. TERMS & NAMES For each term or name, write a sentence explaining its significance.

- **Samuel F. B. Morse**
- **specialization**
- **market revolution**
- **capitalism**
- **entrepreneur**
- **telegraph**
- **John Deere**
- **Cyrus McCormick**

MAIN IDEA

2. TAKING NOTES
Create a time line like the one below, on which you label and date the important innovations in transportation, communication, and manufacturing during the early 19th century.

1825 — **1850**

Which innovation do you think was most important, and why?

CRITICAL THINKING

3. COMPARING AND CONTRASTING
Compare economies of the different regions of the United States in the mid-1800s. Use details from the section to support your answer.

4. DRAWING CONCLUSIONS
Why were the reaper and the steel plow important?

5. ANALYZING EFFECTS
During the 1830s and 1840s, transportation and communication linked the country more than ever before. How did these advances affect ordinary Americans?
Think About:
- the new kinds of transportation
- specific changes in communications
- the new industries of the time period

SECTION 2

Manifest Destiny

MAIN IDEA	WHY IT MATTERS NOW	Terms & Names
Americans moved west, energized by their belief in the rightful expansion of the United States from the Atlantic to the Pacific.	**The South and Southwest are now the fastest-growing regions of the United States.**	**• manifest destiny • Treaty of Fort Laramie • Santa Fe Trail • Oregon Trail • Mormons • Joseph Smith • Brigham Young • "Fifty-Four Forty or Fight!"**

One American's Story

Use the graphic organizer online to take notes about the reasons Americans headed west.

Amelia Stewart Knight's diary of her family's five-month journey to Oregon in 1853 described "the beautiful Boise River, with her green timber," which delighted the family. The last entry in the diary describes when she and her family reached their destination, Oregon.

A PERSONAL VOICE AMELIA STEWART KNIGHT

> **"[M]y eighth child was born. After this we picked up and ferried across the Columbia River, utilizing a skiff, canoes and flatboat. It took three days. Here husband traded two yoke of oxen for a half section of land with one-half acre planted to potatoes and a small log cabin and lean-to with no windows. This is the journey's end."**
>
> —quoted in *Covered Wagon Women*

Knight's situation was by no means unique; probably one in five women who made the trek was pregnant. Her condition, however, did little to lighten her workload. Even young children shouldered important responsibilities on the trail.

Amelia Stewart Knight told of camping by hot springs where she could brew tea without starting a fire.

The Frontier Draws Settlers

Many Americans assumed that the United States would extend its dominion to the Pacific Ocean and create a vast republic that would spread the blessings of democracy and civilization across the continent.

AMERICAN MISSION Thomas Jefferson had dreamed that the United States would become an "empire for liberty" by expanding across the continent "with room enough for our descendants to the thousandth and thousandth generation."

Toward that end, Jefferson's Louisiana Purchase in 1803 had doubled the young nation's size. For a quarter century after the War of 1812, Americans explored this huge territory in limited numbers. Then, in the 1840s, expansion fever gripped the country. Americans began to believe that their movement westward and southward was destined and ordained by God.

The editor of the *United States Magazine and Democratic Review* described the annexation of Texas in 1845 as "the fulfillment of our manifest destiny to overspread the continent allotted by Providence for the free development of our yearly multiplying millions." Many Americans immediately seized on the phrase **"manifest destiny"** to express their belief that the United States' destiny was to expand to the Pacific Ocean and into Mexican territory. They believed that this destiny was manifest, or obvious. (A)

MAIN IDEA

Summarizing
(A) Explain the concept of manifest destiny.

ATTITUDES TOWARD THE FRONTIER Most Americans had practical reasons for moving west. Many settlers endured the trek because of personal economic problems. The panic of 1837, for example, had dire consequences and convinced many people that they would be better off attempting a fresh start in the West.

The abundance of land in the West was the greatest attraction. Whether for farming or speculation, land ownership was an important step toward prosperity. As farmers and miners moved west, merchants followed, seeking new markets.

While Americans had always traded with Europe, the transportation revolution increased opportunities for trade with Asia as well. Several harbors in the Oregon Territory helped expand trade with China and Japan and also served as naval stations for a Pacific fleet.

Settlers and Native Americans

The increasing number of U.S. settlers moving west inevitably affected Native American communities. Most Native Americans tried to maintain strong cultural traditions, even if forced to move from ancestral lands. Some began to assimilate—or become part of—the advancing white culture. Still others, although relatively few in number, fought hard to keep whites away from their homes.

THE BLACK HAWK WAR In the early 1830s, white settlers in western Illinois and eastern Iowa placed great pressure on the Native American people there to move west of the Mississippi River. Consequently, representatives from several Native American tribes visited Chief Black Hawk of the Sauk tribe, and one told of a prophet who had a vision of future events involving Black Hawk.

▲ John Wesley Jarvis painted Black Hawk *(left)* and his son, Whirling Thunder *(right)* in 1833.

A PERSONAL VOICE

"He said that the Big Black Bird Hawk was the man to lead the [Native American] nations and win back the old homes of the people; that when the fight began . . . the warriors would be without number; that back would come the buffalo . . . and that in a little while the white man would be driven to the eastern ocean and across to the farther shore from whence he came."

—tribal elder quoted in *Native American Testimony*

MAIN IDEA

Evaluating Leadership
(B) What motivated Black Hawk to rebel against the United States?

The story convinced Black Hawk to lead a rebellion against the United States. The Black Hawk War started in Illinois and spread to the Wisconsin Territory. It ended in August 1832, when Illinois militia members slaughtered more than 200 Sauk and Fox people. As a result, the Sauk and Fox tribes were forcibly removed to areas west of the Mississippi. (B)

THE OGLALA SIOUX

Following the Fort Laramie Treaty, the federal government gradually reclaimed the Sioux's sacred Black Hills, and since 1889 the Oglala Sioux have lived on the Pine Ridge reservation in South Dakota.

In the 1990s, tourism was the largest source of revenue for Pine Ridge, which boasts some of the most beautiful territory in the Northern Plains. Visitors also come for the annual pow-wow, held in August, and the tribe's Prairie Winds casino.

Nevertheless, with only 20 percent of adults employed and a 61 percent poverty rate, the reservation remains one of the poorest areas in the United States.

MIDDLE GROUND The place that neither the Native Americans nor the settlers dominated, according to historian Richard White, was the middle ground. As long as settlers needed Native Americans as trading partners and guides, relations between settlers and Native Americans could be beneficial. Amelia Stewart Knight described such an encounter on the middle ground.

A PERSONAL VOICE AMELIA STEWART KNIGHT

> **"Traveled 13 miles, over very bad roads, without water. After looking in vain for water, we were about to give up as it was near night, when husband came across a company of friendly Cayuse Indians about to camp, who showed him where to find water. . . . We bought a few potatoes from an Indian, which will be a treat for our supper."**
>
> —quoted in *Covered Wagon Women*

By the 1840s, the middle ground was well west of the Mississippi, because the Indian Removal Act of 1830 and other Indian removal treaties had pushed Native Americans off their eastern lands to make room for the settlers.

FORT LARAMIE TREATY As settlers moved west, small numbers of displaced Native Americans occasionally fought them. The U.S. government responded to the settlers' fears of attack by calling a conference near what is now Laramie, Wyoming. The Cheyenne, Arapaho, Sioux, Crow, and others joined U.S. representatives in swearing "to maintain good faith and friendship in all their mutual intercourse, and to make an effective and lasting peace."

The 1851 **Treaty of Fort Laramie** provided various Native American nations control of the Central Plains, land east of the Rocky Mountains that stretched roughly from the Arkansas River north to Canada. In turn, these Native Americans promised not to attack settlers and to allow the construction of government forts and roads. The government pledged to honor the agreed-upon boundaries and to make annual payments to the Native Americans.

Still the movement of settlers increased. Traditional Native American hunting lands were trampled and depleted of buffalo and elk. The U.S. government repeatedly violated the terms of the treaty. Subsequent treaties demanded that Native Americans abandon their lands and move to reservations. (C)

MAIN IDEA

Analyzing Effects

(C) What were the effects of the U.S. government policies toward Native Americans in the mid-1800s?

Trails West

While the westward movement of many U.S. settlers had disastrous effects on the Native American communities there, the experience was also somewhat perilous for traders and settlers. Nevertheless, thousands made the trek, using a series of old Native American trails and new routes.

THE SANTA FE TRAIL One of the busiest and most well-known avenues of trade was the **Santa Fe Trail,** which led 780 miles from Independence, Missouri, to Santa Fe, New Mexico.

Each spring between 1821 and the 1860s, Missouri traders loaded their covered wagons with cloth, knives, and guns, and set off toward Santa Fe. For about the first 150 miles—to Council Grove, Kansas—wagons traveled alone. After that, fearing attacks by Kiowa and Comanche, among others, the traders banded into

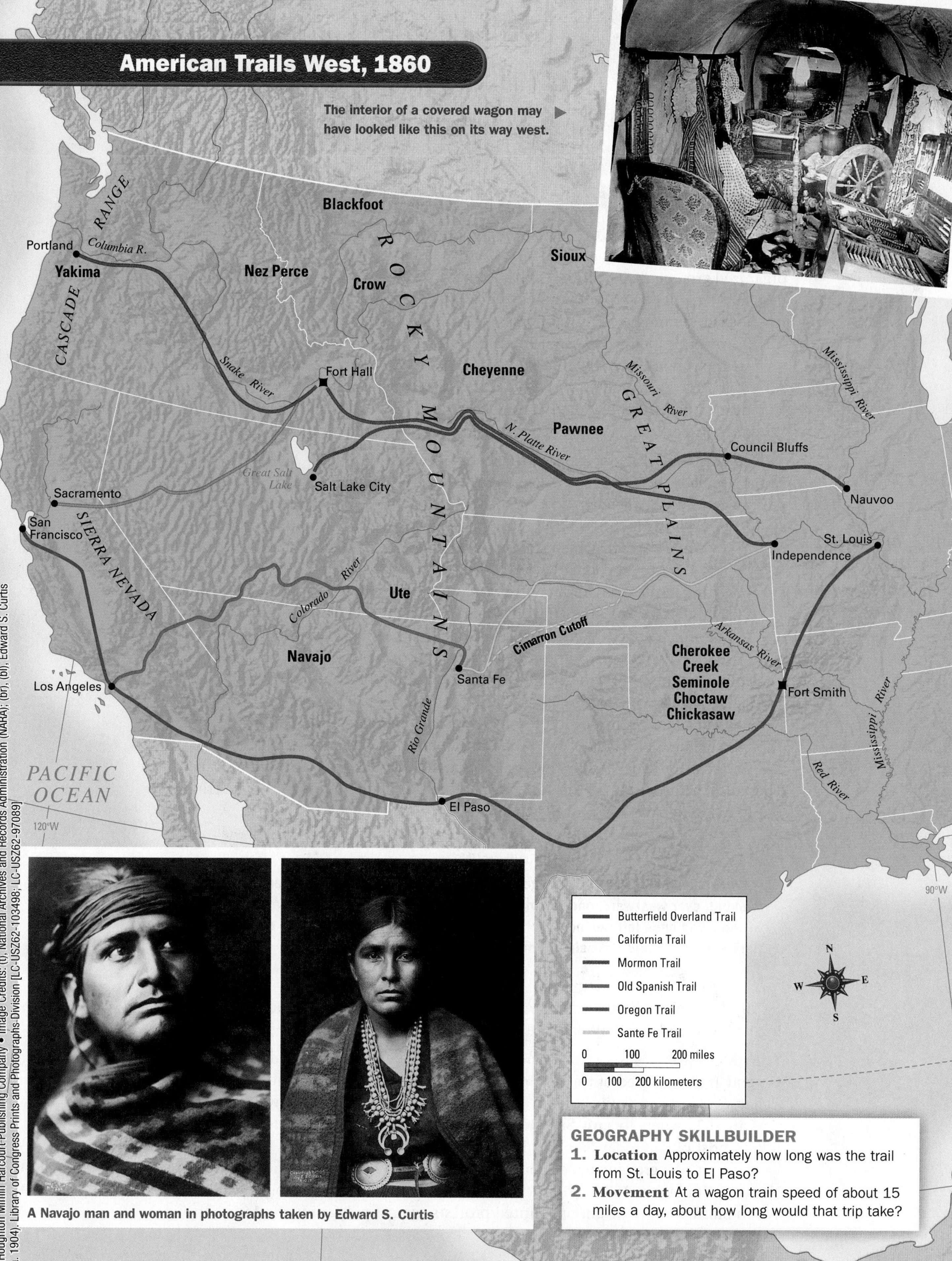

The interior of a covered wagon may have looked like this on its way west.

A Navajo man and woman in photographs taken by Edward S. Curtis

GEOGRAPHY SKILLBUILDER

1. **Location** Approximately how long was the trail from St. Louis to El Paso?
2. **Movement** At a wagon train speed of about 15 miles a day, about how long would that trip take?

Conestoga ▶ wagons were usually pulled by six horses. These wagons were capable of hauling loads up to six tons.

organized groups of up to 100 wagons. Scouts rode along the column to check for danger. At night the traders formed the wagons into squares with their wheels interlocked, forming a corral for horses, mules, and oxen.

Teamwork ended when Santa Fe came into view. Traders charged off on their own as each tried to be the first to enter the Mexican province of New Mexico. After a few days of trading, they loaded their wagons with silver, gold, and furs, and headed back to the United States. These traders established the first visible American presence in New Mexico and in the Mexican province of Arizona.

THE OREGON TRAIL In 1836, Marcus and Narcissa Whitman, Methodist missionaries, made their way into Oregon Territory where they set up mission schools to convert Native Americans to Christianity and educate them. By driving their wagon as far as Fort Boise, they proved that wagons could travel on the **Oregon Trail,** which started in Independence, Missouri, and ended in Portland, Oregon, in the Willamette Valley. Their letters east praising the fertile soil and abundant rainfall attracted hundreds of other Americans to the Oregon Trail. The route from Independence to Portland traced some of the same paths that Lewis and Clark had followed several decades earlier.

"Eastward I go only by force, but westward I go free."

HENRY DAVID THOREAU

Following the Whitmans' lead, some of the Oregon pioneers bought wooden-wheeled covered Conestoga wagons. But most walked, pushing handcarts loaded with a few precious possessions. The trip took months. Fever, diarrhea, and cholera killed many travelers, who were then buried alongside the trail.

Caravans provided protection against possible attack by Native Americans. They also helped combat the loneliness of the difficult journey, as Catherine Haun, who migrated from Iowa, explained.

A Personal Voice CATHERINE HAUN

"We womenfolk visited from wagon to wagon or congenial friends spent an hour walking, ever westward, and talking over our home life back in 'the states'; telling of the loved ones left behind; voicing our hopes for the future . . . and even whispering a little friendly gossip of emigrant life."

—quoted in *Frontier Women*

By 1844, about 5,000 American settlers had arrived in Oregon and were farming its green and fertile Willamette Valley. D

MAIN IDEA

Analyzing Events

D What difficulties were faced by families like the Whitmans and the Hauns?

THE MORMON MIGRATION One group that migrated westward along the Oregon Trail consisted of the **Mormons,** a religious community that would play a major role in the settling of the West. Mormon history began in western New York in 1827 when **Joseph Smith** and five associates established the Church of Jesus Christ of Latter-day Saints in Fayette, New York, in 1830.

Smith and a growing band of followers decided to move west. They settled in Nauvoo, Illinois, in 1839. Within five years, the community numbered 20,000. When Smith's angry neighbors printed protests against polygamy, the Mormons' practice of having more than one wife, Smith destroyed their printing press. As a result, in 1844 he was jailed for treason. An anti-Mormon mob broke into the jail and murdered Smith and his brother.

Smith's successor, **Brigham Young,** decided to move his followers beyond the boundaries of the United States. Thousands of Mormons travelled by wagon north to Nebraska, across Wyoming to the Rockies, and then southwest. In 1847, the Mormons stopped at the edge of the lonely desert near the Great Salt Lake. E

The Mormons awarded plots of land to each family according to its size but held common ownership of two critical resources—water and timberland. Soon they had coaxed settlements and farms from the bleak landscape by irrigating their fields. Salt Lake City blossomed out of the land the Mormons called Deseret.

MAIN IDEA

Analyzing Motives

E Why did the Mormons move farther west in their search for a new home?

Americans Headed West to...

- escape religious presecution
- find new markets for commerce
- claim land for farming, ranching, and mining
- locate harbors on the Pacific
- seek employment and avoid creditors after the panic of 1837
- spread the virtues of democracy

RESOLVING TERRITORIAL DISPUTES The Oregon Territory was only one point of contention between the United States and Britain. In the early 1840s, Great Britain still claimed areas in parts of what are now Maine and Minnesota. The Webster-Ashburton Treaty of 1842 settled these disputes in the East and the Midwest, but the two nations merely continued "joint occupation" of the Oregon Territory.

In 1844, Democrat James K. Polk's presidential platform called for annexation of the entire Oregon Territory. Reflecting widespread support for Polk's views, newspapers adopted the slogan **"Fifty-Four Forty or Fight!"** The slogan referred to the latitude 54°40′, the northern limit of the disputed Oregon Territory. By the mid-1840s, however, the fur trade was in decline, and Britain's interest in the territory waned. On the American side, Polk's advisors deemed the land north of 49° latitude unsuited for agriculture. Consequently, the two countries peaceably agreed in 1846 to extend the mainland boundary with Canada along the forty-ninth parallel westward from the Rocky Mountains to Puget Sound, establishing the current U.S. boundary. Unfortunately, establishing the boundary in the Southwest would not be so easy.

ASSESSMENT

1. TERMS & NAMES For each term or name, write a sentence explaining its significance.

- **manifest destiny**
- **Treaty of Fort Laramie**
- **Santa Fe Trail**
- **Oregon Trail**
- **Mormons**
- **Joseph Smith**
- **Brigham Young**
- **"Fifty-Four Forty or Fight!"**

MAIN IDEA

2. TAKING NOTES
Use a chart like this one to compare the motivations of travelers on the Oregon, Santa Fe, and Mormon trails.

Trail	Motivations
Oregon Trail	
Mormon Trail	
Santa Fe Trail	

Which do you think was the most common motive? Explain.

CRITICAL THINKING

3. EVALUATING
What were the benefits and drawbacks of the belief in manifest destiny? Use specific references to the section to support your response. **Think About:**

- the various reasons for the move westward
- the settlers' point of view
- the impact on Native Americans
- the impact on the nation as a whole

4. ANALYZING PRIMARY SOURCES
John L. O'Sullivan, editor of the *United States Magazine and Democratic Review*, described manifest destiny as meaning that American settlers should "possess the whole of the continent that Providence has given us for the development of the great experiment of liberty and . . . self-government." Do you think the same attitudes exist today? Explain.

GEOGRAPHY SPOTLIGHT

Mapping the Oregon Trail

In 1841, Congress appropriated $30,000 for a survey of the Oregon Trail. John C. Frémont was named to head the expeditions. Frémont earned his nickname "the Pathfinder" by leading four expeditions—which included artists, scientists, and cartographers, among them the German-born cartographer Charles Preuss—to explore the American West between 1842 and 1848. When Frémont submitted the report of his second expedition, Congress immediately ordered the printing of 10,000 copies, which were widely distributed.

The "Topographical Map of the Road from Missouri to Oregon," drawn by Preuss, appeared in seven sheets. Though settlers first used this route in 1836, it was not until 1846 that Preuss published his map to guide them. The long, narrow map shown here is called a "strip" map, a map that shows a thin strip of the earth's surface—in this case, the last stretch of the trail before reaching Fort Wallah-Wallah.

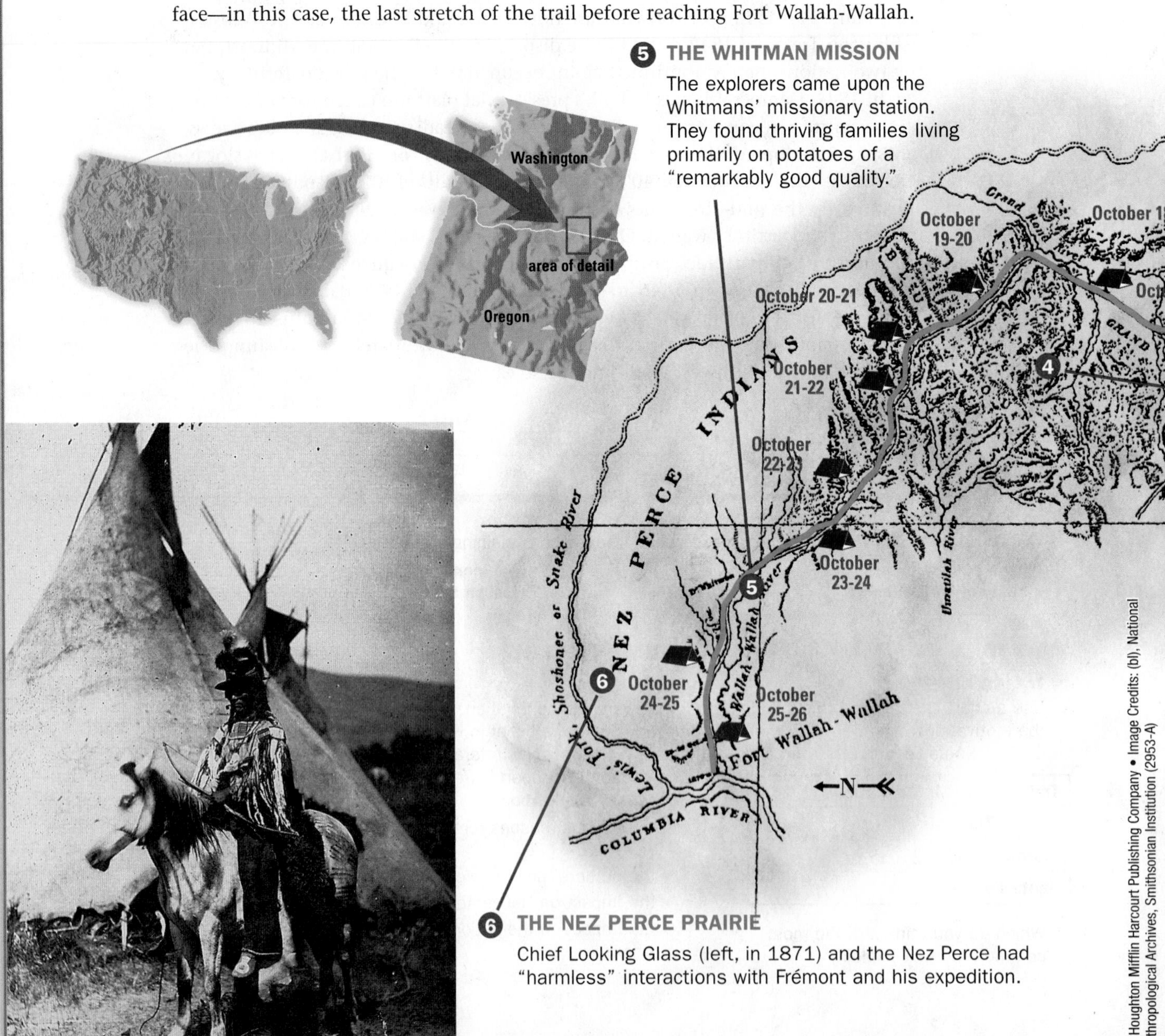

5 THE WHITMAN MISSION

The explorers came upon the Whitmans' missionary station. They found thriving families living primarily on potatoes of a "remarkably good quality."

6 THE NEZ PERCE PRAIRIE

Chief Looking Glass (left, in 1871) and the Nez Perce had "harmless" interactions with Frémont and his expedition.

1 FORT BOISÉE (BOISE)

This post became an important stopping point for settlers along the trail. Though salmon were plentiful in summer, Frémont noted that in the winter Native Americans often were forced to eat "every creeping thing, however loathsome and repulsive," to stay alive.

2 MAP NOTATION

Preuss recorded dates, distances, temperatures, and geographical features as the expedition progressed along the trail.

3 RECORDING NATURAL RESOURCES

On October 13, Frémont traveled through a desolate valley of the Columbia River to a region of "arable mountains," where he observed "nutritious grasses" and good soil that would support future flocks and herds.

4 CROSSING THE MOUNTAINS

Pioneers on the trail cut paths through the Blue Mountains, a wooded range that Frémont believed had been formed by "violent and extensive igneous [volcanic] action."

THINKING CRITICALLY

1. **Analyzing Patterns** Use the map to identify natural obstacles that settlers faced on the Oregon Trail.
2. **Creating a Thematic Map** Do research to find out more about early mapping efforts for other western trails. Then create a settler's map of a small section of one trail. To help you decide what information you should show, pose some questions that a settler might have and that your map will answer. Then, sketch and label your map.

SEE SKILLBUILDER HANDBOOK, PAGE R32.

hmhsocialstudies.com RESEARCH WEB LINKS

Expansion in Texas

MAIN IDEA	WHY IT MATTERS NOW	Terms & Names
Mexico offered land grants to American settlers, but conflict developed over religion and other cultural differences, and the issue of slavery.	Today, the state of Texas shares an important trading partnership with Mexico.	• Stephen F. Austin • land grant • Antonio López de Santa Anna • Texas Revolution • Alamo • Sam Houston • Republic of Texas • annex

One American's Story

hmhsocialstudies.com
TAKING NOTES
Use the graphic organizer online to take notes about American settlements in Texas.

In 1821, **Stephen F. Austin** led the first of several groups of American settlers to a fertile area "as good in every respect as man could wish for, land first rate, plenty of timber, fine water—beautifully rolling" along the Brazos River. However, Austin's plans didn't work out as well as he had hoped; 12 years later, he found himself in a Mexican prison and his new homeland in an uproar. After his release, Austin spoke about the impending crisis between Texas and Mexico.

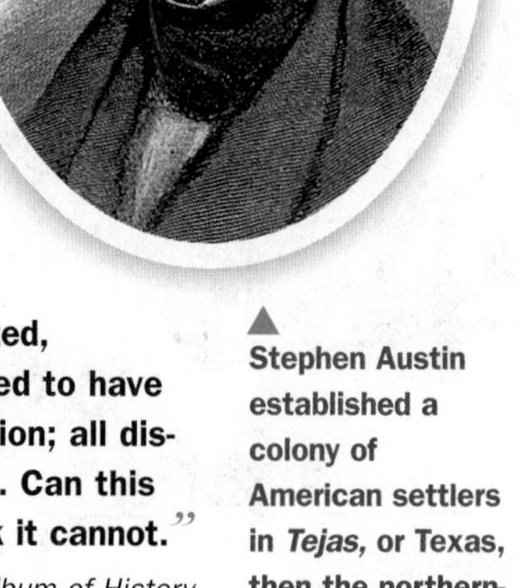

▲ Stephen Austin established a colony of American settlers in *Tejas*, or Texas, then the northernmost province of the Mexican state of Coahuila.

A PERSONAL VOICE STEPHEN F. AUSTIN

"Texas needs peace, and a local government; its inhabitants are farmers, and they need a calm and quiet life. . . . [But] my efforts to serve Texas involved me in the labyrinth of Mexican politics. I was arrested, and have suffered a long persecution and imprisonment. . . . I fully hoped to have found Texas at peace and in tranquillity, but regret to find it in commotion; all disorganized, all in anarchy, and threatened with immediate hostilities. . . . Can this state of things exist without precipitating the country into a war? I think it cannot."

—quoted in *Texas: An Album of History*

Austin's warning proved to be prophetic. The conflict between Texas and Mexico would soon escalate into a bloody struggle.

Americans Settle in the Southwest

During three centuries of Spanish rule of Mexico, only a few thousand Mexican settlers had migrated to the vast landscape of what is now Texas. Despite the region's rich natural resources and a climate conducive to agriculture, a number of problems scared off many potential Mexican settlers. One was the growing friction between Native American and Mexican inhabitants of the area.

THE MISSION SYSTEM Since the earliest Spanish settlements, the Native American and Mexican populations in the Southwest had come into close contact. Before Mexico won its independence in 1821, Spain's system of Roman

Catholic missions in California, New Mexico, and Texas tried to convert Native Americans to Catholicism and to settle them on mission lands. To protect the missions, Spanish soldiers manned nearby *presidios,* or forts.

The mission system declined during the 1820s and 1830s, after Mexico had won its independence. After wresting the missions from Spanish control, the Mexican government offered the surrounding lands to government officials and ranchers. While some Native Americans were forced to remain as unpaid laborers, many others fled the missions, returning to traditional ways. When Mexicans captured Native Americans for forced labor, groups of hostile Comanche and Apache retaliated by sweeping through Texas, terrorizing Mexican settlements and stealing livestock that supported many American settlers and Mexican settlers, or *Tejanos.* **A**

MAIN IDEA

Analyzing Effects

A How did relations between the Mexicans and Native Americans in the Southwest change after 1821?

THE IMPACT OF MEXICAN INDEPENDENCE Trade opportunities between Mexico's northern provinces and the United States multiplied. Tejano livestock, mostly longhorn cattle, provided tallow, hides, and other commercial goods to trade in Santa Fe, New Mexico, north and west of Texas.

Newly free, Mexico sought to improve its economy. Toward that end, the country eased trade restrictions and made trade with the United States more attractive than trade between northern Mexico and other sections of Mexico. Gradually, the ties loosened between Mexico and the northern provinces, which included present-day New Mexico, California, Texas, Arizona, Nevada, and Utah.

Mexico was beginning to discover what Spain had previously learned: owning a vast territory did not necessarily mean controlling it. Mexico City—the seat of Mexican government—lay far from the northern provinces and often seemed indifferent to the problems of settlers in Texas. Native American groups, such as the Apache and the Comanche, continued to threaten the thinly scattered Mexican settlements in New Mexico and Texas. Consequently, the Mexican government began to look for ways to strengthen ties between Mexico City and the northern provinces.

MEXICO INVITES U.S. SETTLERS To prevent border violations by horse thieves and to protect the territory from Native American attacks, the Mexican government encouraged American farmers to settle in Texas. In 1821, and again in 1823 and 1824, Mexico offered enormous **land grants** to agents, who were called *empresarios*. The empresarios, in turn, attracted American settlers, who eagerly bought cheap land in return for a pledge to obey Mexican laws and observe the official religion of Roman Catholicism.

Many Americans as well as Mexicans rushed at the chance. The same restless determination that produced new inventions and manufactured goods fed the American urge to remove any barrier to settlement of the West. The population of Anglo, or English-speaking, settlers from Europe and the United States soon surpassed the population of Tejanos who lived in Texas. Until the 1830s, the Anglo settlers lived as naturalized Mexican citizens. **B**

MAIN IDEA

Analyzing Motives

B What did Mexico hope to gain from Anglo settlement in Texas?

AUSTIN IN TEXAS The most successful empresario, Stephen F. Austin, established a colony between the Brazos and Colorado rivers, where "no drunkard, no gambler, no profane swearer, and no idler" would be allowed. By 1825, Austin had issued 297 land grants to the group that later

NOW & THEN

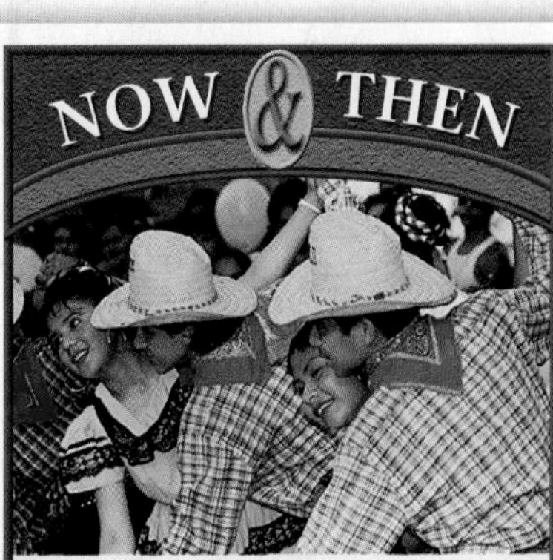

TEJANO CULTURE

The Anglo and Mexican cultures of Texas have shaped one another, especially in terms of music, food, and language.

For example, Tejano music reflects roots in Mexican mariachi as well as American country and western music and is now a $100 million a year industry. As for language, *Tejanos* often speak a mixture of Spanish and English called Spanglish.

As Enrique Madrid, who lives in the border area between Texas and Mexico, says, "We have two very powerful cultures coming to terms with each other every day on the banks of the Rio Grande and creating a new culture."

became known as Texas's Old Three Hundred. Each family received 177 very inexpensive acres of farmland, or 4,428 acres for stock grazing, as well as a 10-year exemption from paying taxes. "I am convinced," Austin said, "that I could take on fifteen hundred families as easily as three hundred."

At the colony's capital in San Felipe, a visiting blacksmith, Noah Smithwick, described an established town, with "weddings and other social gatherings." Smithwick stayed in a simple home but learned that "in the course of time the pole cabin gave place to a handsome brick house and that the rude furnishings were replaced by the best the country boasted." C

In 1836, Mary Austin Holley, Stephen Austin's cousin, wrote admiringly about towns such as Galveston on the Gulf Coast and Bastrop.

MAIN IDEA

Evaluating Leadership

C Why was Stephen Austin's colony so successful?

VIDEO
Independence for Texas

hmhsocialstudies.com

A PERSONAL VOICE MARY AUSTIN HOLLEY

"Bastrop . . . continues to grow rapidly. It is a favorite spot for new settlers, and is quite the rage at present. . . . It is situated on a bend of the [Colorado], sloping beautifully down to the water, with ranges of timber—first oak, then pine, then cedar, rising in regular succession behind it."

—quoted in *Texas: An Album of History*

Word about Texas spread throughout the United States. Posters boldly stated, "Go To Texas!" Confident that Texas eventually would yield great wealth, Americans increasingly discussed extending the U.S. boundaries to the river they called the Rio Grande (known in Mexico as the Rio Bravo). President John Quincy Adams had previously offered to buy Texas for $1 million; President Andrew Jackson later upped the bid to $5 million. Mexico not only refused to sell Texas but also began to regret its hospitality to Anglo immigrants.

KEY PLAYER

SANTA ANNA
1795–1876

Antonio López de Santa Anna began his career fighting for Spain in the war over Mexican independence. Later, he switched sides to fight for Mexico.

Declaring himself the "Napoleon of the West," Santa Anna took control of the government about ten years after Mexico won independence in 1821. He spent the next 34 years alternately serving as president, leading troops into battle, and living in exile. He served as president 11 times.

Santa Anna was a complex man with much charm. He sacrificed his considerable wealth to return again and again to the battlefield and died in poverty and almost forgotten.

Texas Fights for Independence

As Texas's Anglo population surged, tensions grew with Mexico over cultural differences, as well as slavery. The overwhelmingly Protestant settlers spoke English rather than Spanish. Many of the settlers were Southern cotton or sugar farmers who had brought slaves with them. Mexico, which had abolished slavery in 1824, insisted in vain that the Texans free their slaves.

"COME TO TEXAS" In 1830, Mexico sealed its borders and slapped a heavy tax on the importation of American goods. Mexico, however, lacked sufficient troops to police its borders well. Despite restrictions, the Anglo population of Texas doubled between 1830 and 1834. In 1834, Austin won a repeal of the prohibition on immigration. By 1835, more than 1,000 Anglos each month streamed into Texas, scrawling the initials "G.T.T." on their doors to indicate that they had "Gone to Texas." A year later, Texas's population included only 3,500 Tejanos, 12,000 Native Americans, 45,000 Anglos, and 5,000 African Americans. D

Meanwhile, Mexican politics became increasingly unstable. Austin had traveled to Mexico City late in 1833 to present petitions for greater self-government for Texas to Mexican president **Antonio López de Santa Anna.**

MAIN IDEA

Contrasting

D List some of the cultural conflicts caused by the influx of Anglo settlers into Texas.

While Austin was on his way home, Santa Anna suspended the 1824 Mexican constitution and had Austin imprisoned for inciting revolution. After Santa Anna revoked local powers in Texas and other Mexican states, several rebellions erupted, including what would eventually be known as the **Texas Revolution.**

hmhsocialstudies.com
INTERACTIVE
Witness the action of the Battle of San Jacinto.

"REMEMBER THE ALAMO!" Austin had argued with Santa Anna for self-government for Texas, but without success. Determined to force Texas to obey laws he had established, Santa Anna marched toward San Antonio at the head of a 4,000-member army. At the same time, Austin and his followers issued a call for Texans to arm themselves.

MAIN IDEA
Comparing
E Compare the reasons for the Texas Revolution with the reasons for the American Revolution.

Late in 1835, the Texans attacked. They drove the Mexican forces from the **Alamo,** an abandoned mission and fort. In response, Santa Anna swept northward and stormed and destroyed the small American garrison in the Alamo. All 187 U.S. defenders died, including the famous frontiersmen Jim Bowie, who had designed the razor-sharp Bowie knife, and Davy Crockett, who sported a raccoon cap with a long tail hanging down his back. Hundreds of Mexicans also perished. Only a few women and children were spared. **E**

THE LONE STAR REPUBLIC Later in March of 1836, Santa Anna's troops executed 300 rebels at Goliad. The Alamo and Goliad victories would prove costly for Santa Anna. Six weeks after the defeat of the Alamo, on April 21, the Texans

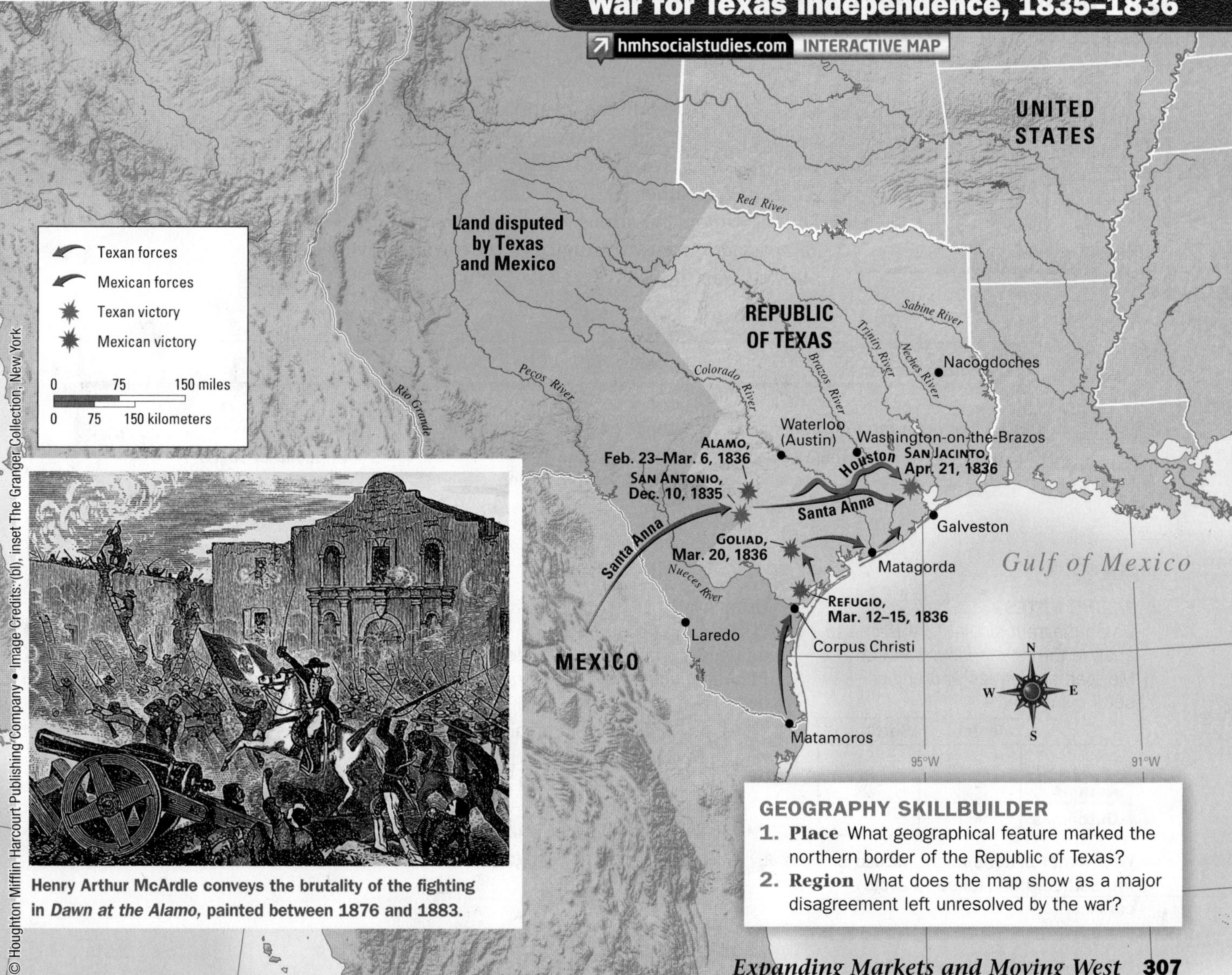

Henry Arthur McArdle conveys the brutality of the fighting in *Dawn at the Alamo,* painted between 1876 and 1883.

GEOGRAPHY SKILLBUILDER

1. **Place** What geographical feature marked the northern border of the Republic of Texas?
2. **Region** What does the map show as a major disagreement left unresolved by the war?

KEY PLAYER

SAM HOUSTON
1793–1863

Sam Houston ran away from home at about age 15 and lived for nearly three years with the Cherokee. He later fought in the U.S. Army, studied law, was elected to Congress, and became governor of Tennessee.

In his memoirs, Houston told of listening in vain for the signal guns indicating that the Alamo still stood.

> "I listened with an acuteness of sense which no man can understand whose hearing has not been sharpened by the teachings of the dwellers of the forest."

struck back. Led by **Sam Houston,** they defeated Santa Anna at the Battle of San Jacinto. With shouts of "Remember the Alamo!" the Texans killed 630 of Santa Anna's soldiers in 18 minutes and captured Santa Anna. The victorious Texans set Santa Anna free after he signed the Treaty of Velasco, which granted independence to Texas. In September 1836, Houston became president of the **Republic of Texas.** The new "Lone Star Republic" set up an army and a navy and proudly flew its new silk flag with the lone gold star.

TEXAS JOINS THE UNION On March 2, 1836, as the battle for the Alamo was raging, Texans had declared their independence from Mexico. Believing that Mexico had deprived them of their fundamental rights, the Texas rebels had likened themselves to the American colonists who had chafed under British rule 60 years earlier. On March 16, they ratified a constitution based on that of the United States. In 1838, Sam Houston invited the United States to **annex,** or incorporate, the Texas republic into the United States. Most people within Texas hoped this would happen. U.S. opinion, however, divided along sectional lines. Southerners sought to extend slavery, already established in Texas. Northerners feared that annexation of more slave territory would tip the uneasy balance in the Senate in favor of slave states—and prompt war with Mexico. (F)

> **MAIN IDEA**
> **Contrasting**
> (F) Explain the differences between the Northern and Southern positions on the annexation of Texas.

Then in 1844, the U.S. presidential election featured a debate on westward expansion. The man who would win the presidency, James K. Polk, a slaveholder, firmly favored annexation of Texas "at the earliest practicable period."

On December 29, 1845, Texas became the 28th state in the Union. A furious Mexican government recalled its ambassador from Washington. Events were moving quickly toward war.

SECTION 3 ASSESSMENT

1. **TERMS & NAMES** For each term or name, write a sentence explaining its significance.
   - **Stephen F. Austin**
   - **land grant**
   - **Antonio López de Santa Anna**
   - **Texas Revolution**
   - **Alamo**
   - **Sam Houston**
   - **Republic of Texas**
   - **annex**

MAIN IDEA

2. **TAKING NOTES**
   Use a diagram similar to this one to analyze the relationship between Mexican authorities and Anglos settling in Texas.

	Mexico	Settlers
Goals		
Actions		
Outcomes		

   What other actions might Mexico or the settlers have taken to avoid conflict?

CRITICAL THINKING

3. **COMPARING**
   Compare and contrast Santa Anna and Austin as leaders. Use details from the section to explain your answer. **Think About:**
   - Santa Anna's role as president of Mexico
   - Santa Anna's qualities as a military leader
   - Austin's settlement in Texas
   - Austin's abilities as a negotiator

4. **SYNTHESIZING**
   Which group or country gained the most from the entry of Texas into the United States? Who lost the most? Support your opinion with specific references to the section.

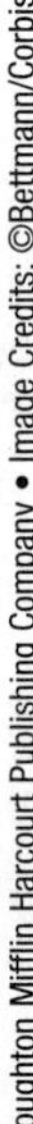

SECTION 4

The War with Mexico

MAIN IDEA

Tensions over the U.S. annexation of Texas led to war with Mexico, resulting in huge territorial gains for the United States.

WHY IT MATTERS NOW

The United States has achieved its goal of expanding across the continent from east to west.

Terms & Names

- **James K. Polk**
- **Zachary Taylor**
- **Stephen Kearny**
- **Republic of California**
- **Winfield Scott**
- **Treaty of Guadalupe Hidalgo**
- **Gadsden Purchase**
- **forty-niners**
- **gold rush**

One American's Story

hmhsocialstudies.com TAKING NOTES

Use the graphic organizer online to take notes about the war with Mexico and its effect on the U.S. border.

Robert E. Lee was born into a prominent Virginia family in 1807. His father had been a hero of the American Revolution. In 1846, the war with Mexico provided the 39-year-old captain with his first combat experience. Among the soldiers whom Lee directed in battle was his younger brother, Sidney Smith Lee. The elder Lee wrote about the battle.

▲ Robert E. Lee followed his father into a military career, graduating from the new U.S. Military Academy at West Point.

A PERSONAL VOICE ROBERT E. LEE

"No matter where I turned, my eyes reverted to [my brother], and I stood by his gun whenever I was not wanted elsewhere. Oh, I felt awfully, and am at a loss what I should have done had he been cut down before me. I thank God that he was saved. . . . [The service from the American battery] was terrific, and the shells thrown from our battery were constant and regular discharges, so beautiful in their flight and so destructive in their fall. It was awful! My heart bled for the inhabitants. The soldiers I did not care so much for, but it was terrible to think of the women and children."

—a letter cited in *R. E. Lee* by Douglas Southall Freeman

In recoiling at the ugliness of the war with Mexico, Lee hardly stood alone. From the start, Americans hotly debated whether the United States should pursue the war.

Polk Urges War

Hostilities between the United States and Mexico, which had flared during the Texas Revolution in 1836, reignited over the American annexation of Texas in 1845. The two countries might have solved these issues peaceably if not for the continuing instability of the Mexican government and the territorial aspirations of the U.S. president, **James K. Polk.**

▲ James Polk, also known as "Polk the Purposeful"

Polk now believed that war with Mexico would bring not only Texas but also New Mexico and California into the Union. The president supported Texas's claims in disputes with Mexico over the Texas-Mexico border. While Texas insisted that its southern border extended to the Rio Grande, Mexico insisted that Texas's border stopped at the Nueces River, 100 miles northeast of the Rio Grande.

SLIDELL'S REJECTION In 1844, Santa Anna was ousted as Mexico's president. The Mexican political situation was confusing and unpredictable. In late 1845, "Polk the Purposeful" sent a Spanish-speaking emissary, John Slidell, to Mexico to purchase California and New Mexico and to gain approval of the Rio Grande as the Texas border. When Slidell arrived, Mexican officials refused to receive him. Hoping for Mexican aggression that would unify Americans behind a war, Polk then issued orders for General **Zachary Taylor** to march to the Rio Grande and blockade the river. Mexicans viewed this action as a violation of their rights.

Many Americans shared Polk's goals for expansion, but public opinion was split over resorting to military action. Slavery would soon emerge as the key issue complicating this debate.

SECTIONAL ATTITUDES TOWARD WAR The idea of war unleashed great public celebrations. Volunteers swarmed recruiting stations, and the advent of daily newspapers, printed on new rotary presses, gave the war a romantic appeal.

Not everyone cheered. The abolitionist James Russell Lowell considered the war a "national crime committed in behoof of slavery, our common sin." Even proslavery spokesman John C. Calhoun saw the perils of expansionism. Mexico, he said, was "the forbidden fruit; the penalty of eating it would be to subject our institutions to political death."

Many Southerners, however, saw the annexation of Texas as an opportunity to extend slavery and increase Southern power in Congress. Furthermore, the Wilmot Proviso, a proposed amendment to a military appropriations bill of 1846, prohibited slavery in lands that might be gained from Mexico. This attack on slavery solidified Southern support for war by transforming the debate on war into a debate on slavery.

Northerners mainly opposed the war. Antislavery Whigs and abolitionists saw the war as a plot to expand slavery and ensure Southern domination of the Union. In a resolution adopted by the Massachusetts legislature, Charles Sumner proclaimed that "the lives of Mexicans are sacrificed in this cause; and a domestic question, which should be reserved for bloodless debate in our own country, is transferred to fields of battle in a foreign land." (A)

MAIN IDEA

Analyzing Effects

(A) How did the issue of slavery affect the debate over the war with Mexico?

The War Begins

As Taylor positioned his forces at the Rio Grande in 1845–1846, John C. Frémont led an exploration party through Mexico's Alta California province, another violation of Mexico's territorial rights. The Mexican government had had enough.

Mexico responded to Taylor's invasion of the territory it claimed by sending troops across the Rio Grande. In a skirmish near Matamoros, Mexican soldiers killed 9 U.S. soldiers. Polk immediately sent a war message to Congress, declaring that by shedding "American blood upon American soil," Mexico had started the war. Representative Abraham Lincoln questioned the truthfulness of the message, asking "whether our citizens, whose blood was shed, as in his message declared, were or were not, at that time, armed officers and soldiers, sent into that settlement by the military order of the President." Lincoln introduced a "Spot Resolution," asking Polk to certify the spot where the skirmish had occurred.

Truthful or not, Polk's message persuaded the House to recognize a state of war with Mexico by a vote of 174 to 14, and the Senate by a vote of 40 to 2, with numerous abstentions. Some antislavery Whigs had tried to oppose the war but were barely allowed to gain the floor of Congress to speak. Since Polk withheld key facts, the full reality of what had happened on the distant Rio Grande was not known. But the theory and practice of manifest destiny had launched the United States into its first war on foreign territory. B

MAIN IDEA

Analyzing Causes

B How did President Polk provoke Mexico to attack U.S. forces?

▲ This 19th-century wood engraving shows Colonel Stephen Kearny capturing Santa Fe, New Mexico.

KEARNY MARCHES WEST In 1846, as part of his plan to seize New Mexico and California, Polk ordered Colonel **Stephen Kearny** to march from Fort Leavenworth, Kansas, across the desert to Santa Fe, New Mexico. Kearny earned the nickname "the Long Marcher" as he and his men crossed 800 miles of barren ground. They were met in Santa Fe by a New Mexican contingent that included upper-class Mexicans who wanted to join the United States. New Mexico fell to the United States without a shot being fired. After dispatching some of his troops south to Mexico, the Long Marcher led the rest on another long trek, this time to southern California. C

MAIN IDEA

Analyzing Motives

C How do Kearny's actions support the idea of manifest destiny?

THE REPUBLIC OF CALIFORNIA By the turn of the 19th century, Spanish settlers had set up more than 20 missions along the California coast. After independence, the Mexican government took over these missions, just as it had done in Texas. By the late 1830s, about 12,000 Mexican settlers had migrated to California to set up cattle ranches, where they pressed Native Americans into service as workers. By the mid-1840s, about 500 U.S. settlers also lived in California.

Polk's offer to buy California in 1845 aroused the indignation of the Mexican government. A group of American settlers, led by Frémont, seized the town of Sonoma in June 1846. Hoisting a flag that featured a grizzly bear, the rebels proudly declared their independence from Mexico and proclaimed the nation of the **Republic of California.** Kearny arrived from New Mexico and joined forces with Frémont and a U.S. naval expedition led by Commodore John D. Sloat. The Mexican troops quickly gave way, leaving U.S. forces in control of California.

THE WAR IN MEXICO For American troops in Mexico, one military victory followed another. Though Mexican soldiers gallantly defended their own soil, their army labored under poor leadership. In contrast, U.S. soldiers served under some of the nation's best officers, such as Captain Robert E. Lee and Captain Ulysses S. Grant, both West Point graduates.

War with Mexico, 1846–1848

hmhsocialstudies.com INTERACTIVE MAP

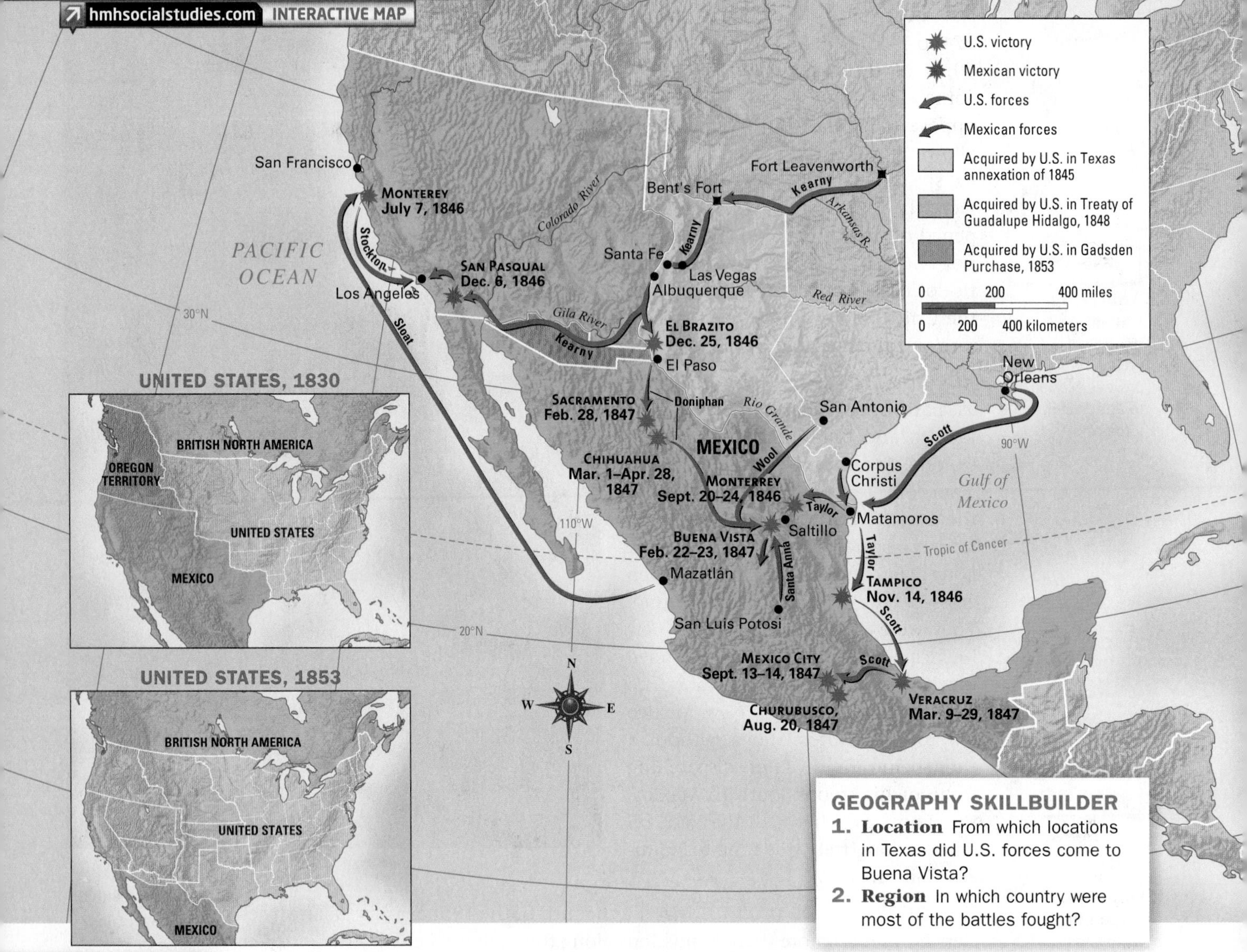

U.S. victory
Mexican victory
U.S. forces
Mexican forces
Acquired by U.S. in Texas annexation of 1845
Acquired by U.S. in Treaty of Guadalupe Hidalgo, 1848
Acquired by U.S. in Gadsden Purchase, 1853

UNITED STATES, 1830

UNITED STATES, 1853

GEOGRAPHY SKILLBUILDER

1. **Location** From which locations in Texas did U.S. forces come to Buena Vista?
2. **Region** In which country were most of the battles fought?

VIDEO
The Mexican-American War
hmhsocialstudies.com

The American invasion of Mexico lasted about a year and featured a pair of colorful generals, Zachary Taylor and **Winfield Scott.** Affectionately nicknamed "Old Rough and Ready" because he sported a casual straw hat and plain brown coat, Taylor attacked and captured Monterrey, Mexico, in September 1846, but allowed the Mexican garrison to escape.

Meanwhile, Polk hatched a bizarre scheme with Santa Anna, who had been living in exile in Cuba. If Polk would help him sneak back to Mexico, Santa Anna promised he would end the war and mediate the border dispute. Polk agreed, but when Santa Anna returned to Mexico, he resumed the presidency, took command of the army and, in February 1847, ordered an attack on Taylor's forces at Buena Vista. Though the Mexican army boasted superior numbers, its soldiers suffered from exhaustion. Taylor's more rested troops pushed Santa Anna into Mexico's interior.

Scott's forces took advantage of Santa Anna's failed strategy and captured Veracruz in March. General Scott always wore a full-dress blue uniform with a yellow sash, which won him the nickname "Old Fuss and Feathers." Scott supervised an amphibious landing at Veracruz, in which an army of 10,000 landed on an island off Veracruz in 200 ships and ferried 67 boats in less than 5 hours. Scott's troops then set off for Mexico City, which they captured on September 14, 1847. Covering 260 miles, Scott's army had lost not a single battle.

America Gains the Spoils of War

For Mexico, the war in which it lost at least 25,000 lives and nearly half its land marked an ugly milestone in its relations with the United States. America's victory came at the cost of about 13,000 lives. Of these, nearly 2,000 died in battle or from wounds and more than 11,000 perished from diseases, such as yellow fever. However, the war enlarged U.S. territory by approximately one-third.

THE TREATY OF GUADALUPE HIDALGO On February 2, 1848, the United States and Mexico signed the **Treaty of Guadalupe Hidalgo.** Mexico agreed to the Rio Grande border for Texas and ceded New Mexico and California to the United States. The United States agreed to pay $15 million for the Mexican cession, which included present-day California, Nevada, New Mexico, Utah, most of Arizona, and parts of Colorado and Wyoming. The treaty guaranteed Mexicans living in these territories freedom of religion, protection of property, bilingual elections, and open borders.

Five years later, in 1853, President Franklin Pierce would authorize his emissary James Gadsden to pay Mexico an additional $10 million for another piece of territory south of the Gila River. Along with the settlement of Oregon and the Treaty of Guadalupe Hidalgo, the **Gadsden Purchase** established the current borders of the lower 48 states. D

ANOTHER PERSPECTIVE

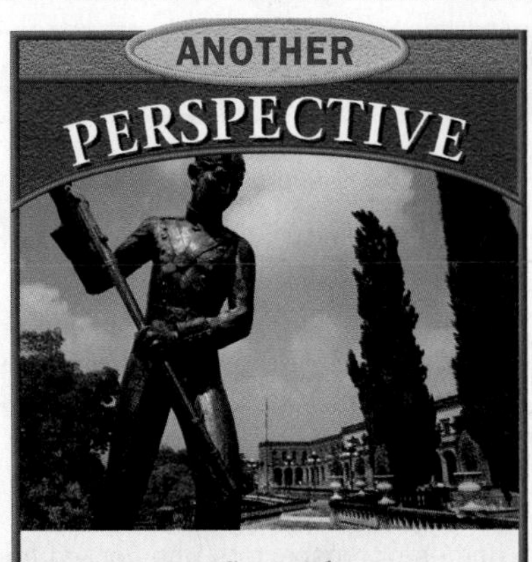

LOS NIÑOS HÉROES

Though most Americans know little about the war with Mexico, Mexicans view the war as a crucial event in their history.

On September 14, 1847, General Winfield Scott captured Mexico City after the hard-fought Battle of Chapultepec, the site of the Mexican military academy. There, six young cadets leaped from Chapultepec Castle to commit suicide rather than surrender to the U.S. Army. A monument *(shown above)* that honors *los Niños Héroes* (the boy heroes) inspires pilgrimages every September.

MAIN IDEA

Summarizing

D Explain the importance of the Treaty of Guadalupe Hidalgo and the Gadsden Purchase.

TAYLOR'S ELECTION IN 1848 In 1848 the Democrats nominated Lewis Cass for president and hesitated about the extension of slavery into America's vast new holdings. A small group of antislavery Democrats nominated Martin Van Buren to lead the Free-Soil Party, which supported a congressional prohibition on the extension of slavery into the territories. Van Buren captured 10 percent of the popular vote and no electoral votes. The Whig nominee, war hero Zachary Taylor, easily won the election. Taylor's victory, however, was soon overshadowed by a glittering discovery in one of America's new territories.

The California Gold Rush

In January 1848, James Marshall, an American carpenter working on John Sutter's property in the California Sierra Nevadas, discovered gold at Sutter's Mill. Word of the chance discovery traveled east.

THE RUSH BEGINS Soon after the news reached San Francisco, residents traveled to the Sacramento Valley in droves to pan for gold. Lacking staff and readers, San Francisco's newspaper, the *Californian,* suspended publication. An editorial in the final issue, dated May 29, complained that the whole country "resounds with the sordid cry of gold, GOLD, GOLD! while the field is left half-plowed, the house half-built, and everything neglected but the manufacture of shovels and pickaxes."

Analyzing Political Cartoons

"THE WAY THEY GO TO CALIFORNIA"

This cartoon lithograph by Nathaniel Currier (1813–1888) was inspired by the California gold rush. Currier was a founder of the Currier and Ives company, which became famous for detailed lithographs of 19th-century daily life.

Here Currier portrays some of the hordes of prospectors who flocked from all over the world to California in 1849. The mob wields picks and shovels, desperate to find any means of transport to the "Golden West." While some miners dive into the water, weighed down by heavy tools, one clever prospector has invented a new type of airship to speed him to the treasure.

SKILLBUILDER
Analyzing Political Cartoons

1. How has the cartoonist added humor to this portrayal of the gold seekers?
2. What clues tell you that this cartoon is about the California gold rush?

SEE SKILLBUILDER HANDBOOK, PAGE R24.

HISTORY

VIDEO
Gold Rush: Dangerous Short-cut to the West

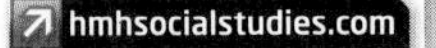
hmhsocialstudies.com

On June 6, 1848, Monterey's Mayor Walter Colton sent a scout to report on what was happening. After the scout returned on June 14, the mayor described the scene that had taken place in the middle of the town's main street.

A PERSONAL VOICE WALTER COLTON

> **"The blacksmith dropped his hammer, the carpenter his plane, the mason his trowel, the farmer his sickle, the baker his loaf, and the tapster his bottle. All were off for the mines. . . . I have only a community of women left, and a gang of prisoners, with here and there a soldier who will give his captain the slip at first chance. I don't blame the fellow a whit; seven dollars a month, while others are making two or three hundred a day!"**
>
> —quoted in *California: A Bicentennial History*

As gold fever traveled eastward, overland migration to California skyrocketed, from 400 in 1848 to 44,000 in 1850. The rest of the world soon caught the fever. Among the so-called **forty-niners,** the prospectors who flocked to California in 1849 in the **gold rush,** were people from Asia, South America, and Europe. E

MAIN IDEA
Comparing
E What common dreams did people who sought gold in California share with those who settled in Oregon?

IMPACT OF GOLD FEVER Because of its location as a supply center, San Francisco became "a pandemonium of a city," according to one traveler. Indeed, the city's population exploded from 1,000 in 1848 to 35,000 in 1850. Ferrying people and supplies, ships clogged San Francisco's harbor with a forest of masts.

Louisa Clapp and her husband, Fayette, left the comforts of a middle-class family in New England to join the gold rush for adventure. After living in San Francisco for more than a year, the Clapps settled in a log cabin in the interior mining town of Rich Bar. While her husband practiced medicine, Louisa tried her hand at mining and found it hardly to her liking.

A PERSONAL VOICE
LOUISA CLAPP

"I have become a mineress; that is, if having washed a pan of dirt with my own hands, and procured therefrom three dollars and twenty-five cents in gold dust . . . will entitle me to the name. I can truly say, with the blacksmith's apprentice at the close of his first day's work at the anvil, that 'I am sorry I learned the trade;' for I wet my feet, tore my dress, spoilt a pair of new gloves, nearly froze my fingers, got an awful headache, took cold and lost a valuable breastpin, in this my labor of love."

—quoted in *They Saw the Elephant*

▲ These miners are prospecting in Spanish Flat, California, in 1852.

GOLD RUSH BRINGS DIVERSITY By 1849, California's population exceeded 100,000. The Chinese were the largest group to come from overseas. Free blacks also came by the hundreds, and many struck it rich. By 1855, the wealthiest African Americans in the country were living in California. The fast-growing population included large numbers of Mexicans as well. The California demographic mix also included slaves—that is until a constitutional convention in 1849 drew up a state constitution that outlawed slavery.

California's application for statehood provoked fiery protest in Congress and became just one more sore point between irate Northerners and Southerners, each intent on winning the sectional argument over slavery. Nevertheless, California did win statehood in 1850.

SECTION 4 ASSESSMENT

1. **TERMS & NAMES** For each term or name, write a sentence explaining its significance.
   - **James K. Polk**
   - **Zachary Taylor**
   - **Stephen Kearny**
   - **Republic of California**
   - **Winfield Scott**
   - **Treaty of Guadalupe Hidalgo**
   - **Gadsden Purchase**
   - **forty-niners**
   - **gold rush**

MAIN IDEA

2. **TAKING NOTES**
   Draw a chart showing how the boundaries of the contiguous United States were formed.

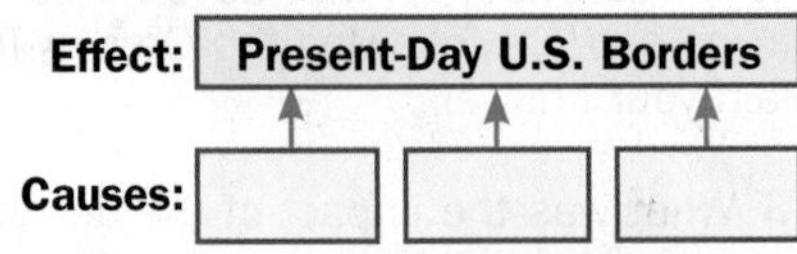

   How did the United States pursue its goal of expanding in the 1840s?

CRITICAL THINKING

3. **EVALUATING**
   How would you evaluate President Polk's attitude and behavior toward Mexico? Use specific references to the chapter to support your response. **Think About:**
   - Polk's position on expansion
   - his actions once in office
   - his relationship with Santa Anna

4. **ANALYZING EFFECTS**
   What were some of the effects of the California gold rush?

5. **EVALUATING DECISIONS**
   Would you have supported the controversial war with Mexico? Why or why not? Explain your answer, including details from the chapter.

VISUAL SUMMARY

EXPANDING MARKETS AND MOVING WEST

UNITED STATES IN 1853

MARKET REVOLUTION
- technological changes
- economic interdependence
- greater economic diversity among the regions of the nation

MANIFEST DESTINY
- the idea of manifest destiny used to justify settling the land
- increasing westward migration

EXPANSION IN TEXAS
- land grants offered by Mexico
- American settlement of Texas
- conflict over cultural differences, and over slavery
- American uprising
- Texas independence
- U.S. annexation of Texas

WAR WITH MEXICO
- tension over annexation of Texas
- war with Mexico
- huge territorial gains for the U.S.
- greater westward movement of settlers

CALIFORNIA GOLD RUSH
- discovery of gold in California
- population and economic boom in California
- California statehood (1850)

UNITED STATES IN 1853

TERMS & NAMES

For each term or name below, write a sentence explaining its connection to the expansion of the U.S. in the mid-19th century.

1. Samuel F. B. Morse
2. manifest destiny
3. Oregon Trail
4. Brigham Young
5. Antonio López de Santa Anna
6. Alamo
7. Sam Houston
8. Republic of Texas
9. James K. Polk
10. Treaty of Guadalupe Hidalgo

MAIN IDEAS

Use your notes and the information in the chapter to answer the following questions.

The Market Revolution

1. What inventions and technological advancements changed lives as part of the market revolution?
2. How did the inventions and innovations of the mid-19th century encourage various regions to specialize in certain industries?

Manifest Destiny

3. Why was the concept of manifest destiny of particular appeal to Americans in the 1840s?
4. What were the factors that drew settlers west during the first half of the 19th century?

Expansion in Texas

5. What made Americans want to settle in Texas?
6. What were the major events that led to Texas joining the Union?

The War with Mexico

7. What developments caused the United States to go to war with Mexico?
8. What effect did the gold rush have on the growth of California?

CRITICAL THINKING

1. **USING YOUR NOTES** What were America's goals and ideals during this period of expansion and economic change? Draw a chart in which you list goals from the period, how they were achieved, and their positive or negative effects.

Goal	How Achieved	Positive/Negative Effects

2. **INTERPRETING MAPS** Review the map in the Geography Spotlight, Mapping the Oregon Trail. In what ways would this map have been helpful to settlers following the Oregon Trail to a new home? Explain your answer.

3. **ANALYZING EFFECTS** What was the impact of the new methods of communication during this period? Use details from the text to support your response.

STANDARDIZED TEST PRACTICE

Use the map and your knowledge of U.S. history to answer questions 1 and 2.

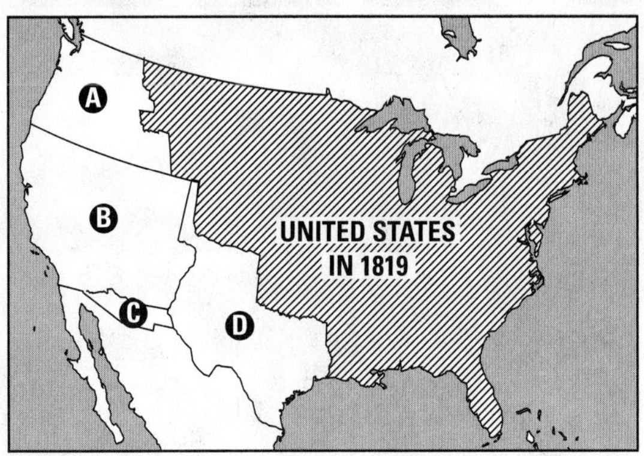

1. Which area on the map corresponds to the label "Mexican Cession, 1848"?

   A Area A
   B Area B
   C Area C
   D Area D

2. Which area on the map corresponds to the label "Oregon territory"?

   F Area A
   G Area B
   H Area C
   J Area D

Use the quotation below and your knowledge of U.S. history to answer question 3.

> **"[T]he right of our manifest destiny to over spread and to possess the whole of the continent which Providence has given us for the development of the great experiment of liberty and . . . development of self government entrusted to us. It is [a] right such as that of the tree to the space of air and the earth suitable for the full expansion of its principle and destiny of growth."**
>
> —John L. O'Sullivan,
> *United States Magazine and Democratic Review*

3. In this passage, the writer uses the term "manifest destiny" to mean that —

   A expansion is not only good but bound to happen.
   B neighboring territories will resent U.S. expansion.
   C America's growth can be compared to a tree.
   D self-government leads to expansion.

4. All of the following were outcomes of the California Gold Rush *except* —

   F increased diversity in the region.
   G the rapid growth of San Francisco.
   H an increase in overland migration.
   J the expansion of slavery in California.

For additional test practice, go online for:

- Diagnostic tests
- Tutorials

INTERACT WITH HISTORY

Think about the issues you explored at the beginning of the chapter. Organize into small groups and hold a debate about the way the United States acquired land from Mexico. Use information from the chapter to support your viewpoint.

FOCUS ON WRITING

Imagine you are a member of Congress, and you believe that the Treaty of Guadalupe Hidalgo is flawed. Write a different version of the treaty for Congress to adopt. For each main point in your treaty, compare it to the Treaty of Guadalupe Hidalgo and explain why your version is better.

MULTIMEDIA ACTIVITY

21ST CENTURY

Visit the links for Chapter Assessment to find out more about the revolution in technology and communication in the first half of the 19th century. What invention most appeals to you, and why? Prepare a multimedia presentation that describes the impact that your favorite invention had on society at the time.

hmhsocialstudies.com

The Real West: Rush for Gold

When gold was discovered in northern California in 1848, it caused a sensation. Gold seekers from the United States and the rest of the world rushed to California to find their fortunes. The conditions of the trip were difficult, as was the labor required to extract the gold from rivers and mines. Although some people became wealthy, many more never found the riches they had expected. So many people arrived so quickly that California became a state within three years of gold being discovered.

Explore some of the history and documents of the California Gold Rush online. You can find a wealth of information, video clips, primary sources, activities, and more at hmhsocialstudies.com.

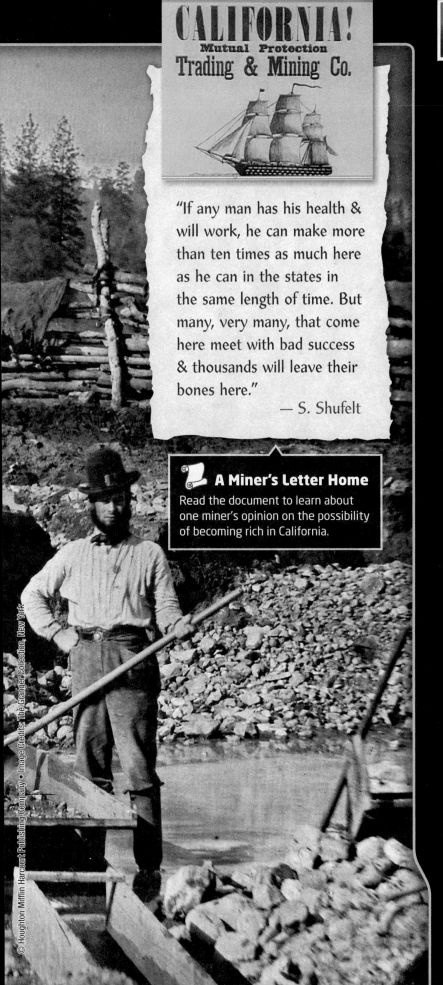

CALIFORNIA!
Mutual Protection
Trading & Mining Co.

"If any man has his health & will work, he can make more than ten times as much here as he can in the states in the same length of time. But many, very many, that come here meet with bad success & thousands will leave their bones here."
— S. Shufelt

A Miner's Letter Home
Read the document to learn about one miner's opinion on the possibility of becoming rich in California.

Heading West
Watch the video to learn about the dangers that overland travelers faced when trying to get to California from the eastern United States.

Search for the Mother Lode
Watch the video to see the various methods that forty-niners used to mine the gold in California.

Statehood
Watch the video to discover the political issues surrounding the admission of California as a free state and its implications for the rest of the nation.

CHAPTER 10

THE UNION IN PERIL

Essential Question

How did conflict over slavery and other regional tensions lead to the Civil War?

ALABAMA COURSE OF STUDY

12 Describe the founding of the first abolitionist societies by Benjamin Rush and Benjamin Franklin and the role played by later critics of slavery, including William Lloyd Garrison, Frederick Douglass, Sojourner Truth, Angelina and Sarah Grimké, Henry David Thoreau, and Charles Sumner.

- Explaining the importance of the Northwest Ordinance of 1787 that banned slavery in new states north of the Ohio River.
- Describing the rise of the Underground Railroad and its leaders, including Harriet Tubman and the impact of Harriet Beecher Stowe's Uncle Tom's Cabin, on the abolitionist movement.

13 Summarize major legislation and court decisions from 1800 to 1861 that led to increasing sectionalism, including the Missouri Compromise of 1820, the Compromise of 1850, the Fugitive Slave Acts, the Kansas-Nebraska Act, and the Dred Scott decision.

- Analyzing the formation of the Republican Party for its impact on the 1860 election of Abraham Lincoln as President of the United States.

Soldiers arrest abolitionist John Brown and his followers at the federal arsenal at Harpers Ferry, Virginia (now West Virginia), 1859. Brown had hoped to steal weapons and use them to instigate a nationwide slave rebellion.

1850 Congress passes Compromise of 1850.

1850 California enters the Union.

1852 Franklin Pierce is elected president.

1852 Harriet Beecher Stowe publishes *Uncle Tom's Cabin.*

1854 Congress approves the Kansas-Nebraska Act.

1854 The Republican Party forms.

USA / WORLD — 1850 | 1852 | 1854

1850 Taipeng Rebellion in China begins.

1853 Crimean War begins.

1854 Charles Dickens's *Hard Times* is published.

Image Credits: (bkgd), ©Corbis; (cl), Society of California Pioneers; (cr), Private Collection/Picture Research Consultants & Archives; (br), ©Hulton Archive/Getty Images

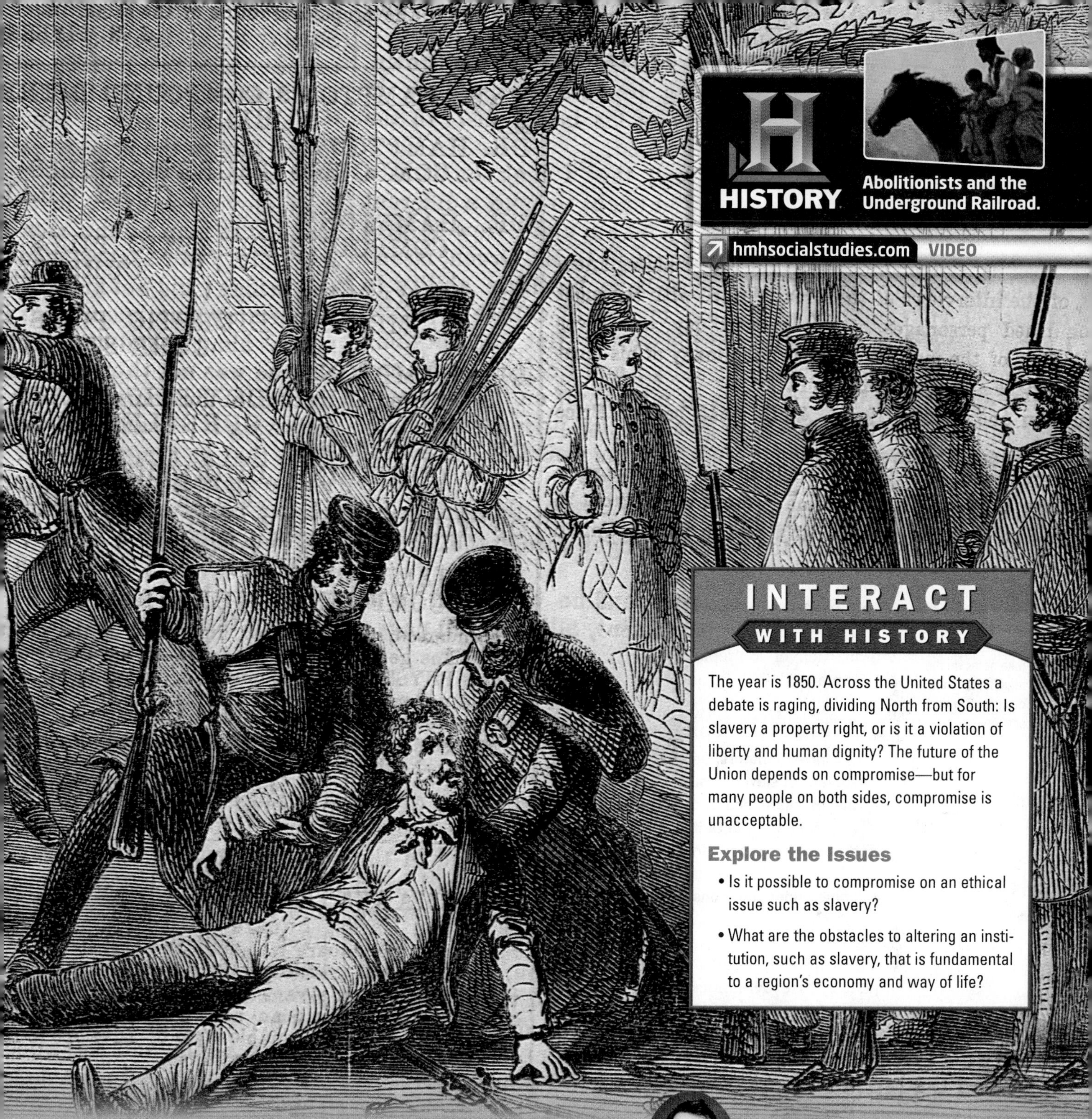

HISTORY Abolitionists and the Underground Railroad.

hmhsocialstudies.com VIDEO

INTERACT WITH HISTORY

The year is 1850. Across the United States a debate is raging, dividing North from South: Is slavery a property right, or is it a violation of liberty and human dignity? The future of the Union depends on compromise—but for many people on both sides, compromise is unacceptable.

Explore the Issues

- Is it possible to compromise on an ethical issue such as slavery?
- What are the obstacles to altering an institution, such as slavery, that is fundamental to a region's economy and way of life?

1856 James Buchanan is elected president.

1857 The Supreme Court rules against Dred Scott.

1859 John Brown attacks the arsenal at Harpers Ferry, Virginia.

1860 Abraham Lincoln is elected president.

1861 The Confederacy is formed.

1856 — 1858 — 1860

1858 The 13.5-ton bell, "Big Ben," is cast in Britain.

1859 Charles Darwin's *Origin of Species* is published.

1861 Russian serfs emancipated by Czar Alexander II.

Image Credits: (bkgd), ©Corbis; (br), ©Stock Montage/Hulton Archive/Getty Images; (bl), ©Corbis

The Divisive Politics of Slavery

MAIN IDEA	WHY IT MATTERS NOW	Terms & Names
The issue of slavery dominated U.S. politics in the early 1850s.	U.S. society continues to be challenged by issues of fairness, equality, race, and class.	• Wilmot Proviso • secession • Compromise of 1850 • popular sovereignty • Stephen A. Douglas • Millard Fillmore

One American's Story

hmhsocialstudies.com
TAKING NOTES

Use the graphic organizer online to take notes on the regional differences discussed in the section.

South Carolina senator John C. Calhoun was so sick that he had missed four months of debate over whether California should enter the Union as a free state. On March 4, 1850, Calhoun, explaining that he was too ill to deliver a prepared speech, asked Senator James M. Mason of Virginia to deliver it for him.

A PERSONAL VOICE JOHN C. CALHOUN

"I have, Senators, believed from the first that the agitation of the subject of slavery would, if not prevented by some timely and effective measure, end in disunion. . . . The agitation has been permitted to proceed . . . until it has reached a period when it can no longer be disguised or denied that the Union is in danger. You have thus had forced upon you the greatest and the gravest question that can ever come under your consideration: How can the Union be preserved?"

—quoted in *The Compromise of 1850*, edited by Edwin C. Rozwenc

▲ John C. Calhoun was vice-president under John Quincy Adams and Andrew Jackson. His last words were: "The South. The poor South."

Senator Calhoun called on the North to give the South "justice, simple justice." He demanded that slavery be allowed throughout the territories won in the war with Mexico. If it was not, he declared, the South would secede, or withdraw, from the Union. Once again, the issue of slavery had brought about a political crisis, deepening the gulf between the North and the South.

Differences Between North and South

Senator Calhoun argued that although the North and the South had been politically equal when the Constitution was adopted, the "perfect equilibrium" between the two sections no longer existed. At any rate, the two sections certainly had developed different ways of life by the 1850s.

INDUSTRY AND IMMIGRATION IN THE NORTH The North industrialized rapidly as factories turned out ever-increasing amounts of products, from textiles and sewing machines to farm equipment and guns. Railroads—with more than 20,000 miles of track laid during the 1850s—carried raw materials eastward and manufactured goods and settlers westward. Small towns like Chicago matured into cities almost overnight, due to the sheer volume of goods and people arriving by railroad. Telegraph wires strung along the railroad tracks provided a network of instant communication for the North.

Immigrants from Europe entered the industrial workplace in growing numbers. Many became voters with a strong opposition to slavery. They feared the expansion of slavery for two main reasons. First, it might bring slave labor into direct competition with free labor, or people who worked for wages. Second, it threatened to reduce the status of white workers who could not successfully compete with slaves.

AGRICULTURE AND SLAVERY IN THE SOUTH Unlike the North, the South remained a predominantly rural society, consisting mostly of plantations and small farms. The Southern economy relied on staple crops such as cotton. Though one-third of the nation's population lived in the South in 1850, the South produced under 10 percent of the nation's manufactured goods. At the same time that Northern railroad lines were expanding, Southerners were mostly using rivers to transport goods. In addition, few immigrants settled in the South, because African Americans, whether enslaved or free, met most of the available need for artisans, mechanics, and laborers. Those immigrants who did settle in the South, however, displayed significant opposition to slavery. For example, German-American newspapers in Texas and in Baltimore, Maryland published editorials in favor of universal voting rights and freedom for African Americans.

MAIN IDEA

Contrasting
A List three ways in which the North and the South differed in the mid 1800s.

The conflict over slavery rattled Southern society. In three Southern states, Mississippi, Louisiana, and South Carolina, African Americans were in the majority. In Alabama and Florida, African Americans composed almost half of the population. While blacks dreamed of an end to slavery, many Southern whites feared that any restriction of slavery would lead to a social and economic revolution. Furthermore, Calhoun warned that such a revolution would condemn blacks as well as whites "to the greatest calamity, and the [South] to poverty, desolation, and wretchedness." A

History Through *Architecture*

GREEK REVIVAL ARCHITECTURE

The Greek Revival was an architectural style that spread throughout the United States between 1825 and 1860. Like ancient Greek temples, many buildings in this style had columns on all four sides. This style was applied to all types of buildings in Greek Revival architecture, from small houses to state capitols. The hot, humid climate of the South encouraged the development of a high porch and with columns rising to the full height of a building. These wide porches were unusual in the cooler climate of Europe but well-suited to tropical regions. In the hands of Greek Revival architects in the South, the porches became grand living spaces where families could find shelter from the summer heat.

Oak Alley Plantation, Louisiana ▼

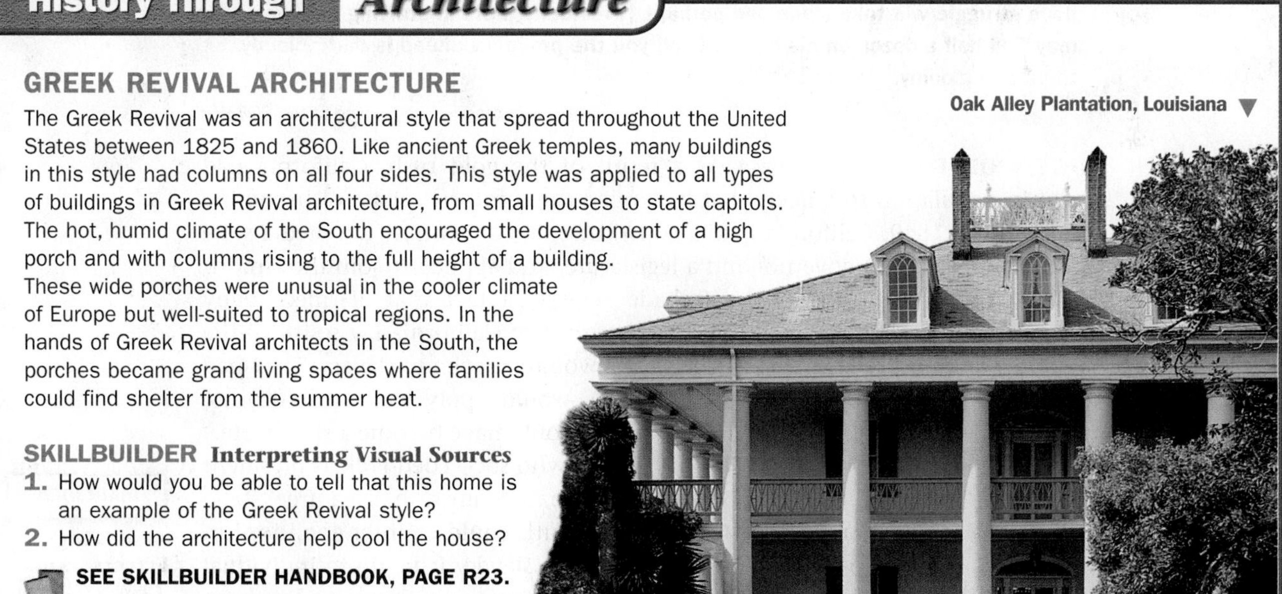

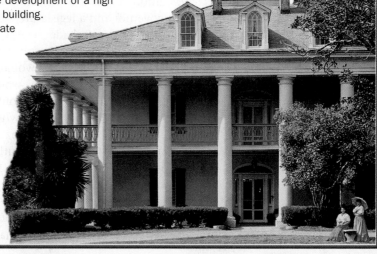

SKILLBUILDER **Interpreting Visual Sources**
1. How would you be able to tell that this home is an example of the Greek Revival style?
2. How did the architecture help cool the house?

SEE SKILLBUILDER HANDBOOK, PAGE R23.

Slavery in the Territories

On August 8, 1846, Pennsylvania Democrat David Wilmot heightened tensions between North and South by introducing an amendment to a military appropriations bill proposing that "neither slavery nor involuntary servitude shall ever exist" in any territory the United States might acquire as a result of the war with Mexico. In strictly practical terms, the **Wilmot Proviso** meant that California, as well as the territories of Utah and New Mexico, would be closed to slavery forever.

THE WILMOT PROVISO The Wilmot Proviso divided Congress along regional lines. Northerners, angry over the refusal of Southern congressmen to vote for internal improvements, such as the building of canals and roads, supported the proviso. They also feared that adding slave territory would give slave states more members in Congress and deny economic opportunity to free workers.

Membership in House of Representatives

Year	Members from Free States	Members from Slave States
1800	77	65
1810	105	81
1820	123	90
1830	142	100
1840	141	91
1850	144	90

Source: *Historical Statistics of the United States*

SKILLBUILDER Interpreting Charts
About what percentage of House members represented free states in 1850?

Southerners, as expected, opposed the proviso, which, some argued, raised complex constitutional issues. Slaves were property, Southerners claimed, and property was protected by the Constitution. Laws like the Wilmot Proviso would undermine such constitutional protections.

Many Southerners feared that if the Wilmot Proviso became law, the inevitable addition of new free states to the Union would shift the balance of power permanently to the North. The House of Representatives approved the proviso, but the Senate rejected it. Congressman Alexander H. Stephens of Georgia issued a dire prediction. B

MAIN IDEA

Analyzing Motives

B Explain why Northerners favored the Wilmot Proviso and why Southerners did not.

A PERSONAL VOICE ALEXANDER H. STEPHENS

"The North is going to stick the Wilmot amendment to every appropriation and then all the South will vote against any measure thus clogged. Finally a tremendous struggle will take place and perhaps [President] Polk in starting one war may find half a dozen on his hands. I tell you the prospect ahead is dark, cloudy, thick and gloomy."

—quoted in *The Coming of the Civil War*

STATEHOOD FOR CALIFORNIA As a result of the gold rush, California had grown in population so quickly that it skipped the territorial phase of becoming a state. In late 1849, California held a constitutional convention, adopted a state constitution, elected a governor and a legislature, and applied to join the Union.

California's new constitution forbade slavery, a fact that alarmed many Southerners. They had assumed that because most of California lay south of the Missouri Compromise line of 36°30′, the state would be open to slavery. They had hoped that the compromise, struck in 1820, would apply to new territories, including California, which would have become a slave state.

California's admission to the Union in 1850 increased tensions between North and South. ▼

STATE OF CALIFORNIA

General Zachary Taylor, who succeeded Polk as president in 1849, supported California's admission as a free state. Moreover, he felt that the South could counter abolitionism most effectively by leaving the slavery issue up to individual territories rather than to Congress. Southerners, however, saw this as a move to block slavery in the territories and as an attack on the Southern way of life—and began to question whether the South should remain in the Union. C

MAIN IDEA

Analyzing Effects

C Why did California's application for statehood cause an uproar?

The Senate Debates

The 31st Congress opened in December 1849 in an atmosphere of distrust and bitterness. The question of California statehood topped the agenda. Of equal concern was the border dispute in which the slave state of Texas claimed the eastern half of New Mexico Territory, where the issue of slavery had not yet been settled. In the meantime, Northerners demanded the abolition of slavery in the District of Columbia, while Southerners accused the North of failing to enforce the Fugitive Slave Act of 1793. As passions rose, some Southerners threatened **secession,** the formal withdrawal of a state from the Union. Could anything be done to prevent the United States from becoming two nations?

CLAY'S COMPROMISE Henry Clay worked night and day to shape a compromise that both the North and the South could accept. Though ill, he visited his old rival Daniel Webster on January 21, 1850, and obtained Webster's support. Eight days later, Clay presented to the Senate a series of resolutions later called the **Compromise of 1850,** which he hoped would settle "all questions in controversy between the free and slave states, growing out of the subject of Slavery."

TERMS OF THE COMPROMISE Clay's compromise (summarized on the chart shown on the next page) contained provisions to appease Northerners as well as Southerners. To satisfy the North, the compromise provided that California be admitted to the Union as a free state. To satisfy the South, the compromise proposed a new and more effective fugitive slave law.

MAIN IDEA

Comparing
D What Northern issues and Southern issues were addressed by the Compromise of 1850?

Other provisions of the compromise had elements that appealed to both regions. For example, a provision that allowed residents of the territories of New Mexico and Utah **popular sovereignty**—the right of residents of a territory to vote for or against slavery—appealed to both North and South. As part of the compromise, the federal government would pay Texas $10 million to surrender its claim to New Mexico. Northerners were pleased because, in effect, it limited slavery in Texas to within its current borders. Southerners were pleased because the money would help defray Texas's expenses and debts from the war with Mexico. D

1 Daniel Webster strongly supported Clay's compromise. He left the Senate before Stephen Douglas could engineer passage of all the provisions of the compromise.

2 Henry Clay offered his compromise to the Senate in January 1850. In his efforts to save the Union, Clay earned the name "the Great Compromiser."

3 John C. Calhoun opposed the compromise. He died two months after Clay proposed it.

On February 5, Clay defended his resolutions and begged both the North and the South to consider them thoughtfully. The alternative was disunion—and, in Clay's opinion, quite possibly war.

A Personal Voice HENRY CLAY

"And such a war as it would be, following the dissolution of the Union! Sir, we may search the pages of history, and none so ferocious, so bloody, so implacable, so exterminating . . . would rage with such violence. . . . I implore gentlemen, I adjure them, whether from the South or the North . . . to pause at the edge of the precipice, before the fearful and dangerous leap be taken into the yawning abyss below."

—quoted in *Voices from the Civil War*

CALHOUN AND WEBSTER RESPOND Clay's speech marked the start of one of the greatest political debates in United States history. Within a month, Calhoun had presented the Southern case for slavery in the territories. He was followed three days later by Daniel Webster, who began his eloquent appeal for national unity by saying, "I wish to speak today, not as a Massachusetts man, nor as a Northern man, but as an American. . . . 'Hear me for my cause.'" He urged Northerners to try to compromise with the South by passing a stricter fugitive slave law, and he warned Southern firebrands to think more cautiously about the danger of secession.

A Personal Voice DANIEL WEBSTER

"I hear with pain, and anguish, and distress, the word *secession,* especially when it falls from the lips of those who are eminently patriotic. . . . Secession! Peaceable secession! . . . There can be no such thing as a peaceable secession. . . . Is the great Constitution under which we live . . . to be thawed and melted away by secession. . . . No, sir! I will not state what might produce the disruption of the states; . . . [What] that disruption must produce . . . [would be] such a war as I will not describe."

—"Seventh of March" speech, quoted in *The American Spirit*

The Compromise of 1850

Calhoun's Goals	Terms of the Compromise	Webster's Goals
Calhoun believed strongly in states' rights over federal power and held the interests of the slaveholding South as his highest priority. He had long believed that "the agitation of the subject of slavery would . . . end in disunion." He blamed the sectional crisis on Northern abolitionists and argued that the South had "no concession or surrender to make" on the issue of slavery.	• California admitted as a free state • Utah and New Mexico territories decide about slavery • Texas-New Mexico boundary dispute resolved; Texas paid $10 million by federal government. • The sale of slaves banned in the District of Columbia. But slavery itself may continue there. • Fugitive Slave Act required people in the free states to help capture and return escaped slaves.	Webster had argued with Northern Whigs that slavery should not be extended into the territories. Upon hearing Calhoun's threat of secession, he took to the Senate floor and endorsed Clay's compromise "for the preservation of the Union. . . . a great, popular, constitutional government, guarded by legislation, by law, by judicature, and defended by the whole affections of the people."

SKILLBUILDER Interpreting Charts
1. How did Calhoun and Webster disagree over states' rights? 2. How did the compromise try to satisfy both sides?

Webster's speech became one of the most famous in the history of the Senate. Spectators packed the Senate chamber for the event.

THE COMPROMISE IS ADOPTED The Senate rejected the proposed compromise in July. Discouraged, Clay left Washington. **Stephen A. Douglas** of Illinois picked up the pro-compromise reins.

To avoid another defeat, Douglas developed a shrewd plan. He unbundled the package of resolutions and reintroduced them one at a time, hoping to obtain a majority vote for each measure individually. Thus, any individual congressman could vote for the provisions that he liked and vote against, or abstain from voting on, those that he disliked. It appeared as though Douglas had found the key to passing the entire compromise.

The unexpected death of President Taylor on July 9 aided Douglas's efforts. Taylor's successor, **Millard Fillmore,** made it clear that he supported the compromise. In the meantime, the South was ready to negotiate. Calhoun's death had removed one obstacle to compromise. Southern leaders came out in favor of Clay's individual proposals as being the best the South could secure without radical action. After eight months of effort, the Compromise of 1850 was voted into law. E

Analyzing Effects

E What was the result of Douglas's unbundling of Clay's resolutions?

President Fillmore embraced the compromise as the "final settlement" of the question of slavery and sectional differences. For the moment, the crisis over slavery in the territories had passed. However, the relief was short-lived. Even as crowds in Washington celebrated the passage of the compromise, the next crisis loomed ominously on the horizon—enforcement of the new fugitive slave law.

KEY PLAYER

STEPHEN A. DOUGLAS
1813–1861

Stephen A. Douglas's political cleverness, oratorical skill, and personal drive earned him the nickname the Little Giant—a reference to the fact that he stood only 5'4" tall.

Using his political skill, Douglas engineered the passage of the Compromise of 1850 when all of the efforts of senatorial warriors, such as Clay, had failed. Douglas later became the well-known opponent of Abraham Lincoln in both a senatorial and a presidential election.

Douglas had been a judge, and then served two terms in the House of Representatives before he was elected to the Senate. However, he never achieved his ultimate political goal: the presidency.

SECTION 1 ASSESSMENT

1. **TERMS & NAMES** For each term or name, write a sentence explaining its significance.
   - **Wilmot Proviso**
   - **secession**
   - **Compromise of 1850**
   - **popular sovereignty**
   - **Stephen A. Douglas**
   - **Millard Fillmore**

MAIN IDEA

2. **TAKING NOTES**
   Create a chart similar to this one. Complete it by indicating each region's position on an issue or trend covered in this section.

Issue or Trend	North	South
1.		
2.		
3.		
4.		
5.		

   How was each region affected by the issue or trend?

CRITICAL THINKING

3. **HYPOTHESIZING**
   Do you think there are any points at which a different action or leader might have resolved the conflict between the North and the South? Support your opinion with references from this section. **Think About:**
   - issues raised by the Wilmot Proviso, California statehood, and the Compromise of 1850
   - constitutional issues raised by Southerners

4. **ANALYZING PRIMARY SOURCES**
   When California applied for statehood in 1850, Mississippi senator Jefferson Davis warned, "For the first time, we are about permanently to destroy the balance of power between the sections." Why might Davis have felt this way?

5. **EVALUATING**
   Do you think the North or the South won more significant concessions in the Compromise of 1850? Explain your answer.

SECTION 2

Protest, Resistance, and Violence

MAIN IDEA

Proslavery and antislavery factions disagreed over the treatment of fugitive slaves and the spread of slavery to the territories.

WHY IT MATTERS NOW

The antislavery leaders became role models for leaders of civil rights movements in the 20th century.

Terms & Names

- **Fugitive Slave Act**
- **personal liberty laws**
- **Underground Railroad**
- **Harriet Tubman**
- **Harriet Beecher Stowe**
- ***Uncle Tom's Cabin***
- **Kansas-Nebraska Act**
- **John Brown**
- **Bleeding Kansas**

One American's Story

hmhsocialstudies.com TAKING NOTES

Use the graphic organizer online to take notes on the major events in the growing conflict between the North and the South.

On June 2, 1854, thousands lined the streets of Boston. Flags flew at half-mast, and a black coffin bearing the words "The Funeral of Liberty" dangled from a window. Federal soldiers, bayonets ready for action, marched a lone African American, Anthony Burns, toward the harbor. Charlotte Forten, a free black, wrote about the day.

▲ **Charlotte Forten was the granddaughter of James Forten, a Philadelphia abolitionist who fought in the Revolutionary War.**

A PERSONAL VOICE CHARLOTTE FORTEN

"Today Massachusetts has again been disgraced. . . . With what scorn must that government be regarded, which cowardly assembles thousands of soldiers to satisfy the demands of slaveholders; to deprive of his freedom a man, created in God's own image, whose sole offense is the color of his skin! . . . A cloud seems hanging over me, over all our persecuted race, which nothing can dispel."

—quoted in *The Underground Railroad*, by Charles L. Blockson

Anthony Burns was being forced back into slavery in Virginia. As a result of his trial, antislavery sentiment in the North soared. "We went to bed one night old-fashioned, conservative, compromise Union Whigs," wrote one Northerner, "and waked up stark mad Abolitionists."

Fugitive Slaves and the Underground Railroad

Burns's return to slavery followed the passage of the **Fugitive Slave Act,** which was a component of the Compromise of 1850. Many people were surprised by the harsh terms of the act. Under the law, alleged fugitives were not entitled to a trial by jury, despite the Sixth Amendment provision calling for a speedy and public jury trial and the right to counsel. Nor could fugitives testify on their own behalf.

A statement by a slave owner was all that was required to have a slave returned. Frederick Douglass bitterly summarized the situation.

A PERSONAL VOICE FREDERICK DOUGLASS

"The colored men's rights are less than those of a jackass. No man can take away a jackass without submitting the matter to twelve men in any part of this country. A black man may be carried away without any reference to a jury. It is only necessary to claim him, and that some villain should swear to his identity. There is more protection there for a horse, for a donkey, or anything, rather than a colored man."

—quoted in *Voices from the Civil War*

Federal commissioners charged with enforcing the law were to receive a $10 fee if they returned an alleged fugitive, but only $5 if they freed him or her, an obvious incentive to "return" people to slavery. Finally, anyone convicted of helping an alleged fugitive was subject to a fine of $1,000, imprisonment for six months, or both.

RESISTING THE LAW Infuriated by the Fugitive Slave Act, some Northerners resisted it by organizing vigilance committees to send endangered African Americans to safety in Canada. Others resorted to violence to rescue fugitive slaves. Nine Northern states passed **personal liberty laws,** which forbade the imprisonment of runaway slaves and guaranteed that they would have jury trials. And Northern lawyers dragged these trials out—often for three or four years—in order to increase slave catchers' expenses. Southern slave owners were enraged by Northern resistance to the Fugitive Slave Act, prompting one Harvard law student from Georgia to tell his mother, "Do not be surprised if when I return home you find me a confirmed disunionist." (A)

MAIN IDEA

Analyzing Effects

(A) What effect did the Fugitive Slave Act have on abolitionist feelings in the North?

With a price of $40,000 on her head, Harriet Tubman was called "Moses" by those she helped escape on the Underground Railroad. ▼

HARRIET TUBMAN AND THE UNDERGROUND RAILROAD As time went on, free African Americans and white abolitionists developed a secret network of people who would, at great risk to themselves, aid fugitive slaves in their escape. This network became known as the **Underground Railroad.** The "conductors" hid fugitives in secret tunnels and false cupboards, provided them with food and clothing, and escorted or directed them to the next "station," often in disguise.

One of the most famous conductors was **Harriet Tubman,** born a slave in 1820 or 1821. As a young girl, she suffered a severe head injury when a plantation overseer hit her with a lead weight. The blow damaged her brain, causing her to lose consciousness several times a day. To compensate for her disability, Tubman increased her strength until she became strong enough to perform tasks that most men could not do. In 1849, after Tubman's owner died, she decided to make a break for freedom and succeeded in reaching Philadelphia.

Shortly after passage of the Fugitive Slave Act, Tubman became a conductor on the Underground Railroad. In all, she made 19 trips back to the South and is said to have helped 300 slaves—including her own parents—flee to freedom. Neither Tubman nor the slaves she helped were ever captured. Later she became an ardent speaker for abolition.

For slaves, escaping from slavery was indeed a dangerous process. It meant traveling on foot at night without any sense of distance or direction except for the North Star and other natural signs. It meant avoiding patrols of armed men on horseback and struggling through forests and across rivers. Often it meant going

KEY PLAYER

HARRIET BEECHER STOWE
1811–1896

Harriet Beecher Stowe was born in Connecticut into a prominent reform family. Her father was a Presbyterian minister and temperance advocate, Lyman Beecher. Her brother, Henry, was a clergyman and abolitionist.

Stowe moved with her family to Cincinnati, where the issue of slavery—once rather remote—became painfully familiar. She never forgot standing on the banks of the Ohio River, watching boats fill with slaves from Kentucky to be shipped to slave markets. Her hatred of slavery grew until she resolved to express herself in writing, and *Uncle Tom's Cabin* resulted. The novel made such an impact that when Abraham Lincoln met Stowe a decade later, during the Civil War, he said, "So this is the little lady who made the big war."

without food for days at a time. Harry Grimes, a slave who ran away from North Carolina, described the difficulties of escaping to the North.

A PERSONAL VOICE HARRY GRIMES

> **"In the woods I lived on nothing. . . . I stayed in the hollow of a big poplar tree for seven months. . . . I suffered mighty bad with the cold and for something to eat. One time a snake come to the tree . . . and I took my axe and chopped him in two. It was . . . the poisonest kind of snake we have. While in the woods all my thoughts was how to get away to a free country."**
>
> —quoted in *The Underground Railroad,* by Charles L. Blockson

Once fugitive slaves reached the North, many elected to remain there and take their chances. Other fugitives continued their journey all the way to Canada to be completely out of reach of slave catchers. Meanwhile, a new abolitionist voice spoke out and brought slavery to the attention of a great many Americans. **B**

MAIN IDEA

Summarizing
B How did the Underground Railroad operate?

UNCLE TOM'S CABIN In 1852, ardent abolitionist **Harriet Beecher Stowe** published ***Uncle Tom's Cabin.*** Stirring strong reactions from North and South alike, the novel became an instant bestseller. More than a million copies had sold by the middle of 1853.

The novel's plot was melodramatic and many of its characters were stereotypes, but *Uncle Tom's Cabin* delivered the message that slavery was not just a political contest, but also a great moral struggle. Readers tensed with excitement as the slave Eliza fled across the frozen Ohio River, clutching her infant son in her arms. They wept bitterly when Simon Legree, a wicked Northern slave owner who moved to the South, bought Uncle Tom and had him whipped to death.

In quick response, Northern abolitionists increased their protests against the Fugitive Slave Act, while Southerners criticized the book as an attack on the South as a whole. The furor over *Uncle Tom's Cabin* had barely begun to settle when a new controversy over slavery drew heated debate.

CAUTION!!
COLORED PEOPLE
OF BOSTON, ONE & ALL,
You are hereby respectfully CAUTIONED and advised, to avoid conversing with the
Watchmen and Police Officers of Boston,
For since the recent ORDER OF THE MAYOR & ALDERMEN, they are empowered to act as
KIDNAPPERS
AND
Slave Catchers,
And they have already been actually employed in KIDNAPPING, CATCHING, AND KEEPING SLAVES. Therefore, if you value your LIBERTY, and the Welfare of the Fugitives among you, Shun them in every possible manner, as so many HOUNDS on the track of the most unfortunate of your race.
Keep a Sharp Look Out for KIDNAPPERS, and have TOP EYE open.
APRIL 24, 1851.

◀ **An abolitionist poster distributed in 1851**

Tension in Kansas and Nebraska

Abolitionist feelings in the North further intensified when the issue of slavery in the territories—supposedly settled by the Compromise of 1850—surfaced once again. Ironically, Senator Stephen Douglas, who had helped to steer the compromise to victory, was the person most responsible for resurrecting the issue.

GEOGRAPHY SKILLBUILDER

1. **Movement** What does this map tell you about the routes of the Underground Railroad?
2. **Place** Name three cities that were destinations on the Underground Railroad.
3. **Location** Why do you think these cities were destinations?

POPULAR SOVEREIGNTY As early as 1844, Douglas was pushing to organize the huge territory west of Iowa and Missouri. In 1854, he developed a proposal to divide the area into two territories, Nebraska and Kansas. His motives were complicated. For one thing, Douglas was pushing for the construction of a railroad between Chicago—his hometown, where he also owned real estate—and San Francisco. To get this route, he had to make a deal with Southerners, who wanted the railroad to start in Memphis or New Orleans.

In addition, Douglas was anxious to organize the western territory because he believed that most of the nation's people wished to see the western lands incorporated into the Union. Along with many other Democrats, Douglas was sure that continued expansion would strengthen his party and unify the nation. He also believed that popular sovereignty—that is, the right of residents of a given territory to vote on slavery for themselves—provided the most fair and democratic way to organize the new state governments. But what Douglas failed to fully understand was how strongly opposed to slavery Northerners had become.

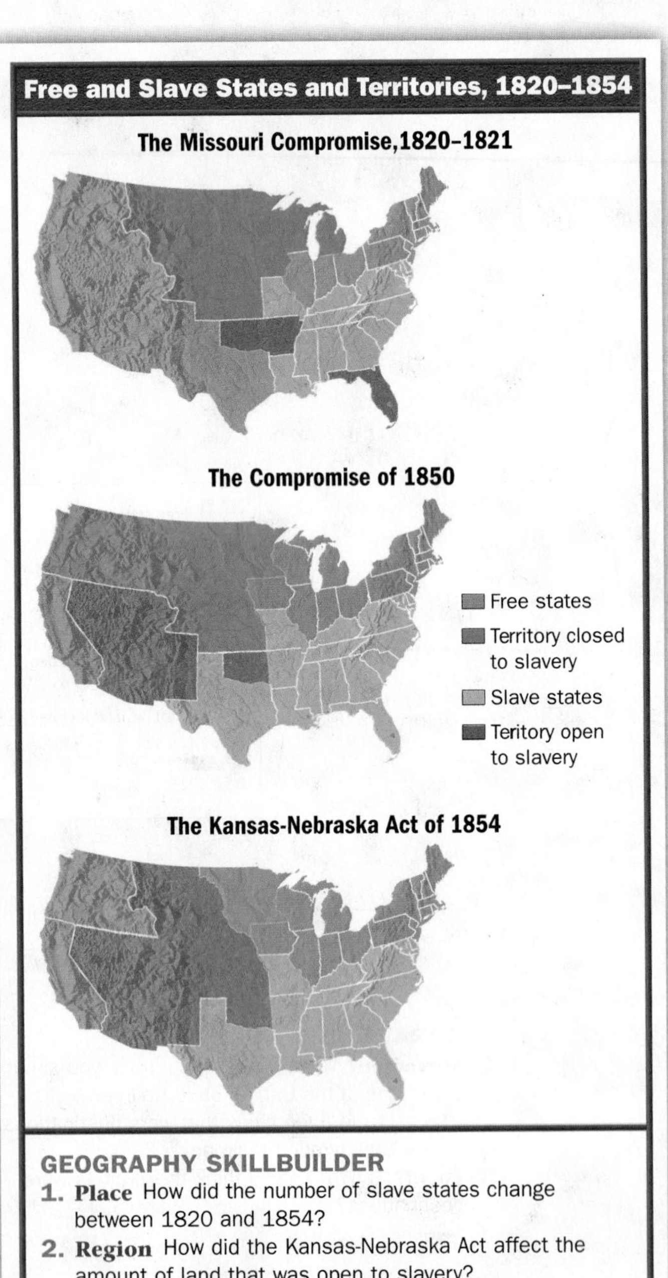

GEOGRAPHY SKILLBUILDER

1. **Place** How did the number of slave states change between 1820 and 1854?
2. **Region** How did the Kansas-Nebraska Act affect the amount of land that was open to slavery?

To Douglas, popular sovereignty seemed like an excellent way to decide whether slavery would be allowed in the Nebraska Territory. The only difficulty was that Nebraska Territory lay north of the Missouri Compromise line of 36°30′ and therefore was legally closed to slavery. Douglas assumed, though, that the territory of Nebraska would enter the Union as two states, one free and one slave, and thus maintain the balance in the Senate between North and South.

Douglas was convinced that slavery could not exist on the open prairies, since none of the crops relying on slave labor could be grown there. However, to win over the South, Douglas decided to support repeal of the Missouri Compromise—which now would make slavery legal north of the 36°30′ line—though he predicted it would cause "a storm" in Congress. His prediction was right. (C)

MAIN IDEA

Analyzing Issues

(C) Explain why popular sovereignty was so controversial.

THE KANSAS–NEBRASKA ACT On January 23, 1854, Douglas introduced a bill in Congress to divide the area into two territories: Nebraska in the north and Kansas in the south. If passed, it would repeal the Missouri Compromise and establish popular sovereignty for both territories. Congressional debate over the bill was bitter. Some Northern congressmen saw the bill as part of a plot to turn the territories into slave states; but nearly

90 percent of Southern congressmen voted for the bill. The bitterness spilled over into the general population, which deluged Congress with petitions both for and against the bill.

In the North, Douglas found himself ridiculed for betraying the Missouri Compromise. Yet he did not waver. He believed strongly that popular sovereignty was the democratic way to resolve the slavery issue.

A PERSONAL VOICE STEPHEN A. DOUGLAS

> **"If the people of Kansas want a slaveholding state, let them have it, and if they want a free state they have a right to it, and it is not for the people of Illinois, or Missouri, or New York, or Kentucky, to complain, whatever the decision of Kansas may be."**
>
> —quoted in *The Civil War*, by Geoffrey C. Ward

With the help of President Franklin Pierce, a Democrat elected in 1852, Douglas steered his proposal through the Senate. After months of struggle and strife, the **Kansas-Nebraska Act** became law in May 1854. All eyes turned westward as the fate of the new territories hung in the balance.

Violence Erupts in "Bleeding Kansas"

The race for the possession of Kansas was on. New York senator William Seward threw down the gauntlet: "Come on, then, gentlemen of the Slave States. . . . We will engage in competition for the virgin soil of Kansas and God give the victory to the side that is stronger in numbers as it is in right."

From both the North and the South, settlers poured into the Kansas Territory. Some were simply farmers in search of new land. Most were sent by emigrant aid societies, groups formed specifically to supply rifles, animals, seed, and farm equipment to antislavery migrants.

This organized party of Kansas-bound armed settlers was one of the groups known as "Free-State batteries."

By March 1855, Kansas had enough settlers to hold an election for a territorial legislature. However, thousands of "border ruffians" from the slave state of Missouri, led by Missouri senator David Atchison, crossed into Kansas with their revolvers cocked and voted illegally. They won a fraudulent majority for the proslavery candidates, who set up a government at Lecompton and promptly issued a series of proslavery acts. Furious over events in Lecompton, abolitionists organized a rival government in Topeka in fall 1855. D

MAIN IDEA

Analyzing Causes

D Why did Kansas become a center of controversy over the issue of slavery?

"THE SACK OF LAWRENCE" Before long, violence surfaced in the struggle for Kansas. Antislavery settlers had founded a town named Lawrence. A proslavery grand jury condemned Lawrence's inhabitants as traitors and called on the local sheriff to arrest them. On May 21, 1856, a proslavery posse of 800 armed men swept into Lawrence to carry out the grand jury's will. The posse burned down the antislavery headquarters, destroyed two newspapers' printing presses, and looted many houses and stores. Abolitionist newspapers dubbed the event "the sack of Lawrence."

hmhsocialstudies.com

INTERACTIVE

Explore the sack of Lawrence

"THE POTTAWATOMIE MASSACRE" The news from Lawrence soon reached **John Brown,** an abolitionist described by one historian as "a man made of the stuff of saints." Brown believed that God had called on him to fight slavery. He also had the mistaken impression that the proslavery posse in Lawrence had killed five men. Brown was set on revenge. On May 24th, he and his followers pulled five men from their beds in the proslavery settlement of Pottawatomie Creek, hacked off their hands, and stabbed them with broadswords. This attack became famous as the "Pottawatomie Massacre" and quickly led to cries for revenge. It became the bloody shirt that proslavery Kansas settlers waved in summoning attacks on Free-Soilers.

The massacre triggered dozens of incidents throughout Kansas. Some 200 people were killed. John Brown fled Kansas but left behind men and women who lived with rifles by their sides. People began calling the territory **Bleeding Kansas,** as it had become a violent battlefield in a civil war.

KEY PLAYER

JOHN BROWN
1800–1859

John Brown was a fiery idealist who believed that God had called on him to fight slavery. He was raised in a deeply religious antislavery family. Brown was never financially successful although he tried a variety of ventures, from farming to land speculation.

By 1849, Brown was living in the black community of North Elba, New York. He supported many abolitionist causes, such as David Walker's *Appeal* and helped finance farms for fugitive slaves.

Brown became a powerful symbol of the moral issue of slavery in the North and reinforced the worst fears of the South. After a number of raids on proslavery settlers in Kansas and a raid on Harpers Ferry, Virginia, Brown was caught. He was hanged for treason in 1859.

VIOLENCE IN THE SENATE Violence was not restricted to Kansas. On May 19, abolitionist senator Charles Sumner from Massachusetts gave in the Senate a fiery speech later called "The Crime Against Kansas." For two days he verbally attacked his colleagues for their support of slavery. Sumner was particularly abusive toward the aged senator Andrew P. Butler of South Carolina, sneering at him for his proslavery beliefs and making fun of his impaired speech.

On May 22, Butler's nephew, Congressman Preston S. Brooks, walked into the Senate chamber and over to Sumner's desk. "I have read your speech twice over, carefully," Brooks said softly. "It is a libel on South Carolina and Mr. Butler, who is a relative of mine." With that, he lifted up his cane and struck Sumner on the head repeatedly before the cane broke. Sumner suffered shock and apparent brain damage and did not return to his Senate seat for over three years.

Southerners applauded and showered Brooks with new canes, including one inscribed with the words, "Hit him again!" Northerners condemned the incident as yet

This 1856 cartoon shows Preston Brooks attacking Charles Sumner in the U.S. Senate chamber.

MAIN IDEA

Summarizing

E Describe Northern and Southern reactions to the incident between Brooks and Sumner.

another example of Southern brutality and antagonism toward free speech. Northerners and Southerners, it appeared, had met an impasse. E

The widening gulf between the North and the South had far-reaching implications for party politics as well. The compromises that had been tried from the time of the Wilmot Proviso until the Kansas-Nebraska Act could not satisfy either the North or the South. The tensions that resulted led to new political alliances as well as to violence. As the two sections grew further apart, the old national parties were torn apart and new political parties emerged.

SECTION 2 ASSESSMENT

1. **TERMS & NAMES** For each term or name, write a sentence explaining its significance.
   - **Fugitive Slave Act**
   - **personal liberty laws**
   - **Underground Railroad**
   - **Harriet Tubman**
   - **Harriet Beecher Stowe**
   - ***Uncle Tom's Cabin***
   - **Kansas-Nebraska Act**
   - **John Brown**
   - **Bleeding Kansas**

MAIN IDEA

2. **TAKING NOTES**
   Create a time line highlighting the major events in the growing conflict between the North and the South. Use a form similar to the one below.

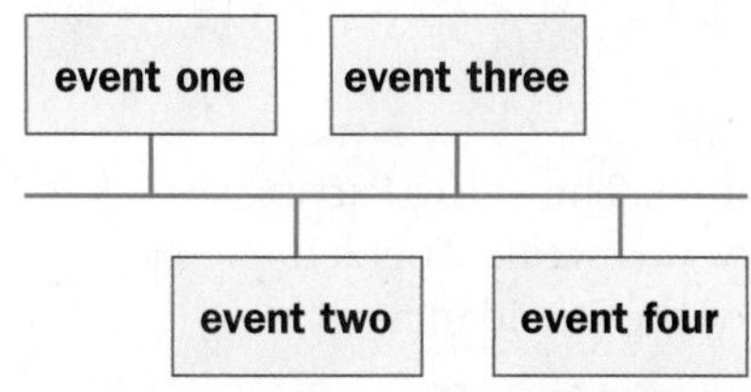

Select one event. Explain how it was representative of North–South conflict.

CRITICAL THINKING

3. **ANALYZING EFFECTS**
   Explain how *Uncle Tom's Cabin* affected the abolitionist cause. Use details from the section to support your answer.
4. **ANALYZING ISSUES**
   Why was the Kansas-Nebraska Act so controversial? Use details from the section to support your answer.
5. **SYNTHESIZING**
   Explain the concept of popular sovereignty and describe Northern and Southern reactions to it as a way of making decisions about slavery in the territories. Use evidence from the text to support your answer. **Think About:**
   - Douglas's view on continued expansion
   - Douglas and the Missouri Compromise
   - the congressional balance of power

SECTION 3

The Birth of the Republican Party

MAIN IDEA	WHY IT MATTERS NOW	Terms & Names
In the mid-1850s, the issue of slavery and other factors split political parties and led to the birth of new ones.	**The Republican and Democratic parties remain the major political forces in the United States today.**	**•Franklin Pierce •nativism •Know-Nothing Party •Free-Soil Party •Republican Party •Horace Greeley •John C. Frémont •James Buchanan**

One American's Story

hmhsocialstudies.com TAKING NOTES

Use the graphic organizer online to take notes on the growth of the Republican Party in the 1850s.

As editor of the *New York Tribune*, Horace Greeley always spoke his mind. A staunch abolitionist, Greeley consistently argued in his columns against popular sovereignty and in favor of forcible resistance to slave catchers.

In March 1855, after Greeley became frustrated with the Whig Party's shifting position on slavery, he issued a call to arms for "the friends of freedom" to "be girding up their loins for future contests" and join a new antislavery political party, the Republican Party.

A PERSONAL VOICE HORACE GREELEY

> **"[The Republicans have] the heart, the conscience and the understanding of the people with them. . . . All that is noble, all that is true, all that is pure, all that is manly, and estimable in human character, goes to swell the power of the anti-slavery party of the North. That party. . . . now embraces every Northern man who does not want to see the government converted into a huge engine for the spread of slavery over the whole continent, every man . . . opposed to . . . the passage of the Kansas-Nebraska bill."**
>
> —quoted in *The Coming of the Civil War*

▲ **Horace Greeley founded the *New York Tribune* in 1841.**

Greeley's appeal accurately reflected the changing national political scene. With the continuing tension over slavery, many Americans needed a national political voice. That voice was to be the Republican Party.

New Political Parties Emerge

By the end of 1856, the nation's political landscape had shifted. The Whig Party had split over the issue of slavery, and the Democratic Party was weak. This left the new Republican Party to move within striking distance of the presidency.

SLAVERY DIVIDES WHIGS Divisions in the Whig Party widened in 1852 when General Winfield Scott became the Whig nominee for president. Scott owed his nomination to Northern Whigs who opposed the Fugitive Slave Act and gave only lukewarm support to the Compromise of 1850. Southern Whigs, however, backed the compromise in order to appear both proslavery and pro-Union. Because of Scott's position, the Whig vote in the South fell from 50 percent in 1848, to 35 percent in 1852, handing the election to the Democratic candidate **Franklin Pierce**.

▲ The 1854 campaign banner for the Know-Nothing Party reflects its members' fear and resentment of immigrants.

In 1854 the Kansas-Nebraska Act brought about the demise of the Whigs, who once again took opposing positions on legislation that involved the issue of slavery. Unable to agree on a national platform, the Southern faction splintered as its members looked for a proslavery, pro-Union party to join, while Whigs in the North sought a political alternative.

NATIVISM One alternative was the American Party which had its roots in a secret organization known as the Order of the Star-Spangled Banner. Members of this society believed in **nativism,** the favoring of native-born Americans over immigrants. Using secret handshakes and passwords, members were told to answer questions about their activities by saying, "I know nothing." When nativists formed the American Party in 1854, it soon became better known as the **Know-Nothing Party.**

Primarily middle-class Protestants, nativists were dismayed not only at the total number of new immigrants but also at the number of Catholics among them. To nativists, the Catholic immigrants who had flooded into the country during the 1830s and 1840s were overly influenced by the Pope and could form a conspiracy to overthrow democracy.

MAIN IDEA

Analyzing Causes

A What impact did the slavery issue have on the Democratic and Whig parties?

While the Democratic Party courted immigrant voters, nativists voted for Know-Nothing candidates. The Know-Nothing Party did surprisingly well at the polls in 1854. However, like the Whig Party, the Know-Nothings split over the issue of slavery in the territories. Southern Know-Nothings looked for another alternative to the Democrats. Meanwhile, Northern Know-Nothings began to edge toward the Republican Party. A

Antislavery Parties Form

Two forerunners of the Republican Party had emerged during the 1840s. In 1844 the tiny abolitionist Liberty Party—whose purpose was to pursue the cause of abolition by passing new laws—received only a small percentage of votes in the presidential election. Yet the Liberty Party won enough votes to throw the election to Democrat James K. Polk instead of Whig candidate Henry Clay.

In 1848 the **Free-Soil Party,** which opposed the extension of slavery into the territories, nominated former Democratic president Martin Van Buren. Although the Free-Soil Party failed to win any electoral votes in 1848, it received 10 percent of the popular vote, thus sending a clear message: even if some Northerners did not favor abolition, they definitely opposed the extension of slavery into the territories.

THE FREE-SOILERS Many Northerners were Free-Soilers without being abolitionists. A number of Northern Free-Soilers supported laws prohibiting black settlement in their communities and denying blacks the right to vote. Free-Soilers objected to slavery's impact on free white workers in the wage-based labor force, upon which the North depended. Abolitionist William Lloyd Garrison considered the Free-Soil Party "a sign of discontent with things political . . . reaching for something better. . . . It is a party for keeping Free Soil and not for setting men free."

Major Political Parties 1850–1860		
Party	**Established**	**Major Platform**
Free-Soil	1848	• against extension of slavery • pro-labor
Know-Nothing	1854 (as American Party)	• anti-immigration • anti-Catholic
Whig	Organized 1834	• pro-business • divided on slavery
Republican	1854	• opposed expansion of slavery into territories
Democratic	1840 (The Democratic-Republican party adopted "Democratic Party" as official name)	• states' rights • limited government • divided on slavery

SKILLBUILDER Interpreting Charts
What issue is addressed by almost all the parties shown on the chart?

Free-Soilers detected a dangerous pattern in such events as the passage of the Fugitive Slave Act and the repeal of the Missouri Compromise. They were convinced that a conspiracy existed on the part of the "diabolical slave power" to spread slavery throughout the United States. Something or someone, according to the Free-Soilers, had to prevent this spread. **B**

MAIN IDEA

Analyzing Motives

B Why did most Free-Soilers object to slavery?

REPUBLICAN PARTY In February 1854, at a school house in Ripon, Wisconsin, some discontented Northern Whigs held a meeting with antislavery Democrats and Free-Soilers to form a new political party. On July 6, the new **Republican Party** was formally organized in Jackson, Michigan. Among its founders was **Horace Greeley.**

The Republican Party was united in opposing the Kansas-Nebraska Act and in keeping slavery out of the territories. Otherwise, it embraced a wide range of opinions. The conservative faction hoped to resurrect the Missouri Compromise. At the opposite extreme were some radical abolitionists. The Republican Party's ability to draw support from such diverse groups provided the party with the strength to win a political tug of war with the other parties.

The main competition for the Republican Party was the Know-Nothing Party. Both parties targeted the same groups of voters. By 1855 the Republicans had set up party organizations in about half of the Northern states, but they lacked a national organization. Then, in quick succession, came the fraudulent territorial election in Kansas in March 1855, and the sack of Lawrence, the Pottawatomie massacre, and the caning of Sumner in 1856. Between "Bleeding Kansas" and "Bleeding Sumner," the Republicans had the issues they needed in order to challenge the Democrats for the presidency in 1856.

The Free-Soilers' banner features John C. Frémont and calls for an end to the spread of "slave power" in the nation.

THE 1856 ELECTION The Republicans chose **John C. Frémont,** the famed "Pathfinder" who had mapped the Oregon Trail and led U.S. troops into California during the war with Mexico, as their candidate in 1856. The Know-Nothings split their allegiance, with Northerners endorsing Frémont and Southerners selecting former U.S. president Millard Fillmore. Although Fillmore had once been a Whig, for all practical purposes, the Whigs had now dissolved.

The Democrats nominated **James Buchanan** of Pennsylvania. Although he was a Northerner, most of his Washington friends were Southerners. Furthermore, as minister to Great Britain he had been out of the country during the disputes over the Kansas-Nebraska Act in 1854. Thus, he had antagonized neither the North nor the South. Buchanan was the only truly national candidate. To balance support between the North and the South, the Democrats chose John C. Breckinridge of Kentucky as Buchanan's running mate.

If Frémont had won, the South might well have seceded then and there. Judge P. J. Scruggs of Mississippi put it bluntly.

A PERSONAL VOICE P. J. SCRUGGS

"The election of Frémont would present, at once, to the people of the South, the question whether they would tamely crouch at the feet of their despoilers, or . . . openly defy their enemies, and assert their independence. In my judgment, anything short of immediate, prompt, and unhesitating secession, would be an act of servility that would seal our doom for all time to come."

—quoted in *The Coming of the Civil War*

Buchanan, however, carried the day. Although he received only 45 percent of the popular vote, he won the entire South except for Maryland. Frémont, who carried 11 of the 16 free states, came in a strong second with 33 percent, while Fillmore brought up the rear with 22 percent.

Analyzing Effects

C Why was the election of 1856 so important to the growth of the Republican Party?

The meaning was clear. First, the Democrats could win the presidency with a national candidate who could compete in the North without alienating Southerners. Second, the Know-Nothings were in decline. Third, the Republicans were a political force in the North. C

The 1856 presidential campaign had been hard-fought. However, the dissension that characterized party politics in the mid-1850s was only a pale preview of the turmoil that would divide the nation before the end of the decade.

SECTION 3 ASSESSMENT

1. **TERMS & NAMES** For each term or name, write a sentence explaining it significance.

- **Franklin Pierce**
- **nativism**
- **Know-Nothing Party**
- **Free-Soil Party**
- **Republican Party**
- **Horace Greeley**
- **John C. Frémont**
- **James Buchanan**

MAIN IDEA

2. **TAKING NOTES**
Show how various events led to the growth of the Republican Party in the 1850s. Use a chart similar to the one below.

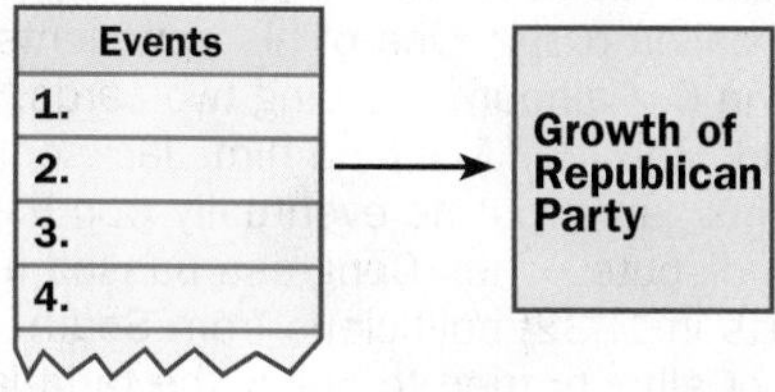

Which event was most important in the rise of the Republican Party?

CRITICAL THINKING

3. **CONTRASTING**
How did the attitudes toward slavery held by abolitionists, Free-Soilers, and Know-Nothings differ? Explain your answer. **Think About:**
   - the ultimate goal of abolitionists
   - the reason Free-Soilers objected to slavery
   - what caused the split in the Know-Nothing Party

4. **SYNTHESIZING**
How did the way in which the Republican Party was formed indicate that the party stood a good chance at success?

5. **ANALYZING ISSUES**
Why might the newly formed Republican Party have chosen John C. Frémont as their first presidential candidate in 1856?

TRACING THEMES

States' Rights

The power struggle between states and the federal government has caused controversy since the country's beginning. At its worst, the conflict resulted in the Civil War. Today, state and federal governments continue to square off on jurisdictional issues.

- In 1996, the Supreme Court ruled that congressional districts in Texas and North Carolina that had been redrawn to increase minority representation were unconstitutional.
- In 2000, the Supreme Court agreed to hear another case in the ongoing—since 1979—dispute between the federal government and the state of Alaska over who has authority to lease offshore land for oil and gas drilling.

Constitutional conflicts between states' rights and federal jurisdiction are pictured here. As you read, see how each issue was resolved.

1787

▼ CONSTITUTIONAL CONVENTION

ISSUE: The Constitution tried to resolve the original debate over states' rights versus federal authority.

At the Constitutional Convention in Philadelphia, delegates wanted to create a federal government that was stronger than the one created by the Articles of Confederation. But delegates disagreed about whether the federal government should have more power than the states. They also disagreed about whether large states should have more power than small states in the national legislature. The convention compromised—the Constitution reserves certain powers for the states, delegates other powers to the federal government, divides some powers between state and federal governments, and tries to balance the differing needs of the states through two houses of Congress.

We the People
Article. 1.

1832

NULLIFICATION ▲

ISSUE: The state of South Carolina moved to nullify, or declare void, a tariff set by Congress.

In the cartoon above, President Andrew Jackson, right, is playing a game called bragg. One of his opponents, Vice-President John C. Calhoun, is hiding two cards, "Nullification" and "Anti-Tariff," behind him. Jackson is doing poorly in this game, but he eventually won the real nullification dispute. When Congress passed high tariffs on imports in 1832, politicians from South Carolina, led by Calhoun, tried to nullify the tariff law, or declare it void. Jackson threatened to enforce the law with federal troops. Congress reduced the tariff to avoid a confrontation, and Calhoun resigned the vice-presidency.

1860

◀ SOUTH CAROLINA'S SECESSION

ISSUE: The conflict over a state's right to secede, or withdraw, from the Union led to the Civil War.

In December 1860, Southern secessionists cheered "secession" enthusiastically in front of the Mills House (left), a hotel in Charleston, South Carolina. South Carolina seceded after the election of Abraham Lincoln, whom the South perceived as anti-states' rights and antislavery. Lincoln took the position that states did not have the right to secede from the Union. In 1861, he ordered that provisions be sent to the federal troops stationed at Fort Sumter in Charleston harbor. South Carolinians fired on the fort—and the Civil War was under way. The Union's victory in the war ended the most serious challenge to federal authority: states did not have the right to secede from the Union.

1957

LITTLE ROCK CENTRAL HIGH SCHOOL ▲

ISSUE: Some Southern governors refused to obey federal desegregation mandates for schools.

In 1957, President Eisenhower mobilized federal troops in Little Rock, Arkansas, to enforce the Supreme Court's 1954 ruling in the case of *Brown* v. *Board of Education of Topeka*. This ruling made segregation in public schools illegal. The Arkansas National Guard escorted nine African-American students into Little Rock Central High School against the wishes of Governor Orval Faubus, who had tried to prevent the students from entering the school. After this incident, Faubus closed the high schools in Little Rock in 1958 and 1959, thereby avoiding desegregation.

THINKING CRITICALLY

CONNECT TO HISTORY

1. **Creating a Chart** For each incident pictured, create a chart that tells who was on each side of the issue, summarizes each position, and explains how the issue was resolved.

CONNECT TO TODAY

2. **Using Primary and Secondary Sources** Research one of the controversies in the bulleted list in the opening paragraph or another states' rights controversy of the 1990s or 2000s. Decide which side you support. Write a paragraph explaining your position on the issue.

SEE SKILLBUILDER HANDBOOK, PAGE R22.

RESEARCH WEB LINKS

Slavery and Secession

MAIN IDEA	WHY IT MATTERS NOW	Terms & Names
A series of controversial events heightened the sectional conflict that brought the nation to the brink of war.	Secession created deep divisions in American society that persist to the present time.	•Dred Scott •Roger B. Taney •Abraham Lincoln •Freeport Doctrine •Harpers Ferry •Confederacy •Jefferson Davis

One American's Story

hmhsocialstudies.com
TAKING NOTES
Use the graphic organizer online to take notes on how the major events discussed in this section sharpened the North-South conflict.

HISTORY
VIDEO
Lincoln's House Divided Speech
hmhsocialstudies.com

On June 16, 1858, the Republican Party of Illinois nominated its state chairman, Abraham Lincoln, to run for the U.S. Senate against Democratic incumbent Stephen A. Douglas. That night Lincoln launched his campaign with a ringing address to the convention. It included a biblical quotation.

A PERSONAL VOICE ABRAHAM LINCOLN

> **"'A house divided against itself cannot stand.' I believe this government cannot endure permanently half *slave* and half *free.* I do not expect the Union to be *dissolved* —I do not expect the house to fall—but I do expect it will cease to be divided. It will become *all* one thing or all the other. Either the *opponents* of slavery will arrest the further spread of it . . . or its *advocates* will push it forward, till it shall become alike lawful in *all* the States, *old* as well as *new, North* as well as *South.*"**
>
> —1858 speech

▲ **This photograph shows Lincoln in about 1858, before the Civil War took its toll.**

Lincoln was correct in that the United States could not survive for long with such a deep gulf between the North and the South—but was he right that the Union would not dissolve? With a weak president in James Buchanan and new legal questions over slavery, the United States faced the future with apprehension. Some suspected that events would lead like a trail of powder to a final explosion.

Slavery Dominates Politics

For strong leaders, slavery was a difficult issue. But it presented even more of a challenge for the indecisive President Buchanan, whose administration was plagued by slavery-related controversies. The first one arose on March 6, 1857.

***DRED SCOTT* DECISION** In 1856 an important legal question came before the Supreme Court. The case concerned **Dred Scott,** a slave from Missouri. Scott's owner had taken him north of the Missouri Compromise line in 1834. For four years they had lived in free territory in Illinois and Wisconsin. Later they returned to Missouri, where Scott's owner died. Scott then began a lawsuit to gain his freedom. He claimed that he had become a free person by living in free territory for several years.

▲ Dred Scott's lawsuit dragged on for years, and set off even more controversy over slavery.

On March 6, 1857, Supreme Court Chief Justice **Roger B. Taney** handed down the decision. (See Historic Decisions of the Supreme Court, *Dred Scott* v. *Sandford.*) The Court ruled that slaves did not have the rights of citizens. Furthermore, said the court, Dred Scott had no claim to freedom, because he had been living in Missouri, a slave state, when he began his suit. Finally, the Court ruled that the Missouri Compromise was unconstitutional. Congress could not forbid slavery in any part of the territories. Doing so would interfere with slaveholders' Fifth Amendment right to own property.

Sectional passions exploded immediately. Southerners cheered the Court's decision. Northerners were stunned. By striking down the Missouri Compromise, the Supreme Court had cleared the way for the extension of slavery. Opponents of slavery now pinned their hopes on the Republican Party. If the Republicans became strong enough, they could still keep slavery in check. (A)

MAIN IDEA

Analyzing Effects

(A) What was the significance of the *Dred Scott* decision?

THE LECOMPTON CONSTITUTION In fall 1857, the proslavery government at Lecompton, Kansas, wrote a constitution and applied for admission to the Union. Free-Soilers—who by this time outnumbered proslavery settlers in Kansas by nearly ten to one—rejected the proposed constitution because it protected the rights of slaveholders. The legislature called for a referendum in which the people could vote on the proslavery constitution. They voted against it.

At this point President Buchanan made a poor decision: he endorsed the proslavery Lecompton constitution. He owed his presidency to Southern support and believed that since Kansas contained only about 200 slaves, the Free-Soilers were overreacting.

Buchanan's endorsement provoked the wrath of Illinois Democrat Stephen A. Douglas, who did not care "whether [slavery] is voted down or voted up." What he cared about was popular sovereignty. Backed by an antislavery coalition of Republicans and Northern Democrats, Douglas persuaded Congress to authorize another referendum on the constitution. In summer 1858, voters rejected the constitution once again. Northerners hailed Douglas as a hero, Southerners scorned him as a traitor, and the two wings of the Democratic Party moved still farther apart. (B)

MAIN IDEA

Analyzing Motives

(B) Why did Buchanan support the Lecompton constitution?

Lincoln-Douglas Debates

That summer witnessed the start of one of Illinois's greatest political contests: the 1858 race for the U.S. Senate between Democratic incumbent Douglas and Republican challenger **Abraham Lincoln.** To many outsiders, it must have seemed like an uneven match. Douglas was a two-term senator with an outstanding record and a large campaign chest. Who was Lincoln?

A self-educated man with a dry wit, Lincoln was known locally as a successful lawyer and politician. Elected as a Whig to one term in Congress in 1846, he broke with his party after the passage of the Kansas-Nebraska Act in 1854 and became a Republican two years later.

LINCOLN CHALLENGES DOUGLAS As the senatorial campaign progressed, the Republican Party decided that Lincoln needed to counteract the "Little Giant's" well-known name and extensive financial resources. As a result, Lincoln challenged Douglas to a series of seven open-air debates to be held throughout Illinois on the issue of slavery in the territories. Douglas accepted the challenge, and the stage was set for some of the most celebrated debates in U.S. history.

The Lincoln-Douglas debates created quite a spectacle, partly due to the opponents' difference in height.

Lincoln and Douglas had very different speaking styles. Douglas exuded self-confidence, pacing back and forth on the stage and dramatically using his fists to pound home his points. Lincoln, on the other hand, delivered his comments solemnly, using direct and plain language.

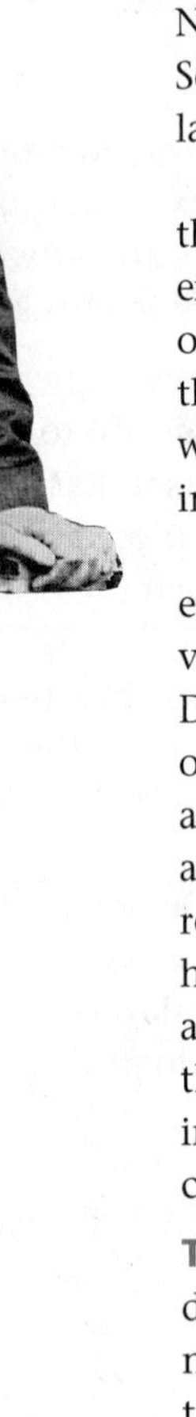

POSITIONS AND ARGUMENTS The two men's positions were simple and consistent. Douglas believed deeply in popular sovereignty, in allowing the residents of a territory to vote for or against slavery. Although he did not think that slavery was immoral, he did believe that it was a backward labor system unsuitable to prairie agriculture. The people, Douglas figured, understood this and would vote Kansas and Nebraska free. However, Lincoln, like many Free-Soilers, believed that slavery was immoral—a labor system based on greed.

The crucial difference between the two was that Douglas believed that popular sovereignty would allow slavery to pass away on its own, while Lincoln doubted that slavery would cease to spread without legislation outlawing it in the territories.

In the course of the debates, each candidate tried to distort the views of the other. Lincoln tried to make Douglas look like a defender of slavery and of the *Dred Scott* decision. In turn, Douglas accused Lincoln of being an abolitionist and an advocate of racial equality. Lincoln responded by saying, "I am not, nor ever have been, in favor of bringing about in any way the social and political equality of the white and black races." He did, however, insist that slavery was a moral, social, and political wrong that should not be allowed to spread.

THE FREEPORT DOCTRINE In their second debate, held at Freeport, Lincoln asked his opponent a crucial question. Could the settlers of a territory vote to exclude slavery before the territory became a state? Everyone knew that the *Dred Scott* decision said no—that territories could not exclude slavery. Popular sovereignty, Lincoln implied, was thus an empty phrase.

Douglas's response to Lincoln's question became later known as the **Freeport Doctrine.** Douglas contended, "Slavery cannot exist a day or an hour anywhere, unless it is supported by local police regulations." If the people of a territory were Free-Soilers, he explained, then all they had to do was elect representatives who would not enforce slave property laws. In other words, regardless of theory or the Supreme Court's ruling, people could get around the *Dred Scott* decision.

MAIN IDEA

Comparing

C Explain the similarities and differences between Lincoln's position on slavery and that of Douglas.

Douglas won the Senate seat, but his response had worsened the split between the Northern and Southern wings of the Democratic Party. As for Lincoln, his attacks on the "vast moral evil" of slavery drew national attention, and some Republicans began thinking of him as an excellent candidate for the presidency in 1860. C

POLITICAL DEBATES

In the mid-19th century, people flocked to public grandstands, where the political candidates debated the issues of the day.

When Lincoln debated Douglas, thousands of people came to listen. Each debate lasted for three hours, and listeners stood the entire time, interrupting the speakers with cheers and an occasional heckle. When the debate ended, spectators adjourned to tables of barbecued meat and ice cream. Torchlit parades ended the day.

The first televised presidential debate, in 1960, featured candidates Kennedy and Nixon. Since then, presidential candidates, including Bush and Gore (above), have made televised debating a cornerstone of presidential campaigning.

Passions Ignite

If 1858 was a year of talk, then 1859 turned out to be a year of action. Most Americans probably would have welcomed a respite from the issue of slavery. Instead, "God's angry man," John Brown, reemerged on the scene and ended all hopes of a compromise over slavery between the North and the South.

HARPERS FERRY While politicians debated the slavery issue, John Brown was studying the slave uprisings that had occurred in ancient Rome and on the French island of Haiti. He believed that the time was ripe for similar uprisings in the United States. Brown secretly obtained financial backing from several prominent Northern abolitionists. On the night of October 16, 1859, he led a band of 21 men, black and white, into **Harpers Ferry,** Virginia (now West Virginia). His aim was to seize the federal arsenal there, distribute the captured arms to slaves in the area, and start a general slave uprising.

Sixty of the town's prominent citizens were held hostage by Brown who hoped that their slaves would then join the insurrection. No slaves came forward. Instead, local troops killed eight of Brown's men. Then a detachment of U.S. Marines, commanded by Colonel Robert E. Lee, raced to Harpers Ferry, stormed the engine house where Brown and his men had barricaded themselves, killed two more of the raiders, and captured Brown. Brown was then turned over to Virginia to be tried for treason.

Historians have long debated Brown's actions. There is no doubt that he hated slavery with all his heart. However, why did he fail to tell slaves in the area about his plans beforehand? Why didn't he provide his men with enough food to last for even one day? In any case, Brown certainly hoped that his actions would arouse Northern fury and start a war for abolition.

JOHN BROWN'S HANGING On December 2, 1859, Brown was hanged for high treason in the presence of federal troops and a crowd of curious observers. Public reaction was immediate and intense. Although Lincoln and Douglas condemned Brown as a murderer, many other Northerners expressed admiration for him and for his cause. Bells tolled at the news of his execution, guns fired salutes, and huge crowds gathered to hear fiery speakers denounce the South. Some Northerners began to call Brown a martyr for the sacred cause of freedom.

History Through Art

JOHN BROWN GOING TO HIS HANGING (1942)

This scene, painted by the African-American artist Horace Pippin in 1942, shows John Brown being transported by wagon to his execution. The artist has focused our attention on the cruelty of Brown's fate.

The abolitionist is shown tied with the rope that will be used to hang him, and sitting on the coffin that will receive his body after death. Brown's dark shape is silhouetted by the large white building behind him, a structure that combines the features of both courthouse and prison.

SKILLBUILDER

Interpreting Visual Sources

1. Why do you think the African-American woman in the right-hand corner is looking away from the scene?
2. How has the artist expressed the hopelessness of the situation?

SEE SKILLBUILDER HANDBOOK, PAGE R23.

The response was equally extreme in the South, where outraged mobs assaulted whites who were suspected of holding antislavery views. Harpers Ferry terrified Southern slaveholders, who were convinced the North was plotting slave uprisings everywhere. Even longtime supporters of the Union called for secession. As one former Unionist explained, "I am willing to take the chances of . . . disunion, sooner than submit any longer to Northern insolence and Northern outrage." D

MAIN IDEA

Analyzing Effects

D Why did Harpers Ferry increase tensions between the North and the South?

Lincoln Is Elected President

Despite the tide of hostility that now flowed between North and South, the Republican Party eagerly awaited its presidential convention in May 1860. When the convention began, almost everyone believed that the party's candidate would be Senator William H. Seward of New York. However, events took a dramatic turn.

THE REPUBLICAN CONVENTION The convention took place in Chicago, which had quickly transformed itself into a convention city with more than 50 hotels and an 18,000-square-foot wooden meeting center named the Wigwam. Republicans flooded into the frontier city in such crowds that despite the preparations, many ended up sleeping on pool tables in the hotels.

The convention opened to a surging crowd of delegates, newsmen, and spectators. The 4,500-person delegate floor overflowed within minutes. To gain seating in the galleries, which were reserved for gentlemen who had come with ladies, determined single men even offered schoolgirls a quarter for their company. The first day of the convention was passed in forming committees, listening to prayers, and gossiping about politics. As events came to a close, campaign managers for the candidates retreated to their headquarters and began bargaining for delegates' votes, some working late into the night.

SEWARD AND LINCOLN Senator William H. Seward appeared to have everything one needed in order to be a successful presidential candidate: the credential of having led antislavery forces in Congress, the financial support of New York political organizations—and a desire to be the center of attention. In fact, Seward himself had little doubt that he would be nominated. Well before the voting took place, Seward drafted his senatorial resignation speech, which he planned to deliver when his nomination became official.

Seward's well-known name and his reputation may have worked against him, however. Abraham Lincoln's being relatively unknown probably won him the nomination. Unlike Seward, Lincoln had not had much chance to offend his fellow Republicans. The delegates rejected Seward and his talk of an "irrepressible conflict" between North and South. On the third ballot, they nominated Lincoln, who seemed more moderate in his views. Although Lincoln pledged to halt the further spread of slavery "as with a chain of steel," he also tried to reassure Southerners that a Republican administration would not "directly, or indirectly, interfere with their slaves, or with them, about their slaves." His reassurances fell on deaf ears. In Southern eyes, he was a "black Republican," whose election would be "the greatest evil that has ever befallen this country."

▲ **Because Lincoln was virtually unknown in the East, his first name was written incorrectly as "Abram" on this 1860 election flag.**

MAIN IDEA

Drawing Conclusions

E How did slavery affect U.S. political parties in 1860?

THE ELECTION OF 1860 Three major candidates vied for office in addition to Lincoln. The Democratic Party split over the issue of slavery. Northern Democrats backed Stephen Douglas and his doctrine of popular sovereignty. Southern Democrats backed Vice-President John C. Breckinridge of Kentucky. Former Know-Nothings and Whigs from the South, along with some moderate Northerners, organized the Constitutional Union Party, which ignored the issue of slavery altogether. They nominated John Bell of Tennessee. **E**

Analyzing *Political Cartoons*

"A POLITICAL RACE"

This cartoon depicts the major candidates in the 1860 presidential election. Three of the candidates, Bell, Breckinridge, and Douglas, are in hot pursuit of the front runner—Republican Abraham Lincoln. It was a close race. Lincoln defeated Douglas in the North. Breckinridge carried most of the South. Because the North had a higher population than the South, Lincoln won the election.

SKILLBUILDER

Analyzing Political Cartoons

1. Who, in the opinion of the artist, is the fittest man in the race?
2. How does this cartoon suggest the course of the election of 1860?

SEE SKILLBUILDER HANDBOOK, PAGE R24.

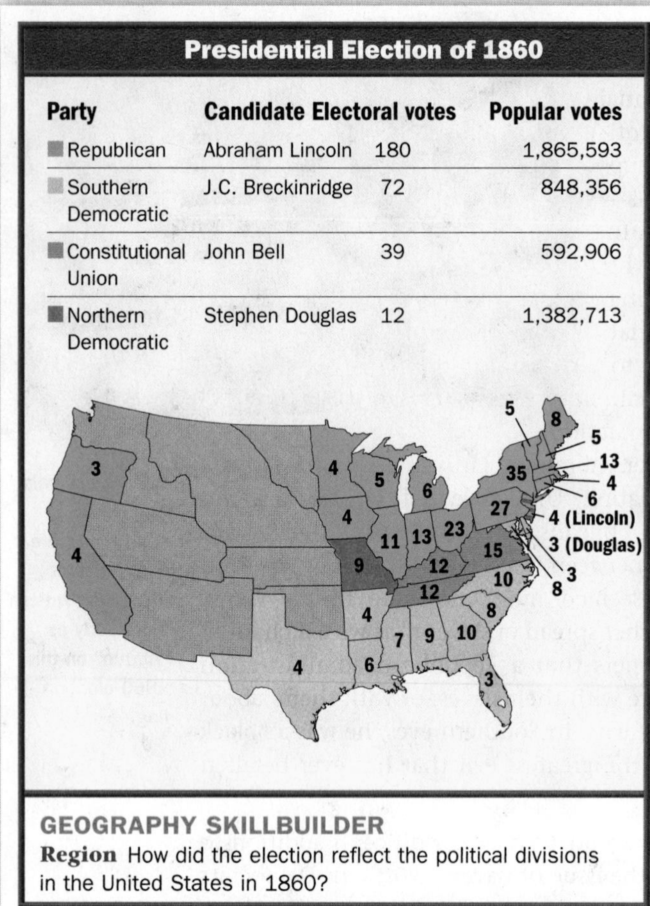

Presidential Election of 1860

Party	Candidate	Electoral votes	Popular votes
Republican	Abraham Lincoln	180	1,865,593
Southern Democratic	J.C. Breckinridge	72	848,356
Constitutional Union	John Bell	39	592,906
Northern Democratic	Stephen Douglas	12	1,382,713

GEOGRAPHY SKILLBUILDER
Region How did the election reflect the political divisions in the United States in 1860?

Lincoln emerged as the winner, but like Buchanan in the previous election, he received less than half the popular vote. In fact, although Lincoln defeated his combined opponents in the electoral vote by 180 to 123, he received no electoral votes from the South. Unlike Buchanan, Lincoln had sectional rather than national support, carrying every free state but not even appearing on the ballot in most of the slave states. The outlook for the Union was grim.

Southern Secession

Lincoln's victory convinced Southerners that they had lost their political voice in the national government. Fearful that Northern Republicans would submit the South to what noted Virginia agriculturist Edmund Ruffin called "the most complete subjection and political bondage," some Southern states decided to act. South Carolina led the way, seceding from the Union on December 20, 1860. Four days later, the news reached William Tecumseh Sherman, superintendent of the Louisiana State Seminary of Learning and Military Academy. In utter dismay, Sherman poured out his fears for the South.

A PERSONAL VOICE WILLIAM TECUMSEH SHERMAN

"This country will be drenched in blood. . . . [T]he people of the North. . . . are not going to let the country be destroyed without a mighty effort to save it. Besides, where are your men and appliances of war to contend against them? . . . You are rushing into war with one of the most powerful, ingeniously mechanical and determined people on earth—right at your doors. . . . Only in spirit and determination are you prepared for war. In all else you are totally unprepared."

—quoted in *None Died in Vain*

Even Sherman underestimated the depth and intensity of the South's commitment. For many Southern planters, the cry of "States' rights!" meant the complete independence of Southern states from federal government control. Most white Southerners also feared that an end to their entire way of life was at hand. Many were desperate for one last chance to preserve the slave labor system and saw secession as the only way. Mississippi followed South Carolina's lead and seceded on January 9, 1861. Florida seceded the next day. Within a few weeks, Alabama, Georgia, Louisiana, and Texas had also seceded. F

MAIN IDEA

Analyzing Effects

F How did Lincoln's election affect the South?

THE SHAPING OF THE CONFEDERACY On February 4, 1861, delegates from the secessionist states met in Montgomery, Alabama, where they formed the **Confederacy,** or Confederate States of America. The Confederate constitution closely resembled that of the United States. The most notable difference was that the Confederate constitution "protected and recognized" slavery in new

▲ **This 1864 playing card bears the portrait of Jefferson Davis, president of the Confederate States of America.**

territories. The new constitution also stressed that each state was to be "sovereign and independent," a provision that would hamper efforts to unify the South.

On February 9, delegates to the Confederate constitutional convention unanimously elected former senator **Jefferson Davis** of Mississippi as president and Alexander Stephens of Georgia as vice-president. Davis had made his position clear, noting that to present a show of strength to the North, the South should "offer no doubtful or divided front." At his inauguration, Davis declared, "The time for compromise has now passed." His listeners responded by singing "Farewell to the Star-Spangled Banner" and "Dixie."

THE CALM BEFORE THE STORM As the nation awaited Lincoln's inauguration in March, its citizens were confused. What would happen now? Seven slave states had seceded and formed a new nation. Eight slave states remained within the Union. Would they secede also?

President Buchanan was uncertain. He announced that secession was illegal, but that it also would be illegal for him to do anything about it. He tied his own hands, but in truth there was not much that he could have done.

One problem was that Washington, D.C. was very much a Southern city. There were secessionists in Congress and in all of the departments of the federal government, as well as in the president's cabinet. Consequently, mass resignations took place. To some people it seemed as if the federal government were melting away. One key question remained in everyone's mind: Would the North allow the South to leave the Union without a fight?

HISTORICAL SPOTLIGHT

SECESSION AND THE BORDER STATES

Four slave states—Maryland, Kentucky, Missouri, and Delaware—were undecided about secession. Lincoln believed that these states would be essential to the success of the Union if war broke out. They had thriving industries and good access to important rail and water routes. Also, bordering North and South made the four states crucial to the movement of troops and supplies. Moreover, Maryland almost surrounded Washington, D.C., the seat of government.

As president, Lincoln faced a choice: free the slaves and make abolitionists happy, or ignore slavery for the moment to avoid alienating the border states. He chose the latter, but that did not prevent violent conflicts between secessionists and Unionists in Maryland, Kentucky, and Missouri. With militia intervention, and some political maneuvering, Lincoln kept the four border states in the Union.

ASSESSMENT

1. **TERMS & NAMES** For each term or name, write a sentence explaining its significance.
   - **Dred Scott**
   - **Roger B. Taney**
   - **Abraham Lincoln**
   - **Freeport Doctrine**
   - **Harpers Ferry**
   - **Confederacy**
   - **Jefferson Davis**

MAIN IDEA

2. **TAKING NOTES**
   List six major events described in this section and explain how each one sharpened the North-South conflict.

Event	Result
1. →	
2. →	
3. →	

CRITICAL THINKING

3. **CONTRASTING**
   How did Lincoln and Douglas disagree about slavery? Which of their views were facts, and which were opinions?

4. **EVALUATING**
   If you had been voting in the presidential election of 1860, for whom would you have voted, other than Abraham Lincoln? Explain your reasoning by using specific references to the chapter.

5. **ANALYZING PRIMARY SOURCES**
   In *Dred Scott* v. *Sandford* of 1857, the Supreme Court found that:

   > **"A free negro of the African race, whose ancestors were brought to this country and sold as slaves, is not a "citizen" within the meaning of the Constitution of the United States."**

   How did the Supreme Court decision add to the tensions over slavery in the 1850s?

DRED SCOTT v. *SANDFORD* (1857)

ORIGINS OF THE CASE Dred Scott's slave master had brought him from the slave state of Missouri to live for a time in free territory and in the free state of Illinois. Eventually they returned to Missouri. Scott believed that because he had lived in free territory, he should be free. In 1854 he sued in federal court for his freedom. The court ruled against him, and he appealed to the Supreme Court.

THE RULING **The Supreme Court ruled that African Americans were not and could never be citizens. Thus, Dred Scott had no right even to file a lawsuit and remained enslaved.**

LEGAL REASONING

The Court's decision, based primarily on Chief Justice Roger Taney's written opinion, made two key findings. First, it held that because Scott was a slave, he was not a citizen and had no right to sue in a United States court.

> **"We think they [slaves] . . . are not included, and were not intended to be included, under the word 'citizens' in the Constitution, and can therefore claim none of the rights and privileges which that instrument provides for and secures to citizens of the United States."**

This could have been the end of the matter, but Taney went further. He said that by banning slavery, Congress was, in effect, taking away property. Such an action, he wrote, violated the Fifth Amendment, which guarantees the right not to be deprived of property without due process of law (such as a hearing). Thus, all congressional efforts to ban slavery in the territories were prohibited.

Justices John McLean and Benjamin Curtis strongly dissented on both points. They showed that the U.S. Constitution, state constitutions, and other laws had recognized African Americans as citizens. They also pointed to the clause in the Constitution giving Congress the power to "make all needful Rules and Regulations" to govern U.S. territories. In their view, this clause gave Congress the power to prohibit slavery in the territories.

◀ **Chief Justice Roger Taney**

LEGAL SOURCES

U.S. CONSTITUTION

U.S. CONSTITUTION, ARTICLE 4, SECTION 2 (1789)

"No Person held to Service or Labor in one State, . . . escaping into another, shall, in Consequence of any Law or Regulation therein, be discharged from such Service or Labor. . . ."

U.S. CONSTITUTION, ARTICLE 4, SECTION 3 (1789)

"The Congress shall have Power to dispose of and make all needful Rules and Regulations respecting the Territory or other Property belonging to the United States. . . ."

U.S. CONSTITUTION, FIFTH AMENDMENT (1791)

"No person shall be . . . deprived of life, liberty, or property, without due process of law. . . ."

RELATED CASES

***ABLEMAN* v. *BOOTH* (1858)**

The Court decided that the Fugitive Slave Act was constitutional and that laws passed in Northern states that prohibited the return of fugitive slaves were unconstitutional.

WHY IT MATTERED

Taney's opinion in *Dred Scott* had far-reaching consequences. Legally, the opinion greatly expanded the reach of slavery. Politically, it heightened the sectional tensions that would lead to the Civil War.

Before the Court decided *Dred Scott,* Americans widely accepted the idea that Congress and the states could limit slavery. As the dissenters argued, many previous acts of Congress had limited slavery—for example, the Northwest Ordinance had banned slavery in the Northwest Territory—and no one had claimed that those acts violated property rights.

Taney's opinion in *Dred Scott,* however, was a major change. This expansion of slaveholders' rights cast doubt on whether free states could prevent slave owners from bringing or even selling slaves into free areas.

As a result, *Dred Scott* intensified the slavery debate as no single event had before. In going beyond what was needed to settle the case before him, Taney's ruling became a political act, and threw into question the legitimacy of the Court. Further, Taney's opinion took the extreme proslavery position and installed it as the national law. It not only negated all the compromises made to date by pro- and anti-slavery forces, but it seemed to preclude any possible future compromises.

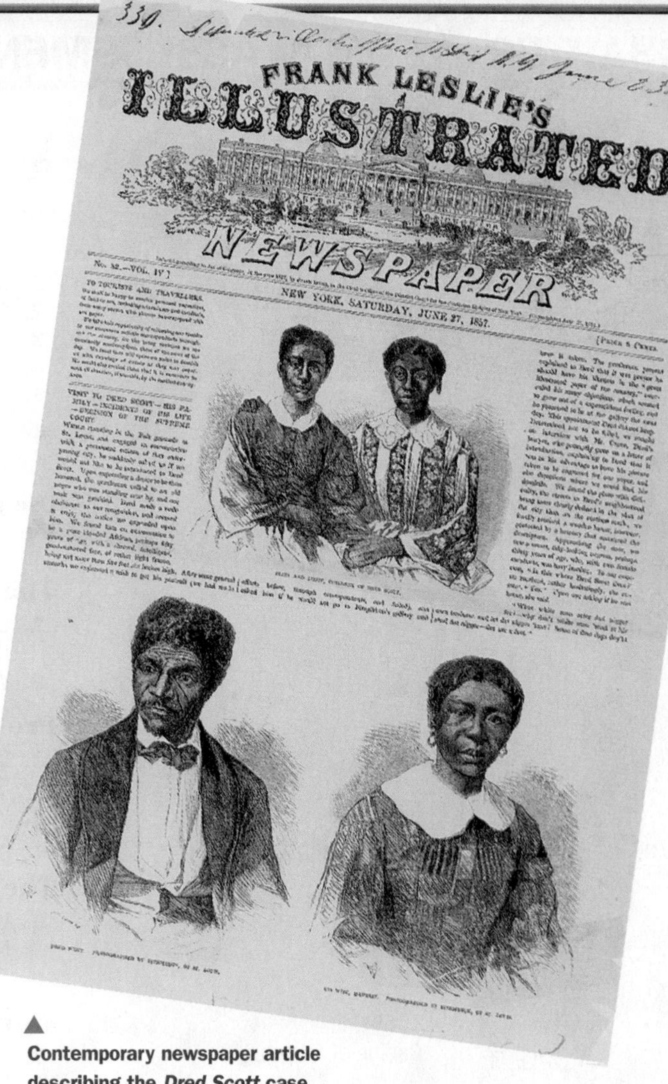
FRANK LESLIE'S ILLUSTRATED NEWSPAPER

NEW YORK, SATURDAY, JUNE 27, 1857.

Contemporary newspaper article describing the *Dred Scott* case.

HISTORICAL IMPACT

It took four years of bitter civil war to find out if Taney's opinion would stand as the law of the land. It would not. Immediately after the Civil War, the federal government moved to abolish slavery with the Thirteenth Amendment (1865) and then to extend state and national citizenship with the Fourteenth Amendment (1868) to "[a]ll persons born or naturalized in the United States." The wording of these amendments was expressly intended to nullify *Dred Scott.*

These amendments meant that *Dred Scott* would no longer be used as a precedent—an earlier ruling that can be used to justify a current one. Instead, it is now pointed to as an important lesson on the limits of the Supreme Court's power, as a key step on the road to the Civil War, and as one of the worst decisions ever made by the Supreme Court.

THINKING CRITICALLY

CONNECT TO HISTORY

1. **Developing Historical Perspective** Use the library to find commentaries on *Dred Scott* written at the time the decision was made. Read two of these commentaries and identify which section—North or South—the writer or speaker came from. Explain how each person's region shaped his or her views.

SEE SKILLBUILDER HANDBOOK, PAGE R11.

CONNECT TO TODAY

2. Visit the links for Historic Decisions of the Supreme Court to research what it means to be a citizen of the United States and what rights that citizenship extends. Research which constitutional amendments, U.S. laws, and Supreme Court decisions guarantee the rights of citizens. Prepare an oral presentation or annotated display to summarize your findings.

CHAPTER 10 ASSESSMENT

VISUAL SUMMARY

THE UNION IN PERIL

1846
Wilmot Proviso

Compromise of 1850

1854
Kansas-Nebraska Act

1856
Bleeding Kansas

1856
Caning of Sumner

1857
Dred Scott v. Sandford

1859
Attack at Harpers Ferry

Election of 1860

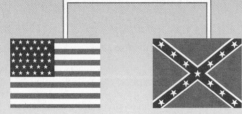

TERMS & NAMES

For each term below, write a sentence explaining its connection to the growing conflict in the 1850s.

1. secession
2. Compromise of 1850
3. popular sovereignty
4. Stephen A. Douglas
5. Fugitive Slave Act
6. Harriet Tubman
7. nativism
8. Horace Greeley
9. John Brown
10. Dred Scott

MAIN IDEAS

Use your notes and the information in the chapter to answer the following questions.

The Divisive Politics of Slavery

1. Describe the economic differences between the North and the South in the 1850s.
2. What were the major terms of the Compromise of 1850?

Protest, Resistance, and Violence

3. Discuss the impacts Harriet Tubman and Harriet Beecher Stowe had on antislavery attitudes in the North.
4. What were the basic provisions and results of the Kansas-Nebraska Act?

The Birth of the Republican Party

5. Why did the Republican Party grow as the Whig and Know-Nothing parties declined in the 1850s?
6. Summarize the results of the election of 1856.

Slavery and Secession

7. Compare and contrast Abraham Lincoln's and Stephen A. Douglas's views about slavery in the territories.
8. Why was the South so upset by Lincoln's election?

CRITICAL THINKING

1. **USING YOUR NOTES** In a chart like the one shown, explain how the following key events led to secession.

KEY EVENT	FUEL FOR SECESSION
Wilmot Proviso of 1846	
Compromise of 1850	
Kansas-Nebraska Act of 1854	
Election of 1860	

2. **DRAWING CONCLUSIONS** John Brown, Harriet Tubman, and Harriet Beecher Stowe all opposed slavery. Explain whether you consider any of these people to be heroes. Defend your viewpoint with references from the chapter.

3. **INTERPRETING MAPS** Review the Underground Railroad map. Think about the terrain and bodies of water that an escaping slave would have faced. In what ways might these physical features have helped or hindered a fugitive's progress?

STANDARDIZED TEST PRACTICE

Use the pie charts and your knowledge of U.S. history to answer question 1.

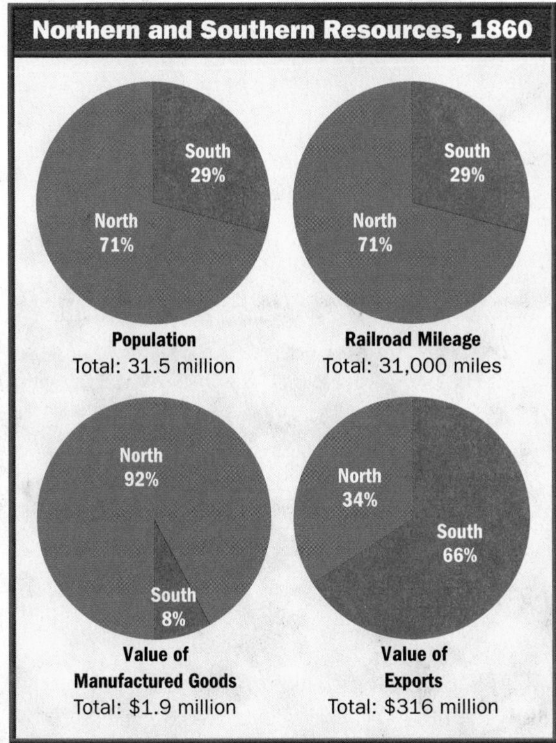

1. Which of the following statements is *not* supported by the pie charts?
   - **A** The South was at a disadvantage in population.
   - **B** The South had no advantages over the North.
   - **C** The North held an advantage in the value of manufactured goods.
   - **D** The North and South had unequal resources.

Use the quotation below and your knowledge of U.S. history to answer question 2.

> **"The State of Ohio is separated from Kentucky just by one river; on either side of it the soil is equally fertile, and the situation equally favourable, and yet everything is different. Here [on the Ohio side] a population devoured by feverish activity, trying every means to make its fortune. . . . There [on the Kentucky side] is a people which makes others work for it and shows little compassion, a people without energy, mettle or the spirit of enterprise. . . . These differences cannot be attributed to any other cause but slavery. It degrades the black population and enervates [saps the energy of] the white."**
>
> —Alexis de Tocqueville, *Journey to America*

2. Why might an abolitionist in the 1850s have been eager to support de Tocqueville's point of view?
   - **F** to publicize the virtues of Ohio
   - **G** to persuade people to settle in Kansas
   - **H** to argue that slavery was bad for slave and master
   - **J** to show that immigrants don't understand American traditions

3. The Wilmot Proviso failed to pass in the Senate because —
   - **A** Northerners controlled the Senate.
   - **B** Southerners controlled the Senate.
   - **C** California was against it.
   - **D** Mexico was in support of it.

For additional test practice, go online for:
- Diagnostic tests
- Tutorials

INTERACT WITH HISTORY

Recall the issues that you explored at the beginning of the chapter. Now that you know more about the road leading to the secession crisis, would you change any of your responses? Write a plan of action in the voice of a presidential adviser.

FOCUS ON WRITING

Imagine it is 1858. You are Abraham Lincoln preparing to debate Stephen Douglas. Write a speech arguing against popular sovereignty. In your speech, use persuasive appeals to convince Illinois voters to oppose popular sovereignty and ultimately to give you their votes in the next election.

MULTIMEDIA ACTIVITY

21ST CENTURY

Visit the links for Chapter Assessment to find out more about John Brown and the raid at Harpers Ferry. Discuss one of the following questions in a short essay.

- How was John Brown regarded by abolitionists?
- Was John Brown's plan destined to fail?

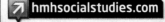

hmhsocialstudies.com

CHAPTER 11 THE CIVIL WAR

Essential Question

What were the strategies, outcomes, and legacies of the Civil War?

ALABAMA COURSE OF STUDY

14 Describe how the Civil War influenced the United States, including the Anaconda Plan and the major battles of Bull Run, Antietam, Vicksburg, and Gettysburg and Sherman's March to the Sea.

- Identifying key Northern and Southern Civil War personalities, including Abraham Lincoln, Jefferson Davis, Ulysses S. Grant, Robert E. Lee, Thomas Jonathan "Stonewall" Jackson, and William Tecumseh Sherman.
- Analyzing the impact of the division of the nation during the Civil War regarding resources, population distribution, and transportation.
- Explaining reasons for border states' remaining in the Union during the Civil War.
- Describing nonmilitary events and life during the Civil War, including the Homestead Act, the Morrill Act, Northern draft riots, the Emancipation Proclamation, and the Gettysburg Address.
- Describing the role of women in American society during the Civil War, including efforts made by Elizabeth Blackwell and Clara Barton.
- Tracing Alabama's involvement in the Civil War.

Union soldiers in the trenches at Petersburg, Virginia, in 1865

USA

1861 Inauguration of President Lincoln

1861 Fort Sumter is taken by the Confederates.

1862 North and South clash at Shiloh.

1863 President Lincoln issues the Emancipation Proclamation.

1863 The Union wins at Gettysburg and Vicksburg.

1861 | 1862 | 1863

WORLD

1861 Victor Emmanuel II proclaims an independent Kingdom of Italy.

1861 Alexander II emancipates the Russian serfs.

1862 Otto von Bismarck is named prime minister of Prussia.

1863 Shir 'Ali Khan becomes emir of Afghanistan.

Image Credits: (bkgd), Library of Congress Prints and Photographs Division [LC-USZC6-48]; (cl), The Granger Collection, New York; (cr), ©Heeb Christian/age footstock

HISTORY Lincoln: An American Icon

hmhsocialstudies.com VIDEO

INTERACT WITH HISTORY

The year is 1861. Seven Southern states have seceded from the Union over the issues of slavery and states' rights. They have formed their own government, called the Confederacy, and raised an army. In March, the Confederate army attacks and seizes Fort Sumter, a Union stronghold in South Carolina. President Lincoln responds by issuing a call for volunteers to serve in the Union army.

Explore the Issues

- Can diplomacy prevent a war between the states?
- What makes a civil war different from a foreign war?
- How might a civil war affect society and the U.S. economy?

1864 **The Confederate vessel *Hunley* makes the first successful submarine attack in history.**

1864 Abraham Lincoln is reelected.

1865 **Lee surrenders to Grant at Appomattox.**

1865 Andrew Johnson becomes president after Lincoln's assassination.

1863 | 1864 | 1865

1864 **Leo Tolstoy writes *War and Peace*.**

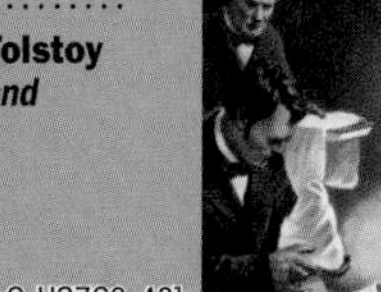

1865 **Joseph Lister pioneers antiseptic surgery.**

Image Credits: Library of Congress Prints and Photographs Division [LC-USZC6-48]; (cl), *Hunley* The Museum of the Confederacy, Richmond, Virginia. Photography by Katherine Wetzel; (bl), *Tolstoy* ©Archivo Iconografico, S.A./Corbis; (br), *Lister* ©Bettmann/Corbis

SECTION 1

The Civil War Begins

MAIN IDEA

The secession of Southern states caused the North and the South to take up arms.

WHY IT MATTERS NOW

The nation's identity was forged in part by the Civil War.

Terms & Names

- **Fort Sumter**
- **Anaconda plan**
- **Bull Run**
- **Stonewall Jackson**
- **George McClellan**
- **Ulysses S. Grant**
- **Shiloh**
- **David G. Farragut**
- ***Monitor***
- ***Merrimack***
- **Robert E. Lee**
- **Antietam**

One American's Story

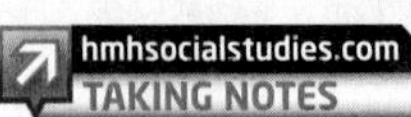

Use the graphic organizer online to take notes about early Civil War battles.

On April 18, 1861, the federal supply ship *Baltic* dropped anchor off the coast of New Jersey. Aboard was Major Robert Anderson, a 35-year army veteran on his way from Charleston, South Carolina, to New York City. That day, Anderson wrote out a report to the secretary of war, describing his most recent command.

A PERSONAL VOICE
ROBERT ANDERSON

"Having defended Fort Sumter for thirty-four hours, until the quarters were entirely burned, the main gates destroyed by fire, . . . the magazine surrounded by flames, . . . four barrels and three cartridges of powder only being available, and no provisions but pork remaining, I accepted terms of evacuation . . . and marched out of the fort . . . with colors flying and drums beating . . . and saluting my flag with fifty guns."

—quoted in *Fifty Basic Civil War Documents*

▲ **Major Anderson *(far left)* and Fort Sumter's Union troops**

The flag that Major Anderson saluted was the Stars and Stripes. After it came down, the Confederates raised their own flag, the Stars and Bars. The confederate attack on Fort Sumter signaled the start of the Civil War.

Confederates Fire on Fort Sumter

The seven southernmost states that had already seceded formed the Confederate States of America on February 4, 1861. Confederate soldiers immediately began taking over federal installations in their states—courthouses, post offices, and especially forts. By the time of Abraham Lincoln's inauguration on March 4, only two Southern forts remained in Union hands. The more important was South Carolina's **Fort Sumter**, on an island in Charleston harbor.

The day after his inauguration, the new president received an urgent dispatch from the fort's commander, Major Anderson. The Confederacy was demanding that he surrender or face an attack, and his supplies of food and ammunition would last six weeks at the most.

LINCOLN'S DILEMMA The news presented Lincoln with a dilemma. If he ordered the navy to shoot its way into Charleston harbor and reinforce Fort Sumter, he would be responsible for starting hostilities, which might prompt the slave states still in the Union to secede. If he ordered the fort evacuated, he would be treating the Confederacy as a legitimate nation. Such an action would anger the Republican Party, weaken his administration, and endanger the Union.

FIRST SHOTS Lincoln executed a clever political maneuver. He would not abandon Fort Sumter, but neither would he reinforce it. He would merely send in "food for hungry men."

Now it was Jefferson Davis who faced a dilemma. If he did nothing, he would damage the image of the Confederacy as a sovereign, independent nation. On the other hand, if he ordered an attack on Fort Sumter, he would turn peaceful secession into war. Davis chose war. At 4:30 A.M. on April 12, Confederate batteries began thundering away. Charleston's citizens watched and cheered as though it were a fireworks display. The South Carolinians bombarded the fort with more than 4,000 rounds before Anderson surrendered. (A)

MAIN IDEA

Analyzing Causes
(A) Why did Jefferson Davis choose to go to war?

VIRGINIA SECEDES News of Fort Sumter's fall united the North. When Lincoln called for 75,000 volunteers to serve for three months, the response was overwhelming. In Iowa, 20 times the state's quota rushed to enlist.

Lincoln's call for troops provoked a very different reaction in the states of the upper South. On April 17, Virginia, unwilling to fight against other Southern states, seceded—a terrible loss to the Union. Virginia was the most heavily populated state in the South and the most industrialized (with a crucial ironworks and navy yard). In May, Arkansas, Tennessee, and North Carolina followed Virginia, bringing the number of Confederate states to 11. However, the western counties of Virginia were antislavery, so they seceded from Virginia and were admitted into the Union as West Virginia in 1863. The four remaining slave states—Maryland, Delaware, Kentucky, and Missouri—remained in the Union, although many of the citizens in those states fought for the Confederacy.

Most Union troops saw the war as a struggle to preserve the Union. ▼

Most Confederate soldiers fought to protect the South from Northern aggression. ▼

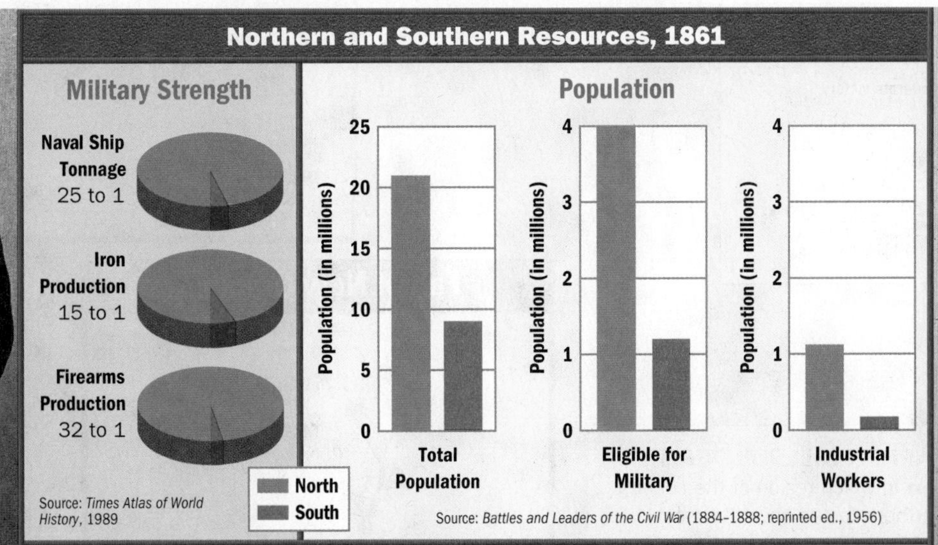

SKILLBUILDER Interpreting Graphs

1. Which side—North or South—had the advantage in terms of industrial production?
2. What do the overall data suggest about the eventual outcome of the war?

Americans Expect a Short War

Northerners and Confederates alike expected a short, glorious war. Soldiers left for the front with bands playing and crowds cheering. Both sides felt that right was on their side.

UNION AND CONFEDERATE STRATEGIES In reality the two sides were unevenly matched. The Union enjoyed enormous advantages in resources over the South—more fighting power, more factories, greater food production, and a more extensive railroad system. In addition, Lincoln proved to be a decisive yet patient leader, skillful at balancing political factions.

> *"The die was cast; war was declared . . . and we were all afraid it would be over and we [would] not be in the fight."*
>
> SAM WATKINS, CONFEDERATE SOLDIER

The Confederacy likewise enjoyed some advantages, notably "King Cotton" (and the profits it earned on the world market), first-rate generals, a strong military tradition, and soldiers who were highly motivated because they were defending their homeland. However, the South had a tradition of local and limited government, and there was resistance to the centralization of government necessary to run a war. Several Southern governors were so obstinate in their assertion of states' rights that they refused to cooperate with the Confederate government. **B**

> **MAIN IDEA**
>
> **Contrasting**
>
> **B** Contrast the strengths of the North and the South.

The two sides pursued different military strategies. The Union, which had to conquer the South to win, devised a three-part plan: (1) the Union navy would blockade Southern ports, so they could neither export cotton nor import much-needed manufactured goods, (2) Union riverboats and armies would move down the Mississippi River and split the Confederacy in two, and (3) Union armies would capture the Confederate capital at Richmond, Virginia.

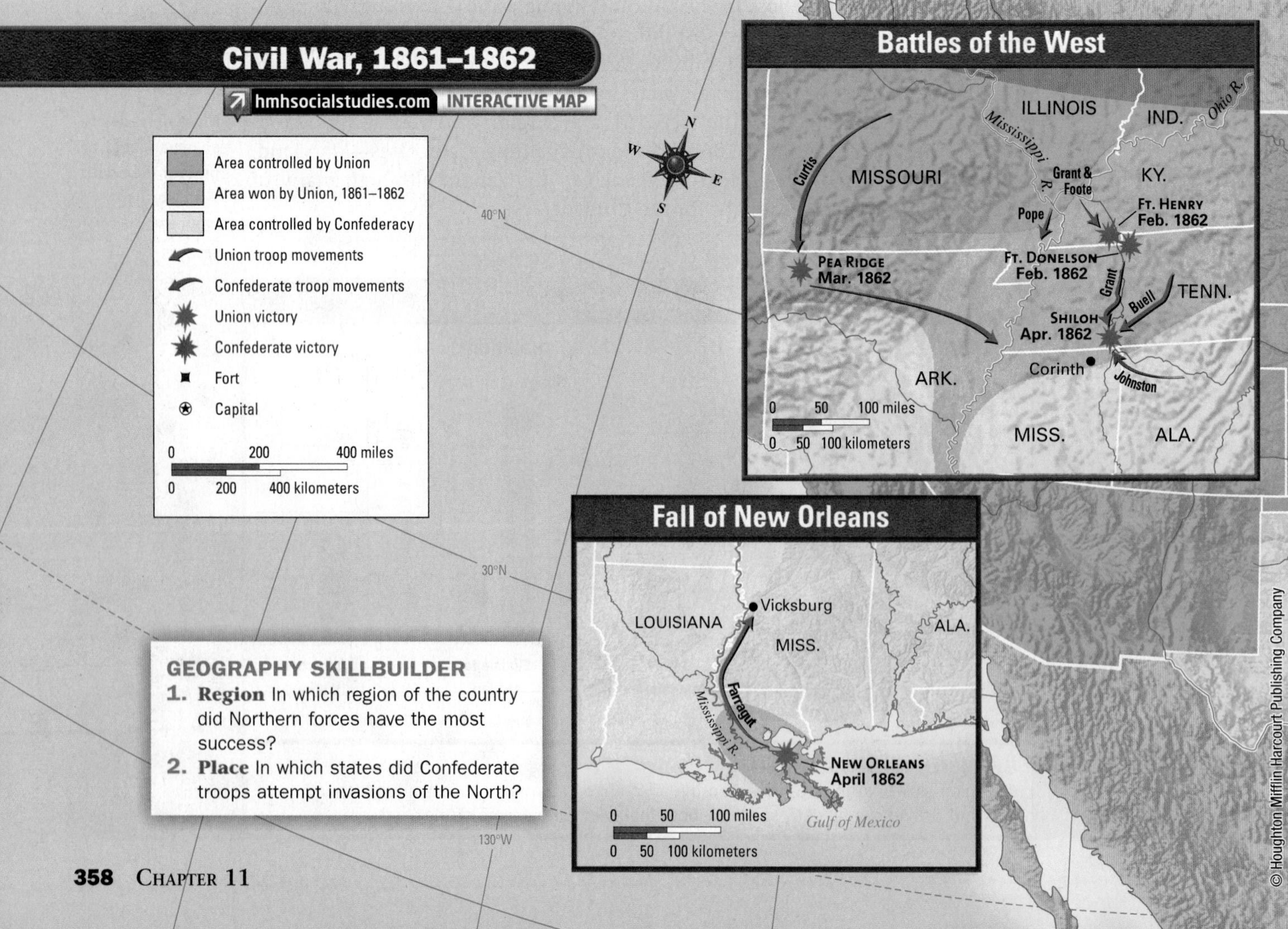

GEOGRAPHY SKILLBUILDER

1. **Region** In which region of the country did Northern forces have the most success?
2. **Place** In which states did Confederate troops attempt invasions of the North?

Northern newspapers dubbed the strategy the **Anaconda plan,** after a snake that suffocates its victims in its coils. Because the Confederacy's goal was its own survival as a nation, its strategy was mostly defensive. However, Southern leaders encouraged their generals to attack—and even to invade the North—if the opportunity arose.

BULL RUN The first major bloodshed occurred on July 21, about three months after Fort Sumter fell. An army of 30,000 inexperienced Union soldiers on its way toward the Confederate capital at Richmond, only 100 miles from Washington, D.C., came upon an equally inexperienced Confederate army encamped near the little creek of **Bull Run,** just 25 miles from the Union capital. Lincoln commanded General Irvin McDowell to attack, noting, "You are green, it is true, but they are green also."

The battle was a seesaw affair. In the morning the Union army gained the upper hand, but the Confederates held firm, inspired by General Thomas J. Jackson. "There is Jackson standing like a stone wall!" another general shouted, originating the nickname **Stonewall Jackson.** In the afternoon Confederate reinforcements arrived and turned the tide of battle into the first victory for the South. The routed Union troops began a panicky retreat to the capital.

HISTORICAL SPOTLIGHT

PICNIC AT BULL RUN

Before the First Battle of Bull Run, the inexperienced soldiers weren't the only ones who expected the war to be a "picnic." In Washington, ladies and gentlemen put on their best clothes and mounted their carriages. Carrying baskets of food and iced champagne, they rode out to observe the first encounter of the war.

The battle did not turn out to be the entertainment viewers expected. When the Confederates forced the Union to retreat, the Northerners were blocked by the carriages of the panicking civilians. After that disaster, no one in the North predicted that the war would be over after just one skirmish.

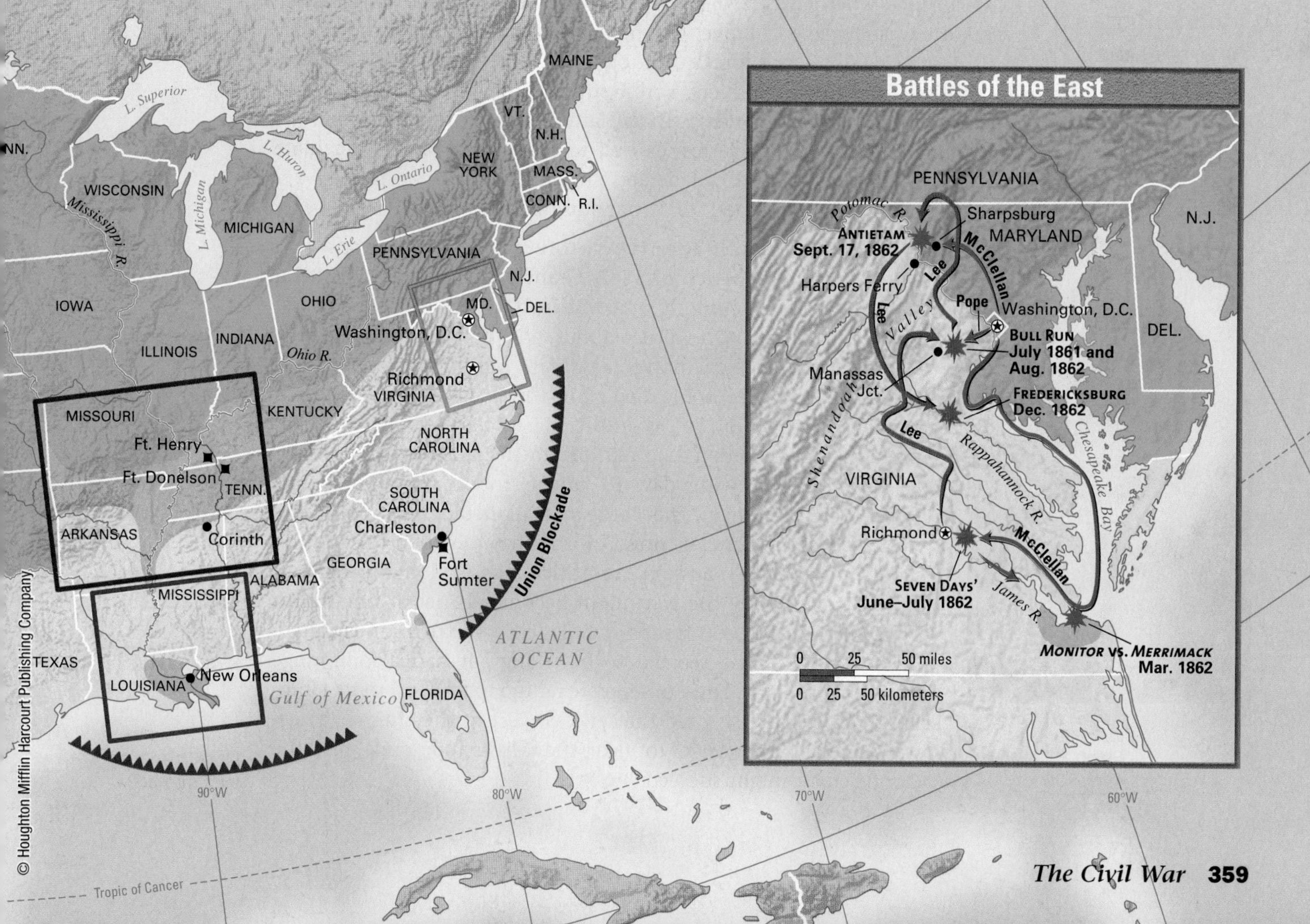

A newspaper reporter described the chaos at the scene.

A Personal Voice

"I saw officers . . . —majors and colonels who had deserted their commands—pass me galloping as if for dear life. . . . For three miles, hosts of Federal troops . . . all mingled in one disorderly rout. Wounded men lying along the banks . . . appealed with raised hands to those who rode horses, begging to be lifted behind, but few regarded such petitions."

—correspondent, New York *World*, July 21, 1861

Fortunately for the Union, the Confederates were too exhausted and disorganized to attack Washington. Still, Confederate morale soared. Bull Run "has secured our independence," declared a Georgia secessionist, and many Southern soldiers, confident that the war was over, left the army and went home. C

MAIN IDEA

Analyzing Effects

C How did Southerners react to the outcome of Bull Run?

Union Armies in the West

Lincoln responded to the defeat at Bull Run by calling for the enlistment of 500,000 men to serve for three years instead of three months. Three days later, he called for an additional 500,000 men. He also appointed General **George McClellan** to lead this new Union army, encamped near Washington. While McClellan drilled his men—soon to be known as the Army of the Potomac—the Union forces in the West began the fight for control of the Mississippi.

"No terms except unconditional and immediate surrender . . ."

ULYSSES S. GRANT

FORTS HENRY AND DONELSON In February 1862 a Union army invaded western Tennessee. At its head was General **Ulysses S. Grant,** a rumpled West Point graduate who had failed at everything he had tried in civilian life—whether as farmer, bill collector, real estate agent, or store clerk. He was, however, a brave, tough, and decisive military commander.

In just 11 days, Grant's forces captured two Confederate forts that held strategic positions on important rivers, Fort Henry on the Tennessee River and Fort Donelson on the Cumberland River. In the latter victory, Grant informed the Southern commander that "no terms except unconditional and immediate surrender can be accepted." The Confederates surrendered and, from then on, people said that Grant's initials stood for "Unconditional Surrender" Grant.

▲ Grant, at Shiloh in 1862

SHILOH One month after the victories at Fort Henry and Fort Donelson, in late March of 1862, Grant gathered his troops near a small Tennessee church named **Shiloh,** which was close to the Mississippi border. On April 6 thousands of yelling Confederate soldiers surprised the Union forces. Many Union troops were shot while making coffee; some died while they were still lying in their blankets. With Union forces on the edge of disaster, Grant reorganized his troops, ordered up reinforcements, and counterattacked at dawn the following day. By midafternoon the Confederate forces were in retreat. The Battle of Shiloh taught both sides a strategic lesson. Generals now realized that they had to send out scouts, dig trenches, and build fortifications. Shiloh also demonstrated how bloody the war might become, as nearly one-fourth of the battle's 100,000 troops were killed, wounded, or captured. Although the battle seemed to be a draw, it had a long-range impact on the war. The Confederate failure to hold on to its Ohio-Kentucky frontier showed that at least part of the Union's three-way strategy, the drive to take the Mississippi and split the Confederacy, might succeed. D

MAIN IDEA

Summarizing

D What did the battle of Shiloh show about the future course of the Civil War?

FARRAGUT ON THE LOWER MISSISSIPPI As Grant pushed toward the Mississippi River, a Union fleet of about 40 ships approached the river's mouth in Louisiana. Its commander was sixty-year-old **David G. Farragut;** its assignment, to seize New Orleans, the Confederacy's largest city and busiest port.

On April 24, Farragut ran his fleet past two Confederate forts in spite of booming enemy guns and fire rafts heaped with burning pitch. Five days later, the U.S. flag flew over New Orleans. During the next two months, Farragut took control of Baton Rouge and Natchez. If the Union captured all the major cities along the lower Mississippi, then Texas, Louisiana, Arkansas, and Tennessee would be cut off. Only Port Hudson, Louisiana, and Vicksburg, Mississippi, perched high on a bluff above the river, still stood in the way.

A Revolution in Warfare

Instrumental in the successes of Grant and Farragut in the West was a new type of war machine: the ironclad ship. This and other advances in technology changed military strategy and contributed to the war's high casualty rate.

IRONCLADS The ironclad ship could splinter wooden ships, withstand cannon fire, and resist burning. Grant used four ironclad ships when he captured Forts Henry and Donelson. On March 9, 1862, two ironclads, the North's ***Monitor*** and the South's ***Merrimack*** (renamed by the South as the *Virginia*) fought an historic duel.

A Union steam frigate, the *Merrimack*, had sunk off the coast of Virginia in 1861. The Confederates recovered the ship, and Confederate secretary of the navy Stephen R. Mallory put engineers to work plating it with iron. When Union secretary of the navy Gideon Welles heard of this development, he was determined to respond in kind. Naval engineer John Ericsson designed a ship, the *Monitor*, that resembled a "gigantic cheese box" on an "immense shingle," with two guns mounted on a revolving turret. On March 8, 1862, the *Merrimack* attacked three wooden Union warships, sinking the first, burning the second, and driving the third aground. The *Monitor* arrived and, the following day, engaged the Confederate vessel. Although the battle was a draw, the era of wooden fighting ships was over. (E)

MAIN IDEA

Evaluating

(E) What advantages did ironclad ships have over wooden ships?

NEW WEAPONS Even more deadly than the development of ironclad ships was the invention of the rifle and the minié ball. Rifles were more accurate than old-fashioned muskets, and soldiers could load rifles more quickly and therefore fire more rounds during battle. The minié ball was a soft lead bullet that was more destructive than earlier bullets. Troops in the Civil War also used primitive hand grenades and land mines.

An engagement between the *Monitor* and the *Merrimack*, March, 9, 1862, painted by J. G. Tanner

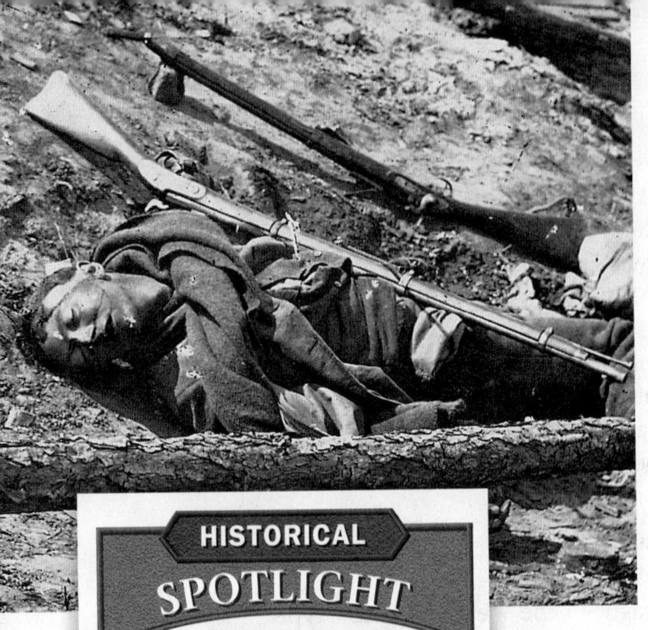

The new technology gradually changed military strategy. Because the rifle and the minié could kill far more people than older weapons, soldiers fighting from inside trenches or behind barricades had a great advantage in mass infantry attacks. (F)

MAIN IDEA

Analyzing Effects
(F) How did technology affect military strategy during the Civil War?

The War for the Capitals

As the campaign in the west progressed and the Union navy tightened its blockade of Southern ports, the third part of the North's three-part strategy—the plan to capture the Confederate capital at Richmond—faltered. One of the problems was General McClellan.

Although he was an excellent administrator and popular with his troops, McClellan was extremely cautious. After five full months of training an army of 120,000 men, he insisted that he could not move against Richmond until he had 270,000 men. He complained that there were only two bridges across the Potomac, not enough for an orderly retreat should the Confederates repulse the Federals. Northern newspapers began to mock his daily bulletins of "All quiet on the Potomac," and even the patient Lincoln commented that he would like to "borrow McClellan's army if the general himself was not going to use it." (G)

MAIN IDEA

Contrasting
(G) Contrast Grant and McClellan as generals.

HISTORICAL SPOTLIGHT

BOYS IN WAR

Both the Union and Confederate armies had soldiers who were under 18 years of age. Union soldier Arthur MacArthur (father of World War II hero Douglas MacArthur) became a colonel when he was only 19.

Examination of some Confederate recruiting lists for 1861–1862 reveals that approximately 5 percent were 17 or younger—with some as young as 13. The percentage of boys in the Union army was lower, perhaps 1.5 percent. These figures, however, do not count the great number of boys who ran away to follow each army without officially enlisting. The young man pictured above was killed at Petersburg, Virginia, shortly before the end of the war.

"ON TO RICHMOND" After dawdling all winter, McClellan finally got under way in the spring of 1862. He transported the Army of the Potomac slowly toward the Confederate capital. On the way he encountered a Confederate army commanded by General Joseph E. Johnston. After a series of battles, Johnston was wounded, and command of the army passed to **Robert E. Lee.**

Lee was very different from McClellan—modest rather than vain, and willing to go beyond military textbooks in his tactics. He had opposed secession. However, he declined an offer to head the Union army and cast his lot with his beloved state of Virginia.

Determined to save Richmond, Lee moved against McClellan in a series of battles known collectively as the Seven Days' Battles, fought from June 25 to July 1, 1862. Although the Confederates had fewer soldiers and suffered higher casualties, Lee's determination and unorthodox tactics so unnerved McClellan that he backed away from Richmond and headed down the peninsula to the sea.

ANTIETAM Now Lee moved against the enemy's capital. On August 29 and 30, his troops won a resounding victory at the Second Battle of Bull Run. A few days later, they crossed the Potomac into the Union state of Maryland. A resident of one Potomac River town described the starving Confederate troops.

A PERSONAL VOICE MARY BEDINGER MITCHELL

"All day they crowded to the doors of our houses, with always the same drawling complaint: 'I've been a-marchin' and a-fightin' for six weeks stiddy, and I ain't had n-a-r-thin' to eat 'cept green apples an' green cawn, an' I wish you'd please to gimme a bite to eat.' . . . That they could march or fight at all seemed incredible."

—quoted in *Battle Cry of Freedom*

At this point McClellan had a tremendous stroke of luck. A Union corporal, exploring a meadow where the Confederates had camped, found a copy of Lee's army orders wrapped around a bunch of cigars! The plan revealed that Lee's and Stonewall Jackson's armies were separated for the moment.

For once McClellan acted aggressively and ordered his men forward after Lee. The two armies fought on September 17 beside a sluggish creek called the **Antietam** (ăn-tē′təm). The clash proved to be the bloodiest single-day battle in American history. Casualties totaled more than 26,000, as many as in the War of 1812 and the war with Mexico combined. Instead of pursuing the battered Confederate army and possibly ending the Civil War, however, McClellan, cautious as always, did nothing. Though the battle itself was a standoff, the South, which had lost a quarter of its men, retreated the next day across the Potomac into Virginia.

▲ Lincoln and McClellan confer at Antietam in 1862.

On November 7, 1862, Lincoln fired McClellan. This solved one problem by getting rid of the general whom Lincoln characterized as having "the slows." However, the president would soon face a diplomatic conflict with Britain and increased pressure from abolitionists.

SECTION 1 ASSESSMENT

1. **TERMS & NAMES** For each term or name, write a sentence explaining its significance.
   - **Fort Sumter**
   - **Anaconda plan**
   - **Bull Run**
   - **Stonewall Jackson**
   - **George McClellan**
   - **Ulysses S. Grant**
   - **Shiloh**
   - **David G. Farragut**
   - ***Monitor***
   - ***Merrimack***
   - **Robert E. Lee**
   - **Antietam**

MAIN IDEA

2. **TAKING NOTES**
   For each month listed below, create a newspaper headline summarizing a key Civil War battle that occurred. Write your headlines in a chart like the one shown.

1861	
Month	**Headline**
• **April**	
• **July**	
1862	
Month	**Headline**
• **February**	
• **April**	
• **September**	

CRITICAL THINKING

3. **HYPOTHESIZING**
   What if Virginia had not seceded from the Union in 1861? Speculate on how this might have affected the course of the war. Support your answer with examples. **Think About:**
   - Virginia's influence on other Southern states
   - Virginia's location and its human and material resources
   - how the North's military strategy might have been different

4. **DRAWING CONCLUSIONS**
   What do you think were General McClellan's major tactical errors? Support your response with details from the text.

5. **EVALUATING DECISIONS**
   Do you think Lincoln's decision to fire McClellan was a good one? Why or why not?

SECTION 2

The Politics of War

MAIN IDEA	WHY IT MATTERS NOW	Terms & Names
By issuing the Emancipation Proclamation, President Lincoln made slavery the focus of the war.	**The Proclamation was a first step toward improving the status of African Americans.**	**• Emancipation Proclamation • habeas corpus • Copperhead • conscription**

One American's Story

hmhsocialstudies.com
TAKING NOTES

Use the graphic organizer online to take notes about political issues during the Civil War.

Shortly after the Civil War began, William Yancey of Alabama and two other Confederate diplomats asked Britain—a major importer of Southern cotton—to formally recognize the Confederacy as an independent nation. The British Secretary of State for Foreign Affairs met with them twice, but in May 1861, Britain announced its neutrality. Insulted, Yancey returned home and told his fellow Southerners not to hope for British aid.

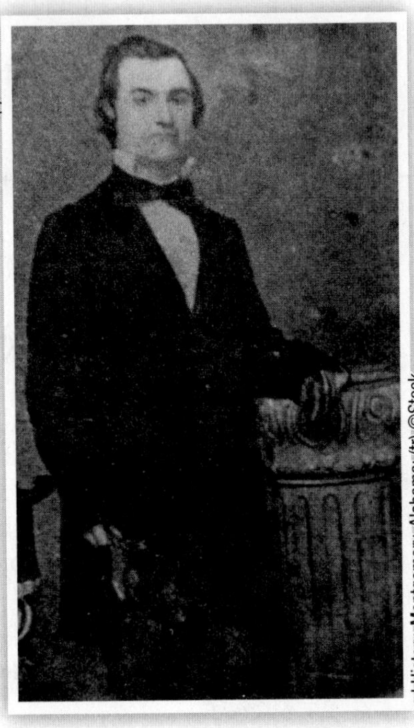

▲ William Yancey, 1851

A PERSONAL VOICE WILLIAM YANCEY

> **"You have no friends in Europe. . . . The sentiment of Europe is anti-slavery, and that portion of public opinion which forms, and is represented by, the government of Great Britain, is abolition. They will never recognize our independence until our conquering sword hangs dripping over the prostrate heads of the North. . . . It is an error to say that 'Cotton is King.' It is not. It is a great and influential factor in commerce, but not its dictator."**
>
> —quoted in *The Civil War: A Narrative*

In spite of Yancey's words, many Southerners continued to hope that economic necessity would force Britain to come to their aid. Meanwhile, abolitionists waged a public opinion war against slavery, not only in Europe, but in the North.

Britain Remains Neutral

A number of economic factors made Britain no longer dependent on Southern cotton. Not only had Britain accumulated a huge cotton inventory just before the outbreak of war, it also found new sources of cotton in Egypt and India. Moreover, when Europe's wheat crop failed, Northern wheat and corn replaced cotton as an essential import. As one magazine put it, "Old King Cotton's dead and buried." Britain decided that neutrality was the best policy—at least for a while.

THE TRENT AFFAIR In the fall of 1861, an incident occurred to test that neutrality. The Confederate government sent two diplomats, James Mason and John Slidell, in a second attempt to gain support from Britain and France. The two men traveled aboard a British merchant ship, the *Trent*. Captain Charles Wilkes of the American warship *San Jacinto* stopped the *Trent* and arrested the two men. The British threatened war against the Union and dispatched 8,000 troops to Canada. Aware of the need to fight just "one war at a time," Lincoln freed the two prisoners, publicly claiming that Wilkes had acted without orders. Britain was as relieved as the United States was to find a peaceful way out of the crisis.

The first page of Lincoln's handwritten copy of the Emancipation Proclamation ▼

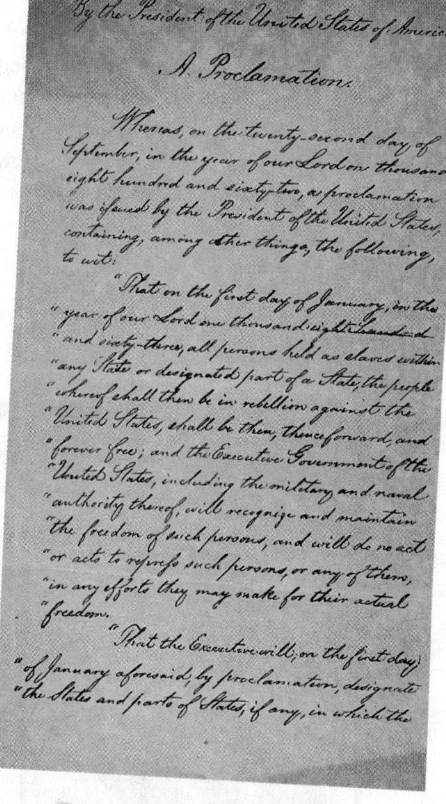
By the President of the United States of America:

A Proclamation.

Whereas, on the twenty-second day of September, in the year of our Lord one thousand eight hundred and sixty-two, a proclamation was issued by the President of the United States, containing, among other things, the following, to wit:

"That on the first day of January, in the "year of our Lord one thousand eight hundred "and sixty-three, all persons held as slaves within "any State or designated part of a State, the people "whereof shall then be in rebellion against the "United States, shall be then, thenceforward, and "forever free; and the Executive Government of the "United States, including the military and naval "authority thereof, will recognize and maintain "the freedom of such persons, and will do no act "or acts to repress such persons, or any of them, "in any efforts they may make for their actual "freedom.

"That the Executive will, on the first day "of January aforesaid, by proclamation, designate "the States and parts of States, if any, in which the

Proclaiming Emancipation

As the South struggled in vain to gain foreign recognition, abolitionist feeling grew in the North. Some Northerners believed that just winning the war would not be enough if the issue of slavery was not permanently settled.

LINCOLN'S VIEW OF SLAVERY Although Lincoln disliked slavery, he did not believe that the federal government had the power to abolish it where it already existed. When Horace Greeley urged him in 1862 to transform the war into an abolitionist crusade, Lincoln replied that although it was his personal wish that all men could be free, his official duty was different: "My paramount object in this struggle is to save the Union, and is not either to save or destroy Slavery."

As the war progressed, however, Lincoln did find a way to use his constitutional war powers to end slavery. Slave labor built fortifications and grew food for the Confederacy. As commander in chief, Lincoln decided that, just as he could order the Union army to seize Confederate supplies, he could also authorize the army to emancipate slaves.

Emancipation offered a strategic benefit. The abolitionist movement was strong in Britain, and emancipation would discourage Britain from supporting the Confederacy. Emancipation was not just a moral issue; it became a weapon of war. (A)

MAIN IDEA

Summarizing

(A) In what way was the Emancipation Proclamation a part of Lincoln's military strategy?

EMANCIPATION PROCLAMATION On January 1, 1863, Lincoln issued his **Emancipation Proclamation**. The following portion captured national attention.

from THE EMANCIPATION PROCLAMATION ABRAHAM LINCOLN

"All persons held as slaves within any State or designated part of a State the people whereof shall then be in rebellion against the United States, shall be then, thenceforward, and forever free. . . . And upon this act, sincerely believed to be an act of justice, warranted by the Constitution upon military necessity, I invoke the considerate judgment of mankind, and the gracious favor of Almighty God."

Lincoln presents the Emancipation Proclamation to his cabinet, 1862. ▼

The Proclamation did not free any slaves immediately because it applied only to areas behind Confederate lines, outside Union control. Since the Proclamation was a military action aimed at the states in rebellion, it did not apply to Southern territory already occupied by Union troops nor to the slave states that had not seceded.

REACTIONS TO THE PROCLAMATION Although the Proclamation did not have much practical effect, it had immense symbolic importance. For many, the Proclamation gave the war a high moral purpose by turning the struggle into a fight to free the slaves. In Washington, D.C., the Reverend Henry M. Turner, a free-born African American, watched the capital's inhabitants receive the news of emancipation.

A PERSONAL VOICE HENRY M. TURNER

> **"Men squealed, women fainted, dogs barked, white and colored people shook hands, songs were sung, and by this time cannons began to fire at the navy yard. . . . Great processions of colored and white men marched to and fro and passed in front of the White House. . . . The President came to the window . . . and thousands told him, if he would come out of that palace, they would hug him to death."**
>
> —quoted in *Voices from the Civil War*

VIDEO
Emancipation Proclamation

hmhsocialstudies.com

Free blacks also welcomed the section of the Proclamation that allowed them to enlist in the Union army. Even though many had volunteered at the beginning of the war, the regular army had refused to take them. Now they could fight and help put an end to slavery.

Not everyone in the North approved of the Emancipation Proclamation, however. The Democrats claimed that it would only prolong the war by antagonizing the South. Many Union soldiers accepted it grudgingly, saying they had no love for abolitionists or African Americans, but they would support emancipation if that was what it took to reunify the nation.

Confederates reacted to the Proclamation with outrage. Jefferson Davis called it the "most execrable [hateful] measure recorded in the history of guilty man." As Northern Democrats had predicted, the Proclamation had made the Confederacy more determined than ever to fight to preserve its way of life.

After the Emancipation Proclamation, compromise was no longer an option. The Confederacy knew that if it lost, its slave-holding society would perish, and the Union knew that it could win only by completely defeating the Confederacy. From January 1863 on, it was a fight to the death. B

KEY PLAYERS

ABRAHAM LINCOLN
1809–1865

Abraham Lincoln was born to illiterate parents, and once said that in his boyhood there was "absolutely nothing to excite ambition for education." Yet he hungered for knowledge.

He educated himself and, after working as rail-splitter, storekeeper, and surveyor, he taught himself law. This led to a career in politics—and eventually to the White House. In Europe at that time, people were more or less fixed in the station into which they had been born. In the United States, Lincoln was free to achieve whatever he could. Small wonder that he fought to preserve the nation he described as "the last best hope of earth."

JEFFERSON DAVIS
1808–1889

Jefferson Davis, who was named after Thomas Jefferson, was born in Kentucky and grew up in Mississippi. After graduating from West Point, he served in the army and then became a planter. He was elected to the U.S. Senate in 1846 and again in 1856, resigning when Mississippi seceded.

His election as president of the Confederacy dismayed him. As his wife Varina wrote, "I thought his genius was military, but as a party manager he would not succeed."

Varina was right. Davis had poor relations with many Confederate leaders, causing them to put their states' welfare above the Confederacy's.

MAIN IDEA

Analyzing Effects

B What effects did the Emancipation Proclamation have on the war?

Both Sides Face Political Problems

Neither side in the Civil War was completely unified. There were Confederate sympathizers in the North, and Union sympathizers in the South. Such divided loyalties created two problems: How should the respective governments handle their critics? How could they ensure a steady supply of fighting men for their armies?

DEALING WITH DISSENT Lincoln dealt forcefully with disloyalty. For example, when a Baltimore crowd attacked a Union regiment a week after Fort Sumter, Lincoln sent federal troops to Maryland. He also suspended in that state the writ of **habeas corpus,** a court order that requires authorities to bring a person held in jail before the court to determine why he or she is being jailed. Lincoln used this same strategy later in the war to deal with dissent in other states. As a result, more than 13,000 suspected Confederate sympathizers in the Union were arrested and held without trial, although most were quickly released. The president also seized telegraph offices to make sure no one used the wires for subversion. When Supreme Court Chief Justice Roger Taney declared that Lincoln had gone beyond his constitutional powers, the president ignored his ruling.

Background
A **copperhead** is a poisonous snake with natural camouflage.

Those arrested included **Copperheads,** or Northern Democrats who advocated peace with the South. Ohio congressman Clement Vallandigham was the most famous Copperhead. Vallandigham was tried and convicted by a military court for urging Union soldiers to desert and for advocating an armistice.

Jefferson Davis at first denounced Lincoln's suspension of civil liberties. Later, however, Davis found it necessary to follow the Union president's example. In 1862, he suspended habeas corpus in the Confederacy.

Lincoln's action in dramatically expanding presidential powers to meet the crises of wartime set a precedent in U.S. history. Since then, some presidents have cited war or "national security" as a reason to expand the powers of the executive branch of government. (C)

MAIN IDEA

Evaluating Leadership
(C) What actions did Lincoln take to deal with dissent?

CONSCRIPTION Although both armies originally relied on volunteers, it didn't take long before heavy casualties and widespread desertions led to **conscription,** a draft that would force certain members of the population to serve in the army. The Confederacy passed a draft law in 1862, and the Union followed suit in 1863. Both laws ran into trouble.

The Confederate law drafted all able-bodied white men between the ages of 18 and 35. (In 1864, as the Confederacy suffered more losses, the limits changed to 17 and 50.) However, those who could afford to were allowed to hire substitutes to serve in their places. The law also exempted planters who owned 20 or more slaves. Poor Confederates howled that it was a "rich man's war but a poor man's fight." In spite of these protests, almost 90 percent of eligible Southern men served in the Confederate army.

The Union law drafted white men between 20 and 45 for three years, although it, too, allowed draftees to hire substitutes. It also provided for commutation, or paying a $300 fee to avoid conscription altogether. In the end, only 46,000 draftees actually went into the army. Ninety-two percent of the approximately 2 million soldiers who served in the Union army were volunteers—180,000 of them African-American.

Vocabulary
commutation: the substitution of one kind of payment for another

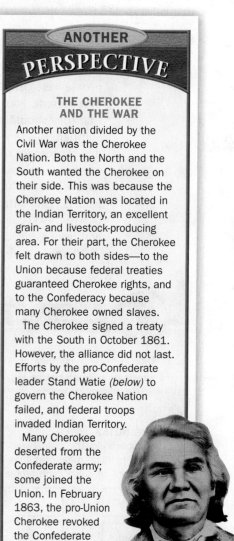

THE CHEROKEE AND THE WAR

Another nation divided by the Civil War was the Cherokee Nation. Both the North and the South wanted the Cherokee on their side. This was because the Cherokee Nation was located in the Indian Territory, an excellent grain- and livestock-producing area. For their part, the Cherokee felt drawn to both sides—to the Union because federal treaties guaranteed Cherokee rights, and to the Confederacy because many Cherokee owned slaves.

The Cherokee signed a treaty with the South in October 1861. However, the alliance did not last. Efforts by the pro-Confederate leader Stand Watie *(below)* to govern the Cherokee Nation failed, and federal troops invaded Indian Territory.

Many Cherokee deserted from the Confederate army; some joined the Union. In February 1863, the pro-Union Cherokee revoked the Confederate treaty.

THE RIOT CONTINUED.

Violence and Pillage.

General Rioting About the City.

The Mob Repulsed by the Police and Military.

LABOR SUSPENDED IN FACTORIES

CITIZENS STONED AND BEATEN.

A Number of the Rioters Supposed to be Killed.

COL. O'BRIEN BEATEN ALMOST TO DEATH.

RAILROAD TRAVEL SUSPENDED.

MAYOR OPDYKE'S HOUSE ATTACKED.

Details of the Riot Throughout the City.

▲ In New York City in July 1863, draft rioters vented their anger on African-American institutions such as this orphanage.

DRAFT RIOTS In 1863 New York City was a tinderbox waiting to explode. Poor people were crowded into slums, crime and disease ran rampant, and poverty was ever-present. Poor white workers—especially Irish immigrants—thought it unfair that they should have to fight a war to free slaves. The white workers feared that Southern blacks would come north and compete for jobs. When officials began to draw names for the draft, angry men gathered all over the city to complain.

For four days, July 13–16, mobs rampaged through the city. The rioters wrecked draft offices, Republican newspaper offices, and the homes of antislavery leaders. They attacked well-dressed men on the street (those likely to be able to pay the $300 commutation fee) and attacked African Americans. By the time federal troops ended the melee, more than 100 persons lay dead.

The draft riots were not the only dramatic development away from the battlefield. Society was also experiencing other types of unrest.

SECTION 2 ASSESSMENT

1. **TERMS & NAMES** For each term or name, write a sentence explaining its significance.
   - **Emancipation Proclamation**
   - **habeas corpus**
   - **Copperhead**
   - **conscription**

MAIN IDEA

2. **TAKING NOTES**
   In a diagram like the one shown, note the political measures that Lincoln took to solve each problem.

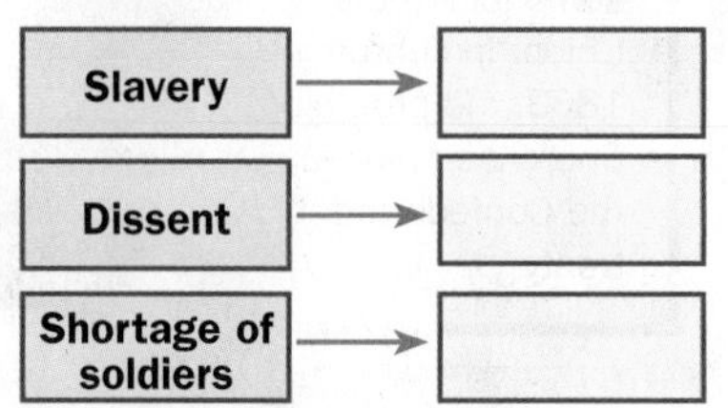

CRITICAL THINKING

3. **EVALUATING LEADERSHIP**
   Do you think that Lincoln's measures to deal with disloyalty and dissent represented an abuse of power? Why or why not? **Think About:**
   - conditions of wartime versus peacetime
   - Lincoln's primary goal
   - Supreme Court Justice Roger Taney's view of Lincoln's powers

4. **ANALYZING PRIMARY SOURCES**

   > **"To fight against slaveholders, without fighting against slavery, is but a half-hearted business, and paralyzes the hands engaged in it."**
   >
   > —Frederick Douglass, quoted in *Battle Cry of Freedom*

   How do you think Lincoln would have replied to Douglass?

SECTION 3

Life During Wartime

MAIN IDEA	WHY IT MATTERS NOW	Terms & Names
The Civil War brought about dramatic social and economic changes in American society.	The expansion of roles for African Americans and women set the stage for later equalities of opportunity.	• Fort Pillow • income tax • Clara Barton • Andersonville

One American's Story

hmhsocialstudies.com TAKING NOTES

Use the graphic organizer online to take notes about economic changes during the Civil War and their effects.

Mary Chesnut, a well-born Southerner whose husband served in the Confederate government, kept a diary describing key war events, such as the attack on Fort Sumter. Her diary paints a vivid picture as well of the marriages and flirtations, hospital work, and dinner parties that comprised daily life in the South.

In 1864, Chesnut found that her social standing could no longer protect her from the economic effects of the war.

A PERSONAL VOICE MARY CHESNUT

"September 19th . . . My pink silk dress I have sold for six hundred dollars, to be paid in installments, two hundred a month for three months. And I sell my eggs and butter from home for two hundred dollars a month. Does it not sound well—four hundred dollars a month, regularly? In what? 'In Confederate money.' Hélas! [Alas!]"

—quoted in *Mary Chesnut's Civil War*

The "Confederate money" Chesnut received was almost worthless. Inflation, or a sharp increase in the cost of living, had devalued Confederate currency to such an extent that $400 was worth only a dollar or two compared to prewar currency. Not all the effects of the Civil War were economic—the war also caused profound social changes.

African Americans Fight for Freedom

African Americans played an important role in the struggle to end slavery. Some served as soldiers, while others took action away from the battlefield.

AFRICAN-AMERICAN SOLDIERS When the Civil War started, it was a white man's war. Neither the Union nor the Confederacy officially accepted African Americans as soldiers.

In 1862, Congress passed a law allowing African Americans to serve in the military. It was only after the Emancipation Proclamation was decreed, however,

▲ Battery A of the 2nd United States Colored Artillery at gun drill

that large-scale enlistment occurred. Although African Americans made up only 1 percent of the North's population, by war's end nearly 10 percent of the Union army was African American. The majority were former slaves from Virginia and other slave states, both Confederate and Union.

Although accepted as soldiers, African Americans suffered discrimination. They served in separate regiments commanded by white officers. Usually African Americans could not rise above the rank of captain—although Alexander T. Augustana, a surgeon, did attain the rank of Lieutenant Colonel. White privates earned $13 a month, plus a $3.50 clothing allowance. Black privates earned only $10 a month, with no clothing allowance. Blacks protested, and several regiments served without pay for months rather than accept the lesser amount. Congress finally equalized the pay of white and African-American soldiers in 1864.

The mortality rate for African-American soldiers was higher than that for white soldiers, primarily because many African Americans were assigned to labor duty in the garrisons, where they were likely to catch typhoid, pneumonia, malaria, or some other deadly disease. Then, too, the Confederacy would not treat captured African-American soldiers as prisoners of war. Many were executed on the spot, and those who were not killed were returned to slavery. A particularly gruesome massacre occurred at **Fort Pillow,** Tennessee, in 1864. Confederate troops killed over 200 African-American prisoners and some whites as they begged for their lives.

Even though most Southerners opposed the idea of African-American soldiers, the Confederacy did consider drafting slaves and free blacks in 1863 and again in 1864. One Louisiana planter argued that since slaves "*caused* the fight," they should share in the burden of battle. Georgia general Howell Cobb responded, "If slaves will make good soldiers our whole theory of slavery is wrong."

HISTORICAL SPOTLIGHT

GLORY FOR THE 54TH MASSACHUSETTS

In July 1863, the African-American 54th Massachusetts Infantry, including two sons of Frederick Douglass, led an assault on Fort Wagner, near Charleston harbor. The attack failed. More than 40 percent of the soldiers were killed. Confederates found the regiment's flag *(above)* under a pile of dead soldiers. Among the dead was the white commander, Colonel Robert G. Shaw. Among the survivors were Douglass's sons and Sergeant William Carney, the first African American to win a Congressional Medal of Honor.

As the New York *Tribune* pointed out, "If this Massachusetts 54th had faltered when its trial came, 200,000 troops for whom it was a pioneer would never have put into the field." Shaw's father declared that his son lay "with his brave, devoted followers. . . . what a bodyguard he has!"

SLAVE RESISTANCE IN THE CONFEDERACY As Union forces pushed deeper into Confederate territory, thousands of slaves sought freedom behind the lines of the Union army. Those who remained on plantations sometimes engaged in sabotage, breaking plows, destroying fences, and neglecting livestock. When Southern plantation owners fled before approaching Union troops, many slaves refused to be dragged along. They waited to welcome the Yankees, who had the power to liberate them. (A)

For whites on farms and plantations in the South, slave resistance compounded the stresses and privations of the war. Fearful of a general slave uprising, Southerners tightened slave patrols and spread rumors about how Union soldiers abused runaways. No general uprising occurred, but slave resistance gradually weakened the plantation system. By 1864 even many Confederates realized that slavery was doomed.

MAIN IDEA

Drawing Conclusions

(A) How did African Americans contribute to the struggle to end slavery?

The War Affects Regional Economies

The decline of the plantation system was not the only economic effect that the Civil War caused. Other effects included inflation and a new type of federal tax. In general, the war expanded the North's economy while shattering that of the South.

SOUTHERN SHORTAGES The Confederacy soon faced a food shortage due to three factors: the drain of manpower into the army, the Union occupation of food-growing areas, and the loss of slaves to work in the fields. Meat became a once-a-week luxury at best, and even such staples as rice and corn were in short supply. Food prices skyrocketed. In 1861 the average family spent $6.65 a month on food. By mid-1863, it was spending $68 a month—if it could find any food to buy. The situation grew so desperate that in 1863 hundreds of women and children—and some men—stormed bakeries and rioted for bread. Mrs. Roger A. Pryor remembered talking to an 18-year-old member of a mob in Richmond on April 2, 1863. (B)

MAIN IDEA

Analyzing Causes

(B) What caused food shortages in the South?

A PERSONAL VOICE MRS. ROGER A. PRYOR

"**As she raised her hand to remove her sunbonnet, her loose calico sleeve slipped up, and revealed a mere skeleton of an arm. She perceived my expression as I looked at it, and hastily pulled down her sleeve with a short laugh. 'This is all that's left of me!' she said. 'It seems real funny, don't it? . . . We are going to the bakeries and each of us will take a loaf of bread. That is little enough for the government to give us after it has taken all our men.'**"

—quoted in *Battle Cry of Freedom*

The mob broke up only when President Jefferson Davis climbed up on a cart, threw down all the money he had, and ordered the crowd to disperse or be shot. The next day, the Confederate government distributed some of its stocks of rice.

The Union blockade of Southern ports created shortages of other items, too, including salt, sugar, coffee, nails, needles, and medicines. One result was that many Confederates smuggled cotton into the North in exchange for gold, food, and other goods. Deploring this trade with the enemy, one Confederate general raged that cotton had made "more damn rascals on both sides than anything else."

NORTHERN ECONOMIC GROWTH Overall, the war's effect on the economy of the North was much more positive. Although a few industries, such as cotton textiles, declined, most boomed. The army's need for uniforms, shoes, guns, and other supplies supported woolen mills, steel foundries, coal mines, and many other industries. Because the draft reduced the available work force, western wheat farmers bought reapers and other labor-saving machines, which benefited the companies that manufactured those machines. (C)

MAIN IDEA

Analyzing Causes

(C) Why was the war less damaging to the economy of the North than to that of the South?

The economic boom had a dark side, though. Wages did not keep up with prices, and many people's standard of living declined. When white male workers went out on strike, employers hired free blacks, immigrants, women, and boys to replace them for lower pay.

ECONOMIC BACKGROUND

CURRENCY AND INFLATION

To raise revenue, both the Union and the Confederacy issued paper money. The Union passed a law declaring that its currency was legal tender, so everyone had to accept it. This national currency succeeded because the public maintained confidence in the Northern economy.

The currency issued by the Confederate treasury (pictured below) was unbacked by gold. Added to this, each state in the Confederacy continued to use its own currency. Because of the war-weakened Southern economy, the public lost faith in Confederate currency—its value plummeted, and prices soared. The Confederacy's war inflation rate reached close to 7,000 percent; prices were 70 times higher at the end of the war than at the beginning. The Union inflation rate was 80 percent.

Northern women—who like many Southern women replaced men on farms and in city jobs—also obtained government jobs for the first time. They worked mostly as clerks, copying ledgers and letters by hand. Although they earned less than men, they remained a regular part of the Washington work force after the war.

Because of the booming economy and rising prices, many businesses in the North made immense profits. This was especially true of those with government contracts, mostly because such contractors often cheated. They supplied uniforms and blankets made of "shoddy"—fibers reclaimed from rags—that came apart in the rain. They passed off spoiled meat as fresh and demanded twice the usual price for guns. This corruption spilled over into the general society. The New York *Herald* commented on the changes in the American character: "The individual who makes the most money—no matter how—and spends the most—no matter for what—is considered the greatest man. . . . The world has seen its iron age, its silver age, its golden age, and its brazen age. This is the age of shoddy."

Congress decided to help pay for the war by tapping its citizens' wealth. In 1863 Congress enacted the tax law that authorized the nation's first **income tax,** a tax that takes a specified percentage of an individual's income.

Soldiers Suffer on Both Sides

Both Union and Confederate soldiers had marched off to war thinking it would prove to be a glorious affair. They were soon disillusioned, not just by heavy casualties but also by poor living conditions, diet, and medical care.

LIVES ON THE LINES Garbage disposal and latrines in army camps were almost unknown. Although army regulations called for washing one's hands and face every day and taking a complete bath once a week, many soldiers failed to do so. As a result, body lice, dysentery, and diarrhea were common.

Army rations were far from appealing. Union troops subsisted on beans, bacon, and hardtack—square biscuits that were supposedly hard enough to stop a bullet. As one Northerner wrote:

> The soldiers' fare is very rough,
> The bread is hard, the beef is tough;
> If they can stand it, it will be,
> Through love of God, a mystery.

Wounded Union troops recuperate after battle near a makeshift field hospital. ▼

Science & Technology

BATTLEFIELD MEDICINE

In the Civil War, weapons technology overtook medical technology. Minié balls, soft lead bullets, caused traumatic wounds that could often be treated only by amputation. As the effects of bacteria were not yet known, surgeons never sterilized instruments, making infection one of soldiers' worst enemies.

Field Hospitals ▼

The badly wounded were taken to field hospitals, like this one at Gettysburg. The surgeon is preparing for an amputation; the man behind the patient administers an anesthetic, probably chloroform.

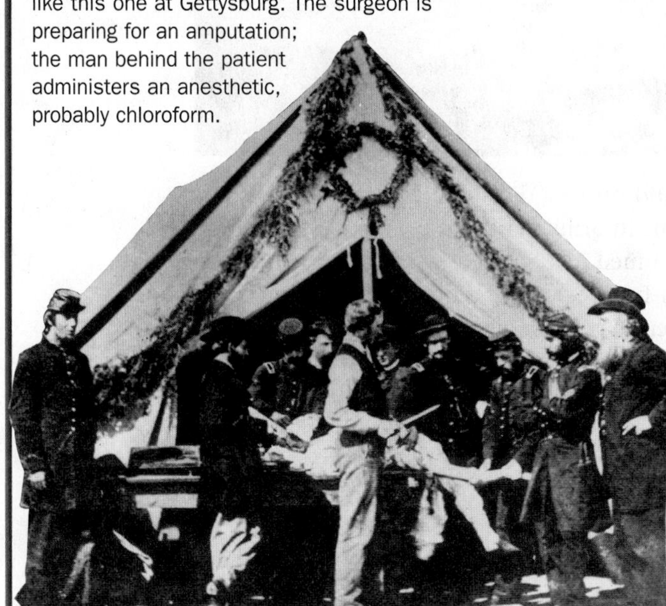

Clara Barton ▶

As a war nurse, Clara Barton collected and distributed supplies and dug bullets out of soldiers' bodies with her penknife. Barton was particularly good at anticipating troop movements and sometimes arrived at the battlefield before the fighting had even begun. Most women, however, served in hospitals rather than at the front lines. On the battlefield soldiers were usually attended by male medics.

Surgeon's Tools ▼

A surgeon's kit might contain cloth for bandages or administering chloroform, opium pills to kill pain, forceps and knives for cleaning wounds, and saws for amputations.

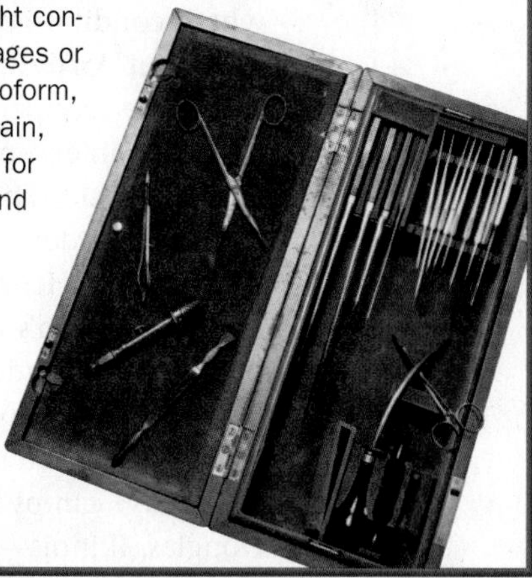

Confederate troops fared equally poorly. A common food was "cush," a stew of small cubes of beef and crumbled cornbread mixed with bacon grease. Fresh vegetables were hardly ever available. Both sides loved coffee, but Southern soldiers had only substitutes brewed from peanuts, dried apples, or corn.

CIVIL WAR MEDICINE Soon after Fort Sumter fell, the federal government set up the United States Sanitary Commission. Its task was twofold: to improve the hygienic conditions of army camps and to recruit and train nurses. The "Sanitary" proved a great success. It sent out agents to teach soldiers such things as how to avoid polluting their water supply. It developed hospital trains and hospital ships to transport wounded men from the battlefield.

At the age of 60, Dorothea Dix became the nation's first superintendent of women nurses. To discourage women looking for romance, Dix insisted applicants be at least 30 and "very plain-looking." Impressed by the work of women nurses he observed, the surgeon general required that at least one-third of Union hospital nurses be women; some 3,000 served. Union nurse **Clara Barton** often cared for the sick and wounded at the front lines. After her courage under fire at Antietam, a surgeon described her as the "angel of the battlefield."

MAIN IDEA

Summarizing

D How did the Sanitary Commission improve medical treatment during the war?

As a result of the Sanitary Commission's work, the death rate among Union wounded, although terrible by 20th-century standards, showed considerable improvement over that of previous wars. **D**

The Confederacy did not have a Sanitary Commission, but thousands of Southern women volunteered as nurses. Sally Tompkins, for example, performed so heroically in her hospital duties that she eventually was commissioned as a captain.

The Confederate prison at Andersonville, Georgia, in 1864 ◀

PRISONS Improvements in hygiene and nursing did not reach the war prisons, where conditions were even worse than in army camps. The worst Confederate prison, at **Andersonville,** Georgia, jammed 33,000 men into 26 acres, or about 34 square feet per man. The prisoners had no shelter from the broiling sun or chilling rain except what they made themselves by rigging primitive tents of blankets and sticks. They drank from the same stream that served as their sewer. About a third of Andersonville's prisoners died. Part of the blame rested with the camp's commander, Henry Wirz (whom the North eventually executed as a war criminal). The South's lack of food and tent canvas also contributed to the appalling conditions. In addition, the prisons were overcrowded because the North had halted prisoner exchanges when the South refused to return African-American soldiers who had been captured in battle.

Prison camps in the North—such as those at Elmira, New York, and at Camp Douglas, Illinois—were only slightly better. Northern prisons provided about five times as much space per man, barracks for sleeping, and adequate food. However, thousands of Confederates, housed in quarters with little or no heat, contracted pneumonia and died. Hundreds of others suffered from dysentery and malnutrition, from which some did not recover. Historians estimate that 15 percent of Union prisoners in Southern prisons died, while 12 percent of Confederate prisoners died in Northern prisons.

A series of battles in the Mississippi Valley and in the East soon sent a fresh wave of prisoners of war flooding into prison camps.

ASSESSMENT

1. **TERMS & NAMES** For each term or name, write a sentence explaining its significance.
   - **Fort Pillow**
   - **income tax**
   - **Clara Barton**
   - **Andersonville**

MAIN IDEA

2. **TAKING NOTES**
   In a two-column chart, list the economic changes that occurred in the North and South as a result of the Civil War. Explain how these changes affected the two regions.

ECONOMIC CHANGES

North	South

CRITICAL THINKING

3. **ANALYZING EFFECTS**
   What effects did the Civil War have on women and African Americans?
   Think About:
   - new opportunities in both the North and the South
   - discriminatory practices that persisted for both groups

4. **SYNTHESIZING**
   Imagine you were one of the Northern women and doctors who convinced the government to establish the Sanitary Commission. What reasons would you have offered to justify this commission? Use details from the text to support your response.

The North Takes Charge

MAIN IDEA	WHY IT MATTERS NOW	Terms & Names
Key victories at Vicksburg and Gettysburg helped the Union wear down the Confederacy.	These victories clinched the North's win and led to the preservation of the Union.	• Gettysburg • Chancellorsville • Vicksburg • Gettysburg Address • William Tecumseh Sherman • Appomattox Court House

One American's Story

hmhsocialstudies.com
TAKING NOTES

Use the graphic organizer online to take notes on major events in the last two years of the Civil War.

Shortly after three o'clock on the afternoon of July 3, 1863, from behind a stone wall on a ridge south of the little town of Gettysburg, Pennsylvania, Union troops watched thousands of Confederate soldiers advance toward them across an open field. Union officer Frank Aretas Haskell described the scene.

▲ A Confederate charge during the battle of Gettysburg

A Personal Voice

FRANK ARETAS HASKELL

"More than half a mile their front extends . . . man touching man, rank pressing rank. . . . The red flags wave, their horsemen gallop up and down, the arms of [thirteen] thousand men, barrel and bayonet, gleam in the sun, a sloping forest of flashing steel. Right on they move, as with one soul, in perfect order without impediment of ditch, or wall, or stream, over ridge and slope, through orchard and meadow, and cornfield, magnificent, grim, irresistible."

—quoted in *The Civil War: An Illustrated History*

An hour later, half of the Confederate force lay dead or wounded, cut down by crossfire from massed Union guns. Because of the North's heavy weaponry, it had become suicide for unprotected troops to assault a strongly fortified position.

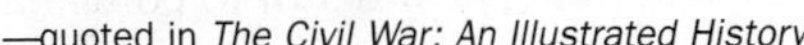

Armies Clash at Gettysburg

The July 3 infantry charge was part of a three-day battle at **Gettysburg,** which many historians consider the turning point of the Civil War. The battle of Gettysburg crippled the South so badly that General Lee would never again possess sufficient forces to invade a Northern state.

Battle of Gettysburg, July 1863

hmhsocialstudies.com INTERACTIVE MAP

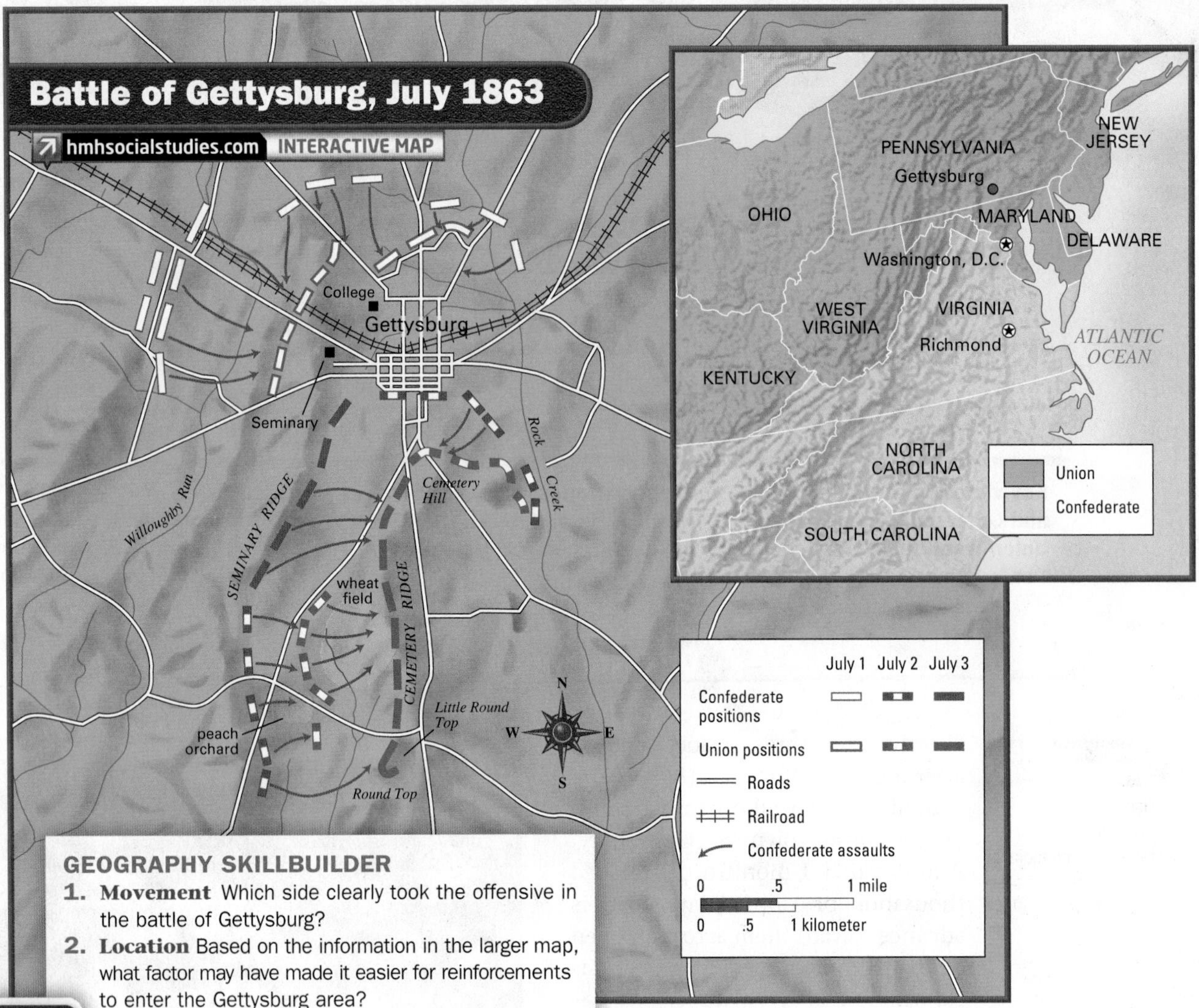

GEOGRAPHY SKILLBUILDER

1. **Movement** Which side clearly took the offensive in the battle of Gettysburg?
2. **Location** Based on the information in the larger map, what factor may have made it easier for reinforcements to enter the Gettysburg area?

VIDEO
Gettysburg Address
hmhsocialstudies.com

PRELUDE TO GETTYSBURG The year 1863 actually had gone well for the South. During the first four days of May, the South defeated the North at **Chancellorsville,** Virginia. Lee outmaneuvered Union general Joseph Hooker and forced the Union army to retreat. The North's only consolation after Chancellorsville came as the result of an accident. As General Stonewall Jackson returned from a patrol on May 2, Confederate guards mistook him for a Yankee and shot him in the left arm. A surgeon amputated his arm the following day. When Lee heard the news, he exclaimed, "He has lost his left arm, but I have lost my right." But the true loss was still to come; Jackson caught pneumonia and died May 10.

Despite Jackson's tragic death, Lee decided to press his military advantage and invade the North. He needed supplies, he hoped that an invasion would force Lincoln to pull troops away from Vicksburg, and he thought that a major Confederate victory on Northern soil might tip the political balance of power in the Union to pro-Southern Democrats. Accordingly, he crossed the Potomac into Maryland and then pushed on into Pennsylvania. (A)

MAIN IDEA

Analyzing Motives

(A) What did Lee hope to gain by invading the North?

GETTYSBURG The most decisive battle of the war was fought near Gettysburg, Pennsylvania. The town was an unlikely spot for a bloody battle—and indeed, no one planned to fight there.

Confederate soldiers led by A. P. Hill, many of them barefoot, heard there was a supply of footwear in Gettysburg and went to find it, and also to meet up with forces under General Lee. When Hill's troops marched toward Gettysburg, they ran into a couple of brigades of Union cavalry under the command of John Buford, an experienced officer from Illinois.

Buford ordered his men to take defensive positions on the hills and ridges surrounding the town, from which they engaged Hill's troops. The shooting attracted more troops and each side sent for reinforcements.

The Northern armies, now under the command of General George Meade, that were north and west of Gettysburg began to fall back under a furious rebel assault. The Confederates took control of the town. Lee knew, however, that the battle would not be won unless the Northerners were also forced to yield their positions on Cemetery Ridge, the high ground south of Gettysburg. B

MAIN IDEA

Analyzing Effects

B Why was it important that the Union held on to the high ground in Gettysburg?

THE SECOND DAY On July 2, almost 90,000 Yankees and 75,000 Confederates stood ready to fight for Gettysburg. Lee ordered General James Longstreet to attack Cemetery Ridge, which was held by Union troops. At about 4:00 P.M., Longstreet's troops advanced from Seminary Ridge, through the peach orchard and wheat field that stood between them and the Union position.

The yelling Rebels overran Union troops who had mistakenly left their positions on Little Round Top, a hill that overlooked much of the southern portion of the battlefield. As a brigade of Alabamans approached the hill, however, Union leaders noticed the undefended position. Colonel Joshua L. Chamberlain, who had been a language professor before the war, led his Maine troops to meet the Rebels, and succeeded in repulsing repeated Confederate attacks. When his soldiers ran short of ammunition and more than a third of the brigade had fallen, Chamberlain ordered a bayonet charge at the Confederates.

The Rebels, exhausted by the uphill fighting and the 25-mile march of the previous day, were shocked by the Union assault and surrendered in droves. Chamberlain and his men succeeded in saving the Union lines from certain rebel artillery attacks from Little Round Top. Although the Union troops had given some ground, their lines still held at the close of day.

THE THIRD DAY Lee was optimistic, however. With one more day of determined attack, he felt he could break the Union defenses. Early in the afternoon of July 3, Lee ordered an artillery barrage on the middle of the Union lines. For two hours, the two armies fired at one another in a vicious exchange that could be heard in Pittsburgh. When the Union

History Through

GETTYSBURG CYCLORAMA (detail) (1884)

Twenty years after the fact, French artist Paul Philippoteaux depicted the battle of Gettysburg in a giant painting. To ensure that the 360-foot-long and 26-foot-high work was realistic, Philippoteaux studied the battle site and interviewed survivors. **What details in the painting contribute to its realism and sense of action?**

"It's all my fault"

GEN. ROBERT E. LEE ON THE FAILURE OF PICKETT'S CHARGE

artillery fell silent, Lee insisted that Longstreet press forward. Longstreet reluctantly ordered his men, including those under the command of General Pickett, to attack the center of the Union lines. Deliberately, they marched across the farmland toward the Union high ground. Suddenly, Northern artillery renewed its barrage. Some of the Confederates had nearly reached the Union lines when Yankee infantry fired on them as well. Devastated, the Confederates staggered back. The Northerners had succeeded in holding the high ground south of Gettysburg.

Lee sent cavalry led by General James E. B. (Jeb) Stuart circling around the right flank of Meade's forces, hoping they would surprise the Union troops from the rear and meet Longstreet's men in the middle. Stuart's campaign stalled, however, when his men clashed with Union forces under David Gregg three miles away.

Not knowing that Gregg had stopped Stuart nor that Lee's army was severely weakened, Union general Meade never ordered a counterattack. After the battle, Lee gave up any hopes of invading the North and led his army in a long, painful retreat back to Virginia through a pelting rain.

The three-day battle produced staggering losses. Total casualties were more than 30 percent. Union losses included 23,000 men killed or wounded. For the Confederacy, approximately 28,000 were killed or wounded. Fly-infested corpses lay everywhere in the July heat; the stench was unbearable. Lee would continue to lead his men brilliantly in the next two years of the war, but neither he nor the Confederacy would ever recover from the loss at Gettysburg or the surrender of Vicksburg, which occurred the very next day. C

MAIN IDEA

Analyzing Effects

C Why was the battle of Gettysburg a disaster for the South?

Grant Wins at Vicksburg

While the Army of the Potomac was turning back the Confederates in central Pennsylvania, Union general Ulysses S. Grant continued his campaign in the west. **Vicksburg,** Mississippi, was one of only two Confederate holdouts preventing the Union from taking complete control of the Mississippi River, an important waterway for transporting goods.

U. S. Grant, photographed in August 1864 ▼

VICKSBURG UNDER SIEGE In the spring of 1863, Grant sent a cavalry brigade to destroy rail lines in central Mississippi and draw attention away from the port city. While the Confederate forces were distracted, Grant was able to land infantry south of Vicksburg late on April 30. In 18 days, Union forces whipped several rebel units and sacked Jackson, the capital of the state.

Their confidence growing with every victory, Grant and his troops rushed to Vicksburg. Two frontal assaults on the city failed; so, in the last week of May 1863, Grant settled in for a siege. He set up a steady barrage of artillery, shelling the city from both the river and the land for several hours a day and forcing its residents to take shelter in caves that they dug out of the yellow clay hillsides.

Food supplies ran so low that people ate dogs and mules. At last some of the starving Confederate soldiers defending Vicksburg sent their commander a petition saying, "If you can't feed us, you'd better surrender."

On July 3, 1863, the same day as Pickett's charge, the Confederate commander of Vicksburg asked Grant for terms of surrender. The city fell on July 4. Five days later Port Hudson, Louisiana, the last Confederate holdout on the Mississippi, also fell—and the Confederacy was cut in two.

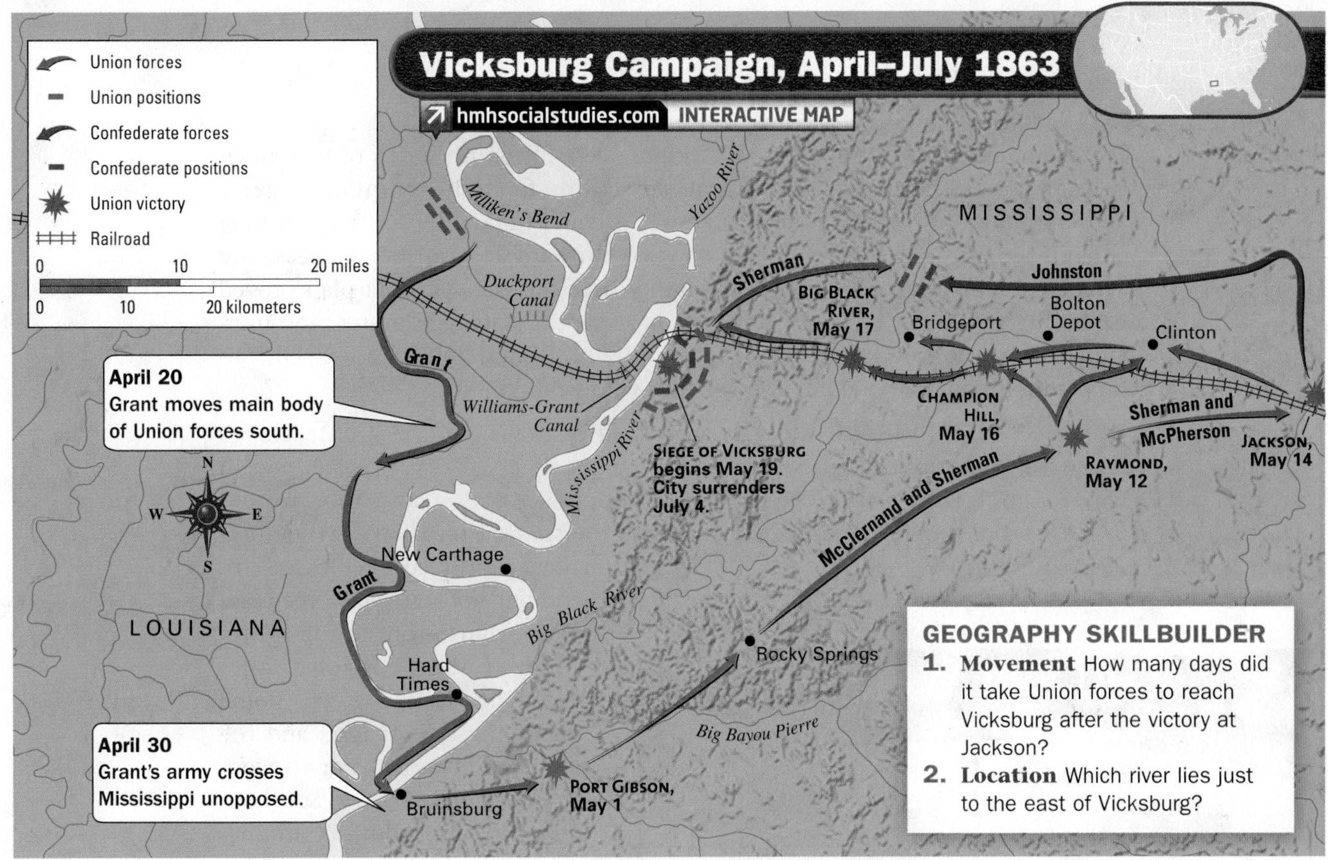

The Gettysburg Address

In November 1863, a ceremony was held to dedicate a cemetery in Gettysburg. The first speaker was Edward Everett, a noted orator, who gave a flowery two-hour oration. Then Abraham Lincoln spoke for a little more than two minutes. According to the historian Garry Wills, Lincoln's **Gettysburg Address** "remade America." Before the war, people said, "The United States *are*." After Lincoln's speech, they said, "The United States *is*."

The Gettysburg Address ABRAHAM LINCOLN

"Four score and seven years ago our fathers brought forth on this continent a new nation, conceived in Liberty, and dedicated to the proposition that all men are created equal.

Now we are engaged in a great civil war, testing whether that nation, or any nation so conceived and so dedicated, can long endure. We are met on a great battlefield of that war. We have come to dedicate a portion of that field, as a final resting place for those who here gave their lives that that nation might live. It is altogether fitting and proper that we should do this.

But, in a larger sense, we can not dedicate—we can not consecrate—we can not hallow—this ground. The brave men, living and dead, who struggled here, have consecrated it, far above our poor power to add or detract. The world will little note, nor long remember what we say here, but it can never forget what they did here. It is for us the living, rather, to be dedicated here to the unfinished work which they who fought here have thus far so nobly advanced. It is rather for us to be here dedicated to the great task remaining before us—that from these honored dead we take increased devotion to that cause for which they gave the last full measure of devotion—that we here highly resolve that these dead shall not have died in vain—that this nation, under God, shall have a new birth of freedom—and that government of the people, by the people, for the people, shall not perish from the earth." D

—*The Gettysburg Address*, November 19, 1863

MAIN IDEA

Summarizing

D What beliefs about the United States did Lincoln express in the Gettysburg Address?

The Confederacy Wears Down

The twin defeats at Gettysburg and Vicksburg cost the South much of its limited fighting power. The Confederacy was already low on food, shoes, uniforms, guns, and ammunition. No longer able to attack, it could hope only to hang on long enough to destroy Northern morale and work toward an armistice—a cease-fire agreement based on mutual consent—rather than a surrender. That plan proved increasingly unlikely, however. Southern newspapers, state legislatures, and individuals began to call openly for an end to the hostilities, and President Lincoln finally found not just one but two generals who would fight.

CONFEDERATE MORALE As war progressed, morale on the Confederacy's home front deteriorated. The Confederate Congress passed a weak resolution in 1863 urging planters to grow fewer cash crops like cotton and tobacco and increase production of food. Farmers resented the tax that took part of their produce and livestock, especially since many rich planters continued to cultivate cotton and tobacco—in some cases even selling crops to the North. Many soldiers deserted after receiving letters from home about the lack of food and the shortage of farm labor to work the farms. In every Southern state except South Carolina, there were soldiers who decided to turn and fight for the North—for example, 2,400 Floridians served in the Union army.

Discord in the Confederate government made it impossible for Jefferson Davis to govern effectively. Members of the Confederate Congress squabbled among themselves. In South Carolina, the governor was upset when troops from his state were placed under the command of officers from another state.

In 1863, North Carolinians who wanted peace held more than 100 open meetings in their state. A similar peace movement sprang up in Georgia in early 1864. Although these movements failed, by mid-1864, Assistant Secretary of War John Campbell was forced to acknowledge that active opposition to the war "in the mountain districts of North Carolina, South Carolina, Georgia, and Alabama menaces the existence of the Confederacy as fatally as . . . the armies of the United States." E

KEY PLAYERS

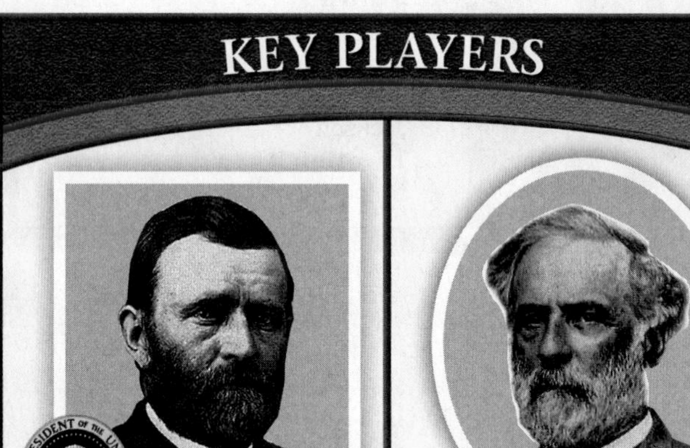

ULYSSES S. GRANT
1822–1885

U. S. Grant once said of himself, "A military life had no charms for me." Yet, a military man was what he was destined to be. He fought in the war with Mexico—even though he termed it "wicked"—because he believed his duty was to serve his country. His next post was in the West, where Grant grew so lonely for his family that he resigned.

When the Civil War began, Grant served as colonel of the Illinois volunteers because General McClellan had been too busy to see him!

However, once Grant began fighting in Tennessee, Lincoln recognized his abilities. When newspapers demanded Grant's dismissal after Shiloh, Lincoln replied, "I can't spare this man. He fights."

ROBERT E. LEE
1807–1870

Lee was an aristocrat. His father had been one of George Washington's best generals, and his wife was the great-granddaughter of Martha Washington. As a man who believed slavery was evil, Lee nonetheless fought for the Confederacy out of loyalty to his beloved home state of Virginia. "I did only what my duty demanded. I could have taken no other course without dishonor," he said.

As a general, Lee was brilliant, but he seldom challenged civilian leaders about their failure to provide his army with adequate supplies. His soldiers—who called him Uncle Robert—almost worshiped him because he insisted on sharing their hardships.

MAIN IDEA

Analyzing Effects

E How did discontent among members of the Confederate Congress affect the war?

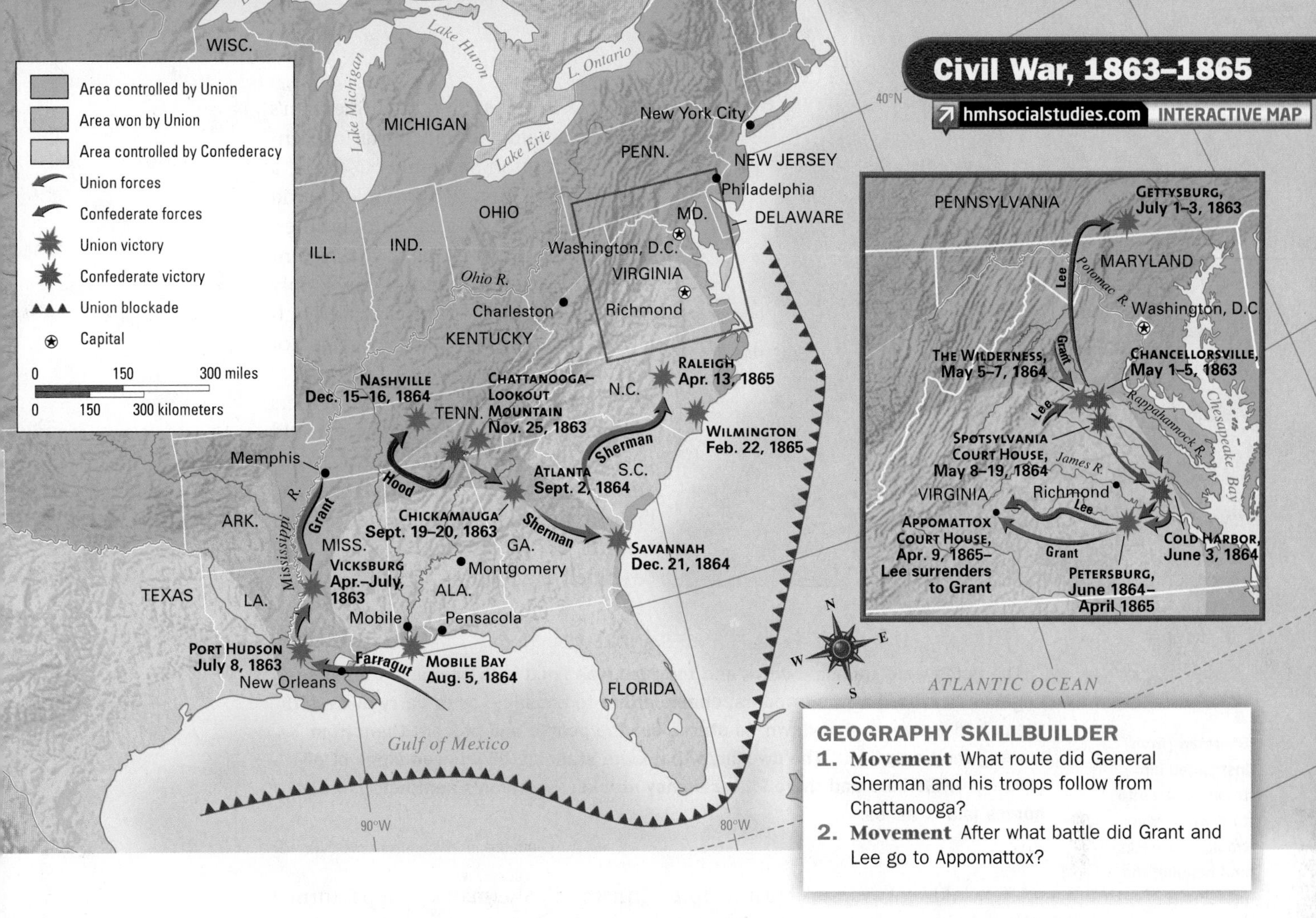

GEOGRAPHY SKILLBUILDER

1. **Movement** What route did General Sherman and his troops follow from Chattanooga?
2. **Movement** After what battle did Grant and Lee go to Appomattox?

GRANT APPOINTS SHERMAN In March 1864, President Lincoln appointed Ulysses S. Grant, the hero of the battle at Vicksburg, commander of all Union armies. Grant in turn appointed **William Tecumseh Sherman** as commander of the military division of the Mississippi. These two appointments would change the course of the war.

Old friends and comrades in arms, both men believed in total war. They believed that it was essential to fight not only the South's armies and government but its civilian population as well. They reasoned, first, that civilians produced the weapons, grew the food, and transported the goods on which the armies relied, and, second, that the strength of the people's will kept the war going. If the Union destroyed that will to fight, the Confederacy would collapse.

GRANT AND LEE IN VIRGINIA Grant's overall strategy was to immobilize Lee's army in Virginia while Sherman raided Georgia. Even if Grant's casualties ran twice as high as those of Lee—and they did—the North could afford it. The South could not.

Starting in May 1864, Grant threw his troops into battle after battle, the first in a wooded area, known as the Wilderness, near Fredericksburg, Virginia. The fighting was brutal, made even more so by the fires spreading through the thick trees. The string of battles continued at Spotsylvania, at Cold Harbor (where Grant lost 7,000 men in one hour), and finally at Petersburg, which would remain under Union attack from June 1864 to April 1865.

During the period from May 4 to June 18, 1864, Grant lost nearly 60,000 men—which the North could replace—to Lee's 32,000 men—which the South could not replace. Democrats and Northern newspapers called Grant a butcher. However, Grant kept going because he had promised Lincoln, "Whatever happens, there will be no turning back."

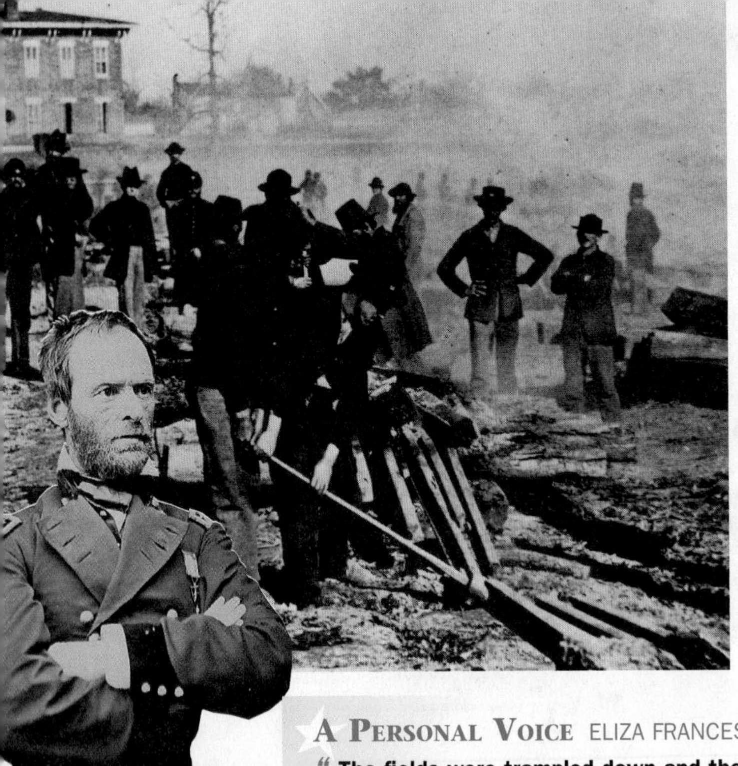

Sherman *(front)* instructed his troops in Atlanta to destroy train tracks by heating and bending the metal rails.

SHERMAN'S MARCH After Sherman's army occupied the transportation center of Atlanta on September 2, 1864, a Confederate army tried to circle around him and cut his railroad supply lines. Sherman decided to fight a different battle. He would abandon his supply lines and march southeast through Georgia, creating a wide path of destruction and living off the land as he went. He would make Southerners "so sick of war that generations would pass away before they would again appeal to it." In mid-November he burned most of Atlanta and set out toward the coast. A Georgia girl described the result.

A PERSONAL VOICE ELIZA FRANCES ANDREWS

"The fields were trampled down and the road was lined with carcasses of horses, hogs, and cattle that the invaders, unable either to consume or to carry away with them, had wantonly shot down, to starve out the people and prevent them from making their crops. . . . The dwellings that were standing all showed signs of pillage . . . while here and there lone chimney stacks, 'Sherman's sentinels,' told of homes laid in ashes."

—quoted in *Voices from the Civil War*

After taking Savannah just before Christmas, Sherman's troops turned north to help Grant "wipe out Lee." Following behind them now were about 25,000 former slaves eager for freedom. As the army marched through South Carolina in 1865, it inflicted even more destruction than it had in Georgia. As one Union private exclaimed, "Here is where treason began and, by God, here is where it shall end!" The army burned almost every house in its path. In contrast, when Sherman's forces entered North Carolina, which had been the last state to secede, they stopped destroying private homes and—anticipating the end of the war—began handing out food and other supplies. F

MAIN IDEA

Analyzing Motives

F What were Sherman's objectives in marching his troops from Atlanta to Savannah?

THE ELECTION OF 1864 As the 1864 presidential election approached, Lincoln faced heavy opposition. Many Democrats, dismayed at the war's length, its high casualty rates, and recent Union losses, joined pro-Southern party members to nominate George McClellan on a platform of an immediate armistice. Still resentful over having been fired by Lincoln, McClellan was delighted to run.

Lincoln's other opponents, the Radical Republicans, favored a harsher proposal than Lincoln's for readmitting the Confederate states. They formed a third political party and nominated John C. Frémont as their candidate. To attract Democrats, Lincoln's supporters dropped the Republican name, retitled themselves the National Union Party, and chose Andrew Johnson, a pro-Union Democrat from Tennessee, as Lincoln's running mate.

Lincoln was pessimistic about his chances. "I am going to be beaten," he said in August, "and unless some great change takes place, badly beaten." However, some great change did take place. On August 5, Admiral David Farragut entered Mobile Bay in Alabama and within three weeks shut down that major Southern port. On September 2, Sherman telegraphed, "Atlanta is ours." By month's end, Frémont had withdrawn from the presidential race. On October 19, General

◀ Thomas Lovell's *Surrender at Appomattox* is a modern rendering of Lee's surrender to Grant.

Philip Sheridan finally chased the Confederates out of the Shenandoah Valley in northern Virginia. The victories buoyed the North, and with the help of absentee ballots cast by Union soldiers, Lincoln won a second term.

THE SURRENDER AT APPOMATTOX By late March 1865, it was clear that the end of the Confederacy was near. Grant and Sheridan were approaching Richmond from the west, while Sherman was approaching from the south. On April 2—in response to news that Lee and his troops had been overcome by Grant's forces at Petersburg—President Davis and his government abandoned their capital, setting it afire to keep the Northerners from taking it. Despite the fire-fighting efforts of Union troops, flames destroyed some 900 buildings and damaged hundreds more.

Lee and Grant met to arrange a Confederate surrender on April 9, 1865, in a Virginia village called **Appomattox** (ăp′ə-măt′əks) **Court House.** At Lincoln's request, the terms were generous. Grant paroled Lee's soldiers and sent them home with their personal possessions, horses, and three days' rations. Officers were permitted to keep their side arms. Within two months all remaining Confederate resistance collapsed. After four long years, at tremendous human and economic costs, the Civil War was over.

SECTION 4 ASSESSMENT

1. **TERMS & NAMES** For each term or name, write a sentence explaining its significance.
   - **Gettysburg**
   - **Chancellorsville**
   - **Vicksburg**
   - **Gettysburg Address**
   - **William Tecumseh Sherman**
   - **Appomattox Court House**

MAIN IDEA

2. **TAKING NOTES**
   Create a time line of the major battles and political events relating to the final two years of the Civil War. Use the dates already plotted on the time line below as a guide.

   May 1863 — **March 1864** — **April 1865**

   Which event was the turning point? Why?

CRITICAL THINKING

3. **EVALUATING**
   Do you think that a general's win-loss record on the battlefield is the best gauge of measuring greatness as a military leader? Why or why not? **Think About:**
   - Grant's campaign in Virginia, Sherman's march to Atlanta, and Lee's surrender
   - Democrats' and Northern newspapers' criticism of Grant
   - the criteria you would use to evaluate a military leader

4. **EVALUATING DECISIONS**
   Grant and Sherman presented a logical rationale for using the strategy of total war. Do you think the end—defeating the Confederacy—justified the means—causing harm to civilians? Explain.

5. **ANALYZING MOTIVES**
   Why do you think Lincoln urged generous terms for a Confederate surrender?

The Legacy of the War

MAIN IDEA	WHY IT MATTERS NOW	Terms & Names
The Civil War settled long-standing disputes over states' rights and slavery.	The federal government established supreme authority, and no state has threatened secession since.	• National Bank Act • Thirteenth Amendment • Red Cross • John Wilkes Booth

One American's Story

hmhsocialstudies.com TAKING NOTES

Use the graphic organizer online to take notes about the consequences of the Civil War.

Garland H. White, a former slave from Virginia, marched with other Yankee soldiers into the Confederate capital of Richmond after it fell. Now chaplain of the 28th United States Colored troops, White was returning to the state where he had once served in bondage. As the soldiers marched along the city streets, thousands of African Americans cheered. A large crowd of soldiers and civilians gathered in the neighborhood where the slave market had been. Garland White remembered the scene.

A Personal Voice GARLAND H. WHITE

> **"I marched at the head of the column, and soon I found myself called upon by the officers and men of my regiment to make a speech, with which, of course, I readily complied. A vast multitude assembled on Broad Street, and I was aroused amid the shouts of 10,000 voices, and proclaimed for the first time in that city freedom to all [humankind]."**
>
> —quoted in *Been in the Storm So Long*

▲ Union troops in the South sometimes came upon slave markets like this one.

Freedom for slaves was not the only legacy of the Civil War. The struggle transformed the nation's economy, its government, the conduct of warfare, and the future careers of many of its participants.

The War Changes the Nation

In 1869 Professor George Ticknor of Harvard commented that since the Civil War, "It does not seem to me as if I were living in the country in which I was born." The Civil War caused tremendous political, economic, technological, and social change in the United States. It also exacted a high price in the cost of human life.

POLITICAL CHANGES Decades before the war, Southern states had threatened secession when federal policies angered them. After the war, the federal government assumed supreme national authority and no state has ever seceded again. The states' rights issue did not go away; it simply led in a different direction from secession. Today, arguments about states' rights versus federal control focus on such issues as whether the state or national government should determine how to use local funds.

In addition to ending the threat of secession, the war greatly increased the federal government's power. Before the Civil War, the federal government had little impact on most people's daily lives. Most citizens dealt only with their county governments. During the war, however, the federal government reached into people's pockets, taxing private incomes. It also required everyone to accept its new paper currency (even those who had previously contracted to be repaid in coins). Most dramatically, the federal government tore reluctant men from their families to fight in the war. After the war, U.S. citizens could no longer assume that the national government in Washington was too far away to bother them. **A**

> **MAIN IDEA**
> **Analyzing Effects**
> **A** How did the power of the federal government increase during the war?

ECONOMIC CHANGES The Civil War had a profound impact on the nation's economy. Between 1861 and 1865, the federal government did much to help business, in part through subsidizing construction of a national railroad system. The government also passed the **National Bank Act** of 1863, which set up a system of federally chartered banks, set requirements for loans, and provided for banks to be inspected. These measures helped make banking safer for investors.

The economy of the Northern states boomed. Northern entrepreneurs had grown rich selling war supplies to the government and thus had money to invest in new businesses after the war. As army recruitment created a labor shortage in the North, the sale of labor-saving agricultural tools such as the reaper increased dramatically. By war's end, large-scale commercial agriculture had taken hold.

The war devastated the South economically. It took away the South's source of cheap labor—slavery—and also wrecked most of the region's industry. It wiped out 40 percent of the livestock, destroyed much of the South's farm machinery and railroads, and left thousands of acres of land uncultivated.

The economic gap between North and South had widened drastically. Before the war, Southern states held 30 percent of the national wealth; in 1870 they held

Though both Union and Confederate soldiers were lucky to escape the war with their lives, thousands—like this young amputee—faced an uncertain future. ▼

The Costs of the Civil War

Deaths

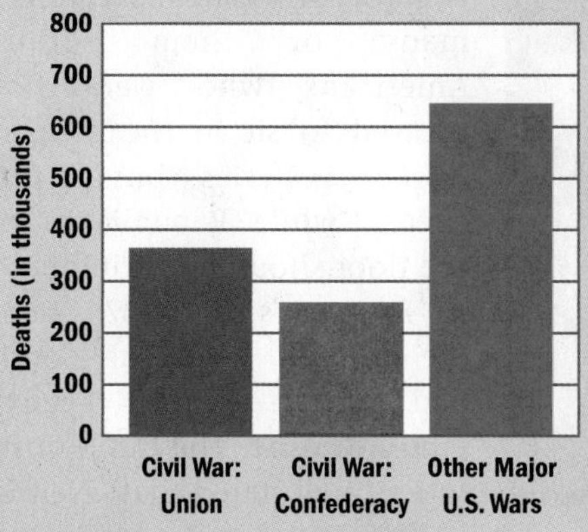

Source: *Warfare and Armed Conflicts: A Statistical Reference to Casualty and Other Figures, 1500-2000*; U.S. Department of Defense

Economic Costs

- Union war costs totaled $2.3 billion.
- Confederate war costs ran to $1 billion.
- Union war costs increased the national debt from $65 million in 1860 to $2.7 billion in 1865.
- Confederate debt ran over $1.8 billion in 1864.
- Union inflation peaked at 182% in 1864.
- Confederate inflation rose to 7,000%.

SKILLBUILDER Interpreting Data
1. Based on the bar graph, how did the combined Union and Confederate losses compare with those of other wars?
2. Why was inflation worse in the Confederacy than in the Union?

only 12 percent. In 1860, Southerners earned about 70 percent of the Northern average; in 1870, they earned less than 40 percent. This economic disparity between the regions would not diminish until the 20th century.

COSTS OF THE WAR The human costs of the Civil War were staggering. They affected almost every American family. Approximately 360,000 Union soldiers and 260,000 Confederates died, nearly as many as in all other American wars combined. Another 275,000 Union soldiers and 225,000 Confederates were wounded. Veterans with missing limbs became a common sight nationwide. In addition, military service had occupied some 2,400,000 men—nearly 10 percent of the nation's population of approximately 31,000,000—for four long years. It disrupted their education, their careers, and their families.

The Civil War's economic costs were just as extensive. Historians estimate that the Union and the Confederate governments spent a combined total of about $3.3 billion during the four years of war, or more than twice what the government had spent in the previous 80 years! The costs did not stop when the war ended. Twenty years later, interest payments on the war debt plus veterans' pensions still accounted for almost two-thirds of the federal budget.

The War Changes Lives

The war not only impacted the nation's economy and politics, it also changed individual lives. Perhaps the biggest change came for African Americans.

NEW BIRTH OF FREEDOM The Emancipation Proclamation, which Lincoln had issued under his war powers, freed only those slaves who lived in the states that were behind Confederate lines and not yet under Union control. The government had to decide what to do about the border states, where slavery was still legal.

The president believed that the only solution would be a constitutional amendment abolishing slavery. The Republican-controlled Senate approved an amendment in the summer of 1864, but the House, with its large Democratic membership, did not. After Lincoln's reelection, the amendment was reintroduced in the House in January of 1865. This time the administration convinced a few Democrats to vote in its favor with promises of government jobs after they left office. The amendment passed with two votes to spare. Spectators—many of them African Americans who were now allowed to sit in the congressional galleries—burst into cheers, while Republicans on the floor shouted in triumph.

By year's end 27 states, including 8 from the South, had ratified the **Thirteenth Amendment.** The U.S. Constitution now stated that "Neither slavery nor involuntary servitude, except as a punishment for crime whereof the party shall have been duly convicted, shall exist within the United States."

A store in Richmond, Virginia, decorated in celebration of Liberation Day, the anniversary of the Emancipation Proclamation ▼

History Through *Photojournalism*

MATHEW BRADY'S PHOTOGRAPHS

The Civil War marked the first time in United States history that photography, a resource since 1839, played a major role in a military conflict. Hundreds of photographers traveled with the troops, working both privately and for the military. The most famous Civil War photographer was Mathew Brady, who employed about 20 photographers to meet the public demand for pictures from the battlefront. This was the beginning of American news photography, or photojournalism.

Many of Brady's photographs are a mix of realism and artificiality. Due to the primitive level of photographic technology, subjects had to be carefully posed and remain still during the long exposure times.

In this 1864 photograph Brady posed a kneeling soldier, offering a canteen of water, beside a wounded soldier with his arm in a sling. Images like this, showing the wounded or the dead, brought home the harsh reality of war to the civilian population. ▼

▲ **"Encampment of the Army of the Potomac" (May 1862). Few photographs of the Civil War are as convincing in their naturalism as this view over a Union encampment. Simply by positioning the camera behind the soldiers, the photographer draws the viewer into the composition. Although we cannot see the soldiers' faces, we are compelled to see through their eyes.**

SKILLBUILDER Interpreting Visual Sources

1. What elements in the smaller photograph seem posed or contrived? What elements are more realistic?
2. How do these photographs compare with more heroic imagery of traditional history painting?

SEE SKILLBUILDER HANDBOOK, PAGE R23.

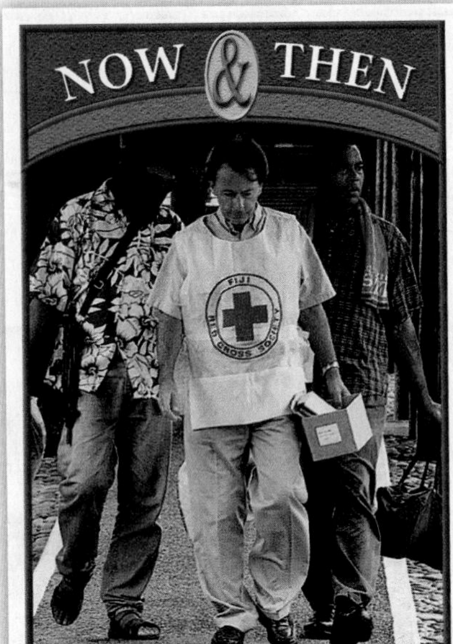

THE RED CROSS

Civil War nurse Clara Barton led the American branch of the Red Cross for 23 years. Today's International Red Cross can be found wherever human suffering occurs, not just in conventional armed conflicts. In Fiji in June 2000, rebels took the country's prime minister and 30 members of parliament hostage. The Red Cross employee above was given safe passage to give hostages medical attention, mattresses, and blankets.

Swiss businessman Henri Dunant first had the idea for the Red Cross when, in 1859, he saw injured soldiers abandoned on the battlefield in Italy. Horrified, he organized local people to provide aid to the wounded. Back in Switzerland, Dunant, and a group of lawyers and doctors, founded an international committee for the relief of wounded soldiers.

CIVILIANS FOLLOW NEW PATHS After the war ended, those who had served—Northerners and Southerners alike—had to find new directions for their lives.

Some war leaders continued their military careers, while others returned to civilian life. William Tecumseh Sherman remained in the army and spent most of his time fighting Native Americans in the West. Robert E. Lee lost Arlington, his plantation, which the Secretary of War of the Union had turned into a cemetery for Union dead. Lee became president of Washington College in Virginia, now known as Washington and Lee University. Lee swore renewed allegiance to the United States, but Congress accidentally neglected to restore his citizenship (until 1975). Still, Lee never spoke bitterly of Northerners or the Union.

Many veterans returned to their small towns and farms after the war. Others, as Grant noted, "found they were not satisfied with the farm, the store, or the workshop of the villages, but wanted larger fields." Many moved to the burgeoning cities or went west in search of opportunity.

Others tried to turn their wartime experience to good. The horrors that Union nurse Clara Barton witnessed during the war inspired her to spend her life helping others. In 1869, Barton went to Europe to rest and recuperate from her work during the war. She became involved in the activities of the International Committee of the Red Cross during the Franco-Prussian War. Returning to the United States, Barton helped found the American **Red Cross** in 1881. **B**

MAIN IDEA

Summarizing

B What were some effects that the war had on individuals?

THE ASSASSINATION OF LINCOLN Whatever plans Lincoln had to reunify the nation after the war, he never got to implement them. On April 14, 1865, five days after Lee surrendered to Grant at Appomattox Court House, Lincoln and his wife went to Ford's Theatre in Washington to see a British comedy, *Our American Cousin*. During the play's third act, a man silently opened the unguarded doors to the presidential box. He crept up behind Lincoln, raised a pistol, and fired, hitting the president in the back of the head.

The assassin, **John Wilkes Booth**—a 26-year-old actor and Southern sympathizer—then leaped down to the stage. In doing so, he caught his spur on one of the flags draped across the front of the box. Booth landed hard on his left leg and broke it. He rose and said something that the audience had trouble understanding. Some thought it was the state motto of Virginia, *"Sic semper tyrannis"*—in English "Thus be it ever to tyrants." Others thought he said, "The South is avenged!" Then he limped offstage into the wings.

Despite a broken leg, Booth managed to escape. Twelve days later, Union cavalry trapped him in a Virginia tobacco barn, and set the building on fire. When Booth still refused to surrender, a shot was fired. He may have been shot by cavalry or by himself, but the cavalry dragged him out. Booth is said to have whispered, "Tell my mother I died for my country. I did what I thought was best." His last words were "Useless, useless."

After Lincoln was shot, he remained unconscious through the night. He died at 7:22 A.M. the following morning, April 15. It was the first time a president of the United States had been assassinated. Secretary of the Navy Gideon Welles recorded the public's immediate reactions in his diary.

A Personal Voice
GIDEON WELLES

"It was a dark and gloomy morning, and rain set in. . . . On the Avenue in front of the White House were several hundred colored people, mostly women and children, weeping and wailing their loss. This crowd did not appear to diminish through the whole of that cold, wet day; they seemed not to know what was to be their fate since their great benefactor was dead, and their hopeless grief affected me more than almost anything else, though strong and brave men wept when I met them."

—quoted in *Voices from the Civil War*

▲ **Lincoln's body lies in state.**

The funeral train that carried Lincoln's body from Washington to his hometown of Springfield, Illinois, took 14 days for its journey. Approximately 7 million Americans, or almost one-third of the entire Union population, turned out to publicly mourn the martyred leader.

The Civil War had ended. Slavery and secession were no more. Now the country faced two different problems: how to restore the Southern states to the Union and how to integrate approximately 4 million newly freed African Americans into national life.

ASSESSMENT

1. **TERMS & NAMES** For each term or name, write a sentence explaining its significance.
   - **National Bank Act**
   - **Thirteenth Amendment**
   - **Red Cross**
   - **John Wilkes Booth**

MAIN IDEA

2. **TAKING NOTES**
   Copy the multiple-effects chart below on your paper and fill it in with consequences of the Civil War.

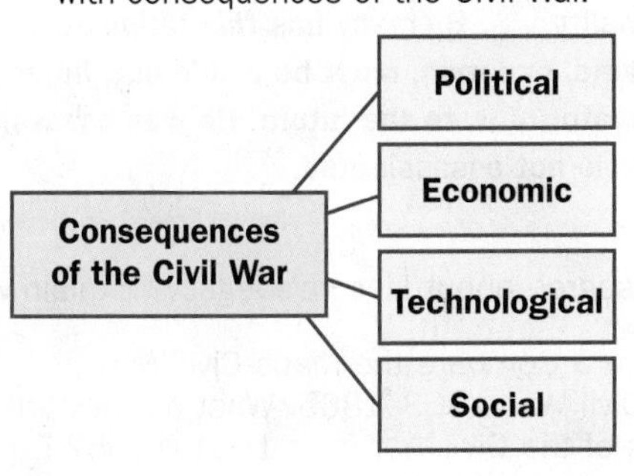

CRITICAL THINKING

3. **HYPOTHESIZING**
   Imagine that you are a member of a group of Southern leaders who must rebuild the South after the war. What would you recommend that the government do to help the South?
   Think About:
   - the economic devastation of the South
   - the human costs of the war
   - the numbers of newly freed slaves

4. **ANALYZING ISSUES**
   What political and social issues from the Civil War era do you think are still issues today? Use details from the text to support your answer.

5. **SYNTHESIZING**
   Write three questions that you have about the lives of African Americans after the Civil War.

CHAPTER 11 ASSESSMENT

VISUAL SUMMARY

THE CIVIL WAR

LONG-TERM CAUSES

- Conflict over slavery in territories
- Economic differences between North and South
- Conflict between states' rights and federal control

IMMEDIATE CAUSES

- Election of Lincoln
- Secession of southern states
- Firing on Fort Sumter

IMMEDIATE EFFECTS

- Abolition of slavery
- Widening gap between economies of North and South
- Physical devastation of the South
- Reunification of the country

LONG-TERM EFFECTS

- Reconstruction of the South
- Industrial boom
- Increased federal authority

TERMS & NAMES

For each term or name below, write a sentence explaining its connection to the Civil War.

1. Ulysses S. Grant
2. Robert E. Lee
3. Emancipation Proclamation
4. conscription
5. income tax
6. Andersonville
7. Gettysburg Address
8. Appomattox Court House
9. Thirteenth Amendment
10. John Wilkes Booth

MAIN IDEAS

Use your notes and the information in the chapter to answer the following questions.

The Civil War Begins

1. What were the military strategies of the North and South at the outset of the Civil War?
2. What advantages did the North have over the South?

The Politics of War

3. How did different groups react to the Emancipation Proclamation? Give examples.

Life During Wartime

4. What acts of protest occurred in both the North and South?

The North Takes Charge

5. In what ways did the South's morale deteriorate?
6. What was Grant and Sherman's rationale for using the strategy of total war?

The Legacy of the War

7. How did the Civil War provide the economic foundation for the United States to become an industrial giant?

CRITICAL THINKING

1. **USING YOUR NOTES** On a continuum like the one shown, mark where Abraham Lincoln's and Jefferson Davis's policies would fall. Support your ratings with evidence from the text.

◀ **less federal control** — **more federal control** ▶

2. **ANALYZING PRIMARY SOURCES** Poet Walt Whitman made the following observation about Lincoln.

> **"He leaves for America's history and biography, so far, not only its most dramatic reminiscence—he leaves, in my opinion, the greatest . . . personality. . . . By many has *this Union* been . . . help'd; but if one name, one man, must be pick'd out, he, most of all, is the conservator of it, to the future. He was assassinated—but the Union is not assassinated."**
>
> —Walt Whitman, *Specimen Days*

Do you agree or disagree about Lincoln's legacy? Explain why.

3. **INTERPRETING MAPS** Compare the maps Civil War, 1861–1862, and Civil War, 1863–1865. What do they tell you about the progress of the Civil War from 1861–1865? Explain.

STANDARDIZED TEST PRACTICE

Use the cartoon and your knowledge of U.S. history to answer question 1.

LINCOLN'S TWO DIFFICULTIES.

LIN. "WHAT? NO MONEY! NO MEN!"

1. According to the cartoon, President Lincoln's "two difficulties" are how to —
   A pay government salaries and build support in Congress.
   B reduce taxes and find good generals.
   C avoid bankruptcy and stop the draft riots.
   D finance the war and find enough soldiers to fight.

2. What technological advance contributed most to the Civil War's high casualty rate?
   F the ironclad ship
   G the minié ball
   H the land mine
   J the camera

3. Which pair of events are listed in the order in which they occurred?
   A Battle of Gettysburg; Battle of Antietam
   B New York City draft riots; First Battle of Bull Run
   C Battle of Gettysburg; fall of Atlanta
   D First Battle of Bull Run; firing on Fort Sumter

4. Which of the following is *not* true of the South after the Civil War?
   F It held 30 percent of the national wealth.
   G Most of its industry was destroyed.
   H Its labor system was dismantled.
   J As much as 40 percent of its livestock was wiped out.

For additional test practice, go online for:

- Diagnostic tests
- Tutorials

INTERACT WITH HISTORY

Think about the issues you explored at the beginning of the chapter. In light of what you now know about the Civil War, consider whether the use of force can preserve a nation. Write a short editorial for an 1861 newspaper supporting or opposing the war. Discuss what might have happened if the North allowed the South to secede.

FOCUS ON WRITING

Imagine that you are a U.S. citizen living during the Civil War, and the Emancipation Proclamation has just been issued. Decide whether you think the proclamation was effective. Write a letter to President Lincoln expressing your point of view.

COLLABORATIVE LEARNING

21ST CENTURY

Use the Internet to find Mary Chesnut's diary of the Civil War. As a group, read several entries and discuss them. Then create three diary entries that Mary Chesnut might have written. Make sure the entries are in keeping with her personality and writing style. Each entry should refer to significant events, issues, or people of the Civil War. Share your group's entries with the class.

MULTIMEDIA CONNECTIONS

DAYS OF DARKNESS: THE GETTYSBURG CIVILIANS

Gettysburg, Pennsylvania, was a sleepy agricultural town of about 2,400 residents when the Civil War arrived on its doorstep in the early summer of 1863. Many of the town's men were elsewhere, either fighting in the war or guarding their livestock in the countryside. This left mostly women and children to endure the battle. For three terrifying days they hid in basements or in tightly shuttered houses. Even after the battle finally ended the horrors continued, as the Gettysburg civilians emerged to find a scene of unimaginable death and destruction.

Explore some of the personal stories and recollections of the Gettysburg civilians online. You can find a wealth of information, video clips, primary sources, activities, and more at hmhsocialstudies.com.

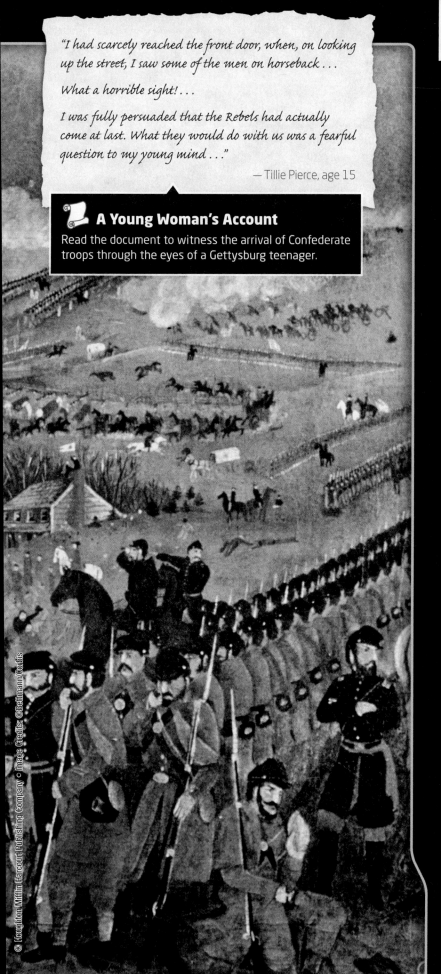

“I had scarcely reached the front door, when, on looking up the street, I saw some of the men on horseback . . .

What a horrible sight! . . .

I was fully persuaded that the Rebels had actually come at last. What they would do with us was a fearful question to my young mind . . .”

— Tillie Pierce, age 15

A Young Woman’s Account

Read the document to witness the arrival of Confederate troops through the eyes of a Gettysburg teenager.

CLICK THROUGH INTER/ACTIVITIES

hmhsocialstudies.com

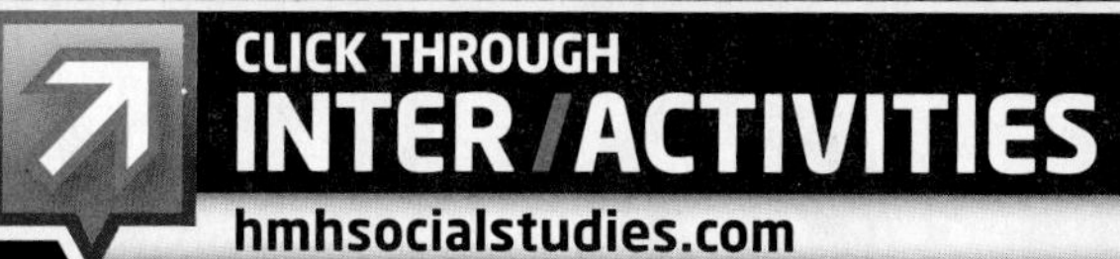

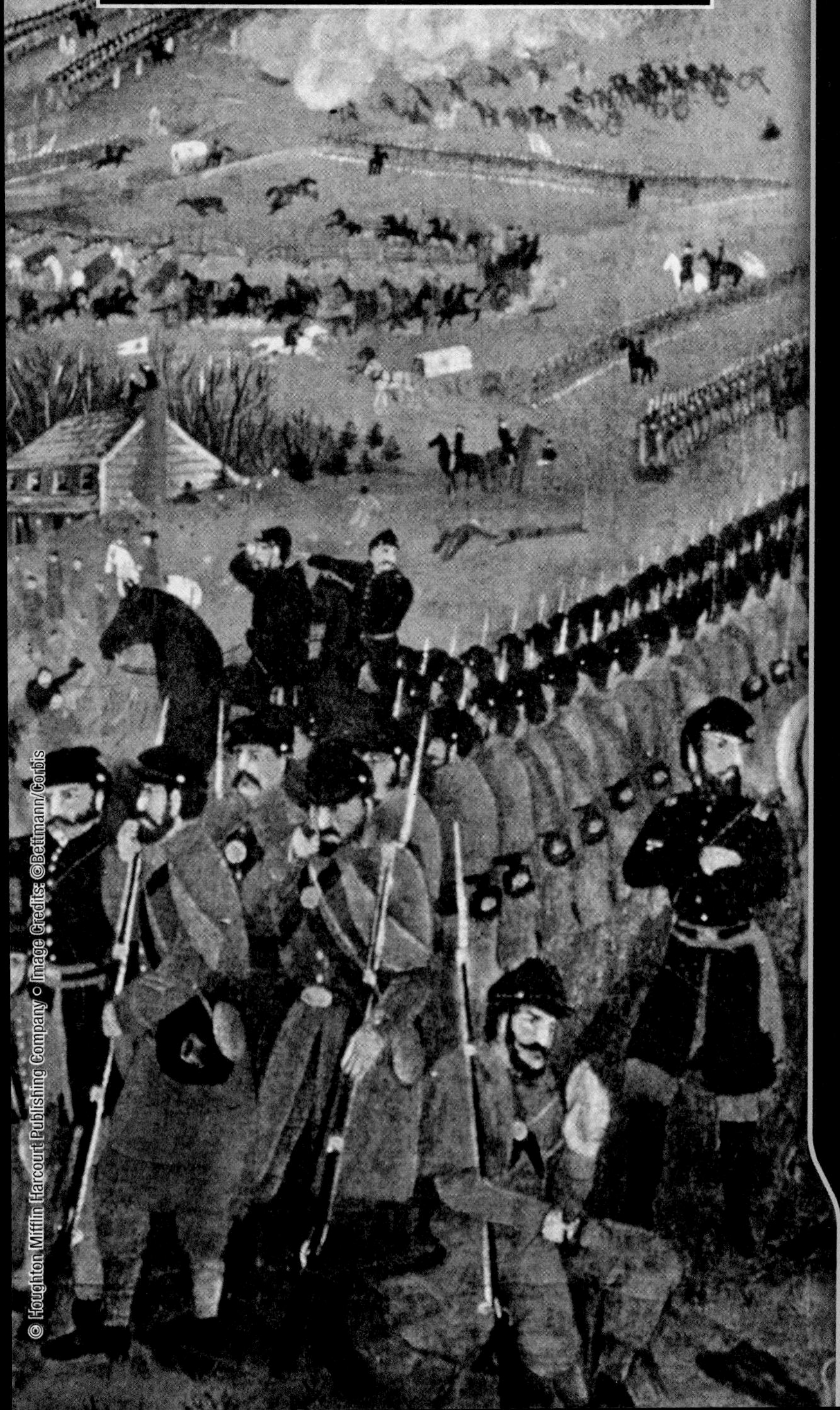

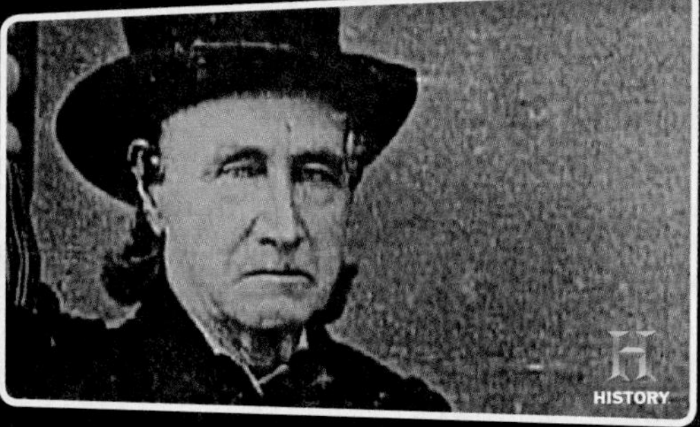

A Citizen-Soldier

Watch the video to meet John Burns, the man who would come to be called the “Citizen Hero of Gettysburg.”

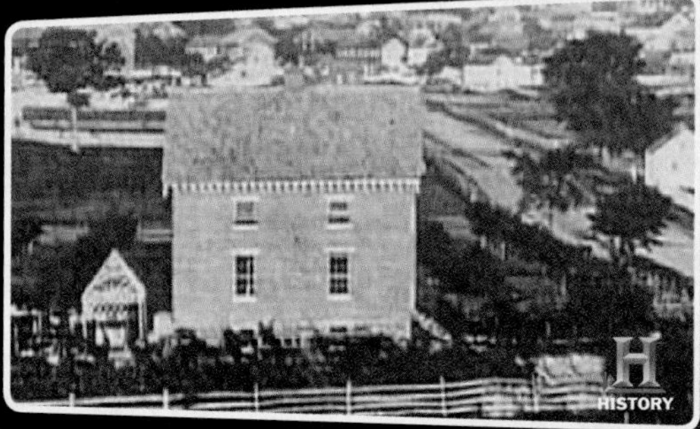

A Family’s Story

Watch the video to discover the story of courage and commitment exhibited by one Gettysburg family.

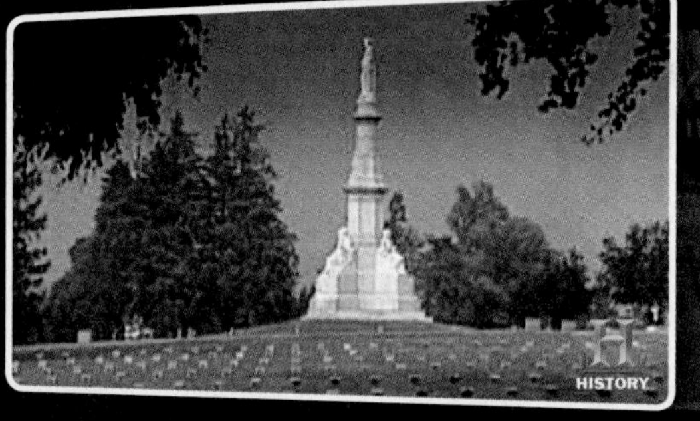

The National Cemetery

Watch the video to learn about the Soldiers’ National Cemetery and the speech President Lincoln gave there.

Reconstruction and Its Effects

Essential Question

What were the political struggles, accomplishments, and failures of Reconstruction in the years following the Civil War?

ALABAMA COURSE OF STUDY

15 Compare congressional and presidential reconstruction plans, including African-American political participation.

- Tracing economic changes in the post-Civil War period for whites and African Americans in the North and South, including the effectiveness of the Freedmen's Bureau.
- Describing social restructuring of the South, including Southern military districts, the role of carpetbaggers and scalawags, the creation of the black codes, and the Ku Klux Klan.
- Describing the Compromise of 1877.
- Summarizing post-Civil War constitutional amendments, including the Thirteenth, Fourteenth, and Fifteenth Amendments.
- Explaining causes for the impeachment of President Andrew Johnson.

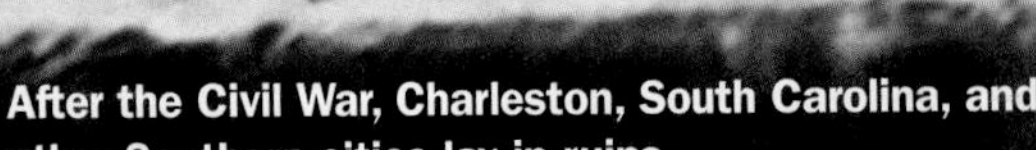

After the Civil War, Charleston, South Carolina, and other Southern cities lay in ruins.

USA

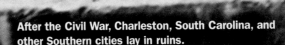

1865 Confederacy surrenders at Appomattox.

1865 Andrew Johnson becomes president after Lincoln's assassination.

1866 President Johnson presses for moderate Reconstruction policies.

1867 U.S. buys Alaska from Russia for $7.2 million.

1868 Congress impeaches President Johnson.

1868 Ulysses S. Grant is elected president.

1864 — 1868

WORLD

1866 Austro-Prussian War is fought.

1869 Mohandas K. Gandhi is born in India.

President Ulysses S. Grant: Scandal and Legacy

hmhsocialstudies.com VIDEO

INTERACT WITH HISTORY

The year is 1865, and at last the Civil War is over. The South's primary labor system, slavery, has been abolished. About 4.5 million African Americans now have their freedom but lack money, property, education, and opportunity. Southern states are beginning the process of readmission to the Union, but the effects of war continue to be felt throughout the South. Rail lines are unusable. Farms, plantations, and factories lie in ruins.

Explore the Issues

- How can Northern resources help the South?
- In what ways can the South rebuild its economy?
- What can the government do to assist African Americans?

1871 U.S. and Great Britain sign Treaty of Washington.

1872 Horace Greeley runs for president as a Liberal Republican.

1872 President Grant is reelected.

1876 Hayes-Tilden presidential election results in deadlock.

1877 Federal troops withdraw from the South.

1877 Rutherford B. Hayes is inaugurated.

1872

1876

1870 Unification of Italy is completed.

1871 Kaiser Wilhelm I unifies Germany.

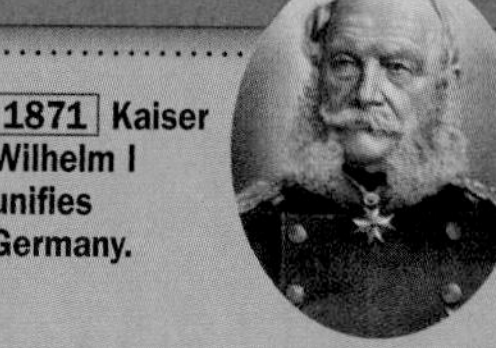

1874 British declare Gold Coast of Africa a colony.

1875 France's National Assembly votes to continue the Third Republic.

Image Credits: (bkgd), ©Mathew B. Brady/Corbis; (c), ©Corbis; (b), ©Hulton Archive/Getty Images

The Politics of Reconstruction

MAIN IDEA	WHY IT MATTERS NOW	Terms & Names
Congress opposed Lincoln's and Johnson's plans for Reconstruction and instead implemented its own plan to rebuild the South.	Reconstruction was an important step in African Americans' struggle for civil rights.	• Andrew Johnson • Reconstruction • Radical Republicans • Thaddeus Stevens • Wade-Davis Bill • Freedmen's Bureau • black codes • Fourteenth Amendment • impeach • Fifteenth Amendment

One American's Story

hmhsocialstudies.com
TAKING NOTES

Use the graphic organizer online to take notes on presidential Reconstruction and congressional Reconstruction.

As a young man, **Andrew Johnson**—who succeeded Abraham Lincoln as president—entered politics in Tennessee. He won several important offices, including those of congressman, governor, and U.S. senator.

After secession, Johnson was the only senator from a Confederate state to remain loyal to the Union. A former slave-owner, by 1863 Johnson supported abolition. He hated wealthy Southern planters, whom he held responsible for dragging poor whites into the war. Early in 1865, he endorsed harsh punishment for the rebellion's leaders.

A Personal Voice ANDREW JOHNSON

"The time has arrived when the American people should understand what crime is, and that it should be punished, and its penalties enforced and inflicted. . . . Treason must be made odious . . . traitors must be punished and impoverished . . . their social power must be destroyed. I say, as to the leaders, punishment. I say leniency, conciliation, and amnesty to the thousands whom they have misled and deceived."

—quoted in *Reconstruction: The Ending of the Civil War*

▲ Andrew Johnson, the 17th president of the United States

On becoming president, Johnson faced not only the issue of whether to punish or pardon former Confederates but also a larger problem: how to bring the defeated Confederate states back into the Union.

Lincoln's Plan for Reconstruction

Reconstruction was the period during which the United States began to rebuild after the Civil War, lasting from 1865 to 1877. The term also refers to the process the federal government used to readmit the Confederate states. Complicating the process was the fact that Abraham Lincoln, Andrew Johnson, and Congress had differing ideas on how Reconstruction should be handled.

LINCOLN'S TEN-PERCENT PLAN Lincoln, before his death, had made it clear that he favored a lenient Reconstruction policy. Lincoln believed that secession was constitutionally impossible and therefore that the Confederate states had never left the Union. He contended that it was individuals, not states, who had rebelled and that the Constitution gave the president the power to pardon individuals. Lincoln wished to make the South's return to the Union as quick and easy as possible.

In December 1863, President Lincoln announced his Proclamation of Amnesty and Reconstruction, also known as the Ten-Percent Plan. The government would pardon all Confederates—except high-ranking Confederate officials and those accused of crimes against prisoners of war—who would swear allegiance to the Union. After ten percent of those on the 1860 voting lists took this oath of allegiance, a Confederate state could form a new state government and gain representation in Congress. (A)

Summarizing

(A) What was President Lincoln's planned approach to Reconstruction?

Under Lincoln's terms, four states—Arkansas, Louisiana, Tennessee, and Virginia—moved toward readmission to the Union. However, Lincoln's moderate Reconstruction plan angered a minority of Republicans in Congress, known as **Radical Republicans.** Led by Senator Charles Sumner of Massachusetts and Representative **Thaddeus Stevens** of Pennsylvania, the Radicals wanted to destroy the political power of former slaveholders. Most of all, they wanted African Americans to be given full citizenship and the right to vote. In 1865, the idea of African-American suffrage was truly radical; no other country that had abolished slavery had given former slaves the vote.

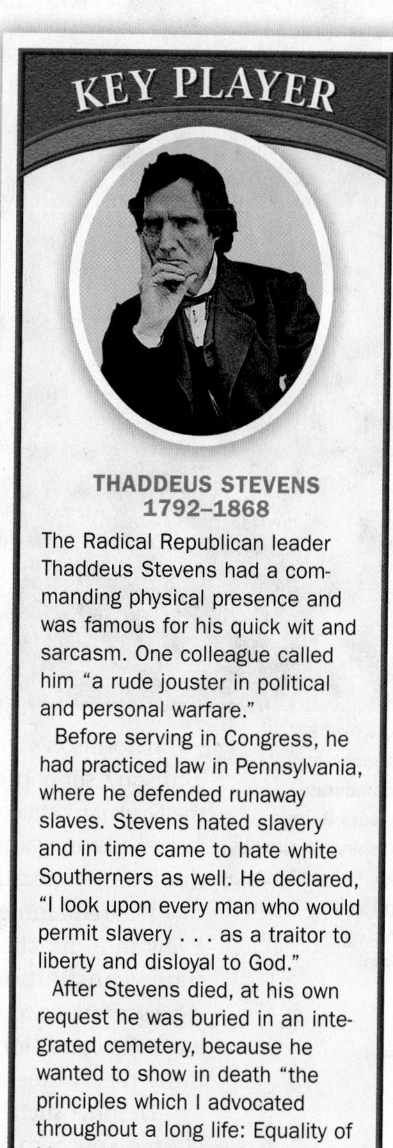

THADDEUS STEVENS
1792–1868

The Radical Republican leader Thaddeus Stevens had a commanding physical presence and was famous for his quick wit and sarcasm. One colleague called him "a rude jouster in political and personal warfare."

Before serving in Congress, he had practiced law in Pennsylvania, where he defended runaway slaves. Stevens hated slavery and in time came to hate white Southerners as well. He declared, "I look upon every man who would permit slavery . . . as a traitor to liberty and disloyal to God."

After Stevens died, at his own request he was buried in an integrated cemetery, because he wanted to show in death "the principles which I advocated throughout a long life: Equality of Man before his Creator."

RADICAL REACTION In July 1864, the Radicals responded to the Ten-Percent Plan by passing the **Wade-Davis Bill,** which proposed that Congress, not the president, be responsible for Reconstruction. It also declared that for a state government to be formed, a majority—not just ten percent—of those eligible to vote in 1860 would have to take a solemn oath to support the Constitution.

Lincoln used a pocket veto to kill the Wade-Davis Bill after Congress adjourned. According to the Constitution, a president has ten days to either sign or veto a bill passed by Congress. If the president does neither, the bill will automatically become law. When a bill is passed less than ten days before the end of a congressional session, the president can prevent its becoming law by simply ignoring, or "pocketing," it. The Radicals called Lincoln's pocket veto an outrage and asserted that Congress had supreme authority over Reconstruction. The stage was set for a presidential-congressional showdown.

Johnson's Plan

Lincoln's assassination in April 1865 left his successor, the Democrat Andrew Johnson, to deal with the Reconstruction controversy. A staunch Unionist, Johnson had often expressed his intent to deal harshly with Confederate leaders. Most white Southerners therefore considered Johnson a traitor to his region, while Radicals believed that he was one of them. Both were wrong.

▲ Former Confederate officers George Washington Custis Lee, Robert E. Lee, and Walter Taylor, photographed in 1865

JOHNSON CONTINUES LINCOLN'S POLICIES In May 1865, with Congress in recess, Johnson announced his own plan, Presidential Reconstruction. He declared that each remaining Confederate state—Alabama, Florida, Georgia, Mississippi, North Carolina, South Carolina, and Texas—could be readmitted to the Union if it would meet several conditions. Each state would have to withdraw its secession, swear allegiance to the Union, annul Confederate war debts, and ratify the Thirteenth Amendment, which abolished slavery.

To the dismay of Thaddeus Stevens and the Radicals, Johnson's plan differed little from Lincoln's. The one major difference was that Johnson wished to prevent most high-ranking Confederates and wealthy Southern landowners from taking the oath needed for voting privileges. The Radicals were especially upset that Johnson's plan, like Lincoln's, failed to address the needs of former slaves in three areas: land, voting rights, and protection under the law. (B)

MAIN IDEA

Contrasting
(B) How did the views of Presidents Lincoln and Johnson on Reconstruction differ from the views of the Radicals?

If Johnson's policies angered Radicals, they relieved most white Southerners. Johnson's support of states' rights instead of a strong central government reassured the Southern states. Although Johnson supported abolition, he was not in favor of former slaves gaining the right to vote—he pardoned more than 13,000 former Confederates because he believed that "white men alone must manage the South."

The remaining Confederate states quickly agreed to Johnson's terms. Within a few months, these states—all except Texas—held conventions to draw up new state constitutions, to set up new state governments, and to elect representatives to Congress. However, some Southern states did not fully comply with the conditions for returning to the Union. For example, Mississippi did not ratify the Thirteenth Amendment.

Despite such instances of noncompliance, in December 1865, the newly elected Southern legislators arrived in Washington to take their seats. Fifty-eight of them had previously sat in the Congress of the Confederacy, six had served in the Confederate cabinet, and four had fought against the United States as Confederate generals. Johnson pardoned them all—a gesture that infuriated the Radicals and made African Americans feel they had been betrayed. In an 1865 editorial, an African-American newspaper publisher responded to Johnson's actions.

A PERSONAL VOICE PHILIP A. BELL

> "**The war does not appear to us to be ended, nor rebellion suppressed. They have commenced reconstruction on disloyal principles. If rebel soldiers are allowed to mumble through oaths of allegiance, and vote Lee's officers into important offices, and if Legislatures, elected by such voters, are allowed to define the provisions of the Amnesty Proclamation, then were our conquests vain. . . . Already we see the fruits of this failure on the part of Government to mete out full justice to the loyal blacks, and retribution to the disloyal whites.**"
>
> —quoted in *Witness for Freedom: African American Voices on Race, Slavery, and Emancipation*

PRESIDENTIAL RECONSTRUCTION COMES TO A STANDSTILL When the 39th Congress convened in December 1865, the Radical Republican legislators, led by Thaddeus Stevens, disputed Johnson's claim that Reconstruction was complete. Many of them believed that the Southern states were not much different from the way they had been before the war. As a result, Congress refused to admit the newly elected Southern legislators.

At the same time, moderate Republicans pushed for new laws to remedy weaknesses they saw in Johnson's plan. In February 1866, Congress voted to continue and enlarge the **Freedmen's Bureau.** The bureau, established by Congress in the last month of the war, assisted former slaves and poor whites in the South by distributing clothing and food. In addition, the Freedmen's Bureau set up more than 40 hospitals, approximately 4,000 schools, 61 industrial institutes, and 74 teacher-training centers.

▲ One important project of the Freedmen's Bureau was establishing primary schools, like the one shown here, for the children of former slaves.

CIVIL RIGHTS ACT OF 1866 Two months later, Congress passed the Civil Rights Act of 1866, which gave African Americans citizenship and forbade states from passing discriminatory laws—**black codes**—that severely restricted African Americans' lives. Mississippi and South Carolina had first enacted black codes in 1865, and other Southern states had rapidly followed suit.

Black codes had the effect of restoring many of the restrictions of slavery by prohibiting blacks from carrying weapons, serving on juries, testifying against whites, marrying whites, and traveling without permits. In some states, African Americans were forbidden to own land. Even worse, in many areas resentful whites used violence to keep blacks from improving their position in society. To many members of Congress, the passage of black codes indicated that the South had not given up the idea of keeping African Americans in bondage. **C**

> **MAIN IDEA**
> **Analyzing Causes**
> **C** How did black codes help bring about the passage of the Civil Rights Act of 1866?

Johnson shocked everyone when he vetoed both the Freedmen's Bureau Act and the Civil Rights Act. Congress, Johnson contended, had gone far beyond anything "contemplated by the authors of the Constitution." These vetoes proved to be the opening shots in a battle between the president and Congress. By rejecting the two acts, Johnson alienated the moderate Republicans who were trying to improve his Reconstruction plan. He also angered the Radicals by appearing to support Southerners who denied African Americans their full rights. Johnson had not been in office a year when presidential Reconstruction ground to a halt.

Congressional Reconstruction

Angered by Johnson's actions, radical and moderate Republican factions decided to work together to shift the control of the Reconstruction process from the executive branch to the legislature, beginning a period of "congressional Reconstruction."

MODERATES AND RADICALS JOIN FORCES In mid-1866, moderate Republicans joined with Radicals to override the president's vetoes of the Civil Rights and Freedmen's Bureau acts. The Civil Rights Act of 1866 became the first major legislation ever enacted over a presidential veto. In addition, Congress drafted the **Fourteenth Amendment,** which provided a constitutional basis for the Civil Rights Act.

The Fourteenth Amendment made "all persons born or naturalized in the United States" citizens of the country. All were entitled to equal protection of the law, and no state could deprive any person of life, liberty, or property without due process of law. The amendment did not specifically give African Americans the vote. However, it did specify that if any state prevented a portion of its male citizens from voting, that state would lose a percentage of its congressional seats equal to the percentage of citizens kept from the polls. Another provision barred most Confederate leaders from holding federal or state offices unless they were permitted to do so by a two-thirds-majority vote of Congress. D

Congress adopted the Fourteenth Amendment and sent it to the states for approval. If the Southern states had voted to ratify it, most Northern legislators and their constituents would have been satisfied to accept them back into the Union. President Johnson, however, believed that the amendment treated former Confederate leaders too harshly and that it was wrong to force states to accept an amendment that their legislators had no part in drafting. Therefore, he advised the Southern states to reject the amendment. All but Tennessee did reject it, and the amendment was not ratified until 1868.

MAIN IDEA

Summarizing

D What were the main benefits that the Fourteenth Amendment offered African Americans?

1866 CONGRESSIONAL ELECTIONS The question of who should control Reconstruction became one of the central issues in the bitter 1866 congressional elections. Johnson, accompanied by General Ulysses S. Grant, went on a speaking tour, urging voters to elect representatives who agreed with his Reconstruction policy. But his train trip from Washington to St. Louis and Chicago and back was a disaster. Johnson offended many voters with his rough language and behavior. His audiences responded by jeering at him and cheering Grant.

In addition, race riots in Memphis, Tennessee, and New Orleans, Louisiana, caused the deaths of at least 80 African Americans. Such violence convinced Northern voters that the federal government must step in to protect former slaves. In the 1866 elections, moderate and Radical Republicans won a landslide victory over Democrats. The Republicans gained a two-thirds majority in Congress, ensuring them the numbers they needed to override presidential vetoes. By March 1867, the 40th Congress was ready to move ahead with its Reconstruction policy. E

MAIN IDEA

Analyzing Effects

E What effect did the election of 1866 have on Republicans' ability to carry out their plan for Reconstruction?

RECONSTRUCTION ACT OF 1867 Radicals and moderates joined in passing the Reconstruction Act of 1867, which did not recognize state governments formed under the Lincoln and Johnson plans—except for that of Tennessee, which had ratified the Fourteenth Amendment and had been readmitted to the Union. The act divided the other ten former Confederate states into five military districts, each headed by a Union general. The voters in the districts—including African-American men—would elect delegates to conventions in which new state

Major Reconstruction Legislation, 1865–1870

Legislation	Provisions
Freedmen's Bureau Acts (1865–1866)	Offered assistance, such as medical aid and education, to freed slaves and war refugees
Civil Rights Act of 1866	Granted citizenship and equal protection under the law to African Americans
Fourteenth Amendment (ratified 1868)	Makes all persons "born or naturalized in the United States" citizens; stipulates that states that prevented male citizens from voting would lose a percentage of their congressional seats; barred most Confederate leaders from holding political offices
Reconstruction Act of 1867	Abolished governments formed in the former Confederate states; divided those states into five military districts; set up requirements for readmission to the Union
Fifteenth Amendment (ratified 1870)	States that no one can be kept from voting because of "race, color, or previous condition of servitude"
Enforcement Act of 1870	Protected the voting rights of African Americans and gave the federal government power to enforce the Fifteenth Amendment

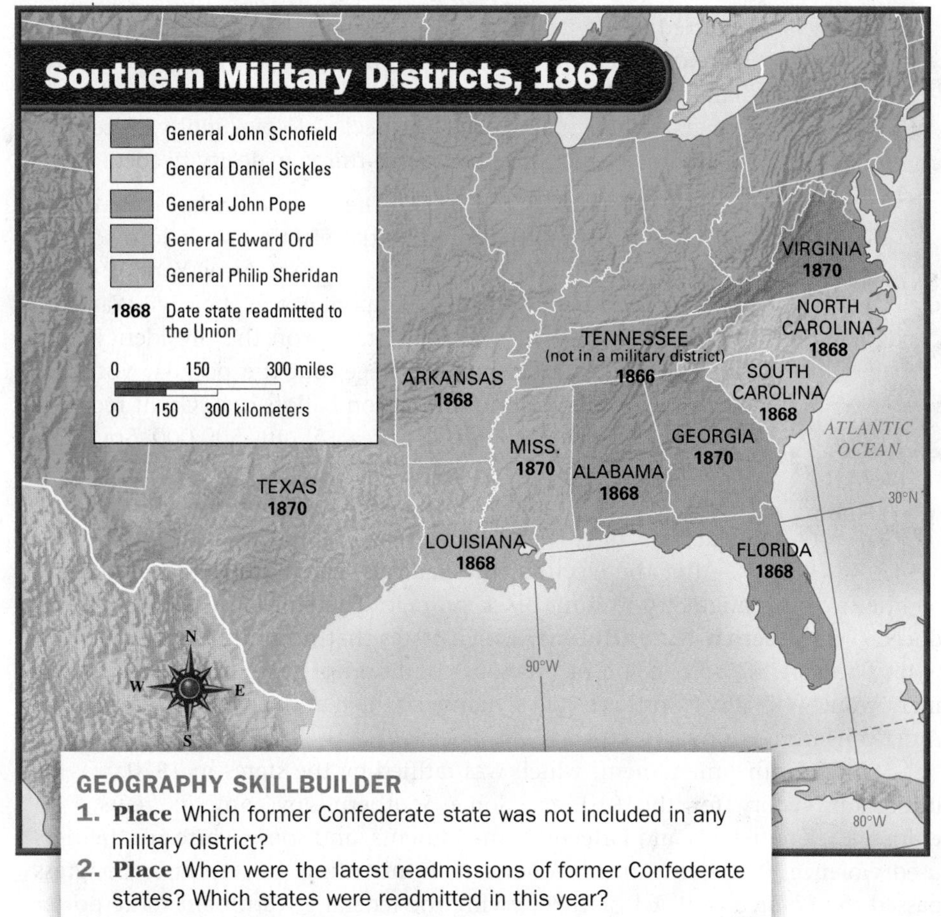

GEOGRAPHY SKILLBUILDER

1. **Place** Which former Confederate state was not included in any military district?
2. **Place** When were the latest readmissions of former Confederate states? Which states were readmitted in this year?

constitutions would be drafted. In order for a state to reenter the Union, its constitution had to ensure African-American men the vote, and the state had to ratify the Fourteenth Amendment.

Johnson vetoed the Reconstruction Act of 1867 because he believed it was in conflict with the Constitution. Congress promptly overrode the veto.

JOHNSON IMPEACHED Radical leaders felt President Johnson was not carrying out his constitutional obligation to enforce the Reconstruction Act. For instance, Johnson removed military officers who attempted to enforce the act. The Radicals looked for grounds on which to **impeach** the president—that is, to formally charge him with misconduct in office. The House of Representatives has the sole power to impeach federal officials, who are then tried in the Senate.

In March 1867, Congress had passed the Tenure of Office Act, which stated that the president could not remove cabinet officers "during the term of the president by whom they may have been appointed" without the consent of the Senate. One purpose of this act was to protect Secretary of War Edwin Stanton, the Radicals' ally.

Johnson, along with many others, was certain that the Tenure of Office Act was unconstitutional. To force a court test of the act, Johnson fired Secretary of War Stanton. His action provided the Radicals with the opportunity they needed—the House brought 11 charges of impeachment against Johnson, 9 of which were based on his violation of the Tenure of Office Act. Johnson's lawyers disputed these charges by pointing out that President Lincoln, not Johnson, had appointed Secretary Stanton, so the act did not apply.

Johnson's trial before the Senate took place from March to May 1868. On the day the final vote was taken at the trial, tension

The lucky holders of tickets like this one could see Johnson's impeachment proceedings in 1868.

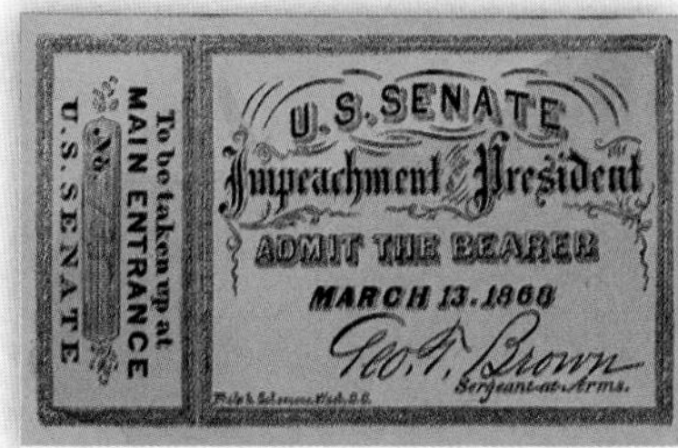

▲ A campaign poster supporting the Republican ticket in the election of 1868

mounted in the jammed Senate galleries. Would the Radicals get the two-thirds vote needed for conviction? People in the Senate chamber held their breath as one by one the senators gave their verdicts. When the last senator declared "Not guilty," the vote was 35 to 19, one short of the two-thirds majority needed.

ULYSSES S. GRANT ELECTED The Democrats knew that they could not win the 1868 presidential election with Johnson, so they nominated the wartime governor of New York, Horatio Seymour. Seymour's Republican opponent was the Civil War hero Ulysses S. Grant. In November, Grant won the presidency by a wide margin in the electoral college, but the popular vote was less decisive. Out of almost 6 million ballots cast, Grant received a majority of only 306,592 votes. About 500,000 Southern African Americans had voted, most of them for Grant, bringing home the importance of the African-American vote to the Republican Party.

After the election, the Radicals feared that pro-Confederate Southern whites might try to limit black suffrage. Therefore, the Radicals introduced the **Fifteenth Amendment,** which states that no one can be kept from voting because of "race, color, or previous condition of servitude." The amendment would also affect Northern states, many of which at this time barred African Americans from voting.

The Fifteenth Amendment, which was ratified by the states in 1870, was an important victory for the Radicals. Some Southern governments refused to enforce the Fourteenth and Fifteenth Amendments, and some white Southerners used violence to prevent African Americans from voting. In response, Congress passed the Enforcement Act of 1870, giving the federal government more power to punish those who tried to prevent African Americans from exercising their rights.

Such political achievements were not, however, the only changes taking place during Reconstruction. The period was also a time of profound social and economic changes in the South.

SECTION 1 ASSESSMENT

1. **TERMS & NAMES** For each term or name, write a sentence explaining its significance.
   - **Andrew Johnson**
   - **Reconstruction**
   - **Radical Republicans**
   - **Thaddeus Stevens**
   - **Wade-Davis Bill**
   - **Freedmen's Bureau**
   - **black codes**
   - **Fourteenth Amendment**
   - **impeach**
   - **Fifteenth Amendment**

MAIN IDEA

2. **TAKING NOTES**
Fill in a chart like the one shown with features of presidential Reconstruction and congressional Reconstruction.

Presidential Reconstruction	Congressional Reconstruction

Why did presidential Reconstruction fail?

CRITICAL THINKING

3. **HYPOTHESIZING**
Describe how Reconstruction might have been different if Abraham Lincoln had lived.

4. **INTERPRETING CHARTS**
Look again at the Major Reconstruction Legislation chart. What was the primary focus of the major Reconstruction legislation?

5. **EVALUATING DECISIONS**
Do you think the Radical Republicans were justified in impeaching President Johnson? Why or why not? **Think About:**
   - the controversy over Reconstruction policies
   - the meaning of the Tenure of Office Act
   - Johnson's vetoes

Reconstructing Society

MAIN IDEA	WHY IT MATTERS NOW	Terms & Names
Various groups contributed to the rebuilding of Southern society after the war.	**Many African-American institutions, including colleges and churches, were established during Reconstruction.**	• **scalawag** • **carpetbagger** • **Hiram Revels** • **sharecropping** • **tenant farming**

One American's Story

hmhsocialstudies.com TAKING NOTES

Use the graphic organizer online to take notes on problems facing the South after the Civil War and solutions that were offered for those problems.

Robert G. Fitzgerald, an African American, was born free in Delaware in 1840. During the Civil War, he served in both the U.S. Army and the U.S. Navy. In 1866, the Freedmen's Bureau sent Fitzgerald to teach in a small Virginia town. His students were former slaves of all ages who were hungry to learn reading, writing, spelling, arithmetic, and geography.

▲ **Robert Fitzgerald**

A PERSONAL VOICE ROBERT G. FITZGERALD

"I came to Virginia one year ago on the 22nd of this month. Erected a school, organized and named the Freedman's Chapel School. Now (June 29th) have about 60 who have been for several months engaged in the study of arithmetic, writing, etc. etc. This morning sent in my report accompanied with compositions from about 12 of my advanced writers instructed from the Alphabet up to their [present] condition, their progress has been surprisingly rapid."

—quoted in *Proud Shoes*

Fitzgerald was one of many who labored diligently against the illiteracy and poverty that slavery had forced upon most African Americans. The need to help former slaves, however, was just one of many issues the nation confronted during Reconstruction.

Conditions in the Postwar South

Under the congressional Reconstruction program, state constitutional conventions met and Southern voters elected new, Republican-dominated governments. In 1868, the former Confederate states of Alabama, Arkansas, Florida, Louisiana, North Carolina, and South Carolina reentered the Union (joining Tennessee, which had reentered earlier). The remaining four former Confederate states completed the process by 1870. However, even after all the states were back in the Union, the Republicans did not end the process of Reconstruction because they wanted to make economic changes in the South.

Clearing battlefields of human remains was just one of many tasks facing Reconstruction governments.

PHYSICAL AND ECONOMIC CONDITIONS Because the Civil War was fought mostly on Southern soil, many of the new Southern state governments faced the challenge of physically rebuilding a battle-scarred region. The Union general William T. Sherman estimated that his troops alone had destroyed about $100 million worth of Confederate property in Georgia and South Carolina. Charred buildings, twisted railroad tracks, demolished bridges, neglected roads, and abandoned farms had to be restored or replaced.

The economic effects of the war were devastating for the South. Property values had plummeted. Those who had invested in Confederate bonds had little hope of recovering their money. Many small farms were ruined or in disrepair. As a result of these and other factors, Southerners of every economic class were poorer than they had been at the start of the war. In one county of Alabama, for example, the wealth per capita among whites dropped from $18,000 in 1860 to about $3,000 in 1870.

Not only were many of the South's economic resources destroyed, but the region's population was devastated. More than one-fifth of the adult white men of the Confederacy died in the war. Many of those who did return from battle were maimed for life. Tens of thousands of Southern African-American men also died, either fighting for the Union or working in Confederate labor camps. (A)

MAIN IDEA

Identifying Problems

(A) What were the main postwar problems that Reconstruction governments in the South had to solve?

PUBLIC WORKS PROGRAMS The Republican governments built roads, bridges, and railroads and established orphanages and institutions for the care of people with mental illnesses and disabilities. They also created the first public school systems that most Southern states had ever had.

These ambitious projects—and the larger state governments that were required to administer them—were expensive. Few financial resources were available, and Northern capitalists were reluctant to invest in the region. To raise money, most Southern state governments increased taxes of all kinds, draining existing resources and slowing the region's recovery.

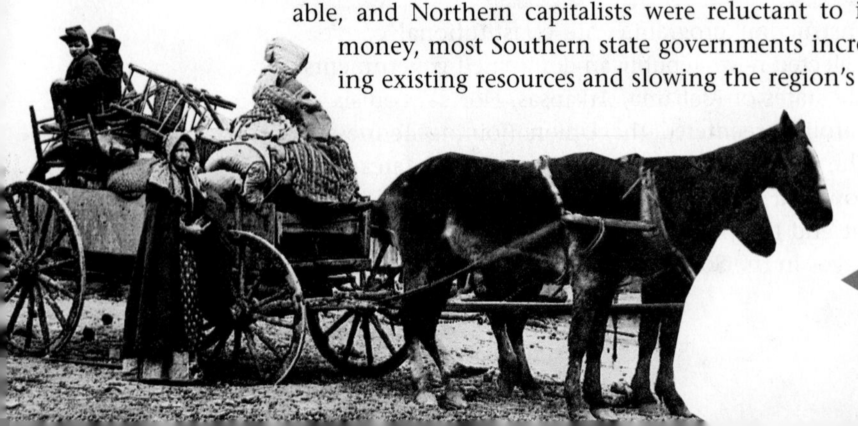

Southern families like this one lost their homes and most of their possessions because of economic problems after the Civil War.

Politics in the Postwar South

Another difficulty facing the new Republican governments was that different groups within the Republican Party in the South often had conflicting goals.

SCALAWAGS AND CARPETBAGGERS Although the terms *scalawag* and *carpetbagger* were negative labels imposed by political enemies, historians still use the terms when referring to the two groups. Democrats, opposed to the Republicans' plan for Reconstruction, called white Southerners who joined the Republican Party **scalawags.** Some scalawags hoped to gain political offices with the help of the African-American vote and then use those offices to enrich themselves. Southern Democrats unfairly pointed to these unscrupulous individuals as representative of all white Southern Republicans. Some so-called scalawags honestly thought that a Republican government offered the best chances for the South to rebuild and industrialize. The majority were small farmers who wanted to improve their economic and political position and to prevent the former wealthy planters from regaining power.

The Democrats used an equally unflattering name for the Northerners who moved to the South after the war—**carpetbaggers.** The name referred to the belief that Northerners arrived with so few belongings that everything could fit in a carpetbag, a small piece of luggage made of carpeting. Most white Southerners believed that the carpetbaggers wanted to exploit the South's postwar turmoil for their own profit. However, like the scalawags, carpetbaggers had mixed motives. Some were Freedmen's Bureau agents, teachers, and ministers who felt a moral duty to help former slaves. Others wanted to buy land or hoped to start new industries legitimately. Still others truly were the dishonest businesspeople whom the Southerners scorned. B

Comparing

B What were some similarities in the goals of scalawags and carpetbaggers? of carpetbaggers and African Americans?

Northerners were thought to carry their belongings in carpetbags such as this one. ▼

Analyzing *Political Cartoons*

UNWELCOME GUEST

Of all the political cartoonists of the 19th century, Thomas Nast (1840–1902) had the greatest and most long-lasting influence. Nast created symbols that have become part of America's visual heritage, symbols that include the Democratic donkey, the Republican elephant, and Santa Claus.

This cartoon from a Southern Democratic newspaper depicts Carl Schurz, a liberal Republican who advocated legal equality for African Americans. Schurz is shown as a carpetbagger trudging down a dusty Southern road as a crowd of people watch his arrival.

SKILLBUILDER Analyzing Political Cartoons

1. Is Schurz shown in a positive or negative light? How can you tell?
2. Why do you think the cartoonist portrays the Southern people standing in a group, far away from Schurz?

SEE SKILLBUILDER HANDBOOK, PAGE R24.

▲ **This woodcut from a newspaper shows freedmen voting in Washington, D.C., June 1867.**

AFRICAN AMERICANS AS VOTERS African Americans—who made up the largest group of Southern Republicans—gained voting rights as a result of the Fifteenth Amendment. During Reconstruction, African-American men registered to vote for the first time; nine out of ten of them supported the Republican Party. Although most former slaves had little experience with politics, and relatively few could read and write, they were eager to exercise their voting rights.

A Personal Voice
WILLIAM BEVERLY NASH

> **"We are not prepared for this suffrage. But we can learn. Give a man tools and let him commence to use them and in time he will earn a trade. So it is with voting. We may not understand it at the start, but in time we shall learn to do our duty."**
>
> —quoted in *The Trouble They Seen: Black People Tell the Story of Reconstruction*

In many areas of the South, almost 90 percent of the qualified African-American voters voted. Early in 1868, a Northerner in Alabama observed that "in defiance of fatigue, hardship, hunger, and threats of employers," African Americans still flocked to the polls.

POLITICAL DIFFERENCES Conflicting goals among Republican Party members led to disunity in the party's ranks. In particular, few scalawags shared the Republican commitment to civil rights and suffrage for African Americans. Over time, many of them returned to the Democratic Party.

In addition, some Republican governors began to appoint white Democrats to office in an attempt to persuade more white voters to vote Republican. This policy backfired—it convinced very few white Democrats to change parties, and it made blacks feel betrayed.

The new status of African Americans required fundamental changes in the attitudes of most Southern whites. Some whites supported the Republicans during Reconstruction and thought that the end of slavery would ultimately benefit the South. In addition, some Southern farmers and merchants thought that investment by Northerners would help the South recover from the war. Many white Southerners, though, refused to accept blacks' new status and resisted the idea of equal rights. A Freedmen's Bureau agent noted that some "Southern whites are quite indignant if they are not treated with the same deference as they were accustomed to" under the system of slavery.

Moreover, white Southerners had to accept defeat and the day-to-day involvement of Northerners in their lives. Eva B. Jones, the wife of a former Confederate officer, understood how difficult that adjustment was for many. In a letter to her mother-in-law, she expressed emotions that were typical of those felt by many ex-Confederates.

MAIN IDEA

Analyzing Motives
C What do you think the former Confederates who emigrated hoped to accomplish?

A PERSONAL VOICE EVA B. JONES

> **"A joyless future of probable ignominy, poverty, and want is all that spreads before us. . . . You see, it is with no resigned spirit that *I* yield to the iron yoke our conqueror forges for his fallen and powerless foe. The degradation of a whole country and a proud people is indeed a mighty, an all-enveloping sorrow."**
>
> —quoted in *The Children of Pride: A True Story of Georgia and the Civil War*

Not all white Southerners were willing to remain in the South. Several thousand planters emigrated to Europe, Mexico, and Brazil after the war. **C**

Former Slaves Face Many Challenges

Amid the turmoil of the South during Reconstruction, African Americans looked forward to new opportunities. Slaves had been forbidden to travel without permission, to marry legally, to attend school, and to live and work as they chose. After the war, the 4 million former slaves gained the chance to take control of their lives.

NEW-WON FREEDOMS At first, many former slaves were cautious about testing the limits of their freedom. One freedman explained, "We was afraid to move. Just like . . . turtles after emancipation. Just stick our heads out to see how the land lay." As the reality of freedom sank in, freed African Americans faced many decisions. Without land, jobs, tools, money, and with few skills besides those of farming, what were they to do? How would they feed and clothe themselves? How and where would they live?

During slavery, slaves were forbidden to travel without a pass. White planters had enforced that rule by patrolling the roads. During Reconstruction, African Americans took advantage of their new freedom to go where they wanted. One former slave from Texas explained the passion for traveling: "They seemed to want to get closer to freedom, so they'd know what it was—like it was a place or a city."

The majority of freed African Americans who moved, however, were not just testing their freedom. Thousands were eager to leave plantations that they associated with oppression and move to Southern towns and cities where they could find jobs. From 1865 to 1870, the African-American population of the ten largest Southern cities doubled.

REUNIFICATION OF FAMILIES Slavery had split many African-American families apart; spouses sometimes lived on different plantations, and children were often separated from their parents. During Reconstruction, many freed African Americans took advantage of their new mobility to search for loved ones. In 1865, for example, one man walked more than 600 miles from Georgia to North Carolina, looking for his wife and children.

Many former slaves bought charts like this one to keep track of their family histories. ▼

Among former slaves, younger generations sometimes helped educate their elders. A young woman in Mt. Meigs, Alabama, teaches her mother to read.

The Freedmen's Bureau worked to reunite families, and African-American newspapers printed poignant "Information Wanted" notices about missing relatives. Tragically, in many cases the lost family members were never found. However, freed persons, who had been denied legal unions under slavery, could now marry legally, and raise children without the fear that someone would sell them. For African Americans, reconstructing their families was an important part of establishing an identity as a free people.

EDUCATION Because slaves had been punished if they tried to learn how to read and write, nearly 80 percent of freed African Americans over the age of 20 were illiterate in 1870. During Reconstruction, however, freed people of all ages—grandparents, parents, and children alike—sought education.

African Americans established educational institutions with assistance from a number of public and private organizations, including the Freedmen's Bureau and African-American churches. One college founded during Reconstruction was Hampton Institute in Hampton, Virginia. By 1870, African Americans had spent more than $1 million on education. Initially, most teachers in black schools were Northern whites, about half of whom were women. However, educated African Americans like Robert G. Fitzgerald also became teachers, and by 1869, black teachers outnumbered whites in these schools.

Some white Southerners, outraged by the idea of educated African Americans, responded violently. In one instance, the former slave Washington Eager was murdered because, as his brother explained, he had become "too big a man . . . he [could] write and read and put it down himself." Despite the threat of violence, freed people were determined to learn. By 1877, more than 600,000 African Americans were enrolled in elementary schools.

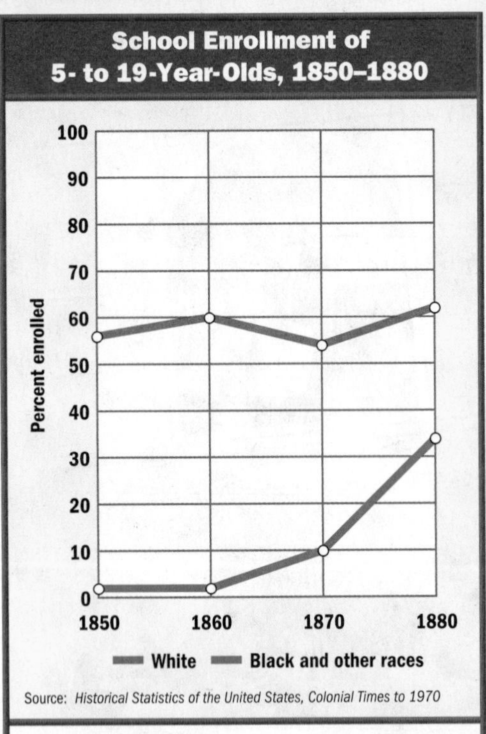

SKILLBUILDER Interpreting Graphs
How might you explain why white school enrollment decreased between 1860 and 1870 while enrollment of others increased?

CHURCHES AND VOLUNTEER GROUPS During slavery many plantation slaves had attended white churches and camp meetings with their owners. Resenting the preachers who urged them to obey their masters, the slaves had also held their own religious gatherings called "praise meetings."

After the war many African Americans founded their own churches, which were usually Baptist or Methodist, and held services similar to the earlier praise meetings. Because churches were the principal institutions that African Americans fully controlled, African-American ministers emerged as influential community leaders. They often played an important role in the broader political life of the country as well.

Besides organizing their own schools and churches, freed African Americans formed thousands of volunteer organizations. They established their own fire companies, trade associations, political organizations, and drama groups, to name just a few. These groups not only fostered independence but also provided financial and emotional support for their members, while offering African Americans opportunities to gain the leadership skills that slavery had often denied them.

POLITICS AND AFRICAN AMERICANS The period from 1865 to 1877 saw growing African-American involvement in politics at all levels. For the first time, African Americans held office in local, state, and federal government. At first, most African Americans in politics were freeborn. Many of these black officeholders were ministers or teachers who had been educated in the North. By 1867, however, former slaves were playing an increasing role in political organizations and were winning a greater number of offices.

Nevertheless, even though there were almost as many black citizens as white citizens in the South, African-American officeholders remained in the minority. Only South Carolina had a black majority in the state legislature. No Southern state elected an African-American governor. Moreover, out of 125 Southerners elected to the U.S. Congress during congressional Reconstruction, only 16 were African Americans. Among these was **Hiram Revels,** the first African-American senator. D

MAIN IDEA

Summarizing

D How did freed African Americans try to improve their lives?

LAWS AGAINST SEGREGATION By the end of 1866, most of the Republican Southern state governments had repealed the black codes. African-American legislators took social equality a step further by proposing bills to desegregate public transportation. In 1871, Texas passed a law prohibiting railroads from making distinctions between groups of passengers, and several other states followed suit. However, many antisegregation laws were not enforced. State orphanages, for example, usually had separate facilities for white and black children.

African Americans themselves focused more on building up the black community than on total integration. By establishing separate African-American institutions—such as schools, churches, and political and social organizations—they were able to focus on African-American leadership and escape the interference of the whites who had so long dominated their lives.

KEY PLAYER

HIRAM REVELS
1822–1901

Hiram Revels of Mississippi (pictured above on the far left, with—left to right—the African-American representatives Benjamin S. Turner of Alabama, Robert C. De Large of South Carolina, Josiah T. Walls of Florida, Jefferson M. Long of Georgia, Joseph H. Rainey of South Carolina, and Robert Brown Elliott of South Carolina) was born of free parents in Fayetteville, North Carolina. Because he could not obtain an education in the South, he attended Knox College in Illinois. As an African Methodist Episcopal minister, he recruited African Americans to fight for the Union during the Civil War and also served as an army chaplain.

In 1865, Revels settled in Mississippi. He served on the Natchez city council and then was elected to Mississippi's state senate in 1869. In 1870, Revels became the first African American elected to the U.S. Senate. Ironically, he held the seat that had once belonged to Jefferson Davis.

Changes in the Southern Economy

When asked to explain the idea of freedom, Garrison Frazier, a former slave turned Baptist minister, said that freedom consisted in "placing us where we could reap the fruit of our own labor." To accomplish this, Frazier said, freed African Americans needed "to have land, and turn it and till it." Few former slaves, however, had enough money to buy land, and those who did have cash were frequently frustrated by whites' refusal to sell property to them.

NOW & THEN

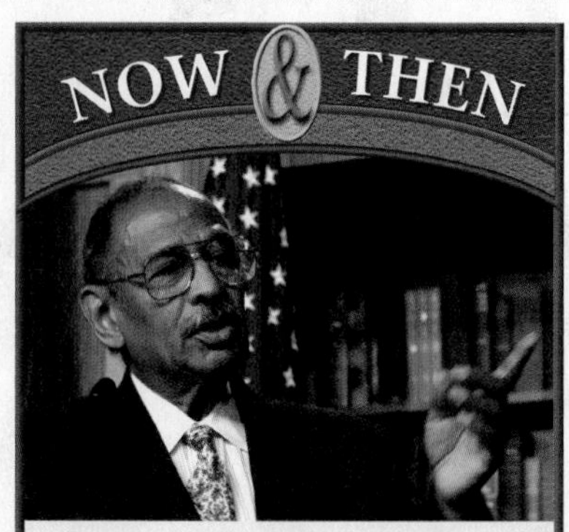

REPARATIONS FOR SLAVERY

In the year 1867, Representative Thaddeus Stevens introduced a bill that, had it been successful, would have granted each freed adult male slave 40 acres of land and $100. Since then, a number of other attempts have been made to legislate reparations—amends, usually financial—for the evils of slavery.

In 1989, Representative John Conyers of Michigan (shown above) proposed the first in a series of bills that would create a commission to study the impact of slavery. If the committee found that reparations were called for, it would recommend appropriate measures for Congress to take. In 1999, Conyers introduced a bill that would require the government to issue a formal apology for slavery. So far, these proposals and others like them have not been passed into law.

However, a group of prominent class-action lawyers met in 2000 to begin studying the issue, intending to bring suit against the government and against businesses that profited from slavery.

Some victims of postslavery racism have actually been granted reparations. Early in 2001, a state commission in Oklahoma awarded $12 million to black survivors and victims' descendants of a deadly 1921 Tulsa race riot.

40 ACRES AND A MULE In January 1865, during the Civil War, General Sherman had promised the freed slaves who followed his army 40 acres per family and the use of army mules. Soon afterward, about 40,000 freed persons settled on 400,000 abandoned or forfeited acres in coastal Georgia and South Carolina. The freed African Americans farmed their plots until August 1865, when President Johnson ordered that the original landowners be allowed to reclaim their land and evict the former slaves.

Many freed African Americans asserted that they deserved part of the planters' land. An Alabama black convention declared, "The property which they hold was nearly all earned by the sweat of *our* brows." Some Radical Republicans agreed. Thaddeus Stevens called for the government to confiscate plantations and to redistribute part of the land to former slaves. However, many Republicans considered it wrong to seize citizens' private property. As a result, Congress either rejected land-reform proposals or passed weak legislation. An example was the 1866 Southern Homestead Act. Although it set aside 44 million acres in the South for freed blacks and loyal whites, the land was swampy and unsuitable for farming. Furthermore, few homesteaders had the resources—seed, tools, plows, and horses—to farm successfully. (E)

> **MAIN IDEA**
> **Identifying Problems**
> (E) What caused land-reform proposals to fail?

RESTORATION OF PLANTATIONS Although African Americans and poor whites wanted to own small farms, the planter class wanted to restore the plantation system, in which many acres were devoted to a single profitable cash crop, such as cotton. Some wealthy Northern merchants and owners of textile mills encouraged the planters in their efforts to reestablish plantations and resume widespread cotton production.

Planters claimed that to make the plantation system work, they needed to have almost complete control over their laborers.

Before the abolition of slavery, planters had forced young and old and men and women to work in the fields for extremely long hours. Now the planters feared that they might not be able to make a profit, since they had to pay their laborers and could no longer force field hands to put in such brutally long workdays. In addition, many former slaveholders deeply resented having to negotiate for the services of former slaves.

Planters also faced a labor shortage, caused by a number of factors. The high death toll of the war had reduced the number of able-bodied workers. Many African-American women and children refused to work in the fields after they were freed. Finally, many freed persons felt that raising cotton under the direction of white overseers was too much like slavery.

As an alternative, some former slaves worked in mills or on railroad-construction crews. Others tried subsistence farming—growing just enough food for their own families. To stop this trend, white planters were determined to keep the former slaves from getting land that they could use to support themselves.

SHARECROPPING AND TENANT FARMING Without their own land, freed African Americans could not grow crops to sell or to feed their families. Economic necessity thus forced many former slaves to sign labor contracts with planters. In exchange for wages, housing, and food, freedmen worked in the fields. Although the Freedmen's Bureau promoted this wage-labor system, the arrangement did not satisfy either freedmen or planters. On the one hand, freedmen thought that the wages were too low and that white employers had too much control over them. On the other hand, planters often lacked sufficient cash to pay workers. These conditions led planters and laborers to experiment with two alternative arrangements: sharecropping and tenant farming.

In the system of **sharecropping,** landowners divided their land and gave each worker—either freed African American or poor white—a few acres, along with seed and tools. At harvest time, each worker gave a share of his crop, usually half, to the landowner. This share paid the owner back and ended the arrangement until it was renewed the following year.

In theory, "croppers" who saved a little and bought their own tools could drive a better bargain with landowners. They might even rent land for cash from the planters, and keep all their harvest, in a system known as **tenant farming.** Eventually they might move up the economic ladder to become outright owners of their farms.

Sharecropping

hmhsocialstudies.com INTERACTIVE

A CYCLE OF POVERTY

Sharecroppers were supposed to have a chance to climb the economic ladder, but by the time they had shared their crops and paid their debts, they rarely had any money left. A sharecropper often became tied to one plantation, having no choice but to work until his or her debts were paid.

1 Sharecroppers are given small plots of land and seed by the landowners.
2 Sharecroppers buy food, clothing, and supplies on credit.
3 They plant a crop. (Yields are low, and the same crop year after year depletes the soil.)
4 Sharecroppers must give the landlords a large share of the harvested crops.
5 Sharecroppers sell what crops remain but are at the mercy of low market prices.
6 Sharecroppers pay off accounts. Some landlords and merchants charge unjust fines for late payments.
7 A few sharecroppers with leftover cash might become tenant farmers.

A sharecropper works a Georgia cotton field in 1870.

SKILLBUILDER Interpreting Charts
How did the sharecropping system make it hard for small farmers to improve their standard of living?

SEE SKILLBUILDER HANDBOOK, PAGE R27.

▲ One successful Southern industry was the manufacture of tobacco products.

The arrangement seldom worked that way in practice, however. Most tenant farmers bought their supplies on credit, often from merchants who charged them inflated prices. Farmers rarely harvested enough crops to pay for both past debts and future supplies. The end result was that very few farmers saved enough cash to buy land.

COTTON NO LONGER KING Another economic change turned Southern agriculture upside down: cotton was no longer king. During the war, demand for Southern cotton had begun to drop as other countries increased their cotton production. As a result, prices plummeted after the war. In 1869, the price of cotton was 16.5 cents per pound. By the late 1870s, the price had fallen to about 8 cents per pound. Instead of diversifying—or varying—their crops, Southern planters tried to make up for the lower prices by growing more cotton—an oversupply that only drove down prices even further.

The South's agricultural problems did lead to attempts to diversify the region's economy. Textile mills sprang up, and a new industry—tobacco-product manufacturing—took hold. Diversification helped raise the average wage in the South, though it was still much lower than that of Northern workers.

At the end of the Civil War, most of the state banks in the South were saddled with Confederate debts—loans made to the Confederate government. The banks awaited repayment that, in most cases, would never come. In the following years, falling cotton prices and mounting planters' debts caused many banks to fail. The only credit that Southerners in rural areas could get was that offered by local merchants. Despite efforts to improve the Southern economy, the devastating economic impact of the Civil War rippled through Southern life into the 20th century. F

Many whites, frustrated by their loss of political power and by the South's economic stagnation, took out their anger on African Americans. In the late 1860s and early 1870s, certain white groups embarked on a campaign to terrorize African Americans into giving up their political rights and their efforts at economic improvement.

MAIN IDEA

Analyzing Causes

F What factors contributed to the stagnation of the Southern economy?

SECTION 2 ASSESSMENT

1. **TERMS & NAMES** For each term or name, write a sentence explaining its significance.
   - **scalawag**
   - **carpetbagger**
   - **Hiram Revels**
   - **sharecropping**
   - **tenant farming**

MAIN IDEA

2. **TAKING NOTES** In a chart like the one shown, list five problems facing the South after the Civil War and at least one attempted solution for each one.

Problem	Attempted Solution

CRITICAL THINKING

3. **FORMING GENERALIZATIONS** How did the Civil War weaken the Southern economy? Give examples to support your answer.

4. **ANALYZING ISSUES** Thaddeus Stevens believed that giving land to former slaves was more important than giving them the vote. Do you agree or disagree? Why?

5. **EVALUATING** Which accomplishment of African Americans during Reconstruction do you consider most significant? Explain your choice. **Think About:**
   - the development of a free African-American community
   - the lingering effects of slavery
   - opportunities for leadership

The Collapse of Reconstruction

MAIN IDEA

Southern opposition to Radical Reconstruction, along with economic problems in the North, ended Reconstruction.

WHY IT MATTERS NOW

The failure of Congress and the Supreme Court to protect the rights of African Americans during Reconstruction delayed blacks' achievement of full civil rights by over a century.

Terms & Names

- **Ku Klux Klan (KKK)**
- **panic of 1873**
- **redemption**
- **Rutherford B. Hayes**
- **Samuel J. Tilden**
- **Compromise of 1877**
- **home rule**

One American's Story

hmhsocialstudies.com TAKING NOTES

Use the graphic organizer online to take notes on the major events that ended Reconstruction.

In 1868, white Georgia legislators, who were in the majority in both houses, expelled 27 black members of the state senate and House of Representatives. The new state constitution gave African Americans the right to vote, they argued, but not to hold office. Outraged by this expulsion, Henry M. Turner, an African-American legislator, addressed the Georgia House of Representatives.

A PERSONAL VOICE HENRY M. TURNER

"Whose Legislature is this? Is it a white man's Legislature or is it a black man's . . . ? . . . It is said that Congress never gave us the right to hold office. I want to know . . . if the Reconstruction measures did not base their action on the ground that no distinction should be made on account of race, color or previous condition! . . . We have built up your country. We have worked in your fields, and garnered your harvests, for two hundred and fifty years! Do we ask you for compensation? . . . We are willing to let the dead past bury its dead; but we ask you, now, for our RIGHTS."

—quoted in *The Trouble They Seen: Black People Tell the Story of Reconstruction*

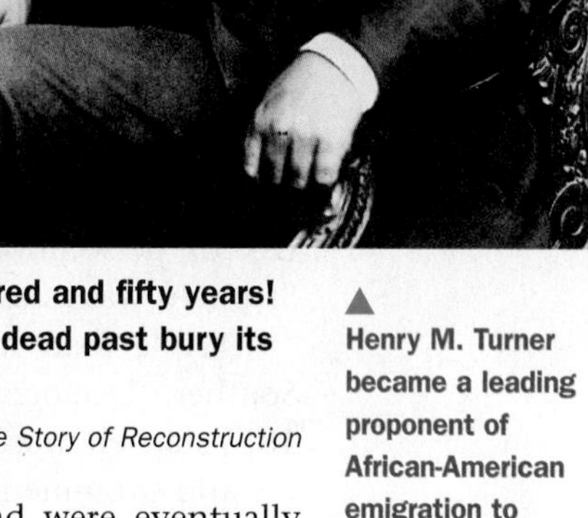

▲ **Henry M. Turner became a leading proponent of African-American emigration to Africa.**

The expelled legislators petitioned the U.S. Congress and were eventually reinstated in office. But by the time Congress acted, more than a year later, the terms of Turner and his colleagues were almost at an end.

Opposition to Reconstruction

White Southerners who took direct action against African-American participation in government were in the minority. Most white Southerners swallowed whatever resentment they felt over African Americans' change in status. However, some bitter Southern whites relied on violence to keep African Americans from participating in politics.

▲ **Klan members wore costumes to conceal their identities and to appear more menacing. These Klan members were captured in an Alabama riot in 1868.**

KU KLUX KLAN Founded as a social club for Confederate veterans, the **Ku Klux Klan (KKK)** started in Tennessee in 1866. As membership in the group spread rapidly through the South, many of the new chapters turned into violent terrorist organizations. By 1868, the Klan existed in practically every Southern state. Its overarching goal was to restore white supremacy. Its method was to prevent African Americans from exercising their political rights. Between 1868 and 1871, the Klan and other secret groups killed thousands of men, women, and children, and burned schools, churches, and property.

Abram Colby, who organized a branch of Georgia's Equal Rights Association and later served as a Republican member of the Georgia legislature, testified before Congress about Klan atrocities.

A PERSONAL VOICE ABRAM COLBY

"[The Klan] broke my door open, took me out of bed, took me to the woods and whipped me three hours or more and left me for dead. They said to me, 'Do you think you will ever vote another damned radical ticket?' . . . I supposed they would kill me anyhow. I said, 'If there was an election tomorrow, I would vote the radical ticket.' They set in and whipped me a thousand licks more, with sticks and straps that had buckles on the ends of them."

—quoted in *Testimony Taken by the Joint Select Committee to Inquire into the Condition of Affairs in the Late Insurrectionary States*

While the vast majority of the Klan's victims were African-American, whites who tried to help African Americans—whether by educating them, renting land to them, or buying their crops—were also in danger.

Another Klan objective was to turn the Republicans, who had established the Reconstruction governments, out of power. The North Carolina state senator John Stephens, a white Republican, answered warnings that his life was in danger by saying that some 3,000 African-American voters had supported him "at the risk of persecution and starvation" and that he would not abandon them. Stephens was assassinated in 1870.

While Klan members tried to conceal their identities when they struck, Southern Democrats openly used violence to intimidate Republicans before the 1875 state election in Mississippi. Democrats rioted and attacked Republican leaders and prominent African Americans. Their terrorist campaign frightened the African-American majority away from the polls, and white Democratic candidates swept the election. The Democrats used similar tactics to win the 1876 elections in Florida, South Carolina, and Louisiana. (A)

MAIN IDEA

Analyzing Motives

(A) What were the goals of the KKK?

ECONOMIC PRESSURE The Klan and other secret groups tried to prevent African Americans from making economic, as well as political, progress. African Americans who owned their own land or who worked in occupations other than agriculture were subject to attacks and destruction of property.

In fact, economic necessity forced most former slaves—who had little money or training in other occupations—to work for whites as wage laborers or sharecroppers. Some white Southerners refused to hire or do business with African Americans who were revealed by election officials to have voted Republican. The fear of economic reprisals kept many former slaves from voting at all.

LEGISLATIVE RESPONSE To curtail Klan violence and Democratic intimidation, Congress passed a series of Enforcement Acts in 1870 and 1871. One act provided for the federal supervision of elections in Southern states. Another act gave the president the power to use federal troops in areas where the Klan was active. However, President Grant was not aggressive in his use of the power given to him by the Enforcement Acts, and in 1882, the Supreme Court ruled that the 1871 Enforcement Act was unconstitutional.

Although federal enforcement of anti-Klan legislation was limited, it did contribute to a decrease in the Klan's activities in the late 1870s. However, the reason for the reduction in Klan violence was the Klan's own success—by 1880, terrorist groups had managed to restore white supremacy throughout the South. The Klan no longer needed such organized activity to limit the political and civil rights of most African Americans. B

MAIN IDEA

Identifying Problems

B Why was the government weak in its ability to confront the Klan?

Vocabulary

amnesty: a pardon granted by a government, especially for political offenses

SHIFTS IN POLITICAL POWER By passing the Enforcement Acts, Congress seemed to shore up Republican power. But shortly after these acts went into effect, Congress passed legislation that severely weakened the Republican Party in the South.

With the Amnesty Act, passed in May 1872, Congress returned the right to vote and the right to hold federal and state offices—revoked by the Fourteenth Amendment—to about 150,000 former Confederates, who would almost certainly vote Democratic. In the same year Congress allowed the Freedmen's Bureau to expire, believing that it had fulfilled its purpose. As a result of these actions, Southern Democrats had an opportunity to shift the balance of political power in their favor.

Scandals and Money Crises Hurt Republicans

As Southern Republicans struggled to maintain their hold on Reconstruction governments, widespread political corruption in the federal government weakened their party. During the early 1870s, scandals plagued the Grant administration. These scandals diverted public attention away from conditions in the South.

FRAUD AND BRIBERY President Grant was considered an honest man. However, he had had no political experience before becoming president and found it difficult to believe that others might use him for their own political advantage. When making political appointments, he often selected friends and acquaintances rather than people of proven ability. Too frequently, Grant's appointees turned out to be dishonest.

Beginning in 1872, a series of long-simmering scandals associated with Grant's administration boiled over. First, a newspaper exposed how the Crédit Mobilier, a construction company working for the Union Pacific Railroad, had skimmed off large profits from the railroad's government contract. Implicated were several top Republicans, including Vice-President Schuyler Colfax.

REPUBLICAN UNITY SHATTERED A group of Republicans, angered by the corruption, called for honest, efficient government. They formed the Liberal Republican Party in 1872, hoping to oust Grant in that year's presidential election.

WORLD STAGE

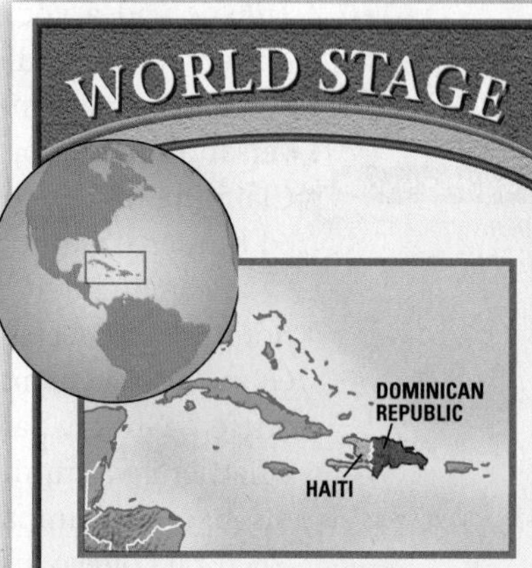

THE DOMINICAN REPUBLIC

Although the United States focused largely on domestic problems during Reconstruction, the nation did have one significant dealing with a foreign power. In 1870, President Grant attempted to annex the Dominican Republic, one of two nations sharing the Caribbean island of Hispaniola (the other being Haiti).

This action aroused a storm of controversy. The plan's supporters believed that annexation would increase Caribbean trade and spread "the blessings of our free institutions." Opponents pointed out that the Dominican Republic was caught up in a civil war and felt that the United States should avoid involvement in the conflict. The Senate rejected the annexation treaty.

Analyzing *Political Cartoons*

SCANDAL IN THE GRANT ADMINISTRATION

Political cartoonists had a field day with Grant's troubles and often criticized the president's refusal to believe that his associates were dishonest. In this cartoon, President Grant pulls packets labeled with the names of various scandals out of a barrel. The caption—"I hope I get to the bottom soon"—suggests that the corruption in Grant's administration runs deep and that there may be more scandals to come.

SKILLBUILDER Analyzing Political Cartoons

1. What political scandals can you identify from the packets lying outside the barrel?
2. Why do you think the cartoonist portrayed Grant as having his head stuck in a barrel?

SEE SKILLBUILDER HANDBOOK, PAGE R24.

U. S. Grant: "I hope I get to the bottom soon."

HISTORY

VIDEO
President Ulysses S. Grant: Scandal and Legacy

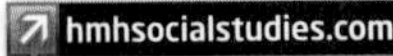

hmhsocialstudies.com

As the 1872 presidential election approached, the Liberal Republicans held a separate convention. They chose Horace Greeley, the editor of the *New York Tribune* and a vocal pre-Civil War abolitionist, as their candidate. He had supported some Radical Republican causes—abolition and the Fourteenth and Fifteenth Amendments. However, he had broken with Radicals by calling for universal amnesty for Confederates and for an end to military rule in the South. Claiming that Reconstruction governments had achieved their purpose, he wanted former slaves to fend for themselves.

Believing that it would take a united effort to oust Grant, the Democrats also nominated Greeley. Nevertheless, Greeley lost the 1872 presidential election to Grant by a wide margin. "I was the worst beaten man that ever ran for that high office," Greeley said, "and I have been assailed so bitterly that I hardly know whether I was running for President or the penitentiary." Physically exhausted by his rigorous campaign, Greeley died a few weeks after the election—before the electoral college made his defeat official.

Although the Liberal Republicans did not win the White House, they did weaken the Radicals' hold over the Republican Party. The breakdown of Republican unity made it even harder for the Radicals to continue to impose their Reconstruction plan on the South.

CONTINUED SCANDAL Despite the rift in the Republican party that resulted from the scandals, corruption in Grant's administration continued. In 1875, the so-called Whiskey Ring was exposed. Internal-revenue collectors and other officials accepted bribes from whiskey distillers who wanted to avoid paying taxes on their product—a conspiracy that defrauded the federal government of millions of dollars. One of the 238 persons indicted in this scandal was Grant's private secretary, General Orville E. Babcock. Grant refused to believe that such a close associate was guilty and helped him escape conviction.

Finally, in 1876, an investigation revealed that Secretary of War William W. Belknap had accepted bribes from merchants who wanted to keep their profitable trading concessions in Indian territory. The House of Representatives impeached Belknap, who promptly resigned. The public also learned that the secretary of the navy had taken bribes from shipbuilders and the secretary of the interior had had shady dealings with land speculators. As the evidence mounted, there was increasing disgust with the blatant corruption in the Grant administration, and Grant did not seek reelection in 1876. **C**

MAIN IDEA

Summarizing
C Give examples of corruption in the Grant administration.

Economic Turmoil

As if political scandals were not enough for the country to deal with, a wave of economic troubles hit the nation in 1873.

This 1873 cartoon portrays the panic as a health officer, sweeping garbage out of Wall Street. The trash is labeled "rotten railways," and "shaky banks," among other things. ▼

THE PANIC OF 1873 The economy had been expanding since the end of the Civil War, and investors became convinced that business profits would continue to increase indefinitely. Eager to take advantage of new business opportunities in the South, Northern and Southern investors borrowed increasing amounts of money and built new facilities as quickly as possible.

Unfortunately, many of those who invested in these new businesses took on more debt than they could afford. A Philadelphia banker named Jay Cooke invested heavily in railroads. Not enough investors bought shares in Cooke's railroad lines to cover his ballooning construction costs, and he could not pay his debts. In September 1873, Cooke's banking firm, the nation's largest dealer in government securities, went bankrupt, setting off a series of financial failures known as the **panic of 1873.** Smaller banks closed, and the stock market temporarily collapsed. Within a year, 89 railroads went broke. By 1875, more than 18,000 companies had folded. The panic triggered a five-year economic depression—a period of reduced business activity and high unemployment—in which 3 million workers lost their jobs. D

MAIN IDEA

Predicting Effects

D What effect do you think the panic of 1873 might have had on the Republican Party?

CURRENCY DISPUTE The economic depression following the panic of 1873 also fueled a dispute over currency. This dispute had its roots in the Civil War. During the war, the federal government had begun to issue greenbacks, paper money that was not backed by equal value in gold. When the war ended, many financial experts advocated withdrawing the greenbacks and returning the nation completely to a currency backed by gold. This action would have reduced the number of dollars in circulation.

In contrast, Southern and Western farmers and manufacturers wanted the government to issue even more greenbacks. They believed that "easy money"—a large money supply—would help them pay off their debts.

In 1875, Congress passed the Specie Resumption Act, which promised to put the country back on the gold standard. This act sparked further debate over monetary policies. As the economy improved, beginning in 1878, the controversy died down. However, the passionate debate over the money question in the 1870s was one of many factors that drew the attention of voters and politicians away from Reconstruction.

Judicial and Popular Support Fades

In 1874, a Southern Democratic senator wrote, "*Radicalism* is dissolving—going to pieces." Indeed, political scandals, economic problems, and the restoration of political rights to former Confederate Democrats seriously weakened the Radical Republicans. In addition, the Supreme Court began to undo some of the social and political changes that the Radicals had made.

SUPREME COURT DECISIONS Although Congress had passed important laws to protect the political and civil rights of African Americans, the Supreme Court began to take away those same protections. During the 1870s, the Court issued a series of decisions that undermined both the Fourteenth and Fifteenth Amendments.

In the *Slaughterhouse* cases of 1873, for example, the Court decided that the Fourteenth Amendment protected only the rights people had by virtue of their citizenship in the United States, such as the right of interstate travel and the right to federal protection when traveling on the high seas and abroad. The Court contended that most of Americans' basic civil rights were obtained through their citizenship in a state and that the amendment did not protect those rights.

Another setback for Reconstruction was *U.S.* v. *Cruikshank* in 1876, in which the Court ruled that the Fourteenth Amendment did not give the federal government the right to punish individual whites who oppressed blacks. The same year, in *U.S.* v. *Reese,* the Court ruled in favor of officials who had barred African Americans from voting, stating that the Fifteenth Amendment did not "confer the right of suffrage on anyone" but merely listed grounds on which states could not deny suffrage. By the late 1870s, the Supreme Court's restrictive rulings had narrowed the scope of these amendments so much that the federal government no longer had much power to protect the rights of African Americans. Although the Supreme Court would later overturn them, these decisions impeded African Americans' efforts to gain equality for years to come. E

MAIN IDEA

Analyzing Effects

E How did the *Slaughterhouse* and *Reese* decisions affect African Americans' pursuit of civil rights?

NORTHERN SUPPORT FADES As the Supreme Court rejected Reconstruction policies in the 1870s, Northern voters grew indifferent to events in the South. Weary of the "Negro question" and sick of "carpetbag government," many Northern voters shifted their attention to such national concerns as the panic of 1873 and the corruption in Grant's administration. In addition, a desire for reconciliation between the regions spread through the North. Although political violence continued in the South and African Americans were denied civil and political rights, the tide of public opinion in the North began to turn against Reconstruction policies.

As both judicial and public support decreased, Republicans began to back away from their commitment to Reconstruction. The impassioned Radicals who had led the fight for congressional Reconstruction, Charles Sumner and Thaddeus Stevens, were dead. Business interests diverted the attention of both moderates and Radicals, and scalawags and carpetbaggers deserted the Republican Party. Moreover, Republicans gradually came to believe that government could not impose the moral and social changes needed for former slaves to make progress in the South. As a result, Republicans slowly retreated from the policies of Reconstruction. F

MAIN IDEA

Analyzing Issues

F Why did Northern attitudes toward Reconstruction change?

Civil Rights Setbacks in the Supreme Court

Date	Decision(s)	Ruling
1873	*Slaughterhouse* cases	Most civil rights were ruled to be state, rather than federal, rights and therefore unprotected by the Fourteenth Amendment.
1876	*U.S.* v. *Cruikshank*	The Fourteenth Amendment was ruled not to grant the federal government power to punish whites who oppressed blacks.
1876	*U.S.* v. *Reese*	The Fifteenth Amendment was determined not to grant voting rights to anyone, but rather to restrict types of voter discrimination.

Democrats "Redeem" the South

Between 1869 and 1875, Democrats recaptured the state governments of Alabama, Arkansas, Georgia, Mississippi, North Carolina, Tennessee, Texas, and Virginia. As a result of **redemption—**as the Democrats called their return to power in the South—and the national election of 1876, congressional Reconstruction came to an end.

ELECTION OF 1876 In 1876, Grant decided not to run for a third term. The Republicans then chose the stodgy governor of Ohio, **Rutherford B. Hayes,** as their candidate. Smelling victory, the Democrats put up one of their ablest leaders, Governor **Samuel J. Tilden** of New York. Tilden had helped clean up the graft that had flourished in New York City under the corrupt Tweed Ring.

As most people had expected, Tilden won the popular vote. However, he fell one short of the number of electoral votes needed to win, and 20 electoral votes were disputed. Congress appointed a commission to deal with the problem. The commission, which had a Republican majority, gave the election to the Republican, Hayes, even though he had received a minority of the popular vote.

For the first time in U.S. history, a candidate who had lost the popular election became president. How did it happen? In the oldest tradition of politics, party leaders made a deal. Although Republicans controlled the electoral commission, Democrats controlled the House of Representatives, which had to approve the election results. Southern Democrats were willing to accept Hayes if they could get something in return.

The price they demanded was, first of all, the withdrawal of federal troops from Louisiana and South Carolina—two of the three Southern states that Republicans still governed. Second, the Democrats wanted federal money to build a railroad from Texas to the West Coast and to improve Southern rivers, harbors, and bridges. Third, they wanted Hayes to appoint a conservative Southerner to the cabinet. In the **Compromise of 1877,** Republican leaders agreed to these demands, and Hayes was peacefully inaugurated. The acceptance of this compromise meant the end of Reconstruction in the South.

HISTORICAL SPOTLIGHT

THE ELECTORAL COLLEGE AND THE 1876 ELECTION

The nation was in such turmoil over the disputed 1876 election that people talked of another civil war. Of the 20 contested electoral votes, 19 came from Florida, South Carolina, and Louisiana. Republican officials in those states threw out election returns from counties where violence kept Republican voters from the polls. The Democrats refused to accept the altered returns, and each party sent its own set of results to Washington, D.C.

Fortunately for the country, the warlike slogans proved to be just political rhetoric. After a joint session of Congress met to witness the counting of electoral votes, which did not settle the dispute, the parties struck a deal—the Compromise of 1877.

TILDEN.
HAYES.
OF THE TWO EVILS
CHOOSE THE LEAST.

▲ An advertisement expresses ambivalence about the two candidates in the 1876 election.

HOME RULE IN THE SOUTH After the 1876 election, Republicans and Democrats disputed the results in Louisiana's and South Carolina's elections, and both states ended up with two rival state governments! When Hayes later removed the federal troops in those states, the Democrats took over. Florida also had questionable election returns, but the state supreme court ruled in favor of the Democrats. As a result, Republicans no longer controlled the government of any Southern state.

The Democrats had achieved their long-desired goal of **home rule—**the ability to run state governments without federal intervention. These so-called Redeemers set out to rescue the South from what they viewed as a decade of mismanagement by Northerners, Republicans, and African Americans. They passed laws that restricted the rights of African Americans, wiped out social programs, slashed taxes, and dismantled public schools. (G)

MAIN IDEA

Analyzing Causes

(G) How did the Compromise of 1877 bring about the end of Reconstruction?

LEGACY OF RECONSTRUCTION Despite the efforts of African Americans and many Radical Republicans, Reconstruction ended without much real progress in the battle against discrimination. Charles Harris, an African-American Union Army veteran and former Alabama legislator, expressed his frustration in an 1877 letter.

A PERSONAL VOICE CHARLES HARRIS

> **"We obey laws; others make them. We support state educational institutions, whose doors are virtually closed against us. We support asylums and hospitals, and our sick, deaf, dumb, or blind are met at the doors by . . . unjust discriminations. . . . From these and many other oppressions . . . our people long to be *free*."**
>
> —quoted in American Colonization Society Papers in the *Congressional Record*

Although Radical Republicans wanted to help the former slaves, they made several serious mistakes. First, they assumed that extending certain civil rights to freed persons would enable them to protect themselves through participation in government, especially in lawmaking. However, Congress did not adequately protect those rights, and the Supreme Court undermined them. Second, the Radicals balked at distributing land to former slaves, which prevented them from becoming

POINT

"Reconstruction was a failure."

Federal and state governments failed to secure the rights guaranteed to former slaves by constitutional amendments.

- State Republican parties could not preserve black-white voter coalitions that would have enabled them to stay in power and continue political reform.
- Radical Republican governments were unable or unwilling to enact land reform or to provide former slaves with the economic resources needed to break the cycle of poverty.
- Racial bias was a national, not a regional, problem. After the Panic of 1873, Northerners were more concerned with economic problems than with the problems of former slaves.
- The Supreme Court undermined the power of the Fourteenth and Fifteenth Amendments.

At the end of Reconstruction, former slaves found themselves once again in a subordinate position in society. The historian Eric Foner concludes, "Whether measured by the dreams inspired by emancipation or the more limited goals of securing blacks' rights as citizens. . . . Reconstruction can only be judged a failure."

COUNTERPOINT

"Reconstruction was a success."

Reconstruction was an attempt to create a social and political revolution despite economic collapse and the opposition of much of the white South. Under these conditions its accomplishments were extraordinary.

- African Americans only a few years removed from slavery participated at all levels of government.
- State governments had some success in solving social problems; for example, they funded public school systems open to all citizens.
- African Americans established institutions that had been denied them during slavery: schools, churches, and families.
- The breakup of the plantation system led to some redistribution of land.
- Congress passed the Fourteenth and Fifteenth Amendments, which helped African Americans to attain full civil rights in the 20th century.

W. E. B. Du Bois summarized the achievements of the period this way: "[I]t was Negro loyalty and the Negro vote alone that restored the South to the Union; established the new democracy, both for white and black."

Despite the loss of ground that followed Reconstruction, African Americans succeeded in carving out a measure of independence within Southern society.

THINKING CRITICALLY

1. **CONNECT TO HISTORY** **Evaluating** What are the two major arguments each side makes as to whether Reconstruction was a success or failure? Which perspective do you agree with, and why?

    **SEE SKILLBUILDER HANDBOOK, PAGE R16.**

2. **CONNECT TO TODAY** **Analyzing Issues** One historian has referred to Reconstruction as "America's Unfinished Revolution." Is the U.S. still dealing with issues left over from that period? Research Reconstruction's legacy using newspapers, magazines, or other sources. Make a short persuasive presentation in class.

economically independent of the landowning planter class. Finally, the Radicals did not fully realize the extent to which deep-seated racism in society would weaken the changes that Congress had tried to make.

But congressional Reconstruction was not a complete failure. The Thirteenth Amendment permanently abolished slavery in all of the states. Furthermore, Radical Republicans did succeed in passing the Fourteenth and Fifteenth Amendments, and although the Supreme Court narrowed the interpretation of the amendments during the 1870s, they remained part of the Constitution. In the 20th century, the amendments provided the necessary constitutional foundation for important civil rights legislation.

During Reconstruction, African Americans had founded many black colleges and volunteer organizations, and the percentage of literate African Americans had gradually increased. The memory of this time of expanding opportunities lived on in the African-American community and inspired the fight to regain civil rights.

◀ **Medical students at Howard University, an African-American institution founded in 1867**

ASSESSMENT

1. **TERMS & NAMES** For each term or name, write a sentence explaining its significance.
   - **Ku Klux Klan (KKK)**
   - **redemption**
   - **Samuel J. Tilden**
   - **home rule**
   - **panic of 1873**
   - **Rutherford B. Hayes**
   - **Compromise of 1877**

MAIN IDEA

2. **TAKING NOTES**
   Re-create the time line below. Fill in the major events that ended Reconstruction.

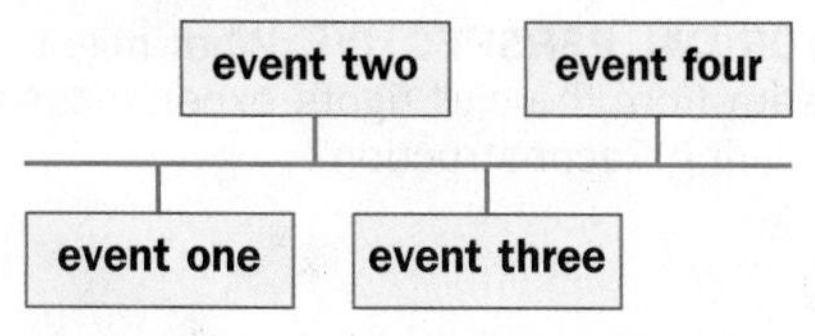

Which event do you think was most significant and why?

CRITICAL THINKING

3. **ANALYZING EFFECTS**
   What were the positive and negative effects of Reconstruction?

4. **EVALUATING LEADERSHIP**
   During Reconstruction, was the presidency weak or strong? Support your answer with details from the text.

5. **EVALUATING DECISIONS**
   Do you think the political deal to settle the election of 1876 was an appropriate solution? Explain why or why not. **Think About:**
   - the causes of the conflict over the election
   - other possible solutions to the controversy
   - the impact of the settlement

CHAPTER 12 ASSESSMENT

VISUAL SUMMARY

Reconstruction and Its Effects

FOUNDATIONS

- Presidents Lincoln and Johnson propose lenient policies toward the former Confederate states.
- Radical Republicans gain control of Congress and pass the Reconstruction Act of 1867.
- Conflict over approach leads Congress to impeach Johnson.

PROGRESS

- States ratify the Fourteenth and Fifteenth Amendments.
- Republicans control most state governments in the South.
- States start public works programs and public schools.
- Former slaves reunite families, work for wages, and build African-American culture.

COLLAPSE

- War debt and low demand for cotton slow the South's recovery.
- African Americans are terrorized by racist violence.
- Supreme Court decisions undermine Fourteenth and Fifteenth Amendments.
- Republican Party is weakened by internal conflict, scandal, and financial panic.
- Republicans withdraw troops from the South to gain Hayes the presidency in 1876.
- Democrats control governments, weaken civil rights, and eliminate public schools and programs.

TERMS & NAMES

For each term or name below, write a sentence explaining its connection to Reconstruction.

1. Andrew Johnson
2. Radical Republicans
3. Freedmen's Bureau
4. Fourteenth Amendment
5. Fifteenth Amendment
6. carpetbagger
7. Hiram Revels
8. sharecropping
9. Ku Klux Klan (KKK)
10. Rutherford B. Hayes

MAIN IDEAS

Use your notes and the information in the chapter to answer the following questions.

The Politics of Reconstruction

1. How did Andrew Johnson's plan to reconstruct the Confederate states differ from Lincoln's?
2. How did the Civil Rights Act of 1866 become law?
3. Why did the Radicals want to impeach Andrew Johnson?

Reconstructing Society

4. What three groups made up the Republican Party in the South during Reconstruction?
5. In what ways did emancipated slaves exercise their freedom?
6. How did white landowners in the South reassert their economic power in the decade following the Civil War?

The Collapse of Reconstruction

7. How did Southern whites regain political power during Reconstruction?
8. What economic and political developments weakened the Republican Party during Grant's second term?
9. What significance did the victory by Rutherford B. Hayes in the 1876 presidential race have for Reconstruction?

CRITICAL THINKING

1. **USING YOUR NOTES** In a chart like the one below, list the results of the national elections of 1866, 1868, 1870, 1872, and 1876. Then note how each result affected Reconstruction.

Year	Results	Significance

2. **ANALYZING ISSUES** How do you think Reconstruction could have been made more effective in rebuilding the South and ensuring the rights of the freed slaves?

3. **EVALUATING** Do you think the changes in the South during Reconstruction benefited Southerners? Support your opinion.

4. **DEVELOPING HISTORICAL PERSPECTIVE** What might Americans today learn from the civil rights experiences of African Americans during Reconstruction?

STANDARDIZED TEST PRACTICE

Use the quotation below and your knowledge of U.S. history to answer question 1.

> **"On the coast of South Carolina, after a year of experimenting on the willingness of the freedmen to work and their ability to support themselves, a plan was begun of cutting up the large estates into twenty and forty acre plots, to be sold to the freedmen at government prices. . . . This plan was eminently fair and just; it was also a radical abolishment of slavery. It made the freedman owner of his own labor, and also an owner of a fair share of the land. . . . At the first sale of these lands, the freedmen came up promptly and bought largely, showing the thrift and shrewdness of men worthy of citizenship."**
>
> —**James McCune Smith,** quoted in *Witness for Freedom: African American Voices on Race, Slavery, and Emancipation*

1. According to the point of view expressed in the quotation, the best way to help former slaves was to —

A encourage plantation owners to hire former slaves.

B allow plantation owners to buy back their land.

C assist former slaves in gaining ownership of land.

D divide large plantations into smaller plots.

2. In the Reconstruction Act of 1867, Congress set requirements for the readmission of former Confederate states into the Union. Which of the following problems did the act address?

F Southern states did not allow African Americans to vote.

G Southern states had little money to pay for public works projects.

H Former slaves needed education.

J Confederate bonds and money were worthless.

3. Which of the following items was responsible for finally ending Reconstruction in the South?

A ratification of the Fifteenth Amendment

B the Compromise of 1877

C President Grant's failure to win reelection

D the decisions of the Supreme Court in the 1870s

hmhsocialstudies.com TEST PRACTICE

For additional test practice, go online for:

• Diagnostic tests • Tutorials

INTERACT WITH HISTORY

Recall the issues that you explored at the beginning of the chapter. Now that you have read more about efforts to reconstruct the South, what is your opinion of how the government handled Reconstruction? Write an opinion statement. Consider the following questions:

- What goals did the government actually set for Reconstruction?
- How could the government have pursued its goals more effectively?
- What additional goals should the government have set? Why?

FOCUS ON WRITING

During Reconstruction, many leaders felt that it was the president's responsibility to restore the Union. Others felt it was the responsibility of Congress. Write a persuasive essay expressing your view on who should oversee Reconstruction in the former Confederacy. Be sure to include evidence that supports your position while also highlighting the negative aspects of the alternative plan for Reconstruction.

COLLABORATIVE LEARNING

In a small group read and discuss the "One American's Story" at the beginning of Section X. Then create a presentation that Robert Fitzgerald might have used to convince Northerners to support the Freedmen's Bureau and schools for former slaves. What if Fitzgerald had had access to 21st-century technology? Use audio, video, or computer software to make the presentation more effective. Present the final product to your class.

UNIT

4

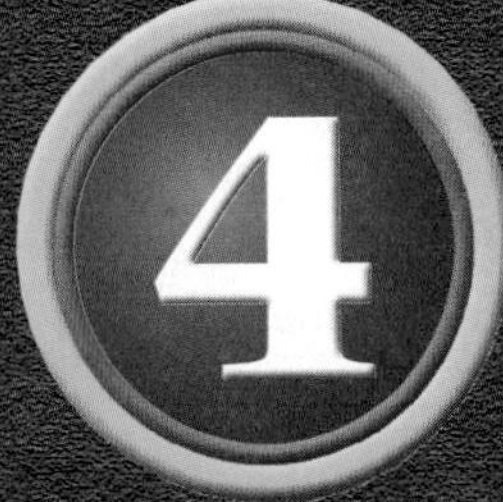

Migration and Industrialization 1877–1917

UNIT PROJECT

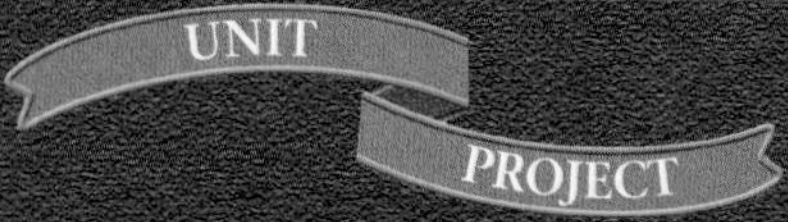

Oral Report

This unit describes how the United States transformed itself from a rural, agricultural society to an urban, industrial one. Prepare an oral report that summarizes one or more of the factors that caused this change. Create visuals to accompany your report.

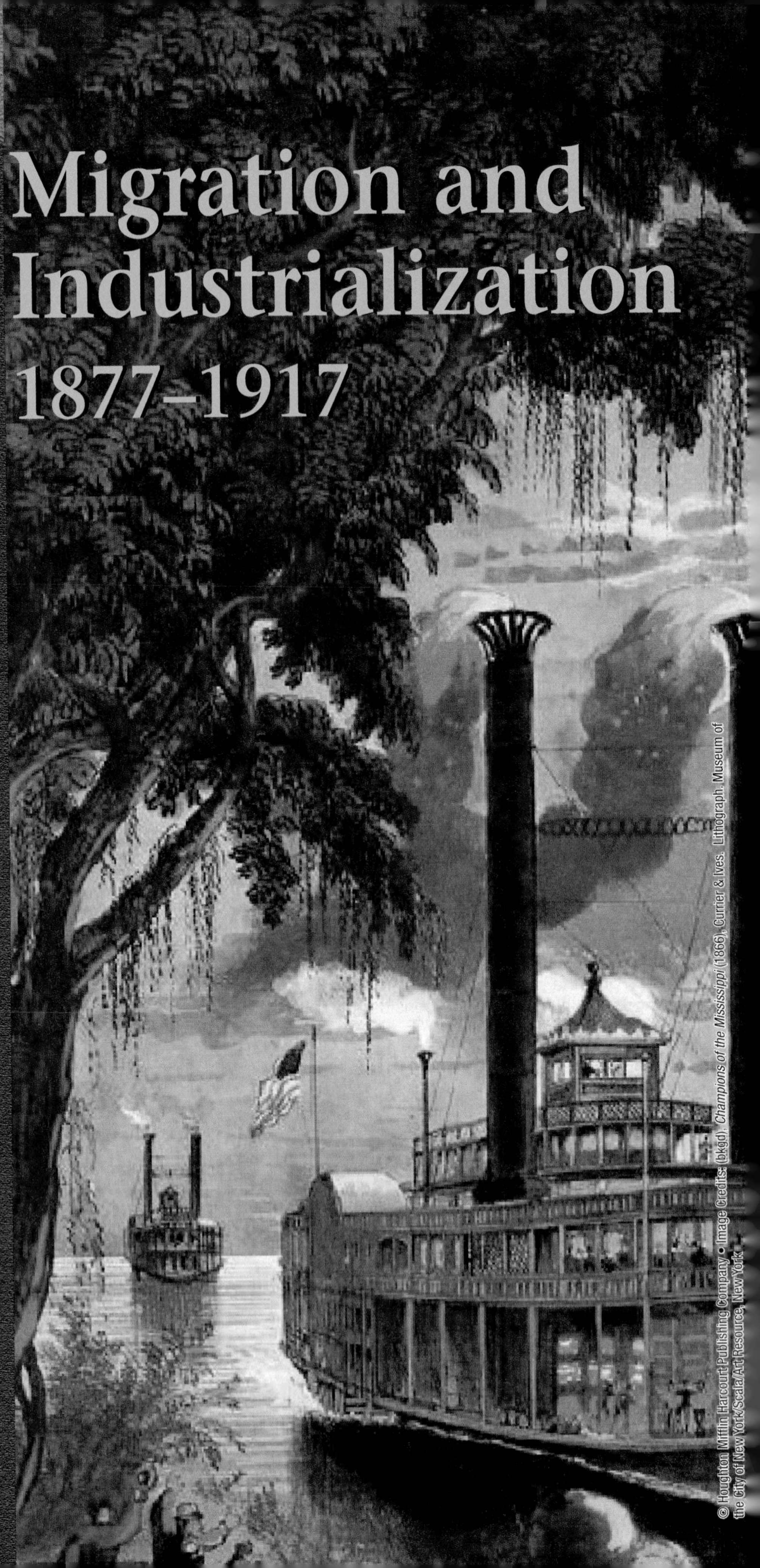

Champions of the Mississippi **by Currier and Ives**

QUEEN OF THE WEST

ALABAMA *A New South Emerges*

In the decades following the Civil War, industrialization swept across the northern United States. Although many former Confederate states continued to depend on agriculture, they also embraced the industrial age. Mechanization and factory-based production in the South caught the eye of journalists, who started calling the region the New South. Although Alabama lacked financing and skilled labor immediately after the war, the state joined its southern neighbors in this late 19th-century transformation.

A girl manages a machine at the Barker Cotton Mills in Mobile.

Industry

Before the Civil War, Alabama's economy was based on raising livestock and growing crops, especially cotton. The state had significant natural resources, including iron ore, coal, and limestone. These rich deposits attracted investors to Alabama, and mining and industry grew in the 1880s. By the end of the decade, the state was the second-largest iron ore producer in the nation and had more than 50 blast furnaces running.

Cotton also played a key role in the state's industrialization. More than 9,000 Alabamians worked in cotton mills by the end of the century. Cottonseeds were used to produce soap, fertilizer, oil, and food for livestock. Many new flour mills, brickyards, grist mills, and furniture factories also opened in Alabama during this period. Between 1880 and 1900, the number of factories in the state increased from 2,000 to 5,500. Transportation advances, especially the building of more railroad lines, proved important to the growth of industry.

Urbanization

Despite these economic changes, a vast majority of Alabamians still lived on farms at the end of the century. Industrialization, however, was beginning to encourage urban growth within the state. This trend continued in the 20th century. Birmingham, founded in 1871, became a leading business center and crude iron producer with nearly 40,000 residents just three decades later. Called the "Magic City" because of its rapid growth, Birmingham was a symbol of the economic transformation of the New South. Other towns in Alabama also grew due to new factories and closeness to coal and iron deposits. Anniston, for example, became the state's fourth-largest city and a top industrial center by 1900, producing sewer pipes, locomotive brakes, and cotton textiles.

Industrialization led to efforts to improve Alabama's urban areas. The increased prosperity of cities such as Montgomery, Huntsville, and Gadsden allowed for innovations such as electric streetcars, streetlights, and telephone exchanges. The port city of Mobile recovered after years of decline in the 1890s and early 1900s. This was due to municipal improvements; growing timber exports and banana imports; and a new, deeper shipping channel.

Birmingham became known as the "Magic City" because of how quickly it grew. State-of-the-art streetcars helped move people around the bustling city.

Immigration and Migration

From the mid-1800s through the early 1900s, millions of immigrants arrived in the United States. Though Alabama was not a leading destination for the new arrivals, the state's foreign-born population did increase. In the 1880s, the industrial plants of Birmingham attracted immigrants from Ireland, Scotland, England, the Netherlands, and Italy. Baldwin County on the eastern shore of Mobile Bay also increased in diversity after settlers from Germany, Greece, Italy, and French Canada arrived to farm and fish.

Like the rest of the nation, Alabama's population grew rapidly in the late 19th and early 20th centuries. In just 40 years, from 1870 to 1910, the number of residents in the state more than doubled from 996,992 to 2,138,093. Alabama's growth rate then slowed, likely due to many African Americans leaving the South beginning in 1915, a movement called the Great Migration. Between 1915 and 1940, 1.7 million African-American Alabamians moved to cities in the North and West seeking economic opportunity and racial tolerance. Alabama's non-white population in fact decreased in the decade between 1910 and 1920.

Aerial depiction of Birmingham in 1885

Exploring Further...

Conduct online research to find images related to industrialization or urbanization in Alabama between 1877 and 1914. Select at least five images and prepare a slide show. Provide a short paragraph for each image that includes

- its date.
- its location.
- a description of what appears in the image.
- how the image reflects the industrial and/or urban growth of Alabama.

CHAPTER 13

CHANGES ON THE WESTERN FRONTIER

Essential Question

How did westward migration after the Civil War affect the United States?

ALABAMA COURSE OF STUDY

14 Describe how the Civil War influenced the United States, including the Anaconda Plan and the major battles of Bull Run, Antietam, Vicksburg, and Gettysburg and Sherman's March to the Sea.

- Describing nonmilitary events and life during the Civil War, including the Homestead Act, the Morrill Act, Northern draft riots, the Emancipation Proclamation, and the Gettysburg Address.

Until the 1860s, the migratory Indians of Montana—including the Blackfeet shown here—followed the buffalo herds and traded peacefully with whites in the region.

USA

1870 Red Cloud, chief of the Oglala Sioux, states his people's case in Washington, D.C.

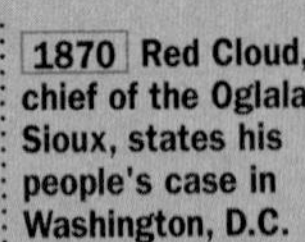

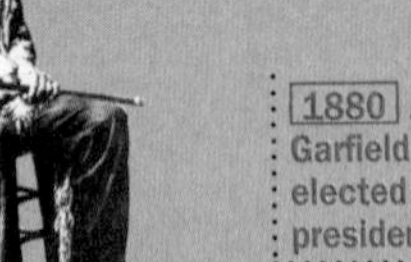

1880 James Garfield is elected president.

1881 Garfield is assassinated. Chester Arthur becomes president.

1884 Grover Cleveland is elected president.

1870

1880

WORLD

1869 Suez Canal is opened.

1872 Secret ballot is adopted in Britain.

1881 French occupy Tunisia.

Image Credits: (bkgd), National Anthropological Archives, Smithsonian Institution (4703); (cl), The Granger Collection, New York; (cr), ©MPI/HultonArchive/Getty Images; (br), ©HultonDeutsch Collection/Corbis

HISTORY

Sitting Bull: Chief of the Lakota Nation

hmhsocialstudies.com VIDEO

INTERACT WITH HISTORY

It is the late 1890s. The American West is the last frontier. Ranchers, cowboys, and miners have changed forever the lives of the Native Americans who hunted on the Western plains. Now westward fever intensifies as "boomers" rush to grab "free" farm land with the government's blessing.

Explore the Issues

- What might be some ways to make a living on the Western frontier?
- If native peoples already live in your intended home, how will you co-exist?
- How might settlers and Native Americans differ regarding use of the land?

1889 Oklahoma opened for settlement; the land rush begins.

1890 Sioux are massacred at Wounded Knee.

1893 Diminished U.S. gold reserve triggers the panic of 1893.

1896 William McKinley is elected president.

1896 William Jennings Bryan runs for president.

1890

1900

1893 France takes over Indochina.

1899 Berlin Conference divides Africa among European nations.

1900 Boxer Rebellion takes place in China.

Image Credits: (bkgd), National Anthropological Archives, Smithsonian Institution (4703); (bl), ©Bettmann/Corbis; (br), ©Blank Archives/Hulton Archive/Getty Images

SECTION 1

Cultures Clash on the Prairie

MAIN IDEA	WHY IT MATTERS NOW	Terms & Names
The cattle industry boomed in the late 1800s, as the culture of the Plains Indians declined.	**Today, ranchers and Plains Indians work to preserve their cultural traditions.**	**•Great Plains •Treaty of Fort Laramie •Sitting Bull •George A. Custer •assimilation •Dawes Act •Battle of Wounded Knee •longhorn •Chisholm Trail •long drive**

One American's Story

hmhsocialstudies.com
TAKING NOTES
Use the graphic organizer online to take notes on cultures in the American West.

Zitkala-Ša was born a Sioux in 1876. As she grew up on the Great Plains, she learned the ways of her people. When Zitkala-Ša was eight years old she was sent to a Quaker school in Indiana. Though her mother warned her of the "white men's lies," Zitkala-Ša was not prepared for the loss of dignity and identity she experienced, which was symbolized by the cutting of her hair.

A PERSONAL VOICE ZITKALA-ŠA

> **"I cried aloud . . . and heard them gnaw off one of my thick braids. Then I lost my spirit. Since the day I was taken from my mother I had suffered extreme indignities. . . . And now my long hair was shingled like a coward's! In my anguish I moaned for my mother, but no one came. . . . Now I was only one of many little animals driven by a herder."**
>
> —*The School Days of an Indian Girl*

Zitkala-Ša experienced firsthand the clash of two very different cultures that occurred as ever-growing numbers of white settlers moved onto the Great Plains. In the resulting struggle, the Native American way of life was changed forever.

The Culture of the Plains Indians

Zitkala-Ša knew very little about the world east of the Mississippi River. Most Easterners knew equally little about the West, picturing a vast desert occupied by savage tribes. That view could not have been more inaccurate. In fact, distinctive and highly developed Native American ways of life existed on the **Great Plains**, the grassland extending through the west-central portion of the United States. (See map, Shrinking Native American Lands, and Battle Sites.)

To the east, near the lower Missouri River, tribes such as the Osage and Iowa had, for more than a century, hunted and planted crops and settled in small villages. Farther west, nomadic tribes such as the Sioux and Cheyenne gathered wild foods and hunted buffalo. Peoples of the Plains, abiding by tribal law, traded and produced beautifully crafted tools and clothing.

THE HORSE AND THE BUFFALO After the Spanish brought horses to New Mexico in 1598, the Native American way of life began to change. As the native peoples acquired horses—and then guns—they were able to travel farther and hunt more efficiently. By the mid-1700s, almost all the tribes on the Great Plains had left their farms to roam the plains and hunt buffalo.

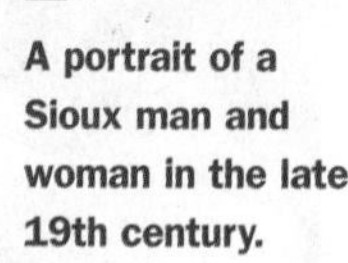

▲ A portrait of a Sioux man and woman in the late 19th century.

Their increased mobility often led to war when hunters in one tribe trespassed on other tribes' hunting grounds. For the young men of a tribe, taking part in war parties and raids was a way to win prestige. A Plains warrior gained honor by killing his enemies, as well as by "counting coup." This practice involved touching a live enemy with a coup stick and escaping unharmed. And sometimes warring tribes would call a truce so that they could trade goods, share news, or enjoy harvest festivals. Native Americans made tepees from buffalo hides and also used the skins for clothing, shoes, and blankets. Buffalo meat was dried into jerky or mixed with berries and fat to make a staple food called pemmican. While the horse gave Native Americans speed and mobility, the buffalo provided many of their basic needs and was central to life on the Plains. (See chart, Importance of the Buffalo.) (A)

Vocabulary
coup: a feat of bravery performed in battle

MAIN IDEA

Summarizing
(A) How did the horse influence Native American life on the Great Plains?

FAMILY LIFE Native Americans on the plains usually lived in small extended family groups with ties to other bands that spoke the same language. Young men trained to become hunters and warriors. The women helped butcher the game and prepared the hides that the men brought back to the camp; young women sometimes chose their own husbands.

The Plains Indian tribes believed that powerful spirits controlled events in the natural world. Men or women who showed particular sensitivity to the spirits became medicine men or women, or shamans. Children learned proper behavior and culture through stories and myths, games, and good examples. Despite their communal way of life, however, no individual was allowed to dominate the group. Leaders ruled by counsel rather than by force, and land was held in common for the use of the whole tribe.

This Yankton Sioux coup stick was used by warriors. ▼

Settlers Push Westward

The culture of the white settlers differed in many ways from that of the Native Americans on the plains. Unlike Native Americans, who believed that land could not be owned, the settlers believed that owning land, making a mining claim, or starting a business would give them a stake in the country. They argued that the Native Americans had forfeited their rights to the land because they hadn't settled down to "improve" it. Concluding that the plains were "unsettled," migrants streamed westward along railroad and wagon trails to claim the land.

THE LURE OF SILVER AND GOLD The prospect of striking it rich was one powerful attraction of the West. The discovery of gold in Colorado in 1858 drew tens of thousands of miners to the region.

Most mining camps and tiny frontier towns had filthy, ramshackle living quarters. Rows of tents and shacks with dirt "streets" and wooden sidewalks had replaced unspoiled picturesque landscapes. Fortune seekers of every description —including Irish, German, Polish, Chinese, and African-American men—crowded the camps and boomtowns. A few hardy, business-minded women tried their luck too, working as laundresses, freight haulers, or miners. Cities such as Virginia City, Nevada, and Helena, Montana, originated as mining camps on Native American land.

HISTORY
VIDEO
Sitting Bull: Chief of the Lakota Nation
hmhsocialstudies.com

The Government Restricts Native Americans

While allowing more settlers to move westward, the arrival of the railroads also influenced the government's policy toward the Native Americans who lived on the plains. In 1834, the federal government had passed an act that designated the entire Great Plains as one enormous reservation, or land set aside for Native American tribes. In the 1850s, however, the government changed its policy and created treaties that defined specific boundaries for each tribe. Most Native Americans spurned the government treaties and continued to hunt on their traditional lands, clashing with settlers and miners—with tragic results. B

MAIN IDEA
Analyzing Issues
B What was the government's policy toward Native American land?

KEY PLAYER

SITTING BULL
1831–1890

As a child, Sitting Bull was known as Hunkesni, or Slow; he earned the name Tatanka Iyotanka (Sitting Bull) after a fight with the Crow, a traditional enemy of the Sioux.

Sitting Bull led his people by the strength of his character and purpose. He was a warrior, spiritual leader, and medicine man, and he was determined that whites should leave Sioux territory. His most famous fight was at the Little Bighorn River. About his opponent, George Armstrong Custer, he said, "They tell me I murdered Custer. It is a lie. . . . He was a fool and rode to his death."

After Sitting Bull's surrender to the federal government in 1881, his dislike of whites did not change. He was killed by Native American police at Standing Rock Reservation in December 1890.

MASSACRE AT SAND CREEK One of the most tragic events occurred in 1864. Most of the Cheyenne, assuming they were under the protection of the U.S. government, had peacefully returned to Colorado's Sand Creek Reserve for the winter. Yet General S. R. Curtis, U.S. Army commander in the West, sent a telegram to militia colonel John Chivington that read, "I want no peace till the Indians suffer more." In response, Chivington and his troops descended on the Cheyenne and Arapaho—about 200 warriors and 500 women and children—camped at Sand Creek. The attack at dawn on November 29, 1864 killed over 150 inhabitants, mostly women and children.

DEATH ON THE BOZEMAN TRAIL The Bozeman Trail ran directly through Sioux hunting grounds in the Bighorn Mountains. The Sioux chief, Red Cloud (Mahpiua Luta), had unsuccessfully appealed to the government to end white settlement on the trail. In December 1866, the warrior Crazy Horse ambushed Captain William J. Fetterman and his company at Lodge Trail Ridge. Over 80 soldiers were killed. Native Americans called this fight the Battle of the Hundred Slain. Whites called it the Fetterman Massacre.

Skirmishes continued until the government agreed to close the Bozeman Trail. In return, the **Treaty of Fort Laramie,** in which the Sioux agreed to live on a reservation along the Missouri River, was forced on the leaders of the Sioux in 1868. **Sitting Bull** (Tatanka Iyotanka), leader of the Hunkpapa Sioux, had never signed it. Although the Ogala and Brule Sioux did sign the treaty, they expected to continue using their traditional hunting grounds.

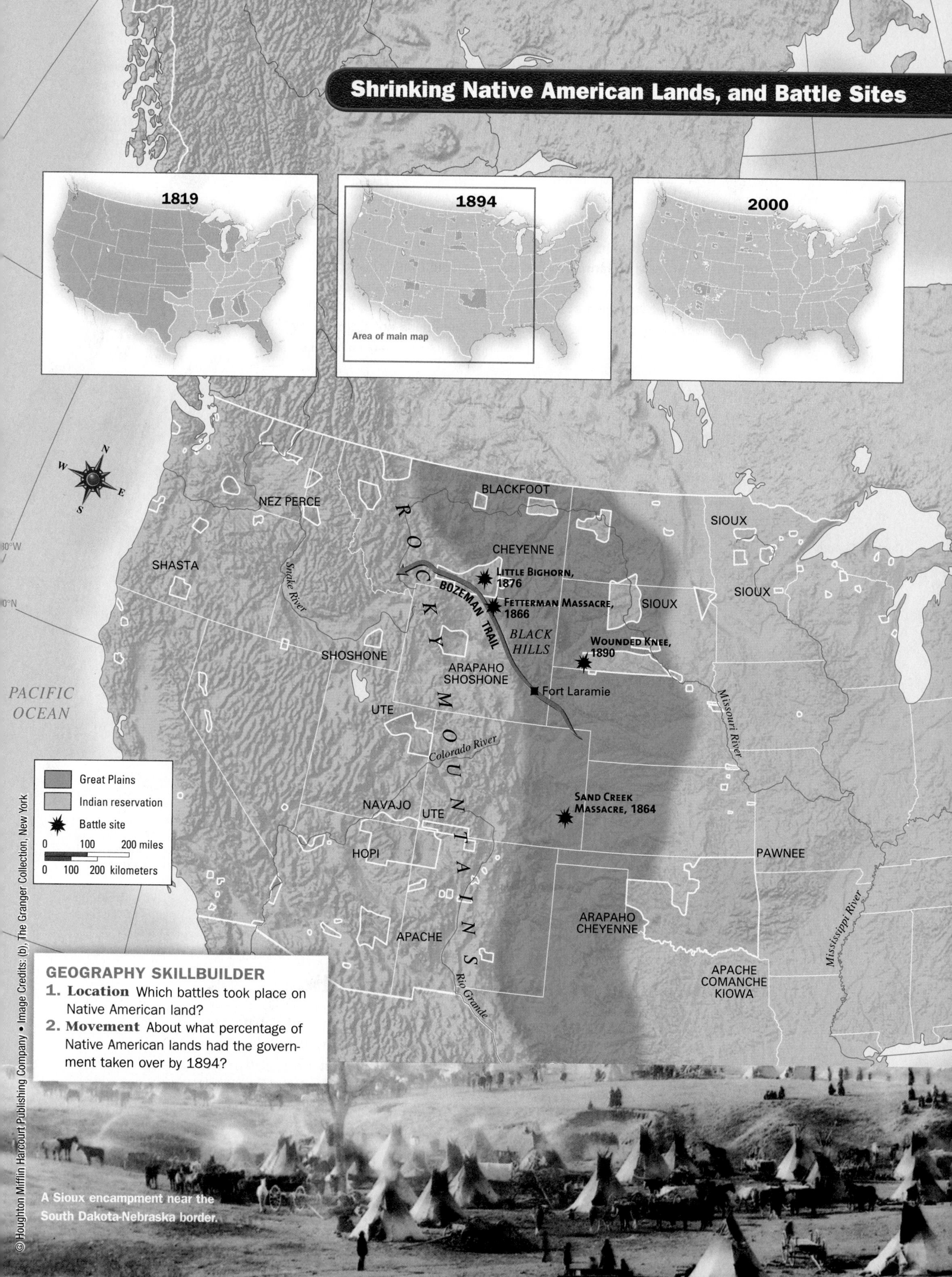

GEOGRAPHY SKILLBUILDER

1. **Location** Which battles took place on Native American land?
2. **Movement** About what percentage of Native American lands had the government taken over by 1894?

A Sioux encampment near the South Dakota-Nebraska border.

Bloody Battles Continue

The Treaty of Fort Laramie provided only a temporary halt to warfare. The conflict between the two cultures continued as settlers moved westward and Native American nations resisted the restrictions imposed upon them. A Sioux warrior explained why.

The Winchester '76 rifle used by government troops, and a Sioux war bow.

A PERSONAL VOICE GALL, A HUNKPAPA SIOUX

> **"[We] have been taught to hunt and live on the game. You tell us that we must learn to farm, live in one house, and take on your ways. Suppose the people living beyond the great sea should come and tell you that you must stop farming, and kill your cattle, and take your houses and lands, what would you do? Would you not fight them?"**
>
> —quoted in *Bury My Heart at Wounded Knee*

RED RIVER WAR In late 1868, war broke out yet again as the Kiowa and Comanche engaged in six years of raiding that finally led to the Red River War of 1874–1875. The U.S. Army responded by herding the people of friendly tribes onto reservations while opening fire on all others. General Philip Sheridan, a Union Army veteran, gave orders "to destroy their villages and ponies, to kill and hang all warriors, and to bring back all women and children." With such tactics, the army crushed resistance on the southern plains.

GOLD RUSH Within four years of the Treaty of Fort Laramie, miners began searching the Black Hills for gold. The Sioux, Cheyenne, and Arapaho protested to no avail. In 1874, when Colonel **George A. Custer** reported that the Black Hills had gold "from the grass roots down," a gold rush was on. Red Cloud and Spotted Tail, another Sioux chief, vainly appealed again to government officials in Washington.

Colonel George Armstrong Custer, 1865

CUSTER'S LAST STAND In early June 1876, the Sioux and Cheyenne held a sun dance, during which Sitting Bull had a vision of soldiers and some Native Americans falling from their horses. When Colonel Custer and his troops reached the Little Bighorn River, the Native Americans were ready for them.

Led by Crazy Horse, Gall, and Sitting Bull, the warriors—with raised spears and rifles—outflanked and crushed Custer's troops. Within an hour, Custer and all of the men of the Seventh Cavalry were dead. By late 1876, however, the Sioux were beaten. Sitting Bull and a few followers took refuge in Canada, where they remained until 1881. Eventually, to prevent his people's starvation, Sitting Bull was forced to surrender. Later, in 1885, he appeared in William F. "Buffalo Bill" Cody's Wild West Show. C

Analyzing Effects
C What were the results of Custer's last stand?

The Government Supports Assimilation

The Native Americans still had supporters in the United States, and debate over the treatment of Native Americans continued. The well-known writer Helen Hunt Jackson, for example, exposed the government's many broken promises in her 1881 book *A Century of Dishonor*. At the same time many sympathizers supported **assimilation,** a plan under which Native Americans would give up their beliefs and way of life and become part of the white culture.

THE DAWES ACT In 1887, Congress passed the **Dawes Act** aiming to "Americanize" the Native Americans. The act broke up the reservations and gave some of the reservation land to individual Native Americans—160 acres to each head of household and 80 acres to each unmarried adult. The government would sell the remainder of the reservations to settlers, and the resulting income would be used by Native Americans to buy farm implements. By 1932, whites had taken about two-thirds of the territory that had been set aside for Native Americans. In the end, the Native Americans received no money from the sale of these lands.

THE DESTRUCTION OF THE BUFFALO Perhaps the most significant blow to tribal life on the plains was the destruction of the buffalo. Tourists and fur traders shot buffalo for sport. U.S. General Sheridan noted with approval that buffalo hunters were destroying the Plains Indians' main source of food, clothing, shelter, and fuel. In 1800, approximately 65 million buffalo roamed the plains; by 1890, fewer than 1000 remained. In 1900, the United States sheltered, in Yellowstone National Park, a single wild herd of buffalo.

The Battle of Wounded Knee

The Sioux continued to suffer poverty and disease. In desperation, they turned to a Paiute prophet who promised that if the Sioux performed a ritual called the Ghost Dance, Native American lands and way of life would be restored.

The Ghost Dance movement spread rapidly among the 25,000 Sioux on the Dakota reservation. Alarmed military leaders ordered the arrest of Sitting Bull. In December 1890, about 40 Native American police were sent to arrest him. Sitting Bull's friend and bodyguard, Catch-the-Bear, shot one of them. The police then killed Sitting Bull. In the aftermath, Chief Big Foot led the fearful Sioux away.

WOUNDED KNEE On December 28, 1890, the Seventh Cavalry—Custer's old regiment—rounded up about 350 starving and freezing Sioux and took them to a camp at Wounded Knee Creek in South Dakota. The next day, the soldiers demanded that the Native Americans give up all their weapons. A shot was fired; from which side, it was not clear. The soldiers opened fire with deadly cannon.

Importance of the Buffalo
The buffalo provided the Plains Indians with more than just a high-protein food source.
1800 65,000,000
1870 1,000
2000 260,000
THE SKULL of the buffalo was considered sacred and was used in many Native American rituals.
THE HORNS were carved into bowls and spoons.
THE BONES of the buffalo were made into hide scrapers, tool handles, sled runners, and hoe blades. The hoofs were ground up and used as glue.
THE HIDE was by far the most precious part of the buffalo. Native American clothing, tepees, and even arrow shields were made from buffalo hide.

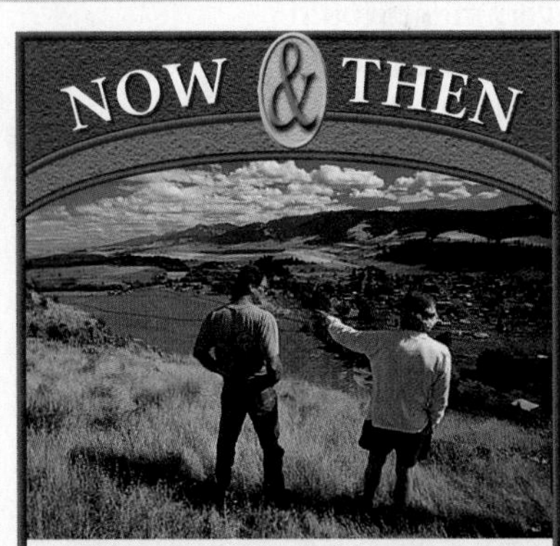

NEZ PERCE IN OREGON

Forced off their tribal lands in Wallowa County, Oregon, in 1877, the Nez Perce are returning almost 120 years later. 1999 figures put the number of Nez Perce in the Oregon area at around 3,000.

In 1997, Wallowa community leaders obtained a grant to develop the Wallowa Band Nez Perce Trail Interpretive Center—a cultural center that hosts powwows and other activities to draw tourists.

"I never thought I'd see the day," said Earl (Taz) Conner, a direct descendant of Chief Joseph, the best known of the Nez Perce. And, in the words of Soy Redthunder, another tribe member, "[We] look at it as homecoming."

Within minutes, the Seventh Cavalry slaughtered as many as 300 mostly unarmed Native Americans, including several children. The soldiers left the corpses to freeze on the ground. This event, the **Battle of Wounded Knee,** brought the Indian wars—and an entire era—to a bitter end. **D**

MAIN IDEA

Analyzing Causes

D What events led to the Battle of Wounded Knee?

A PERSONAL VOICE BLACK ELK

"I did not know then how much was ended. When I look back . . . I can still see the butchered women and children lying heaped and scattered all along the crooked gulch. . . . And I can see that something else died there in the bloody mud, and was buried in the blizzard. A people's dream died there. It was a beautiful dream."

—*Black Elk Speaks*

Cattle Becomes Big Business

As the great herds of buffalo disappeared, and Native Americans were forced onto smaller and less desirable reservations, horses and cattle flourished on the plains. As cattle ranchers opened up the Great Plains to big business, ranching from Texas to Kansas became a profitable investment.

VAQUEROS AND COWBOYS American settlers had never managed large herds on the open range, and they learned from their Mexican neighbors how to round up, rope, brand, and care for the animals. The animals themselves, the Texas **longhorns,** were sturdy, short-tempered breeds accustomed to the dry grasslands of southern Spain. Spanish settlers raised longhorns for food and brought horses to use as work animals and for transportation.

As American as the cowboy seems today, his way of life stemmed directly from that of those first Spanish ranchers in Mexico. The cowboy's clothes, food, and vocabulary were heavily influenced by the Mexican *vaquero,* who was the first to wear spurs, which he attached with straps to his bare feet and used to control his horse. His *chaparreras,* or leather overalls, became known as chaps. He ate *charqui,* or "jerky"—dried strips of meat. The Spanish *bronco caballo,* or "rough horse" that ran wild, became known as a bronco or bronc. The strays, or *mesteños,* were the same mustangs that the American cowboy tamed and prized. The Mexican *rancho* became the American ranch. Finally, the English words *corral* and

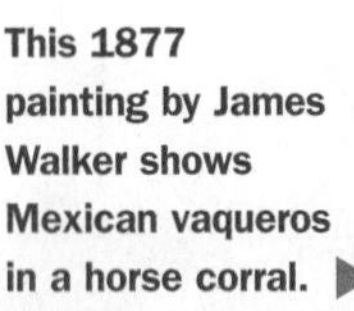

This 1877 painting by James Walker shows Mexican vaqueros in a horse corral. ▶

MAIN IDEA

Drawing Conclusions

E What does the American cowboy tradition owe to the Mexican vaquero?

rodeo were borrowed from Spanish. In his skills, dress, and speech, the Mexican vaquero was the true forerunner of the American "buckaroo" or cowboy. **E**

Despite the plentiful herds of Western cattle, cowboys were not in great demand until the railroads reached the Great Plains. Before the Civil War, ranchers for the most part didn't stray far from their homesteads with their cattle. There were, of course, some exceptions. During the California gold rush in 1849, some hardy cattlemen on horseback braved a long trek, or drive, through Apache territory and across the desert to collect $25 to $125 a head for their cattle. In 1854, two ranchers drove their cattle 700 miles to Muncie, Indiana, where they put them on stock cars bound for New York City. When the cattle were unloaded in New York, the stampede that followed caused a panic on Third Avenue. Parts of the country were not ready for the mass transportation of animals.

GROWING DEMAND FOR BEEF After the Civil War, the demand for beef skyrocketed, partly due to the rapidly growing cities. The Chicago Union Stock Yards opened in 1865, and by spring 1866, the railroads were running regularly through Sedalia, Missouri. From Sedalia, Texas ranchers could ship their cattle to Chicago and markets throughout the East. They found, however, that the route to Sedalia presented several obstacles: including thunderstorms and rain-swollen rivers. Also, in 1866, farmers angry about trampled crops blockaded cattle in Baxter Springs, Kansas, preventing them from reaching Sedalia. Some herds then had to be sold at cut-rate prices, others died of starvation. **F**

MAIN IDEA

Summarizing

F What developments led to the rapid growth of the cattle industry?

THE COW TOWN The next year, cattlemen found a more convenient route. Illinois cattle dealer Joseph McCoy approached several Western towns with plans to create a shipping yard where the trails and rail lines came together. The tiny Kansas town of Abilene enthusiastically agreed to the plan. McCoy built cattle pens, a three-story hotel, and helped survey the **Chisholm Trail**—the major cattle route from San Antonio, Texas, through Oklahoma to Kansas. Thirty-five thousand head of cattle were shipped out of the yard in Abilene during its first

VIDEO
Wild West: Cattle Drive

hmhsocialstudies.com

Cattle Trails and the Railroads, 1870s–1890s

hmhsocialstudies.com INTERACTIVE MAP

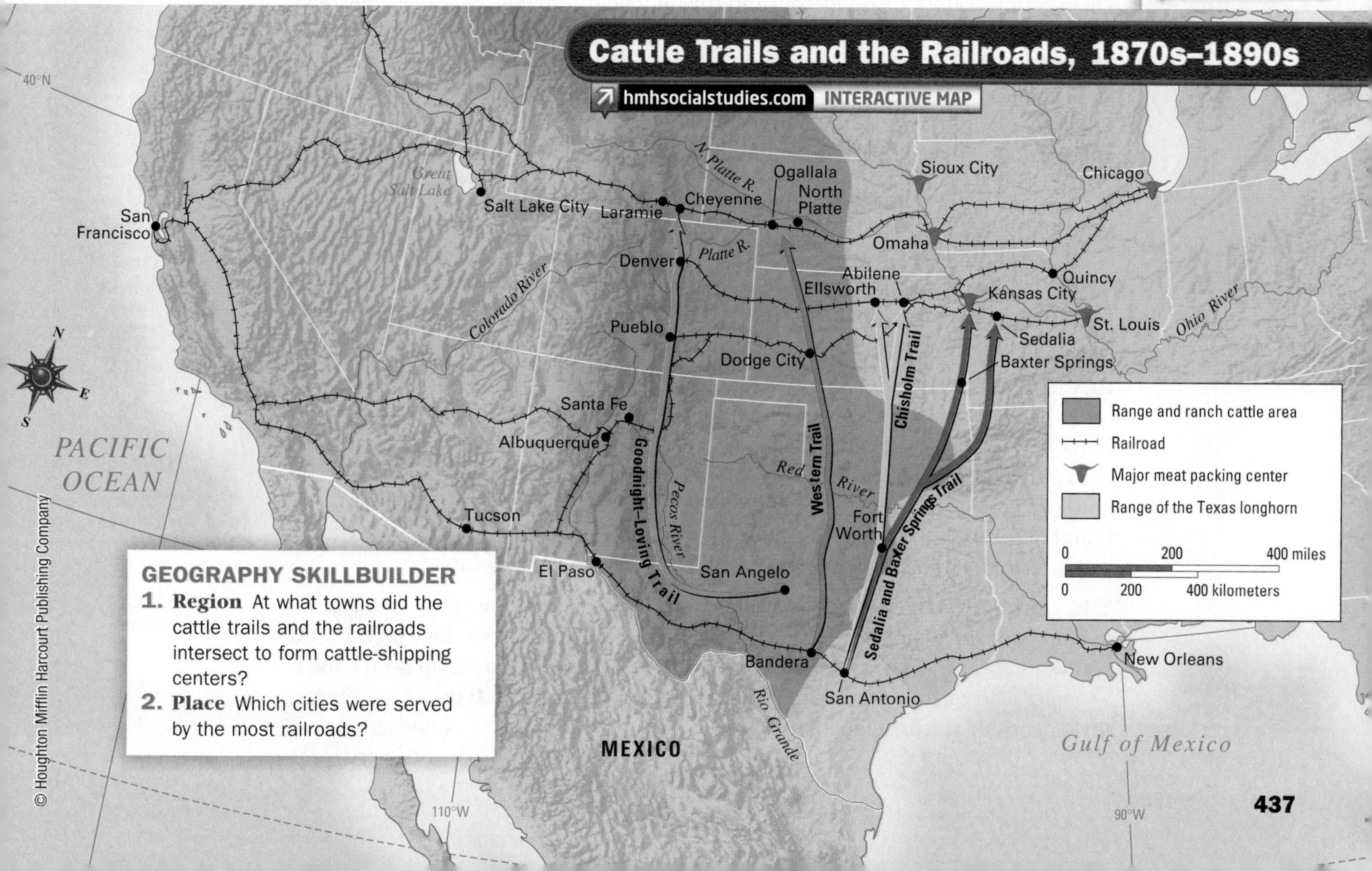

Range and ranch cattle area
Railroad
Major meat packing center
Range of the Texas longhorn

0 200 400 miles
0 200 400 kilometers

GEOGRAPHY SKILLBUILDER

1. **Region** At what towns did the cattle trails and the railroads intersect to form cattle-shipping centers?
2. **Place** Which cities were served by the most railroads?

History Through Art

STAMPEDED BY LIGHTNING (1908)

Painter and sculptor Frederic Remington is best known for his romantic and spirited depictions of the Western frontier. Remington liked to paint in a single dominant color. Native Americans, cowboys at work, and other familiar Western scenes were all subjects of Remington's work.

What do you learn about the work of the cowboy in this painting?

year in operation. The following year, business more than doubled, to 75,000 head. Soon ranchers were hiring cowboys to drive their cattle to Abilene. Within a few years, the Chisholm Trail had worn wide and deep.

A Day in the Life of a Cowboy

The meeting of the Chisholm Trail and the railroad in Abilene ushered in the heyday of the cowboy. As many as 55,000 worked the plains between 1866 and 1885. Although folklore and postcards depicted the cowboy as Anglo-American, about 25 percent of them were African American, and at least 12 percent were Mexican. The romanticized American cowboy of myth rode the open range, herding cattle and fighting villains. Meanwhile, the real-life cowboy was doing nonstop work.

A DAY'S WORK A cowboy worked 10 to 14 hours a day on a ranch and 14 or more on the trail, alert at all times for dangers that might harm or upset the herds. Some cowboys were as young as 15; most were broken-down by the time they were 40. A cowboy might own his saddle, but his trail horse usually belonged to his boss. He was an expert rider and roper. His gun might be used to protect the herd from wild or diseased animals rather than to hurt or chase outlaws.

ROUNDUP The cowboy's season began with a spring roundup, in which he and other hands from the ranch herded all the longhorns they could find on the open range into a large corral. They kept the herd penned there for several days, until the cattle were so hungry that they preferred grazing to running away. Then the cowboys sorted through the herd, claiming the cattle that were marked with the brand of their ranch and calves that still needed to be branded. After the herd was gathered and branded, the trail boss chose a crew for the long drive.

THE LONG DRIVE This overland transport, or **long drive,** of the animals often lasted about three months. A typical drive included one cowboy for every 250 to 300 head of cattle; a cook who also drove the chuck wagon and set up camp; and a wrangler who cared for the extra horses. A trail boss earned $100 or more a month for supervising the drive and negotiating with settlers and Native Americans.

During the long drive, the cowboy was in the saddle from dawn to dusk. He slept on the ground and bathed in rivers. He risked death and loss every day of the drive, especially at river crossings, where cattle often hesitated and were swept away. Because lightning was a constant danger, cowboys piled their spurs, buckles, and other metal objects at the edge of their camp to avoid attracting lightning bolts. Thunder, or even a sneeze, could cause a stampede. G

MAIN IDEA

Comparing
G How did the cowboy's life differ from the myth about it?

LEGENDS OF THE WEST Legendary figures like James Butler "Wild Bill" Hickok and Martha Jane Burke (Calamity Jane) actually never dealt with cows. Hickok served as a scout and a spy during the Civil War and, later, as a marshal in Abilene, Kansas. He was a violent man who was shot and killed while holding a pair of aces and a pair of eights in a poker game, a hand still known as the "dead man's hand." Calamity Jane was an expert sharpshooter who dressed as a man. She may have been a scout for Colonel George Custer.

HISTORICAL SPOTLIGHT

THE WILD WEST SHOW

In the 1880s, William F. Cody toured the country with a show called Buffalo Bill's Wild West. The show featured trick riding and roping exhibitions. It thrilled audiences with mock battles between cowboys and Indians.

Wild Bill Hickok, Annie Oakley, Calamity Jane (shown here), and even Sitting Bull toured in Wild West shows. Their performances helped make Western life a part of American mythology.

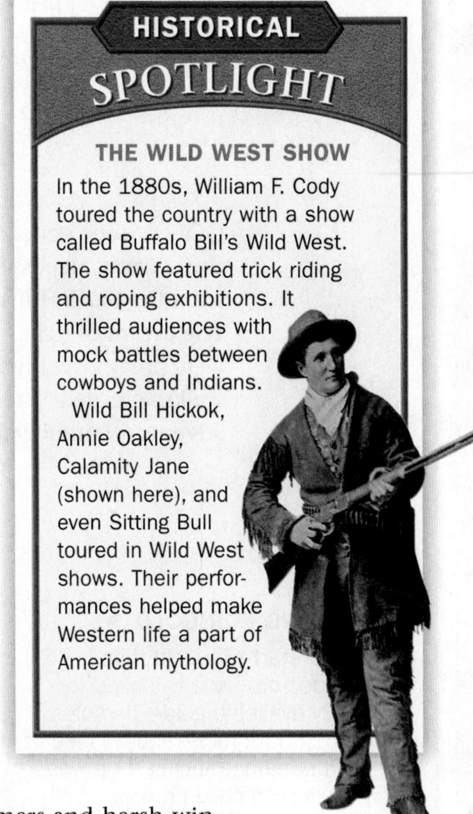

The End of the Open Range

Almost as quickly as cattle herds multiplied and ranching became big business, the cattle frontier met its end. Overgrazing of the land, extended bad weather, and the invention of barbed wire were largely responsible.

Between 1883 and 1887 alternating patterns of dry summers and harsh winters wiped out whole herds. Most ranchers then turned to smaller herds of high-grade stock that would yield more meat per animal. Ranchers fenced the land with barbed wire, invented by Illinois farmer Joseph F. Glidden. It was cheap and easy to use and helped to turn the open plains into a series of fenced-in ranches. The era of the wide-open West was over.

SECTION 1 ASSESSMENT

1. **TERMS & NAMES** For each term or name, write a sentence explaining its significance.
   - **Great Plains**
   - **Treaty of Fort Laramie**
   - **Sitting Bull**
   - **George A. Custer**
   - **assimilation**
   - **Dawes Act**
   - **Battle of Wounded Knee**
   - **longhorn**
   - **Chisholm Trail**
   - **long drive**

MAIN IDEA

2. **TAKING NOTES**
   Fill in supporting details about the culture of the Plains Indians.

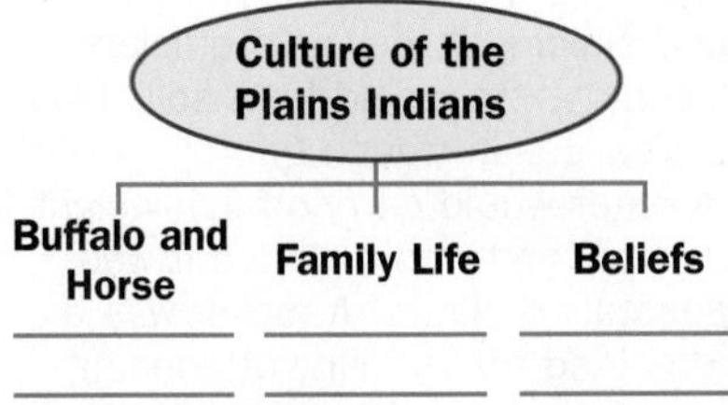

CRITICAL THINKING

3. **MAKING INFERENCES**
   Why do you think the assimilation policy of the Dawes Act failed? Support your opinion with information from the text.
   Think About:
   - the experience of Native Americans such as Zitkala-Ša
   - the attitudes of many white leaders toward Native Americans
   - the merits of owning property
   - the importance of cultural heritage

4. **ANALYZING CAUSES**
   What economic opportunities drew large numbers of people to the Great Plains beginning in the mid-1800s?

5. **DRAWING CONCLUSIONS**
   Identify the reasons for the rise and the decline of the cattle industry.

DAILY LIFE 1849–1900

Gold Mining

GOLD! Some struck it rich—some struck out. Between the Civil War and the turn of the century, deposits of the precious yellow metal were discovered in scattered sites from the Black Hills of South Dakota and Cripple Creek, Colorado, to Nome, Alaska. The dream of riches lured hundreds of thousands of prospectors into territories that were previously inhabited only by native peoples. The fortune seekers came from all walks: grizzled veterans from the California gold rush of 1849, youths seeking adventure, middle-class professionals, and even some families.

PANNING FOR GOLD ▶

At the start of a gold rush, prospectors usually looked for easily available gold—particles eroded from rocks and washed downstream. Panning for it was easy—even children could do it. They scooped up mud and water from the streambed in a flat pan and swirled it. The circular motion of the water caused the sand to wash over the side and the remaining minerals to form layers according to weight. Gold, which is heavier than most other minerals, sank to the bottom.

◀ SLUICES AND ROCKERS

In 1898, prospectors like this mother and son in Fairbanks, Alaska, found sluicing to be more efficient than panning, since it could extract gold from soil. They would shovel soil into a sluice—a trough through which water flowed—and the water would carry off lightweight materials. The gold sank to the bottom, where it was caught in wooden ridges called cleats. A rocker was a portable sluice that combined the mobility of panning with the efficiency of sluicing.

IN THE BOWELS OF THE EARTH

Although surface gold could be extracted by panning and sluicing, most gold was located in veins in underground rock. Mining these deposits involved digging tunnels along the veins of gold and breaking up tons of ore—hard and dangerous work. Tunnels often collapsed, and miners who weren't killed were trapped in utter darkness for days.

Heat was a problem, too. As miners descended into the earth, the temperature inside the mine soared. At a depth of about 2,000 feet, the temperature of the water that invariably flooded the bottom of a mine could be 160°F.

Cave-ins and hot water weren't the only dangers that miners faced. The pressure in the underground rock sometimes became so intense that it caused deadly explosions.

A FAMILY AFFAIR

This early placer, or surface, mine at Cripple Creek attracted many women and children. It grew out of the vision of a young rancher, Bob Womack. He had found gold particles washed down from higher land and was convinced that the Cripple Creek area was literally a gold mine.

Because Womack was generally disliked, the community ignored him. When a German count struck gold there, however, business boomed. Womack died penniless—but the mines produced a $400 million bonanza.

DATA FILE

BOOM TO BUST

Gold-rush towns could blossom out of the wilderness virtually overnight—but they could also die out almost as quickly.

LONG ODDS

These statistics for the Klondike gold rush, from 1896 to 1899, show the incredible odds against striking it rich.

100,000 people set out for the Klondike.
40,000 people make it.
20,000 stake claims.
4,000 prospectors find gold.
200 become rich.

DEADLY DIGGING

An estimated 7,500 people died while digging for gold and silver during the Western gold rushes. That was more than the total number of people who died in the Indian wars.

THINKING CRITICALLY

CONNECT TO HISTORY

1. **Creating Graphs** Use the Data File to create a bar graph that shows the percentage of people who set out for the Klondike who did not get there, got there, staked claims, found gold, and became rich.

 **SEE SKILLBUILDER HANDBOOK, PAGE R30.**

CONNECT TO TODAY

2. **Researching Ghost Towns** Research the history of a ghost town from boom to bust. Present a short report on life in the town and its attempts to survive beyond the gold rush.

hmhsocialstudies.com
RESEARCH WEB LINKS

Settling on the Great Plains

MAIN IDEA	WHY IT MATTERS NOW	Terms & Names
Settlers on the Great Plains transformed the land despite great hardships.	**The Great Plains region remains the breadbasket of the United States.**	**• Homestead Act • exoduster • soddy • Morrill Act • bonanza farm**

One American's Story

Use the graphic organizer online to take notes about settling the Great Plains.

When Esther Clark Hill was a girl on the Kansas prairie in the 1800s, her father often left the family to go on hunting or trading expeditions. His trips left Esther's mother, Allena Clark, alone on the farm.

Esther remembered her mother holding on to the reins of a runaway mule team, "her black hair tumbling out of its pins and over her shoulders, her face set and white, while one small girl clung with chattering teeth to the sides of the rocking wagon." The men in the settlement spoke admiringly about "Leny's nerve," and Esther thought that daily life presented a challenge even greater than driving a runaway team.

▲ **Plains settlers, like this woman depicted in Harvey Dunn's painting *Pioneer Woman*, had to be strong and self-reliant.**

A PERSONAL VOICE ESTHER CLARK HILL

"I think, as much courage as it took to hang onto the reins that day, it took more to live twenty-four hours at a time, month in and out, on the lonely and lovely prairie, without giving up to the loneliness."

—quoted in *Pioneer Women*

As the railroads penetrated the frontier and the days of the free-ranging cowboy ended, hundreds of thousands of families migrated west, lured by vast tracts of cheap, fertile land. In their effort to establish a new life, they endured extreme hardships and loneliness.

Settlers Move Westward to Farm

It took over 250 years—from the first settlement at Jamestown until 1870—to turn 400 million acres of forests and prairies into flourishing farms. Settling the second 400 million acres took only 30 years, from 1870 to 1900. Federal land policy and the completion of transcontinental railroad lines made this rapid settlement possible.

RAILROADS OPEN THE WEST From 1850 to 1871, the federal government made huge land grants to the railroads—170 million acres, worth half a billion dollars—for laying track in the West. In one grant, both the Union Pacific and the Central Pacific received 10 square miles of public land for every mile of track laid in a state and 20 square miles of land for every mile of track laid in a territory.

In the 1860s, the two companies began a race to lay track. The Central Pacific moved eastward from Sacramento, and the Union Pacific moved westward from Omaha. Civil War veterans, Irish and Chinese immigrants, African Americans, and Mexican Americans did most of the grueling labor. In late 1868, workers for the Union Pacific cut their way through the solid rock of the mountains, laying up to eight miles of track a day. Both companies had reached Utah by the spring of 1869. Fifteen years later, the country boasted five transcontinental railroads. The rails to the East and West Coasts were forever linked.

The railroad companies sold some of their land to farmers for two to ten dollars an acre. Some companies successfully sent agents to Europe to recruit buyers. By 1880, 44 percent of the settlers in Nebraska and more than 70 percent of those in Minnesota and Wisconsin were immigrants. (A)

MAIN IDEA

Analyzing Causes

(A) How did the railroads help open the West?

GOVERNMENT SUPPORT FOR SETTLEMENT Another powerful attraction of the West was the land itself. In 1862, Congress passed the **Homestead Act**, offering 160 acres of land free to any citizen or intended citizen who was head of the household. From 1862 to 1900, up to 600,000 families took advantage of the government's offer. Several thousand settlers were **exodusters**—African Americans who moved from the post-Reconstruction South to Kansas.

Despite the massive response by homesteaders, or settlers on this free land, private speculators and railroad and state government agents sometimes used the law for their own gain. Cattlemen fenced open lands, while miners and woodcutters claimed national resources. Only about 10 percent of the land was actually settled by the families for whom it was intended. In addition, not all plots of land were of equal value. Although 160 acres could provide a decent living in the fertile soil of Iowa or Minnesota, settlers on drier Western land required larger plots to make farming worthwhile.

Vocabulary
speculator: a person who buys or sells something that involves a risk on the chance of making a profit

Eventually, the government strengthened the Homestead Act and passed more legislation to encourage settlers. In 1889, a major land giveaway in what is now Oklahoma attracted thousands of people. In less than a day, land-hungry settlers claimed 2 million acres in a massive land rush. Some took possession of the land before the government officially declared it open. Because these settlers claimed land sooner than they were supposed to, Oklahoma came to be known as the Sooner State. (B)

MAIN IDEA

Analyzing Effects

(B) In what ways did government policies encourage settlement of the West?

Posters like the one shown here drew hundreds of thousands of settlers to the West. Among the settlers were thousands of exodusters—freed slaves who had left the South.

Ho for Kansas!
Brethren, Friends, & Fellow Citizens:
I feel thankful to inform you that the
REAL ESTATE
AND
Homestead Association,
Will Leave Here the
15th of April, 1878,
In pursuit of Homes in the Southwestern Lands of America, at Transportation Rates, cheaper than ever was known before.
For full information inquire of
Benj. Singleton, better known as old Pap,
NO. 5 NORTH FRONT STREET.
Beware of Speculators and Adventurers, as it is a dangerous thing to fall in their hands.
Nashville, Tenn., March 18, 1878.

THE CLOSING OF THE FRONTIER As settlers gobbled up Western land, Henry D. Washburn and fellow explorer Nathaniel P. Langford asked Congress to help protect the wilderness from settlement. In 1870, Washburn, who was surveying land in northwestern Wyoming, described the area's geysers and bubbling springs as: "objects new in experience . . . possessing unlimited grandeur and beauty."

In 1872, the government created Yellowstone National Park. Seven years later, the Department of the Interior forced railroads to give up their claim to Western landholdings that were equal in area to New York, New Jersey, Pennsylvania, Delaware, Maryland, and Virginia combined. Even so, by 1880, individuals had bought more than 19 million acres of government-owned land. Ten years later, the Census Bureau declared that the country no longer had a continuous frontier line—the frontier no longer existed. To many, the frontier was what had made America unique. In an 1893 essay entitled "The Significance of the Frontier in American History," the historian Frederick Jackson Turner agreed.

Background
The U.S. Census Bureau is the permanent collector of timely, relevant data about the people and economy of the United States.

A Personal Voice FREDERICK JACKSON TURNER

"American social development has been continually beginning over again on the frontier. This perennial rebirth, this fluidity of American life, this expansion westward with its new opportunities, its continuous touch with the simplicity of primitive society, furnish the forces dominating American character."

—"The Significance of the Frontier in American History"

Today many historians question Turner's view. They think he gave too much importance to the frontier in the nation's development and in shaping a special American character. C

MAIN IDEA

Summarizing
C What was Turner's view of the role of the American frontier in 1893?

Settlers Meet the Challenges of the Plains

The frontier settlers faced extreme hardships—droughts, floods, fires, blizzards, locust plagues, and occasional raids by outlaws and Native Americans. Yet the number of people living west of the Mississippi River grew from 1 percent of the nation's population in 1850 to almost 30 percent by the turn of the century.

Vocabulary
locust: any of numerous grasshoppers that travel in large swarms, often doing great damage to crops

DUGOUTS AND SODDIES Since trees were scarce, most settlers built their homes from the land itself. Many pioneers dug their homes into the sides of ravines or small hills. A stovepipe jutting from the ground was often the only clear sign of such a dugout home.

Those who moved to the broad, flat plains often made freestanding houses by stacking blocks of prairie turf. Like a dugout, a sod home, or **soddy**, was warm in

A pioneer family stands in front of their soddy near Coburg, Nebraska, in 1887. ▶

winter and cool in summer. Soddies were small, however, and offered little light or air. They were havens for snakes, insects, and other pests. Although they were fireproof, they leaked continuously when it rained.

WOMEN'S WORK Virtually alone on the flat, endless prairie, homesteaders had to be almost superhumanly self-sufficient. Women often worked beside the men in the fields, plowing the land and planting and harvesting the predominant crop, wheat. They sheared the sheep and carded wool to make clothes for their families. They hauled water from wells that they had helped to dig, and made soap and candles from tallow. At harvest time, they canned fruits and vegetables. They were skilled in doctoring—from snakebites to crushed limbs. Women also sponsored schools and churches in an effort to build strong communities.

TECHNICAL SUPPORT FOR FARMERS Establishing a homestead was challenging. Once accomplished, it was farming the prairie, year in and year out, that became an overwhelming task. In 1837, John Deere had invented a steel plow that could slice through heavy soil. In 1847, Cyrus McCormick began to mass-produce a reaping machine. But a mass market for these devices didn't fully develop until the late 1800s with the migration of farmers onto the plains.

Other new and improved devices made farm work speedier—the spring-tooth harrow to prepare the soil (1869), the grain drill to plant the seed (1841), barbed wire to fence the land (1874), and the corn binder (1878). Then came a reaper that could cut and thresh wheat in one pass. By 1890, there were more than 900 manufacturers of farm equipment. In 1830, producing a bushel of grain took about 183 minutes. By 1900, with the use of these machines, it took only 10 minutes. These inventions made more grain available for a wider market. D

MAIN IDEA

Summarizing

D How did new inventions change farming in the West?

AGRICULTURAL EDUCATION The federal government supported farmers by financing agricultural education. The **Morrill Act** of 1862 and 1890 gave federal land to the states to help finance agricultural colleges, and the Hatch Act of 1887 established agricultural experiment stations to inform farmers of new developments. Agricultural researchers developed grains for arid soil and techniques for dry farming, which helped the land to retain moisture. These innovations enabled the dry eastern plains to flourish and become "the breadbasket of the nation."

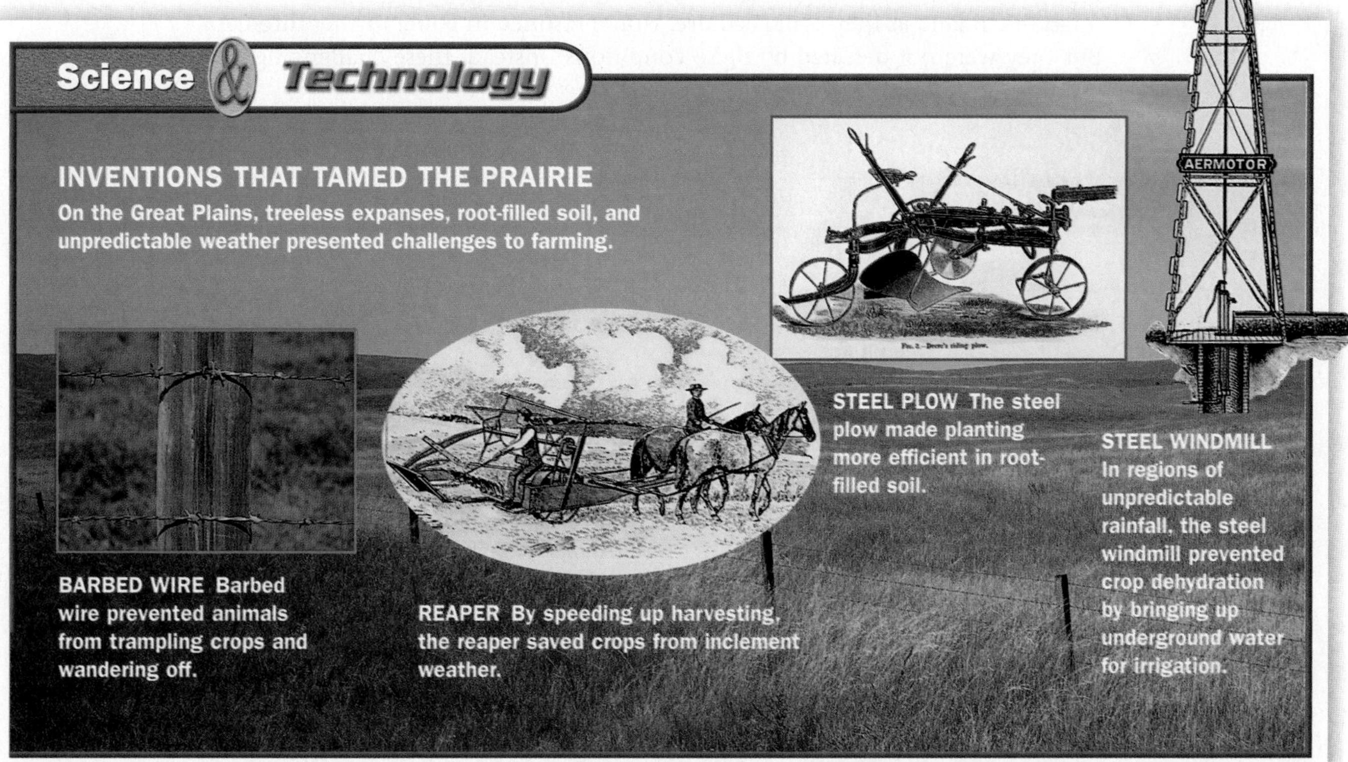

Science & Technology

INVENTIONS THAT TAMED THE PRAIRIE

On the Great Plains, treeless expanses, root-filled soil, and unpredictable weather presented challenges to farming.

BARBED WIRE Barbed wire prevented animals from trampling crops and wandering off.

REAPER By speeding up harvesting, the reaper saved crops from inclement weather.

STEEL PLOW The steel plow made planting more efficient in root-filled soil.

STEEL WINDMILL In regions of unpredictable rainfall, the steel windmill prevented crop dehydration by bringing up underground water for irrigation.

▲ Bonanza farms like this one required the labor of hundreds of farm hands and horses.

FARMERS IN DEBT Elaborate machinery was expensive, and farmers often had to borrow money to buy it. When prices for wheat were higher, farmers could usually repay their loans. When wheat prices fell, however, farmers needed to raise more crops to make ends meet. This situation gave rise to a new type of farming in the late 1870s. Railroad companies and investors created **bonanza farms**, enormous single-crop spreads of 15,000–50,000 acres. The Cass-Cheney-Dalrymple farm near Cassleton, North Dakota, for example, covered 24 square miles. By 1900, the average farmer had nearly 150 acres under cultivation. Some farmers mortgaged their land to buy more property, and as farms grew bigger, so did farmers' debts. Between 1885 and 1890, much of the plains experienced drought, and the large single-crop operations couldn't compete with smaller farms, which could be more flexible in the crops they grew. The bonanza farms slowly folded into bankruptcy.

Vocabulary
mortgage: to legally pledge property to a creditor as security for the payment of a loan or debt

Farmers also felt pressure from the rising cost of shipping grain. Railroads charged Western farmers a higher fee than they did farmers in the East. Also, the railroads sometimes charged more for short hauls, for which there was no competing transportation, than for long hauls. The railroads claimed that they were merely doing business, but farmers resented being taken advantage of. "No other system of taxation has borne as heavily on the people as those extortions and inequalities of railroad charges" wrote Henry Demarest Lloyd in an article in the March 1881 edition of *Atlantic Monthly*.

Vocabulary
extortion: illegal use of one's official position or powers to obtain property or funds

Many farmers found themselves growing as much grain as they could grow, on as much land as they could acquire, which resulted in going further into debt. But they were not defeated by these conditions. Instead, these challenging conditions drew farmers together in a common cause.

ASSESSMENT

1. **TERMS & NAMES** For each term or name, write a sentence explaining its significance.
   - **Homestead Act**
   - **exoduster**
   - **soddy**
   - **Morrill Act**
   - **bonanza farm**

MAIN IDEA

2. **TAKING NOTES**
   Create a time line of four events that shaped the settling of the Great Plains.

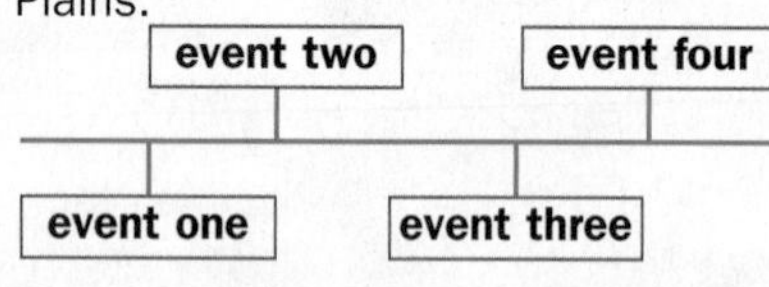

   How might history be different if one of these events hadn't happened?

CRITICAL THINKING

3. **EVALUATING**
   How successful were government efforts to promote settlement of the Great Plains? Give examples to support your answer. **Think About:**
   - the growth in population on the Great Plains
   - the role of railroads in the economy
   - the Homestead Act

4. **DRAWING CONCLUSIONS**
   Review the changes in technology that influenced the life of settlers on the Great Plains in the late 1800s. Explain how you think settlement of the plains would have been different without these inventions.

5. **IDENTIFYING PROBLEMS**
   How did the railroads take advantage of farmers?

SECTION 3

Farmers and the Populist Movement

MAIN IDEA	WHY IT MATTERS NOW	Terms & Names
Farmers united to address their economic problems, giving rise to the Populist movement.	**Many of the Populist reform issues, such as income tax and legally protected rights of workers, are now taken for granted.**	**• Oliver Hudson Kelley • Grange • Farmers' Alliances • Populism • bimetallism • gold standard • William McKinley • William Jennings Bryan**

One American's Story

hmhsocialstudies.com
TAKING NOTES
Use the graphic organizer online to take notes about the Populist Party.

As a young adult in the early 1870s, Mary Elizabeth Lease left home to teach school on the Kansas plains. After marrying farmer Charles Lease, she joined the growing Farmers' Alliance movement and began speaking on issues of concern to farmers. Lease joked that her tongue was "loose at both ends and hung on a swivel," but her golden voice and deep blue eyes hypnotized her listeners.

A PERSONAL VOICE MARY ELIZABETH LEASE

"What you farmers need to do is to raise less corn and more Hell! We want the accursed foreclosure system wiped out. . . . We will stand by our homes and stay by our firesides by force if necessary, and we will not pay our debts to the loan-shark companies until the Government pays its debts to us."

—quoted in "The Populist Uprising"

Farmers had endured great hardships in helping to transform the plains from the "Great American Desert" into the "breadbasket of the nation," yet every year they reaped less and less of the bounty they had sowed with their sweat.

▲ **Mary Elizabeth Lease, the daughter of Irish immigrants, was a leader of the Populist Party.**

Farmers Unite to Address Common Problems

In the late 1800s, many farmers were trapped in a vicious economic cycle. Prices for crops were falling, and farmers often mortgaged their farms so that they could buy more land and produce more crops. Good farming land was becoming scarce, though, and banks were foreclosing on the mortgages of increasing numbers of farmers who couldn't make payments on their loans. Moreover, the railroads were taking advantage of farmers by charging excessive prices for shipping and storage.

Analyzing *Political Cartoons*

THE PLIGHT OF THE FARMERS

Farmers were particularly hard hit in the decades leading to the financial panic of 1893. They regarded big business interests as insurmountable enemies who were bringing them to their knees and leaving them with debts at every turn. This cartoon is a warning of the dangers confronting not only the farmers but the entire nation.

SKILLBUILDER Analyzing Political Cartoons

1. How does this cartoon depict the plight of the farmers?
2. Who does the cartoonist suggest is responsible for the farmers' plight?

SEE SKILLBUILDER HANDBOOK, PAGE R24.

ECONOMIC DISTRESS The troubles of the farmers were part of a larger economic problem affecting the entire nation. During the Civil War, the United States had issued almost $500 million in paper money, called greenbacks. Greenbacks could not be exchanged for silver or gold money. They were worth less than hard money of the same face value. Hard money included both coins and paper money printed in yellow ink that could be exchanged for gold. After the war, the government began to take the greenbacks out of circulation.

Retiring the greenbacks caused some discontent. It increased the value of the money that stayed in circulation. It meant that farmers who had borrowed money had to pay back their loans in dollars that were worth more than the dollars they had borrowed. At the same time they were receiving less money for their crops. Between 1867 and 1887, for example, the price of a bushel of wheat fell from $2.00 to 68 cents. In effect, farmers lost money at every turn. (A)

> **MAIN IDEA**
> **Analyzing Issues**
> (A) Why did farmers think that an increased money supply would help solve their economic problems?

Throughout the 1870s, the farmers and other debtors pushed the government to issue more money into circulation. Those tactics failed—although the Bland-Allison Act of 1878 required the government to buy and coin at least $2 million to $4 million worth of silver each month. It wasn't enough to support the increase in the money supply that the farmers wanted.

PROBLEMS WITH THE RAILROADS Meanwhile, farmers paid outrageously high prices to transport grain. Lack of competition among the railroads meant that it might cost more to ship grain from the Dakotas to Minneapolis by rail than from Chicago to England by boat. Also, railroads made secret agreements with middlemen—grain brokers and merchants—that allowed the railroads to control grain storage prices and to influence the market price of crops.

Many farmers mortgaged their farms for credit with which to buy seed and supplies. Suppliers charged high rates of interest, sometimes charging more for items bought on credit than they did for cash purchases. Farmers got caught in a cycle of credit that meant longer hours and more debt every year. It was time for reform. (B)

> **MAIN IDEA**
> **Analyzing Causes**
> (B) What were some of the causes of farmers' economic problems?

THE FARMERS' ALLIANCES To push effectively for reforms, however, farmers needed to organize. In 1867, **Oliver Hudson Kelley** started the Patrons of

Husbandry, an organization for farmers that became popularly known as the **Grange**. Its original purpose was to provide a social outlet and an educational forum for isolated farm families. By the 1870s, however, Grange members spent most of their time and energy fighting the railroads. The Grange's battle plan included teaching its members how to organize, how to set up farmers' cooperatives, and how to sponsor state legislation to regulate railroads.

Vocabulary
regulate: to control or direct according to a rule or law

The Grange gave rise to other organizations, such as **Farmers' Alliances.** These groups included many others who sympathized with farmers. Alliances sent lecturers from town to town to educate people about topics such as lower interest rates on loans and government control over railroads and banks. Spellbinding speakers such as Mary Elizabeth Lease helped get the message across.

Membership grew to more than 4 million—mostly in the South and the West. The Southern Alliance, including white Southern farmers, was the largest. About 250,000 African Americans belonged to the Colored Farmers' National Alliance. Some alliance members promoted cooperation between black and white alliances, but most members accepted the separation of the organizations.

HISTORICAL SPOTLIGHT

THE COLORED FARMERS' NATIONAL ALLIANCE

A white Baptist missionary, R. M. Humphrey, organized the Colored Farmers' National Alliance in 1886 in Houston, Texas. Like their counterparts in the white alliances, members of the local colored farmers' alliances promoted cooperative buying and selling. Unlike white organizations, however, the black alliances had to work mostly in secret to avoid racially motivated violence at the hands of angry landowners and suppliers.

The Rise and Fall of Populism

Leaders of the alliance movement realized that to make far-reaching changes, they would need to build a base of political power. **Populism**—the movement of the people—was born with the founding of the Populist, or People's, Party, in 1892. On July 2, 1892, a Populist Party convention in Omaha, Nebraska, demanded reforms to lift the burden of debt from farmers and other workers and to give the people a greater voice in their government.

THE POPULIST PARTY PLATFORM The economic reforms proposed by the Populists included an increase in the money supply, which would produce a rise in prices received for goods and services; a graduated income tax; and a federal loan program. The proposed governmental reforms included the election of U.S. senators by popular vote, single terms for the president and the vice-president, and a secret ballot to end vote fraud. Finally, the Populists called for an eight-hour workday and restrictions on immigration.

The proposed changes were so attractive to struggling farmers and desperate laborers that in 1892 the Populist presidential candidate won almost 10 percent of the total vote. In the West, the People's Party elected five senators, three governors, and about 1,500 state legislators. The Populists' programs eventually became the platform of the Democratic Party and kept alive the concept that the government is responsible for reforming social injustices. C

MAIN IDEA
Summarizing
C What was the Populist Party platform?

THE PANIC OF 1893 During the 1880s, farmers were overextended with debts and loans. Railroad construction had expanded faster than markets. In February 1893, the Philadelphia and Reading Railroad went bankrupt, followed by the Erie, the Northern Pacific, the Union Pacific, and the Santa Fe. The government's gold supply had worn thin, partly due to its obligation to purchase silver. People panicked and traded paper money for gold. The panic also spread to Wall Street, where the prices of stocks fell rapidly. The price of silver then plunged, causing silver mines to close. By the end of the year, over 15,000 businesses and 500 banks had collapsed.

WILLIAM JENNINGS BRYAN 1860–1925

William Jennings Bryan might be considered a patron saint of lost causes, largely because he let beliefs, not politics, guide his actions. He resigned his position as secretary of state (1913–1915) under Woodrow Wilson, for example, to protest the president's movement away from neutrality regarding the war in Europe.

Near the end of his life, he went to Tennessee to assist the prosecution in the Scopes "monkey trial," contesting the teaching of evolution in public schools. He is perhaps best characterized by a quote from his own "Cross of Gold" speech: "The humblest citizen in all the land, when clad in the armor of a righteous cause, is stronger than all the hosts of error."

Investments declined, and consumer purchases, wages, and prices also fell. Panic deepened into depression as 3 million people lost their jobs. By December 1894, a fifth of the work force was unemployed. Many farm families suffered both hunger and unemployment. **D**

MAIN IDEA

Analyzing Causes

D What caused the panic of 1893?

SILVER OR GOLD Populists watched as the two major political parties became deeply divided in a struggle between different regions and economic interests. Business owners and bankers of the industrialized Northeast were Republicans; the farmers and laborers of the agrarian South and West were Democrats.

The central issue of the campaign was which metal would be the basis of the nation's monetary system. On one side were the "silverites," who favored **bimetallism**, a monetary system in which the government would give citizens either gold or silver in exchange for paper currency or checks. On the other side were President Cleveland and the "gold bugs," who favored the **gold standard**—backing dollars solely with gold.

The backing of currency was an important campaign issue because people regarded paper money as worthless if it could not be turned in for gold or silver. Because silver was more plentiful than gold, backing currency with both metals, as the silverites advocated, would make more currency (with less value per dollar) available. Supporters of bimetallism hoped that this measure would stimulate the stagnant economy. Retaining the gold standard would provide a more stable, but expensive, currency.

BRYAN AND THE "CROSS OF GOLD" Stepping into the debate, the Populist Party called for bimetallism and free coinage of silver. Yet their strategy was undecided: should they join forces with sympathetic candidates in the major parties and risk losing their political identity, or should they nominate their own candidates and risk losing the election?

As the 1896 campaign progressed, the Republican Party stated its firm commitment to the gold standard and nominated Ohioan **William McKinley** for president. After much debate, the Democratic Party came out in favor of a combined gold and silver standard, including unlimited coinage of silver. At the Democratic convention, former Nebraska congressman **William Jennings Bryan**, editor of the *Omaha World-Herald*, delivered an impassioned address to the assembled

Gold Bugs and Silverites

	Gold Bugs	Silverites
Who They Were	bankers and businessmen	farmers and laborers
What They Wanted	gold standard less money in circulation	bimetallism more money in circulation
Why	Loans would be repaid in stable money.	Products would be sold at higher prices.
Effects	DEFLATION • Prices fall. • Value of money increases. • Fewer people have money.	INFLATION • Prices rise. • Value of money decreases. • More people have money.

delegates. An excerpt of what has become known as the "Cross of Gold" speech follows.

A PERSONAL VOICE WILLIAM JENNINGS BRYAN

> **"Having behind us the producing masses of this nation and the world, supported by the commercial interests, the laboring interests, and the toilers everywhere, we will answer their demand for a gold standard by saying to them: You shall not press down upon the brow of labor this crown of thorns, you shall not crucify mankind upon a cross of gold."**
>
> —Democratic convention speech, Chicago, July 8, 1896

▲ **William Jennings Bryan's "Cross of Gold" speech inspired many cartoonists.**

Bryan won the Democratic nomination. When the Populist convention met two weeks later, the delegates were both pleased and frustrated. They liked Bryan and the Democratic platform, but they detested the Democratic vice-presidential candidate, Maine banker Arthur Sewall. Nor did they like giving up their identity as a party. They compromised by endorsing Bryan, nominating their own candidate, Thomas Watson of Georgia, for vice-president, and keeping their party organization intact. (E)

MAIN IDEA

Analyzing Issues
(E) Why was the metal that backed paper currency such an important issue in the 1896 presidential campaign?

THE END OF POPULISM Bryan faced a difficult campaign. His free-silver stand had led gold bug Democrats to nominate their own candidate. It also weakened his support in cities, where consumers feared inflation because it would make goods more expensive. In addition, Bryan's meager funds could not match the millions backing McKinley. Bryan tried to make up for lack of funds by campaigning in 27 states and sometimes making 20 speeches a day. McKinley, on the other hand, campaigned from his front porch, while thousands of well-known people toured the country speaking on his behalf.

McKinley got approximately 7 million votes and Bryan about 6.5 million. As expected, McKinley carried the East, while Bryan carried the South and the farm vote of the Middle West. The voters of the industrial Middle West, with their fear of inflation, brought McKinley into office.

With McKinley's election, Populism collapsed, burying the hopes of the farmers. The movement left two powerful legacies, however: a message that the downtrodden could organize and have political impact, and an agenda of reforms, many of which would be enacted in the 20th century.

SECTION 3 ASSESSMENT

1. **TERMS & NAMES** For each term or name, write a sentence explaining its significance.
   - **Oliver Hudson Kelley**
   - **Grange**
   - **Farmers' Alliances**
   - **Populism**
   - **bimetallism**
   - **gold standard**
   - **William McKinley**
   - **William Jennings Bryan**

MAIN IDEA

2. **TAKING NOTES**
Identify the causes of the rise of the Populist Party and the effects the party had.

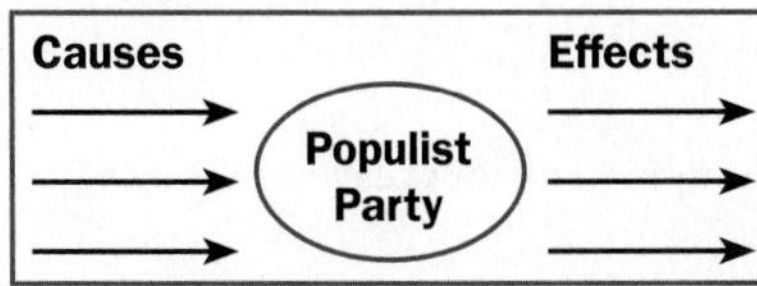

Which effect has the most impact today? Explain.

CRITICAL THINKING

3. **EVALUATING**
What do you think were the most significant factors in bringing an end to the Populist Party? **Think about:**
   - monetary policy
   - third-party status
   - source of popular support
   - popular participation policy

4. **MAKING INFERENCES**
How did the Grange and the Farmers' Alliances pave the way for the Populist Party?

Literature of the West

1850–1900 After gold was discovered in California, Americans came to view the West as a region of unlimited possibility. Those who could not venture there in person enjoyed reading about the West in colorful tales by writers such as Mark Twain (Samuel Clemens) and Bret Harte. Dime novels, cheaply bound adventure stories that sold for a dime, were also enormously popular in the second half of the 19th century.

Since much of the West was Spanish-dominated for centuries, Western literature includes legends and songs of Hispanic heroes and villains. It also includes the haunting words of Native Americans whose lands were taken and cultures threatened as white pioneers moved west.

▲ Mark Twain

THE CELEBRATED JUMPING FROG OF CALAVERAS COUNTY

The American humorist Samuel Clemens—better known as Mark Twain—was a would-be gold and silver miner who penned tales of frontier life. "The Celebrated Jumping Frog of Calaveras County" is set in a California mining camp. Most of the tale is told by Simon Wheeler, an old-timer given to exaggeration.

> "Well, Smiley kep' the beast in a little lattice box, and he used to fetch him downtown sometimes and lay for a bet. One day a feller—a stranger in the camp, he was—come acrost him with his box, and says:
>
> "'What might it be that you've got in the box?'
>
> "And Smiley says, sorter indifferent-like, 'It might be a parrot, or it might be a canary, maybe, but it ain't—it's only just a frog.'
>
> "And the feller took it, and looked at it careful, and turned it round this way and that, and says, 'H'm—so 'tis. Well, what's *he* good for?'
>
> "'Well,' Smiley says, easy and careless, 'he's good enough for *one* thing, I should judge—he can outjump any frog in Calaveras County.'
>
> "The feller took the box again, and took another long, particular look, and give it back to Smiley, and says, very deliberate, 'Well,' he says, 'I don't see no p'ints about that frog that's any better'n any other frog.'
>
> "'Maybe you don't,' Smiley says. 'Maybe you understand frogs and maybe you don't understand 'em; maybe you've had experience, and maybe you ain't only a amature, as it were. Anyways, I've got my opinion, and I'll resk forty dollars that he can outjump any frog in Calaveras County.'"

—Mark Twain, "The Celebrated Jumping Frog of Calaveras County" (1865)

THE BALLAD OF GREGORIO CORTEZ

In the border ballads, or *corridos,* of the American Southwest, few figures are as famous as the Mexican vaquero, Gregorio Cortez. This excerpt from a ballad about Cortez deals with a confrontation between Cortez and a group of Texas lawmen. Although he is hotly pursued, Cortez has an amazingly long run before being captured.

. . . And in the county of Kiansis
They cornered him after all;
Though they were more than
three hundred
He leaped out of their corral.

Then the Major Sheriff said,
As if he was going to cry,
"Cortez, hand over your weapons;
We want to take you alive."

Then said Gregorio Cortez,
And his voice was like a bell,
"You will never get my
weapons
Till you put me in a cell."

Then said Gregorio Cortez,
With his pistol in his hand,
"Ah, so many mounted Rangers
Just to take one Mexican!"

—Anonymous, "The Ballad of Gregorio Cortez," translated by Américo Paredes

▲ Chief Satanta

CHIEF SATANTA'S SPEECH AT THE MEDICINE LODGE CREEK COUNCIL

Known as the Orator of the Plains, Chief Satanta represented the Kiowa people in the 1867 Medicine Lodge Creek negotiations with the U.S. government. The speech from which this excerpt is taken was delivered by Satanta in Spanish but was translated into English and widely published in leading newspapers of the day.

All the land south of the Arkansas belongs to the Kiowas and Comanches, and I don't want to give away any of it. I love the land and the buffalo and will not part with it. I want you to understand well what I say. Write it on paper. Let the Great Father [U.S. president] see it, and let me hear what he has to say. I want you to understand also, that the Kiowas and Comanches don't want to fight, and have not been fighting since we made the treaty. I hear a great deal of good talk from the gentlemen whom the Great Father sends us, but they never do what they say. I don't want any of the medicine lodges [schools and churches] within the country. I want the children raised as I was. When I make peace, it is a long and lasting one—there is no end to it. . . . A long time ago this land belonged to our fathers; but when I go up to the river I see camps of soldiers on its banks. These soldiers cut down my timber; they kill my buffalo; and when I see that, my heart feels like bursting; I feel sorry. I have spoken.

—Chief Satanta, speech at the Medicine Lodge Creek Council (1867)

THINKING CRITICALLY

1. **Comparing and Contrasting** Compare and contrast the views these selections give of the American frontier in the second half of the 19th century. Use details from the selections to help explain your answer.

SEE SKILLBUILDER HANDBOOK, PAGE R8.

2. **hmhsocialstudies.com** INTERNET ACTIVITY

From the gauchos of the Argentine pampas to the workers on Australian sheep stations, many nations have had their own versions of the cowboys of the American West. Use the links for American Literature to research one such nation. Prepare a bulletin-board display that shows the similarities and differences between Western cowboys and their counterparts in that country.

CHAPTER 13 ASSESSMENT

TERMS & NAMES

For each term or name below, write a sentence explaining its connection to changes on the Great Plains.

1. Homestead Act
2. Sitting Bull
3. assimilation
4. Morrill Act
5. exoduster
6. George A. Custer
7. William Jennings Bryan
8. William McKinley
9. Populism
10. Grange

MAIN IDEAS

Use your notes and the information in the chapter to answer the following questions.

Cultures Clash on the Prairie

1. Identify three differences between the culture of the Native Americans and the culture of the white settlers on the Great Plains.
2. How effective was the Dawes Act in promoting the assimilation of Native Americans into white culture?
3. Why did the cattle industry become a big business in the late 1800s?
4. How did cowboy culture reflect the ethnic diversity of the United States?

Settling on the Great Plains

5. What measures did the government take to support settlement of the frontier?
6. How did settlers overcome the challenges of living on the Great Plains?

Farmers and the Populist Movement

7. What economic problems confronted American farmers in the 1890s?
8. According to farmers and other supporters of free silver, how would bimetallism help the economy?

CRITICAL THINKING

1. **USING YOUR NOTES** Create a cause/effect diagram identifying the reasons that agricultural output from the Great Plains increased during the late 1800s.

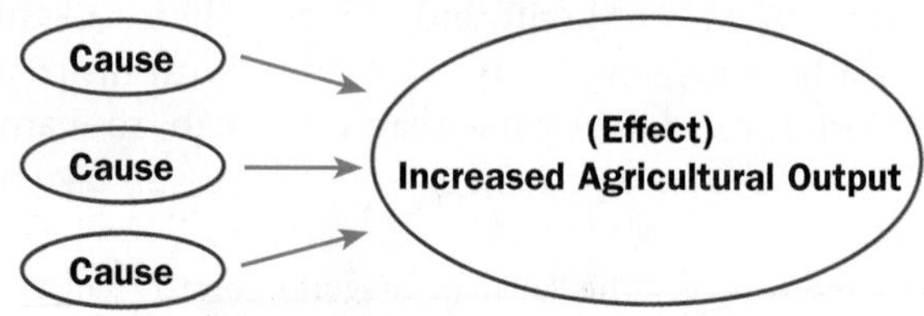

2. **ANALYZING MOTIVES** In 1877, Nez Perce Chief Joseph said, "My people have always been the friends of white men. Why are you in such a hurry?" Why do you think white people hurried to settle the West, with so little regard for Native Americans? Give evidence from the chapter to support your position.
3. **INTERPRETING CHARTS** Look at the Gold Bugs and Silverites chart. What would be the result of the policies favored by the gold bugs? by the silverites?

VISUAL SUMMARY CHANGES ON THE WESTERN FRONTIER

CLASH OF CULTURES ON THE FRONTIER

NATIVE AMERICANS
Native Americans of the plains hunted, farmed, and traded in traditional ways. Plains peoples relied on the buffalo for a variety of survival needs.

MINERS
Discoveries of gold and other precious metals led to the growth of mining camps and boomtowns in the Rocky Mountains and to the west.

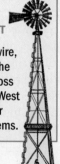

RANCHERS AND COWHANDS
Ranchers and cowboys ushered in the era of the long drive and the roundup. Texas longhorn cattle took the place of the buffalo as the dominant animal on the Great Plains.

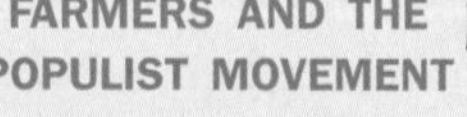

FARMERS AND THE POPULIST MOVEMENT
New settlement, barbed wire, and bad weather ended the cattle boom. Farmers across the South, Midwest, and West organized to address their common economic problems.

HOMESTEADERS
Hundreds of thousands of homesteaders settled on the plains, claiming land grants from the U.S. government.

STANDARDIZED TEST PRACTICE

Use the flowchart and your knowledge of U.S. history to answer question 1.

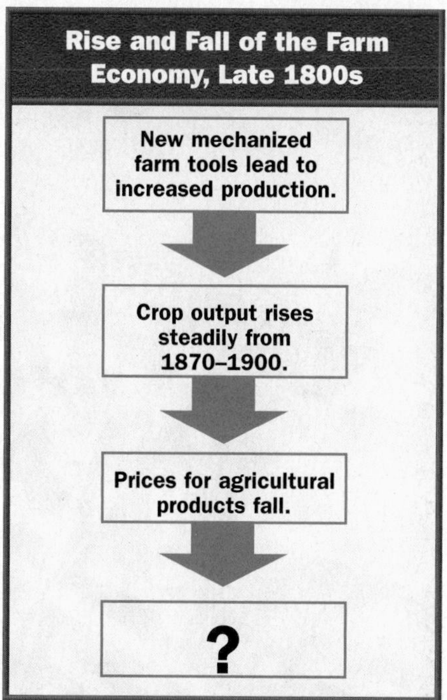

Rise and Fall of the Farm Economy, Late 1800s
New mechanized farm tools lead to increased production.
Crop output rises steadily from 1870–1900.
Prices for agricultural products fall.
?

1. Which effect accurately completes the flowchart?
   - **A** Farmers have less money to repay loans, and many lose their farms.
   - **B** Small farmers live off the land, so are not affected by the economy.
   - **C** Wealthy farmers hoard gold, rather than depend on paper money.
   - **D** The government subsidizes farmers to help them pay their bills.

Use the quotation and your knowledge of U.S. history to answer question 2.

> **"[We] have been taught to hunt and live on the game. You tell us that we must learn to farm, live in one house, and take on your ways. Suppose the people living beyond the great sea should come and tell you that you must stop farming, and kill your cattle, and take your houses and lands, what would you do? Would you not fight them?"**
>
> —Gall, a Hunkpapa Sioux, quoted in *Bury My Heart at Wounded Knee*

2. What was Gall's view of future relations between the Plains Indians and the settlers?
   - **F** peaceful coexistence
   - **G** further conflict
   - **H** mutual respect
   - **J** equality before the law

3. How did the invention of barbed wire change the look of the Western frontier?
   - **A** It endangered wildlife.
   - **B** It ended the cattle frontier.
   - **C** It increased cattle stocks.
   - **D** It enriched the cow towns.

For additional test practice, go online for:
- Diagnostic tests
- Tutorials

INTERACT WITH HISTORY

Think about the issues you explored at the beginning of the chapter. Suppose you are a frontier settler. Write a letter to the family members you left behind describing your journey west and how you are living now. Use information from the chapter to provide some vivid impressions of life on the frontier.

FOCUS ON WRITING

You are a historian studying the development of the American West. Write an essay explaining how Americans settled the West in the late 1800s and how the region changed as a result. Use specific examples to support your main idea.

COLLABORATIVE LEARNING

21st CENTURY

Work in pairs to research federal policy toward Native Americans between 1830 and 1890. Then work together to create a time line identifying key events that shaped the policy and the relationships between whites and Native Americans during the time period. Begin your time line with the passage of the Indian Removal Act in 1830 and end it with the Battle of Wounded Knee in 1890.

CHAPTER 14

A NEW INDUSTRIAL AGE

Essential Question

What impact did scientific discoveries and manufacturing processes have on the nature of work, the American labor movement, and American businesses?

Laborers blasted tunnels and constructed bridges to send the railroad through the rugged Sierra Nevada mountains.

USA

1869 Central Pacific and Union Pacific complete the transcontinental railroad.

1876 Alexander Graham Bell invents the telephone.

1877 *Munn* v. *Illinois* establishes government regulation of railroads.

Mother Jones supports the Great Strike of 1877.

1879 Thomas A. Edison invents a workable light bulb.

1884 Grover Cleveland is elected president.

1870

1880

WORLD

1870 Franco-Prussian War breaks out.

1875 British labor unions win right to strike.

1882 United States restricts Chinese immigration.

1883 Germany becomes the first nation to provide national health insurance.

Image Credits: (bkgd), Courtesy California State Railroad Museum; (br), National Museum of American History, Smithsonian Institution, Electrical Collections (791641); (bl), Underwood Photo Archives

INTERACT WITH HISTORY

The year is 1863 and railroad construction is booming. In six years, the U.S. will be linked by rail from coast to coast. Central Pacific Railroad employs mainly Chinese immigrants to blast tunnels, lay track, and drive spikes, all for low wages. You are a journalist assigned to describe this monumental construction project for your readers.

Explore the Issues

- What dangers do the railroad workers encounter?
- How will businesses and the general public benefit from the transcontinental railroad?
- How might railroad construction affect the environment?

1886 Haymarket riot turns public sentiment against unions.

1890 Congress passes the Sherman Antitrust Act.

1894 President Cleveland sends federal troops to Illinois to end the Pullman strike.

1896 William McKinley is elected president.

1900 William McKinley is reelected.

1890

1900

1890 Colonization of sub-Saharan Africa peaks.

1893 Women in New Zealand gain voting rights.

1896 First modern Olympic Games are held in Athens, Greece.

Image Credits: Courtesy California State Railroad Museum; (bl), (br), The Granger Collection, New York

SECTION 1

The Expansion of Industry

MAIN IDEA	WHY IT MATTERS NOW	Terms & Names
At the end of the 19th century, natural resources, creative ideas, and growing markets fueled an industrial boom.	**Technological developments of the late 19th century paved the way for the continued growth of American industry.**	**• Edwin L. Drake • Bessemer process • Thomas Alva Edison • Christopher Sholes • Alexander Graham Bell**

One American's Story

hmhsocialstudies.com
TAKING NOTES

Use the graphic organizer online to take notes on the causes of the industrial boom and their impact on industrialization.

One day, Pattillo Higgins noticed bubbles in the springs around Spindletop, a hill near Beaumont in southeastern Texas. This and other signs convinced him that oil was underground. If Higgins found oil, it could serve as a fuel source around which a vibrant industrial city would develop.

Higgins, who had been a mechanic and a lumber merchant, couldn't convince geologists or investors that oil was present, but he didn't give up. A magazine ad seeking investors got one response—from Captain Anthony F. Lucas, an experienced prospector who also believed that there was oil at Spindletop. When other investors were slow to send money, Higgins kept his faith, not only in Spindletop, but in Lucas.

▲ Pattillo Higgins

A PERSONAL VOICE PATTILLO HIGGINS

"Captain Lucas, . . . these experts come and tell you this or that can't happen because it has never happened before. You believe there is oil here, . . . and I think you are right. I know there is oil here in greater quantities than man has ever found before."

—quoted in *Spindletop*

In 1900, the two men found investors, and they began to drill that autumn. After months of difficult, frustrating work, on the morning of January 10, 1901, oil gushed from their well. The Texas oil boom had begun.

Natural Resources Fuel Industrialization

After the Civil War, the United States was still largely an agricultural nation. By the 1920s—a mere 60 years later—it had become the leading industrial power in the world. This immense industrial boom was due to several factors, including: a wealth of natural resources, government support for business, and a growing urban population that provided both cheap labor and markets for new products.

BLACK GOLD Though eastern Native American tribes had made fuel and medicine from crude oil long before Europeans arrived on the continent, early American settlers had little use for oil. In the 1840s, Americans began using kerosene to light lamps after the Canadian geologist Abraham Gesner discovered how to distill the fuel from oil or coal.

It wasn't until 1859, however, when **Edwin L. Drake** successfully used a steam engine to drill for oil near Titusville, Pennsylvania, that removing oil from beneath the earth's surface became practical. This breakthrough started an oil boom that spread to Kentucky, Ohio, Illinois, Indiana, and, eventually, Texas. Petroleum-refining industries arose in Cleveland and Pittsburgh as entrepreneurs rushed to transform the oil into kerosene. Gasoline, a byproduct of the refining process, originally was thrown away. But after the automobile became popular, gasoline became the most important form of oil.

Vocabulary
entrepreneur: a person who organizes, operates, and assumes the risk for a business venture

BESSEMER STEEL PROCESS Oil was not the only natural resource that was plentiful in the United States. There were also abundant deposits of coal and iron. In 1887, prospectors discovered iron ore deposits more than 100 miles long and up to 3 miles wide in the Mesabi Range of Minnesota. At the same time, coal production skyrocketed—from 33 million tons in 1870 to more than 250 million tons in 1900.

Iron is a dense metal, but it is soft and tends to break and rust. It also usually contains other elements, such as carbon. Removing the carbon from iron produces a lighter, more flexible, and rust-resistant metal—steel. The raw materials needed to make steel were readily available; all that was needed was a cheap and efficient manufacturing process. The **Bessemer process,** developed independently by the British manufacturer Henry Bessemer and American ironmaker William Kelly around 1850, soon became widely used. This technique involved injecting air into molten iron to remove the carbon and other impurities. By 1880, American manufacturers were using the new method to produce more than 90 percent of the nation's steel. In this age of rapid change and innovation, even

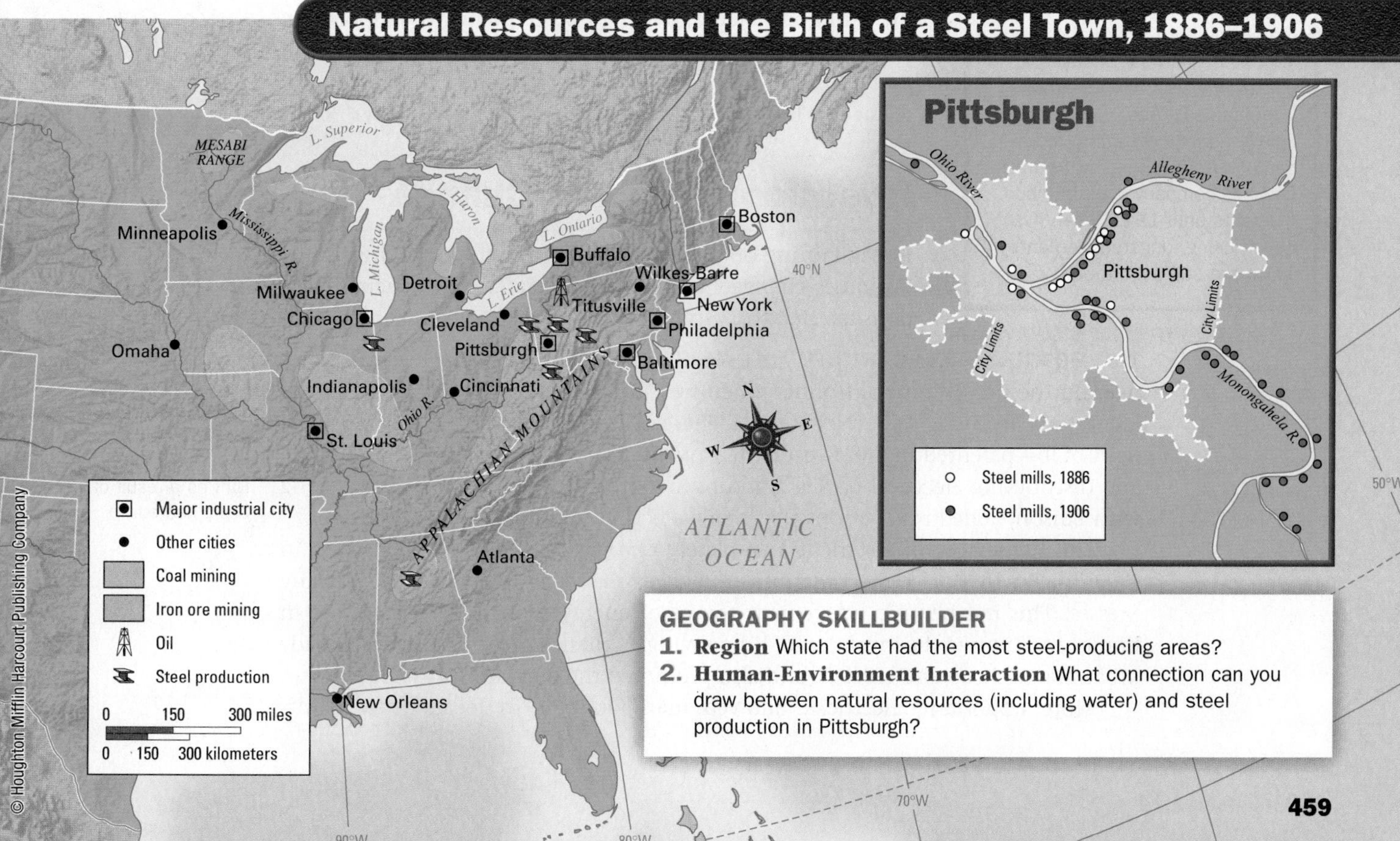

GEOGRAPHY SKILLBUILDER

1. **Region** Which state had the most steel-producing areas?
2. **Human-Environment Interaction** What connection can you draw between natural resources (including water) and steel production in Pittsburgh?

The Technological Explosion, 1826–1903

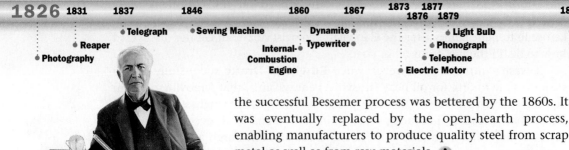

1826 ● Photography
1831 ● Reaper
1837 ● Telegraph
1846 ● Sewing Machine
1860 ● Internal-Combustion Engine
1867 ● Dynamite
1867 ● Typewriter
1873 ● Electric Motor
1876 ● Telephone
1877 ● Phonograph
1879 ● Light Bulb
1895 ● Radio
1895 ● Motion Pictures
1895 ● X-Ray
1903 ● Airplane

HISTORICAL SPOTLIGHT

ILLUMINATING THE LIGHT BULB

Shortly after moving into a long wooden shed at Menlo Park, Thomas Alva Edison and his associates set to work to develop the perfect incandescent bulb. Arc lamps already lit some city streets and shops, using an electric current passing between two sticks of carbon, but they were glaring and inefficient.

Edison hoped to create a long-lasting lamp with a soft glow, and began searching for a filament that would burn slowly and stay lit. Edison tried wires, sticks, blades of grass, and even hairs from his assistants' beards. Finally, a piece of carbonized bamboo from Japan did the trick. Edison's company used bamboo filaments until 1911, when it began using tungsten filaments, which are still used today.

the successful Bessemer process was bettered by the 1860s. It was eventually replaced by the open-hearth process, enabling manufacturers to produce quality steel from scrap metal as well as from raw materials. **A**

MAIN IDEA

Summarizing

A What natural resources were most important for industrialization?

NEW USES FOR STEEL The railroads, with thousands of miles of track, became the biggest customers for steel, but inventors soon found additional uses for it. Joseph Glidden's barbed wire and McCormick's and Deere's farm machines helped transform the plains into the food producer of the nation.

Steel changed the face of the nation as well, as it made innovative construction possible. One of the most remarkable structures was the Brooklyn Bridge. Completed in 1883, it spanned 1,595 feet of the East River in New York City. Its steel cables were supported by towers higher than any man-made and weight-bearing structure except the pyramids of Egypt. Like those ancient marvels, the completed bridge was called a wonder of the world.

Around this time, setting the stage for a new era of expansion upward as well as outward, William Le Baron Jenney designed the first skyscraper with a steel frame—the Home Insurance Building in Chicago. Before Jenney had his pioneering idea, the weight of large buildings was supported entirely by their walls or by iron frames, which limited the buildings' height. With a steel frame to support the weight, however, architects could build as high as they wanted. As structures soared into the air, not even the sky seemed to limit what Americans could achieve.

Inventions Promote Change

By capitalizing on natural resources and their own ingenuity, inventors changed more than the landscape. Their inventions affected the very way people lived and worked.

THE POWER OF ELECTRICITY In 1876, **Thomas Alva Edison** became a pioneer on the new industrial frontier when he established the world's first research laboratory in Menlo Park, New Jersey. There Edison perfected the incandescent light bulb—patented in 1880—and later invented an entire system for producing and distributing electrical power. Another inventor, George Westinghouse, along with Edison, added innovations that made electricity safer and less expensive.

Vocabulary
incandescent: giving off visible light as a result of being heated

The harnessing of electricity completely changed the nature of business in America. By 1890, electric power ran numerous machines, from fans to printing presses. This inexpensive, convenient source of energy soon became available in homes and spurred the invention of time-saving appliances. Electric streetcars made urban travel cheap and efficient and also promoted the outward spread of cities.

More important, electricity allowed manufacturers to locate their plants

MAIN IDEA

Analyzing Effects

B How did electricity change American life?

wherever they wanted—not just near sources of power, such as rivers. This enabled industry to grow as never before. Huge operations, such as the Armour and Swift meatpacking plants, and the efficient processes that they used became the models for new consumer industries. **B**

INVENTIONS CHANGE LIFESTYLES Edison's light bulb was only one of several revolutionary inventions. **Christopher Sholes** invented the typewriter in 1867 and changed the world of work. Next to the light bulb, however, perhaps the most dramatic invention was the telephone, unveiled by **Alexander Graham Bell** and Thomas Watson in 1876. It opened the way for a worldwide communications network.

▲ The typewriter shown here dates from around 1890.

The typewriter and the telephone particularly affected office work and created new jobs for women. Although women made up less than 5 percent of all office workers in 1870, by 1910 they accounted for nearly 40 percent of the clerical work force. New inventions also had a tremendous impact on factory work, as well as on jobs that traditionally had been done at home. For example, women had previously sewn clothing by hand for their families. With industrialization, clothing could be mass-produced in factories, creating a need for garment workers, many of whom were women.

Industrialization freed some factory workers from backbreaking labor and helped improve workers' standard of living. By 1890, the average workweek had been reduced by about ten hours. However, many laborers felt that the mechanization of so many tasks reduced human workers' worth. As consumers, though, workers regained some of their lost power in the marketplace. The country's expanding urban population provided a vast potential market for the new inventions and products of the late 1800s.

SECTION 1 ASSESSMENT

1. **TERMS & NAMES** For each term or name, write a sentence explaining its significance.
   - **Edwin L. Drake**
   - **Bessemer process**
   - **Thomas Alva Edison**
   - **Christopher Sholes**
   - **Alexander Graham Bell**

MAIN IDEA

2. **TAKING NOTES**
   In a chart like the one below, list resources, ideas, and markets that affected the industrial boom of the 19th century. In the second column, note how each item contributed to industrialization.

Resources, Ideas, Markets	Impact

CRITICAL THINKING

3. **MAKING INFERENCES**
   Do you think that consumers gained power as industry expanded in the late 19th century? Why or why not?

4. **HYPOTHESIZING**
   If the U.S. had been poor in natural resources, how would industrialization have been affected?

5. **ANALYZING EFFECTS**
   Which invention or development described in this section had the greatest impact on society? Justify your choice. **Think About:**
   - the applications of inventions
   - the impact of inventions on people's daily lives
   - the effect of inventions on the workplace

GEOGRAPHY SPOTLIGHT

Industry Changes the Environment

By the mid-1870s, new ideas and technology were well on the way to changing almost every aspect of American life. The location of Cleveland, Ohio, on the shores of Lake Erie, gave the city access to raw materials and made it ripe for industrialization. What no one foresaw were the undesirable side effects of rapid development and technological progress.

1 FROM HAYSTACKS TO SMOKESTACKS

In 1874, parts of Cleveland were still rural, with farms like the one pictured dotting the landscape. The smokestacks of the Standard Oil refinery in the distance, however, indicate that industrialization had begun.

2 REFINING THE LANDSCAPE

Industries like the Standard Oil refinery shown in this 1889 photo soon became a source of prosperity for both Cleveland and the entire country. The pollution they belched into the atmosphere, however, was the beginning of an ongoing problem: how to balance industrial production and environmental concerns.

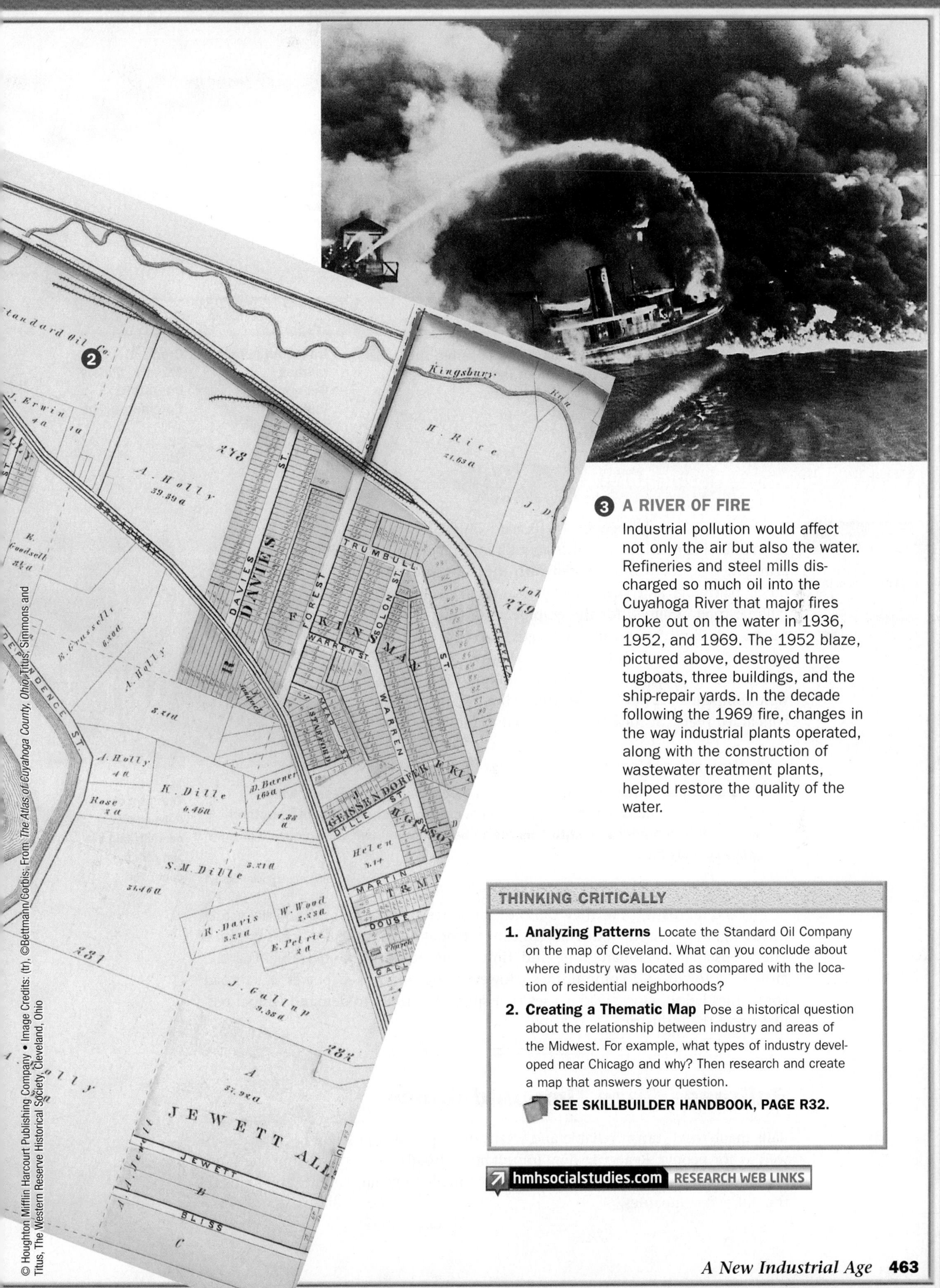

3 A RIVER OF FIRE

Industrial pollution would affect not only the air but also the water. Refineries and steel mills discharged so much oil into the Cuyahoga River that major fires broke out on the water in 1936, 1952, and 1969. The 1952 blaze, pictured above, destroyed three tugboats, three buildings, and the ship-repair yards. In the decade following the 1969 fire, changes in the way industrial plants operated, along with the construction of wastewater treatment plants, helped restore the quality of the water.

THINKING CRITICALLY

1. **Analyzing Patterns** Locate the Standard Oil Company on the map of Cleveland. What can you conclude about where industry was located as compared with the location of residential neighborhoods?
2. **Creating a Thematic Map** Pose a historical question about the relationship between industry and areas of the Midwest. For example, what types of industry developed near Chicago and why? Then research and create a map that answers your question.

SEE SKILLBUILDER HANDBOOK, PAGE R32.

hmhsocialstudies.com RESEARCH WEB LINKS

The Age of the Railroads

MAIN IDEA	WHY IT MATTERS NOW	Terms & Names
The growth and consolidation of railroads benefited the nation but also led to corruption and required government regulation.	**Railroads made possible the expansion of industry across the United States.**	**•transcontinental railroad •George M. Pullman •Crédit Mobilier •*Munn* v. *Illinois* •Interstate Commerce Act**

One American's Story

hmhsocialstudies.com
TAKING NOTES

Use the graphic organizer online to take notes on the effects of the rapid growth of the railroads.

In October 1884, the economist Richard Ely visited the town of Pullman, Illinois, to write about it for *Harper's* magazine. At first, Ely was impressed with the atmosphere of order, planning, and well-being in the town George M. Pullman had designed for the employees of his railroad-car factory. But after talking at length with a dissatisfied company officer, Ely concluded the town had a fatal flaw: it too greatly restricted its residents. Pullman employees were compelled to obey rules in which they had no say. Ely concluded that "the idea of Pullman is un-American."

▲ **The town of Pullman was carefully laid out and strictly controlled.**

A PERSONAL VOICE RICHARD T. ELY

"It is benevolent, well-wishing feudalism [a medieval social system], which desires the happiness of the people, but in such way as shall please the authorities. . . . If free American institutions are to be preserved, we want no race of men reared as underlings."

—"Pullman: A Social Study"

As the railroads grew, they came to influence many facets of American life, including, as in the town of Pullman, the personal lives of the country's citizens. They caused the standard time and time zones to be set and influenced the growth of towns and communities. However, the unchecked power of railroad companies led to widespread abuses that spurred citizens to demand federal regulation of the industry.

Railroads Span Time and Space

Rails made local transit reliable and westward expansion possible for business as well as for people. Realizing how important railroads were for settling the West and developing the country, the government made huge land grants and loans to the railroad companies.

A NATIONAL NETWORK By 1856, the railroads extended west to the Mississippi River, and three years later, they crossed the Missouri. Just over a decade later, crowds across the United States cheered as the Central Pacific and Union Pacific Railroads met at Promontory, Utah, on May 10, 1869. A golden spike marked the spanning of the nation by the first **transcontinental railroad.** Other transcontinental lines followed, and regional lines multiplied as well. At the start of the Civil War, the nation had had about 30,000 miles of track. By 1890, that figure was nearly six times greater.

ROMANCE AND REALITY The railroads brought the dreams of available land, adventure, and a fresh start within the grasp of many Americans. This romance was made possible, however, only by the harsh lives of railroad workers.

The Central Pacific Railroad employed thousands of Chinese immigrants. The Union Pacific hired Irish immigrants and desperate, out-of-work Civil War veterans to lay track across treacherous terrain while enduring attacks by Native Americans. Accidents and diseases disabled and killed thousands of men each year. In 1888, when the first railroad statistics were published, the casualties totaled more than 2,000 employees killed and 20,000 injured.

RAILROAD TIME In spite of these difficult working conditions, the railroad laborers helped to transform the diverse regions of the country into a united nation. Though linked in space, each community still operated on its own time, with noon when the sun was directly overhead. Noon in Boston, for example, was almost 12 minutes later than noon in New York. Travelers riding from Maine to California might reset their watches 20 times.

In 1869, to remedy this problem, Professor C. F. Dowd proposed that the earth's surface be divided into 24 time zones, one for each hour of the day. Under his plan, the United States would contain four zones: the Eastern, Central, Mountain, and Pacific time zones. The railroad companies endorsed Dowd's plan enthusiastically, and many towns followed suit.

Finally, on November 18, 1883, railroad crews and towns across the country synchronized their watches. In 1884, an international conference set worldwide time zones that incorporated railroad time. The U.S. Congress, however, didn't officially adopt railroad time as the standard for the nation until 1918. As strong a unifying force as the railroads were, however, they also opened the way for abuses that led to social and economic unrest. (A)

MAIN IDEA

Analyzing Effects

(A) What were the effects of railroad expansion?

HISTORICAL SPOTLIGHT

CHINESE IMMIGRANTS AND THE RAILROADS

Although the railroads paid all their employees poorly, Asians usually earned less than whites. The average pay for whites working a ten-hour day was $40 to $60 a month plus free meals. Chinese immigrants hired by the Central Pacific performed similar tasks from dawn to dusk for about $35 a month—and they had to supply their own food.

The immigrants' working conditions were miserable. In 1866, for example, the railroad hired them to dig a tunnel through a granite mountain. For five months of that year, the Chinese lived and worked in camps surrounded by banks of snow. The total snowfall reached over 40 feet. Hundreds of the men were buried in avalanches or later found frozen, still clutching their shovels or picks.

Opportunities and Opportunists

The growth of the railroads influenced the industries and businesses in which Americans worked. Iron, coal, steel, lumber, and glass industries grew rapidly as they tried to keep pace with the railroads' demand for materials and parts. The rapid spread of railroad lines also fostered the growth of towns, helped establish new markets, and offered rich opportunities for both visionaries and profiteers.

ANOTHER PERSPECTIVE

ON THE WRONG TRACK

While the railroads captured the imagination of most 19th-century Americans, there were those who didn't get on the bandwagon. The writer Herman Melville raged against the smoke-belching iron horse and the waves of change it set in motion as vehemently as his character Captain Ahab raged against the white whale and the sea in *Moby-Dick*. "Hark! here comes that old dragon again—that gigantic gadfly . . . snort! puff! scream! Great improvements of the age," Melville fumed. "Who wants to travel so fast? My grandfather did not, and he was no fool."

NEW TOWNS AND MARKETS By linking previously isolated cities, towns, and settlements, the railroads promoted trade and interdependence. As part of a nationwide network of suppliers and markets, individual towns began to specialize in particular products. Chicago soon became known for its stockyards and Minneapolis for its grain industries. These cities prospered by selling large quantities of their products to the entire country. New towns and communities also grew up along the railroad lines. Cities as diverse as Abilene, Kansas; Flagstaff, Arizona; Denver, Colorado; and Seattle, Washington, owed their prosperity, if not their very existence, to the railroads. (B)

MAIN IDEA

Summarizing

(B) How did the railroads affect cities?

PULLMAN The railroads helped cities not only grow up but branch out. In 1880, for example, **George M. Pullman** built a factory for manufacturing sleepers and other railroad cars on the Illinois prairie. The nearby town that Pullman built for his employees followed in part the models of earlier industrial experiments in Europe. Whereas New England textile manufacturers had traditionally provided housing for their workers, the town of Pullman provided for almost all of workers' basic needs. Pullman residents lived in clean, well-constructed brick houses and apartment buildings with at least one window in every room—a luxury for city dwellers. In addition, the town offered services and facilities such as doctors' offices, shops, and an athletic field.

hmhsocialstudies.com

INTERACTIVE

Explore the impact of the railroads on Chicago.

As Richard Ely observed, however, the town of Pullman remained firmly under company control. Residents were not allowed to loiter on their front steps or to drink alcohol. Pullman hoped that his tightly controlled environment would ensure a stable work force. However, Pullman's refusal to lower rents after cutting his employees' pay led to a violent strike in 1894.

CRÉDIT MOBILIER Pullman created his company town out of the desire for control and profit. In some other railroad magnates, or powerful and influential industrialists, these desires turned into self-serving corruption. In one of the most infamous schemes, stockholders in the Union Pacific Railroad formed, in 1864, a construction company called **Crédit Mobilier** (krĕd′ĭt mō-bēl′yər). The stockholders gave this company a contract to lay track at two to three times the actual cost—and pocketed the profits. They donated shares of stock to about 20 representatives in Congress in 1867.

A congressional investigation of the company, spurred by reports in the *New York Sun*, eventually found that the officers of the Union Pacific had taken up to $23 million in stocks, bonds, and cash. Testimony implicated such well-known and respected federal officials as Vice-President Schuyler Colfax and Congressman James Garfield, who later became president. Although these public figures kept their profits and received little more than a slap on the wrist, the reputation of the Republican Party was tarnished. (C)

MAIN IDEA

Summarizing

(C) How did railroad owners use Crédit Mobilier to make huge, undeserved profits?

Pullman cars brought luxury to the rails, as shown in this advertisement from around 1890. ▼

The Grange and the Railroads

Farmers were especially disturbed by what they viewed as railroad corruption. The Grangers—members of the Grange, a farmers' organization founded in 1867—began demanding governmental control over the railroad industry.

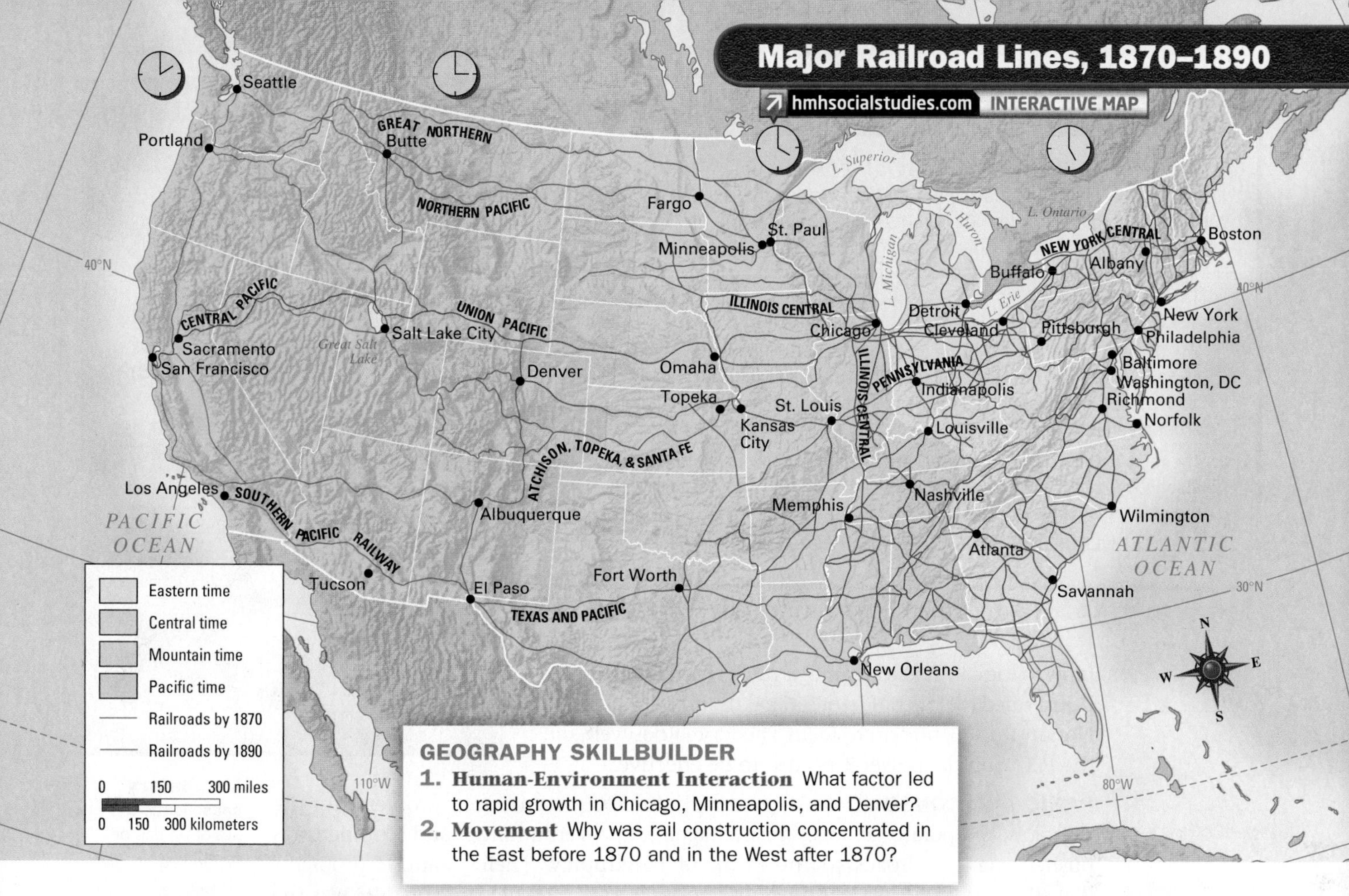

GEOGRAPHY SKILLBUILDER

1. **Human-Environment Interaction** What factor led to rapid growth in Chicago, Minneapolis, and Denver?
2. **Movement** Why was rail construction concentrated in the East before 1870 and in the West after 1870?

Background
Price fixing occurs when companies within an industry all agree to charge the same price for a given service, rather than competing to offer the lowest price.

RAILROAD ABUSES Farmers were angry with railroad companies for a host of reasons. They were upset by misuse of government land grants, which the railroads sold to other businesses rather than to settlers, as the government intended. The railroads also entered into formal agreements to fix prices, which helped keep farmers in their debt. In addition, they charged different customers different rates, often demanding more for short hauls—for which there was no alternative carrier—than they did for long hauls.

GRANGER LAWS In response to these abuses by the railroads, the Grangers took political action. They sponsored state and local political candidates, elected legislators, and successfully pressed for laws to protect their interests. In 1871 Illinois authorized a commission "to establish maximum freight and passenger rates and prohibit discrimination." Grangers throughout the West, Midwest, and Southeast convinced state legislators to pass similar laws, called Granger laws.

The railroads fought back, challenging the constitutionality of the regulatory laws. In 1877, however, in the case of ***Munn v. Illinois,*** the Supreme Court upheld the Granger laws by a vote of seven to two. The states thus won the right to regulate the railroads for the benefit of farmers and consumers. The Grangers also helped establish an important principle—the federal government's right to regulate private industry to serve the public interest. D

MAIN IDEA

Analyzing Issues
D How did the Grangers, who were largely poor farmers, do battle with the giant railroad companies?

INTERSTATE COMMERCE ACT The Grangers' triumph was short-lived, however. In 1886, the Supreme Court ruled that a state could not set rates on interstate commerce—railroad traffic that either came from or was going to another state. In response to public outrage, Congress passed the **Interstate Commerce Act** in 1887. This act reestablished the right of the federal government to supervise railroad activities and established a five-member Interstate Commerce Commission (ICC) for that purpose. The ICC had difficulty regulating railroad rates because of a long legal process and resistance from the railroads. The final

Analyzing *Political Cartoons*

"THE MODERN COLOSSUS OF (RAIL) ROADS"

Joseph Keppler drew this cartoon in 1879, featuring the railroad "giants" William Vanderbilt (top), Jay Gould (bottom right), and Cyrus W. Fields (bottom left). The three magnates formed a railroad trust out of their Union Pacific, New York Central, and Lake Shore & Dependence lines.

SKILLBUILDER Analyzing Political Cartoons

1. The title of this cartoon is a pun on the Colossus of Rhodes, a statue erected in 282 B.C. on an island near Greece. According to legend, the 100-foot-tall statue straddled Rhodes's harbor entrance. Do you think the artist means the comparison as a compliment or a criticism? Why?
2. The reins held by the railroad magnates attach not only to the trains but also to the tracks and the railroad station. What does this convey about the magnates' control of the railroads?

SEE SKILLBUILDER HANDBOOK, PAGE R24.

blow to the commission came in 1897, when the Supreme Court ruled that it could not set maximum railroad rates. Not until 1906, under President Theodore Roosevelt, did the ICC gain the power it needed to be effective.

PANIC AND CONSOLIDATION Although the ICC presented few problems for the railroads, corporate abuses, mismanagement, overbuilding, and competition pushed many railroads to the brink of bankruptcy. Their financial problems played a major role in a nationwide economic collapse. The panic of 1893 was the worst depression up to that time: by the end of 1893, around 600 banks and 15,000 businesses had failed, and by 1895, 4 million people had lost their jobs. By the middle of 1894, a quarter of the nation's railroads had been taken over by financial companies. Large investment firms such as J. P. Morgan & Company reorganized the railroads. As the 20th century dawned, seven powerful companies held sway over two-thirds of the nation's railroad tracks.

Vocabulary
consolidation: the act of uniting or combining

SECTION 2 ASSESSMENT

1. **TERMS & NAMES** For each term or name, write a sentence explaining its significance.
   - **transcontinental railroad**
   - **George M. Pullman**
   - **Crédit Mobilier**
   - ***Munn* v. *Illinois***
   - **Interstate Commerce Act**

MAIN IDEA

2. **TAKING NOTES**
   In a chart like the one below, fill in effects of the rapid growth of railroads.

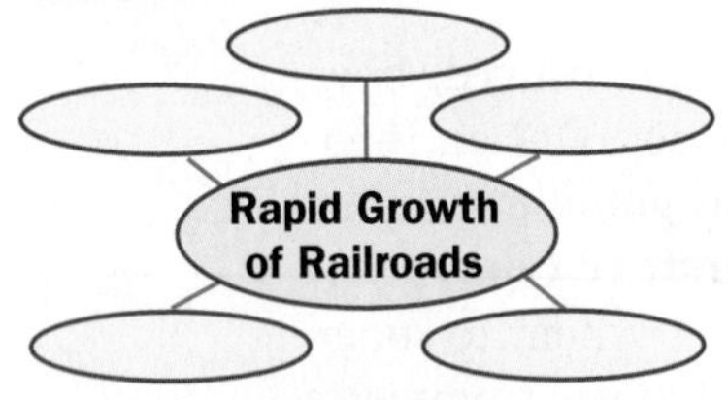

How did the growth of railroads affect people's everyday lives? How did it affect farmers?

CRITICAL THINKING

3. **MAKING INFERENCES**
   Do you think the government and private citizens could have done more to curb the corruption and power of the railroads? Give examples to support your opinion.
   Think About:
   - why the railroads had power
   - the rights of railroad customers and workers
   - the scope of government regulations
4. **SYNTHESIZING**
   The federal government gave land and made loans to the railroad companies. Why was the government so eager to promote the growth of railroads?
5. **ANALYZING MOTIVES**
   Reread the Another Perspective feature on railroads. Why do you think that some Americans disliked this new means of transportation?

SECTION 3

Big Business and Labor

MAIN IDEA

The expansion of industry resulted in the growth of big business and prompted laborers to form unions to better their lives.

WHY IT MATTERS NOW

Many of the strategies used today in industry and in the labor movement, such as consolidation and the strike, have their origins in the late 19th century.

Terms & Names

- **Andrew Carnegie**
- **vertical and horizontal integration**
- **Social Darwinism**
- **John D. Rockefeller**
- **Sherman Antitrust Act**
- **Samuel Gompers**
- **American Federation of Labor (AFL)**
- **Eugene V. Debs**
- **Industrial Workers of the World (IWW)**
- **Mary Harris Jones**

One American's Story

hmhsocialstudies.com TAKING NOTES

Use the graphic organizer online to take notes on the achievements and setbacks of the labor movement between 1876 and 1911.

Born in Scotland to penniless parents, **Andrew Carnegie** came to this country in 1848, at age 12. Six years later, he worked his way up to become private secretary to the local superintendent of the Pennsylvania Railroad. One morning, Carnegie single-handedly relayed messages that unsnarled a tangle of freight and passenger trains. His boss, Thomas A. Scott, rewarded Carnegie by giving him a chance to buy stock. Carnegie's mother mortgaged the family home to make the purchase possible. Soon Carnegie received his first dividend.

▲ Nineteenth-century industrialist Andrew Carnegie gave money to build public libraries, hoping to help others write their own rags-to-riches stories.

A PERSONAL VOICE ANDREW CARNEGIE

"One morning a white envelope was lying upon my desk, addressed in a big John Hancock hand, to 'Andrew Carnegie, Esquire.' . . . All it contained was a check for ten dollars upon the Gold Exchange Bank of New York. I shall remember that check as long as I live. . . . It gave me the first penny of revenue from capital—something that I had not worked for with the sweat of my brow. 'Eureka!' I cried. 'Here's the goose that lays the golden eggs.'"

—*Autobiography of Andrew Carnegie*

Andrew Carnegie was one of the first industrial moguls to make his own fortune. His rise from rags to riches, along with his passion for supporting charities, made him a model of the American success story.

Carnegie's Innovations

By 1865, Carnegie was so busy managing the money he had earned in dividends that he happily left his job at the Pennsylvania Railroad. He entered the steel business in 1873 after touring a British steel mill and witnessing the awesome spectacle of the Bessemer process in action. By 1899, the Carnegie Steel Company

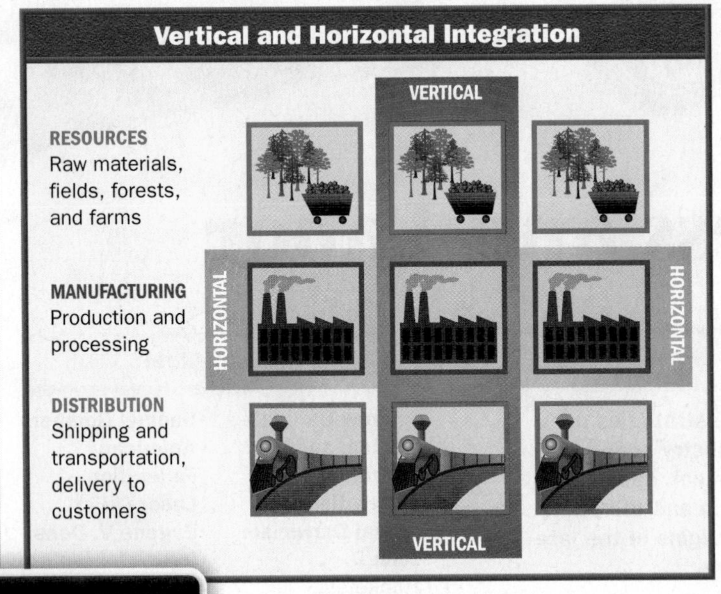

manufactured more steel than all the factories in Great Britain.

NEW BUSINESS STRATEGIES Carnegie's success was due in part to management practices that he initiated and that soon became widespread. First, he continually searched for ways to make better products more cheaply. He incorporated new machinery and techniques, such as accounting systems that enabled him to track precise costs. Second, he attracted talented people by offering them stock in the company, and he encouraged competition among his assistants.

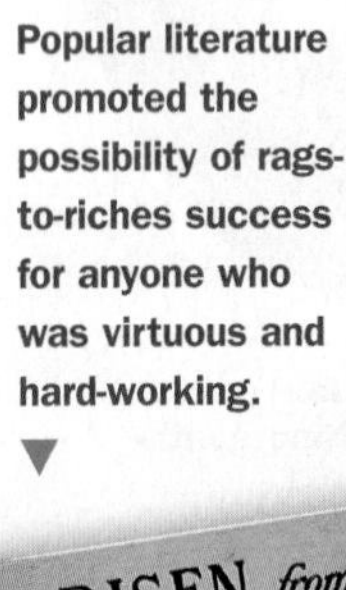

VIDEO
Great Minds in Business: Andrew Carnegie

hmhsocialstudies.com

In addition to improving his own manufacturing operation, Carnegie attempted to control as much of the steel industry as he could. He did this mainly by **vertical integration,** a process in which he bought out his suppliers—coal fields and iron mines, ore freighters, and railroad lines—in order to control the raw materials and transportation systems. Carnegie also attempted to buy out competing steel producers. In this process, known as **horizontal integration,** companies producing similar products merge. Having gained control over his suppliers and having limited his competition, Carnegie controlled almost the entire steel industry. By the time he sold his business in 1901, Carnegie's companies produced by far the largest portion of the nation's steel. (A)

MAIN IDEA

Summarizing
(A) What were Andrew Carnegie's management and business strategies?

Social Darwinism and Business

Andrew Carnegie explained his extraordinary success by pointing to his hard work, shrewd investments, and innovative business practices. Late-19th-century social philosophers offered a different explanation for Carnegie's success. They said it could be explained scientifically by a new theory—Social Darwinism.

Popular literature promoted the possibility of rags-to-riches success for anyone who was virtuous and hard-working. ▼

PRINCIPLES OF SOCIAL DARWINISM The philosophy called **Social Darwinism** grew out of the English naturalist Charles Darwin's theory of biological evolution. In his book *On the Origin of Species*, published in 1859, Darwin described his observations that some individuals of a species flourish and pass their traits along to the next generation, while others do not. He explained that a process of "natural selection" weeded out less-suited individuals and enabled the best-adapted to survive.

The English philosopher Herbert Spencer used Darwin's biological theories to explain the evolution of human society. Soon, economists found in Social Darwinism a way to justify the doctrine of laissez faire (a French term meaning "allow to do"). According to this doctrine, the marketplace should not be regulated. William G. Sumner, a political science professor at Yale University, promoted the theory that success and failure in business were governed by natural law and that no one had the right to intervene.

A NEW DEFINITION OF SUCCESS The premise of the survival and success of the most capable naturally made sense to the 4,000 millionaires who had emerged since the Civil War. Because the theory supported the notion of individual responsibility and blame, it also appealed to the Protestant work ethic of many Americans. According to Social Darwinism, riches were a sign of God's favor, and therefore the poor must be lazy or inferior people who deserved their lot in life.

Fewer Control More

Although some business owners endorsed the "natural law" in theory, in practice most entrepreneurs did everything they could to control the competition that threatened the growth of their business empires.

GROWTH AND CONSOLIDATION Many industrialists took the approach "If you can't beat 'em, join 'em." They often pursued horizontal integration in the form of mergers. A merger usually occurred when one corporation bought out the stock of another. A firm that bought out all its competitors could achieve a monopoly, or complete control over its industry's production, wages, and prices.

One way to create a monopoly was to set up a holding company, a corporation that did nothing but buy out the stock of other companies. Headed by banker J. P. Morgan, United States Steel was one of the most successful holding companies. In 1901, when it bought the largest manufacturer, Carnegie Steel, it became the world's largest business.

Corporations such as the Standard Oil Company, established by **John D. Rockefeller,** took a different approach to mergers: they joined with competing companies in trust agreements. Participants in a trust turned their stock over to a group of trustees—people who ran the separate companies as one large corporation. In return, the companies were entitled to dividends on profits earned by the trust. Trusts were not legal mergers, however. Rockefeller used a trust to gain total control of the oil industry in America. B

MAIN IDEA

Summarizing

B What strategies enabled big businesses to eliminate competition?

ROCKEFELLER AND THE "ROBBER BARONS" In 1870, Rockefeller's Standard Oil Company of Ohio processed two or three percent of the country's crude oil. Within a decade, it controlled 90 percent of the refining business. Rockefeller reaped huge profits by paying his employees extremely low wages and driving his competitors out of business by selling his oil at a lower price than it cost to produce it. Then, when he controlled the market, he hiked prices far above original levels.

Alarmed at the tactics of industrialists, critics began to call them robber barons. But industrialists were also philanthropists. Although Rockefeller kept most of his assets, he still gave away over $500 million, establishing the Rockefeller Foundation, providing funds to found the University of Chicago, and creating a medical institute that helped find a cure for yellow fever.

KEY PLAYER

JOHN D. ROCKEFELLER 1839–1937

At the height of John Davison Rockefeller's power, an associate noted that he "always sees a little farther than the rest of us—and then he sees around the corner."

Rockefeller's father was a flashy peddler of phony cancer cures with a unique approach to raising children. "I cheat my boys every chance I get. . . . I want to make 'em sharp," he boasted.

It seems that this approach succeeded with the oldest son, John D., who was sharp enough to land a job as an assistant bookkeeper at the age of 16. Rockefeller was very proud of his own son, who succeeded him in the family business. At the end of his life, Rockefeller referred not to his millions but to John D., Jr., as "my greatest fortune."

This 1900 cartoon, captioned "What a funny little government!" is a commentary on the power of the Standard Oil empire. John D. Rockefeller holds the White House in his hand.

Andrew Carnegie donated about 90 percent of the wealth he accumulated during his lifetime; his fortune still supports the arts and learning today. "It will be a great mistake for the community to shoot the millionaires," he said, "for they are the bees that make the most honey, and contribute most to the hive even after they have gorged themselves full." C

MAIN IDEA

Evaluating
C Do you agree with Carnegie's defense of millionaires? Why or why not?

SHERMAN ANTITRUST ACT Despite Carnegie's defense of millionaires, the government was concerned that expanding corporations would stifle free competition. In 1890, the **Sherman Antitrust Act** made it illegal to form a trust that interfered with free trade between states or with other countries.

Prosecuting companies under the Sherman Act was not easy, however, because the act didn't clearly define terms such as *trust*. In addition, if firms such as Standard Oil felt pressure from the government, they simply reorganized into single corporations. The Supreme Court threw out seven of the eight cases the federal government brought against trusts. Eventually, the government stopped trying to enforce the Sherman act, and the consolidation of businesses continued.

BUSINESS BOOM BYPASSES THE SOUTH Industrial growth concentrated in the North, where natural and urban resources were plentiful. The South was still trying to recover from the Civil War, hindered by a lack of capital—money for investment. After the war, people were unwilling to invest in risky ventures. Northern businesses already owned 90 percent of the stock in the most profitable Southern enterprise, the railroads, thereby keeping the South in a stranglehold. The South remained mostly agricultural, with farmers at the mercy of railroad rates. Entrepreneurs suffered not only from excessive transportation costs, but also from high tariffs on raw materials and imported goods, and from a lack of skilled workers. The post-Reconstruction South seemed to have no way out of economic stagnation. However, growth in forestry and mining, and in the tobacco, furniture, and textile industries, offered hope. D

MAIN IDEA

Synthesizing
D How did economic factors limit industrialization in the South?

In this photograph, taken by Lewis Hine in 1912, a young sweatshop laborer in New York City carries piecework home.

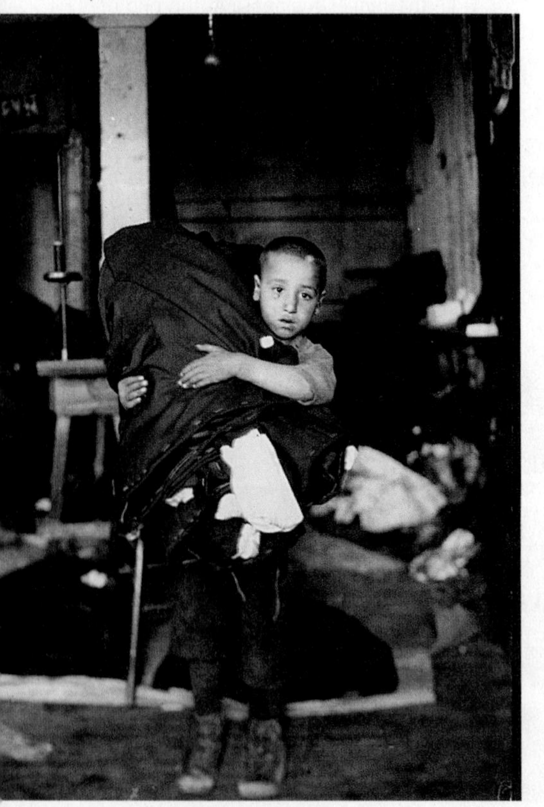

Labor Unions Emerge

As business leaders merged and consolidated their forces, it seemed necessary for workers to do the same. Although Northern wages were generally higher than Southern wages, exploitation and unsafe working conditions drew workers together across regions in a nationwide labor movement. Laborers—skilled and unskilled, female and male, black and white—joined together in unions to try to improve their lot.

LONG HOURS AND DANGER One of the largest employers, the steel mills, often demanded a seven-day workweek. Seamstresses, like factory workers in most industries, worked 12 or more hours a day, six days a week. Employees were not entitled to vacation, sick leave, unemployment compensation, or reimbursement for injuries suffered on the job.

Yet injuries were common. In dirty, poorly ventilated factories, workers had to perform repetitive, mind-dulling tasks, sometimes with dangerous or faulty equipment. In 1882, an average of 675 laborers were killed in work-related accidents each week. In addition, wages were so low that most families could not survive unless everyone held a job. Between 1890 and 1910, for example, the number of women working for wages doubled, from 4 million to more than 8 million. Twenty percent of the boys and 10 percent of the girls under age 15—some as young as five years old—also held full-time jobs. With little time or energy left for school, child laborers forfeited their futures to help their families make ends meet.

In sweatshops, or workshops in tenements rather than in factories, workers had little choice but to put up with the conditions. Sweatshop employment, which was tedious and required few skills, was often the only avenue open to women and children. Jacob Riis described the conditions faced by "sweaters."

A PERSONAL VOICE JACOB RIIS

"The bulk of the sweater's work is done in the tenements, which the law that regulates factory labor does not reach. . . . In [them] the child works unchallenged from the day he is old enough to pull a thread. There is no such thing as a dinner hour; men and women eat while they work, and the 'day' is lengthened at both ends far into the night."

—*How the Other Half Lives*

Not surprisingly, sweatshop jobs paid the lowest wages—often as little as 27 cents for a child's 14-hour day. In 1899, women earned an average of $267 a year, nearly half of men's average pay of $498. The very next year Andrew Carnegie made $23 million—with no income tax.

EARLY LABOR ORGANIZING Skilled workers had formed small, local unions since the late 1700s. The first large-scale national organization of laborers, the National Labor Union (NLU), was formed in 1866 by ironworker William H. Sylvis. The refusal of some NLU local chapters to admit African Americans led to the creation of the Colored National Labor Union (CNLU). Nevertheless, NLU membership grew to 640,000. In 1868, the NLU persuaded Congress to legalize an eight-hour day for government workers. (E)

MAIN IDEA

Analyzing Issues

(E) How did industrial working conditions contribute to the growth of the labor movement?

NLU organizers concentrated on linking existing local unions. In 1869, Uriah Stephens focused his attention on individual workers and organized the Noble Order of the Knights of Labor. Its motto was "An injury to one is the concern of all." Membership in the Knights of Labor was officially open to all workers, regardless of race, gender, or degree of skill. Like the NLU, the Knights supported an eight-hour workday and advocated "equal pay for equal work" by men and women. They saw strikes, or refusals to work, as a last resort and instead advocated arbitration. At its height in 1886, the Knights of Labor had about 700,000 members. Although the Knights declined after the failure of a series of strikes, other unions continued to organize.

Vocabulary

arbitration: a method of settling disputes in which both sides submit their differences to a mutually approved judge

Union Movements Diverge

As labor activism spread, it diversified. Two major types of unions made great gains under forceful leaders.

CRAFT UNIONISM One form of labor organization was craft unionism, which included skilled workers from one or more trades. Jewish immigrant **Samuel Gompers** led the Cigar Makers' International Union to join other craft unions in 1886. The **American Federation of Labor (AFL),**

HISTORICAL SPOTLIGHT

AFRICAN AMERICANS AND THE LABOR MOVEMENT

Angered by their exclusion from the NLU, African American laborers formed the Colored National Labor Union (CNLU) in 1869. Led by Isaac Meyers, a caulker from Baltimore, the CNLU emphasized cooperation between management and labor and the importance of political reform.

The CNLU disbanded in the early 1870s, but many African-American laborers found a home in the Knights of Labor, the first union to welcome blacks and whites alike. The Great Strike of 1877 brought whites and African Americans together, but the labor movement remained largely divided along racial lines.

Management often hired African Americans as strikebreakers, which intensified white unions' resistance to accepting blacks. African Americans continued to organize on their own, but discrimination and their small numbers relative to white unions hurt black unions' effectiveness.

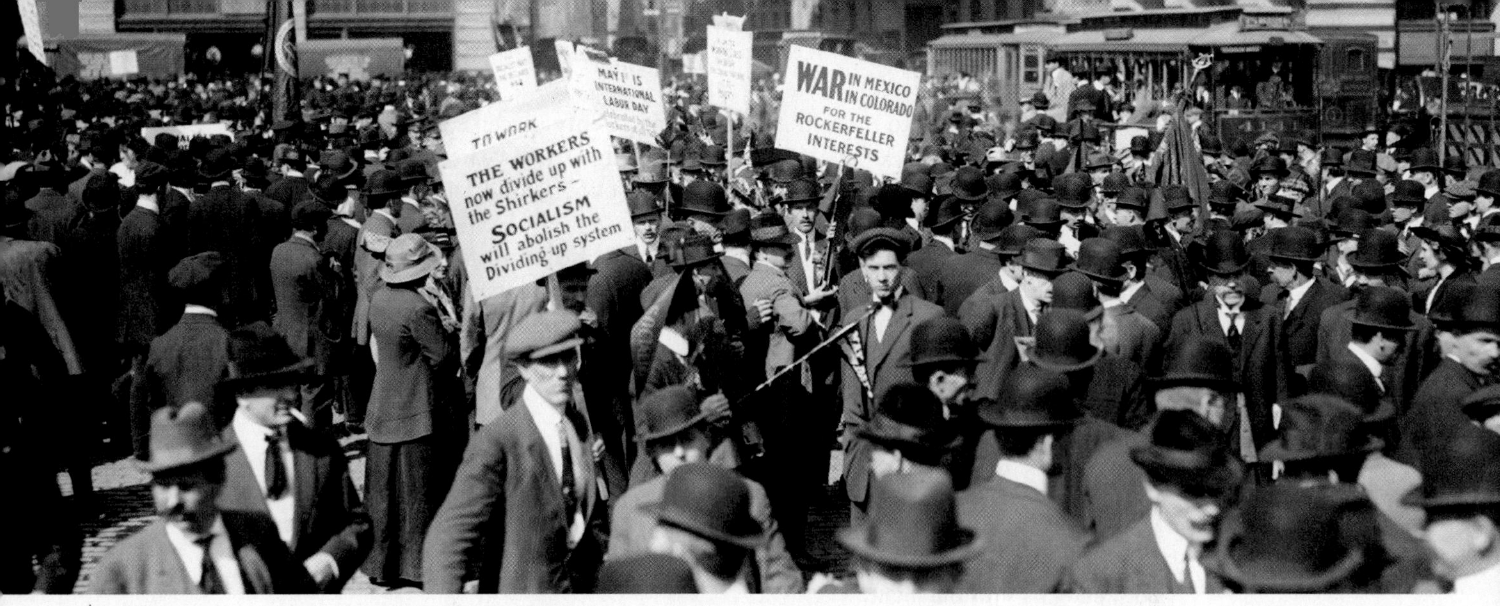

In New York City's Union Square in 1914, IWW members protest violence against striking coal miners in Colorado.

with Gompers as its president, focused on collective bargaining, or negotiation between representatives of labor and management, to reach written agreements on wages, hours, and working conditions. Unlike the Knights of Labor, the AFL used strikes as a major tactic. Successful strikes helped the AFL win higher wages and shorter workweeks. Between 1890 and 1915, the average weekly wages in unionized industries rose from $17.50 to $24, and the average workweek fell from almost 54.5 hours to just under 49 hours.

INDUSTRIAL UNIONISM Some labor leaders felt that unions should include all laborers—skilled and unskilled—in a specific industry. This concept captured the imagination of **Eugene V. Debs,** who attempted to form such an industrial union—the American Railway Union (ARU). Most of the new union's members were unskilled and semiskilled laborers, but skilled engineers and firemen joined too. In 1894, the new union won a strike for higher wages. Within two months, its membership climbed to 150,000, dwarfing the 90,000 enrolled in the four skilled railroad brotherhoods. Though the ARU, like the Knights of Labor, never recovered after the failure of a major strike, it added to the momentum of union organizing. (F)

> *"The strike is the weapon of the oppressed."*
> EUGENE V. DEBS

MAIN IDEA

Contrasting
(F) How did craft unions and industrial unions differ?

SOCIALISM AND THE IWW In an attempt to solve the problems faced by workers, Eugene Debs and some other labor activists eventually turned to socialism, an economic and political system based on government control of business and property and equal distribution of wealth. Socialism, carried to its extreme form—communism, as advocated by the German philosopher Karl Marx—would result in the overthrow of the capitalist system. Most socialists in late-19th-century America drew back from this goal, however, and worked within the labor movement to achieve better conditions for workers. In 1905, a group of radical unionists and socialists in Chicago organized the **Industrial Workers of the World (IWW),** or the Wobblies. Headed by William "Big Bill" Haywood, the Wobblies included miners, lumberers, and cannery and dock workers. Unlike the ARU, the IWW welcomed African Americans, but membership never topped 100,000. Its only major strike victory occurred in 1912. Yet the Wobblies, like other industrial unions, gave dignity and a sense of solidarity to unskilled workers.

OTHER LABOR ACTIVISM IN THE WEST In April 1903, about 1,000 Japanese and Mexican workers organized a successful strike in the sugar-beet fields of Ventura County, California. They formed the Sugar Beet and Farm Laborers' Union of Oxnard. In Wyoming, the State Federation of Labor supported a union of Chinese and Japanese miners who sought the same wages and treatment as other union miners. These small, independent unions increased both the overall strength of the labor movement and the tension between labor and management.

Strikes Turn Violent

Industry and government responded forcefully to union activity, which they saw as a threat to the entire capitalist system.

THE GREAT STRIKE OF 1877 In July 1877, workers for the Baltimore and Ohio Railroad (B&O) struck to protest their second wage cut in two months. The work stoppage spread to other lines. Most freight and even some passenger traffic, covering over 50,000 miles, was stopped for more than a week. After several state governors asked President Rutherford B. Hayes to intervene, saying that the strikers were impeding interstate commerce, federal troops ended the strike.

THE HAYMARKET AFFAIR Encouraged by the impact of the 1877 strike, labor leaders continued to press for change. On the evening of May 4, 1886, 3,000 people gathered at Chicago's Haymarket Square to protest police brutality—a striker had been killed and several had been wounded at the McCormick Harvester plant the day before. Rain began to fall at about 10 o'clock, and the crowd was dispersing when police arrived. Then someone tossed a bomb into the police line. Police fired on the workers; seven police officers and several workers died in the chaos that followed. No one ever learned who threw the bomb, but the three speakers at the demonstration and five other radicals were charged with inciting a riot. All eight were convicted; four were hanged and one committed suicide in prison. After Haymarket, the public began to turn against the labor movement. G

MAIN IDEA

Analyzing Causes

G How did the 1877 strike and Haymarket cause the public to resent the labor movement?

THE HOMESTEAD STRIKE Despite the violence and rising public anger, workers continued to strike. The writer Hamlin Garland described conditions at the Carnegie Steel Company's Homestead plant in Pennsylvania.

A PERSONAL VOICE HAMLIN GARLAND

"Everywhere . . . groups of pale, lean men slouched in faded garments, grimy with the soot and grease of the mills. . . . A roar as of a hundred lions, a thunder as of cannons, . . . jarring clang of falling iron. . . !"

—quoted in *McClure's Magazine*

The steelworkers finally called a strike on June 29, 1892, after the company president, Henry Clay Frick, announced his plan to cut wages. Frick hired armed

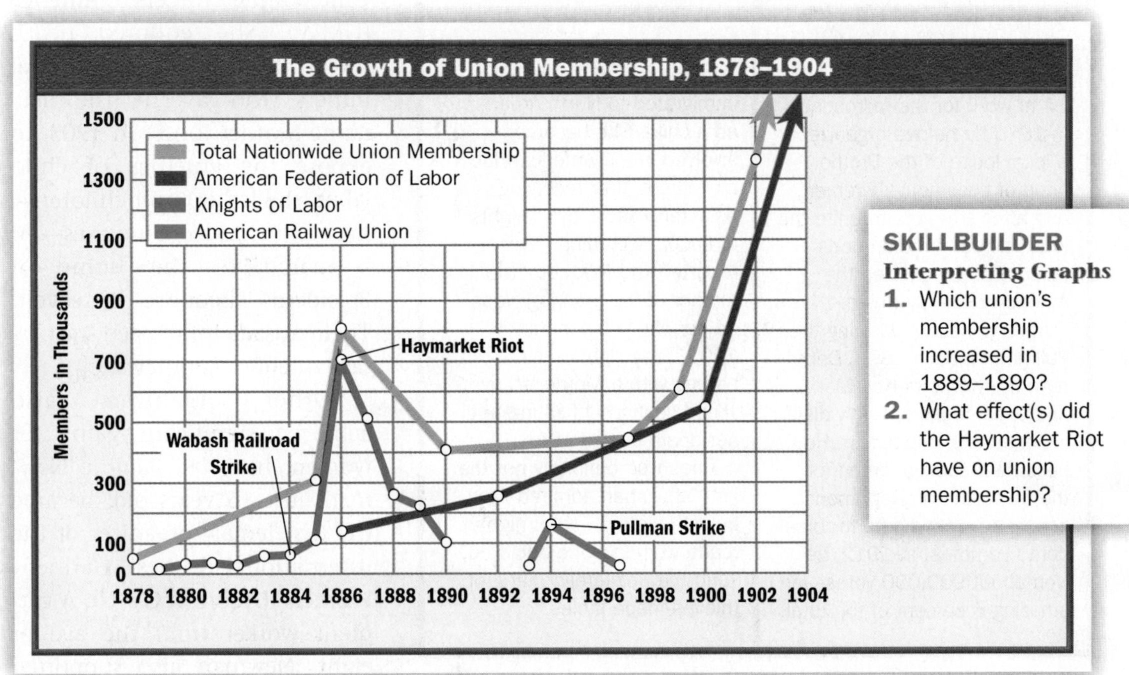

SKILLBUILDER

Interpreting Graphs

1. Which union's membership increased in 1889–1890?
2. What effect(s) did the Haymarket Riot have on union membership?

guards from the Pinkerton Detective Agency to protect the plant so that he could hire scabs, or strikebreakers, to keep it operating. In a pitched battle that left at least three detectives and nine workers dead, the steelworkers forced out the Pinkertons and kept the plant closed until the Pennsylvania National Guard arrived on July 12. The strike continued until November, but by then the union had lost much of its support and gave in to the company. It would take 45 years for steelworkers to mobilize once again.

THE PULLMAN COMPANY STRIKE Strikes continued in other industries, however. During the panic of 1893 and the economic depression that followed, the Pullman company laid off more than 3,000 of its 5,800 employees and cut the wages of the rest by 25 to 50 percent, without cutting the cost of its employee housing. After paying their rent, many workers took home less than $6 a week. A strike was called in the spring of 1894, when the Pullman company failed to restore wages or decrease rents. Eugene Debs asked for arbitration, but Pullman refused to negotiate with the strikers. So the ARU began boycotting Pullman trains.

After Pullman hired strikebreakers, the strike turned violent, and President Grover Cleveland sent in federal troops. In the bitter aftermath, Debs was jailed. Pullman fired most of the strikers, and the railroads blacklisted many others, so they could never again get railroad jobs.

WOMEN ORGANIZE Although women were barred from many unions, they united behind powerful leaders to demand better working conditions, equal pay for equal work, and an end to child labor. Perhaps the most prominent organizer in the women's labor movement was **Mary Harris Jones.** Jones supported the Great Strike of 1877 and later organized for the United Mine Workers of America (UMW). She endured death threats and jail with the coal miners, who gave her the nickname Mother Jones. In 1903, to expose the cruelties of child labor, she led 80 mill children—many with hideous injuries—on a march to the home of President Theodore Roosevelt. Their crusade influenced the passage of child labor laws.

Other organizers also achieved significant gains for women. In 1909, Pauline Newman, just 16 years old, became the first female organizer of the International Ladies' Garment Workers' Union (ILGWU). A garment worker from the age of eight, Newman also supported

KEY PLAYERS

EUGENE V. DEBS
1855–1926

Born in Indiana, Eugene V. Debs left home at the age of 14 to work for the railroads. In 1875 he helped organize a local lodge of the Brotherhood of Locomotive Firemen, and after attempts to unite the local railroad brotherhoods failed, Debs organized the American Railway Union.

While in prison following the Pullman strike in 1894, Debs read the works of Karl Marx and became increasingly disillusioned with capitalism. He became a spokesperson for the Socialist Party of America and was its candidate for president five times. In 1912, he won about 900,000 votes—an amazing 6 percent of the total.

MOTHER JONES
1830–1930

Mary Harris "Mother" Jones was a native of Ireland who immigrated to North America as a child. She became involved in the American labor movement after receiving assistance from the Knights of Labor. According to a reporter who followed "the mother of the laboring class" on her children's march in 1903, "She fights their battles with a Mother's Love." Jones continued fighting until her death at age 100.

Jones was definitely not the kind of woman admired by industrialists. "God almighty made women," she declared, "and the Rockefeller gang of thieves made ladies."

the "Uprising of the 20,000," a 1909 seamstresses' strike that won labor agreements and improved working conditions for some strikers.

The public could no longer ignore conditions in garment factories after a fire broke out at the Triangle Shirtwaist factory in New York City on March 25, 1911. The fire spread swiftly through the oil-soaked machines and piles of cloth, engulfing the eighth, ninth, and tenth floors. As workers attempted to flee, they discovered that the company had locked all but one of the exit doors to prevent theft. The unlocked door was blocked by fire. The factory had no sprinkler system, and the single fire escape collapsed almost immediately. In all, 146 women died; some were found huddled with their faces raised to a small window. Public outrage flared after a jury acquitted the factory owners of manslaughter. In response, the state of New York set up a task force to study factory working conditions. (H)

MAIN IDEA

Summarizing
(H) What factors made the Triangle Shirtwaist fire so lethal?

▲ **The fire department's ladders reached only to the sixth floor, two floors below the burning Triangle Shirtwaist Company.**

MANAGEMENT AND GOVERNMENT PRESSURE UNIONS

The more powerful the unions became, the more employers came to fear them. Management refused to recognize unions as representatives of the workers. Many employers forbade union meetings, fired union members, and forced new employees to sign "yellow-dog contracts," swearing that they would not join a union.

Finally, industrial leaders, with the help of the courts, turned the Sherman Antitrust Act against labor. All a company had to do was say that a strike, picket line, or boycott would hurt interstate trade, and the state or federal government would issue an injunction against the labor action. Legal limitations made it more and more difficult for unions to be effective. Despite these pressures, workers—especially those in skilled jobs—continued to view unions as a powerful tool. By 1904, the AFL had about 1,700,000 members in its affiliated unions; by the eve of World War I, AFL membership would climb to over 2 million.

ASSESSMENT

1. **TERMS & NAMES** For each term or name, write a sentence explaining its significance.
   - **Andrew Carnegie**
   - **vertical and horizontal integration**
   - **Social Darwinism**
   - **John D. Rockefeller**
   - **Sherman Antitrust Act**
   - **Samuel Gompers**
   - **American Federation of Labor (AFL)**
   - **Eugene V. Debs**
   - **Industrial Workers of the World (IWW)**
   - **Mary Harris Jones**

MAIN IDEA

2. **TAKING NOTES**
   Make a time line of the notable achievements and setbacks of the labor movement between 1876 and 1911.

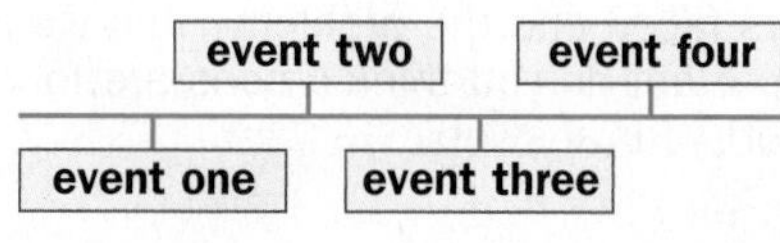

   In what ways did strikes threaten industry?

CRITICAL THINKING

3. **EVALUATING LEADERSHIP**
   Do you think that the tycoons of the late 19th century are best described as ruthless robber barons or as effective captains of industry?
   Think About:
   - their management tactics and business strategies
   - their contributions to the economy
   - their attitude toward competition

4. **DRAWING CONCLUSIONS**
   Does the life of Andrew Carnegie support or counter the philosophy of Social Darwinism? Explain.

5. **HYPOTHESIZING**
   If the government had supported unions instead of management in the late 19th century, how might the lives of workers have been different?

CHAPTER 14 ASSESSMENT

VISUAL SUMMARY

A New Industrial Age

LONG-TERM CAUSES

- abundant natural resources
- harnessing of early power sources such as water and coal
- invention of the steam engine
- construction of roads, canals, and railroads in early 1800s

IMMEDIATE CAUSES

- expansion of railroads in late 1800s
- cheap labor supply provided by increasing immigration
- burst of technological innovation
- new management techniques and business strategies
- investment capital

BIG BUSINESS BOOMS

1880–1914

IMMEDIATE EFFECTS

- growth of large corporations
- new and plentiful manufactured goods
- poor working conditions in factories and sweatshops
- increased labor activism

LONG-TERM EFFECTS

- regional economies are linked
- labor movement wins shorter workweek

TERMS & NAMES

For each term or name below, write a sentence explaining its connection to the industrialization of the late 19th century.

1. Thomas Alva Edison
2. Alexander Graham Bell
3. George M. Pullman
4. transcontinental railroad
5. Interstate Commerce Act
6. Andrew Carnegie
7. Sherman Antitrust Act
8. Samuel Gompers
9. American Federation of Labor (AFL)
10. Mary Harris Jones

MAIN IDEAS

Use your notes and the information in the chapter to answer the following questions.

The Expansion of Industry

1. How did the growth of the steel industry influence the development of other industries?
2. How did inventions and developments in the late 19th century change the way people worked?

The Age of the Railroads

3. Why did people, particularly farmers, demand regulation of the railroads in the late 19th century?
4. Why were attempts at railroad regulation often unsuccessful?

Big Business and Labor

5. Why were business leaders such as John D. Rockefeller called robber barons?
6. Why did the South industrialize more slowly than the North did?
7. Why did workers form unions in the late 19th century?
8. What factors limited the success of unions?

CRITICAL THINKING

1. **USING YOUR NOTES** In a chart like the one shown, list what you see as the overall costs and benefits of industrialization.

INDUSTRIALIZATION	
Costs	Benefits

2. **RECOGNIZING BIAS** In 1902 George Baehr, head of the Philadelphia and Reading Railway Company, said, "The rights and interests of the labor man will be protected and cared for not by the labor agitators but by the Christian men to whom God in his infinite wisdom has given the control of the property interests of the country." What bias does this statement reveal? How does Baehr's view reflect Social Darwinism?

3. **IDENTIFYING PROBLEMS** Consider the problems that late-19th-century workers faced and the problems that workers face today. How important do you think unions are for present-day workers? Support your answer.

STANDARDIZED TEST PRACTICE

Use the quotation below and your knowledge of U.S. history to answer question 1.

> **"No man, however benevolent, liberal, and wise, can use a large fortune so that it will do half as much good in the world as it would if it were divided into moderate sums and in the hands of workmen who had earned it by industry and frugality."**
>
> —Rutherford B. Hayes, from *The Diary and Letters of Rutherford Birchard Hayes*

1. Which of the following people could best be described by Rutherford B. Hayes's words *benevolent*, *liberal*, and *a large fortune?*
   - **A** Thomas Edison
   - **B** Eugene V. Debs
   - **C** Charles Darwin
   - **D** Andrew Carnegie

2. The American Federation of Labor (AFL) differed from the Knights of Labor in that the Knights of Labor focused on —
   - **F** collective bargaining and aggressive use of strikes.
   - **G** organizing only unskilled workers.
   - **H** arbitration and use of strikes as a last resort.
   - **J** winning a shorter workweek.

3. How did the railroads both benefit from and contribute to the industrialization of the United States?
   - **A** The railroads needed government protection, and their development helped government grow.
   - **B** The railroads used new inventions and brought people to see the inventions.
   - **C** The railroads used steel and coal and delivered both to new markets.
   - **D** The railroads needed passengers, and passengers needed to get to new industries.

4. In the 19th century, government attempts to regulate industry in the United States included the Interstate Commerce Act (1887) and the Sherman Antitrust Act (1890). What posed the biggest obstacle to enforcement of these laws?
   - **F** the business tactics of industrialists
   - **G** the use of vertical integration
   - **H** the rulings of the Supreme Court
   - **J** the theory of Social Darwinism

For additional test practice, go online for:

- Diagnostic tests
- Tutorials

INTERACT WITH HISTORY

Recall the issues that you explored at the beginning of the chapter. Consider how your answer might be different based on what you now know about the effects of railroad expansion and business consolidation. Then write a newspaper editorial about the Great Strike of 1877, supporting the position of either the railroad owners or the striking workers.

FOCUS ON WRITING

Imagine you are a union leader in a factory. If your demands for better working conditions are not met, all of the employees will stop work and go on strike. Write a persuasive letter in which you urge your employer to adopt specific reforms to improve working conditions.

COLLABORATIVE LEARNING

21ST CENTURY

In a small group read and discuss the "One American's Story" at the beginning of the section. Consider the following question: What qualities did Pattillo Higgins have that made him successful? Then make a poster describing Pattillo Higgins's personal qualities and how they helped him to achieve his dream. What present-day figures share Higgins's traits? Add images of these people, with captions, to the poster and display it in your classroom.

CHAPTER 15 IMMIGRANTS AND URBANIZATION

Essential Question

What were the economic, social, and political effects of immigration?

The intersection of Orchard and Hester Streets on New York City's Lower East Side, center of Jewish immigrant life in 1905.

USA

1877 Rutherford B. Hayes is elected president.

1880 James A. Garfield is elected president.

1881 Chester A. Arthur succeeds Garfield after Garfield's assassination.

1884 Grover Cleveland is elected president.

1888 Benjamin Harrison is elected president.

1892 Grover Cleveland is elected to a second term.

1880 — 1890

WORLD

1876 Porfirio Díaz seizes power in Mexico.

1884 Berlin Conference meets to divide Africa among European nations.

1885 Indian National Congress forms.

1893 France establishes Indochina.

Image Credits: (bkgd), The Granger Collection, New York; (bl), ©Bettmann/Corbis; (bc), (br), The Granger Collection, New York

HISTORY Ellis Island: Arrival

hmhsocialstudies.com VIDEO

INTERACT WITH HISTORY

The year is 1880. New York City's swelling population has created a housing crisis. Immigrant families crowd into apartments that lack light, ventilation, and sanitary facilities. Children have nowhere to play except in the streets and are often kept out of school to work and help support their families. You are a reformer who wishes to help immigrants improve their lives.

Explore the Issues

- How can immigrants gain access to the services they need?
- What skills do newcomers need?
- How might immigrants respond to help from an outsider?

1896 William McKinley is elected president.

1898 Hawaii is annexed by the United States.

1900 McKinley is reelected.

1901 The Commonwealth of Australia is founded.

1903 The Wright Brothers achieve the first successful airplane flight.

1905 Workers revolt in St. Petersburg, Russia.

1908 Oil is discovered in Persia.

1910 The appearance of Halley's comet causes widespread panic.

1912 Woodrow Wilson is elected president.

1912 Qing dynasty in China is overthrown.

1914 Panama Canal opens.

1900 1910

Image Credits: (bkgd), The Granger Collection, New York; (b), The Granger Collection, New York

The New Immigrants

MAIN IDEA	WHY IT MATTERS NOW	Terms & Names
Immigration from Europe, Asia, the Caribbean, and Mexico reached a new high in the late 19th and early 20th centuries.	**This wave of immigration helped make the United States the diverse society it is today.**	**• Ellis Island • Angel Island • melting pot • nativism • Chinese Exclusion Act • Gentlemen's Agreement**

One American's Story

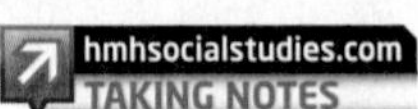

Use the graphic organizer online to take notes about immigration to the United States.

In 1871, 14-year-old Fong See came from China to "Gold Mountain"—the United States. Fong See stayed, worked at menial jobs, and saved enough money to buy a business. Despite widespread restrictions against the Chinese, he became a very successful importer and was able to sponsor many other Chinese who wanted to enter the United States. Fong See had achieved the American dream. However, as his great-granddaughter Lisa See recalls, he was not satisfied.

A PERSONAL VOICE LISA SEE

"He had been trying to achieve success ever since he had first set foot on the Gold Mountain. His dream was very 'American.' He wanted to make money, have influence, be respected, have a wife and children who loved him. In 1919, when he traveled to China, he could look at his life and say he had achieved his dream. But once in China, he suddenly saw his life in a different context. In America, was he really rich? Could he live where he wanted? . . . Did *Americans* care what he thought? . . . The answers played in his head—no, no, no."

—*On Gold Mountain*

Despite Fong See's success, he could not, upon his death in 1957, be buried next to his Caucasian wife because California cemeteries were still segregated.

Through the "Golden Door"

Millions of immigrants like Fong See entered the United States in the late 19th and early 20th centuries, lured by the promise of a better life. Some of these immigrants sought to escape difficult conditions—such as famine, land shortages, or religious or political persecution. Others, known as "birds of passage," intended to immigrate temporarily to earn money, and then return to their homelands.

Background
From 1815 to 1848, a wave of revolutions—mostly sparked by a desire for constitutional governments—shook Europe. In 1830, for example, the Polish people rose up against their Russian rulers.

EUROPEANS Between 1870 and 1920, approximately 20 million Europeans arrived in the United States. Before 1890, most immigrants came from countries in western and northern Europe. Beginning in the 1890s, however, increasing numbers came from southern and eastern Europe. In 1907 alone, about a million people arrived from Italy, Austria-Hungary, and Russia.

Why did so many leave their homelands? Many of these new immigrants left to escape religious persecution. Whole villages of Jews were driven out of Russia by pogroms, organized attacks often encouraged by local authorities. Other Europeans left because of rising population. Between 1800 and 1900, the population in Europe doubled to nearly 400 million, resulting in a scarcity of land for farming. Farmers competed with laborers for too few industrial jobs. In the United States, jobs were supposedly plentiful. In addition, a spirit of reform and revolt had spread across Europe in the 19th century. Influenced by political movements at home, many young European men and women sought independent lives in America.

CHINESE AND JAPANESE While waves of Europeans arrived on the shores of the East Coast, Chinese immigrants came to the West Coast in smaller numbers. Between 1851 and 1883, about 300,000 Chinese arrived. Many came to seek their fortunes after the discovery of gold in 1848 sparked the California gold rush. Chinese immigrants helped build the nation's railroads, including the first transcontinental line. When the railroads were completed, they turned to farming, mining, and domestic service. Some, like Fong See, started businesses. However, Chinese immigration was sharply limited by a congressional act in 1882.

In 1884, the Japanese government allowed Hawaiian planters to recruit Japanese workers, and a Japanese emigration boom began. The United States' annexation of Hawaii in 1898 resulted in increased Japanese immigration to the West Coast. Immigration continued to increase as word of comparatively high American wages spread. The wave peaked in 1907, when 30,000 left Japan for the United States. By 1920, more than 200,000 Japanese lived on the West Coast.

VIDEO
Italians in America: Old World, New Land

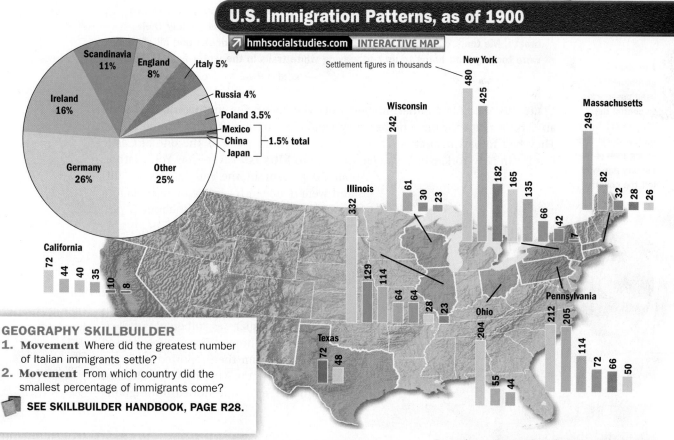

U.S. Immigration Patterns, as of 1900

hmhsocialstudies.com INTERACTIVE MAP

Scandinavia 11%
England 8%
Italy 5%
Russia 4%
Poland 3.5%
Mexico, China, Japan 1.5% total
Ireland 16%
Germany 26%
Other 25%

Settlement figures in thousands

California: 72, 44, 40, 35, 10, 8
Texas: 72, 48
Illinois: 332, 129, 114, 64, 64, 28, 23
Wisconsin: 242, 61, 30, 23
New York: 480, 425, 182, 165, 135, 66, 42, 7
Massachusetts: 249, 82, 32, 28, 26
Ohio: 204, 55, 44
Pennsylvania: 212, 205, 114, 72, 66, 50

GEOGRAPHY SKILLBUILDER

1. **Movement** Where did the greatest number of Italian immigrants settle?
2. **Movement** From which country did the smallest percentage of immigrants come?

SEE SKILLBUILDER HANDBOOK, PAGE R28.

THE WEST INDIES AND MEXICO Between 1880 and 1920, about 260,000 immigrants arrived in the eastern and southeastern United States from the West Indies. They came from Jamaica, Cuba, Puerto Rico, and other islands. Many West Indians left their homelands because jobs were scarce and the industrial boom in the United States seemed to promise work for everyone.

Mexicans, too, immigrated to the United States to find work, as well as to flee political turmoil. The 1902 National Reclamation Act, which encouraged the irrigation of arid land, created new farmland in Western states and drew Mexican farm workers northward. After 1910, political and social upheavals in Mexico prompted even more immigration. About 700,000 people—7 percent of the population of Mexico at the time—came to the U.S. over the next 20 years. A

MAIN IDEA

Analyzing Causes

A What reasons did people from other parts of the world have for immigrating to the United States?

Life in the New Land

No matter what part of the globe immigrants came from, they faced many adjustments to an alien—and often unfriendly—culture.

A DIFFICULT JOURNEY By the 1870s, almost all immigrants traveled by steamship. The trip across the Atlantic Ocean from Europe took approximately one week, while the Pacific crossing from Asia took nearly three weeks.

Many immigrants traveled in steerage, the cheapest accommodations in a ship's cargo holds. Rarely allowed on deck, immigrants were crowded together in the gloom, unable to exercise or catch a breath of fresh air. They often had to sleep in louse-infested bunks and share toilets with many other passengers. Under these conditions, disease spread quickly, and some immigrants died before they reached their destination. For those who survived, the first glimpse of America could be breathtaking.

A PERSONAL VOICE ROSA CAVALLERI

> "***America!*** **. . . We were so near it seemed too much to believe. Everyone stood silent—like in prayer. . . . Then we were entering the harbor. The land came so near we could almost reach out and touch it. . . . Everyone was holding their breath. Me too. . . . Some boats had bands playing on their decks and all of them were tooting their horns to us and leaving white trails in the water behind them.**"
>
> —quoted in *Rosa: The Life of an Italian Immigrant*

ELLIS ISLAND After initial moments of excitement, the immigrants faced the anxiety of not knowing whether they would be admitted to the United States. They had to pass inspection at immigration stations, such as the one at Castle Garden in New York, which was later moved to **Ellis Island** in New York Harbor. About 20 percent of the immigrants at Ellis Island were detained for a day or more before being inspected. However, only about 2 percent of those were denied entry.

The processing of immigrants on Ellis Island was an ordeal that might take five hours or more. First, they had to pass a physical examination by a doctor. Anyone with a serious health problem or a contagious disease, such as tuberculosis, was promptly sent home. Those who passed the medical exam then reported to a government inspector. The inspector checked documents and questioned immigrants

European governments used passports to control the number of professionals and young men of military age who left the country. ▼

Vocabulary
tuberculosis: a bacterial infection, characterized by fever and coughing, that spreads easily

Many immigrants, like these arriving at Ellis Island, were subjected to tests such as the one below. To prove their mental competence, they had to identify the four faces looking left in 14 seconds. Can you do it?

TESTS FOR DETECTION OF DEFECTIVES.

FIG. 4.—Moon Section of "V. C." test. The subject should be able to point out the four moons that are looking to the left in fourteen seconds, if he is directed to begin at the upper right hand corner and proceed systematically along each line, left to right.

A. B. C. D. E.

FIG. 5.—The Key Section of the "V. C." test. The time element has not been worked out for this section, but it is hardly the less valuable. "A" is shown the subject and he is asked to find the nearest like it in Fig. 1, "B" is shown and he is asked to find it in Fig. 3, "C" is shown and he is asked to find it in Fig. 4, "D" is shown and he is asked to find it in Fig. 2, and "E" is shown and he is asked to find it in Fig. 4.

to determine whether they met the legal requirements for entering the United States. The requirements included proving they had never been convicted of a felony, demonstrating that they were able to work, and showing that they had some money (at least $25 after 1909). One inspector, Edward Ferro, an Italian immigrant himself, gave this glimpse of the process.

Vocabulary
felony: any one of the most serious crimes under the law, including murder, rape, and burglary

A Personal Voice EDWARD FERRO

"The language was a problem of course, but it was overcome by the use of interpreters. . . . It would happen sometimes that these interpreters—some of them—were really softhearted people and hated to see people being deported, and they would, at times, help the aliens by interpreting in such a manner as to benefit the alien and not the government."

—quoted in *I Was Dreaming to Come to America*

From 1892 to 1924, Ellis Island was the chief immigration station in the United States. An estimated 17 million immigrants passed through its noisy, bustling facilities.

ANGEL ISLAND While European immigrants arriving on the East Coast passed through Ellis Island, Asians—primarily Chinese—arriving on the West Coast gained admission at **Angel Island** in San Francisco Bay. Between 1910 and 1940, about 50,000 Chinese immigrants entered the United States through Angel Island. Processing at Angel Island stood in contrast to the procedure at Ellis Island. Immigrants endured harsh questioning and a long detention in filthy, ramshackle buildings while they waited to find out whether they would be admitted or rejected. (B)

MAIN IDEA
Identifying Problems
(B) What difficulties did immigrants face in gaining admission to the United States?

VIDEO
Angel Island: Ellis Island of the West
hmhsocialstudies.com

COOPERATION FOR SURVIVAL Once admitted to the country, immigrants faced the challenges of finding a place to live, getting a job, and getting along in daily life while trying to understand an unfamiliar language and culture. Many immigrants sought out people who shared their cultural values, practiced their religion, and spoke their native language. The ethnic communities were life rafts for immigrants. People pooled their money to build churches or synagogues. They formed social clubs and aid societies. They founded orphanages and homes for the elderly, and established cemeteries. They even published newspapers in their own languages.

Vocabulary
synagogue: place of meeting for worship and religious instruction in the Jewish faith

Committed to their own cultures but also trying hard to grow into their new identities, many immigrants came to think of themselves as "hyphenated" Americans. As hard as they tried to fit in, these new Polish- and Italian- and Chinese-Americans felt increasing friction as they rubbed shoulders with people born and raised in the United States. Native-born people often disliked the immigrants' unfamiliar customs and languages, and viewed them as a threat to the American way of life. C

MAIN IDEA
Summarizing
C How did immigrants deal with challenges they faced?

Immigration Restrictions

Many native-born Americans thought of their country as a **melting pot,** a mixture of people of different cultures and races who blended together by abandoning their native languages and customs. Many new immigrants, however, did not wish to give up their cultural identities. As immigration increased, strong anti-immigrant feelings emerged.

THE RISE OF NATIVISM One response to the growth in immigration was **nativism,** or overt favoritism toward native-born Americans. Nativism gave rise to anti-immigrant groups and led to a demand for immigration restrictions.

Many nativists believed that Anglo-Saxons—the Germanic ancestors of the English—were superior to other ethnic groups. These nativists did not object to immigrants from the "right" countries. Prescott F. Hall, a founder in 1894 of the Immigration Restriction League, identified desirable immigrants as "British, German, and Scandinavian stock, historically free, energetic, progressive." Nativists thought that problems were caused by immigrants from the "wrong" countries—"Slav, Latin, and Asiatic races, historically down-trodden . . . and stagnant."

Vocabulary
progressive: favoring advancement toward better conditions or new ideas

Nativists sometimes objected more to immigrants' religious beliefs than to their ethnic backgrounds. Many native-born Americans were Protestants and thought that Roman Catholic and Jewish immigrants would undermine the democratic institutions established by the country's Protestant founders. The American Protective Association, a nativist group founded in 1887, launched vicious anti-Catholic attacks, and many colleges, businesses, and social clubs refused to admit Jews.

Chinese immigrants wait outside the hospital on Angel Island in San Francisco Bay, 1910. ▼

In 1897, Congress—influenced by the Immigration Restriction League—passed a bill requiring a literacy test for immigrants. Those who could not read 40 words in English or their native language would be refused entry. Although President Cleveland vetoed the bill, it was a powerful statement of public sentiment. In 1917, a similar bill would be passed into law in spite of President Woodrow Wilson's veto.

ANTI-ASIAN SENTIMENT Nativism also found a foothold in the labor movement, particularly in the West, where native-born workers feared that jobs would go to Chinese immigrants, who would accept lower wages. The depression of 1873 intensified anti-Chinese sentiment in California. Work was scarce, and labor groups exerted political pressure on the government to restrict Asian immigration. The founder of the Workingmen's Party, Denis Kearney, headed the anti-Chinese movement in California. He made hundreds of speeches throughout the state, each ending with the message, "The Chinese must go!"

In 1882, Congress slammed the door on Chinese immigration for ten years by passing the **Chinese Exclusion Act.** This act banned entry to all Chinese except students, teachers, merchants, tourists, and government officials. In 1892, Congress extended the law for another ten years. In 1902, Chinese immigration was restricted indefinitely; the law was not repealed until 1943.

▲ Fear and resentment of Chinese immigrants sometimes resulted in mob attacks, like the one shown here.

THE GENTLEMEN'S AGREEMENT The fears that had led to anti-Chinese agitation were extended to Japanese and other Asian people in the early 1900s. In 1906, the local board of education in San Francisco segregated Japanese children by putting them in separate schools. When Japan raised an angry protest at this treatment of its emigrants, President Theodore Roosevelt worked out a deal. Under the **Gentlemen's Agreement** of 1907–1908, Japan's government agreed to limit emigration of unskilled workers to the United States in exchange for the repeal of the San Francisco segregation order.

Although doorways for immigrants had been all but closed to Asians on the West Coast, cities in the East and the Midwest teemed with European immigrants—and with urban opportunities and challenges.

ASSESSMENT

1. **TERMS & NAMES** For each term or name, write a sentence explaining its significance.
   - **Ellis Island**
   - **Angel Island**
   - **melting pot**
   - **nativism**
   - **Chinese Exclusion Act**
   - **Gentlemen's Agreement**

MAIN IDEA

2. **TAKING NOTES**
   Create a diagram such as the one below. List two or more causes of each effect.

Causes ⟶	Effects
1. 2. 3.	Immigrants leave their home countries.
1. 2. 3.	Immigrants face hardships in the United States.
1. 2. 3.	Some nativists want to restrict immigration.

CRITICAL THINKING

3. **IDENTIFYING PROBLEMS**
   Which group of immigrants do you think faced the greatest challenges in the United States? Why?
4. **ANALYZING EFFECTS**
   What were the effects of the massive influx of immigrants to the U.S. in the late 1800s?
5. **EVALUATING**
   What arguments can you make against nativism and anti-immigrant feeling? **Think About:**
   - the personal qualities of immigrants
   - the reasons for anti-immigrant feeling
   - the contributions of immigrants to the United States

TRACING THEMES

Diversity and the National Identity

Before the first Europeans arrived, a variety of cultural groups—coastal fishing societies, desert farmers, plains and woodland hunters—inhabited North America. With the arrival of Europeans and Africans, the cultural mix grew more complex. Although this diversity has often produced tension, it has also been beneficial. As different groups learned from one another about agriculture, technology, and social customs, American culture became a rich blend of cultures from around the world.

1610s–1870s

◀ SPANISH NORTH AMERICA

Spanish missionaries in the Southwest tried to impose their culture upon Native Americans. However, many Native Americans retained aspects of their original cultures even as they took on Spanish ways. For example, today many Pueblo Indians of New Mexico perform ancient ceremonies, such as the Corn Dance, in addition to celebrating the feast days of Catholic saints. Later, the first cowboys—descendants of the Spanish—would introduce to white Americans cattle-ranching techniques developed in Mexico.

1776

THE DECLARATION OF INDEPENDENCE ▶

The signers of the Declaration of Independence were descendants of immigrants. The founders' ancestors had come to North America in search of economic opportunity and freedom of religious expression. When the Second Continental Congress declared a "United States" in 1776, they acknowledged that the country would contain diverse regions and interests. Thus the founders placed on the presidential seal the motto *"E Pluribus Unum"*—"out of many, one."

1862–1863

THE EMANCIPATION PROCLAMATION ▲

At the midpoint of the Civil War, President Abraham Lincoln issued the Emancipation Proclamation, freeing all slaves in areas of the Union that were in rebellion. Although the Proclamation could not be enforced immediately, it was a strong statement of opposition to slavery, and it paved the way for African Americans' citizenship.

1886

THE STATUE OF LIBERTY ▶

Jewish poet Emma Lazarus wrote the famous lines inscribed at the foot of the Statue of Liberty, "Give me your tired, your poor,/Your huddled masses yearning to breathe free, . . ." The statue's dedication took place during the most extensive wave of immigration the United States has ever known.

Many native-born Americans felt that the newcomers should fully immerse themselves in their new culture. However, most immigrants combined American language and customs with their traditional ways. As immigrants celebrated Independence Day and Thanksgiving, they introduced into American culture new celebrations, such as Chinese New Year and Cinco de Mayo.

2000

◀ 21ST-CENTURY DIVERSITY

In 1998, three countries (Mexico, China, and India) contributed a third of the total number of immigrants to the United States. The rest of 1998's immigrants came from countries as diverse as Vietnam, Sudan, and Bosnia.

American athletes at the 2000 Olympic Games in Sydney, Australia, reflected the increasing diversity of the U.S., pointing toward a future in which there may no longer be a majority racial or ethnic group.

THINKING CRITICALLY

CONNECT TO HISTORY

1. **Analyzing Motives** Why do you think some groups have tried to suppress the culture of others over the course of history? Why have many groups persisted in retaining their cultural heritage?

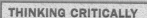

SEE SKILLBUILDER HANDBOOK, PAGE R6.

CONNECT TO TODAY

2. **Predicting Effects** Research current U.S. policy on immigration. How might this policy affect cultural diversity? Write a short editorial from one of the following viewpoints:
   - U.S. immigration policy needs to change.
   - U.S. immigration policy should be maintained.

The Challenges of Urbanization

MAIN IDEA	WHY IT MATTERS NOW	Terms & Names
The rapid growth of cities forced people to contend with problems of housing, transportation, water, and sanitation.	Consequently, residents of U.S. cities today enjoy vastly improved living conditions.	• urbanization • Americanization movement • tenement • mass transit • Social Gospel movement • settlement house • Jane Addams

One American's Story

hmhsocialstudies.com TAKING NOTES

Use the graphic organizer online to take notes about urbanization and its problems.

In 1870, at age 21, Jacob Riis left his native Denmark for the United States. Riis found work as a police reporter, a job that took him into some of New York City's worst slums, where he was shocked at the conditions in the overcrowded, airless, filthy tenements. Riis used his talents to expose the hardships of New York City's poor.

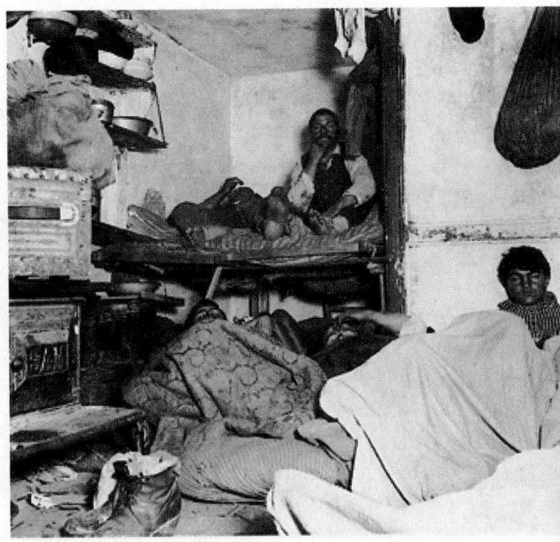

▲ As many as 12 people slept in rooms such as this one in New York City, photographed by Jacob Riis around 1889.

A Personal Voice JACOB RIIS

"Be a little careful, please! The hall is dark and you might stumble over the children pitching pennies back there. Not that it would hurt them; kicks and cuffs are their daily diet. They have little else. . . . Close [stuffy]? Yes! What would you have? All the fresh air that ever enters these stairs comes from the hall-door that is forever slamming. . . . Here is a door. Listen! That short hacking cough, that tiny, helpless wail—what do they mean? . . . The child is dying with measles. With half a chance it might have lived; but it had none. That dark bedroom killed it."

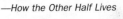

—*How the Other Half Lives*

Making a living in the late 19th and early 20th centuries was not easy. Natural and economic disasters had hit farmers hard in Europe and in the United States, and the promise of industrial jobs drew millions of people to American cities. The urban population exploded from 10 million to 54 million between 1870 and 1920. This growth revitalized the cities but also created serious problems that, as Riis observed, had a powerful impact on the new urban poor.

Urban Opportunities

The technological boom in the 19th century contributed to the growing industrial strength of the United States. The result was rapid **urbanization,** or growth of cities, mostly in the regions of the Northeast and Midwest.

IMMIGRANTS SETTLE IN CITIES Most of the immigrants who streamed into the United States in the late 19th century became city dwellers because cities were the cheapest and most convenient places to live. Cities also offered unskilled laborers steady jobs in mills and factories. By 1890, there were twice as many Irish residents in New York City as in Dublin, Ireland. By 1910, immigrant families made up more than half the total population of 18 major American cities.

The **Americanization movement** was designed to assimilate people of wide-ranging cultures into the dominant culture. This social campaign was sponsored by the government and by concerned citizens. Schools and voluntary associations provided programs to teach immigrants skills needed for citizenship, such as English literacy and American history and government. Subjects such as cooking and social etiquette were included in the curriculum to help the newcomers learn the ways of native-born Americans. (A)

MAIN IDEA

Analyzing Motives

(A) Why did native-born Americans start the Americanization movement?

Despite these efforts, many immigrants did not wish to abandon their traditions. Ethnic communities provided the social support of other immigrants from the same country. This enabled them to speak their own language and practice their customs and religion. However, these neighborhoods soon became overcrowded, a problem that was intensified by the arrival of new transplants from America's rural areas.

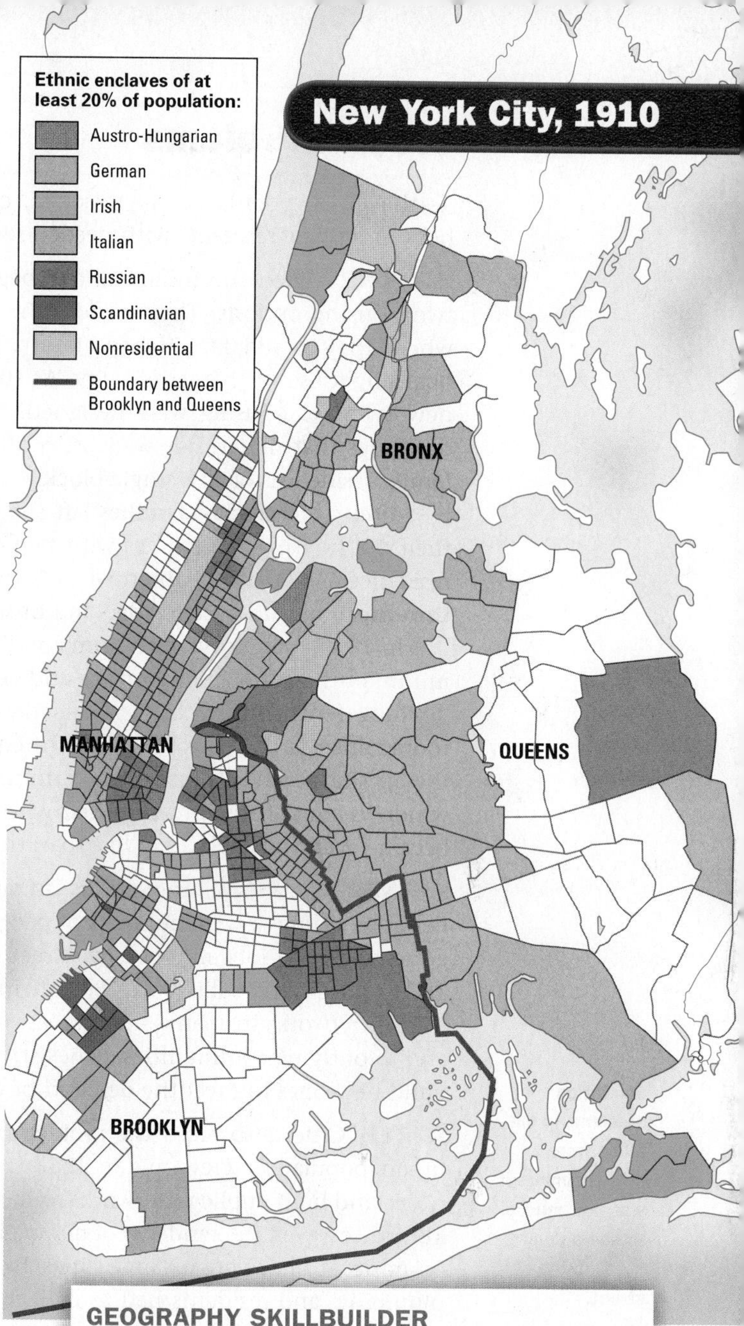

New York City, 1910

GEOGRAPHY SKILLBUILDER

1. **Place** What general pattern of settlement do you notice?
2. **Movement** Which ethnic group settled in the largest area of New York City?

MIGRATION FROM COUNTRY TO CITY Rapid improvements in farming technology during the second half of the 19th century were good news for some farmers but bad news for others. Inventions such as the McCormick reaper and the steel plow made farming more efficient but meant that fewer laborers were needed to work the land. As more and more farms merged, many rural people moved to cities to find whatever work they could.

Many of the Southern farmers who lost their livelihoods were African Americans. Between 1890 and 1910, about 200,000 African Americans moved north and west, to cities such as Chicago and Detroit, in an effort to escape racial violence, economic hardship, and political oppression. Many found conditions only somewhat better than those they had left behind. Segregation and discrimination were often the reality in Northern cities. Job competition between blacks and white immigrants caused further racial tension.

Urban Problems

As the urban population skyrocketed, city governments faced the problems of how to provide residents with needed services and safe living conditions.

HOUSING When the industrial age began, working-class families in cities had two housing options. They could either buy a house on the outskirts of town, where they would face transportation problems, or rent cramped rooms in a boardinghouse in the central city. As the urban population increased, however, new types of housing were designed. For example, row houses—single-family dwellings that shared side walls with other similar houses—packed many single-family residences onto a single block.

After working-class families left the central city, immigrants often took over their old housing, sometimes with two or three families occupying a one-family residence. As Jacob Riis pointed out, these multifamily urban dwellings, called **tenements,** were overcrowded and unsanitary.

In 1879, to improve such slum conditions, New York City passed a law that set minimum standards for plumbing and ventilation in apartments. Landlords began building tenements with air shafts that provided an outside window for each room. Since garbage was picked up infrequently, people sometimes dumped it into the air shafts, where it attracted vermin. To keep out the stench, residents nailed windows shut. Though established with good intent, these new tenements soon became even worse places to live than the converted single-family residences. B

MAIN IDEA

Identifying Problems

B What housing problems did urban working-class families face?

TRANSPORTATION Innovations in **mass transit,** transportation systems designed to move large numbers of people along fixed routes, enabled workers to go to and from jobs more easily. Street cars were introduced in San Francisco in 1873 and electric subways in Boston in 1897. By the early 20th century, mass-transit networks in many urban areas linked city neighborhoods to one another and to outlying communities. Cities struggled to repair old transit systems and to build new ones to meet the demand of expanding populations.

WATER Cities also faced the problem of supplying safe drinking water. As the urban population grew in the 1840s and 1850s, cities such as New York and Cleveland built public waterworks to handle the increasing demand. As late as the 1860s, however, the residents of many cities had grossly inadequate piped water—or none at all. Even in large cities like New York, homes seldom had indoor plumbing, and residents had to collect water in pails from faucets on the street and heat it for bathing. The necessity of improving water quality to control diseases such as cholera and typhoid fever was obvious. To make city water safer, filtration was introduced in the 1870s and chlorination in 1908. However, in the early 20th century, many city dwellers still had no access to safe water.

Vocabulary
chlorination: a method of purifying water by mixing it with the chemical chlorine

Sanitation problems in big cities were overwhelming. It was not unusual to see a dead horse in the street. ▼

SANITATION As the cities grew, so did the challenge of keeping them clean. Horse manure piled up on the streets, sewage flowed through open gutters, and factories spewed foul smoke into the air. Without dependable trash collection, people dumped their garbage on the streets. Although private contractors called scavengers were hired to sweep the streets, collect garbage, and clean outhouses, they

MAIN IDEA

Analyzing Effects

C How did conditions in cities affect people's health?

often did not do the jobs properly. By 1900, many cities had developed sewer lines and created sanitation departments. However, the task of providing hygienic living conditions was an ongoing challenge for urban leaders. **C**

CRIME As the populations of cities increased, pickpockets and thieves flourished. Although New York City organized the first full-time, salaried police force in 1844, it and most other city law enforcement units were too small to have much impact on crime.

FIRE The limited water supply in many cities contributed to another menace: the spread of fires. Major fires occurred in almost every large American city during the 1870s and 1880s. In addition to lacking water with which to combat blazes, most cities were packed with wooden dwellings, which were like kindling waiting to be ignited. The use of candles and kerosene heaters also posed a fire hazard. In San Francisco, deadly fires often broke out during earthquakes. Jack London described the fires that raged after the San Francisco earthquake of 1906.

A PERSONAL VOICE JACK LONDON

> **"On Wednesday morning at a quarter past five came the earthquake. A minute later the flames were leaping upward. In a dozen different quarters south of Market Street, in the working-class ghetto, and in the factories, fires started. There was no opposing the flames. . . . And the great water-mains had burst. All the shrewd contrivances and safeguards of man had been thrown out of gear by thirty seconds' twitching of the earth-crust."**
>
> —"The Story of an Eye-witness"

At first, most city firefighters were volunteers and not always available when they were needed. Cincinnati, Ohio, tackled this problem when it established the nation's first paid fire department in 1853. By 1900, most cities had full-time professional fire departments. The introduction of a practical automatic fire sprinkler in 1874 and the replacement of wood as a building material with brick, stone, or concrete also made cities safer.

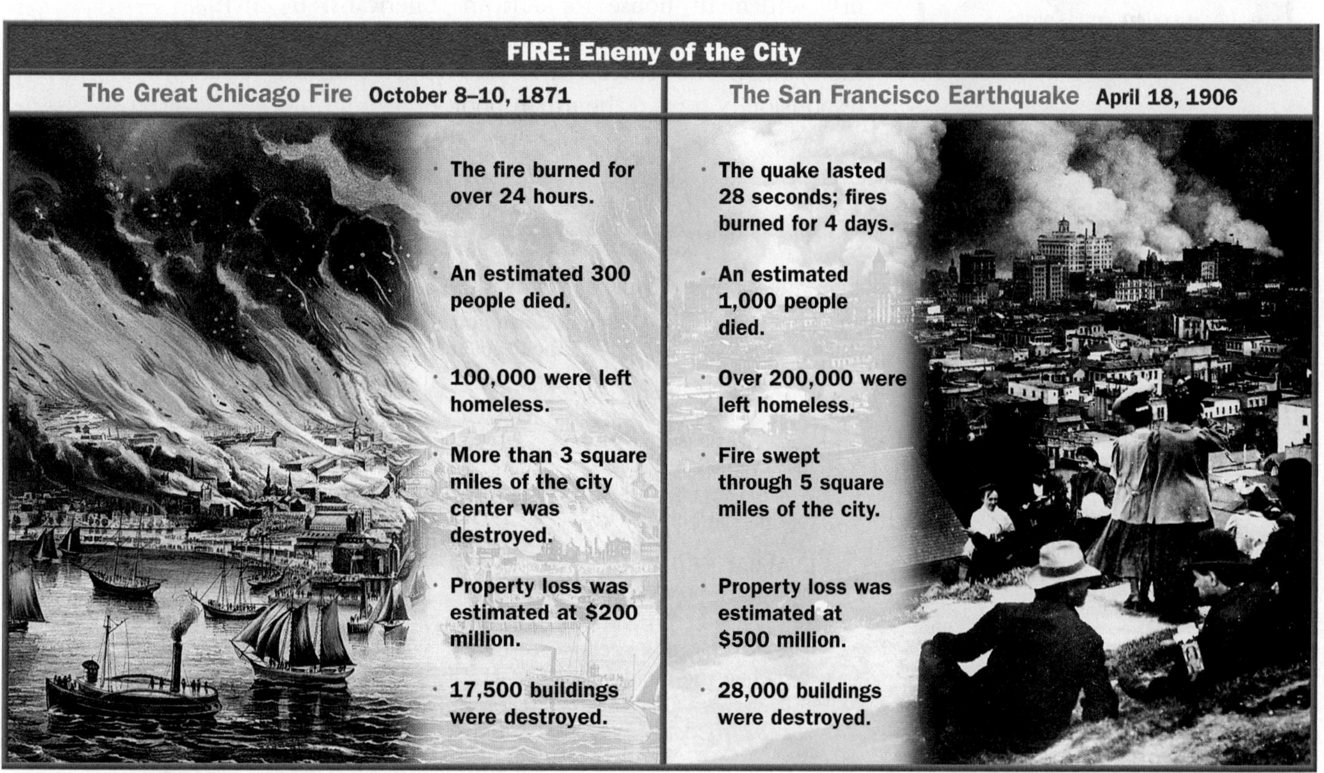

FIRE: Enemy of the City
The Great Chicago Fire October 8–10, 1871
• The fire burned for over 24 hours.
• An estimated 300 people died.
• 100,000 were left homeless.
• More than 3 square miles of the city center was destroyed.
• Property loss was estimated at $200 million.
• 17,500 buildings were destroyed.
The San Francisco Earthquake April 18, 1906
• The quake lasted 28 seconds; fires burned for 4 days.
• An estimated 1,000 people died.
• Over 200,000 were left homeless.
• Fire swept through 5 square miles of the city.
• Property loss was estimated at $500 million.
• 28,000 buildings were destroyed.

KEY PLAYER

JANE ADDAMS
1860–1935

During a trip to England, Jane Addams visited Toynbee Hall, the first settlement house. Addams believed that settlement houses could be effective because there, workers would "learn from life itself" how to address urban problems. She cofounded Chicago's Hull House in 1889.

Addams was also an antiwar activist, a spokesperson for racial justice, and an advocate for quality-of-life issues, from infant mortality to better care for the aged. In 1931, she was a co-winner of the Nobel Peace Prize.

Until the end of her life, Addams insisted that she was just a "very simple person." But many familiar with her accomplishments consider her a source of inspiration.

Reformers Mobilize

As problems in cities mounted, concerned Americans worked to find solutions. Social welfare reformers targeted their efforts at relieving urban poverty.

THE SETTLEMENT HOUSE MOVEMENT An early reform program, the **Social Gospel movement,** preached salvation through service to the poor. Inspired by the message of the Social Gospel movement, many 19th-century reformers responded to the call to help the urban poor. In the late 1800s, a few reformers established **settlement houses,** community centers in slum neighborhoods that provided assistance to people in the area, especially immigrants. Many settlement workers lived at the houses so that they could learn firsthand about the problems caused by urbanization and help create solutions.

Run largely by middle-class, college-educated women, settlement houses provided educational, cultural, and social services. They provided classes in such subjects as English, health, and painting, and offered college extension courses. Settlement houses also sent visiting nurses into the homes of the sick and provided whatever aid was needed to secure "support for deserted women, insurance for bewildered widows, damages for injured operators, furniture from the clutches of the installment store."

Settlement houses in the United States were founded by Charles Stover and Stanton Coit in New York City in 1886. **Jane Addams**—one of the most influential members of the movement—and Ellen Gates Starr founded Chicago's Hull House in 1889. In 1890, Janie Porter Barrett founded Locust Street Social Settlement in Hampton, Virginia—the first settlement house for African Americans. By 1910, about 400 settlement houses were operating in cities across the country. The settlement houses helped cultivate social responsibility toward the urban poor.

ASSESSMENT

1. TERMS & NAMES For each term or name, write a sentence explaining its significance.

- **urbanization**
- **Americanization movement**
- **tenement**
- **mass transit**
- **Social Gospel movement**
- **settlement house**
- **Jane Addams**

MAIN IDEA

2. TAKING NOTES
Re-create the spider map below on your paper. List urban problems on the vertical lines. Fill in details about attempts that were made to solve each problem.

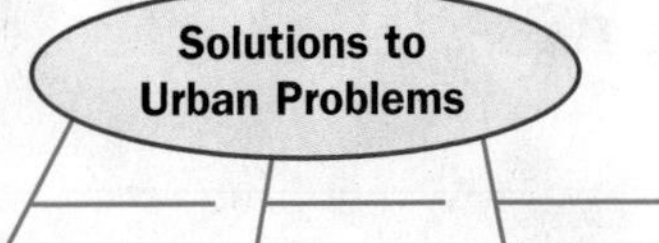

CRITICAL THINKING

3. ANALYZING MOTIVES
Why did immigrants tend to group together in cities?

4. EVALUATING
Which solution (or attempted solution) to an urban problem discussed in this section do you think had the most impact? Why?

5. ANALYZING EFFECTS
What effects did the migration from rural areas to the cities in the late 19th century have on urban society?
Think About:

- why people moved to cities
- the problems caused by rapid urban growth
- the differences in the experiences of whites and blacks

Politics in the Gilded Age

MAIN IDEA	WHY IT MATTERS NOW	Terms & Names
Local and national political corruption in the 19th century led to calls for reform.	**Political reforms paved the way for a more honest and efficient government in the 20th century and beyond.**	**• political machine • graft • Boss Tweed • patronage • civil service • Rutherford B. Hayes • James A. Garfield • Chester A. Arthur • Pendleton Civil Service Act • Grover Cleveland • Benjamin Harrison**

One American's Story

hmhsocialstudies.com
TAKING NOTES
Use the graphic organizer online to take notes about political corruption in the Gilded Age.

Mark Twain described the excesses of the late 19th century in a satirical novel, *The Gilded Age*, a collaboration with the writer Charles Dudley Warner. The title of the book has since come to represent the period from the 1870s to the 1890s. Twain mocks the greed and self-indulgence of his characters, including Philip Sterling.

A Personal Voice
MARK TWAIN AND CHARLES DUDLEY WARNER

"There are many young men like him [Philip Sterling] in American society, of his age, opportunities, education and abilities, who have really been educated for nothing and have let themselves drift, in the hope that they will find somehow, and by some sudden turn of good luck, the golden road to fortune. . . . He saw people, all around him, poor yesterday, rich to-day, who had come into sudden opulence by some means which they could not have classified among any of the regular occupations of life."

—*The Gilded Age*

A luxurious apartment building rises behind a New York City shantytown in 1889.

Twain's characters find that getting rich quick is more difficult than they had thought it would be. Investments turn out to be worthless; politicians' bribes eat up their savings. The glittering exterior of the age turns out to hide a corrupt political core and a growing gap between the few rich and the many poor.

The Emergence of Political Machines

In the late 19th century, cities experienced rapid growth under inefficient government. In a climate influenced by dog-eat-dog Social Darwinism, cities were receptive to a new power structure, the political machine, and a new politician, the city boss.

THE POLITICAL MACHINE An organized group that controlled the activities of a political party in a city, the **political machine** also offered services to voters and businesses in exchange for political or financial support. In the decades after the Civil War, political machines gained control of local government in Baltimore, New York, San Francisco, and other major cities.

The machine was organized like a pyramid. At the pyramid's base were local precinct workers and captains, who tried to gain voters' support on a city block or in a neighborhood and who reported to a ward boss. At election time, the ward boss worked to secure the vote in all the precincts in the ward, or electoral district. Ward bosses helped the poor and gained their votes by doing favors or providing services. As Martin Lomasney, elected ward boss of Boston's West End in 1885, explained, "There's got to be in every ward somebody that any bloke can come to . . . and get help. Help, you understand; none of your law and your justice, but help." At the top of the pyramid was the city boss, who controlled the activities of the political party throughout the city. Precinct captains, ward bosses, and the city boss worked together to elect their candidates and guarantee the success of the machine. (A)

MAIN IDEA

Summarizing

(A) In what way did the structure of the political machine resemble a pyramid?

THE ROLE OF THE POLITICAL BOSS Whether or not the boss officially served as mayor, he controlled access to municipal jobs and business licenses, and influenced the courts and other municipal agencies. Bosses like Roscoe Conkling in New York used their power to build parks, sewer systems, and waterworks, and gave money to schools, hospitals, and orphanages. Bosses could also provide government support for new businesses, a service for which they were often paid extremely well.

It was not only money that motivated city bosses. By solving urban problems, bosses could reinforce voters' loyalty, win additional political support, and extend their influence.

▲ A corrupt 19th-century boss robs the city treasury by easily cutting government red tape, or bureaucracy.

IMMIGRANTS AND THE MACHINE Many precinct captains and political bosses were first-generation or second-generation immigrants. Few were educated beyond grammar school. They entered politics early and worked their way up from the bottom. They could speak to immigrants in their own language and understood the challenges that newcomers faced. More important, the bosses were able to provide solutions. The machines helped immigrants with naturalization (attaining full citizenship), housing, and jobs—the newcomers' most pressing needs. In return, the immigrants provided what the political bosses needed—votes. (B)

MAIN IDEA

Analyzing Motives

(B) Why did immigrants support political machines?

"Big Jim" Pendergast, an Irish-American saloonkeeper, worked his way up from precinct captain to Democratic city boss in Kansas City by aiding Italian, African-American, and Irish voters in his ward. By 1900, he controlled Missouri state politics as well.

A PERSONAL VOICE JAMES PENDERGAST

"I've been called a boss. All there is to it is having friends, doing things for people, and then later on they'll do things for you. . . . You can't coerce people into doing things for you—you can't make them vote for you. I never coerced anybody in my life. Wherever you see a man bulldozing anybody he don't last long."

—quoted in *The Pendergast Machine*

Municipal Graft and Scandal

While the well-oiled political machines provided city dwellers with services, many political bosses fell victim to corruption as their influence grew.

ELECTION FRAUD AND GRAFT When the loyalty of voters was not enough to carry an election, some political machines turned to fraud. Using fake names, party faithfuls cast as many votes as were needed to win.

Once a political machine got its candidates into office, it could take advantage of numerous opportunities for **graft,** the illegal use of political influence for personal gain. For example, by helping a person find work on a construction project for the city, a political machine could ask the worker to bill the city for more than the actual cost of materials and labor. The worker then "kicked back" a portion of the earnings to the machine. Taking these kickbacks, or illegal payments for their services, enriched the political machines—and individual politicians.

Political machines also granted favors to businesses in return for cash and accepted bribes to allow illegal activities, such as gambling, to flourish. Politicians were able to get away with shady dealings because the police rarely interfered. Until about 1890, police forces were hired and fired by political bosses.

THE TWEED RING SCANDAL William M. Tweed, known as **Boss Tweed,** became head of Tammany Hall, New York City's powerful Democratic political machine, in 1868. Between 1869 and 1871, Boss Tweed led the Tweed Ring, a group of corrupt politicians, in defrauding the city.

One scheme, the construction of the New York County Courthouse, involved extravagant graft. The project cost taxpayers $13 million, while the actual construction cost was $3 million. The difference went into the pockets of Tweed and his followers.

Thomas Nast, a political cartoonist, helped arouse public outrage against Tammany Hall's graft, and the Tweed Ring was finally broken in 1871. Tweed was indicted on 120 counts of fraud and extortion and was sentenced to 12 years in jail. His sentence was reduced to one year, but after leaving jail, Tweed was quickly arrested on another charge. While serving a second sentence, Tweed escaped. He was captured in Spain when officials identified him from a Thomas Nast cartoon. By that time, political corruption had become a national issue.

▲ **Boss Tweed, head of Tammany Hall.**

Vocabulary
extortion: illegal use of one's official position to obtain property or funds

Analyzing *Political Cartoons*

"THE TAMMANY TIGER LOOSE"

Political cartoonist Thomas Nast ridiculed Boss Tweed and his machine in the pages of *Harper's Weekly*. Nast's work threatened Tweed, who reportedly said, "I don't care so much what the papers write about me—my constituents can't read; but . . . they can see pictures!"

SKILLBUILDER Analyzing Political Cartoons

1. Under the Tammany tiger's victim is a torn paper that reads "LAW." What is its significance?
2. Boss Tweed and his cronies, portrayed as noblemen, watch from the stands on the left. The cartoon's caption reads "What are you going to do about it?" What effect do you think Nast wanted to have on his audience?

SEE SKILLBUILDER HANDBOOK, PAGE R24.

Civil Service Replaces Patronage

RUTHERFORD B. HAYES (1877–1881)

" Nobody ever left the presidency with less regret . . . than I do."

JAMES A. GARFIELD (1881)

"Assassination can be no more guarded against than death by lightning."

CHESTER A. ARTHUR (1881–1885)

" There doesn't seem to be anything else for an ex-president to do but . . . raise big pumpkins."

The desire for power and money that made local politics corrupt in the industrial age also infected national politics.

PATRONAGE SPURS REFORM Since the beginning of the 19th century, presidents had complained about the problem of **patronage,** or the giving of government jobs to people who had helped a candidate get elected. In Andrew Jackson's administration, this policy was known as the spoils system. People from cabinet members to workers who scrubbed the steps of the Capitol owed their jobs to political connections. As might be expected, some government employees were not qualified for the positions they filled. Moreover, political appointees, whether qualified or not, sometimes used their positions for personal gain.

Reformers began to press for the elimination of patronage and the adoption of a merit system of hiring. Jobs in **civil service**—government administration—should go to the most qualified persons, reformers believed. It should not matter what political views they held or who recommended them. C

MAIN IDEA

Analyzing Causes

C How did patronage contribute to government incompetence and fraud?

REFORM UNDER HAYES, GARFIELD, AND ARTHUR Civil service reform made gradual progress under Presidents Hayes, Garfield, and Arthur. Republican president **Rutherford B. Hayes,** elected in 1876, could not convince Congress to support reform, so he used other means. Hayes named independents to his cabinet. He also set up a commission to investigate the nation's customhouses, which were notorious centers of patronage. On the basis of the commission's report, Hayes fired two of the top officials of New York City's customhouse, where jobs were controlled by the Republican Party. These firings enraged the Republican New York senator and political boss Roscoe Conkling and his supporters, the Stalwarts.

When Hayes decided not to run for reelection in 1880, a free-for-all broke out at the Republican convention, between the Stalwarts—who opposed changes in the spoils system—and reformers. Since neither Stalwarts nor reformers could win a majority of delegates, the convention settled on an independent presidential candidate, Ohio congressman **James A. Garfield.** To balance out Garfield's ties to reformers, the Republicans nominated for vice-president **Chester A. Arthur,** one of Conkling's supporters. Despite Arthur's inclusion on the ticket, Garfield angered the Stalwarts by giving reformers most of his patronage jobs once he was elected.

On July 2, 1881, as President Garfield walked through the Washington, D.C., train station, he was shot two times by a mentally unbalanced lawyer named Charles Guiteau, whom Garfield had turned down for a job. The would-be assassin announced, "I did it and I will go to jail for it. I am a Stalwart and Arthur is now president." Garfield finally died from his wounds on September 19. Despite his ties to the Stalwarts, Chester Arthur turned reformer when he became president. His first message to Congress urged legislators to pass a civil service law.

The resulting **Pendleton Civil Service Act** of 1883 authorized a bipartisan civil service commission to make appointments to federal jobs through a merit system based on candidates' performance on an examination. By 1901, more than 40 percent of all federal jobs had been classified as civil service positions, but the Pendleton Act had mixed consequences. On the one hand, public administration became more honest and efficient. On the other hand, because officials could no longer pressure employees for campaign contributions, politicians turned to other sources for donations.

Business Buys Influence

MAIN IDEA

Analyzing Effects

D What were the positive and the negative effects of the Pendleton Civil Service Act?

With employees no longer a source of campaign contributions, politicians turned to wealthy business owners. Therefore, the alliance between government and big business became stronger than ever. D

HARRISON, CLEVELAND, AND HIGH TARIFFS Big business hoped the government would preserve, or even raise, the tariffs that protected domestic industries from foreign competition. The Democratic Party, however, opposed high tariffs because they increased prices. In 1884, the Democratic Party won a presidential election for the first time in 28 years with candidate **Grover Cleveland.** As president, Cleveland tried to lower tariff rates, but Congress refused to support him.

In 1888, Cleveland ran for reelection on a low-tariff platform against the former Indiana senator **Benjamin Harrison,** the grandson of President William Henry Harrison. Harrison's campaign was financed by large contributions from companies that wanted tariffs even higher than they were. Although Cleveland won about 100,000 more popular votes than Harrison, Harrison took a majority of the electoral votes and the presidency. He signed the McKinley Tariff Act of 1890, which raised tariffs on manufactured goods to their highest level yet.

In 1892, Cleveland was elected again—the only president to serve two nonconsecutive terms. He supported a bill for lowering the McKinley Tariff but refused to sign it because it also provided for a federal income tax. The Wilson-Gorman Tariff became law in 1894 without the president's signature. In 1897, William McKinley was inaugurated president and raised tariffs once again.

The attempt to reduce the tariff had failed, but the spirit of reform was not dead. New developments in areas ranging from technology to mass culture would help redefine American society as the United States moved into the 20th century.

ASSESSMENT

1. **TERMS & NAMES** For each term or name, write a sentence explaining its significance.
   - **political machine**
   - **graft**
   - **Boss Tweed**
   - **patronage**
   - **civil service**
   - **Rutherford B. Hayes**
   - **James A. Garfield**
   - **Chester A. Arthur**
   - **Pendleton Civil Service Act**
   - **Grover Cleveland**
   - **Benjamin Harrison**

MAIN IDEA

2. **TAKING NOTES**
   In a chart like the one shown, list examples of corruption in 19th-century politics.

CRITICAL THINKING

3. **EVALUATING LEADERSHIP**
   Reread A Personal Voice by James Pendergast. Explain whether you agree or disagree that machine politicians did not coerce people.

4. **ANALYZING CAUSES**
   Why do you think tariff reform failed? Support your response with evidence from the chapter.

5. **HYPOTHESIZING**
   How do you think politics in the United States would have been different if the Pendleton Civil Service Act had not been passed?
   THINK ABOUT:
   - the act's impact on federal workers
   - the act's impact on political fundraising
   - Republican Party conflicts

CHAPTER 15 ASSESSMENT

TERMS & NAMES

For each term or name below, write a sentence explaining its connection to immigration and urbanization.

1. Ellis Island
2. Gentlemen's Agreement
3. Americanization movement
4. Jane Addams
5. political machine
6. graft
7. Boss Tweed
8. patronage
9. Rutherford B. Hayes
10. Pendleton Civil Service Act

MAIN IDEAS

Use your notes and the information in the chapter to answer the following questions.

The New Immigrants

1. What trends or events in other countries prompted people to move to the United States in the late 19th and early 20th centuries?
2. What difficulties did many of these new immigrants face?

The Challenges of Urbanization

3. Why did cities in the United States grow rapidly in the decades following the Civil War?
4. What problems did this rapid growth pose for cities?
5. What solutions to urban problems did the settlement-house movement propose?

Politics in the Gilded Age

6. Why did machine politics become common in big cities in the late 19th century?
7. What government problems arose as a result of patronage?
8. Summarize the views of Grover Cleveland and Benjamin Harrison on tariffs.

CRITICAL THINKING

1. **USING YOUR NOTES** In a diagram like the one below, show one result of and one reaction against (a) the increase in immigration and (b) the increase in machine politics.

		Result		Reaction
Increased Immigration	→	______	→	______
Increased Machine Politics	→	______	→	______

2. **EVALUATING** In the 1860s, Horace Greeley—editor of the *New York Tribune*—remarked, "We cannot all live in the cities, yet nearly all seem determined to do so." Why do you think this was true at the end of the 19th century? Do you think it is still true? Why or why not?

3. **COMPARING** How were politicians like Boss Tweed similar to industrial magnates like Carnegie and Rockefeller?

VISUAL SUMMARY: IMMIGRANTS AND URBANIZATION

IMMIGRATION AND MIGRATION

- Poverty and persecution cause millions of people to leave Europe, China, Japan, the Caribbean, and Mexico for the United States.
- Immigrants are forced to adapt to a new language and culture.
- Changes in agriculture cause people to migrate from the rural U.S. to the cities in search of work.
- Many immigrants and migrants face discrimination in their efforts to find jobs and housing.

URBANIZATION

- The influx of immigrants and migrants causes a population boom in cities.
- City services, such as housing, transportation, water, and sanitation, are stretched to the limit.
- Reformers try to fix urban problems through education, training, charity, and political action.

POLITICS

- Political machines develop to take advantage of the needs of immigrants and the urban poor.
- City politicians use fraud and graft to maintain political power.
- Corruption in national politics results in the call for civil service jobs to be awarded on the basis of merit.
- Big business's growing influence on politics defeats tariff reform that would aid wage-earners.

STANDARDIZED TEST PRACTICE

Use the quotation and your knowledge of U.S. history to answer question 1.

> **"The Chinese . . . ask for fair treatment. . . . Since the first restriction law was passed the United States has received as immigrants more than two million Austro-Hungarians, two million Italians and a million and a half Russians and Finns. Each of these totals is from five to seven times the whole amount of Chinese immigration of all classes during thirty years of free immigration. . . . The question is not now of the admission of laborers, but whether other Chinese who are entitled to come under both law and treaty shall receive the same courtesies as people of other nations, and shall be relieved from many harassing regulations. They must no longer be detained, photographed and examined as if they were suspected of crime."**
>
> —Ng Poon Chew, from *The Treatment of the Exempt Classes of Chinese in the United States*

1. The information in the passage supports which *one* of the following points of view?
   - **A** European immigration should be restricted.
   - **B** Chinese laborers should be allowed to immigrate.
   - **C** All immigrants are treated like criminals.
   - **D** Chinese immigrants and European immigrants should be treated the same.

Use the cartoon and your knowledge of U.S. history to answer question 2.

TAMMANY RING
WHO STOLE THE PEOPLES MONEY ? "— DO TELL . N.Y.TIMES.
'TWAS HIM

2. The cartoon suggests that Boss Tweed (the large figure at left) —
   - **F** was solely responsible for stealing the people's money.
   - **G** did not steal the people's money.
   - **H** had help from his associates in stealing the people's money.
   - **J** was loyal to his associates.

hmhsocialstudies.com TEST PRACTICE

For additional test practice, go online for:

- Diagnostic tests
- Tutorials

INTERACT WITH HISTORY

Think about the issues you explored at the beginning of the chapter. With what you have learned about the challenges faced by immigrants in the 19th century, consider the following question: What were the best solutions attempted by government and reformers in the 1800s? Create a pamphlet promoting the reform, improvement, or government solution you chose.

FOCUS ON WRITING

Imagine you are a senator and the Senate is about to vote on the Chinese Exclusion Act. Prepare a persuasive speech arguing against the new law. For the first part of your speech, explain why this law is unjust and unfair to the Chinese. For the second part, address the concerns of those in favor of the act and provide an alternate solution for the issues prompting the Chinese Exclusion Act.

COLLABORATIVE LEARNING

Organize into small groups and discuss stories of immigration or the experiences of recent immigrants to the U.S. that you have heard or read about. With the group, create a multimedia presentation of these stories. Use pictures, text, and sound to represent the stories.

HISTORY

MULTIMEDIA CONNECTIONS

Ellis Island

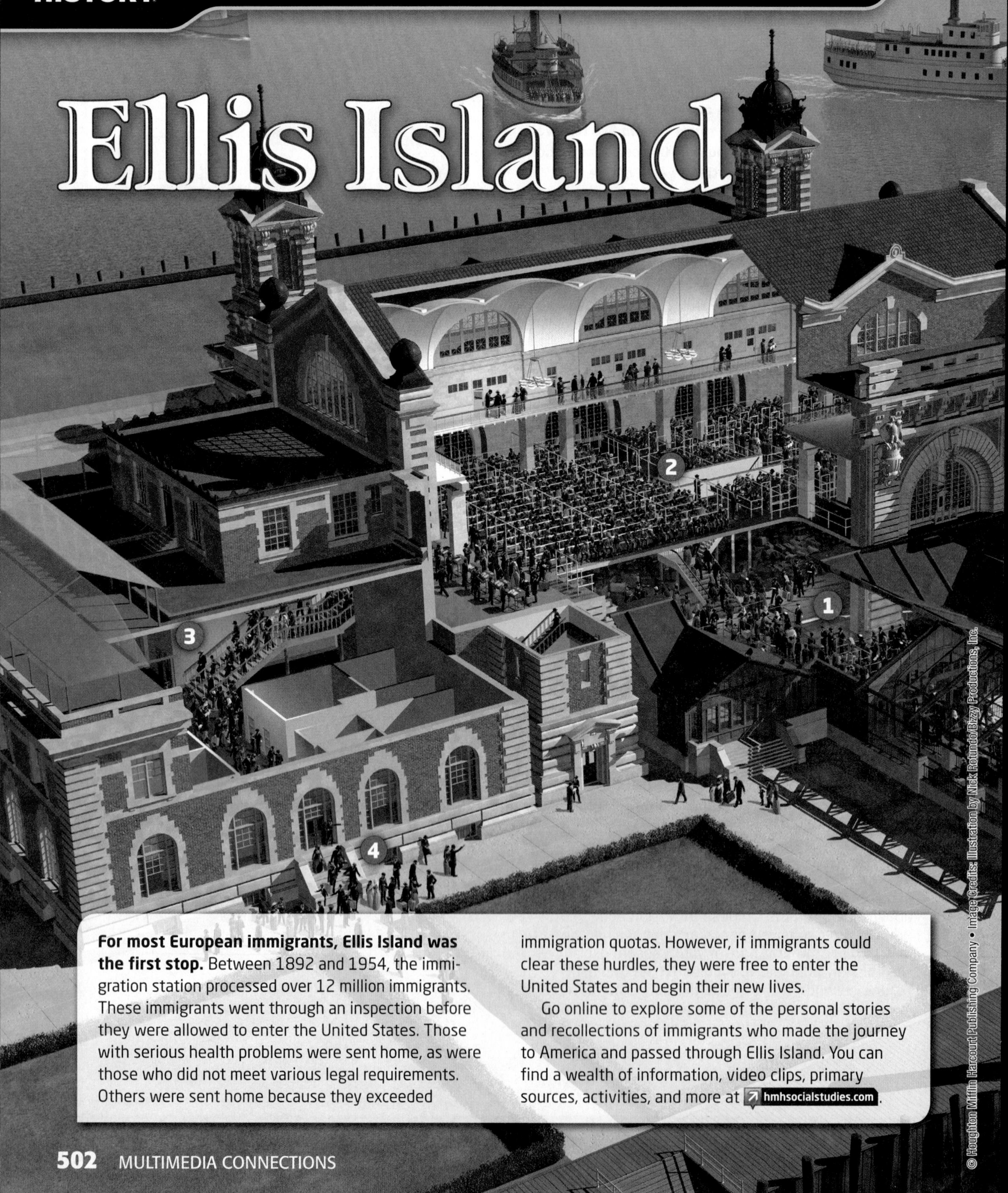

For most European immigrants, Ellis Island was the first stop. Between 1892 and 1954, the immigration station processed over 12 million immigrants. These immigrants went through an inspection before they were allowed to enter the United States. Those with serious health problems were sent home, as were those who did not meet various legal requirements. Others were sent home because they exceeded immigration quotas. However, if immigrants could clear these hurdles, they were free to enter the United States and begin their new lives.

Go online to explore some of the personal stories and recollections of immigrants who made the journey to America and passed through Ellis Island. You can find a wealth of information, video clips, primary sources, activities, and more at hmhsocialstudies.com.

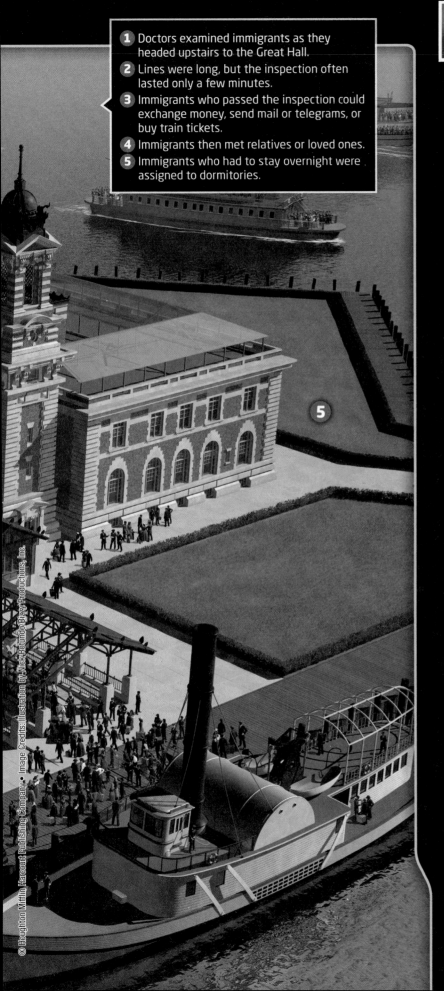

1 Doctors examined immigrants as they headed upstairs to the Great Hall.

2 Lines were long, but the inspection often lasted only a few minutes.

3 Immigrants who passed the inspection could exchange money, send mail or telegrams, or buy train tickets.

4 Immigrants then met relatives or loved ones.

5 Immigrants who had to stay overnight were assigned to dormitories.

5

CLICK THROUGH
INTER ACTIVITIES
hmhsocialstudies.com

The Golden Door

Watch the video to see how and why immigrants traveled to the United States.

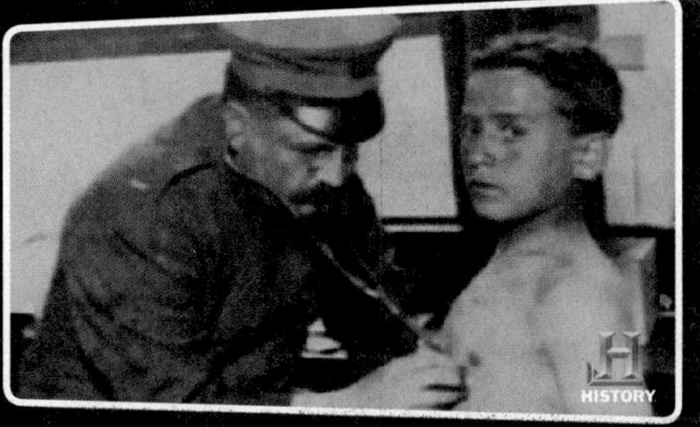

Examination

Watch the video to see the physical examination that immigrants experienced at Ellis Island.

Quotas

Watch the video to see how immigration quotas affected immigrants trying to come to the United States.

CHAPTER 16

LIFE AT THE TURN OF THE 20TH CENTURY

Essential Question

What were the significant trends in areas such as technology, education, race relations, and mass culture at the turn of the 20th century?

ALABAMA COURSE OF STUDY

15 Compare congressional and presidential reconstruction plans, including African-American political participation.

• Explaining the impact of Jim Crow laws and Plessey versus Ferguson on the social and political structure of the New South after Reconstruction.

The World's Columbian Exposition, commemorating the 400th anniversary of Columbus sailing to the Americas.

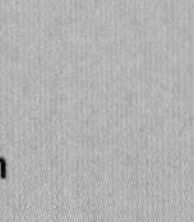

USA

1883 Construction of the Brooklyn Bridge is completed.

1888 Electric trolleys are first introduced.

1892 Ida B. Wells crusades against lynching.

1896 Supreme Court establishes "separate-but-equal" doctrine in *Plessy* v. *Ferguson*.

1880 | 1885 | 1890 | 1895

WORLD

1878 Bicycle touring club is founded in Europe.

1884 Fifteen-nation conference on the division of Africa convenes in Berlin.

1889 Barnum & Bailey Circus opens in London.

Image Credits: (bkgd), Stock Montage; (bl), (br), The Granger Collection, New York

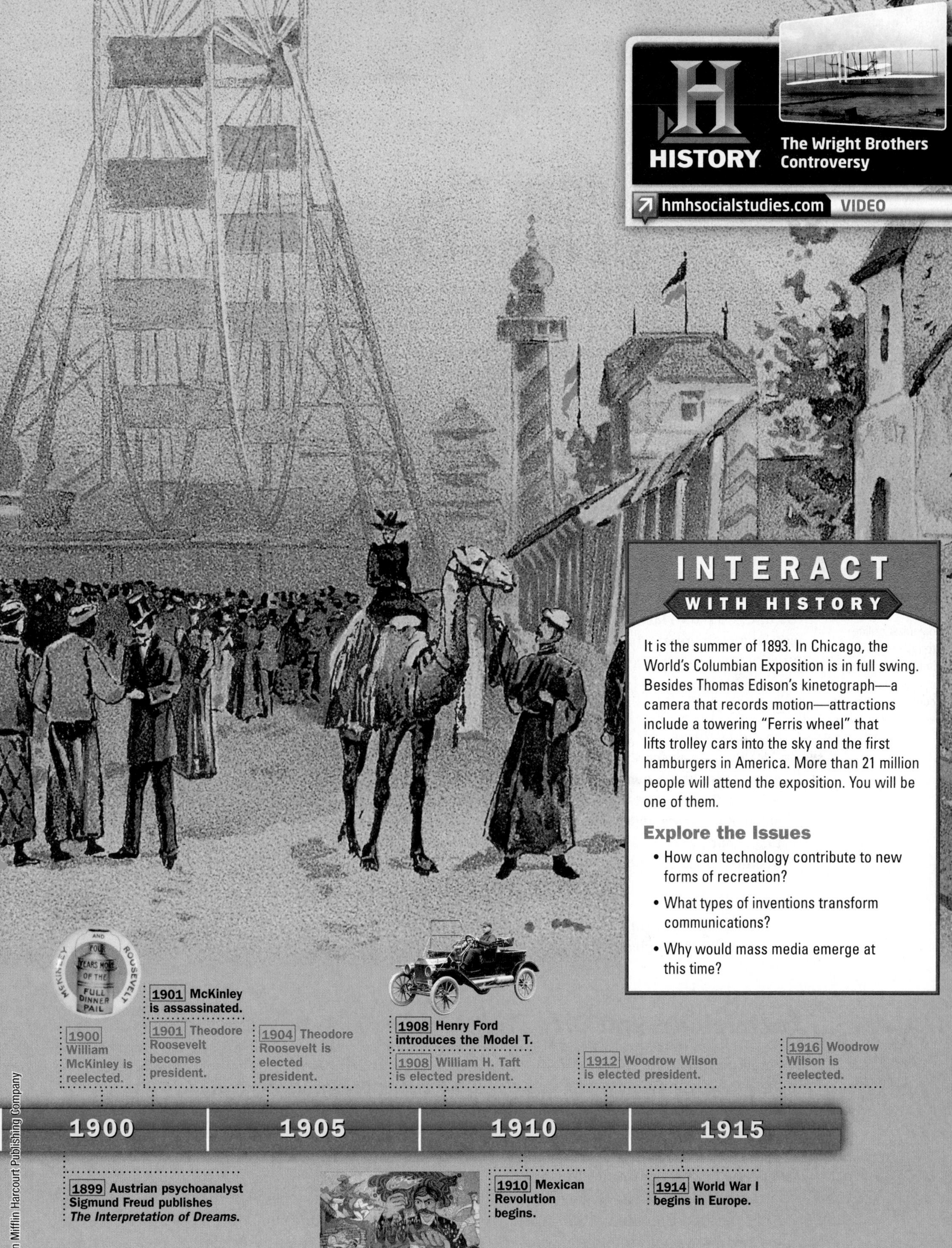

HISTORY

The Wright Brothers Controversy

hmhsocialstudies.com VIDEO

INTERACT WITH HISTORY

It is the summer of 1893. In Chicago, the World's Columbian Exposition is in full swing. Besides Thomas Edison's kinetograph—a camera that records motion—attractions include a towering "Ferris wheel" that lifts trolley cars into the sky and the first hamburgers in America. More than 21 million people will attend the exposition. You will be one of them.

Explore the Issues

- How can technology contribute to new forms of recreation?
- What types of inventions transform communications?
- Why would mass media emerge at this time?

1901 McKinley is assassinated.

1900 William McKinley is reelected.

1901 Theodore Roosevelt becomes president.

1904 Theodore Roosevelt is elected president.

1908 Henry Ford introduces the Model T.

1908 William H. Taft is elected president.

1912 Woodrow Wilson is elected president.

1916 Woodrow Wilson is reelected.

1900 | 1905 | 1910 | 1915

1899 Austrian psychoanalyst Sigmund Freud publishes *The Interpretation of Dreams*.

1910 Mexican Revolution begins.

1914 World War I begins in Europe.

Image Credits: (bkgd), Stock Montage; (bl), ©Bettmann/Corbis; (br), ©Three Lions/Hulton Archive/Getty Images; (bc), ©Charles & Josette Lenars/Corbis

Science and Urban Life

MAIN IDEA

Advances in science and technology helped solve urban problems, including overcrowding.

WHY IT MATTERS NOW

American cities continue to depend on the results of scientific and technological research.

Terms & Names

- **Louis Sullivan**
- **Daniel Burnham**
- **Frederick Law Olmsted**
- **Orville and Wilbur Wright**
- **George Eastman**

One American's Story

hmhsocialstudies.com TAKING NOTES

Use the graphic organizer online to take notes on important changes in city design, communications, and transportation.

The Brooklyn Bridge, connecting Brooklyn to the island of Manhattan in New York City, opened in 1883. It took 14 years to build. Each day, laborers descended to work in a caisson, or watertight chamber, that took them deep beneath the East River. E. F. Farrington, a mechanic who worked on the bridge, described the working conditions.

A PERSONAL VOICE E. F. FARRINGTON

"Inside the caisson everything wore an unreal, weird appearance. There was a confused sensation in the head . . . What with the flaming lights, the deep shadows, the confusing noise of hammers, drills, and chains, the half-naked forms flitting about . . . one might, if of a poetic temperament, get a realizing sense of Dante's Inferno."

—quoted in *The Great Bridge*

In 1883, New Yorkers celebrated the opening of the world's longest suspension bridge, the 1,595-foot-long Brooklyn Bridge.

Four years later, trains ran across the bridge 24 hours a day and carried more than 30 million travelers each year.

Technology and City Life

Engineering innovations, such as the Brooklyn Bridge, laid the groundwork for modern American life. Cities in every industrial area of the country expanded both outward and upward. In 1870, only 25 American cities had populations of 50,000 or more; by 1890, 58 cities could make that claim. By the turn of the 20th century, due to the increasing number of industrial jobs, four out of ten Americans made their homes in cities.

In response to these changes, technological advances began to meet the nation's needs for communication, transportation, and space. One remedy for more urban space was to build toward the sky.

SKYSCRAPERS Architects were able to design taller buildings because of two factors: the invention of elevators and the development of internal steel skeletons to bear the weight of buildings. In 1890–1891, architect **Louis Sullivan** designed the ten-story Wainwright Building in St. Louis. He called the new breed of skyscraper a "proud and soaring thing." The tall building's appearance was graceful because its steel framework supported both floors and walls.

The skyscraper became America's greatest contribution to architecture, "a new thing under the sun," according to the architect Frank Lloyd Wright, who studied under Sullivan. Skyscrapers solved the practical problem of how to make the best use of limited and expensive space. The unusual form of another skyscraper, the Flatiron Building, seemed perfect for its location at one of New York's busiest intersections. **Daniel Burnham** designed this slender 285-foot tower in 1902. The Flatiron Building and other new buildings served as symbols of a rich and optimistic society. (A)

MAIN IDEA

Analyzing Causes
(A) How did new technologies make the building of skyscrapers practical?

ELECTRIC TRANSIT As skyscrapers expanded upward, changes in transportation allowed cities to spread outward. Before the Civil War, horses had drawn the earliest streetcars over iron rails embedded in city streets. In some cities during the 1870s and 1880s, underground moving cables powered streetcar lines. Electricity, however, transformed urban transportation.

In 1888 Richmond, Virginia, became the first American city to electrify its urban transit. Other cities followed. By the turn of the twentieth century, intricate networks of electric streetcars—also called trolley cars—ran from outlying neighborhoods to downtown offices and department stores.

New railroad lines also fed the growth of suburbs, allowing residents to commute to downtown jobs. New York's northern suburbs alone supplied 100,000 commuters each day to the central business district.

A few large cities moved their streetcars far above street level, creating elevated or "el" trains. Other cities, like New York, built subways by moving their rail lines underground. These streetcars, elevated trains, and subways enabled cities to annex suburban developments that mushroomed along the advancing transportation routes. (B)

MAIN IDEA

Summarizing
(B) How did electric transit impact urban life?

ENGINEERING AND URBAN PLANNING Steel-cable suspension bridges, like the Brooklyn Bridge, also brought cities' sections closer together. Sometimes these bridges provided recreational opportunities. In his design for the Brooklyn Bridge, for example, John Augustus Roebling provided an elevated promenade whose "principal use will be to allow people of leisure, and old and young invalids, to promenade over the bridge on fine days." This need for open spaces in the midst of crowded commercial cities inspired the emerging science of urban planning.

Vocabulary
promenade: a public place for walking

City planners sought to restore a measure of serenity to the environment by designing recreational areas. Landscape architect **Frederick Law Olmsted** spearheaded the movement for planned urban parks.

In 1857 Olmsted, along with English-born architect Calvert Vaux, helped draw up a plan for "Greensward," which was selected to become Central Park, in New York City. Olmsted envisioned the park as a rustic haven in the center of the busy city. The finished park featured boating and

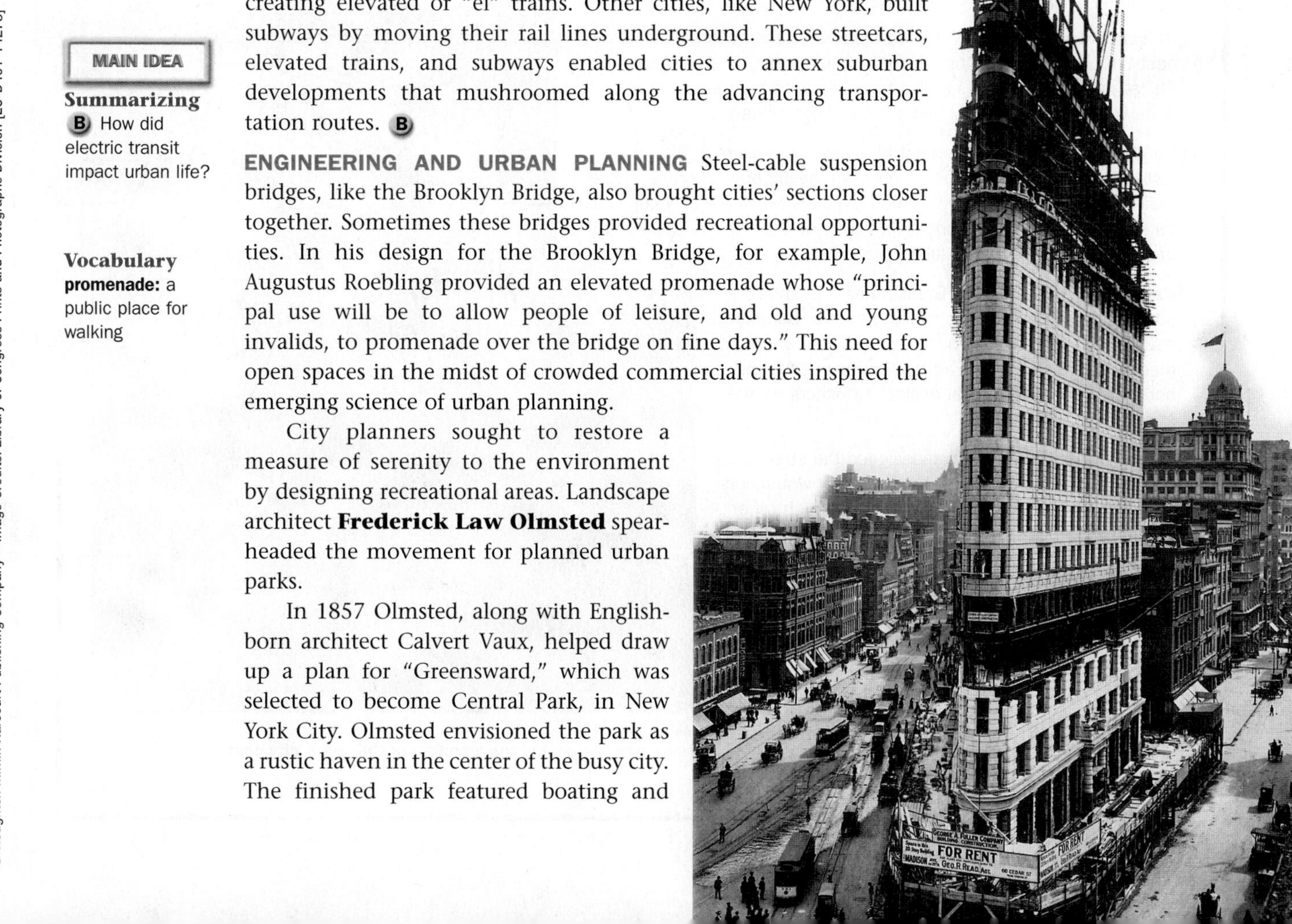

The Flatiron Building, shown here under construction, stands at the intersection of Fifth Avenue and 23rd Street in New York City. ▼

tennis facilities, a zoo, and bicycle paths. Olmsted hoped that the park's beauty would soothe the city's inhabitants and let them enjoy a "natural" setting.

A PERSONAL VOICE FREDERICK LAW OLMSTED

> **"The main object and justification [of the park] is simply to produce a certain influence in the minds of people and through this to make life in the city healthier and happier. The character of this influence . . . is to be produced by means of scenes, through observation of which the mind may be more or less lifted out of moods and habits."**
>
> —quoted in *Frederick Law Olmsted's New York*

In the 1870s, Olmsted planned landscaping for Washington, D.C., and St. Louis. He also drew the initial designs for "the Emerald Necklace," Boston's parks system. Boston's Back Bay area, originally a 450-acre swamp, was drained and developed by urban planners into an area of elegant streets and cultural attractions, including Olmsted's parks.

CITY PLANNING By contrast, Chicago, with its explosive growth from 30,000 people in 1850 to 300,000 in 1870, represented a nightmare of unregulated expansion. Fortunately for the city, a local architect, Daniel Burnham, was intrigued

History Through *Architecture*

THE CHICAGO PLAN

This map from Daniel Burnham's original plan of Chicago looks deceptively like an ordinary map today. But at the time, it was almost revolutionary in its vision, and it inspired city planners all over the country.

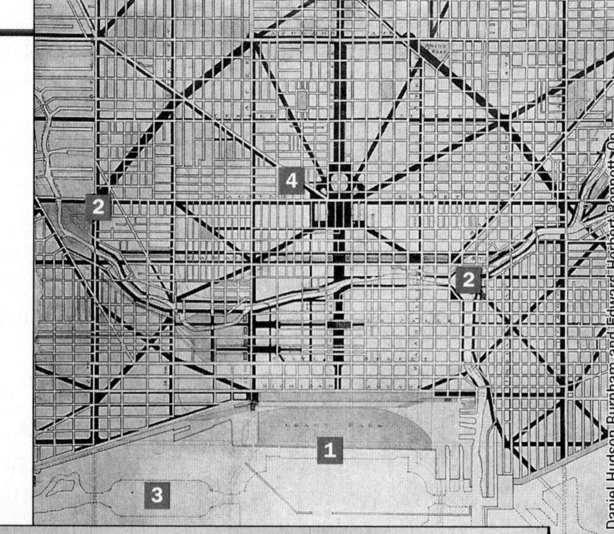

1 **Chicago's Lakefront** First, Burnham designed the "White City" to host the 1893 World's Columbian Exposition. His greatest legacy to Chicago may have been his idea for a lakefront park system, complete with beaches, playing fields, and playgrounds.

2 **Neighborhood Parks** Though not all cities could claim a lakefront vista for recreation, most cities sprinkled neighborhood parks where their residents needed them. Urban planners provided for local parks—such as Lincoln Park in Chicago—so that "the sweet breath of plant life" would be available to everyone.

3 **Harbors For Cities** On the Great Lakes, the shipping business depended on accessible harbors. Burnham saw the advantage of harbors for recreation and commercial purposes, but he advocated moving the harbors away from the central business districts to free space for public use.

4 **The Civic Center** Burnham redesigned the street pattern to create a group of long streets that would converge on a grand plaza, a practice reflected in other American cities. The convergence of major thoroughfares at a city's center helped create a unified city from a host of neighborhoods.

▲ **Unity was the goal of the architect of Chicago's city center.**

SKILLBUILDER Interpreting Visual Sources

1. Why did Chicago's location make it a good choice for urban planning?
2. How was Chicago's importance as a shipping center maintained?

SEE SKILLBUILDER HANDBOOK, PAGE R23.

by the prospect of remaking the city. His motto was "Make no little plans. They have no magic to stir men's blood." He oversaw the transformation of a swampy area near Lake Michigan into a glistening White City for Chicago's 1893 World's Columbian Exposition. Majestic exhibition halls, statues, the first Ferris wheel, and a lagoon greeted more than 21 million visitors who came to the city.

Many urban planners saw in Burnham's White City glorious visions of future cities. Burnham, however, left Chicago an even more important legacy: an overall plan for the city, crowned by elegant parks strung along Lake Michigan. As a result, Chicago's lakefront today features curving banks of grass and sandy beaches instead of a jumbled mass of piers and warehouses. C

MAIN IDEA

Summarizing
C List three major changes in cities near the turn of the century. What effect did each have?

THE GARDEN CITY

Urban planning in the United States had European counterparts. In *Tomorrow: A Peaceful Path to Social Reform* (1898), for example, the British city planner Ebenezer Howard wrote of a planned residential community called a garden city.

Howard wanted to combine the benefits of urban life with easy access to nature. His city plan was based on concentric circles—with a town at the center and a wide circle of rural land on the perimeter. The town center included a garden, concert hall, museum, theater, library, and hospital.

The circle around the town center included a park, a shopping center, a conservatory, a residential area, and industry. Six wide avenues radiated out from the town center. In 1903, Letchworth, England served as the model for Howard's garden city.

New Technologies

New developments in communication brought the nation closer together. In addition to a railroad network that now spanned the nation, advances in printing, aviation, and photography helped to speed the transfer of information.

A REVOLUTION IN PRINTING By 1890, the literacy rate in the United States had risen to nearly 90 percent. Publishers turned out ever-increasing numbers of books, magazines, and newspapers to meet the growing demand of the reading public. A series of technological advances in printing aided their efforts.

American mills began to produce huge quantities of cheap paper from wood pulp. The new paper proved durable enough to withstand high-speed presses. The electrically powered web-perfecting press, for example, printed on both sides of a continuous paper roll, rather than on just one side. It then cut, folded, and counted the pages as they came down the line. Faster production and lower costs made newspapers and magazines more affordable. People could now buy newspapers for a penny a copy.

AIRPLANES In the early 20th century, brothers **Orville** and **Wilbur Wright,** bicycle manufacturers from Dayton, Ohio, experimented with new engines powerful enough to keep "heavier-than-air" craft aloft. First the Wright brothers built a glider. Then they commissioned a four-cylinder internal combustion engine, chose a propeller, and designed a biplane with a 40′4″ wingspan. Their first successful flight—on December 17, 1903, at Kitty Hawk, North Carolina—covered 120 feet and lasted 12 seconds. Orville later described the take-off.

Vocabulary
internal combustion engine: an engine in which fuel is burned within the engine rather than in an external furnace

A PERSONAL VOICE ORVILLE WRIGHT

> **"After running the motor a few minutes to heat it up, I released the wire that held the machine to the track, and the machine started forward into the wind. Wilbur ran at the side of the machine . . . to balance it. . . . Unlike the start on the 14th, made in a calm, the machine, facing a 27-mile wind, started very slowly. . . . One of the life-saving men snapped the camera for us, taking a picture just as the machine had reached the end of the track and had risen to a height of about two feet."**
>
> —quoted in *Smithsonian Frontiers of Flight*

Orville (*right*) and Wilbur Wright at home in Dayton, Ohio, in 1909.

Science & Technology

AVIATION PIONEERS

In 1892, Orville and Wilbur Wright opened a bicycle shop in Dayton, Ohio. They used the profits to fund experiments in aeronautics, the construction of aircraft. In 1903, the Wright brothers took a gasoline-powered airplane that they had designed to a sandy hill outside Kitty Hawk, North Carolina.

The airplane was powered by a 4-cylinder 12-horse-power piston engine, designed and constructed by the bicycle shop's mechanic, Charles Taylor. The piston—a solid cylinder fit snugly into a hollow cylinder that moves back and forth under pressure—was standard until jet-propelled aircraft came into service in the 1940s. ▶

The engine is the heaviest component in airplane construction. The design of lighter engines was the most important development in early aviation history. ▶

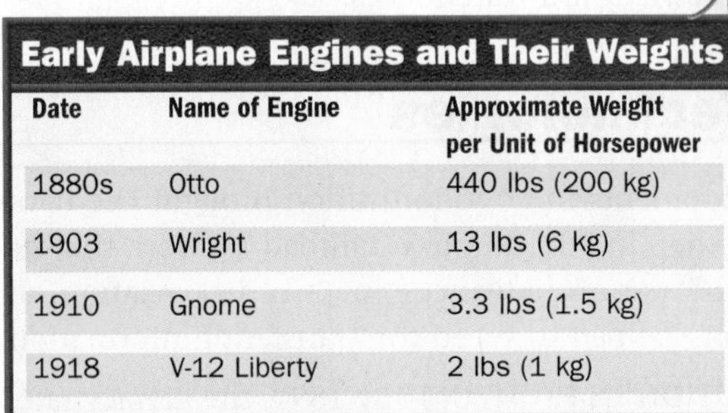

Early Airplane Engines and Their Weights

Date	Name of Engine	Approximate Weight per Unit of Horsepower
1880s	Otto	440 lbs (200 kg)
1903	Wright	13 lbs (6 kg)
1910	Gnome	3.3 lbs (1.5 kg)
1918	V-12 Liberty	2 lbs (1 kg)
1944	Wright Cyclone	1.1 lbs (0.5 kg)

Source: *The History of Invention*, Trevor I. Williams

VIDEO
The Wright Brothers Controversy

◀ **On December 17, Orville Wright made the first successful flight of a powered aircraft in history. The public paid little attention. But within two years, the brothers were making 30-minute flights. By 1908, the pioneer aviators had signed a contract for production of the Wright airplane with the U.S. Army.**

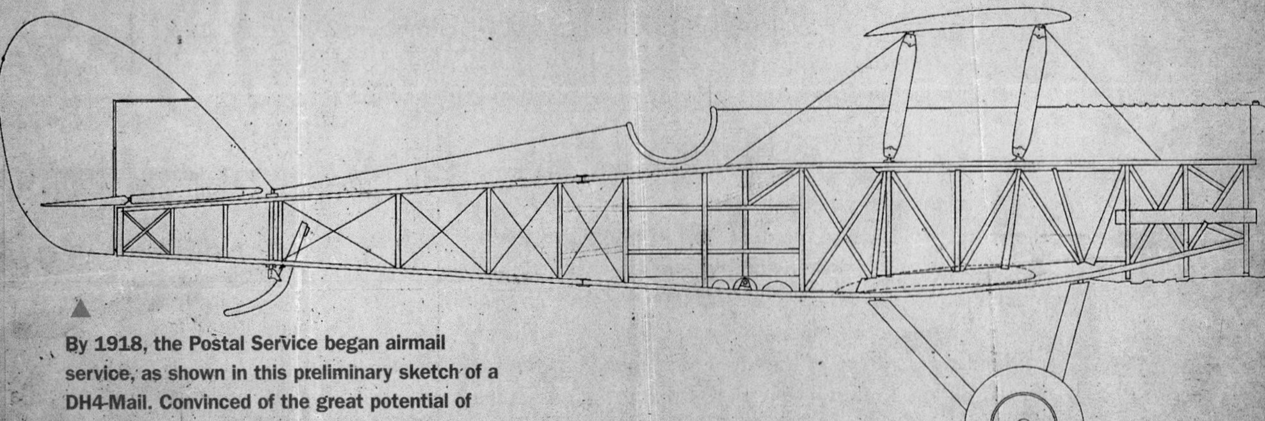

▲ **By 1918, the Postal Service began airmail service, as shown in this preliminary sketch of a DH4-Mail. Convinced of the great potential of flight, the government established the first transcontinental airmail service in 1920.**

Within two years, the Wright brothers had increased their flights to 24 miles. By 1920, convinced of the great potential of flight, the U.S. government had established the first transcontinental airmail service.

PHOTOGRAPHY EXPLOSION Before the 1880s, photography was a professional activity. Because of the time required to take a picture and the weight of the equipment, a photographer could not shoot a moving object. In addition, photographers had to develop their shots immediately.

New techniques eliminated the need to develop pictures right away. **George Eastman** developed a series of more convenient alternatives to the heavy glass plates previously used. Now, instead of carrying their darkrooms around with them, photographers could use flexible film, coated with gelatin emulsions, and could send their film to a studio for processing. When professional photographers were slow to begin using the new film, Eastman decided to aim his product at the masses.

In 1888, Eastman introduced his Kodak camera. The purchase price of $25 included a 100-picture roll of film. After taking the pictures, the photographer would send the camera back to Eastman's Rochester, New York, factory. For $10, the pictures were developed and returned with the camera reloaded. Easily held and operated, the Kodak prompted millions of Americans to become amateur photographers. The camera also helped to create the field of photojournalism. Reporters could now photograph events as they occurred. When the Wright brothers first flew their simple airplane at Kitty Hawk, an amateur photographer captured the first successful flight on film.

KEY PLAYER

GEORGE EASTMAN
1854–1932

In 1877, when George Eastman took up photography as a hobby, he had to lug more than 100 pounds of equipment for one day's outing. To lighten his load, he replaced heavy glass plates with film that could be rolled onto a spool.

In 1888, Eastman sold his first roll-film camera. Eastman called his new camera (shown at left) the Kodak, because the made-up name was short and memorable. It was popularized by the slogan "You Press the Button, We Do the Rest."

SECTION 1 ASSESSMENT

1. **TERMS & NAMES** For each term or name, write a sentence explaining its significance.
   - **Louis Sullivan**
   - **Daniel Burnham**
   - **Frederick Law Olmsted**
   - **Orville and Wilbur Wright**
   - **George Eastman**

MAIN IDEA

2. **TAKING NOTES**
   Using a three-column chart, such as the one below, list three important changes in city design, communication, and transportation.

City Design	Communication	Transportation
1.	1.	1.
2.	2.	2.
3.	3.	3.

Which change had the greatest impact on urban life? Why?

CRITICAL THINKING

3. **HYPOTHESIZING**
   If you had been an urban planner at the turn of the century, what new ideas would you have included in your plan for the ideal city?
   Think About:
   - Olmsted's plans for Central Park
   - Burnham's ideas for Chicago
   - the concept of the garden city

4. **EVALUATING**
   Which scientific or technological development described in this section had the greatest impact on American culture? Use details from the text to justify your choice.

5. **SUMMARIZING**
   How did bridge building contribute to the growth of cities?

SECTION 2

Expanding Public Education

MAIN IDEA	WHY IT MATTERS NOW	Terms & Names
Reforms in public education led to a rise in national literacy and the promotion of public education.	**The public education system is the foundation of the democratic ideals of American society.**	**• Booker T. Washington • Tuskegee Normal and Industrial Institute • W. E. B. Du Bois • Niagara Movement**

One American's Story

hmhsocialstudies.com
TAKING NOTES
Use the graphic organizer online to take notes on developments in education at the turn of the 20th century.

William Torrey Harris was an educational reformer who saw the public schools as a great instrument "to lift all classes of people into . . . civilized life." As U.S. commissioner of education from 1889 to 1906, Harris promoted the ideas of great educators like Horace Mann and John Dewey—particularly the belief that schools exist for the children and not the teachers. Schools, according to Harris, should properly prepare students for full participation in community life.

A Personal Voice WILLIAM TORREY HARRIS

"Every [educational] method must . . . be looked at from two points of view: first, its capacity to secure the development of rationality or of the true adjustment of the individual to the social whole; and, second, its capacity to strengthen the individuality of the pupil and avoid the danger of obliterating the personality of the child by securing blind obedience in place of intelligent cooperation, and by mechanical memorizing in place of rational insight."

—quoted in *Public Schools and Moral Education*

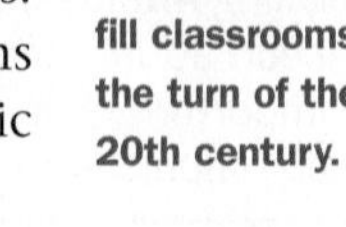

Compulsory attendance laws, though slow to be enforced, helped fill classrooms at the turn of the 20th century.

Many other middle-class reformers agreed with Harris and viewed the public schools as training grounds for employment and citizenship. People believed that economic development depended on scientific and technological knowledge. As a result, they viewed education as a key to greater security and social status. Others saw the public schools as the best opportunity to assimilate the millions of immigrants entering American society. Most people also believed that public education was necessary for a stable and prosperous democratic nation.

Expanding Public Education

Although most states had established public schools by the Civil War, many school-age children still received no formal schooling. The majority of students who went to school left within four years, and few went to high school.

SCHOOLS FOR CHILDREN Between 1865 and 1895, states passed laws requiring 12 to 16 weeks annually of school attendance by students between the ages of 8 and 14. The curriculum emphasized reading, writing, and arithmetic. However, the emphasis on rote memorization and the uneven quality of teachers drew criticism. Strict rules and physical punishment made many students miserable.

One 13-year-old boy explained to a Chicago school inspector why he hid in a warehouse basement instead of going to school.

A Personal Voice

"**They hits ye if yer don't learn, and they hits ye if ye whisper, and they hits ye if ye have string in yer pocket, and they hits ye if yer seat squeaks, and they hits ye if ye don't stan' up in time, and they hits ye if yer late, and they hits ye if ye ferget the page.**"

—anonymous schoolboy quoted in *The One Best System*

MAIN IDEA

Drawing Conclusions

A Why did American children begin attending school at a younger age?

In spite of such problems, children began attending school at a younger age. Kindergartens, which had been created outside the public school system to offer childcare for employed mothers, became increasingly popular. The number of kindergartens surged from 200 in 1880 to 3,000 in 1900, and, under the guidance of William Torrey Harris, public school systems began to add kindergartens to their programs. **A**

Although the pattern in public education in this era was one of growth, opportunities differed sharply for white and black students. In 1880, about 62 percent of white children attended elementary school, compared to about 34 percent of African-American children. Not until the 1940s would public school education become available to the majority of black children living in the South.

THE GROWTH OF HIGH SCHOOLS In the new industrial age, the economy demanded advanced technical and managerial skills. Moreover, business leaders like Andrew Carnegie pointed out that keeping workers loyal to capitalism required society to "provide ladders upon which the aspiring can rise."

By early 1900, more than half a million students attended high school. The curriculum expanded to include courses in science, civics, and social studies. And new vocational courses prepared male graduates for industrial jobs in drafting, carpentry, and mechanics, and female graduates for office work.

Expanding Education/Increasing Literacy

Year	Students Enrolled	Literacy in English (% of Population age 10 and over)
1871	7.6 million	80%
1880	9.9 million	83%
1890	12.7 million	87%
1900	15.5 million	89%
1910	17.8 million	92%
1920	21.6 million	94%

(figure) =1,000,000 students

Sources: *Statistical Abstract of the United States, 1921; Historical Statistics of the United States.*

SKILLBUILDER
Interpreting Graphs

1. By how much did the illiteracy rate drop from 1871 to 1920?
2. Does the number of immigrants during this period make the reduction more or less impressive? Why?

RACIAL DISCRIMINATION African Americans were mostly excluded from public secondary education. In 1890, fewer than 1 percent of black teenagers attended high school. More than two-thirds of these students went to private schools, which received no government financial support. By 1910, about 3 percent of African Americans between the ages of 15 and 19 attended high school, but a majority of these students still attended private schools.

EDUCATION FOR IMMIGRANTS Unlike African Americans, immigrants were encouraged to go to school. Of the nearly 10 million European immigrants settled in the United States between 1860 and 1890, many were Jewish people fleeing poverty and systematic oppression in eastern Europe. Most immigrants sent their children to America's free public schools, where they quickly became "Americanized." Years after she became a citizen, the Russian Jewish immigrant Mary Antin recalled the large numbers of non-English-speaking immigrant children. By the end of the school year, they could recite "patriotic verses in honor of George Washington and Abraham Lincoln . . . with plenty of enthusiasm."

Some people resented the suppression of their native languages in favor of English. Catholics were especially concerned because many public school systems had mandatory readings from the (Protestant) King James Version of the Bible. Catholic communities often set up parochial schools to give their children a Catholic education.

Thousands of adult immigrants attended night school to learn English and to qualify for American citizenship. Employers often offered daytime programs to Americanize their workers. At his Model T plant in Highland Park, Michigan, Henry Ford established a "Sociology Department," because "men of many nations must be taught American ways, the English language, and the right way to live." Ford's ideas were not universally accepted. Labor activists often protested that Ford's educational goals were aimed at weakening the trade union movement by teaching workers not to confront management. B

Vocabulary
parochial school: a school supported by a church parish

MAIN IDEA
Summarizing
B What institutions encouraged European immigrants to become assimilated?

NOW & THEN

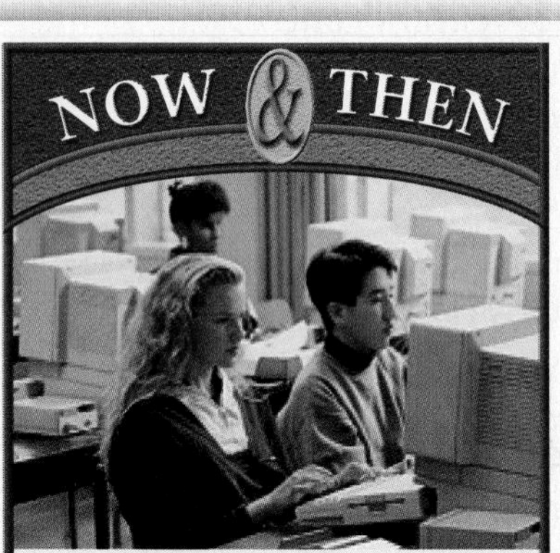

TECHNOLOGY AND SCHOOLS

In 1922,Thomas Edison predicted that motion pictures would eventually replace textbooks. More recently, it has been predicted that computers will replace traditional classrooms and texts. Computers are used for video course sharing, in which students in many locations participate in the same class. Teachers are using electronic interactive whiteboards to help them lead and record presentations and discussions. Students are also using computers to access and share scientific data and to communicate with peers around the world.

Expanding Higher Education

Although the number of students attending high school had increased by the turn of the century, only a minority of Americans had high school diplomas. At the same time, an even smaller minority—only 2.3 percent—of America's young people attended colleges and universities.

CHANGES IN UNIVERSITIES Between 1880 and 1920, college enrollments more than quadrupled. And colleges instituted major changes in curricula and admission policies. Industrial development changed the nation's educational needs. The research university emerged—offering courses in modern languages, the physical sciences, and the new disciplines of psychology and sociology. Professional schools in law and medicine were established. Private colleges and universities required entrance exams, but some state universities began to admit students by using the high school diploma as the entrance requirement.

HIGHER EDUCATION FOR AFRICAN AMERICANS After the Civil War, thousands of freed African Americans pursued higher education, despite their exclusion from white institutions. With the help of the Freedmen's Bureau and other groups, blacks founded Howard, Atlanta, and Fisk Universities, all of which opened between 1865 and 1868. Private donors could not, however, financially support or educate a sufficient number of black college graduates to meet the needs of the segregated communities. By 1900, out of about 9 million African Americans, only 3,880 were in attendance at colleges or professional schools. C

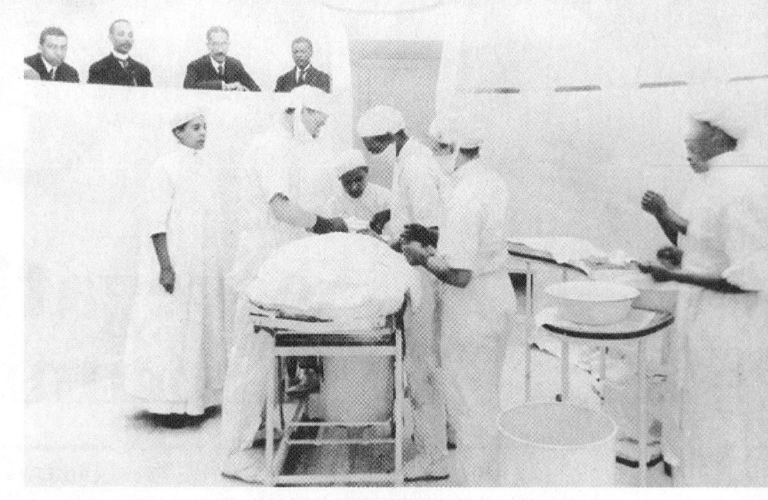

▲ Medical students and their professors work in the operating theater of the Moorland-Spingarn Research Center at Howard University.

MAIN IDEA

Synthesizing

C Describe the state of higher education for African Americans at the turn of the century.

The prominent African American educator, **Booker T. Washington,** believed that racism would end once blacks acquired useful labor skills and proved their economic value to society. Washington, who was born enslaved, graduated from Virginia's Hampton Institute. By 1881, he headed the **Tuskegee Normal and Industrial Institute,** now called Tuskegee University, in Alabama. Tuskegee aimed to equip African Americans with teaching diplomas and useful skills in agricultural, domestic, or mechanical work. "No race," Washington said, "can prosper till it learns that there is as much dignity in tilling a field as in writing a poem."

By contrast, **W. E. B. Du Bois,** the first African American to receive a doctorate from Harvard (in 1895), strongly disagreed with Washington's gradual approach. In 1905, Du Bois founded the **Niagara Movement,** which insisted that blacks should seek a liberal arts education so that the African-American community would have well-educated leaders.

Du Bois proposed that a group of educated blacks, the most "talented tenth" of the community, attempt to achieve immediate inclusion into mainstream American life. "We are Americans, not only by birth and by citizenship," Du Bois argued, "but by our political ideals. . . . And the greatest of those ideals is that ALL MEN ARE CREATED EQUAL."

By the turn of the 20th century, millions of people received the education they needed to cope with a rapidly changing world. At the same time, however, racial discrimination remained a thorn in the flesh of American society.

SECTION 2 ASSESSMENT

1. **TERMS & NAMES** For each term or name, write a sentence explaining its significance.
   - **Booker T. Washington**
   - **Tuskegee Normal and Industrial Institute**
   - **W. E. B. Du Bois**
   - **Niagara Movement**

MAIN IDEA

2. **TAKING NOTES**
   In a chart like the one below, list at least three developments in education at the turn of the 20th century and their major results.

Development	Result
1.	
2.	
3.	

Which educational development do you think was most important? Explain your choice.

CRITICAL THINKING

3. **HYPOTHESIZING**
   How might the economy and culture of the United States have been different without the expansion of public schools? **Think About:**
   - the goals of public schools and whether those goals have been met
   - why people supported expanding public education
   - the impact of public schools on the development of private schools

4. **COMPARING**
   Compare and contrast the views of Booker T. Washington and W. E. B. Du Bois on the subject of the education of African Americans.

SECTION 3

Segregation and Discrimination

MAIN IDEA

African Americans led the fight against voting restrictions and Jim Crow laws.

WHY IT MATTERS NOW

Today, African Americans have the legacy of a century-long battle for civil rights.

Terms & Names

- Ida B. Wells
- poll tax
- grandfather clause
- segregation
- Jim Crow laws
- *Plessy* v. *Ferguson*
- debt peonage

One American's Story

hmhsocialstudies.com TAKING NOTES

Use the graphic organizer online to take notes on important events in race relations at the turn of the 20th century.

Born into slavery shortly before emancipation, **Ida B. Wells** moved to Memphis in the early 1880s to work as a teacher. She later became an editor of a local paper. Racial justice was a persistent theme in Wells's reporting. The events of March 9, 1892 turned that theme into a crusade. Three African-American businessmen, friends of Wells, were lynched—illegally executed without trial. Wells saw lynching for what it was.

▲ Ida B. Wells moved north to continue her fight against lynching by writing, lecturing, and organizing for civil rights.

A PERSONAL VOICE IDA B. WELLS

"Thomas Moss, Calvin McDowell, and Lee Stewart had been lynched in Memphis . . . [where] no lynching had taken place before. . . . This is what opened my eyes to what lynching really was. An excuse to get rid of Negroes who were acquiring wealth and property and thus keep the race terrorized."

—quoted in *Crusade for Justice*

African Americans were not the only group to experience violence and racial discrimination. Native Americans, Mexican residents, and Chinese immigrants also encountered bitter forms of oppression, particularly in the American West.

African Americans Fight Legal Discrimination

As African Americans exercised their newly won political and social rights during Reconstruction, they faced hostile and often violent opposition from whites. African Americans eventually fell victim to laws restricting their civil rights but never stopped fighting for equality. For at least ten years after the end of Reconstruction in 1877, African Americans in the South continued to vote and occasionally to hold political office. By the turn of the 20th century, however, Southern states had adopted a broad system of legal policies of racial discrimination and devised methods to weaken African-American political power.

VOTING RESTRICTIONS All Southern states imposed new voting restrictions and denied legal equality to African Americans. Some states, for example, limited the vote to people who could read, and required registration officials to administer a literacy test to test reading. Blacks trying to vote were often asked more difficult questions than whites, or given a test in a foreign language. Officials could pass or fail applicants as they wished.

▲ This theater in Leland, Mississippi, was segregated under the Jim Crow laws.

Another requirement was the **poll tax**, an annual tax that had to be paid before qualifying to vote. Black as well as white sharecroppers were often too poor to pay the poll tax. To reinstate white voters who may have failed the literacy test or could not pay the poll tax, several Southern states added the **grandfather clause** to their constitutions. The clause stated that even if a man failed the literacy test or could not afford the poll tax, he was still entitled to vote if he, his father, or his grandfather had been eligible to vote before January 1, 1867. The date is important because before that time, freed slaves did not have the right to vote. The grandfather clause therefore did not allow them to vote.

JIM CROW LAWS During the 1870s and 1880s, the Supreme Court failed to overturn the poll tax or the grandfather clause, even though the laws undermined all federal protections for African Americans' civil rights. At the same time that blacks lost voting rights, Southern states passed racial **segregation** laws to separate white and black people in public and private facilities. These laws came to be known as **Jim Crow laws** after a popular old minstrel song that ended in the words "Jump, Jim Crow." Racial segregation was put into effect in schools, hospitals, parks, and transportation systems throughout the South.

Vocabulary
minstrel: one of a troupe of entertainers in blackface presenting a comic variety show

PLESSY* v. *FERGUSON Eventually a legal case reached the U.S. Supreme Court to test the constitutionality of segregation. In 1896, in ***Plessy* v. *Ferguson***, the Supreme Court ruled that the separation of races in public accommodations was legal and did not violate the Fourteenth Amendment. The decision established the doctrine of "separate but equal," which allowed states to maintain segregated facilities for blacks and whites as long as they provided equal service. The decision permitted legalized racial segregation for almost 60 years. (See Historic Decisions of the Supreme Court, *Plessy* v. *Ferguson*.) A

MAIN IDEA

Analyzing Effects
A How did the *Plessy* v. *Ferguson* ruling affect the civil rights of African Americans?

Turn-of-the-Century Race Relations

African Americans faced not only formal discrimination but also informal rules and customs, called racial etiquette, that regulated relationships between whites and blacks. Usually, these customs belittled and humiliated African Americans, enforcing their second-class status. For example, blacks and whites never shook hands, since shaking hands would have implied equality. Blacks also had to yield the sidewalk to white pedestrians, and black men always had to remove their hats for whites.

Some moderate reformers, like Booker T. Washington, earned support from whites. Washington suggested that whites and blacks work together for social progress.

A PERSONAL VOICE BOOKER T. WASHINGTON

"To those of the white race . . . I would repeat what I say to my own race. . . . Cast down your bucket among these people who have, without strikes and labour wars, tilled your fields, cleared your forests, builded your railroads and cities, and brought forth treasures from the bowels of the earth. . . . In all things that are purely social we can be as separate as the fingers, yet one as the hand in all things essential to mutual progress."

—Atlanta Exposition address, 1895

Washington hoped that improving the economic skills of African Americans would pave the way for long-term gains. People like Ida B. Wells and W. E. B. Du Bois, however, thought that the problems of inequality were too urgent to postpone. B

VIOLENCE African Americans and others who did not follow the racial etiquette could face severe punishment or death. All too often, blacks who were accused of violating the etiquette were lynched. Between 1882 and 1892, more than 1,400 African-American men and women were shot, burned, or hanged without trial in the South. Lynching peaked in the 1880s and 1890s but continued well into the 20th century.

HISTORICAL SPOTLIGHT

WASHINGTON *VS.* DU BOIS

Booker T. Washington argued for a gradual approach to racial equality—suggesting that "it is at the bottom of life we must begin, and not at the top."

Ten years later, W. E. B. Du Bois denounced this view of gradual equality. Du Bois demanded full social and economic equality for African Americans, declaring that "persistent manly agitation is the way to liberty."

In 1909 the Niagara Movement, founded by Du Bois in 1905, became the National Association for the Advancement of Colored People (NAACP), with Du Bois as the editor of its journal, *The Crisis*. He wrote, "We refuse to surrender . . . leadership . . . to cowards and trucklers. We are men; we will be treated as men." The NAACP continues the fight for racial equality today.

MAIN IDEA

Summarizing

B What were Booker T. Washington's views about establishing racial equality?

DISCRIMINATION IN THE NORTH Most African Americans lived in the segregated South, but by 1900, a number of blacks had moved to Northern cities. Many blacks migrated to Northern cities in search of better-paying jobs and social equality. But after their arrival, African Americans found that there was racial discrimination in the North as well. African Americans found themselves forced into segregated neighborhoods. They also faced discrimination in the workplace. Labor unions often discouraged black membership, and employers hired African-American labor only as a last resort and fired blacks before white employees.

Sometimes the competition between African Americans and working-class whites became violent, as in the New York City race riot of 1900. Violence erupted after a young black man, believing that his wife was being mistreated by a white policeman, killed the policeman. Word of the killing spread, and whites retaliated by attacking blacks. Northern blacks, however, were not alone in facing discrimination. Non-whites in the West also faced oppression. C

MAIN IDEA

Contrasting

C How did conditions for African Americans in the North differ from their circumstances in the South?

Discrimination in the West

Western communities were home to people of many backgrounds working and living side by side. Native Americans still lived in the Western territories claimed by the United States. Asian immigrants went to America's Pacific Coast in search of wealth and work. Mexicans continued to inhabit the American Southwest. African Americans were also present, especially in former slave-holding areas, such as Texas. Still, racial tensions often made life difficult.

MEXICAN WORKERS In the late 1800s, the railroads hired more Mexicans than members of any other ethnic group to construct rail lines in the Southwest.

Mexican track workers for the Southern Pacific railroad posed for this group photo taken sometime between 1910 and 1915.

Mexicans were accustomed to the region's hot, dry climate. But the work was grueling, and the railroads made them work for less money than other ethnic groups.

Mexicans were also vital to the development of mining and agriculture in the Southwest. When the 1902 National Reclamation Act gave government assistance for irrigation projects, many southwest desert areas bloomed. Mexican workers became the major labor force in the agricultural industries of the region.

Vocabulary
peon: a worker bound in servitude to a landlord creditor

Some Mexicans, however, as well as African Americans in the Southwest, were forced into **debt peonage,** a system that bound laborers into slavery in order to work off a debt to the employer. Not until 1911 did the Supreme Court declare involuntary peonage a violation of the Thirteenth Amendment.

EXCLUDING THE CHINESE By 1880, more than 100,000 Chinese immigrants lived in the United States. White people's fear of job competition with the Chinese immigrants often pushed the Chinese into segregated schools and neighborhoods. As you have read, strong opposition to Chinese immigration developed, and not only in the West.

Racial discrimination posed terrible legal and economic problems for nonwhites throughout the United States at the turn of the century. More people, however, whites in particular, had leisure time for new recreational activities, as well as money to spend on a growing arrray of consumer products.

SECTION 3 ASSESSMENT

1. **TERMS & NAMES** For each term or name, write a sentence explaining its significance.
   - **Ida B. Wells**
   - **poll tax**
   - **grandfather clause**
   - **segregation**
   - **Jim Crow laws**
   - ***Plessy* v. *Ferguson***
   - **debt peonage**

MAIN IDEA

2. **TAKING NOTES**
Review the section, and find five key events to place on a time line as shown.

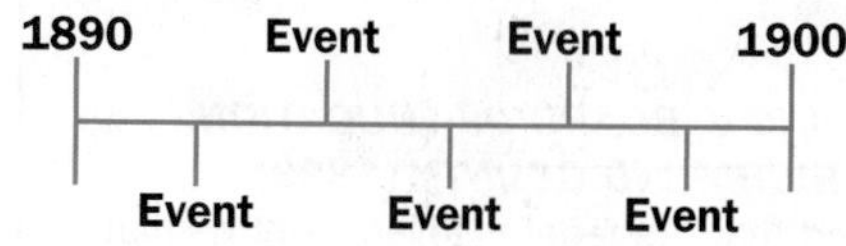

Which of these events do you think was most important? Why?

CRITICAL THINKING

3. **IDENTIFYING PROBLEMS**
How did segregation and discrimination affect the lives of African Americans at the turn of the 20th century?

4. **COMPARING**
What did some African-American leaders do to fight discrimination?

5. **CONTRASTING**
How did the challenges and opportunities for Mexicans in the United States differ from those for African Americans? **Think About:**
   - the types of work available to each group
   - the effects of government policies on each group
   - the effect of the legal system on each group

PLESSY v. *FERGUSON* (1896)

ORIGINS OF THE CASE In 1892, Homer Plessy took a seat in the "Whites Only" car of a train and refused to move. He was arrested, tried, and convicted in the District Court of New Orleans for breaking Louisiana's segregation law. Plessy appealed, claiming that he had been denied equal protection under the law. The Supreme Court handed down its decision on May 18, 1896.

THE RULING **The Court ruled that separate-but-equal facilities for blacks and whites did not violate the Constitution.**

LEGAL REASONING

Plessy claimed that segregation violated his right to equal protection under the law. Moreover he claimed that, being "of mixed descent," he was entitled to "every recognition, right, privilege and immunity secured to the citizens of the United States of the white race."

Justice Henry B. Brown, writing for the majority, ruled:

> **"The object of the [Fourteenth] amendment was . . . undoubtedly to enforce the absolute equality of the two races before the law, but . . . it could not have been intended to abolish distinctions based upon color, or to enforce social, as distinguished from political equality, or a commingling of the two races upon terms unsatisfactory to either. Laws permitting, and even requiring, their separation in places where they are liable to be brought into contact do not necessarily imply the inferiority of either race to the other."**

In truth, segregation laws did perpetrate an unequal and inferior status for African Americans. Justice John Marshall Harlan understood this fact and dissented from the majority opinion. He wrote, "In respect of civil rights, all citizens are equal before the law." He condemned the majority for letting "the seeds of race hate . . . be planted under the sanction of law." He also warned that "The thin disguise of 'equal' accommodations . . . will not mislead any one, nor atone for the wrong this day done."

Justice John Marshall Harlan

LEGAL SOURCES

LEGISLATION

U.S. CONSTITUTION, FOURTEENTH AMENDMENT (1868)
"No state shall . . . deny to any person within its jurisdiction the equal protection of the laws."

LOUISIANA ACTS 1890, NO. 111
". . . that all railway companies carrying passengers in their coaches in this State, shall provide equal but separate accommodations for the white, and colored races."

RELATED CASES

CIVIL RIGHTS CASES (1883)
The Court ruled that the Fourteenth Amendment could not be used to prevent private citizens from discriminating against others on the basis of race.

***WILLIAMS* v. *MISSISSIPPI* (1898)**
The Court upheld a state literacy requirement for voting that, in effect, kept African Americans from the polls.

***CUMMING* v. *BOARD OF EDUCATION OF RICHMOND COUNTY* (1899)**
The Court ruled that the federal government cannot prevent segregation in local school facilities because education is a local, not federal, issue.

▲ **One result of Jim Crow laws was separate drinking fountains for whites and African Americans.**

WHY IT MATTERED

In the decades following the Civil War [1861–1865], Southern state legislatures passed laws that aimed to limit civil rights for African Americans. The Black Codes of the 1860s, and later Jim Crow laws, were intended to deprive African Americans of their newly won political and social rights granted during Reconstruction.

Plessy was one of several Supreme Court cases brought by African Americans to protect their rights against segregation. In these cases, the Court regularly ignored the Fourteenth Amendment and upheld state laws that denied blacks their rights. *Plessy* was the most important of these cases because the Court used it to establish the separate-but-equal doctrine.

As a result, city and state governments across the South—and in some other states—maintained their segregation laws for more than half of the 20th century. These laws limited African Americans' access to most public facilities, including restaurants, schools, and hospitals. Without exception, the facilities reserved for whites were superior to those reserved for nonwhites. Signs reading "Colored Only" and "Whites Only" served as constant reminders that facilities in segregated societies were separate but not equal.

HISTORICAL IMPACT

It took many decades to abolish legal segregation. During the first half of the 20th century, the National Association for the Advancement of Colored People (NAACP) led the legal fight to overturn *Plessy*. Although they won a few cases over the years, it was not until 1954 in *Brown* v. *Board of Education* that the Court overturned any part of *Plessy*. In that case, the Supreme Court said that separate-but-equal was unconstitutional in public education, but it did not completely overturn the separate-but-equal doctrine.

In later years, the Court did overturn the separate-but-equal doctrine, and it used the *Brown* decision to do so. For example, in 1955, Rosa Parks was convicted for violating a Montgomery, Alabama, law for segregated seating on buses. A federal court overturned the conviction, finding such segregation unconstitutional. The case was appealed to the Supreme Court, which upheld without comment the lower court's decision. In doing so in this and similar cases, the Court signaled that the reasoning behind *Plessy* no longer applied.

▲ **As secretary of the Montgomery chapter of the NAACP, Rosa Parks had protested segregation through everyday acts long before Sepember 1955.**

THINKING CRITICALLY

CONNECT TO TODAY

1. **Analyzing Primary Sources** Read the part of the Fourteenth Amendment reprinted in this feature. Write a paragraph explaining what you think "equal protection of the laws" means. Use evidence to support your ideas.

SEE SKILLBUILDER HANDBOOK, PAGE R22.

CONNECT TO HISTORY 

2. Visit the links for Historic Decisions of the Supreme Court to research and read Justice Harlan's entire dissent in *Plessy* v. *Ferguson*. Based on his position, what view might Harlan have taken toward laws that denied African Americans the right to vote? Write a paragraph or two expressing what Harlan would say about those laws.

The Dawn of Mass Culture

MAIN IDEA	WHY IT MATTERS NOW	Terms & Names
As Americans had more time for leisure activities, a modern mass culture emerged.	Today, the United States has a worldwide impact on mass culture.	• Joseph Pulitzer • William Randolph Hearst • Ashcan school • Mark Twain • rural free delivery (RFD)

One American's Story

hmhsocialstudies.com TAKING NOTES

Use the graphic organizer online to take notes on the development of mass culture.

Along the Brooklyn seashore, on a narrow sandbar just nine miles from busy Manhattan, rose the most famous urban amusement center, Coney Island. In 1886, its main developer, George Tilyou, bragged, "If Paris is France, then Coney Island . . . is the world." Indeed, tens of thousands of visitors mobbed Coney Island after work each evening and on Sundays and holidays. When Luna Park, a spectacular amusement park on Coney Island, opened in May 1903, a reporter described the scene.

A PERSONAL VOICE BRUCE BLEN

"[Inside the park was] an enchanted, storybook land of trellises, columns, domes, minarets, lagoons, and lofty aerial flights. And everywhere was life—a pageant of happy people; and everywhere was color—a wide harmony of orange and white and gold. . . . It was a world removed—shut away from the sordid clatter and turmoil of the streets."

—quoted in *Amusing the Million*

▲ The sprawling amusement center at Coney Island became a model for urban amusement parks.

Coney Island offered Americans a few hours of escape from the hard work week. A schoolteacher who walked fully dressed into the ocean explained her unusual behavior by saying, "It has been a hard year at school, and when I saw the big crowd here, everyone with the brakes off, the spirit of the place got the better of me." The end of the 19th century saw the rise of a "mass culture" in the United States.

American Leisure

Middle-class Americans from all over the country shared experiences as new leisure activities, nationwide advertising campaigns, and the rise of a consumer culture began to level regional differences. As the 19th century drew to a close, many Americans fought off city congestion and dull industrial work by enjoying amusement parks, bicycling, new forms of theater, and spectator sports.

AMUSEMENT PARKS To meet the recreational needs of city dwellers, Chicago, New York City, and other cities began setting aside precious green space for outdoor enjoyment. Many cities built small playgrounds and playing fields throughout their neighborhoods for their citizens' enjoyment.

"Eight hours for work, eight hours for rest, eight hours for what we will"

THE CARPENTERS' UNION, WORCESTER, MASSACHUSETTS

Some amusement parks were constructed on the outskirts of cities. Often built by trolley-car companies that sought more passengers, these parks boasted picnic grounds and a variety of rides. The roller coaster drew daredevil customers to Coney Island in 1884, and the first Ferris wheel drew enthusiastic crowds to the World's Columbian Exposition in Chicago in 1893. Clearly, many Americans were ready for new and innovative forms of entertainment—and a whole panorama of recreational activities soon became available.

BICYCLING AND TENNIS With their huge front wheels and solid rubber tires, the first American bicycles challenged their riders. Because a bump might toss the cyclist over the handlebars, bicycling began as a male-only sport. However, the 1885 manufacture of the first commercially successful "safety bicycle," with its smaller wheels and air-filled tires, made the activity more popular. And the Victor safety bicycle, with a dropped frame and no crossbar, held special appeal to women.

Abandoning their tight corsets, women bicyclists donned shirtwaists (tailored blouses) and "split" skirts in order to cycle more comfortably. This attire soon became popular for daily wear. The bicycle also freed women from the scrutiny of the ever-present chaperone. The suffragist Susan B. Anthony declared, "I think [bicycling] has done more to emancipate women than anything else in the world. . . . It gives women a feeling of freedom and self-reliance." Fifty thousand men and women had taken to cycles by 1888. Two years later 312 American firms turned out 10 million bikes in one year. (A)

MAIN IDEA

Making Inferences

(A) How did the mass production of bicycles change women's lives?

Americans took up the sport of tennis as enthusiastically as they had taken up cycling. The modern version of this sport originated in North Wales in 1873. A year later, the United States saw its first tennis match. The socialite Florence Harriman recalled that in the 1880s her father returned from England with one of New York's first tennis sets. At first, neighbors thought the elder Harriman had installed the nets to catch birds.

Hungry or thirsty after tennis or cycling? Turn-of-the-century enthusiasts turned to new snacks with recognizable brand names. They could munch on a Hershey chocolate bar, first sold in 1900, and wash down the chocolate with a Coca-Cola®. An Atlanta pharmacist originally formulated the drink as a cure for headaches in 1886. The ingredients included extracts from Peruvian coca leaves as well as African cola nuts.

Bicycling and other new sports became fads in the late 1800s. ▼

The Negro Leagues were first formed in 1920.

SPECTATOR SPORTS Americans not only participated in new sports, but became avid fans of spectator sports, especially boxing and baseball. Though these two sports had begun as popular informal activities, by the turn of the 20th century they had become profitable businesses. Fans who couldn't attend an important boxing match jammed barbershops and hotel lobbies to listen to telegraphed transmissions of the contest's highlights.

BASEBALL New rules transformed baseball into a professional sport. In 1845, Alexander J. Cartwright, an amateur player, organized a club in New York City and set down regulations that used aspects of an English sport called rounders. Five years later, 50 baseball clubs had sprung up in the United States, and New York alone boasted 12 clubs in the mid-1860s.

In 1869, a professional team named the Cincinnati Red Stockings toured the country. Other clubs soon took to the road, which led to the formation of the National League in 1876 and the American League in 1900. In the first World Series, held in 1903, the Boston Pilgrims beat the Pittsburgh Pirates. African-American baseball players, who were excluded from both leagues because of racial discrimination, formed their own clubs and two leagues—the Negro National League and the Negro American League.

The novelist Mark Twain called baseball "the very symbol . . . and visible expression of the drive and push and rush and struggle of the raging, tearing, booming nineteenth century." By the 1890s, baseball had a published game schedule, official rules, and a standard-sized diamond. B

MAIN IDEA

Drawing Conclusions

B Why do you think sports were so popular among Americans at the turn of the century?

The Spread of Mass Culture

As increasing numbers of Americans attended school and learned to read, the cultural vistas of ordinary Americans expanded. Art galleries, libraries, books, and museums brought new cultural opportunities to more people. Other advances fostered mass entertainment. New media technology led to the release of hundreds of motion pictures. Mass-production printing techniques gave birth to thousands of books, magazines, and newspapers.

MASS CIRCULATION NEWSPAPERS Looking for ways to captivate readers' attention, American newspapers began using sensational headlines. For example, to introduce its story about the horrors of the Johnstown, Pennsylvania flood of 1889, in which more than 2,000 people died, one newspaper used the headline "THE VALLEY OF DEATH."

Joseph Pulitzer, a Hungarian immigrant who had bought the *New York World* in 1883, pioneered popular innovations, such as a large Sunday edition, comics, sports coverage, and women's news. Pulitzer's paper emphasized "sin, sex, and sensation" in an attempt to surpass his main competitor, the wealthy **William Randolph Hearst**, who had purchased the New York *Morning Journal* in 1895. Hearst, who already owned the San Francisco *Examiner*, sought to outdo Pulitzer by filling the *Journal* with exaggerated tales of personal scandals, cruelty, hypnotism, and even an imaginary conquest of Mars. C

MAIN IDEA

Drawing Conclusions

C How did the *World* and the *Journal* attract readers?

The escalation of their circulation war drove both papers to even more sensational news coverage. By 1898, the circulation of each paper had reached more than one million copies a day.

PROMOTING FINE ARTS By 1900, at least one art gallery graced every large city. Some American artists, including Philadelphian Thomas Eakins, began to embrace realism, an artistic school that attempted to portray life as it is really lived. Eakins had studied anatomy with medical students and used painstaking geometric perspective in his work. By the 1880s, Eakins was also using photography to make realistic studies of people and animals.

In the early 20th century, the **Ashcan school** of American art, led by Eakins's student Robert Henri, painted urban life and working people with gritty realism and no frills. Both Eakins and the Ashcan school, however, soon were challenged by the European development known as abstract art, a direction that most people found difficult to understand.

In many cities, inhabitants could walk from a new art gallery to a new public library, sometimes called "the poor man's university." By 1900, free circulating libraries in America numbered in the thousands.

History Through Art

THE CHAMPION SINGLE SCULLS (MAX SCHMITT IN A SINGLE SCULL) (1871)

This painting by Thomas Eakins is an example of the realist movement—an artistic school that aimed at portraying people and environments as they really are.

What realistic details do you see portrayed in this painting?

▲ Highly popular dime novels often featured adventure stories.

POPULAR FICTION As literacy rates rose, scholars debated the role of literature in society. Some felt that literature should uplift America's literary tastes, which tended toward crime tales and Western adventures.

Most people preferred to read light fiction. Such books sold for a mere ten cents, hence their name, "dime novels." Dime novels typically told glorified adventure tales of the West and featured heroes like Edward Wheeler's *Deadwood Dick*. Wheeler published his first Deadwood Dick novel in 1877 and in less than a decade produced over 30 more. D

MAIN IDEA

Analyzing Causes

D What factors contributed to the popularity of dime novels?

Some readers wanted a more realistic portrayal of American life. Successful writers of the era included Sarah Orne Jewett, Theodore Dreiser, Stephen Crane, Jack London, and Willa Cather. Most portrayed characters less polished than the upper-class men and women of Henry James's and Edith Wharton's novels. Samuel Langhorne Clemens, the novelist and humorist better known as **Mark Twain,** inspired a host of other young authors when he declared his independence of "literature and all that bosh." Yet, some of his books have become classics of American literature. *The Adventures of Huckleberry Finn*, for example, remains famed for its rendering of life along the Mississippi River.

Although art galleries and libraries attempted to raise cultural standards, many Americans had scant interest in high culture—and others did not have access to it. African Americans, for example, were excluded from visiting many museums and other white-controlled cultural institutions.

New Ways to Sell Goods

Along with enjoying new leisure activities, Americans also changed the way they shopped. Americans at the turn of the 20th century witnessed the beginnings of the shopping center, the development of department and chain stores, and the birth of modern advertising.

URBAN SHOPPING Growing city populations made promising targets for enterprising merchants. The nation's earliest form of a shopping center opened in Cleveland, Ohio, in 1890. The glass-topped arcade contained four levels of jewelry, leather goods, and stationery shops. The arcade also provided band music on Sundays so that Cleveland residents could spend their Sunday afternoons strolling through the elegant environment and gazing at the window displays.

Retail shopping districts formed where public transportation could easily bring shoppers from outlying areas. To anchor these retail shopping districts, ambitious merchants started something quite new, the modern department store.

THE DEPARTMENT STORE Marshall Field of Chicago first brought the department store concept to America. While working as a store clerk, Field found that paying close attention to women customers could increase sales considerably. In 1865, Field opened his own store, featuring several floors of specialized departments. Field's motto was "Give the lady what she wants." Field also pioneered the bargain basement, selling bargain goods that were "less expensive but reliable."

THE CHAIN STORE Department stores prided themselves on offering a variety of personal services. New chain stores—retail stores offering the same merchandise under the same ownership—sold goods for less by buying in quantity and limiting personal service. In the 1870s, F. W. Woolworth found that if he offered an item at a very low price, "the consumer would purchase it on the spur of the

Vocabulary
consumer: a person who purchases goods or services for direct use or ownership

moment" because "it was only a nickel." By 1911, the Woolworth chain boasted 596 stores and sold more than a million dollars in goods a week.

ADVERTISING An explosion in advertising also heralded modern consumerism. Expenditures for advertising were under $10 million a year in 1865 but increased tenfold, to $95 million, by 1900. Patent medicines grabbed the largest number of advertising lines, followed by soaps and baking powders. In addition to newspapers and magazines, advertisers used ingenious methods to push products. Passengers riding the train between New York and Philadelphia in the 1870s might see signs for Dr. Drake's Plantation Bitters on barns, houses, billboards, and even rocks.

CATALOGS AND RFD Montgomery Ward and Sears Roebuck brought retail merchandise to small towns. Ward's catalog, launched in 1872, grew from a single sheet the first year to a booklet with ordering instructions in ten languages. Richard Sears started his company in 1886. Early Sears catalogs stated that the company received "hundreds of orders every day from young and old who never [before] sent away for goods." By 1910, about 10 million Americans shopped by mail. The United States Post Office boosted mail-order businesses. In 1896 the Post Office introduced a **rural free delivery (RFD)** system that brought packages directly to every home.

The turn of the 20th century saw prosperity that caused big changes in Americans' daily lives. At the same time, the nation's growing industrial sector faced problems that called for reform.

NOW & THEN

CATALOG SHOPPING

Catalogs were a novelty when Sears and Montgomery Ward arrived on the scene. However, by the mid-1990s, more than 13 billion catalogs filled the mailboxes of Americans.

Today, the world of mail-order business is changing. After over 100 years of operation, Montgomery Ward filed for bankruptcy on December 28, 2000.

Online shopping is challenging mail-order commerce today. Online retail sales grew from $500 million in 1998 to nearly $89 billion in 2007. What do online shoppers order? Computer equipment, computer software, and electronic appliances make up about 25 percent of online spending.

ASSESSMENT

1. **TERMS & NAMES** For each term or name, write a sentence explaining its significance.
   - **Joseph Pulitzer**
   - **William Randolph Hearst**
   - **Ashcan school**
   - **Mark Twain**
   - **rural free delivery (RFD)**

MAIN IDEA

2. **TAKING NOTES**
   Re-create the spider diagram below. Add examples to each category.

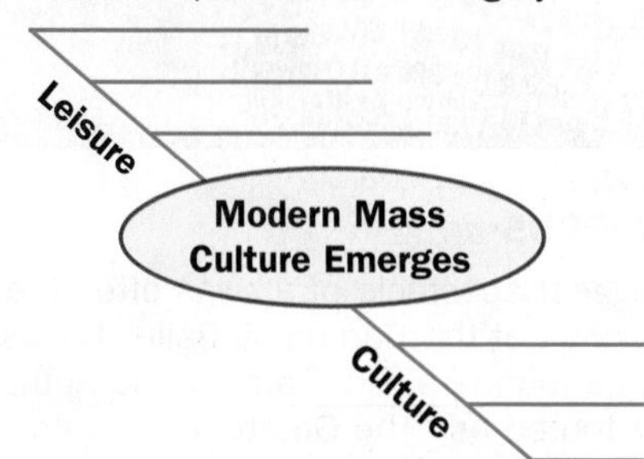

Why is mass culture often described as a democratic phenomenon?

CRITICAL THINKING

3. **SUMMARIZING**
   How did American methods of selling goods change at the turn of the 20th century?
   Think About:
   - how city people did their shopping
   - how rural residents bought goods
   - how merchants advertised their products

4. **ANALYZING VISUAL SOURCES**
   This cartoon shows the masters of the "new journalism." According to the cartoonist, where were Pulitzer and Hearst leading American journalism?

DAILY LIFE

1877–1917

Going to the Show

As Americans moved from rural areas to cities, they looked for new ways to spend their weekend and evening leisure time. Live theatrical performances brought pleasure to cities and small towns alike. Stars, popular performers who could attract large audiences, compensated for the less-talented supporting actors. Audiences could choose from a wide range of music, drama, circus, and the latest in entertainment—moving pictures.

◄ VAUDEVILLE THEATER

Performances that included song, dance, juggling, slapstick comedy, and sometimes chorus lines of female performers were characteristic of vaudeville. Promoters sought large audiences with varied backgrounds. Writing in *Scribner's Magazine* in October 1899, actor Edwin Milton Royle hailed vaudeville theater as "an American invention" that offered something to attract nearly everyone.

Until the 1890s, African-American performers filled roles mainly in minstrel shows that featured exaggerated imitations of African-American music and dance and reinforced racist stereotypes of blacks. By the turn of the century, however, minstrel shows had largely been replaced by more sophisticated musicals, and many black performers entertained in vaudeville.

Bill "Bojangles" Robinson was a popular tap dancer.

▲ THE CIRCUS

The biggest spectacle of all was often the annual visit of the Barnum & Bailey Circus, which its founders, P. T. Barnum and Anthony Bailey, touted as "The Greatest Show on Earth." Established in 1871, the circus arrived by railroad and staged a parade through town to advertise the show.

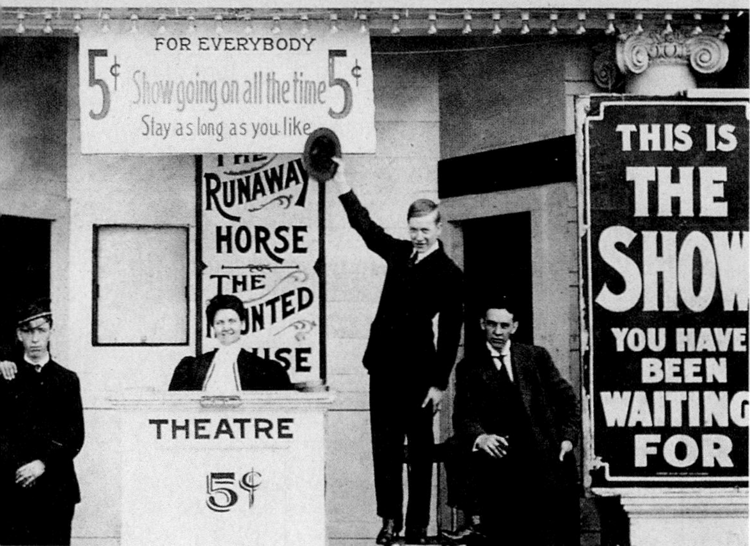

▲ **THE SILVER SCREEN**

The first films, one-reel, ten-minute sequences, consisted mostly of vaudeville skits or faked newsreels. In 1903, the first modern film—an eight-minute silent feature called *The Great Train Robbery*—debuted in five-cent theaters called nickelodeons. By showing a film as often as 16 times a day, entrepreneurs could generate greater profits than by a costly stage production. By 1907, an estimated 3,000 nickelodeons dotted the country.

◀ **RAGTIME MUSIC**

A blend of African-American spirituals and European musical forms, ragtime originated in the 1880s in the saloons of the South. African-American pianist and composer Scott Joplin's ragtime compositions made him famous in the first decade of the 1900s. Ragtime led later to jazz, rhythm and blues, and rock 'n' roll. These forms of popular American culture spread worldwide, creating new dances and fashions that emulated the image of "loud, loose, American rebel."

DATA FILE

A LOOK AT THE FACTS

A shorter workweek allowed many Americans more time for leisure activities, and they certainly took advantage of it.

- In 1890, an average of 60,000 fans attended professional baseball games daily.
- In 1893, a crowd of 50,000 attended the Princeton-Yale football game.
- *A Trip to Chinatown,* one of the popular new musical comedies, ran for an amazing 650 performances in the 1890s.
- In 1900, 3 million phonograph records of Broadway-produced musical comedies were sold.
- The love of the popular musicals contributed to the sale of $42 million worth of musical instruments in 1900.
- By 1900, almost 500 men's social clubs existed. Nine hundred college fraternity and sorority chapters had over 150,000 members.

Changes in the U.S. Workweek

Year	Hours per week
1860	66
1890	60
1920	51

Source: *Historical Statistics of the United States*

THINKING CRITICALLY

CONNECT TO HISTORY

1. **Interpreting Data** Study the statistics in the Data File. What summary statements about the culture and attitudes of this time period can you make? Is this a time in history when you would like to have lived? Why or why not?

 **SEE SKILLBUILDER HANDBOOK, PAGE R27.**

CONNECT TO TODAY

2. **Chronological Order** Trace the development and impact on the rest of the world of one area—music, theater, or film—of popular American culture. Use a time line from the turn of the 20th to the 21st century with "United States developments" on one side and "world impacts" on the other.

hmhsocialstudies.com RESEARCH WEB LINKS

CHAPTER 16 ASSESSMENT

TERMS & NAMES

For each term or name, write a sentence explaining its connection to late 19th-century American life.

1. Louis Sullivan
2. Orville and Wilbur Wright
3. Booker T. Washington
4. W. E. B. Du Bois
5. Niagara Movement
6. Ida B. Wells
7. Jim Crow laws
8. *Plessy* v. *Ferguson*
9. debt peonage
10. rural free delivery

MAIN IDEAS

Use your notes and the information in the chapter to answer the following questions.

Science and Urban Life

1. How did new technology promote urban growth around the turn of the century?
2. In what ways did methods of communication improve in the late 19th and early 20th centuries?

Expanding Public Education

3. How did late 19th century public schools change?
4. Why did some immigrants oppose sending their children to public schools?

Segregation and Discrimination

5. In what ways was racial discrimination reinforced by the federal government's actions and policies?
6. How did Mexicans help make the Southwest prosperous in the late 19th century?

Dawn of Mass Culture

7. What leisure activities flourished at the turn of the 20th century?
8. What innovations in retail methods changed the way Americans shopped during this time period?

CRITICAL THINKING

1. **USING YOUR NOTES** Create a table similar to the one shown, listing at least six important trends at the turn of the century, along with a major impact of each.

Trend	Impact
1.	
2.	
3.	
4.	
5.	
6.	

2. **DRAWING CONCLUSIONS** How had changes in technology affected urban life by the turn of the 20th century?

3. **INTERPRETING GRAPHS** Look at the graph, Expanding Education/Increasing Literacy. Which year reported the greatest gain in the literacy rate? What do you think were the implications on society of a more literate population?

VISUAL SUMMARY LIFE AT THE TURN OF THE 20TH CENTURY

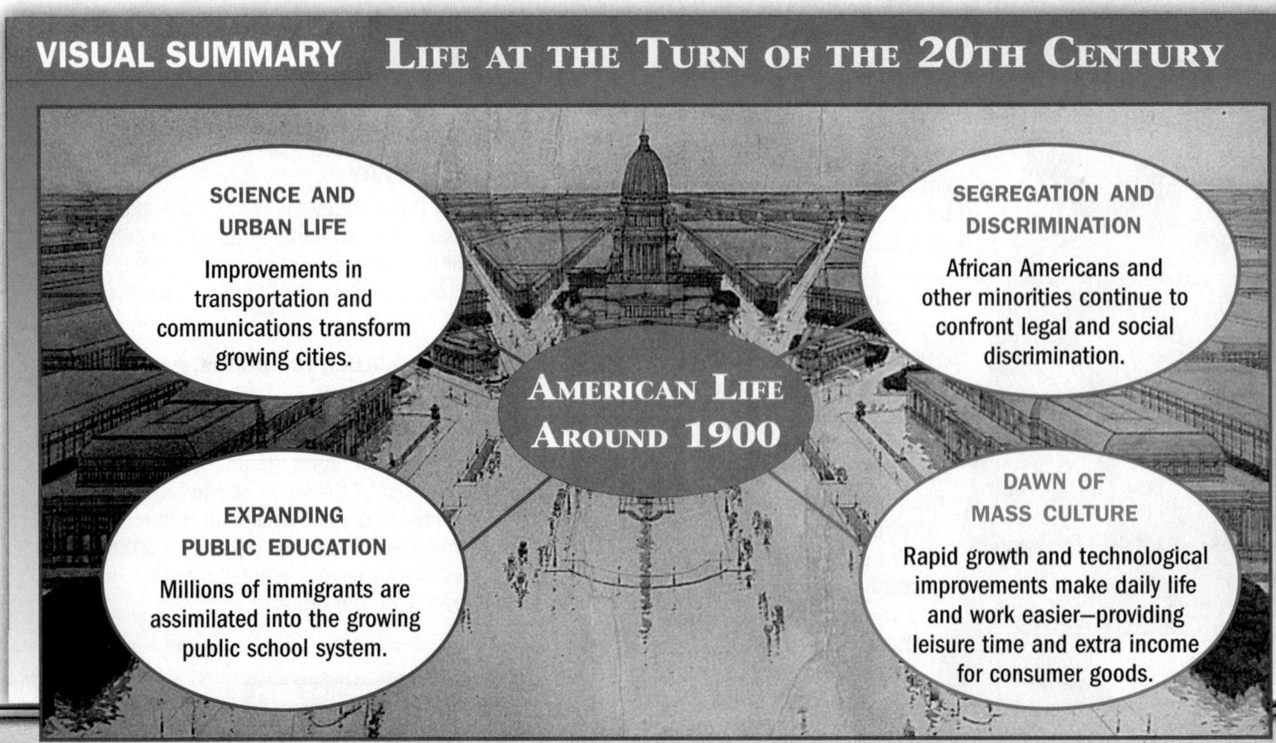

SCIENCE AND URBAN LIFE
Improvements in transportation and communications transform growing cities.
SEGREGATION AND DISCRIMINATION
African Americans and other minorities continue to confront legal and social discrimination.
AMERICAN LIFE AROUND 1900
EXPANDING PUBLIC EDUCATION
Millions of immigrants are assimilated into the growing public school system.
DAWN OF MASS CULTURE
Rapid growth and technological improvements make daily life and work easier—providing leisure time and extra income for consumer goods.

STANDARDIZED TEST PRACTICE

Use the quotation below and your knowledge of U.S. history to answer question 1.

> "**We boast of the freedom enjoyed by our people above all other peoples. But it is difficult to reconcile that boast with a state of the law which, practically, puts the brand of servitude and degradation upon a large class of our fellow-citizens, our equals before the law.**"
>
> —Justice John Marshall Harlan in the dissenting opinion in *Plessy* v. *Ferguson*

1. Justice Harlan used this reasoning for what purpose?
   - **A** to celebrate American democracy
   - **B** to justify segregation
   - **C** to denounce the "separate-but-equal" argument
   - **D** to demonstrate that equality before the law is not practical

2. Which of the following was *not* an outcome of expanding public education in the early 20th century?
   - **F** the establishment of public high schools and colleges
   - **G** the growth of equal education for all
   - **H** a rise in the literacy rate
   - **J** the founding of kindergartens

3. The turn of the 20th century brought shorter work hours and more leisure time to many urban Americans. Which of the following bar graphs correctly reflects these factors?

A

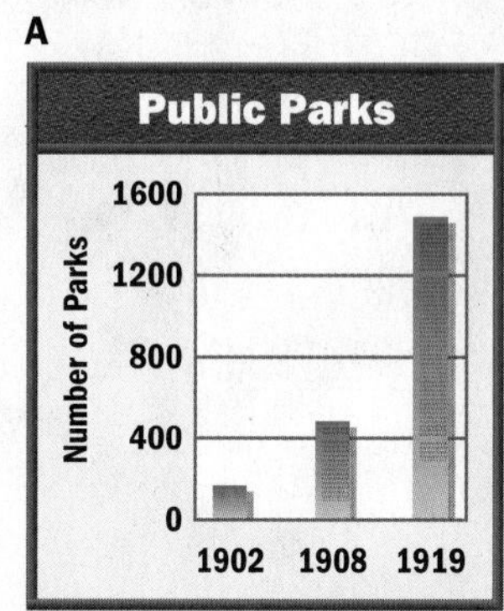

B

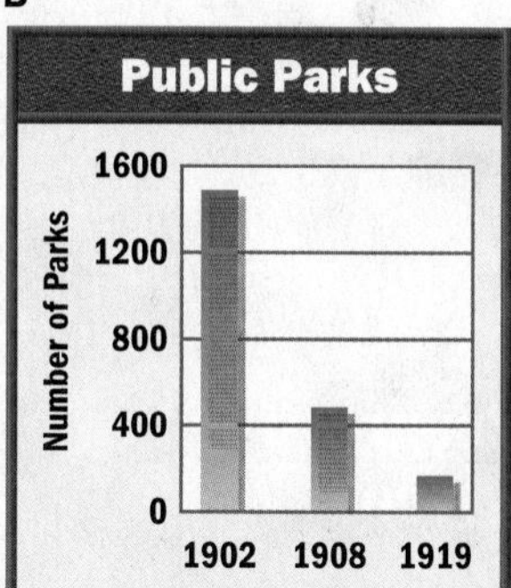

C

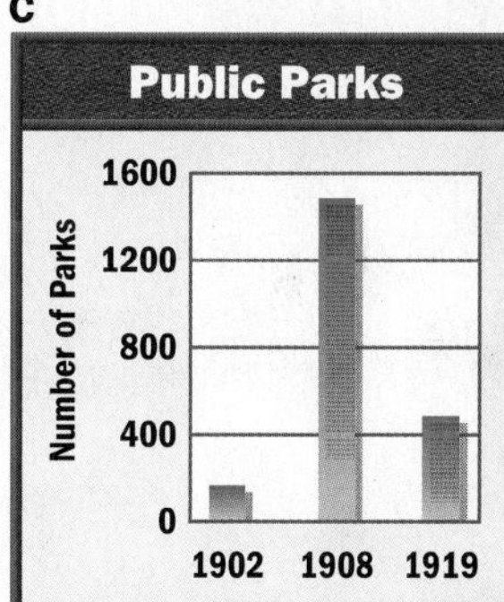

D

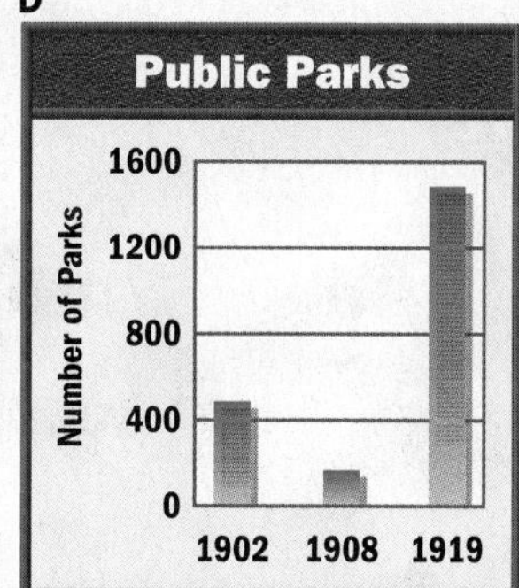

hmhsocialstudies.com TEST PRACTICE

For additional test practice, go online for:

- Diagnostic tests
- Tutorials

INTERACT WITH HISTORY

Recall the issues that you explored at the beginning of the chapter. Now that you know more about the role of technology in people's lives, would you change any of your responses? Discuss your ideas with a small group. Then make a cause-and-effect chart about one technological innovation of the era and its lasting impact on society.

FOCUS ON WRITING

Imagine you are a newspaper editor in 1896. Write an editorial explaining what you think of the Supreme Court ruling in *Plessy* v. *Ferguson*. Be sure to address the "separate but equal" argument.

MULTIMEDIA ACTIVITY

21ST CENTURY

Visit the links for Chapter Assessment to find out more about the World's Columbian Exposition held in Chicago in 1893. In a small group, make a list of the "famous firsts," such as the first elevated railway, introduced at the exposition. Illustrate your list, adding pictures and informative captions, on a colorful poster for display in the classroom.

hmhsocialstudies.com

Modern America Emerges 1890–1920

CHAPTER 17
The Progressive Era
1890–1920

CHAPTER 18
America Claims an Empire
1890–1920

News Story

As you read, identify a person, issue, or event that interests you. Plan and write an illustrated news story about the subject you have chosen. Use your text as well as information that you research in the library and on the Internet.

The Statue of Liberty **by Francis Hopkinson Smith**

ALABAMA Constitutional Change

Following the Civil War, amendments to the United States Constitution gave citizenship and the right to vote to formerly enslaved people. In order to return to the Union, Alabama approved a constitution in 1868 allowing African Americans to vote. The Republican Party gained control of the state legislature with the support of African-American voters. A few years later, Democrats regained power in Alabama as support for Reconstruction decreased. Although committed to maintaining white power, the new leadership did not eliminate African-American voting rights in the 1875 constitution. White leaders feared that the federal government would reject such obvious discrimination.

African Americans voting in Reconstruction elections

Motives for Change

Though African Americans were legally allowed to vote, Alabama Democrats devised ways to prevent African Americans from voting Republicans back into power. One common method was not allowing ballots to be read to voters who could not read. Also, political districts were drawn so that African-American voters were in particular districts, called gerrymandering. Some white politicians were still concerned that these limits were not enough and called for formal constitutional restrictions against African-American suffrage.

Around the same time, mill workers, miners, and tenant farmers protested against business elites during the populist revolt of the 1890s. Large landowners, industrial elites, and wealthy bankers in Alabama wanted to protect their economic power from changes demanded by populists. The state's elite classes also tried to lower tax rates for landowners and big business. They also wanted the state government to have more power than local governments. To achieve this agenda, Alabama lawmakers set up a referendum in 1901 calling for a constitutional convention.

Provisions of the 1901 Constitution

Delegates to the 1901 convention spent three months drafting a new constitution, which then had to be approved by Alabama voters. In November the document gained ratification by a margin of 108,613 votes to 81,734. The state's Black Belt counties, a region with a majority African-American population, voted in favor of ratification. However, it was no secret that the new constitution would protect white supremacy. Scholars believe that fraudulent methods, such as intimidating voters and miscounting ballots, were used to approve the constitution in the Black Belt counties.

The 1901 constitution, whether rightly ratified or not, established reading requirements and poll taxes that mostly ended the voting rights of African Americans. Because the restrictions affected poor and illiterate people of all races, the constitution provided loopholes that allowed some working-class white men to vote. Alabama's new governmental document also reduced property taxes for big business and large landowners, while concentrating power in the state legislature. Alabama's elites got everything they had wanted in the 1901 constitution.

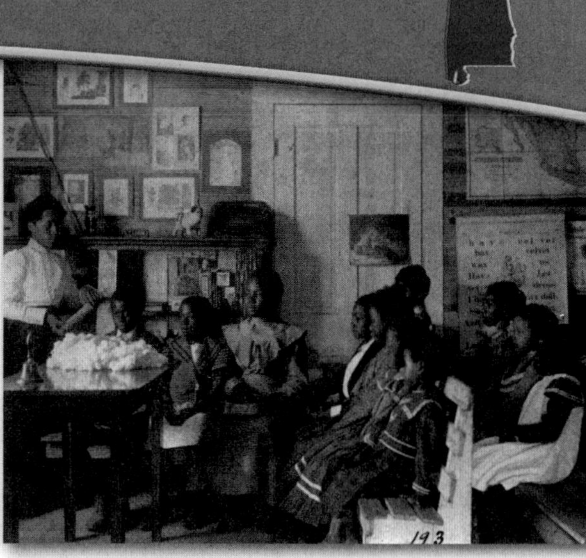

Under the 1901 constitution, segregated schools became the norm in Alabama.

Impact

In achieving the goals of its authors, the 1901 constitution had a harsh impact on thousands of Alabamians. Nearly all African Americans and a large percentage of poor whites lost the right to have any say in how the state would be governed. The new constitution also segregated the state's schools. Moreover, the constitution led to the extension of Jim Crow laws to housing, buses, and even cemeteries. The state was allowed to isolate African Americans into a second-class existence.

The 1901 constitution's requirements also placed large burdens on local governments. Counties were forced to secure constitutional amendments to perform basic tasks, such as adjusting local property tax rates or removing dead farm animals. This shift of local matters to state authority has resulted in more than 800 amendments to Alabama's constitution. It is the longest constitution in the world. Limits on property taxes in the 1901 constitution benefited powerful business interests. However, property tax limits weakened funding for education and forced the increase of sales taxes—a burden that fell mostly on the lower classes.

It did not take long before Alabamians wanted constitutional reform. Governor Emmet O'Neal in 1915 and Governor Thomas Kilby in 1923 led unsuccessful efforts for constitutional change.

A farmer plows his field in Coffee County, Alabama.

Exploring Further...

Research the creation of Alabama's 1901 constitution and write a one-page report. Your report should include the following questions.

- Which interests in Alabama wanted a new constitution?
- Why did these interests want a new constitution?
- How did the 1901 constitution gain ratification?

Make sure to include the effects of the 1901 constitution on

- voting in Alabama.
- state and local governments.

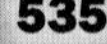

CHAPTER 17 THE PROGRESSIVE ERA

Essential Question

How did the progressive movement try to bring about social change?

ALABAMA COURSE OF STUDY

4 Describe the political system of the United States based on the Constitution of the United States.

• Interpreting the Preamble to the Constitution of the United States; separation of powers; federal system; elastic clause; the Bill of Rights; and the Thirteenth, Fourteenth, Fifteenth, and Nineteenth Amendments as key elements of the Constitution of the United States.

11 Evaluate the impact of American social and political reform on the emergence of a distinct culture.

• Explaining the influence of Elizabeth Cady Stanton, Dorothea Lynde Dix, and Susan B. Anthony on the development of social reform movements prior to the Civil War.

A 1916 suffrage parade.

USA

1896 William McKinley is elected president.

1900 William McKinley is reelected.

1901 McKinley is assassinated; Theodore Roosevelt becomes president.

1904 Theodore Roosevelt is elected president.

1890 | 1900

WORLD

1889 Eiffel Tower opens for visitors.

1898 Marie Curie discovers radium.

1899 Boer War in South Africa begins.

1901 Commonwealth of Australia is created.

Image Credits: (bkgd), (bc), ©Bettmann/Corbis; (bl), ©Michael Maslin Historic Photographs/Corbis

INTERACT WITH HISTORY

It is the dawn of the 20th century, and the reform movement is growing. Moral reformers are trying to ban alcoholic beverages. Political reformers work toward fair government and business practices. Women fight for equal wages and the right to vote. Throughout society, social and economic issues take center stage.

Explore the Issues

- What types of actions might pressure big business to change?
- How can individuals bring about change in their government?
- How might reformers recruit others?

1908 William H. Taft is elected president.

1909 W. E. B. Du Bois helps found the National Association for the Advancement of Colored People (NAACP).

1910 Mexican revolution begins.

1912 Woodrow Wilson is elected president.

1912 China's Qin dynasty topples.

1914 World War I begins in Europe.

1916 Woodrow Wilson is reelected.

1919 Eighteenth Amendment outlaws alcoholic beverages.

1919 Mohandas Gandhi becomes leader of the independence movement in India.

1920 Nineteenth Amendment grants women the right to vote.

1910

1920

Image Credits: (bkgd), ©Bettmann/Corbis; (br), The Granger Collection, New York; (bl), ©Bettmann/Corbis; (bc), ©Peter Ruhe/Gandhiserve Foundation

The Origins of Progressivism

MAIN IDEA

Political, economic, and social change in late 19th century America led to broad progressive reforms.

WHY IT MATTERS NOW

Progressive reforms in areas such as labor and voting rights reinforced democratic principles that continue to exist today.

Terms & Names

- **progressive movement**
- **Florence Kelley**
- **prohibition**
- **muckraker**
- **scientific management**
- **Robert M. La Follette**
- **initiative**
- **referendum**
- **recall**
- **Seventeenth Amendment**

One American's Story

hmhsocialstudies.com TAKING NOTES

Use the graphic organizer online to take notes about progressive reform organizations.

Camella Teoli was just 12 years old when she began working in a Lawrence, Massachusetts, textile mill to help support her family. Soon after she started, a machine used for twisting cotton into thread tore off part of her scalp. The young Italian immigrant spent seven months in the hospital and was scarred for life.

Three years later, when 20,000 Lawrence mill workers went on strike for higher wages, Camella was selected to testify before a congressional committee investigating labor conditions such as workplace safety and underage workers. When asked why she had gone on strike, Camella answered simply, "Because I didn't get enough to eat at home." She explained how she had gone to work before reaching the legal age of 14.

▲ Mill workers on strike in 1912 in Lawrence, Massachusetts

A PERSONAL VOICE CAMELLA TEOLI

"I used to go to school, and then a man came up to my house and asked my father why I didn't go to work, so my father says I don't know whether she is 13 or 14 years old. So, the man say You give me $4 and I will make the papers come from the old country [Italy] saying [that] you are 14. So, my father gave him the $4, and in one month came the papers that I was 14. I went to work, and about two weeks [later] got hurt in my head."

—at congressional hearings, March 1912

After nine weeks of striking, the mill workers won the sympathy of the nation as well as five to ten percent pay raises. Stories like Camella's set off a national investigation of labor conditions, and reformers across the country organized to address the problems of industrialization.

Four Goals of Progressivism

At the dawn of the new century, middle-class reformers addressed many of the problems that had contributed to the social upheavals of the 1890s. Journalists and writers exposed the unsafe conditions often faced by factory workers, including women and children. Intellectuals questioned the dominant role of large corporations in American society. Political reformers struggled to make government more responsive to the people. Together, these reform efforts formed the **progressive movement,** which aimed to restore economic opportunities and correct injustices in American life.

Even though reformers never completely agreed on the problems or the solutions, each of their progressive efforts shared at least one of the following goals:

- protecting social welfare
- promoting moral improvement
- creating economic reform
- fostering efficiency

PROTECTING SOCIAL WELFARE Many social welfare reformers worked to soften some of the harsh conditions of industrialization. The Social Gospel and settlement house movements of the late 1800s, which aimed to help the poor through community centers, churches, and social services, continued during the Progressive Era and inspired even more reform activities.

The Young Men's Christian Association (YMCA), for example, opened libraries, sponsored classes, and built swimming pools and handball courts. The Salvation Army fed poor people in soup kitchens, cared for children in nurseries, and sent "slum brigades" to instruct poor immigrants in middle-class values of hard work and temperance.

Vocabulary
temperance: refraining from alcohol consumption

In addition, many women were inspired by the settlement houses to take action. **Florence Kelley** became an advocate for improving the lives of women and children. She was appointed chief inspector of factories for Illinois after she had helped to win passage of the Illinois Factory Act in 1893. The act, which prohibited child labor and limited women's working hours, soon became a model for other states.

FLORENCE KELLEY
1859–1932

The daughter of an antislavery Republican congressman from Pennsylvania, Florence Kelley became a social reformer whose sympathies lay with the powerless, especially working women and children. During a long career, Kelley pushed the government to solve America's social problems.

In 1899, Kelley became general secretary of the National Consumers' League, where she lobbied to improve factory conditions. "Why," Kelley pointedly asked while campaigning for a federal child-labor law, "are seals, bears, reindeer, fish, wild game in the national parks, buffalo, [and] migratory birds all found suitable for federal protection, but not children?"

PROMOTING MORAL IMPROVEMENT Other reformers felt that morality, not the workplace, held the key to improving the lives of poor people. These reformers wanted immigrants and poor city dwellers to uplift themselves by improving their personal behavior. **Prohibition,** the banning of alcoholic beverages, was one such program.

Prohibitionist groups feared that alcohol was undermining American morals. Founded in Cleveland in 1874, the Woman's Christian Temperance Union (WCTU) spearheaded the crusade for prohibition. Members advanced their cause by entering saloons, singing, praying, and urging saloonkeepers to stop selling alcohol. As momentum grew, the Union was transformed by Frances Willard from a small midwestern religious group in 1879 to a national organization. Boasting 245,000 members by 1911, the WCTU became the largest women's group in the nation's history. (A)

MAIN IDEA

Analyzing Motives
(A) Why did the prohibition movement appeal to so many women?

In the 1890s, Carry Nation worked for prohibition by walking into saloons, scolding the customers, and using her hatchet to destroy bottles of liquor.

WCTU members followed Willard's "do everything" slogan and began opening kindergartens for immigrants, visiting

HISTORICAL SPOTLIGHT

ANTI-SALOON LEAGUE

Quietly founded by progressive women in 1895, the Anti-Saloon League called itself "the Church in action against the saloon." Whereas early temperance efforts had asked individuals to change their ways, the Anti-Saloon League worked to pass laws to force people to change and to punish those who drank.

The Anti-Saloon League endorsed politicians who opposed "Demon Rum," no matter which party they belonged to or where they stood on other issues. It also organized statewide referendums to ban alcohol. Between 1900 and 1917, voters in nearly half of the states—mostly in the South and the West—prohibited the sale, production, and use of alcohol. Individual towns, city wards, and rural areas also voted themselves "dry."

inmates in prisons and asylums, and working for suffrage. The WCTU reform activities, like those of the settlement-house movement, provided women with expanded public roles, which they used to justify giving women voting rights.

Sometimes efforts at prohibition led to trouble with immigrant groups. Such was the case with the Anti-Saloon League, founded in 1895. As members sought to close saloons to cure society's problems, tension arose between them and many immigrants, whose customs often included the consumption of alcohol. Additionally, saloons filled a number of roles within the immigrant community such as cashing paychecks and serving meals.

CREATING ECONOMIC REFORM As moral reformers sought to change individual behavior, a severe economic panic in 1893 prompted some Americans to question the capitalist economic system. As a result, some Americans, especially workers, embraced socialism. Labor leader Eugene V. Debs, who helped organize the American Socialist Party in 1901, commented on the uneven balance among big business, government, and ordinary people under the free-market system of capitalism.

A PERSONAL VOICE EUGENE V. DEBS

> **"Competition was natural enough at one time, but do you think you are competing today? Many of you think you are competing. Against whom? Against [oil magnate John D.] Rockefeller? About as I would if I had a wheelbarrow and competed with the Santa Fe [railroad] from here to Kansas City."**
>
> —*Debs: His Life, Writings and Speeches*

Though most progressives distanced themselves from socialism, they saw the truth of many of Debs's criticisms. Big business often received favorable treatment from government officials and politicians and could use its economic power to limit competition.

Journalists who wrote about the corrupt side of business and public life in mass circulation magazines during the early 20th century became known as **muckrakers** (mŭk′rāk′r). (The term refers to John Bunyan's "Pilgrim's Progress," in which a character is so busy using a rake to clean up the muck of this world that he does not raise his eyes to heaven.) In her "History of the Standard Oil Company," a monthly serial in *McClure's Magazine*, the writer Ida M. Tarbell described the company's cutthroat methods of eliminating competition. "Mr. Rockefeller has systematically played with loaded dice," Tarbell charged, "and it is doubtful if there has been a time since 1872 when he has run a race with a competitor and started fair." B

MAIN IDEA

Evaluating

B What contribution did muckrakers make to the reform movement?

FOSTERING EFFICIENCY Many progressive leaders put their faith in experts and scientific principles to make society and the workplace more efficient. In defending an Oregon law that limited women factory and laundry workers to a ten-hour day, lawyer Louis D. Brandeis paid little attention to legal argument. Instead, he focused on data produced by social scientists documenting the high costs of long working hours for both the individual and society. This type of argument—the "Brandeis brief"—would become a model for later reform litigation.

Within industry, Frederick Winslow Taylor began using time and motion studies to improve efficiency by breaking manufacturing tasks into simpler parts. "Taylorism" became a management fad, as industry reformers applied these **scientific management** studies to see just how quickly each task could be performed.

Workers at the Ford flywheel factory cope with the demanding pace of the assembly line to earn five dollars a day—a good wage in 1914.

However, not all workers could work at the same rate, and although the introduction of the assembly lines did speed up production, the system required people to work like machines. This caused a high worker turnover, often due to injuries suffered by fatigued workers. To keep automobile workers happy and to prevent strikes, Henry Ford reduced the workday to eight hours and paid workers five dollars a day. This incentive attracted thousands of workers, but they exhausted themselves. As one homemaker complained in a letter to Henry Ford in 1914, "That $5 is a blessing—a bigger one than you know but oh they earn it."

Such efforts at improving efficiency, an important part of progressivism, targeted not only industry, but government as well. C

MAIN IDEA

Contrasting
C Contrast the goals of scientific management with other progressive reforms.

"Everybody will be able to afford [a car], and about everyone will have one."

HENRY FORD, 1909

Cleaning Up Local Government

Cities faced some of the most obvious social problems of the new industrial age. In many large cities, political bosses rewarded their supporters with jobs and kickbacks and openly bought votes with favors and bribes. Efforts to reform city politics stemmed in part from the desire to make government more efficient and more responsive to its constituents. But those efforts also grew from distrust of immigrants' participation in politics.

REFORMING LOCAL GOVERNMENT Natural disasters sometimes played an important role in prompting reform of city governments. In 1900, a hurricane and tidal wave almost demolished Galveston, Texas. The politicians on the city council botched the huge relief and rebuilding job so badly that the Texas legislature appointed a five-member commission of experts to take over. Each expert took charge of a different city department, and soon Galveston was rebuilt. This success prompted the city to adopt the commission idea as a form of government, and by 1917, 500 cities had followed Galveston's example.

Another natural disaster—a flood in Dayton, Ohio, in 1913—led to the widespread adoption of the council-manager form of government. Staunton, Virginia, had already pioneered this system, in which people elected a city council to make laws. The council in turn appointed a manager, typically a person with training and experience in public administration, to run the city's departments. By 1925, managers were administering nearly 250 cities.

REFORM MAYORS In some cities, mayors such as Hazen Pingree of Detroit, Michigan (1890–1897), and Tom Johnson of Cleveland, Ohio (1901–1909), introduced progressive reforms without changing how government was organized.

Concentrating on economics, Pingree instituted a fairer tax structure, lowered fares for public transportation, rooted out corruption, and set up a system of work relief for the unemployed. Detroit city workers built schools, parks, and a municipal lighting plant.

Johnson was only one of 19 socialist mayors who worked to institute progressive reforms in America's cities. In general, these mayors focused on dismissing corrupt and greedy private owners of utilities—such as gasworks, waterworks, and transit lines—and converting the utilities to publicly owned enterprises. Johnson believed that citizens should play a more active role in city government. He held meetings in a large circus tent and invited them to question officials about how the city was managed. D

MAIN IDEA

Summarizing

D How did city government change during the Progressive Era?

Reform at the State Level

Local reforms coincided with progressive efforts at the state level. Spurred by progressive governors, many states passed laws to regulate railroads, mines, mills, telephone companies, and other large businesses.

HISTORICAL SPOTLIGHT

JAMES S. HOGG, TEXAS GOVERNOR (1891–1895)

Among the most colorful of the reform governors was James S. Hogg of Texas. Hogg helped to drive illegal insurance companies from the state and championed antitrust legislation. His chief interest, however, was in regulating the railroads. He pointed out abuses in rates—noting, for example, that it cost more to ship lumber from East Texas to Dallas than to ship it all the way to Nebraska. A railroad commission, established largely as a result of his efforts, helped increase milling and manufacturing in Texas by lowering freight rates.

REFORM GOVERNORS Under the progressive Republican leadership of **Robert M. La Follette,** Wisconsin led the way in regulating big business. "Fighting Bob" La Follette served three terms as governor before he entered the U.S. Senate in 1906. He explained that, as governor, he did not mean to "smash corporations, but merely to drive them out of politics, and then to treat them exactly the same as other people are treated."

La Follette's major target was the railroad industry. He taxed railroad property at the same rate as other business property, set up a commission to regulate rates, and forbade railroads to issue free passes to state officials. Other reform governors who attacked big business interests included Charles B. Aycock of North Carolina and James S. Hogg of Texas.

PROTECTING WORKING CHILDREN As the number of child workers rose dramatically, reformers worked to protect workers and to end child labor. Businesses hired children because they performed unskilled jobs for lower wages and because children's small hands made them more adept at handling small parts and tools. Immigrants and rural migrants often sent their children to work because they viewed their children as part of the family economy. Often wages were so low for adults that every family member needed to work to pull the family out of poverty.

In industrial settings, however, children were more prone to accidents caused by fatigue. Many developed serious health problems and suffered from stunted growth. E

MAIN IDEA

Analyzing Causes

E Why did reformers seek to end child labor?

Formed in 1904, the National Child Labor Committee sent investigators to gather evidence of children working in harsh conditions. They then organized exhibitions with photographs and statistics to dramatize the children's plight. They were joined by labor union members who argued that child labor lowered wages for all workers. These groups pressured

History Through *Photojournalism*

IMAGES OF CHILD LABOR

In 1908, Lewis Hine quit his teaching job to document child labor practices. Hine's photographs and descriptions of young laborers—some only three years old—were widely distributed and displayed in exhibits. His compelling images of exploitation helped to convince the public of the need for child labor regulations.

Hine devised a host of clever tactics to gain access to his subjects, such as learning shop managers' schedules and arriving during their lunch breaks. While talking casually with the children, he secretly scribbled notes on paper hidden in his pocket.

Because of their small size, spindle boys and girls *(top)* were forced to climb atop moving machinery to replace parts. For four-year-old Mary *(left)*, shucking two pots of oysters was a typical day's work.

SKILLBUILDER **Interpreting Visual Sources**

1. Lewis Hine believed in the power of photography to move people to action. What elements of these photographs do you find most striking?
2. Why do you think Hine was a successful photographer?

 **SEE SKILLBUILDER HANDBOOK, PAGE R23.**

national politicians to pass the Keating-Owen Act in 1916. The act prohibited the transportation across state lines of goods produced with child labor.

Two years later the Supreme Court declared the act unconstitutional due to interference with states' rights to regulate labor. Reformers did, however, succeed in nearly every state by effecting legislation that banned child labor and set maximum hours.

EFFORTS TO LIMIT WORKING HOURS The Supreme Court sometimes took a more sympathetic view of the plight of workers. In the 1908 case of *Muller* v. *Oregon*, Louis D. Brandeis—assisted by Florence Kelley and Josephine Goldmark—persuasively argued that poor working women were much more economically insecure than large corporations. Asserting that women required the state's protection against powerful employers, Brandeis convinced the Court to uphold an Oregon law limiting women to a ten-hour workday. Other states responded by enacting or strengthening laws to reduce women's hours of work. A similar Brandeis brief in *Bunting* v. *Oregon* in 1917 persuaded the Court to uphold a ten-hour workday for men.

Progressives also succeeded in winning workers' compensation to aid the families of workers who were hurt or killed on the job. Beginning with Maryland in 1902, one state after another passed legislation requiring employers to pay benefits in death cases.

REFORMING ELECTIONS In some cases, ordinary citizens won state reforms. William S. U'Ren prompted his state of Oregon to adopt the secret ballot (also called the Australian ballot), the initiative, the referendum, and the recall. The initiative and referendum gave citizens the power to create laws. Citizens could petition to place an **initiative**—a bill originated by the people rather than lawmakers—on the ballot. Then voters, instead of the legislature, accepted or rejected the initiative by **referendum,** a vote on the initiative. The **recall** enabled voters to remove public officials from elected positions by forcing them to face another election before the end of their term if enough voters asked for it. By 1920, 20 states had adopted at least one of these procedures.

In 1899, Minnesota passed the first mandatory statewide primary system. This enabled voters, instead of political machines, to choose candidates for public office through a special popular election. About two-thirds of the states had adopted some form of direct primary by 1915.

DIRECT ELECTION OF SENATORS It was the success of the direct primary that paved the way for the **Seventeenth Amendment** to the Constitution. Before 1913, each state's legislature had chosen its own United States senators, which put even more power in the hands of party bosses and wealthy corporation heads. To force senators to be more responsive to the public, progressives pushed for the popular election of senators. At first, the Senate refused to go along with the idea, but gradually more and more states began allowing voters to nominate senatorial candidates in direct primaries. As a result, Congress approved the Seventeenth Amendment in 1912. Its ratification in 1913 made direct election of senators the law of the land. (F)

Government reform—including efforts to give Americans more of a voice in electing their legislators and creating laws—drew increased numbers of women into public life. It also focused renewed attention on the issue of woman suffrage.

MAIN IDEA

Summarizing
(F) Summarize the impact of the direct election of senators.

ASSESSMENT

1. **TERMS & NAMES** For each term or name, write a sentence explaining its significance.
   - **progressive movement**
   - **Florence Kelley**
   - **prohibition**
   - **muckraker**
   - **scientific management**
   - **Robert M. La Follette**
   - **initiative**
   - **referendum**
   - **recall**
   - **Seventeenth Amendment**

MAIN IDEA

2. **TAKING NOTES**
   Copy the web below on your paper. Fill it in with examples of organizations that worked for reform in the areas named.

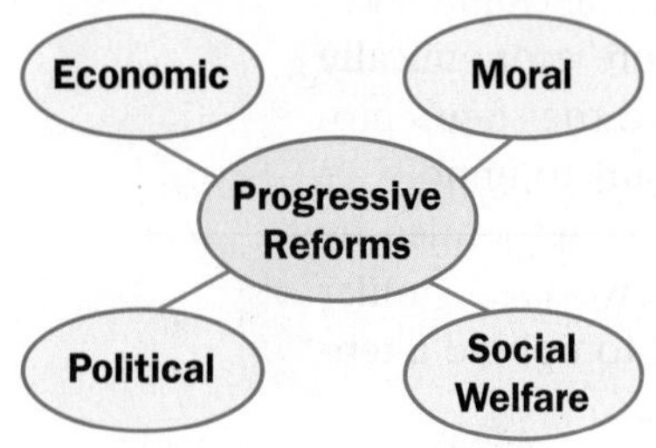

   Which group was most successful and why?

CRITICAL THINKING

3. **FORMING GENERALIZATIONS**
   In what ways might Illinois, Wisconsin, and Oregon all be considered trailblazers in progressive reform? Support your answers. **Think About:**
   - legislative and electoral reforms at the state level
   - the leadership of William U'Ren and Robert La Follette
   - Florence Kelley's appointment as chief inspector of factories for Illinois

4. **INTERPRETING VISUAL SOURCES**
   This cartoon shows Carry Nation inside a saloon that she has attacked. Do you think the cartoonist had a favorable or unfavorable opinion of this prohibitionist? Explain.

SECTION 2

Women in Public Life

MAIN IDEA

As a result of social and economic change, many women entered public life as workers and reformers.

WHY IT MATTERS NOW

Women won new opportunities in labor and education that are enjoyed today.

Terms & Names

- **NACW**
- **suffrage**
- **Susan B. Anthony**
- **NAWSA**

One American's Story

hmhsocialstudies.com TAKING NOTES

Use the graphic organizer online to take notes about women and work in the late 1800s.

In 1879, Susette La Flesche, a young Omaha woman, traveled east to translate into English the sad words of Chief Standing Bear, whose Ponca people had been forcibly removed from their homeland in Nebraska. Later, she was invited with Chief Standing Bear to go on a lecture tour to draw attention to the Ponca's situation.

A PERSONAL VOICE SUSETTE LA FLESCHE

"We are thinking men and women. . . . We have a right to be heard in whatever concerns us. Your government has driven us hither and thither like cattle. . . . Your government has no right to say to us, Go here, or Go there, and if we show any reluctance, to force us to do its will at the point of the bayonet. . . . Do you wonder that the Indian feels outraged by such treatment and retaliates, although it will end in death to himself?"

—quoted in *Bright Eyes*

▲ Susette La Flesche

La Flesche testified before congressional committees and helped win passage of the Dawes Act of 1887, which allowed individual Native Americans to claim reservation land and citizenship rights. Her activism was an example of a new role for American women, who were expanding their participation in public life.

Women in the Work Force

Before the Civil War, married middle-class women were generally expected to devote their time to the care of their homes and families. By the late 19th century, however, only middle-class and upper-class women could afford to do so. Poorer women usually had no choice but to work for wages outside the home.

FARM WOMEN On farms in the South and the Midwest, women's roles had not changed substantially since the previous century. In addition to household tasks such as cooking, making clothes, and laundering, farm women handled a host of other chores such as raising livestock. Often the women had to help plow and plant the fields and harvest the crops.

WOMEN IN INDUSTRY As better-paying opportunities became available in towns, and especially cities, women had new options for finding jobs, even though men's labor unions excluded them from membership. At the turn of the century,

Telephone operators manually connect phone calls in 1915.

NOW & THEN

TELEPHONE OPERATORS

Today, when Americans use the telephone, an automated voice often greets them with instructions about which buttons to press. In the 19th century, every telephone call had to be handled by a telephone operator, a person who connected wires through a switchboard.

Young men, the first telephone operators, proved unsatisfactory. Patrons complained that the male operators used profane language and talked back to callers. Women soon largely replaced men as telephone operators, and were willing to accept the ten-dollar weekly wage.

Department stores advertised shopping by telephone as a convenience. One ad in the Chicago telephone book of 1904 declared, "Every [telephone] order, inquiry, or request will be quickly and intelligently cared for." The ad pictured a line of female telephone operators.

one out of five American women held jobs; 25 percent of them worked in manufacturing.

The garment trade claimed about half of all women industrial workers. They typically held the least skilled positions, however, and received only about half as much money as their male counterparts or less. Many of these women were single and were assumed to be supporting only themselves, while men were assumed to be supporting families.

Women also began to fill new jobs in offices, stores, and classrooms. These jobs required a high school education, and by 1890, women high school graduates outnumbered men. Moreover, new business schools were preparing bookkeepers and stenographers, as well as training female typists to operate the new machines. (A)

MAIN IDEA

Analyzing Causes

(A) What kinds of job opportunities prompted more women to complete high school?

DOMESTIC WORKERS Many women without formal education or industrial skills contributed to the economic survival of their families by doing domestic work, such as cleaning for other families. After almost 2 million African-American women were freed from slavery, poverty quickly drove nearly half of them into the work force. They worked on farms and as domestic workers, and migrated by the thousands to big cities for jobs as cooks, laundresses, scrubwomen, and maids. Altogether, roughly 70 percent of women employed in 1870 were servants.

Unmarried immigrant women also did domestic labor, especially when they first arrived in the United States. Many married immigrant women contributed to the family income by taking in piecework or caring for boarders at home.

Women Lead Reform

Dangerous conditions, low wages, and long hours led many female industrial workers to push for reforms. Their ranks grew after 146 workers, mostly Jewish and Italian immigrant girls, died in a 1911 fire in the Triangle Shirtwaist Factory in New York City. Middle- and upper-class women also entered the public sphere. By 1910, women's clubs, at which these women discussed art or literature, were nearly half a million strong. These clubs sometimes grew into reform groups that addressed issues such as temperance or child labor.

WOMEN IN HIGHER EDUCATION Many of the women who became active in public life in the late 19th century had attended the new women's colleges. Vassar

College—with a faculty of 8 men and 22 women—accepted its first students in 1865. Smith and Wellesley Colleges followed in 1875. Though Columbia, Brown, and Harvard Colleges refused to admit women, each university established a separate college for women.

Although women were still expected to fulfill traditional domestic roles, women's colleges sought to grant women an excellent education. In her will, Smith College's founder, Sophia Smith, made her goals clear.

A PERSONAL VOICE SOPHIA SMITH

"[It is my desire] to furnish for my own sex means and facilities for education equal to those which are afforded now in our College to young men. . . . It is not my design to render my sex any the less feminine, but to develop as fully as may be the powers of womanhood & furnish women with means of usefulness, happiness, & honor now withheld from them."

—quoted in *Alma Mater*

MAIN IDEA

Analyzing Effects

B What social and economic effects did higher education have on women?

By the late 19th century, marriage was no longer a woman's only alternative. Many women entered the work force or sought higher education. In fact, almost half of college-educated women in the late 19th century never married, retaining their own independence. Many of these educated women began to apply their skills to needed social reforms. **B**

WOMEN AND REFORM Uneducated laborers started efforts to reform workplace health and safety. The participation of educated women often strengthened existing reform groups and provided leadership for new ones. Because women were not allowed to vote or run for office, women reformers strove to improve conditions at work and home. Their "social housekeeping" targeted workplace reform, housing reform, educational improvement, and food and drug laws.

In 1896, African-American women founded the National Association of Colored Women, or **NACW,** by merging two earlier organizations. Josephine Ruffin identified the mission of the African-American women's club movement as "the moral education of the race with which we are identified." The NACW managed nurseries, reading rooms, and kindergartens.

After the Seneca Falls convention of 1848, women split over the Fourteenth and Fifteenth Amendments, which granted equal rights including the right to vote to African American men, but excluded women. **Susan B. Anthony,** a leading proponent of woman **suffrage,** the right to vote, said "[I] would sooner cut off my right hand than ask the ballot for the black man and not for women." In 1869 Anthony and Elizabeth Cady Stanton had founded the National Women Suffrage Association (NWSA), which united with another group in 1890 to

Suffragists recruit supporters for a march.

KEY PLAYER

SUSAN B. ANTHONY
1820–1906

Born to a strict Quaker family, Susan B. Anthony was not allowed to enjoy typical childhood entertainment such as music, games, and toys. Her father insisted on self-discipline, education, and a strong belief system for all of his eight children. At an early age, Anthony developed a positive view of womanhood from a teacher named Mary Perkins who educated the children in their home.

After voting illegally in the presidential election of 1872, Anthony was fined $100 at her trial. "Not a penny shall go to this unjust claim," she defiantly declared. She never paid the fine.

become the National American Woman Suffrage Association, or **NAWSA.** Other prominent leaders included Lucy Stone and Julia Ward Howe, the author of "The Battle Hymn of the Republic."

Woman suffrage faced constant opposition. The liquor industry feared that women would vote in support of prohibition, while the textile industry worried that women would vote for restrictions on child labor. Many men simply feared the changing role of women in society.

A THREE–PART STRATEGY FOR SUFFRAGE Suffragist leaders tried three approaches to achieve their objective. First, they tried to convince state legislatures to grant women the right to vote. They achieved a victory in the territory of Wyoming in 1869, and by the 1890s Utah, Colorado, and Idaho had also granted voting rights to women. After 1896, efforts in other states failed.

Second, women pursued court cases to test the Fourteenth Amendment, which declared that states denying their male citizens the right to vote would lose congressional representation. Weren't women citizens, too? In 1871 and 1872, Susan B. Anthony and other women tested that question by attempting to vote at least 150 times in ten states and the District of Columbia. The Supreme Court ruled in 1875 that women were indeed citizens—but then denied that citizenship automatically conferred the right to vote.

Third, women pushed for a national constitutional amendment to grant women the vote. Stanton succeeded in having the amendment introduced in California, but it was killed later. For the next 41 years, women lobbied to have it reintroduced, only to see it continually voted down. (C)

> **MAIN IDEA**
> **Making Inferences**
> (C) Why did suffragist leaders employ a three-part strategy for gaining the right to vote?

Before the turn of the century, the campaign for suffrage achieved only modest success. Later, however, women's reform efforts paid off in improvements in the treatment of workers and in safer food and drug products—all of which President Theodore Roosevelt supported, along with his own plans for reforming business, labor, and the environment.

ASSESSMENT

1. **TERMS & NAMES** For each term or name, write a sentence explaining its significance.
   - **NACW**
   - **suffrage**
   - **Susan B. Anthony**
   - **NAWSA**

MAIN IDEA

2. **TAKING NOTES**
   In a chart like the one below, fill in details about working women in the late 1800s.

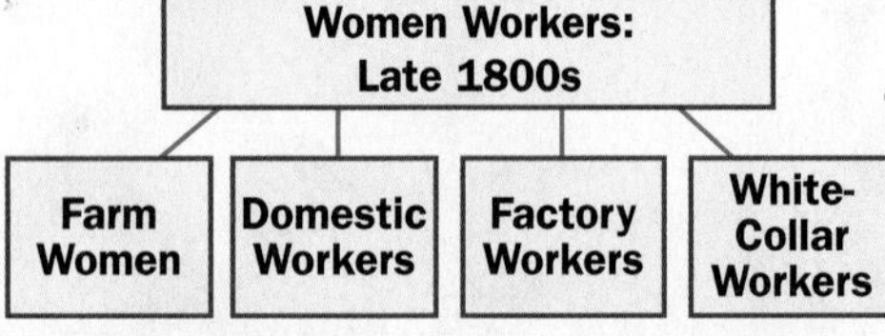

   What generalizations can you make about women workers at this time?

CRITICAL THINKING

3. **SYNTHESIZING**
   What women and movements during the Progressive Era helped dispel the stereotype that women were submissive and nonpolitical?

4. **MAKING INFERENCES**
   Why do you think some colleges refused to accept women in the late 19th century?

5. **ANALYZING ISSUES**
   Imagine you are a woman during the Progressive Era. Explain how you might recruit other women to support the following causes: improving education, housing reform, food and drug laws, the right to vote. **Think About:**
   - the problems that each movement was trying to remedy
   - how women benefited from each cause

SECTION 3

Teddy Roosevelt's Square Deal

MAIN IDEA

As president, Theodore Roosevelt worked to give citizens a Square Deal through progressive reforms.

WHY IT MATTERS NOW

As part of his Square Deal, Roosevelt's conservation efforts made a permanent impact on environmental resources.

Terms & Names

- **Upton Sinclair**
- ***The Jungle***
- **Theodore Roosevelt**
- **Square Deal**
- **Meat Inspection Act**
- **Pure Food and Drug Act**
- **conservation**
- **NAACP**

One American's Story

Use the graphic organizer online to take notes about Theodore Roosevelt's presidency.

When muckraking journalist **Upton Sinclair** began research for a novel in 1904, his focus was the human condition in the stockyards of Chicago. Sinclair intended his novel to reveal "the breaking of human hearts by a system [that] exploits the labor of men and women for profits." What most shocked readers in Sinclair's book ***The Jungle*** (1906), however, was the sickening conditions of the meatpacking industry.

A PERSONAL VOICE UPTON SINCLAIR

"There would be meat that had tumbled out on the floor, in the dirt and sawdust, where the workers had tramped and spit uncounted billions of consumption [tuberculosis] germs. There would be meat stored in great piles in rooms; . . . and thousands of rats would race about on it. . . . A man could run his hand over these piles of meat and sweep off handfuls of the dried dung of rats. These rats were nuisances, and the packers would put poisoned bread out for them; they would die, and then rats, bread, and meat would go into the hoppers together."

—*The Jungle*

Upton Sinclair poses with his son at the time of the writing of *The Jungle*.

President **Theodore Roosevelt,** like many other readers, was nauseated by Sinclair's account. The president invited the author to visit him at the White House, where Roosevelt promised that "the specific evils you point out shall, if their existence be proved, and if I have the power, be eradicated."

A Rough-Riding President

Theodore Roosevelt was not supposed to be president. In 1900, the young governor from New York was urged to run as McKinley's vice-president by the state's political bosses, who found Roosevelt impossible to control. The plot to nominate Roosevelt worked, taking him out of state office. However, as vice-president,

▲ When the president spared a bear cub on a hunting expedition, a toymaker marketed a popular new product, the teddy bear.

Roosevelt stood a heartbeat away from becoming president. Indeed, President McKinley had served barely six months of his second term before he was assassinated, making Roosevelt the most powerful person in the government.

ROOSEVELT'S RISE Theodore Roosevelt was born into a wealthy New York family in 1858. An asthma sufferer during his childhood, young Teddy drove himself to accomplish demanding physical feats. As a teenager, he mastered marksmanship and horseback riding. At Harvard College, Roosevelt boxed and wrestled.

At an early age, the ambitious Roosevelt became a leader in New York politics. After serving three terms in the New York State Assembly, he became New York City's police commissioner and then assistant secretary of the U.S. Navy. The aspiring politician grabbed national attention, advocating war against Spain in 1898. His volunteer cavalry brigade, the Rough Riders, won public acclaim for its role in the battle at San Juan Hill in Cuba. Roosevelt returned a hero and was soon elected governor of New York and then later won the vice-presidency.

THE MODERN PRESIDENCY When Roosevelt was thrust into the presidency in 1901, he became the youngest president ever at 42 years old. Unlike previous presidents, Roosevelt soon dominated the news with his many exploits. While in office, Roosevelt enjoyed boxing, although one of his opponents blinded him in the left eye. On another day, he galloped 100 miles on horseback, merely to prove the feat possible.

In politics, as in sports, Roosevelt acted boldly, using his personality and popularity to advance his programs. His leadership and publicity campaigns helped create the modern presidency, making him a model by which all future presidents would be measured. Citing federal responsibility for the national welfare, Roosevelt thought the government should assume control whenever states proved incapable of dealing with problems. He explained, "It is the duty of the president to act upon the theory that he is the steward of the people, and . . . to assume that he has the legal right to do whatever the needs of the people demand, unless the Constitution or the laws explicitly forbid him to do it."

Teddy Roosevelt enjoyed an active lifestyle, as this 1902 photo reveals. ▶

MAIN IDEA

Synthesizing
A What actions and characteristics of Teddy Roosevelt contributed to his reputation as the first modern president?

Roosevelt saw the presidency as a "bully pulpit," from which he could influence the news media and shape legislation. If big business victimized workers, then President Roosevelt would see to it that the common people received what he called a **Square Deal.** This term was used to describe the various progressive reforms sponsored by the Roosevelt administration. **A**

Using Federal Power

Roosevelt's study of history—he published the first of his 44 books at the age of 24—convinced him that modern America required a powerful federal government. "A simple and poor society can exist as a democracy on the basis of sheer individualism," Roosevelt declared, "but a rich and complex industrial society cannot so exist." The young president soon met several challenges to his assertion of federal power.

TRUSTBUSTING By 1900, trusts—legal bodies created to hold stock in many companies—controlled about four-fifths of the industries in the United States. Some trusts, like Standard Oil, had earned poor reputations with the public by the use of unfair business practices. Many trusts lowered their prices to drive competitors out of the market and then took advantage of the lack of competition to jack prices up even higher. Although Congress had passed the Sherman Antitrust Act in 1890, the act's vague language made enforcement difficult. As a result, nearly all the suits filed against the trusts under the Sherman Act were ineffective.

President Roosevelt did not believe that all trusts were harmful, but he sought to curb the actions of those that hurt the public interest. The president concentrated his efforts on filing suits under the Sherman Antitrust Act. In 1902, Roosevelt made newspaper headlines as a trustbuster when he ordered the Justice Department to sue the Northern Securities Company, which had established a monopoly over northwestern railroads. In 1904, the Supreme Court dissolved the company. Although the Roosevelt administration filed 44 antitrust suits, winning a number of them and breaking up some of the trusts, it was unable to slow the merger movement in business.

VIDEO
Teddy Roosevelt vs. Corporate America

hmhsocialstudies.com

Analyzing *Political Cartoons*

"THE LION-TAMER"

As part of his Square Deal, President Roosevelt aggressively used the Sherman Antitrust Act of 1890 to attack big businesses engaging in unfair practices. His victory over his first target, the Northern Securities Company, earned him a reputation as a hard-hitting trustbuster committed to protecting the public interest. This cartoon shows Roosevelt trying to tame the wild lions that symbolize the great and powerful companies of 1904.

SKILLBUILDER Analyzing Political Cartoons

1. What do the lions stand for?
2. Why are all the lions coming out of a door labeled "Wall St."?
3. What do you think the cartoonist thinks about trustbusting? Cite details from the cartoon that support your interpretation.

SEE SKILLBUILDER HANDBOOK, PAGE R24.

THE LION-TAMER

1902 COAL STRIKE When 140,000 coal miners in Pennsylvania went on strike and demanded a 20 percent raise, a nine-hour workday, and the right to organize a union, the mine operators refused to bargain. Five months into the strike, coal reserves ran low. Roosevelt, seeing the need to intervene, called both sides to the White House to talk, and eventually settled the strike. Irked by the "extraordinary stupidity and bad temper" of the mine operators, he later confessed that only the dignity of the presidency had kept him from taking one owner "by the seat of the breeches" and tossing him out of the window.

Faced with Roosevelt's threat to take over the mines, the opposing sides finally agreed to submit their differences to an arbitration commission—a third party that would work with both sides to mediate the dispute. In 1903, the commission issued its compromise settlement. The miners won a 10 percent pay hike and a shorter, nine-hour workday. With this, however, they had to give up their demand for a closed shop—in which all workers must belong to the union—and their right to strike during the next three years.

> *"In life, as in a football game, the principle . . . is: Hit the line hard."*
> THEODORE ROOSEVELT

President Roosevelt's actions had demonstrated a new principle. From then on, when a strike threatened the public welfare, the federal government was expected to intervene. In addition, Roosevelt's actions reflected the progressive belief that disputes could be settled in an orderly way with the help of experts, such as those on the arbitration commission. B

MAIN IDEA

Analyzing Effects

B What was significant about the way the 1902 coal strike was settled?

RAILROAD REGULATION Roosevelt's real goal was federal regulation. In 1887, Congress had passed the Interstate Commerce Act, which prohibited wealthy railroad owners from colluding to fix high prices by dividing the business in a given area. The Interstate Commerce Commission (ICC) was set up to enforce the new law but had little power. With Roosevelt's urging, Congress passed the Elkins Act in 1903, which made it illegal for railroad officials to give, and shippers to receive, rebates for using particular railroads. The act also specified that railroads could not change set rates without notifying the public.

Vocabulary

collude: to act together secretly to achieve an illegal or deceitful purpose

The Hepburn Act of 1906 strictly limited the distribution of free railroad passes, a common form of bribery. It also gave the ICC power to set maximum railroad rates. Although Roosevelt had to compromise with conservative senators who opposed the act, its passage boosted the government's power to regulate the railroads.

NOW & THEN

MEAT INSPECTION

During the Progressive Era, people worried about the kinds of things that might fall—or walk—into a batch of meat being processed. Today, Americans worry more about contamination by unseen dangers, such as E. coli bacteria, mad cow disease, and antibiotics or other chemicals that may pose long-range health risks to people.

In July 1996, Congress passed the most extensive changes in standards for meat inspection since the Meat Inspection Act of 1906. The costs of the new, more scientific inspections amount to about a tenth of a penny per pound of meat. The FDA has also adopted restrictions on importation of feed and livestock from other countries to prevent the spread of disease.

Health and the Environment

President Roosevelt's enthusiasm and his considerable skill at compromise led to laws and policies that benefited both public health and the environment. He wrote, "We recognize and are bound to war against the evils of today. The remedies are partly economic and partly spiritual, partly to be obtained by laws, and in greater part to be obtained by individual and associated effort."

REGULATING FOODS AND DRUGS After reading *The Jungle* by Upton Sinclair, Roosevelt responded to the public's clamor for action. He appointed a commission of experts to investigate the meatpacking industry. The commission issued a scathing report backing up Sinclair's account of the disgusting conditions in the industry. True to his word, in 1906 Roosevelt pushed for passage of the **Meat Inspection Act,**

Coal Mining in the Early 1900s

hmhsocialstudies.com INTERACTIVE

Coal played a key role in America's industrial boom around the turn of the century, providing the United States with about 90 percent of its energy. Miners often had to dig for coal hundreds of feet below the earth's surface. The work in these mines was among the hardest and most dangerous in the world. Progressive Era reforms helped improve conditions for miners, as many won wage increases and shorter work hours.

The coal mines employed thousands of children, like this boy pictured in 1909. In 1916, progressives helped secure passage of a child labor law that forbade interstate commerce of goods produced by children under the age of 14.

Most underground mines had two shafts—an elevator shaft (shown here) for transporting workers and coal, and an air shaft for ventilation.

Like these men working in 1908, miners typically spent their days in dark, cramped spaces underground.

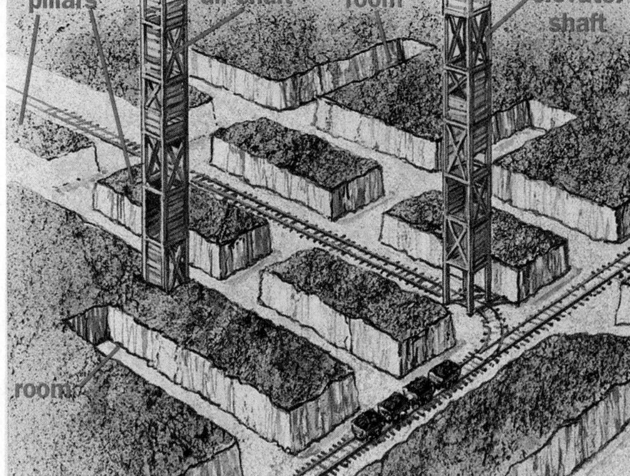

Most mines used a room-and-pillar method for extracting coal. This entailed digging out "rooms" of coal off a series of tunnels, leaving enough coal behind to form a pillar that prevented the room from collapsing.

The miners' main tool was the pick. Many also used drilling machines.

Donkeys or mules pulled the coal cars to the elevators, which transported the coal to the surface.

Government workers inspect meat as it moves through the packinghouse. ▶

which dictated strict cleanliness requirements for meatpackers and created the program of federal meat inspection that was in use until it was replaced by more sophisticated techniques in the 1990s.

The compromise that won the act's passage, however, left the government paying for the inspections and did not require companies to label their canned goods with date-of-processing information. The compromise also granted meatpackers the right to appeal negative decisions in court.

PURE FOOD AND DRUG ACT Before any federal regulations were established for advertising food and drugs, manufacturers had claimed that their products accomplished everything from curing cancer to growing hair. In addition, popular children's medicines often contained opium, cocaine, or alcohol. In a series of lectures across the country, Dr. Harvey Washington Wiley, chief chemist at the Department of Agriculture, criticized manufacturers for adding harmful preservatives to food and brought needed attention to this issue.

A typical late-19th-century product advertisement. ▼

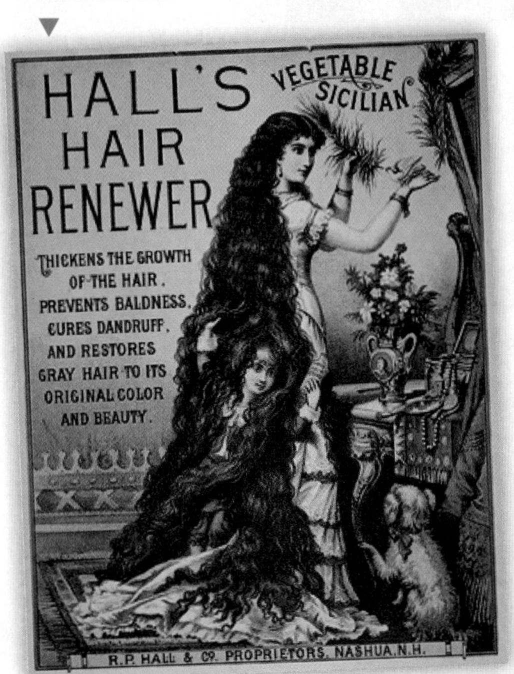

HALL'S
VEGETABLE SICILIAN
HAIR
RENEWER
THICKENS THE GROWTH OF THE HAIR.
PREVENTS BALDNESS.
CURES DANDRUFF,
AND RESTORES GRAY HAIR TO ITS ORIGINAL COLOR AND BEAUTY.
R.P. HALL & CO. PROPRIETORS, NASHUA, N.H.

In 1906, Congress passed the **Pure Food and Drug Act,** which halted the sale of contaminated foods and medicines and called for truth in labeling. Although this act did not ban harmful products outright, its requirement of truthful labels reflected the progressive belief that given accurate information, people would act wisely. C

MAIN IDEA

Comparing

C What similarities did the Meat Inspection Act and Pure Food and Drug Act share?

CONSERVATION AND NATURAL RESOURCES Before Roosevelt's presidency, the federal government had paid very little attention to the nation's natural resources. Despite the establishment of the U.S. Forest Bureau in 1887 and the subsequent withdrawal from public sale of 45 million acres of timberlands for a national forest reserve, the government stood by while private interests gobbled up the shrinking wilderness.

In the late 19th century Americans had shortsightedly exploited their natural environment. Pioneer farmers leveled the forests and plowed up the prairies. Ranchers allowed their cattle to overgraze the Great Plains. Coal companies cluttered the land with refuse from mines. Lumber companies ignored the effect of their logging operations on flood control and neglected to plant trees to replace those they had cut down. Cities dumped untreated sewage and industrial wastes into rivers, poisoning the streams and creating health hazards.

CONSERVATION MEASURES Roosevelt condemned the view that America's resources were endless and made conservation a primary concern. John Muir, a naturalist and writer with whom Roosevelt camped in California's Yosemite National Park in 1903, persuaded the president to set aside 148 million acres of forest reserves. Roosevelt also set aside 1.5 million acres of water-power sites and another 80 million acres of land that experts from the U.S. Geological Survey would explore for mineral and water resources. Roosevelt also established more than 50 wildlife sanctuaries and several national parks.

True to the Progressive belief in using experts, in 1905 the president named Gifford Pinchot as head of the U.S. Forest Service. A professional conservationist, Pinchot had administrative skill as well as the latest scientific and technical information. He advised Roosevelt to conserve forest and grazing lands by keeping large tracts of federal land exempt from private sale.

Conservationists like Roosevelt and Pinchot, however, did not share the views of Muir, who advocated complete preservation of the wilderness. Instead, **conservation** to them meant that some wilderness areas would be preserved while others would be developed for the common good. Indeed, Roosevelt's federal water projects transformed some dry wilderness areas to make agriculture possible. Under the National Reclamation Act of 1902, known as the Newlands

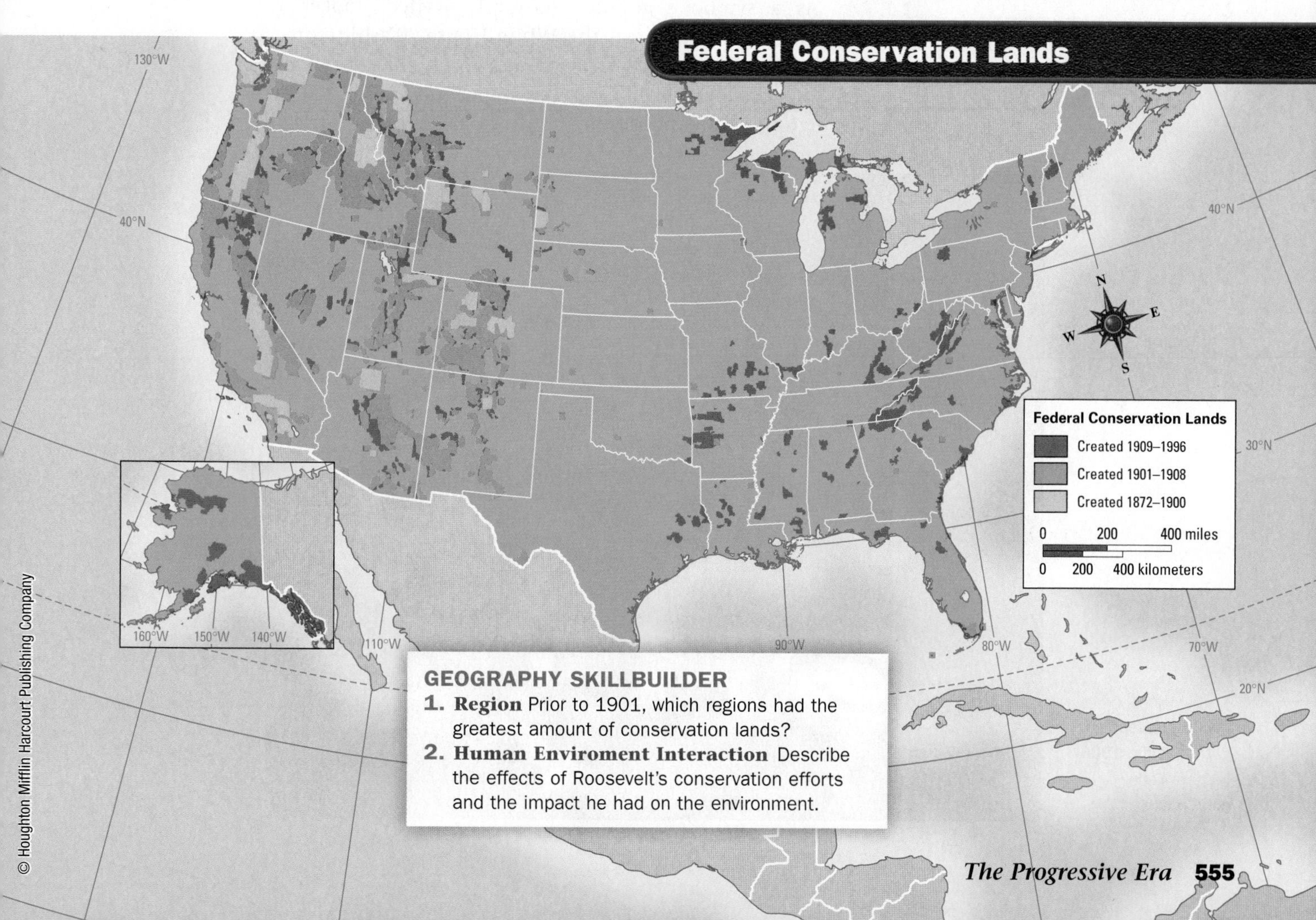

GEOGRAPHY SKILLBUILDER

1. **Region** Prior to 1901, which regions had the greatest amount of conservation lands?
2. **Human Enviroment Interaction** Describe the effects of Roosevelt's conservation efforts and the impact he had on the environment.

Act, money from the sale of public lands in the West funded large-scale irrigation projects, such as the Roosevelt Dam in Arizona and the Shoshone Dam in Wyoming. The Newlands Act established the precedent that the federal government would manage the precious water resources of the West. D

MAIN IDEA

Summarizing

D Summarize Roosevelt's approach to environmental problems.

HISTORICAL SPOTLIGHT

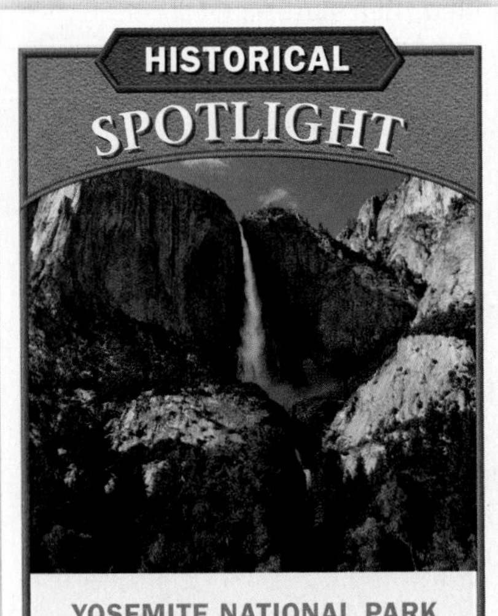

YOSEMITE NATIONAL PARK

The naturalist John Muir visited the Yosemite region of central California in 1868 and made it his home base for a period of six years while he traveled throughout the West.

Muir was the first to suggest that Yosemite's spectacular land formations had been shaped by glaciers. Today the park's impressive cliffs, waterfalls, lakes, and meadows draw sports enthusiasts and tourists in all seasons.

Roosevelt and Civil Rights

Roosevelt's concern for the land and its inhabitants was not matched in the area of civil rights. Though Roosevelt's father had supported the North, his mother, Martha, may well have been the model for the Southern belle Scarlett O'Hara in Margaret Mitchell's famous novel, *Gone with the Wind*. In almost two terms as president, Roosevelt—like most other progressives—failed to support civil rights for African Americans. He did, however, support a few individual African Americans.

Despite opposition from whites, Roosevelt appointed an African American as head of the Charleston, South Carolina, customhouse. In another instance, when some whites in Mississippi refused to accept the black postmistress he had appointed, he chose to close the station rather than give in. In 1906, however, Roosevelt angered many African Americans when he dismissed without question an entire regiment of African-American soldiers accused of conspiracy in protecting others charged with murder in Brownsville, Texas.

As a symbolic gesture, Roosevelt invited Booker T. Washington to dinner at the White House. Washington—head of the Tuskegee Normal and Industrial Institute, an all-black training school—was then the African-American leader most respected by powerful whites. Washington faced opposition, however, from other African

Civil rights leaders gather at the 1905 Niagara Falls conference. ▶

Vocabulary
accommodation: adapting or making adjustments in order to satisfy someone else

Americans, such as W. E. B. Du Bois, for his accommodation of segregationists and for blaming black poverty on blacks and urging them to accept discrimination.

Persistent in his criticism of Washington's ideas, Du Bois renewed his demands for immediate social and economic equality for African Americans. In his 1903 book *The Souls of Black Folk*, Du Bois wrote of his opposition to Washington's position.

A PERSONAL VOICE W. E. B. DU BOIS

"**So far as Mr. Washington preaches Thrift, Patience, and Industrial Training for the masses, we must hold up his hands and strive with him. . . . But so far as Mr. Washington apologizes for injustice, North or South, does not rightly value the privilege and duty of voting, belittles the emasculating effects of caste distinctions, and opposes the higher training and ambition of our brighter minds,—so far as he, the South, or the Nation, does this,—we must unceasingly and firmly oppose them.**"

—*The Souls of Black Folk*

Du Bois and other advocates of equality for African Americans were deeply upset by the apparent progressive indifference to racial injustice. In 1905 they held a civil rights conference in Niagara Falls, and in 1909 a number of African Americans joined with prominent white reformers in New York to found the **NAACP**—the National Association for the Advancement of Colored People. The NAACP, which had over 6,000 members by 1914, aimed for nothing less than full equality among the races. That goal, however, found little support in the Progressive Movement, which focused on the needs of middle-class whites. The two presidents who followed Roosevelt also did little to advance the goal of racial equality.

Background
The Niagara Movement was comprised of 29 black intellectuals. They met secretly in 1905 to compose a civil rights manifesto.

KEY PLAYER

W. E. B. DU BOIS
1868–1963

In 1909, W. E. B. Du Bois helped to establish the NAACP and entered into the forefront of the early U.S. civil rights movement. However, in the 1920s, he faced a power struggle with the NAACP's executive secretary, Walter White.

Ironically, Du Bois had retreated to a position others saw as dangerously close to that of Booker T. Washington. Arguing for a separate economy for African Americans, Du Bois made a distinction, which White rejected, between enforced and voluntary segregation. By mid-century, Du Bois was outside the mainstream of the civil rights movement. His work remained largely ignored until after his death in 1963.

SECTION 3 ASSESSMENT

1. **TERMS & NAMES** For each term or name, write a sentence explaining its significance.
   - **Upton Sinclair**
   - ***The Jungle***
   - **Theodore Roosevelt**
   - **Square Deal**
   - **Meat Inspection Act**
   - **Pure Food and Drug Act**
   - **conservation**
   - **NAACP**

MAIN IDEA

2. **TAKING NOTES**
Create five problem-solution diagrams like the one below to show how the following problems were addressed during Roosevelt's presidency: (a) 1902 coal strike, (b) Northern Securities Company monopoly, (c) unsafe meat processing, (d) exploitation of the environment, and (e) racial injustice.

Problems → **Solutions**

Write headlines announcing the solutions.

CRITICAL THINKING

3. **FORMING GENERALIZATIONS**
In what ways do you think the progressive belief in using experts played a role in shaping Roosevelt's reforms? Refer to details from the text. **Think About:**
   - Roosevelt's use of experts to help him tackle political, economic, and environmental problems
   - how experts' findings affected legislative actions

4. **EVALUATING**
Research the coal strike of 1902. Do you think Roosevelt's intervention was in favor of the strikers or of the mine operators? Why?

5. **ANALYZING ISSUES**
Why did W. E. B. Du Bois oppose Booker T. Washington's views on racial discrimination?

The Muckrakers

1902–1917 The tradition of the investigative reporter uncovering corruption was established early in the 20th century by the writers known as muckrakers. Coined by President Theodore Roosevelt, the term *muckraker* alludes to the English author John Bunyan's famous 17th-century religious allegory *The Pilgrim's Progress*, which features a character too busy raking up the muck to see a heavenly crown held over him. The originally negative term soon was applied to many writers whose reform efforts Roosevelt himself supported. The muckraking movement spilled over from journalism as writers such as Upton Sinclair made use of the greater dramatic effects of fiction.

◀ **IDA M. TARBELL**

Ida M. Tarbell's "The History of the Standard Oil Company" exposed the ruthlessness with which John D. Rockefeller had turned his oil business into an all-powerful monopoly. Her writing added force to the trustbusting reforms of the early 20th century. Here Tarbell describes how Standard Oil used lower transportation rates to drive out smaller refineries, such as Hanna, Baslington and Company.

> Mr. Hanna had been refining since July, 1869. . . . Some time in February, 1872, the Standard Oil Company asked [for] an interview with him and his associates. They wanted to buy his works, they said. "But we don't want to sell," objected Mr. Hanna. "You can never make any more money, in my judgment," said Mr. Rockefeller. "You can't compete with the Standard. We have all the large refineries now. If you refuse to sell, it will end in your being crushed." Hanna and Baslington were not satisfied. They went to see . . . General Devereux, manager of the Lake Shore road. They were told that the Standard had special rates; that it was useless to try to compete with them. General Devereux explained to the gentlemen that the privileges granted the Standard were the legitimate and necessary advantage of the larger shipper over the smaller. . . . General Devereux says they "recognised the propriety" of his excuse. They certainly recognised its authority. They say that they were satisfied they could no longer get rates to and from Cleveland which would enable them to live, and "reluctantly" sold out. It must have been reluctantly, for they had paid $75,000 for their works, and had made thirty per cent. a year on an average on their investment, and the Standard appraiser allowed them $45,000.

—Ida M. Tarbell, "The History of the Standard Oil Company" (1904)

LINCOLN STEFFENS ▶

Lincoln Steffens is usually named as a leading figure of the muckraking movement. He published exposés of business and government corruption in *McClure's Magazine* and other magazines. These articles were then collected in two books: *The Shame of the Cities* and *The Struggle for Self-Government*. Below is a section from an article Steffens wrote to expose voter fraud in Philadelphia.

> The police are forbidden by law to stand within thirty feet of the polls, but they are at the box and they are there to see that the [Republican political] machine's orders are obeyed and that repeaters whom they help to furnish are permitted to vote without "intimidation" on the names they, the police, have supplied. The editor of an anti-machine paper who was looking about for himself once told me that a ward leader who knew him well asked him into a polling place. "I'll show you how it's done," he said, and he had the repeaters go round and round voting again and again on the names handed them on slips. . . . The business proceeds with very few hitches; there is more jesting than fighting. Violence in the past has had its effect; and is not often necessary nowadays, but if it is needed the police are there to apply it.

—Lincoln Steffens, *The Shame of the Cities* (1904)

UPTON SINCLAIR

Upton Sinclair's chief aim in writing *The Jungle* was to expose the shocking conditions that immigrant workers endured. The public, however, reacted even more strongly to the novel's revelations of unsanitary conditions in the meatpacking industry. Serialized in 1905 and published in book form one year later, *The Jungle* prompted a federal investigation that resulted in passage of the Meat Inspection Act in 1906.

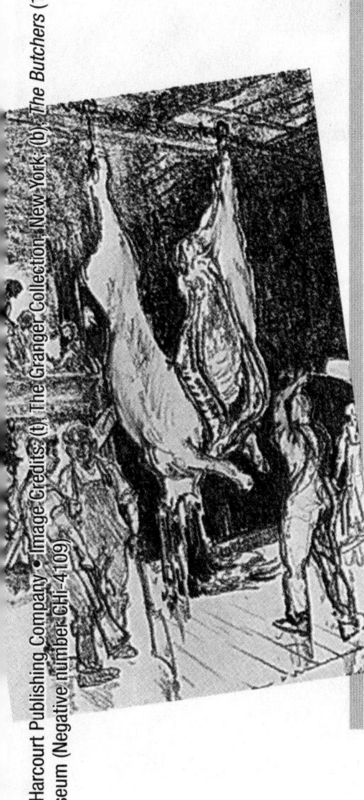

> Jonas had told them how the meat that was taken out of pickle would often be found sour, and how they would rub it up with [baking] soda to take away the smell, and sell it to be eaten on free-lunch counters; also of all the miracles of chemistry which they performed, giving to any sort of meat, fresh or salted, whole or chopped, any color and any flavor and any odor they chose. . . .
>
> It was only when the whole ham was spoiled that it came into the department of Elzbieta. Cut up by the two-thousand-revolutions-a-minute flyers, and mixed with half a ton of other meat, no odor that ever was in a ham could make any difference. There was never the least attention paid to what was cut up for sausage; there would come all the way back from Europe old sausage that had been rejected, and that was moldy and white—it would be dosed with borax and glycerine, and dumped into the hoppers, and made over again for home consumption.

—Upton Sinclair, *The Jungle* (1906)

THINKING CRITICALLY

1. **Comparing and Contrasting** State the main idea of each of these selections. What role do details play in making the passages convincing?

   SEE SKILLBUILDER HANDBOOK, PAGE R8.

2. hmhsocialstudies.com INTERNET ACTIVITY 21ST CENTURY

   Visit the links for American Literature: The Muckrakers to learn more about the muckrakers. What topics did they investigate? How did they affect public opinion? What legal changes did they help to bring about? Write a summary of the muckrakers' impact on society.

Progressivism Under Taft

MAIN IDEA	WHY IT MATTERS NOW	Terms & Names
Taft's ambivalent approach to progressive reform led to a split in the Republican Party and the loss of the presidency to the Democrats.	Third-party candidates continue to wrestle with how to become viable candidates.	• Gifford Pinchot • William Howard Taft • Payne-Aldrich Tariff • Bull Moose Party • Woodrow Wilson

One American's Story

Use the graphic organizer online to take notes about difficulties during Taft's presidency.

Early in the 20th century, Americans' interest in the preservation of the country's wilderness areas intensified. Writers proclaimed the beauty of the landscape, and new groups like the Girl Scouts gave city children the chance to experience a different environment. The desire for preservation clashed with business interests that favored unrestricted development. **Gifford Pinchot** (pĭn′shō′), head of the U.S. Forest Service under President Roosevelt, took a middle ground. He believed that wilderness areas could be scientifically managed to yield public enjoyment while allowing private development.

▲ Gifford Pinchot

A PERSONAL VOICE GIFFORD PINCHOT

"The American people have evidently made up their minds that our natural resources must be conserved. That is good. But it settles only half the question. For whose benefit shall they be conserved—for the benefit of the many, or for the use and profit of the few? . . . There is no other question before us that begins to be so important, or that will be so difficult to straddle, as the great question between special interest and equal opportunity, between the privileges of the few and the rights of the many, between government by men for human welfare and government by money for profit."

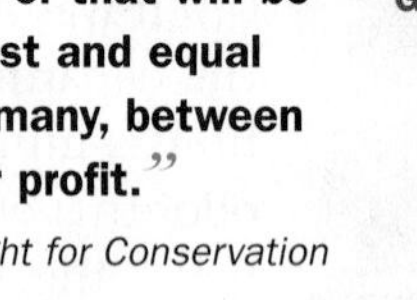

—*The Fight for Conservation*

President Roosevelt, a fellow conservationist, favored Pinchot's multi-use land program. However, when he left office in 1909, this approach came under increasing pressure from business people who favored unrestricted commercial development.

Taft Becomes President

After winning the election in 1904, Roosevelt pledged not to run for reelection in 1908. He handpicked his secretary of war, **William Howard Taft,** to run against William Jennings Bryan, who had been nominated by the Democrats for the third time. Under the slogan "Vote for Taft this time, You can vote for Bryan any time," Taft and the Republicans won an easy victory.

TAFT STUMBLES As president, Taft pursued a cautiously progressive agenda, seeking to consolidate rather than to expand Roosevelt's reforms. He received little credit for his accomplishments, however. His legal victories, such as busting 90 trusts in a four-year term, did not bolster his popularity. Indeed, the new president confessed in a letter to Roosevelt that he never felt like the president. "When I am addressed as 'Mr. President,'" Taft wrote, "I turn to see whether you are not at my elbow."

The cautious Taft hesitated to use the presidential bully pulpit to arouse public opinion. Nor could he subdue troublesome members of his own party. Tariffs and conservation posed his first problems.

THE PAYNE–ALDRICH TARIFF Taft had campaigned on a platform of lowering tariffs, a staple of the progressive agenda. When the House passed the Payne Bill, which lowered rates on imported manufactured goods, the Senate proposed an alternative bill, the Aldrich Bill, which made fewer cuts and increased many rates. Amid cries of betrayal from the progressive wing of his party, Taft signed the **Payne-Aldrich Tariff,** a compromise that only moderated the high rates of the Aldrich Bill. This angered progressives who believed Taft had abandoned progressivism. The president made his difficulties worse by clumsily attempting to defend the tariff, calling it "the best [tariff] bill the Republican party ever passed."

DIFFICULT DECISIONS

CONTROLLING RESOURCES

Historically, conservationists such as Gifford Pinchot have stood for the balanced use of natural resources, preserving some and using others for private industry. Free-market advocates like Richard Ballinger pressed for the private development of wilderness areas. Preservationists such as John Muir advocated preserving all remaining wilderness.

1. Examine the pros and cons of each position. With which do you agree? What factors do you think should influence decisions about America's wilderness areas?
2. If you'd been asked in 1902 to decide whether to develop or preserve America's wilderness areas, what would you have decided? Why?

DISPUTING PUBLIC LANDS Next, Taft angered conservationists by appointing as his secretary of the interior Richard A. Ballinger, a wealthy lawyer from Seattle. Ballinger, who disapproved of conservationist controls on western lands, removed 1 million acres of forest and mining lands from the reserved list and returned it to the public domain.

When a Department of the Interior official was fired for protesting Ballinger's actions, the fired worker published a muckraking article against Ballinger in *Collier's Weekly* magazine. Pinchot added his voice. In congressional testimony he accused Ballinger of letting commercial interests exploit the natural resources that rightfully belonged to the public. President Taft sided with Ballinger and fired Pinchot from the U.S. Forest Service. (A)

MAIN IDEA

Analyzing Issues

(A) How did Taft's appointee Richard Ballinger anger conservationists?

The Republican Party Splits

Taft's cautious nature made it impossible for him to hold together the two wings of the Republican Party: progressives who sought change and conservatives who did not. The Republican Party began to fragment.

PROBLEMS WITHIN THE PARTY Republican conservatives and progressives split over Taft's support of the political boss Joseph Cannon, House Speaker from Illinois. A rough-talking, tobacco-chewing politician, "Uncle Joe" often disregarded seniority in filling committee slots. As chairman of the House Rules Committee, which decides what bills Congress considers, Cannon often weakened or ignored progressive bills.

Reform-minded Republicans decided that their only alternative was to strip Cannon of his power. With the help of Democrats, they succeeded in March 1910 with a resolution that called for the entire House to elect the Committee on Rules and excluded the Speaker from membership in the committee.

William Howard Taft

KEY PLAYER

WILLIAM HOWARD TAFT
1857–1930

William Howard Taft never wanted to be president. After serving one term, Taft left the White House, which he called "the lonesomest place in the world," and taught constitutional law at Yale for eight years.

In 1921, President Harding named Taft chief justice of the Supreme Court. The man whose family had nicknamed him "Big Lub" called this appointment the highest honor he had ever received. As chief justice, Taft wrote that "in my present life I don't remember that I ever was President."

However, Americans remember Taft for, among many other things, initiating in 1910 the popular presidential custom of throwing out the first ball of the major league baseball season.

By the midterm elections of 1910, however, the Republican Party was in shambles, with the progressives on one side and the "old guard" on the other. Voters voiced concern over the rising cost of living, which they blamed on the Payne-Aldrich Tariff. They also believed Taft to be against conservation. When the Republicans lost the election, the Democrats gained control of the House of Representatives for the first time in 18 years.

Vocabulary
"old guard": conservative members of a group

THE BULL MOOSE PARTY After leaving office, Roosevelt headed to Africa to shoot big game. He returned in 1910 to a hero's welcome, and responded with a rousing speech proposing a "New Nationalism," under which the federal government would exert its power for "the welfare of the people."

By 1912, Roosevelt had decided to run for a third term as president. The primary elections showed that Republicans wanted Roosevelt, but Taft had the advantage of being the incumbent—that is, the holder of the office. At the Republican convention in June 1912, Taft supporters maneuvered to replace Roosevelt delegates with Taft delegates in a number of delegations. Republican progressives refused to vote and formed a new third party, the Progressive Party. They nominated Roosevelt for president.

The Progressive Party became known as the **Bull Moose Party**, after Roosevelt's boast that he was "as strong as a bull moose." The party's platform called for the direct election of senators and the adoption in all states of the initiative, referendum, and recall. It also advocated woman suffrage, workmen's compensation, an eight-hour workday, a minimum wage for women, a federal law against child labor, and a federal trade commission to regulate business. **B**

MAIN IDEA

Contrasting
B What were the differences between Taft's and Roosevelt's campaign platforms?

The split in the Republican ranks handed the Democrats their first real chance at the White House since the election of Grover Cleveland in 1892. In the 1912 presidential election, they put forward as their candidate a reform governor of New Jersey named **Woodrow Wilson**.

Democrats Win in 1912

Under Governor Woodrow Wilson's leadership, the previously conservative New Jersey legislature had passed a host of reform measures. Now, as the Democratic presidential nominee, Wilson endorsed a progressive platform called the New Freedom. It demanded even stronger antitrust legislation, banking reform, and reduced tariffs.

The split between Taft and Roosevelt, former Republican allies, turned nasty during the fall campaign. Taft labeled Roosevelt a "dangerous egotist," while Roosevelt branded Taft a "fathead" with the brain of a "guinea pig." Wilson distanced himself, quietly gloating, "Don't interfere when your enemy is destroying himself."

The election offered voters several choices: Wilson's New Freedom, Taft's conservatism, Roosevelt's progressivism, or the Socialist Party policies of Eugene V. Debs. Both Roosevelt and Wilson supported a stronger government role in economic affairs but differed over strategies. Roosevelt supported government action to supervise big business but did not oppose all business monopolies, while Debs called for an end to capitalism. Wilson supported small business and free-market competition and characterized all business monopolies as evil. In a speech, Wilson explained why he felt that all business monopolies were a threat.

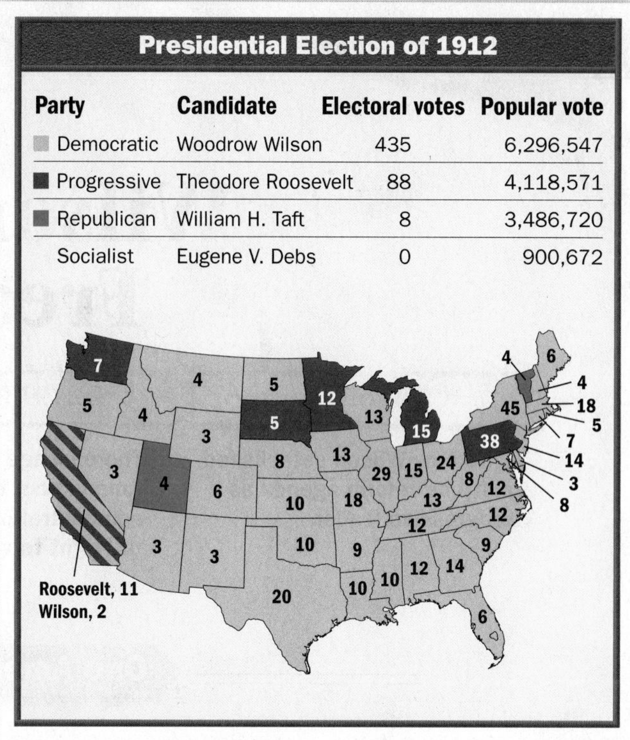

Presidential Election of 1912

Party	Candidate	Electoral votes	Popular vote
Democratic	Woodrow Wilson	435	6,296,547
Progressive	Theodore Roosevelt	88	4,118,571
Republican	William H. Taft	8	3,486,720
Socialist	Eugene V. Debs	0	900,672

A Personal Voice
WOODROW WILSON

> **"If the government is to tell big business men how to run their business, then don't you see that big business men have to get closer to the government even than they are now? Don't you see that they must capture the government, in order not to be restrained too much by it? . . . I don't care how benevolent the master is going to be, I will not live under a master. That is not what America was created for. America was created in order that every man should have the same chance as every other man to exercise mastery over his own fortunes."**
>
> —quoted in *The New Freedom*

MAIN IDEA

Predicting Effects

C What might be one of Wilson's first issues to address as president?

Although Wilson captured only 42 percent of the popular vote, he won an overwhelming electoral victory and a Democratic majority in Congress. As a third-party candidate, Roosevelt defeated Taft in both popular and electoral votes. But reform claimed the real victory, with more than 75 percent of the vote going to the reform candidates—Wilson, Roosevelt, and Debs. In victory, Wilson could claim a mandate to break up trusts and to expand the government's role in social reform. **C**

SECTION 4 ASSESSMENT

1. **TERMS & NAMES** For each term or name, write a sentence explaining its significance.
   - **Gifford Pinchot**
   - **William Howard Taft**
   - **Payne-Aldrich Tariff**
   - **Bull Moose Party**
   - **Woodrow Wilson**

MAIN IDEA

2. **TAKING NOTES**
   Re-create the chart below on your paper. Then fill in the causes Taft supported that made people question his leadership.

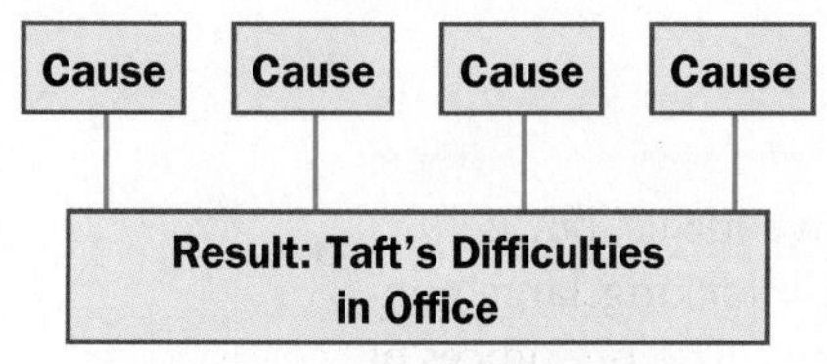

   Which causes do you think would upset most people today? Explain.

CRITICAL THINKING

3. **HYPOTHESIZING**
   What if Roosevelt had won another term in office in 1912? Speculate on how this might have affected the future of progressive reforms. Support your answer. **Think About:**
   - Roosevelt's policies that Taft did not support
   - the power struggles within the Republican Party
   - Roosevelt's perception of what is required of a president

4. **EVALUATING**
   Both Roosevelt and Taft resorted to mudslinging during the 1912 presidential campaign. Do you approve or disapprove of negative campaign tactics? Support your opinion.

Section 5

Wilson's New Freedom

MAIN IDEA	WHY IT MATTERS NOW	Terms & Names
Woodrow Wilson established a strong reform agenda as a progressive leader.	**The passage of the Nineteenth Amendment during Wilson's administration granted women the right to vote.**	**• Carrie Chapman Catt • Clayton Antitrust Act • Federal Trade Commission (FTC) • Federal Reserve System • Nineteenth Amendment**

One American's Story

hmhsocialstudies.com
TAKING NOTES

Use the graphic organizer online to take notes about progressivism during Wilson's first term.

On March 3, 1913, the day of Woodrow Wilson's inauguration, 5,000 woman suffragists marched through hostile crowds in Washington, D.C. Alice Paul and Lucy Burns, the parade's organizers, were members of the National American Woman Suffrage Association (NAWSA). As police failed to restrain the rowdy gathering and congressmen demanded an investigation, Paul and Burns could see the momentum building for suffrage.

By the time Wilson began his campaign for a second term in 1916, the NAWSA's president, **Carrie Chapman Catt**, saw victory on the horizon. Catt expressed her optimism in a letter to her friend Maud Wood Park.

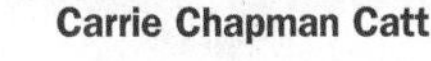

Carrie Chapman Catt

A PERSONAL VOICE CARRIE CHAPMAN CATT

"I do feel keenly that the turn of the road has come. . . . I really believe that we might pull off a campaign which would mean the vote within the next six years if we could secure a Board of officers who would have sufficient momentum, confidence and working power in them. . . . Come! My dear Mrs. Park, gird on your armor once more."

—letter to Maud Wood Park

Catt called an emergency suffrage convention in September 1916, and invited President Wilson, who cautiously supported suffrage. He told the convention, "There has been a force behind you that will . . . be triumphant and for which you can afford. . . . to wait." They did have to wait, but within four years, the passage of the suffrage amendment became the capstone of the progressive movement.

Wilson Wins Financial Reforms

Like Theodore Roosevelt, Woodrow Wilson claimed progressive ideals, but he had a different idea for the federal government. He believed in attacking large concentrations of power to give greater freedom to average citizens. The prejudices of his Southern background, however, prevented him from using federal power to fight off attacks directed at the civil rights of African Americans.

WILSON'S BACKGROUND Wilson spent his youth in the South during the Civil War and Reconstruction. The son, grandson, and nephew of Presbyterian ministers, he received a strict upbringing. Before entering politics, Wilson worked as a lawyer, a history professor, and later as president of Princeton University. In 1910, Wilson became the governor of New Jersey. As governor, he supported progressive legislation programs such as a direct primary, worker's compensation, and the regulation of public utilities and railroads.

As America's newly elected president, Wilson moved to enact his program, the "New Freedom," and planned his attack on what he called the triple wall of privilege: the trusts, tariffs, and high finance.

TWO KEY ANTITRUST MEASURES "Without the watchful . . . resolute interference of the government," Wilson said, "there can be no fair play between individuals and such powerful institutions as the trusts. Freedom today is something more than being let alone." During Wilson's administration, Congress enacted two key antitrust measures. The first, the **Clayton Antitrust Act** of 1914, sought to strengthen the Sherman Antitrust Act of 1890. The Clayton Act prohibited corporations from acquiring the stock of another if doing so would create a monopoly; if a company violated the law, its officers could be prosecuted.

The Clayton Act also specified that labor unions and farm organizations not only had a right to exist but also would no longer be subject to antitrust laws. Therefore, strikes, peaceful picketing, boycotts, and the collection of strike benefits became legal. In addition, injunctions against strikers were prohibited unless the strikers threatened damage that could not be remedied. Samuel Gompers, president of the American Federation of Labor (AFL), saw great value to workers in the Clayton Act. He called it a Magna Carta for labor, referring to the English document, signed in 1215, in which the English king recognized that he was bound by the law and that the law granted rights to his subjects.

Vocabulary
injunction: a court order prohibiting a party from a specific course of action

The second major antitrust measure, the Federal Trade Commission Act of 1914, set up the **Federal Trade Commission (FTC).** This "watchdog" agency was given the power to investigate possible violations of regulatory statutes, to require periodic reports from corporations, and to put an end to a number of unfair business practices. Under Wilson, the FTC administered almost 400 cease-and-desist orders to companies engaged in illegal activity. (A)

MAIN IDEA
Summarizing
(A) What was the impact of the two antitrust measures?

A NEW TAX SYSTEM In an effort to curb the power of big business, Wilson worked to lower tariff rates, knowing that supporters of big business hadn't allowed such a reduction under Taft.

Wilson lobbied hard in 1913 for the Underwood Act, which would substantially reduce tariff rates for the first time since the Civil War. He summoned Congress to a special session to plead his case, and established a precedent of delivering the State of the Union message in person. Businesses lobbied too, looking to block tariff reductions. When manufacturing lobbyists—people hired by manufacturers to present their case to government officials—descended on the capital to urge senators to vote no, passage seemed unlikely. Wilson denounced the lobbyists and urged voters to monitor their senators' votes. Because of the new president's use of the bully pulpit, the Senate voted to cut tariff rates even more deeply than the House had done.

DEREGULATION

In recent years the railroad, airline, and telecommunications industries have all been deregulated, or permitted to compete without government control. It is hoped that this will improve their efficiency and lower prices.

During the Progressive Era, reformers viewed regulation as a necessary role of government to ensure safety and fairness for consumers as well as industrial competitors. Opponents of regulation, however, believed that government regulation caused inefficiency and high prices.

Modern critics of deregulation argue that deregulated businesses may skimp on safety. They may also neglect hard-to-serve populations, such as elderly, poor, or disabled people, while competing for more profitable customers.

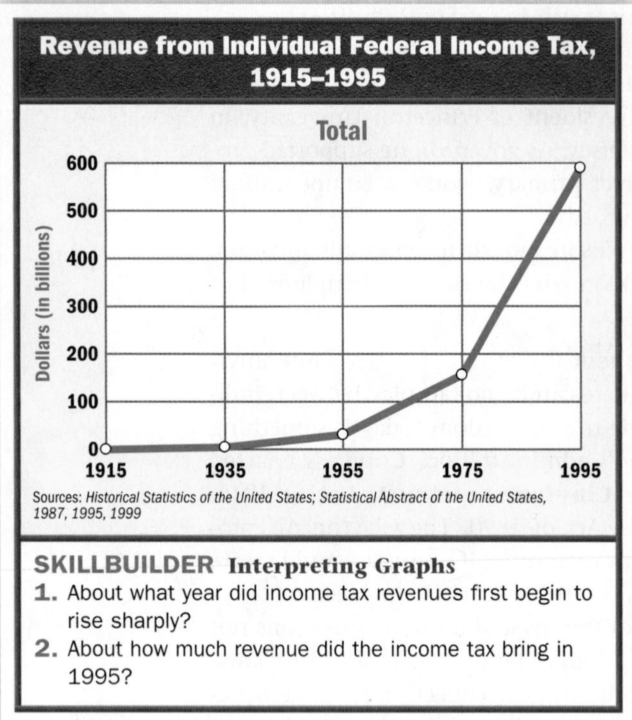

Sources: *Historical Statistics of the United States; Statistical Abstract of the United States*, 1987, 1995, 1999

SKILLBUILDER Interpreting Graphs

1. About what year did income tax revenues first begin to rise sharply?
2. About how much revenue did the income tax bring in 1995?

FEDERAL INCOME TAX With lower tariff rates, the federal government had to replace the revenue that tariffs had previously supplied. Ratified in 1913, the Sixteenth Amendment legalized a federal income tax, which provided revenue by taxing individual earnings and corporate profits.

Under this graduated tax, larger incomes were taxed at higher rates than smaller incomes. The tax began with a modest tax on family incomes over $4,000, and ranged from 1 percent to a maximum of 6 percent on incomes over $500,000. Initially, few congressmen realized the potential of the income tax, but by 1917, the government was receiving more money on the income tax than it had ever gained from tariffs. Today, income taxes on corporations and individuals represent the federal government's main source of revenue.

FEDERAL RESERVE SYSTEM Next, Wilson turned his attention to financial reform. The nation needed a way to strengthen the ways in which banks were run, as well as a way to quickly adjust the amount of money in circulation. Both credit availability and money supply had to keep pace with the economy.

Wilson's solution was to establish a decentralized private banking system under federal control. The Federal Reserve Act of 1913 divided the nation into 12 districts and established a regional central bank in each district. These "banker's banks" then served the other banks within the district.

The federal reserve banks could issue new paper currency in emergency situations, and member banks could use the new currency to make loans to their customers. Federal reserve banks could transfer funds to member banks in trouble, saving the banks from closing and protecting customers' savings. By 1923, roughly 70 percent of the nation's banking resources were part of the **Federal Reserve System**. One of Wilson's most enduring achievements, this system still serves as the basis of the nation's banking system. (B)

MAIN IDEA

Evaluating

(B) Why were tariff reform and the Federal Reserve System important?

Women Win Suffrage

While Wilson pushed hard for reform of trusts, tariffs, and banking, determined women intensified their push for the vote. The educated, native-born, middle-class women who had been active in progressive movements had grown increasingly impatient about not being allowed to vote. As of 1910, women had federal voting rights only in Wyoming, Utah, Colorado, Washington, and Idaho.

Determined suffragists pushed on, however. They finally saw success come within reach as a result of three developments: the increased activism of local groups, the use of bold new strategies to build enthusiasm for the movement, and the rebirth of the national movement under Carrie Chapman Catt.

LOCAL SUFFRAGE BATTLES The suffrage movement was given new strength by growing numbers of college-educated women. Two Massachusetts organizations, the Boston Equal Suffrage Association for Good Government and the College Equal Suffrage League, used door-to-door campaigns to reach potential supporters. Founded by Radcliffe graduate Maud Wood Park, the Boston group spread the message of suffrage to poor and working-class women. Members also took trolley tours where, at each stop, crowds would gather to watch the unusual sight of a woman speaking in public.

Many wealthy young women who visited Europe as part of their education became involved in the suffrage movement in Britain. Led by Emmeline Pankhurst, British suffragists used increasingly bold tactics, such as heckling government officials, to advance their cause. Inspired by their activism, American women returned to the United States armed with similar approaches in their own campaigns for suffrage.

CATT AND THE NATIONAL MOVEMENT Susan B. Anthony's successor as president of NAWSA was Carrie Chapman Catt, who served from 1900 to 1904 and resumed the presidency in 1915. When Catt returned to NAWSA after organizing New York's Women Suffrage Party, she concentrated on five tactics: (1) painstaking organization; (2) close ties between local, state, and national workers; (3) establishing a wide base of support; (4) cautious lobbying; and (5) gracious, ladylike behavior.

Although suffragists saw victories, the greater number of failures led some suffragists to try more radical tactics. Lucy Burns and Alice Paul formed their own more radical organization, the Congressional Union, and its successor, the National Woman's Party. They pressured the federal government to pass a suffrage amendment, and by 1917 Paul had organized her followers to mount a round-the-clock picket line around the White House. Some of the picketers were arrested, jailed, and even force-fed when they attempted a hunger strike.

These efforts, and America's involvement in World War I, finally made suffrage inevitable. Patriotic American women who headed committees, knitted socks for soldiers, and sold liberty bonds now claimed their overdue reward for supporting the war effort. In 1919, Congress passed the **Nineteenth Amendment,** granting women the right to vote. The amendment won final ratification in August 1920—72 years after women had first convened and demanded the vote at the Seneca Falls convention in 1848. C

MAIN IDEA

Analyzing Events

C Why do you think women won the right to vote in 1920, after earlier efforts had failed?

WORLD STAGE

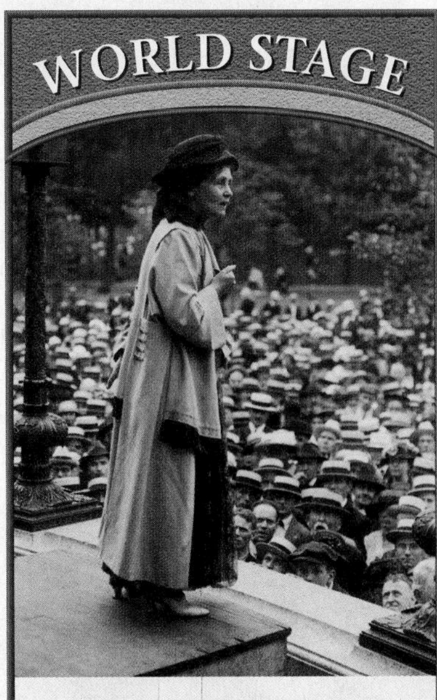

EMMELINE PANKHURST

American women struggling for suffrage received valuable tutoring from their English counterparts, whose bold maneuvers had captured media coverage.

The noted British suffragist Emmeline Pankhurst, who helped found the National Women's Social and Political Union, often engaged in radical tactics. Pankhurst and other suffragists staged parades, organized protest meetings, endured hunger strikes, heckled candidates for Parliament, and spat on policemen who tried to quiet them. They were often imprisoned for their activities, before Parliament granted them the right to vote in 1928.

The Limits of Progressivism

Despite Wilson's economic and political reforms, he disappointed Progressives who favored social reform. In particular, on racial matters Wilson appeased conservative Southern Democratic voters but disappointed his Northern white and black supporters. He placed segregationists in charge of federal agencies, thereby expanding racial segregation in the federal government, the military, and Washington, D.C.

Vocabulary

appease: pacify by granting concessions

WILSON AND CIVIL RIGHTS Like Roosevelt and Taft, Wilson retreated on civil rights once in office. During the presidential campaign of 1912, he won the support of the NAACP's black intellectuals and white liberals by promising to treat blacks equally and to speak out against lynching.

History Through *Architecture*

FROM SPLENDOR TO SIMPLICITY

The progressive movement, which influenced numerous aspects of society, also impacted the world of American architecture. One of the most prominent architects of the time was Frank Lloyd Wright, who studied under the renowned designer Louis Sullivan. In the spirit of progressivism, Wright sought to design buildings that were orderly, efficient, and in harmony with the world around them.

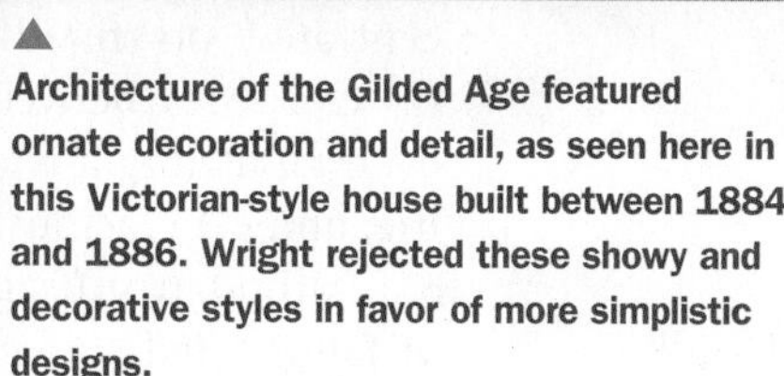

▲ **Architecture of the Gilded Age featured ornate decoration and detail, as seen here in this Victorian-style house built between 1884 and 1886. Wright rejected these showy and decorative styles in favor of more simplistic designs.**

▲ **Wright's "prairie style" design features a low, horizontal, and well-defined structure made predominantly of wood, concrete, brick, and other simple materials. Shown here is the Robie House (1909), one of Wright's most famous prairie-style structures, which incorporates these architectural qualities.**

SKILLBUILDER Interpreting Visual Sources

1. What are the most striking differences between the two houses? Cite examples that contrast the two buildings.
2. How does Wright's style reflect the progressive spirit?

SEE SKILLBUILDER HANDBOOK, PAGE R23.

As president, however, Wilson opposed federal antilynching legislation, arguing that these crimes fell under state jurisdiction. In addition, the Capitol and the federal offices in Washington, D.C., which had been desegregated during Reconstruction, resumed the practice of segregation shortly after Wilson's election.

Wilson appointed to his cabinet fellow white Southerners who extended segregation. Secretary of the Navy Josephus Daniels, for example, proposed at a cabinet meeting to do away with common drinking fountains and towels in his department. According to an entry in Daniel's diary, President Wilson agreed because he had "made no promises in particular to negroes, except to do them justice." Segregated facilities, in the president's mind, were just.

African Americans and their liberal white supporters in the NAACP felt betrayed. Oswald Garrison Villard, a grandson of the abolitionist William Lloyd Garrison, wrote to Wilson in dismay, "The colored men who voted and worked for you in the belief that their status as American citizens was safe in your hands are deeply cast down." Wilson's response—that he had acted "in the interest of the negroes" and "with the approval of some of the most influential negroes I know"—only widened the rift between the president and some of his former supporters.

On November 12, 1914, the president's reception of an African-American delegation brought the confrontation to a bitter climax. William Monroe Trotter, editor-in-chief of the *Guardian*, an African-American Boston newspaper, led the delegation. Trotter complained that African Americans from 38 states had asked the president to reverse the segregation of government employees, but that segregation had since increased. Trotter then commented on Wilson's inaction.

A PERSONAL VOICE WILLIAM MONROE TROTTER

> **"Only two years ago you were heralded as perhaps the second Lincoln, and now the Afro-American leaders who supported you are hounded as false leaders and traitors to their race. . . . As equal citizens and by virtue of your public promises we are entitled at your hands to freedom from discrimination, restriction, imputation, and insult in government employ. Have you a 'new freedom' for white Americans and a new slavery for your 'Afro-American fellow citizens'? God forbid!"**
>
> —address to President Wilson, November 12, 1914

Wilson found Trotter's tone infuriating. After an angry Trotter shook his finger at the president to emphasize a point, the furious Wilson demanded that the delegation leave. Wilson's refusal to extend civil rights to African Americans pointed to the limits of progressivism under his administration. America's involvement in the war raging in Europe would soon reveal other weaknesses. D

Analyzing Effects
D What actions of Wilson disappointed civil rights advocates?

THE TWILIGHT OF PROGRESSIVISM After taking office in 1913, Wilson had said, "There's no chance of progress and reform in an administration in which war plays the principal part." Yet he found that the outbreak of World War I in Europe in 1914 demanded America's involvement. Meanwhile, distracted Americans and their legislators allowed reform efforts to stall. As the pacifist and reformer Jane Addams mournfully reflected, "The spirit of fighting burns away all those impulses . . . which foster the will to justice."

International conflict was destined to be part of Wilson's presidency. During the early years of his administration, Wilson had dealt with issues of imperialism that had roots in the late 19th century. However, World War I dominated most of his second term as president. The Progressive Era had come to an end.

SECTION 5 ASSESSMENT

1. **TERMS & NAMES** For each term or name, write a sentence explaining its significance.
   - **Carrie Chapman Catt**
   - **Clayton Antitrust Act**
   - **Federal Trade Commission (FTC)**
   - **Federal Reserve System**
   - **Nineteenth Amendment**

MAIN IDEA

2. **TAKING NOTES**
Create a time line of key events relating to Progressivism during Wilson's first term. Use the dates already plotted on the time line below as a guide.

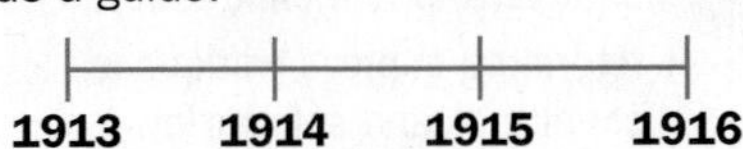

Write a paragraph explaining which event you think best demonstrates progressive reform.

CRITICAL THINKING

3. **ANALYZING PRIMARY SOURCES**
Wilson said, "Without the watchful . . . resolute interference of the government, there can be no fair play between individuals and . . . the trusts." How does this statement reflect Wilson's approach to reform? Support your answer. **Think About:**
   - the government's responsibility to the public
   - the passage of two key antitrust measures

4. **ANALYZING MOTIVES**
Why do you think Wilson failed to push for equality for African Americans, despite his progressive reforms? **Think About:**
   - progressive presidents before Wilson
   - Wilson's background
   - the primary group of people progressive reforms targeted

CHAPTER 17 ASSESSMENT

TERMS & NAMES

For each term or name below, write a sentence explaining its connection to the Progressive Era.

1. progressive movement
2. muckraker
3. suffrage
4. Susan B. Anthony
5. Theodore Roosevelt
6. NAACP
7. Gifford Pinchot
8. Woodrow Wilson
9. Clayton Antitrust Act
10. Federal Reserve System

MAIN IDEAS

Use your notes and the information in the chapter to answer the following questions.

The Origins of Progressivism

1. What were the four goals that various progressive reform movements struggled to achieve?
2. What kind of state labor laws resulted from progressives' lobbying to protect workers?
3. How did government change during the Progressive Era? How were these changes important?

Women in Public Life

4. In the late 1890s, what job opportunities were available to uneducated women without industrial skills?
5. Give two examples of national women's organizations committed to social activism. Briefly describe their progressive missions.

Teddy Roosevelt's Square Deal

6. What scandalous practices did Upton Sinclair expose in his novel *The Jungle*? How did the American public, Roosevelt, and Congress respond?
7. How did Roosevelt earn his reputation as a trust-buster?

Progressivism Under Taft

8. As a progressive, how did Taft compare with Roosevelt?
9. Why did the Republican Party split during Taft's administration?

Wilson's New Freedom

10. How did the Clayton Antitrust Act benefit labor?
11. Cite two examples of social welfare legislation that Wilson opposed during his presidency and the arguments he used to defend his position.

CRITICAL THINKING

1. **USING YOUR NOTES** Create a Venn diagram to show some of the similarities and differences between Roosevelt's Square Deal and Wilson's New Freedom.

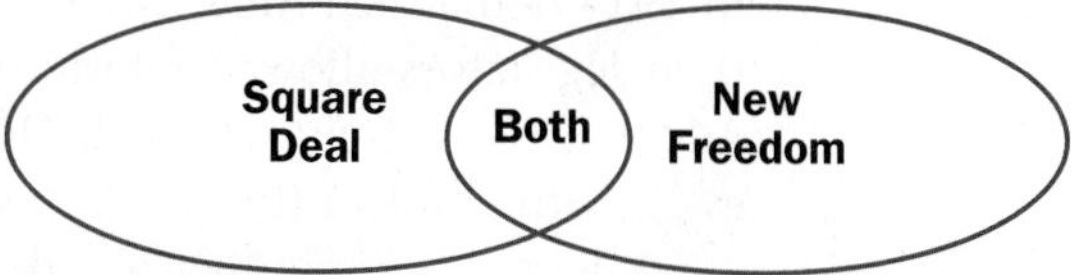

2. **DEVELOPING HISTORICAL PERSPECTIVE** What social, political, and economic trends in American life do you think caused the reform impulse during the Progressive Era? Support your answer with details from the text.

VISUAL SUMMARY THE PROGRESSIVE ERA

PROGRESSIVISM

ECONOMIC
- Roosevelt establishes a Square Deal
- new tax system is instituted
- Roosevelt breaks up trusts

SOCIAL & MORAL
- women fight for the right to vote
- Eighteenth Amendment bans alcoholic beverages
- Social services for women, children, and the poor

POLITICAL
- elections are reformed
- citizens given greater voice in government: recall, initiative, referendum

INDUSTRY
- National Child Labor Committee organizes to end child labor
- reformers improve workplace conditions and set maximum working hours

HEALTH & ENVIRONMENT
- conservationists establish wilderness conservation areas and preserve natural resources
- Pure Food and Drug Act protects consumers

STANDARDIZED TEST PRACTICE

Use the quotation and your knowledge of U.S. history to answer question 1.

> **"Labor began to organize itself in Trade Unions and to confront the industrialists with a stiff bargaining power. These developments were to lead to a period of protest and reform in the early twentieth century. The gains conferred by large-scale industry were great and lasting, but the wrongs that had accompanied their making were only gradually righted."**
>
> —Winston Churchill, *The Great Republic: A History of America*

1. In the passage, Winston Churchill attempts to explain what prompted Progressive Era reformers. The passage explains the actions of which of the following labor reform leaders?

A Maria Mitchell
B Carry Nation
C Susan B. Anthony
D Florence Kelley

2. The muckrakers served Progressivism by —

F informing people about abuses so that they could protest.
G enacting legislation to prevent political corruption.
H cleaning up unhealthy meat processing plants.
J filing and prosecuting antitrust lawsuits.

3. In the presidential election of 1912, three candidates attempted to win the liberal, progressive vote. Which candidate for president in 1912 ran on a conservative platform?

A Woodrow Wilson
B William Taft
C Theodore Roosevelt
D Eugene V. Debs

hmhsocialstudies.com TEST PRACTICE

For additional test practice, go online for:

- Diagnostic tests
- Tutorials

INTERACT WITH HISTORY

Think about the issues you explored at the beginning of the chapter. As a class, discuss what progressive reformers did to bring about changes in government and society. Consider what else they might have done to be more effective. Rank their efforts in order of effectiveness and offer suggestions for improvement.

FOCUS ON WRITING

Conservation of natural resources became a focus of federal attention in the early 1900s. Write an explanation of the two different perspectives on conservation advocated by Gifford Pinchot and John Muir. Then decide which position you agree with and explain why.

COLLABORATIVE LEARNING

21st CENTURY

Imagine you are a reporter covering a 1912 congressional hearing investigating labor conditions in a textile mill. Work with a partner to write two newspaper articles—one that shows bias in favor of the mill workers, and one that shows bias in favor of the mill. Share the articles with the class and analyze how language can affect the reporting of information.

CHAPTER 18

AMERICA CLAIMS AN EMPIRE

Essential Question

Which individuals and events moved the United States into the role of a world power?

This lithograph of Roosevelt leading the Rough Riders at San Juan Hill shows the men on horseback, although they actually fought on foot.

1893 Business groups, aided by U.S. marines, overthrow Hawaii's Queen Liliuokalani.

1898 ***U.S.S. Maine*** **explodes and sinks. The Spanish-American War begins.**

1901 Theodore Roosevelt becomes president after McKinley is assassinated.

USA
WORLD

1890

1900

1895 Guglielmo Marconi develops the technology that led to the modern radio.

1898 Marie Curie discovers radium.

1900 In China, the Boxers rebel.

1903 Panama declares its independence from Colombia.

Image Credits: (bkgd), ©Corbis; (bl), ©Bettmann/Corbis; (br), ©Hulton Archive/Getty Images

HISTORY TR and the Spanish-American War

hmhsocialstudies.com VIDEO

INTERACT WITH HISTORY

In the late 1890s, American newspapers are running sensational stories about Spain's harsh rule of Cuba. Such articles anger Americans. Among those willing to fight for Cuba's freedom are a group of volunteers, the Rough Riders. Led by future president Theodore Roosevelt, the Rough Riders become a model for others to follow.

Explore the Issues

- When should the U.S. intervene in the affairs of another country?
- In what ways do dramatic headlines influence American opinion?

1908 William Howard Taft is elected president.

1912 Woodrow Wilson is elected president.

1914 The Panama Canal opens.

1917 Puerto Ricans become U.S. citizens.

1917 The United States enters World War I.

1910 | **1920**

1910 The Mexican Revolution begins.

1914 World War I begins in Europe.

1917 Mexico revises and adopts its constitution.

Image Credits: (bkgd), ©Corbis; (c), ©Underwood & Underwood/Corbis; (b), ©Corbis

SECTION 1

Imperialism and America

MAIN IDEA	WHY IT MATTERS NOW	Terms & Names
Beginning in 1867 and continuing through the century, global competition caused the United States to expand.	**During this time period, the United States acquired Hawaii and Alaska, both of which became states in 1959.**	**•Queen Liliuokalani •imperialism •Alfred T. Mahan •William Seward •Pearl Harbor •Sanford B. Dole**

One American's Story

hmhsocialstudies.com TAKING NOTES

Use the graphic organizer online to take notes on events and concepts that illustrate the roots of imperialism.

In 1893 **Queen Liliuokalani** (lə-lē′ə-ō-kə-lä′nē) realized that her reign in Hawaii had come to an end. More than 160 U.S. sailors and marines stood ready to aid the *haoles* (white foreigners) who planned to overthrow the Hawaiian monarchy. In an eloquent statement of protest, the proud monarch surrendered to the superior force of the United States.

▲ **Hawaii's "Queen Lil" announced that if restored to power, she would behead those who had conspired to depose her.**

A PERSONAL VOICE QUEEN LILIUOKALANI

"I, Liliuokalani, . . . do hereby solemnly protest against any and all acts done against myself and the constitutional government of the Hawaiian Kingdom. . . . Now, to avoid any collision of armed forces and perhaps the loss of life, I do under this protest . . . yield my authority until such time as the Government of the United States shall . . . undo the action of its representatives and reinstate me in the authority which I claim as the constitutional sovereign of the Hawaiian Islands."

—quoted in *Those Kings and Queens of Old Hawaii*

U.S. ambassador to Hawaii John L. Stevens informed the State Department, "The Hawaiian pear is now fully ripe, and this is the golden hour for the United States to pluck it." The annexation of Hawaii was only one of the goals of America's empire builders in the late 19th century.

American Expansionism

Americans had always sought to expand the size of their nation, and throughout the 19th century they extended their control toward the Pacific Ocean. However, by the 1880s, many American leaders had become convinced that the United States should join the imperialist powers of Europe and establish colonies overseas. **Imperialism**—the policy in which stronger nations extend their economic, political, or military control over weaker territories—was already a trend around the world.

GLOBAL COMPETITION European nations had been establishing colonies for centuries. In the late 19th century Africa had emerged as a prime target of European expansionism. By the early 20th century, only two countries in all of Africa—Ethiopia and Liberia—remained independent. (A)

MAIN IDEA

Analyzing Effects

(A) How did European imperialism affect Africa?

Imperialists also competed for territory in Asia, especially in China. In its late-19th-century reform era, Japan replaced its old feudal order with a strong central government. Hoping that military strength would bolster industrialization, Japan joined European nations in competition for China in the 1890s.

Most Americans gradually warmed to the idea of expansion overseas. With a belief in manifest destiny, they already had pushed the U.S. border to the Pacific Ocean. Three factors fueled the new American imperialism:

- desire for military strength
- thirst for new markets
- belief in cultural superiority

DESIRE FOR MILITARY STRENGTH Seeing that other nations were establishing a global military presence, American leaders advised that the United States build up its own military strength. One such leader was Admiral **Alfred T. Mahan** of the U.S. Navy. Mahan urged government officials to build up American naval power in order to compete with other powerful nations. As a result of the urging of Mahan and others, the United States built nine steel-hulled cruisers between 1883 and 1890. The construction of modern battleships such as the *Maine* and the *Oregon* transformed the country into the world's third largest naval power.

KEY PLAYER

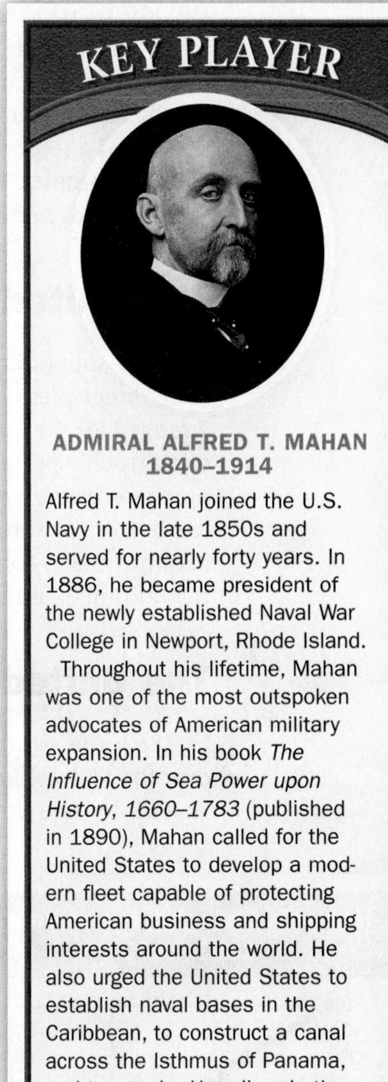

ADMIRAL ALFRED T. MAHAN 1840–1914

Alfred T. Mahan joined the U.S. Navy in the late 1850s and served for nearly forty years. In 1886, he became president of the newly established Naval War College in Newport, Rhode Island.

Throughout his lifetime, Mahan was one of the most outspoken advocates of American military expansion. In his book *The Influence of Sea Power upon History, 1660–1783* (published in 1890), Mahan called for the United States to develop a modern fleet capable of protecting American business and shipping interests around the world. He also urged the United States to establish naval bases in the Caribbean, to construct a canal across the Isthmus of Panama, and to acquire Hawaii and other Pacific islands.

THIRST FOR NEW MARKETS In the late 19th century, advances in technology enabled American farms and factories to produce far more than American citizens could consume. Now the United States needed raw materials for its factories and new markets for its agricultural and manufactured goods. Imperialists viewed foreign trade as the solution to American overproduction and the related problems of unemployment and economic depression.

Background

In the late 1800s, new farm machinery greatly improved grain production. For example, plows, harrows, threshing machines, and reapers increased corn production by 264 percent and the wheat harvest by 252 percent.

In the early 1900s, the Navy's Great White Fleet, so named because its ships were painted white, was a sign of America's growing military power. ▶

BELIEF IN CULTURAL SUPERIORITY Cultural factors also were used to justify imperialism. Some Americans combined the philosophy of Social Darwinism—a belief that free-market competition would lead to the survival of the fittest—with a belief in the racial superiority of Anglo-Saxons. They argued that the United States had a responsibility to spread Christianity and "civilization" to the world's "inferior peoples." This viewpoint narrowly defined "civilization" according to the standards of only one culture.

The United States Acquires Alaska

An early supporter of American expansion was **William Seward,** Secretary of State under presidents Abraham Lincoln and Andrew Johnson. In 1867, Seward arranged for the U.S. to buy Alaska from the Russians for $7.2 million. Seward had some trouble persuading the House of Representatives to approve funding for the purchase. Some people thought it was silly to buy what they called "Seward's Icebox" or "Seward's folly." Time showed how wrong they were. In 1959, Alaska became a state. For about two cents an acre, the United States had acquired a land rich in timber, minerals, and, as it turned out, oil. **B**

MAIN IDEA

Developing Historical Perspective

B How did time prove that the purchase of Alaska was not an act of folly?

The United States Takes Hawaii

In 1867, the same year in which Alaska was purchased, the United States took over the Midway Islands, which lie in the Pacific Ocean about 1300 miles north of Hawaii. No one lived on the islands, so the event did not attract much attention.

Hawaii was another question. The Hawaiian Islands had been economically important to the United States for nearly a century. Since the 1790s, American merchants had stopped there on their way to China and East India. In the 1820s, Yankee missionaries founded Christian schools and churches on the islands. Their children and grandchildren became sugar planters who sold most of their crop to the United States.

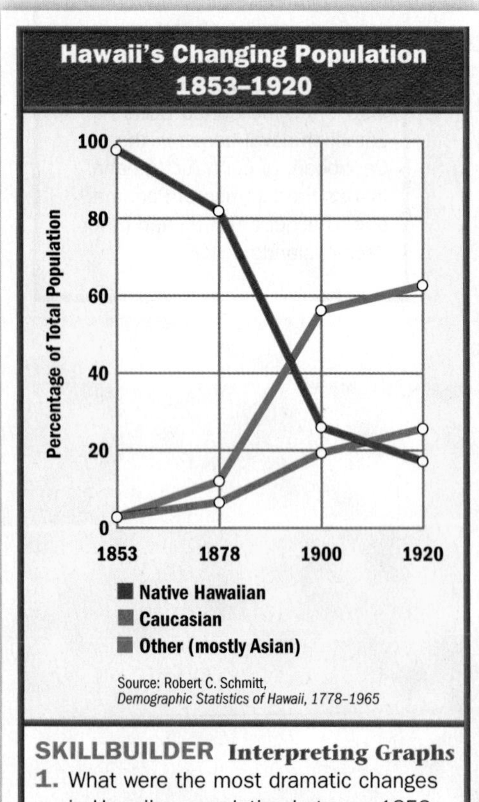

Source: Robert C. Schmitt, *Demographic Statistics of Hawaii, 1778–1965*

SKILLBUILDER Interpreting Graphs

1. What were the most dramatic changes in Hawaiian population between 1853 and 1920?
2. How might these changes have affected the political climate there?

THE CRY FOR ANNEXATION In the mid-19th century, American-owned sugar plantations accounted for about three-quarters of the islands' wealth. Plantation owners imported thousands of laborers from Japan, Portugal, and China. By 1900, foreigners and immigrant laborers outnumbered native Hawaiians about three to one.

White planters profited from close ties with the United States. In 1875, the United States agreed to import Hawaiian sugar duty-free. Over the next 15 years, Hawaiian sugar production increased nine times. Then the McKinley Tariff of 1890 provoked a crisis by eliminating the duty-free status of Hawaiian sugar. As a result, Hawaiian sugar growers faced competition in the American market. American planters in Hawaii called for the United States to annex the islands so they wouldn't have to pay the duty.

Vocabulary

annex: to incorporate territory into an existing country or state

U.S. military and economic leaders already understood the value of the islands. In 1887, they pressured Hawaii to allow the United States to build a naval base at **Pearl Harbor,** the kingdom's best port. The base became a refueling station for American ships.

THE END OF A MONARCHY Also in that year, Hawaii's King Kalakaua had been strong-armed by white business leaders. They forced him to amend Hawaii's constitution, effectively limiting voting rights to only wealthy landowners. But when Kalakaua died in 1891, his sister Queen Liliuokalani came to power with a "Hawaii for Hawaiians" agenda. She proposed removing the property-owning qualifications for voting. To prevent this from happening, business groups—encouraged by Ambassador John L. Stevens—organized a revolution. With the help of marines, they overthrew the queen and set up a government headed by **Sanford B. Dole.**

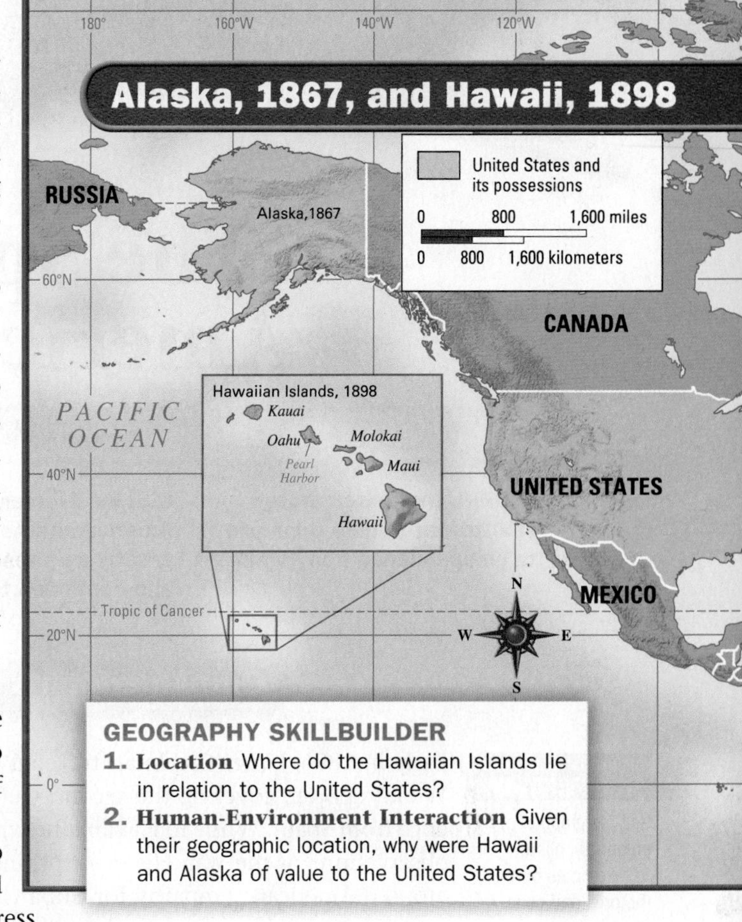

GEOGRAPHY SKILLBUILDER

1. **Location** Where do the Hawaiian Islands lie in relation to the United States?
2. **Human-Environment Interaction** Given their geographic location, why were Hawaii and Alaska of value to the United States?

President Cleveland directed that the queen be restored to her throne. When Dole refused to surrender power, Cleveland formally recognized the Republic of Hawaii. But he refused to consider annexation unless a majority of Hawaiians favored it.

Analyzing Events

C What factors led to the annexation of Hawaii in 1898?

In 1897, William McKinley, who favored annexation, succeeded Cleveland as president. On August 12, 1898, Congress proclaimed Hawaii an American territory, although Hawaiians had never had the chance to vote. In 1959, Hawaii became the 50th state of the United States. C

SECTION 1 ASSESSMENT

1. **TERMS & NAMES** For each term or name, write a sentence explaining its significance.
   - **Queen Liliuokalani**
   - **imperialism**
   - **Alfred T. Mahan**
   - **William Seward**
   - **Pearl Harbor**
   - **Sanford B. Dole**

MAIN IDEA

2. **TAKING NOTES**
   Copy this web on your paper and fill it in with events and concepts that illustrate the roots of imperialism.

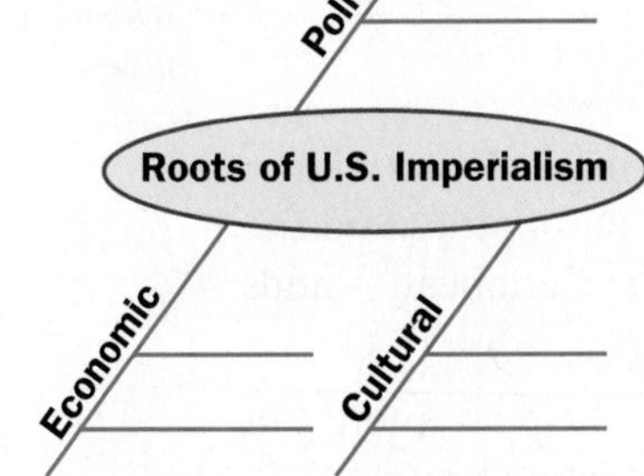

Choose one event to explain further in a paragraph.

CRITICAL THINKING

3. **DRAWING CONCLUSIONS**
   Manifest destiny greatly influenced American policy during the first half of the 19th century. How do you think manifest destiny set the stage for American imperialism at the end of the century?

4. **EVALUATING**
   In your opinion, did Sanford B. Dole and other American planters have the right to stage a revolt in Hawaii in 1893? **Think About:**
   - American business interests in Hawaii
   - the rights of native Hawaiians

5. **ANALYZING PRIMARY SOURCES**
   In the following passage, how does Indiana Senator Albert J. Beveridge explain the need for the U.S. to acquire new territories?

"Fate has written our policy for us; the trade of the world must and shall be ours. . . . We will establish trading posts throughout the world as distributing points for American products. . . Great colonies governing themselves, flying our flag and trading with us, will grow about our posts of trade."

—quoted in *Beveridge and the Progressive Era*

The Spanish-American War

SECTION 2

MAIN IDEA	WHY IT MATTERS NOW	Terms & Names
In 1898, the United States went to war to help Cuba win its independence from Spain.	**U.S. involvement in Latin America and Asia increased greatly as a result of the war and continues today.**	**•José Martí •Valeriano Weyler •yellow journalism •*U.S.S. Maine* •George Dewey •Rough Riders •San Juan Hill •Treaty of Paris**

One American's Story

hmhsocialstudies.com
TAKING NOTES
Use the graphic organizer online to take notes on the pros and cons of annexing the Philippines.

Early in 1896, James Creelman traveled to Cuba as a *New York World* reporter, covering the second Cuban war for independence from Spain. While in Havana, he wrote columns about his observations of the war. His descriptions of Spanish atrocities aroused American sympathy for Cubans.

A Personal Voice JAMES CREELMAN

> **"No man's life, no man's property is safe [in Cuba]. American citizens are imprisoned or slain without cause. American property is destroyed on all sides. . . . Wounded soldiers can be found begging in the streets of Havana. . . . The horrors of a barbarous struggle for the extermination of the native population are witnessed in all parts of the country. Blood on the roadsides, blood in the fields, blood on the doorsteps, blood, blood, blood! . . . Is there no nation wise enough, brave enough to aid this blood-smitten land?"**
>
> —*New York World,* May 17, 1896

Newspapers during that period often exaggerated stories like Creelman's to boost their sales as well as to provoke American intervention in Cuba.

Cuban rebels burn the town of Jaruco in March 1896.

Cubans Rebel Against Spain

By the end of the 19th century, Spain—once the most powerful colonial nation on earth—had lost most of its colonies. It retained only the Philippines and the island of Guam in the Pacific, a few outposts in Africa, and the Caribbean islands of Cuba and Puerto Rico in the Americas.

AMERICAN INTEREST IN CUBA The United States had long held an interest in Cuba, which lies only 90 miles south of Florida. In 1854, diplomats recommended to President Franklin Pierce that the United States buy Cuba from Spain. The Spanish responded by saying that they would rather see Cuba sunk in the ocean.

But American interest in Cuba continued. When the Cubans rebelled against Spain between 1868 and 1878, American sympathies went out to the Cuban people.

The Cuban revolt against Spain was not successful, but in 1886 the Cuban people did force Spain to abolish slavery. After the emancipation of Cuba's slaves, American capitalists began investing millions of dollars in large sugar cane plantations on the island.

THE SECOND WAR FOR INDEPENDENCE Anti-Spanish sentiment in Cuba soon erupted into a second war for independence. **José Martí,** a Cuban poet and journalist in exile in New York, launched a revolution in 1895. Martí organized Cuban resistance against Spain, using an active guerrilla campaign and deliberately destroying property, especially American-owned sugar mills and plantations. Martí counted on provoking U.S. intervention to help the rebels achieve *Cuba Libre!*—a free Cuba.

Vocabulary
guerrilla: a member of a military force that harasses the enemy

Public opinion in the United States was split. Many business people wanted the government to support Spain in order to protect their investments. Other Americans, however, were enthusiastic about the rebel cause. The cry "Cuba Libre!" was, after all, similar in sentiment to Patrick Henry's "Give me liberty or give me death!" (A)

MAIN IDEA

Analyzing Motives
(A) Why did José Martí encourage Cuban rebels to destroy sugar mills and plantations?

KEY PLAYER

JOSÉ MARTÍ
1853–1895

The Cuban political activist José Martí dedicated his life to achieving independence for Cuba. Expelled from Cuba at the age of 16 because of his revolutionary activities, Martí earned a master's degree and a law degree. He eventually settled in the United States.

Wary of the U.S. role in the Cuban struggle against the Spanish, Martí warned, "I know the Monster, because I have lived in its lair." His fears of U.S. imperialism turned out to have been well-founded. U.S. troops occupied Cuba on and off from 1906 until 1922.

Martí died fighting for Cuban independence in 1895. He is revered today in Cuba as a hero and martyr.

War Fever Escalates

In 1896, Spain responded to the Cuban revolt by sending General **Valeriano Weyler** to Cuba to restore order. Weyler tried to crush the rebellion by herding the entire rural population of central and western Cuba into barbed-wire concentration camps. Here civilians could not give aid to rebels. An estimated 300,000 Cubans filled these camps, where thousands died from hunger and disease.

HEADLINE WARS Weyler's actions fueled a war over newspaper circulation that had developed between the American newspaper tycoons William Randolph Hearst and Joseph Pulitzer. To lure readers, Hearst's *New York Journal* and Pulitzer's *New York World* printed exaggerated accounts—by reporters such as James Creelman—of "Butcher" Weyler's brutality. Stories of poisoned wells and of children being thrown to the sharks deepened American sympathy for the rebels. This sensational style of writing, which exaggerates the news to lure and enrage readers, became known as **yellow journalism.**

Hearst and Pulitzer fanned war fever. When Hearst sent the gifted artist Frederic Remington to Cuba to draw sketches of reporters' stories, Remington informed the publisher that a war between the United States and Spain seemed very unlikely. Hearst reportedly replied, "You furnish the pictures and I'll furnish the war."

THE DE LÔME LETTER American sympathy for "Cuba Libre!" grew with each day's headlines. When President William McKinley took office in 1897, demands for American intervention in Cuba were on the rise. Preferring to avoid war with Spain, McKinley tried diplomatic means to resolve the crisis. At first, his efforts appeared to succeed. Spain recalled General Weyler, modified the policy regarding concentration camps, and offered Cuba limited self-government.

In February 1898, however, the *New York Journal* published a private letter written by Enrique Dupuy de Lôme, the Spanish minister to the United States. A Cuban rebel had stolen the letter from a Havana post office and leaked it to the newspaper, which was thirsty for scandal. The de Lôme letter criticized President McKinley, calling him "weak" and "a bidder for the admiration of the crowd." The embarrassed Spanish government apologized, and the minister resigned. Still, Americans were angry over the insult to their president.

THE *U.S.S. MAINE* EXPLODES Only a few days after the publication of the de Lôme letter, American resentment toward Spain turned to outrage. Early in 1898, President McKinley had ordered the ***U.S.S. Maine*** to Cuba to bring home American citizens in danger from the fighting and to protect American property. On February 15, 1898, the ship blew up in the harbor of Havana. More than 260 men were killed.

At the time, no one really knew why the ship exploded; however, American newspapers claimed that the Spanish had blown up the ship. The *Journal*'s headline read "The warship *Maine* was split in two by an enemy's secret infernal machine." Hearst's paper offered a reward of $50,000 for the capture of the Spaniards who supposedly had committed the outrage. (B)

MAIN IDEA

Summarizing

(B) What events increased the tension between the United States and Spain?

War with Spain Erupts

Now there was no holding back the forces that wanted war. "Remember the *Maine!*" became the rallying cry for U.S. intervention in Cuba. It made no difference that the Spanish government agreed, on April 9, to almost everything the United States demanded, including a six-month cease-fire.

▲ **When the *U.S.S. Maine* exploded in the harbor of Havana, newspapers like the *New York Journal* were quick to place the blame on Spain.**

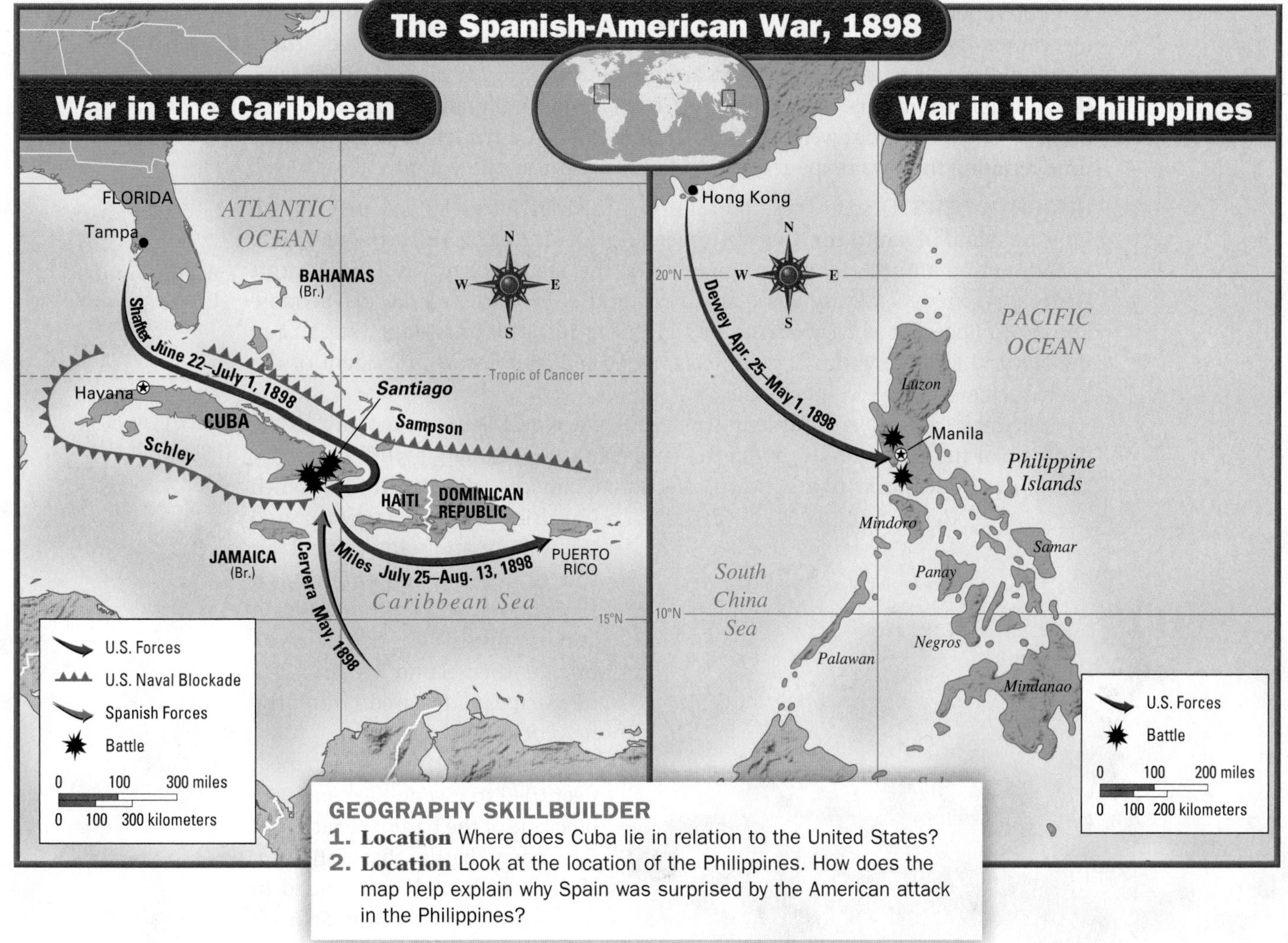

GEOGRAPHY SKILLBUILDER

1. **Location** Where does Cuba lie in relation to the United States?
2. **Location** Look at the location of the Philippines. How does the map help explain why Spain was surprised by the American attack in the Philippines?

MAIN IDEA

Analyzing Events

C How did the Spanish try to avoid war with the United States?

Despite the Spanish concessions, public opinion favored war. On April 11, McKinley asked Congress for authority to use force against Spain. After a week of debate, Congress agreed, and on April 20 the United States declared war. **C**

THE WAR IN THE PHILIPPINES The Spanish thought the Americans would invade Cuba. But the first battle of the war took place in a Spanish colony on the other side of the world—the Philippine Islands.

On April 30, the American fleet in the Pacific steamed to the Philippines. The next morning, Commodore **George Dewey** gave the command to open fire on the Spanish fleet at Manila, the Philippine capital. Within hours, Dewey's men had destroyed every Spanish ship there. Dewey's victory allowed U.S. troops to land in the Philippines.

Dewey had the support of the Filipinos who, like the Cubans, also wanted freedom from Spain. Over the next two months, 11,000 Americans joined forces with Filipino rebels led by Emilio Aguinaldo. In August, Spanish troops in Manila surrendered to the United States.

THE WAR IN THE CARIBBEAN In the Caribbean, hostilities began with a naval blockade of Cuba. Admiral William T. Sampson effectively sealed up the Spanish fleet in the harbor of Santiago de Cuba.

Dewey's victory at Manila had demonstrated the superiority of United States naval forces. In contrast, the army maintained only a small professional force, supplemented by a larger inexperienced and ill-prepared volunteer force. About

125,000 Americans had volunteered to fight. The new soldiers were sent to training camps that lacked adequate supplies and effective leaders. Moreover, there were not enough modern guns to go around, and the troops were outfitted with heavy woolen uniforms unsuitable for Cuba's tropical climate. In addition, the officers—most of whom were Civil War veterans—had a tendency to spend their time recalling their war experiences rather than training the volunteers.

ROUGH RIDERS Despite these handicaps, American forces landed in Cuba in June 1898 and began to converge on the port city of Santiago. The army of 17,000 included four African-American regiments of the regular army and the **Rough Riders,** a volunteer cavalry under the command of Leonard Wood and Theodore Roosevelt. Roosevelt, a New Yorker, had given up his job as Assistant Secretary of the Navy to lead the group of volunteers. He would later become president of the United States.

Background
The Rough Riders trained as cavalry but fought on foot because their horses didn't reach Cuba in time.

The most famous land battle in Cuba took place near Santiago on July 1. The first part of the battle, on nearby Kettle Hill, featured a dramatic uphill charge by the Rough Riders and two African-American regiments, the Ninth and Tenth Cavalries. Their victory cleared the way for an infantry attack on the strategically important **San Juan Hill.** Although Roosevelt and his units played only a minor role in the second victory, U.S. newspapers declared him the hero of San Juan Hill.

Two days later, the Spanish fleet tried to escape the American blockade of the harbor at Santiago. The naval battle that followed, along the Cuban coast, ended in the destruction of the Spanish fleet. On the heels of this victory, American troops invaded Puerto Rico on July 25.

▲ These African-American troops prepare for battle during the Spanish-American War.

TREATY OF PARIS The United States and Spain signed an armistice, a cease-fire agreement, on August 12, ending what Secretary of State John Hay called "a splendid little war." The actual fighting in the war had lasted only 15 weeks.

On December 10, 1898, the United States and Spain met in Paris to agree on a treaty. At the peace talks, Spain freed Cuba and turned over the islands of Guam in the Pacific and Puerto Rico in the West Indies to the United States. Spain also sold the Philippines to the United States for $20 million. D

MAIN IDEA
Summarizing
D What were the terms of the Treaty of Paris?

DEBATE OVER THE TREATY The **Treaty of Paris** touched off a great debate in the United States. Arguments centered on whether or not the United States had the right to annex the Philippines, but imperialism was the real issue. President McKinley told a group of Methodist ministers that he had prayed for guidance on Philippine annexation and had concluded "that there was nothing left for us to do but to take them all [the Philippine Islands], and to educate the Filipinos, and uplift and Christianize them." McKinley's need to justify imperialism may have clouded his memory—most Filipinos had been Christian for centuries.

Other prominent Americans presented a variety of arguments—political, moral, and economic—against annexation. Some felt that the treaty violated the Declaration of Independence by denying self-government to the newly acquired territories. The African-American educator Booker T. Washington argued that the United States should settle race-related issues at home before taking on social problems elsewhere. The labor leader Samuel Gompers feared that Filipino immigrants would compete for American jobs.

On February 6, 1899, the annexation question was settled with the Senate's approval of the Treaty of Paris. The United States now had an empire that included Guam, Puerto Rico, and the Philippines. The next question Americans faced was how and when the United States would add to its dominion.

This lithograph criticizes American foreign policy in 1898. In the cartoon, Uncle Sam is riding a bicycle with wheels labeled "western hemisphere" and "eastern hemisphere." He has abandoned his horse, on whose saddle appears "Monroe Doctrine," because the horse is too slow.

SECTION 2 ASSESSMENT

1. TERMS & NAMES For each term or name, write a sentence explaining its significance.

- **José Martí**
- **Valeriano Weyler**
- **yellow journalism**
- ***U.S.S. Maine***
- **George Dewey**
- **Rough Riders**
- **San Juan Hill**
- **Treaty of Paris**

MAIN IDEA

2. TAKING NOTES
In 1898, a debate raged in the United States over whether the U.S. had the right to annex the Philippines. Use a graphic organizer like the one below to summarize the pros and cons of this debate.

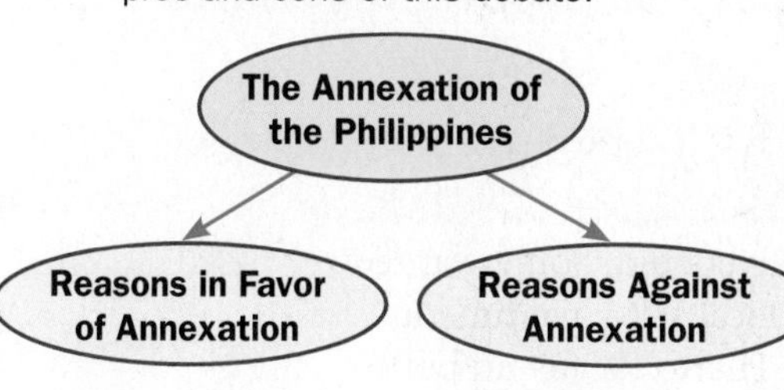

Which side do you support? Why?

CRITICAL THINKING

3. MAKING INFERENCES
What do you think were the unstated editorial policies of yellow journalism? Support your answer with evidence from the text.
Think About:
- James Creelman's account of Spanish atrocities against Cubans
- Hearst's remark to Remington
- the *Journal* headline about the explosion of the battleship *Maine*

4. ANALYZING EFFECTS
Many anti-imperialists worried that imperialism might threaten the American democratic system. How might this happen?

5. DRAWING CONCLUSIONS
In 1898 Theodore Roosevelt resigned his post as Assistant Secretary of the Navy to organize the Rough Riders. Why do you think Roosevelt was willing to take this risk? How do you think this decision affected his political career?

Acquiring New Lands

MAIN IDEA	WHY IT MATTERS NOW	Terms & Names
In the early 1900s, the United States engaged in conflicts in Puerto Rico, Cuba, and the Philippines.	**Today, the United States maintains a strong military and political presence in strategic worldwide locations.**	**•Foraker Act •Platt Amendment •protectorate •Emilio Aguinaldo •John Hay •Open Door notes •Boxer Rebellion**

One American's Story

hmhsocialstudies.com TAKING NOTES

Use the graphic organizer online to take notes on key events relating to U.S. relations with Cuba, Puerto Rico, and the Philippines.

When Puerto Rico became part of the United States after the Spanish-American War, many Puerto Ricans feared that the United States would not give them the measure of self-rule that they had gained under the Spanish. Puerto Rican statesman and publisher Luis Muñoz Rivera was one of the most vocal advocates of Puerto Rican self-rule. Between 1900 and 1916, he lived primarily in the United States and continually worked for the independence of his homeland. Finally, in 1916, the U.S. Congress, facing possible war in Europe and wishing to settle the issue of Puerto Rico, invited Muñoz Rivera to speak. On May 5, 1916, Muñoz Rivera stood before the U.S. House of Representatives to discuss the future of Puerto Rico.

▲ Luis Muñoz Rivera

A PERSONAL VOICE LUIS MUÑOZ RIVERA

"You, citizens of a free fatherland, with its own laws, its own institutions, and its own flag, can appreciate the unhappiness of the small and solitary people that must await its laws from your authority. . . . when you acquire the certainty that you can found in Puerto Rico a republic like that founded in Cuba and Panama . . . give us our independence and you will stand before humanity as . . . a great creator of new nationalities and a great liberator of oppressed peoples."

—quoted in *The Puerto Ricans*

Muñoz Rivera returned to Puerto Rico where he died in November 1916. Three months later, the United States made Puerto Ricans U.S. citizens.

Ruling Puerto Rico

Not all Puerto Ricans wanted independence, as Muñoz Rivera did. Some wanted statehood, while still others hoped for some measure of local self-government as an American territory. As a result, the United States gave Puerto Ricans no promises regarding independence after the Spanish-American War.

MILITARY RULE During the Spanish-American War, United States forces, under General Nelson A. Miles, occupied the island. As his soldiers took control, General Miles issued a statement assuring Puerto Ricans that the Americans were there to "bring you protection, not only to yourselves but to your property, to promote your prosperity, and to bestow upon you the immunities and blessings of the liberal institutions of our government." For the time being, Puerto Rico would be controlled by the military until Congress decided otherwise.

RETURN TO CIVIL GOVERNMENT Although many Puerto Ricans had dreams of independence or statehood, the United States had different plans for the island's future. Puerto Rico was strategically important to the United States, both for maintaining a U.S. presence in the Caribbean and for protecting a future canal that American leaders wanted to build across the Isthmus of Panama. In 1900, Congress passed the **Foraker Act,** which ended military rule and set up a civil government. The act gave the president of the United States the power to appoint Puerto Rico's governor and members of the upper house of its legislature. Puerto Ricans could elect only the members of the legislature's lower house. (A)

MAIN IDEA

Analyzing Issues

(A) Why was Puerto Rico important to the United States?

In 1901, in the Insular Cases, the U.S. Supreme Court ruled that the Constitution did not automatically apply to people in acquired territories. Congress, however, retained the right to extend U.S. citizenship, and it granted that right to Puerto Ricans in 1917. It also gave them the right to elect both houses of their legislature.

NOW & THEN

PUERTO RICO

Ever since their transfer under the Treaty of Paris from Spain to the United States, Puerto Ricans have debated their status, as shown above. In 1967, 1993, and 1998, Puerto Ricans rejected both statehood and independence in favor of commonwealth, a status given the island in 1952.

As members of a commonwealth, Puerto Ricans are U.S. citizens. They can move freely between the island and the mainland and are subjected to the military draft but cannot vote in U.S. presidential elections. A majority of Puerto Ricans have rejected statehood because they fear it would mean giving up their Latino culture.

Cuba and the United States

When the United States declared war against Spain in 1898, it recognized Cuba's independence from Spain. It also passed the Teller Amendment, which stated that the United States had no intention of taking over any part of Cuba. The Treaty of Paris, which ended the war, further guaranteed Cuba the independence that its nationalist leaders had been demanding for years.

AMERICAN SOLDIERS Though officially independent, Cuba was occupied by American troops when the war ended. José Martí, the Cuban patriot who had led the movement for independence from Spain, had feared that the United States would merely replace Spain and dominate Cuban politics. In some ways, Martí's prediction came true. Under American occupation, the same officials who had served Spain remained in office. Cubans who protested this policy were imprisoned or exiled.

Background

Yellow fever damages many body parts, especially the liver. Dr. Carlos Finlay discovered that the disease is carried by mosquitoes. Clearing out the mosquitos' breeding places helped eliminate the disease in Cuba.

On the other hand, the American military government provided food and clothing for thousands of families, helped farmers put land back into cultivation, and organized elementary schools. Through improvement of sanitation and medical research, the military government helped eliminate yellow fever, a disease that had killed hundreds of Cubans each year.

PLATT AMENDMENT In 1900 the newly formed Cuban government wrote a constitution for an independent Cuba. The constitution, however, did not specify the relationship between Cuba and the United States. Consequently, in 1901, the United States insisted that Cuba add to its constitution several provisions, known as the **Platt Amendment,** stating that

- Cuba could not make treaties that might limit its independence or permit a foreign power to control any part of its territory
- the United States reserved the right to intervene in Cuba
- Cuba was not to go into debt that its government could not repay
- the United States could buy or lease land on the island for naval stations and refueling stations

The United States made it clear that its army would not withdraw until Cuba adopted the Platt Amendment. In response, a torchlight procession marched on the residence of Governor-General Leonard Wood in protest. Some protestors even called for a return to arms to defend their national honor against this American insult. The U.S. government stood firm, though, and Cubans reluctantly ratified the new constitution. In 1903, the Platt Amendment became part of a treaty between the two nations, and it remained in effect for 31 years. Under the terms of the treaty, Cuba became a U.S. **protectorate,** a country whose affairs are partially controlled by a stronger power.

Vocabulary
ratify: to make valid by approving

PROTECTING AMERICAN BUSINESS INTERESTS The most important reason for the United States to maintain a strong political presence in Cuba was to protect American businesses that had invested in the island's sugar, tobacco, and mining industries, as well as in its railroads and public utilities.

Analyzing *Political Cartoons*

"WELL, I HARDLY KNOW WHICH TO TAKE FIRST!"

Throughout the early 1900s, the United States intervened in the affairs of its Latin American neighbors several times. American troops withdrew from Cuba in 1902 but later returned three times to quell popular uprisings against conservative leaders. The U.S. also intervened in Nicaragua and Haiti. Not surprisingly, few Latin Americans welcomed United States intervention. As the cartoon shows, the United States had a different point of view.

WELL, I HARDLY KNOW WHICH TO TAKE FIRST!

SKILLBUILDER
Analyzing Political Cartoons

1. What is on the bill of fare, or menu, in this restaurant?
2. Which president does the waiter portray?
3. What seems to be Uncle Sam's attitude toward the offerings on the menu?

SEE SKILLBUILDER HANDBOOK, PAGE R24.

Although many businesspeople were convinced that annexing and imposing colonial rule on new territories was necessary to protect American business interests, some were concerned about colonial entanglements. The industrialist Andrew Carnegie argued against the taking of nations as colonies.

A PERSONAL VOICE ANDREW CARNEGIE

"The exports of the United States this year [1898] are greater than those of any other nation in the world. Even Britain's exports are less, yet Britain 'possesses' . . . a hundred 'colonies' . . . scattered all over the world. The fact that the United States has none does not prevent her products and manufactures from invading . . . all parts of the world in competition with those of Britain."

—quoted in *Distant Possessions*

Despite such concerns, the U.S. state department continued to push for control of its Latin American neighbors. In the years to come, the United States would intervene time and again in the affairs of other nations in the Western Hemisphere.

Filipinos Rebel

In the Philippines, Filipinos reacted with outrage to the Treaty of Paris, which called for American annexation of the Philippines. The rebel leader **Emilio Aguinaldo** (ĕ-mēl′yō ä′gē-näl′dō) believed that the United States had promised independence. When he and his followers learned the terms of the treaty, they vowed to fight for freedom.

PHILIPPINE–AMERICAN WAR In February 1899, the Filipinos, led by Aguinaldo, rose in revolt. The United States assumed almost the same role that Spain had played, imposing its authority on a colony that was fighting for freedom. When Aguinaldo turned to guerrilla tactics, the United States forced Filipinos to live in designated zones, where poor sanitation, starvation, and disease killed thousands. This was the very same practice that Americans had condemned Spain for using in Cuba.

▲ **U.S. military action in the Philippines resulted in suffering for Filipino civilians. About 200,000 people died as a result of malnutrition, disease, and such guerrilla tactics as the burning of villages.**

During the occupation, white American soldiers looked on the Filipinos as inferiors. However, many of the 70,000 U.S. troops sent to the Philippines were African Americans. When African-American newspapers questioned why blacks were helping to spread racial prejudice to the Philippines, some African-American soldiers deserted to the Filipino side and developed bonds of friendship with the Filipinos.

Contrasting

B What were the aims of the Filipinos? of the Americans?

It took the Americans nearly three years to put down the rebellion. About 20,000 Filipino rebels died fighting for independence. The war claimed 4,000 American lives and cost $400 million—20 times the price the United States had paid to purchase the islands. B

AFTERMATH OF THE WAR After suppressing the rebellion, the United States set up a government similar to the one it had established for Puerto Rico. The U.S. president would appoint a governor, who would then appoint the upper house of the legislature. Filipinos would elect the lower house. Under American rule, the Philippines moved gradually toward independence and finally became an independent republic on July 4, 1946.

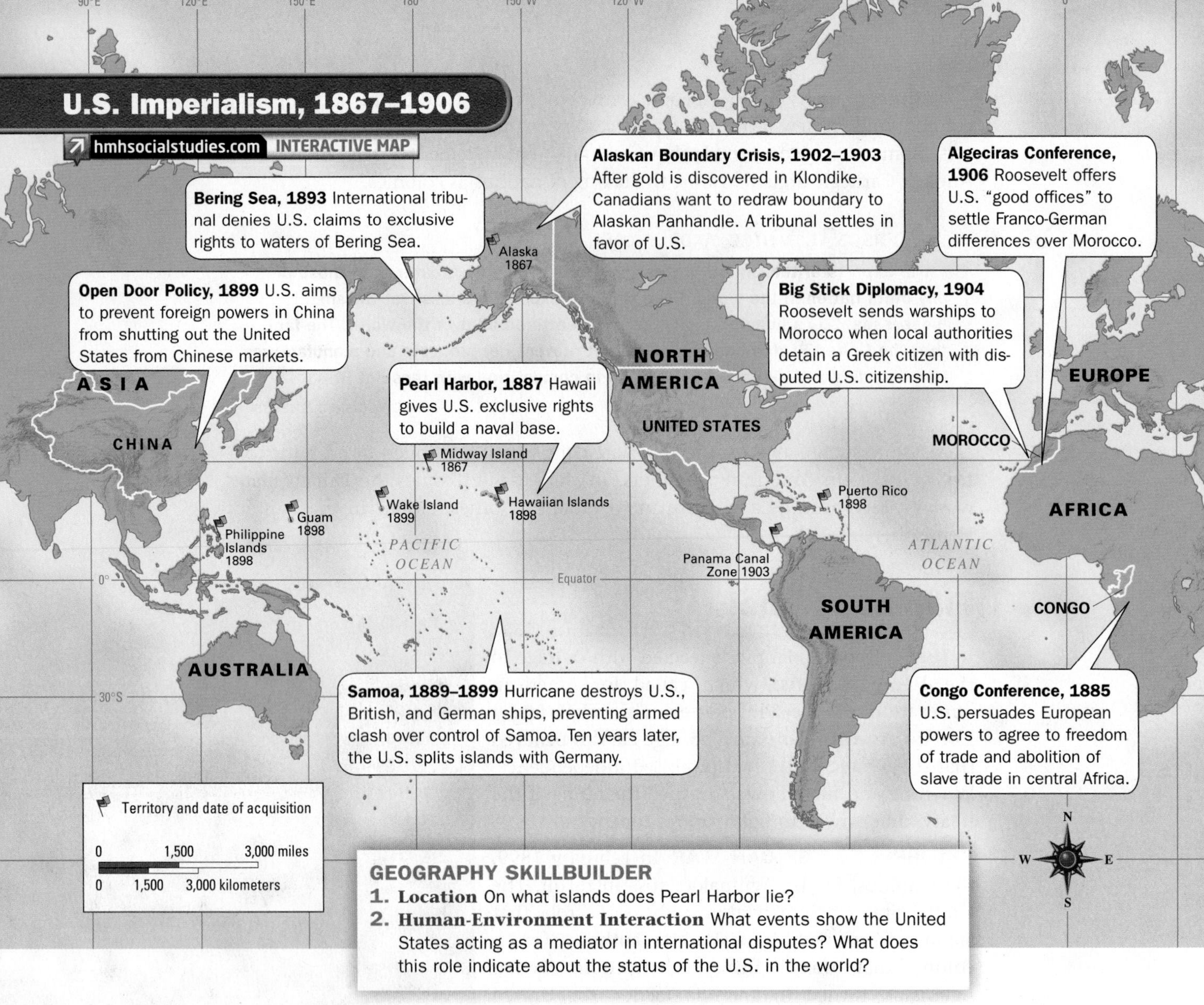

U.S. Imperialism, 1867–1906
hmhsocialstudies.com INTERACTIVE MAP
Bering Sea, 1893 International tribunal denies U.S. claims to exclusive rights to waters of Bering Sea.
Alaskan Boundary Crisis, 1902–1903 After gold is discovered in Klondike, Canadians want to redraw boundary to Alaskan Panhandle. A tribunal settles in favor of U.S.
Algeciras Conference, 1906 Roosevelt offers U.S. "good offices" to settle Franco-German differences over Morocco.
Open Door Policy, 1899 U.S. aims to prevent foreign powers in China from shutting out the United States from Chinese markets.
Big Stick Diplomacy, 1904 Roosevelt sends warships to Morocco when local authorities detain a Greek citizen with disputed U.S. citizenship.
Pearl Harbor, 1887 Hawaii gives U.S. exclusive rights to build a naval base.
Alaska 1867
Midway Island 1867
Wake Island 1899
Hawaiian Islands 1898
Guam 1898
Philippine Islands 1898
Puerto Rico 1898
Panama Canal Zone 1903
ASIA
CHINA
NORTH AMERICA
UNITED STATES
EUROPE
MOROCCO
AFRICA
CONGO
SOUTH AMERICA
AUSTRALIA
PACIFIC OCEAN
ATLANTIC OCEAN
Equator
Samoa, 1889–1899 Hurricane destroys U.S., British, and German ships, preventing armed clash over control of Samoa. Ten years later, the U.S. splits islands with Germany.
Congo Conference, 1885 U.S. persuades European powers to agree to freedom of trade and abolition of slave trade in central Africa.
Territory and date of acquisition
0 1,500 3,000 miles
0 1,500 3,000 kilometers

GEOGRAPHY SKILLBUILDER

1. **Location** On what islands does Pearl Harbor lie?
2. **Human-Environment Interaction** What events show the United States acting as a mediator in international disputes? What does this role indicate about the status of the U.S. in the world?

Foreign Influence in China

U.S. imperialists saw the Philippines as a gateway to the rest of Asia, particularly to China. China was seen as a vast potential market for American products. It also presented American investors with new opportunities for large-scale railroad construction.

Weakened by war and foreign intervention, China had become known as the "sick man of Asia." France, Germany, Britain, Japan, and Russia had established prosperous settlements along the coast of China. They also had carved out spheres of influence, areas where each nation claimed special rights and economic privileges.

JOHN HAY'S OPEN DOOR NOTES The United States began to fear that China would be carved into colonies and American traders would be shut out. To protect American interests, U.S. Secretary of State **John Hay** issued, in 1899, a series of policy statements called the **Open Door notes.** The notes were letters addressed to the leaders of imperialist nations proposing that the nations share their trading rights with the United States, thus creating an open door. This meant that no single nation would have a monopoly on trade with any part of China. The other imperialist powers reluctantly accepted this policy. C

MAIN IDEA

Analyzing Causes

C Why did Secretary of State John Hay issue the policy statements known as the Open Door notes?

▲
During the Boxer Rebellion, shown here in this Chinese print, Chinese patriots demanded that all foreigners be expelled from the country. The Boxers surrounded the European section of Beijing and kept it under siege for several months.

VIDEO
China:
Boxer Uprising

hmhsocialstudies.com

THE BOXER REBELLION IN CHINA Although China kept its freedom, Europeans dominated most of China's large cities. Resentment simmered beneath the surface as some Chinese formed secret societies pledged to rid the country of "foreign devils." The most famous of these secret groups were the Boxers, so named by Westerners because members practiced martial arts.

Vocabulary
martial arts: combat or self-defense arts that originated in East Asia, such as judo or karate

The Boxers killed hundreds of missionaries and other foreigners, as well as Chinese converts to Christianity. In August 1900, troops from Britain, France, Germany, and Japan joined about 2,500 American soldiers and marched on the Chinese capital. Within two months, the international forces put down the **Boxer Rebellion.** Thousands of Chinese people died during the fighting.

PROTECTING AMERICAN RIGHTS After the Boxer Rebellion, the United States feared that European nations would use their victory to take even greater control of China. To prevent this, John Hay issued a second series of Open Door notes, announcing that the United States would "safeguard for the world the principle of equal and impartial trade with all parts of the Chinese Empire." This policy paved the way for greater American influence in Asia.

The Open Door policy reflected three deeply held American beliefs about the United States industrial capitalist economy. First, Americans believed that the growth of the U.S. economy depended on exports. Second, they felt the United States had a right to intervene abroad to keep foreign markets open. Third, they feared that the closing of an area to American products, citizens, or ideas threatened U.S. survival. These beliefs became the bedrock of American foreign policy.

WORLD STAGE

THE BOXER PROTOCOL

On September 7, 1901, China and 11 other nations signed the Boxer Protocol—a final settlement of the Boxer Rebellion.

The Qing government agreed to execute some Chinese officials, to punish others, and to pay about $332 million in damages. The United States was awarded a settlement of $24.5 million. It used about $4 million to pay American citizens for actual losses incurred during the rebellion. In 1908, the U.S. government returned the rest of the money to China to be used for the purpose of educating Chinese students in their own country and in the United States.

The Impact of U.S. Territorial Gains

In 1900, Republican William McKinley, a reluctant but confirmed imperialist, was elected to a second term against Democrat William Jennings Bryan, who staunchly opposed imperialism. McKinley's reelection confirmed that a majority of Americans favored his policies. Under McKinley, the United States had gained an empire.

Yet even before McKinley was reelected, an Anti-Imperialist League had sprung into being. The league included some of the most prominent people in America, such as former president Grover Cleveland, industrial leader Andrew Carnegie, the social worker Jane Addams, and many leading writers. Anti-imperialists had different and sometimes conflicting reasons for their opposition, but all agreed that it was wrong for the United States to rule other people without their consent. The novelist Mark Twain questioned the motives for imperialism in a satirical piece written in 1901.

A PERSONAL VOICE MARK TWAIN

"Shall we go on conferring our Civilization upon the peoples that sit in darkness, or shall we give those poor things a rest? . . . Extending the Blessings of Civilization to our Brother who Sits in Darkness has been a good trade and has paid well, on the whole; and there is money in it yet . . . but not enough, in my judgment, to make any considerable risk advisable."

—quoted in *To the Person Sitting in Darkness*

▲ **Mark Twain**

As a novelist, Twain had great influence on American culture but little influence on foreign policy. In the early 20th century, the United States under President Theodore Roosevelt and President Woodrow Wilson would continue to exert its power around the globe.

SECTION 3 ASSESSMENT

1. **TERMS & NAMES** For each term or name, write a sentence explaining its significance.
   - **Foraker Act**
   - **Platt Amendment**
   - **protectorate**
   - **Emilio Aguinaldo**
   - **John Hay**
   - **Open Door notes**
   - **Boxer Rebellion**

MAIN IDEA

2. **TAKING NOTES**
   Create a time line of key events relating to U.S. relations with Cuba, Puerto Rico, and the Philippines. Use the dates already plotted on the time line below as a guide.

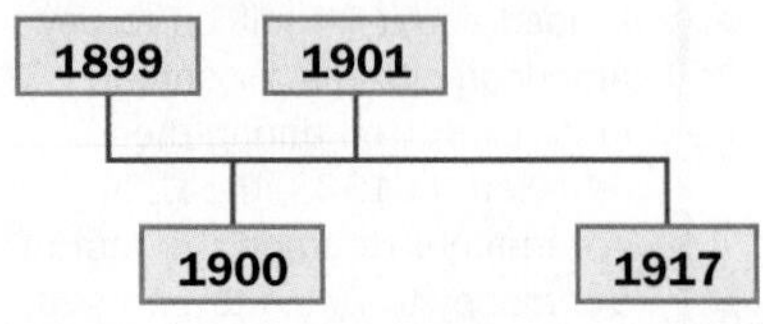

   Which event do you think was most significant? Why?

CRITICAL THINKING

3. **EVALUATING**
   How did American rule of Puerto Rico harm Puerto Ricans? How did it help Puerto Ricans? Do you think the benefits outweighed the harmful effects? Why or why not?

4. **COMPARING**
   How was U.S. policy toward China different from U.S. policy toward the Philippines? To what can you attribute the difference?

5. **ANALYZING ISSUES**
   How did U.S. foreign policy at the turn of the century affect actions taken by the United States toward China? **Think About:**
   - why the United States wanted access to China's markets
   - the purpose of the Open Door notes
   - the U.S. response to the Boxer Rebellion

America as a World Power

MAIN IDEA	WHY IT MATTERS NOW	Terms & Names
The Russo-Japanese War, the Panama Canal, and the Mexican Revolution added to America's military and economic power.	**American involvement in conflicts around 1900 led to involvement in World War I and later to a peacekeeper role in today's world.**	**•Panama Canal •Roosevelt Corollary •dollar diplomacy •Francisco "Pancho" Villa •Emiliano Zapata •John J. Pershing**

One American's Story

hmhsocialstudies.com
TAKING NOTES
Use the graphic organizer online to take notes on how Teddy Roosevelt and Woodrow Wilson used American power around the world.

Joseph Bucklin Bishop, a policy adviser to the canal's chief engineer, played an important role in the building of the Panama Canal. As editor of the *Canal Record*, a weekly newspaper that provided Americans with updates on the project, Bishop described a frustrating problem that the workers encountered.

A PERSONAL VOICE JOSEPH BUCKLIN BISHOP

"The Canal Zone was a land of the fantastic and the unexpected. No one could say when the sun went down what the condition of the Cut would be when [the sun] rose. For the work of months or even years might be blotted out by an avalanche of earth or the toppling over of a mountain of rock. It was a task to try men's souls; but it was also one to kindle in them a joy of combat . . . and a faith in ultimate victory which no disaster could shake."

—quoted in *The Impossible Dream: The Building of the Panama Canal*

Workers digging the Panama Canal faced hazardous landslides and death from disease.

The building of the Panama Canal reflected America's new role as a world power. As a technological accomplishment, the canal represented a confident nation's refusal to let any physical obstacle stand in its way.

Teddy Roosevelt and the World

The assassination of William McKinley in 1901 thrust Vice-President Theodore Roosevelt into the role of a world leader. Roosevelt was unwilling to allow the imperial powers of Europe to control the world's political and economic destiny. In 1905, building on the Open Door notes to increase American influence in East Asia, Roosevelt mediated a settlement in a war between Russia and Japan.

ROOSEVELT THE PEACEMAKER In 1904, Russia and Japan, Russia's neighbor in East Asia, were both imperialist powers, and they were competing for control of Korea. The Japanese took the first action in what would become the Russo-Japanese War with a sudden attack on the Russian Pacific fleet. To everyone's surprise, Japan destroyed it. Japan then proceeded to destroy a second fleet sent as reinforcement. Japan also won a series of land battles, securing Korea and Manchuria.

As a result of these battles, Japan began to run out of men and money, a fact that it did not want to reveal to Russia. Instead, Japanese officials approached President Roosevelt in secret and asked him to mediate peace negotiations. Roosevelt agreed, and in 1905, Russian and Japanese delegates convened in Portsmouth, New Hampshire.

The first meeting took place on the presidential yacht. Roosevelt had a charming way of greeting people with a grasp of the hand, a broad grin, and a hearty "Dee-lighted." Soon the opposing delegates began to relax and cordially shook hands.

The Japanese wanted Sakhalin Island, off the coast of Siberia, and a large sum of money from Russia. Russia refused. Roosevelt persuaded Japan to accept half the island and forgo the cash payment. In exchange, Russia agreed to let Japan take over Russian interests in Manchuria and Korea. The successful efforts in negotiating the Treaty of Portsmouth won Roosevelt the 1906 Nobel Peace Prize.

As U.S. and Japanese interests expanded in East Asia, the two nations continued diplomatic talks. In later agreements, they pledged to respect each other's possessions and interests in East Asia and the Pacific. (A)

KEY PLAYER

THEODORE ROOSEVELT
1858–1919

Rimless glasses, a bushy mustache, and prominent teeth made Roosevelt easy for cartoonists to caricature. His great enthusiasm for physical activity—boxing, tennis, swimming, horseback riding, and hunting—provided cartoonists with additional material. Some cartoons portrayed Roosevelt with the toy teddy bear that he inspired.

Roosevelt had six children, who became notorious for their rowdy antics. Their father once sent a message through the War Department, ordering them to call off their "attack" on the White House. Roosevelt thrived on the challenges of the presidency. He wrote, "I do not believe that anyone else has ever enjoyed the White House as much as I have."

MAIN IDEA

Analyzing Effects

(A) What were the results of Roosevelt's negotiations with the Japanese and Russians?

PANAMA CANAL By the time Roosevelt became president, many Americans, including Roosevelt, felt that the United States needed a canal cutting across Central America. Such a canal would greatly reduce travel time for commercial and military ships by providing a shortcut between the Atlantic and Pacific oceans. (See Geography Spotlight, The Panama Canal.) As early as 1850, the United States and Britain had agreed to share the rights to such a canal. In the Hay-Pauncefote Treaty of 1901, however, Britain gave the United States exclusive rights to build and control a canal through Central America.

Engineers identified two possible routes for the proposed canal. One, through Nicaragua, posed fewer obstacles because much of it crossed a large lake. The other route crossed through Panama (then a province of Colombia) and was shorter and filled with mountains and swamps. In the late 1800s, a French company had tried to build a canal in Panama. After ten years, the company gave up. It sent an agent, Philippe Bunau-Varilla, to Washington to convince the United States to buy its claim. In 1903, the president and Congress decided to use the Panama route and agreed to buy the French company's route for $40 million.

Before beginning work on the **Panama Canal,** the United States had to get permission from Colombia, which then ruled Panama. When these negotiations broke down, Bunau-Varilla helped organize a Panamanian rebellion against Colombia. On November 3, 1903, nearly a dozen U.S. warships were present as Panama declared its independence. Fifteen days later, Panama and the United

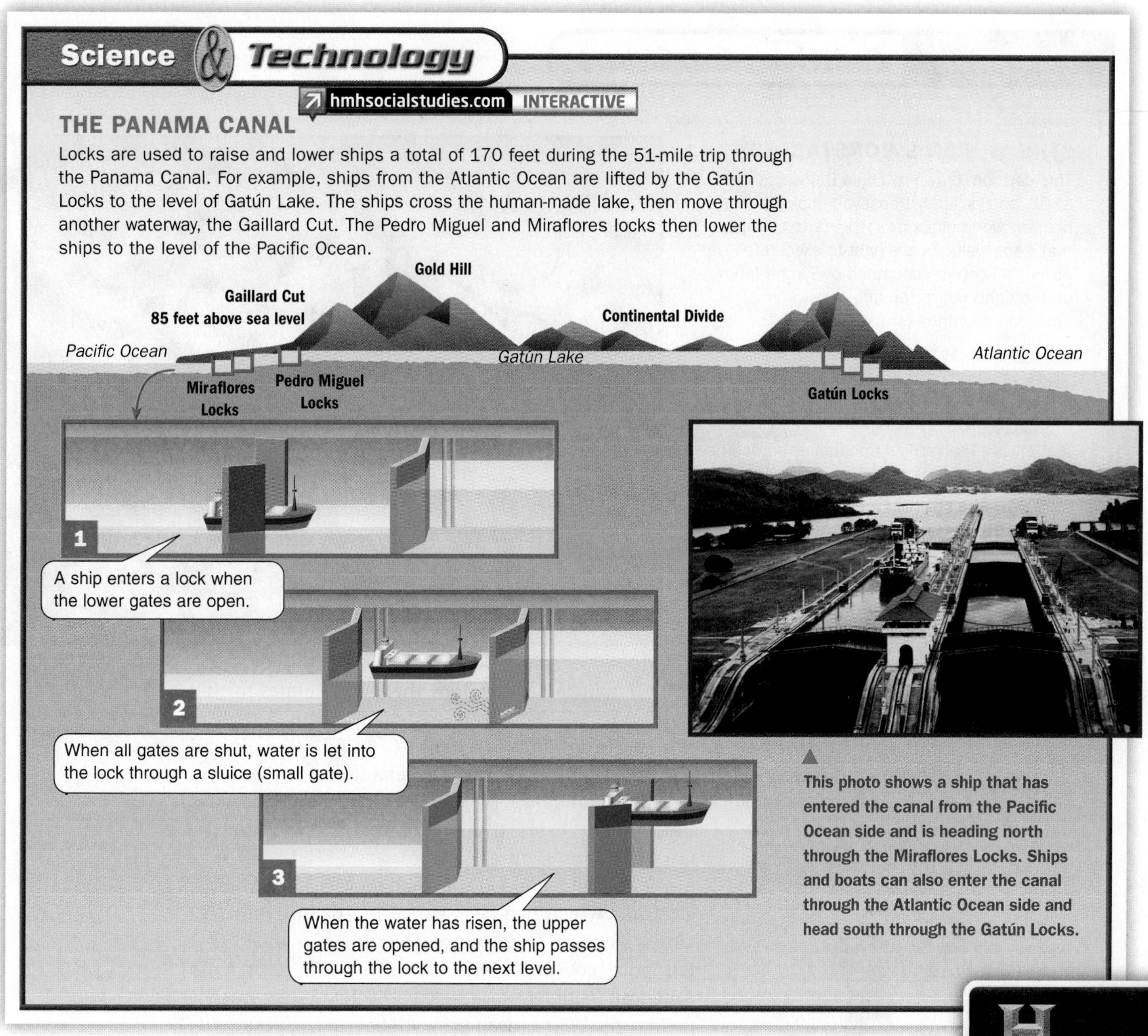
Science & Technology
hmhsocialstudies.com INTERACTIVE
THE PANAMA CANAL
Locks are used to raise and lower ships a total of 170 feet during the 51-mile trip through the Panama Canal. For example, ships from the Atlantic Ocean are lifted by the Gatún Locks to the level of Gatún Lake. The ships cross the human-made lake, then move through another waterway, the Gaillard Cut. The Pedro Miguel and Miraflores locks then lower the ships to the level of the Pacific Ocean.
Gold Hill
Gaillard Cut
85 feet above sea level
Continental Divide
Pacific Ocean
Gatún Lake
Atlantic Ocean
Miraflores Locks
Pedro Miguel Locks
Gatún Locks
1
A ship enters a lock when the lower gates are open.
2
When all gates are shut, water is let into the lock through a sluice (small gate).
3
When the water has risen, the upper gates are opened, and the ship passes through the lock to the next level.

This photo shows a ship that has entered the canal from the Pacific Ocean side and is heading north through the Miraflores Locks. Ships and boats can also enter the canal through the Atlantic Ocean side and head south through the Gatún Locks.

HISTORY

VIDEO
Panama Canal: Locks
hmhsocialstudies.com

States signed a treaty in which the United States agreed to pay Panama $10 million plus an annual rent of $250,000 for an area of land across Panama, called the Canal Zone. The payments were to begin in 1913.

CONSTRUCTING THE CANAL Construction of the Panama Canal ranks as one of the world's greatest engineering feats. Builders fought diseases, such as yellow fever and malaria, and soft volcanic soil that proved difficult to remove from where it lay. Work began in 1904 with the clearing of brush and draining of swamps. By 1913, the height of the construction, more than 43,400 workers were employed. Some had come from Italy and Spain; three-quarters were blacks from the British West Indies. More than 5,600 workers on the canal died from accidents or disease. The total cost to the United States was about $380 million. B

MAIN IDEA

Identifying Problems

B What problems did canal workers encounter in constructing the canal?

On August 15, 1914, the canal opened for business, and more than 1,000 merchant ships passed through during its first year. U.S.-Latin American relations, however, had been damaged by American support of the rebellion in Panama. The resulting ill will lasted for decades, despite Congress's paying Colombia $25 million in 1921 to compensate the country for its lost territory.

Analyzing *Political Cartoons*

"THE WORLD'S CONSTABLE"

This cartoon, drawn by Louis Dalrymple in 1905, shows Teddy Roosevelt implementing his new world diplomacy. The cartoon implies that Roosevelt has the right to execute police power to keep the countries of Europe (shown on the right) out of the affairs of Latin American countries (shown on the left).

SKILLBUILDER
Analyzing Political Cartoons

1. How does the cartoonist portray President Roosevelt?
2. Why is "The World's Constable" a good title for this cartoon?

SEE SKILLBUILDER HANDBOOK, PAGE R24.

THE ROOSEVELT COROLLARY Financial factors drew the United States further into Latin American affairs. In the late 19th century, many Latin American nations had borrowed huge sums from European banks to build railroads and develop industries. Roosevelt feared that if these nations defaulted on their loans, Europeans might intervene. He was determined to make the United States the predominant power in the Caribbean and Central America.

Roosevelt reminded European powers of the Monroe Doctrine, which had been issued in 1823 by President James Monroe. The Monroe Doctrine demanded that European countries stay out of the affairs of Latin American nations. Roosevelt based his Latin America policy on a West African proverb that said, "Speak softly and carry a big stick." In his December 1904 message to Congress, Roosevelt added the **Roosevelt Corollary** to the Monroe Doctrine. He warned that disorder in Latin America might "force the United States . . . to the exercise of an international police power." In effect, the corollary said that the United States would now use force to protect its economic interests in Latin America.

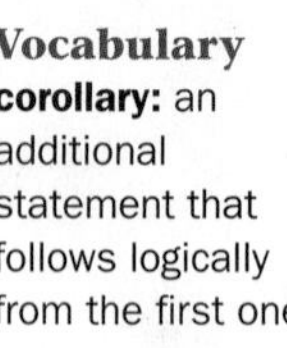

Vocabulary
corollary: an additional statement that follows logically from the first one

"Speak softly and carry a big stick; you will go far."
THEODORE ROOSEVELT

DOLLAR DIPLOMACY During the next decade, the United States exercised its police power on several occasions. For example, when a 1911 rebellion in Nicaragua left the nation near bankruptcy, President William H. Taft, Roosevelt's successor, arranged for American bankers to loan Nicaragua enough money to pay its debts. In return, the bankers were given the right to recover their money by collecting Nicaragua's customs duties. The U.S. bankers also gained control of Nicaragua's state-owned railroad system and its national bank. When Nicaraguan citizens heard about this deal, they revolted against President Adolfo Díaz. To prop up

Díaz's government, some 2,000 marines were sent to Nicaragua. The revolt was put down, but some marine detachments remained in the country until 1933.

The Taft administration followed the policy of using the U.S. government to guarantee loans made to foreign countries by American businesspeople. This policy was called **dollar diplomacy** by its critics and was often used to justify keeping European powers out of the Caribbean.

Woodrow Wilson's Missionary Diplomacy

The Monroe Doctrine, issued by President James Monroe in 1823, had warned other nations against expanding their influence in Latin America. The Roosevelt Corollary asserted, in 1904, that the United States had a right to exercise international police power in the Western Hemisphere. In 1913, President Woodrow Wilson gave the Monroe Doctrine a moral tone.

According to Wilson's "missionary diplomacy," the United States had a moral responsibility to deny recognition to any Latin American government it viewed as oppressive, undemocratic, or hostile to U.S. interests. Prior to this policy, the United States recognized any government that controlled a nation, regardless of that nation's policies or how it had come to power. Wilson's policy pressured nations in the Western Hemisphere to establish democratic governments. Almost immediately, the Mexican Revolution put Wilson's policy to the test.

THE MEXICAN REVOLUTION Mexico had been ruled for more than three decades by a military dictator, Porfirio Díaz. A friend of the United States, Díaz had long encouraged foreign investments in his country. As a result, foreigners, mostly Americans, owned a large share of Mexican oil wells, mines, railroads, and ranches. While foreign investors and some Mexican landowners and politicians had grown rich, the common people of the country were desperately poor.

VIDEO
The Peasant Revolution
hmhsocialstudies.com

In 1911, Mexican peasants and workers led by Francisco Madero overthrew Díaz. Madero promised democratic reforms, but he proved unable to satisfy the conflicting demands of landowners, peasants, factory workers, and the urban middle class. After two years, General Victoriano Huerta took over the government. Within days Madero was murdered. Wilson refused to recognize the government that Huerta formed. He called it "a government of butchers." C

MAIN IDEA

Analyzing Motives
C Why did President Wilson refuse to recognize Huerta's government?

INTERVENTION IN MEXICO Wilson adopted a plan of "watchful waiting," looking for an opportunity to act against Huerta. The opportunity came in April 1914, when one of Huerta's officers arrested a small group of American sailors in Tampico, on Mexico's eastern shore. The Mexicans quickly released them and apologized, but Wilson used the incident as an excuse to intervene in Mexico and ordered U.S. Marines to occupy Veracruz, an important Mexican port. Eighteen Americans and at least 200 Mexicans died during the invasion.

The incident brought the United States and Mexico close to war. Argentina, Brazil, and Chile stepped in to mediate the conflict. They proposed that Huerta step down and that U.S. troops withdraw without paying Mexico for damages. Mexico rejected the plan, and Wilson refused to recognize a government that had come to power as a result of violence. The Huerta regime soon collapsed, however, and Venustiano Carranza, a nationalist leader, became president in 1915. Wilson withdrew the troops and formally recognized the Carranza government.

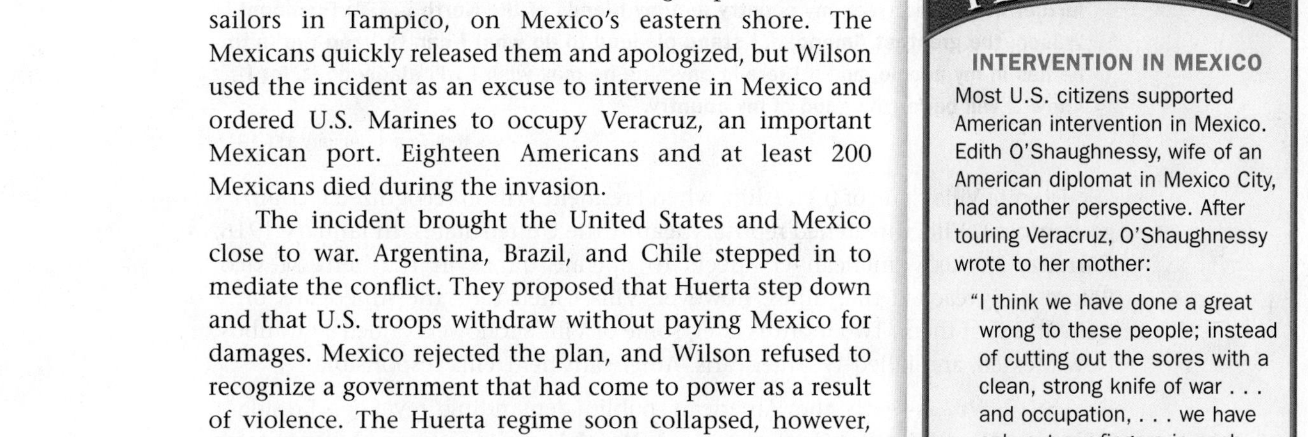

ANOTHER PERSPECTIVE

INTERVENTION IN MEXICO

Most U.S. citizens supported American intervention in Mexico. Edith O'Shaughnessy, wife of an American diplomat in Mexico City, had another perspective. After touring Veracruz, O'Shaughnessy wrote to her mother:

> "I think we have done a great wrong to these people; instead of cutting out the sores with a clean, strong knife of war . . . and occupation, . . . we have only put our fingers in each festering wound and inflamed it further."

History Through Art

ZAPATISTAS (1931)

José Orozco, one of Mexico's foremost artists, painted these Zapatistas (followers of Zapata), to honor the peasant men and women who fought in the Mexican revolution. Orozco did many paintings in support of the revolution. **What aspects of the image does the artist use to convey strength and unity?**

REBELLION IN MEXICO Carranza was in charge, but like others before him, he did not have the support of all Mexicans. Rebels under the leadership of **Francisco "Pancho" Villa** (vē′ə) and **Emiliano Zapata** (ĕ-mēl-yä′nō zə-pä′tə) opposed Carranza's provisional government. Zapata—son of a mestizo peasant—was dedicated to land reform. "It is better to die on your feet than live on your knees," Zapata told the peasants who joined him. Villa, a fierce nationalist, had frequently courted the support and aid of the United States.

A PERSONAL VOICE PANCHO VILLA

> **"[A]s long as I have anything to do with the affairs in Mexico there will be no further friction between my country and my friends of the North . . . To President Wilson, the greatest American, I stand pledged to do what I can to keep the faith he has in my people, and if there is anything he may wish I will gladly do it, for I know it will be for the good of my country."**
>
> —*New York Times*, January 11, 1915

Despite Villa's talk of friendship, when President Wilson recognized Carranza's government, Villa threatened reprisals against the United States. In January 1916, Carranza invited American engineers to operate mines in northern Mexico. Before they reached the mines, however, Villa's men took the Americans off a train and shot them. Two months later, some of Villa's followers raided Columbus, New Mexico, and killed 17 Americans. Americans held Villa responsible.

CHASING VILLA With the American public demanding revenge, President Wilson ordered Brigadier General **John J. Pershing** and an expeditionary force of about 15,000 soldiers into Mexico to capture Villa dead or alive. For almost a year, Villa eluded Pershing's forces. Wilson then called out 150,000 National Guardsmen and stationed them along the Mexican border. In the meantime,

Mexicans grew angrier over the U.S. invasion of their land. In June 1916, U.S. troops clashed with Carranza's army, resulting in deaths on both sides.

Carranza demanded the withdrawal of U.S. troops, but Wilson refused. War seemed imminent. However, in the end, both sides backed down. The United States, facing war in Europe, needed peace on its southern border. In February 1917, Wilson ordered Pershing to return home. Later that year, Mexico adopted a constitution that gave the government control of the nation's oil and mineral resources and placed strict regulations on foreign investors.

▲ **Pancho Villa directs a column of his troops through northern Mexico in 1914.**

Although Carranza had called for the constitution of 1917, he failed to carry out its measures. Instead, he ruled oppressively until 1920 when a moderate named Alvaro Obregón came to power. Obregón's presidency marked the end of civil war and the beginning of reform.

U.S. intervention in Mexican affairs provided a clear model of American imperialist attitudes in the early years of the 20th century. Americans believed in the superiority of free-enterprise democracy, and the American government attempted to extend the reach of this economic and political system, even through armed intervention.

The United States pursued and achieved several foreign policy goals in the early 20th century. First, it expanded its access to foreign markets in order to ensure the continued growth of the domestic economy. Second, the United States built a modern navy to protect its interests abroad. Third, the United States exercised its international police power to ensure dominance in Latin America.

SECTION 4 ASSESSMENT

1. **TERMS & NAMES** For each term or name below, write a sentence explaining its significance.
   - **Panama Canal**
   - **Roosevelt Corollary**
   - **dollar diplomacy**
   - **Francisco "Pancho" Villa**
   - **Emiliano Zapata**
   - **John J. Pershing**

SUMMARIZING

2. **TAKING NOTES**
   In a two-column chart, list ways Teddy Roosevelt and Woodrow Wilson used American power around the world during their presidencies.

Using American Power	
Roosevelt	Wilson

Choose one example and discuss its impact with your classmates.

CRITICAL THINKING

3. **COMPARING AND CONTRASTING**
   What do you think were the similarities and differences between Roosevelt's Big Stick policy and Wilson's missionary diplomacy? Use evidence from the text to support your response. **Think About:**
   - the goal of each of these foreign policies
   - how the policies defined the role of U.S. intervention in international affairs
   - how the policies were applied

4. **EVALUATING DECISIONS**
   In your opinion, should the United States have become involved in the affairs of Colombia, Nicaragua, and Mexico during the early 1900s? Support your answer with details. **Think About:**
   - the effect of the Roosevelt Corollary
   - the results of dollar diplomacy
   - the implication of Wilson's missionary diplomacy

GEOGRAPHY SPOTLIGHT

The Panama Canal: Funnel for Trade

By the late 19th century, the U.S. position in global trade was firmly established. A glance at a world map during that time revealed the trade advantages of cutting through the world's great landmasses at two strategic points. The first cut, through the Isthmus of Suez in Egypt, was completed in 1869 and was a spectacular success. A second cut, this one through Panama, in Central America, would be especially advantageous to the United States. Such a cut, or canal, would substantially reduce the sailing time between the nation's Atlantic and Pacific ports.

It took the United States ten years, from 1904 to 1914, to build the Panama Canal. By 1999, more than 700,000 vessels, flying the flags of about 70 nations, had passed through its locks. In the year 2000, Panama assumed full control of the canal.

INTERCOASTAL TRADE ▲

The first boat through the canal heralded the arrival of increased trade between the Atlantic and Pacific ports of the United States.

NUMBERS TELL THE STORY ▶

A ship sailing from New York to San Francisco by going around South America travels 13,000 miles; the canal shortens the journey to 5,200 miles.

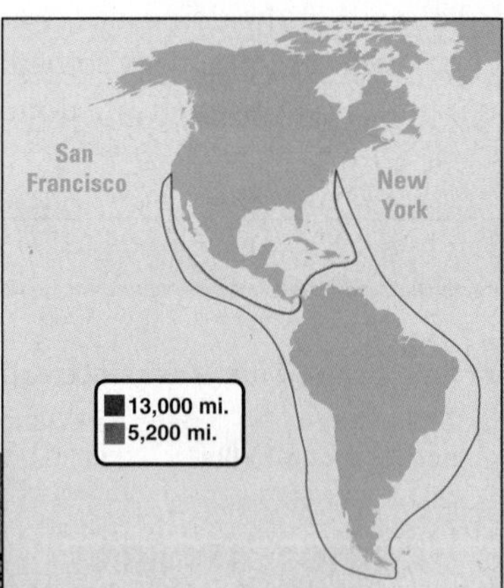

◀ OCEANGOING VESSELS

Ships, like this one, must be of a certain dimension in order to fit through the canal's locks. These container ships must be no more than 106 feet across and 965 feet in length, with a draft (the depth of the vessel below the water line when fully loaded) of no more than 39.5 feet. Each ship pays a toll based on its size, its cargo, and the number of passengers it carries.

◀ **NEW YORK CITY**

New York City and other U.S. Atlantic ports accounted for about 60 percent of the traffic using the Panama Canal in the early decades of its existence.

NEW ORLEANS ▲

Since its founding in 1718, New Orleans has served as a major port for the products of the areas along the Mississippi River. In 1914, the Panama Canal brought Pacific markets into its orbit.

New York

to Europe

to Africa

New Orleans

Panama Canal

to South America

Panama is a narrow stretch of land—or isthmus —that connects North and South America. In building the canal, engineers took advantage of natural waterways. Moving ships through the mountains of the Continental Divide required the use of massive locks. Locks allow a section of the canal to be closed off so that the water level can be raised or lowered.

THINKING CRITICALLY

1. **Analyzing Patterns** On a world map, identify the route that ships took to get from New York City to San Francisco before the Panama Canal opened. How did this route change after the opening of the canal?
2. **Creating a Model** Use clay to shape a model of a cross-section of the Panama Canal as shown in the Science and Technology feature about the Panama Canal. For the locks, use foam blocks or pieces of wood that you have glued together. Paint the model, and then label each part of the canal.

 **SEE SKILLBUILDER HANDBOOK, PAGE R31.**

hmhsocialstudies.com RESEARCH WEB LINKS

CHAPTER 18 ASSESSMENT

VISUAL SUMMARY

AMERICA CLAIMS AN EMPIRE

CAUSES

- Economic competition among industrial nations
- Political and military competition, including the creation of a strong naval force
- A belief in Anglo-Saxon superiority

AMERICAN IMPERIALISM

EFFECTS

- The U.S. purchased Alaska in 1867.
- The U.S. annexed Hawaii in 1898.

- In 1898, the U.S. helped Cuba win independence from Spain.
- In the Treaty of Paris, the U.S. gained Puerto Rico, Guam, and the Philippine Islands.

- Following the Spanish-American War, the U.S.
  —reorganized the government of Puerto Rico
  —established a protectorate over Cuba
  —crushed a revolt in Philippines
- In 1899, the Open Door policy established U.S. trading rights in China.

- In the early 1900s, President Roosevelt initiated plans for the Panama Canal and asserted the right of the U.S. to exercise police power in the Western Hemisphere.
- President Wilson pressured Mexico and other countries in the Western Hemisphere to establish democratic governments.

TERMS & NAMES

For each term or name below, write a sentence explaining its significance to U.S. foreign policy between 1890 and 1920.

1. Queen Liliuokalani
2. imperialism
3. José Martí
4. yellow journalism
5. *U.S.S. Maine*
6. protectorate
7. Open Door notes
8. Boxer Rebellion
9. Panama Canal
10. Roosevelt Corollary

MAIN IDEAS

Use your notes and the information in the chapter to answer the following questions.

Imperialism and America

1. What three factors spurred American imperialism?
2. How did Queen Liliuokalani's main goal conflict with American imperialists' goals?

The Spanish-American War

3. Why was American opinion about Cuban independence divided?
4. Briefly describe the terms of the Treaty of Paris of 1898.

Acquiring New Lands

5. Why was the U.S. interested in events in Puerto Rico?
6. What sparked the Boxer Rebellion in 1900, and how was it crushed?
7. What three key beliefs about America's industrial capitalist economy were reflected in the Open Door policy?

America as a World Power

8. What conflict triggered the war between Russia and Japan?
9. Why is the construction of the Panama Canal considered one of the world's greatest engineering feats?
10. Explain the key difference between Woodrow Wilson's moral diplomacy and Teddy Roosevelt's "big stick" diplomacy.

CRITICAL THINKING

1. **USING YOUR NOTES** Create a Venn diagram like the one below to show the similarities and differences between José Martí of Cuba and Emilio Aguinaldo of the Philippines.

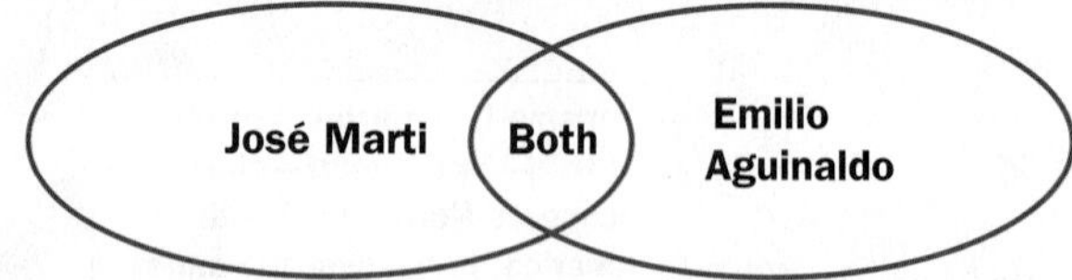

2. **HYPOTHESIZING** Would Cuba have won its independence in the late 19th century if the United States had not intervened there? Support your opinion with details from the text.

3. **INTERPRETING MAPS** Review the Spanish American War in the Caribbean map and the U.S. Imperialism map. Why do you think American naval bases in the Caribbean and the Pacific were beneficial to the United States?

STANDARDIZED TEST PRACTICE

Use the cartoon and your knowledge of U.S. history to answer question 1.

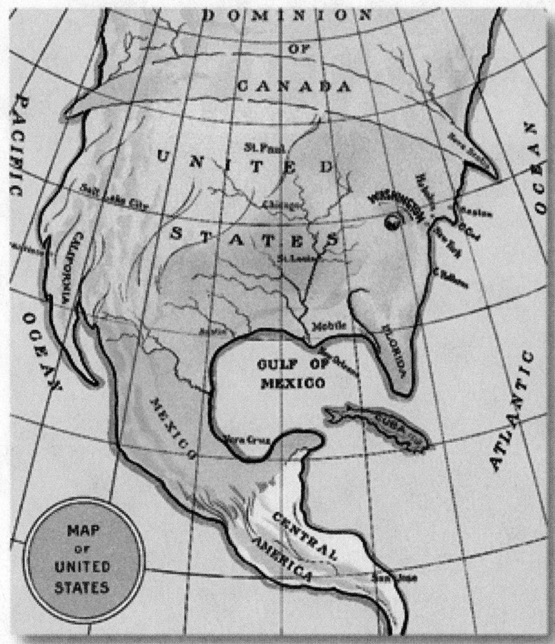

1. What is the cartoonist's point of view concerning the relationship between the United States and Cuba?
   - **A** The United States wishes to be friends with Cuba.
   - **B** The United States will devour Cuba.
   - **C** The United States is wasting its time fighting over such a small area.
   - **D** The United States has no interest in Cuba.

Use the map and your knowledge of U.S. history to answer question 2.

2. How did the building of the Panama Canal support United States efforts to become a world power?
   - **F** It gave the United States a colony in Central America.
   - **G** It prevented Japan and China from attacking Hawaii.
   - **H** It opened up a new avenue for trade with China.
   - **J** By providing a shortcut between the Atlantic Ocean and Pacific Ocean, it opened up new trading opportunities.

For additional test practice, go online for:

- Diagnostic tests
- Tutorials

INTERACT WITH HISTORY

Recall the issues that you explored at the beginning of the chapter. Suppose you are a journalist at the end of the Spanish-American War. You work for William Randolph Hearst's *New York Journal*. Write a newspaper editorial that presents your point of view about whether or not the Senate should ratify the Treaty of Paris, thus annexing the Philippines.

FOCUS ON WRITING

Imagine you are a worker helping to build the Panama Canal. Write a diary entry giving details about the work you are doing, the hardships you face, and why you think the project is worthwhile.

MULTIMEDIA ACTIVITY

21st CENTURY

Use the *Electronic Library of Primary Sources* and Internet resources to research opinions on imperialism between 1895 and 1920.

- Choose a document, incident, or piece of writing about imperialism. Decide if you support it or disagree with it.
- Write a speech that presents your point of view. Decide how you will make your arguments clear and convincing while also addressing opposing concerns.
- Practice your speech aloud and then present it to the class.

RAND McNALLY

World Atlas

CONTENTS

Complete Legend for Physical and Political Maps

Symbols

Lake
Salt Lake
Seasonal Lake
River
Waterfall
Canal
Mountain Peak
Highest Mountain Peak

Cities

■ Los Angeles	City over 1,000,000 population
▣ Calgary	City of 250,000 to 1,000,000 population
• Haifa	City under 250,000 population
✪ *Paris*	National Capital
★ Vancouver	Secondary Capital (State, Province, or Territory)

Type Styles Used to Name Features

CHINA	Country
ONTARIO	State, Province, or Territory
PUERTO RICO (U.S.)	Possession
ATLANTIC OCEAN	Ocean or Sea
Alps	Physical Feature
Borneo	Island

Boundaries

International Boundary
Secondary Boundary

Land Elevation and Water Depths

Land Elevation

Meters	Feet
3,000 and over	9,840 and over
2,000 - 3,000	6,560 - 9,840
500 - 2,000	1,640- 6,560
200 - 500	656 - 1,640
0 - 200	0 - 656

Water Depth

Meters	Feet
Less than 200	Less than 656
200 - 2,000	656 - 6,560
Over 2,000	Over 6,560

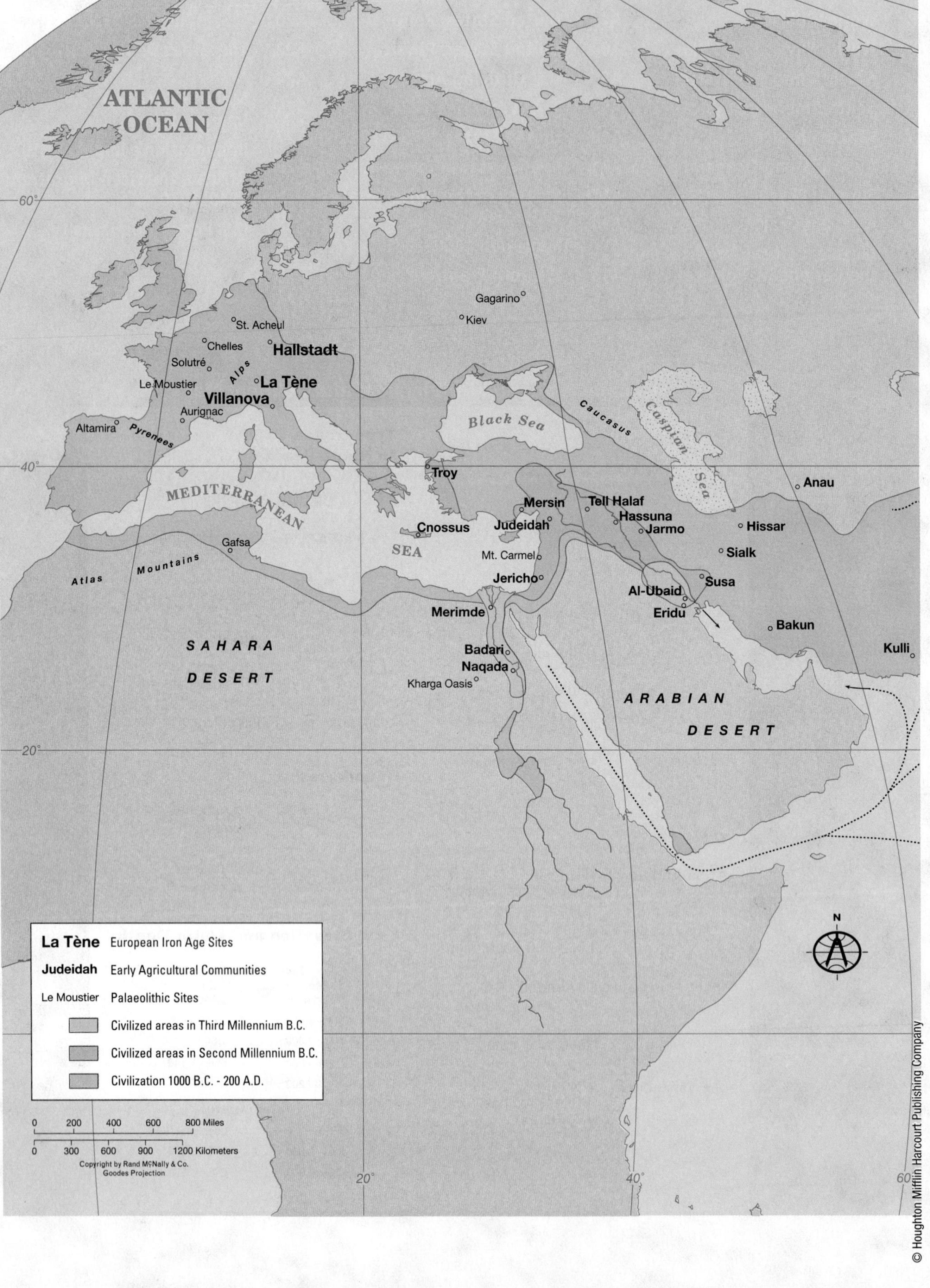
ARCTIC OCEAN
ATLANTIC OCEAN
60°
40°
20°
20°
40°
60°
Gagarino
Kiev
St. Acheul
Chelles
Hallstadt
Solutré
Alps
La Tène
Le Moustier
Villanova
Aurignac
Altamira
Pyrenees
Black Sea
Caucasus
Caspian Sea
Troy
Anau
MEDITERRANEAN SEA
Mersin
Tell Halaf
Hassuna
Jarmo
Judeidah
Hissar
Cnossus
Gafsa
Mt. Carmel
Sialk
Atlas Mountains
Jericho
Susa
Al-Ubaid
Eridu
Merimde
Bakun
Kulli
SAHARA DESERT
Badari
Naqada
Kharga Oasis
ARABIAN DESERT
N
La Tène European Iron Age Sites
Judeidah Early Agricultural Communities
Le Moustier Palaeolithic Sites
Civilized areas in Third Millennium B.C.
Civilized areas in Second Millennium B.C.
Civilization 1000 B.C. - 200 A.D.
0 200 400 600 800 Miles
0 300 600 900 1200 Kilometers
Copyright by Rand McNally & Co.
Goodes Projection

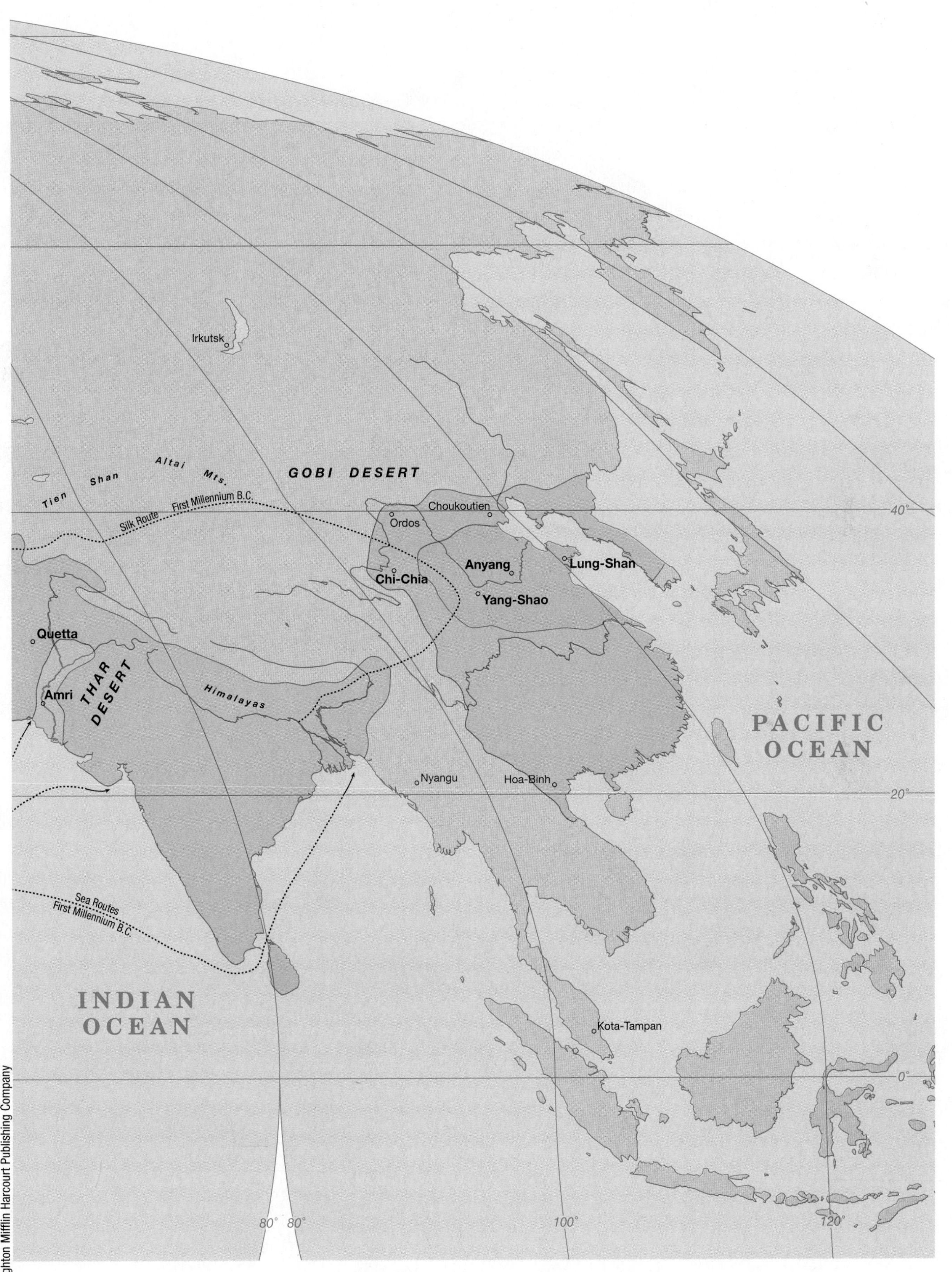
Irkutsk
Tien Shan
Altai Mts.
GOBI DESERT
Silk Route First Millennium B.C.
Choukoutien
Ordos
Anyang
Lung-Shan
Chi-Chia
Yang-Shao
Quetta
Amri
THAR DESERT
Himalayas
PACIFIC OCEAN
Nyangu
Hoa-Binh
Sea Routes First Millennium B.C.
INDIAN OCEAN
Kota-Tampan
40°
20°
0°
80°
80°
100°
120°

ARCTIC OCEAN
GREENLAND
(Den.)
Baffin Bay
Arctic Circle
ICELAND
FAROE IS. (Den.)
UNITED KINGDOM
IRELAND
London
FRANCE
Madrid
PORTUGAL
SPAIN
Azores (Port.)
Casablanca
MOROCCO
RUSSIA
ALASKA (U.S.)
Yukon
Anchorage
Aleutian Islands
CANADA
Hudson Bay
Newfoundland
Vancouver
Missouri
Montréal
Ottawa
Chicago
UNITED STATES
New York
Washington, D.C.
Colorado
Mississippi
Los Angeles
Houston
Gulf of Mexico
MIDWAY IS. (U.S.)
Tropic of Cancer
Hawaiian Islands (U.S.)
MEXICO
Mexico City
BAHAMAS
CUBA
HAITI
DOM. REP.
PUERTO RICO (U.S.)
JAMAICA
BELIZE
GUAT.
HOND.
EL SAL.
NIC.
COSTA RICA
PANAMA
Caribbean Sea
ATLANTIC
Canary Islands (Sp.)
W. SAHARA
MAURITANIA
MALI
CAPE VERDE
SENEGAL
GAMBIA
GUINEA-BISSAU
GUINEA
SIERRA LEONE
LIBERIA
COTE D'IVOIRE
BURK. FASO
GHANA
Niger
PACIFIC
Caracas
TRINIDAD AND TOBAGO
VENEZUELA
GUYANA
SURINAME
FRENCH GUIANA
COLOMBIA
Equator
KIRIBATI
Galapagos Islands (Ecuador)
ECUADOR
Amazon
BRAZIL
PERU
Lima
OCEAN
OCEAN
SAMOA
AMERICAN SAMOA
COOK ISLANDS (N.Z.)
TONGA
FRENCH POLYNESIA
BOLIVIA
ST. HELENA (U.K.)
PARAGUAY
Rio de Janeiro
Tropic of Capricorn
Easter Island (Chile)
ARGENTINA
Santiago
URUGUAY
Buenos Aires
CHILE
N
0 1000 2000 Miles
0 1000 2000 3000 Kilometers
Copyright by Rand McNally & Co.
Robinson Projection
M-101519-2
FALKLAND IS. (U.K.)
South Georgia (U.K.)
South Orkney Is. (U.K.)
South Shetland Is. (U.K.)
Antarctic Circle
Weddell Sea

National Capital
Major Cities

ARCTIC OCEAN
Greenland
Baffin Island
Baffin Bay
Jan Mayen
Arctic Circle
Iceland
Faroe Is.
British Isles
London
Yukon
Mt. McKinley 20,320 Ft. 6,194m
Mackenzie
Canadian Shield
Hudson Bay
NORTH AMERICA
Rocky Mountains
Great Plains
Aleutian Islands
Vancouver
Newfoundland
St. Lawrence
Appalachian Mts.
Washington, D.C.
Cape Hatteras
Mississippi
Colorado
Los Angeles
Azores
Iberian Peninsula
Atlas Mts.
Midway Is.
Baja California
Gulf of Mexico
ATLANTIC
Canary Islands
Tropic of Cancer
Hawaiian Islands
Yucatan Peninsula
Cuba
Hispaniola
Puerto Rico
Jamaica
Caribbean Sea
Cape Verde Islands
Cape Verde
Niger
PACIFIC
Trinidad
Orinoco
OCEAN
Palmyra
Equator
Galapagos Islands
Amazon
Amazon Basin
SOUTH AMERICA
Kiribati
OCEAN
Marquesas Is.
Andes
Samoa Islands
Mato Grosso Plateau
St. Helena
Cook Islands
Tonga Is.
Tahiti
Tropic of Capricorn
Rio de Janeiro
Easter Island
Paraná
Mt. Aconcagua 22,831 Ft. 6,959m
Archipiélago Juan Fernández
Buenos Aires
N
Chatham Is.
Patagonia
0 1000 2000 Miles
0 1000 2000 3000 Kilometers
Copyright by Rand McNally & Co.
Robinson Projection
M-101520-1
Falkland Is.
South Georgia
Tierra del Fuego
Cape Horn
South Sandwich Is.
South Orkney Is.
South Shetland Is.
Antarctic Circle
Antarctic Peninsula
Weddell Sea
Ross Sea
Marie Byrd Land
Vinson Massif 16,066 Ft. 4,897m
180° 165° 150° 135° 120° 105° 90° 75° 60° 45° 30° 15°
75° 60° 45° 30° 15° 0° 15° 30° 45° 60° 75°

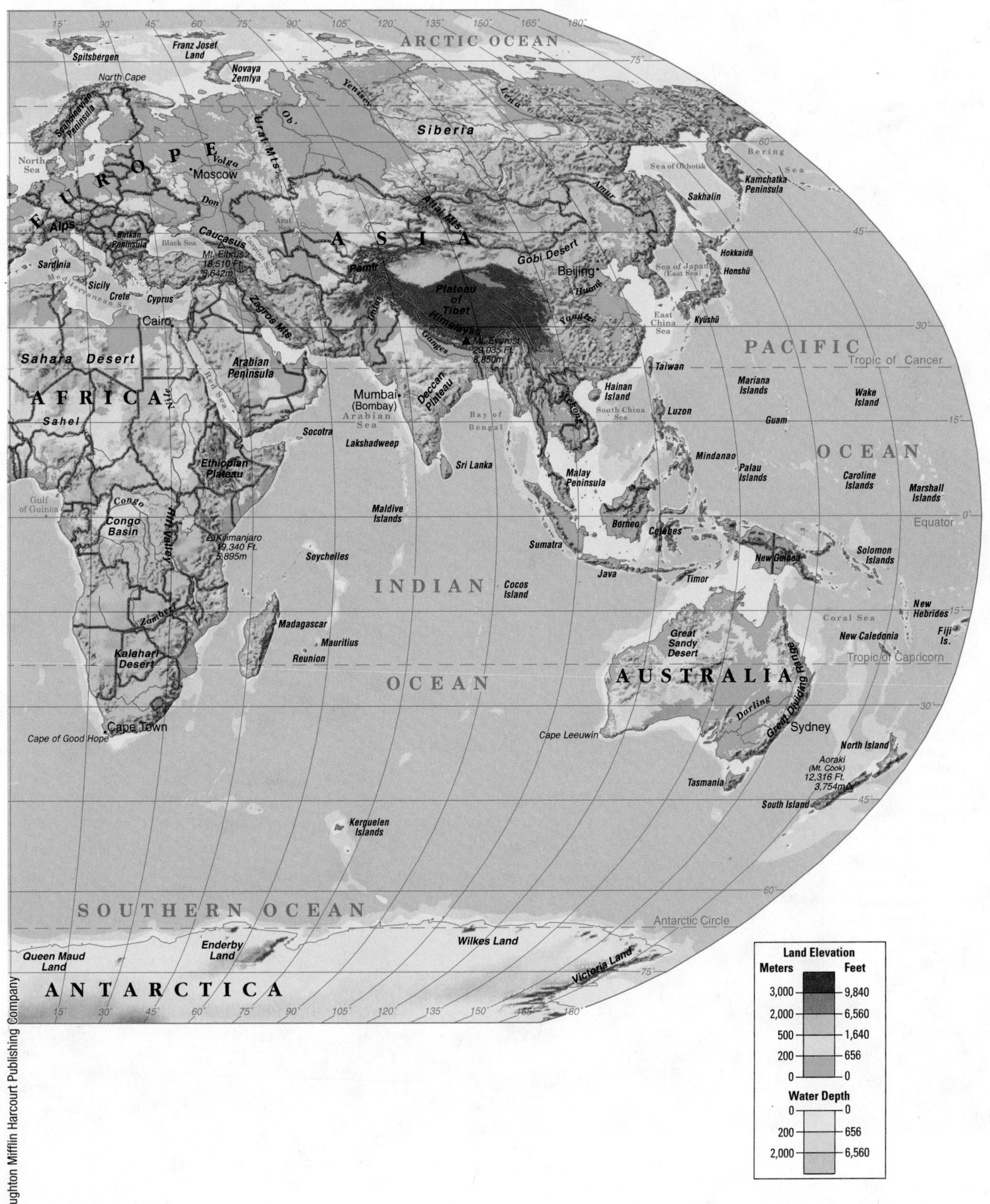
ARCTIC OCEAN
Spitsbergen
Franz Josef Land
North Cape
Novaya Zemlya
Scandinavian Peninsula
Yenisey
Lena
Ob'
Ural Mts.
Siberia
North Sea
EUROPE
Volga
Moscow
Bering Sea
Sea of Okhotsk
Kamchatka Peninsula
Sakhalin
Amur
Don
Altai Mts.
Alps
Balkan Peninsula
Black Sea
Caucasus
Aral Sea
Caspian Sea
ASIA
Mt. Elbrus 18,510 Ft. 5,642m
Gobi Desert
Hokkaidō
Sardinia
Pamir
Beijing
Sea of Japan (East Sea)
Honshū
Mediterranean Sea
Sicily
Crete
Cyprus
Plateau of Tibet
Huang
Cairo
Zagros Mts.
Indus
Himalayas
Yangtze
East China Sea
Kyūshū
Ganges
Mt. Everest 29,035 Ft. 8,850m
PACIFIC
Tropic of Cancer
Sahara Desert
Arabian Peninsula
Taiwan
Red Sea
Mariana Islands
AFRICA
Nile
Mumbai (Bombay)
Deccan Plateau
Hainan Island
Wake Island
Mekong
Sahel
Arabian Sea
Bay of Bengal
South China Sea
Luzon
Guam
Socotra
Lakshadweep
OCEAN
Ethiopian Plateau
Sri Lanka
Mindanao
Palau Islands
Caroline Islands
Marshall Islands
Malay Peninsula
Gulf of Guinea
Congo
Maldive Islands
Equator
Congo Basin
Rift Valley
Borneo
Celebes
Kilimanjaro 19,340 Ft. 5,895m
Sumatra
Seychelles
New Guinea
Solomon Islands
Java
Timor
INDIAN
Cocos Island
Zambezi
New Hebrides
Coral Sea
Madagascar
Great Sandy Desert
New Caledonia
Fiji Is.
Mauritius
Kalahari Desert
Reunion
Tropic of Capricorn
Great Dividing Range
AUSTRALIA
OCEAN
Darling
Cape Town
Sydney
Cape of Good Hope
Cape Leeuwin
North Island
Aoraki (Mt. Cook) 12,316 Ft. 3,754m
Tasmania
South Island
Kerguelen Islands
SOUTHERN OCEAN
Antarctic Circle
Enderby Land
Wilkes Land
Queen Maud Land
Victoria Land
ANTARCTICA
Land Elevation
Meters
Feet
3,000
9,840
2,000
6,560
500
1,640
200
656
0
0
Water Depth
0
0
200
656
2,000
6,560

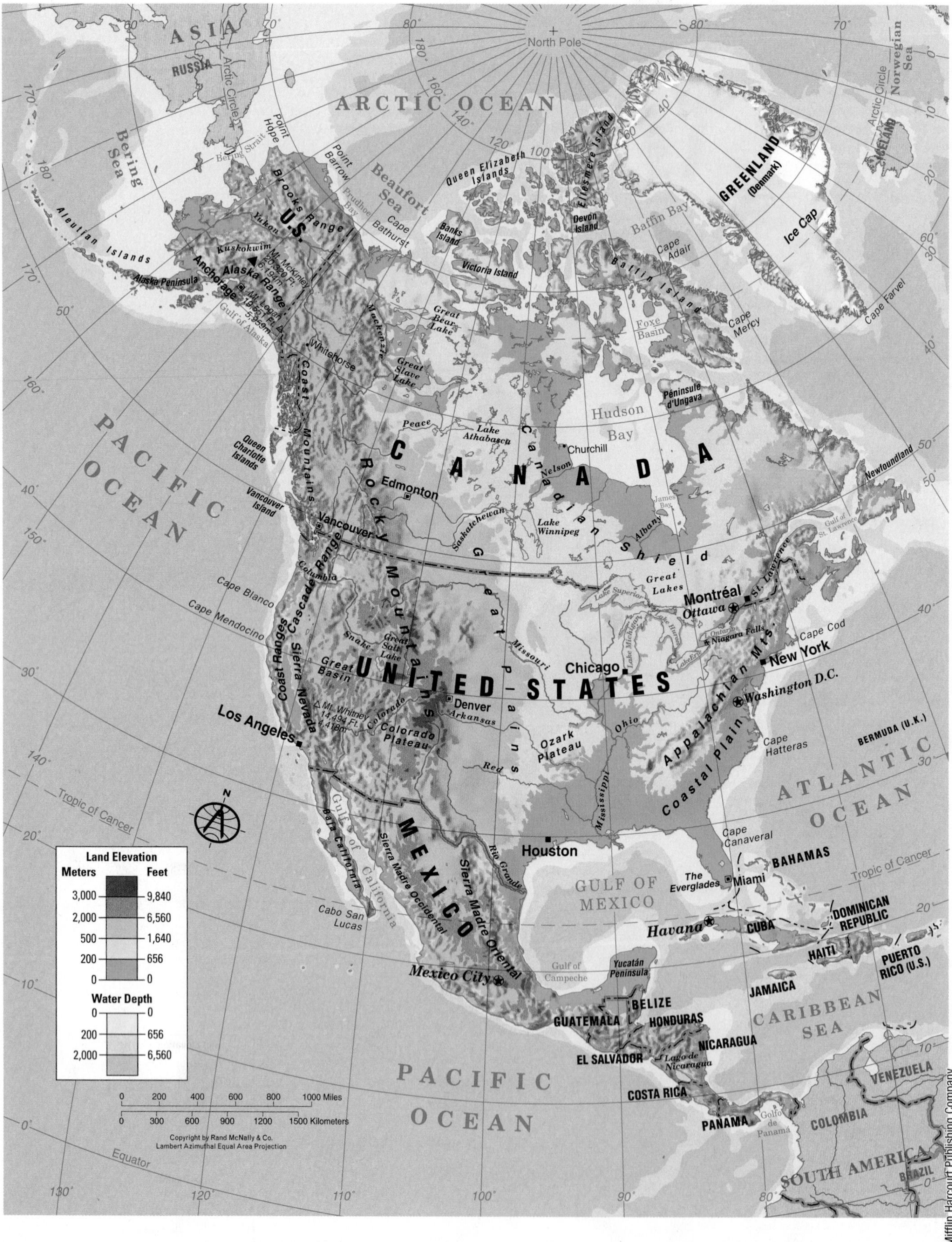
ARCTIC OCEAN
North Pole
ASIA
RUSSIA
Arctic Circle
Bering Sea
Bering Strait
Point Hope
Point Barrow
Prudhoe Bay
Beaufort Sea
Cape Bathurst
Brooks Range
U.S.
Yukon
Kuskokwim
Mt. McKinley 20,320 Ft. 6,194m
Alaska Range
Anchorage
Mt. Logan 19,551 Ft. 5,959m
Gulf of Alaska
Aleutian Islands
Alaska Peninsula
Queen Elizabeth Islands
Ellesmere Island
Devon Island
Banks Island
Victoria Island
Great Bear Lake
Great Slave Lake
Mackenzie
Whitehorse
Coast Mountains
Baffin Bay
Baffin Island
Cape Adair
Foxe Basin
Cape Mercy
GREENLAND (Denmark)
Ice Cap
Cape Farvel
ICELAND
Norwegian Sea
Péninsule d'Ungava
Hudson Bay
Churchill
Nelson
James Bay
Peace
Lake Athabasca
Canadian Shield
CANADA
Edmonton
Saskatchewan
Lake Winnipeg
Albany
Newfoundland
Gulf of St. Lawrence
St. Lawrence
Queen Charlotte Islands
Vancouver Island
Vancouver
PACIFIC OCEAN
Rocky Mountains
Great Plains
Cascade Range
Columbia
Cape Blanco
Cape Mendocino
Coast Ranges
Sierra Nevada
Snake
Great Salt Lake
Great Basin
Mt. Whitney 14,494 Ft. 4,418m
Colorado
Colorado Plateau
Denver
Arkansas
Missouri
Great Lakes
Lake Superior
Lake Michigan
Lake Huron
Lake Ontario
Lake Erie
Niagara Falls
Montréal
Ottawa
Chicago
New York
Cape Cod
UNITED STATES
Washington D.C.
Appalachian Mts.
Ohio
Ozark Plateau
Red
Mississippi
Coastal Plain
Cape Hatteras
BERMUDA (U.K.)
ATLANTIC OCEAN
Los Angeles
Tropic of Cancer
Houston
Rio Grande
Cape Canaveral
BAHAMAS
The Everglades
Miami
GULF OF MEXICO
Havana
CUBA
DOMINICAN REPUBLIC
HAITI
PUERTO RICO (U.S.)
JAMAICA
CARIBBEAN SEA
Baja California
Gulf of California
Cabo San Lucas
Sierra Madre Occidental
Sierra Madre Oriental
MEXICO
Mexico City
Gulf of Campeche
Yucatán Peninsula
BELIZE
GUATEMALA
HONDURAS
NICARAGUA
Lago de Nicaragua
EL SALVADOR
COSTA RICA
PANAMA
Golfo de Panamá
VENEZUELA
COLOMBIA
SOUTH AMERICA
BRAZIL
Equator
Land Elevation
Meters
Feet
3,000
9,840
2,000
6,560
500
1,640
200
656
0
0
Water Depth
0
0
200
656
2,000
6,560
0 200 400 600 800 1000 Miles
0 300 600 900 1200 1500 Kilometers
Copyright by Rand McNally & Co.
Lambert Azimuthal Equal Area Projection

ATLANTIC OCEAN
CARIBBEAN SEA
GULF OF MEXICO
NORTH AMERICA
CUBA
DOMINICAN REPUBLIC
HAITI
JAMAICA
PUERTO RICO (U.S.)
Greater Antilles
Lesser Antilles
MEXICO
BELIZE
Gulf of Honduras
HONDURAS
GUATEMALA
EL SALVADOR
NICARAGUA
COSTA RICA
PANAMA
Gulf of Panama
Cristóbal Colón Peak 18,948 Ft. 5,775m
Caracas
TRINIDAD AND TOBAGO
Llanos
Orinoco
VENEZUELA
GUYANA
SURINAME
FRENCH GUIANA
Cape Orange
Magdalena
Bogotá
COLOMBIA
Galapagos Islands (Ec.)
ECUADOR
Chimborazo 20,703 Ft. 6,310m
Putumayo
Japurá
Negro
Manaus
Amazon
Ilha de Marajó
Belém
Equator
Amazon Basin
Juruá
Madeira
Tapajós
Tocantins
BRAZIL
Selvas
Ucayali
PERU
Andes
Recife
Mt. Huascarán 22,133 Ft. 6,746m
Lima
Mato Grosso Plateau
São Francisco
Mt. Illampu 21,066 Ft. 6,421m
Lake Titicaca
BOLIVIA
Cordillera Oriental
Brasília
Serra do Espinhaço
Mt. Sajama 21,463 Ft. 6,542m
Gran Chaco
Paraná
Atacama Desert
PARAGUAY
São Paulo
Rio de Janeiro
Tropic of Capricorn
Isla San Ambrosio (Chile)
Isla San Felix (Chile)
Mt. Ojos del Salado 22,615 Ft. 6,893m
ARGENTINA
URUGUAY
PACIFIC OCEAN
Archipiélago Juan Fernández (Chile)
Mt. Aconcagua 22,831 Ft. 6,959m
Santiago
Buenos Aires
Río de la Plata
Pampas
CHILE
San Matías Gulf
Península Valdés
Chiloé
Patagonia
San Jorge Gulf
Point Medanoso
Grand Bay
West Falkland
East Falkland
FALKLAND ISLANDS (U.K.)
Strait of Magellan
Tierra del Fuego
Cape Horn
South Georgia (U.K.)
Drake Passage
South Shetland Islands (U.K.)
South Orkney Islands (U.K.)
South Sandwich Islands (U.K.)
Land Elevation
Meters Feet
3,000 9,840
2,000 6,560
500 1,640
200 656
0 0
Water Depth
0 0
200 656
2,000 6,560
0 200 400 600 800 1000 Miles
0 300 600 900 1200 1500 Kilometers
Copyright by Rand McNally & Co.
Lambert Azimuthal Equal Area Projection
N
RAND McNALLY

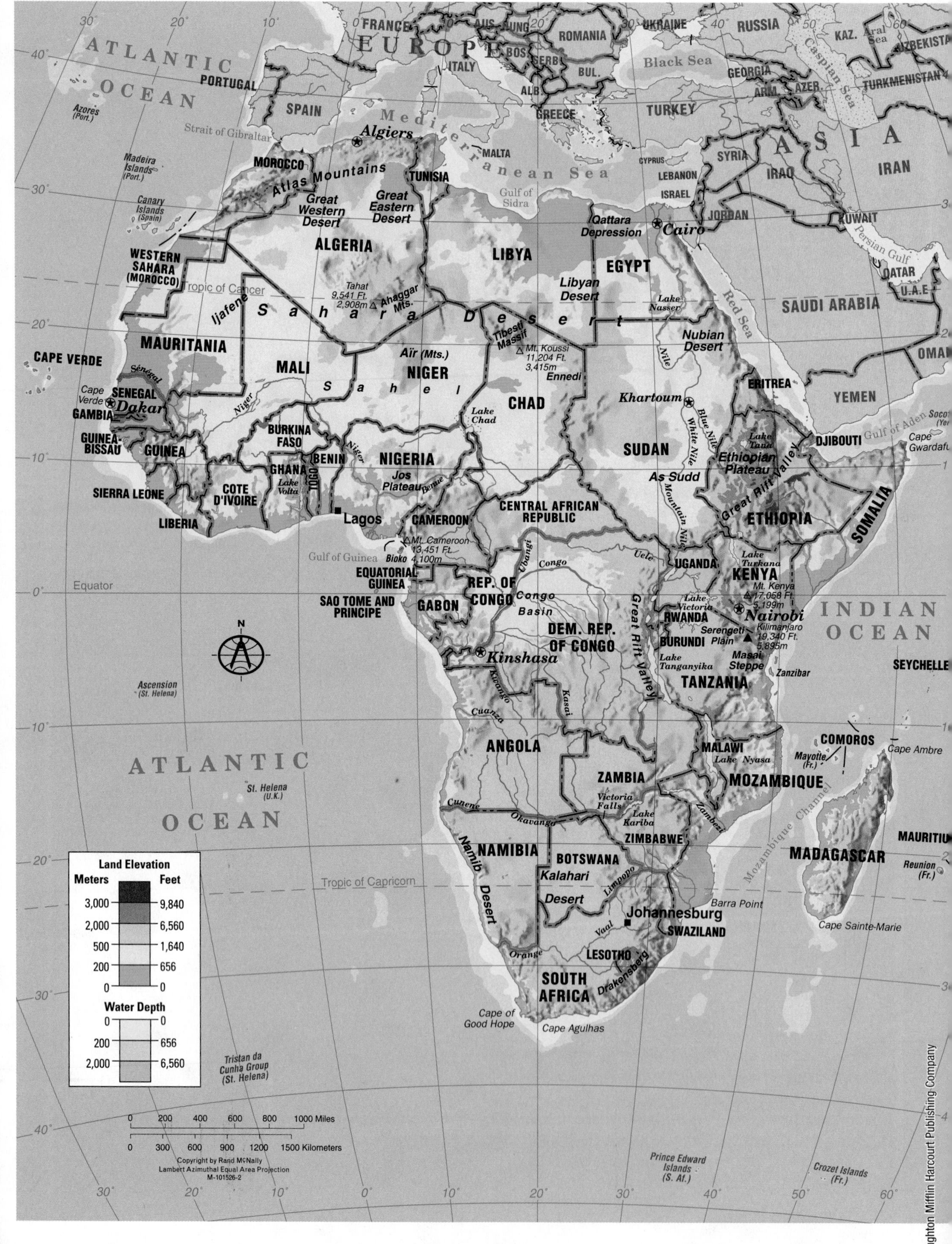

RAND McNALLY

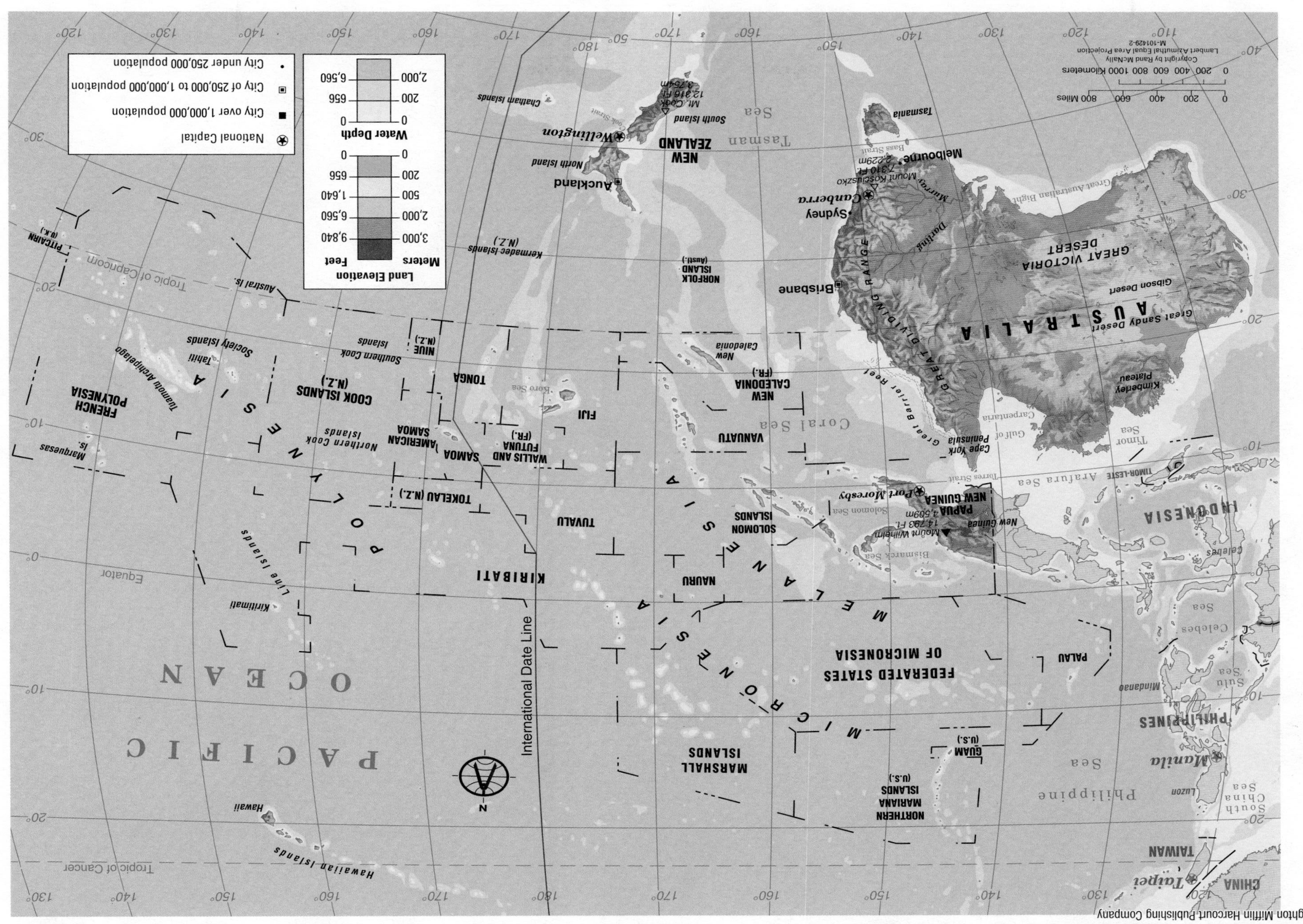
PACIFIC OCEAN
MICRONESIA
MELANESIA
POLYNESIA
AUSTRALIA
GREAT VICTORIA DESERT
Great Sandy Desert
Gibson Desert
Kimberley Plateau
GREAT DIVIDING RANGE
Great Barrier Reef
Cape York Peninsula
Gulf of Carpentaria
Great Australian Bight
Darling
Murray
Mount Kosciuszko 7,310 Ft. 2,229m
Brisbane
Sydney
Canberra
Melbourne
Bass Strait
Tasmania
Tasman Sea
Coral Sea
Timor Sea
Arafura Sea
Torres Strait
TIMOR-LESTE
INDONESIA
New Guinea
PAPUA NEW GUINEA
Mount Wilhelm 14,793 Ft. 4,509m
Port Moresby
Bismarck Sea
Solomon Sea
SOLOMON ISLANDS
VANUATU
NEW CALEDONIA (FR.)
New Caledonia
NORFOLK ISLAND (Austl.)
NEW ZEALAND
North Island
South Island
Auckland
Wellington
Cook Strait
Mt. Cook 12,316 Ft. 3,754m
Chatham Islands
Kermadec Islands (N.Z.)
FIJI
Koro Sea
TONGA
NIUE (N.Z.)
Southern Cook Islands
COOK ISLANDS (N.Z.)
Northern Cook Islands
AMERICAN SAMOA
SAMOA
WALLIS AND FUTUNA (FR.)
TOKELAU (N.Z.)
TUVALU
KIRIBATI
NAURU
Line Islands
Kiritimati
Equator
Society Islands
Tahiti
Tuamotu Archipelago
FRENCH POLYNESIA
Marquesas Is.
Austral Is.
PITCAIRN (U.K.)
Tropic of Capricorn
Tropic of Cancer
Hawaiian Islands
Hawaii
MARSHALL ISLANDS
FEDERATED STATES OF MICRONESIA
PALAU
GUAM (U.S.)
NORTHERN MARIANA ISLANDS (U.S.)
Philippine Sea
PHILIPPINES
Manila
Luzon
Mindanao
Sulu Sea
Celebes Sea
Celebes
South China Sea
TAIWAN
Taipei
CHINA
International Date Line
N
Land Elevation
Meters Feet
3,000 9,840
2,000 6,560
500 1,640
200 656
0 0
Water Depth
0 0
200 656
2,000 6,560
National Capital
City over 1,000,000 population
City of 250,000 to 1,000,000 population
City under 250,000 population
0 200 400 600 800 Miles
0 200 400 600 800 1000 Kilometers
Copyright by Rand McNally
Lambert Azimuthal Equal Area Projection
M-101429-2

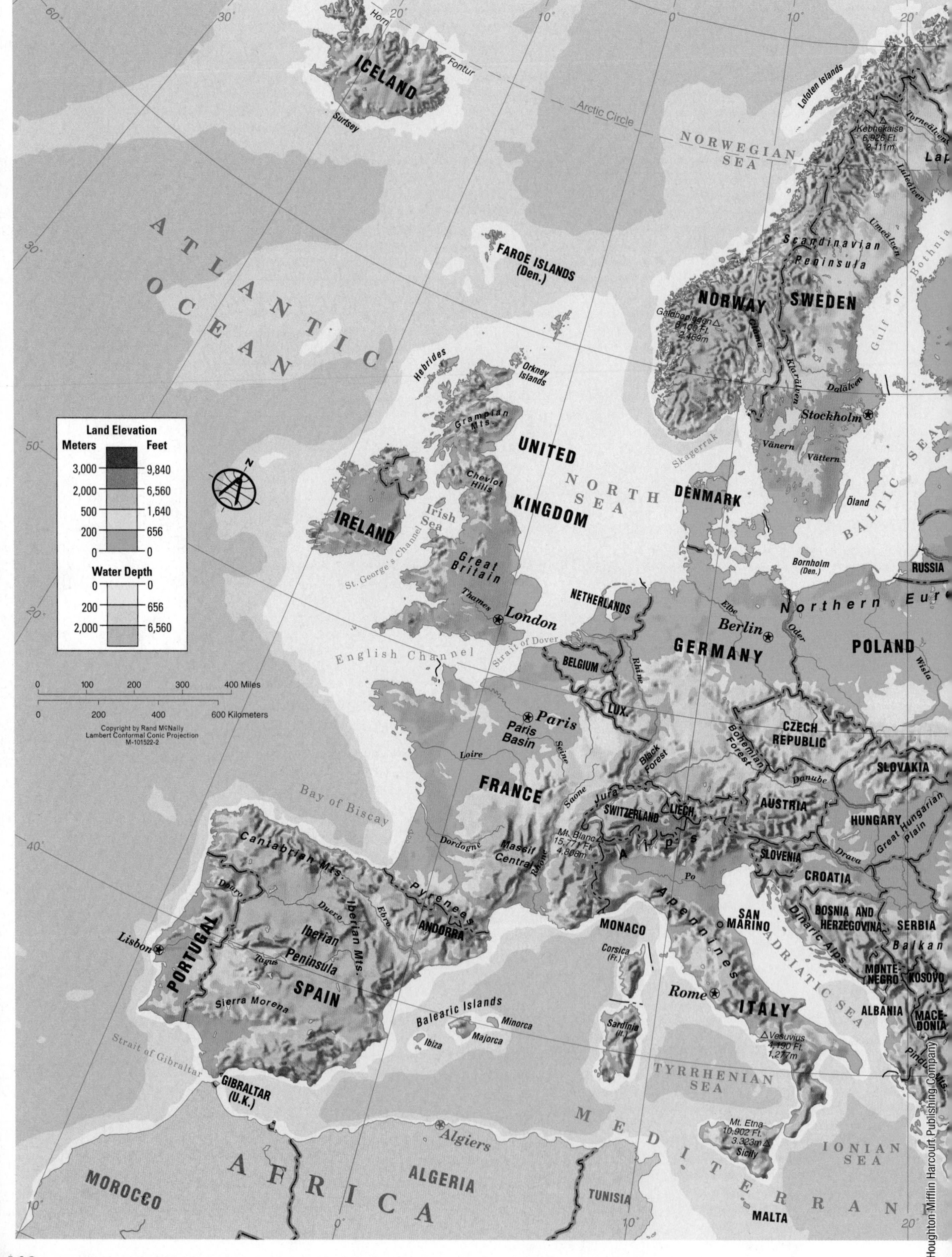
Land Elevation
Meters
Feet
3,000
9,840
2,000
6,560
500
1,640
200
656
0
0
Water Depth
0
0
200
656
2,000
6,560
0
100
200
300
400 Miles
0
200
400
600 Kilometers
Copyright by Rand McNally
Lambert Conformal Conic Projection
M-101522-2
ICELAND
Horn
Fontur
Surtsey
Arctic Circle
NORWEGIAN SEA
ATLANTIC OCEAN
FAROE ISLANDS (Den.)
Lofoten Islands
Kebnekaise 6,926 Ft. 2,111m
Torneälven
Luleälven
Umeälven
Scandinavian Peninsula
Gulf of Bothnia
NORWAY
SWEDEN
Galdhopiggen 8,100 Ft. 2,469m
Glåma
Klarälven
Dalälven
Stockholm
Vänern
Vättern
Öland
BALTIC SEA
Skagerrak
DENMARK
Bornholm (Den.)
RUSSIA
Hebrides
Orkney Islands
Grampian Mts.
UNITED KINGDOM
NORTH SEA
Cheviot Hills
IRELAND
Irish Sea
St. George's Channel
Great Britain
Thames
London
Strait of Dover
English Channel
NETHERLANDS
BELGIUM
LUX.
Elbe
Oder
Berlin
Northern European
GERMANY
POLAND
Wisła
Rhine
CZECH REPUBLIC
Bohemian Forest
Black Forest
Danube
SLOVAKIA
Paris
Paris Basin
Seine
Loire
FRANCE
Saône
Jura
SWITZERLAND
LIECH.
AUSTRIA
HUNGARY
Great Hungarian Plain
Bay of Biscay
Mt. Blanc 15,771 Ft. 4,808m
Alps
Dordogne
Massif Central
Rhône
SLOVENIA
Drava
Po
CROATIA
Cantabrian Mts.
Douro
Duero
Iberian Mts.
Ebro
Pyrenees
ANDORRA
Iberian Peninsula
Lisbon
PORTUGAL
Tagus
SPAIN
Sierra Morena
MONACO
Corsica (Fr.)
SAN MARINO
Apennines
Dinaric Alps
BOSNIA AND HERZEGOVINA
SERBIA
Balkan
ADRIATIC SEA
MONTENEGRO
KOSOVO
Rome
ITALY
ALBANIA
MACEDONIA
Balearic Islands
Minorca
Majorca
Ibiza
Sardinia (It.)
Vesuvius 4,190 Ft. 1,277m
Pindus Mts.
Strait of Gibraltar
GIBRALTAR (U.K.)
TYRRHENIAN SEA
Mt. Etna 10,902 Ft. 3,323m
Sicily
IONIAN SEA
Algiers
MEDITERRANEAN
AFRICA
MOROCCO
ALGERIA
TUNISIA
MALTA

Murmansk
Kola Peninsula
Ponoy
WHITE SEA
Timan Ridge
Pechora
Mezen
Ural Mountains
Ob'
Irtysh
FINLAND
Onega
Northern Dvina
Northern Uvals (Uplands)
Kama
Sukhona
Lake Onega
Lake Ladoga
Helsinki
RUSSIA
Rybinsk Res.
ESTONIA
Lake Peipus
ASIA
Valdai Hills
Moscow
Oka
LATVIA
Plain
Central Russian Upland
Khopër
Don
Ural
KAZAKHSTAN
Syr Darya
Neman
BELARUS
Caspian Depression
Aral Sea
Pripyat
Dnieper Lowland
Kiev
UKRAINE
Dnieper
Donets Basin
Volga
UZBEKISTAN
Amu Darya
Dniester
MOLDOVA
CASPIAN SEA
TURKMENISTAN
Sea of Azov
Crimean Peninsula
Transylvanian Alps
Caucasus
Mt. Elbrus 18,510 Ft. 5,642m
GEORGIA
Baku
BLACK SEA
Danube
ARMENIA
AZERBAIJAN
AZER.
BULGARIA
Istanbul
Tehran
TURKEY
IRAN
GREECE
AEGEAN SEA
IRAQ
SYRIA
Euphrates
Tigris
Rhodes
CYPRUS
LEBANON
Crete
SEA

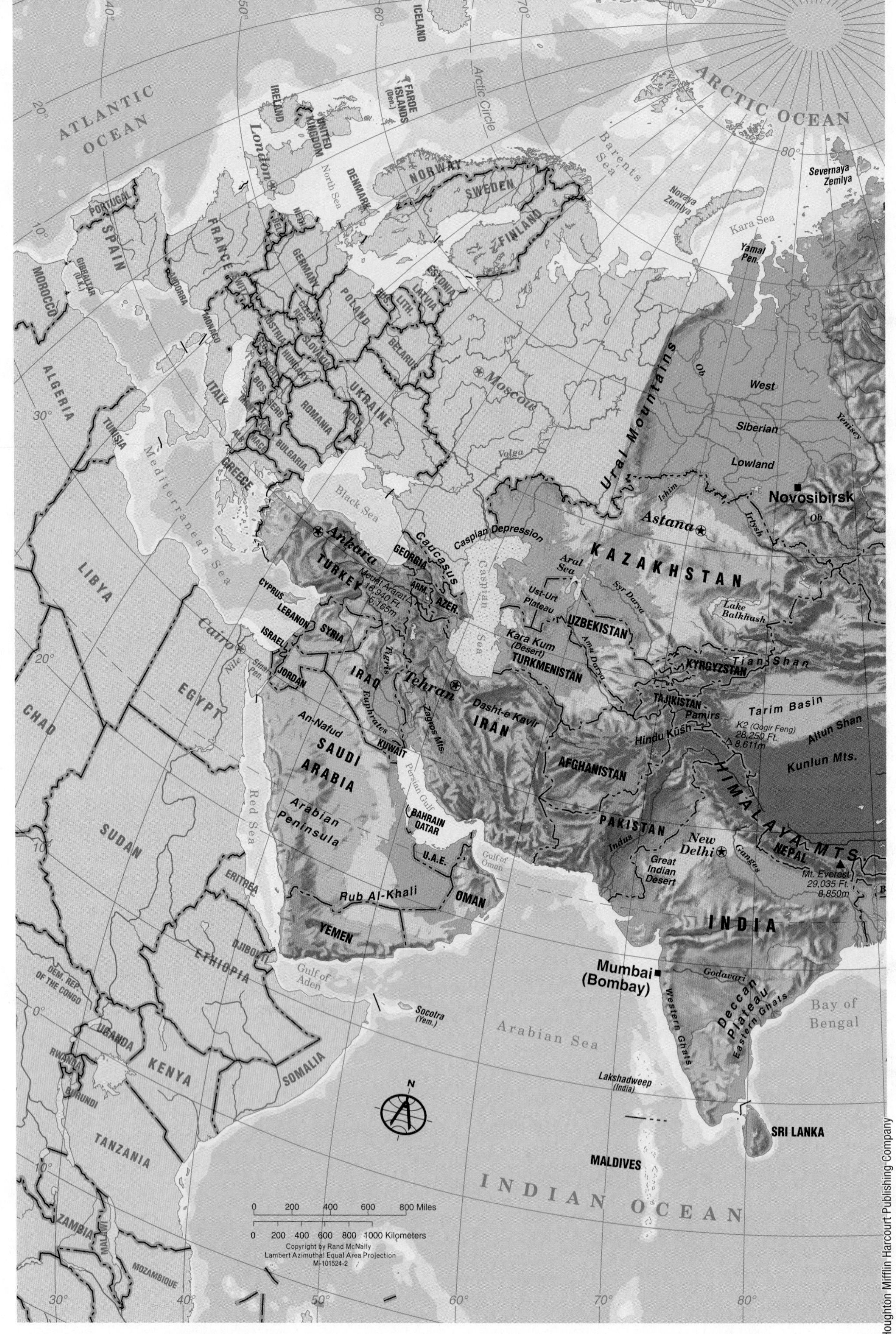
ARCTIC OCEAN
ATLANTIC OCEAN
ICELAND
FAROE ISLANDS (Den.)
IRELAND
UNITED KINGDOM
London
North Sea
DENMARK
NORWAY
SWEDEN
FINLAND
Arctic Circle
Barents Sea
Novaya Zemlya
Severnaya Zemlya
Kara Sea
Yamal Pen.
PORTUGAL
SPAIN
FRANCE
GERMANY
POLAND
ESTONIA
LATVIA
LITH.
BELARUS
UKRAINE
CZECH REP.
AUSTRIA
SLOVAKIA
HUNGARY
ROMANIA
MOLD.
BULGARIA
ITALY
GREECE
ALB.
MACE.
BOS.
SERB.
MONACO
ANDORRA
GIBRALTAR (U.K.)
MOROCCO
ALGERIA
TUNISIA
LIBYA
EGYPT
CHAD
SUDAN
ERITREA
DJIBOUTI
ETHIOPIA
SOMALIA
KENYA
UGANDA
RWANDA
BURUNDI
TANZANIA
DEM. REP. OF THE CONGO
ZAMBIA
MALAWI
MOZAMBIQUE
Mediterranean Sea
Moscow
Volga
Ural Mountains
Ob
West Siberian Lowland
Yenisey
Novosibirsk
Irtysh
Ishim
Astana
KAZAKHSTAN
Caspian Depression
Caucasus
Black Sea
Ankara
TURKEY
GEORGIA
ARM.
AZER.
Mount Ararat 16,940 Ft. 5,165m
Caspian Sea
Aral Sea
Ust-Urt Plateau
Syr Darya
Lake Balkhash
UZBEKISTAN
Kara Kum (Desert)
TURKMENISTAN
Amu Darya
KYRGYZSTAN
Tian Shan
TAJIKISTAN
Pamirs
Tarim Basin
K2 (Qogir Feng) 28,250 Ft. 8,611m
Altun Shan
Kunlun Mts.
Hindu Kush
HIMALAYA MTS.
NEPAL
Mt. Everest 29,035 Ft. 8,850m
CYPRUS
LEBANON
SYRIA
ISRAEL
JORDAN
Cairo
Nile
Sinai Pen.
IRAQ
Tigris
Euphrates
Tehran
Dasht-e Kavir
IRAN
Zagros Mts.
An-Nafud
SAUDI ARABIA
KUWAIT
Persian Gulf
BAHRAIN
QATAR
U.A.E.
Gulf of Oman
OMAN
Arabian Peninsula
Rub Al-Khali
YEMEN
Red Sea
Gulf of Aden
Socotra (Yem.)
AFGHANISTAN
PAKISTAN
Indus
New Delhi
Ganges
Great Indian Desert
INDIA
Mumbai (Bombay)
Godavari
Deccan Plateau
Western Ghats
Eastern Ghats
Bay of Bengal
Arabian Sea
Lakshadweep (India)
MALDIVES
SRI LANKA
INDIAN OCEAN
N
0 200 400 600 800 Miles
0 200 400 600 800 1000 Kilometers
Copyright by Rand McNally
Lambert Azimuthal Equal Area Projection
M-101524-2
RAND McNALLY

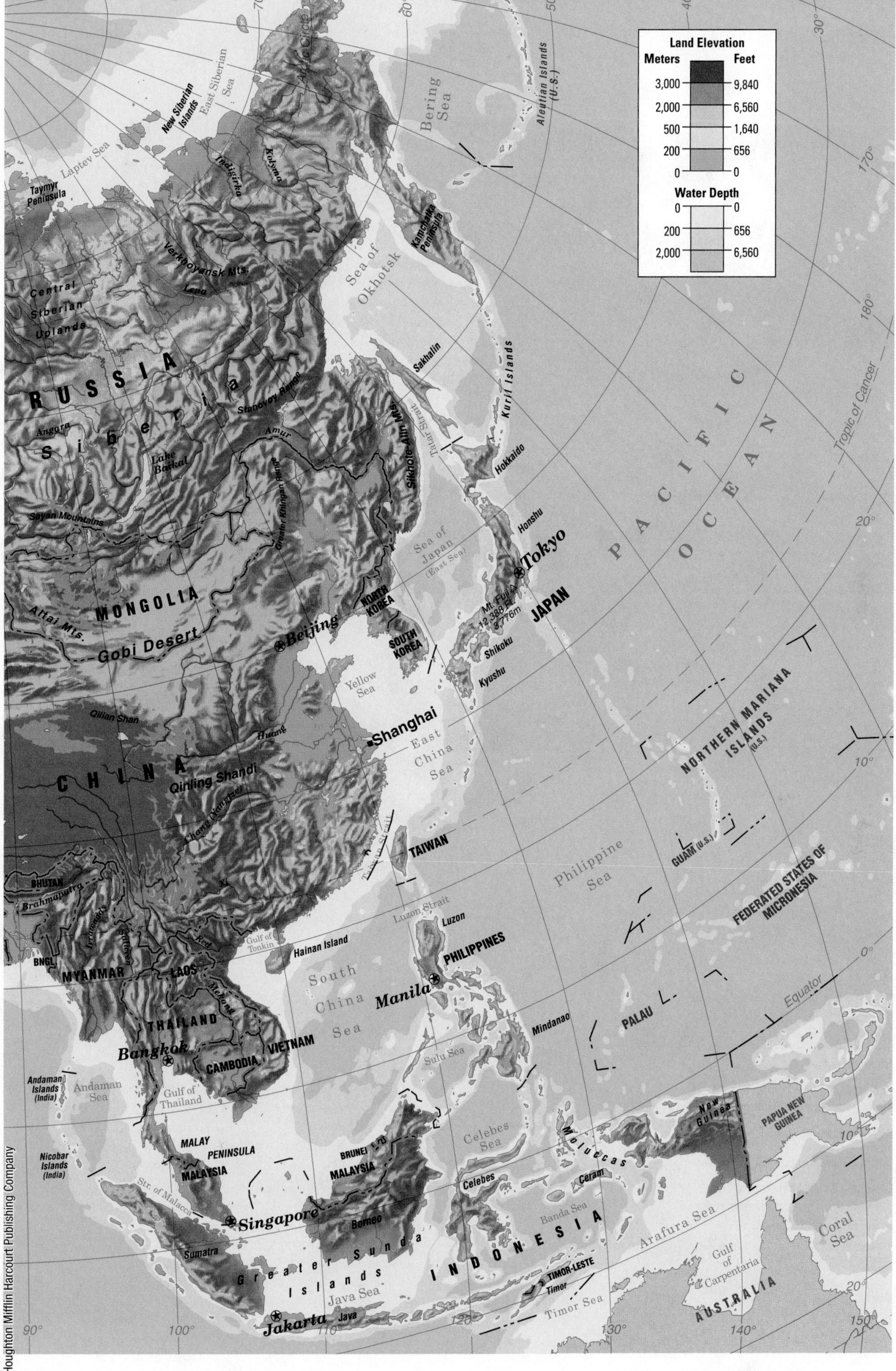
Land Elevation
Meters
Feet
3,000
9,840
2,000
6,560
500
1,640
200
656
0
0
Water Depth
0
0
200
656
2,000
6,560
East Siberian Sea
New Siberian Islands
Laptev Sea
Taymyr Peninsula
Arctic Circle
Bering Sea
Aleutian Islands (U.S.)
Indigirka
Kolyma
Kamchatka Peninsula
Sea of Okhotsk
Verkhoyansk Mts.
Lena
Central Siberian Uplands
RUSSIA
Siberia
Stanovoy Range
Sakhalin
Kuril Islands
Angara
Lake Baikal
Amur
Tatar Strait
Sikhote-Alin Mts.
Hokkaido
Sayan Mountains
Greater Khingan Range
PACIFIC OCEAN
Tropic of Cancer
Honshu
Sea of Japan (East Sea)
Tokyo
NORTH KOREA
Mt. Fuji 12,388 ft. 3,776m
JAPAN
MONGOLIA
Altai Mts.
Gobi Desert
Beijing
SOUTH KOREA
Shikoku
Kyushu
Yellow Sea
Qilian Shan
Huang
Shanghai
East China Sea
NORTHERN MARIANA ISLANDS (U.S.)
CHINA
Qinling Shandi
Chang (Yangtze)
Taiwan Strait
TAIWAN
GUAM (U.S.)
Philippine Sea
FEDERATED STATES OF MICRONESIA
BHUTAN
Brahmaputra
Irrawaddy
Salween
Red
Gulf of Tonkin
Hainan Island
Luzon Strait
Luzon
PHILIPPINES
BNGL.
MYANMAR
LAOS
South China Sea
Manila
Mekong
THAILAND
VIETNAM
PALAU
Mindanao
Equator
Bangkok
CAMBODIA
Sulu Sea
Andaman Islands (India)
Andaman Sea
Gulf of Thailand
New Guinea
PAPUA NEW GUINEA
Celebes Sea
Moluccas
MALAY PENINSULA
BRUNEI
Nicobar Islands (India)
MALAYSIA
MALAYSIA
Celebes
Ceram
Str. of Malacca
Singapore
Borneo
Banda Sea
Arafura Sea
Coral Sea
Sumatra
Greater Sunda Islands
INDONESIA
Gulf of Carpentaria
TIMOR-LESTE
Timor
Java Sea
Timor Sea
AUSTRALIA
Jakarta
Java
90°
100°
110°
120°
130°
140°
150°
0°
10°
20°
30°
40°
50°
60°
70°
170°
180°

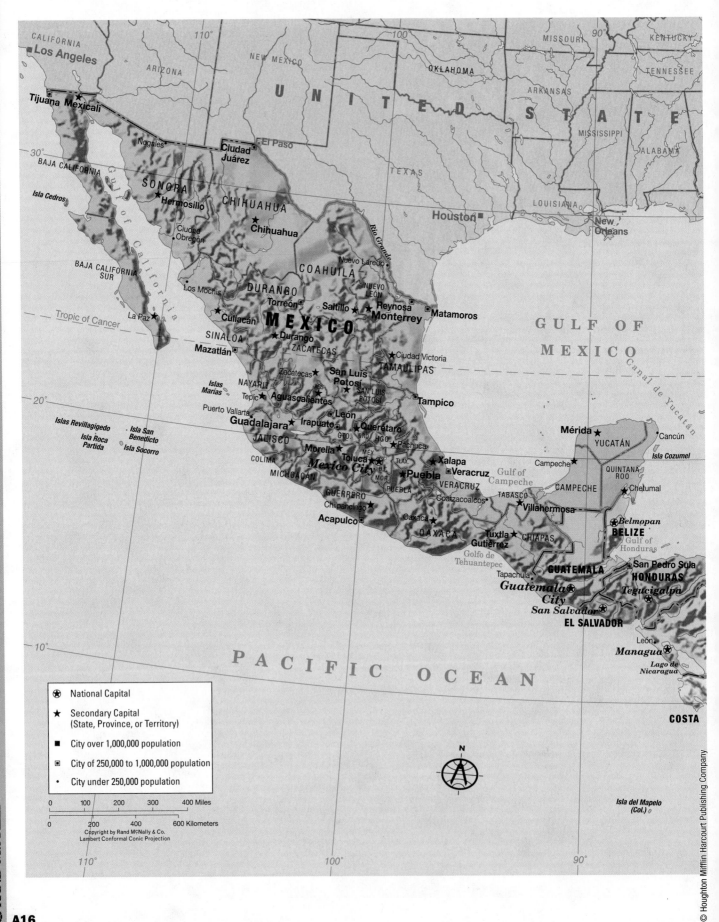

CALIFORNIA
Los Angeles
ARIZONA
NEW MEXICO
OKLAHOMA
MISSOURI
KENTUCKY
TENNESSEE
ARKANSAS
UNITED STATES
MISSISSIPPI
ALABAMA
TEXAS
LOUISIANA
Houston
New Orleans
El Paso
Tijuana
Mexicali
Nogales
Ciudad Juárez
BAJA CALIFORNIA
Isla Cedros
SONORA
Hermosillo
Gulf of California
CHIHUAHUA
Chihuahua
Ciudad Obregón
Rio Grande
BAJA CALIFORNIA SUR
Los Mochis
Nuevo Laredo
COAHUILA
DURANGO
NUEVO LEÓN
Torreón
Saltillo
Reynosa
Monterrey
Matamoros
La Paz
Tropic of Cancer
Culiacán
MEXICO
SINALOA
Durango
Mazatlán
ZACATECAS
Ciudad Victoria
TAMAULIPAS
GULF OF MEXICO
Canal de Yucatán
Zacatecas
San Luis Potosí
Islas Marías
NAYARIT
AGS.
SAN LUIS POTOSÍ
Tepic
Aguascalientes
Tampico
Puerto Vallarta
León
Islas Revillagigedo
Guadalajara
Irapuato
Querétaro
Isla San Benedicto
Isla Roca Partida
Isla Socorro
JALISCO
GTO.
QRO.
HGO.
Pachuca
Mérida
YUCATÁN
Cancún
Isla Cozumel
Morelia
COLIMA
Toluca
MÉX.
D.F.
TLAX.
Mexico City
Xalapa
Campeche
MICHOACÁN
MOR.
Puebla
Veracruz
Gulf of Campeche
QUINTANA ROO
PUEBLA
VERACRUZ
CAMPECHE
Chetumal
GUERRERO
Coatzacoalcos
TABASCO
Villahermosa
Chilpancingo
Acapulco
Oaxaca
Belmopan
BELIZE
OAXACA
Tuxtla Gutiérrez
CHIAPAS
Gulf of Honduras
Golfo de Tehuantepec
Tapachula
GUATEMALA
San Pedro Sula
HONDURAS
Guatemala City
Tegucigalpa
San Salvador
EL SALVADOR
León
Managua
Lago de Nicaragua
PACIFIC OCEAN
COSTA
Isla del Mapelo (Col.)
110°
100°
90°
30°
20°
10°

- ⊛ National Capital
- ★ Secondary Capital (State, Province, or Territory)
- ■ City over 1,000,000 population
- ▣ City of 250,000 to 1,000,000 population
- • City under 250,000 population

N

0 100 200 300 400 Miles
0 200 400 600 Kilometers

Lambert Conformal Conic Projection

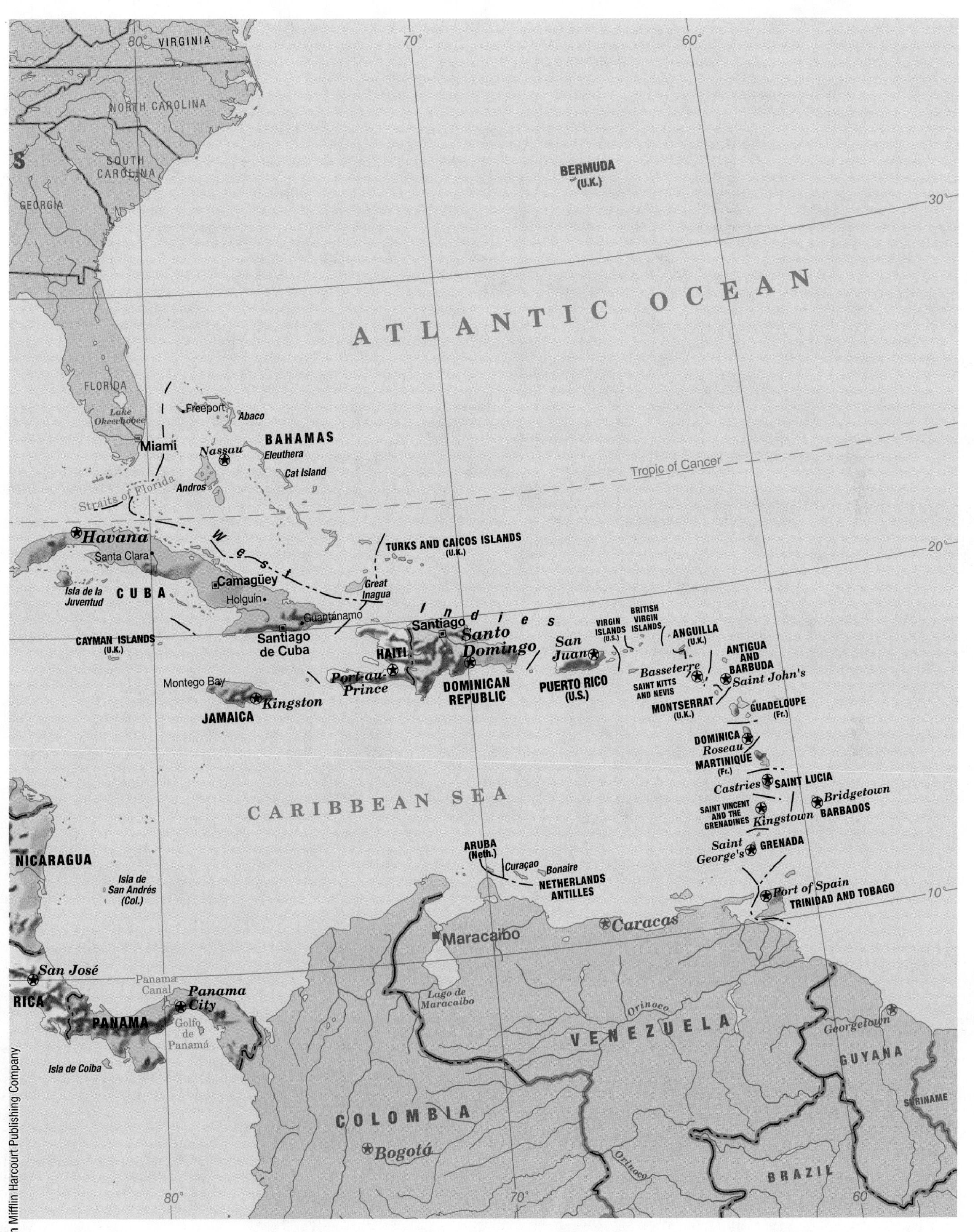
VIRGINIA
NORTH CAROLINA
SOUTH CAROLINA
GEORGIA
BERMUDA (U.K.)
ATLANTIC OCEAN
FLORIDA
Lake Okeechobee
Freeport
Abaco
BAHAMAS
Miami
Nassau
Eleuthera
Cat Island
Andros
Straits of Florida
Tropic of Cancer
West Indies
Havana
Santa Clara
TURKS AND CAICOS ISLANDS (U.K.)
Camagüey
Isla de la Juventud
CUBA
Holguín
Great Inagua
Guantánamo
Santiago
Santo Domingo
CAYMAN ISLANDS (U.K.)
Santiago de Cuba
HAITI
San Juan
VIRGIN ISLANDS (U.S.)
BRITISH VIRGIN ISLANDS
ANGUILLA (U.K.)
Montego Bay
Port-au-Prince
DOMINICAN REPUBLIC
PUERTO RICO (U.S.)
Basseterre
SAINT KITTS AND NEVIS
ANTIGUA AND BARBUDA
Saint John's
Kingston
JAMAICA
MONTSERRAT (U.K.)
GUADELOUPE (Fr.)
DOMINICA
Roseau
MARTINIQUE (Fr.)
SAINT LUCIA
Castries
Bridgetown
CARIBBEAN SEA
SAINT VINCENT AND THE GRENADINES
Kingstown
BARBADOS
Saint George's
GRENADA
ARUBA (Neth.)
Curaçao
Bonaire
NETHERLANDS ANTILLES
NICARAGUA
Isla de San Andrés (Col.)
Port of Spain
TRINIDAD AND TOBAGO
Caracas
Maracaibo
San José
RICA
Panama Canal
Panama City
PANAMA
Golfo de Panamá
Isla de Coiba
Lago de Maracaibo
Orinoco
VENEZUELA
Georgetown
GUYANA
SURINAME
COLOMBIA
Bogotá
BRAZIL
80°
70°
60°
30°
20°
10°

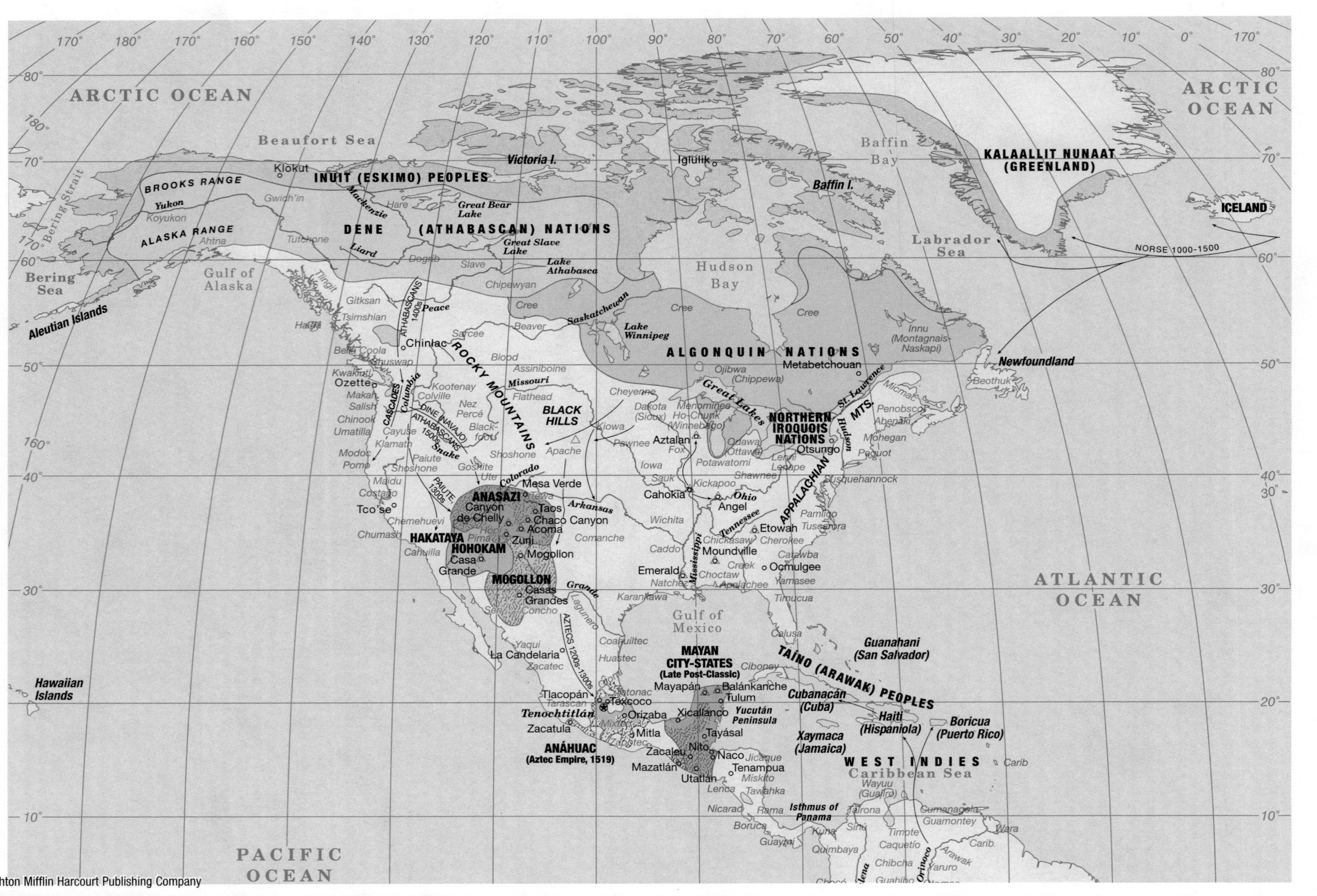
ARCTIC OCEAN
Beaufort Sea
Bering Sea
Gulf of Alaska
Hudson Bay
Baffin Bay
Labrador Sea
ATLANTIC OCEAN
PACIFIC OCEAN
Gulf of Mexico
Caribbean Sea
KALAALLIT NUNAAT (GREENLAND)
ICELAND
NORSE 1000-1500
Newfoundland
INUIT (ESKIMO) PEOPLES
DENE (ATHABASCAN) NATIONS
ALGONQUIN NATIONS
NORTHERN IROQUOIS NATIONS
BROOKS RANGE
ALASKA RANGE
ROCKY MOUNTAINS
APPALACHIAN MTS.
CASCADES
BLACK HILLS
Victoria I.
Baffin I.
Aleutian Islands
Hawaiian Islands
Great Bear Lake
Great Slave Lake
Lake Athabasca
Lake Winnipeg
Great Lakes
ATHABASCANS 1400s
DINE (NAVAJO) ATHABASCANS 1500s
PAIUTE 1300s
AZTECS 1200s-1300s
ANASAZI
HAKATAYA
HOHOKAM
MOGOLLON
MAYAN CITY-STATES (Late Post-Classic)
ANÁHUAC (Aztec Empire, 1519)
TAÍNO (ARAWAK) PEOPLES
WEST INDIES
Guanahani (San Salvador)
Cubanacán (Cuba)
Haiti (Hispaniola)
Xaymaca (Jamaica)
Boricua (Puerto Rico)
Yucután Peninsula
Isthmus of Panama
Klokut
Iglulik
Chinlac
Ozette
Tco'se
Metabetchouan
Aztalan
Cahokia
Angel
Etowah
Moundville
Ocmulgee
Emerald
Otsungo
Mesa Verde
Taos
Canyon de Chelly
Chaco Canyon
Acoma
Zuni
Mogollon
Casa Grande
Casas Grandes
La Candelaria
Tlacopán
Texcoco
Tenochtitlán
Zacatula
Orizaba
Mitla
Xicallanco
Mayapán
Balánkanche
Tulum
Tayásal
Nito
Naco
Zacaleu
Tenampua
Mazatlán
Utatlán
Yukon
Mackenzie
Liard
Peace
Saskatchewan
Columbia
Snake
Colorado
Missouri
Arkansas
Grande
Ohio
Tennessee
Mississippi
St. Lawrence
Hudson
Orinoco
Koyukon
Ahtna
Gwich'in
Tutchone
Hare
Dogrib
Slave
Chipewyan
Cree
Innu (Montagnais-Naskapi)
Beothuk
Micmac
Penobscot
Abenaki
Mohegan
Pequot
Susquehannock
Tlingit
Gitksan
Tsimshian
Haida
Bella Coola
Shuswap
Kwakiutl
Makah
Salish
Chinook
Umatilla
Modoc
Pomo
Maidu
Costano
Chumash
Chemehuevi
Cahuilla
Kootenay
Colville
Nez Percé
Cayuse
Klamath
Paiute
Shoshone
Black-foot
Sarcee
Beaver
Blood
Assiniboine
Flathead
Goshute
Ute
Hopi
Pima
Tewa
Apache
Comanche
Kiowa
Cheyenne
Dakota (Sioux)
Pawnee
Iowa
Sauk
Fox
Menominee
Ho-Chunk (Winnebago)
Ojibwa (Chippewa)
Odawa (Ottawa)
Potawatomi
Kickapoo
Shawnee
Lenni Lenape
Wichita
Caddo
Natchez
Karankawa
Chickasaw
Choctaw
Creek
Apalachee
Cherokee
Catawba
Yamasee
Timucua
Calusa
Pamlico
Tuscarora
Yaqui
Zacatec
Seri
Concho
Lagunero
Coahuiltec
Huastec
Totonac
Tarascan
Mixtec
Zapotec
Ciboney
Jicaque
Miskito
Lenca
Tawahka
Nicarao
Rama
Boruca
Guaymí
Kuna
Sinú
Quimbaya
Tairona
Wayuu (Guajiro)
Cumanagoto
Guamontey
Timote
Caquetío
Chibcha
Carib
Arawak
Yaruro
Wara

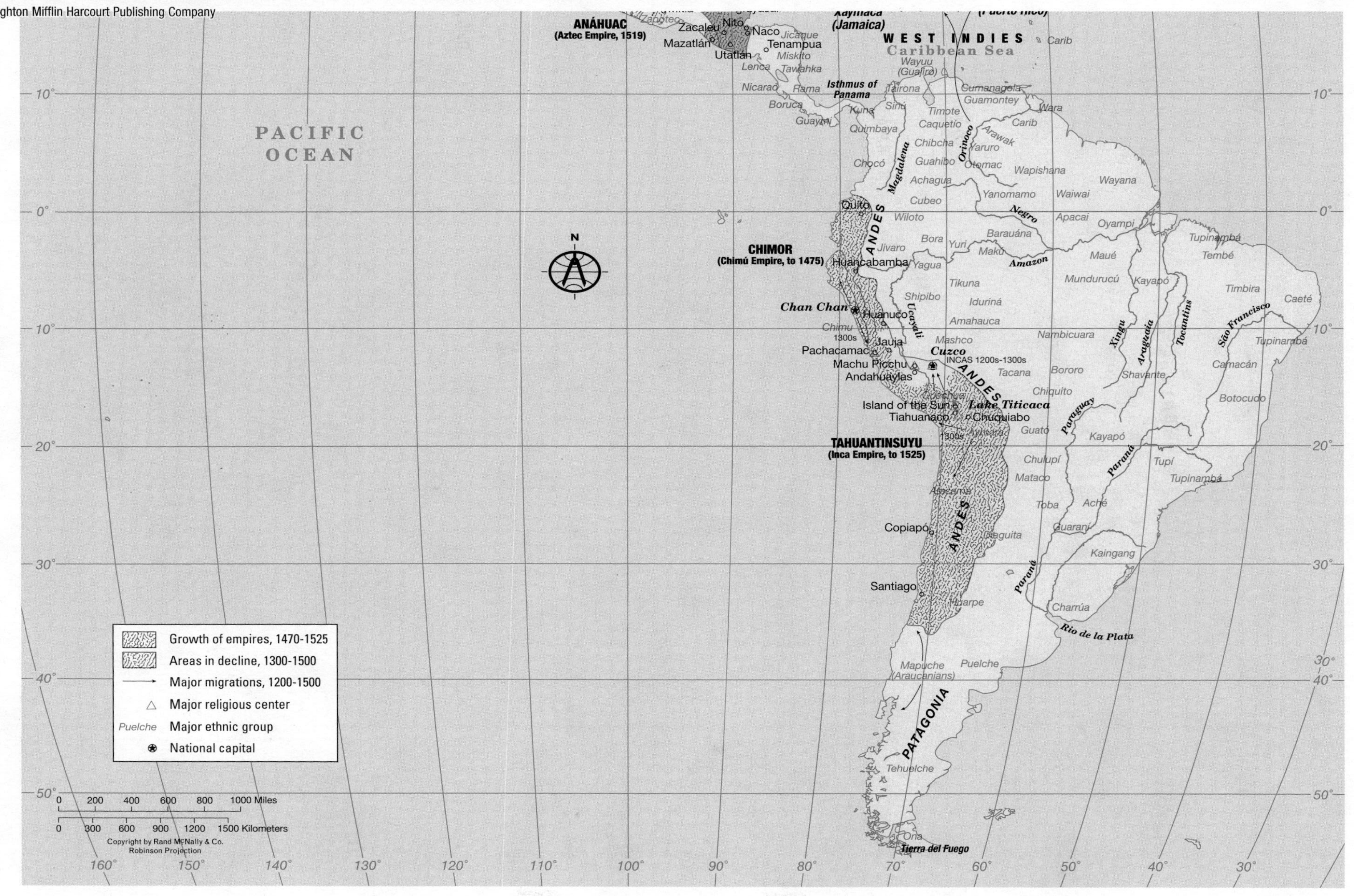

PACIFIC OCEAN
ANÁHUAC
(Aztec Empire, 1519)
Zacaleu
Nito
Naco
Mazatlán
Utatlán
Tenampua
Jicaque
Miskito
Lenca
Tawahka
Nicarao
Rama
Boruca
Guaymí
Isthmus of Panama
Xaymaca
(Jamaica)
WEST INDIES
Caribbean Sea
Carib
Wayuu
(Guajiro)
Tairona
Cumanagota
Guamontey
Kuna
Sinú
Timote
Wara
Quimbaya
Caquetío
Carib
Arawak
Chibcha
Yaruro
Orinoco
Magdalena
Chocó
Guahibo
Otomac
Wapishana
Wayana
Achagua
Yanomamo
Waiwai
Cubeo
Quito
ANDES
Wiloto
Negro
Apacai
Oyampi
Tupinambá
Tembé
CHIMOR
(Chimú Empire, to 1475)
Jívaro
Bora
Yurí
Barauána
Makú
Maué
Huancabamba
Yagua
Amazon
Mundurucú
Kayapó
Timbira
Caeté
Tikuna
Chan Chan
Shipibo
Iduriná
Huanuco
Ucayali
Amahauca
Chimu
1300s
Jauja
Mashco
Nambicuara
Xingu
Araguaia
Tocantins
São Francisco
Tupinambá
Pachacamac
Cuzco
INCAS 1200s-1300s
Machu Picchu
Andahuaylas
Tacana
Bororo
Shavante
Camacán
Botocudo
ANDES
Chiquito
Island of the Sun
Lake Titicaca
Tiahuanaco
Chuquiabo
Guató
Paraguay
1300s
Aymara
Kayapó
TAHUANTINSUYU
(Inca Empire, to 1525)
Chulupí
Paraná
Tupí
Tupinambá
Mataco
Toba
Aché
Copiapó
ANDES
Guaraní
Diaguita
Kaingang
Santiago
Paraná
Huarpe
Charrúa
Río de la Plata
Mapuche
(Araucanians)
Puelche
PATAGONIA
Tehuelche
Ona
Tierra del Fuego
Growth of empires, 1470-1525
Areas in decline, 1300-1500
Major migrations, 1200-1500
Major religious center
Puelche Major ethnic group
National capital
0 200 400 600 800 1000 Miles
0 300 600 900 1200 1500 Kilometers
Copyright by Rand McNally & Co.
Robinson Projection
N
10°
0°
10°
20°
30°
40°
50°
160°
150°
140°
130°
120°
110°
100°
90°
80°
70°
60°
50°
40°
30°

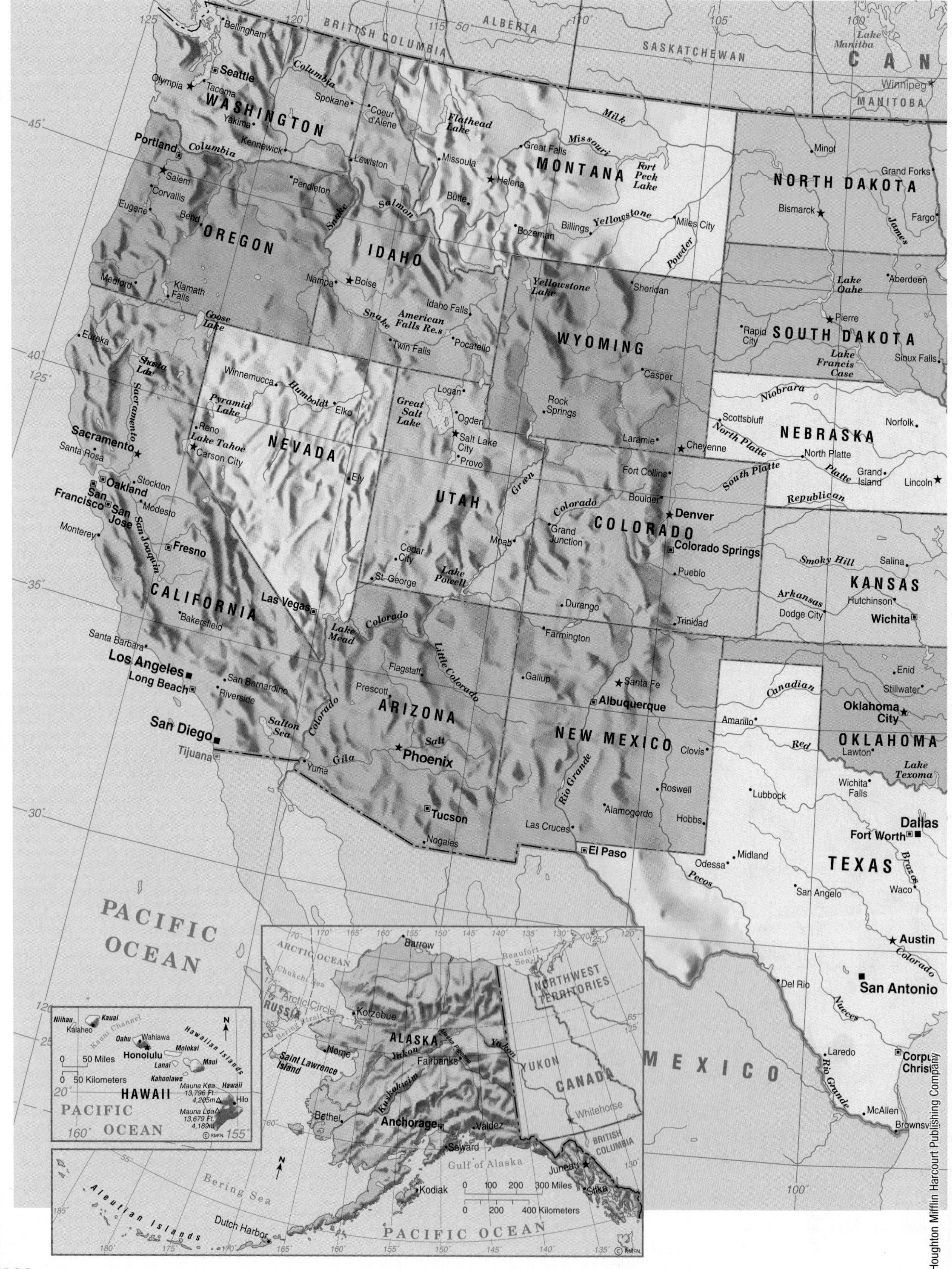
BRITISH COLUMBIA
ALBERTA
SASKATCHEWAN
MANITOBA
CAN
Lake Manitoba
Winnipeg
Bellingham
Seattle
Olympia
Tacoma
WASHINGTON
Yakima
Spokane
Coeur d'Alene
Kennewick
Columbia
Portland
Salem
Corvallis
Eugene
Bend
OREGON
Pendleton
Medford
Klamath Falls
Lewiston
Missoula
Flathead Lake
Great Falls
Missouri
Milk
MONTANA
Fort Peck Lake
Helena
Butte
Salmon
Snake
Billings
Yellowstone
Miles City
Bozeman
Powder
IDAHO
Nampa
Boise
Idaho Falls
American Falls Res.
Twin Falls
Pocatello
Goose Lake
Eureka
Shasta Lake
Sacramento
Winnemucca
Humboldt
Elko
Pyramid Lake
Reno
Lake Tahoe
Carson City
NEVADA
Santa Rosa
Oakland
Stockton
San Francisco
San Jose
Modesto
Monterey
San Joaquin
Fresno
CALIFORNIA
Las Vegas
Bakersfield
Santa Barbara
Los Angeles
Long Beach
San Bernardino
Riverside
Salton Sea
San Diego
Tijuana
Yuma
Gila
Ely
Logan
Great Salt Lake
Ogden
Salt Lake City
Provo
UTAH
Cedar City
St. George
Lake Powell
Moab
Green
Lake Mead
Colorado
Flagstaff
Prescott
Little Colorado
ARIZONA
Salt
Phoenix
Tucson
Nogales
Yellowstone Lake
Sheridan
WYOMING
Casper
Rock Springs
Laramie
Cheyenne
Fort Collins
Boulder
Denver
Grand Junction
COLORADO
Colorado Springs
Pueblo
Durango
Trinidad
Farmington
Gallup
Santa Fe
Albuquerque
NEW MEXICO
Rio Grande
Roswell
Alamogordo
Las Cruces
Hobbs
Clovis
El Paso
Minot
Grand Forks
NORTH DAKOTA
Bismarck
Fargo
James
Lake Oahe
Aberdeen
Pierre
Rapid City
SOUTH DAKOTA
Lake Francis Case
Sioux Falls
Niobrara
Scottsbluff
North Platte
NEBRASKA
Norfolk
Platte
Grand Island
Lincoln
South Platte
Republican
Smoky Hill
Salina
KANSAS
Arkansas
Hutchinson
Dodge City
Wichita
Enid
Stillwater
Canadian
Oklahoma City
Amarillo
OKLAHOMA
Red
Lawton
Lake Texoma
Wichita Falls
Lubbock
Dallas
Fort Worth
Midland
Odessa
Pecos
TEXAS
Brazos
San Angelo
Waco
Austin
Colorado
Del Rio
San Antonio
Nueces
Laredo
Corpus Christi
Rio Grande
McAllen
Brownsville
MEXICO
PACIFIC OCEAN
ARCTIC OCEAN
Barrow
Beaufort Sea
Chukchi Sea
NORTHWEST TERRITORIES
Arctic Circle
RUSSIA
Bering Strait
Kotzebue
ALASKA
Nome
Saint Lawrence Island
Yukon
Fairbanks
Alaska Range
Kuskokwim
YUKON
CANADA
Whitehorse
Bethel
Anchorage
Valdez
Seward
BRITISH COLUMBIA
Gulf of Alaska
Juneau
Sitka
Kodiak
Bering Sea
Aleutian Islands
Dutch Harbor
PACIFIC OCEAN
0 100 200 300 Miles
0 200 400 Kilometers
Niihau
Kauai
Kalaheo
Kauai Channel
Oahu
Wahiawa
Honolulu
Molokai
Lanai
Maui
Kahoolawe
Hawaiian Islands
0 50 Miles
0 50 Kilometers
HAWAII
Hawaii
Mauna Kea 13,796 Ft. 4,205m
Hilo
Mauna Loa 13,679 Ft. 4,169m
PACIFIC OCEAN
© RMN.

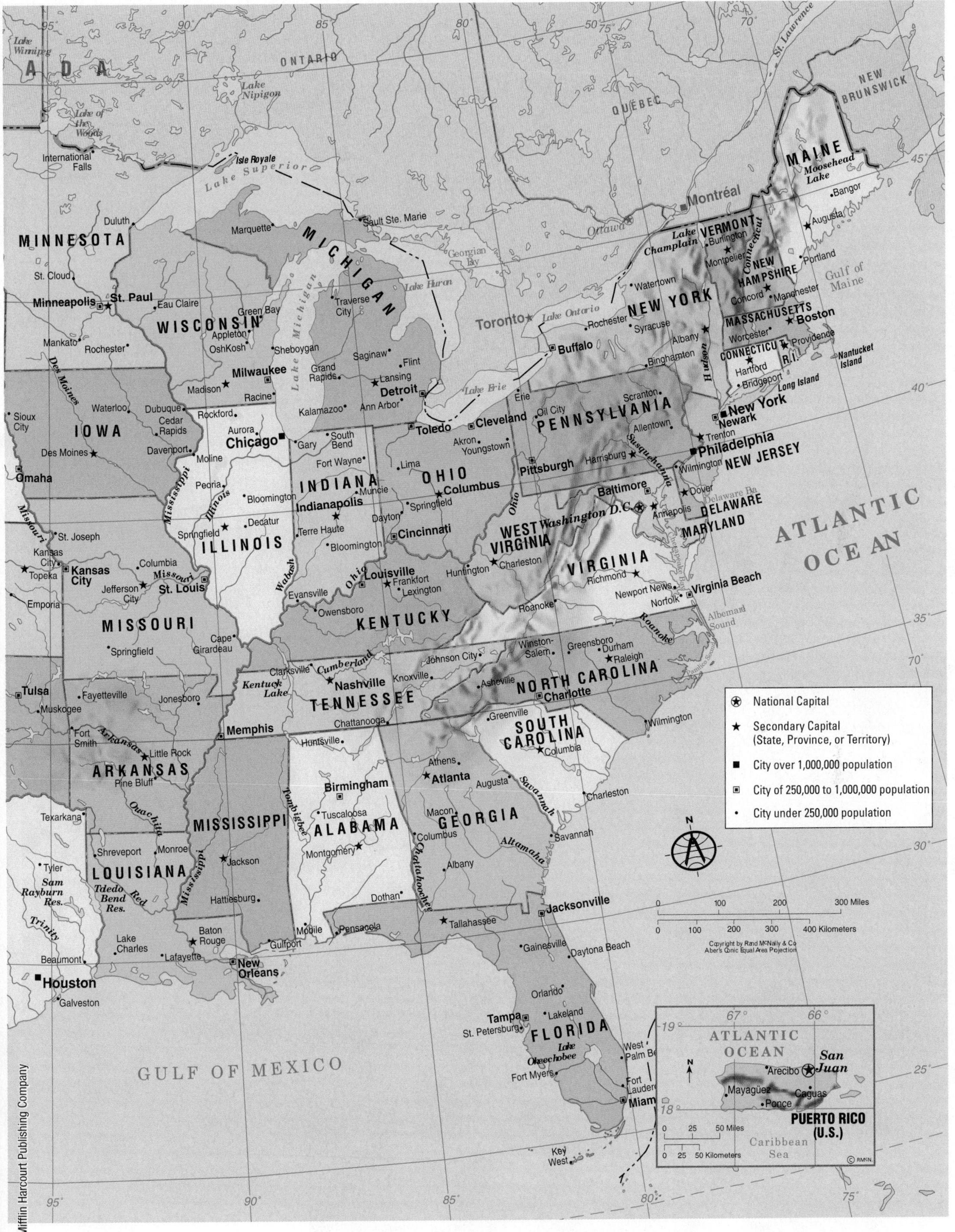
ONTARIO
QUÉBEC
NEW BRUNSWICK
Lake Winnipeg
Lake Nipigon
Lake of the Woods
International Falls
Isle Royale
Lake Superior
Sault Ste. Marie
Georgian Bay
Lake Huron
Lake Michigan
Lake Ontario
Lake Erie
Lake Champlain
Moosehead Lake
Montréal
Ottawa
Toronto
St. Lawrence
Gulf of Maine
MINNESOTA
Duluth
St. Cloud
Minneapolis
St. Paul
Mankato
Rochester
WISCONSIN
Eau Claire
Green Bay
Appleton
OshKosh
Sheboygan
Milwaukee
Madison
Racine
MICHIGAN
Marquette
Traverse City
Saginaw
Flint
Grand Rapids
Lansing
Detroit
Kalamazoo
Ann Arbor
IOWA
Sioux City
Waterloo
Dubuque
Cedar Rapids
Des Moines
Davenport
Omaha
ILLINOIS
Rockford
Aurora
Chicago
Moline
Peoria
Bloomington
Springfield
Decatur
INDIANA
Gary
South Bend
Fort Wayne
Muncie
Indianapolis
Terre Haute
Bloomington
Evansville
OHIO
Toledo
Cleveland
Akron
Youngstown
Lima
Columbus
Springfield
Dayton
Cincinnati
PENNSYLVANIA
Erie
Oil City
Scranton
Allentown
Pittsburgh
Harrisburg
Philadelphia
NEW YORK
Watertown
Rochester
Syracuse
Buffalo
Albany
Binghamton
New York
Long Island
VERMONT
Burlington
Montpelier
NEW HAMPSHIRE
Concord
Manchester
MAINE
Bangor
Augusta
Portland
MASSACHUSETTS
Worcester
Boston
CONNECTICUT
Hartford
Bridgeport
R.I.
Providence
Nantucket Island
NEW JERSEY
Newark
Trenton
Wilmington
DELAWARE
Dover
MARYLAND
Baltimore
Annapolis
Washington D.C.
WEST VIRGINIA
Charleston
Huntington
VIRGINIA
Richmond
Newport News
Norfolk
Virginia Beach
Roanoke
Albemarle Sound
Pamlico Sound
MISSOURI
St. Joseph
Kansas City
Columbia
Jefferson City
St. Louis
Springfield
Cape Girardeau
Topeka
Emporia
KENTUCKY
Louisville
Frankfort
Lexington
Owensboro
TENNESSEE
Clarksville
Nashville
Knoxville
Johnson City
Chattanooga
Memphis
Kentucky Lake
NORTH CAROLINA
Winston-Salem
Greensboro
Durham
Raleigh
Asheville
Charlotte
Wilmington
SOUTH CAROLINA
Greenville
Columbia
Charleston
GEORGIA
Athens
Atlanta
Augusta
Macon
Columbus
Savannah
Albany
ALABAMA
Huntsville
Birmingham
Tuscaloosa
Montgomery
Dothan
Mobile
MISSISSIPPI
Jackson
Hattiesburg
Gulfport
ARKANSAS
Fayetteville
Jonesboro
Fort Smith
Little Rock
Pine Bluff
Texarkana
LOUISIANA
Shreveport
Monroe
Baton Rouge
Lake Charles
Lafayette
New Orleans
Toledo Bend Res.
Sam Rayburn Res.
Tulsa
Muskogee
Tyler
Beaumont
Houston
Galveston
FLORIDA
Pensacola
Tallahassee
Jacksonville
Gainesville
Daytona Beach
Orlando
Tampa
Lakeland
St. Petersburg
Lake Okeechobee
West Palm Beach
Fort Myers
Fort Lauderdale
Miami
Key West
ATLANTIC OCEAN
GULF OF MEXICO
National Capital
Secondary Capital (State, Province, or Territory)
City over 1,000,000 population
City of 250,000 to 1,000,000 population
City under 250,000 population
0 100 200 300 Miles
0 100 200 300 400 Kilometers
Copyright by Rand McNally & Co
Albers Conic Equal Area Projection
ATLANTIC OCEAN
San Juan
Arecibo
Mayagüez
Ponce
Caguas
PUERTO RICO (U.S.)
Caribbean Sea
0 25 50 Miles
0 25 50 Kilometers

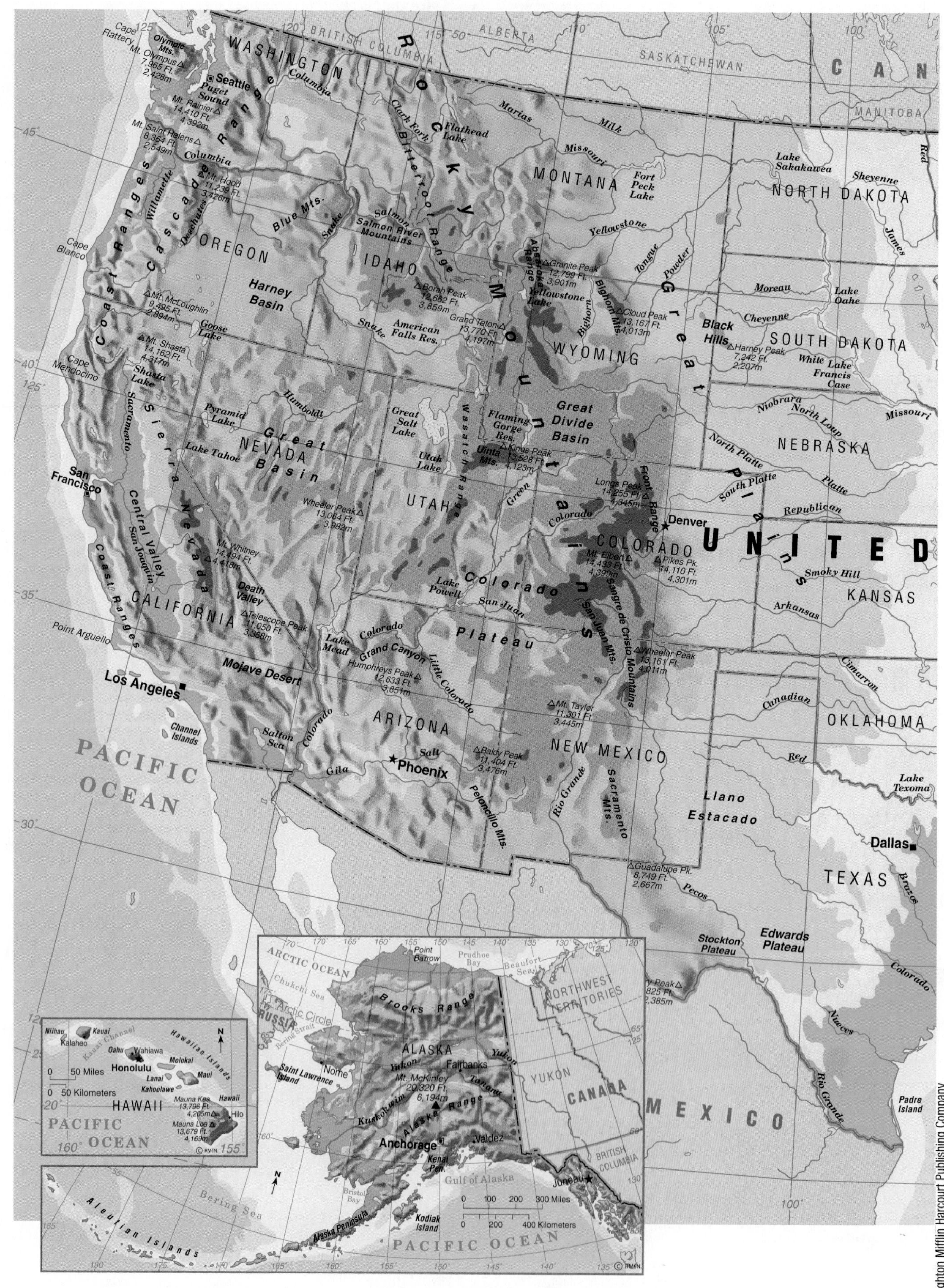
WASHINGTON
OREGON
IDAHO
MONTANA
WYOMING
NORTH DAKOTA
SOUTH DAKOTA
NEBRASKA
KANSAS
COLORADO
UTAH
NEVADA
CALIFORNIA
ARIZONA
NEW MEXICO
OKLAHOMA
TEXAS
UNITED
CAN
MEXICO
BRITISH COLUMBIA
ALBERTA
SASKATCHEWAN
MANITOBA
PACIFIC OCEAN
Rocky Mountains
Great Plains
Coast Ranges
Cascade Range
Sierra Nevada
Great Basin
Colorado Plateau
Cape Flattery
Olympic Mts.
Mt. Olympus 7,965 Ft. 2,428m
Seattle
Puget Sound
Mt. Rainier 14,410 Ft. 4,392m
Mt. Saint Helens 8,364 Ft. 2,549m
Mt. Hood 11,239 Ft. 3,426m
Columbia
Willamette
Deschutes
Blue Mts.
Cape Blanco
Harney Basin
Mt. McLoughlin 9,495 Ft. 2,894m
Goose Lake
Mt. Shasta 14,162 Ft. 4,317m
Shasta Lake
Cape Mendocino
Sacramento
Pyramid Lake
Humboldt
Lake Tahoe
San Francisco
Central Valley
San Joaquin
Mt. Whitney 14,494 Ft. 4,418m
Death Valley
Telescope Peak 11,050 Ft. 3,368m
Point Arguello
Los Angeles
Channel Islands
Mojave Desert
Salton Sea
Clark Fork
Flathead Lake
Bitterroot Range
Salmon
Salmon River Mountains
Snake
Borah Peak 12,662 Ft. 3,859m
American Falls Res.
Grand Teton 13,770 Ft. 4,197m
Marias
Milk
Missouri
Fort Peck Lake
Yellowstone
Absaroka Range
Granite Peak 12,799 Ft. 3,901m
Yellowstone Lake
Bighorn
Bighorn Mts.
Cloud Peak 13,167 Ft. 4,013m
Tongue
Powder
Great Salt Lake
Wasatch Range
Utah Lake
Uinta Mts.
Flaming Gorge Res.
Kings Peak 13,528 Ft. 4,123m
Great Divide Basin
Green
Wheeler Peak 13,064 Ft. 3,982m
Longs Peak 14,255 Ft. 4,345m
Front Range
Denver
Mt. Elbert 14,433 Ft. 4,399m
Pikes Pk. 14,110 Ft. 4,301m
Lake Powell
San Juan
San Juan Mts.
Sangre de Cristo Mountains
Wheeler Peak 13,161 Ft. 4,011m
Lake Mead
Grand Canyon
Humphreys Peak 12,633 Ft. 3,851m
Little Colorado
Mt. Taylor 11,301 Ft. 3,445m
Baldy Peak 11,404 Ft. 3,476m
Gila
Salt
Phoenix
Peloncillo Mts.
Rio Grande
Sacramento Mts.
Guadalupe Pk. 8,749 Ft. 2,667m
Pecos
Llano Estacado
Lake Sakakawea
Sheyenne
James
Red
Moreau
Lake Oahe
Cheyenne
Black Hills
Harney Peak 7,242 Ft. 2,207m
White
Lake Francis Case
Niobrara
North Loup
North Platte
South Platte
Platte
Republican
Smoky Hill
Arkansas
Cimarron
Canadian
Lake Texoma
Dallas
Brazos
Stockton Plateau
Edwards Plateau
Nueces
Padre Island
Colorado
ARCTIC OCEAN
Chukchi Sea
Arctic Circle
Point Barrow
Prudhoe Bay
Beaufort Sea
Brooks Range
NORTHWEST TERRITORIES
ALASKA
Bering Strait
Saint Lawrence Island
Nome
Yukon
Fairbanks
Tanana
Mt. McKinley 20,320 Ft. 6,194m
Kuskokwim
Alaska Range
YUKON
CANADA
Anchorage
Valdez
Kenai Pen.
Gulf of Alaska
BRITISH COLUMBIA
Juneau
Bristol Bay
Bering Sea
Alaska Peninsula
Kodiak Island
Aleutian Islands
PACIFIC OCEAN
0 100 200 300 Miles
0 200 400 Kilometers
Niihau
Kauai
Kalaheo
Kauai Channel
Oahu
Wahiawa
Honolulu
Hawaiian Islands
Molokai
Lanai
Maui
Kahoolawe
Hawaii
Mauna Kea 13,796 Ft. 4,205m
Mauna Loa 13,679 Ft. 4,169m
Hilo
HAWAII
PACIFIC OCEAN
0 50 Miles
0 50 Kilometers
© RMcN.
RAND McNALLY

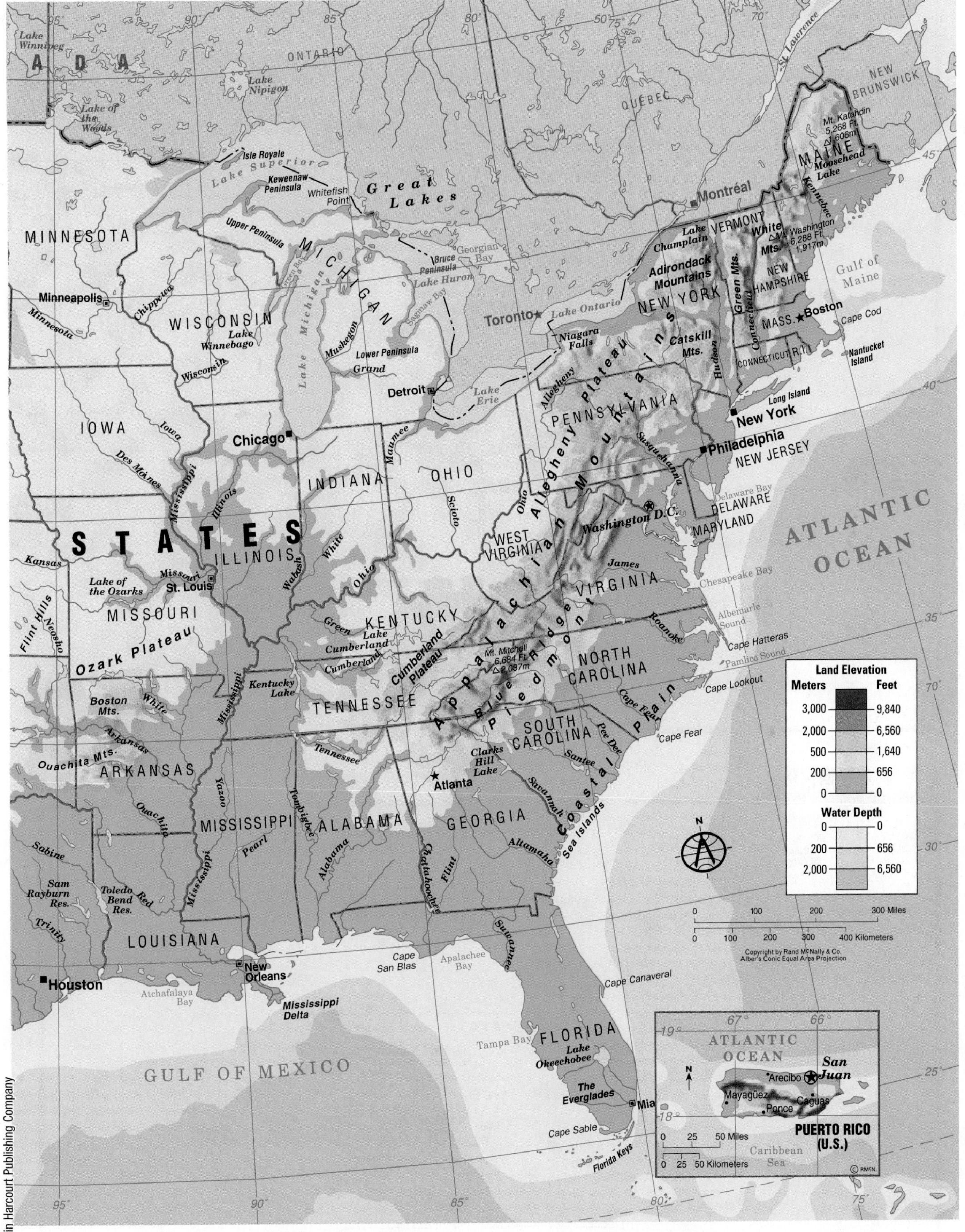

Lake Winnipeg
ONTARIO
Lake Nipigon
Lake of the Woods
QUÉBEC
St. Lawrence
NEW BRUNSWICK
Mt. Katahdin 5,268 Ft. 1,606m
MAINE
Moosehead Lake
Kennebec
Isle Royale
Lake Superior
Keweenaw Peninsula
Whitefish Point
Great Lakes
Montréal
MINNESOTA
Upper Peninsula
MICHIGAN
Bruce Peninsula
Georgian Bay
Lake Huron
Green Bay
Lake Michigan
Saginaw Bay
Lake Champlain
VERMONT
White Mts.
Mt. Washington 6,288 Ft. 1,917m
Adirondack Mountains
Green Mts.
NEW HAMPSHIRE
Gulf of Maine
Minneapolis
Minnesota
Chippewa
WISCONSIN
Lake Winnebago
Wisconsin
Muskegon
Lower Peninsula
Grand
Toronto
Lake Ontario
NEW YORK
Niagara Falls
Catskill Mts.
Hudson
Connecticut
MASS.
Boston
Cape Cod
CONNECTICUT
R.I.
Nantucket Island
Detroit
Lake Erie
Allegheny
Allegheny Plateau
Long Island
New York
IOWA
Iowa
Chicago
Maumee
PENNSYLVANIA
Susquehanna
Philadelphia
NEW JERSEY
Des Moines
Mississippi
Illinois
INDIANA
OHIO
Scioto
Ohio
Allegheny Mountains
Washington D.C.
Delaware Bay
DELAWARE
MARYLAND
ATLANTIC OCEAN
STATES
Kansas
ILLINOIS
Wabash
White
WEST VIRGINIA
Appalachian Mountains
Missouri
St. Louis
Lake of the Ozarks
James
VIRGINIA
Chesapeake Bay
Flint Hills
Neosho
MISSOURI
Green
KENTUCKY
Lake Cumberland
Cumberland Plateau
Albemarle Sound
Roanoke
Ozark Plateau
Cumberland
Mt. Mitchell 6,684 Ft. 2,037m
Blue Ridge
NORTH CAROLINA
Cape Hatteras
Pamlico Sound
Kentucky Lake
Piedmont
Cape Lookout
Cape Fear
Boston Mts.
TENNESSEE
SOUTH CAROLINA
Pee Dee
Coastal Plain
Arkansas
Ouachita Mts.
ARKANSAS
Tennessee
Clarks Hill Lake
Santee
Atlanta
Yazoo
Tombigbee
Savannah
Ouachita
MISSISSIPPI
ALABAMA
GEORGIA
Sea Islands
Sabine
Pearl
Alabama
Chattahoochee
Flint
Altamaha
Sam Rayburn Res.
Toledo Bend Res.
Red
Trinity
LOUISIANA
Suwannee
Cape San Blas
Apalachee Bay
Houston
New Orleans
Atchafalaya Bay
Mississippi Delta
Cape Canaveral
Tampa Bay
FLORIDA
Lake Okeechobee
GULF OF MEXICO
The Everglades
Miami
Cape Sable
Florida Keys
Land Elevation
Meters
Feet
3,000
9,840
2,000
6,560
500
1,640
200
656
0
0
Water Depth
0
0
200
656
2,000
6,560
N
0
100
200
300 Miles
0
100
200
300
400 Kilometers
Copyright by Rand McNally & Co.
Albers Conic Equal Area Projection
ATLANTIC OCEAN
San Juan
Arecibo
Mayagüez
Caguas
Ponce
PUERTO RICO (U.S.)
0 25 50 Miles
0 25 50 Kilometers
Caribbean Sea
© RMCN.
95°
90°
85°
80°
75°
70°
50°
45°
40°
35°
30°
25°
67°
66°
19°
18°

Guam

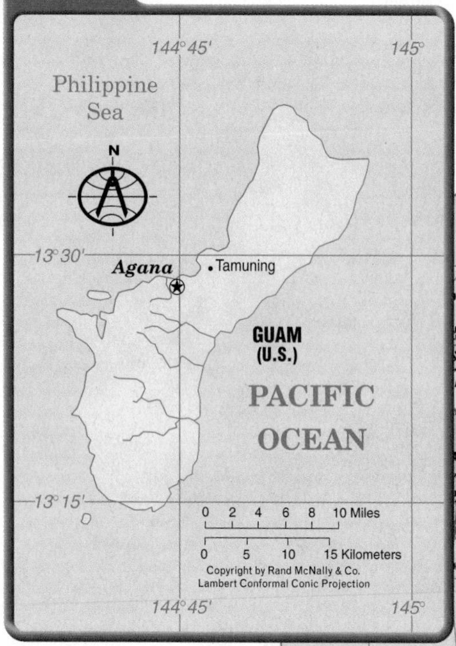

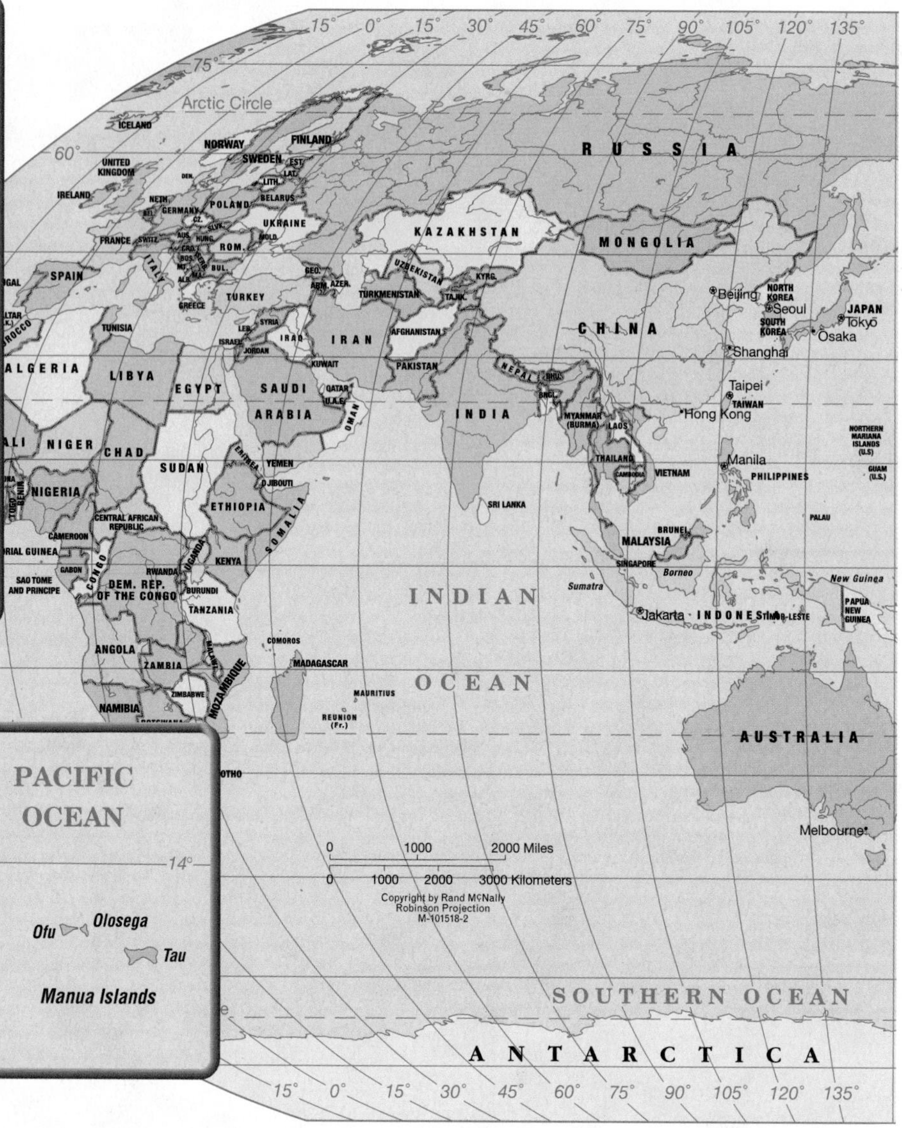

144° 45'
145°
Philippine Sea
N
13° 30'
Agana
Tamuning
GUAM (U.S.)
PACIFIC OCEAN
13° 15'
0 2 4 6 8 10 Miles
0 5 10 15 Kilometers
Copyright by Rand McNally & Co.
Lambert Conformal Conic Projection

Arctic Circle
ICELAND
NORWAY
FINLAND
SWEDEN
UNITED KINGDOM
IRELAND
POLAND
BELARUS
UKRAINE
FRANCE
SPAIN
ITALY
ROM.
BUL.
GREECE
TURKEY
R U S S I A
KAZAKHSTAN
MONGOLIA
UZBEKISTAN
TURKMENISTAN
AFGHANISTAN
IRAN
IRAQ
SYRIA
ISRAEL
JORDAN
KUWAIT
PAKISTAN
C H I N A
Beijing
NORTH KOREA
Seoul
SOUTH KOREA
JAPAN
Tokyo
Osaka
Shanghai
Taipei
TAIWAN
Hong Kong
NEPAL
INDIA
MYANMAR (BURMA)
LAOS
THAILAND
CAMBODIA
VIETNAM
Manila
PHILIPPINES
NORTHERN MARIANA ISLANDS (U.S.)
GUAM (U.S.)
PALAU
SRI LANKA
BRUNEI
MALAYSIA
SINGAPORE
Borneo
Sumatra
Jakarta
INDONESIA
TIMOR-LESTE
New Guinea
PAPUA NEW GUINEA
TUNISIA
ALGERIA
LIBYA
EGYPT
SAUDI ARABIA
QATAR
U.A.E.
OMAN
YEMEN
DJIBOUTI
ERITREA
SUDAN
ETHIOPIA
SOMALIA
NIGER
CHAD
NIGERIA
CENTRAL AFRICAN REPUBLIC
CAMEROON
GABON
CONGO
DEM. REP. OF THE CONGO
SAO TOME AND PRINCIPE
UGANDA
KENYA
RWANDA
BURUNDI
TANZANIA
ANGOLA
ZAMBIA
MALAWI
MOZAMBIQUE
ZIMBABWE
NAMIBIA
COMOROS
MADAGASCAR
MAURITIUS
REUNION (Fr.)
INDIAN OCEAN
AUSTRALIA
Melbourne
SOUTHERN OCEAN
A N T A R C T I C A
0 1000 2000 Miles
0 1000 2000 3000 Kilometers
Copyright by Rand McNally
Robinson Projection
M-101518-2

Samoa

171°
170°
0 5 10 15 20 25 Miles
0 10 20 30 40 Kilometers
Copyright by Rand McNally & Co
Lambert Conformal Conic Projection
PACIFIC OCEAN
14°
N
AMERICAN SAMOA
Pago Pago
Aunuu
Tutuila
Ofu
Olosega
Tau
Manua Islands

Pacific Islands

NORTHERN MARIANA ISLANDS (U.S.)
GUAM (U.S.)
HAWAII
P A C I F I C O C E A N
N
Koror
CAROLINE ISLANDS
MARSHALL ISLANDS
FEDERATED STATES OF MICRONESIA
PALAU
INTERNATIONAL DATE LINE
0 200 400 600 800 1000 Miles
0 300 600 900 1200 1500 Kilometers
Copyright by Rand McNally & Co.
Lambert Azimuthal Equal Area Projection
Equator
NAURU
KIRIBATI
PHOENIX ISLANDS
INDON.
SOLOMON ISLANDS
PAPUA NEW GUINEA
Port Moresby
Honiara
TUVALU
TOKELAU (N.Z.)
SANTA CRUZ ISLANDS
WALLIS AND FUTUNA (Fr.)
SAMOA
Apia
AMERICAN SAMOA
FRENCH POLYNESIA
CORAL SEA
Gulf of Carpentaria
VANUATU
Port Vila
FIJI
Suva
COOK ISLANDS (N.Z.)
Cairns
TONGA
NIUE (N.Z.)
AUSTRALIA
NEW CALEDONIA (Fr.)
Nouméa

RAND McNALLY

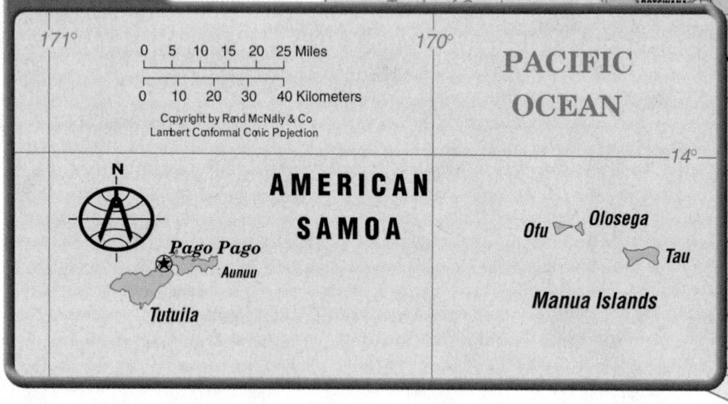

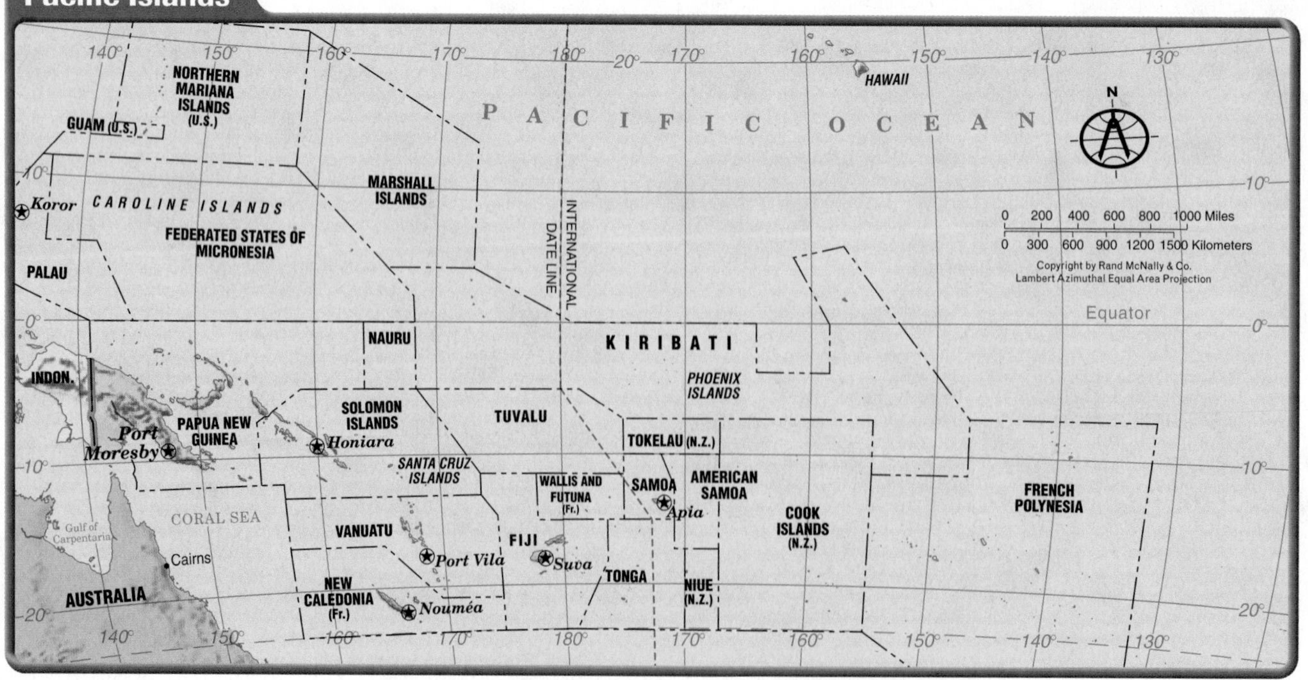

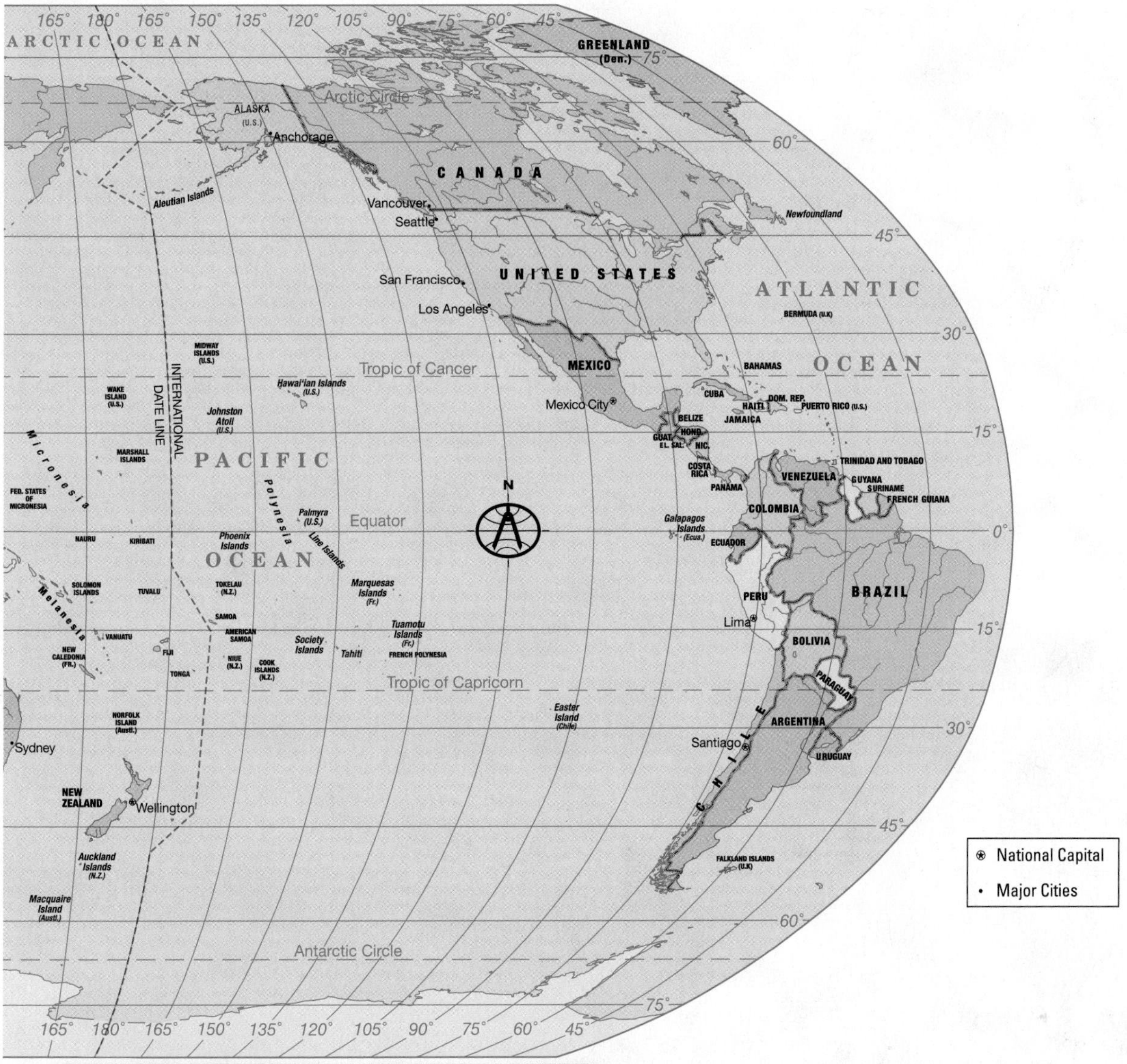

ARCTIC OCEAN
GREENLAND (Den.)
Arctic Circle
ALASKA (U.S.)
Anchorage
Aleutian Islands
CANADA
Vancouver
Seattle
Newfoundland
San Francisco
UNITED STATES
Los Angeles
ATLANTIC OCEAN
BERMUDA (U.K.)
MIDWAY ISLANDS (U.S.)
INTERNATIONAL DATE LINE
Tropic of Cancer
MEXICO
BAHAMAS
CUBA
DOM. REP.
HAITI
PUERTO RICO (U.S.)
JAMAICA
WAKE ISLAND (U.S.)
Hawai'ian Islands (U.S.)
Johnston Atoll (U.S.)
Mexico City
BELIZE
HOND.
GUAT.
EL SAL.
NIC.
COSTA RICA
PANAMA
TRINIDAD AND TOBAGO
VENEZUELA
GUYANA
SURINAME
FRENCH GUIANA
Micronesia
MARSHALL ISLANDS
PACIFIC OCEAN
Polynesia
FED. STATES OF MICRONESIA
Palmyra (U.S.)
Equator
Galapagos Islands (Ecua.)
COLOMBIA
ECUADOR
NAURU
KIRIBATI
Phoenix Islands
Line Islands
SOLOMON ISLANDS
TUVALU
TOKELAU (N.Z.)
Marquesas Islands (Fr.)
PERU
BRAZIL
Melanesia
SAMOA
AMERICAN SAMOA
VANUATU
FIJI
NEW CALEDONIA (FR.)
TONGA
NIUE (N.Z.)
COOK ISLANDS (N.Z.)
Society Islands
Tahiti
Tuamotu Islands (Fr.)
FRENCH POLYNESIA
Lima
BOLIVIA
Tropic of Capricorn
PARAGUAY
NORFOLK ISLAND (Austl.)
Easter Island (Chile)
ARGENTINA
CHILE
Santiago
URUGUAY
Sydney
NEW ZEALAND
Wellington
Auckland Islands (N.Z.)
Macquaire Island (Austl.)
FALKLAND ISLANDS (U.K.)
Antarctic Circle

National Capital
Major Cities

Puerto Rico and the U.S. Virgin Islands

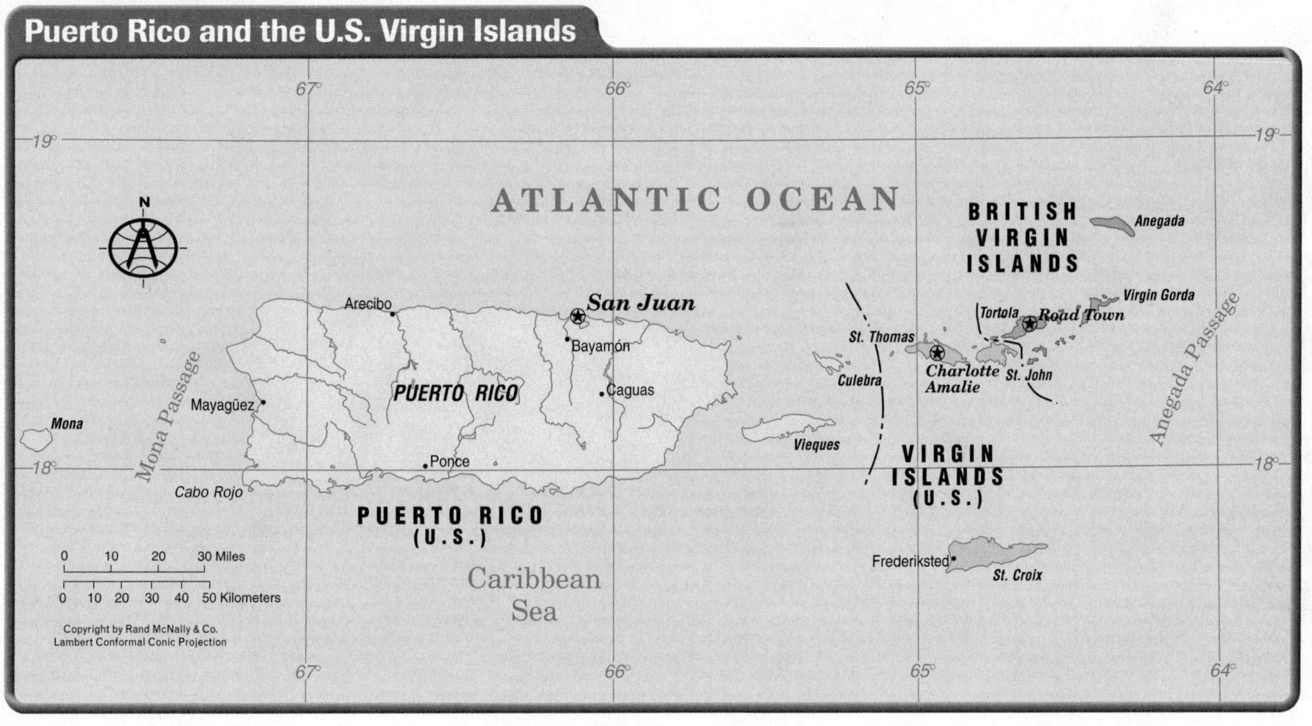

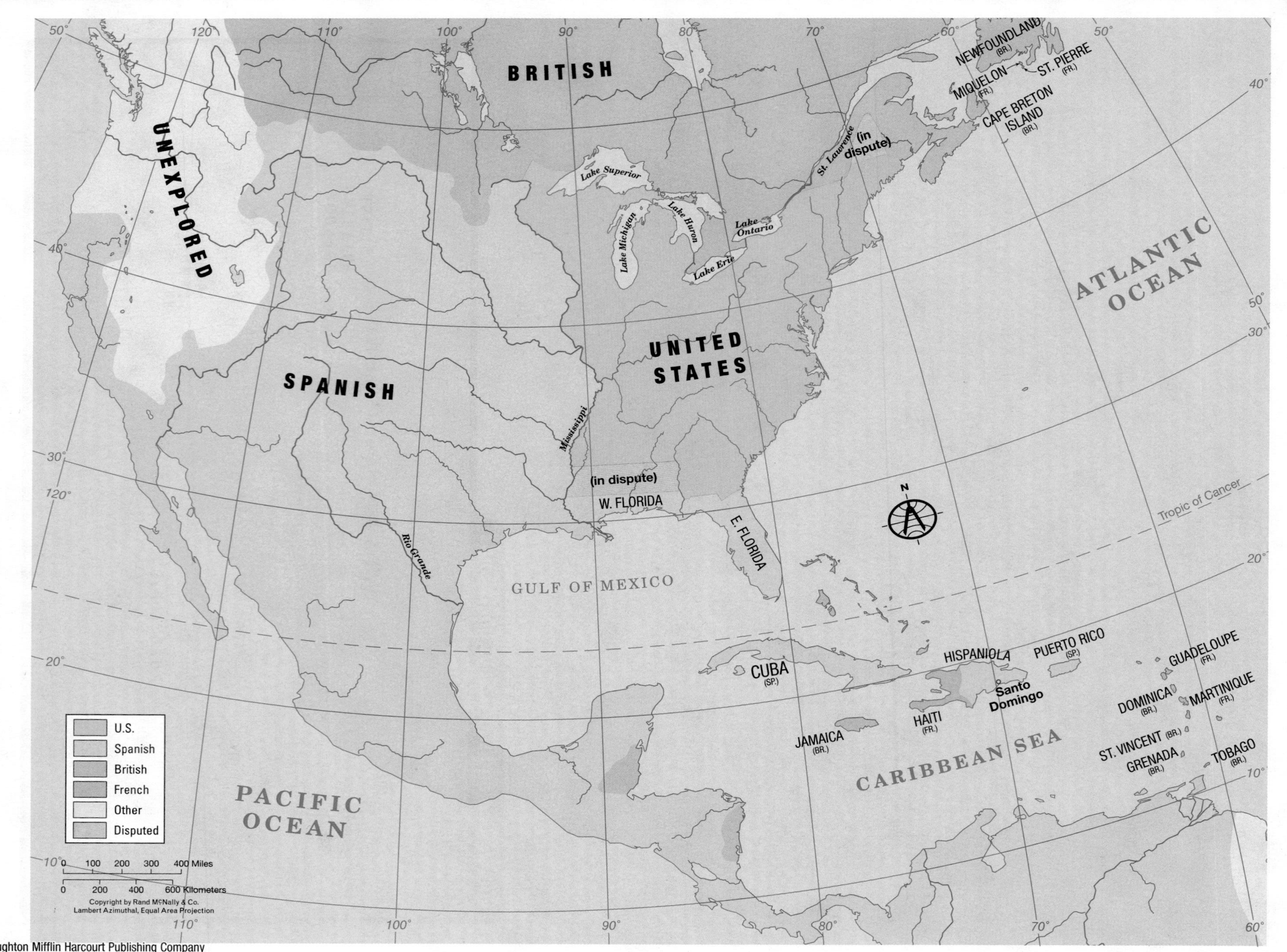
BRITISH
UNEXPLORED
SPANISH
UNITED STATES
NEWFOUNDLAND (BR.)
MIQUELON (FR.)
ST. PIERRE (FR.)
CAPE BRETON ISLAND (BR.)
St. Lawrence
(in dispute)
Lake Superior
Lake Michigan
Lake Huron
Lake Ontario
Lake Erie
ATLANTIC OCEAN
Mississippi
(in dispute)
W. FLORIDA
E. FLORIDA
Rio Grande
GULF OF MEXICO
Tropic of Cancer
CUBA (SP.)
HISPANIOLA
PUERTO RICO (SP.)
Santo Domingo
HAITI (FR.)
JAMAICA (BR.)
GUADELOUPE (FR.)
DOMINICA (BR.)
MARTINIQUE (FR.)
ST. VINCENT (BR.)
GRENADA (BR.)
TOBAGO (BR.)
CARIBBEAN SEA
PACIFIC OCEAN
U.S.
Spanish
British
French
Other
Disputed
0 100 200 300 400 Miles
0 200 400 600 Kilometers
Copyright by Rand McNally & Co.
Lambert Azimuthal, Equal Area Projection
N

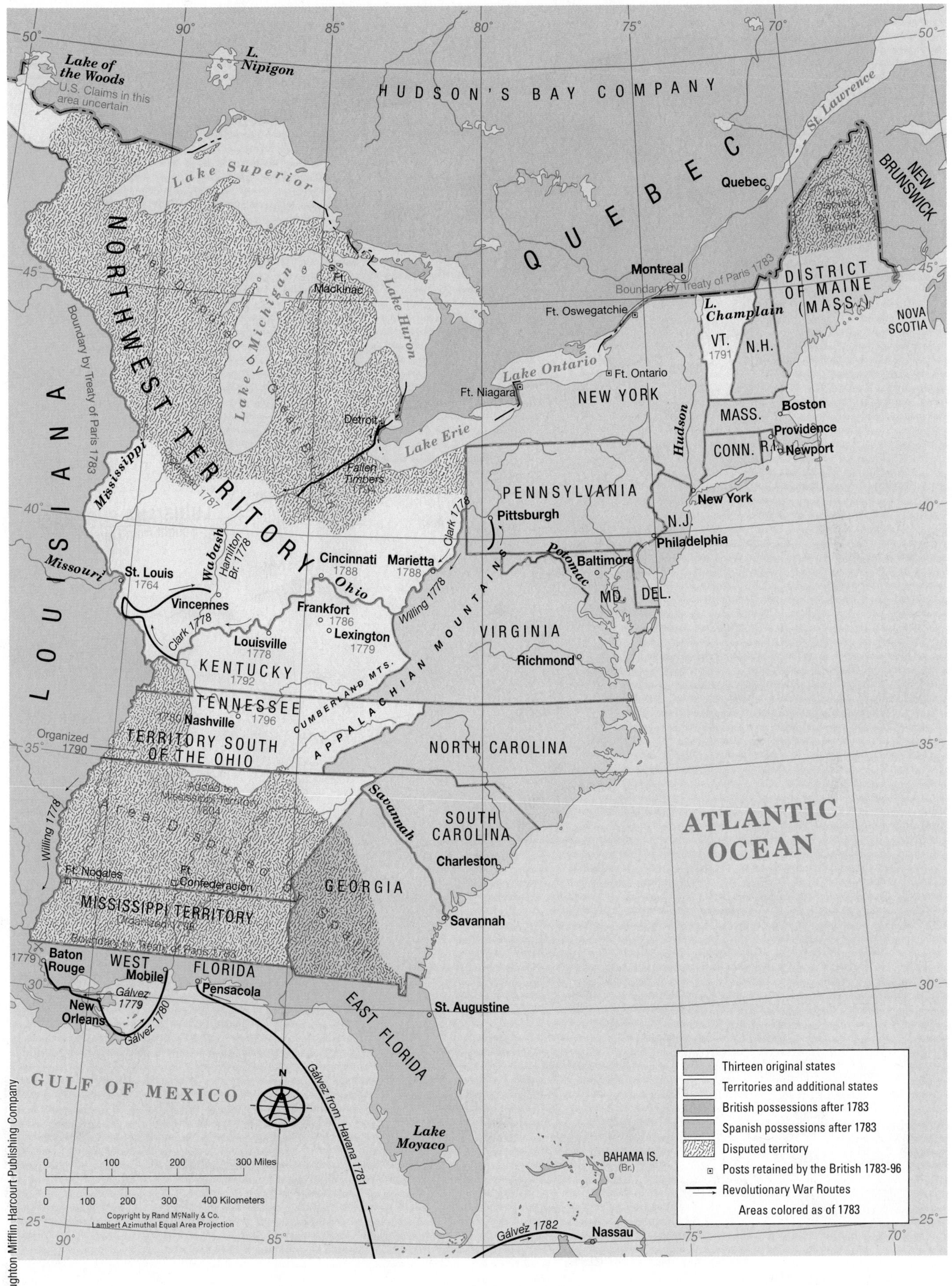
Lake of the Woods
U.S. Claims in this area uncertain
L. Nipigon
HUDSON'S BAY COMPANY
Lake Superior
QUEBEC
Quebec
St. Lawrence
NEW BRUNSWICK
Area Disputed by Great Britain
NORTHWEST TERRITORY
Organized 1787
Ft. Mackinac
Lake Michigan
Lake Huron
Montreal
Boundary by Treaty of Paris 1783
DISTRICT OF MAINE (MASS.)
NOVA SCOTIA
Ft. Oswegatchie
L. Champlain
VT. 1791
N.H.
Lake Ontario
Ft. Ontario
Ft. Niagara
NEW YORK
LOUISIANA
Boundary by Treaty of Paris 1783
Mississippi
Detroit
Lake Erie
Fallen Timbers 1794
MASS.
Boston
Providence
CONN.
R.I.
Newport
Hudson
PENNSYLVANIA
New York
Pittsburgh
N.J.
Philadelphia
Clark 1778
Missouri
St. Louis 1764
Wabash
Hamilton Br. 1778
Cincinnati 1788
Marietta 1788
Ohio
Potomac
Baltimore
MD.
DEL.
Vincennes
Frankfort 1786
Lexington 1779
Willing 1778
Clark 1778
Louisville 1778
VIRGINIA
Richmond
APPALACHIAN MOUNTAINS
KENTUCKY 1792
CUMBERLAND MTS.
TENNESSEE 1796
1780 Nashville
Organized 1790
TERRITORY SOUTH OF THE OHIO
NORTH CAROLINA
Added to Mississippi Territory 1804
Area Disputed by Spain
Savannah
SOUTH CAROLINA
ATLANTIC OCEAN
Willing 1778
Charleston
Ft. Nogales
Ft. Confederación
GEORGIA
MISSISSIPPI TERRITORY
Organized 1798
Savannah
Boundary by Treaty of Paris 1783
1779
Baton Rouge
WEST FLORIDA
Mobile
Gálvez 1779
New Orleans
Gálvez 1780
Pensacola
EAST FLORIDA
St. Augustine
GULF OF MEXICO
N
Gálvez from Havana 1781
Lake Moyaco
BAHAMA IS. (Br.)
Gálvez 1782
Nassau
0 100 200 300 Miles
0 100 200 300 400 Kilometers
Copyright by Rand McNally & Co.
Lambert Azimuthal Equal Area Projection
Thirteen original states
Territories and additional states
British possessions after 1783
Spanish possessions after 1783
Disputed territory
Posts retained by the British 1783-96
Revolutionary War Routes
Areas colored as of 1783
RAND McNALLY

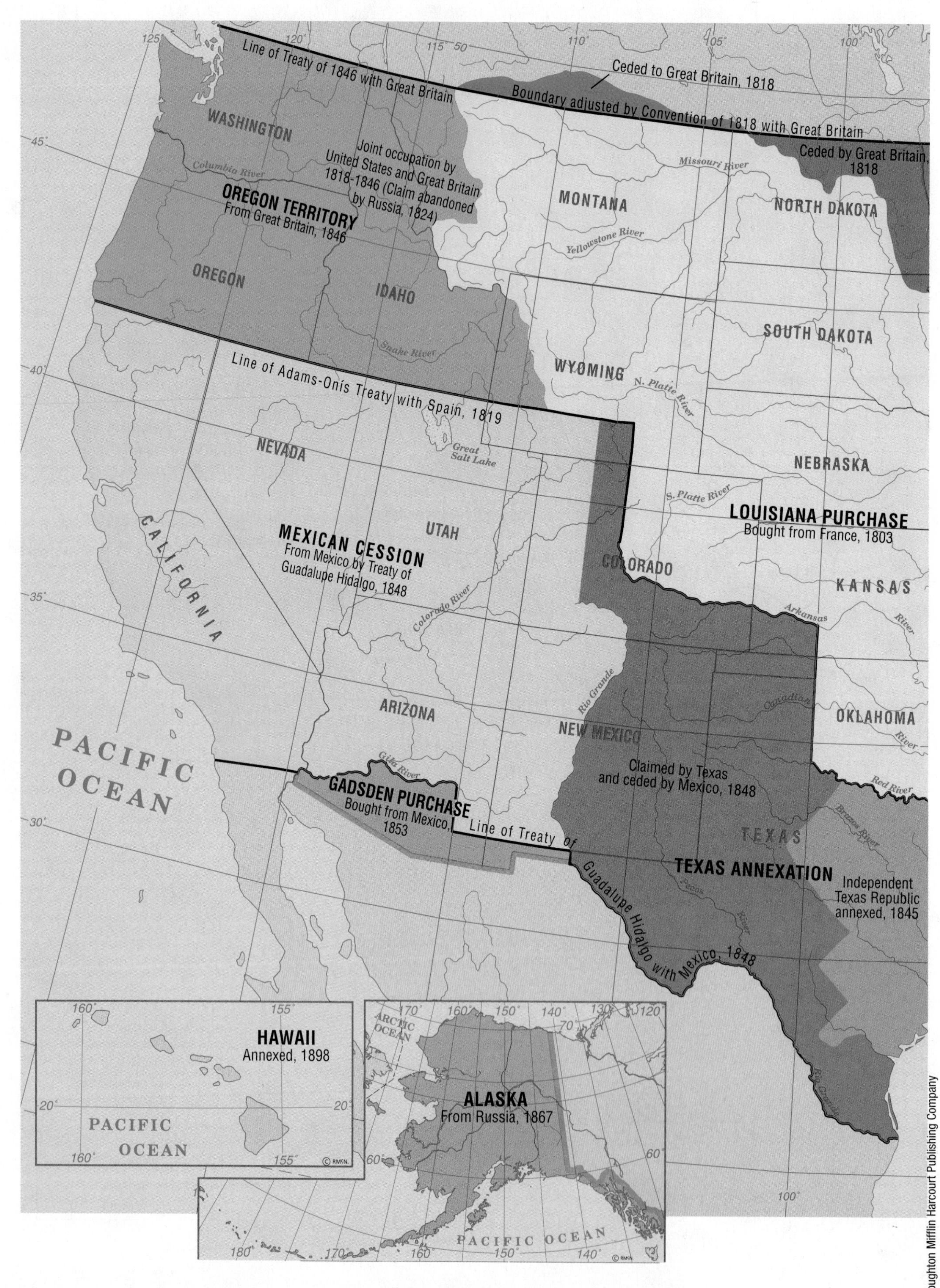
Line of Treaty of 1846 with Great Britain
Ceded to Great Britain, 1818
Boundary adjusted by Convention of 1818 with Great Britain
Ceded by Great Britain, 1818
WASHINGTON
Joint occupation by United States and Great Britain 1818-1846 (Claim abandoned by Russia, 1824)
OREGON TERRITORY
From Great Britain, 1846
OREGON
IDAHO
MONTANA
NORTH DAKOTA
SOUTH DAKOTA
WYOMING
Columbia River
Missouri River
Yellowstone River
Snake River
N. Platte River
Line of Adams-Onís Treaty with Spain, 1819
NEVADA
Great Salt Lake
NEBRASKA
S. Platte River
LOUISIANA PURCHASE
Bought from France, 1803
MEXICAN CESSION
From Mexico by Treaty of Guadalupe Hidalgo, 1848
UTAH
CALIFORNIA
COLORADO
KANSAS
Colorado River
Arkansas River
Rio Grande
ARIZONA
NEW MEXICO
Canadian River
OKLAHOMA
PACIFIC OCEAN
Gila River
GADSDEN PURCHASE
Bought from Mexico, 1853
Claimed by Texas and ceded by Mexico, 1848
Red River
Brazos River
TEXAS
Line of Treaty of Guadalupe Hidalgo with Mexico, 1848
TEXAS ANNEXATION
Independent Texas Republic annexed, 1845
Pecos River
HAWAII
Annexed, 1898
PACIFIC OCEAN
ARCTIC OCEAN
ALASKA
From Russia, 1867
PACIFIC OCEAN

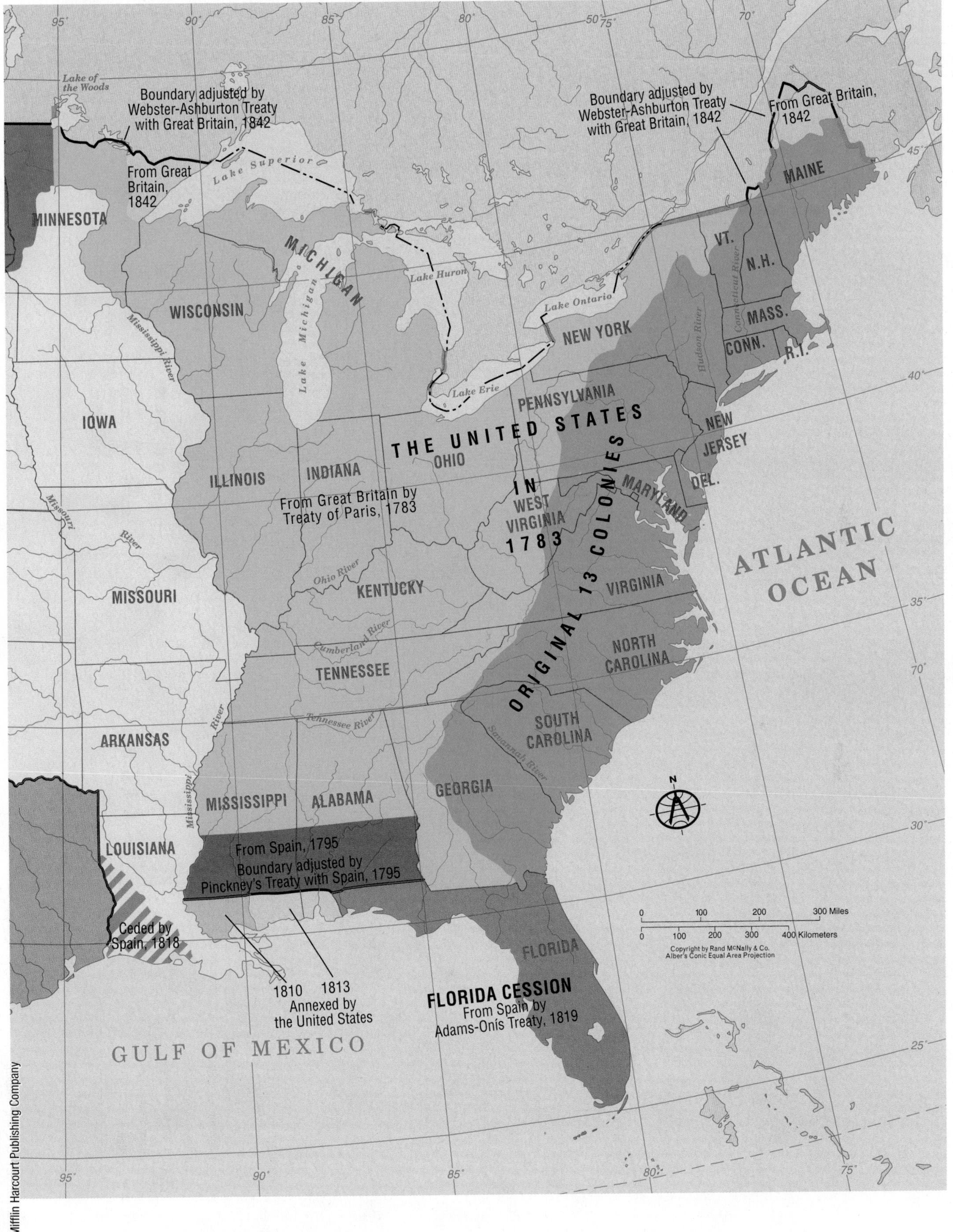
Lake of the Woods
Boundary adjusted by Webster-Ashburton Treaty with Great Britain, 1842
From Great Britain, 1842
Lake Superior
Boundary adjusted by Webster-Ashburton Treaty with Great Britain, 1842
From Great Britain, 1842
MAINE
MINNESOTA
MICHIGAN
VT.
N.H.
Lake Huron
WISCONSIN
Lake Michigan
Lake Ontario
MASS.
NEW YORK
CONN.
R.I.
Lake Erie
PENNSYLVANIA
IOWA
THE UNITED STATES IN 1783
NEW JERSEY
OHIO
ILLINOIS
INDIANA
ORIGINAL 13 COLONIES
MARYLAND
DEL.
From Great Britain by Treaty of Paris, 1783
WEST VIRGINIA
ATLANTIC OCEAN
Ohio River
KENTUCKY
VIRGINIA
MISSOURI
Cumberland River
NORTH CAROLINA
TENNESSEE
Tennessee River
SOUTH CAROLINA
ARKANSAS
Mississippi River
Missouri River
Hudson River
Connecticut River
Savannah River
GEORGIA
MISSISSIPPI
ALABAMA
LOUISIANA
From Spain, 1795
Boundary adjusted by Pinckney's Treaty with Spain, 1795
Ceded by Spain, 1818
0 100 200 300 Miles
0 100 200 300 400 Kilometers
Copyright by Rand McNally & Co.
Alber's Conic Equal Area Projection
FLORIDA
1810 1813
Annexed by the United States
FLORIDA CESSION
From Spain by Adams-Onís Treaty, 1819
GULF OF MEXICO

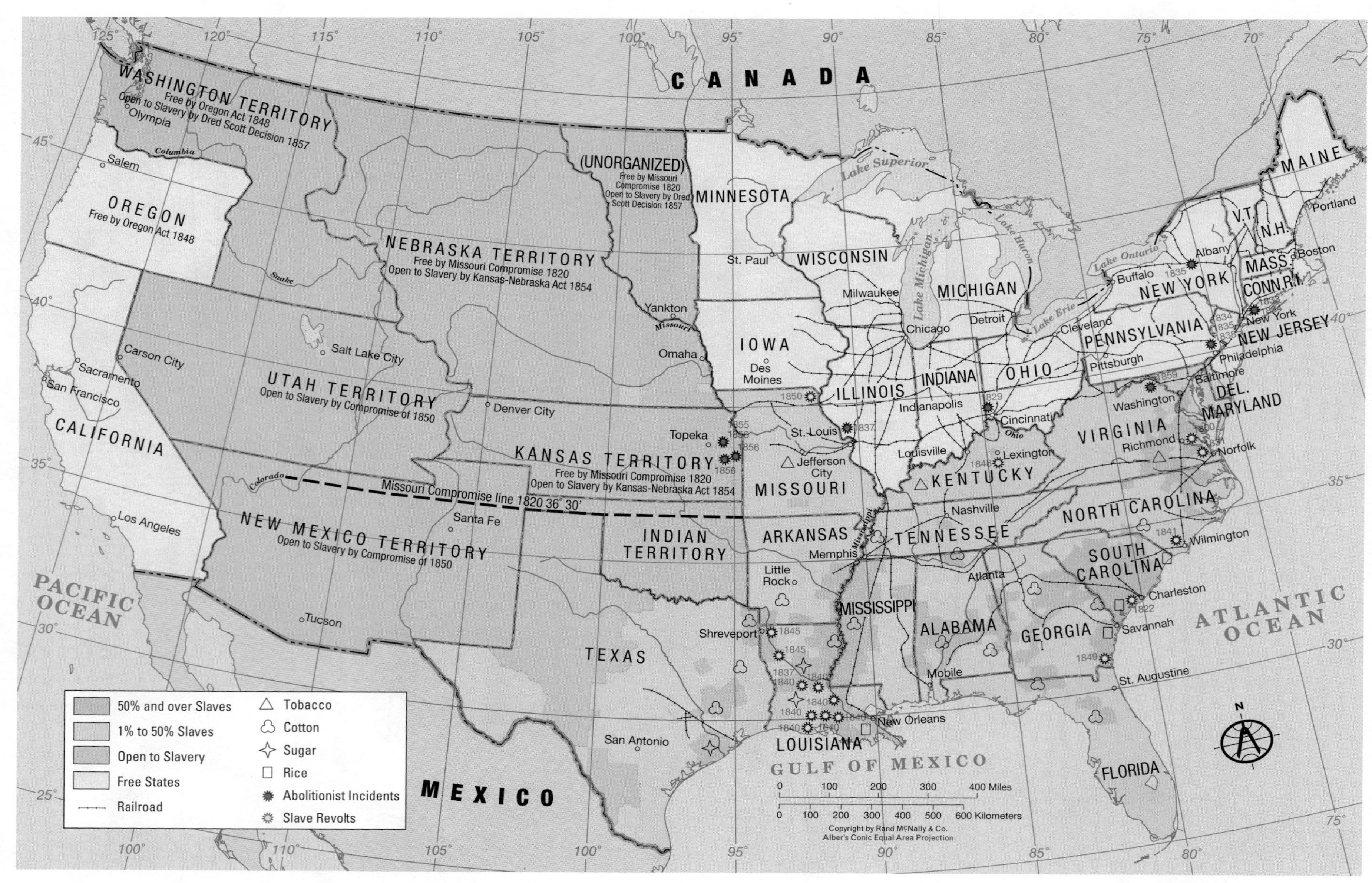
CANADA
WASHINGTON TERRITORY
Free by Oregon Act 1848
Open to Slavery by Dred Scott Decision 1857
OREGON
Free by Oregon Act 1848
(UNORGANIZED)
Free by Missouri Compromise 1820
Open to Slavery by Dred Scott Decision 1857
NEBRASKA TERRITORY
Free by Missouri Compromise 1820
Open to Slavery by Kansas-Nebraska Act 1854
UTAH TERRITORY
Open to Slavery by Compromise of 1850
KANSAS TERRITORY
Free by Missouri Compromise 1820
Open to Slavery by Kansas-Nebraska Act 1854
Missouri Compromise line 1820 36° 30'
NEW MEXICO TERRITORY
Open to Slavery by Compromise of 1850
INDIAN TERRITORY
CALIFORNIA
TEXAS
MINNESOTA
WISCONSIN
IOWA
MICHIGAN
ILLINOIS
INDIANA
OHIO
MISSOURI
ARKANSAS
KENTUCKY
TENNESSEE
MISSISSIPPI
ALABAMA
GEORGIA
LOUISIANA
FLORIDA
SOUTH CAROLINA
NORTH CAROLINA
VIRGINIA
MARYLAND
DEL.
PENNSYLVANIA
NEW JERSEY
NEW YORK
CONN.
R.I.
MASS.
V.T.
N.H.
MAINE
MEXICO
PACIFIC OCEAN
ATLANTIC OCEAN
GULF OF MEXICO
Lake Superior
Lake Michigan
Lake Huron
Lake Erie
Lake Ontario
Columbia
Snake
Missouri
Colorado
Mississippi
Ohio
Olympia
Salem
Carson City
Sacramento
San Francisco
Los Angeles
Salt Lake City
Tucson
Santa Fe
Denver City
Yankton
Omaha
Topeka
St. Paul
Des Moines
Milwaukee
Chicago
Detroit
Cleveland
Buffalo
Albany
Portland
Boston
New York
Philadelphia
Pittsburgh
Baltimore
Washington
Richmond
Norfolk
Wilmington
Charleston
Savannah
St. Augustine
Indianapolis
Cincinnati
Louisville
Lexington
St. Louis
Jefferson City
Nashville
Memphis
Little Rock
Atlanta
Mobile
New Orleans
Shreveport
San Antonio
1850
1837
1829
1848
1855
1856
1859
1835
1834
1800
1831
1841
1822
1849
1845
1840
50% and over Slaves
1% to 50% Slaves
Open to Slavery
Free States
Railroad
Tobacco
Cotton
Sugar
Rice
Abolitionist Incidents
Slave Revolts
0 100 200 300 400 Miles
0 100 200 300 400 500 600 Kilometers
Copyright by Rand McNally & Co.
Alber's Conic Equal Area Projection
N
125° 120° 115° 110° 105° 100° 95° 90° 85° 80° 75° 70°
45° 40° 35° 30° 25°

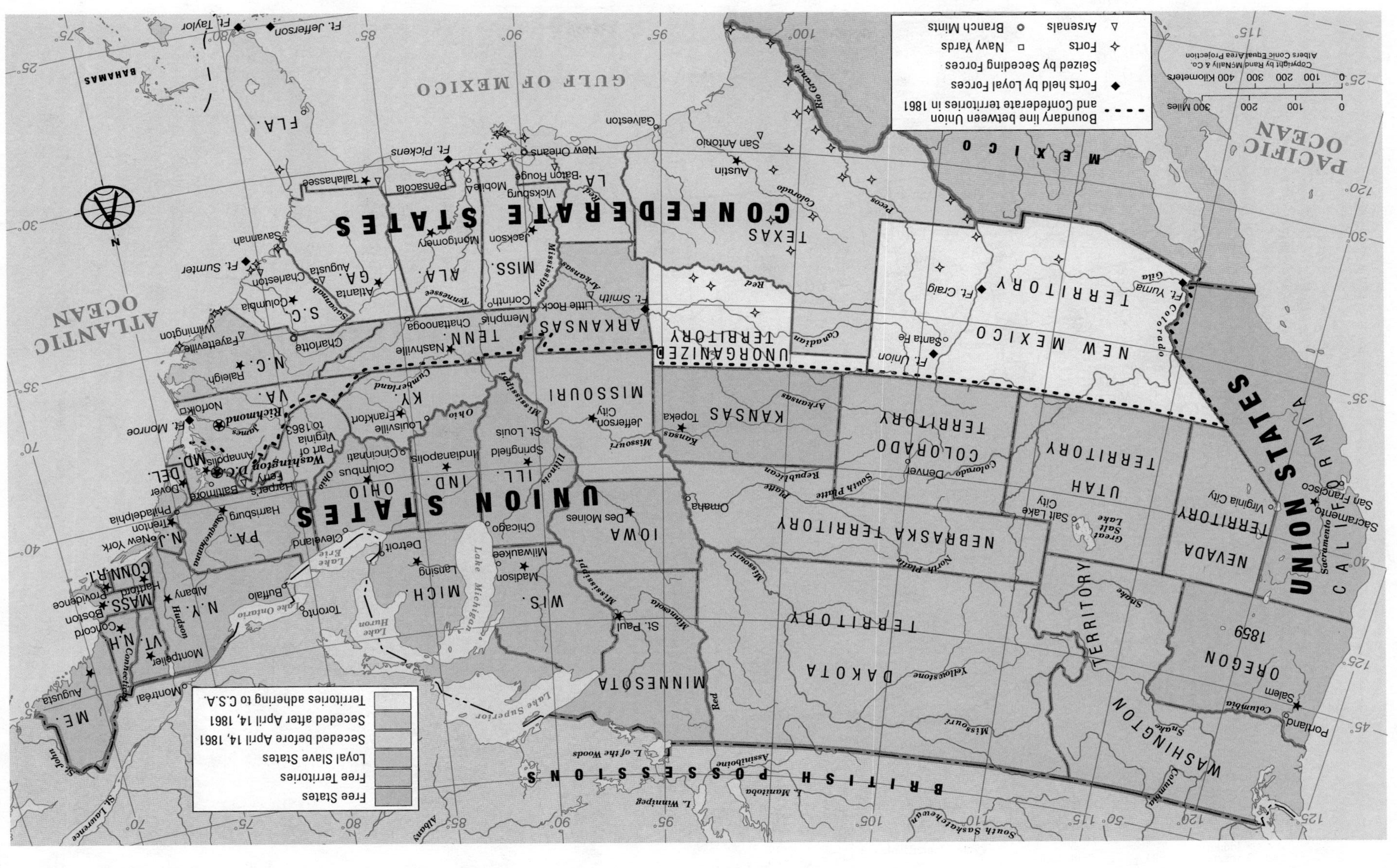
Free States
Free Territories
Loyal Slave States
Seceded before April 14, 1861
Seceded after April 14, 1861
Territories adhering to C.S.A.
Boundary line between Union and Confederate territories in 1861
Forts held by Loyal Forces
Seized by Seceding Forces
Forts
Navy Yards
Arsenals
Branch Mints
UNION STATES
CONFEDERATE STATES
BRITISH POSSESSIONS
MEXICO
ATLANTIC OCEAN
PACIFIC OCEAN
GULF OF MEXICO
BAHAMAS
WASHINGTON TERRITORY
OREGON 1859
CALIFORNIA
NEVADA TERRITORY
UTAH TERRITORY
COLORADO TERRITORY
NEBRASKA TERRITORY
DAKOTA TERRITORY
NEW MEXICO TERRITORY
UNORGANIZED TERRITORY
KANSAS
MINNESOTA
IOWA
MISSOURI
WIS.
MICH.
ILL.
IND.
OHIO
KY.
TENN.
ARKANSAS
TEXAS
LA.
MISS.
ALA.
GA.
FLA.
S.C.
N.C.
VA.
Part of Virginia to 1863
MD.
DEL.
PA.
N.J.
N.Y.
VT.
N.H.
MASS.
CONN.
R.I.
ME.
Washington D.C.
Richmond
Ft. Sumter
Ft. Pickens
Ft. Monroe
Ft. Jefferson
Ft. Taylor
Ft. Smith
Ft. Union
Ft. Craig
Ft. Yuma
Harper's Ferry
300 Miles
400 Kilometers
Copyright by Rand McNally & Co.
Albers Conic Equal Area Projection

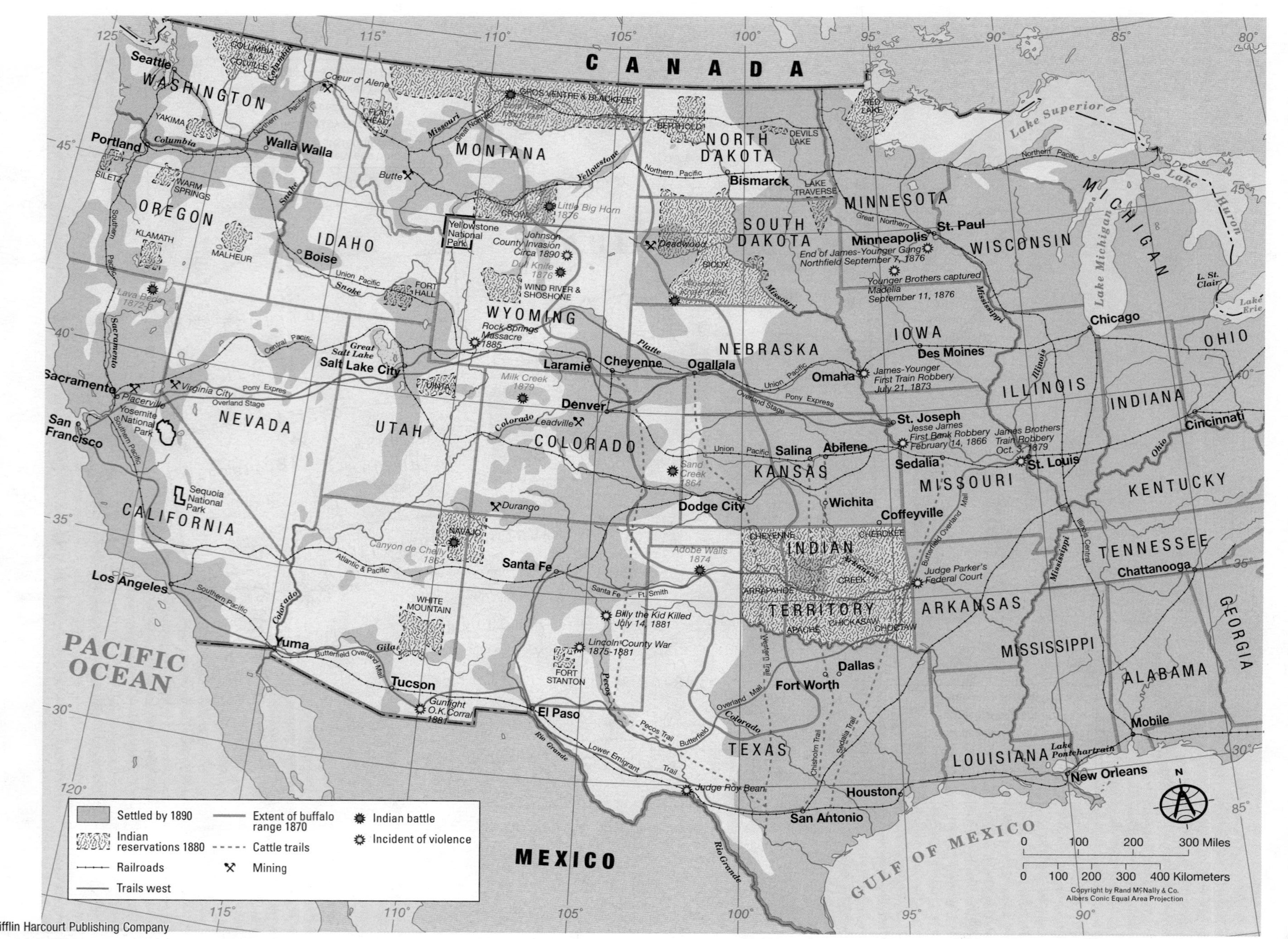
CANADA
MEXICO
PACIFIC OCEAN
GULF OF MEXICO
WASHINGTON
OREGON
IDAHO
MONTANA
WYOMING
NEVADA
UTAH
CALIFORNIA
COLORADO
NORTH DAKOTA
SOUTH DAKOTA
NEBRASKA
KANSAS
MINNESOTA
IOWA
MISSOURI
WISCONSIN
ILLINOIS
MICHIGAN
INDIANA
OHIO
KENTUCKY
TENNESSEE
ARKANSAS
MISSISSIPPI
ALABAMA
GEORGIA
LOUISIANA
TEXAS
INDIAN TERRITORY
Seattle
Portland
Walla Walla
Boise
Butte
Sacramento
San Francisco
Los Angeles
Yuma
Tucson
Salt Lake City
Laramie
Cheyenne
Denver
Leadville
Durango
Santa Fe
El Paso
Ogallala
Dodge City
Salina
Abilene
Wichita
Coffeyville
Omaha
Des Moines
St. Joseph
Sedalia
St. Louis
Bismarck
Minneapolis
St. Paul
Chicago
Cincinnati
Chattanooga
Mobile
New Orleans
Houston
San Antonio
Dallas
Fort Worth
Little Big Horn 1876
Johnson County Invasion Circa 1890
Dull Knife 1876
Rock Springs Massacre 1885
Milk Creek 1879
Sand Creek 1864
Adobe Walls 1874
Billy the Kid Killed July 14, 1881
Lincoln County War 1875–1881
Gunfight O.K. Corral 1881
Judge Roy Bean
Judge Parker's Federal Court
Lava Beds 1872–3
Canyon de Chelly 1864
End of James-Younger Gang Northfield September 7, 1876
Younger Brothers captured Madelia September 11, 1876
James-Younger First Train Robbery July 21, 1873
Jesse James First Bank Robbery February 14, 1866
James Brothers Train Robbery Oct. 3, 1879
Yellowstone National Park
Yosemite National Park
Sequoia National Park
Lake Superior
Lake Michigan
Lake Huron
Lake Erie
L. St. Clair
Lake Pontchartrain
Great Salt Lake
Northern Pacific
Great Northern
Union Pacific
Central Pacific
Southern Pacific
Atlantic & Pacific
Illinois Central
Pony Express
Overland Stage
Butterfield Overland Mail
Overland Mail
Western Trail
Chisholm Trail
Sedalia Trail
Pecos Trail
Lower Emigrant Trail
Santa Fe
Ft. Smith
Columbia
Snake
Missouri
Yellowstone
Platte
Colorado
Gila
Rio Grande
Pecos
Arkansas
Mississippi
Ohio
Illinois
Sacramento
Coeur d'Alene
Virginia City
Deadwood
Placerville
YAKIMA
COLUMBIA & COLVILLE
FLAT HEAD
GROS VENTRE & BLACKFEET
BERTHOLD
DEVILS LAKE
LAKE TRAVERSE
RED LAKE
SIOUX
CROW
WARM SPRINGS
SILETZ
KLAMATH
MALHEUR
FORT HALL
WIND RIVER & SHOSHONE
UINTA
NAVAJO
WHITE MOUNTAIN
FORT STANTON
CHEYENNE
CHEROKEE
CREEK
ARAPAHOE
CHICKASAW
CHOCTAW
APACHE
Settled by 1890
Indian reservations 1880
Railroads
Trails west
Extent of buffalo range 1870
Cattle trails
Mining
Indian battle
Incident of violence
0 100 200 300 Miles
0 100 200 300 400 Kilometers
Copyright by Rand McNally & Co.
Albers Conic Equal Area Projection
N
125°
120°
115°
110°
105°
100°
95°
90°
85°
80°
45°
40°
35°
30°

The Civil War

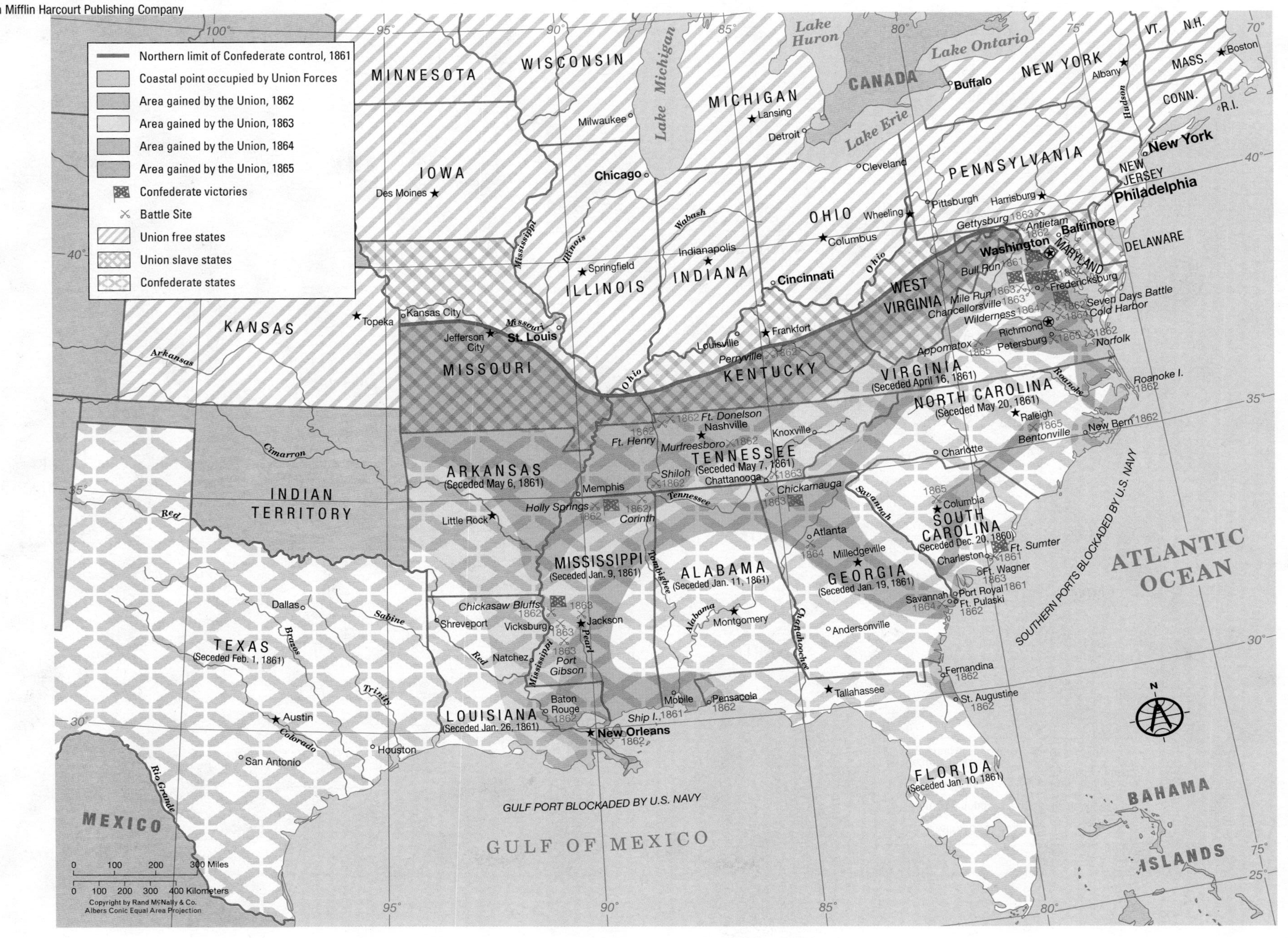
Northern limit of Confederate control, 1861
Coastal point occupied by Union Forces
Area gained by the Union, 1862
Area gained by the Union, 1863
Area gained by the Union, 1864
Area gained by the Union, 1865
Confederate victories
Battle Site
Union free states
Union slave states
Confederate states
MINNESOTA
WISCONSIN
MICHIGAN
IOWA
ILLINOIS
INDIANA
OHIO
PENNSYLVANIA
NEW YORK
VT.
N.H.
MASS.
CONN.
R.I.
NEW JERSEY
DELAWARE
MARYLAND
KANSAS
MISSOURI
KENTUCKY
WEST VIRGINIA
VIRGINIA (Seceded April 16, 1861)
NORTH CAROLINA (Seceded May 20, 1861)
TENNESSEE (Seceded May 7, 1861)
SOUTH CAROLINA (Seceded Dec. 20, 1860)
GEORGIA (Seceded Jan. 19, 1861)
ALABAMA (Seceded Jan. 11, 1861)
MISSISSIPPI (Seceded Jan. 9, 1861)
ARKANSAS (Seceded May 6, 1861)
LOUISIANA (Seceded Jan. 26, 1861)
TEXAS (Seceded Feb. 1, 1861)
FLORIDA (Seceded Jan. 10, 1861)
INDIAN TERRITORY
CANADA
MEXICO
BAHAMA ISLANDS
ATLANTIC OCEAN
GULF OF MEXICO
Lake Huron
Lake Ontario
Lake Erie
Lake Michigan
SOUTHERN PORTS BLOCKADED BY U.S. NAVY
GULF PORT BLOCKADED BY U.S. NAVY
Boston
Albany
Buffalo
New York
Philadelphia
Harrisburg
Pittsburgh
Gettysburg 1863
Antietam 1862
Baltimore
Washington
Bull Run 1861
Fredericksburg
Mile Run 1863
Chancellorsville 1863
Wilderness 1864
Seven Days Battle
Cold Harbor
Richmond
Petersburg 1865
Norfolk
Appomatox 1865
Roanoke I. 1862
Raleigh
Bentonville 1865
New Bern 1862
Charlotte
Columbia 1865
Charleston
Ft. Sumter 1861
Ft. Wagner 1863
Port Royal 1861
Savannah 1864
Ft. Pulaski 1862
Fernandina 1862
St. Augustine 1862
Tallahassee
Andersonville
Milledgeville
Atlanta 1864
Chickamauga 1863
Chattanooga 1863
Knoxville
Nashville
Ft. Donelson 1862
Ft. Henry 1862
Murfreesboro 1862
Shiloh 1862
Memphis
Holly Springs 1862
Corinth 1862
Little Rock
Chickasaw Bluffs 1862
Vicksburg 1863
Jackson 1863
Port Gibson 1863
Natchez
Shreveport
Baton Rouge 1862
New Orleans 1862
Ship I. 1861
Mobile
Pensacola 1862
Montgomery
Frankfort
Louisville
Perryville 1862
Cincinnati
Columbus
Wheeling
Cleveland
Detroit
Lansing
Indianapolis
Springfield
Chicago
Milwaukee
Des Moines
St. Louis
Jefferson City
Kansas City
Topeka
Dallas
Austin
San Antonio
Houston
Ohio
Mississippi
Missouri
Illinois
Wabash
Tennessee
Tombigbee
Alabama
Chattahoochee
Savannah
Roanoke
Hudson
Pearl
Red
Sabine
Trinity
Brazos
Colorado
Rio Grande
Arkansas
Cimarron
0 100 200 300 Miles
0 100 200 300 400 Kilometers
Copyright by Rand McNally & Co.
Albers Conic Equal Area Projection
N

U.S. Industries 1920

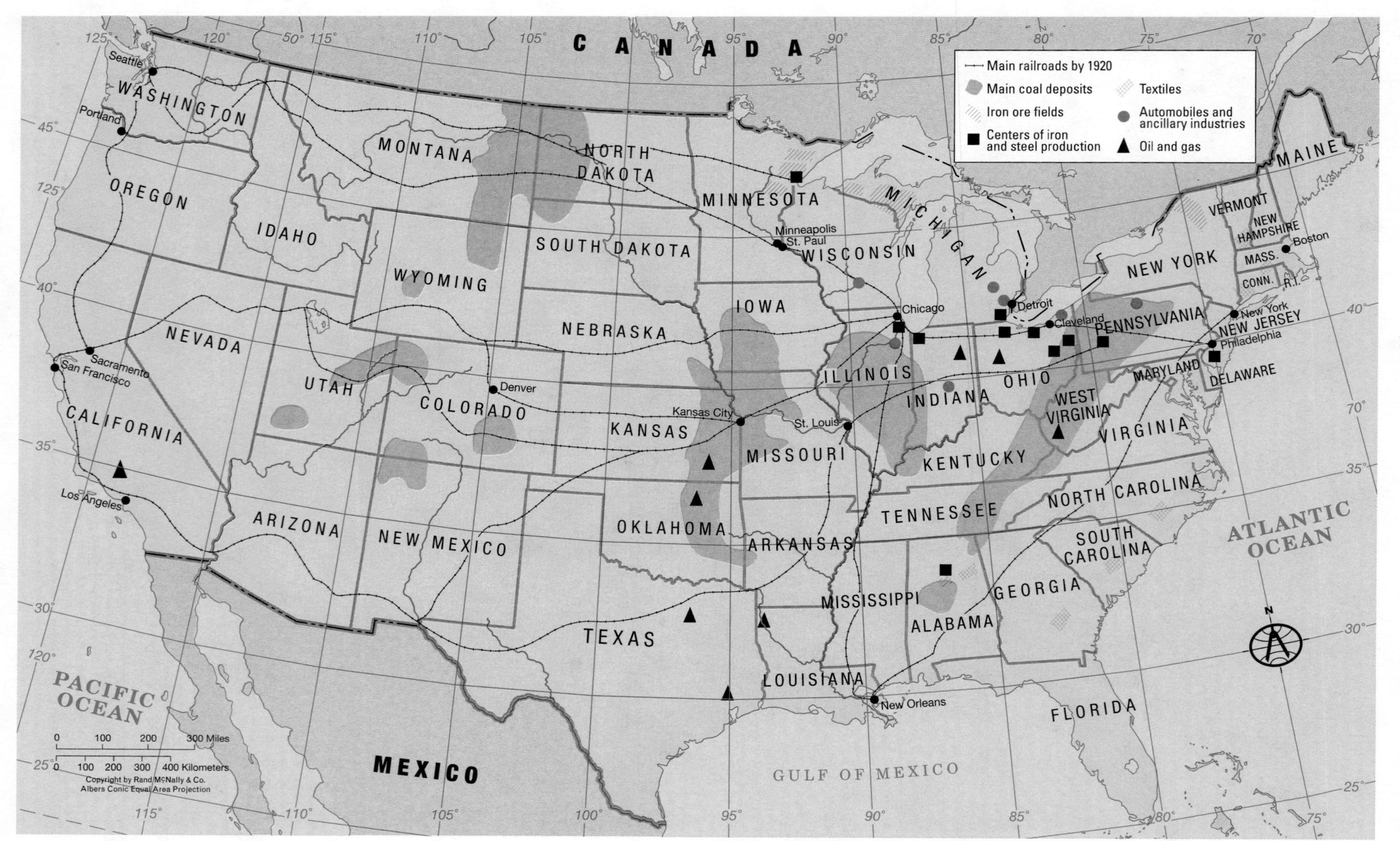

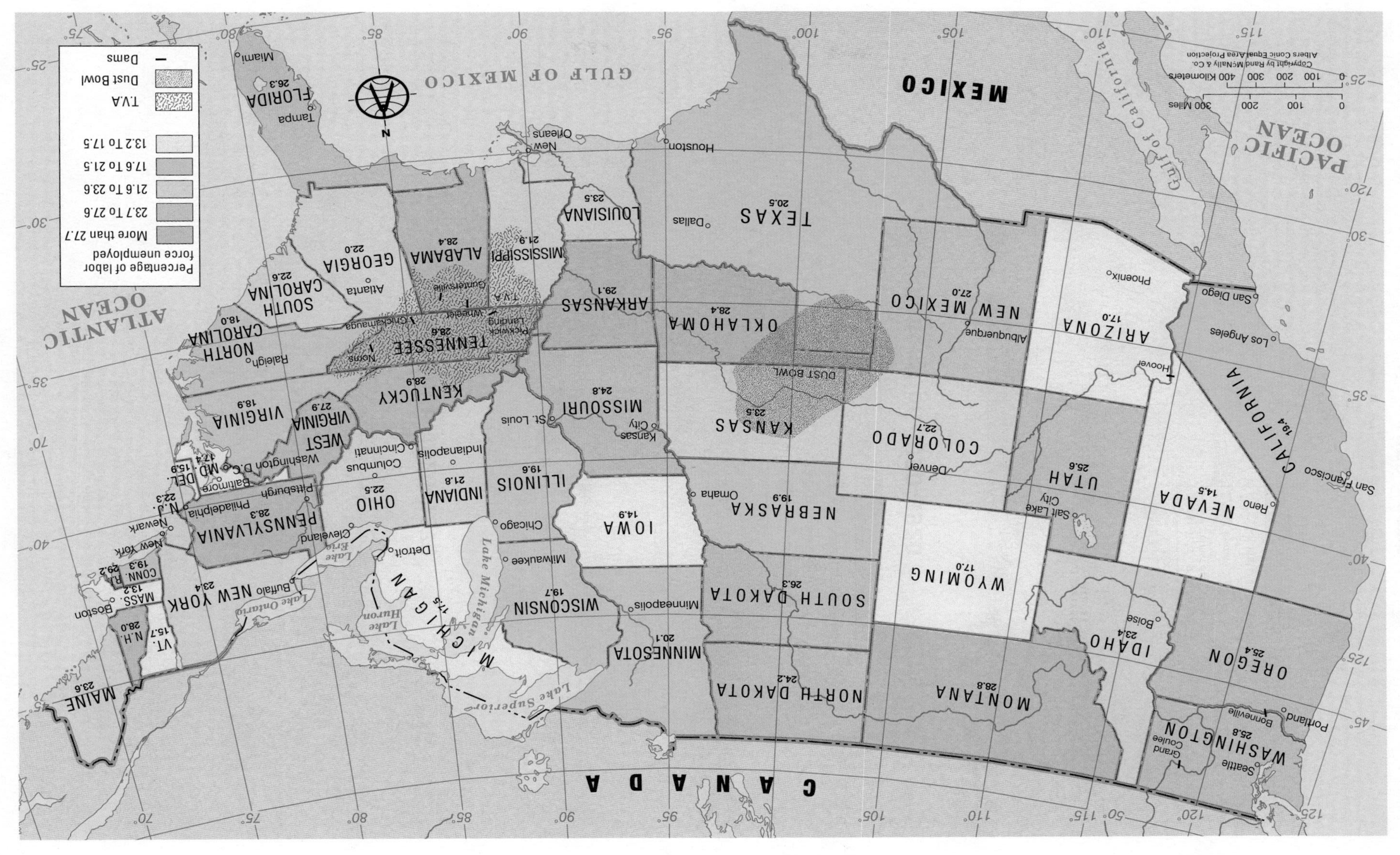
Percentage of labor force unemployed
More than 27.7
23.7 To 27.6
21.6 To 23.6
17.6 To 21.5
13.2 To 17.5
T.V.A
Dust Bowl
Dams
CANADA
MEXICO
ATLANTIC OCEAN
PACIFIC OCEAN
GULF OF MEXICO
Gulf of California
WASHINGTON 25.8
OREGON 25.4
CALIFORNIA 19.4
NEVADA 14.5
IDAHO 23.4
MONTANA 28.8
WYOMING 17.0
UTAH 25.6
ARIZONA 17.0
COLORADO 22.7
NEW MEXICO 27.0
NORTH DAKOTA 24.2
SOUTH DAKOTA 26.3
NEBRASKA 19.9
KANSAS 23.5
OKLAHOMA 28.4
TEXAS 20.5
MINNESOTA 20.1
IOWA 14.9
MISSOURI 24.8
ARKANSAS 29.1
LOUISIANA 23.5
WISCONSIN 19.7
ILLINOIS 19.6
MICHIGAN 17.5
INDIANA 21.8
OHIO 22.5
KENTUCKY 28.9
TENNESSEE 28.6
MISSISSIPPI 21.9
ALABAMA 28.4
GEORGIA 22.0
FLORIDA 26.3
SOUTH CAROLINA 22.6
NORTH CAROLINA 18.0
VIRGINIA 18.9
WEST VIRGINIA 27.9
PENNSYLVANIA 28.3
NEW YORK 23.4
N.J. 22.3
DEL. 15.9
MD. 17.4
VT. 15.7
N.H. 28.0
MAINE 23.6
MASS. 13.2
CONN. 19.3
R.I. 29.2
DUST BOWL
T.V.A.
Grand Coulee
Bonneville
Hoover
Pickwick Landing
Wheeler
Guntersville
Chickamauga
Norris
Seattle
Portland
Boise
Reno
San Francisco
Los Angeles
San Diego
Salt Lake City
Phoenix
Denver
Albuquerque
Omaha
Kansas City
Dallas
Houston
New Orleans
Minneapolis
Milwaukee
Chicago
St. Louis
Indianapolis
Cincinnati
Columbus
Detroit
Cleveland
Pittsburgh
Buffalo
Philadelphia
Baltimore
Washington D.C.
Newark
New York
Boston
Raleigh
Atlanta
Tampa
Miami
Lake Superior
Lake Michigan
Lake Huron
Lake Erie
Lake Ontario
0 100 200 300 Miles
0 100 200 300 400 Kilometers
Copyright by Rand McNally & Co.
Albers Conic Equal-Area Projection

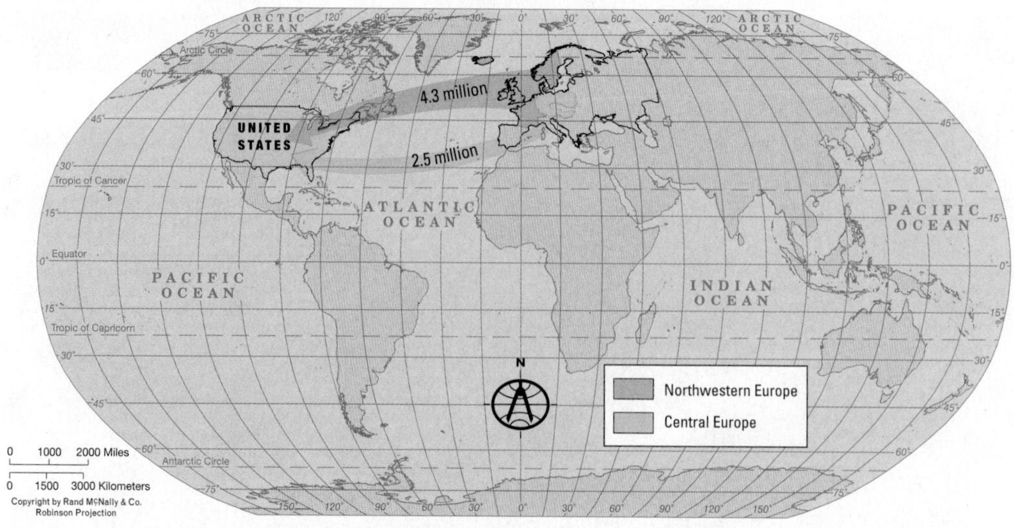

Immigration 1820–1870

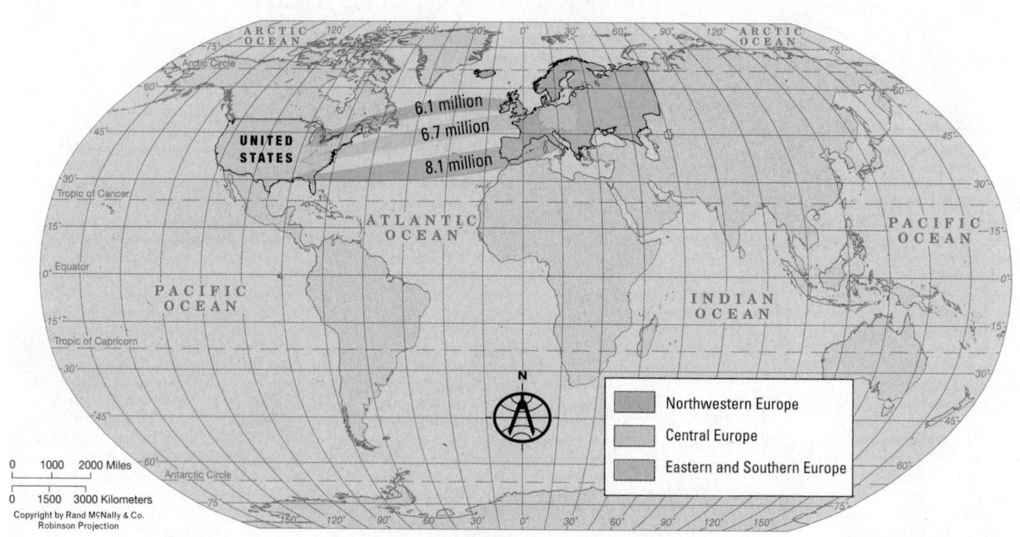

Immigration 1880–1920

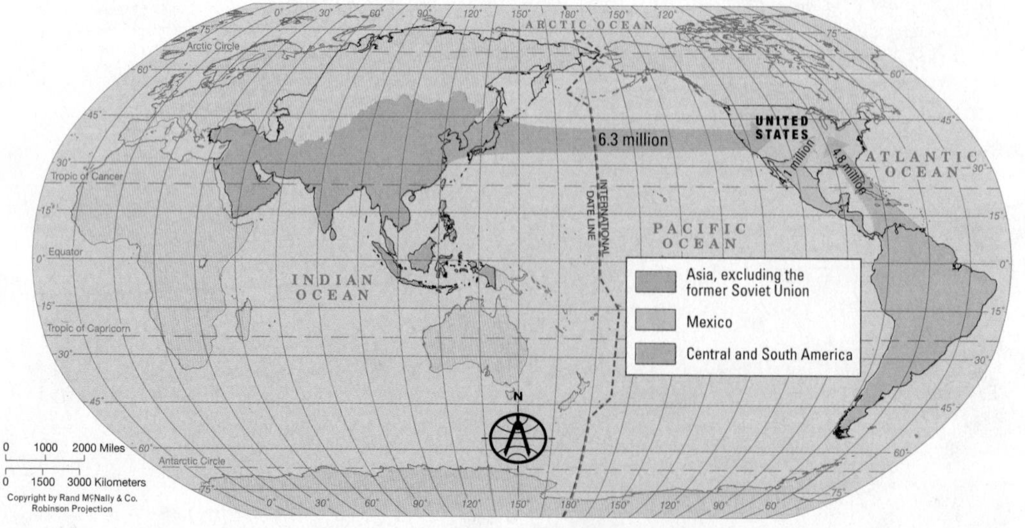

Immigration 1960s–1990s

Immigration's Impact 1910

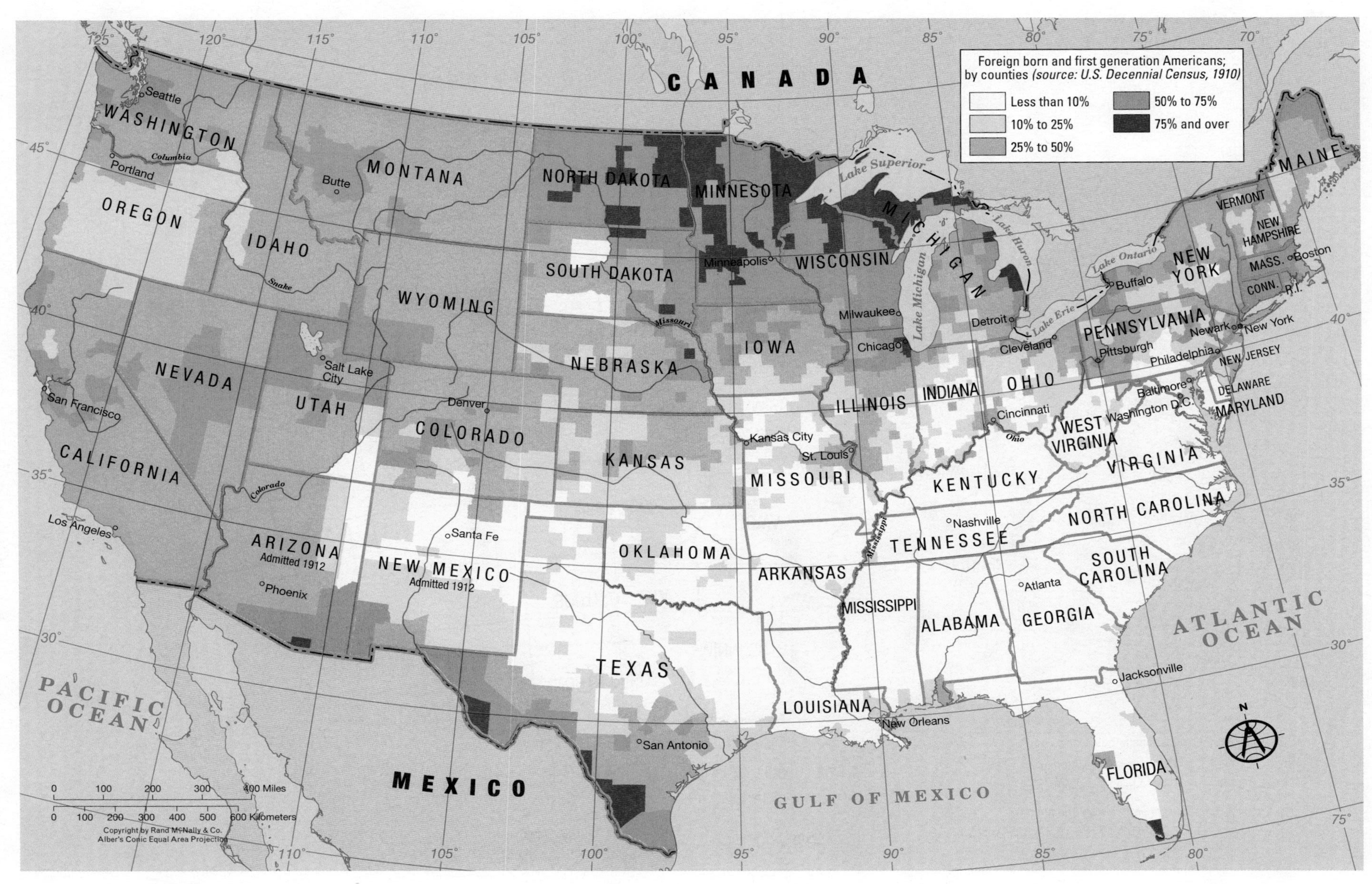

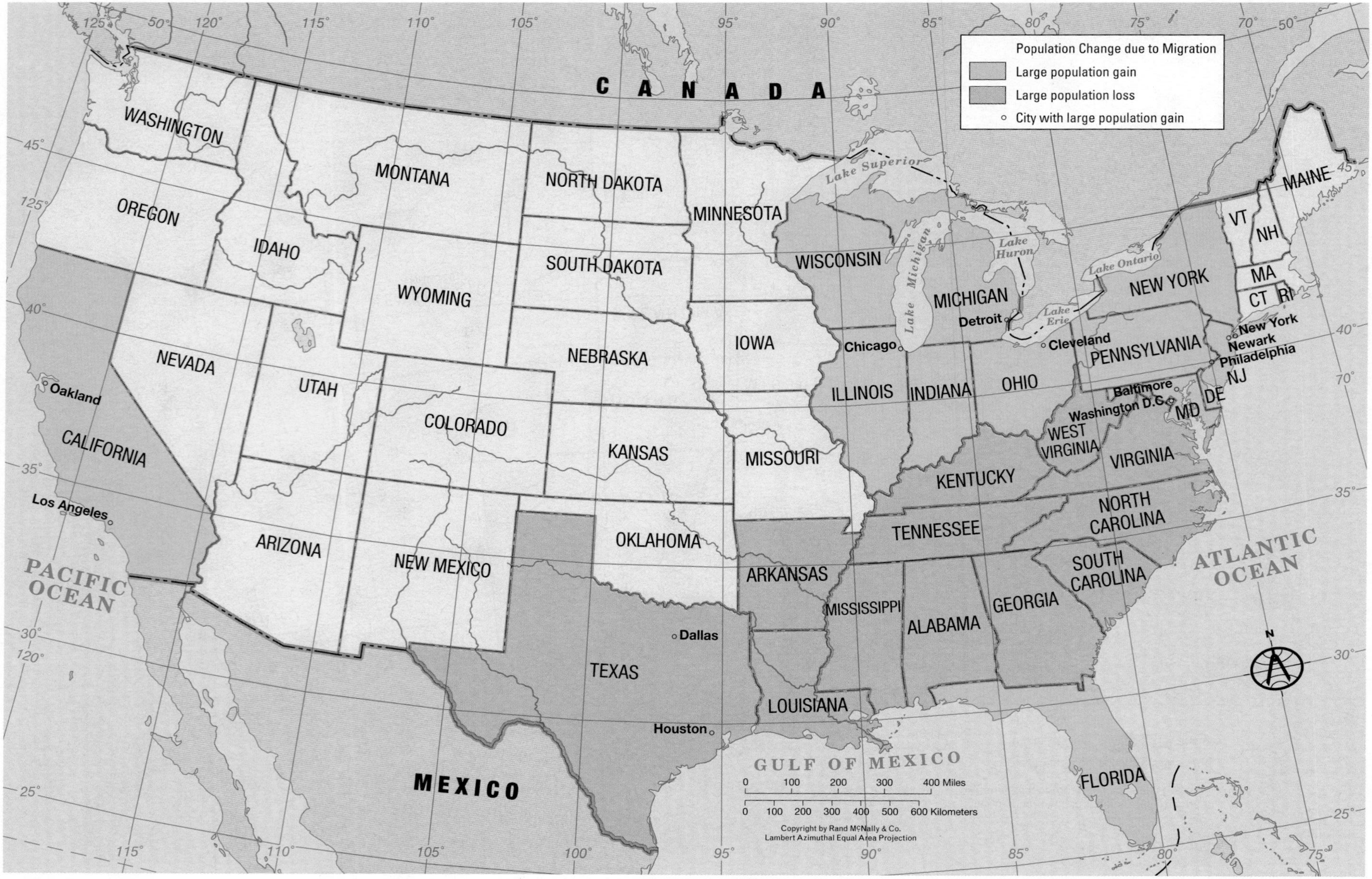

African-American Migration 1940–1970

Population Change due to Migration
- Large population gain
- Large population loss
- City with large population gain

CANADA

WASHINGTON OREGON IDAHO MONTANA WYOMING NORTH DAKOTA SOUTH DAKOTA NEBRASKA MINNESOTA IOWA WISCONSIN MICHIGAN NEVADA UTAH COLORADO KANSAS MISSOURI ILLINOIS INDIANA OHIO CALIFORNIA ARIZONA NEW MEXICO OKLAHOMA TEXAS ARKANSAS LOUISIANA MISSISSIPPI ALABAMA GEORGIA FLORIDA TENNESSEE KENTUCKY WEST VIRGINIA VIRGINIA NORTH CAROLINA SOUTH CAROLINA PENNSYLVANIA NEW YORK VT NH MAINE MA CT RI NJ DE MD

Oakland, Los Angeles, Dallas, Houston, Chicago, Detroit, Cleveland, Washington D.C., Baltimore, Philadelphia, Newark, New York

Lake Superior, Lake Michigan, Lake Huron, Lake Erie, Lake Ontario

PACIFIC OCEAN, ATLANTIC OCEAN, GULF OF MEXICO, MEXICO

0 100 200 300 400 Miles
0 100 200 300 400 500 600 Kilometers

Copyright by Rand McNally & Co.
Lambert Azimuthal Equal Area Projection

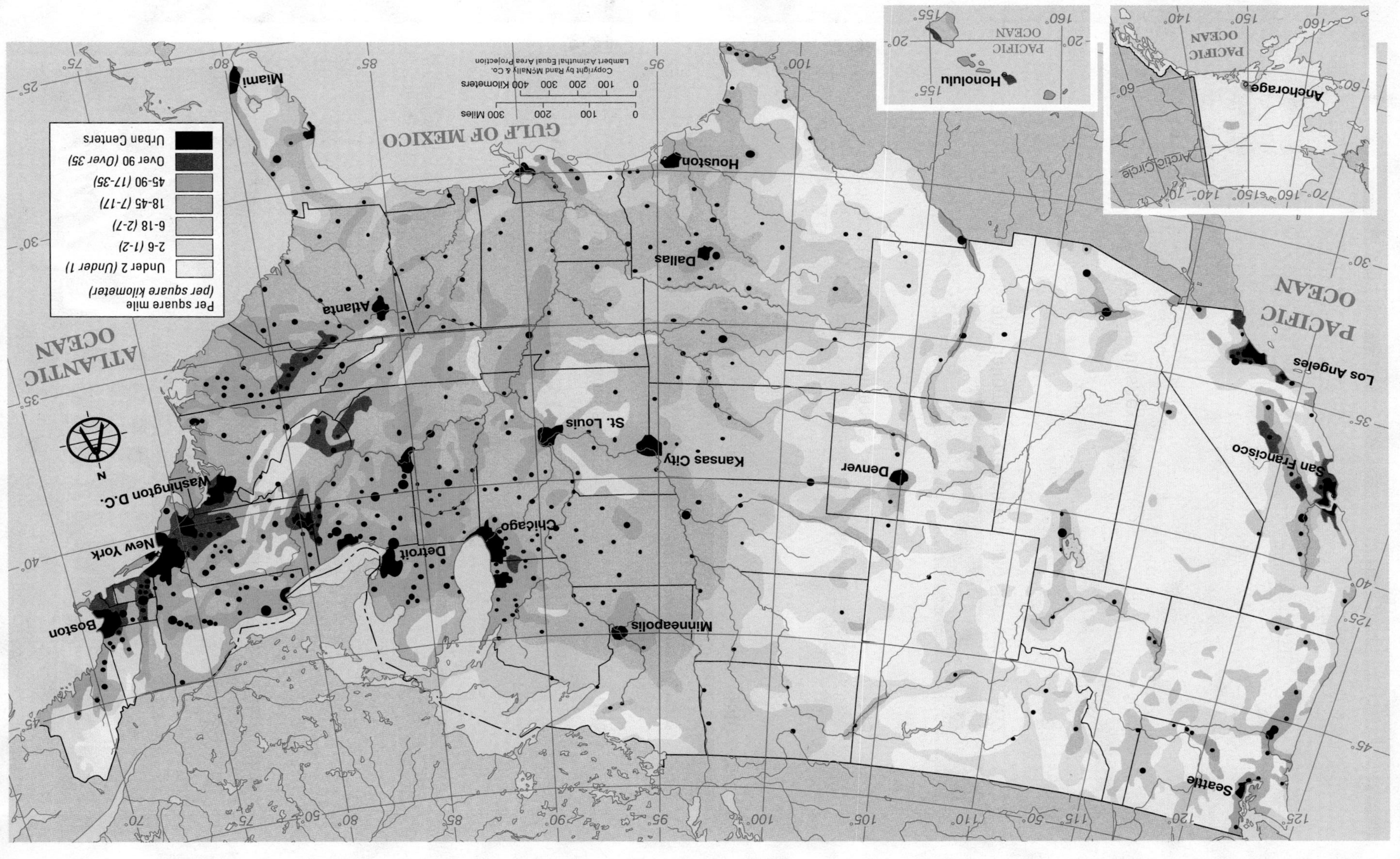
Per square mile
(per square kilometer)
Under 2 (Under 1)
2-6 (1-2)
6-18 (2-7)
18-45 (7-17)
45-90 (17-35)
Over 90 (Over 35)
Urban Centers
ATLANTIC OCEAN
GULF OF MEXICO
PACIFIC OCEAN
N
Boston
New York
Washington D.C.
Detroit
Chicago
Atlanta
Miami
Minneapolis
St. Louis
Kansas City
Dallas
Houston
Denver
Seattle
San Francisco
Los Angeles
Honolulu
Anchorage
Arctic Circle
0 100 200 300 Miles
0 100 200 300 400 Kilometers
Copyright by Rand McNally & Co.
Lambert Azimuthal Equal Area Projection

REFERENCE SECTION

 Skillbuilder Handbook

1.1 Finding Main Ideas

DEFINING THE SKILL

Finding main ideas means identifying words that sum up the single most important thought in an entire paragraph or section. To find the main idea of a passage, identify the topic. Then, as you read, ask, What central idea do the many details explain or support?

APPLYING THE SKILL

This excerpt from President Richard M. Nixon's memoirs is about wiretapping, or bugging—planting a concealed microphone to get information. The diagram that follows identifies and organizes information in the passage.

HOW TO FIND MAIN IDEAS

Strategy 1 Identify the topic by looking at the title, or by looking for key words. This passage repeats the words *bugged, bugging, tapped,* and *wiretap.*

Strategy 2 Look for a topic sentence. Ask whether any one sentence sums up the point of the whole passage. In this passage, the second sentence states Nixon's attitude toward bugging.

Strategy 3 Look for details or examples. The many examples support the attitude that wiretapping was a common practice.

NIXON ON WIRETAPPING 1

I had been in politics too long, and seen everything from dirty tricks to vote fraud. 2 I could not muster much moral outrage over a political 1 bugging.

Larry O'Brien [director of the Democratic National Committee] might affect astonishment and horror, but he knew as well as I did that political bugging had been around nearly since the invention of the wiretap. 3 As recently as 1970 a former member of Adlai Stevenson's [Democratic candidate for president in 1952 and 1956] campaign staff had publicly stated that he had tapped the [John F.] Kennedy organization's phone lines at the 1960 Democratic convention. 3 Lyndon Johnson felt that the Kennedys had had him tapped; 3 Barry Goldwater said that his 1964 campaign had been bugged; 3 and Edgar Hoover [director of the FBI, 1924–1972] told me that in 1968 Johnson had ordered my campaign plane bugged.

Source: Richard Nixon, *The Memoirs of Richard Nixon* (New York: Grosset & Dunlap, 1978), pp. 628–629.

Make a Diagram

State the topic and list the supporting details in a chart. Use the information you record to help you state the main idea.

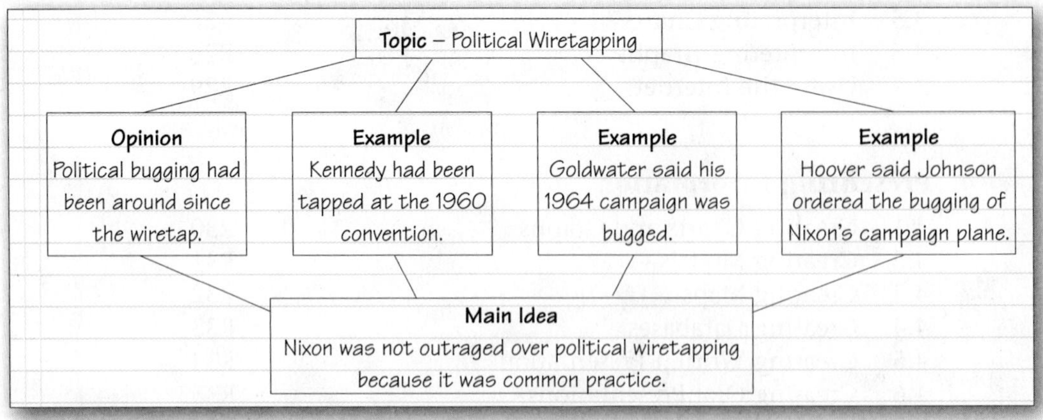

1.2 Following Chronological Order

DEFINING THE SKILL

Chronological order is "time order"—the sequence of events in time. Chronology may be either relative or absolute. Relative chronology relates one event to another. This helps historians to see causes, effects, and other relationships between events. Absolute chronology ties events to an exact time or date, pinpointing dates in one universal framework—the passage of time.

APPLYING THE SKILL

The following paragraph is about several events leading up to the Watergate scandal that brought down the Nixon administration. The time line that follows puts the events of the passage in chronological order.

HOW TO FOLLOW CHRONOLOGICAL ORDER

Strategy 1 Look for clue words about time. These are words like *initial, first, next, then, before, after, finally,* and *by that time.*

Strategy 2 Use specific dates provided in the text.

Strategy 3 Watch for references to previous historical events that are included in the background. Usually a change in verb tense will indicate a previous event.

The Pentagon Papers

The (1) initial event that many historians believe led to Watergate took place on (2) June 13, 1971, when the *New York Times* began publishing articles called the Pentagon Papers, which divulged government secrets about the U.S. involvement in Vietnam. The information had been leaked by a former Defense Department official, Daniel Ellsberg. The Justice Department asked the courts to suppress publication of the articles, but on (2) July 30, 1971, the Supreme Court ruled that the information could be published. (1) Two months later, in September, a group of special White House agents known as the plumbers burglarized the office of Ellsberg's psychiatrist in a vain attempt to find evidence against Ellsberg. President Nixon (3) had authorized the creation of the plumbers in 1971, after the Pentagon Papers were published, to keep government secrets from leaking to the media and to help ensure his reelection in November 1972.

Make a Time Line

If the events in a passage are numerous and complex, make a time line to represent them. The time line here lists the events from the passage above in time order.

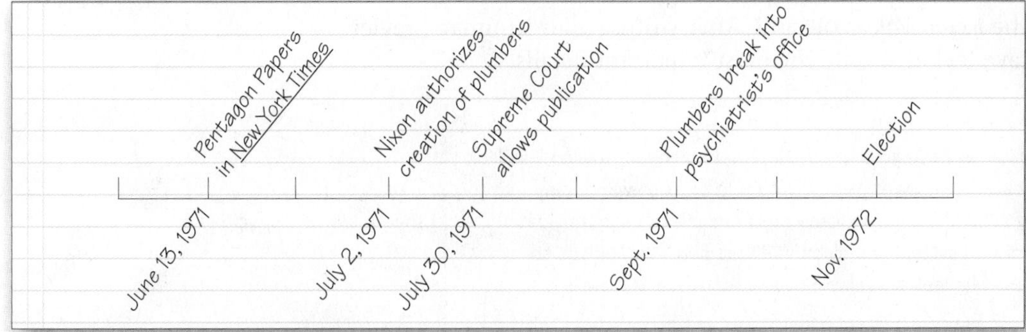

1.3 Clarifying; Summarizing

DEFINING THE SKILL

Clarifying means checking to be sure you clearly understand what you have read. One way to do this is by asking yourself questions. In your answers, you might restate in your own words what you have read.

When you **summarize,** you condense what you have read into fewer words, stating only the main idea and the most important supporting details. It is important to use your own words in a summary.

APPLYING THE SKILL

The excerpt below describes a major oil spill. Following the excerpt is a summary that condenses the key information in the passage into a few sentences.

HOW TO SUMMARIZE

Strategy 1 Look for topic sentences stating the main ideas. These are often at the beginning of a section or paragraph. In a summary, rewrite the main ideas in your own words.

Strategy 2 Include only the most important facts and statistics. Pay attention to numbers, dates, quantities, and other data.

Strategy 3 Clarify understanding by asking questions. Also, look up any words you do not recognize.

THE *EXXON VALDEZ* OIL SPILL

1 In March 1989, the oil tanker *Exxon Valdez* ran aground in Prince William Sound along the coast of Alaska, dumping about 2 11 million gallons of crude oil into the sea. Within days, 1,800 miles of coastline were fouled with thick black oil that coated rocks and beaches. At least 10 percent of the area's birds, sea otters, and other animals were killed, and commercial fisheries estimated that they would lose at least 50 percent of the season's catch.

The captain of the *Exxon Valdez* was found guilty of 3 negligence, and attempts were made to clean up the spill. 2 Ten years later, however, scientists found that pools of oil buried in coves were still poisoning shellfish, otters, and ducks, while several bird species failed to reproduce.

2 Between 1989 and 1994, Exxon spent about $2.1 billion in efforts to clean up Prince William Sound. In the meantime, some 34,000 commercial fishers and other Alaskans sued the company for damages, claiming that the oil spill had ruined their livelihoods.

Write a Summary

You can write your summary in a paragraph. The paragraph below summarizes the passage about the *Exxon Valdez* oil spill. After writing your summary, review it to see that you have included only the most important details.

In 1989, the *Exxon Valdez* ran aground off the Alaskan coast, spilling 11 million gallons of oil. The water and coastline for hundreds of miles were badly polluted, and many animals died. Alaskans sued the oil company for lost income. Exxon spent $2.1 billion for a cleanup effort and was subject to litigation from people who lost their livelihoods because of the spill.

1.4 Identifying Problems

DEFINING THE SKILL

Identifying problems means recognizing and understanding difficulties faced by particular people or groups at particular times. Being able to focus on specific problems helps historians understand the motives for actions and the forces underlying historical events.

APPLYING THE SKILL

The following passage tells about the experience of newcomers to Northern cities, like Boston and Philadelphia, in the late 1800s. Below the passage is a chart that organizes the information the passage contains.

HOW TO IDENTIFY PROBLEMS

Strategy 1 Look for problems that are implied but not stated. Problems are sometimes stated indirectly. This sentence implies that many immigrants settled in the cities because of limited opportunities elsewhere.

Strategy 2 Look for difficulties people faced.

Strategy 3 Evaluate solutions to problems.

Strategy 4 Recognize that sometimes the solution to one problem may cause another problem.

IMMIGRANT LIFE IN THE CITIES

1 The lure that drew many immigrants to America and its cities often was the same one that had attracted settlers to the West—opportunity. In the nation's industrialized centers people saw a chance to 2 escape poverty, find work, and carve out a better life.

Cities offered unskilled laborers steady jobs in mills and factories and provided the social support of neighborhoods of people with the same ethnic background. 3 Living among people who shared their background enabled the newcomers to speak their own language while learning about their new home. 4 Overcrowding soon became a problem, however—one that was intensified by the migration of people from America's rural areas.

Make a Chart

The chart below summarizes the problems and solutions in the passage. The chart details what the problems were, what steps people took to solve the problems, and how those solutions affected them.

Problems	Solutions	Outcomes
poverty	coming to U.S. cities	jobs available
lack of opportunity	coming to U.S. cities	jobs, housing, communities
lack of work skills	factory and mill jobs requiring low level of training	enough jobs for the time being
unfamiliarity with language	living in ethnic communities	community but overcrowding

1.5 Analyzing Motives

DEFINING THE SKILL

Analyzing motives in history means examining the reasons why a person, group, or government took a particular action. These reasons often go back to the needs, emotions, and prior experiences of the person or group, as well as their plans, circumstances, and objectives.

APPLYING THE SKILL

The following paragraphs tell how the early Mormons were treated and why they moved west in the mid-1800s. The diagram below the passage summarizes the Mormons' motives for that journey.

HOW TO ANALYZE MOTIVES

Strategy 1 Look for different kinds of motives. Some motives are negative, and others are positive.

Strategy 2 Look for the influence of important individuals or leaders in motivating others.

Strategy 3 Look for basic needs and human emotions as powerful motivators. Such needs and emotions include food and shelter, greed, ambition, compassion, and fear.

The Mormon Migration

Some of the Mormons' beliefs alarmed and angered other Americans. 1 Plagued by persecution and violence and seeking to convert Native Americans, Mormon church founder Joseph Smith led his followers west to a small community in Illinois. Conflict soon developed again when Smith allowed male members to have more than one wife. This idea infuriated many of Smith's neighbors, and he was eventually murdered by a mob.

2 The Mormons rallied around a new leader, Brigham Young, who urged them to move farther west. There they encountered a desert area near a salt lake, just beyond the mountains of what was then part of Mexico. The salty water was useless for crops and animals. Because the land was not desirable to others, 3 Young realized that his people might be safe there. The Mormons began to build Salt Lake City.

Make a Diagram

In the center of the diagram, list the important actions from the passage. Around it, list motives in different categories.

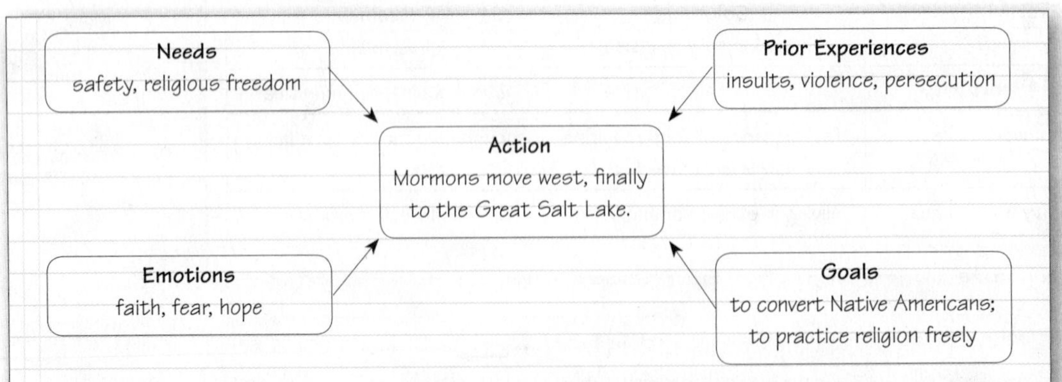

1.6 Analyzing Causes and Effects

DEFINING THE SKILL

A **cause** is an action in history that prompts something to happen. An **effect** is a historical event or condition that is the result of the cause. A single event may have several causes. It is also possible for one cause to result in several effects. Historians identify cause-and-effect relationships to help them understand why historical events took place.

APPLYING THE SKILL

The following paragraphs describe the early events leading to the Battle of Little Bighorn. The diagram that follows the passage summarizes the chain of causes and effects.

HOW TO IDENTIFY CAUSES AND EFFECTS

Strategy ❶ Look for reasons behind the events. Here the discovery of gold motivated white Americans to move into Sioux territory.

Strategy ❷ Look for clue words indicating cause. These include *because, due to, since,* and *therefore.*

Strategy ❸ Look for clue words indicating consequences. These include *brought about, led to, as a result, thus, consequently,* and *responded.* Remember that a cause may have several effects.

Broken Treaties

The Treaty of Fort Laramie (1868) had promised the Sioux that they could live forever in Paha Sapa, the Black Hills area of what is now South Dakota and Wyoming. The area was sacred to the Sioux. It was the center of their land and the place where warriors went to await visions from their guardian spirits.

Unfortunately for the Sioux, the Black Hills contained large deposits of gold. ❶ As soon as white Americans learned that gold had been discovered, they poured into the Native Americans' territory and began staking claims.

❷ Because the Sioux valued their land so highly, they appealed to the government to enforce the treaty terms and remove the miners. The government ❸ responded by offering to purchase the land from the Sioux. When the Sioux refused, the government sent in the Seventh Cavalry to remove the Native Americans.

Make a Cause-and-Effect Diagram

Starting with the first cause in a series, fill in the boxes until you reach the end result.

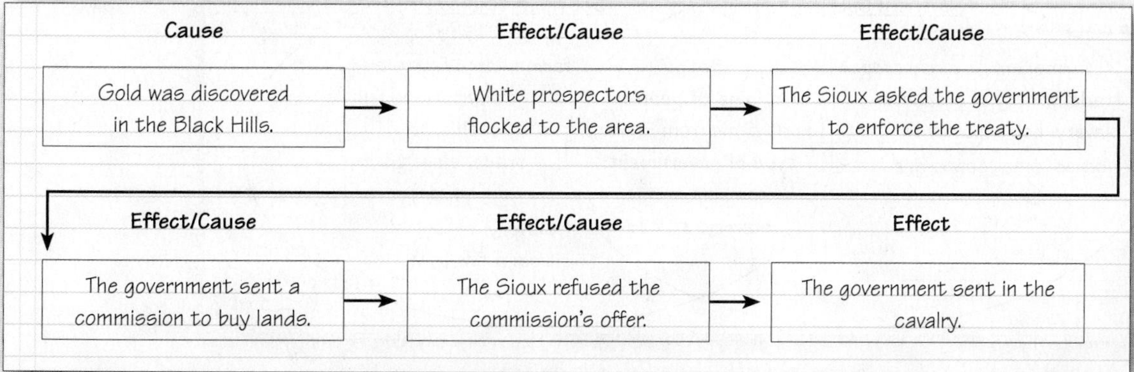
Cause
Gold was discovered in the Black Hills.
Effect/Cause
White prospectors flocked to the area.
Effect/Cause
The Sioux asked the government to enforce the treaty.
Effect/Cause
The government sent a commission to buy lands.
Effect/Cause
The Sioux refused the commission's offer.
Effect
The government sent in the cavalry.

1.7 Comparing; Contrasting

DEFINING THE SKILL

Comparing involves looking at the similarities and differences between two or more things. **Contrasting** means examining only the differences between them. Historians might compare and contrast events, personalities, beliefs, institutions, works of art, or many other types of things in order to give them a context for the period of history they are studying.

APPLYING THE SKILL

The following passage describes life in colonial America during the last half of the 1600s. The Venn diagram below shows the similarities and differences between the Northern and Southern colonies.

HOW TO COMPARE AND CONTRAST

Strategy (1) Look for clue words that show how two things differ. Clue words include *different, differ, unlike, by contrast, however,* and *on the other hand.*

Strategy (2) Look for clue words indicating that two things are alike. Clue words include *both, all, like, as, likewise,* and *similarly.*

Strategy (3) Look for features that two things have in common.

Life in the Early American Colonies

Not long after the English colonies were established, it became apparent that two very (1) different ways of life were developing in the Northern and Southern colonies. In the South, both (2) rich plantation owners and poorer frontier farmers sought land. Virginia and Maryland became known as the tobacco colonies. (3) Large farms, but few towns, appeared there.

Slavery existed in (3) all the colonies, but it became a vital source of labor in the South. (1) By contrast, the New England and middle colonies did not rely on slave labor or single staple crops, such as tobacco or rice. Most people were farmers, but they grew a wide variety of crops. The New England colonies traded actively with the islands of the West Indies. In addition to foods, they exported all kinds of other items, ranging from barrels to horses. In return, they imported sugar and molasses. (3) All this trade resulted in the growth of small towns and larger port cities.

Make a Venn Diagram

Use the two ovals to contrast the Northern and Southern colonies and the overlapping area to show what the two regions have in common.

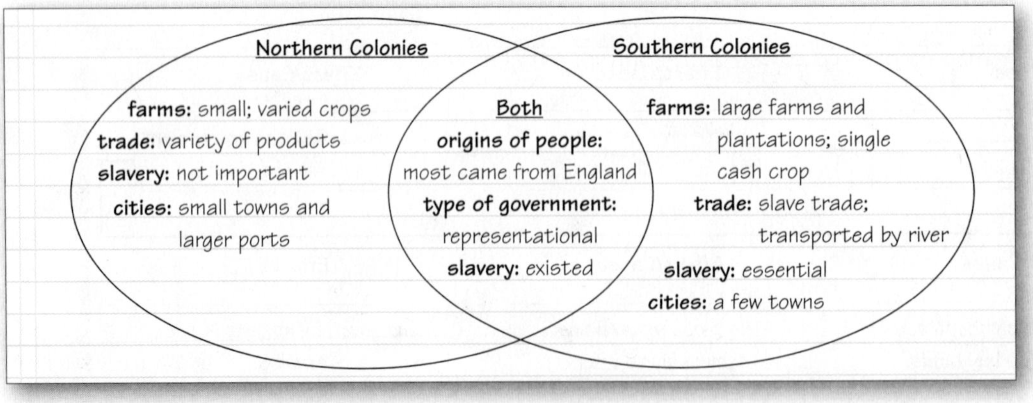

Northern Colonies
farms: small; varied crops
trade: variety of products
slavery: not important
cities: small towns and larger ports

Both
origins of people: most came from England
type of government: representational
slavery: existed

Southern Colonies
farms: large farms and plantations; single cash crop
trade: slave trade; transported by river
slavery: essential
cities: a few towns

1.8 Distinguishing Fact from Opinion

DEFINING THE SKILL

Facts are dates, statistics, and accounts of events, or they are statements that are generally known to be true. Facts can be checked for accuracy.
Opinions are the judgments, beliefs, and feelings of a writer or speaker.

APPLYING THE SKILL

The following excerpt describes the 1886 Haymarket affair in Chicago. The chart summarizes the facts and opinions.

HOW TO DISTINGUISH FACT FROM OPINION

Strategy ❶ Look for specific events, dates, and statistics that can be verified.

Strategy ❷ Look for assertions, claims, hypotheses, and judgments. Here a speaker at the event is expressing an opinion.

Strategy ❸ Look for judgments the historian makes about events. Here the writer states the opinion that the event was a disaster and then backs up this opinion by explaining the negative consequences of the event.

The Haymarket Affair

❶ At ten o'clock another speaker stepped forward, the main burden of his address being that ❷ there was no hope of improving the condition of workingmen through legislation; it must be through their own efforts. . . .

The speaker hurried to a conclusion, but at that point 180 police officers entered the square and headed for the wagon that had served as a speakers' platform. The captain in charge called on the meeting to disperse. . . .

❶ At that moment someone threw a bomb into the ranks of the policemen gathered about the speakers. After the initial shock and horror, the police opened fire on the 300 or 400 people who remained. One policeman had been killed by the bomb, and more than 60 injured. One member of the crowd was killed by police fire, and at least 12 were wounded. . . .

❸ In almost every . . . way Haymarket was a disaster. It vastly augmented [increased] the already considerable paranoia of most Americans in regard to anarchists, socialists, communists, and radicals in general. It increased hostility toward . . . foreigners. . . . It caused a serious impairment of freedom of speech in every part of the country.

Source: Page Smith, *The Rise of Industrial America* (New York: Penguin, 1990), pp. 244–256.

Make a Chart

List the facts you learn in a passage as well as the opinions that are expressed.

Facts	Opinions
Just after 10:00, as a speaker was finishing up, someone threw a bomb into the group of 180 policemen surrounding the speakers. More than 60 police were injured, and about 13 civilians were injured or killed when police fired into the crowd.	speaker: Workers must improve their own situations since legislation can't do it for them. historian: Nothing good came of the Haymarket affair; and in fact it had many negative consequences: • increased paranoia about radicals • increased hostility toward foreigners • impaired freedom of speech

1.9 Making Inferences

DEFINING THE SKILL

Making inferences from a piece of historical writing means drawing conclusions based on facts, examples, opinions, and the author's use of language. To make inferences, use clues in the text and your own personal experience, historical knowledge, and common sense.

APPLYING THE SKILL

The following passage is from a speech by President Ronald Reagan promoting his economic program. The chart below lists some inferences that can be drawn from the first paragraph.

HOW TO MAKE INFERENCES

Strategy 1 From the facts in the text and historical knowledge, you can infer that Reagan is blaming the Democrats for the poor economy.

Strategy 2 Look for clues about the writer's opinion. From Reagan's language and the goals of his program, you can infer that he sees government spending and taxation as a major cause of the economic crisis.

Strategy 3 Note opinionated language. You can infer from words such as *exaggerated* and *inaccurate* that Reagan disagrees with criticism of his plan.

On the Program for Economic Recovery

1 All of us are aware of the punishing inflation which has for the first time in 60 years held to double-digit figures for 2 years in a row. Interest rates have reached absurd levels of more than 20 percent and over 15 percent for those who would borrow to buy a home. . . . Almost 8 million Americans are out of work. . . .

2 I am proposing a comprehensive four-point program . . . aimed at reducing the growth in government spending and taxing, reforming and eliminating regulations which are unnecessary and unproductive or counterproductive, and encouraging a consistent monetary policy aimed at maintaining the value of the currency.

Now, I know that 3 exaggerated and inaccurate stories about these cuts have disturbed many people. . . . Those who, through no fault of their own, must depend on the rest of us—the poverty stricken, the disabled, the elderly, all those with true need—can rest assured that the social safety net of programs they depend on are exempt from any cuts.

Make a Chart

Record clues in the text as well as what you know about the topic on the basis of your own experience, knowledge, and common sense.

Clues in the Text: Facts, Examples, Language	Personal Experience, Historical Knowledge, Common Sense	Inference
• inflation in double digits • Interest rates over 20% • 8 milion unemployed • Inflation is "punishing" • Interest rates "absurd"	• Reagan defeated Democratic incumbent Jimmy Carter in the 1980 election.	Reagan blames the Democrats for the current economic problems.

2.1 Developing Historical Perspective

DEFINING THE SKILL

Historical perspective is an understanding of events and people in the context of their times. Using historical perspective can help you avoid judging the past solely in terms of present-day norms and values.

APPLYING THE SKILL

The following passage is the opening portion of an address by President Theodore Roosevelt. Below it is a chart that summarizes the information from a historical perspective.

HOW TO DEVELOP HISTORICAL PERSPECTIVE

Strategy ❶ Identify any historical figures, occasions, events, and dates.

Strategy ❷ Notice words, phrases, and settings that reflect the period. Here the language used by the president reflects the optimism of the Progressive Era.

Strategy ❸ Explain how people's actions and words reflect attitudes, values, and passions of the era. Here Roosevelt equates a strong nation with "manly virtues."

❶ INAUGURAL ADDRESS, 1905
President Theodore Roosevelt

My fellow-citizens, no people on earth have more cause to be thankful than ours, and this is said . . . with gratitude to the Giver of Good who has blessed us with the conditions which have enabled us to achieve so large a measure of well-being and happiness. To us as a people it has been granted to lay the foundations of our national life in a ❷ new continent. We are the ❷ heirs of the ages, and yet we have had to pay few of the penalties which in old countries are exacted by the dead hand of a bygone civilization. We have not been obliged to fight for our existence against any alien race; and yet our life has called for the ❸ vigor and effort without which the manlier and hardier virtues wither away. . . . [The] success which we confidently believe the future will bring, should cause in us no feeling of vainglory, but rather a deep and abiding realization of all which life has offered us; a full acknowledgment of the responsibility which is ours; and a fixed determination to show that under a free government a mighty people can thrive best, alike as regards the things of the body and the things of the soul.

Write a Summary

In a chart, list key words, phrases, and details from the passage, and then write a short paragraph summarizing the basic values and attitudes it conveys.

Key Phrases	Attitudes	Roosevelt's Inaugural Address
• Giver of Good • blessed us • heirs of the ages • bygone civilization • manlier and hardier virtues • mighty people • things of the body and things of the soul	• belief in God • optimistic about the future • grateful for the past	Theodore Roosevelt reveals a strong and resilient optimism about the American nation. His confidence is grounded in deep religious faith in God (the "Giver of Good") and God's plan for the nation. Roosevelt clearly believes in the ability of the American people to solve whatever problems they face as they move into a bright future. Roosevelt's faith and appeal to the manly virtues reflects typical attitudes and values of the 19th- and early 20th-century Americans.

2.2 Formulating Historical Questions

DEFINING THE SKILL

Formulating historical questions entails asking questions about events and trends—what caused them, what made them important, and so forth. The ability to formulate historical questions is an important step in doing research. Formulating questions will help you to guide and focus your research as well as to understand maps, graphs, and other historical sources.

APPLYING THE SKILL

At a women's rights convention in the mid-1800s, the delegates adopted a "Declaration of Sentiments" that set forth a number of grievances. The following passage is a description of that event. Below is a web diagram that organizes historical questions about the event.

HOW TO FORMULATE HISTORICAL QUESTIONS

Strategy 1 Ask about the basic facts of the event. Who were the leaders? What did they do? Where and when did the event take place?

Strategy 2 Ask about the cause of an event. Why did an event take place?

Strategy 3 Ask about historical influences on a speaker or event. What other historical events was it similar to? How was it different?

Strategy 4 Ask about the results produced by various causes. What were the results of the event?

Seneca Falls, 1848

1 Elizabeth Cady Stanton and Lucretia Mott decided to act on their resolution to hold a women's rights convention. In 1848, more than 300 women and men convened at Seneca Falls, New York, the small town that gave the convention its name. Before the convention, Stanton and Mott spent a day composing an agenda and a 2 detailed statement of grievances. Stanton carefully modeled this "Declaration of Sentiments" on the 3 Declaration of Independence. 4 The participants approved all measures unanimously, except for one: women's right to vote. This measure passed by a narow margin due to Stanton's insistence. The franchise for women, though it passed, remained a controversial topic.

Make a Web Diagram

Using a web diagram, ask a broad question about the event described above. Then ask specific questions to help you explore the first.

2.3 Hypothesizing

DEFINING THE SKILL

Hypothesizing means developing a possible explanation for historical events. A hypothesis is a tentative assumption about what happened in the past or what might happen in the future. A hypothesis takes available information, links it to previous experience and knowledge, and comes up with a possible explanation, conclusion, or prediction.

APPLYING THE SKILL

As the Cold War came to an end, people offered various hypotheses to explain why the Soviet Union broke up and to predict what would replace it. Read this passage and form your own hypothesis. Below the passage is a chart that presents a hypothesis and the facts used to support it.

HOW TO FORM A HYPOTHESIS

Strategy ❶ Identify the events, pattern, or trend you want to explain. Develop a hypothesis that might explain the event. You might hypothesize that Gorbachev's new policies would deeply affect politics in the Soviet Union and Eastern Europe.

Strategy ❷ Determine what facts you have about the situation. These facts support various hypotheses about how Gorbachev's policies affected politics both inside and outside the Soviet Union.

The Cold War Ends

In March 1985, Mikhail Gorbachev became the general secretary of the Communist Party in the Soviet Union. ❶ He initiated a new policy of openness and reform within the USSR, putting an end to the collective ownership of resources, most government censorship, and controlled elections. ❷ A dramatic increase in nationalism on the part of the non-Russian republics followed the open elections, and in December 1991, all republics except Russia declared independence. ❷ The USSR was replaced by a loose federation of 12 republics called the Commonwealth of Independent States. ❷ Gorbachev's new policies led to massive changes in Eastern Europe, as the satellite states, with his encouragement, moved toward democracy.

Make a Chart

Use a chart to summarize your hypothesis about Gorbachev's reforms and the facts that support it. Then you can see what additional information you need to help prove or disprove it.

Hypothesis	Facts that support the hypothesis	Additional information needed
Gorbachev's new policies would help lead to Western victory in the Cold War.	• increase in nationalism in non-Russian republics • USSR replaced by a loose federation • Satellite states moved towards democracy	• Were democratic reforms put into effect? • Did free elections result in greater stability? • Did the end of collective ownership advance private enterprise?

2.4 Analyzing Issues

DEFINING THE SKILL

Analyzing issues in history means taking apart complicated issues to identify the different points of view in economic, social, political, or moral debates.

APPLYING THE SKILL

The following passage describes working conditions in U.S. factories in the late 1800s and early 1900s. Notice how the cluster diagram below it helps you to analyze the issue of child labor.

HOW TO ANALYZE ISSUES

Strategy 1 Identify the central point of view and how it is defended.

Strategy 2 Look for facts and statistics. The numbers supplied by facts and statistics can help you decide on a position.

Strategy 3 Look for the other side to an issue. You need to look at all sides of an issue before deciding what you think.

Children at Work

1 Wages for most factory workers were so low that many families could not survive unless all their members, including children, worked. 2 Between 1890 and 1910, 20 percent of boys and 10 percent of girls under age 15—some as young as five years old—held full-time jobs. 2 A typical work week was 12 hours a day, six days a week. Many of these children worked from dawn to dusk, wasted by hunger and exhaustion that made them prone to crippling accidents. With little time or energy left for school, child laborers gave up their futures to help their families make ends meet.

3 Nonetheless, factory owners and some parents praised child labor for keeping children out of mischief. They believed that idleness for children was bad and that work provided healthy occupation. Meanwhile, the reformer Jacob Riis and others worked for decent conditions, better wages, and laws that restricted child labor.

Make a Cluster Diagram

In order to better analyze an issue, make a diagram and distinguish the facts as well as the different points of view.

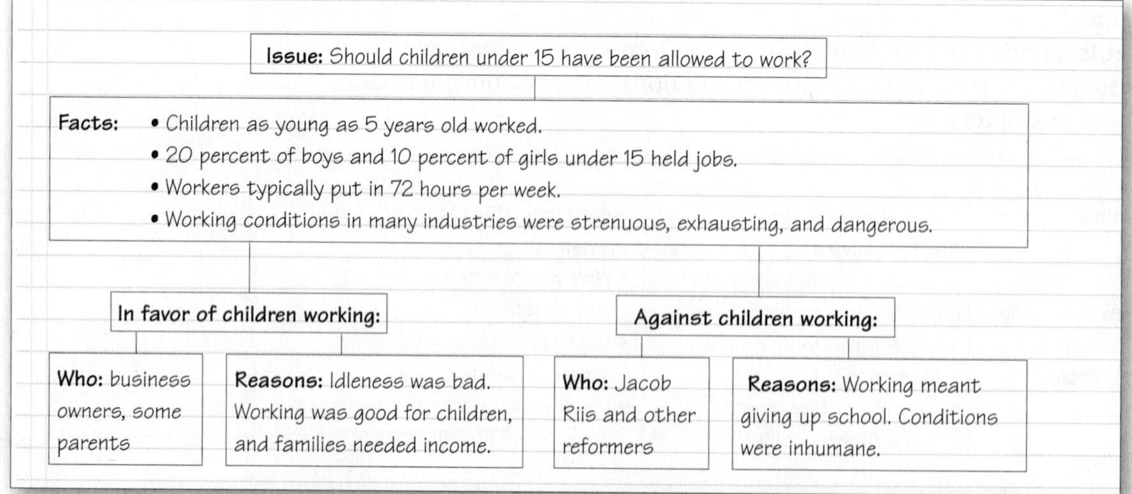

Issue: Should children under 15 have been allowed to work?
Facts:
• Children as young as 5 years old worked.
• 20 percent of boys and 10 percent of girls under 15 held jobs.
• Workers typically put in 72 hours per week.
• Working conditions in many industries were strenuous, exhausting, and dangerous.
In favor of children working:
Who: business owners, some parents
Reasons: Idleness was bad. Working was good for children, and families needed income.
Against children working:
Who: Jacob Riis and other reformers
Reasons: Working meant giving up school. Conditions were inhumane.

2.5 Analyzing Assumptions and Biases

DEFINING THE SKILL

An **assumption** is a belief or an idea that is taken for granted. Some assumptions are based on evidence; some are based on feelings. A **bias** is a prejudiced point of view. Historical accounts that are biased reflect the personal prejudices of the author or historian and tend to be one-sided.

APPLYING THE SKILL

The following passage is from *The Americans at Home* by the Scottish minister David Macrae, who wrote the book after visiting the United States in the 1860s. The chart below the excerpt helps to summarize information about the writer's assumptions and biases.

HOW TO ANALYZE ASSUMPTIONS AND BIASES

Strategy 1 Identify the author and information about him or her. Does the author belong to a special-interest group, religious organization, political party, or social movement that might promote a one-sided or slanted viewpoint on the subject?

Strategy 2 Examine the evidence. Is what the author relates consistent with other accounts or supported by factual data?

Strategy 3 Look for words, phrases, statements, or images that might convey a positive or negative slant, and thus reveal the author's bias.

The Americans at Home

1 by David Macrae

[T]he American girls are very delightful. 2 And in one point they fairly surpass the majority of English girls—they are all educated and well informed. . . . The admirable educational system . . . covering the whole area of society, has given them education whether they are rich or poor, has furnished them with a great deal of information, and has quickened their desire for more. . . . 3 Their tendency is perhaps to talk too much, and . . . it seemed to me sometimes to make no perceptible difference whether they knew anything of the subject they talked about or not. But they usually know a little of everything; and their general intelligence and vivacity make them very delightful companions.

Make a Chart

For each of the heads listed on the left-hand side of the chart, summarize what information you can find in the passage.

David Macrae's Impression of American Girls	
speaker	David Macrae
date	1860s
occasion	Macrae's visit to the United States
tone	humorous, light-hearted
assumptions	The author assumes that girls are to be measured by companionship abilities.
bias	The author seems to have a prejudice that girls are inferior to boys or men.

2.6 Evaluating Decisions and Courses of Action

DEFINING THE SKILL

Evaluating decisions means making judgments about the decisions that historical figures made. Historians evaluate decisions on the basis of their moral implications and their costs and benefits from different points of view. **Evaluating alternative courses** of action means carefully judging the choices that historical figures had in order to better understand why they made the decisions they did.

APPLYING THE SKILL

The following passage describes the decisions President John F. Kennedy had to make when he learned of Soviet missile bases in Cuba. Below the passage is a chart in which one possible alternative decision is analyzed.

HOW TO EVALUATE DECISIONS

Strategy 1 Look at decisions made by individuals or by groups. Notice the decisions Kennedy made in response to Soviet actions.

Strategy 2 Look at the outcome of the decisions.

Strategy 3 Analyze a decision in terms of the alternatives that were possible. Both Kennedy and Khrushchev faced the alternatives of either escalating or defusing the crisis.

The Cuban Missile Crisis

During the summer of 1962, the flow of Soviet weapons into Cuba—including nuclear missiles—greatly increased. (1) President Kennedy responded cautiously at first, issuing a warning that the United States would not tolerate the presence of offensive nuclear weapons in Cuba.

(1) On the evening of October 22, after the president learned that the Soviets were building missile bases in Cuba, he delivered a public ultimatum: any missile attack from Cuba would trigger an all-out attack on the Soviet Union. Soviet ships continued to head toward the island, while the U.S. military prepared to invade Cuba. To avoid confrontation, (2) the Soviet premier, Khrushchev, offered to remove the missiles from Cuba in exchange for a pledge not to invade the island. Kennedy agreed, and the crisis ended.

(3) Some people criticized Kennedy for practicing brinkmanship when private talks might have resolved the crisis without the threat of nuclear war. Others believed he had been too soft and had passed up an ideal chance to invade Cuba and to oust its communist leader, Fidel Castro.

Make a Chart

Make a chart evaluating an alternative course of action regarding the Cuban missile crisis based on its possible pros and cons.

alternative	pros	cons	evaluation
Negotiate a settlement quietly without threatening nuclear war.	1. Avoid the threat of nuclear war 2. Avoid frightening U.S. citizens	1. The U.S. would not look like a strong world leader. 2. The government would lose favor with Cuban exiles living in the U.S.	your answer: Would this have been a good choice? Why or why not?

2.7 Forming Opinions (Evaluating)

DEFINING THE SKILL

Forming opinions, or evaluating, means deciding what your own thoughts or feelings are and making judgments about events and people in history. Opinions should be supported with facts and examples.

APPLYING THE SKILL

The following passage includes comments on the French Revolution by Gouverneur Morris, one of the participants in the Constitutional Convention, and by Thomas Jefferson.

HOW TO FORM AN OPINION AND SUPPORT IT WITH FACTS

Strategy 1 Decide what you think about a subject after reading all the information available to you. After reading this description, you might decide that political causes either do or do not sometimes justify violence.

Strategy 2 Support your opinion with facts, quotations, and examples, including references to similar events in other historical eras.

Strategy 3 Look for the opinions of historians and other experts. Consider their opinions when forming your own.

A Scene of Mob Violence

Gouverneur Morris was a visitor to Paris during the early days of the French Revolution. In the following journal entry he describes a scene of revolutionary mob violence: **1** "The head and body of Mr. de Foulon are introduced in triumph. . . . His crime [was] to have accepted a place in the Ministry. This mutilated form of an old man of seventy-five is shown to Bertier, his son-in-law, the intend't. [another official] of Paris, and afterwards **2** he also is put to death and cut to pieces. . . ." Such violence was common during the French Revolution and shocked a good many Americans. **3** However, Thomas Jefferson was a supporter of the Revolution, saying, "The liberty of the whole earth was depending on the issue of the contest, and . . . rather than it should have failed, I would have seen half the earth desolated."

Make a Chart

Summarize your opinion and supporting information in a chart. List facts, quotations, and examples.

Opinion: The French Revolution was especially violent and cruel.		
facts:	**quotations:**	**examples:**
• Violence escalated. • Jacobins launched Reign of Terror. • Moderates sent to guillotine. • Jacobins declared war on other countries.	"he also is put to death and cut to pieces"	Jacobins beheaded Louis XVI

2.8 Drawing Conclusions

DEFINING THE SKILL

Drawing conclusions involves considering the implications of what you have read and forming a final statement about its meaning or consequences. To draw conclusions, you need to look closely at facts and then use your own experience and common sense to decide what those facts mean.

APPLYING THE SKILL

The following passage tells about employment trends in the 1990s. The highlighted text indicates information from which conclusions can be drawn. In the diagram below, the information and conclusions are organized in a clear way.

HOW TO DRAW CONCLUSIONS

Strategy ❶ Use the facts to draw a conclusion. Conclusion: In general, the economy was good in the mid-1990s.

Strategy ❷ Read carefully to understand all the facts. Conclusion: Income expectations were lower.

Strategy ❸ Ask questions of the material. How did the use of temporary workers affect job security? (It reduced it.) What did employment statistics for young people indicate? (Jobs were harder for young people to find.)

Job Outlook in the Mid-1990s

Several trends emerged in the workplace of the 1990s. ❶ Inflation was at its lowest level since the 1960s, and 10 million new jobs created between 1993 and 1996 helped lower the unemployment rate to 5.1 percent in 1996. ❷ Median household income adjusted for inflation, however, declined from $33,585 to $31,241, even though there were many households in which both parents worked.

In addition, ❸ many jobs once done by permanent employees of a company were done by temporary workers, who were paid only for the time they were needed and who typically received no benefits. Three out of four young Americans thought they would earn less in their lifetimes than their parents did. Unemployment in their age group continued at the same rate, while the unemployment rate for other adults had fallen. ❸ In 1993, about one in seven workers between the ages of 16 and 25 was out of work, double the national average.

Make a Diagram

Summarize the data and your conclusion about the above passage in a diagram.

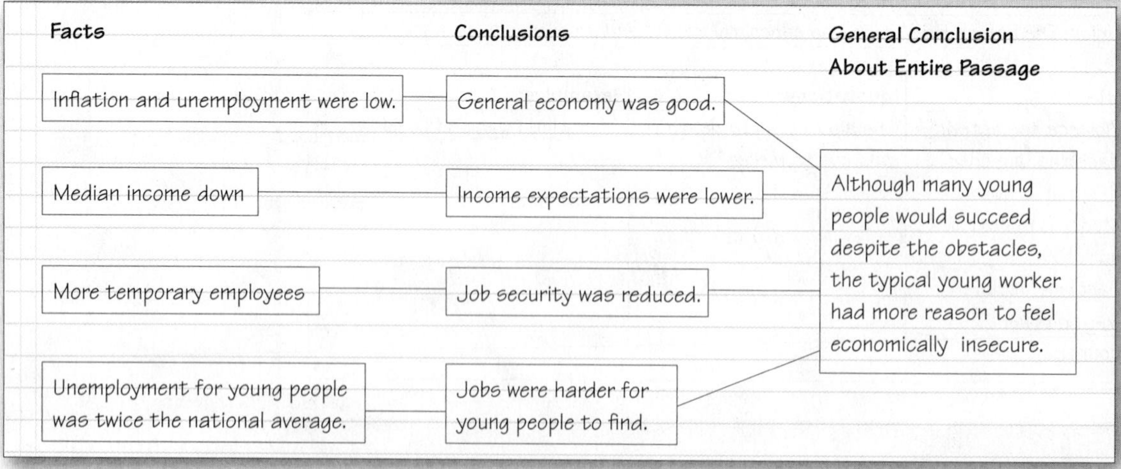
Facts
Conclusions
General Conclusion About Entire Passage
Inflation and unemployment were low.
General economy was good.
Median income down
Income expectations were lower.
More temporary employees
Job security was reduced.
Unemployment for young people was twice the national average.
Jobs were harder for young people to find.
Although many young people would succeed despite the obstacles, the typical young worker had more reason to feel economically insecure.

2.9 Synthesizing

DEFINING THE SKILL

Synthesizing is the skill historians use in developing interpretations of the past. Like detective work, synthesizing involves putting together clues, information, and ideas to form an overall picture of a historical event.

APPLYING THE SKILL

The following passage describes the earliest inhabitants of the Americas. The highlighted text indicates how some information leads toward a synthesis—an overall picture.

HOW TO SYNTHESIZE

Strategy 1 Read carefully to understand the facts.

Strategy 2 Look for explanations that link the facts together. This assertion is based on the evidence provided in the next couple of sentences.

Strategy 3 Consider what you already know in order to accept statements as reasonable.

Strategy 4 Bring together the information you have gathered to arrive at a new understanding of the subject.

The First Americans

From the (1) discovery of chiseled arrowheads and charred bones at ancient sites, it appears that the earliest Americans lived as big-game hunters. (2) People gradually shifted to hunting smaller game and gathering available plants. They collected nuts and wild rice. They invented snares, as well as bows and arrows, to hunt small animals, and they wove nets to catch fish.

Between 10,000 and 15,000 years ago, a revolution took place in what is now central Mexico. (3) People began to raise plants as food. Maize may have been the first domesticated plant. Agriculture eventually spread to other regions.

The rise of agriculture brought tremendous changes to the Americas. Agriculture made it possible for people to remain in one place. It also enabled them to accumulate and store surplus food. As their surplus increased, people had the time to develop skills and more complex ideas about the world. (4) From this agricultural base rose larger, more stable, and increasingly complex societies.

Make a Cluster Diagram

Use a cluster diagram to organize the facts, opinions, examples, and interpretations that you have brought together to form a synthesis.

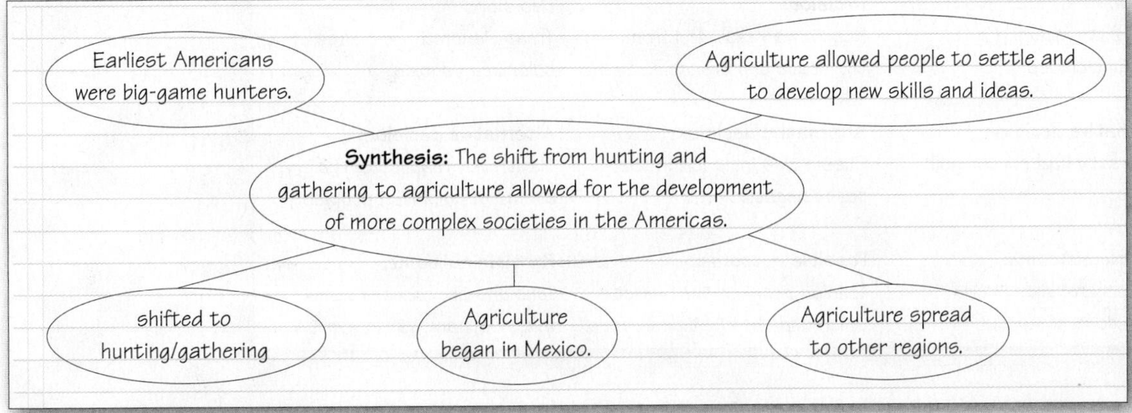

2.10 Making Predictions

DEFINING THE SKILL

Making predictions entails identifying situations that leaders or groups face or have faced in the past, and then suggesting what course of action they might take as well as what might happen as a result of that action. Making predictions about the effects of past events helps you to understand how events in the past shape the future. Making predictions about the effects of proposed actions, such as proposed legislation, helps you to evaluate possible courses of action.

APPLYING THE SKILL

The following passage discusses the central weaknesses of the Treaty of Versailles, which ended World War I. Below the passage is a chart that lists decisions made by those who framed the treaty, along with alternative decisions and predictions of possible outcomes.

HOW TO MAKE PREDICTIONS

Strategy ❶ Identify the decisions.

Strategy ❷ Decide what other decisions might have been made.

Strategy ❸ Predict the outcomes of the alternative decisions.

Weaknesses of the Treaty of Versailles

❶ First, the treaty humiliated Germany. The war-guilt clause, which forced Germany to accept blame for the war and pay financial reparations, caused Germans of all political viewpoints to detest the treaty.

❷ Second, Russia, which had fought with the Allies, was excluded from the peace conference. Russia had suffered almost the same number of casualties as Germany—the two countries had by far the highest casualty rates of the war. Russia lost more territory than Germany did. The Union of Soviet Socialist Republics, as Russia was called after 1922, grew determined to regain its lost territory.

❸ Third, the treaty ignored the claims of colonized people for self-determination. For example, the Allies dismissed the claims of the Vietnamese, who wanted freedom from French colonial rule.

Make a Chart

Record decisions made as well as alternative decisions and possible outcomes.

Decision: The treaty included a war-guilt clause.	**Decision:** Russia was excluded from the peace conference.	**Decision:** Treaty ignored the claims of colonized peoples.
Alternative decision: The treaty had no war-guilt clause.	**Alternative decision:** Russia was included in the peace negotiations.	**Alternative decision:** The treaty respected the claims of colonized peoples.
Possible outcome: Germany rebuilds. World War II does not occur.	**Possible outcome:** Tension between the Soviet Union and the West decreases.	**Possible outcome:** Tensions are reduced worldwide; Vietnam War is averted.

2.11 Forming Generalizations

DEFINING THE SKILL

Forming generalizations means making broad judgments based on the information in texts. When you form generalizations, you need to be sure they are valid. They must be based on sufficient evidence, and they must be consistent with the information given.

APPLYING THE SKILL

The following three excerpts deal with Herbert Hoover and his relation to the Great Depression. Notice how the information in the web diagram below supports the generalization drawn.

HOW TO FORM GENERALIZATIONS

Strategy 1 Determine what information the sources have in common. All the sources suggest that people blamed Hoover for the Great Depression.

Strategy 2 State your generalization in sentence form. A generalization often needs a qualifying word, such as *most*, *many*, or *some*, to make it valid.

On President Hoover and the Great Depression

1 "By 1930, people were calling the shantytowns in American cities Hoovervilles. . . . Homeless people called the newspapers in which they wrapped themselves 'Hoover blankets.' Empty pockets turned inside out were 'Hoover flags.'"

—*The Americans*

"[My aunt] told me . . . . 1 People were starving because of Herbert Hoover. My mother was out of work because of Herbert Hoover. Men were killing themselves because of Herbert Hoover."

—Russell Baker

1 "If someone bit an apple and found a worm in it, Hoover would get the blame."

—Will Rogers

Make a Web Diagram

Use a web diagram to record relevant information and make a valid generalization.

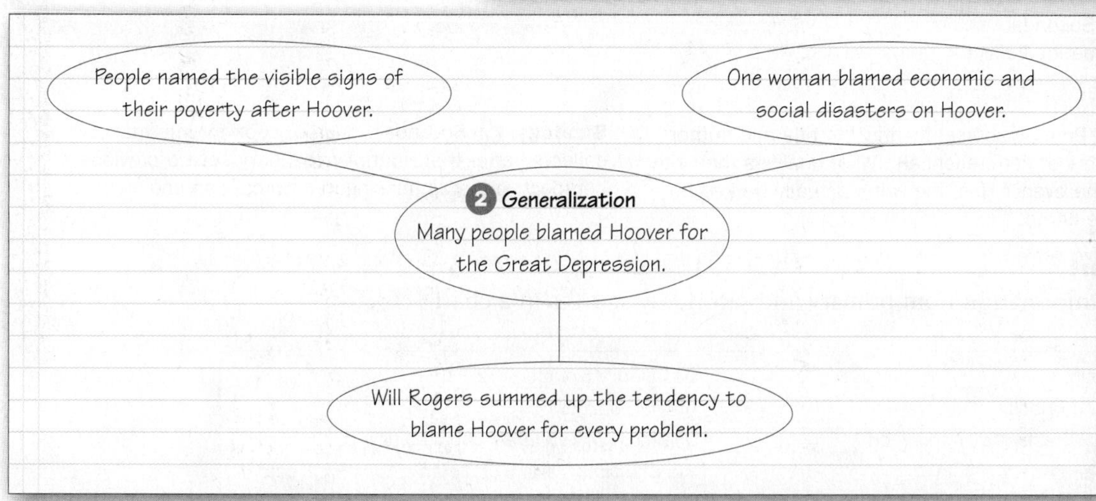
People named the visible signs of their poverty after Hoover.
One woman blamed economic and social disasters on Hoover.
2 Generalization
Many people blamed Hoover for the Great Depression.
Will Rogers summed up the tendency to blame Hoover for every problem.

3.1 Primary and Secondary Sources

DEFINING THE SKILL

Primary sources are accounts written or created by people who were present at historical events, either as participants or as observers. These include letters, diaries, journals, speeches, some news articles, eyewitness accounts, government data, statutes, court opinions, and autobiographies.

Secondary sources are based on primary sources and are produced by people who were not present at the original events. They often combine information from a number of different accounts. Secondary sources include history books, historical essays, some news articles, and biographies.

APPLYING THE SKILL

The following passage describes the explosion of the first atomic bomb in 1945. It is mainly a secondary source, but it quotes an eyewitness account that is a primary source.

❶

The First Atomic Bomb

As the time to test the bomb drew near, the air around Los Alamos crackled with rumors and fears. ❷ At one end of the scale were fears that the bomb wouldn't work at all. At the other end was the prediction that the explosion would set fire to the atmosphere, which would mean the end of the earth.

On July 16, 1945, the first atomic bomb was detonated in the desert near Alamogordo, New Mexico. ❸ In his book *What Little I Remember*, Otto Frisch, a Manhattan Project scientist, described what happened next:

"[T]hat object on the horizon which looked like a small sun was still too bright to look at. . . . After another ten seconds or so it had grown and . . . was slowly rising into the sky from the ground, with which it remained connected by a lengthening grey stem of swirling dust. . . ."

❹ That blinding flash was followed by a deafening roar as a tremendous shock wave rolled across the trembling desert. The bomb not only worked, but it was more powerful than most had dared hope.

HOW TO LOCATE AND IDENTIFY PRIMARY AND SECONDARY SOURCES

Strategy ❶ Locating sources: The catalog in your school library or a local public library lists resources alphabetically by subject, title, and author. Most of these are secondary sources but may contain copies or excerpts of primary sources. Articles in a general encyclopedia such as *World Book* or *Encyclopedia Americana* can give you an overview of a topic and usually provide references to additional sources.

Strategy ❷ Secondary source: Look for information collected from several sources.

Strategy ❸ Primary source: Identify the title and author and evaluate his or her credentials. What qualifies the writer to report on the event? Here the writer actually worked on developing the bomb.

Strategy ❹ Secondary source: Look for information collected after the event. A secondary source provides a perspective that is missing in a primary source.

Make a Chart

Summarize information from primary and secondary sources in a chart.

Primary Source	Secondary Source
Author: Otto Frisch	Author: unknown
Qualifications: scientist working on Manhattan Project	Qualifications; had access to multiple accounts of the time leading up to and following event
Information: detailed description, sensory observations, feeling of awe	Information: description of range of points of view and of information available only after event

3.2 Visual, Audio, Multimedia Sources

DEFINING THE SKILL

Visual sources can be paintings, illustrations, photographs, political cartoons, and advertisements. **Audio sources** include recorded speeches, interviews, press conferences, and radio programs. Movies, CD-ROMs, television, and computer software are the newest kind of historical sources, called **multimedia sources.** These sources are rich with historical details and sometimes convey the feelings and points of view of an era better than words do.

APPLYING THE SKILL

The following photograph shows a group of college students and civil rights activists joined in song as they protest unfair voting laws in 1964.

1 In the summer of 1964, college students volunteered to go to Mississippi to help register that state's African-American voters.

HOW TO INTERPRET VISUAL SOURCES

Strategy 1 Identify the subject and the source. A title or caption often gives a description of a photo or other visual source. This photograph shows volunteers who worked in the 1964 voting rights drive in Mississippi.

Strategy 2 Identify important visual details. In this photograph, white and black college students are holding hands and singing. Behind them is a bus.

Strategy 3 Make inferences from the visual details. Holding hands and singing together suggest fellowship and unity—the students are showing solidarity in the fight for civil rights.

Make a Chart

Summarize your interpretation of the photograph in a simple chart.

Subject	A diverse group of college students.
Details	Bus, joined hands, white and black Americans side by side, singing
Inferences	The subjects share a belief in racial equality, freedom, and solidarity. Some or all of the group may have traveled to Mississippi together on the bus.

3.3 Analyzing Political Cartoons

DEFINING THE SKILL

Political cartoons use humor to make a serious point. Political cartoons often express a point of view on an issue better than words do. Understanding signs and symbols will help you to interpret political cartoons.

Like many text sources that express a point of view, cartoons are often **biased,** or unfairly weighted toward one point of view. To identify a cartoon's bias, look for exaggerations and caricature. Try to restate the message of the cartoon in words, then identify overgeneralizations and opinions stated as facts.

APPLYING THE SKILL

The following political cartoon shows President Calvin Coolidge playing the saxophone while big business dances. The chart below it summarizes historical information gained from interpreting the visual source.

HOW TO INTERPRET VISUAL SOURCES

Strategy 1 Identify the subject. This cartoon deals with President Calvin Coolidge's relationship with big business.

Strategy 2 Identify important symbols and details. Big business is shown as a carefree flapper of the 1920s. The president's saxophone is labeled "Praise," suggesting his positive attitude toward the fun-loving flapper.

Strategy 3 Interpret the message. The image implies that serving big business interests is important to the president.

Strategy 4 Analyze the point of view. The cartoonist suggests that the relationship between the president and big business is too cozy.

Strategy 5 Identify bias. The president is caricatured by being depicted engaging in frivolity and at the service of big business. The cartoon charges that the president does not take his responsibilities seriously.

Make a Chart

Summarize your interpretation of the cartoon in a simple chart.

Subject: Coolidge's Relationship with big business		
Point of View	**Symbols/Details**	**Message**
Satirical of the Coolidge administration and of big business	Flapper: big business, carefree and overgrown	Big business and the president are too close. Business is having too good a time—with the president's help.
	President: playing a tune for business	

3.4 Interpreting Maps

DEFINING THE SKILL

Maps are representations of features on the earth's surface. Historians use maps to locate historical events, to demonstrate how geography has influenced history, and to illustrate patterns and distributions of human activity and its environmental effects.

Political maps show political units, from countries, states, and provinces to counties, districts, and towns. **Physical maps** show mountains, hills, plains, rivers, lakes, and oceans. They may include elevations of land and depths of water. **Historical maps** illustrate such things as economic activity, political alliances, migrations, battles, and population density. While reading maps, historians pose questions and use the following features to find answers:

A **compass rose** indicates the map's orientation on the globe. It may show all four cardinal directions (N, S, E, W) or just one, north.

Lines indicate boundaries between political areas, roads and highways, routes of exploration or migration, and rivers and other waterways. Lines may vary in width and color.

Symbols or icons represent real objects or events. Cities, towns, and villages often appear as dots. A capital city is often shown as a star within a circle. An area's products or resources may be indicated by symbols. Battles are often shown by starbursts, troop movements by arrows.

Labels designate key places, such as cities, states, bodies of water, and events.

Lines of longitude and latitude appear on maps to indicate the absolute location of the area shown. Lines of latitude show distance north or south of the equator, measured in degrees. Lines of longitude show distance in degrees east or west of the prime meridian, which runs through Greenwich, England.

A **legend or key** is a small table in which the symbols, types of lines, and special colors that appear in the map are listed and explained.

Sometimes **colors** are used to indicate areas under different political or cultural influence. Colors and **shading** are also used to show distributions, patterns, and such features as altitudes.

A **map's scale** shows the ratio between a unit of length on the map and a unit of distance on the earth. A typical scale shows a one-inch segment and indicates the number of miles that length represents on the map. A map on which an inch represents 500 miles has a scale of 1:31,680,000.

Continued on page R26.

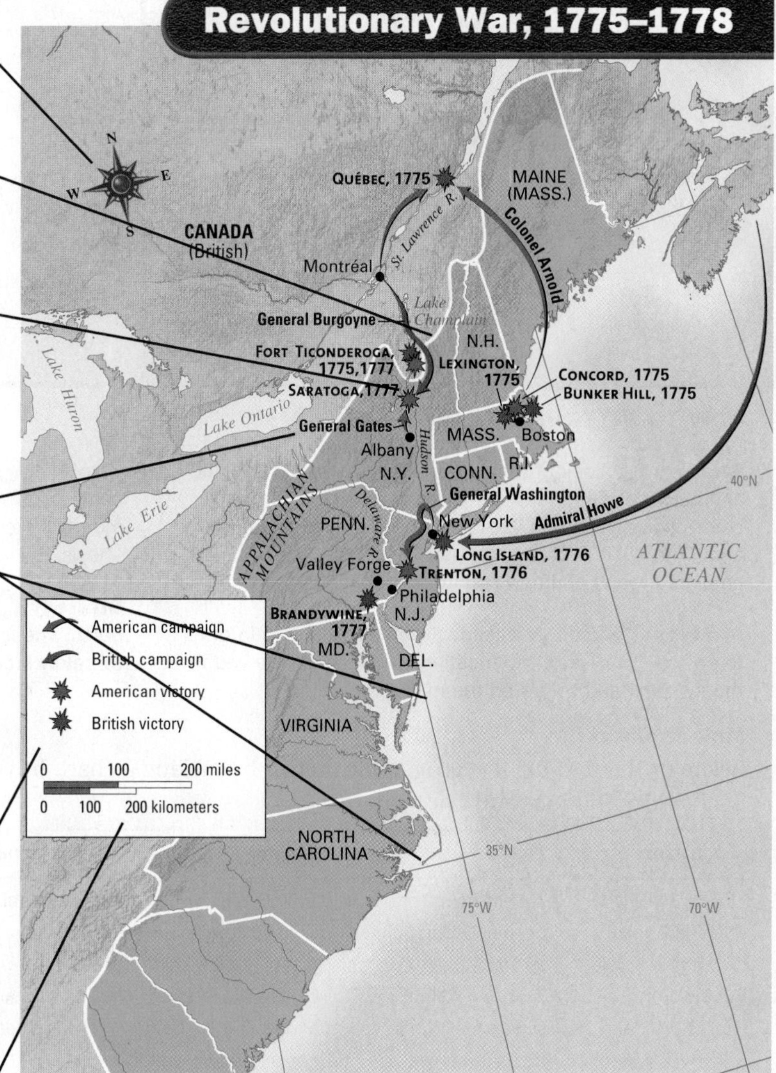

Distributions on a map are where certain symbols, such as those for cities, fall. Sometimes distributions show patterns, such as a cluster, a line, or a wide circle. On this map, for example, the battle symbols show a pattern of being fought near rivers or ports.

APPLYING THE SKILL

The historical maps below show land claims in Europe in 1915 and 1923. Together they show the political effects of World War I.

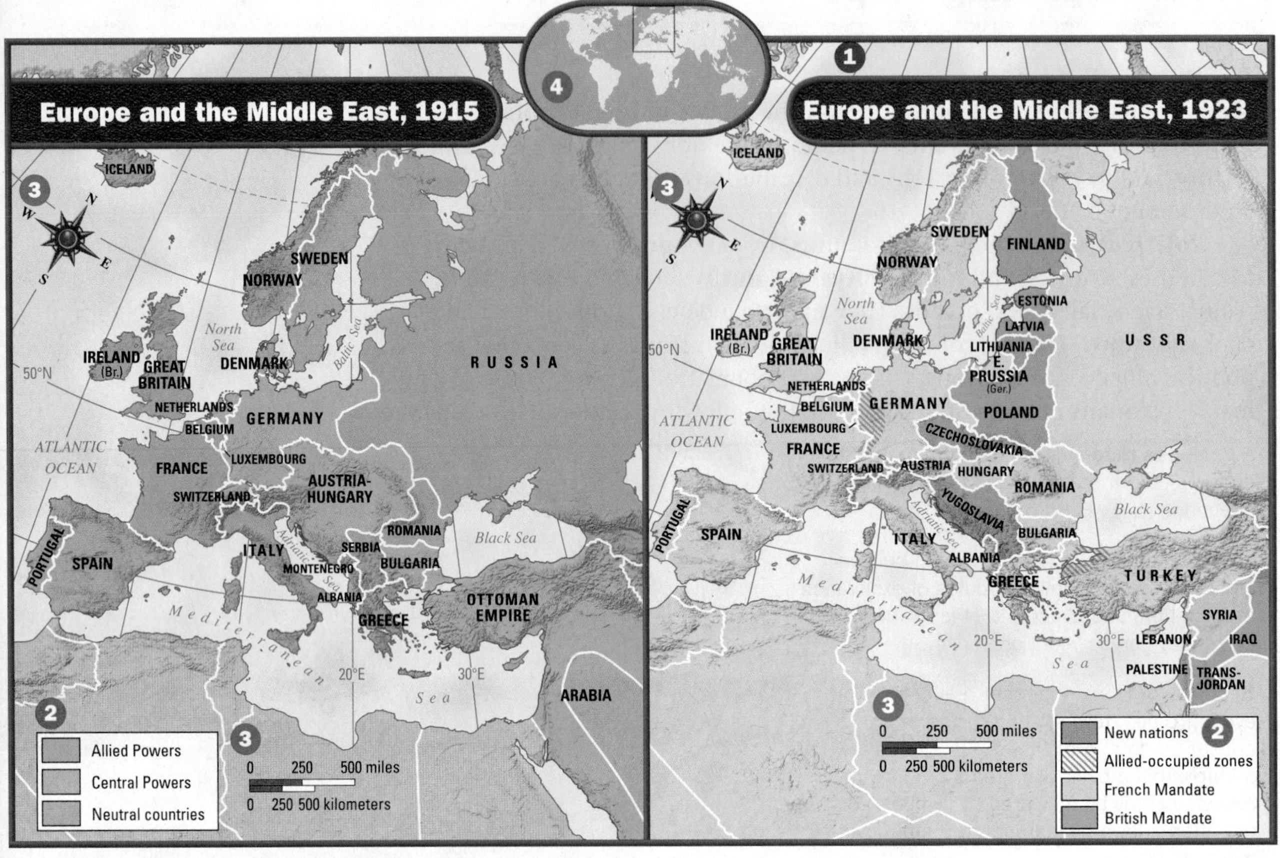

HOW TO INTERPRET A HISTORICAL MAP

Strategy 1 Look at the map's title to learn the subject and purpose of the map. Here the maps show Europe before and after World War I. Pose a historical question about the subject of the map, such as "How were old empires divided and new countries formed?"

Strategy 2 Use the legend to interpret the map in order to answer your historical question. The legend tells you what the symbols and colors on the map mean.

Strategy 3 Look at the scale and compass rose. The scale shows you what distances are represented. On these maps, 1.4 cm represents 500 miles. The compass rose shows you which direction on the map is north.

Strategy 4 Find where the map area is located on the earth. These maps span a large area from the Arctic Circle to below latitude 30° N, and from 10° W to 40° E.

Make a Chart

Relate the map to the five geographic themes by making a chart. In your chart, also analyze distributions and find patterns.

Location:	Place:	Region:	Movement:	Human-Environment Interaction:
Europe and the Middle East; from the Arctic Circle to below 30° North and from 10° West to 40° East	A continent that is a peninsula surrounded by the Mediterranean Sea, the Atlantic Ocean, the North Sea, as well as western-most Asia	The old empires of the Central Powers are distributed within Central Europe and the Middle East. The new nations and mandates are in Eastern Europe and the Middle East.	Political boundaries shifted after the war. New nations and mandates were established.	The new boundaries fall along rivers, bodies of water, and mountain ranges. There is a pattern. The pattern shows that the new countries form a narrow strip from North to South.

3.5 Interpreting Charts

DEFINING THE SKILL

Charts are visual presentations of material. Historians use charts to organize, simplify, and summarize information in a way that makes it more meaningful or memorable.

Simple charts are used to consolidate or compare information. **Tables** are used to organize numbers, percentages, or other information into columns and rows for easy reference. Diagrams provide visual clues to the meaning of the information they contain. Illustrated diagrams are sometimes called **infographics.**

APPLYING THE SKILL

The following diagram gives a visual representation of how the economy functions. The paragraph below summarizes the information contained in the diagram.

HOW TO INTERPRET CHARTS

Strategy 1 Identify the symbols. Here the symbols represent individuals, producers, government, and the product market.

Strategy 2 Look for the main idea. The arrows show the cycle of supply and demand in a free enterprise system of economy. Here individuals are at the top of the chart, indicating that they begin the cycle by creating a demand for goods and services.

Strategy 3 Follow the arrows to study the chart. Read the description of each image in the diagram. Together, the images show the flow of economic activity from producers to individuals and back. The government affects the cycle by regulating and stabilizing economic activity.

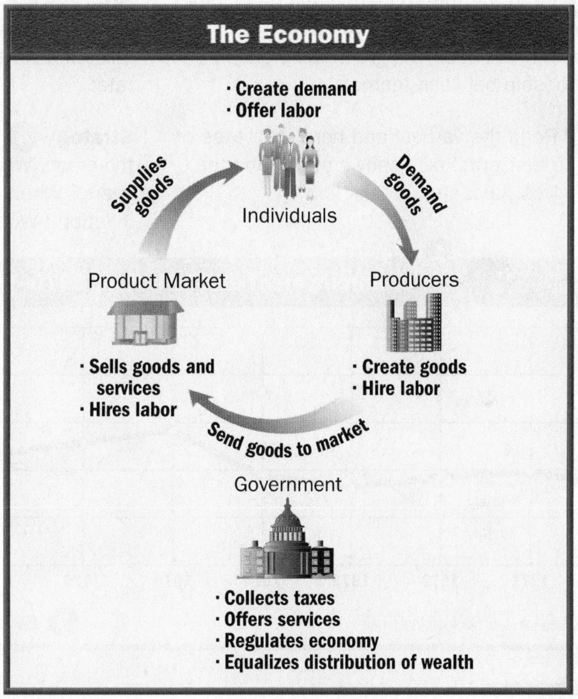

The Economy

Write a Summary

Write a paragraph to summarize what you learned from the diagram.

Individuals want or need products or services. Producers try to fulfill that demand by hiring workers (labor) to produce the good or service. Producers then make the goods and services available for sale on the market. During this process, the government regulates economic activity and equalizes the distribution of wealth, among other functions. Once goods are sent to stores or other distribution centers, people must be hired (labor) to sell the goods.

3.6 Interpreting Graphs

DEFINING THE SKILL

Graphs show statistical information in a visual manner. Historians use graphs to visualize and compare amounts, ratios, economic trends, and changes over time.

Line graphs typically show quantities on the vertical axis (up the left side) and time in various units on the horizontal axis (across the bottom). **Pie graphs** are useful for showing relative proportions. The circle represents the whole and the slices represent the parts belonging to various subgroups. **Bar graphs** are commonly used to display information about quantities.

APPLYING THE SKILL

The image below shows a double line graph. The lines show the rate of inflation as compared with the rate of unemployment from 1970 to 1980.

HOW TO INTERPRET A GRAPH

Strategy 1 Read the title to identify the main idea of the graph. When two subjects are shown, such as unemployment and inflation, the graph will probably show a relationship between them.

Strategy 2 Read the vertical and horizontal axes of the graph. The horizontal axis shows years, and the vertical axis gives percents.

Strategy 3 Look at the legend. Find out what each symbol in the graph represents. In this graph the gold line represents the inflation rate and the purple line represents the unemployment rate.

Strategy 4 Summarize the information shown in each part of the graph. What trends do you see in the line graph over certain years? When did unemployment rise and fall? What about inflation? What can you infer from the patterns?

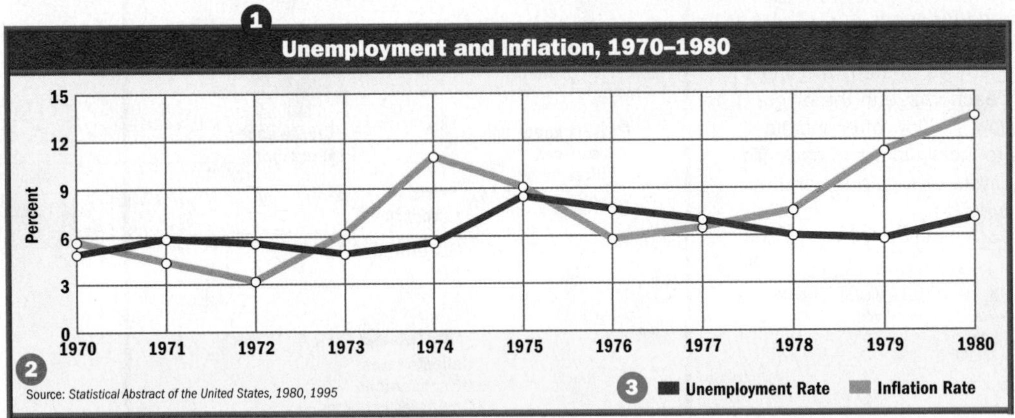

Write a Summary

Write a paragraph to summarize what you learned from the graph.

Unemployment declined between 1976 and 1979 but rose between 1974 and 1975, while inflation declined between 1975 and 1976 and rose in the periods 1973–1974 and 1977–1980. From the graph it appears that unemployment rises or falls following inflation rate changes, but less dramatically.

3.7 Using the Internet

DEFINING THE SKILL

The **Internet** is a network of computers associated with universities, libraries, news organizations, government agencies, businesses, and private individuals worldwide. Every page of information on the Internet has its own address, or **URL.**

The international collection of sites known as the **World Wide Web** is a source of information about current events as well as research on historical subjects. This textbook contains many suggestions for using the World Wide Web. You can begin by entering the URL for Holt McDougal's site: hmhsocialstudies.com.

APPLYING THE SKILL

The computer screen below shows the home page of the Library of Congress.

HOW TO USE THE INTERNET

Strategy 1 Go directly to a Web page. If you know the address of a particular Web page, type the address in the strip at the top of the screen and press RETURN. After a few seconds, that page will appear on your screen.

If you want to research the Web for information on a topic, visit a general search site such as www.google.com or www.yahoo.com. The following sites have information that may be useful in your research:

Library of Congress—www.loc.gov

National Archives and Records Administration—www.nara.gov

Smithsonian Institution—www.si.org

PBS—www.pbs.org

National Geographic—www.nationalgeographic.com

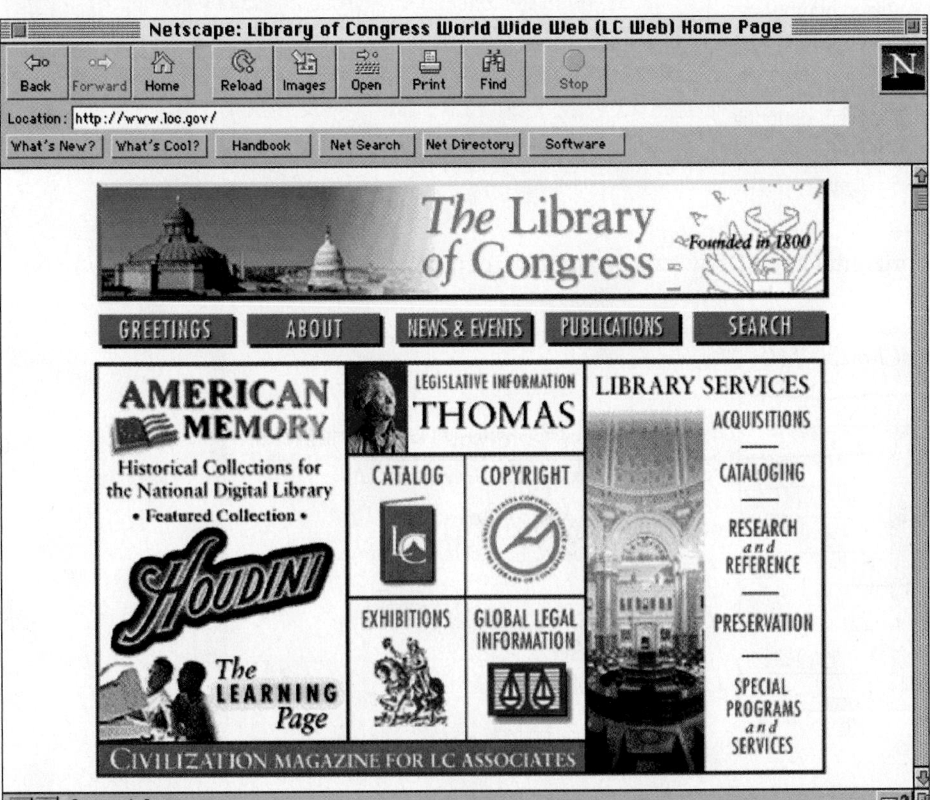

Strategy 2 Learn about the page. Click on one of the topics across the top of the page to learn more about the Library of Congress and how to use its Web site.

Strategy 3 Explore the features of the page. Click on any one of the images or topics to find out more about a specific subject.

4.1 Creating Charts and Graphs

DEFINING THE SKILL

Charts and **graphs** are visual representations of information. (See Skillbuilders 3.5 and 3.6.) Three types of graphs are **bar graphs, line graphs,** and **pie graphs.** Use a bar graph to display information about quantities and to compare related quantities. Use a line graph to show a change in a single quantity over time. Use a pie graph to show relative proportions among parts of a single thing. Charts can be used to condense and organize written information or lists.

APPLYING THE SKILL

The following passage includes data about American commuting choices between 1960 and 1990. The bar graph below shows how the information in the passage might be represented.

HOW TO CREATE A BAR GRAPH

Strategy 1 Use a title that sums up the information; include a time span.

Strategy 2 Note dates and the percentages. Dates will form the horizontal axis of your graph; percentages will form the vertical axis.

Strategy 3 Organize the data. Group numbers that provide information about the same year.

Strategy 4 Decide how best to represent the information. Sketch a graph and a legend, denoting the meanings of any colors and symbols.

American Commuting Choices, 1960–1990

In 1960, 64% of the population traveled to work by car, truck, or van; 12% took public transportation; 7% worked at home; and 17% got to work by other means. In 1990, 87% traveled to work by car, truck, or van; 5% took public transportation; 3% worked at home; and 5% went to work by other means.

Create a Bar Graph

Clearly label vertical and horizontal axes. Draw bars accurately. Include a legend.

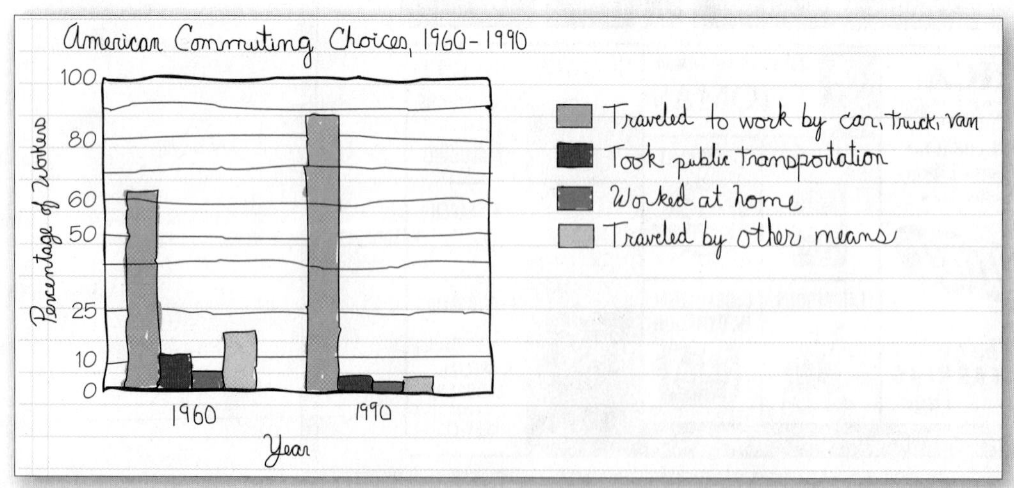

4.2 Creating Models

DEFINING THE SKILL

Models, like maps, are visual representations of information. Historians make models of geographical areas, villages, cities, inventions, buildings, and other physical objects of historical importance. A model can be a two-dimensional representation, such as a poster or a diagram that explains how something happened. It also can be a three-dimensional representation or even a computer-created image.

APPLYING THE SKILL

The following image is a two-dimensional model of the tunnel system used by the Vietcong during the Vietnam War. Examine the strategies used in making this model to learn how to create your own.

HOW TO CREATE A MODEL

Strategy 1 Gather the information you need to understand the situation or event. Here the creator has gathered information about the tunnel system from various reference sources.

Strategy 2 Think about symbols you may want to use. Since the model should give information in a visual way, think about ways you can use color, pictures, or other visuals to tell the story.

Strategy 3 Gather the supplies you will need to create the model. For this model, the creator might have used computer software or colored markers or pencils.

Strategy 4 Visualize and sketch an idea for your model. Once you have created a picture in your mind from either written text or other images, make an actual sketch to plan how your model might look.

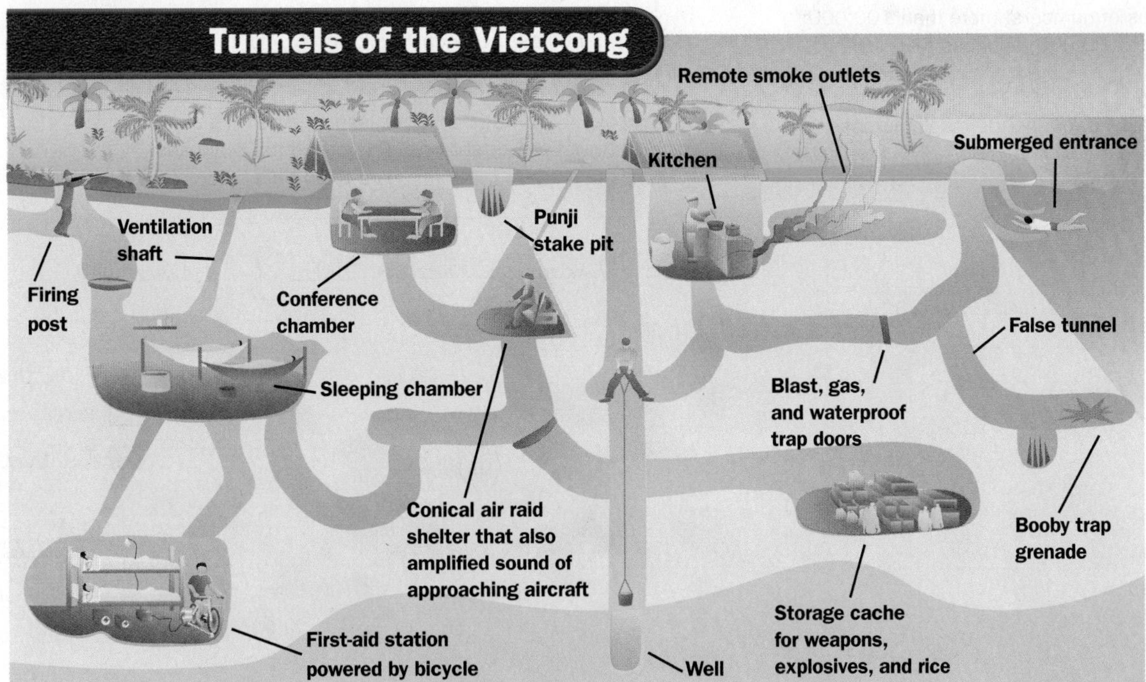

4.3 Creating Maps

DEFINING THE SKILL

Maps are scale representations, usually of land surfaces. (See Skillbuilder 3.4.) Creating a map involves representing geographical data visually. When you draw a map, it is easiest to use an existing map as a guide. You can include data on climate and population and on patterns or distributions of human activity.

APPLYING THE SKILL

The following chart shows the numbers of 1995 immigrants who planned to settle in the southwestern states of the United States. The map below depicts the data given in the chart.

Immigrants, by State of Intended Residence, 1995

Arizona	7,700	Nevada	4,306	Texas	49,963
California	166,482	New Mexico	2,758	Utah	2,831
Colorado	7,713				

HOW TO CREATE A MAP

Strategy 1 Determine what map you should use as a guide. Find a map of the Southwest that you can re-create.

Strategy 2 Decide how best to show the data. These data can be grouped in three broad categories of numbers: more than 100,000; 10,000 to 100,000; and less than 10,000.

Strategy 3 Select a title that identifies the geographical area and the map's purpose. Include a date or time span.

Strategy 4 Draw and label the lines of latitude and longitude. Use the guide map's scale and a ruler to help you correctly space the lines of latitude and longitude.

Strategy 5 Draw the subject of your map, following your guide map carefully. Color or mark the map to show its purpose. Use each color or symbol to represent similar information.

Strategy 6 Include a key or legend explaining colors, symbols, or shading. Reproduce the scale and compass rose from the map you used as a guide.

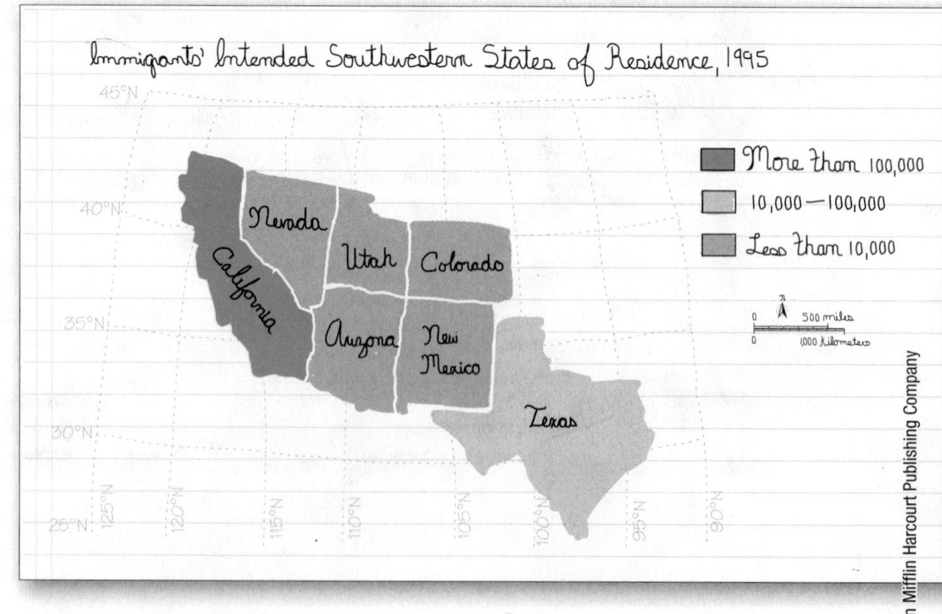

4.4 Creating Databases

DEFINING THE SKILL

A **database** is a collection of data, or information, that is organized so that you can find and retrieve information on a specific topic quickly and easily. Once a computerized database is set up, you can search it to find specific information without going through the entire database. The database will provide a list of all stored information related to your topic. Learning how to use a database will help you learn how to create one.

APPLYING THE SKILL

The chart below is a database for some of the significant legislation passed during President Johnson's Great Society program.

1 Significant Great Society Legislation

❷ Legislation	Date	Significance
❸ Economic Opportunity Act	1964	❹ created Job Corps and other programs to help the poor
Civil Rights Act	1964	outlawed discrimination in public accommodations
Medical Care Act	1965	❹ established Medicare and Medicaid programs to help the elderly and the poor
Higher Education Act	1965	provided low-interest loans for college students
Truth in Packaging Act	1966	set standards for labeling consumer products
Highway Safety Act	1966	required states to set up highway safety programs
Demonstration Cities and Metropolitan Area Redevelopment Act	1966	❹ provided funds to rebuild poor neighborhoods
Air Quality Act	1967	set federal air pollution guidelines

HOW TO CREATE A DATABASE

Strategy ❶ Identify the topic of the database. The keywords, or most important words, in the title are "Great Society" and "Legislation." These words were used to begin the research for this database.

Strategy ❷ Identify the kind of data you need to enter in your database. These will be the column headings—or categories—of your database. The keywords "Legislation," "Date," and "Significance," were chosen to categorize this research.

Strategy ❸ Once you find the data you want to include, identify the entries under each heading.

Strategy ❹ Use the database to help you find the information quickly. For example, in this database you could search by the word "poor" for programs related to anti-poverty measures.

4.5 Creating Written Presentations

DEFINING THE SKILL

Written presentations are in-depth reports on a topic in history. Often, written presentations take a stand on an issue or try to support a specific conclusion. To successfully report on an event or make a point, your writing needs to be clear, concise, and supported by factual details.

APPLYING THE SKILL

The following is a written presentation about the main goals of progressivism. Use the strategies listed below to help you learn to create a written presentation.

HOW TO CREATE A WRITTEN PRESENTATION

Strategy 1 Identify a topic that you wish to research, focusing on one or more questions that you hope to answer about the topic. Then research the topic using library resources and the Internet.

Strategy 2 Formulate a hypothesis. This will serve as the main idea, or thesis, of your presentation. Analyze the information in your sources and develop a hypothesis that answers your questions about the topic.

Strategy 3 Organize the facts and supporting details around your main idea. These facts and examples should be presented in a way that helps you build a logical case to prove your point.

Strategy 4 To express your ideas clearly, use standard grammar, spelling, sentence structure, and punctuation. Proofread your work to make sure it is well-organized and grammatically correct.

For more on how to create a historical research paper and other written presentations, see the ***Writing for Social Studies*** handbook.

Make an Outline

Creating an outline like the one shown here will help you organize your ideas and produce an effective written presentation.

1 The Goals of Progressivism

1. 2 All progressive reforms had one of four goals.
   A. Protecting Social Welfare
      3 1. Social Gospel movement sought to help the poor.
      2. Settlement houses provided aid to poor city dwellers.
   B. Promoting Moral Improvement
      1. Reformers sought to improve Americans' personal behavior.
      2. WCTU worked for prohibition.
   C. Creating Economic Reform
      1. Writers criticized capitalism.
      2. American Socialist Party formed.
      3. Muckrakers exposed corruption in business and government.
   D. Fostering Efficiency
      1. Emergence of scientific management in the workplace
      2. Development of the assembly line

The Goals of Progressivism

As America approached the 20th century a number of citizens tried to reform society. Their efforts formed what became known as the progressive movement. Progressive reformers had the following four goals, social welfare, moral improvement, economic reform, and efficiency.

Many reformers sought to promote social welfare—especially in the crowded, run-down, and unhealthy areas of the cities. The Social Gospel movement inspired followers to erect churches in poor communities. It also persuaded business leaders to treat workers more fair. Other reformers established settlement house in slum neighborhoods which provided educational, cultural, and social services to people—especially to immigrants.

Another group of reformers felt that the lives of poor people could be improved through moral instruction. These reformers offer programs to improve personal behavior. The Women's Christian Temperence Union, for instance, promoted prohibition. It believed that alcohol was the root of many of society's problems.

Other progressives, such as Henry George and Edward Bellamy, blamed the competitive nature of capitalism for creating a large underclass. Some Americans, especially workers, embraced socialism. In 1898, Eugene Debs helped organize the american socialist party. Advocated communal living and a classless society. During the early 20th century, journalists exposed the corrupt side of business and politics known as muckrakers.

Meanwhile, some tried to make American society more efficient. Frederick Winslow Taylor popularized scientific management, the effort to improve efficiency in the workplace by applying scientific principles. Out of this concept emerged the assembly line, which required workers to perform the same task over and over, and thus sped up production.

Through their hard work, the progressives reformed many levels of society and helped Americans live better lives.

Use punctuation marks for their correct purposes. A colon precedes a list.

Use the correct parts of speech. An adverb modifies a verb.

Check for common agreement errors. Subjects and verbs must agree in person and number.

Use consistent verb tense. Use past tense for events in the past.

Check spelling with both an electronic spell checker and a dictionary.

Capitalize all proper nouns, including names of political parties.

Use correct sentence structure. Every sentence needs a subject and a verb.

Be sure sentence structure leads clearly from one phrase to the next. Correct misplaced modifiers.

4.6 Creating Oral Presentations

DEFINING THE SKILL

An **oral presentation** is a speech or talk given before an audience. Oral presentations can be given to inform an audience about a certain topic or persuade an audience to think or act in a certain way. You can learn how to give effective oral presentations by examining some of the more famous ones in history.

APPLYING THE SKILL

The following is an excerpt from a student's speech supporting Southern secession. Use the strategies listed below to help you learn to create an oral presentation.

HOW TO CREATE AN ORAL PRESENTATION

Strategy 1 Choose one central idea or theme and organize your presentation to support it. Here, the writer calls for the United States government to allow the Southern states to secede.

Strategy 2 Use words or images to persuade your audience. In this speech, the writer has used a metaphor of family conflict to express the antagonism between North and South.

Strategy 3 Make sure your arguments support your central idea or theme. In this speech, the writer's arguments all support the main theme.

> 1 The Southern states should be allowed to secede. 3 Since it was the states that helped create the national government, surely the states have the right to declare their independence from that government.
>
> The industrial North will never understand the needs of the farmers and plantation owners of the South. 2 The South and the North are like two brothers whose lives and attitudes have become so different that they can no longer live under the same roof. Why should they be forced to remain together?

Giving an Oral Presentation

When you give an oral presentation, make sure to

- maintain eye contact with your audience.
- use gestures and body language to emphasize your main points and to help express your ideas.
- pace yourself. Do not rush to finish your presentation.
- vary your tone of voice to help bring out the meaning of your words.

4.7 Creating Visual Presentations

DEFINING THE SKILL

A **visual presentation** of history uses visual sources to explain a particular historical event. Such sources could include paintings, maps, charts and graphs, costume drawings, photographs, political cartoons, and advertisements. Movies, CD-ROMs, television, and computer software are among the visual sources called multimedia sources because they also include sound. (See Skillbuilder 3.2.) Visual sources can provide much insight into various eras and events of the past. Creating a visual presentation will help you to become more familiar with the many different sources of historical information available.

APPLYING THE SKILL

The image below shows a student using a computer to create a visual presentation. Use the strategies listed below to help you plan out the steps needed to compile a clear, engaging, and informative presentation.

HOW TO CREATE A VISUAL PRESENTATION

Strategy 1 Identify the topic of your presentation and decide which types of visuals will most effectively convey your information. For example, you might want to use slides and posters along with a map. If you want to include multimedia sources, you could use documentary film or television footage of an event.

Strategy 2 Conduct research to determine what visual sources are available. Some topics, such as wars, may have more visual source material than others. You can create your own visual sources, such as a graph or chart, to accompany what you find.

Strategy 3 Write a script for the presentation. A narration of events to accompany the visuals will tie the various sources together and aid you in telling the story.

Strategy 4 Record the presentation. A video recording will preserve the presentation for future viewing and allow you to show it to different groups of people.

Facts About the States

Alabama
4,447,100 people
52,237 sq. mi.
Rank in area: 30
Entered Union in 1819

Alaska
626,932 people
615,230 sq. mi.
Rank in area: 1
Entered Union in 1959

Arizona
5,130,632 people
114,006 sq. mi.
Rank in area: 6
Entered Union in 1912

Arkansas
2,673,400 people
53,182 sq. mi.
Rank in area: 28
Entered Union in 1836

California
33,871,648 people
158,869 sq. mi.
Rank in area: 3
Entered Union in 1850

Colorado
4,301,261 people
104,100 sq. mi.
Rank in area: 8
Entered Union in 1876

Connecticut
3,405,565 people
5,544 sq. mi.
Rank in area: 48
Entered Union in 1788

Delaware
783,600 people
2,396 sq. mi.
Rank in area: 49
Entered Union in 1787

District of Columbia
572,059 people
68 sq. mi.

Florida
15,982,378 people
59,928 sq. mi.
Rank in area: 23
Entered Union in 1845

Georgia
8,186,453 people
58,977 sq. mi.
Rank in area: 24
Entered Union in 1788

Hawaii
1,211,537 people
6,459 sq. mi.
Rank in area: 47
Entered Union in 1959

Idaho
1,293,953 people
83,574 sq. mi.
Rank in area: 14
Entered Union in 1890

Illinois
12,419,293 people
57,918 sq. mi.
Rank in area: 25
Entered Union in 1818

Indiana
6,080,485 people
36,420 sq. mi.
Rank in area: 38
Entered Union in 1816

Iowa
2,926,324 people
56,276 sq. mi.
Rank in area: 26
Entered Union in 1846

Kansas
2,688,418 people
82,282 sq. mi.
Rank in area: 15
Entered Union in 1861

Kentucky
4,041,769 people
40,411 sq. mi.
Rank in area: 37
Entered Union in 1792

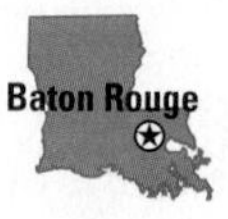

Louisiana
4,468,976 people
49,651 sq. mi.
Rank in area: 31
Entered Union in 1812

Maine
1,274,923 people
33,741 sq. mi.
Rank in area: 39
Entered Union in 1820

Maryland
5,296,486 people
12,297 sq. mi.
Rank in area: 42
Entered Union in 1788

Massachusetts
6,349,097 people
9,241 sq. mi.
Rank in area: 45
Entered Union in 1788

Michigan
9,938,444 people
96,705 sq. mi.
Rank in area: 11
Entered Union in 1837

Minnesota
4,919,479 people
86,943 sq. mi.
Rank in area: 12
Entered Union in 1858

Mississippi
2,844,658 people
48,286 sq. mi.
Rank in area: 32
Entered Union in 1817

Missouri
5,595,211 people
69,709 sq. mi.
Rank in area: 21
Entered Union in 1821

Montana
902,195 people
147,046 sq. mi.
Rank in area: 4
Entered Union in 1889

Population figures are according to the Census 2000.

Nebraska
1,711,263 people
77,538 sq. mi.
Rank in area: 16
Entered Union in 1867

Nevada
1,998,257 people
110,567 sq. mi.
Rank in area: 7
Entered Union in 1864

New Hampshire
1,235,786 people
9,283 sq. mi.
Rank in area: 44
Entered Union in 1788

New Jersey
8,414,350 people
8,215 sq. mi.
Rank in area: 46
Entered Union in 1787

New Mexico
1,819,046 people
121,598 sq. mi.
Rank in area: 5
Entered Union in 1912

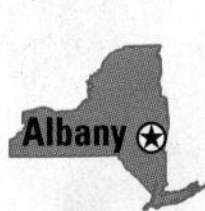

New York
18,976,457 people
53,989 sq. mi.
Rank in area: 27
Entered Union in 1788

North Carolina
8,049,313 people
52,672 sq. mi.
Rank in area: 29
Entered Union in 1789

North Dakota
642,200 people
70,704 sq. mi.
Rank in area: 18
Entered Union in 1889

Ohio
11,353,140 people
44,828 sq. mi.
Rank in area: 34
Entered Union in 1803

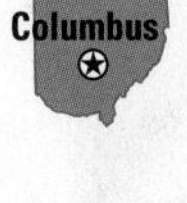

Oklahoma
3,450,654 people
69,903 sq. mi.
Rank in area: 20
Entered Union in 1907

Oregon
3,421,399 people
97,132 sq. mi.
Rank in area: 10
Entered Union in 1859

Pennsylvania
12,281,054 people
46,058 sq. mi.
Rank in area: 33
Entered Union in 1787

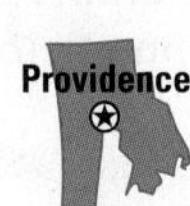

Rhode Island
1,048,319 people
1,231 sq. mi.
Rank in area: 50
Entered Union in 1790

South Carolina
4,012,012 people
31,189 sq. mi.
Rank in area: 40
Entered Union in 1788

South Dakota
754,844 people
77,121 sq. mi.
Rank in area: 17
Entered Union in 1889

Tennessee
5,689,283 people
42,146 sq. mi.
Rank in area: 36
Entered Union in 1796

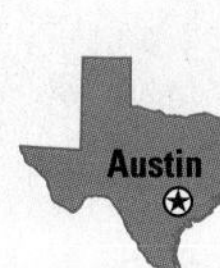

Texas
20,851,820 people
267,277 sq. mi.
Rank in area: 2
Entered Union in 1845

Utah
2,233,169 people
84,904 sq. mi.
Rank in area: 13
Entered Union in 1896

Vermont
608,827 people
9,615 sq. mi.
Rank in area: 43
Entered Union in 1791

Virginia
7,078,515 people
42,326 sq. mi.
Rank in area: 35
Entered Union in 1788

Washington
5,894,121 people
70,637 sq. mi.
Rank in area: 19
Entered Union in 1889

West Virginia
1,808,344 people
24,231 sq. mi.
Rank in area: 41
Entered Union in 1863

Wisconsin
5,363,675 people
64,599 sq. mi.
Rank in area: 22
Entered Union in 1848

Wyoming
493,782 people
97,818 sq. mi.
Rank in area: 9
Entered Union in 1890

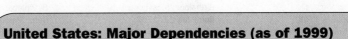

United States: Major Dependencies (as of 1999)

American Samoa 63,781 people; 90 sq. mi.

Guam 151,968 people; 217 sq. mi.

Commonwealth of Puerto Rico 3,889,507 people; 3,508 sq. mi.

Virgin Islands of the United States 119,615 people; 171 sq. mi.

Presidents of the United States

Dates given are for term in office.

Here are some little-known facts about the presidents of the United States:

- First president born in the new United States: **Martin Van Buren** (8th president)
- Only president who was a bachelor: **James Buchanan**
- First left-handed president: **James A. Garfield**
- Largest president: **William Howard Taft** (6 feet, 2 inches; 332 pounds)
- Youngest president: **Theodore Roosevelt** (42 years old)
- Oldest president: **Ronald Reagan** (77 years old when he left office in 1989)
- First president born west of the Mississippi River: **Herbert Hoover** (born in West Branch, Iowa)
- First president born in the 20th century: **John F. Kennedy** (born May 29, 1917)

1 George Washington
1789–1797
No Political Party
Birthplace: Virginia
Born: February 22, 1732
Died: December 14, 1799

2 John Adams
1797–1801
Federalist
Birthplace: Massachusetts
Born: October 30, 1735
Died: July 4, 1826

3 Thomas Jefferson
1801–1809
Democratic-Republican
Birthplace: Virginia
Born: April 13, 1743
Died: July 4, 1826

4 James Madison
1809–1817
Democratic-Republican
Birthplace: Virginia
Born: March 16, 1751
Died: June 28, 1836

5 James Monroe
1817–1825
Democratic-Republican
Birthplace: Virginia
Born: April 28, 1758
Died: July 4, 1831

6 John Quincy Adams
1825–1829
Republican
Birthplace: Massachusetts
Born: July 11, 1767
Died: February 23, 1848

7 Andrew Jackson
1829–1837
Democrat
Birthplace: South Carolina
Born: March 15, 1767
Died: June 8, 1845

8 Martin Van Buren
1837–1841
Democrat
Birthplace: New York
Born: December 5, 1782
Died: July 24, 1862

9 William H. Harrison
1841
Whig
Birthplace: Virginia
Born: February 9, 1773
Died: April 4, 1841

10 John Tyler
1841–1845
Whig
Birthplace: Virginia
Born: March 29, 1790
Died: January 18, 1862

11 James K. Polk
1845–1849
Democrat
Birthplace: North Carolina
Born: November 2, 1795
Died: June 15, 1849

12 Zachary Taylor
1849–1850
Whig
Birthplace: Virginia
Born: November 24, 1784
Died: July 9, 1850

13 **Millard Fillmore**
1850–1853
Whig
Birthplace: New York
Born: January 7, 1800
Died: March 8, 1874

14 **Franklin Pierce**
1853–1857
Democrat
Birthplace: New Hampshire
Born: November 23, 1804
Died: October 8, 1869

15 **James Buchanan**
1857–1861
Democrat
Birthplace: Pennsylvania
Born: April 23, 1791
Died: June 1, 1868

16 **Abraham Lincoln**
1861–1865
Republican
Birthplace: Kentucky
Born: February 12, 1809
Died: April 15, 1865

17 **Andrew Johnson**
1865–1869
Democrat
Birthplace: North Carolina
Born: December 29, 1808
Died: July 31, 1875

18 **Ulysses S. Grant**
1869–1877
Republican
Birthplace: Ohio
Born: April 27, 1822
Died: July 23, 1885

19 **Rutherford B. Hayes**
1877–1881
Republican
Birthplace: Ohio
Born: October 4, 1822
Died: January 17, 1893

20 **James A. Garfield**
1881
Republican
Birthplace: Ohio
Born: November 19, 1831
Died: September 19, 1881

21 **Chester A. Arthur**
1881–1885
Republican
Birthplace: Vermont
Born: October 5, 1829
Died: November 18, 1886

22 **24** **Grover Cleveland**
1885–1889, 1893–1897
Democrat
Birthplace: New Jersey
Born: March 18, 1837
Died: June 24, 1908

23 **Benjamin Harrison**
1889–1893
Republican
Birthplace: Ohio
Born: August 20, 1833
Died: March 13, 1901

25 **William McKinley**
1897–1901
Republican
Birthplace: Ohio
Born: January 29, 1843
Died: September 14, 1901

26 **Theodore Roosevelt**
1901–1909
Republican
Birthplace: New York
Born: October 27, 1858
Died: January 6, 1919

27 **William H. Taft**
1909–1913
Republican
Birthplace: Ohio
Born: September 15, 1857
Died: March 8, 1930

28 **Woodrow Wilson**
1913–1921
Democrat
Birthplace: Virginia
Born: December 29, 1856
Died: February 3, 1924

29 **Warren G. Harding**
1921–1923
Republican
Birthplace: Ohio
Born: November 2, 1865
Died: August 2, 1923

30 Calvin Coolidge
1923–1929
Republican
Birthplace: Vermont
Born: July 4, 1872
Died: January 5, 1933

31 Herbert C. Hoover
1929–1933
Republican
Birthplace: Iowa
Born: August 10, 1874
Died: October 20, 1964

32 Franklin D. Roosevelt
1933–1945
Democrat
Birthplace: New York
Born: January 30, 1882
Died: April 12, 1945

33 Harry S. Truman
1945–1953
Democrat
Birthplace: Missouri
Born: May 8, 1884
Died: December 26, 1972

34 Dwight D. Eisenhower
1953–1961
Republican
Birthplace: Texas
Born: October 14, 1890
Died: March 28, 1969

35 John F. Kennedy
1961–1963
Democrat
Birthplace: Massachusetts
Born: May 29, 1917
Died: November 22, 1963

36 Lyndon B. Johnson
1963–1969
Democrat
Birthplace: Texas
Born: August 27, 1908
Died: January 22, 1973

37 Richard M. Nixon
1969–1974
Republican
Birthplace: California
Born: January 9, 1913
Died: April 22, 1994

38 Gerald R. Ford
1974–1977
Republican
Birthplace: Nebraska
Born: July 14, 1913
Died: December 26, 2006

39 James E. Carter, Jr.
1977–1981
Democrat
Birthplace: Georgia
Born: October 1, 1924

40 Ronald W. Reagan
1981–1989
Republican
Birthplace: Illinois
Born: February 6, 1911
Died: June 4, 2004

41 George H. W. Bush
1989–1993
Republican
Birthplace: Massachusetts
Born: June 12, 1924

42 William J. Clinton
1993–2001
Democrat
Birthplace: Arkansas
Born: August 19, 1946

43 George W. Bush
2001–2009
Republican
Birthplace: Connecticut
Born: July 6, 1946

44 Barack H. Obama
2009–
Democrat
Birthplace: Hawaii
Born: August 4, 1961

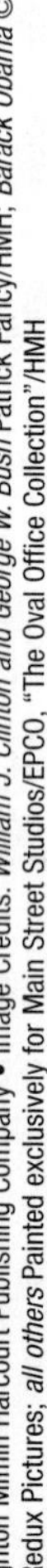

GLOSSARY

The Glossary is an alphabetical listing of many of the key terms from the chapters, along with their meanings. The definitions listed in the Glossary are the ones that apply to the way the words are used in this textbook. The Glossary gives the part of speech of each word. The following abbreviations are used:

adj. **= adjective** ***n.*** **= noun** ***v.*** **= verb**

PRONUNCIATION KEY

Symbol	Examples	Symbol	Examples	Symbol	Examples
ă	**a**t, g**a**s	m	**m**an, see**m**	v	**v**an, sa**v**e
ā	**a**pe, d**ay**	n	**n**ight, mitte**n**	w	**w**eb, t**w**ice
ä	f**a**ther, b**a**rn	ng	si**ng**, a**n**ger	y	**y**ard, law**y**er
âr	f**air**, d**are**	ŏ	**o**dd, n**o**t	z	**z**oo, rea**s**on
b	**b**ell, ta**b**le	ō	**o**pen, r**oa**d, gr**ow**	zh	trea**s**ure, gara**ge**
ch	**ch**in, lun**ch**	ô	**aw**ful, b**ough**t, h**o**rse	ə	**a**wake, ev**e**n, penc**i**l,
d	**d**ig, bore**d**	oi	c**oi**n, b**oy**		pil**o**t, foc**u**s
ĕ	**e**gg, t**e**n	o͝o	l**oo**k, f**u**ll	ər	p**er**form, lett**er**
ē	**e**vil, s**ee**, m**ea**l	o͞o	r**oo**t, gl**ue**, thr**ough**		
f	**f**all, lau**gh**, **ph**rase	ou	**ou**t, c**ow**	**Sounds in Foreign Words**	
g	**g**old, bi**g**	p	**p**ig, ca**p**	KH	*German* i**ch**, au**ch**;
h	**h**it, in**h**ale	r	**r**ose, sta**r**		*Scottish* lo**ch**
hw	**wh**ite, every**wh**ere	s	**s**it, fa**ce**	N	*French* e**n**tre, bo**n**, fi**n**
ĭ	**i**nch, f**i**t	sh	**sh**e, ma**sh**	œ	*French* f**eu**, c**oeu**r;
ī	**i**dle, m**y**, tr**ie**d	t	**t**ap, hoppe**d**		*German* sch**ö**n
îr	d**ear**, h**ere**	th	**th**ing, wi**th**	ü	*French* **u**tile, r**ue**;
j	**j**ar, **g**em, ba**dge**	*th*	**th**en, o**th**er		*German* gr**ü**n
k	**k**eep, **c**at, lu**ck**	ŭ	**u**p, n**u**t		
l	**l**oad, ratt**le**	ûr	f**ur**, **ear**n, b**ir**d, w**or**m		

STRESS MARKS

′ This mark indicates that the preceding syllable receives the primary stress. For example, in the word *lineage,* the first syllable is stressed: [lĭn′ē-ĭj].

′ This mark is used only in words in which more than one syllable is stressed. It indicates that the preceding syllable is stressed, but somewhat more weakly than the syllable receiving the primary stress. In the word *consumerism,* for example, the second syllable receives the primary stress, and the fourth syllable receives a weaker stress: [kən-so͞o′mə-rĭz′əm].

A

abolition *n.* movement to end slavery.

Adams-Onís [ăd′əmz-ō-nēs′] **Treaty** *n.* an 1819 agreement in which Spain gave over control of the territory of Florida to the United States.

Adena [ə-dē′nə] *n.* a Mound Builder society that was centered in the Ohio River valley and flourished from about 700 B.C. to A.D. 100.

Alamo, the [ăl′ə-mō′] *n.* a mission and fort in San Antonio, Texas, where Mexican forces massacred rebellious Texans in 1836.

Alien and Sedition [ā′lē-ən] [sĭ-dĭsh′ən] **Acts** *n.* a series of four laws enacted in 1798 to reduce the political power of recent immigrants to the United States.

American Federation of Labor (AFL) *n.* an alliance of trade and craft unions, formed in 1886.

Americanization [ə-mĕr′ĭ-kə-nĭ-zā′shən] **movement** *n.* education program designed to help immigrants assimilate to American culture.

American System *n.* a pre-Civil War set of measures designed to unify the nation and strengthen its economy by means of protective tariffs, a national bank, and such internal improvements as the development of a transportation system.

Anaconda [ăn′ə-kŏn′də] **plan** *n.* a three-part strategy by which the Union proposed to defeat the Confederacy in the Civil War.

Anasazi [ä′nə-sä′zē] *n.* a Native American group that lived on the mesa tops, cliff sides, and canyon bottoms of the Four Corners region (where the present-day states of Arizona, New Mexico, Colorado, and Utah meet) from about A.D. 100 to 1300.

annex [ə-nĕks′] *v.* to incorporate a territory into an existing political unit, such as a state or a nation.

antebellum [ăn′tē-bĕl′əm] *adj.* belonging to the period before the Civil War.

Antifederalist [ăn′tē-fĕd′ər-ə-lĭst] *n.* an opponent of a strong central government.

Appomattox [ăp′ə-măt′əks] **Court House** *n.* town near Appomattox, Virginia, where Lee surrendered to Grant on April 9, 1865, thus ending the Civil War. (37°N 79°W)

apprentice [ə-prĕn′tĭs] *n.* a worker learning a trade or craft, usually under the supervision of a master.

arbitration *n.* a method of settling disputes in which both sides submit their differences to a mutually approved judge.

armistice [är′mĭ-stĭs] *n.* a truce, or agreement to end an armed conflict.

Articles of Confederation [kən-fĕd′ə-rā′shən] *n.* a document, adopted by the Second Continental Congress in 1777 and finally approved by the states in 1781, that outlined the form of government of the new United States.

Ashcan school *n.* a group of early 20th-century American artists who often painted realistic pictures of city life—such as tenements and homeless people—thus earning them their name.

assimilation [ə-sĭm′ə-lā′shən] *n.* a minority group's adoption of the beliefs and way of life of the dominant culture.

Aztec [ăz′tĕk′] *n.* a Native American people that settled in the Valley of Mexico in the 1200s A.D. and later developed a powerful empire.

B

Bank of the United States *n.* either of the two national banks, funded by the federal government and private investors, established by Congress, the first in 1791 and the second in 1816.

Battle of Wounded Knee [wo͞on′dĭd nē′] *n.* the massacre by U.S. soldiers of 300 unarmed Native Americans at Wounded Knee Creek, South Dakota, in 1890.

Benin [bə-nĭn′] *n.* a West African kingdom that flourished in the Niger Delta region (in what is now Nigeria) from the 14th to the 17th century.

Bessemer [bĕs′ə-mər] **process** *n.* a cheap and efficient process for making steel, developed around 1850.

Bill of Rights *n.* the first ten amendments to the U.S. Constitution, added in 1791 and consisting of a formal list of citizens' rights and freedoms.

bimetallism [bī-mĕt′l-ĭz′əm] *n.* the use of both gold and silver as a basis for a national monetary system.

black codes *n.* the discriminatory laws passed throughout the post-Civil-War South which severely restricted African Americans' lives, prohibiting such activities as traveling without permits, carrying weapons, serving on juries, testifying against whites, and marrying whites.

Bleeding Kansas *n.* a name applied to the Kansas Territory in the years before the Civil War, when the territory was a battleground between proslavery and antislavery forces.

blockade [blŏ-kād′] *n.* the use of ships or troops to prevent movement into and out of a port or region controlled by a hostile nation.

bonanza [bə-năn′zə] **farm** *n.* an enormous farm on which a single crop is grown.

Boston Massacre [bô′stən măs′ə-kər] *n.* a clash between British soldiers and Boston colonists in 1770, in which five of the colonists were killed.

Boston Tea Party *n.* the dumping of 18,000 pounds of tea into Boston Harbor by colonists in 1773 to protest the Tea Act.

Boxer Rebellion *n.* a 1900 rebellion in which members of a Chinese secret society sought to free their country from Western influence.

Bull Moose Party *n.* a name given to the Progressive Party, formed to support Theodore Roosevelt's candidacy for the presidency in 1912.

C

cabinet [kăb′ə-nĭt] *n.* the group of department heads who serve as the president's chief advisers.

capitalism [kăp′ĭ-tl-ĭz′əm] *n.* an economic system in which private individuals and corporations control the means of production and use them to earn profits.

carpetbagger [kär′pĭt-băg′ər] *n.* a Northerner who moved to the South after the Civil War.

cash crop *n.* a crop grown by a farmer for sale rather than for personal use.

checks and balances *n.* the provisions in the U.S. Constitution that prevent any branch of the U.S. government from dominating the other two branches.

Chinese Exclusion Act *n.* a law, enacted in 1882, that prohibited all Chinese except students, teachers, merchants, tourists, and government officials from entering the United States.

Chisholm [chĭz′əm] **Trail** *n.* the major cattle route from San Antonio, Texas, through Oklahoma to Kansas.

chlorination *n.* a method of purifying water by mixing it with chemical chlorine.

civil disobedience [dĭs′ə-bē′dē-əns] *n.* the refusal to obey those laws which are seen as unjust in an effort to bring about a change in governmental policy. Henry David Thoreau wrote about civil disobedience in the 19th century, and the tactic was promoted by Martin Luther King, Jr., during the Civil Rights Era.

civil service *n.* the nonmilitary branches of government administration.

Clayton Antitrust [klāt′n ăn′tē-trŭst′] **Act** *n.* a law, enacted in 1914, that made certain monopolistic business practices illegal and protected the rights of labor unions and farm organizations.

colonization [kŏl′ə-nĭ-zā′shən] *n.* the establishment of outlying settlements by a parent country.

Columbian Exchange [kə-lŭm′bē-ən ĭks-chānj′] *n.* the transfer—beginning with Columbus's first voyage—of plants, animals, and diseases between the Western Hemisphere and the Eastern Hemisphere.

committees of correspondence [kôr′ĭ-spŏn′dəns] *n.* one of the groups set up by American colonists to exchange information about British threats to their liberties.

Common Sense *n.* a pamphlet by Thomas Paine, published in 1776, that called for separation of the colonies from Britain.

Compromise [kŏm′prə-mīz′] **of 1850** *n.* a series of congressional measures intended to settle the major disagreements between free states and slave states.

Compromise of 1877 *n.* a series of congressional measures under which the Democrats agreed to accept the Republican candidate Rutherford B. Hayes as president, even though he had lost the popular vote. The measures included the withdrawal of federal troops from Southern states, federal money for improving Southern infrastructure, and the appointment of a conservative Southern cabinet member.

Confederacy [kən-fĕd′ər-ə-sē] *n.* the Confederate States of America, a confederation formed in 1861 by the Southern states after their secession from the Union.

confederation [kən-fĕd′ə-rā′shən] *n.* an alliance permitting states or nations to act together on matters of mutual concern.

conquistador [kŏng-kē′stə-dôr′] *n.* one of the Spaniards who traveled to the Americas as an explorer and conqueror in the 16th century.

conscription [kən-skrĭp′shən] *n.* the drafting of citizens for military service.

conservation [kŏn′sûr-vā′shən] *n.* the planned management of natural resources, involving the protection of some wilderness areas and the development of others for the common good.

consolidation [kən-sŏl′ĭ-dā′shən] *n.* the act of uniting or combining.

Copperhead [kŏp′ər-hĕd′] *n.* a Northern Democrat who advocated making peace with the Confederacy during the Civil War.

cottage industry *n.* a system of production in which manufacturers provide the materials for goods to be produced in the home.

cotton gin *n.* a machine for cleaning the seeds from cotton fibers, invented by Eli Whitney in 1793.

Crédit Mobilier [krĕd′ĭt mō-bēl′yər] *n.* a construction company formed in 1864 by owners of the Union Pacific Railroad, who used it to fraudulently skim off railroad profits for themselves.

Crusades [kro͞o-sādz′] *n.* a series of Christian military expeditions to the Middle East between A.D. 1096 and 1270, intended to drive the Muslims from the Holy Land.

cult of domesticity [dō′mĕ-stĭs′ĭ-tē] *n.* a belief that married women should restrict their activities to their home and family.

D

Dawes [dôz] **Act** *n.* a law, enacted in 1887, that was intended to "Americanize" Native Americans by distributing reservation land to individual owners.

debt peonage [dĕt′ pē′ə-nĭj] *n.* a system in which workers are bound in servitude until their debts are paid.

Declaration [dĕk′lə-rā′shən] **of Independence** *n.* the document, written by Thomas Jefferson in 1776, in which the delegates of the Continental Congress declared the colonies' independence from Britain.

Democratic-Republican *n.* political party known for its support of strong state governments, founded by Thomas Jefferson in 1792 in opposition to the Federalist Party.

division of labor *n.* the assignment of different tasks and responsibilities to different groups or individuals.

dollar diplomacy [dĭ-plō′mə-sē] *n.* the U.S. policy of using the nation's economic power to exert influence over other countries.

E

egalitarianism [ĭ-găl′ĭ-târ′ē-ə-nĭz′əm] *n.* the belief that all people should have equal political, economic, social, and civil rights.

electoral [ĭ-lĕk′tər-əl] **college** *n.* a group selected by the states to elect the president and the vice-president, in which each state's number of electors is equal to the number of its senators and representatives in Congress.

emancipation *n.* the freeing of slaves.

Emancipation Proclamation [prŏk′lə-mā′shən] *n.* an executive order issued by Abraham Lincoln on January 1, 1863, freeing the slaves in all regions behind Confederate lines.

embargo [ĕm-bär′gō] *n.* a government ban on trade with one or more other nations.

encomienda [ĕng-kô-myĕn′dä] *n.* a system in which Spanish authorities granted colonial landlords the service of Native Americans as forced laborers.

Enlightenment [ĕn-līt′n-mənt] *n.* an 18th-century intellectual movement that emphasized the use of reason and the scientific method as means of obtaining knowledge.

entrepreneur [ŏn′trə-prə-nûr′] *n.* a person who organizes, operates, and assumes the risk for a business venture.

Erie Canal [îr′ē kə-năl′] *n.* a 363-mile-long artificial waterway connecting the Hudson River with Lake Erie, built between 1817 and 1825.

excise [ĕk′sīz′] **tax** *n.* a tax on the production, sale, or consumption of goods produced within a country.

executive [ĭg-zĕk′yə-tĭv] **branch** *n.* the branch of government that administers and enforces the laws.

exoduster [ĕk′sə-dŭs′tər] *n.* an African American who migrated from the South to Kansas in the post-Reconstruction years.

extortion *n.* illegal use of one's official position to obtain property or funds.

F

Farmers' Alliances *n.* groups of farmers, or those in sympathy with farming issues, who sent lecturers from town to town to educate people about agricultural and rural issues.

federalism *n.* a political system in which a national government and constituent units, such as state governments, share power.

Federalists [fĕd′ər-ə-lĭst] *n.* supporters of the Constitution and of a strong national government.

Federalist, The *n.* a series of essays defending and explaining the Constitution, written by Alexander Hamilton, James Madison, and John Jay.

Federal Reserve System *n.* a national banking system, established in 1913, that controls the U.S. money supply and the availability of credit in the country.

Federal Trade Commission (FTC) *n.* a federal agency established in 1914 to investigate and stop unfair business practices.

Fifteenth Amendment *n.* an amendment to the U.S. Constitution, adopted in 1870, that prohibits the denial of voting rights to people because of their race or color or because they have previously been slaves.

"Fifty-Four Forty or Fight!" *n.* a slogan used in the 1844 presidential campaign as a call for the U.S. annexation of the entire Oregon Territory.

Foraker [fôr′ə-kər] **Act** *n.* legislation passed by Congress in 1900, in which the U.S. ended military rule in Puerto Rico and set up a civil government.

forty-niner *n.* one of the people who migrated to California in search of riches after gold was discovered there in 1848.

Fourteenth Amendment *n.* an amendment to the U.S. Constitution, adopted in 1868, that makes all persons born or naturalized in the United States—including former slaves—citizens of the country and guarantees equal protection of the laws.

Freedmen's Bureau [frēd-mĕnz byŏŏr′ō] *n.* a federal agency set up to help former slaves after the Civil War.

Freeport Doctrine [frē′pôrt′ dŏk′trĭn] *n.* the idea, expressed by Stephen Douglas in 1858, that any territory could exclude slavery by simply refusing to pass laws supporting it.

Free-Soil Party *n.* a political party formed in 1848 to oppose the extension of slavery into U.S. territories.

French and Indian War *n.* a conflict in North America, lasting from 1754 to 1763, that was a part of a worldwide struggle between France and Britain and that ended with the defeat of France and the transfer of French Canada to Britain.

Fugitive [fyōō′jĭ-tĭv] **Slave Act** *n.* a law enacted as part of the Compromise of 1850, designed to ensure that escaped slaves would be returned into bondage.

G

Gadsden [gădz′dən] **Purchase** *n.* an 1853 purchase by the United States of land from Mexico, establishing the present U.S.-Mexico boundary.

gag rule *n.* a rule limiting or preventing debate on an issue.

Gentlemen's Agreement *n.* A 1907–1908 agreement between the U.S. and Japanese governments to limit Japanese immigration to the United States.

Gettysburg Address [gĕt′ēz-bûrg′ ə-drĕs′] *n.* a famous speech delivered by Abraham Lincoln in November 1863, at the dedication of a national cemetery on the site of the Battle of Gettysburg.

Glorious Revolution *n.* the transfer of the British monarchy from James II to William and Mary in 1688–1689.

gold rush *n.* a movement of many people to a region in which gold has been discovered.

gold standard *n.* a monetary system in which the basic unit of currency is defined in terms of a set amount of gold.

graft *n.* the illegal use of political influence for personal gain.

grandfather clause *n.* a provision that exempts certain people from a law on the basis of previously existing circumstances—especially a clause formerly in some Southern states' constitutions that exempted whites from the strict voting requirements used to keep African Americans from the polls.

Grange [grānj] *n.* the Patrons of Husbandry—a social and educational organization through which farmers attempted to combat the power of the railroads in the late 19th century.

Great Awakening *n.* a revival of religious feeling in the American colonies during the 1730s and 1750s.

Great Compromise [kŏm′prə-mīz′] *n.* the Constitutional Convention's agreement to establish a two-house national legislature, with all states having equal representation in one house and each state having representation based on its population in the other house.

Great Plains *n.* the vast grassland that extends through the central portion of North America, from Texas northward to Canada, east of the Rocky Mountains.

H

habeas corpus [hā′bē-əs kôr′pəs] *n.* a court order requiring authorities to bring a prisoner before the court so that the court can determine whether the prisoner is being held legally.

headright [hĕd′rīt′] **system** *n.* the Virginia Company's policy of granting 50 acres of land to each settler and to each family member who accompanied him.

hierarchy [hī′ə-rär′kē] *n.* a social ordering by rank or class.

Hohokam [hə-hō′kəm] *n.* a Native American group that lived in the valleys of the Salt and Gila rivers (in what is now Arizona) from about 300 B.C. to A.D. 1400.

home rule *n.* a state's powers of governing its citizens without federal government involvement.

Homestead [hōm′stĕd′] **Act** *n.* a U.S. law enacted in 1862, that provided 160 acres in the West to any citizen or intended citizen who was head of household and would cultivate the land for five years; a law whose passage led to record numbers of U.S. settlers claiming private property which previously had been reserved by treaty and by tradition for Native American nomadic dwelling and use; the same law strengthened in 1889 to encourage individuals to exercise their private property rights and develop homesteads out of the vast government lands.

Hopewell [hōp′wĕl′] *n.* a Mound Builder society that was centered in the Ohio River valley and flourished from about 200 B.C. to A.D. 400.

horizontal integration [hôr′ĭ-zŏn′tl ĭn′tĭ-grā′shən] *n.* the merging of companies that make similar products.

I

impeach *v.* to formally charge an official with misconduct in office. The House of Representatives has the sole power to impeach federal officials.

imperialism [ĭm-pîr′ē-ə-lĭz′əm] *n.* the policy of extending a nation's authority over other countries by economic, political, or military means.

impressment [ĭm-prĕs′mənt] *n.* the forcible seizure of men for military service.

Inca [ĭng′kə] *n.* a Native American people that around A.D. 1400 created an empire reaching nearly 2,500 miles along the west coast of South America.

incandescent [ĭn′kən-dĕs′ənt] *adj.* giving off visible light as a result of being heated.

income tax *n.* a tax on earnings.

indentured [ĭn-dĕn′chərd] **servant** *n.* a person who has contracted to work for another for a limited period, often in return for travel expenses, shelter, and sustenance.

Indian Removal Act *n.* a law, enacted in 1830, that forced Native American peoples east of the Mississippi to move to lands in the West.

Industrial Revolution *n.* the change in social and economic organization that resulted from the replacement of hand tools with machines and from the development of large-scale industrial production.

Industrial Workers of the World (IWW) *n.* a labor organization for unskilled workers, formed by a group of radical unionists and socialists in 1905.

inflation [ĭn-flā′shən] *n.* an increase in prices or decline in purchasing power caused by an increase in the supply of money.

initiative [ĭ-nĭsh′ə-tĭv] *n.* a procedure by which a legislative measure can be originated by the people rather than by lawmakers.

interchangeable [ĭn′tər-chān′jə-bəl] **parts** *n.* standardized parts that can be used in place of one another.

Interstate [ĭn′tər-stāt′] **Commerce Act** *n.* a law, enacted in 1887, that reestablished the federal government's right to supervise railroad activities and created a five-member Interstate Commerce Commission to do so.

Intolerable [ĭn-tŏl′ər-ə-bəl] **Acts** *n.* a series of laws enacted by Parliament in 1774 to punish Massachusetts colonists for the Boston Tea Party.

Iroquois [ĭr′ə-kwoi′] *n.* a group of Native American peoples inhabiting the woodlands of the Northeast.

Islam [ĭs-läm′] *n.* a religion founded in Arabia in A.D. 622 by the prophet Muhammad; its believers are called Muslims.

J

Jim Crow laws *n.* laws enacted by Southern state and local governments to separate white and black people in public and private facilities.

joint-stock companies *n.* businesses in which investors pool their wealth for a common purpose.

journeyman [jûr′nē-mən] *n.* in the apprentice system, a skilled worker employed by a master.

judicial [jo͞o-dĭsh′əl] **branch** *n.* the branch of government that interprets the laws and the Constitution.

judicial review *n.* the Supreme Court's power to declare an act of Congress unconstitutional.

Judiciary [jo͞o-dĭsh′ ē-ĕr′ē] **Act of 1789** *n.* a law that established the federal court system and the number of Supreme Court justices and that provided for the appeal of certain state court decisions to the federal courts.

Judiciary [jo͞o-dĭsh′ē-ĕr′ē] **Act of 1801** *n.* a law that increased the number of federal judges, allowing President John Adams to fill most of the new posts with Federalists.

Jungle, The *n.* a novel by Upton Sinclair, published in 1906, that portrays the dangerous and unhealthy conditions prevalent in the meatpacking industry at that time.

K

Kansas-Nebraska Act *n.* a law, enacted in 1854, that established the territories of Kansas and Nebraska and gave their residents the right to decide whether to allow slavery.

Kashaya Pomo [kə-shä′yə pō′mō] *n.* a Native American people that formerly inhabited the coastal marshlands of what is now California.

King Philip's War *n.* a conflict, in the years 1675–1676, between New England colonists and Native American groups allied under the leadership of the Wampanoag chief Metacom.

kinship [kĭn′shĭp′] *n.* the ties between members of a family.

Know-Nothing Party *n.* a name given to the American Party, formed in the 1850s to curtail the political influence of immigrants.

Kongo [kŏng′gō] *n.* a group of small kingdoms along the Zaire River in West-Central Africa, united under a single leader in the late 1400s.

Ku Klux Klan [ko͞o′ klŭks klăn′] **(KKK)** *n.* a secret organization that used terrorist tactics in an attempt to restore white supremacy in Southern states after the Civil War.

Kwakiutl [kwä′kē-o͞ot′l] *n.* a Native American people that formerly inhabited the northwestern coastal region of North America.

L

land grant *n.* a gift of public land to an individual or organization.

Land Ordinance [ôr′dn-əns] **of 1785** *n.* a law that established a plan for surveying and selling the federally owned lands west of the Appalachian Mountains.

legislative [lĕj′ĭ-slā′tĭv] **branch** *n.* the branch of government that makes laws.

lineage [lĭn′ē-ĭj] *n.* a group of people descended from a common ancestor.

long drive *n.* the moving of cattle over trails to a shipping center.

longhorn [lông′hôrn′] *n.* a breed of sturdy, long-horned cattle brought by the Spanish to Mexico and suited to the dry conditions of the Southwest.

Louisiana Purchase *n.* the 1803 purchase by the United States of France's Louisiana Territory—extending from the Mississippi River to the Rocky Mountains—for $15 million.

Loyalists [loi′ə-lĭst] *n.* colonists who supported the British government during the American Revolution.

M

manifest destiny [măn′ə-fĕst′ dĕs′tə-nē] *n.* the 19th-century belief that the United States would inevitably expand westward to the Pacific Ocean and into Mexican territory.

Marbury* v. *Madison [mär′bûr-ē vûr′səs măd′ĭ-sən] *n.* an 1803 case in which the Supreme Court ruled that it had the power to abolish legislative acts by declaring them unconstitutional; this power came to be known as judicial review.

market revolution *n.* the major change in the U.S. economy produced by people's beginning to buy and sell goods rather than make them for themselves.

martial [mär′shəl] **law** *n.* temporary rule by military rather than civilian authority.

mass production *n.* the production of goods in large quantities, made possible by the use of machinery and the division of labor.

mass transit *n.* transportation systems designed to move large numbers of people along fixed routes.

master *n.* a skilled artisan, usually one owning a business and employing others.

Maya [mä′yə] *n.* a Native American people whose civilization flourished in Guatemala and the Yucatán Peninsula between about A.D. 250 and 900.

McCulloch* v. *Maryland *n.* an 1819 case in which the Supreme Court ruled that Maryland had no right to tax the Bank of the United States, thereby strengthening the power of the federal government's control over the economy.

Meat Inspection Act *n.* a law, enacted in 1906, that established strict cleanliness requirements for meatpackers and created a federal meat-inspection program.

melting pot *n.* a mixture of people from different cultures and races who blend together by abandoning their native languages and cultures.

mercantilism [mûr′kən-tē-lĭz′əm] *n.* an economic system in which nations seek to increase their wealth and power by obtaining large amounts of gold and silver and by establishing a favorable balance of trade.

Merrimack [mĕr′ə-măk′] *n.* an ironclad ship used by the South in the Civil War.

mestizo [mĕs-tē′zō] *adj.* of mixed Spanish and Native American ancestry.

middle passage *n.* the voyage that brought enslaved Africans to the West Indies and later to North America.

midnight judge *n.* one of the judges appointed by John Adams in the last hours of his administration.

minutemen [mĭn′ĭt-mĕn′] *n.* Patriot civilian soldiers just before and during the Revolutionary War, pledged to be ready to fight at a minute's notice.

Mississippian [mĭs′ĭ-sĭp′ē-ən] *n.* the last and most complex of the Mound Builder societies, inhabiting the Ohio and Mississippi valleys from about A.D. 700 into the 1500s.

Missouri Compromise [kŏm′prə-mīz′] *n.* a series of agreements passed by Congress in 1820–1821 to maintain the balance of power between slave states and free states.

Monitor [mŏn′ĭ-tər] *n.* an ironclad ship used by the North in the Civil War.

Monroe Doctrine [mən-rō′ dŏk′trĭn] *n.* a policy of U.S. opposition to any European interference in the affairs of the Western Hemisphere, announced by President Monroe in 1823.

Mormons [môr′mən] *n.* members of a church founded by Joseph Smith and his associates in 1830.

Morrill [môr′əl] **Acts** *n.* laws enacted in 1862 and 1890 to help create agricultural colleges by giving federal land to states.

muckraker [mŭk′rā′kər] *n.* one of the magazine journalists who exposed the corrupt side of business and public life in the early 1900s.

Munn* v. *Illinois [mŭn′ vûr′səs ĭl′ə-noi′] *n.* an 1877 case in which the Supreme Court upheld states' regulation of railroads for the benefit of farmers and consumers, thus establishing the right of government to regulate private industry to serve the public interest.

N

NAACP [ĕn′ dŭb′əl ā′ sē′ pē′] *n.* the National Association for the Advancement of Colored People—an organization founded in 1909 to promote full racial equality.

NACW *n.* the National Association of Colored Women—a social service organization founded in 1896.

National Bank Act *n.* legislation passed in 1863 to make banking safer for investors. Its provisions included a system of federally chartered banks, new requirements for loans, and a system for the inspection of banks.

nationalism *n.* a devotion to the interests and culture of one's nation.

National Road *n.* a federally funded road begun in 1811 and by 1838 extending from Cumberland, Maryland to Vandalia, Illinois.

National Trades' Union *n.* the first national association of trade unions, formed in 1834.

Navigation [năv′ĭ-gā′shən] **Acts** *n.* a series of laws enacted by Parliament, beginning in 1651, to tighten England's control of trade in its American colonies.

NAWSA *n.* the National American Woman Suffrage Association—an organization founded in 1890 to gain voting rights for women.

neutrality *n.* a refusal to take part in a war between other nations.

Niagara Movement *n.* founded by W. E. B. Du Bois in 1905 to promote the education of African Americans in the liberal arts.

Nineteenth Amendment *n.* an amendment to the U.S. Constitution, adopted in 1920, that gives women the right to vote.

nomadic *adj.* having no fixed home, moving from place to place according to seasons and availability of food and water.

Northwest Ordinance [ôr′dn-əns] **of 1787** *n.* a law that established a procedure for the admission of new states to the Union.

nuclear [no͞o′klē-ər] **family** *n.* a household made up of a mother, a father, and their children.

nullification [nŭl′ə-fĭ-kā′shən] *n.* a state's refusal to recognize an act of Congress that it considers unconstitutional.

O

Olive Branch Petition [pə-tĭsh′ən] *n.* a document sent by the Second Continental Congress to King George III, proposing a reconciliation between the colonies and Britain.

Olmec [ŏl′mĕk] *n.* a Native American people whose civilization flourished in what is now southern Mexico in the period 1200–400 B.C.

Open Door notes *n.* messages sent by Secretary of State John Hay in 1899 to Germany, Russia, Great Britain, France, Italy, and Japan, asking the countries not to interfere with U.S. trading rights in China.

Oregon Trail *n.* a route from Independence, Missouri, to Oregon City, Oregon, used by pioneers traveling to the Oregon Territory.

P

Panama Canal [păn′ə-mä′ kə-năl′] *n.* an artificial waterway cut through the Isthmus of Panama to provide a shortcut between the Atlantic and Pacific oceans, opened in 1914.

panic of 1837 *n.* a U.S. financial crisis in which banks closed and the credit system collapsed, resulting in many bankruptcies and high unemployment.

panic of 1873 *n.* a series of financial failures that triggered a five-year depression in the United States.

Parliament [pär′lə-mənt] *n.* the legislative body of England.

Patriots [pā′trē-ət] *n.* colonists who supported American independence from Britain.

patronage [pā′trə-nĭj] *n.* an officeholder's power to appoint people—usually those who have helped him or her get elected—to positions in government.

Payne-Aldrich Tariff [pān′ ôl′drĭch tăr′ĭf] *n.* a set of tax regulations, enacted by Congress in 1909, that failed to significantly reduce tariffs on manufactured goods.

Pendleton [pĕn′dl-tən] **Civil Service Act** *n.* a law, enacted in 1883, that established a bipartisan civil service commission to make appointments to government jobs by means of the merit system.

Pequot [pē′kwŏt′] **War** *n.* a 1637 conflict in which the Pequot nation battled Connecticut colonists and their Narragansett allies.

personal liberty laws *n.* statutes, passed in nine Northern states in the 1850s, that forbade the imprisonment of runaway slaves and guaranteed jury trials for fugitive slaves.

plantation [plăn-tā′shən] *n.* a large farm on which the labor of slaves or other workers is used to grow a single crop, such as sugar cane or cotton.

Platt [plăt] **Amendment** *n.* a series of provisions that, in 1901, the United States insisted Cuba add to its new constitution, commanding Cuba to stay out of debt and giving the United States the right to intervene in the country and the right to buy or lease Cuban land for naval and fueling stations.

Plessy* v. *Ferguson [plĕs′ē vûr′səs fûr′gə-sən] *n.* an 1896 case in which the Supreme Court ruled that separation of the races in public accommodations was legal, thus establishing the "separate but equal" doctrine.

political machine *n.* an organized group that controls a political party in a city and offers services to voters and businesses in exchange for political and financial support.

poll [pōl] **tax** *n.* an annual tax that formerly had to be paid in some Southern states by anyone wishing to vote.

popular sovereignty [sŏv′ər-ĭn-tē] *n.* a system in which the residents vote to decide an issue.

Populism [pŏp′yə-lĭz′əm] *n.* a late-19th-century political movement demanding that people have a greater voice in government and seeking to advance the interests of farmers and laborers.

Powhatan [pou′ə-tăn′] *n.* a group of Native American peoples that lived in eastern Virginia at the time of the first English settlements there.

Proclamation [prŏk′lə-mā′shən] **of 1763** *n.* an order in which Britain prohibited its American colonists from settling west of the Appalachian Mountains.

profiteering [prŏf′ĭ-tîr′ĭng] *n.* the selling of goods in short supply at inflated prices.

progressive [prə-grĕs′ĭv] **movement** *n.* an early-20th-century reform movement seeking to return control of the government to the people, to restore economic opportunities, and to correct injustices in American life.

prohibition [prō′ə-bĭsh′ən] *n.* the banning of the manufacture, sale, and possession of alcoholic beverages.

proprietor [prə-prī′ĭ-tər] *n.* an owner—particularly one of those granted ownership of, and full governing rights over, certain of the English colonies in North America.

protective tariff [prə-tĕk′tĭv tăr′ĭf] *n.* a tax on imported goods that is intended to protect a nation's businesses from foreign competition.

protectorate [prə-tĕk′tə-rĭt] *n.* a country whose affairs are partially controlled by a stronger power.

Pueblo [pwĕb′lō] *n.* a group of Native American peoples—descendants of the Anasazi—inhabiting the deserts of the Southwest.

Pure Food and Drug Act *n.* a law enacted in 1906 to halt the sale of contaminated foods and drugs and to ensure truth in labeling.

Puritans [pyŏŏr′ĭ-tnz] *n.* members of a group that wanted to eliminate all traces of Roman Catholic ritual and traditions in the Church of England.

Q

Quakers [kwā′kərz] *n.* members of the Society of Friends, a religious group persecuted for its beliefs in 17th-century England.

R

Radical Republican [răd′ĭ-kəl rĭ-pŭb′lĭ-kən] *n.* one of the congressional Republicans who, after the Civil War, wanted to destroy the political power of former slaveholders and to give African Americans full citizenship and the right to vote.

ratification [răt′ə-fĭ-kā′shən] *n.* the official approval of the Constitution, or of an amendment, by the states.

recall [rĭ-kôl′] *n.* a procedure for removing a public official from office by a vote of the people.

Reconstruction [rē′kən-strŭk′shən] *n.* the period of rebuilding that followed the Civil War, during which the defeated Confederate states were readmitted to the Union.

Red Cross *n.* an international organization that provides relief to people in times of war or natural disaster. Clara Barton founded the American branch in 1881.

redemption [rĭ-dĕmp′shən] *n.* the Southern Democrats' term for their return to power in the South in the 1870s.

referendum [rĕf′ə-rĕn′dəm] *n.* a procedure by which a proposed legislative measure can be submitted to a vote of the people.

Reformation [rĕf′ər-mā′shən] *n.* a religious movement in 16th-century Europe, growing out of a desire for reform in the Roman Catholic Church and leading to the establishment of various Protestant churches.

Renaissance [rĕn′ĭ-säns′] *n.* a period of European history, lasting from about 1400 to 1600, during which renewed interest in classical culture led to far-reaching changes in art, learning, and views of the world.

republic [rĭ-pŭb′lĭk] *n.* a government in which the citizens rule through elected representatives.

Republican Party *n.* the modern political party that was formed in 1854 by opponents of slavery in the territories.

republicanism [rĭ-pŭb′lĭ-kə-nĭz′əm] *n.* the belief that government should be based on the consent of the people.

Republic of California *n.* the nation proclaimed by American settlers in California when they declared their independence from Mexico in 1846.

Republic of Texas *n.* the nation established in 1836 when American settlers in the Mexican province of Texas declared and fought for their independence, also commonly known at that time as the "Lone Star Republic."

revival [rĭ-vī′vəl] *n.* a religious gathering designed to reawaken faith through impassioned preaching.

Roosevelt Corollary [rō′zə-vĕlt′ kôr′ə-lĕr-ē] *n.* an extension of the Monroe Doctrine, announced by President Theodore Roosevelt in 1904, under which the United States claimed the right to protect its economic interests by means of military intervention in the affairs of Western Hemisphere nations.

Rough Riders *n.* a volunteer cavalry regiment, commanded by Leonard Wood and Theodore Roosevelt, that served in the Spanish-American War.

royal colony *n.* a colony under the direct control of the English monarch.

rural free delivery (RFD) *n.* the free government delivery of mail and packages to homes in rural areas, begun in 1896.

S

salutary neglect [săl′yə-tĕr′ē nĭ-glĕkt′] *n.* an English policy of relaxing the enforcement of regulations in its colonies in return for the colonies' continued economic loyalty.

Santa Fe [săn′tə fā′] **Trail** *n.* a route from Independence, Missouri, to Santa Fe, New Mexico, used by traders in the early and mid-1800s.

savanna [sə-văn′ə] *n.* a dry grassland dotted with trees and bushes, found in sub-Saharan Africa and other tropical or subtropical regions.

scalawag [skăl′ə-wăg′] *n.* a white Southerner who joined the Republican Party after the Civil War.

scientific management *n.* the application of scientific principles to increase efficiency in the workplace.

secession [sĭ-sĕsh′ən] *n.* the formal withdrawal of a state from the Union.

Second Continental Congress *n.* the Continental Congress that convened in May 1775, approved the Declaration of Independence, and served as the only agency of national government during the Revolutionary War.

Second Great Awakening *n.* a 19th-century religious movement in which individual responsibility for seeking salvation was emphasized, along with the need for personal and social improvement.

sectionalism [sĕk′shə-nə-lĭz′əm] *n.* the placing of the interests of one's own region ahead of the interests of the nation as a whole.

segregation [sĕg′rĭ-gā′shən] *n.* the separation of people on the basis of race.

Seneca Falls [sĕn′ĭ-kə fôlz′] **Convention** *n.* a women's rights convention held in Seneca Falls, New York, in 1848.

Separatist [sĕp′ər-ə-tĭst] *n.* a member of one of the Puritan groups that, denying the possibility of reform within the Church of England, established their own independent congregations.

settlement house *n.* a community center providing assistance to residents—particularly immigrants—in a slum neighborhood.

Seventeenth Amendment *n.* an amendment to the U.S. Constitution, adopted in 1913, that provides for the election of U.S. senators by the people rather than by state legislatures.

sharecropping [shâr′krŏp′ĭng] *n.* a system in which landowners give farm workers land, seed, and tools in return for a part of the crops they raise.

Shays's [shā′zəz] **Rebellion** *n.* an uprising of debt-ridden Massachusetts farmers protesting increased state taxes in 1787.

Sherman Antitrust [shûr′mən ăn′tē-trŭst′] **Act** *n.* a law, enacted in 1890, that was intended to prevent the creation of monopolies by making it illegal to establish trusts that interfered with free trade.

slave *n.* a person who becomes the property of others.

Social Darwinism [sō′shəl där′wĭ-nĭz′əm] *n.* an economic and social philosophy—supposedly based on the biologist Charles Darwin's theory of evolution by natural selection—holding that a system of unrestrained competition will ensure the survival of the fittest.

Social Gospel [gŏs′pəl] **movement** *n.* a 19th-century reform movement based on the belief that Christians have a responsibility to help improve working conditions and alleviate poverty.

soddy [sŏd′ē] *n.* a home built of blocks of turf.

Songhai [sông′hī′] *n.* an empire that, at the height of its power in the 1500s, controlled much of West Africa.

specialization [spĕsh′ə-lĭ-zā′shən] *n.* in farming, the raising of one or two crops for sale rather than a variety of foods for personal use.

spoils system *n.* the practice of winning candidates' rewarding their supporters with government jobs.

Square Deal *n.* President Theodore Roosevelt's program of progressive reforms designed to protect the common people against big business.

Stamp Act *n.* a 1765 law in which Parliament established the first direct taxation of goods and services within the British colonies in North America.

Stono [stō′nō] **Rebellion** *n.* a 1739 uprising of slaves in South Carolina, leading to the tightening of already harsh slave laws.

strike *n.* a work stoppage intended to force an employer to respond to demands.

suffrage [sŭf′rĭj] *n.* the right to vote.

Sugar Act *n.* a trade law enacted by Parliament in 1764 in an attempt to reduce smuggling in the British colonies in North America.

T

Taino [tī′nō] *n.* a Native American people of the Caribbean islands—the first group encountered by Columbus and his men when they reached the Americas.

Tariff of Abominations [ə-bŏm′ə-nā′shənz] *n.* John C. Calhoun's name for an 1828 tariff increase that seemed to Southerners to be enriching the North at their expense.

Tariff of 1816 *n.* a protective tariff designed to aid American industries.

telegraph [tĕl′ĭ-grăf′] *n.* a device for the electrical transmission of coded messages over wires.

temperance [tĕm′pər-əns] **movement** *n.* an organized effort to prevent the drinking of alcoholic beverages.

tenant [tĕn′ənt] **farming** *n.* a system in which farm workers supply their own tools and rent farmland for cash.

tenement [tĕn′ə-mənt] *n.* a multifamily urban dwelling, usually overcrowded and unsanitary.

Texas Revolution *n.* the 1836 rebellion in which Texas gained its independence from Mexico.

Thirteenth Amendment *n.* an amendment to the U.S. Constitution, adopted in 1865, that has abolished slavery and involuntary servitude.

Three-Fifths Compromise [kŏm′prə-mīz′] *n.* the Constitutional Convention's agreement to count three-fifths of a state's slaves as population for purposes of representation and taxation.

Townshend [toun′zənd] **Acts** *n.* a series of laws enacted by Parliament in 1767, establishing indirect taxes on goods imported from Britain by the British colonies in North America.

Trail of Tears [tîrz] *n.* the marches in which the Cherokee people were forcibly removed from Georgia to the Indian Territory in 1838–1840, with thousands of the Cherokee dying on the way.

transcendentalism [trăn′sĕn-dĕn′tl-ĭz′əm] *n.* a philosophical and literary movement of the 1800s that emphasized living a simple life and celebrated the truth found in nature and in personal emotion and imagination.

transcontinental [trăns′kŏn-tə-nĕn′tl] **railroad** *n.* a railroad line linking the Atlantic and Pacific coasts of the United States, completed in 1869.

Treaty of Fort Laramie *n.* the treaty requiring the Sioux to live on a reservation along the Missouri River.

Treaty of Ghent [gĕnt] *n.* the 1814 treaty that ended the War of 1812.

Treaty of Guadalupe Hidalgo [gwäd′l-o͞op′ hĭ-däl′gō] *n.* the 1848 treaty ending the U.S. war with Mexico, in which Mexico ceded California and New Mexico to the United States.

Treaty of Paris (1783) *n.* the treaty that ended the Revolutionary War, confirming the independence of the United States and setting the boundaries of the new nation.

Treaty of Paris (1898) *n.* the treaty ending the Spanish-American War, in which Spain freed Cuba, turned over the islands of Guam and Puerto Rico to the United States, and sold the Philippines to the United States for $20 million.

Treaty of Tordesillas [tôr′də-sē′əs] *n.* the 1494 treaty in which Spain and Portugal agreed to divide the lands of the Western Hemisphere between them.

triangular [trī-ăng′gyə-lər] **trade** *n.* the transatlantic system of trade in which goods and people, including slaves, were exchanged between Africa, England, Europe, the West Indies, and the colonies in North America.

Tuskegee [tŭs-kē′gē] **Normal and Industrial Institute** *n.* founded in 1881, and led by Booker T. Washington, to equip African Americans with teaching diplomas and useful skills in the trades and agriculture.

two-party system *n.* a political system dominated by two major parties.

U

Uncle Tom's Cabin *n.* a best-selling novel by Harriet Beecher Stowe, published in 1852, that portrayed slavery as a great moral evil.

Underground Railroad *n.* a system of routes along which runaway slaves were helped to escape to Canada or to safe areas in the free states.

urbanization [ûr′bə-nĭ-zā′shən] *n.* the growth of cities.

USS *Maine* *n.* a U.S. warship that mysteriously exploded and sank in the harbor of Havana, Cuba, on February 15, 1898.

utopian [yo͞o-tō′pē-ən] **community** *n.* an experimental community designed to be a perfect society, in which its members could live together in harmony.

V

vertical integration [vûr′tĭ-kəl ĭn′tĭ-grā′shən] *n.* a company's taking over its suppliers and distributors and transportation systems to gain total control over the quality and cost of its product.

W

Wade-Davis [wād′ dā′vəs] **Bill** *n.* a bill, passed in 1864 and vetoed by President Lincoln, that would have given Congress control of Reconstruction.

war hawk *n.* one of the members of Congress who favored war with Britain in the early years of the 19th century.

Whig [hwĭg] **Party** *n.* the political party formed in 1834 to oppose the policies of Andrew Jackson.

Wilmot Proviso [wĭl′mət prə-vī′zō] *n.* an amendment to an 1846 military appropriations bill, proposing that none of the territory acquired in the war with Mexico would be open to slavery.

X

XYZ Affair *n.* a 1797 incident in which French officials demanded a bribe from U.S. diplomats.

Y

yellow journalism [jûr′nə-lĭz′əm] *n.* the use of sensationalized and exaggerated reporting by newspapers or magazines to attract readers.

Spanish Glossary

A

abolition [abolición] *s.* movimiento para acabar con la esclavitud.

Adams-Onís Treaty [Tratado de Adams-Onís] *s.* acuerdo de 1819 por el cual España le entregó el control del territorio de Florida a Estados Unidos

Adena *s.* sociedad constructora de túmulos asentada en el valle del río Ohio entre los años 700 a.C. y 100 d.C., aproximadamente; se conoce por sus grandes tumbas cónicas.

Alamo, the [El Álamo] *s.* misión y fuerte situado en San Antonio, Texas, en donde fuerzas mexicanas masacraron a rebeldes texanos en 1836.

Alien and Sedition Acts [Leyes de Extranjeros y de Sedición] *s.* cuatro leyes aprobadas en 1798 para reducir el poder político de los nuevos inmigrantes a EE.UU.

American Federation of Labor (AFL) [Federación Norteamericana del Trabajo] *s.* sindicato de trabajadores calificados creado en 1886 y dirigido por Samuel Gompers.

Americanization movement [movimiento de americanización] *s.* programa educativo ideado para facilitar la asimilación de los inmigrantes a la cultura estadounidense.

American System [Sistema Americano] *s.* programa económico previo a la Guerra Civil diseñado para fortalecer y unificar a Estados Unidos por medio de aranceles proteccionistas, un banco nacional y un sistema de transporte eficiente.

Anaconda plan [plan Anaconda] *s.* estrategia de tres pasos durante la Guerra Civil, mediante la cual la Unión propuso derrotar a la Confederación; su nombre viene de una serpiente que aprieta a sus víctimas.

Anasazi *s.* grupo amerindio que vivió cerca de la región de Four Corners —donde Arizona, New Mexico, Colorado y Utah se unen— de los años 100 a 1400 d.C., aproximadamente.

annex [anexar] *v.* incorporar un territorio a una unidad política existente tal como un estado o país.

antebellum *adj.* previo a la Guerra Civil.

Antifederalist [antifederalista] *s.* oponente de la Constitución y de un gobierno central fuerte.

Appomattox Court House *s.* pueblo cerca de Appomattox, Virginia, donde Lee se rindió a Grant el 9 de abril de 1865. (37°N 79°O)

apprentice [aprendiz] *s.* trabajador que aprende un oficio, por lo general supervisado por un maestro.

arbitration [arbitraje] *s.* método de resolver disputas en el cual ambos lados someten sus diferencias a un juez elegido por las dos partes.

armistice [armisticio] *s.* tregua o acuerdo para terminar un conflicto armado.

Articles of Confederation [Artículos de la Confederación] *s.* documento aprobado por el Segundo Congreso Continental en 1777 y ratificado por los estados finalmente en 1781. Detallaba la forma del gobierno de los nuevos Estados Unidos.

Ashcan School *s.* grupo de artistas estadounidenses de principios del siglo XX que a menudo pintaban escenas realistas de la vida urbana —como arrabales y gente sin hogar— ganándose así el nombre de la escuela del basurero.

assimilation [asimilación] *s.* adopción, por parte de un grupo minoritario, de las creencias y estilo de vida de la cultura dominante.

Aztec [azteca] *s.* pueblo amerindio que colonizó el Valle de México en 1200 d.C. y desarrolló un gran imperio.

B

Bank of the United States (BUS) [Banco de Estados Unidos] *s.* cualquiera de los dos bancos nacionales establecidos por el Congreso, el primero en 1791 y el segundo en 1816.

Battle of Wounded Knee [Batalla de Wounded Knee] *s.* masacre de 300 indígenas desarmados en Wounded Knee Creek, South Dakota, en 1890.

Benin *s.* reino de África occidental que existió en la actual Nigeria; floreció en los bosques del delta del Níger del siglo 14 al 17.

Bessemer process [método Bessemer] *s.* técnica más eficiente y barata de fabricar acero, desarrollada hacia 1850.

Bill of Rights [Carta de Derechos] *s.* primeras diez enmiendas a la Constitución que identifican los derechos de los ciudadanos; se adoptaron en 1791.

bimetallism [bimetalismo] *s.* sistema monetario nacional que utiliza el oro y la plata para respaldar la moneda.

Black Codes [códigos negros] *s.* leyes discriminatorias aprobadas en el Sur después de la Guerra Civil, las cuales restringían severamente la vida de los afroamericanos, prohibiéndoles actividades como viajar sin permiso, llevar armas, participar como jurado, testificar contra los blancos y casarse con blancos.

Bleeding Kansas [Kansas sangrante] *s.* nombre dado al Territorio de Kansas en los años previos a la Guerra Civil, cuando era un campo de batalla entre las fuerzas en pro y en contra de la esclavitud.

blockade [bloqueo] *s.* acto de sellar un puerto o región para prevenir la entrada o salida durante tiempos de guerra.

bonanza farm [granja de bonanza] *s.* extensa granja dedicada a un solo cultivo.

Boston Massacre [Masacre de Boston] *s.* choque entre soldados británicos y colonos en Boston en 1770, durante el cual cinco colonos fueron asesinados.

Boston Tea Party [Motín del Té de Boston] *s.* protesta en 1773 contra el impuesto británico sobre el té; los colonos arrojaron 18,000 libras de té al puerto de Boston.

Boxer Rebellion [Rebelión de los Boxer] *s.* rebelión encabezada en 1900 por los Boxer, sociedad secreta de China, para detener la difusión de la influencia occidental.

Bull Moose Party [Partido Bull Moose] *s.* apodo del Partido Progresista, bajo el que Theodore Roosevelt aspiró, sin éxito, a la presidencia en 1912.

C

cabinet [gabinete] *s.* jefes de departamentos que son asesores directos del presidente.

capitalism [capitalismo] *s.* sistema económico en el que individuos y corporaciones privadas controlan los medios de producción para obtener ganancias.

carpetbagger *s.* norteños que se trasladaron al Sur después de la Guerra Civil.

cash crop [cosecha comercial] *s.* cosecha que se cultiva para su venta más que para uso del granjero.

checks and balances [control y compensación de poderes] *s.* sistema en el cual cada rama del gobierno controla o restringe a las demás ramas.

Chinese Exclusion Act [Ley de Exclusión de Chinos] *s.* ley de 1882 que prohibía la inmigración de ciudadanos chinos, con la excepción de estudiantes, maestros, comerciantes, turistas y funcionarios gubernamentales.

Chisholm Trail [Sendero Chisholm] *s.* la ruta principal de ganado que iba desde San Antonio, Texas, por Oklahoma hasta Kansas.

chlorination [cloración] *s.* purificación del agua al mezclarla químicamente con cloro.

civil disobedience [desobediencia civil] *s.* rechazo a cumplir leyes que parecían injustas, con el objeto de lograr un cambio en la política de gobierno. En el siglo 19, Henry David Thoreau escribió sobre la desobediencia civil, y dicha táctica fue promovida por Martin Luther King, Jr. durante la era de los Derechos civiles.

civil service [servicio civil] *s.* cualquier servicio gubernamental en el que se obtiene un cargo mediante exámenes públicos.

Clayton Antitrust Act [Ley Antitrust Clayton] *s.* ley de 1914 que declaraba ilegales ciertas prácticas empresariales injustas y protegía el derecho de los sindicatos y organizaciones agrícolas.

colonization [colonización] *s.* establecimiento de asentamientos remotos controlados por otro país.

Columbian Exchange [Transferencia Colombina] *s.* transferencia —iniciada con el primer viaje de Colón a las Américas— de plantas, alimentos, animales y enfermedades entre el Hemisferio Occidental y el Hemisferio Oriental.

committees of correspondence [comités de correspondencia] *s.* red de comunicación escrita entre colonos para mantenerse al tanto de las actividades británicas.

Common Sense [Sentido común] *s.* folleto escrito en 1776 por Thomas Paine que exhortaba la separación de las colonias británicas.

Compromise of 1850 [Compromiso de 1850] *s.* serie de medidas del Congreso para resolver los desacuerdos que surgieron a raíz de la esclavitud entre los estados libres y esclavistas.

Compromise of 1877 [Compromiso de 1877] *s.* serie de medidas tomadas por el Congreso por medio de las cuales los demócratas acordaban aceptar al candidato republicano Rutherford B. Hayes como presidente, aunque éste hubiera perdido el voto popular. Las medidas incluían el retiro de tropas federales de los estados del Sur, el uso de dinero federal para mejorar la infraestructura en el Sur y la designación de un miembro de gabinete que sea sureño y conservador.

Confederacy [Estados Confederados de América] *s.* confederación formada en 1861 por los estados del Sur después de que se separaron de la unión.

confederation [confederación] *s.* grupo de estados o naciones unidos para actuar en torno a asuntos de interés mutuo.

conquistador *s.* explorador y colonizador español de las Américas en el siglo 16.

conscription [conscripción] *s.* servicio militar obligatorio de ciertos miembros de la población.

conservation [conservación] *s.* práctica de preservar algunas zonas naturales y desarrollar otras por el bien común.

consolidation [consolidación] *s.* acto de unir o combinar.

Copperhead *s.* nombre de una serpiente venenosa aplicado a los norteños que simpatizaban con el Sur durante la Guerra Civil.

Cottage industry [industria doméstica] *s.* sistema de producción en el cual los fabricantes proveen materiales para ser producidos en las casas.

cotton gin [desmotadora] *s.* máquina para quitar las semillas de las fibras del algodón, inventada por Eli Whitney en 1793.

Crédit Mobilier *s.* compañía constructora formada en 1864 por los dueños de la Union Pacific Railroad; quienes la usaron ilegalmente para obtener ganancias.

Crusades [Cruzadas] *s.* serie de expediciones militares cristianas al Oriente Medio entre los años 1096 y 1270 d.C., con el fin de rescatar del dominio islámico la "Tierra Santa" alrededor de Jerusalén.

cult of domesticity [culto a la domesticidad] *s.* creencia de que la mujer casada debe restringir sus actividades al hogar y la familia.

D

Dawes Act [Ley Dawes] *s.* ley aprobada por el Congreso en 1887 para "americanizar" a los indígenas distribuyendo a individuos la tierra de las reservaciones.

debt peonage [deuda por peonaje] *s.* sistema de servidumbre en el que una persona es obligada a trabajar para pagar una deuda.

Declaration of Independence [Declaración de Independencia] *s.* documento escrito por Thomas Jefferson en 1776 en el cual los delegados del Congreso Continental declaron la independencia de las colonias de Gran Bretaña.

Democratic-Republican [Demócrata-Republicano] *s.* partido político conocido por su apoyo a un fuerte gobierno estatal. Fue fundado por Thomas Jefferson en 1792 en oposición al Federalist Party [Partido Federalista].

division of labor [división del trabajo] *s.* práctica cultural de asignar diferentes tareas y responsabilidades a diferentes grupos o individuos.

dollar diplomacy [diplomacia del dólar] *s.* política de usar el poder económico o la influencia económica de Estados Unidos para alcanzar sus objetivos de política exterior en otros países.

E

egalitarianism [igualitarismo] *s.* creencia de que todas las personas deben tener igualdad de derechos políticos, económicos, sociales y civiles.

electoral college [colegio electoral] *s.* asamblea elegida por votantes para elegir formalmente al presidente y vicepresidente. Cada estado tiene un número de electores equivalente a los miembros de sus senadores y representantes en el Congreso.

emancipation [emancipación] *s.* proceso de liberarse de la esclavitud.

Emancipation Proclamation [Proclama de Emancipación] *s.* orden ejecutiva de Abraham Lincoln el 1° de enero de 1863 que abolía la esclavitud en los estados confederados.

embargo *s.* orden gubernamental que prohíbe el comercio con otra nación.

encomienda *s.* institución colonial de España en las Américas que repartía indígenas a los conquistadores para hacer trabajos forzados.

Enlightenment [Ilustración] *s.* movimiento intelectual del siglo 18 que enfatizaba la razón y los métodos científicos para obtener conocimientos.

entrepreneur [empresario] *s.* persona que organiza, opera y asume todo el riesgo de una ventura de negocios.

Erie Canal [canal del Erie] *s.* vía acuática artificial de 363 millas en New York, construida entre 1817 y 1825 para conectar el río Hudson y el lago Erie.

excise tax [impuesto al consumo] *s.* impuesto a la producción, venta o consumo de artículos producidos en el país.

executive branch [rama ejecutiva] *s.* rama gubernamental cuya función es administrar y aplicar las leyes (presidente o gobernador).

exoduster *s.* afroamericano que emigró del Sur a Kansas después de la Reconstrucción.

extortion [extorsión] *s.* uso ilegal de un cargo público para obtener dinero o propiedad.

F

Farmers' Alliances [Alianzas de granjeros] *s.* grupos de granjeros o simpatizantes de éstos, que enviaban a oradores a viajar de pueblo a pueblo para educar a la gente sobre cuestiones agrarias y rurales.

federalism [federalismo] *s.* sistema político gubernamental en el cual el poder se comparte entre un gobierno nacional y las entidades que lo constituyen, como los gobiernos estatales.

Federalists [federalistas] *s.* partidarios de la Constitución y de un gobierno nacional fuerte.

Federalist, The [El Federalista] *s.* ensayos escritos por Madison, Hamilton y Jay que apoyan y explican la Constitución.

Federal Reserve System [Sistema de la Reserva Federal] *s.* sistema bancario nacional establecido por Woodrow Wilson en 1913 que controla el dinero circulante del país.

Federal Trade Commission (FTC) [Comisión Federal de Comercio] *s.* agencia federal establecida en 1914 para investigar y parar prácticas empresariales injustas.

Fifteenth Amendment [Enmienda 15] *s.* enmienda a la Constitución, adoptada en 1870, que establece que a nadie puede negársele el derecho al voto por motivos de raza, color o por haber sido esclavo.

"Fifty-Four Forty or Fight!" *s.* consigna de la campaña presidencial de 1844 en pro de la anexión del Territorio de Oregon; se refería a la latitud del límite norte del territorio.

Foraker Act [Ley Foraker] *s.* legislación que el Congreso aprobó en 1900 para acabar con el gobierno militar en Puerto Rico y autorizar un gobierno civil.

forty-niner [viajero del 49] *s.* buscador de oro que llegó a California después de 1848 atraído por el oro.

Fourteen Points [los catorce puntos] *s.* plan del presidente Wilson en pro de la paz mundial tras la I Guerra Mundial.

Fourteenth Amendment [Enmienda 14] *s.* enmienda a la constitución adoptada en 1868 que hace ciudadano a toda persona nacida o naturalizada en Estados Unidos, incluso a antiguos esclavos, y garantiza igualdad de protección bajo la ley.

Freedmen's Bureau [Oficina de libertos] *s.* agencia federal formada después de la Guerra Civil para ayudar a personas que habían sido esclavos antes.

Freeport Doctrine [Doctrina Freeport] *s.* posición que tomó en 1858 Stephen Douglas de que cualquier territorio podría excluir la esclavitud con sólo negarse a promulgar leyes en su favor.

Free-Soil Party [Partido de las Tierras Libres] *s.* partido político formado en 1848 que se oponía a la extensión de la esclavitud a los territorios.

French and Indian War [Guerra contra Franceses e Indígenas] *s.* guerra librada en Norteamérica (1757-1763) como parte de un conflicto mundial entre Francia y Gran Bretaña; finalizó con la derrota de Francia y el traspaso del Canadá francés a Gran Bretaña.

Fugitive Slave Act [Ley de los Esclavos Fugitivos] *s.* ley aprobada como parte del Compromiso de 1850 que imponía duras sanciones a quien ayudara a escapar de la esclavitud.

G

Gadsden Purchase [Compra de Gadsden] *s.* compra de tierras de México en 1853 por parte de Estados Unidos que estableció la frontera actual entre los dos países.

gag rule [ley de la mordaza] *s.* orden que limita o previene el debate sobre un determinado asunto.

Gentlemen's Agreement [Acuerdo de Caballeros] *s.* acuerdo concertado durante 1907 y 1908, mediante el cual el gobierno de Japón limitaron la inmigración a Estados Unidos.

Gettysburg Address [Discurso de Gettysburg] *s.* famoso discurso de Abraham Lincoln durante la Guerra Civil al inaugurar un cementerio nacional en el campo de batalla de Gettysburg, Pennsylvania, el 19 de noviembre de 1863.

Glorious Revolution [Revolución Gloriosa] *s.* revolución incruenta en 1688-89 en la que William y Mary le quitaron el trono de Inglaterra a James II.

gold rush [fiebre del oro] *s.* llegada de gente a una región donde se ha descubierto oro.

gold standard [patrón de oro] *s.* sistema monetario en el cual la unidad básica de moneda se define en relación a una cantidad fija de oro.

graft [corrupción] *s.* uso ilegal de un cargo político con el fin de ganancia personal.

grandfather clause [cláusula del abuelo] *s.* estipulación que exime de cumplir una ley a ciertas personas por circunstancias previas; específicamente, cláusula de la constitución de algunos estados sureños que eximía a los blancos de los estrictos requisitos que impedían que los afroamericanos votaran.

Grange [la Granja] *s. The Patrons of Husbandry*—organización de granjeros que intentaron, a partir de la década de 1870, combatir el poder de los ferrocarriles.

Great Awakening [Gran Despertar] *s.* serie de grandes asambleas religiosas en las décadas de 1730 y 1750.

Great Compromise [Gran Compromiso] *s.* plan constitucional para una legislatura de dos cámaras: una que da igual representación a todos los estados y una que basa la representación en la población.

Great Plains [Grandes Praderas] *s.* vasta pradera que se extiende a través de Norteamérica, de Texas a Canadá en dirección norte y hacia el este de las Montañas Rocosas.

H

habeas corpus *s.* orden judicial que manda comparecer a las autoridades ante un juez u otro funcionario de un tribunal para explicar que un preso está detenido legalmente.

headright system [sistema de reparto de tierras por cabeza] *s.* sistema empleado en Virginia que otorgaba cincuenta acres de tierra a cada colono y otro tanto por cada acompañante.

hierarchy [jerarquía] *s.* orden social determinado por rango o clase.

Hohokam *s.* grupo amerindio que vivió en los valles de los ríos Salt y Gila (hoy Arizona) entre los años 300 a.C. y 1400 d.C., aproximadamente.

home rule [gobierno local] *s.* poder de los estados de gobernar a sus ciudadanos sin intervención federal.

Homestead Act [Ley de la Heredad] *s.* ley aprobada en 1862 que otorgaba 160 acres de tierra en el Oeste a cualquier ciudadano or ciudadano futuro que fuera cabeza de familia y que cultivara la tierra por cinco años; ley cuya aprobación llevó a un gran número de colonos estadounidenses a reclamar como propiedad privada tierra que había sido reservada por tratados y tradiciones para la vivienda de indígenas americanos; la misma ley, reforzada en 1889, dio incentivas para que los individuos ejercieran su derecho de propiedad privada y desarrollaran viviendas.

Hopewell *s.* sociedad constructora de túmulos asentada en el valle del río Ohio entre los años 200 a.C. y 400 d.C., aproximadamente; se conoce por sus grandes tumbas cónicas.

horizontal integration [integración horizontal] *s.* proceso mediante el cual compañías que fabrican productos similares se unen y reducen la competencia.

I

impeach [acusar] *v.* culpar oficialmente a un funcionario por su conducta inapropiada como tal. La Cámara de Representantes tiene el poder exclusivo de acusar a funcionarios federales.

imperialism [imperialismo] *s.* política de controlar países por medios económicos, políticos o militares.

impressment [leva] *s.* práctica de reclutar hombres a la fuerza para prestar servicio militar.

Inca *s.* pueblo amerindio creador de un imperio que abarcó casi 2,500 millas a lo largo de la costa occidental de Suramérica, a partir del año 1400 d.C., aproximadamente.

incandescent [incandescente] *adj.* que emite luz visible como resultado de haber sido calentado

income tax [impuesto sobre la renta] *s.* impuesto que retiene un porcentaje específico de ingresos.

indentured servant [sirviente por contrato] *s.* inmigrante que, a cambio de un pasaje para las Américas, era contratado a trabajar por un periodo límite.

Indian Removal Act [Ley de Traslado de los Indígenas] *s.* ley aprobada por el Congreso en 1830 que ordenaba el traslado obligatorio de todas las tribus indígenas del este del Mississippi a tierras del oeste.

Industrial Revolution [Revolución Industrial] *s.* cambios en la organización social y económica como resultado del remplazo del trabajo manual por máquinas y el desarrollo de fábricas de producción a gran escala.

Industrial Workers of the World (IWW) *s.* sindicato de trabajadores de mano de obra no calificada creado en 1905.

inflation [inflación] *s.* fenómeno económico en el que hay un aumento constante en los precios por el incremento del dinero circulante; reduce el poder adquisitivo.

initiative [iniciativa] *s.* reforma gubernamental que permite a los ciudadanos presentar proyectos de ley en el Congreso o en cuerpos legislativos estatales.

interchangeable parts [piezas uniformes] *s.* piezas que se pueden usar de manera intercambiable y que se producen en masa.

Interstate Commerce Act [Ley de Comercio Interestatal] *s.* ley de 1887 que restablecía el derecho del gobierno federal a supervisar los ferrocarriles; creó una Comisión de Comercio Interestatal de cinco miembros.

Intolerable Acts [Leyes Intolerables] *s.* cuatro leyes aprobadas por el Parlamento en 1774 con el fin de castigar a Boston por el Motín del Té de Boston.

Iroquois [iroqueses] *s.* grupo de pueblos amerindios que vivían en los bosques del Noreste.

Islam [islamismo] *s.* religión fundada en Arabia por el profeta Mahoma en el año 622; a sus seguidores se les llama musulmanes.

J

Jim Crow laws [leyes Jim Crow] *s.* leyes impuestas por los gobiernos estatales y municipales del Sur con el fin de separar a blancos y afroamericanos en instalaciones públicas y privadas.

joint-stock company [sociedad de capitales] *s.* institución empresarial tipo corporación en la que inversionistas unen riquezas con un fin común; se usaron para financiar la exploración de las Américas.

journeyman [oficial] *s.* artesano que trabaja al servicio de un maestro.

judicial branch [rama judicial] *s.* rama gubernamental cuya función es interpretar las leyes y la Constitución (Suprema Corte).

judicial review [revisión judicial] *s.* poder de la Suprema Corte de declarar inconstitucional una ley del Congreso.

Judiciary Act of 1789 [Ley Judicial de 1789] *s.* ley que estableció el sistema de tribunales federales y la Suprema Corte que permitió la apelación a cortes federales de ciertas decisiones tomadas por cortes estatales.

Judiciary Act of 1801 [Ley Judicial de 1801] *s.* ley aprobada con el fin de incrementar el número de jueces federalistas.

Jungle, The *[La jungla] s.* novela publicada en 1906 por el periodista Upton Sinclair que denunciaba la insalubridad de la industria de carne en aquella época; llevó a reformas nacionales.

K

Kansas-Nebraska Act [Ley Kansas y Nebraska] *s.* ley aprobada en 1854 que buscaba un acuerdo sobre la extensión de la esclavitud a los territorios de Kansas y Nebraska.

Kashaya Pomo *s.* pueblo amerindio que floreció hace 500 años en lo que hoy es California; vivía en las tierras pantanosas de la costa.

King Philip's War [Guerra del Rey Felipe] *s.* conflicto, en los años 1675 y 1676, entre los colonos de Nueva Inglaterra y grupos amerindios aliados bajo la dirección del cacique Metacom de los wampanoagas.

kinship [parentesco] *s.* lazos indisolubles entre los miembros de una misma familia o tribu.

Know-Nothing Party *s.* nombre dado en la década de 1850 al Partido Americano, un grupo que quería reducir la influencia política de los inmigrantes.

Kongo *s.* serie de pequeños reinos unidos bajo un líder a finales del siglo 15 en las selvas tropicales a lo largo del río Zaire (Congo) en África Central-Occidental.

Ku Klux Klan *s.* sociedad secreta de hombres blancos en los estados sureños después de la Guerra Civil que desató terror para restaurar la supremacía blanca.

Kwakiutl *s.* pueblo amerindio que vivía en la región costera del Noroeste.

L

land grant [concesión de tierras] *s.* lote grande de tierras dado por el gobierno a un agente para su reventa, por lo general con el fin de estimular el desarrollo.

Land Ordinance of 1785 [Ordenanza de Tierras de 1785] *s.* ley que estableció un plan para la agrimensura y venta de las tierras públicas al oeste de los montes Apalaches.

legislative branch [rama legislativa] *s.* rama gubernamental compuesta por representantes elegidos que promulgan leyes (Congreso).

lineage [linaje] *s.* línea de descendencia de una generación a otra —de abuelo, a hija, a nieto, por ejemplo— con un antepasado común.

long drive [arreo de ganado] *s.* proceso mediante el cual los vaqueros llevaban por tierra ganado hacia el mercado.

longhorn *s.* resistente raza de ganado vacuno de cuernos largos llevada por los españoles a México, muy apta para las condiciones de esa región.

Louisiana Purchase [Compra de Louisiana] *s.* compra de terrenos a Francia por 15 millones de dólares en 1803 de las tierras desde el río Mississippi hasta las montañas Rocosas.

Loyalists [realistas] *s.* colonos que apoyaban al gobierno británico durante la Revolución Norteamericana.

M

manifest destiny [destino manifiesto] *s.* término usado en la década de 1840 para describir la creencia de que Estados Unidos estaba inexorablemente destinado a adquirir más territorio, especialmente mediante su expansión hacia el oeste.

Marbury* v. *Madison *s.* caso de 1803 en que la Suprema Corte decidió que tenía el poder de abolir decretos legislativos declarándolos inconstitucionales; ese poder se conoce como revisión judicial.

market revolution [revolución mercantil] *s.* gran cambio económico que llevó a comprar y vender productos en lugar de hacerlos en el hogar.

martial law [ley marcial] *s.* gobierno impuesto por fuerzas militares.

mass production [producción en masa] *s.* producción de artículos en grandes cantidades, con máquinas y división del trabajo.

mass transit [transporte público] *s.* sistemas de transporte diseñados para llevar grandes números de personas por rutas fijas.

master [maestro] *s.* experto artesano; por lo general era dueño de un negocio y empleaba a otros.

Maya *s.* pueblo amerindio que desarrolló una rica cultura en Guatemala y la península de Yucatán entre los años 250 y 900 d.C.

McCulloch* v. *Maryland [McCulloch vs. Maryland] *s.* caso realizado en 1819, en el cual la Corte Suprema de Justicia estableció que Maryland no tenía derecho a cobrarle impuestos al Banco de los Estados Unidos, y consecuentemente fortaleció el poder de control que tenía el gobierno federal sobre la economía.

Meat Inspection Act [Ley de Inspección de la Carne] *s.* ley de 1906 que establecía estrictos requisitos sanitarios en las empacadoras de carne, así como un programa federal de inspección de carnes.

melting pot [crisol de culturas] *s.* mezcla de personas de diferentes culturas y razas que se amalgaman y abandonan su idioma y cultura natal.

mercantilism [mercantilismo] *s.* sistema económico en que un país aumenta su riqueza y poder al incrementar su posesión de oro y plata, y al exportar más productos de los que importa.

Merrimack *s.* buque blindado que usó el Sur durante la Guerra Civil.

mestizo *adj.* con mezcla de español e indígena.

middle passage [travesía intermedia] *s.* tramo de África a las Antillas; parte del triángulo comercial de esclavos.

midnight judge [juez de media noche] *s.* uno de los jueces designados por John Adams en las últimas horas de su gobierno.

minutemen [civil armado] *s.* soldados civiles patriotas que lucharon justo antes y durante la Revolución, quienes prometían estar listos para luchar al primer llamado.

Mississippian [misisipiense] *s.* última sociedad constructora de túmulos, que se extendió al este del río Mississippi del siglo 8 al 16.

Missouri Compromise [Acuerdo de Missouri] *s.* serie de acuerdos aprobados por el Congreso en 1820–1821 para mantener un equilibrio seccional entre los estados esclavistas y los estados libres.

Monitor *s.* buque blindado que usó el Norte durante la Guerra Civil.

Monroe Doctrine [Doctrina Monroe] *s.* declaración del presidente Monroe en 1823 que establecía que Estados Unidos no permitiría la interferencia europea en los asuntos del Hemisferio Occidental.

Mormons [mormones] *s.* miembros de una comunidad religiosa fundada por Joseph Smith, que terminó estableciéndose en Utah.

Morrill Acts [Leyes Morrill] *s.* leyes aprobadas en 1862 y 1890 que otorgaban tierras federales a los estados para financiar universidades agrícolas.

muckraker *s.* uno de los reporteros de revistas que desenmascaraban el lado corrupto de las empresas y de la vida pública a principios del siglo 20.

Munn* v. *Illinois *s.* caso de la Suprema Corte en 1877; estableció el derecho del gobierno federal a regular la industria privada en beneficio del interés público.

N

NAACP *s.* National Association for the Advancement of Colored People (Asociación Nacional para el Avance de la Gente de Color), organización fundada en 1909 y dedicada a la igualdad racial.

NACW *s.* National Association of Colored Women (Asociación Nacional de Mujeres de Color), organización de servicio social fundada en 1896.

National Bank Act [Ley del Banco Nacional] *s.* ley aprobada en 1863 para garantizarles a los inversionistas la seguridad de las actividades bancarias. Entre sus medidas establecía un sistema de bancos federales, nuevos requisitos para préstamos y un sistema de inspección de bancos.

nationalism [nacionalismo] *s.* devoción a los intereses y la cultura de la nación propia.

National Labor Relations Board (NLRB) [Junta Nacional de Relaciones Laborales] *s.* agencia creada en 1935 con el fin de prevenir prácticas laborales injustas y mediar en disputas laborales.

National Road [Carretera Nacional] *s.* carretera financiada por el gobierno cuya construcción se inició en 1811; iba desde Cumberland, Maryland, hasta Vandalia, Illinois.

National Trades' Union [Unión Nacional de Sindicatos] *s.* primera asociación nacional de sindicatos, creada en 1834.

nativism [patriotería] *s.* favoritismo de los intereses de las personas nacidas en un lugar sobre los de las personas extranjeras.

Navigation Acts [Leyes de Navegación] *s.* serie de leyes aprobadas a partir de 1651 que imponían un control más rígido del comercio en las colonias inglesas.

NAWSA *s.* National American Woman Suffrage Association (Asociación Nacional Americana del Sufragio Femenino), creada en 1890 para obtener derechos electorales para la mujer.

neutrality [neutralidad] *s.* política de una nación de no participar directa ni indirectamente en una guerra entre otras naciones.

Niagara Movement [Movimiento Niágara] *s.* fundado en 1905 por W. E. B. Du Bois para promover la enseñanza de humanidades entre los afroamericanos.

Nineteenth Amendment [Enmienda 19] *s.* enmienda a la Constitución adoptada en 1920 que le otorga a la mujer el derecho de votar.

nomadic [nómade] *adj.* que no tiene hogar fijo, que se muda de un lugar a otro según las estaciones y la disponibilidad de comida y agua.

Northwest Ordinance of 1787 [Ordenanza del Noroeste de 1787] *s.* procedimiento para la admisión de nuevos estados a la Unión.

nuclear family [familia nuclear] *s.* unidad formada por padre, madre e hijos.

nullification [anulación] *s.* rechazo de un estado a reconocer cualquier ley del Congreso que considere inconstitucional.

O

Olive Branch Petition [Petición del Ramo de Olivo] *s.* documento enviado por el Segundo Congreso Continental al rey George III; proponía una reconciliación entre las colonias y Gran Bretaña.

Olmec [olmeca] *s.* pueblo amerindio que creó una próspera civilización a lo largo de la costa del golfo de México, entre los años 1200 y 400 a.C.

Open Door notes [notas de Puertas Abiertas] *s.* notas que el Secretario de Estado John Hay envió a Gran Bretaña, Francia, Alemania, Italia, Japón y Rusia, instándolos a no interponerse entre el comercio de Estados Unidos y China.

Oregon Trail [Sendero de Oregon] *s.* camino que va de Independence, Missouri, a la ciudad de Oregon, Oregon.

P

Panama Canal [canal de Panamá] *s.* canal artificial construido a través del istmo de Panamá para abrir paso entre los océanos Atlántico y Pacífico; se abrió en 1914.

panic of 1837 [pánico de 1837] *s.* serie de clausuras de bancos y colapso del sistema crediticio; causó muchas quiebras y desempleo.

panic of 1873 [pánico de 1873] *s.* serie de fracasos económicos que provocaron una depresión de cinco años en Estados Unidos.

Parliament [Parlamento] *s.* cuerpo legislativo de Inglaterra.

Patriots [patriotas] *s.* colonos que apoyaban la independencia norteamericana de Gran Bretaña.

patronage [clientelismo] *s.* sistema de otorgar empleos a personas que ayudan a la elección de un candidato.

Payne-Aldrich Tariff [Arancel Payne-Aldrich] *s.* serie de reglamentos de impuestos, aprobados por el Congreso en 1909, que no logró reducir mucho los aranceles de productos manufacturados.

Pendleton Civil Service Act [Ley Pendleton] *s.* ley de 1883 que autorizaba nombrar empleados del servicio civil por mérito.

Pequot War [Guerra de los Pequot] *s.* conflicto librado en 1637 entre la tribu pequot y colonos asentados en Connecticut, que se aliaron con la tribu narrangansett.

personal liberty laws [leyes de libertad personal] *s.* estatutos aprobados en los estados del Norte que prohibían encarcelar a esclavos fugitivos y les permitían ser juzgados por un jurado.

plantation [plantación] *s.* finca grande en la que se cultiva una sola cosecha, como caña de azúcar o algodón, usando esclavos u otros trabajadores.

Platt Amendment [Enmienda Platt] *s.* serie de medidas implantadas por Estados Unidos en 1901, las cuales debieron ser incluidas por Cuba en su nueva constitución para quedar libre de su deuda y por las que Estados Unidos obtenía el derecho a intervenir en el país y a comprar o alquilar el territorio cubano para establecer estaciones navales y de combustible.

Plessy* v. *Ferguson *s.* caso de 1896 en que la Suprema Corte declaró legal la separación de razas en instalaciones públicas y estableció la doctrina de "separados aunque iguales".

political machine [maquinaria política] *s.* grupo organizado que controla un partido político en una ciudad y ofrece servicios a los votantes y negocios a cambio de apoyo político y financiero.

poll tax [impuesto para votar] *s.* impuesto anual que los ciudadanos debían pagar en algunos estados sureños para poder votar.

popular sovereignty [soberanía popular] *s.* sistema en el cual los ciudadanos votan para decidir sobre un tema.

Populism [populismo] *s.* movimiento político de finales del siglo 19 que exigía la voz popular en el gobierno y que representaba los intereses de los granjeros y promovía una reforma del sistema monetario.

Powhatan *s.* grupo de pueblos amerindios que vivía en el este de Virginia cuando se establecieron las primeras colonias inglesas.

Proclamation of 1763 [Proclama de 1763] *s.* decreto británico que prohibía que los colonos se instalaran al oeste de los montes Apalaches.

profiteering [acaparamiento] *s.* retención de un producto para provocar su escasez y venderlo más caro.

progressive [progresista] *s.* que favorece el avance hacia mejores condiciones o nuevas ideas.

progressive movement [movimiento progresista] *s.* movimiento reformista de comienzos del siglo 20 cuyos objetivos eran mejorar el bienestar social, promover la moralidad, incrementar la justicia económica y devolver a la ciudadanía el control del gobierno.

prohibition [prohibición] *s.* prohibición de bebidas alcohólicas.

proprietor [propietario] *s.* dueño y gobernante de una colonia.

protective tariff [arancel proteccionista] *s.* impuesto aplicado a productos importados para proteger las empresas nacionales de la competencia extranjera.

protectorate [protectorado] *s.* nación cuyo gobierno y asuntos son controlados por una potencia más fuerte.

Pueblo *s.* amerindios descendientes de los anasazi; viven en los desiertos del Suroeste.

Pure Food and Drug Act [Ley de Pureza de Alimentos y Drogas] *s.* ley de 1906 que paró la venta de alimentos y drogas contaminadas y demandó etiquetas fidedignas.

Puritans [puritanos] *s.* miembros de la Iglesia Anglicana que deseaban eliminar las tradiciones católicas y simplificar los servicios religiosos.

Q

Quakers [cuáqueros] *s.* miembros de una secta religiosa considerada radical en el siglo 17, también conocida como Sociedad de Amigos.

R

Radical Republican [republicano radical] *s.* uno de los republicanos del Congreso después de la Guerra Civil que querían destruir el poder político de los antiguos dueños de esclavos y darles a los afroamericanos total ciudadanía y derecho a votar.

ratification [ratificación] *s.* aprobación oficial de la Constitución, o de una enmienda, por parte de los estados.

recall [destitución] *s.* reforma gubernamental que permite a los votantes deponer a funcionarios públicos elegidos.

Reconstruction [Reconstrucción] *s.* período de reconstrucción después de la Guerra Civil y readmisión a la Unión de los estados de la Confederación que habían sido derrotados; de 1865 a 1877.

Red Cross [Cruz Roja] *s.* organización internacional que provee ayuda a la gente en tiempos de guerra o de desastres naturales. En 1881, Clara Barton fundó la sede estadounidense.

redemption [redención] *s.* término usado por los demócratas sureños para referirse a su recuperación del poder en el Sur en la década de 1870.

referendum [referendo] *s.* procedimiento que permite someter al voto popular propuestas legislativas.

Reformation [Reforma] *s.* movimiento religioso en la Europa de comienzos del siglo 16, encaminado a reformar la Iglesia Católica Romana; condujo a la formación del protestantismo.

Renaissance [Renacimiento] *s.* período de la historia europea, que se extendió aproximadamente desde 1400 a 1600, durante el cual un renovado interés en la cultura clásica originó cambios trascendentales en las artes, el aprendizaje y la visión del mundo.

republic [república] *s.* gobierno en el que los ciudadanos mandan por medio de sus representantes elegidos.

republicanism [republicanismo] *s.* creencia de que los gobiernos deben basarse en el consentimiento del pueblo.

Republican Party [Partido Republicano] *s.* partido actual, formado en 1854 por oponentes de la esclavitud en los territorios.

Republic of California [República de California] *s.* nación proclamada por los colonos estadounidenses en California, al declarar éstos su independencia de México en 1846.

Republic of Texas [república de Texas] *s.* nación fundada en 1836, cuando los colonos estadounidenses de la provincia mexicana de Tejas lucharon y declararon su independencia. En esa época se la conocía también como la "República de la Estrella Solitaria".

revival [renovación religiosa] *s.* emotivas reuniones religiosas para revivir la fe, con apasionados sermones.

Roosevelt Corollary [Corolario de Roosevelt] *s.* declaración de 1904 del presidente Theodore Roosevelt en que advertía que Estados Unidos intervendría militarmente en los asuntos de cualquier nación del Hemisferio Occidental para proteger sus intereses económicos si fuera necesario.

Rough Riders *s.* regimiento de caballería voluntario comandado por Leonard Wood y Theodore Roosevelt en la Guerra Española-Norteamericana-Cubana.

royal colony [colonia real] *s.* colonia sujeta al control directo de la corona británica.

rural free delivery (RFD) [correo rural gratuito] *s.* entrega gubernamental gratis de correo y paquetes a zonas rurales; se inició en 1896.

S

salutary neglect [indiferencia saludable] *s.* aplicación poco estricta de las leyes comerciales por parte del gobierno británico a cambio de lealtad comercial de las colonias.

Santa Fe Trail [Sendero de Santa Fe] *s.* camino que va de Independence, Missouri, a Santa Fe, New Mexico.

savanna [sabana] *s.* pastizal plano y seco con árboles y arbustos espaciados; común en África central y otras regiones tropicales y subtropicales.

scalawag *s.* término despectivo para referirse a los sureños blancos que se unieron al Partido Republicano y apoyaron la Reconstrucción después de la Guerra Civil.

scientific management [administración científica] *s.* aplicación de principios científicos para simplificar y facilitar las tareas laborales.

secession [secesión] *s.* retiro formal de un estado de la Unión federal.

Second Continental Congress [Segundo Congreso Continental] *s.* nueva convocatoria del Congreso Continental que se inició en 1775 y redactó la Declaración de Independencia.

Second Great Awakening [Segundo Gran Despertar] *s.* movimiento religioso del siglo 19 que ponía énfasis en la responsabilidad individual para lograr la salvación y la superación personal y social.

sectionalism [regionalismo] *s.* preocupación por los intereses de una región por encima de los de la nación como un todo.

segregation [segregación] *s.* separación de la gente según su raza.

Seneca Falls Convention [convención de Seneca Falls] *s.* convención de derechos femeninos celebrada en 1848 en Seneca Falls, New York.

Separatist [separatista] *s.* miembro de la Iglesia Anglicana que rechazó su reforma y formó una congregación independiente.

settlement house [casa de beneficencia] *s.* centro comunitario en un barrio pobre que ayudaba a los residentes, particularmente a los inmigrantes.

Seventeenth Amendment [Enmienda 17] *s.* enmienda a la Constitución adoptada en 1913; dispone que los senadores federales sean elegidos por los votantes y no por cuerpos legislativos estatales.

sharecropping [aparcería] *s.* sistema en el cual se da a los agricultores tierra, semillas, herramientas y alimentos para vivir, así como una parte de la cosecha, por cultivar la tierra.

Shays's Rebellion [Rebelión de Shays] *s.* sublevación de granjeros endeudados de Massachusetts en 1787, en protesta por los impuestos estatales.

Sherman Antitrust Act [Ley Antitrust Sherman] *s.* ley contra los monopolios de 1890 que declaró ilegal la formación de consorcios que obstruyeran el libre comercio.

slave [esclavo] *s.* persona que se convierte en propiedad de otra.

Social Darwinism [darvinismo social] *s.* conjunto de creencias políticas y económicas basadas en la teoría del biólogo Charles Darwin sobre la selección natural o supervivencia del más apto; favorecía una competencia libre, no regulada, y creía que los individuos o grupos triunfaban porque eran genéticamente superiores.

Social Gospel movement [movimiento del Evangelio Social] *s.* movimiento de reforma del siglo 19 basado en la noción de que los cristianos tenían la responsabilidad social de mejorar las condiciones laborales y aliviar la pobreza urbana.

soddy [choza de tepe] *s.* casa provisional hecha de césped, muy común en las llanuras, donde la madera era escasa.

Songhai *s.* imperio que, en la cúspide de su poderío durante el siglo 16, controlaba gran parte de África occidental.

specialization [especialización] *s.* producción de un número limitado de productos agrícolas para venta nacional o internacional.

spoils system [sistema de prebendas] *s.* práctica de los candidatos ganadores de dar empleos u otras recompensas a sus simpatizantes.

Square Deal *s.* programa de reformas progresistas del presidente Theodore Roosevelt para proteger a la gente común y corriente de las grandes empresas.

Stamp Act [Ley del Timbre] *s.* primer impuesto directo aplicado en 1765 por Gran Bretaña a una variedad de artículos y servicios, tales como documentos legales y periódicos.

Stono Rebellion [Rebelión de Stono] *s.* rebelión de esclavos en la colonia de South Carolina en 1739; en consecuencia se hicieron más estrictas las leyes pertinentes a los esclavos.

strike [huelga] *s.* interrupción del trabajo para presionar a un patrono a responder a ciertas demandas.

suffrage [sufragio] *s.* derecho a votar.

Sugar Act [Ley del Azúcar] *s.* ley británica de 1764 que aplicó un impuesto comercial a la melaza, el azúcar y otras importaciones para reducir el contrabando en las colonias.

T

Taino [taíno] *s.* pueblo amerindio que Colón y su tripulación vieron al arribar a la isla hoy conocida como San Salvador, el 12 de octubre de 1492.

Tariff of Abominations [Arancel Abominable] *s.* nombre que le dio Henry Clay a un aumento de aranceles estipulado en 1828, debido al cual los sureños creían que el norte se estaba enriqueciendo a sus expensas.

Tariff of 1816 [Arancel de 1816] *s.* arancel proteccionista para proteger las jóvenes industrias estadounidenses.

telegraph [telégrafo] *s.* aparato que convierte un mensaje codificado en impulsos eléctricos que viajan por un hilo metálico.

temperance movement [movimiento de templanza] *s.* campaña para prohibir el consumo y la venta de alcohol.

tenant farming [agricultura de arrendatarios] *s.* sistema en el que los agricultores, llamados arrendatarios, ponen sus propias herramientas y animales, y pagan dinero por el arriendo de tierra para cultivar.

tenement [casa de pisos] *s.* vivienda urbana de varias familias, usualmente sobrepoblada y poco sanitaria.

Texas Revolution [Revolución de Texas] *s.* rebelión de 1836 con la que Texas se independizó de México.

Thirteenth Amendment [Enmienda 13] *s.* enmienda a la Constitución, ratificada en 1865, que ha abolido la esclavitud y la servidumbre involuntaria.

Three-Fifths Compromise [Acuerdo de los Tres Quintos] *s.* acuerdo constitucional de considerar como población las tres quintas partes de los esclavos de un estado para efectos de representación y cobro de impuestos.

Townshend Acts [Leyes Townshend] *s.* serie de leyes promulgadas por el Parlamento en 1767 que establecían impuestos indirectos a los artículos de Gran Bretaña importados a las colonias.

Trail of Tears [Sendero de las Lágrimas] *s.* marcha obligada del pueblo cherokee desde Georgia hasta el Territorio Indio entre 1838 y 1840, durante la cual murieron miles de ellos.

transcendentalism [trascendentalismo] *s.* movimiento filosófico y literario que proponía llevar una vida sencilla y celebrar la verdad implícita de la naturaleza, la emoción personal y la imaginación.

transcontinental railroad [ferrocarril transcontinental] *s.* línea férrea finalizada en 1869 que unía la costa Atlántica y la costa Pacífica.

Treaty of Fort Laramie [Tratado del Fuerte Laramie] *s.* tratado que requería que los sioux vivieran en una reservación a lo largo del río Missouri.

Treaty of Ghent [Tratado de Gante] *s.* tratado firmado en 1814 que puso fin a la Guerra de 1812.

Treaty of Guadalupe Hidalgo [Tratado de Guadalupe Hidalgo] *s.* tratado de 1848 que puso fin a la guerra entre Estados Unidos y México, mediante el cual Estados Unidos obtuvo enormes tierras en el Oeste y el Suroeste.

Treaty of Paris (1783) [Tratado de París] *s.* tratado que puso fin a la Guerra Revolucionaria Norteamericana y estableció las fronteras de la nueva nación.

Treaty of Paris (1898) [Tratado de París] *s.* tratado el cual puso fin a la guerra entre España y Estados Unidos. Por medio de este tratado España liberó a Cuba, cedió las islas de Guam y Puerto Rico a Estados Unidos y vendió las Filipinas a este país por 20 millones de dólares.

Treaty of Tordesillas [Tratado de Tordesillas] *s.* tratado de 1494 que dividió las Américas entre España y Portugal mediante una línea vertical imaginaria en el Atlántico; cada país tenía poder sobre un lado de la línea.

triangular trade [triángulo comercial de esclavos] *s.* sistema transatlántico de comercio en el cual la mercancía, incluidos los esclavos, se intercambiaba entre África, Inglaterra, Europa, las Indias Occidentales y las colonias de Norteamérica.

Tuskegee Normal and Industrial Institute [Instituto Normal e Industrial Tuskegee] *s.* fundado en 1881 y dirigido por Booker T. Washington para otorgar diplomas de magisterio y enseñar destrezas comerciales y agrícolas a los afroamericanos.

two-party system [bipartidismo] *s.* sistema político dominado por dos partidos.

U

Uncle Tom's Cabin [La cabaña del tío Tom] *s.* novela famosa (1852) escrita por Harriet Beecher Stowe, que causó intenso furor al retratar la esclavitud como una gran perversión moral.

Underground Railroad [Ferrocarril Subterráneo] *s.* red secreta de personas que ayudaban a los esclavos fugitivos a escapar a lo largo de diversas rutas hacia Canadá o hacia zonas seguras en los estados libres.

urbanization [urbanización] *s.* movimiento de personas a una ciudad.

U.S.S. *Maine* *s.* buque de guerra estadounidense que explotó y naufragó misteriosamente el 15 de febrero de 1898 en el puerto de La Habana, Cuba.

utopian community [comunidad utópica] *s.* comunidad formada por un grupo experimental que vivía unido y buscaba crear un lugar perfecto.

V

vertical integration [integración vertical] *s.* proceso mediante el cual una compañía se adueña de sus proveedores y distribuidores así como de los sistemas de transporte, con lo que obtiene control total sobre la calidad y el costo de su producción.

W

Wade-Davis Bill [proyecto de ley Wade-Davis] *s.* proyecto de ley, aprobado en 1864 y vetado por el presidente Lincoln, que daba al Congreso control de la Reconstrucción.

war hawk [halcón de guerra] *s.* uno de los miembros del Congreso que apoyó la guerra con Gran Bretaña a comienzos del siglo 19.

Whig Party [Partido Liberal] *s.* miembro de un partido político establecido en 1834 en oposición a Andrew Jackson.

Wilmot Proviso [Cláusula Wilmot] *s.* enmienda a un proyecto de ley de fondos militares de 1846; proponía que ninguna porción del territorio adquirido en la guerra con México debía abrirse a la esclavitud.

X

XYZ Affair [Asunto XYZ] *s.* incidente diplomático de 1797 en el que funcionarios franceses trataron de sobornar a funcionarios estadounidenses para entrevistarse con un alto ministro francés.

Y

yellow journalism [prensa amarillista] *s.* uso de métodos sensacionalistas en periódicos o revistas para atraer o influenciar lectores.

Index

A *p* in italics following a page number refers to an illustration on the page. An *m* or a *c* in italics following a page number refers to a map or chart on the page.

A

C

D

E

F

G

H

K

L

M

N

O

P

Q

R

S

T

U

X

Y

Z

ACKNOWLEDGMENTS

TEXT ACKNOWLEDGMENTS

Excerpt from "El Corrido de Gregorio Cortez" from *With His Pistol in His Hand: A Border Ballad and Its Hero* by Améico Parades. Text copyright © 1958, renewed 1986. Reprinted by permission of the author and the University of Texas Press.

Houghton Mifflin Harcourt Publishing Company has made every effort to locate the copyright holders for selections used in this book and to make full acknowledgment for their use. Omissions brought to our attention will be corrected in a subsequent edition.

ART CREDITS

COVER, BACK COVER, AND FRONTISPIECE

Abigail Adams: © Bettmann/Corbis
American Flag: © Izzy Schwartz/PhotoDisc/Getty Images
Abraham Lincoln: Ambrotype (1858), Abraham Byers. © Bettmann/Corbis
Harriet Tubman: © National Geographic Image Collection
George Washington: © Christie's Images/Corbis

Maps

Atlas maps by Rand McNally A2–A39
Unless otherwise indicated below, all other maps, locators, and globe locators by GeoNova LLC.

Master Elements

American flag photo used in Section Opener banners throughout book © Izzy Schwartz/PhotoDisc/Getty Images.

Supreme Court Facade used in "Historic Decisions of the Supreme Court" feature © PhotoDisc/Getty Images.

The presidential seal is used throughout by permission of The Office of the Counsel to the President, The White House, Washington, D.C.
Unless otherwise indicated, photograph provided by The Granger Collection, New York.

REVIEWERS (*continued*)

Manuscript Reviewers
(*continued from page iii*)

Bruce Campbell
Bemidji High School
Bemidji, Minnesota

Al Celaya
Robert E. Lee High School
Tyler, Texas

Anne E. Connor
Westridge School
Pasadena, California

James Crider
Downers Grove South High School
Downers Grove, Illinois

Marci Smith Deal
Hurst-Euless-Bedford Independent School District
Bedford, Texas

Eric DeMeulanaere
Burton Academic High School
San Francisco, California

Gail Dent
Lincoln High School
San Francisco, California

Dr. Simone Dorman
Burton Academic High School
San Francisco, California

Kenward Goode
Robert E. Lee High School
Tyler, Texas

Gary Gregus
Shakopee High School
Shakopee, Minnesota

Patti Harrlod
Edmond Memorial High School
Edmond, Oklahoma

Terry Holt
South Rowan High School
China Grove, North Carolina

Al Juengling
Lamar High School
Chicago, Illinois

James Lee
Lamar High School
Arlington, Texas

Judith Mahnke
Wallenberg High School
San Francisco, California

Gary Marksbury
Lakewood High School
Lakewood, California

Terry McRae
Robert E. Lee High School
Tyler, Texas

Peyton Mullins
Robert E. Lee High School
Tyler, Texas

Brenda Sims Palmer
Lehigh High School
Lehigh Acres, Florida

David Pasternak
Edison Technical High School
Rochester, New York

Dean Pedersen
North Fayette High School
West Union, Iowa

Lindy Poling
Millbrook High School
Raleigh, North Carolina

Kent Rettig
Pensacola High School
Pensacola, Florida

Diane Ring
St. Charles High School
St. Charles, Illinois

Susan Roe
C. E. Jordan High School
Durham, North Carolina

Tom Sewell
Inglemoor High School
Bothell, Washington

Mary Smith
Secondary Social Studies Coordinator
Cypress-Fairbanks Independent School District
Houston, Texas

Clara Spence
Millikan High School
Long Beach, California

Wayne Sylvester
Pentucket High School
Westbury, Massachusetts

Bill Von Vihl
Conifer High School
Conifer, Colorado

Pattie Willbanks
Robert E. Lee High School
Tyler, Texas

Nancy Williams
Jersey Village High School
Houston, Texas

Student Board
(*continued from page iii*)

Kevin Dodd
Lanier High School
Austin, Texas

Melissa Dugan
Mount Lebanon High School
Mount Lebanon, Pennsylvania

Denise Ford
Douglas Byrd Sr. High School
Cumberland County, North Carolina

Rebecca Freeman
Foshay Learning Center
Los Angeles, California

Tonya Gieseking
Broad Ripple High School
Indianapolis, Indiana

Yolande Godfrey
Ocean Township High School
Ocean Township, New Jersey

Norma Jaquez
Odessa High School
Ector County, Texas

Mary McCarthy
Penfield High School
Penfield, New York

Dan McKinley
Bulkeley High School
Hartford, Connecticut

Kris Miller
Midland High School
Cabell County, West Virginia

Brandi Nicholas
Meadowdale High School
Dayton, Ohio

Michael Pancherz
Clark Lake High School
Houston, Texas

Elizabeth Porter
Burnsville High School
Burnsville, Minnesota

Edwin Reyes
Miami Palmetto High School
Dade County, Florida

Misty Sisk
Jackson High School
Jacksonville, Florida

Christopher Sizemore
Community High School
Ann Arbor, Michigan

Jennifer Vasquez
Gilbert High School
Gilbert, Arizona

Everett Wheeler-Bell
East High School
Denver, Colorado

LuKisha Williams
Mackenzie High School
Detroit, Michigan